PLACES R·A·T·E·D ALMANAC

PLACES R·A·T·E·D

5TH EDITION

David Savageau and Geoffrey Loftus

Macmillan • USA

ACKNOWLEDGEMENTS

This revision of *Places Rated Almanac* could not have been done without the insights and criticisms of many people. Their affiliations and the data they have generously made available to us are cited throughout.

Thanks also to: Aviation DataBanks; CMG Information Services; Judith Kinney, researcher; National Golf Foundation; Thomas Nast, cartographer; PHH Technology Services; Quality Resource Systems; and Karyl Savageau, researcher.

Finally, special thanks are due Woods & Poole Economics, Inc., of Washington, DC, for their population, income, and job forecasts. The use of this information, and the conclusions drawn from it, are solely the responsibility of the authors.

PUBLISHER'S NOTE

Macmillan Travel
A Simon & Schuster Macmillan Company
1633 Broadway
New York, NY 10019

Find us online at **http://www.mgr.com/travel** or on America Online at Keyword: **Frommer's**

ISBN 0-02-861233-7

Library of Congress Catalog Card No. 96-79148

Manufactured in the United States of America

10 9 8 7 6 5 4 3 2

CONTENTS

CRIME 257

ARTS 278

HEATH CARE 317

INTRODUCTION

[illegible] question another [illegible] state or somewhere in North America that suited [illegible] than the one where you're living now, and you didn't know of it?

From time to time most people tell pollsters they would rather live somewhere other than where they are. Most of us change our address 11 times throughout our lives, but we do it by simply moving from one house to another within the same city. However, each year 8 million North Americans move to another state or province. Among them, they have millions of reasons for relocating a long distance, and they have one thing in common—the need for information.

Like its four predecessors, this edition of *Places Rated Almanac* is meant for people who are mulling over a relocation as well as for anyone who enjoys learning about cities and towns and what they have to offer. As an almanac, it provides thousands of facts—found neither in standard guidebooks nor in chamber of commerce blandishments—about all 351 officially defined metropolitan areas where three out of four of us live.

But *Places Rated Almanac* is more than a collection of interesting, odd, and useful information about metropolitan areas. It also rates and ranks these metro areas on nine factors that greatly influence the quality of place: costs of living, job outlook, transportation, education, health care, crime, the arts, recreation, and climate. *Places Rated Almanac* might be considered a self-help book with one difference: Instead of pointing the way toward inner peace or upward mobility as most such books do, it helps you decide whether geographical mobility might be the route to a more satisfying life.

Where you live affects your happiness and personal success. It just may be that your present location doesn't fit your needs and preferences. After all, given the extraordinary variety that North American cities offer, what are the odds that the place where you happen to live is the right one for you?

[illegible] may very well [illegible]

FINDING YOUR [illegible]

Places Rated Almanac contains thousands of useful facts and many descriptive sections. It is organized so that readers can find specific items of interest. Each chapter has five parts:

The **introductory** section gives basic information on the chapter's topic, interspersed with facts and figures to help you evaluate metro areas.

Scoring: The system used to rank metro areas for the chapter's topic is described, and one or more metro areas are drawn as "scoring examples" to show why one performs better than the other.

Rankings: The metro areas are listed in their rank order, from best to worst, along with their standard score. Metro areas that are tied get the same rank and are listed in alphabetical order.

Place Profiles: Arranged alphabetically by metro area, these capsule comparisons cover all the elements used to grade the metro areas. These Place Profiles can be columns of information (like the recreation or the arts profiles) or page-wide charts (like the transportation or the crime profiles). The climate profiles have their own special format. All are designed to help you see differences among metro areas at a glance.

Et Cetera: This section expands on the quality-of-life features mentioned in the introductory section. It also contains information on other topics ranging all the way from lists of metro-area professional sports championships, high school graduation requirements, and state and provincial holidays, to essays on traffic laws and tax bites.

The final chapter, "Putting It All Together," adds up the standard scores to identify North America's best all-around metro areas. Here, too, examples of using personal preferences to devise your own scoring system are given.

Postal Abbreviations

Places Rated Almanac uses standard U.S. Post Office and Canada Post abbreviations at the end of metro-area names. Here is a guide.

AB Alberta
AK Alaska
AL Alabama
AR Arkansas
AZ Arizona
BC British Columbia
CA California
CO Colorado
CT Connecticut
DC District of Columbia
DE Delaware
FL Florida
GA Georgia
HI Hawaii
IA Iowa
ID Idaho
IL Illinois
IN Indiana
KS Kansas
KY Kentucky
LA Louisiana
MA Massachusetts
MB Manitoba
MD Maryland
ME Maine
MI Michigan
MN Minnesota
MO Missouri
MS Mississippi
MT Montana
NB New Brunswick
NC North Carolina
ND North Dakota
NE Nebraska
NF Newfoundland
NH New Hampshire
NJ New Jersey
NM New Mexico
NS Nova Scotia
NV Nevada
NY New York
OH Ohio
OK Oklahoma
ON Ontario
OR Oregon
PA Pennsylvania
PQ Quebec
RI Rhode Island
SC South Carolina
SD South Dakota
SK Saskatchewan
TN Tennessee
TX Texas
UT Utah
VA Virginia
VT Vermont
WA Washington
WI Wisconsin
WV West Virginia
WY Wyoming

RATING PLACES: A CONTINENTAL PASTIME

"The tradition of hating New York started long before it began asking the rest of us to pay its bills while condescendingly viewing us as amusing rustics," Mike Royko once wrote in a *Chicago Sun-Times* column. "Actually, I like New York," he continued. "There are better reasons to hate cities like Cleveland or Indianapolis or Detroit or Dallas. But I do dislike New Yorkers."

It may seem the utmost of brass, this business of judging places. Yet everyone does it, privately. Some suspect that culture in Omaha or Des Moines or Saskatoon is a contradiction. Others surmise that daily life in Miami consists of surviving drug-trade shoot-outs, that cold and windy Winnipeg is no place for the seasonally depressed, that Waco has more than a few berserk evangelists walking about, and people in Los Angeles spend most of their waking hours behind a steering wheel waiting for the Big One.

Judging places from best to worst with numbers may seem the highest effrontery of all. Ultimately, how can intangible things like friendliness and optimism be measured with statistics? Yet numeracy is almost as strong a North American character trait as literacy. When it comes to choosing where to live, people have been digesting statistics for a long, long time.

To sell newcomers on settling in colonial Maryland instead of neighboring Virginia, seventeenth-century promoters put together figures showing heavier livestock, more plentiful game, and lower mortality from foul air and Indian attacks.

California for Health, Wealth, and Residence, just one volume in a library of post–Civil War guides touting the West's superior quality of life, compiled data to show the climate along the southern Pacific coast to be the world's best. Not so, countered the Union Pacific Railroad's land office in 1871; settlers will find the most "genial and healthy" seasons in western Kansas.

In this century, the statistical nets were flung even wider. "There are plenty of Americans who regard Kansas as almost barbaric," noted H. L. Mencken in 1931, "just as there are other Americans who shudder whenever they think of Arkansas, Ohio, Indiana, Oklahoma, Texas, or California." Mencken wrote these words in his *American Mercury* magazine to introduce his formula for statistically measuring the progress of civilization in each of the states. He mixed the numbers of Boy Scouts and *Atlantic Monthly* subscribers with lynchings and pellagra cases, added a dash of Who's Who listing along with rates for divorce and murder, threw in figures for rainfall and gasoline consumption, and found that, hands down, Mississippi was the worst American state.

METROPOLITAN AREAS

Places Rated Almanac employs a system that is more useful than any that considers only states or provinces, because broad-brush averages hide local realities. For persons who can live anywhere they wish, there may be more differences between the Texas metro areas of Houston and Amarillo than there are between the Lone Star State and Alberta, Canada.

Places Rated Almanac focuses on metropolitan areas, the smallest units of urban geography for which there is the largest amount of comparable data. From Abilene to Yuma; from huge Los Angeles-Long Beach (pop. 9,233,210) to tiny Enid (pop. 56,873); from foggy St. John's to sunny San Diego, these 351 metro areas cover a lot of ground.

Here you'll find agricultural centers and fashion markets, college towns and mill towns and cow towns, bedroom communities, financial centers, resorts and retirement colonies, and cultural havens right next to ports of entry and industrial giants.

For more than 50 years, metropolitan areas have been defined by detailed government standards. Broadly speaking, an area qualifies as "metropolitan" by the following rules:

United States—any city with a population of at least 50,000, or an urbanized area (embracing one or more towns) of at least 50,000, located in a county or counties with a total population of at least 100,000 (75,000 in New England).

Population Growth, 1990-1997

Fastest Growing	Percent Growth
Laredo, TX	36.4%
Las Vegas, NV-AZ	35.3
McAllen-Edinburg-Mission, TX	29.5
Naples, FL	26.9
Punta Gorda, FL	26.7
Las Cruces, NM	24.4
Boise City, ID	24.0
Olympia, WA	22.8
Orlando, FL	22.7
[illegible] Chapel Hill, NC	22.1
[illegible]	21.9
[illegible]	[illegible]
New Lon[illegible]	[illegible]
New Bedford, MA	[illegible]
Alexandria, LA	−2.8
Champaign-Urbana, IL	−2.8
Fitchburg-Leominster, MA	−2.6
Steubenville-Weirton, OH-WV	−2.5
Bangor, ME	−2.3
New Haven-Meriden, CT	−2.1
Springfield, MA	−2.1
Cumberland, MD-WV	−1.5
Wheeling, WV-OH	−1.5
Pine Bluff, AR	−1.4
Jacksonville, NC	−0.7

Source: Woods & Poole Economics, Inc., Compusearch Market and Social Research Ltd., population estimates.

Canada—an urban area of at least 100,000 people located in the midst of surrounding urban and rural areas that have strong economic and social ties with the urban area as determined by the number of people commuting there to work.

In either case, the metro area's boundaries coincide with those of the surrounding county or counties (in Canada and in New England, metro areas are defined by groups of towns and cities).

Most are within single states and provinces. However, 40 cross state lines. Washington includes not just the District of Columbia, but 5 counties in suburban Maryland, 11 counties and 6 independent cities in northern Virginia, and 2 counties in West Virginia's eastern panhandle. Memphis takes in 3 counties in Tennessee, another across the river in Arkansas, and another in Mississippi. Ottawa-Hull, the only Canadian metro area in more than one province, embraces cities in Ontario and *villes* across the river in Quebec.

There are ample reasons for focusing on metro areas rather than on cities, counties, or states. Thanks to the four-lane highway, cities, counties, and states are less relevant to our daily personal geography. It's common to live in one community, commute to work in another, eat at the restaurants, shop at the stores, and take

Population Size

Largest	1997 Population
Los Angeles–Long Beach, CA	9,206,426
New York, NY	8,592,030
Chicago, IL	7,749,799
Philadelphia, PA-NJ	5,025,289
Washington, DC-MD-VA-WV	4,643,394
Toronto, ON	4,377,587
Detroit, MI	4,355,241
Houston, TX	3,853,138
Atlanta, GA	3,530,445
Montreal, PQ	3,332,939
Boston, MA-NH	3,246,676
Riverside–San Bernardino, CA	3,080,701

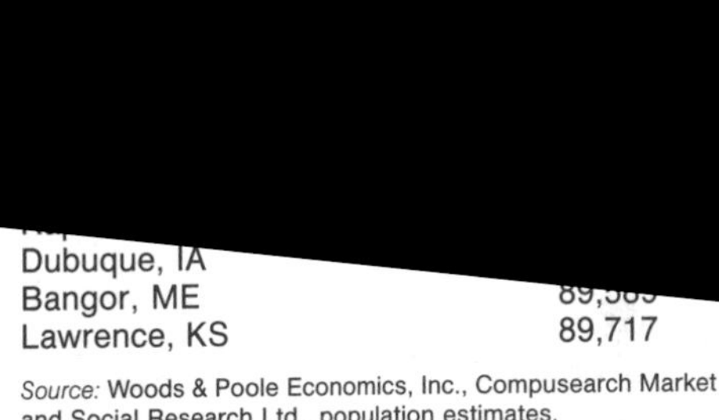

[illegible]	1997 Population
Dubuque, IA	[illegible]
Bangor, ME	89,5[illegible]
Lawrence, KS	89,717

Source: Woods & Poole Economics, Inc., Compusearch Market and Social Research Ltd., population estimates.

advantage of the recreation assets of all the towns around. We pay taxes or fees to water, sewer, park, and school districts that often cross city lines. And every so often we keep or throw out of office our local representative whose district seems to encompass everything in sight.

The perimeters of metro areas supersede the anachronistic political boundaries of incorporated areas and include not just the troubled and depressed older city cores but also the newer parts of suburbia with their sleek new malls, mirror-windowed office parks, low-rise factories, and choice neighborhoods.

Greater Newark, for example, includes affluent Morris County. Buffalo-Niagara Falls includes quaint and tony Lewiston. Cleveland embraces Shaker Heights, and Boston, with its 129 cities and towns, takes in a wealthy fringe of high-tech industries. In the Appendix at the end of this book, a "Metropolitan Place Finder" lists not only the cities after which metro areas are named but suburban and rural towns within the area's boundaries.

Metropolitan Complexes (MCs)

Metro areas stand on their own, but many are contiguous and blend together to form "metropolitan complexes." *Places Rated* identifies 177 metropolitan areas that can be grouped into 59 metropolitan complexes using three criteria: (1) they are parts of the same television market as defined by *The A. C. Nielsen Company* in the U.S. or the *Bureau of Broadcast Measurement* in Canada, (2) their daily newspapers, according to the *Standard Rate*

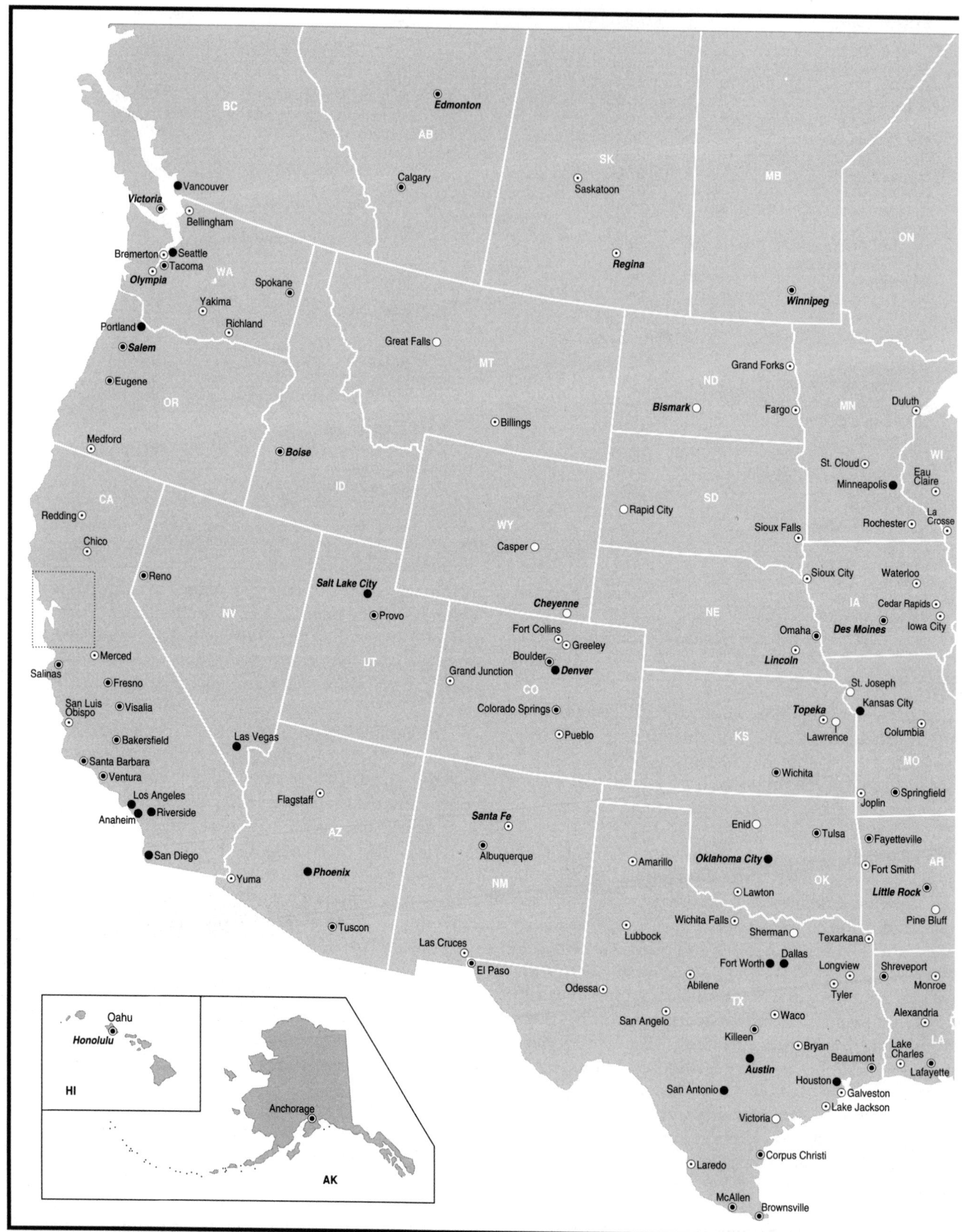
BC
AB
SK
MB
ON
Edmonton
Calgary
Saskatoon
Regina
Winnipeg
Vancouver
Victoria
Bellingham
Bremerton
Seattle
Tacoma
Olympia
WA
Spokane
Yakima
Richland
Portland
Salem
Eugene
OR
Medford
Great Falls
MT
Billings
ND
Bismark
Grand Forks
Fargo
MN
Duluth
Boise
ID
WY
Casper
SD
Rapid City
Sioux Falls
St. Cloud
Minneapolis
Eau Claire
WI
Rochester
La Crosse
CA
Redding
Chico
Reno
NV
Salt Lake City
Provo
UT
Cheyenne
Fort Collins
Greeley
Boulder
Denver
Grand Junction
CO
Colorado Springs
Pueblo
NE
Omaha
Lincoln
Sioux City
Waterloo
IA
Cedar Rapids
Des Moines
Iowa City
Merced
Salinas
Fresno
San Luis Obispo
Visalia
Bakersfield
Las Vegas
Santa Barbara
Ventura
Los Angeles
Anaheim
Riverside
San Diego
Flagstaff
AZ
Phoenix
Yuma
Tuscon
Santa Fe
Albuquerque
NM
Las Cruces
El Paso
KS
Topeka
Lawrence
Wichita
St. Joseph
Kansas City
Columbia
MO
Springfield
Joplin
Enid
Tulsa
Oklahoma City
OK
Lawton
Amarillo
Lubbock
Wichita Falls
Sherman
Fayetteville
Fort Smith
AR
Little Rock
Pine Bluff
Texarkana
Dallas
Fort Worth
Longview
Tyler
Shreveport
Monroe
Abilene
Odessa
San Angelo
TX
Waco
Killeen
Bryan
Austin
Beaumont
Houston
Galveston
Lake Jackson
San Antonio
Victoria
Corpus Christi
Laredo
McAllen
Brownsville
Alexandria
Lake Charles
Lafayette
LA
Oahu
Honolulu
HI
Anchorage
AK

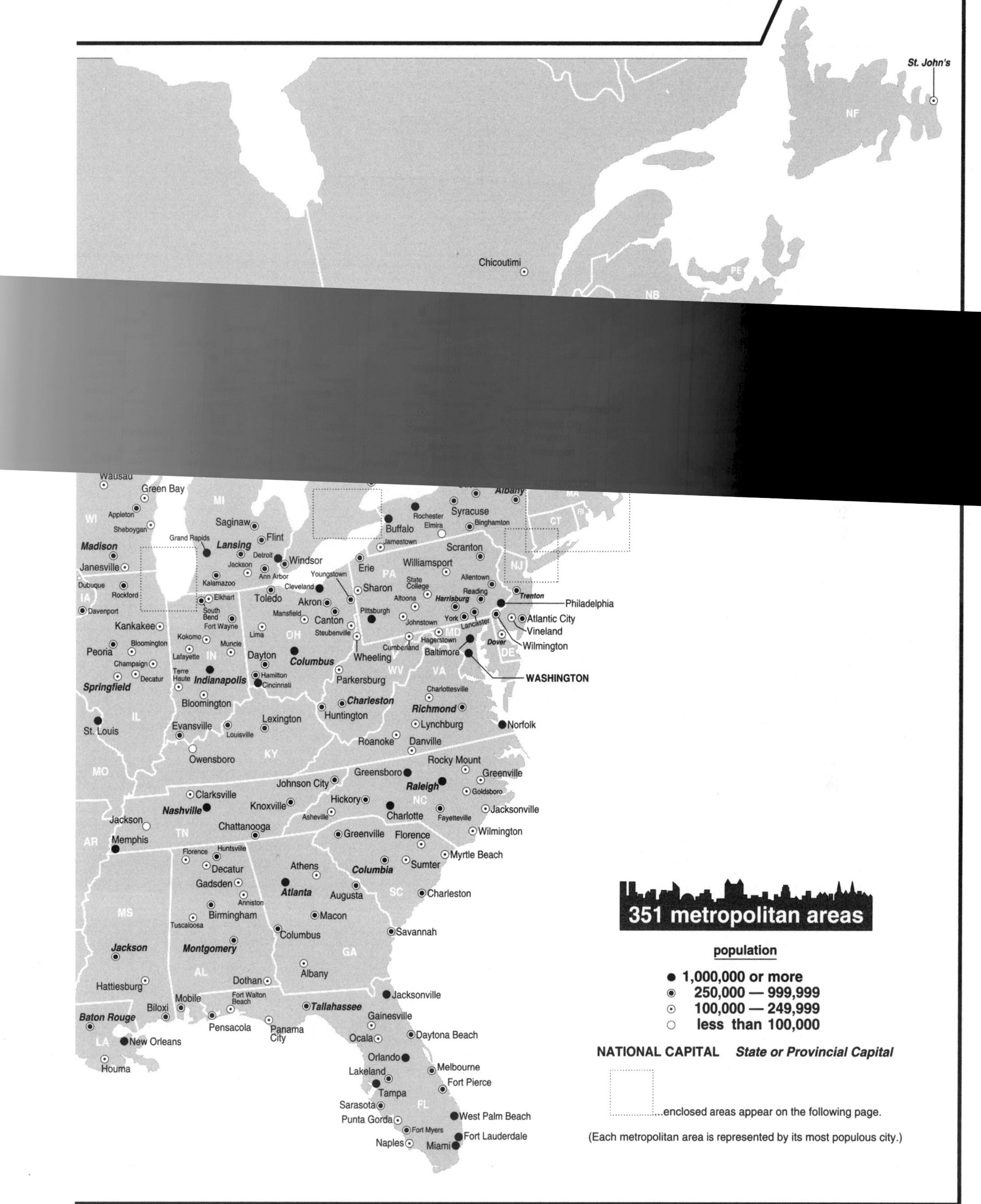
St. John's
NF
PE
NB
Chicoutimi
Wausau
Green Bay
MI
WI
Appleton
Sheboygan
Madison
Janesville
Dubuque
Rockford
IA
Davenport
Saginaw
Flint
Grand Rapids
Lansing
Detroit
Windsor
Jackson
Ann Arbor
Kalamazoo
Elkhart
South Bend
Fort Wayne
Kankakee
Peoria
Bloomington
Champaign
Decatur
Springfield
Kokomo
Muncie
Lafayette
IN
Terre Haute
Indianapolis
Bloomington
Toledo
Lima
Cleveland
Akron
Canton
Mansfield
Youngstown
Sharon
Steubenville
OH
Dayton
Columbus
Hamilton
Cincinnati
Albany
MA
CT
RI
Rochester
Syracuse
Buffalo
Elmira
Binghamton
Jamestown
Scranton
Erie
PA
Williamsport
State College
Allentown
Reading
Altoona
Harrisburg
Pittsburgh
Johnstown
York
Lancaster
NJ
Trenton
Philadelphia
Atlantic City
Vineland
Wilmington
Dover
DE
MD
Hagerstown
Cumberland
Baltimore
WASHINGTON
Wheeling
WV
Parkersburg
VA
Charlottesville
Charleston
Richmond
Huntington
Lynchburg
Norfolk
Roanoke
Danville
St. Louis
IL
Evansville
Louisville
Lexington
Owensboro
KY
MO
Greensboro
Rocky Mount
Greenville
Raleigh
Goldsboro
Johnson City
Clarksville
Nashville
Knoxville
Hickory
Asheville
Charlotte
NC
Fayetteville
Jacksonville
Wilmington
Jackson
TN
Chattanooga
AR
Memphis
Greenville
Florence
Myrtle Beach
Florence
Huntsville
Decatur
Gadsden
Anniston
Athens
Atlanta
Sumter
Columbia
Augusta
SC
Charleston
MS
Tuscaloosa
Birmingham
Macon
Columbus
Savannah
GA
Jackson
Montgomery
AL
Dothan
Albany
Hattiesburg
Jacksonville
Mobile
Fort Walton Beach
Tallahassee
Biloxi
Baton Rouge
Pensacola
Panama City
Gainesville
Daytona Beach
Ocala
LA
New Orleans
Houma
Orlando
Melbourne
Lakeland
Fort Pierce
Tampa
FL
Sarasota
Punta Gorda
West Palm Beach
Fort Myers
Fort Lauderdale
Naples
Miami
351 metropolitan areas
population
1,000,000 or more
250,000 — 999,999
100,000 — 249,999
less than 100,000
NATIONAL CAPITAL
State or Provincial Capital
...enclosed areas appear on the following page.
(Each metropolitan area is represented by its most populous city.)

Thomas Nast, Cartographer

extracted areas

(from preceding pages)

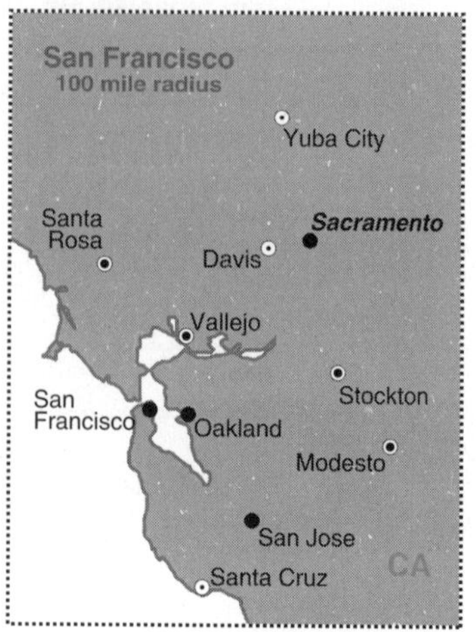

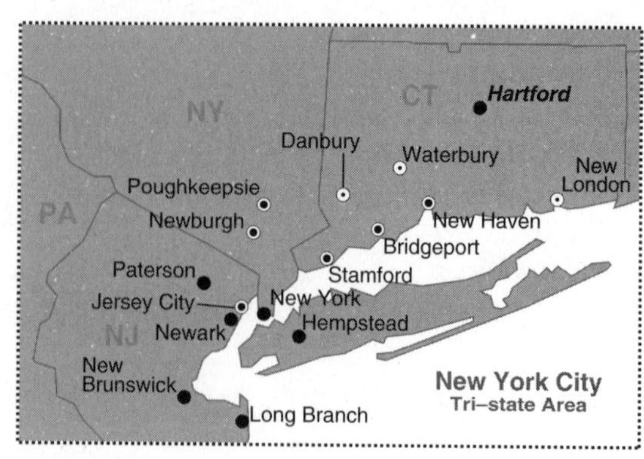

population

- ● 1,000,000 or more
- ◉ 250,000 — 999,999
- ⊙ 100,000 — 249,999
- ○ less than 100,000

(State or Provincial Capital)

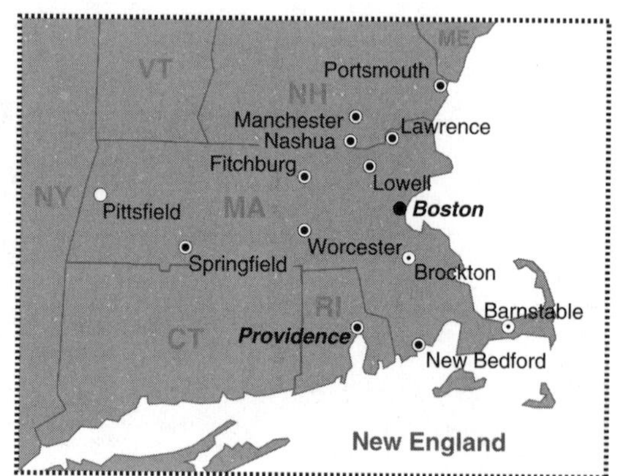

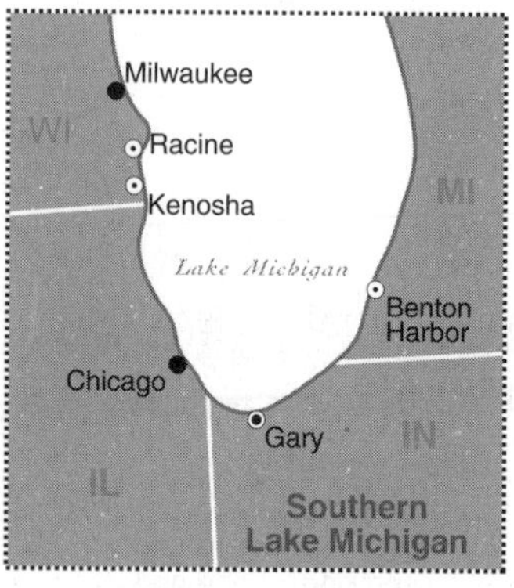

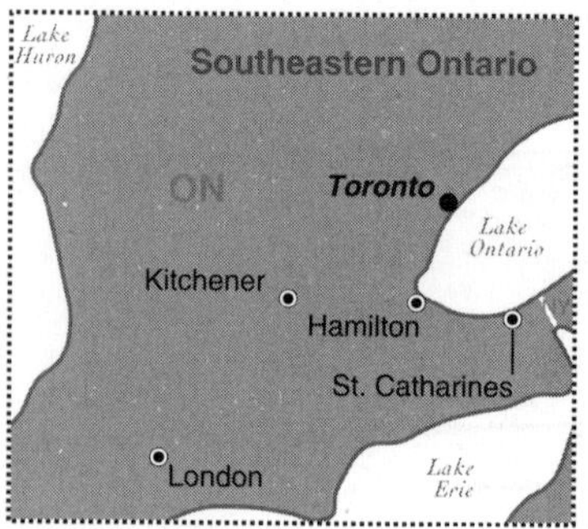

(Each metropolitan area is represented by its most populous city.)

Thomas Nast, Cartographer

and Data Service, significantly invade each other's turf, and (3) many of their workers commute from one to another.

Every weekday morning, for instance, some 40,000 persons in greater Ann Arbor back out of their driveways and drive to an I-94 East access ramp for the commute to their jobs in greater Detroit. Both metro areas are contiguous to one another. Both are part of the same Nielsen TV market, and about one in four households in Ann Arbor gets the *Detroit News.* Given these connections, it's natural that Ann Arbor shares in Detroit's big-city amenities.

It is no different with Waco and Killeen-Temple's connection in central Texas, or that of Albuquerque and Santa Fe in north-central New Mexico or Little Rock and Pine Bluff in Arkansas. The largest metropolitan complex—New York-Northern New Jersey-Long Island—embraces 15 separate areas with a total population of almost 20 million persons.

The list on the following pages shows the county definitions of the metropolitan areas in this edition of *Places Rated Almanac.* Areas that are part of metropolitan complexes are indicated with a • after their names. The chances are good that you live in one of the official metropolitan areas profiled here.

[illegible] Metropolitan Areas

[illegible]	[illegible]	[illegible]	[illegible]
[illegible]	[illegible]	[illegible]	[illegible]
Albany, [illegible] Dougherty and Lee counties	[illegible]	[illegible]	[illegible]
Albany–Schenectady–Troy, NY• Albany, Montgomery, Rensselaer, Saratoga, Schenectady and Schoharie counties	891,897	863,279	+ 3.3
Albuquerque, NM• Bernalillo, Sandoval and Valencia counties	704,607	615,289	+14.5
Alexandria, LA Rapides Parish	127,883	131,503	− 2.8
Allentown–Bethlehem–Easton, PA• Carbon, Lehigh and Northampton counties	618,112	596,545	+ 3.6
Altoona, PA• Blair County	131,804	130,598	+ 0.9
Amarillo, TX Potter and Randall counties	202,974	187,437	+ 8.3
Anchorage, AK Anchorage Borough	268,734	227,594	+18.1
Ann Arbor, MI• Lenawee, Livingston and Washtenaw counties	528,762	492,118	+ 7.4
Anniston, AL Calhoun County	119,012	116,114	+ 2.5
Appleton–Oshkosh–Neenah, WI• Calumet, Outagamie and Winnebago counties	346,912	316,014	+ 9.8
Asheville, NC Buncombe and Madison counties	209,331	192,480	+ 8.8
Athens, GA• Clarke, Madison and Oconee counties	138,373	126,810	+ 9.1
Atlanta, GA• Barrow, Bartow, Carroll, Cherokee, Clayton, Cobb, Coweta, DeKalb, Douglas,	3,530,445	2,977,677	+18.6
[illegible] Atlantic and Cape [illegible] counties	[illegible]	[illegible]	[illegible]
Augusta–Aiken, GA–SC Columbia, McDuffie and Richmond counties, GA; Aiken and Edgefield counties, SC	477,165	417,817	+14.2
Austin–San Marcos, TX Bastrop, Caldwell, Hays, Travis and Williamson counties	1,032,007	850,555	+21.3
Bakersfield, CA Kern County	633,245	549,317	+15.3
Baltimore, MD• Anne Arundel, Baltimore, Carroll, Harford, Howard, Queen Anne's counties and Baltimore city	2,534,042	2,389,292	+ 6.1
Bangor, ME 3 cities and 11 towns in Penobscot and Waldo counties	89,589	91,741	− 2.3
Barnstable–Yarmouth, MA• 10 towns in Barnstable County	147,927	135,413	+ 9.2
Baton Rouge, LA Ascension, East Baton Rouge, Livingston and West Baton Rouge parishes	577,101	529,305	+ 9.0
Beaumont–Port Arthur, TX Hardin, Jefferson and Orange counties	377,561	361,243	+ 4.5
Bellingham, WA• Whatcom County	154,297	129,002	+19.6
Benton Harbor, MI• Berrien County	162,548	161,355	+ 0.7
Bergen–Passaic, NJ• Bergen and Passaic counties	1,301,422	1,279,011	+ 1.8
Billings, MT Yellowstone County	124,639	113,513	+ 9.8

•Identifies a metro area that is part of a Metropolitan Complex.

Source: Woods & Poole Economics Inc. population estimates (U.S.) and Compusearch Social Research Ltd. population estimates (Canada).

Metro Areas and County Components	Population 1997	Population 1990	Percent Growth
Biloxi–Gulfport–Pascagoula, MS* Hancock, Harrison and Jackson counties	349,486	312,238	+11.9
Binghamton, NY Broome and Tioga counties	263,404	264,598	− 0.5
Birmingham, AL* Blount, Jefferson, St. Clair and Shelby counties	897,306	841,719	+ 6.6
Bismarck, ND Burleigh and Morton counties	89,778	83,907	+ 7.0
Bloomington, IN* Monroe County	118,729	109,300	+ 8.6
Bloomington–Normal, IL* McLean County	140,978	129,613	+ 8.8
Boise City, ID Ada and Canyon counties	369,803	298,126	+24.0
Boston, MA–NH* Suffolk County and 18 cities and 108 towns in Bristol, Essex, Middlesex, Norfolk, Plymouth and Worcester counties, MA, and Rockingham County, NH	3,246,676	3,227,098	+ 0.6
Boulder–Longmont, CO* Boulder County	258,772	226,079	+14.5
Brazoria, TX* Brazoria County	225,279	192,603	+17.0
Bremerton, WA* Kitsap County	227,171	192,008	+18.3
Bridgeport, CT* 5 cities and 10 towns in Fairfield and New Haven counties	442,156	443,732	− 0.4
Brockton, MA* 1 city and 13 towns in Bristol, Norfolk and Plymouth counties	240,298	236,624	+ 1.6
Brownsville–Harlingen–San Benito, TX* Cameron County	307,986	261,877	+17.6
Bryan–College Station, TX Brazos County	138,878	121,941	+13.9
Buffalo–Niagara Falls, NY* Erie and Niagara counties	1,196,896	1,190,202	+ 0.6
Burlington, VT 4 cities and 15 towns in Chittenden, Franklin and Grand Isle counties	161,160	151,969	+ 6.0
Calgary, AB 2 cities, 2 towns and 5 minor civil divisions	836,508	738,275	+13.3
Canton–Massillon, OH* Carroll and Stark counties	404,177	394,468	+ 2.5
Casper, WY Natrona County	64,624	61,210	+ 5.6
Cedar Rapids, IA* Linn County	181,308	169,164	+ 7.2
Champaign–Urbana, IL Champaign County	168,208	173,034	− 2.8
Charleston, WV* Kanawha and Putnam counties	256,445	250,355	+ 2.4
Charleston–North Charleston, SC Berkeley, Charleston and Dorchester counties	539,104	509,022	+ 5.9
Charlotte–Gastonia–Rock Hill, NC–SC* Cabarrus, Gaston, Lincoln, Mecklenburg, Rowan and Union counties, NC; York County, SC	1,330,347	1,168,549	+13.8
Charlottesville, VA Albemarle, Fluvanna, Greene counties, and Charlottesville city	145,438	131,985	+10.2
Chattanooga, TN–GA Hamilton and Marion counties, TN; Catoosa, Dade and Walker counties, GA	452,791	424,701	+ 6.6
Cheyenne, WY Laramie County	78,316	73,123	+ 7.1
Chicago, IL* Cook, DeKalb, DuPage, Grundy, Kane, Kendall, Lake, McHenry and Will counties	7,749,799	7,426,046	+ 4.4
Chico–Paradise, CA Butte County	198,206	183,519	+ 8.0
Chicoutimi–Jonquiere, PQ 4 *villes* and 6 minor civil divisions	161,965	160,575	+ 0.9
Cincinnati, OH–KY–IN* Brown, Clermont, Hamilton and Warren counties, OH; Boone, Campbell, Gallatin, Grant, Kenton and Pendleton counties, KY; Dearborn and Ohio counties, IN	1,624,828	1,529,283	+ 6.2
Clarksville–Hopkinsville, TN–KY* Montgomery County, TN; Christian County, KY	192,532	170,422	+13.0
Cleveland–Lorain–Elyria, OH* Ashtabula, Cuyahoga, Geauga, Lake, Lorain and Medina counties	2,249,179	2,203,539	+ 2.1
Colorado Springs, CO* El Paso County	468,642	397,314	+18.0
Columbia, MO Boone County	125,287	112,729	+11.1
Columbia, SC Lexington and Richland counties	518,782	456,093	+13.7
Columbus, GA–AL Chattahoochee, Harris and Muscogee counties, GA; Russell County, AL	278,609	261,292	+ 6.6
Columbus, OH Delaware, Fairfield, Franklin, Licking, Madison and Pickaway counties	1,490,732	1,350,398	+10.4
Corpus Christi, TX Nueces and San Patricio counties	381,900	350,555	+ 8.9
Cumberland, MD–WV Allegany County, MD; Mineral County, WV	100,031	101,566	− 1.5

*Identifies a metro area that is part of a Metropolitan Complex.

Source: Woods & Poole Economics Inc. population estimates (U.S.) and Compusearch Social Research Ltd. population estimates (Canada).

Metro Areas and County Components	Population 1997	Population 1990	Percent Growth
Dallas, TX• Collin, Dallas, Denton, Ellis, Henderson, Hunt, Kaufman and Rockwall counties	3,046,797	2,689,598	+13.3
Danbury, CT• 1 city and 11 towns in Fairfield and Litchfield counties	201,348	193,908	+ 3.8
Danville, VA Pittsylvania County and Danville city	110,428	108,972	+ 1.3
[illegible] Rock [illegible] [illegible]	[illegible]	351,027	+ 2.5
[illegible] Lawrence and [illegible] counties	[illegible]	[illegible]	[illegible]
Decatur, IL Macon County	116,146	[illegible]	[illegible]
Denver, CO• Adams, Arapahoe, Denver, Douglas and Jefferson counties	1,906,354	1,628,439	+17.1
Des Moines, IA Dallas, Polk and Warren counties	428,117	394,370	+ 8.6
Detroit, MI• Lapeer, Macomb, Monroe, Oakland, St. Clair and Wayne counties	4,355,241	4,269,631	+ 2.0
Dothan, AL Dale and Houston counties	141,820	131,192	+ 8.1
Dover, DE Kent County	124,024	111,649	+11.1
Dubuque, IA Dubuque County	88,642	86,416	+ 2.6
Duluth-Superior, MN-WI St. Louis County, MN; Douglas County, WI	242,027	240,219	+ 0.8
Dutchess County, NY• Dutchess County	263,249	259,989	+ 1.3
Eau Claire, WI Chippewa and Eau Claire counties	145,851	137,682	+ 5.9
Edmonton, AB 5 cities, 8 towns and 22 minor civil divisions	901,225	827,613	+ 8.9
El Paso, TX• El Paso County	701,103	596,262	+17.6
Elkhart-Goshen, IN• Elkhart County	169,574	156,366	+ 8.4
Elmira, NY Chemung County	94,976	95,294	− 0.3
Enid, OK Garfield County	56,788	56,642	+ 0.3
Erie, PA Erie County	281,747	275,804	+ 2.2
Eugene-Springfield, OR Lane County	306,136	284,061	+ 7.8
Evansville-Henderson, IN-KY Posey, Vanderburgh and Warrick counties, IN; Henderson County, KY	290,923	279,250	+ 4.2
Fargo-Moorhead, ND-MN Cass County, ND; Clay County, MN	165,869	153,684	+ 7.9
Fayetteville, NC Cumberland County	290,295	275,395	+ 5.4
Fayetteville-Springdale-Rogers, AR Benton and Washington counties	258,349	212,436	+21.6
[illegible]minster, MA• [illegible]	134,698	138,272	− 2.6
[illegible] counties	[illegible]	[illegible]	[illegible]
Florence, SC Florence County	[illegible]	[illegible]	[illegible]
Fort Collins-Loveland, CO• Larimer County	225,691	187,064	[illegible]
Fort Lauderdale, FL• Broward County	1,470,959	1,261,852	+16.6
Fort Myers-Cape Coral, FL• Lee County	403,453	338,301	+19.3
Fort Pierce-Port St. Lucie, FL• Martin and St. Lucie counties	296,860	254,332	+16.7
Fort Smith, AR-OK Crawford and Sebastian counties, AR; Sequoyah County, OK	195,803	176,132	+11.2
Fort Walton Beach, FL• Okaloosa County	170,026	144,480	+17.7
Fort Wayne, IN Adams, Allen, DeKalb, Huntington, Wells and Whitley counties	475,167	457,107	+ 4.0
Fort Worth-Arlington, TX• Hood, Johnson, Parker and Tarrant counties	1,587,369	1,367,751	+16.1
Fresno, CA• Fresno and Madera counties	867,858	760,895	+14.1
Gadsden, AL• Etowah County	101,651	99,793	+ 1.9
Gainesville, FL Alachua County	201,182	182,232	+10.4
Galveston-Texas City, TX• Galveston County	243,991	218,320	+11.8
Gary, IN• Lake and Porter counties	620,987	605,769	+ 2.5
Glens Falls, NY• Warren and Washington counties	123,561	118,969	+ 3.9
Goldsboro, NC• Wayne County	111,240	104,847	+ 6.1

•Identifies a metro area that is part of a Metropolitan Complex.

Source: Woods & Poole Economics Inc. population estimates (U.S.) and Compusearch Social Research Ltd. population estimates (Canada).

Metro Areas and County Components	Population 1997	Population 1990	Percent Growth
Grand Forks, ND–MN Grand Forks County, ND; Polk County, MN	104,254	103,091	+ 1.1
Grand Junction, CO Mesa County	104,989	93,763	+12.0
Grand Rapids–Muskegon–Holland, MI Allegan, Kent, Muskegon and Ottawa counties	1,022,945	941,765	+ 8.6
Great Falls, MT Cascade County	81,422	77,717	+ 4.8
Greeley, CO• Weld County	146,468	131,982	+11.0
Green Bay, WI• Brown County	217,700	195,304	+11.5
Greensboro–Winston-Salem–High Point, NC Alamance, Davidson, Davie, Forsyth, Guilford, Randolph, Stokes and Yadkin counties	1,150,522	1,053,596	+ 9.2
Greenville, NC Pitt County	125,253	108,932	+15.0
Greenville–Spartanburg–Anderson, SC Anderson, Cherokee, Greenville, Pickens and Spartanburg counties	916,632	833,571	+10.0
Hagerstown, MD• Washington County	132,670	121,857	+ 8.9
Halifax, NS 2 cities, 1 town, 2 minor civil divisions and 5 census subdivisions	347,635	315,621	+10.1
Hamilton, ON• 3 cities, 4 towns, and 1 minor civil division	640,645	591,783	+ 8.3
Hamilton–Middletown, OH• Butler County	329,902	292,980	+12.6
Harrisburg–Lebanon–Carlisle, PA• Cumberland, Dauphin, Lebanon and Perry counties	626,870	589,678	+ 6.3
Hartford, CT 4 cities and 55 towns in Hartford, Litchfield, Middlesex, New London, Tolland and Windham counties	1,148,011	1,158,217	− 0.9
Hattiesburg, MS Forrest and Lamar counties	106,816	98,804	+ 8.1
Hickory–Morganton–Lenoir, NC• Alexander, Burke, Caldwell and Catawba counties	318,226	293,183	+ 8.5
Honolulu, HI Honolulu County	878,033	838,198	+ 4.8
Houma, LA Lafourche and Terrebonne parishes	188,223	182,840	+ 2.9
Houston, TX• Chambers, Fort Bend, Harris, Liberty, Montgomery and Waller counties	3,853,138	3,342,330	+15.3
Huntington–Ashland, WV–KY–OH• Cabell and Wayne counties, WV; Boyd, Carter and Greenup counties, KY; Lawrence County, OH	318,106	312,447	+ 1.8
Huntsville, AL• Limestone and Madison counties	328,150	294,469	+11.4
Indianapolis, IN• Boone, Hamilton, Hancock, Hendricks, Johnson, Madison, Marion, Morgan and Shelby counties	1,512,641	1,385,415	+ 9.2
Iowa City, IA• Johnson County	103,495	96,426	+ 7.3
Jackson, MI Jackson County	153,891	150,119	+ 2.5
Jackson, MS Hinds, Madison and Rankin counties	425,282	396,311	+ 7.3
Jackson, TN Madison County	85,080	78,226	+ 8.8
Jacksonville, FL Clay, Duval, Nassau and St. Johns counties	1,003,309	912,713	+ 9.9
Jacksonville, NC Onslow County	148,851	149,858	− 0.7
Jamestown, NY• Chautauqua County	142,643	141,975	+ 0.5
Janesville–Beloit, WI• Rock County	147,113	139,856	+ 5.2
Jersey City, NJ• Hudson County	549,144	553,015	− 0.7
Johnson City–Kingsport–Bristol, TN–VA Carter, Hawkins, Sullivan, Unicoi and Washington counties, TN; Scott and Washington counties and Bristol city, VA	463,477	436,762	+ 6.1
Johnstown, PA• Cambria and Somerset counties	239,028	241,137	− 0.9
Joplin, MO Jasper and Newton counties	148,345	135,074	+ 9.8
Kalamazoo–Battle Creek, MI Calhoun, Kalamazoo and Van Buren counties	450,616	430,388	+ 4.7
Kankakee, IL• Kankakee County	101,946	96,526	+ 5.6
Kansas City, MO–KS• Cass, Clay, Clinton, Jackson, Lafayette, Platte and Ray counties, MO; Johnson, Leavenworth, Miami and Wyandotte counties, KS	1,679,353	1,587,093	+ 5.8
Kenosha, WI• Kenosha County	139,836	128,712	+ 8.6
Killeen–Temple, TX• Bell and Coryell counties	292,910	255,764	+14.5
Kitchener, ON• 3 cities and 2 minor civil divisions	404,419	347,474	+16.4

•Identifies a metro area that is part of a Metropolitan Complex.

Source: Woods & Poole Economics Inc. population estimates (U.S.) and Compusearch Social Research Ltd. population estimates (Canada).

Metro Areas and County Components	Population 1997	Population 1990	Percent Growth
Knoxville, TN Anderson, Blount, Knox, Loudon, Sevier and Union counties	654,391	587,812	+11.3
Kokomo, IN* Howard and Tipton counties	100,426	97,091	+ 3.4
La Crosse, WI–MN La Crosse County, WI; Houston County, MN	124,510	116,665	+ 6.7
[illegible], IN [illegible]	174,310	161,620	+ 7.9
[illegible]	[illegible]	[illegible]	[illegible]
Lancaster, PA Lancaster County	[illegible]	[illegible]	[illegible]
Lansing–East Lansing, MI Clinton, Eaton and Ingham counties	448,750	[illegible]	[illegible]
Laredo, TX Webb County	183,486	134,542	+36.4
Las Cruces, NM* Dona Ana County	169,787	136,505	+24.4
Las Vegas, NV–AZ Clark and Nye counties, NV; Mohave County, AZ	1,174,150	867,802	+35.3
Lawrence, KS* Douglas County	89,717	82,193	+ 9.2
Lawrence, MA–NH* 2 cities and 21 towns in Essex County, MA, and Rockingham County, NH	369,619	354,038	+ 4.4
Lawton, OK Comanche County	117,720	111,391	+ 5.7
Lewiston–Auburn, ME 2 cities and 7 towns in Androscoggin County	90,717	93,735	− 3.2
Lexington, KY Bourbon, Clark, Fayette, Jessamine, Madison, Scott and Woodford counties	444,776	407,431	+ 9.2
Lima, OH Allen and Auglaize counties	156,506	154,485	+ 1.3
Lincoln, NE Lancaster County	232,268	214,424	+ 8.3
Little Rock–North Little Rock, AR* Faulkner, Lonoke, Pulaski and Saline counties	558,536	514,023	+ 8.7
London, ON 2 cities, 1 town and 9 minor civil divisions	420,971	373,966	+12.6
Long Island, NY* Nassau and Suffolk counties	2,661,116	2,608,670	+ 2.0
Longview–Marshall, TX Gregg, Harrison and Upshur counties	205,603	193,942	+ 6.0
Los Angeles–Long Beach, CA* Los Angeles County	9,206,426	8,881,260	+ 3.7
Louisville, KY–IN Bullitt, Jefferson and Oldham counties, KY; Clark, Floyd, Harrison and Scott counties, IN	995,287	950,457	+ 4.7
Lowell, MA–NH* 1 city and 10 towns in Middlesex County, MA, and Hillsborough County, NH	287,130	281,071	+ 2.2
Lubbock, TX Lubbock County	233,425	222,823	+ 4.8
[illegible]	207,673	194,479	+ 6.8
[illegible]	[illegible]	[illegible]	[illegible]
[illegible] 1 city and [illegible] borough, Merrimack and Rockingham counties	[illegible]	[illegible]	[illegible]
Mansfield, OH Crawford and Richland counties	176,167	174,011	+ 1.2
McAllen–Edinburg–Mission, TX* Hidalgo County	501,087	386,901	+29.5
Medford–Ashland, OR Jackson County	170,310	147,308	+15.6
Melbourne–Titusville–Palm Bay, FL* Brevard County	457,019	403,141	+13.4
Memphis, TN–AR–MS Fayette, Shelby and Tipton counties, TN; Crittenden County, AR; DeSoto County, MS	1,089,919	1,009,923	+ 7.9
Merced, CA* Merced County	199,432	179,904	+10.9
Miami, FL* Dade County	2,060,197	1,943,471	+ 6.0
Middlesex–Somerset–Hunterdon, NJ* Hunterdon, Middlesex and Somerset counties	1,090,723	1,022,582	+ 6.7
Milwaukee–Waukesha, WI* Milwaukee, Ozaukee, Washington and Waukesha counties	1,466,324	1,434,444	+ 2.2
Minneapolis–St. Paul, MN–WI* Anoka, Carver, Chisago, Dakota, Hennepin, Isanti, Ramsey, Scott, Sherburne, Washington and Wright counties, MN; Pierce and St. Croix counties, WI	2,791,990	2,548,233	+ 9.6
Mobile, AL* Baldwin and Mobile counties	523,747	478,065	+ 9.6

*Identifies a metro area that is part of a Metropolitan Complex.

Source: Woods & Poole Economics Inc. population estimates (U.S.) and Compusearch Social Research Ltd. population estimates (Canada).

Metro Areas and County Components	Population 1997	Population 1990	Percent Growth
Modesto, CA• Stanislaus County	423,410	375,306	+12.8
Monmouth–Ocean, NJ• Monmouth and Ocean counties	1,058,880	988,666	+ 7.1
Monroe, LA Ouachita Parish	148,270	142,154	+ 4.3
Montgomery, AL Autauga, Elmore and Montgomery counties	319,940	293,149	+ 9.1
Montreal, PQ 2 cities, 76 *villes* and 27 minor civil divisions	3,332,939	3,088,159	+ 7.9
Muncie, IN• Delaware County	119,812	119,672	+ 0.1
Myrtle Beach, SC Horry County	172,399	144,892	+19.0
Naples, FL• Collier County	195,702	154,199	+26.9
Nashua, NH• 1 city and 12 towns in Hillsborough County	179,406	168,604	+ 6.4
Nashville, TN• Cheatham, Davidson, Dickson, Robertson, Rutherford, Sumner, Williamson and Wilson counties	1,131,587	988,708	+14.5
New Bedford, MA• 1 city and 7 towns in Bristol and Plymouth counties	170,561	175,580	− 2.9
New Haven–Meriden, CT• 3 cities and 14 towns in Middlesex and New Haven counties	519,184	530,245	− 2.1
New London–Norwich, CT–RI 3 cities and 19 towns in Middlesex, New London, Windham counties, CT, and Washington County, RI	282,103	290,881	− 3.0
New Orleans, LA• Jefferson, Orleans, Plaquemines, St. Bernard, St. Charles, St. James, St. John the Baptist and St. Tammany parishes	1,331,283	1,283,947	+ 3.7
New York, NY• Bronx, Kings, New York, Putnam, Queens, Richmond, Rockland and Westchester counties	8,592,030	8,546,511	+ 0.5
Newark, NJ• Essex, Morris, Sussex, Union and Warren counties	1,939,507	1,915,883	+ 1.2
Newburgh, NY–PA• Orange and Pike counties	361,213	337,436	+ 7.0
Norfolk–Virginia Beach–Newport News, VA–NC Gloucester, Isle of Wight, James City, Mathews and York counties, VA; Currituck County, NC; Chesapeake, Hampton, Newport News, Norfolk, Poquoson, Portsmouth, Suffolk, Virginia Beach and Williamsburg cities, VA	1,563,195	1,450,896	+ 7.7
Oakland, CA• Alameda and Contra Costa counties	2,281,934	2,087,720	+ 9.3
Ocala, FL Marion County	237,455	196,884	+20.6
Odessa–Midland, TX Ector and Midland counties	243,158	225,465	+ 7.8
Oklahoma City, OK Canadian, Cleveland, Logan, McClain, Oklahoma and Pottawatomie counties	1,022,002	959,862	+ 6.5
Olympia, WA• Thurston County	200,190	163,022	+22.8
Omaha, NE–IA• Pottawattamie, Cass, Douglas, Sarpy and Washington counties	675,404	641,359	+ 5.3
Orange County, CA• Orange County	2,688,925	2,417,740	+11.2
Orlando, FL• Lake, Orange, Osceola and Seminole counties	1,520,244	1,239,110	+22.7
Oshawa, ON• 1 city and 2 towns	279,830	232,777	+20.2
Ottawa–Hull, ON–PQ 5 cities, 5 *villes*, 1 town and 12 minor civil divisions	1,025,165	913,934	+12.2
Owensboro, KY Daviess County	92,005	87,264	+ 5.4
Panama City, FL Bay County	146,692	127,309	+15.2
Parkersburg–Marietta, WV–OH Wood County, WV; Washington County, OH	151,685	149,173	+ 1.7
Pensacola, FL• Escambia and Santa Rosa counties	388,263	345,464	+12.4
Peoria–Pekin, IL• Peoria, Tazewell and Woodford counties	346,673	339,809	+ 2.0
Philadelphia, PA–NJ• Bucks, Chester, Delaware, Montgomery and Philadelphia counties, PA; Burlington, Camden, Gloucester and Salem counties, NJ	5,025,289	4,925,579	+ 2.0
Phoenix–Mesa, AZ Maricopa and Pinal counties	2,637,129	2,245,539	+17.4
Pine Bluff, AR• Jefferson County	84,157	85,374	− 1.4
Pittsburgh, PA Allegheny, Beaver, Butler, Fayette, Washington and Westmoreland counties	2,411,452	2,395,146	+ 0.7
Pittsfield, MA 1 city and 9 towns in Berkshire County	84,916	88,682	− 4.2

•Identifies a metro area that is part of a Metropolitan Complex.

Source: Woods & Poole Economics Inc. population estimates (U.S.) and Compusearch Social Research Ltd. population estimates (Canada).

Metro Areas and County Components	Population 1997	Population 1990	Percent Growth
Portland, ME 3 cities and 17 towns in Cumberland and York counties	227,439	221,554	+ 2.7
Portland–Vancouver, OR–WA• Clackamas, Columbia, Multnomah, Washington and Yamhill counties, OR; Clark County, WA	1,756,943	1,526,542	+15.1
Portsmouth–Rochester, NH–ME• 4 cities and 27 towns in Rockingham and Strafford counties, NH, and York [illegible]	221,211	223,441	− 1.0
[illegible]	[illegible]	[illegible]	[illegible]
Pueblo, CO Pueblo County	[illegible]	[illegible]	[illegible]
Punta Gorda, FL Charlotte County	142,831	112,753	+26.7
Quebec City, PQ 20 *villes* and 25 minor civil divisions	687,758	637,480	+ 7.9
Racine, WI• Racine County	182,743	175,473	+ 4.1
Raleigh–Durham–Chapel Hill, NC• Chatham, Durham, Franklin, Johnston, Orange and Wake counties	1,055,334	864,160	+22.1
Rapid City, SD Pennington County	87,492	81,692	+ 7.1
Reading, PA• Berks County	351,499	337,454	+ 4.2
Redding, CA Shasta County	167,904	148,670	+12.9
Regina, SK 1 city, 4 towns and 12 minor civil divisions	199,386	190,529	+ 4.6
Reno, NV Washoe County	292,012	256,325	+13.9
Richland–Kennewick–Pasco, WA Benton and Franklin counties	178,018	151,213	+17.7
Richmond–Petersburg, VA Charles City, Chesterfield, Dinwiddie, Goochland, Hanover, Henrico, New Kent, Powhatan and Prince George counties; Colonial Heights, Hopewell, Petersburg and Richmond cities	953,050	869,667	+ 9.6
Riverside–San Bernardino, CA• Riverside and San Bernardino counties	3,080,701	2,630,454	+17.1
Roanoke, VA Botetourt and Roanoke counties; Roanoke and Salem cities	232,338	225,075	+ 3.2
Rochester, MN Olmsted County	116,665	106,960	+ 9.1
Rochester, NY Genesee, Livingston, Monroe, Ontario, Orleans and Wayne counties	1,100,554	1,064,699	+ 3.4
Rockford, IL Boone, Ogle and Winnebago counties	352,025	330,516	+ 6.5
Rocky Mount, NC• Edgecombe and Nash counties	144,386	133,709	+ 8.0
[illegible]	[illegible]	[illegible]	+13.3
St. Cloud, MN• Benton and Stearns counties	[illegible]	[illegible]	[illegible]
Saint John, NB 1 city, 3 towns and 17 minor civil divisions	129,992	124,185	+ 4.7
St. John's, NF 2 cities and 17 towns	184,068	169,797	+ 8.4
St. Joseph, MO• Andrew and Buchanan counties	97,565	97,773	− 0.2
St. Louis, MO–IL Crawford, Franklin, Jefferson, Lincoln, St. Charles, St. Louis and Warren counties, MO; St. Louis city, MO; Clinton, Jersey, Madison, Monroe and St. Clair counties, IL	2,585,491	2,496,110	+ 3.6
Salem, OR• Marion and Polk counties	318,004	279,566	+13.7
Salinas, CA Monterey County	372,851	357,191	+ 4.4
Salt Lake City–Ogden, UT• Davis, Salt Lake and Weber counties	1,258,039	1,076,638	+16.8
San Angelo, TX Tom Green County	102,060	98,272	+ 3.9
San Antonio, TX Bexar, Comal, Guadalupe and Wilson counties	1,504,333	1,327,540	+13.3
San Diego, CA San Diego County	2,797,473	2,513,362	+11.3
San Francisco, CA• Marin, San Francisco and San Mateo counties	1,664,916	1,603,269	+ 3.8
San Jose, CA• Santa Clara County	1,611,913	1,497,929	+ 7.6
San Luis Obispo–Atascadero–Paso Robles, CA San Luis Obispo County	237,608	218,112	+ 8.9

•Identifies a metro area that is part of a Metropolitan Complex.

Source: Woods & Poole Economics Inc. population estimates (U.S.) and Compusearch Social Research Ltd. population estimates (Canada).

Metro Areas and County Components	Population 1997	Population 1990	Percent Growth
Santa Barbara–Santa Maria–Lompoc, CA Santa Barbara County	390,082	370,348	+ 5.3
Santa Cruz–Watsonville, CA• Santa Cruz County	244,171	229,444	+ 6.4
Santa Fe, NM• Los Alamos and Santa Fe counties	139,435	117,627	+18.5
Santa Rosa, CA• Sonoma County	441,458	390,118	+13.2
Sarasota–Bradenton, FL• Manatee and Sarasota counties	557,040	492,522	+13.1
Saskatoon, SK 1 city, 9 towns and 11 minor civil divisions	222,821	207,974	+ 7.1
Savannah, GA Bryan, Chatham and Effingham counties	282,981	259,040	+ 9.2
Scranton–Wilkes-Barre–Hazleton, PA Columbia, Lackawanna, Luzerne and Wyoming counties	635,430	638,965	− 0.6
Seattle–Bellevue–Everett, WA• Island, King and Snohomish counties	2,273,003	2,047,988	+11.0
Sharon, PA• Mercer County	123,317	121,034	+ 1.9
Sheboygan, WI• Sheboygan County	107,827	104,091	+ 3.6
Sherbrooke, PQ 4 *villes* and 10 minor civil divisions	148,406	137,436	+ 8.0
Sherman–Denison, TX Grayson County	99,005	94,989	+ 4.2
Shreveport–Bossier City, LA Bossier, Caddo and Webster parishes	382,431	375,245	+ 1.9
Sioux City, IA–NE Woodbury County, IA; Dakota County, NE	120,882	115,271	+ 4.9
Sioux Falls, SD Lincoln and Minnehaha counties	154,564	139,789	+10.6
South Bend, IN• St. Joseph County	257,974	247,503	+ 4.2
Spokane, WA Spokane County	398,146	362,910	+ 9.7
Springfield, IL Menard and Sangamon counties	198,146	189,874	+ 4.4
Springfield, MA 5 cities and 24 towns in Franklin, Hampden and Hampshire counties	575,884	587,948	− 2.1
Springfield, MO Christian, Greene and Webster counties	306,029	265,345	+15.3
Stamford–Norwalk, CT• 2 cities and 6 towns in Fairfield County	332,721	330,063	+ 0.8
State College, PA Centre County	133,953	125,145	+ 7.0
Steubenville–Weirton, OH–WV• Jefferson County, OH; Brooke and Hancock counties, WV	138,714	142,277	− 2.5
Stockton–Lodi, CA• San Joaquin County	530,920	484,336	+ 9.6
Sudbury, ON 1 city, 5 towns and 1 minor civil division	165,418	156,018	+ 6.0
Sumter, SC Sumter County	109,135	101,469	+ 7.6
Syracuse, NY• Cayuga, Madison, Onondaga and Oswego counties	764,697	743,938	+ 2.8
Tacoma, WA• Pierce County	665,778	590,531	+12.7
Tallahassee, FL Gadsden and Leon counties	264,114	234,903	+12.4
Tampa–St. Petersburg–Clearwater, FL• Hernando, Hillsborough, Pasco and Pinellas counties	2,301,290	2,075,585	+10.9
Terre Haute, IN Clay, Vermillion and Vigo counties	151,052	147,573	+ 2.4
Texarkana, TX–Texarkana, AR Bowie County, TX; Miller County, AR	124,979	120,324	+ 3.9
Thunder Bay, ON 1 city and 7 minor civil divisions	124,927	124,116	+ 0.7
Toledo, OH Fulton, Lucas and Wood counties	615,583	614,387	+ 0.2
Topeka, KS• Shawnee County	167,809	161,324	+ 4.0
Toronto, ON• 8 cities, 16 towns and 4 minor civil divisions	4,377,587	3,802,322	+15.1
Trenton, NJ• Mercer County	331,971	326,161	+ 1.8
Trois-Rivieres, PQ 4 *villes* and 6 minor civil divisions	143,397	134,915	+ 6.3
Tucson, AZ Pima County	788,247	668,140	+18.0
Tulsa, OK Creek, Osage, Rogers, Tulsa and Wagoner counties	760,075	710,736	+ 6.9
Tuscaloosa, AL• Tuscaloosa County	162,783	151,017	+ 7.8
Tyler, TX Smith County	165,085	151,446	+ 9.0
Utica–Rome, NY• Herkimer and Oneida counties	317,174	316,911	+ 0.1
Vallejo–Fairfield–Napa, CA• Napa and Solano counties	503,528	454,702	+10.7
Vancouver, BC• 8 cities, 9 district municipalities and 21 minor civil divisions	1,812,165	1,560,271	+16.1

•Identifies a metro area that is part of a Metropolitan Complex.

Source: Woods & Poole Economics Inc. population estimates (U.S.) and Compusearch Social Research Ltd. population estimates (Canada).

Metro Areas and County Components	Population 1997	Population 1990	Percent Growth
Ventura, CA• Ventura County	744,211	670,347	+11.0
Victoria, BC 2 cities, 2 towns, 4 district municipalities and 11 minor civil divisions	316,939	281,849	+12.4
Victoria, TX Victoria County	82,888	74,567	+11.2
Vineland–Millville–Bridgeton, NJ• Cumberland County	140,423	138,212	+ 1.6
Visalia–Tulare–Porterville, CA• [illegible]	356,136	313,979	+13.4
[illegible]	[illegible]	[illegible]	[illegible]
[illegible] doun, Prince William, Spotsylvania, Stafford and Warren counties, VA; Alexandria, Fairfax, Falls Church, Fredericksburg, Manassas and Manassas Park cities, VA; Berkeley and Jefferson counties, WV	[illegible]	[illegible]	[illegible]
Waterbury, CT• 1 city and 9 towns in Litchfield and New Haven counties	220,789	222,011	− 0.6
Waterloo–Cedar Falls, IA Black Hawk County	125,164	123,934	+ 1.0
Wausau, WI Marathon County	123,584	115,714	+ 6.8
West Palm Beach–Boca Raton, FL• Palm Beach County	1,040,082	870,007	+19.5
Wheeling, WV–OH• Marshall and Ohio counties, WV; Belmont County, OH	156,550	158,952	− 1.5
Wichita, KS Butler, Harvey and Sedgwick counties	518,192	486,411	+ 6.5
Wichita Falls, TX Archer and Wichita counties	131,508	130,171	+ 1.0
Williamsport, PA Lycoming County	121,246	118,778	+ 2.1
Wilmington, NC Brunswick and New Hanover counties	208,280	172,231	+20.9
Wilmington–Newark, DE–MD• [illegible]	553,196	515,425	+ 7.3
[illegible]	[illegible]	[illegible]	[illegible]
[illegible] Hampden and Worcester counties, MA, and Windham County, CT	[illegible]	[illegible]	[illegible]
Yakima, WA Yakima County	209,349	189,369	+10.6
Yolo, CA• Yolo County	159,088	142,060	+12.0
York, PA• York County	368,952	340,751	+ 8.3
Youngstown–Warren, OH• Columbiana, Mahoning and Trumbull counties	609,607	601,296	+ 1.4
Yuba City, CA• Sutter and Yuba counties	138,945	123,517	+12.5
Yuma, AZ Yuma County	148,142	121,543	+21.9

•Identifies a metro area that is part of a Metropolitan Complex.

Source: Woods & Poole Economics Inc. population estimates (U.S.) and Compusearch Social Research Ltd. population estimates (Canada).

Decisions, Decisions

Some twenty-five years ago a group of futurists, academics, and government scientists got together at a hotel in northern Virginia for a conference sponsored by the U.S. Environmental Protection Agency. Their job was to discover just how to define "Quality of Life."

The players quickly split into three groups over the issue. One group thought that defining quality of life for all people at all times was impossible and shouldn't be tried at all. A second group disagreed, maintaining that livability *could* be quantified and defined—but *should not*—because measuring a touchy thing like quality of life makes places unwilling competitors of each other and often leads to wrong conclusions. The third group held that judging local livability can be done as long as you make clear what your statistical yardsticks are and go on to use them consistently.

Although the first and second positions may indeed be valid, *Places Rated Almanac* sides with the third.

Rating Places: One Way

This is a book of current statistics about North American metropolitan areas. Certainly it is a more objective source of information about urban livability than the hearsay opinions that people share at a dinner party, a rest stop on the Interstate, an airport bar, or news group on the Internet. Each of the 351 metro areas is rated by 9 factors that anyone thinking of moving would think were highly important.

- The **Costs of Living** chapter looks at household incomes and taxes, and it also measures the costs of such important items as housing, food, health care, and college tuition.
- **Transportation** is rated by local commuting time, public transit, and the diverse intercity travel options by air, rail, and interstate highway.
- The **Jobs** chapter weighs prospects for employment growth to the year 2000 in nine basic areas, including manufacturing, trade, services, finance, and government.
- Each metro area's collection of colleges and universities produces a **Higher Education** rating.
- **Climate** is rated on mildness; that is, how close temperatures remain to 65 degrees Fahrenheit throughout the year. Brightness and Stability also are part of the rating.
- A metro area's **Crime** rating is determined by the average annual number of violent and property crimes per 100,000 people over the past five years.
- The chapter on **The Arts** compares cultural assets, among them art museums and public libraries, opera and ballet companies and symphony orchestras.
- The supply of health-care facilities and practitioners, plus available special options, forms the basis for a metro area's **Health Care** rating.
- **Recreation** also rates assets, from good restaurants to public golf courses, zoos, professional

sports, ocean coastlines, and national parks acreage.

Some readers may fault *Places Rated*'s choice of criteria. Admittedly, its yardsticks for health care, public transportation, options for higher education, and performing arts amenities all favor bigger places over smaller ones. On the other hand, the methods for scoring safety from crime and high living costs favor smaller places over big ones. *Places Rated*'s standards for climate and outdoor recreation assets are certainly not everyone's. But they have nothing to do with population size.

Here are gathered the most up-to-date figures for [illegible] instances, the informa- [illegible] areas are [illegible] portraits. An economic rebound in many [illegible] metro areas continues to draw native sons and daughters back from the Sun Belt.

Likewise, the deepest slump in California in decades may be over and many of the thousands who emigrated to other, more promising areas may decide to return. With so much in life that is unpredictable, you'd be wise to supplement *Places Rated Almanac* with your own independent verification.

Rating Places: Your Way

At the end of this book, in "Putting It All Together," costs of living, climate, housing, crime, health care, transportation, education, the arts, recreation, and jobs get equal weight when identifying metro areas with across-the-board strengths.

You may not agree with this equal-weight system. You may give more importance to forecasted job growth than to a relative lack of crime or an outstanding calendar of performing arts events. For you, low living costs may be much more important than an ocean coastline, an abundance of medical specialists, or an active higher education scene. To identify which factors are more important and which factors are less, you may want to take stock of your preferences.

YOUR PREFERENCE INVENTORY

[illegible] 72 pairs of [illegible] statements aren't [illegible] wrong answers, only those that are best for you. Although the inventory takes about 15 minutes to finish, there is no time limit. Before you start, you might want to photocopy the inventory and ask your spouse or a friend to take it independently. Comparing your preference inventory with another person's can be an interesting exercise.

Directions

For each numbered item, decide which of two statements is more important to you when choosing a place to live. Mark the box next to that statement. Be sure to make a choice for all items.

1. E. ☐ The number of days over 90 degrees,

   or

   A. ☐ Average residential property taxes.

2. F. ☐ The number of murders,

   or

   D. ☐ Variety of public school districts.

3. H. ☐ The number of medical specialists,

   or

   B. ☐ Quality of public transportation.

4. G. ☐ New books added by local libraries,

   or

   E. ☐ Elevation, wind speed, and humidity.

5. A. ☐ The cost of food and clothing,

   or

   B. ☐ How long it takes to commute to work.

6. G. ☐ Libraries and art museums,

   or

   I. ☐ Local college sports.

7. H. ☐ Air quality throughout the year,

   or

   E. ☐ Risk of earthquakes and tornadoes.

8. A. ☐ The typical sales price of homes,

   or

   F. ☐ Local property crime rates.

9\. C. ☐ Forecasted job growth,
or
D. ☐ The pupil/teacher ratio in public schools.

10\. G. ☐ Museums and professional theaters,
or
F. ☐ The number of auto thefts in a year.

11\. I. ☐ The number of public golf courses,
or
B. ☐ Freeway traffic congestion.

12\. H. ☐ Local emergency medical care,
or
G. ☐ Fine-arts radio and TV broadcasting.

13\. G. ☐ Libraries and museums,
or
A. ☐ The cost of living.

14\. A. ☐ The cost of food and clothing,
or
C. ☐ The outlook for employment growth.

15\. H. ☐ Family medical services,
or
D. ☐ The size of public school districts.

16\. G. ☐ Fine-arts radio and TV broadcasting,
or
C. ☐ Job opportunities in the service sector.

17\. C. ☐ Local threat of unemployment,
or
E. ☐ Annual number of clear and cloudy days.

18\. I. ☐ Movie theaters and good restaurants,
or
D. ☐ Variety of public and private colleges.

19\. B. ☐ The supply of public transit,
or
A. ☐ Median prices of homes.

20\. A. ☐ State income tax and sales tax bite,
or
H. ☐ Medical schools and teaching hospitals.

21\. A. ☐ The cost of health care,
or
I. ☐ Access to public golf courses.

22\. G. ☐ Fine-arts radio and TV broadcasting,
or
B. ☐ Airline service and interstate highways.

23\. H. ☐ Supply of family medical practitioners,
or
I. ☐ Good restaurants and movie theaters.

24\. F. ☐ The violent crime rate,
or
E. ☐ Annual amounts of rain and snow.

25\. D. ☐ Pupil/teacher ratio in public schools,
or
E. ☐ Annual number of clear and cloudy days.

26\. I. ☐ Local professional sports teams,
or
F. ☐ Number of robberies and assaults.

27\. H. ☐ Hospitals affiliated with medical schools,
or
F. ☐ Number of burglaries during the year.

28\. D. ☐ Local support of public schools,
or
G. ☐ Dance companies and professional theaters.

29\. I. ☐ Nearby water recreation,
or
C. ☐ New manufacturing jobs by 2000.

30\. I. ☐ Nearby national parks and forests,
or
E. ☐ Number of stormy days during the year.

31\. C. ☐ The mix of white- and blue-collar jobs,
or
F. ☐ Number of robberies in a year.

32\. B. ☐ Airlines serving the local airport,
or
F. ☐ Number of auto thefts in a year.

33\. B. ☐ Buses, subways, and commuter railroads,
or
D. ☐ Local colleges and universities.

34\. A. ☐ State income and sales tax bite,
or
H. ☐ General hospitals and family doctors.

35\. D. ☐ Dollars/student in public schools,
or
A. ☐ Cost of utilities and property taxes.

36\. B. ☐ Interstate highways and airline service,
or
E. ☐ How cold the winters are.

37. H. ☐ Supply of medical specialists,

or

E. ☐ Number of annual rainy and snowy days.

38. F. ☐ Local auto thefts and burglaries,

or

A. ☐ Local household income and taxes.

39. G. ☐ Fine-arts radio and TV broadcasting,

or

B. ☐ Average daily commuting time.

42. E. ☐ Seasonal temperature variation,

or

A. ☐ Typical property taxes.

43. H. ☐ Medical schools and teaching hospitals,

or

G. ☐ Operas and symphony orchestras.

44. I. ☐ Opportunities for pari-mutuel betting,

or

B. ☐ Freeway traffic congestion.

45. C. ☐ Mix of white- and blue-collar jobs,

or

D. ☐ Alternatives to public schools.

46. E. ☐ Seasonal temperature variation,

or

C. ☐ Forecasted growth of employment.

47. F. ☐ Auto thefts, muggings, and shootings,

or

E. ☐ Annual number of freezing days.

48. A. ☐ Cost of heating a home,

or

D. ☐ Variety of private K-12 schools.

49. C. ☐ Expected white-collar job growth,

or

F. ☐ Annual property crime rate.

50. C. ☐ The number of new jobs created by 2000,

or

A. ☐ Annual state income and sales tax bite.

51. G. ☐ Classical music broadcasting,

or

B. ☐ Freeway traffic congestion.

52. H. ☐ Primary medical care,

or

I. ☐ Nearby state parks and forests.

53. D. ☐ Variety of private K-12 schools,

or

E. ☐ Local wind speed and humidity.

56. I. ☐ Golf, bowling, movies, and eating out,

or

D. ☐ Variety of public and private colleges.

57. G. ☐ The number of books in public libraries,

or

C. ☐ The threat of unemployment.

58. I. ☐ Professional sports home teams,

or

E. ☐ Annual amounts of rain and snow.

59. G. ☐ Operas and symphonies,

or

E. ☐ How cold the winters are.

60. A. ☐ Median price of homes,

or

G. ☐ Local performing arts bookings.

61. F. ☐ The violent crime rate,

or

G. ☐ Variety of performing arts.

62. F. ☐ Burglaries and auto thefts,

or

H. ☐ Specialized medical care.

63. C. ☐ Job outlook from now to the year 2000,

or

B. ☐ Freeway traffic congestion.

64. F. ☐ The property crime rate,

or

I. ☐ Nearby national parks and forests.

65. H. ☐ Supply of medical specialists,

or

C. ☐ Forecast for white-collar job growth.

66. D. ☐ Higher education opportunities,

or

G. ☐ Number of public libraries.

67. B. ☐ Access to interstate highways,

or

D. ☐ Private alternatives to public schools.

68. I. ☐ Movie theaters and good restaurants,

or

A. ☐ The cost of food and clothing.

69. H. ☐ The number of doctors in family practice,

or

D. ☐ Choice of public school districts.

70. B. ☐ Airlines serving the area,

or

F. ☐ Burglaries and auto thefts there.

71. H. ☐ Quality of doctors and hospitals,

or

B. ☐ Quality of public transit.

72. H. ☐ Local medical specialists who see patients,

or

C. ☐ Prospects for white-collar job growth.

Plotting Your Preference Profile

It is important that you make a choice for each of the 72 items. Have you left any unchecked? If not, you're ready to draw your Preference Profile.

First Step. Count all the marks you've made in the boxes next to the letter A. Enter the number of "A" statements on the line next to the words "Costs of Living" on your Preference Profile. Then count the statements for each of the other letters. Enter their totals in their respective places of your Preference Profile.

Second Step. Now plot your totals on the blank chart. Place a dot on the appropriate line for each of the numbers and connect the dots to form a line graph of your results (see the Sample Preference Profile below).

Analyzing Your Preference Profile

Each of the factors in your Preference Profile—the costs of living, transportation, job outlook, higher education, climate, crime, the arts, health care, and recreation—is not only a big concern when choosing a place to live; it also has a complete chapter in this book. The purpose of the Preference Inventory is to help you decide the relative importance of each of these nine factors to you personally.

If your scores are high for one or two of these factors, you may want to give extra attention to the chapters devoted to them. Likewise, if your scores are low for any of the nine factors, you may not need to give as much consideration to them as you would to those with high scores. Bear in mind that the inventory orders your preferences in a hierarchy, that each of the factors has some importance to you, and that none should be completely ignored.

SAMPLE PREFERENCE PROFILE

A Costs of Living 11 D Higher Education 10 G The Arts 12
B Transportation 6 E Climate 6 H Health Care 5
C Jobs 8 F Crime 4 I Recreation 10

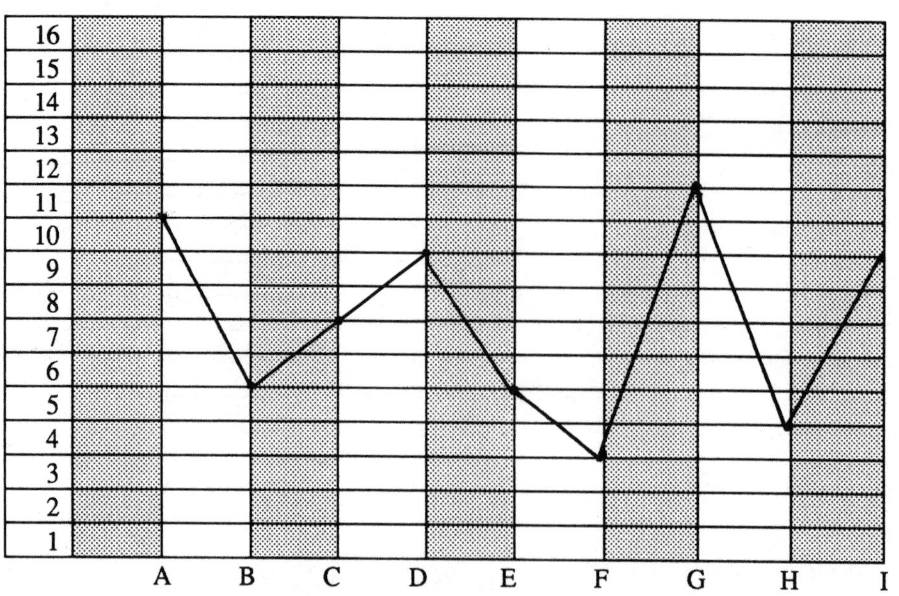

YOUR PREFERENCE PROFILE

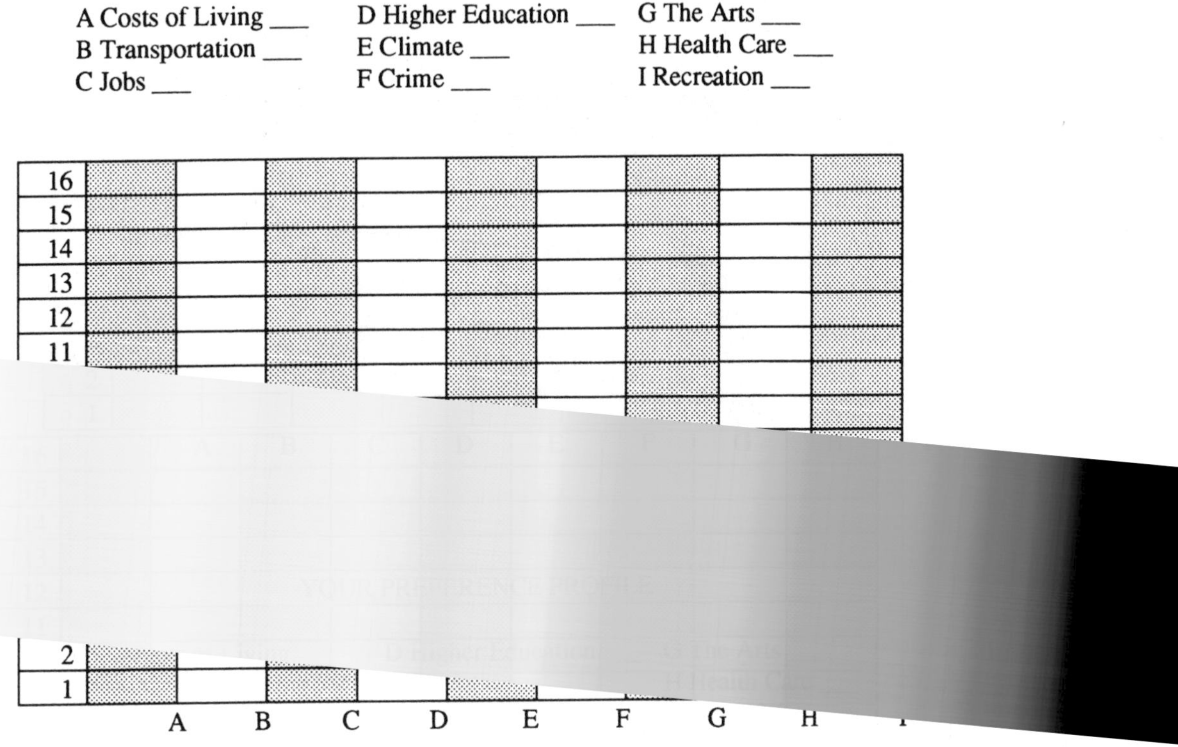

A Costs of Living ___
B Transportation ___
C Jobs ___
D Higher Education ___
E Climate ___
F Crime ___
G The Arts ___
H Health Care ___
I Recreation ___

	A	B	C	D	E	F	G	H	I
16									
15									
14									
13									
12									
11									
10									
9									
8									
7									
6									
5									
4									
3									
2									
1									

YOUR PREFERENCE PROFILE

A Costs of Living ___
B Transportation ___
C Jobs ___
D Higher Education ___
E Climate ___
F Crime ___
G The Arts ___
H Health Care ___
I Recreation ___

	A	B	C	D	E	F	G	H	I
16									
15									
14									
13									
12									
11									
10									
9									
8									
7									
6									
5									
4									
3									
2									
1									

COSTS OF LIVING

In the view of economists, we're all living resources looking for our highest valued use. We switch jobs readily if the money is right. If the prospects are promising, we'll even change careers. And we may risk these changes even if it means packing up and moving far away.

We also flee living costs that have gotten so high we can't afford them. Metro areas attract people because of expanding job opportunities, sure. But they also draw new people because cost-of-living factors like taxes and housing look like bargains.

This is nothing new. For centuries, Americans have moved from rich places where the benefits of good incomes are made empty by high costs of living to places where cheap land and no taxes more than make up for the drawback of paltry incomes.

"Money's no problem," an accountant will tell you. "Lack of money . . . now *that's* a problem." As is the case for most people, your own short-term economic worries may center on the price of hamburger, jeans, gasoline, or haircuts. Over the long run, your concerns may center around tax bites and boosting your household's income at least to the level where it can provide basic day-to-day necessities.

SCRAPING BY ON $58,900 A YEAR

Do average household incomes reflect local living costs? For the most part, they do. According to economists at the Labor Department, two-thirds of the variation in personal incomes between Cincinnati and San Francisco, for example, relates to their different costs of living. The other third reflects their different employers, worker skills, and prevailing wages.

Households aren't always families. One in four are composed either of one person or of several people unrelated to each other (including millions of POSSLQs—Persons of Opposite Sex Sharing Living Quarters). There are 14 million single-parent households with at least one child present, two million of them headed by men. The rest comprise married couples, some with children, some childless, and some whose children have scattered from the nest.

The average household income among 351 metro areas is $58,900 a year according to estimates by the Washington, DC–based firm of Woods & Poole Economics, Inc., and *Places Rated*. These incomes range from $100,000 in suburban Long Island, NY, to less than $43,000 in the poorer parts of south Texas and the Rio Grande valley.

COSTS OF LIVING: NINE FACTORS

"It's a black hole," the *Wall Street Journal* commented on what is meant by costs of living. So what if the Consumer Price Index has gone up ninefold since World War II; what does all that have to do with the high price of getting by in San Francisco as opposed to Peoria?

Several years ago, a special committee appointed by the Department of Labor to look into better ways to

Metro Area Household Incomes

The money coming into households isn't all from wages and salaries. It also includes interest from savings, dividends from stock holdings, government transfer payments, rents, and a multitude of other sources. If these typical incomes seem high, bear in mind that typical households now have two employed persons in them.

Highest	
Long Island, NY	$100,200
Bergen–Passaic, NJ	$96,500
San Francisco, CA	93,300
Trenton, NJ	93,300
Somerset–Hunterdon, NJ	92,300
[illegible]	91,500
Las Cruces, NM	[illegible]
Goldsboro, NC	[illegible]
Lawrence, KS	45,800
Jacksonville, NC	45,900
Hattiesburg, MS	46,000
Flagstaff, AZ–UT	46,100
Sumter, SC	46,700
Cumberland, MD–WV	46,900
Anniston, AL	47,000
Brownsville–Harlingen–San Benito, TX	47,000

Source: Woods & Poole Economics, Inc. Figures are rounded to nearest hundred dollars.

measure cost-of-living variations among places threw in the towel. Given the infinite range of consumer tastes and household tactics for saving a dollar, the only way to pin down why life in one place was more expensive than in another was to focus on the weather's effect on clothing costs and household utility bills, then look at taxes.

Taxes certainly do make a difference. But clothing and home energy bills? Not that much. According to one national retailer, the price difference between cotton and synthetic Sun Belt wardrobes and woolen and down-filled Frost Belt clothing amounts to about one percent of a household's budget. As for the comparative costs of keeping warm in Duluth and staying cool in Dallas, often the only difference is the season during which local residents pay most of their bill.

One firm that counsels transferred employees adopts an 80/20 rule. In its experience, 80 percent of the difference in living costs between where you've come from and where you're going comes down to two things: homeownership (mortgage, insurance, and utilities) and taxes. The other 20 percent comes from prices for everything from a splint for a broken thumb to frozen orange juice, soap flakes, and a shampoo, trim, and blow-dry at a salon.

Taxes—$4,064

In a calendar year, mid-May marks the mythical Tax Freedom point on which we stop handing over all of our earnings to federal, state, and local tax collectors and start pocketing that money for ourselves. Looking at it another way, we spend 2 hours and 47 minutes of every 8-hour working day earning enough money to pay taxes, according to the District of Columbia–based Tax Foundation.

No matter where you live, Social Security taxes hit you with the same impact. So can federal personal income taxes. But state and local taxes vary tremendously. To determine the relative tax bite among metro areas, *Places Rated* focuses on three common levies: state personal income taxes, state and local sales taxes, and

[illegible] employment.

Among 351 metro areas, [illegible] percent, or $1,965, of a four-person household's budget. Canadian provincial income taxes take the biggest bites in North America. In the United States, income taxes are highest in the District of Columbia, Hawaii, Maryland, New York, Oregon, and Wisconsin. In seven states—Alaska, Florida, Nevada, South Dakota, Texas, Washington, and Wyoming—there is no tax on earnings at all.

What these latter pass up on April 15, however, they collect with a vengeance every time a purchase is made at the store. Without an income tax, there is an overdependence on **sales taxes**—especially in Florida, Texas, and Washington—to make up the difference. Around the continent, this levy averages a shade less than 1 percent of the household's budget. As with income taxes, the sales tax bite is greatest throughout Canada.

Property taxes take 2.51 percent, or $1,510, of the household's budget. Critics during the late 1970s likened them to a ransom homeowners paid to keep the house off the tax assessor's auction block. Using this analogy, homeowners in parts of Long Island, NY, buy their homes back every 20 years, since the effective tax rate (a tax on the home's full value) approaches 5 percent. Down in Mobile County, AL, on the other hand, the ransom period is 222 years because of an extremely low effective rate of 0.45 percent.

Property taxes can vary enormously and can be madly confusing to homeowners. In California, two houses on the same block with identical prices and physical characteristics can have substantially different, yet legally impeccable, tax bills if one of them was sold before the approval of Proposition 13 and the other after. In Texas, a home's value can be assessed at different levels at different times of the year by different assessors.

Expensive Housing

For all the price decline since the real estate market peaked on the Pacific coast in 1990 and in the Northeast in the late 1980s, average resale prices still top $200,000 in these twelve markets.

Metro Area	Average Home Price	Property Taxes
Honolulu, HI	$332,000	$1,575
San Francisco, CA	256,800	1,975
San Jose, CA	251,500	2,200
Santa Cruz–Watsonville, CA	235,000	2,050
Stamford–Norwalk, CT	223,500	4,175
Orange County, CA	215,500	2,040
Vancouver, BC	215,500	1,600
Bergen–Passaic, NJ	215,000	4,250
Salinas, CA	213,500	1,785
Victoria, BC	210,000	2,200
Long Island, NY	210,000	4,250
Ventura, CA	210,000	2,010

Cheap Housing

It's hard to imagine some areas of the country experiencing the 350 percent home price inflation that other markets saw in the decades between 1970 and 1990. Here are twelve where typical resale prices might seem like bargains.

Metro Area	Average Home Price	Property Taxes
Steubenville–Weirton, OH–WV	$58,000	$ 875
Johnstown, PA	58,500	1,285
Texarkana, TX–Texarkana, AR	58,500	965
Duluth–Superior, MN–WI	59,500	895
Pine Bluff, AR	59,500	865
Wheeling, WV–OH	59,500	465
Waterloo–Cedar Falls, IA	61,500	775
Enid, OK	62,500	615
Huntington–Ashland, WV–KY–OH	63,500	425
Janesville–Beloit, WI	64,500	1,350
Danville, VA	65,000	965
Fort Smith, AR–OK	65,500	850

Source: Data Quick, Inc., National Association of Realtors, Royal LePage Real Estate Services. Figures are rounded to nearest five hundred dollars.

Home Mortgage—$12,061

Paying off a mortgage is the biggest single item in the household's budget. Based on average metro area home prices, mortgage payments claim 20.10 percent of the budget. Small wonder most newcomers start out renting. While it contributes nothing to net worth, renting permits a household to avoid much of cost-of-living differences among areas. This style of housing tenure also offers greater flexibility.

Utilities—$4,262

Covering everything from water and telephone to piped-in natural gas and electricity, utilities take about 7.10 percent of a four-person household's expenses in metro areas. Utility bills around the continent vary widely for several reasons. Customer density, distance from oil and coal fuel sources, age of the power plant, and the type and size of equipment used in generating electricity all play a part in the charges to consumers.

Food—$9,459

Groceries and dining out claim another 15.77 percent. The costs for food at home don't vary widely in the United States except in New York where not a leaf of cabbage reaches the supermarket except by truck, or in Anchorage and Honolulu where a great many packaged goods arrive by container ship. While prices for prepared foods don't vary enough to hit budgets with differing effect, prices for fresh fruits, vegetables, and dairy products do.

Transportation—$10,172

After mortgage payments, transportation is the largest item on the budget since the typical household has two cars. This item claims 16.95 percent and covers everything from new cars to tires and gasoline, from auto body work to the fare you'd pay if you took the bus. Since there is a national market for cars, meaning you can buy one anywhere for a similar price, the cost of purchasing one doesn't vary much by location. What does vary are taxes, insurance, title and registration fees, and gasoline excise taxes.

Health Care—$4,417

At 7.36 percent, health care's importance on a household budget is on par with home heating and lighting, water, and telephone. It covers everything from an over-the-counter cold remedy to a semiprivate hospital room. To measure part of the cost in each metro area, *Places Rated* looks at the amounts five doctors charge their patients for specific services:

- Family practitioner—office outpatient visit
- Internist—routine EKG with interpretation and report
- Psychiatrist—individual psychotherapy, 75–80 minutes
- Surgeon—arthroscopically aided treatment of tibial fracture
- Ophthalmologist—exam for glaucoma

While Canadian households do not budget for physician treatment or a hospital stay, they do pay for dental care and for some drugs. Indeed, about three out of every ten health-care dollars spent in that country come out of consumers' pockets.

Other—$3,283

Places Rated uses this blanket term to cover college tuition and recreation, which can take in everything from a health club membership, weekday play at an 18-hole public golf course, overnight camping at a state park, and movie tickets. It claims 5.47 percent of the household's budget.

CAVEATS

It is impossible to put a dollar figure on every single item in a typical four-person household's budget. *Places*

Rated makes a reasonable attempt to price nine major budget categories. Together, these account for 80 percent of the total.

Let's admit here that pricing living costs for all people for all the time can't be done with accuracy. The number of unique items that fill a market basket trundled by a household over a year is close to one thousand. Some of us trade at Wal-mart, others at convenience stores, some by mail order and others at Price Club, BJs Wholesale, and Burlington Coat Factory. Still others of us rent our housing rather than buy it, or can do without not just two cars, but any car period.

anywhere you

To help you answer that question,

at nine factors that, aside from savings and investments, account for most of a typical four-person household's budget: (1) state income taxes, (2) state and local sales taxes, (3) property taxes, (4) home mortgage, (5) utilities, (6) food, (7) health care, (8) transportation, and (9) other.

importance in a

penses. The home mortgage index,

weighted at 20.10 percent, the health care index at 7.04 percent, the food index at 15.76 percent, the transportation index at 16.95 percent.

RANKINGS: Costs of Living

To rank metro areas for costs of living, nine factors are weighted according to their relative importance in a typical four-person household's budget: (1) state income taxes, (2) state and local sales taxes, (3) property taxes, (4) home mortgage, (5) utilities, (6) food, (7) health care, (8) transportation, and (9) other. The sum of these weighted indexes is then normalized such that the 50th percentile is the average for all metro areas. Lower scores indicate more expensive metro areas. Higher scores indicate less expensive metro areas. Places with tie scores get the same rank and are listed in alphabetical order.

Metro Areas from Least to Most Expensive

Places Rated Rank		Places Rated Score
1.	Texarkana, TX–Texarkana, AR	99.30
2.	Casper, WY	99.17
3.	Enid, OK	99.06
4.	Wichita Falls, TX	97.86
5.	Fort Smith, AR–OK	97.49
6.	Bryan–College Station, TX	97.09
7.	Alexandria, LA	97.01
8.	Victoria, TX	96.98
9.	Pine Bluff, AR	96.84
10.	McAllen–Edinburg–Mission, TX	96.77
10.	Sherman–Denison, TX	96.77
12.	Anniston, AL	96.29
12.	San Angelo, TX	96.29
14.	Killeen–Temple, TX	96.28
15.	Clarksville–Hopkinsville, TN–KY	95.52
16.	Danville, VA	95.46
17.	Lawton, OK	95.28
18.	Steubenville–Weirton, OH–WV	95.16
19.	Houma, LA	94.71
19.	Monroe, LA	94.71
21.	Waterloo–Cedar Falls, IA	94.63
22.	Wheeling, WV–OH	94.62
23.	Gadsden, AL	94.29
24.	Waco, TX	94.10
25.	Beaumont–Port Arthur, TX	93.85
26.	Abilene, TX	93.46
27.	Huntington–Ashland, WV–KY–OH	93.25
28.	Lake Charles, LA	93.18
29.	Amarillo, TX	93.14
30.	Tyler, TX	93.04
31.	Lubbock, TX	92.61
32.	Laredo, TX	92.00
33.	Grand Forks, ND–MN	91.96

Places Rated Rank		Places Rated Score
34.	Florence, SC	91.77
35.	Longview–Marshall, TX	91.19
36.	Joplin, MO	91.03
37.	Brownsville–Harlingen–San Benito, TX	91.02
38.	Florence, AL	90.61
39.	Dothan, AL	90.10
40.	Parkersburg–Marietta, WV–OH	89.86
41.	El Paso, TX	89.38
42.	Shreveport–Bossier City, LA	89.18
43.	Topeka, KS	89.10
44.	Hattiesburg, MS	89.02
45.	Lafayette, LA	88.86
46.	Cheyenne, WY	88.67
47.	Biloxi–Gulfport–Pascagoula, MS	88.46
48.	Elkhart–Goshen, IN	88.04
49.	Duluth–Superior, MN–WI	87.76
50.	San Antonio, TX	87.68
51.	Great Falls, MT	87.14
52.	Dubuque, IA	86.52
53.	St. Joseph, MO	86.33
54.	Kokomo, IN	85.83
55.	Johnstown, PA	85.62
56.	Fayetteville, NC	85.46
57.	Janesville–Beloit, WI	85.41
58.	Rapid City, SD	85.40
59.	Columbus, GA–AL	85.38
60.	Bismarck, ND	84.20
61.	Jackson, MS	84.02
62.	Macon, GA	83.84
63.	Fort Wayne, IN	83.58
64.	Billings, MT	83.55
65.	Eau Claire, WI	83.08
66.	Wausau, WI	83.02
67.	Sioux Falls, SD	82.85
68.	Sharon, PA	82.59
69.	Fayetteville–Springdale–Rogers, AR	82.55
70.	Evansville–Henderson, IN–KY	82.53
71.	Muncie, IN	82.51
72.	Decatur, AL	82.42
73.	Owensboro, KY	82.35
74.	Sumter, SC	82.18
75.	Chattanooga, TN–GA	82.01
76.	South Bend, IN	81.96
77.	Altoona, PA	81.77
78.	Terre Haute, IN	80.35
79.	Jackson, TN	80.28
80.	Oklahoma City, OK	80.04
81.	Odessa–Midland, TX	79.89
82.	Brazoria, TX	79.85
83.	Lynchburg, VA	79.24
84.	Albany, GA	79.23
85.	Johnson City–Kingsport–Bristol, TN	78.72
86.	Mobile, AL	78.50
87.	Tuscaloosa, AL	78.39
88.	Goldsboro, NC	78.29
89.	Williamsport, PA	78.24
90.	Erie, PA	77.85

Places Rated Rank		Places Rated Score
91.	Benton Harbor, MI	76.41
92.	Ocala, FL	76.36
93.	Fargo–Moorhead, ND–MN	76.13
94.	Jacksonville, NC	75.80
95.	Greenville, NC	75.72
96.	Youngstown–Warren, OH	75.14
97.	Lafayette, IN	74.81
98.	Galveston–Texas City, TX	74.49
99.	Corpus Christi, TX	74.33
100.	Davenport–Moline–Rock Island, IA–IL	74.22
101.	Hickory–Morganton–Lenoir, NC	73.81
102.	Fort Pierce–Port St. Lucie, FL	73.27
103.	Springfield, MO	72.95
104.	New Orleans, LA	72.86
105.	Baton Rouge, LA	71.61
106.	Lawrence, KS	71.33
107.	Knoxville, TN	71.13
108.	Sheboygan, WI	70.91
109.	Saginaw–Bay City–Midland, MI	70.63
110.	Augusta–Aiken, GA–SC	70.22
111.	Decatur, IL	69.86
112.	Tulsa, OK	69.55
113.	Lincoln, NE	68.46
114.	Rocky Mount, NC	68.28
115.	Peoria–Pekin, IL	67.85
116.	Little Rock–North Little Rock, AR	67.28
117.	Bloomington, IN	66.74
118.	Roanoke, VA	66.21
119.	Kankakee, IL	66.19
120.	Charleston, WV	65.97
121.	Wichita, KS	65.51
122.	Springfield, IL	65.42
123.	La Crosse, WI–MN	64.79
124.	Cumberland, MD–WV	64.06
125.	Columbia, SC	63.89
126.	Scranton–Wilkes-Barre–Hazleton, PA	63.34
127.	Panama City, FL	62.60
128.	Appleton–Oshkosh–Neenah, WI	62.34
129.	Bangor, ME	62.25
129.	Kalamazoo–Battle Creek, MI	62.25
131.	Montgomery, AL	61.67
132.	St. Cloud, MN	61.64
133.	Fort Worth–Arlington, TX	61.39
134.	Yakima, WA	61.38
135.	Gainesville, FL	61.25
136.	Pueblo, CO	61.04
137.	Memphis, TN–AR–MS	60.74
138.	Melbourne–Titusville–Palm Bay, FL	60.72
139.	Grand Junction, CO	60.67
140.	Athens, GA	60.54
141.	Flint, MI	60.51
142.	Las Cruces, NM	60.27
143.	Charleston–North Charleston, SC	59.88
144.	Punta Gorda, FL	59.05
145.	Asheville, NC	56.72
146.	Lakeland–Winter Haven, FL	55.67

Places Rated Rank		Places Rated Score
147.	Racine, WI	55.62
148.	Omaha, NE–IA	55.54
149.	Lexington, KY	55.42
150.	Daytona Beach, FL	55.20
151.	Louisville, KY–IN	54.85
152.	Kenosha, WI	54.49
153.	Elmira, NY	54.16
154.	Pensacola, FL	53.63
155.	Tampa–St. Petersburg–Clearwater, FL	53.35
156.	Yuma, AZ	53.31
157.	Jackson, MI	53.29
158.	Richland–Kennewick–Pasco, WA	53.03
159.	Greenville–Spartanburg–Anderson, SC	52.77
160.	Bloomington–Normal, IL	52.48
161.	Cedar Rapids, IA	52.29
162.	Jamestown, NY	52.20
163.	Mansfield, OH	51.92
164.	Spokane, WA	51.79
165.	Nashville, TN	51.77
166.	Utica–Rome, NY	51.68
167.	Houston, TX	51.35
168.	Sioux City, IA–NE	51.30
169.	Grand Rapids–Muskegon–Holland, MI	51.03
170.	Visalia–Tulare–Porterville, CA	50.98
171.	Lima, OH	50.57
172.	Lewiston–Auburn, ME	50.53
173.	Des Moines, IA	50.01
173.	Myrtle Beach, SC	50.01
175.	Lansing–East Lansing, MI	49.84
176.	Columbia, MO	49.83
177.	Iowa City, IA	49.77
178.	Rockford, IL	49.57
179.	Fort Walton Beach, FL	49.53
180.	Yuba City, CA	49.18
181.	Indianapolis, IN	48.65
182.	Toledo, OH	48.32
183.	Champaign–Urbana, IL	48.23
184.	Harrisburg–Lebanon–Carlisle, PA	47.79
185.	Canton–Massillon, OH	47.63
186.	Redding, CA	47.54
187.	State College, PA	47.32
188.	Syracuse, NY	46.58
189.	Kansas City, MO–KS	45.33
190.	Gary, IN	44.80
191.	Bakersfield, CA	44.57
192.	Glens Falls, NY	44.05
193.	Dallas, TX	43.88
194.	York, PA	43.37
195.	Orlando, FL	43.18
196.	Savannah, GA	43.14
197.	Merced, CA	43.06
198.	Wilmington, NC	43.03
199.	Rochester, MN	42.94
200.	Medford–Ashland, OR	42.67
201.	Boise City, ID	42.63
202.	Atlanta, GA	42.61
203.	Greeley, CO	42.12
204.	Chicoutimi–Jonquiere, PQ	41.71
205.	Dayton–Springfield, OH	41.62

Places Rated Rank		Places Rated Score
206.	Birmingham, AL	41.31
207.	Provo–Orem, UT	40.78
208.	Tallahassee, FL	39.71
209.	Huntsville, AL	39.46
210.	Green Bay, WI	39.40
211.	Reading, PA	39.15
212.	Colorado Springs, CO	39.05
213.	Hamilton–Middletown, OH	38.36
214.	Fort Collins–Loveland, CO	38.12
215.	Austin–San Marcos, TX	37.98
[illegible]	[illegible] NY	37.98
[illegible]	[illegible]	[illegible]
226.	Saskatoon, SK	34.22
227.	Jacksonville, FL	34.19
228.	Pittsfield, MA	33.72
229.	Tucson, AZ	33.52
230.	Regina, SK	32.88
231.	Norfolk–Virginia Beach–Newport News, VA	32.79
232.	Olympia, WA	32.41
233.	Greensboro–Winston-Salem–High Point, NC	31.86
234.	Tacoma, WA	31.83
235.	Charlotte–Gastonia–Rock Hill, NC–SC	31.54
236.	Lancaster, PA	31.29
237.	Chico–Paradise, CA	30.50
238.	Fort Lauderdale, FL	30.38
239.	Richmond–Petersburg, VA	29.97
240.	Columbus, OH	29.75
241.	Cincinnati, OH–KY–IN	29.70
242.	Bellingham, WA	29.64
243.	Trois-Rivieres, PQ	29.55
244.	Bremerton, WA	28.52
244.	Edmonton, AB	28.52
246.	Sarasota–Bradenton, FL	28.26
247.	Charlottesville, VA	28.19
248.	Detroit, MI	27.72
249.	Minneapolis–St. Paul, MN–WI	27.52
250.	New Bedford, MA	27.37
251.	Las Vegas, NV–AZ	27.32
252.	Calgary, AB	27.21
253.	Salt Lake City–Ogden, UT	27.20
254.	Hagerstown, MD	27.16
255.	Allentown–Bethlehem–Easton, PA	26.78

Places Rated Rank		Places Rated Score
256.	Fort Myers–Cape Coral, FL	26.03
257.	Saint John, NB	25.48
258.	Phoenix–Mesa, AZ	25.41
259.	Burlington, VT	25.38
260.	Portland, ME	25.04
261.	Flagstaff, AZ–UT	24.87
262.	Albuquerque, NM	23.19
263.	Albany–Schenectady–Troy, NY	22.95
264.	Dutchess County, NY	22.84
265.	Denver, CO	22.82
266.	Wilmington–Newark, DE–MD	22.67
[illegible]	[illegible]	[illegible]
275.	Vineland–[illegible] NJ	[illegible]
276.	St. John's, NF	19.96
277.	Providence–Fall River–Warwick, RI	19.66
278.	Milwaukee–Waukesha, WI	19.64
279.	Anchorage, AK	19.16
280.	Raleigh–Durham–Chapel Hill, NC	18.42
281.	Halifax, NS	17.88
282.	Lawrence, MA–NH	17.36
283.	Springfield, MA	17.21
284.	Montreal, PQ	16.86
285.	Windsor, ON	16.79
286.	Hartford, CT	16.49
287.	Sudbury, ON	16.47
288.	Winnipeg, MB	16.36
289.	Newburgh, NY–PA	16.34
290.	Madison, WI	15.94
291.	Bridgeport, CT	15.89
292.	Lowell, MA–NH	15.76
293.	Baltimore, MD	15.58
294.	Brockton, MA	15.51
295.	Trenton, NJ	15.49
296.	Waterbury, CT	15.39
297.	Philadelphia, PA–NJ	15.12
298.	Fitchburg–Leominster, MA	14.75
299.	Oshawa, ON	14.67
300.	Quebec City, PQ	14.48
301.	Reno, NV	14.46
302.	St. Catharines–Niagara, ON	14.43
303.	Manchester, NH	14.39

Places Rated Rank		Places Rated Score
304.	Sherbrooke, PQ	14.28
305.	Atlantic City–Cape May, NJ	14.08
306.	Thunder Bay, ON	13.31
307.	New London–Norwich, CT–RI	13.24
308.	Nashua, NH	12.81
309.	Yolo, CA	12.76
310.	Worcester, MA–CT	12.74
311.	London, ON	12.68
312.	New Haven–Meriden, CT	12.19
313.	Ottawa–Hull, ON–PQ	11.75
314.	Kitchener, ON	11.65
315.	Vallejo–Fairfield–Napa, CA	11.58
[illegible]	Portland–Vancouver, OR–WA	11.50
[illegible]	[illegible]	10.98
[illegible]	[illegible]	[illegible]
326.	Los Angeles–Long Beach, CA	6.57
327.	Barnstable–Yarmouth, MA	6.48
328.	Monmouth–Ocean, NJ	6.22
329.	San Luis Obispo–Atascadero–Paso Robles, CA	5.81
330.	Washington, DC–MD–VA–WV	5.68
331.	San Diego, CA	4.91
332.	Newark, NJ	4.49
333.	Middlesex–Somerset–Hunterdon, NJ	4.38
334.	New York, NY	4.31
335.	Santa Barbara–Santa Maria–Lompoc, CA	4.15
336.	Toronto, ON	3.77
337.	Victoria, BC	3.49
338.	Santa Rosa, CA	3.36
338.	Ventura, CA	3.36
340.	Oakland, CA	3.28
341.	Boston, MA–NH	3.23
342.	Vancouver, BC	3.15
343.	Salinas, CA	3.10
344.	Orange County, CA	2.87
345.	Bergen–Passaic, NJ	1.93
346.	Santa Cruz–Watsonville, CA	1.92
347.	Stamford–Norwalk, CT	1.66
348.	Long Island, NY	1.44
349.	San Jose, CA	1.23
350.	San Francisco, CA	1.09
351.	Honolulu, HI	0.28

PLACE PROFILES: Costs of Living

The following profiles detail cost-of-living factors used to rank metro areas. At the top of each page are average figures in American dollars for North America's 351 metro areas. Underneath this header, metro areas are listed with their cost indexes relative to the average.

The first column to the right of each metro area's name shows local household income. The second column indexes income and sales taxes paid by a $60,000 a year, two-paycheck couple with two children, plus property taxes on a home with a local average sales price. The third column indexes annual mortgage payments for that home, plus utilities and food costs. The next column shows health care, transportation, and other cost indexes. The last two columns are the *Places Rated* score and rank.

The data come mainly from Places Rated Partnership tax and consumer price surveys through the fall of 1996. In addition, a number of sources were used: Advisory Commission on Intergovernmental Relations, *Significant Features of Fiscal Federalism* (state income and sales taxes), 1996; American Association of Realtors, *Existing Home Sales* (home sales prices) 3rd quarter, 1996; American Automobile Association, *Digest of Motor* Laws (state motor vehicle license, registration fees, and gasoline excise taxes), 1996; American Gas Association, *Gas Facts* (natural gas heating bills), 1996; Canadian Real Estate Association, *MLS Resale Data* (home sales prices), summer 1996; Commerce Clearing House, *Canadian Master Tax Guide* and *State Tax Guide* (state and provincial income and sales taxes), 1996; Compusearch Social Research, Ltd. (Canadian metro area household income estimates), 1996; Data Quick, Inc. (unpublished home sales prices and property taxes), fall 1996; Fodor's Travel Publications, *Mobil Travel Guides* (state park fees, dining-out costs), 1996; Minnesota Department of Revenue, *Comparison of Individual Income Tax Burdens by State* (income taxes), 1996; Royal LePage Real Estate Services, *Survey of Canadian House Prices* (home sales prices), 1996; Sports Directories, Inc., *National Golf Course Directory* (public golf course fees), 1996; Statistics Canada, *Consumer Prices and Price Indexes*, December 1995, and *Inter-City Indexes of Retail Price Differentials*, September 1995; U.S. Department of Defense, Office of Civilian Health and Medical Program of the Uniformed Services, *CMAC Pricing File* (health care costs), 1996; U.S. Department of Energy, *Electric Sales and Revenue* (electricity costs), 1996; U.S. Department of Labor, Bureau of Labor Statistics, *Consumer Expenditure Survey* and *CPI Detailed Report* and *Relative Importance of Components in the Consumer Price Index* (budget expense weights), 1996; U.S. General Services Administration, *Federal Travel Directory* (local *per diems* for food away from home), August 1996; and Woods & Poole Economics, Inc. (U.S. metro area household income estimates), 1996.

A check mark (✓) preceding a metro area's name highlights it as one of the lowest 35 places for costs of living.

Metro Area Average	Household Income $58,900	Income Taxes: $1,969 Sales Taxes: $585 Property Taxes: $1,510	Mortgage: $12,061 Utilities: $4,262 Food: $9,459	Health Care: $4,417 Transportation: $10,172 Other: $3,283	Places Rated Score	Places Rated Rank
✓ Abilene, TX	$53,500	0 129 82	59 79 92	97 105 95	93.46	26
Akron, OH	$59,000	96 108 109	100 118 97	105 98 95	37.37	219
Albany, GA	$49,800	119 95 62	66 93 95	98 100 98	79.23	84
Albany–Schenectady–Troy, NY	$61,500	153 120 142	108 105 104	111 107 103	22.95	263
Albuquerque, NM	$57,000	83 95 72	133 110 98	101 98 101	23.19	262
✓ Alexandria, LA	$50,600	64 116 24	58 76 96	99 99 96	97.01	7
Allentown–Bethlehem–Easton, PA	$63,000	85 103 135	110 113 107	109 101 104	26.78	255

Metro Area Average	Household Income $58,900	Income Taxes: $1,969 Sales Taxes: $585 Property Taxes: $1,510	Mortgage: $12,061 Utilities: $4,262 Food: $9,459	Health Care: $4,417 Transportation: $10,172 Other: $3,283	Places Rated Score	Places Rated Rank
Altoona, PA	$49,500	85 103 96	56 112 100	101 99 98	81.77	77
✓ Amarillo, TX	$55,500	0 129 78	61 77 95	98 103 95	93.14	29
Anchorage, AK	$82,400	0 0 104	127 107 121	123 110 121	19.16	279
[illegible]	[illegible]	117 103 [illegible]	111 116 107	122 103 109	20.97	271
[illegible]	[illegible]	[illegible]	[illegible]	98 [illegible] [illegible]	96.29	12
[illegible]	[illegible]	[illegible]	[illegible]	[illegible]	[illegible]	[illegible]
Asheville, NC	[illegible]	[illegible]	[illegible]	[illegible]	[illegible]	[illegible]
Athens, GA	$48,500	119 95 67	[illegible] 90 101	[illegible] [illegible] 97	[illegible]	[illegible]
Atlanta, GA	$68,600	119 95 77	99 95 102	107 99 102	42.61	202
Atlantic City–Cape May, NJ	$70,900	65 103 162	131 123 103	111 109 107	14.08	305
Augusta–Aiken, GA–SC	$56,100	119 95 64	76 90 96	100 98 100	70.22	110
Austin–San Marcos, TX	$58,000	0 129 136	115 77 95	102 102 98	37.98	215
Bakersfield, CA	$77,700	83 120 82	92 90 109	111 106 105	44.57	191
Baltimore, MD	$71,400	164 86 125	140 93 104	111 102 99	15.58	293
Bangor, ME	$50,000	125 103 119	69 102 103	99 102 102	62.25	129
Barnstable–Yarmouth, MA	$65,100	150 86 150	164 128 108	111 108 108	6.48	327
Baton Rouge, LA	$56,900	64 116 31	82 79 101	102 103 99	71.61	105
✓ Beaumont–Port Arthur, TX	$53,900	0 129 71	56 84 93	103 103 99	93.85	25
Bellingham, WA	$54,300	0 138 112	127 81 104	105 99 108	29.64	242
Benton Harbor, MI	$56,500	117 103 68	55 112 100	108 102 101	76.41	91
Bergen–Passaic, NJ	$93,700	65 103 281	221 123 110	118 111 108	1.93	345

Metro Area Average	Household Income $58,900	Income Taxes: $1,969 Sales Taxes: $585 Property Taxes: $1,510	Mortgage: $12,061 Utilities: $4,262 Food: $9,459	Health Care: $4,417 Transportation: $10,172 Other: $3,283	Places Rated Score	Places Rated Rank
Billings, MT	$56,800	106 0 61	64 88 104	99 103 103	83.55	64
Biloxi–Gulfport–Pascagoula, MS	$49,100	81 120 77	68 75 101	98 95 97	88.46	47
Binghamton, NY	$54,700	153 120 124	85 114 104	105 103 106	37.80	217
Birmingham, AL	$61,000	99 95 51	111 84 96	101 99 101	41.31	206
Bismarck, ND	$55,500	43 99 64	63 105 104	97 100 102	84.20	60
Bloomington, IN	$47,300	96 86 64	77 110 101	98 98 95	66.74	117
Bloomington–Normal, IL	$62,100	85 116 82	79 132 101	102 98 102	52.48	160
Boise City, ID	$62,800	142 86 87	107 74 99	100 98 101	42.63	201
Boston, MA–NH	$68,900	150 86 241	187 132 115	114 112 107	3.23	341
Boulder–Longmont, CO	$71,500	102 103 84	184 91 106	104 103 100	8.31	324
Brazoria, TX	$55,900	0 129 88	69 83 97	105 104 99	79.85	82
Bremerton, WA	$57,900	0 138 110	131 79 105	105 100 103	28.52	244
Bridgeport, CT	$108,700	94 103 153	123 126 105	120 103 109	15.89	291
Brockton, MA	$67,500	150 86 122	119 132 110	114 109 104	15.51	294
Brownsville–Harlingen–San Benito, TX	$45,600	0 129 87	65 75 90	97 102 97	91.02	37
✓ Bryan–College Station, TX	$40,900	0 129 76	54 88 92	98 99 95	97.09	6
Buffalo–Niagara Falls, NY	$57,700	153 120 140	84 105 109	104 107 104	37.98	215
Burlington, VT	$61,300	77 86 112	120 113 107	100 100 109	25.38	259
Calgary, AB	$61,700	242 0 105	125 93 112	36 113 106	27.21	252
Canton–Massillon, OH	$54,300	96 108 105	90 110 97	105 98 95	47.63	185
✓ Casper, WY	$61,800	0 95 47	52 86 104	100 96 100	99.17	2

Metro Area Average	Household Income $58,900	Income Taxes: $1,969 Sales Taxes: $585 Property Taxes: $1,510	Mortgage: $12,061 Utilities: $4,262 Food: $9,459	Health Care: $4,417 Transportation: $10,172 Other: $3,283	Places Rated Score	Places Rated Rank
Cedar Rapids, IA	$61,400	124 95 72	85 119 95	98 99 93	52.29	161
Champaign–Urbana, IL	$50,800	85 116 88	85 131 100	101 97 99	48.23	183
Charleston, WV	$56,200	116 103 50	79 92 100	101 103 93	65.97	120
Charleston–North Charleston, SC	$48,300	122 [illegible]	91 [illegible]	96 [illegible]	59.88	143
[illegible]		[illegible]	[illegible]	99		
Cheyenne, WY	$58,000	0 95 57	67 88 103	100 102 98	88.67	46
Chicago, IL	$77,600	85 116 142	150 128 102	118 103 103	10.02	321
Chico–Paradise, CA	$47,600	83 120 69	112 98 105	105 107 106	30.50	237
Chicoutimi–Jonquiere, PQ	$46,600	256 258 99	59 120 112	36 140 110	41.71	204
Cincinnati, OH–KY–IN	$62,700	96 108 124	110 109 103	105 100 101	29.70	241
✓ Clarksville–Hopkinsville, TN–KY	$46,200	0 118 36	72 73 95	98 93 99	95.52	15
Cleveland–Lorain–Elyria, OH	$64,300	96 108 130	119 131 104	105 102 100	20.75	273
Colorado Springs, CO	$56,000	102 103 46	115 83 99	104 99 97	39.05	212
Columbia, MO	$53,400	102 107 82	93 100 99	105 95 101	49.83	176
Columbia, SC	$56,800	122 101 67	89 83 96	96 94 100	63.89	125
Columbus, GA–AL	$51,200	119 95 61	63 89 97	100 97 99	85.38	59
Columbus, OH	$59,000	96 108 121	107 108 104	105 103 103	29.75	240
Corpus Christi, TX	$53,500	0 129 105	84 76 91	100 98 93	74.33	99
Cumberland, MD–WV	$45,600	164 86 84	77 86 96	105 97 97	64.06	124

Metro Area Average	Household Income $58,900	Income Taxes: $1,969 Sales Taxes: $585 Property Taxes: $1,510	Mortgage: $12,061 Utilities: $4,262 Food: $9,459	Health Care: $4,417 Transportation: $10,172 Other: $3,283	Places Rated Score	Places Rated Rank
Dallas, TX	$70,100	0 129 140	100 86 99	105 104 101	43.88	193
Danbury, CT	$108,700	94 103 204	165 119 106	120 104 106	6.68	325
✓ Danville, VA	$46,400	112 60 63	51 86 98	98 99 99	95.46	16
Davenport–Moline–Rock Island, IA–IL	$56,700	124 95 68	61 114 101	101 100 97	74.22	100
Dayton–Springfield, OH	$59,100	96 108 100	92 116 100	104 100 101	41.62	205
Daytona Beach, FL	$46,300	0 120 91	97 82 98	105 101 101	55.20	150
Decatur, AL	$52,900	99 95 38	71 77 97	100 101 99	82.42	72
Decatur, IL	$56,300	85 116 76	63 137 100	101 97 97	69.86	111
Denver, CO	$67,300	102 103 64	131 95 101	104 105 99	22.82	265
Des Moines, IA	$63,800	124 95 82	89 108 100	99 97 103	50.01	173
Detroit, MI	$70,600	117 103 97	96 116 108	122 109 108	27.72	248
Dothan, AL	$49,800	99 95 39	64 81 95	98 98 99	90.10	39
Dover, DE	$51,300	119 0 79	105 107 108	108 100 104	36.53	222
Dubuque, IA	$56,600	124 95 56	59 89 98	98 100 102	86.52	52
Duluth–Superior, MN–WI	$49,600	142 120 59	44 97 102	104 106 102	87.76	49
Dutchess County, NY	$67,400	153 120 152	105 121 110	111 101 109	22.84	264
Eau Claire, WI	$53,700	154 103 91	53 102 100	101 98 99	83.08	65
Edmonton, AB	$55,600	242 0 132	118 94 123	36 114 108	28.52	244
El Paso, TX	$48,700	0 129 89	65 83 96	99 99 100	89.38	41
Elkhart–Goshen, IN	$61,500	96 86 48	63 101 95	98 95 96	88.04	48
Elmira, NY	$53,000	153 120 104	65 114 107	102 108 102	54.16	153

Metro Area Average	Household Income $58,900	Income Taxes: $1,969 Sales Taxes: $585 Property Taxes: $1,510	Mortgage: $12,061 Utilities: $4,262 Food: $9,459	Health Care: $4,417 Transportation: $10,172 Other: $3,283	Places Rated Score	Places Rated Rank
✓ Enid, OK	$51,000	128 99 40	48 89 93	97 90 96	99.06	3
Erie, PA	$55,600	85 103 105	53 111 100	109 101 101	77.85	90
Eugene–Springfield, OR	$51,600	178 0 89	110 75 97	103 102 98	37.02	220
Evansville–Henderson, IN–KY	$57,200	96 86 51	65 104 98	101 96 96	82.53	70
Fargo–Moorhead, ND–MN	$54,300	43 99 65	77 96 100	104 94 99	76.13	93
Flagstaff, AZ–UT	$44,000	77 103 96	111 112 103	106 112 104	24.87	261
Flint, MI	$57,400	117 103 79	67 112 105	108 104 103	60.51	141
Florence, AL	$48,100	99 95 38	65 78 96	100 97 98	90.61	38
✓ Florence, SC	$52,700	122 101 64	61 84 95	96 92 98	91.77	34
Fort Collins–Loveland, CO	$57,400	102 103 89	107 82 102	104 104 99	38.12	214
Fort Lauderdale, FL	$65,500	0 120 144	117 80 100	118 102 106	30.38	238
Fort Myers–Cape Coral, FL	$59,600	0 120 141	132 80 98	111 100 98	26.03	256
Fort Pierce–Port St. Lucie, FL	$62,000	0 120 77	76 90 98	111 100 99	73.27	102
✓ Fort Smith, AR–OK	$49,700	113 95 56	51 83 95	97 94 98	97.49	5
Fort Walton Beach, FL	$54,400	0 120 110	98 87 99	102 103 103	49.53	179
Fort Wayne, IN	$63,000	96 86 55	66 102 97	101 95 94	83.58	63
Fort Worth–Arlington, TX	$62,800	0 129 130	84 86 100	102 103 99	61.39	133
Fresno, CA	$59,300	83 120 71	99 97 108	107 108 107	37.52	218

Metro Area Average	Household Income $58,900	Income Taxes: $1,969 Sales Taxes: $585 Property Taxes: $1,510	Mortgage: $12,061 Utilities: $4,262 Food: $9,459	Health Care: $4,417 Transportation: $10,172 Other: $3,283	Places Rated Score	Places Rated Rank
✓ Gadsden, AL	$47,300	99 95 37	60 84 94	98 95 98	94.29	23
Gainesville, FL	$50,800	0 120 74	89 99 98	105 99 99	61.25	135
Galveston–Texas City, TX	$58,700	0 129 115	73 80 98	104 104 100	74.49	98
Gary, IN	$59,500	96 86 84	89 123 101	101 101 101	44.80	190
Glens Falls, NY	$53,600	153 120 140	79 107 103	105 103 104	44.05	192
Goldsboro, NC	$44,100	140 112 82	62 99 96	97 97 101	78.29	88
✓ Grand Forks, ND–MN	$46,600	43 99 56	56 97 102	104 99 100	91.96	33
Grand Junction, CO	$50,500	102 103 69	78 91 104	104 106 99	60.67	139
Grand Rapids–Muskegon–Holland, MI	$63,600	117 103 110	82 100 104	108 100 102	51.03	169
Great Falls, MT	$52,300	106 0 58	60 87 105	99 102 106	87.14	51
Greeley, CO	$53,300	102 103 71	101 92 101	104 103 98	42.12	203
Green Bay, WI	$63,200	154 103 140	92 102 96	101 100 100	39.40	210
Greensboro–Winston-Salem–High Point, NC	$58,500	140 112 129	111 97 99	98 98 96	31.86	233
Greenville, NC	$51,500	140 112 89	71 97 97	97 92 95	75.72	95
Greenville–Spartanburg–Anderson, SC	$51,900	122 101 87	98 84 99	96 95 97	52.77	159
Hagerstown, MD	$49,900	164 86 111	122 82 100	105 98 100	27.16	254
Halifax, NS	$55,000	298 309 125	111 108 117	36 128 105	17.88	281
Hamilton, ON	$56,600	306 258 122	143 107 110	36 124 106	10.52	319
Hamilton–Middletown, OH	$57,600	96 108 104	96 119 100	105 99 100	38.36	213
Harrisburg–Lebanon–Carlisle, PA	$61,100	85 103 116	76 116 99	109 107 101	47.79	184
Hartford, CT	$75,600	94 103 158	122 131 104	114 102 109	16.49	286

Metro Area Average	Household Income $58,900	Income Taxes: $1,969 Sales Taxes: $585 Property Taxes: $1,510	Mortgage: $12,061 Utilities: $4,262 Food: $9,459	Health Care: $4,417 Transportation: $10,172 Other: $3,283	Places Rated Score	Places Rated Rank
Hattiesburg, MS	$44,700	81 120 59	66 88 98	98 93 98	89.02	44
Hickory–Morganton–Lenoir, NC	$53,400	140 112 84	66 99 98	97 97 102	73.81	101
Honolulu, HI	$82,400	177 69 104	354 94 141	114 121 116	0.28	351
✓ Houma, LA	$48,100	64 116 24	59 82 95	98 100 99	94.71	19
Houston, TX	$66,400	0 129 132	88 90 98	108 106 100	51.35	167
		124 95 77	84 119 97	98 100 100	49.77	177
Jackson, MI	$52,500	117 103 91	75 117 101	108 101 100	53.29	157
Jackson, MS	$57,500	81 120 65	71 88 99	98 94 97	84.02	61
Jackson, TN	$53,700	0 118 48	83 92 95	97 93 99	80.28	79
Jacksonville, FL	$59,200	0 120 137	115 90 101	105 101 101	34.19	227
Jacksonville, NC	$44,600	140 112 91	67 101 95	97 93 100	75.80	94
Jamestown, NY	$50,000	153 120 122	71 107 106	102 105 103	52.20	162
Janesville–Beloit, WI	$57,000	154 103 89	50 105 102	100 98 97	85.41	57
Jersey City, NJ	$62,100	65 103 250	130 123 110	118 110 110	10.98	317
Johnson City–Kingsport–Bristol, TN–VA	$47,400	0 118 52	87 76 97	98 96 97	78.72	85
Johnstown, PA	$48,700	85 103 85	43 118 99	103 106 100	85.62	55
Joplin, MO	$48,000	102 107 61	65 83 95	97 92 96	91.03	36
Kalamazoo–Battle Creek, MI	$58,100	117 103 8	77 111 104	108 101 100	62.25	129

Metro Area Average	Household Income $58,900	Income Taxes: $1,969 Sales Taxes: $585 Property Taxes: $1,510	Mortgage: $12,061 Utilities: $4,262 Food: $9,459	Health Care: $4,417 Transportation: $10,172 Other: $3,283	Places Rated Score	Places Rated Rank
Kankakee, IL	$55,600	85 116 76	64 135 101	101 99 100	66.19	119
Kansas City, MO–KS	$63,600	102 107 86	94 102 98	106 98 102	45.33	189
Kenosha, WI	$57,200	154 103 115	72 104 100	106 102 103	54.49	152
✓ Killeen–Temple, TX	$47,300	0 129 90	61 83 92	98 93 94	96.28	14
Kitchener, ON	$56,000	306 258 115	139 111 117	36 122 107	11.65	314
Knoxville, TN	$55,100	0 118 65	93 76 95	97 97 96	71.13	107
Kokomo, IN	$58,600	96 86 64	58 112 98	98 96 97	85.83	54
La Crosse, WI–MN	$55,700	154 103 112	65 104 98	104 100 100	64.79	123
Lafayette, IN	$53,700	96 86 67	67 112 99	98 98 98	74.81	97
Lafayette, LA	$48,700	64 116 25	64 86 96	100 101 102	88.86	45
✓ Lake Charles, LA	$52,400	64 116 26	60 82 99	100 100 102	93.18	28
Lakeland–Winter Haven, FL	$49,400	0 120 94	94 88 98	105 101 99	55.67	146
Lancaster, PA	$64,200	85 103 139	97 116 99	101 108 106	31.29	236
Lansing–East Lansing, MI	$57,300	117 103 90	80 109 103	108 103 101	49.84	175
✓ Laredo, TX	$48,900	0 129 96	71 76 91	96 93 96	92.00	32
Las Cruces, NM	$43,300	83 95 51	86 101 96	101 99 98	60.27	142
Las Vegas, NV–AZ	$61,700	0 112 69	122 79 106	111 120 97	27.32	251
Lawrence, KS	$44,500	92 99 75	76 92 96	100 97 100	71.33	106
Lawrence, MA–NH	$70,100	150 86 110	122 122 112	114 105 104	17.36	282
✓ Lawton, OK	$49,000	128 99 48	55 90 93	97 91 101	95.28	17
Lewiston–Auburn, ME	$52,500	125 103 109	85 94 103	99 103 103	50.53	172

Metro Area Average	Household Income $58,900	Income Taxes: $1,969 Sales Taxes: $585 Property Taxes: $1,510	Mortgage: $12,061 Utilities: $4,262 Food: $9,459	Health Care: $4,417 Transportation: $10,172 Other: $3,283	Places Rated Score	Places Rated Rank
Lexington, KY	$56,200	129 112 84	93 75 99	100 96 103	55.42	149
Lima, OH	$55,500	96 108 88	86 112 98	104 98 99	50.57	171
Lincoln, NE	$57,800	99 103 97	76 97 95	95 97 99	68.46	113
Little Rock–North Little Rock, AR	$56,500	113 95 66	76 102 96	94 100 99	67.28	116
London, ON	$53,300	306 258 145	131 112 113	36 121 [illegible]	12.68	311
[illegible]	[illegible]	[illegible] 112 72	[illegible] 94 98	100 100 99	54.85	151
Lowell, MA–NH	$84,000	150 86 122	126 122 112	114 104 104	15.76	292
✓ Lubbock, TX	$54,400	0 129 80	61 89 95	97 99 96	92.61	31
Lynchburg, VA	$52,300	112 60 74	72 88 98	98 98 93	79.24	83
Macon, GA	$54,100	119 95 64	65 93 99	100 95 97	83.84	62
Madison, WI	$65,600	154 103 158	129 113 101	105 103 102	15.94	290
Manchester, NH	$68,600	0 0 235	139 124 102	105 104 102	14.39	303
Mansfield, OH	$49,700	96 108 93	84 120 97	104 96 96	51.92	163
✓ McAllen–Edinburg–Mission, TX	$43,000	0 129 89	59 76 93	95 97 98	96.77	10
Medford–Ashland, OR	$51,200	178 0 84	97 84 96	103 104 103	42.67	200
Melbourne–Titusville–Palm Bay, FL	$53,600	0 120 114	88 86 98	105 100 102	60.72	138
Memphis, TN–AR–MS	$61,400	0 118 79	100 76 101	97 100 94	60.74	137
Merced, CA	$53,800	83 120 62	95 100 105	107 105 104	43.06	197

Metro Area	Household Income	Income Taxes	Sales Taxes	Property Taxes	Mortgage	Utilities	Food	Health Care	Transportation	Other	Places Rated Score	Places Rated Rank
Average	$58,900	$1,969	$585	$1,510	$12,061	$4,262	$9,459	$4,417	$10,172	$3,283		
Miami, FL	$61,000	0	120	163	127	80	102	118	105	109	22.39	268
Middlesex–Somerset–Hunterdon, NJ	$89,600	65	103	197	187	123	110	118	108	107	4.38	333
Milwaukee–Waukesha, WI	$69,300	154	103	167	118	105	102	107	104	103	19.64	278
Minneapolis–St. Paul, MN–WI	$73,200	142	120	89	108	107	99	104	107	102	27.52	249
Mobile, AL	$51,100	99	95	35	71	85	99	99	102	104	78.50	86
Modesto, CA	$60,100	83	120	76	110	76	104	109	105	105	36.10	223
Monmouth–Ocean, NJ	$79,700	65	103	205	176	109	107	113	106	105	6.22	328
✓ Monroe, LA	$48,000	64	116	29	61	78	99	99	97	101	94.71	19
Montgomery, AL	$57,200	99	95	43	88	85	97	98	103	98	61.67	131
Montreal, PQ	$50,500	256	258	145	102	113	114	36	142	111	16.86	284
Muncie, IN	$51,600	96	86	65	60	104	97	101	100	97	82.51	71
Myrtle Beach, SC	$47,600	122	101	80	97	92	99	96	97	99	50.01	173
Naples, FL	$82,100	0	120	112	180	80	100	111	103	103	10.18	320
Nashua, NH	$68,600	0	0	243	144	124	102	105	104	102	12.81	308
Nashville, TN	$63,100	0	118	62	108	80	101	97	101	98	51.77	165
New Bedford, MA	$57,500	150	86	89	107	112	105	114	102	102	27.37	250
New Haven–Meriden, CT	$69,900	94	103	171	134	129	106	117	103	109	12.19	312
New London–Norwich, CT–RI	$67,500	94	103	163	138	127	102	114	100	102	13.24	307
New Orleans, LA	$56,800	64	112	37	73	96	102	106	102	100	72.86	104
New York, NY	$78,500	153	120	205	153	133	139	129	121	129	4.31	334
Newark, NJ	$88,800	65	103	177	185	123	110	118	110	110	4.49	332

Metro Area Average	Household Income $58,900	Income Taxes: $1,969 Sales Taxes: $585 Property Taxes: $1,510	Mortgage: $12,061 Utilities: $4,262 Food: $9,459	Health Care: $4,417 Transportation: $10,172 Other: $3,283	Places Rated Score	Places Rated Rank
Newburgh, NY–PA	$66,200	153 120 175	107 131 111	111 112 106	16.34	289
Norfolk–Virginia Beach–Newport News, VA	$56,400	112 60 103	108 101 103	103 103 102	32.79	231
Oakland, CA	$74,300	83 120 140	209 107 111	124 110 108	3.28	340
Ocala, FL	$46,800	0 120 77	82 78 100	102 99 98	76.36	92
Odessa–Midland, TX	$60,600	0 129 110	71 84 92	103 100 100	79.89	81
		[illegible] 120 135	[illegible] 92 109	119 112 109	2.87	344
Orlando, FL	$58,600	0 120 115	105 94 100	105 100 101	43.18	195
Oshawa, ON	$63,400	306 258 158	122 109 110	36 123 106	14.67	299
Ottawa–Hull, ON–PQ	$62,400	306 258 155	129 110 116	36 127 112	11.75	313
Owensboro, KY	$50,500	129 112 63	67 76 98	98 101 97	82.35	73
Panama City, FL	$48,000	0 120 85	85 92 100	102 104 101	62.60	127
Parkersburg–Marietta, WV–OH	$49,900	116 103 31	55 98 100	104 100 95	89.86	40
Pensacola, FL	$49,700	0 120 100	96 84 99	105 102 100	53.63	154
Peoria–Pekin, IL	$60,100	85 116 72	66 120 102	105 99 102	67.85	115
Philadelphia, PA–NJ	$72,600	85 103 188	119 122 110	113 111 109	15.12	297
Phoenix–Mesa, AZ	$60,400	77 103 62	121 96 104	109 111 100	25.41	258
✓ Pine Bluff, AR	$47,900	113 95 57	44 99 94	94 99 98	96.84	9
Pittsburgh, PA	$61,000	85 103 131	85 128 104	112 108 105	34.40	225

Metro Area Average	Household Income $58,900	Income Taxes: $1,969 Sales Taxes: $585 Property Taxes: $1,510	Mortgage: $12,061 Utilities: $4,262 Food: $9,459	Health Care: $4,417 Transportation: $10,172 Other: $3,283	Places Rated Score	Places Rated Rank
Pittsfield, MA	$59,900	150 86 97	93 117 101	114 102 103	33.72	228
Portland, ME	$62,400	125 103 124	118 96 105	104 104 100	25.04	260
Portland–Vancouver, OR–WA	$63,500	178 0 124	157 79 102	106 109 104	11.50	316
Portsmouth–Rochester, NH–ME	$75,000	0 0 253	151 120 103	105 105 103	10.93	318
Providence–Fall River–Warwick, RI–MA	$60,300	85 120 150	116 110 107	110 112 103	19.66	277
Provo–Orem, UT	$56,900	135 103 87	102 83 96	100 103 101	40.78	207
Pueblo, CO	$48,100	102 103 44	88 88 98	104 100 95	61.04	136
Punta Gorda, FL	$47,500	0 120 92	93 84 98	105 100 99	59.05	144
Quebec City, PQ	$48,800	256 258 154	107 115 119	36 143 110	14.48	300
Racine, WI	$66,700	154 103 107	71 104 102	106 103 103	55.62	147
Raleigh–Durham–Chapel Hill, NC	$62,300	140 112 139	138 96 100	98 98 101	18.42	280
Rapid City, SD	$55,000	0 97 74	66 104 100	95 100 100	85.40	58
Reading, PA	$62,500	85 103 122	83 117 105	109 109 106	39.15	211
Redding, CA	$52,000	83 120 49	100 74 105	105 107 102	47.54	186
Regina, SK	$53,100	266 275 178	94 78 110	36 121 105	32.88	230
Reno, NV	$75,000	0 112 79	147 100 102	111 117 103	14.46	301
Richland–Kennewick–Pasco, WA	$60,000	0 138 92	97 84 102	105 101 103	53.03	158
Richmond–Petersburg, VA	$66,900	112 60 111	110 102 100	102 105 102	29.97	239
Riverside–San Bernardino, CA	$60,900	83 120 100	116 101 105	120 110 103	22.44	267
Roanoke, VA	$59,400	112 60 78	81 88 99	98 102 93	66.21	118
Rochester, MN	$68,000	142 120 72	86 108 98	104 106 103	42.94	199

Metro Area Average	Household Income $58,900	Income Taxes: $1,969 Sales Taxes: $585 Property Taxes: $1,510	Mortgage: $12,061 Utilities: $4,262 Food: $9,459	Health Care: $4,417 Transportation: $10,172 Other: $3,283	Places Rated Score	Places Rated Rank
Rochester, NY	$64,100	153 120 145	82 119 110	107 106 106	35.01	224
Rockford, IL	$58,800	85 116 81	75 137 101	105 103 101	49.57	178
Rocky Mount, NC	$51,100	140 112 109	72 92 98	97 97 100	68.28	114
Sacramento, CA	$62,700	83 120 84	127 96 107	112 109 105	20.61	274
Saginaw–Bay City–Midland, MI	$58,800	117 103 75	59 113 103	108 102 102	70.63	109
[illegible]		326 109	115 120	144 110		
St. Joseph, MO	$50,700	102 107 67	64 93 93	99 94 98	86.33	53
St. Louis, MO–IL	$67,100	102 107 85	130 116 106	107 99 99	20.79	272
Salem, OR	$52,700	178 0 104	101 80 94	102 107 104	36.84	221
Salinas, CA	$73,600	83 120 118	219 104 106	113 110 107	3.10	343
Salt Lake City–Ogden, UT	$62,900	135 103 97	122 85 99	100 102 101	27.20	253
✓ San Angelo, TX	$54,500	0 129 86	58 85 96	96 96 98	96.29	12
San Antonio, TX	$56,400	0 129 92	71 78 96	100 97 97	87.68	50
San Diego, CA	$66,500	83 120 116	187 119 110	112 113 106	4.91	331
San Francisco, CA	$90,600	83 120 130	269 107 112	124 115 111	1.09	350
San Jose, CA	$87,300	83 120 145	263 103 108	123 114 110	1.23	349
San Luis Obispo–Atascadero–Paso Robles, CA	$54,300	83 120 118	180 116 108	113 111 108	5.81	329
Santa Barbara–Santa Maria–Lompoc, CA	$76,800	83 120 111	207 100 107	113 109 106	4.15	335

Metro Area Average	Household Income $58,900	Income Taxes: $1,969 Sales Taxes: $585 Property Taxes: $1,510	Mortgage: $12,061 Utilities: $4,262 Food: $9,459	Health Care: $4,417 Transportation: $10,172 Other: $3,283	Places Rated Score	Places Rated Rank
Santa Cruz–Watsonville, CA	$75,800	83 120 135	244 104 109	113 110 110	1.92	346
Santa Fe, NM	$64,100	83 95 89	168 111 104	101 109 103	9.41	322
Santa Rosa, CA	$70,500	83 120 120	212 102 108	116 112 111	3.36	338
Sarasota–Bradenton, FL	$69,300	0 120 97	133 78 101	105 102 101	28.26	246
Saskatoon, SK	$48,400	266 275 158	90 86 108	36 123 103	34.22	226
Savannah, GA	$56,600	119 95 81	105 100 100	100 94 96	43.14	196
Scranton–Wilkes-Barre–Hazleton, PA	$54,500	85 103 112	65 114 102	109 102 101	63.34	126
Seattle–Bellevue–Everett, WA	$74,600	0 138 140	180 74 108	110 108 106	9.01	323
Sharon, PA	$48,200	85 103 100	52 111 100	103 101 98	82.59	68
Sheboygan, WI	$61,000	154 103 96	63 105 103	101 100 94	70.91	108
Sherbrooke, PQ	$42,400	256 258 145	122 114 113	36 129 107	14.28	304
✓ Sherman–Denison, TX	$52,600	0 129 78	58 84 94	97 97 94	96.77	10
Shreveport–Bossier City, LA	$52,400	64 116 27	70 76 98	101 98 97	89.18	42
Sioux City, IA–NE	$56,000	124 95 85	87 105 100	98 100 99	51.30	168
Sioux Falls, SD	$64,600	0 97 81	73 99 99	95 97 98	82.85	67
South Bend, IN	$57,900	96 86 71	64 103 96	98 97 97	81.96	76
Spokane, WA	$51,000	0 138 99	102 78 106	104 100 99	51.79	164
Springfield, IL	$59,000	85 116 67	77 107 101	104 96 99	65.42	122
Springfield, MA	$60,000	150 86 134	123 115 102	114 104 104	17.21	283
Springfield, MO	$52,400	102 107 62	76 86 95	105 96 99	72.95	103
Stamford–Norwalk, CT	$108,700	94 103 276	231 127 105	120 104 110	1.66	347

Metro Area Average	Household Income $58,900	Income Taxes: $1,969 Sales Taxes: $585 Property Taxes: $1,510	Mortgage: $12,061 Utilities: $4,262 Food: $9,459	Health Care: $4,417 Transportation: $10,172 Other: $3,283	Places Rated Score	Places Rated Rank
State College, PA	$51,700	85 103 87	89 103 100	103 103 107	47.32	187
✓ Steubenville–Weirton, OH–WV	$47,900	96 108 57	43 111 98	104 98 95	95.16	18
Stockton–Lodi, CA	$60,900	83 120 89	126 100 106	109 106 107	21.73	269
Sudbury, ON	$53,500	306 258 125	119 120 114	36 120 104	16.47	287
Sumter, SC	$45,400	122 101 68	64 104 98	96 93 101	82.18	74
[illegible] Clearwater, FL	[illegible]	[illegible] 120 119	[illegible] 80 102	[illegible] 103 96	[illegible]	[illegible]
Terre Haute, IN	$48,100	96 86 65	61 111 95	98 100 96	80.35	78
✓ Texarkana, TX–Texarkana, AR	$48,300	113 95 63	43 80 94	97 97 95	99.30	1
Thunder Bay, ON	$52,800	306 258 145	126 120 113	36 120 109	13.31	306
Toledo, OH	$59,400	96 108 95	76 137 99	104 102 99	48.32	182
Topeka, KS	$59,600	92 99 67	64 86 98	100 92 101	89.10	43
Toronto, ON	$67,500	306 258 155	193 107 116	36 126 107	3.77	336
Trenton, NJ	$90,500	65 103 188	123 126 108	113 106 109	15.49	295
Trois–Rivieres, PQ	$43,000	256 258 131	82 116 113	36 134 105	29.55	243
Tucson, AZ	$50,300	77 103 67	118 85 103	106 104 96	33.52	229
Tulsa, OK	$55,900	128 99 63	83 89 93	97 90 103	69.55	112
Tuscaloosa, AL	$50,600	99 95 54	69 85 96	101 101 101	78.39	87
✓ Tyler, TX	$57,800	0 129 103	61 85 91	99 95 100	93.04	30

Metro Area Average	Household Income $58,900	Income Taxes: $1,969	Sales Taxes: $585	Property Taxes: $1,510	Mortgage: $12,061	Utilities: $4,262	Food: $9,459	Health Care: $4,417	Transportation: $10,172	Other: $3,283	Places Rated Score	Places Rated Rank
Utica–Rome, NY	$49,000	153	120	124	67	107	108	105	108	104	51.68	166
Vallejo–Fairfield–Napa, CA	$77,700	83	120	105	150	103	109	116	109	109	11.58	315
Vancouver, BC	$61,300	268	219	105	222	99	111	36	119	107	3.15	342
Ventura, CA	$77,700	83	120	133	215	99	109	116	108	108	3.36	338
Victoria, BC	$55,600	268	219	145	215	97	118	36	116	105	3.49	337
✓ Victoria, TX	$57,100	0	129	89	61	78	90	100	92	95	96.98	8
Vineland–Millville–Bridgeton, NJ	$61,500	65	103	152	116	128	103	111	105	102	20.36	275
Visalia–Tulare–Porterville, CA	$77,700	83	120	51	92	88	106	105	105	104	50.98	170
✓ Waco, TX	$51,300	0	129	81	60	84	92	97	99	97	94.10	24
Washington, DC–MD–VA–WV	$84,600	169	99	175	170	96	116	118	114	108	5.68	330
Waterbury, CT	$69,900	94	103	135	129	125	103	120	102	104	15.39	296
✓ Waterloo–Cedar Falls, IA	$50,600	124	95	51	47	104	98	98	96	101	94.63	21
Wausau, WI	$61,700	154	103	91	56	101	102	101	96	95	83.02	66
West Palm Beach–Boca Raton, FL	$87,100	0	120	155	135	80	99	111	102	108	21.59	270
✓ Wheeling, WV–OH	$48,700	116	103	30	44	101	99	104	101	100	94.62	22
Wichita, KS	$59,900	92	99	84	77	109	96	100	95	98	65.51	121
✓ Wichita Falls, TX	$55,800	0	129	85	58	86	95	97	92	95	97.86	4
Williamsport, PA	$52,800	85	103	91	55	117	100	109	99	99	78.24	89
Wilmington, NC	$48,900	140	112	124	97	100	98	97	95	99	43.03	198
Wilmington–Newark, DE–MD	$70,100	119	0	94	127	107	112	108	101	103	22.67	266
Windsor, ON	$52,500	306	258	111	122	108	108	36	122	104	16.79	285

Metro Area Average	Household Income $58,900	Income Taxes: $1,969 Sales Taxes: $585 Property Taxes: $1,510	Mortgage: $12,061 Utilities: $4,262 Food: $9,459	Health Care: $4,417 Transportation: $10,172 Other: $3,283	Places Rated Score	Places Rated Rank
Winnipeg, MB	$48,400	277 219 215	114 122 109	36 118 106	16.36	288
Worcester, MA–CT	$61,800	150 86 149	140 106 105	114 104 105	12.74	310
Yakima, WA	$55,400	0 138 91	91 83 104	105 99 100	61.38	134
Yolo, CA	$77,700	83 120 92	150 95 107	112 110 109	12.76	309
York, PA	$62,200	85 103 117	85 119 99	103 104 103	43.37	194

Et Cetera

TAXES

Question: Where in North America can you find rock-bottom property taxes, no sales taxes, no taxes on any of your sources of income, no niggling nickel-and-dime fees for registering a car or taking out a license to catch largemouth bass, and no inheritance taxes for your heirs to pay?

Answer: Dream on. This ideal tax haven would have to combine the low property taxes of Louisiana, Alberta's absence of retail sales taxes, and South Dakota's forgiveness of taxes on personal income. Unfortunately, you just can't find all these terrific tax breaks in one place. Although federal income taxes take nearly the same bite whether you live in New Bedford, New Orleans, or New York, state taxes can differ dramatically around the country. Sales taxes, excise taxes, license taxes, income taxes, property taxes, death taxes, gift taxes, and head taxes are just some of the forms that state taxes take. Depending on where you live, you may encounter all of them or only a few.

Property Taxes. Taxes on land and the buildings on it—whether they are homes, farms, industrial plants, or commercial buildings—are the biggest source of cash for local governments. They are imposed not by states but by the tens of thousands of cities, townships, counties, school districts, sanitary districts, hospital districts, and other assessing jurisdictions in the nation.

The states' role is to specify the maximum rate on the market value of the property, or a percentage of it, as the legal standard for local assessors to follow. The local assessor determines the value to be taxed. If you think the valuation is too high, you have a limited right of appeal. You can't escape property taxes in any state except Alaska (where you must be over 65 to take advantage of that break), but you can find significantly low rates in certain parts of the country. Nationally, the average bills on homes amount to 1.25 percent of their market value, whereas the average bills in Alabama, Arizona, Hawaii, Louisiana, New Mexico, and West Virginia are based on less than half that rate.

Sales Taxes. If people had a choice of raising income taxes or raising sales taxes, they would opt for the latter by a big margin according to recent polls. Sometimes called retail taxes or consumption taxes, sales taxes are collected at the retail level on the purchase of goods. After income taxes, they account for the second largest source of revenue for state governments.

Among the states, the average sales tax is 5 percent.

Throughout Canada, the rate is much higher. If you're living in California, you're paying America's highest state rate: 7.25 percent. If you're from Newfoundland, you're paying North America's highest rate: 12 percent. Canada also imposes a 7 percent value-added tax—the Goods and Services Tax, or GST—payable by consumers in addition to the province's sales tax.

Alaska has no statewide sales tax but local governments may levy the tax. Hawaii has a general excise tax; New Mexico a gross receipts tax. Alberta, Delaware, Montana, New Hampshire, and Oregon collect no sales taxes at all. To a four-person family, this could mean a savings of hundreds of dollars. But you can avoid paying almost that much in areas where such basics as food, medicine, and clothing are exempted.

Personal Income Taxes. When the first federal income tax went into effect in 1913, two states—Mississippi and Wisconsin—were already collecting income taxes on their own. It was only during the 1920s and 1930s that the majority of states began to raise cash by tapping personal incomes. Today, 41 states impose the tax; two (New Hampshire and Tennessee) apply it only to income from interest and dividends; and seven (Alaska, Florida, Nevada, South Dakota, Texas, Washington, and Wyoming) don't tax incomes at all.

THE HIGH COST OF COLLEGE

Some say that in the future white-collar workplace, only those who have college degrees will get the nod for new slots in management training, or even entry-level jobs behind the counter or in the mail room.

But coming up with four years of tuition and fees to help their children launch a career is breaking a lot of middle-income families. To go away to college and make it through in standard time, most students need at least two out of these three sources of money (aside from parental largesse): a scholarship, a student loan, and a part-time job.

The best way to cut costs at the very start is to do some sharp thinking when choosing a college. If you are planning on college, consider your options. You can:

- Live at home, enroll in a low-cost two-year college that offers courses applicable toward a bachelor's degree, and then transfer to a local four-year state college for your junior and senior years. This is the least expensive way to get a college education.
- Enroll in a public four-year college or university in your home state. The tuition will definitely be higher than that of a two-year college. And if you decide to live on campus, it will cost you $4,500 more per year than attending college while living at home.
- Enroll in a public college or university outside your home state. This will mean paying stiff tuition charges. But establishing legal residency could save you a significant amount. Tuitions in California public colleges, for example, are one-fifth what you'd pay in several northeastern states.

Public College In-State Tuition Charges

UNITED STATES	**$3,100**
Alabama	2,490
Alaska	2,410
Arizona	2,230
Arkansas	2,310
California	3,190
Colorado	2,800
Connecticut	4,420
Delaware	4,500
District of Columbia	1,230
Florida	2,110
Georgia	2,320
Hawaii	1,780
Idaho	1,870
Illinois	3,770
Indiana	3,380
Iowa	2,910
Kansas	2,380
Kentucky	2,430
Louisiana	2,610
Maine	3,920
Maryland	3,920
Massachusetts	4,870
Michigan	4,400
Minnesota	3,440
Mississippi	2,890
Missouri	3,290
Montana	2,490
Nebraska	2,430
Nevada	1,890
New Hampshire	4,720
New Jersey	4,450
New Mexico	2,170
New York	3,490
North Carolina	1,770
North Dakota	2,650
Ohio	4,020
Oklahoma	1,980
Oregon	3,610
Pennsylvania	5,320
Rhode Island	4,390
South Carolina	3,560
South Dakota	3,020
Tennessee	2,240
Texas	1,900
Utah	2,310
Vermont	6,790
Virginia	4,450
Washington	3,170
West Virginia	2,320
Wisconsin	2,910
Wyoming	2,250
CANADA	$2,200
Alberta	1,720
British Columbia	2,270
Manitoba	1,930
New Brunswick	2,580
Newfoundland	1,900
Nova Scotia	2,750
Ontario	2,460
Quebec	1,590
Saskatchewan	2,250

Source: National Center for Education Statistics, Statistics Canada.

Note: Costs are in American dollars. United States data are weighted averages; Canadian figures are for undergraduate study at the largest university in each province.

- Register at a private college or university. This is the most expensive option, even if you live at home.

PAYING FOR POWER

Aside from how old the power plant is and how far it is from oil and coal fuel sources, the biggest factors that play a part in charges to consumers are who owns the company, and how the electricity is generated.

The Energy Department's latest price comparison of electricity shows that, in general, publicly owned (municipal) electric power companies charge much lower rates than their larger, privately owned counterparts. Moreover, utilities that operate nuclear power plants tend to charge the consumer much higher rates than

not being allowed to operate ...

During 1996, the billions of kilowatt hours produced by nuclear reactors counted for 16 percent of the total North American electrical output. Over half the electricity consumed in Connecticut, Maine, Nebraska, Ontario, and South Carolina is generated from nuclear power plants.

The following list shows the 32 states and 3 provinces in which nuclear power plants are found. The generating capacity, or power output, for a typical reactor is 1,000 megawatts (one million kilowatts) of electricity, or enough to supply the needs of a city of 600,000 people at any given moment. The date of operation—actual or planned—is also given for each unit along with its county location.

Alabama: 7,279 megawatts total capacity
Houston County: Farley #1 (1977), Farley #2 (1981). Jackson County: Bellefonte #1 (indefinite), Bellefonte #2 (indefinite). Morgan County: Browns Ferry #1 (1974), Browns Ferry #2 (1975), Browns Ferry #3 (1977).

Arizona: 3,810 megawatts total capacity
Maricopa County: Palo Verde #1 (1986), Palo Verde #2 (1986), Palo Verde #3 (1988).

Arkansas: 1,762 megawatts total capacity
Pope County: Arkansas Nuclear #1 (1974), Arkansas Nuclear #2 (1980).

California: 5,694 megawatts total capacity
San Diego County: San Onofre #2 (1983), San Onofre #3 (1984). San Luis Obispo County: Diablo Canyon #1 (1985), Diablo Canyon #2 (1986).

Connecticut: 3,262 megawatts total capacity
Middlesex County: Haddam Neck (1968). New London County: Millstone #1 (1970), Millstone #2 (1975), Millstone #3 (1986).

Florida: 3,856 megawatts total capacity
Citrus County: Crystal River #3 (1977). Dade

North American Sales Tax Rates

State	Rate	Exemptions Food	Exemptions Drugs
Alabama	4%		•
Arizona	5	•	•
Arkansas	4.5		•
California	6	•	•
Colorado	3	•	•
Connecticut*	6	•	•
District of Columbia	7.5	•	•
Florida	6	•	•
Georgia	4		•
Hawaii*	4		•
Idaho*	5		•
Illinois	6.25	1%	1%
Indiana*	5	•	•
Iowa	5	•	•
Kansas	4.9		•
Kentucky	6	•	•
New York	4	•	•
North Carolina	4		•
North Dakota	5	•	•
Ohio	5	•	•
Oklahoma	4.5		•
Pennsylvania*	6	•	•
Rhode Island*	7	•	•
South Carolina	5		•
South Dakota	4		•
Tennessee	6		•
Texas	6.25	•	•
Utah	4.875		•
Vermont*	5	•	•
Virginia*	3.5		•
Washington	6.5	•	•
West Virginia*	6		•
Wisconsin	5	•	•
Wyoming	4		•
CANADA			
British Columbia*	7%	•	•
Manitoba*	7	•	•
New Brunswick*	11	•	•
Newfoundland*	12	•	•
Nova Scotia*	11	•	•
Ontario*	8	•	•
Quebec*	8	•	•
Saskatchewan*	9	•	•

Source: Commerce Clearing House, *Canadian Master Tax Guide* and *State Tax Guide*. Alaska, Alberta, Delaware, Montana, New Hampshire, and Oregon have no general sales tax.

* Indicates a single tax rate throughout the state or province. All other states permit local additions to their base tax rate.

• Indicates food or drugs are exempt.

Note: HI, ID, KS, SD, VT, and WY tax food, but allow an income tax credit to compensate poor households.

State Income Tax Rates

State	Tax Rate Low	Tax Rate High	Brackets	Income Brackets Low	Income Brackets High	Personal Exemption Single	Personal Exemption Married	Personal Exemption Child
Alabama	2.0	5.0	3	500	3,000	1,500	3,000	300
Arizona	3.0	5.6	5	10,000	150,000	2,100	4,200	2,300
Arkansas	1.0	7.0	6	2,999	25,000	20 (c)	40 (c)	20
California	1.0	9.3	6	4,831	219,872	66 (c)	132 (c)	66
Colorado	5.0 flat rate							
Connecticut	3.0	4.5	2	2,250	2,250	12,000 (b)	24,000 (b)	0
Delaware	0.0	7.1	7	2,000	40,000	100 (c)	200 (c)	100
District of Columbia	6.0	9.5	3	10,000	20,000	1,370	2,740	1,370
Georgia	1.0	6.0	6	750	7,000	1,500	3,000	1,500
Hawaii	2.0	10.0	8	1,500	20,500	1,040	2,080	1,040
Idaho	2.0	8.2	8	1,000	20,000	2,550 (d)	5,100 (d)	2,550
Illinois	3.0 flat rate			1,000	2,000	1,000		
Indiana	3.4 flat rate			1,000	2,000	1,000		
Iowa (a)	0.4	9.98	9	1,081	48,645	20 (c)	40 (c)	40
Kansas	4.4	7.75	3	20,000	30,000	2,000	4,000	2,000
Kentucky	2.0	6.0	5	3,000	8,000	20 (c)	40 (c)	20
Louisiana	2.0	6.0	3	10,000	50,000	4,500 (a)	9,000 (a)	1,000
Maine (a)	2.0	8.5	4	4,150	16,500	2,100	4,200	2,100
Maryland	2.0	5.0	4	1,000	3,000	1,200	2,400	1,200
Massachusetts	5.95 flat rate			2,200	4,400	1,000		
Michigan (a)	4.4 flat rate			2,400	4,800	2,400		
Minnesota (a)	6.0	8.5	3	16,070	52,790	2,550 (d)	5,100 (d)	2,550
Mississippi	3.0	5.0	3	5,000	10,000	6,000	9,500	1,500
Missouri	1.5	6.0	10	1,000	9,000	1,200	2,400	400
Montana (a)	2.0	11.0	10	1,800	64,900	1,480	2,960	1,480
Nebraska (a)	2.62	6.99	4	2,400	26,500	69 (c)	138 (c)	69
New Jersey	1.4	6.37	6	20,000	75,000	1,000	2,000	1,500
New Mexico	1.7	8.5	7	5,500	65,000	2,550 (d)	5,100 (d)	2,550
New York	4.0	7.000	4	5,500	11,000	0	0	1,000
North Carolina	6.0	7.75	3	12,750	60,000	2,550 (d)	5,100 (d)	
North Dakota	2.67	12.0	8	3,000	50,000	2,550 (d)	5,100 (d)	2,550
Ohio	0.743	7.5	9	5,000	200,000	750	1,500	750
Oklahoma	0.5	7.0	8	1,000	10,000	1,000	2,000	1,000
Oregon (a)	5.0	9.0	3	2,150	5,400	120 (c)	240 (c)	120
Pennsylvania	2.8 flat rate							
Rhode Island	27.5% Federal tax liability							
South Carolina	2.5	7.0	6	2,250	11,250	2,550 (d)	5,100 (d)	
Utah	2.55	7.0	6	750	3,750	1,913 (d)	3,825 (d)	1,913
Vermont	25.0% Federal tax liability							
Virginia	2.0	5.75	4	3,000	17,000	800	1,600	800
West Virginia	3.0	6.5	5	10,000	60,000	2,000	4,000	2,000
Wisconsin	4.9	6.93	3	7,500	15,000	0	0	50

Source: Federation of Tax Administrators.

Note: Tax rates and brackets are for single individual returns. Alaska, Florida, Nevada, South Dakota, Texas, Washington, and Wyoming do not tax personal income. New Hampshire and Tennessee tax income from interest and dividends.

(a) Combined personal exemptions and standard deduction.

(b) Combined personal exemptions and standard deduction. An additional tax credit is allowed ranging from 75% to 0% based on state-adjusted gross income. Exemption amounts are phased out for higher income taxpayers until they are eliminated for households earning over $71,000. For tax years beginning after 1996, the tax bracket amount increases to $4,500.

(c) Tax credits.

(d) These states allow personal exemption or standard deductions as provided in the Internal Revenue Code. Utah allows a personal exemption equal to three-fourths the federal exemptions. Amounts reported include the 1996 index adjustment.

County: Turkey Point #3 (1972), Turkey Point #4 (1973). St. Lucie County: St. Lucie #1 (1976), St. Lucie #2 (1983).

Georgia: 3,800 megawatts total capacity
Appling County: Hatch #1 (1975), Hatch #2 (1979). Burke County: Vogtle #1 (1987), Vogtle #2 (1989).

Illinois: 12,815 megawatts total capacity
Byron County: Byron #1 (1985), Byron #2 (1987). De Witt County: Clinton (1987). Grundy County: Dresden #2 (1970), Dresden #3 (1971). Lake County: Zion #1 (1973), Zion #2 (1974). La Salle County: La Salle #1 (1984), La Salle #2 (1984). Rock Island County: Quad Cities #1 (1972), Quad Cities #2 (1972). Will County: Braidwood #1 (1988), Braidwood #2 (1988).

Iowa: 545 megawatts total capacity
Linn County: Duane Arnold (1975).

Kansas: 1,150 megawatts total capacity
Coffee County: Wolf Creek (1985).

Louisiana: 2,044 megawatts total capacity
St. Charles Parish: Waterford #3 (1985). West Feliciana Parish: River Bend (1986).

Maine: 825 megawatts total capacity

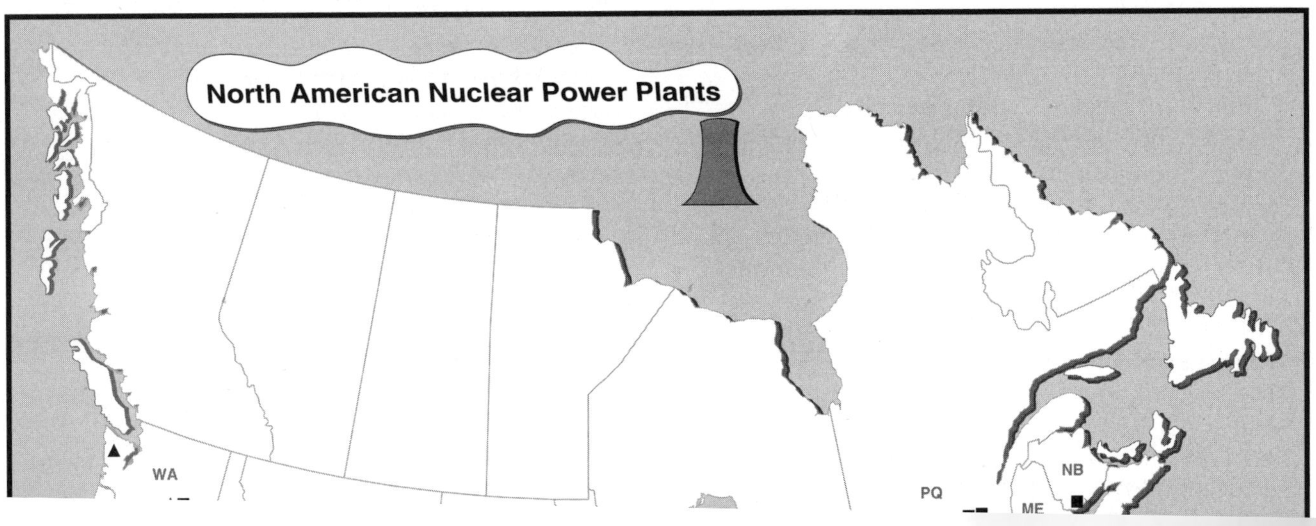

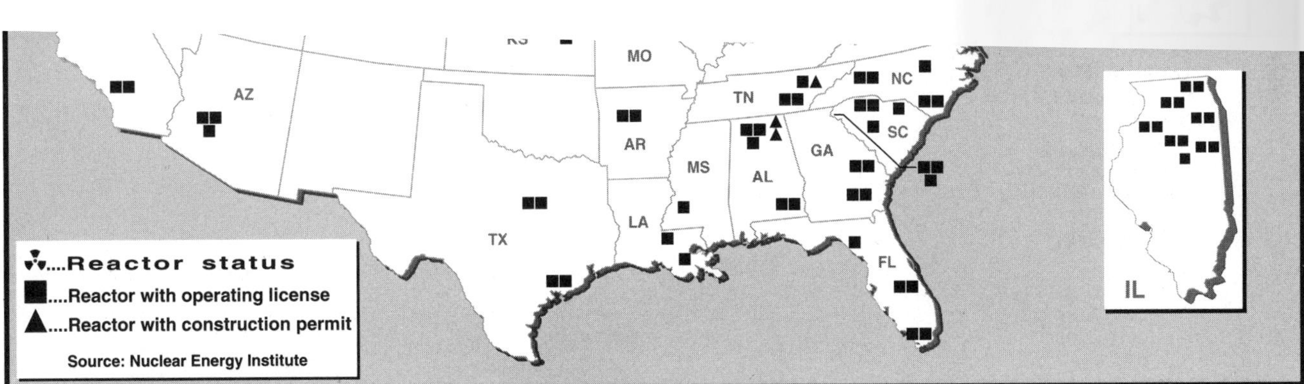

Thomas Nast, Cartographer

Lincoln County: Maine Yankee (1972).

Maryland: 1,650 megawatts total capacity
Calvert County: Calvert Cliffs #1 (1975), Calvert Cliffs #2 (1977).

Massachusetts: 545 megawatts total capacity
Plymouth County: Pilgrim (1972).

Michigan: 4,078 megawatts total capacity
Berrien County: Cook #1 (1975), Cook #2 (1978). Charlevoix County: Big Rock Point (1965). Monroe County: Fermi #2 (1988). Van Buren County: Palisades (1971).

Minnesota: 1,605 megawatts total capacity
Goodhue County: Prairie Island #1 (1973), Prairie Island #2 (1974). Wright County: Monticello (1971).

Mississippi: 1,250 megawatts total capacity
Claiborne County: Grand Gulf (1985).

Missouri: 1,120 megawatts total capacity
Callaway County: Callaway (1984).

Nebraska: 1,246 megawatts total capacity
Namaha County: Cooper (1974). Washington County: Fort Calhoun (1973).

New Brunswick: 633 megawatts total capacity
Point Lepreau: Point Lepreau (1983).

New Hampshire: 650 megawatts total capacity
Rockingham County: Seabrook (1990).

New Jersey: 3,922 megawatts total capacity
Ocean County: Oyster Creek (1969). Salem County: Hope Creek (1986). Salem #1 (1977), Salem #2 (1981).

New York: 4,623 megawatts total capacity
Oswego County: Nine Mile Point #1 (1969), Nine Mile Point #2 (1988). Suffolk County: Fitzpatrick (1975). Wayne County: Ginna (1970). Westchester County: Indian Point #2 (1973), Indian Point #3 (1976).

North Carolina: 4,842 megawatts total capacity
Brunswick County: Brunswick #1 (1977), Bruns-

wick #2 (1975). Mecklenburg County: McGuire #1 (1981), McGuire #2 (1984). Wake County: Harris (1987).

Ohio: 3,270 megawatts total capacity
Lake County: Perry #1 (1987), Perry #2 (indefinite). Ottawa County: Davis–Besse (1977).

Ontario: 4,310 megawatts total capacity
Newcastle: Darlington A (1990), Darlington B (1992). Pickering: Pickering A (1972), Pickering B (1981). Tiverton: Bruce A (1971), Bruce B (1976).

Pennsylvania: 8,009 Total Capacity
Beaver County: Beaver Valley #1 (1976), Beaver Valley #2 (1987). Luzerne County: Susquehanna #1 (1983), Susquehanna #2 (1985). Montgomery County: Limerick #1 (1986), Limerick #2 (1990). York County: Peach Bottom #2 (1974), Peach Bottom #3 (1974).

Quebec: 638 megawatts total capacity
Becancour: Gentilly #2 (1983).

South Carolina: 6,435 megawatts total capacity
Darlington County: Robinson #2 (1971). Fairfield County: Summer (1984). Oconee County: Oconee #1 (1973), Oconee #2 (1973), Oconee #3 (1974). York County: Catawba (1986).

Tennessee: 4,650 megawatts total capacity
Hamilton County: Sequoyah #1 (1981), Sequoyah #2 (1982). Rhea County: Watts Bar #1 (indefinite), Watts Bar #2 (indefinite).

Texas: 4,800 megawatts total capacity
Matagorda County: South Texas Project #1 (1988), South Texas Project #2 (1989). Somervell County: Comanche Peak #1 (1990), Comanche Peak #2 (1993).

Vermont: 514 megawatts total capacity
Windham County: Vermont Yankee (1972).

Virginia: 3,414 megawatts total capacity
Louisa County: North Anna #1 (1978), North Anna #2 (1980). Surry County: Surry #1 (1972), Surry #2 (1973).

Washington: 1,000 megawatts total capacity
Benton County: WPPSS #2 (1984).

Wisconsin: 1,505 megawatts total capacity
Kewaunee County: Kewaunee (1974). Manitowoc County: Point Beach #1 (1970), Point Beach #2 (1972).

If you travel often enough, you might take for granted expressway networks, airline routes, and passenger rails that lace up the continent's different points. But not all metro areas are transportation hubs with highway, rail, and air-route access.

Population size has something to do with an area's transportation assets, but so do the accidents of geography. There are 28 metro areas bigger than Denver, but because the Mile-High City is plunked down at the edge of the Rocky Mountains halfway between Chicago and Southern California, and midway from Houston to Seattle, only four other airports in North America are busier than Denver International.

Intercity travel is only part of the picture. Some metro areas have efficient public transit fleets relied on by hundreds of thousands of commuters each working day. In other metro areas, aging diesel buses with optimistic schedules lurch along routes that rarely reach any neighborhoods but those close to downtown. Still other metro areas have no public transit at all.

GETTING AROUND TOWN

If you are moving to Atlanta, can your family get by without a second car if MARTA's routes reach your new neighborhood? If you are being transferred to company headquarters in downtown Cleveland, will it be more convenient to carpool or ride the RTA rails if you settle in Shaker Heights? How much time will you expect to spend each day getting to and from work? Becoming familiar with the local transportation features of a particular metro area will help you answer some of these questions.

The Commuting Life

Every weekday morning, in cities and towns all over, traffic trickles out of suburban streets, flows into arterial roads, and floods freeways to capacity with people bound for work. According to transportation experts, the morning rush hour lasts 118 minutes, between 7:01 and 8:59. Most workers travel by automobile, alone. One out of 5 belongs to a car pool, and one out of 15 opts for public transit.

The evening rush hour lasts longer, 150 minutes, from 4:30 to 7:00. There are more traffic delays at this time than in the morning when people so purposefully leave home and arrive at work in the shortest possible time. In the evening, many commuters stop for a drink, go shopping, run errands, or just dawdle. After all, one can't be fired for being late for supper. In fact, traffic experts say, even if you head straight home, the evening trip not only seems longer than the trip to work but actually is—20 percent longer.

How much time do metro-area workers spend going to and from the job each day? To allow for the longer trip home in the evening, *Places Rated* multiplies the average journey-to-work figure by 2.2 to estimate the round-trip time in each of the metro areas.

Daily commuting time increases with city size. Workers in Bismarck, ND, for instance, putting in 220 working days a year, spend about 100 hours commuting. Workers residing on Staten Island spend 325 hours

Getting to Work and Back

Longest Commute

1. New York, NY	75.8 minutes
2. Long Island, NY	64.6
3. Washington, DC–MD–VA–WV	63.0
4. Chicago, IL	61.5
5. Riverside–San Bernardino, CA	59.3
6. Newburgh, NY	58.5
7. Monmouth–Ocean, NJ	57.5
8. Oakland, CA	57.5
9. Houston, TX	56.9
10. Vallejo–Fairfield–Napa, CA	56.8

Shortest Commute

1. Bismarck, ND	27.1
2. Grand Forks, ND–MN	27.4
3. Cheyenne, WY	29.5
4. Dubuque, IA	30.1
5. Fargo–Moorhead, ND–MN	30.7
6. Enid, OK	30.8
7. Great Falls, MT	30.9
8. Sheboygan, WI	31.5
9. Rochester, MN	31.6
10. Waterloo–Cedar Falls, IA	31.9

Source: Derived from U.S. Bureau of the Census, 1990 Census of Population and Housing.

The Busiest Intercity Rail Routes

Service aboard trains in VIA Rail Canada's St. Lawrence Corridor and AMTRAK's Northeast Corridor account for half of each country's passenger rail traffic.

AMTRAK Northeast Corridor	Annual Passengers
NortheastDirect (Boston–Washington)	5,510,000
Metroliners (New York–Washington)	2,025,000
New York–Philadelphia	1,711,000
New York–Albany–Niagara Falls	1,071,000
New York–Philadelphia–Harrisburg	550,000
AMTRAK Intercity	
Chicago–Salt Lake City–Oakland	638,000
Chicago–Seattle/Portland	453,000
Chicago–Milwaukee	447,000
New York–Charleston–Miami/Tampa	421,000
Chicago–Detroit–Pontiac/Toledo	395,000
AMTRAK Western	
Santa Barbara–LAX–San Diego	1,629,000
Oakland–Bakersfield	554,000
Los Angeles–Seattle	452,000
San Jose–Roseville	367,000
Seattle–Portland–Eugene	127,000
VIA The Corridor	
Montreal–Toronto	924,000
Toronto–Windsor	656,000
Toronto–Ottawa	524,000

Source: AMTRAK, VIA Rail Canada.

taking the ferry to and from their Manhattan jobs. The contrast between Bismarck and Staten Island, then, is more than one between a prairie state capital and a section of the continent's largest city. Based on commuting time alone, Bismarckers have more free time than Staten Islanders, the equivalent of six 40-hour weeks each year.

Public Mass Transit

One reason for the long commute in big cities is the often exhausting job of making linked transit trips to get to work. The average duration of an *unlinked* transit trip—a direct route, with no transfers—is about 15 minutes. But many big-city commuters have to make linked trips—driving to a park-and-ride or kiss-and-ride lot; boarding a train, ferry, or bus; and sometimes switching again before finally getting to work.

Still, in larger cities where the tab for daily parking in a downtown garage nears $20, where rush-hour traffic approaches gridlock, where distances are long and time always seems short, public transit really counts. In many a large city—Houston and Phoenix, for example—daily driving over long distances is a way of life unrelieved by rapid public transit; taking the bus is the only alternative. In other places such as Atlanta, Toronto, Washington, and San Francisco, large local bus fleets are complemented by rapid transit rail systems.

Depending on where they want to go, New York City commuters can choose from bus, heavy rail, light rail, commuter railroad, ferryboat, and even aerial tramway service. New York straphangers may not always enjoy their subway ride to work, but few among the jostled riders aboard a rocking, grimy IRT car would ever envy a Houston driver who has missed his or her exit on the Katy Freeway at rush hour.

By bus. In most cities, public transit and "the bus" are synonymous. Unlike rapid rail and trolley networks, a bus system requires no expensive construction, and routes can be easily changed to meet demand.

Each of the continent's 1,500 transit systems with fixed-route service puts motor buses on the street, but these systems vary in size and type of operation. Several large systems—CTA (Chicago), TTC (Toronto), WMATA (Washington, DC), and NYCTA (New York), for example—operate thousands of GMC, Orion, and Flyer buses around the clock with less than one minute between buses on the heaviest routes during morning and evening rush hours. At the other extreme are the one- and two-bus shoppers' specials that run loops in the central business district of smaller metro areas.

By rail. Although buses can meet the demand for public transit nearly everywhere, rail lines are more efficient in carrying large numbers of rush-hour commuters in the major cities. Several kinds of rail service are available in the big metro areas, from rapid rail to trolley car to commuter train.

Rapid rail lines. Due to their exclusive rights-of-way, these are unaffected by traffic jams. Their trains and trams not only carry thousands of people but carry them quickly. The average speed of buses during peak rush hour, nationwide, is 12 miles per hour. Rapid rail

North America's Top 30 Airport Pairs

Passenger traffic between 30 airports accounts for 10 percent of all passenger traffic between all commercial airports in North America.

From/To	From/To	Passengers
Honolulu (HNL)	Kahului, Maui (OGG)	3,383,578
Las Vegas (LAS)	Los Angeles (LAX)	2,884,740
Honolulu (HNL)	Los Angeles (LAX)	2,639,497
Los Angeles (LAX)	San Francisco (SFO)	2,621,127
Atlanta (ATL)	Dallas/Fort Worth (DFW)	2,264,934
Los Angeles (LAX)	New York (JFK)	2,201,128
Chicago (ORD)	New York (LGA)	2,071,694
Los Angeles (LAX)	Phoenix (PHX)	2,016,640
Chicago (ORD)	Los Angeles (LAX)	1,973,180
Atlanta (ATL)	Orlando (MCO)	1,946,440
Honolulu (HNL)	Lihue, Kauai (LIH)	1,910,263
Dallas/Fort Worth (DFW)	Los Angeles (LAX)	1,564,031
Honolulu (HNL)	Kona (KOA)	1,549,602
Dallas/Fort Worth (DFW)	Houston (IAH)	1,528,085
Atlanta (ATL)	Newark (EWR)	1,517,936
San Francisco (SFO)	Seattle (SEA)	1,477,860
Chicago (ORD)	Minneapolis/ St. Paul (MSP)	1,476,744
Honolulu (HNL)	San Francisco (SFO)	1,469,124
Atlanta (ATL)	Tampa (TPA)	1,468,115
Detroit (DTW)	Chicago (ORD)	1,440,665

Source: Derived from Federal Aviation Administration origin and destination surveys. Figures include both jet and commuter passengers. The heaviest traffic between a Canadian city pair is that of Montreal and Toronto at 1.1 million passengers.

systems average more than 20 miles per hour. There are two types of rapid rail lines in use today in 24 metro areas: heavy rail, which accounts for 2.5 billion passenger trips in a year, and light rail, which accounts for 150 million passenger trips. Both are electrically powered, and both may be found in the same city.

Heavy rail systems—known locally as subways, elevated rail or ELs—have high-level platform stations. The cars are individually powered through the third rail, and are hitched together to form longer trains during rush hours. New York City's heavy rail system, composed of two separate networks, is the world's largest, with 6,248 cars traveling more than 450 miles of track; Philadelphia also has two systems. Sixteen metro areas have heavy rail systems.

Light rail cars. Powered by overhead electrical wires, these travel at half the speed of heavy rail cars. Because their tracks are laid aboveground, they are less expen-

Top North American Airlines

In 1926, a transcontinental flight cost $400 and took 32 hours including 14 stops for refueling. The same flight today takes less than 6 hours. Seventy years ago 14 airlines operated in North America and together carried some 7,000 passengers. Several survived and are now giants.

Airline	Aircraft	Annual Flights
Delta	563	992,970
American	667	942,683
USAir	443	862,358
United	544	745,414
Northwest	358	537,667
Southwest	178	506,967
Continental	289	470,487
Trans World	182	264,492
Air Canada	105	146,998

Trolley coaches. Trolleys are streetcar-type railways that travel on city streets with semiprivate or exclusive rights-of-way. They are a less efficient form of travel than rapid rail since the trams are at the mercy of automobile traffic and, in some cities, must stop for streetlights. Another disadvantage is that their routes cannot be altered. These systems have been largely replaced by bus; in fact, only nine metro areas in North America have trolley coach operations.

Commuter railroads. Trains have been an important form of transportation from more distant suburbs to the central part of major cities since the nineteenth century. Using both locomotive-hauled and self-propelled passenger cars, this service is marked by multi-trip tickets, station-to-station fares, railroad employment practices, and usually only one or two stations in the central business district.

Twenty-four commuter railroads in 15 metro areas carry nearly 1.5 million commuters to and from work. The largest commuter railroad network, made up of seven firms, is found in New York and uses 1,650 cars to move 525,000 riders in a typical weekday. In Chicago, the next largest commuter railroad center, nine carriers operating 850 cars transport 300,000 workers in a typical day.

INTERCITY TRAVEL

"You can't get there from here" is the punch line of the old joke about the lost city sharper who asked directions of a bemused farmer. The line has little meaning in today's metropolitan areas, given the networks of well-

Some Days . . .

You'll stand the best chance of dodging airport jams if you fly on Thursday afternoon and Saturday night.

The worst travel days used to be Friday and Sunday. Now they are Tuesday and Wednesday because more people take advantage of special fares requiring midweek travel.

. . . You're Better Off in Large Hubs

The Federal Aviation Administration (FAA) rates each metro area for its share of airline service:

A metro area is a . . .	if passengers leaving its airport(s) total
large hub	1% or more
medium hub	0.25% to 0.99%
small hub	0.05% to 0.24%
nonhub	less than 0.05%
	of all U.S. airline passengers in a year.

There's one big advantage to living in a large hub besides having a wider choice of carriers with more frequent nonstop flights to more destinations. Flying between large hubs is cheaper.

The cost of an airline ticket into and out of Bismarck, ND (a nonhub), or Charleston, WV (a small hub), helps subsidize the same airline's small profit from a New York vacationer's air travel to Miami or a Los Angeles conventioneer's trip to Chicago. When airlines skirmish with bargain fares between large hubs, travelers in the smaller hubs end up paying part of the tab.

Decoding the Interstate

The numbers in the middle of the red, white, and blue shield-shaped signs along the interstate system were developed in 1957 by the American Association of State Highway Transportation officials. There are 34 odd-numbered routes running north and south and 27 even-numbered routes running east and west. The lowest-numbered routes are in the West and the South; I-5, for example, lies along the nation's West Coast and I-10 runs along the southern border.

In cities, these one- or two-digit numbers don't change as long as they are part of the major traffic stream. Beltways around the city, on the other hand, carry three numbers; the main route number with an even-numbered prefix. For example, I-495, an 88-mile-long route around Boston, and I-287, a 94-mile-long loop skirting New York City, are the two longest beltways in the interstate system. If a main route carries an odd-numbered prefix (such as I-195 in Miami or I-780 in San Francisco), the route is a spur that connects with the main route at only one end.

Three-digit route numbers are never used twice in the same state. In New York, I-90 runs through Schenectady, Syracuse, Rochester, and Buffalo, and the beltways off this main route in those cities are numbered, respectively, I-890, I-690, I-490, and I-290. This rule isn't carried across state lines, however. Two cities on I-10 but in different states, Houston and New Orleans, have the identical beltway number of I-610.

traveled highways, railroads, and airways that connect these places.

Or does it? Obviously, you can't ramp on to the Interstate or board AMTRAK if your destination is Anchorage or Honolulu. For that matter, you can't get to Bloomington, Brazoria, or Bremerton by the same means. When it comes to intercity travel options, some metro areas are better off than others.

National Highways

When President Franklin Roosevelt idly penciled three east-west and five north-south lines on a U.S. map back in 1938 as part of a proposed national highway system, he probably had no idea that his drawing would be so important in determining whether many rural towns would grow and many others would decline. He was thinking of a 34,000-mile network of multilane toll roads.

Although the concept of collecting tolls was soon dropped by the Bureau of Public Roads, the basic routes on his map foresaw the Interstate Highway System, a river of economic life to cities and towns along the way and possibly a cause of stagnation for those that were bypassed.

The interstate system is now a complete 42,500-mile road network, at least four traffic lanes wide, linking together nearly every American city with a population of more than 50,000. Even though interstate routes account for only 1 percent of all road and street mileage in the United States, they carry 25 percent of all the traffic. One in six U.S. metro areas isn't on the interstate network; in Canada, half of the metro areas aren't on that country's counterpart, the 4,800-mile Trans-Canada Highway.

Boarding Pass, Please

It's getting to be an old saying in the South that when you die and are enroute to heaven or hell, you'll have to make connections in Atlanta. Atlanta's airport, Hartsfield International, is now the world's busiest.

Like other airports that are reached by scheduled airlines, Hartsfield is a twentieth-century urban landmark in the same way the railroad station was a sign of the times in the late nineteenth century. Most of the 296 airports served by major airlines in the United States and Canada are quiet, even desolate places.

But some like Hartsfield resemble self-contained cities and, of the nearly 600 million people who board domestic flights, one in 10 travel between 30 of these airports in the continent's large hubs. Both Hartsfield and Chicago's O'Hare International Airport board more passengers than the 200 smallest airports combined.

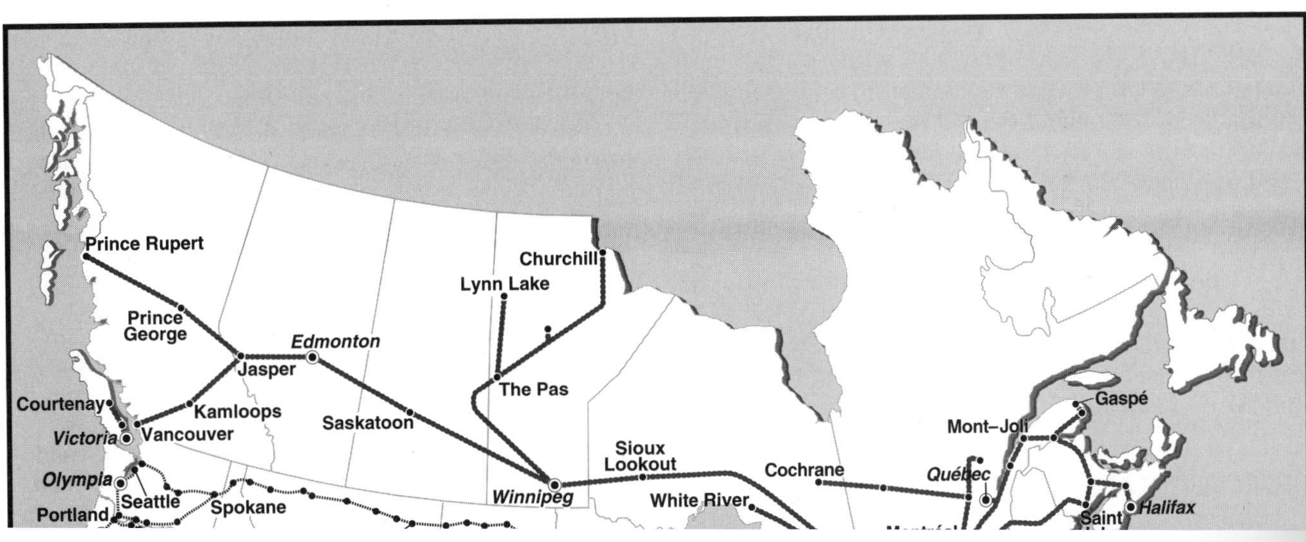

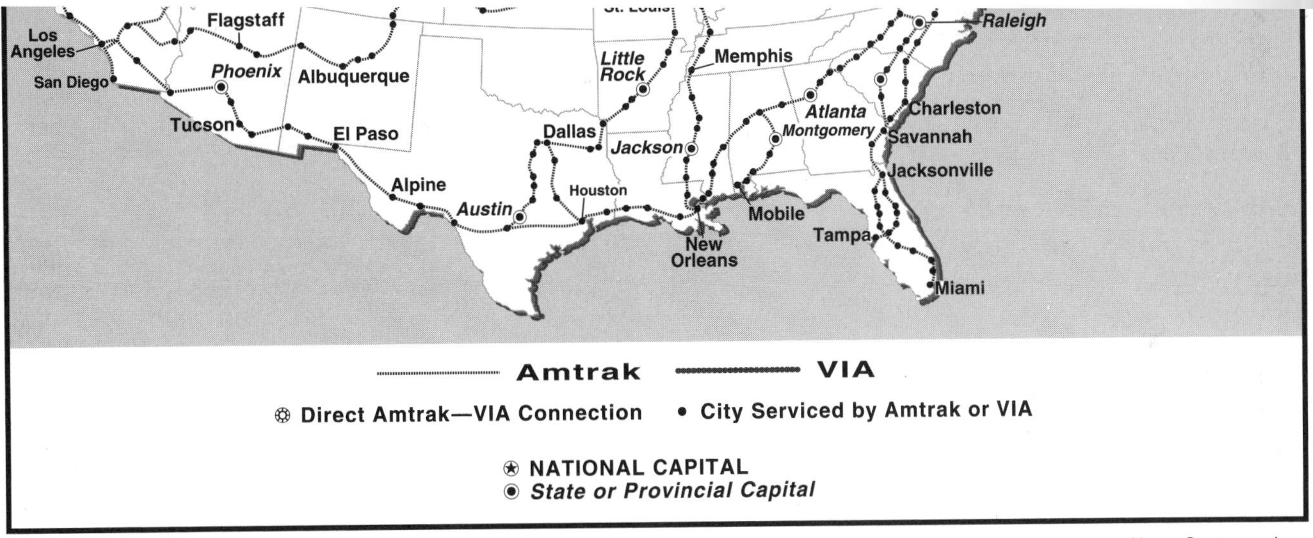

Thomas Nast, Cartographer

Riding the Rails

Seventy years ago, 8 out of 10 people who had to get from one North American city to another did it aboard a train. There were 20,000 different ones from which to choose, if you didn't care where you were going. The Twentieth Century Limited, El Capitan, Blue Streak—each had a unique, trademarked name. They still do—Desert Wind, Sunset Limited, Empire Builder, Texas Eagle, Bonaventure, Canadian—but today there are just 280 of them. Over the years, their share of the commercial intercity passenger traffic has dwindled to 2 percent.

If passenger trains are ever to rise again, the renaissance will be caused not by high gasoline prices and spot fuel shortages but by intolerable congestion on intercity highways. Railroads have a priceless asset: existing tracks and rights-of-way into the continent's population centers.

The National Railroad Passenger Corporation, a profit-making body, was created by Congress to subsidize the passenger business of its member railroads. Better known as AMTRAK, it started operation in 1971. Today it carries virtually all of the 25 million passengers who board U.S. intercity trains each year. VIA, Canada's intercity rail counterpart, also carries nearly all of that country's train passengers.

The passenger rails don't reach everywhere, however. Although AMTRAK's and VIA's timetables boast stops at hundreds of cities and towns from Halifax, NS, to San Diego, CA, 166 of the 351 metro areas aren't on the route system. The metro areas bypassed include such large places as Calgary, Tulsa, Louisville, and Des Moines.

By far the biggest markets for train service are in the U.S. northeast corridor and the St. Lawrence corridor in Canada. But the fastest-growing markets are on the West Coast, particularly for the two-hour-and-forty-minute run between Los Angeles and San Diego and for the six-hour San Francisco-Bakersfield route.

SCORING: TRANSPORTATION

Would a shopper in Syracuse or San Angelo have a better chance of finding a seat on a bus? Which airport—Calgary's or Denver's—has departures to more nonstop destinations? Which metro area, Seattle or New York, is nearer the greatest number of other metro areas?

To derive a score for each metro area, *Places Rated* considers three broad factors: (1) **Connectivity**, or a combination of the number of nonstop jet and commuter airline destinations and the number of passenger rail departures, (2) **Commute**, or a combination of local transit revenue miles and the average minutes it takes to get to work and back, and (3) **Centrality**, or a measurement of how near a metro area is to all other metro areas by a combination of latitude and longitude, national highways, and passenger rail directions.

Each factor is weighted differently—connectivity is 60 percent of the final score, commute is 30 percent, and centrality 10 percent. The sum of these weighted scores for each metro area is then normalized such that the 50th percentile point is the average for all metro areas.

RANKINGS: Transportation

Three broad criteria are used to rate each metro area for transportation: (1) its supply of public transit and its daily commute, (2) its connectivity with other metro areas via national highways, scheduled air service, and passenger rail service, and (3) its centrality, or relative nearness to all other metro areas. Places that are tied get the same rank and are listed in alphabetical order.

Metro Areas from Best to Worst

Places Rated Rank		Places Rated Score
1.	Chicago, IL	98.92
2.	Philadelphia, PA–NJ	98.40
3.	New York, NY	98.34
4.	Toronto, ON	98.29
5.	Montreal, PQ	98.11
6.	Baltimore, MD	97.86
7.	New Haven–Meriden, CT	96.72
8.	Newark, NJ	96.59
9.	Trenton, NJ	96.53
10.	Oshawa, ON	95.60
11.	Windsor, ON	95.58
12.	Washington, DC–MD–VA–WV	95.49
13.	St. Louis, MO–IL	95.25
14.	Minneapolis–St. Paul, MN–WI	95.22
15.	Pittsburgh, PA	95.10
16.	Denver, CO	94.95
17.	St. Cloud, MN	94.42
18.	Los Angeles–Long Beach, CA	94.30
19.	Wilmington–Newark, DE–MD	94.11
20.	Kitchener, ON	93.89
21.	Boston, MA–NH	93.79
22.	Hamilton, ON	93.41
23.	Salt Lake City–Ogden, UT	93.17
24.	Gary, IN	92.72
25.	Ottawa–Hull, ON–PQ	92.70
26.	Detroit, MI	92.68
27.	Atlanta, GA	92.55
28.	Cincinnati, OH–KY–IN	91.63
29.	Bridgeport, CT	91.41
29.	Middlesex–Somerset–Hunterdon, NJ	91.41
31.	Cleveland–Lorain–Elyria, OH	91.36
32.	Milwaukee–Waukesha, WI	90.33
33.	Athens, GA	88.99
34.	London, ON	88.91
35.	Sheboygan, WI	87.81
36.	Bergen–Passaic, NJ	87.79
37.	Atlantic City–Cape May, NJ	87.78
38.	Houston, TX	87.74
39.	Charlotte–Gastonia–Rock Hill, NC–SC	87.72
40.	Springfield, MA	87.69
41.	San Diego, CA	87.26
42.	Tampa–St. Petersburg–Clearwater, FL	87.05
43.	Fort Lauderdale, FL	86.40
44.	San Francisco, CA	86.33
45.	Quebec City, PQ	86.06
46.	Kansas City, MO–KS	85.98
47.	Topeka, KS	85.69
48.	Winnipeg, MB	85.57
49.	San Jose, CA	85.28
50.	Portland–Vancouver, OR–WA	85.09
51.	Phoenix–Mesa, AZ	85.03
52.	Flint, MI	84.94
53.	Lincoln, NE	84.60
54.	Miami, FL	84.56
55.	Orange County, CA	84.50
56.	Albany–Schenectady–Troy, NY	83.87
57.	Calgary, AB	83.64
58.	Bellingham, WA	83.51
59.	Monmouth–Ocean, NJ	83.41
60.	Seattle–Bellevue–Everett, WA	83.40
61.	Hartford, CT	83.19
62.	Greeley, CO	83.13
63.	Stamford–Norwalk, CT	82.70
64.	Sarasota–Bradenton, FL	82.45
65.	Las Vegas, NV–AZ	82.42
66.	Memphis, TN–AR–MS	82.19
67.	Providence–Fall River–Warwick, RI–MA	82.07
68.	Indianapolis, IN	81.97
69.	Greensboro–Winston-Salem–High Point, NC	81.36
69.	Kenosha, WI	81.36
71.	Buffalo–Niagara Falls, NY	81.30

Places Rated Rank		Places Rated Score
72.	Fort Collins–Loveland, CO	81.16
73.	San Antonio, TX	81.14
74.	Oakland, CA	80.86
75.	Orlando, FL	80.72
76.	Champaign–Urbana, IL	80.60
77.	Dutchess County, NY	80.57
78.	Edmonton, AB	80.30
79.	Raleigh–Durham–Chapel Hill, NC	79.27
80.	Daytona Beach, FL	79.17
81.	Boulder–Longmont, CO	79.04
82.	Bloomington–Normal, IL	79.02
83.	Syracuse, NY	78.93
84.	Akron, OH	78.78
85.	Vineland–Millville–Bridgeton, [illegible]	78.51
93.	Olympia, WA	[illegible]
94.	Regina, SK	75.59
95.	Vancouver, BC	74.93
96.	Hagerstown, MD	74.79
97.	Reno, NV	74.73
98.	Yolo, CA	74.60
99.	Nashville, TN	74.36
100.	Hickory–Morganton–Lenoir, NC	74.11
101.	Jersey City, NJ	74.04
102.	St. Catharines–Niagara, ON	73.91
103.	Rochester, NY	73.88
104.	Columbus, OH	73.77
105.	Lakeland–Winter Haven, FL	72.45
106.	Worcester, MA–CT	71.64
107.	St. Joseph, MO	71.48
108.	Muncie, IN	71.13
109.	Long Island, NY	71.01
110.	Dayton–Springfield, OH	71.00
111.	Bloomington, IN	70.80
112.	Jacksonville, FL	70.71
113.	Waterbury, CT	70.68
114.	Austin–San Marcos,	0.56
115.	Kankakee, IL	70.30
116.	St. John's, NF	70.22
117.	Lancaster, PA	70.12
118.	Sacramento, CA	70.09
119.	Salem, OR	70.08
120.	Ventura, CA	70.04
121.	Louisville, KY–IN	69.42
122.	Reading, PA	69.37
123.	New Bedford, MA	68.83
124.	Utica–Rome, NY	68.62
125.	Richmond–Petersburg, VA	68.51
126.	Victoria, BC	68.28
127.	Norfolk–Virginia Beach–Newport News, VA–NC	67.87

Places Rated Rank		Places Rated Score
128.	Tacoma, WA	67.37
129.	Saskatoon, SK	67.03
130.	Spokane, WA	66.97
131.	Santa Cruz–Watsonville, CA	66.96
132.	West Palm Beach–Boca Raton, FL	65.70
133.	Santa Rosa, CA	65.34
134.	Santa Fe, NM	65.15
135.	Danbury, CT	65.05
136.	Harrisburg–Lebanon–Carlisle, PA	64.81
137.	El Paso, TX	64.19
138.	Fresno, CA	63.80
139.	Barnstable–Yarmouth, MA	63.09
140.	Birmingham, AL	62.81
151.	Allentown–Bethlehem–Easton, PA	60.20
152.	Toledo, OH	60.08
153.	Clarksville–Hopkinsville, TN–KY	59.98
154.	Galveston–Texas City, TX	59.78
155.	Pueblo, CO	59.62
156.	Wichita, KS	59.45
157.	Little Rock–North Little Rock, AR	59.38
158.	Thunder Bay, ON	59.27
159.	Davenport–Moline–Rock Island, IA–IL	59.07
160.	Santa Barbara–Santa Maria–Lompoc, CA	58.54
161.	Lawrence, KS	57.98
162.	Melbourne–Titusville–Palm Bay, FL	57.96
163.	Fitchburg–Leominster, MA	57.90
164.	Lawrence, MA–NH	57.40
165.	Fargo–Moorhead, ND–MN	57.11
166.	Brazoria, TX	55.15
167.	Grand Rapids–Muskegon–Holland, MI	54.94
168.	Sudbury, ON	54.67
169.	Charleston, WV	54.65
170.	Des Moines, IA	54.48
171.	South Bend, IN	54.17
172.	Green Bay, WI	53.56
173.	Vallejo–Fairfield–Napa, CA	52.91
174.	Appleton–Oshkosh–Neenah, WI	52.51
175.	Tulsa, OK	51.72
176.	Lubbock, TX	51.08
177.	Fort Myers–Cape Coral, FL	50.91
177.	Kokomo, IN	50.91
179.	La Crosse, WI–MN	50.73
180.	Racine, WI	50.64

Places Rated Rank		Places Rated Score
181.	Sioux Falls, SD	50.30
182.	Jamestown, NY	50.23
183.	Tuscaloosa, AL	49.86
184.	Cedar Rapids, IA	49.81
185.	Bremerton, WA	49.57
186.	Erie, PA	49.37
187.	Madison, WI	49.29
188.	Lowell, MA–NH	49.16
189.	Burlington, VT	48.55
190.	Lansing–East Lansing, MI	48.39
191.	Greenville–Spartanburg–Anderson, SC	48.29
192.	Rocky Mount, NC	48.18
193.	Peoria–Pekin, IL	48.10
194.	Billings, MT	48.05
195.	Anchorage, AK	47.39
204.	Goldsboro, NC	[illegible]
205.	Pensacola, FL	43.02
206.	Nashua, NH	42.45
207.	Iowa City, IA	42.30
208.	Amarillo, TX	42.10
209.	Brockton, MA	41.84
210.	Waterloo–Cedar Falls, IA	41.39
211.	Portland, ME	41.12
212.	Columbia, SC	40.44
213.	Pine Bluff, AR	39.54
214.	Sioux City, IA–NE	39.27
215.	Tallahassee, FL	38.68
216.	Newburgh, NY–PA	38.48
217.	Evansville–Henderson, IN–KY	38.44
218.	Mobile, AL	38.23
219.	Lexington, KY	37.74
220.	Savannah, GA	37.61
221.	Pittsfield, MA	37.42
222.	Glens Falls, NY	37.13
223.	Salinas, CA	36.77
224.	Biloxi–Gulfport–Pascagoula, MS	36.74
225.	Gainesville, FL	36.54
226.	Rochester, MN	35.87
227.	Knoxville, TN	35.80
228.	Jackson, MS	35.61
229.	Scranton–Wilkes-Barre–Hazleton, PA	35.51
230.	Bismarck, ND	35.47
231.	Binghamton, NY	34.95
232.	Shreveport–Bossier City, LA	33.51
233.	Roanoke, VA	33.20
234.	Dubuque, IA	33.02
235.	Saint John, NB	32.82
236.	Yuba City, CA	32.61
237.	Johnstown, PA	31.99
238.	Naples, FL	31.86

Places Rated Rank		Places Rated Score
239.	Waco, TX	31.01
240.	Wausau, WI	30.57
241.	Cheyenne, WY	29.92
242.	Elkhart-Goshen, IN	29.75
243.	Bakersfield, CA	29.47
244.	Honolulu, HI	28.92
245.	Manchester, NH	27.96
246.	Huntington-Ashland, WV-KY-OH	27.88
247.	Fayetteville, NC	27.80
248.	New London-Norwich, CT-RI	27.53
249.	Janesville-Beloit, WI	27.50
250.	Lafayette, IN	27.32
251.	Punta Gorda, FL	27.16
252.	Visalia-Tulare-Porterville, CA	27.12
253.	Elmira, NY	26.71
254.	Springfield, MO	26.67
255.	Fayetteville-Springdale-Rogers, AR	25.71
256.	Lynchburg, VA	25.67
256.	Sherbrooke, PQ	25.67
258.	Corpus Christi, TX	25.58
259.	Grand Junction, CO	25.35
260.	Duluth-Superior, MN-WI	24.80
261.	Richland-Kennewick-Pasco, WA	24.48
262.	Redding, CA	24.31
263.	Abilene, TX	24.30
264.	Merced, CA	24.06
265.	Charlottesville, VA	23.85
266.	Odessa-Midland, TX	23.43
267.	Fort Walton Beach, FL	23.17
268.	Modesto, CA	22.76
269.	Medford-Ashland, OR	22.23
270.	York, PA	22.00
271.	Rockford, IL	21.50
272.	Jackson, MI	21.48
273.	Wichita Falls, TX	21.19
274.	Brownsville-Harlingen-San Benito, TX	21.13
275.	Rapid City, SD	20.82

Places Rated Rank		Places Rated Score
276.	Flagstaff, AZ-UT	20.57
277.	Altoona, PA	20.27
278.	Monroe, LA	20.09
279.	Columbus, GA-AL	20.04
280.	Saginaw-Bay City-Midland, MI	19.99
281.	Myrtle Beach, SC	19.88
282.	Yakima, WA	19.88
283.	Williamsport, PA	19.72
284.	Charleston-North Charleston, SC	19.15
285.	Chicoutimi-Jonquiere, PQ	19.06
286.	State College, PA	18.80
287.	Montgomery, AL	18.62
288.	Beaumont-Port Arthur, TX	18.31
289.	Decatur, IL	17.91
290.	Chico-Paradise, CA	17.89
291.	Gadsden, AL	17.81
292.	Fort Pierce-Port St. Lucie, FL	17.61
293.	Asheville, NC	17.51
294.	Killeen-Temple, TX	17.46
295.	Yuma, AZ	17.17
296.	San Luis Obispo-Atascadero-Paso Robles, CA	16.83
297.	Chattanooga, TN-GA	16.62
298.	San Angelo, TX	16.59
299.	Youngstown-Warren, OH	16.20
300.	Laredo, TX	16.17
301.	Eau Claire, WI	15.84
302.	Columbia, MO	15.53
303.	Lafayette, LA	14.76
304.	Baton Rouge, LA	14.07
305.	Huntsville, AL	13.96
306.	Wilmington, NC	12.66
307.	Johnson City-Kingsport-Bristol, TN-VA	12.46
308.	Florence, SC	11.44
309.	Albany, GA	11.21
310.	Lake Charles, LA	11.10
311.	Casper, WY	11.00
312.	Danville, VA	10.90

Places Rated Rank		Places Rated Score
313.	Lawton, OK	9.89
314.	Alexandria, LA	9.23
315.	Parkersburg-Marietta, WV-OH	9.01
316.	Owensboro, KY	7.49
317.	Enid, OK	6.52
318.	Sharon, PA	6.47
319.	Stockton-Lodi, CA	6.03
320.	Lima, OH	5.97
321.	Lewiston-Auburn, ME	5.62
322.	McAllen-Edinburg-Mission, TX	5.38
323.	Anniston, AL	5.36
324.	Joplin, MO	5.32
325.	Jackson, TN	5.27
326.	Sumter, SC	5.18
327.	Hattiesburg, MS	5.14
328.	Augusta-Aiken, GA-SC	4.93
329.	Cumberland, MD-WV	4.79
330.	Panama City, FL	4.76
331.	Texarkana, TX-Texarkana, AR	4.65
332.	Mansfield, OH	4.64
333.	Longview-Marshall, TX	4.57
334.	Bryan-College Station, TX	4.27
335.	Trois-Rivieres, PQ	3.68
336.	Dothan, AL	3.46
337.	Tyler, TX	3.39
338.	Jacksonville, NC	3.26
339.	Terre Haute, IN	3.14
340.	Fort Smith, AR-OK	2.88
341.	Wheeling, WV-OH	2.87
342.	Dover, DE	2.74
343.	Decatur, AL	2.43
344.	Ocala, FL	2.34
345.	Macon, GA	2.22
346.	Greenville, NC	1.85
347.	Steubenville-Weirton, OH-WV	1.53
348.	Victoria, TX	1.42
349.	Sherman-Denison, TX	0.36
350.	Florence, AL	0.35
351.	Houma, LA	0.10

PLACE PROFILES: Transportation

The following pages detail local commuting time, mass transit, and intercity travel assets in each metro area.

Sources for the information include American Public Transit Association, *Transit Fact Book,* 1996; Canadian Urban Transit Association, *Canadian Transit Fact Book,* 1996; Community Transportation Association of America, *Directory of UMTA-Funded Rural and Specialized Transit Systems,* 1995; Jane's Information Group, *Jane's Urban Transport Systems,* 1996; National Railroad Passenger Corporation, *AMTRAK's America,* 1996, and AMTRAK *Timetable,* Spring 1996; Official Airline Guides, Inc., *Travel Planner,* Summer 1996; Pentrex Publishing Company, *Passenger Train Journal;* Statistics Canada, Aviation Statistics Center, *Aviation Bulletins,* 1996; U.S. Department of Transportation, Federal Aviation Administration, unpublished 298C non-stop destination data for commuter carriers and T100 non-stop destination data for jet carriers; Federal Transit Administration, *National Transit Database,* 1996; and VIA Rail Canada *Timetable,* Spring 1996.

The first entry, **Daily Commute,** is the minutes workers spend getting to and from the job, regardless of the mode of transportation. These minutes are journey-to-work figures multiplied by 2.2 to represent a round-trip whose return half takes slightly longer than the first half. The source for U.S. metro areas is the 1990 Census of Population. Figures for Canadian metro areas are *Places Rated* estimates.

Next to the heading **Public Transit** is the name of the local transit agency or the name of the largest agency if there is more than one. Under the heading is the number of mass transit vehicles from all local agencies on the street at rush hour.

A major part of a metro area's freeways are also heavily traveled routes of the country's **Interstate Highways**. These highways are intercity travel assets, too. Accordingly, each main route in the system that reaches the metro area is listed. The source is U.S. Department of Transportation, Federal Highway Administration, unpublished "Interstate System Log and Finder List," their outbound direction and the name of the city termination as of Spring 1996.

Next to the heading **Domestic Air Service** is the FAA's hub classification for the metro area: large hub, medium hub, small hub, or nonhub. Hub classifications for Canadian airports are derived by *Places Rated* from their share in total North American passenger enplanements.

The airport's name comes underneath followed by the airport's three-letter international identifier enclosed in parentheses and the airport's distance and direction from the central business district. Below the airport's name are the number of nonstop jet destinations with more than 5,000 outbound passengers per year and the top three markets listed in order of passengers enplaned. A similar listing is given for

Abilene, TX
Daily Commute: 32.3 minutes
Public Transit: *AT*
10 city buses
Interstate Highway: I–20
Domestic Airline Service (Nonhub)
Abilene Regional (ABI) 3 miles SE
1 nonstop commuter destination:
Dallas (DFW)
Places Rated Score: 24.30 Places Rated Rank: 263

Akron, OH
Daily Commute: 44.6 minutes
Public Transit: *METRO*
152 city buses
Interstate Highways: I–76, I–77
Domestic Airline Service (Part of Cleveland hub)
Akron–Canton Regional (CAK) 12 miles SE
3 nonstop jet destinations:
Pittsburgh (PIT)
Chicago (ORD)
Charlotte (CLT)
4 nonstop commuter destinations:
Cincinnati (CVG)
Pittsburgh (PIT)
Detroit (DTW)
Places Rated Score: 78.78 Places Rated Rank: 84

Albany, GA
Daily Commute: 36.5 minutes
Public Transit: *ATS*
8 city buses
Domestic Airline Service (Nonhub)
Dougherty County (ABY) 4 miles SW
1 nonstop jet destination:
Atlanta (ATL)
Places Rated Score: 11.21 Places Rated Rank: 309

Albany–Schenectady–Troy, NY
Daily Commute: 43.9 minutes
Public Transit: *CDTA*
205 city buses
Interstate Highways: I–87, I–88, I–90
AMTRAK Weekly Departures:
7 E Boston
7 N Montreal
54 S New York
7 S Washington
7 W Chicago
10 W Niagara Falls
7 W Toronto
Domestic Airline Service (Small hub)
Albany County (ALB) 8 miles NW
16 nonstop jet destinations:
Chicago (ORD)
Pittsburgh (PIT)
Atlanta (ATL)
9 nonstop commuter destinations:
New York (JFK)
Baltimore (BWI)
New York (LGA)
Places Rated Score: 83.87 Places Rated Rank: 56

Albuquerque, NM
Daily Commute: 43.2 minutes
Public Transit: *Sun Tran*
104 city buses
Interstate Highways: I–25, I–40
AMTRAK Weekly Departures:
7 E Chicago
7 W Los Angeles
Domestic Airline Service (Medium hub)
Albuquerque International (ABQ) 5 miles SE
36 nonstop jet destinations:
Phoenix (PHX)
Dallas (DFW)
Denver (DIA)
5 nonstop commuter destinations:
Farmington (FMN)
Roswell (ROW)
Salt Lake City (SLC)
Places Rated Score: 76.74 Places Rated Rank: 91

Alexandria, LA
Daily Commute: 43.6 minutes
Public Transit: *ATRANS*
10 city buses
Interstate Highway: I–49
Domestic Airline Service (Nonhub)
Alexandria Esler Regional (ESF) 15 miles NE
2 nonstop jet destinations:
Dallas (DFW)

Houston (IAH)
2 nonstop commuter destinations:
Dallas (DFW)
Memphis (MEM)
Places Rated Score: 9.23 Places Rated Rank: 314

Allentown–Bethlehem–Easton, PA
Daily Commute: 44.8 minutes
Public Transit: *LANTA*
54 city buses
Interstate Highway: I–78
Domestic Airline Service (Small hub)
Lehigh Valley International (ABE) 4 miles NE
7 nonstop jet destinations:
Pittsburgh (PIT)
Chicago (ORD)
Detroit (DTW)
6 nonstop commuter destinations:
Philadelphia (PHL)
Baltimore (BWI)
Washington (DCA)
Places Rated Score: 60.20 Places Rated Rank: 151

Altoona, PA
Daily Commute: 35.0 minutes
Public Transit: *AMTRAN*
43 city buses
AMTRAK Weekly Departures:
14 E New York
14 W Pittsburgh
Domestic Airline Service (Nonhub)
Altoona/Blair County (AOO) 12 miles S
1 nonstop commuter destination:
Pittsburgh (PIT)
Places Rated Score: 20.27 Places Rated Rank: 277

Amarillo, TX
Daily Commute: 37.1 minutes
Public Transit: *ACT*
13 city buses
Interstate Highways: I–27, I–40
Domestic Airline Service (Small hub)
Amarillo International (AMA) 9 miles E
7 nonstop jet destinations:
Dallas (DAL)
Dallas (DFW)
Phoenix (PHX)
2 nonstop commuter destinations:
Dallas (DFW)
Denver (DIA)
Places Rated Score: 42.10 Places Rated Rank: 208

Anchorage, AK
Daily Commute: 39.2 minutes
Public Transit: *AT*
40 city buses
Domestic Airline Service (Medium hub)
Anchorage International (ANC) 5 miles SW
27 nonstop jet destinations:
Seattle (SEA)
Salt Lake City (SLC)
Denver (DIA)
9 nonstop commuter destinations:
Kenai (ENA)
Kodiak (ADQ)
Homer (HOM)
Places Rated Score: 47.39 Places Rated Rank: 195

Ann Arbor, MI
Daily Commute: 46.8 minutes
Public Transit: *AATA*
58 city buses
Interstate Highway: I–94
AMTRAK Weekly Departures:
21 E Pontiac
21 W Chicago
Domestic Airline Service
Nearest is Detroit (DTW) 25 miles E
Places Rated Score: 78.23 Places Rated Rank: 86

Anniston, AL
Daily Commute: 40.0 minutes
Interstate Highway: I–20
AMTRAK Weekly Departures:
7 N New York
7 S New Orleans
Domestic Airline Service (Nonhub)
Anniston Metropolitan (ANB) 3 miles SW
1 nonstop commuter destination
Atlanta (ATL)
Places Rated Score: 5.36 Places Rated Rank: 323

Appleton–Oshkosh–Neenah, WI
Daily Commute: 33.8 minutes
Public Transit: *Valley Transit/OTS*
45 city buses
Domestic Airline Service (Part of Green Bay hub)
Outagamie County (ATW) 5 miles W
3 nonstop jet destinations:
Chicago (ORD)
Milwaukee (MKE)
Atlanta (ATL)
3 nonstop commuter destinations:
Minneapolis (MSP)
Cincinnati (CVG)
Milwaukee (MKE)
Places Rated Score: 52.51 Places Rated Rank: 174

Asheville, NC
Daily Commute: 41.1 minutes
Public Transit: *City Coach*
13 city buses
Interstate Highways: I–26, I–40
Domestic Airline Service (Small hub)
Asheville Regional (AVL) 12 miles S
2 nonstop jet destinations:
Charlotte (CLT)
Atlanta (ATL)
3 nonstop commuter destinations:
Charlotte (CLT)
Cincinnati (CVG)
Nashville (BNA)
Places Rated Score: 17.51 Places Rated Rank: 293

✓ Athens, GA
Daily Commute: 37.8 minutes
Public Transit: *ATS*
16 city buses
Domestic Airline Service (Part of Atlanta hub)
Athens/Ben Epps (AHN) 3 miles E
1 nonstop commuter destination:
Charlotte (CLT)
Places Rated Score: 88.99 Places Rated Rank: 33

✓ Atlanta, GA
Daily Commute: 55.8 minutes
Public Transit: *MARTA*
591 city buses
238 heavy rail cars
Interstate Highways: I–20, I–75, I–85
AMTRAK Weekly Departures:
7 N New York
7 S New Orleans
Domestic Airline Service (Large hub)
Hartsfield Atlanta International (ATL) 9 miles S
126 nonstop jet destinations:
Dallas (DFW)
Orlando (MCO)
Chicago (ORD)
1 nonstop commuter destination:
Nashville (BNA)
Places Rated Score: 92.55 Places Rated Rank: 27

Atlantic City–Cape May, NJ
Daily Commute: 42.8 minutes
Public Transit: *NJTC*
152 city buses
AMTRAK Weekly Departures:
7 N New York

7 S Miami
Domestic Airline Service (Part of Philadelphia hub)
Atlantic City International (ACY) 9 miles NW
7 nonstop jet destinations:
Detroit (DTW)
Boston (BOS)
Fort Lauderdale (FLL)
1 nonstop commuter destination:
Philadelphia (PHL)
Places Rated Score: 87.78 Places Rated Rank: 37

Augusta–Aiken, GA–SC
Daily Commute: 47.1 minutes
Public Transit: *APT*
24 city buses
Interstate Highway: I–20
Domestic Airline Service (Nonhub)
Augusta Bush Field (AGS) 8 miles S
1 nonstop jet destination:
Atlanta (ATL)
1 nonstop commuter destination:

Domestic Airline Service (Medium hub)
Robert Mueller Municipal (AUS) 4 miles NE
31 nonstop jet destinations:
Dallas (DFW)
Dallas (DAL)
Houston (IAH)
3 nonstop commuter destinations:
Corpus Christi (CRP)
Tyler (TYR)
Beaumont (BPT)
Places Rated Score: 70.56 Places Rated Rank: 114

Bakersfield, CA
Daily Commute: 42.2 minutes
Public Transit: *GET*
54 city buses
AMTRAK Weekly Departures:
21 N San Francisco
Domestic Airline Service (Nonhub)
Meadows Field (BFL) 4 miles NW
2 nonstop jet destinations:
Los Angeles (LAX)
Dallas (DFW)
3 nonstop commuter destinations:
Los Angeles (LAX)
San Francisco (SFO)
Sacramento (SMF)
Places Rated Score: 29.47 Places Rated Rank: 243

✓ Baltimore, MD
Daily Commute: 55.9 minutes
Public Transit: *MTA/MARC*
897 city buses
107 commuter rail
48 heavy rail cars
30 light rail cars
Interstate Highways: I–70, I–83, I–95, I–97
AMTRAK Weekly Departures:
62 N Boston
7 N Montreal
136 N New York
14 N Springfield
7 S Charlotte
7 S Miami
7 S New Orleans
8 S Newport News
13 S Richmond
7 S Tampa
182 S Washington
Domestic Airline Service (Part of Washington hub)
Baltimore–Washington International (BWI) 10 miles S
52 nonstop jet destinations:
Chicago (ORD)
Cleveland (CLE)
St. Louis (STL)
27 nonstop commuter destinations:
Philadelphia (PHL)
New York (JFK)
Salisbury (SBY)
Places Rated Score: 97.86 Places Rated Rank: 6

Bangor, ME
Daily Commute: 32.0 minutes
Public Transit: *The Bus*
10 city buses
Interstate Highway: I–95
Domestic Airline Service (Nonhub)

Domestic Airline Service (Part of Boston hub)
Barnstable Municipal (HYA)
3 nonstop commuter destinations:
Boston (BOS)
Nantucket (ACK)
Newark (EWR)
Places Rated Score: 63.09 Places Rated Rank: 139

Baton Rouge, LA
Daily Commute: 48.9 minutes
Public Transit: *CTC*
37 city buses
Interstate Highways: I–10, I–12
Domestic Airline Service (Small hub)
Baton Rouge Metropolitan (BTR) 8 miles N
4 nonstop jet destinations:
Atlanta (ATL)
Dallas (DFW)
Houston (IAH)
1 nonstop commuter destination:
Dallas (DFW)
Nashville (BNA)
Places Rated Score: 14.07 Places Rated Rank: 304

Beaumont–Port Arthur, TX
Daily Commute: 42.5 minutes
Public Transit: *BMT/PAT*
18 city buses
Interstate Highway: I–10
AMTRAK Weekly Departures:
3 E Miami
3 W Los Angeles
Domestic Airline Service (Nonhub)
Beaumont Jefferson County (BPT) 10 miles SE
2 nonstop jet destinations:
Dallas (DFW)
Houston (IAH)
2 nonstop commuter destinations:
Dallas (DFW)
Austin (AUS)
Places Rated Score: 18.31 Places Rated Rank: 288

Bellingham, WA
Daily Commute: 36.1 minutes
Public Transit: *WTA*
23 city buses

Interstate Highway: I–5
AMTRAK Weekly Departures:
7 N Vancouver
7 S Seattle
Domestic Airline Service (Part of Vancouver hub)
Bellingham International (BLI) 4 miles NW
1 nonstop commuter destination:
Seattle (SEA)
Places Rated Score: 83.51 Places Rated Rank: 58

Benton Harbor, MI
Daily Commute: 37.0 minutes
Public Transit: *TCTA*
2 city buses
Interstate Highways: I–94, I–96
AMTRAK Weekly Departures:
21 E Pontiac
6 E Toronto
28 W Chicago
Domestic Airline Service
Nearest is South Bend (SBN) 33 miles SE
Places Rated Score: 44.77 Places Rated Rank: 201

Bergen–Passaic, NJ
Daily Commute: 53.2 minutes
Public Transit: *NJTC*
459 city buses
Interstate Highways: I–80, I–95
Domestic Airline Service
Nearest is Newark (EWR) 14 miles S
Places Rated Score: 87.79 Places Rated Rank: 36

Billings, MT
Daily Commute: 34.1 minutes
Public Transit: *MET*
16 city buses
Interstate Highways: I–90, I–94
Domestic Airline Service (Small hub)
Billings Logan International (BIL) 2 miles NW
7 nonstop jet destinations:
Salt Lake City (SLC)
Denver (DIA)
Minneapolis (MSP)
Places Rated Score: 48.05 Places Rated Rank: 194

Biloxi–Gulfport–Pascagoula, MS
Daily Commute: 44.5 minutes
Public Transit: *Mississippi Coast*
24 city buses
Interstate Highway: I–10
AMTRAK Weekly Departures:
3 E Miami
3 W Los Angeles
Domestic Airline Service (Part of New Orleans hub)
Gulfport–Biloxi Regional (GPT) 3 miles N
2 nonstop jet destinations:
Atlanta (ATL)
Houston (IAH)
2 nonstop commuter destinations:
Memphis (MEM)
Dallas (DFW)
Places Rated Score: 36.74 Places Rated Rank: 224

Binghamton, NY
Daily Commute: 37.2 minutes
Public Transit: *Broome County*
36 city buses
Interstate Highways: I–81, I–88
Domestic Airline Service (Nonhub)
Binghamton Regional/Edwin Link (BGM) 7 miles N
2 nonstop jet destinations:
Pittsburgh (PIT)
Newark (EWR)
5 nonstop commuter destinations:
Baltimore (BWI)
Detroit (DTW)
Washington (IAD)
Places Rated Score: 34.95 Places Rated Rank: 231

Birmingham, AL
Daily Commute: 49.4 minutes
Public Transit: *MAX*
79 city buses
Interstate Highways: I–20, I–59, I–65
AMTRAK Weekly Departures:
3 N New York
3 S New Orleans
Domestic Airline Service (Small hub)
Birmingham Municipal (BHM) 5 miles NE
17 nonstop jet destinations:
Atlanta (ATL)
Dallas (DFW)
Charlotte (CLT)
4 nonstop commuter destinations:
Orlando (MCO)
Cincinnati (CVG)
Nashville (BNA)
Places Rated Score: 62.81 Places Rated Rank: 140

Bismarck, ND
Daily Commute: 27.1 minutes
Interstate Highway: I–94
Domestic Airline Service (Nonhub)
Bismarck Municipal (BIS) 3 miles SE
2 nonstop jet destinations:
Minneapolis (MSP)
Denver (DIA)
Places Rated Score: 35.47 Places Rated Rank: 230

Bloomington, IN
Daily Commute: 37.8 minutes
Public Transit: *BPT*
15 city buses
Domestic Airline Service
Nearest is Indianapolis (IND) 40 miles NE
Places Rated Score: 70.80 Places Rated Rank: 111

Bloomington–Normal, IL
Daily Commute: 33.9 minutes
Public Transit: *B–N PTS*
14 city buses
Interstate Highways: I–39, I–55, I–74
AMTRAK Weekly Departures:
29 N Chicago
7 S Kansas City
3 S Los Angeles
5 S Springfield
14 S St. Louis
Domestic Airline Service (Part of Peoria hub)
Bloomington/Normal (BMI) 3 miles E
2 nonstop jet destinations:
St. Louis (STL)
Chicago (ORD)
2 nonstop commuter destinations:
Detroit (DTW)
Minneapolis (MSP)
Places Rated Score: 79.02 Places Rated Rank: 82

Boise City, ID
Daily Commute: 36.6 minutes
Public Transit: *Boise Urban Stages*
26 city buses
Interstate Highway: I–84
AMTRAK Weekly Departures:
3 E Chicago
3 W Seattle
Domestic Airline Service (Small hub)
Boise Air Terminal (BOI) 4 miles SW
20 nonstop jet destinations:
Salt Lake City (SLC)
Seattle (SEA)
Portland (PDX)
Places Rated Score: 61.26 Places Rated Rank: 147

✓ Boston, MA–NH
Daily Commute: 51.8 minutes
Public Transit: *MBTA*

832 city buses
406 heavy rail cars
291 commuter rail
177 light rail cars
23 trolly coaches
7 ferries

Interstate Highways: I–90, I–93, I–95

AMTRAK Weekly Departures:
1 S New York
8 S Newport News
5 S Richmond
42 S Washington
7 W Albany

Domestic Airline Service (Large hub)
Boston Logan International (BOS) 3 miles NE
68 nonstop jet destinations:
New York (LGA)
Chicago (ORD)
Atlanta (ATL)
19 nonstop commuter destinations:
New York (JFK)

Places Rated Score: 79.04 Places Rated Rank: 81

Brazoria, TX

Daily Commute: 51.5 minutes
Domestic Airline Service
Nearest is Houston (HOU) 50 miles NE
Places Rated Score: 55.15 Places Rated Rank: 166

Bremerton, WA

Daily Commute: 51.5 minutes
Public Transit: *Kitsap Transit*
76 city buses
5 ferries
Domestic Airline Service
Nearest is Seattle (SEA) 35 miles SE
Places Rated Score: 49.57 Places Rated Rank: 185

✓ Bridgeport, CT

Daily Commute: 44.7 minutes
Public Transit: *GBTD*
47 city buses
Interstate Highway: I–95
AMTRAK Weekly Departures:
30 N Boston
7 N Springfield
5 S New York
1 S Richmond
36 S Washington
Domestic Airline Service (Part of New York–Tri-State hub)
Igor Sikorsky Memorial (BDR) 4 miles S
3 nonstop commuter destinations:
Islip (ISP)
Baltimore (BWI)
Philadelphia (PHL)
Places Rated Score: 91.41 Places Rated Rank: 30

Brockton, MA

Daily Commute: 57.6 minutes
Public Transit: *BAT*
48 city buses
Domestic Airline Service
Nearest is Boston (BOS) 25 miles N
Places Rated Score: 41.84 Places Rated Rank: 209

Brownsville–Harlingen–San Benito, TX

Daily Commute: 36.5 minutes
Public Transit: *BUS*
12 city buses
Domestic Airline Service (Part of McAllen hub)
South Padre Island International (BRO) 4 miles E
1 nonstop jet destination:
Houston (IAH)
Places Rated Score: 21.13 Places Rated Rank: 274

Bryan–College Station, TX

Daily Commute: 32.3 minutes
Public Transit: *Brazos Transit*
8 city buses
Domestic Airline Service (Nonhub)
Easterwood Field (CLL) 3 miles S
2 nonstop jet destinations:
Dallas (DFW)
Houston (HOU)
Places Rated Score: 4.27 Places Rated Rank: 334

Buffalo–Niagara Falls, NY

Daily Commute: 41.9 minutes

Greater Buffalo International
18 nonstop jet destinations:
Chicago (ORD)
Newark (EWR)
New York (LGA)
8 nonstop commuter destinations:
New York (JFK)
Baltimore (BWI)
Albany (ALB)
Places Rated Score: 81.30 Places Rated Rank: 71

Burlington, VT

Daily Commute: 37.0 minutes
Public Transit: *Chittenden TA*
24 city buses
Interstate Highway: I–89
AMTRAK Weekly Departures:
7 N Montreal
7 S Washington
Domestic Airline Service (Small hub)
Burlington International (BTV) 3 miles E
6 nonstop jet destinations:
Chicago (ORD)
Philadelphia (PHL)
Newark (EWR)
6 nonstop commuter destinations:
New York (LGA)
Boston (BOS)
Washington (IAD)
Places Rated Score: 48.55 Places Rated Rank: 189

Calgary, AB

Daily Commute: 42.0 minutes
Public Transit: *Calgary Transit*
472 city buses
72 light rail coaches
National Highways: AB–2, TC–1
Domestic Airline Service (Large hub)
Calgary International (YYC) 9 miles NE
52 nonstop destinations:
Vancouver (YVR)
Toronto (YYZ)
Edmonton (YEG)
Places Rated Score: 83.64 Places Rated Rank: 57

Canton–Massillon, OH

Daily Commute: 41.3 minutes

Public Transit: *RTA Proline*
29 city buses
Interstate Highway: I–77
AMTRAK Weekly Departures:
7 E Washington
7 W Chicago
Domestic Airline Service
Nearest is Akron (CAK) 12 miles N
Places Rated Score: 76.01 Places Rated Rank: 92

Casper, WY
Daily Commute: 32.6 minutes
Interstate Highway: I–25
Domestic Airline Service (Nonhub)
Natrona County International (CPR) 8 miles NW
2 nonstop commuter destinations:
Salt Lake City (SLC)
Denver (DIA)
Places Rated Score: 11.00 Places Rated Rank: 311

Cedar Rapids, IA
Daily Commute: 34.1 minutes
Public Transit: *Five Seasons Transit*
34 city buses
Interstate Highway: I–80
Domestic Airline Service (Small hub)
Cedar Rapids Municipal (CID) 8 miles SW
4 nonstop jet destinations:
Chicago (ORD)
St. Louis (STL)
Denver (DIA)
4 nonstop commuter destinations:
Minneapolis (MSP)
Cincinnati (CVG)
Kansas City (MCI)
Places Rated Score: 49.81 Places Rated Rank: 184

Champaign–Urbana, IL
Daily Commute: 31.9 minutes
Public Transit: *MTD*
67 city buses
Interstate Highways: I–57, I–72, I–74
AMTRAK Weekly Departures:
12 N Chicago
7 S Carbondale
5 S New Orleans
Domestic Airline Service (Nonhub)
University of Illinois/Willard (CMI) 6 miles SW
2 nonstop jet destinations:
Chicago (ORD)
St. Louis (STL)
3 nonstop commuter destinations:
Detroit (DTW)
Indianapolis (IND)
Minneapolis (MSP)
Places Rated Score: 80.60 Places Rated Rank: 76

Charleston, WV
Daily Commute: 42.9 minutes
Public Transit: *KRT*
43 city buses
Interstate Highways: I–64, I–77, I–79
AMTRAK Weekly Departures:
3 E Washington
3 W Chicago
Domestic Airline Service (Nonhub)
Charleston/Yeager Field (CRW) 4 miles NE
4 nonstop jet destinations:
Pittsburgh (PIT)
Atlanta (ATL)
Charlotte (CLT)
5 nonstop commuter destinations:
Cincinnati (CVG)
Washington (DCA)
Charlotte (CLT)
Places Rated Score: 54.65 Places Rated Rank: 169

Charleston–North Charleston, SC
Daily Commute: 48.5 minutes
Public Transit: *SCE&G*
34 city buses
Interstate Highway: I–26
AMTRAK Weekly Departures:
7 N New York
7 S Miami
Domestic Airline Service (Small hub)
Charleston International (CHS) 13 miles NW
8 nonstop jet destinations:
Atlanta (ATL)
Charlotte (CLT)
Greensboro (GSO)
2 nonstop commuter destinations:
Washington (IAD)
Raleigh–Durham (RDU)
Places Rated Score: 19.15 Places Rated Rank: 284

Charlotte–Gastonia–Rock Hill, NC–SC
Daily Commute: 46.7 minutes
Public Transit: *CTS*
130 city buses
Interstate Highways: I–77, I–85
AMTRAK Weekly Departures:
14 N New York
7 N Raleigh
7 S New Orleans
Domestic Airline Service (Large hub)
Charlotte–Douglas International (CLT) 6 miles W
85 nonstop jet destinations:
Atlanta (ATL)
New York (LGA)
Philadelphia (PHL)
34 nonstop commuter destinations:
Hilton Head (HHH)
New Bern (EWN)
Cincinnati (CVG)
Places Rated Score: 87.72 Places Rated Rank: 39

Charlottesville, VA
Daily Commute: 40.9 minutes
Public Transit: *CTS*
11 city buses
Interstate Highway: I–64
AMTRAK Weekly Departures:
7 N New York
3 N Washington
7 S New Orleans
3 W Chicago
Domestic Airline Service (Nonhub)
Charlottesville–Albemarle (CHO) 8 miles N
5 nonstop commuter destinations:
Charlotte (CLT)
Baltimore (BWI)
Cincinnati (CVG)
Places Rated Score: 23.85 Places Rated Rank: 265

Chattanooga, TN–GA
Daily Commute: 46.6 minutes
Public Transit: *CARTA*
52 city buses
2 cable inclines
Interstate Highways: I–24, I–75
Domestic Airline Service (Nonhub)
Chattanooga Lovell Field (CHA) 8 miles E
2 nonstop jet destinations:
Atlanta (ATL)
Charlotte (CLT)
4 nonstop commuter destinations:
Cincinnati (CVG)
Memphis (MEM)
Nashville (BNA)
Places Rated Score: 16.62 Places Rated Rank: 297

Cheyenne, WY
Daily Commute: 29.5 minutes
Interstate Highways: I–25, I–80
AMTRAK Weekly Departures:
3 E Chicago

3 W Seattle
Domestic Airline Service (Nonhub)
Cheyenne Municipal (CYS) 1 mile N
1 nonstop commuter destination:
Denver (DIA)
Places Rated Score: 29.92 Places Rated Rank: 241

✓ Chicago, IL
Daily Commute: 61.5 minutes
Public Transit: *RTA-CTA*
2,312 city buses
952 commuter rail
804 heavy rail cars
Interstate Highways: I-55, I-57, I-80, I-88, I-90, I-94
AMTRAK Weekly Departures:
7 E New York
21 E Pontiac
6 E Toronto
10 E Washington
41 N Milwaukee

126 nonstop jet destinations:
New York (LGA)
Los Angeles (LAX)
Denver (DIA)
7 nonstop commuter destinations:
Lansing (LAN)
Springfield (SPI)
Peoria (PIA)
Midway (MDW) 11 miles SW
107 nonstop jet destinations:
Detroit (DTW)
St. Louis (STL)
Cleveland (CLE)
4 nonstop commuter destinations:
Cincinnati (CVG)
Grand Rapids (GRR)
Des Moines (DSM)
Places Rated Score: 98.92 Places Rated Rank: 1

Chico-Paradise, CA
Daily Commute: 36.5 minutes
Public Transit: *CAT*
12 city buses
AMTRAK Weekly Departures:
7 N Seattle
7 S Los Angeles
Domestic Airline Service
Nearest is Redding (RDD) 69 miles NW
Places Rated Score: 17.89 Places Rated Rank: 290

Chicoutimi-Jonquiere, PQ
Daily Commute: 36.5 minutes
Public Transit: *CITS*
30 city buses
Domestic Airline Service (Nonhub)
Bagotville (YBG) 11 miles SE
2 nonstop jet destinations:
Quebec (YQB)
Montreal (YUL)
Places Rated Score: 19.06 Places Rated Rank: 285

✓ Cincinnati, OH-KY-IN
Daily Commute: 48.9 minutes
Public Transit: *SORTA*
408 city buses
Interstate Highways: I-71, I-74, I-75
AMTRAK Weekly Departures:
3 E Washington
3 W Chicago
Domestic Airline Service (Large hub)
Cincinnati/Northern Kentucky International (CVG) 13 miles SW
74 nonstop jet destinations:
Chicago (ORD)
Atlanta (ATL)
Salt Lake City (SLC)
60 nonstop commuter destinations:
Toronto (YYZ)
Detroit (DTW)
Lexington (LEX)
Places Rated Score: 91.63 Places Rated Rank: 28

Clarksville-Hopkinsville, TN-KY
Daily Commute: 40.6 minutes
Public Transit: *CTS*
6 city buses
Interstate Highway: I-24

7 E New York
7 E Washington
14 W Chicago
Domestic Airline Service (Medium hub)
Cleveland-Hopkins International (CLE) 10 miles SW
52 nonstop jet destinations:
Chicago (ORD)
Baltimore (BWI)
Chicago (MDW)
6 nonstop commuter destinations:
Cincinnati (CVG)
Nashville (BNA)
Washington (IAD)
Places Rated Score: 91.36 Places Rated Rank: 31

Colorado Springs, CO
Daily Commute: 39.8 minutes
Public Transit: *CST*
39 city buses
Interstate Highway: I-25
Domestic Airline Service (Small hub)
Colorado Springs Municipal (COS) 6 miles SE
22 nonstop jet destinations:
Denver (DIA)
Dallas (DFW)
Phoenix (PHX)
Places Rated Score: 62.04 Places Rated Rank: 143

Columbia, MO
Daily Commute: 35.6 minutes
Public Transit: *CATS*
13 city buses
Interstate Highway: I-70
Domestic Airline Service (Nonhub)
Columbia Regional (COU) 12 miles S
1 nonstop jet destination:
St. Louis (STL)
Places Rated Score: 15.53 Places Rated Rank: 302

Columbia, SC
Daily Commute: 44.4 minutes
Public Transit: *SCE&G*
35 city buses
Interstate Highways: I-20, I-26, I-77
AMTRAK Weekly Departures:
7 N New York

7 S Tampa
Domestic Airline Service (Small hub)
Columbia Metropolitan (CAE) 7 miles S
6 nonstop jet destinations:
Atlanta (ATL)
Charlotte (CLT)
Miami (MIA)
2 nonstop commuter destinations:
Cincinnati (CVG)
Nashville (BNA)
Places Rated Score: 40.44 Places Rated Rank: 212

Columbus, GA–AL
Daily Commute: 38.6 minutes
Public Transit: *METRA*
24 city buses
Interstate Highway: I–185
Domestic Airline Service (Nonhub)
Columbus Metropolitan (CSG) 7 miles NE
1 nonstop jet destination:
Atlanta (ATL)
3 nonstop commuter destinations:
Charlotte (CLT)
Memphis (MEM)
Nashville (BNA)
Places Rated Score: 20.04 Places Rated Rank: 279

Columbus, OH
Daily Commute: 45.6 minutes
Public Transit: *COTA*
264 city buses
Interstate Highways: I–70, I–71
Domestic Airline Service (Medium hub)
Port Columbus International (CMH) 7 miles NE
31 nonstop jet destinations:
Atlanta (ATL)
Chicago (MDW)
Chicago (ORD)
10 nonstop commuter destinations:
Cincinnati (CVG)
Pittsburgh (PIT)
Nashville (BNA)
Places Rated Score: 73.77 Places Rated Rank: 104

Corpus Christi, TX
Daily Commute: 41.4 minutes
Public Transit: *CCRTA*
57 city buses
Interstate Highway: I–37
Domestic Airline Service (Small hub)
Corpus Christi International (CRP) 10 miles NW
4 nonstop jet destinations:
Dallas (DFW)
Houston (HOU)
Houston (IAH)
1 nonstop commuter destination:
Austin (AUS)
Places Rated Score: 25.58 Places Rated Rank: 258

Cumberland, MD–WV
Daily Commute: 40.5 minutes
Public Transit: *ACTA*
11 city buses
Interstate Highway: I–68
AMTRAK Weekly Departures:
7 E Washington
7 W Chicago
Domestic Airline Service (Nonhub)
Wiley Ford (CBE) 3 miles S
1 nonstop commuter destination:
Pittsburgh (PIT)
Places Rated Score: 4.79 Places Rated Rank: 329

Dallas, TX
Daily Commute: 52.9 minutes
Public Transit: *DART*
740 city buses
111 light rail cars
Interstate Highways: I–20, I–30, I–35E, I–45
AMTRAK Weekly Departures:
3 N Chicago
3 W Los Angeles
Domestic Airline Service (Large hub)
Dallas/Fort Worth International (DFW) 12 miles NW
115 nonstop jet destinations:
Atlanta (ATL)
Chicago (ORD)
Denver (DIA)
28 nonstop commuter destinations:
Fort Smith (FSM)
Lafayette (LFT)
Abilene (ABI)
Dallas Love Field (DAL) 6 miles NW
15 nonstop jet destinations:
Houston (HOU)
San Antonio (SAT)
Austin (AUS)
Places Rated Score: 62.20 Places Rated Rank: 142

Danbury, CT
Daily Commute: 55.0 minutes
Public Transit: *HART*
15 city buses
35 commuter rail
Interstate Highway: I–84
Domestic Airline Service
Nearest is Bridgeport (BDR) 29 miles SE
Places Rated Score: 65.05 Places Rated Rank: 135

Danville, VA
Daily Commute: 41.1 minutes
Public Transit: *DTS*
8 city buses
AMTRAK Weekly Departures:
7 N New York
7 S New Orleans
Domestic Airline Service
Nearest is Greensboro (GSO) 45 miles SW
Places Rated Score: 10.90 Places Rated Rank: 312

Davenport–Moline–Rock Island, IA–IL
Daily Commute: 37.2 minutes
Public Transit: *Metro Link/CitiBus*
71 city buses
Interstate Highways: I–74, I–80, I–88
AMTRAK Weekly Departures:
7 E Chicago
7 S Quincy
Domestic Airline Service (Small hub)
Quad-City (MLI) 4 miles S
3 nonstop jet destinations:
St. Louis (STL)
Chicago (ORD)
Denver (DIA)
1 nonstop commuter destination:
Minneapolis (MSP)
Places Rated Score: 59.07 Places Rated Rank: 159

Dayton–Springfield, OH
Daily Commute: 42.1 minutes
Public Transit: *RTA/SCAT*
179 city buses
26 trolly coaches
Interstate Highways: I–70, I–75
Domestic Airline Service (Medium hub)
James M. Cox International (DAY) 13 miles N
16 nonstop jet destinations:
Chicago (ORD)
Atlanta (ATL)
St. Louis (STL)
8 nonstop commuter destinations:
Cincinnati (CVG)
Pittsburgh (PIT)
Detroit (DTW)
Places Rated Score: 71.00 Places Rated Rank: 110

Daytona Beach, FL
Daily Commute: 45.0 minutes
Public Transit: *VOTRAN*
30 city buses
Interstate Highways: I–4, I–95
AMTRAK Weekly Departures:
14 N New York
10 S Miami
7 S Tampa
Domestic Airline Service (Part of Orlando hub)
Daytona Beach Regional (DAB) 3 miles SW
4 nonstop jet destinations:
Atlanta (ATL)
Charlotte (CLT)
Newark (EWR)
2 nonstop commuter destinations:
Orlando (MCO)
Miami (MIA)
Places Rated Score: 79.17 Places Rated Rank: 80

Decatur, AL
Daily Commute: 47.0 minutes

Decatur Regional (DCU) 4 miles E
1 nonstop jet destination:
St. Louis (STL)
1 nonstop commuter destination:
Chicago (ORD)
Places Rated Score: 17.91 Places Rated Rank: 289

✓ Denver, CO
Daily Commute: 48.1 minutes
Public Transit: *RTD*
685 city buses
10 light rail cars
Interstate Highways: I–25, I–70, I–76
AMTRAK Weekly Departures:
9 E Chicago
3 N Seattle
3 W Los Angeles
4 W Oakland
Domestic Airline Service (Large hub)
Denver International (DIA) 23 miles NE
100 nonstop jet destinations:
Chicago (ORD)
Dallas (DFW)
Los Angeles (LAX)
26 nonstop commuter destinations:
Grand Junction (GJT)
Rapid City (RAP)
Durango (DRO)
Places Rated Score: 94.95 Places Rated Rank: 16

Des Moines, IA
Daily Commute: 38.0 minutes
Public Transit: *METRO*
76 city buses
Interstate Highways: I–35, I–80
Domestic Airline Service (Small hub)
Des Moines Municipal (DSM) 3 miles SW
8 nonstop jet destinations:
Chicago (ORD)
Denver (DIA)
St. Louis (STL)
5 nonstop commuter destinations:
Cincinnati (CVG)
Kansas City (MCI)
Minneapolis (MSP)
Places Rated Score: 54.48 Places Rated Rank: 170

✓ Detroit, MI
Daily Commute: 50.9 minutes
Public Transit: *DOT/SMART*
639 city buses
Interstate Highways: I–75, I–94, I–96
AMTRAK Weekly Departures:
7 E Toronto
21 W Chicago
Domestic Airline Service (Large hub)
Detroit Metropolitan (DTW) 20 miles SW
77 nonstop jet destinations:
Chicago (ORD)
Minneapolis (MSP)
Atlanta (ATL)
35 nonstop commuter destinations:
Flint (FNT)
Cincinnati (CVG)
Lansing (LAN)
Places Rated Score: 92.68 Places Rated Rank: 26

Dothan, AL
Daily Commute: 37.0 minutes

Nearest is Philadelphia (PHL) [illegible] miles NE
Places Rated Score: 2.74 Places Rated Rank: 342

Dubuque, IA
Daily Commute: 30.1 minutes
Public Transit: *KeyLine*
16 city buses
Domestic Airline Service (Nonhub)
Dubuque Municipal (DBQ) 9 miles S
1 nonstop jet destination:
Chicago (ORD)
1 nonstop commuter destination:
Minneapolis (MSP)
Places Rated Score: 33.02 Places Rated Rank: 234

Duluth–Superior, MN–WI
Daily Commute: 37.0 minutes
Public Transit: *DTA*
71 city buses
Interstate Highway: I–35
Domestic Airline Service (Nonhub)
Duluth International (DLH) 7 miles NW
2 nonstop commuter destinations:
Minneapolis (MSP)
Chicago (ORD)
Places Rated Score: 24.80 Places Rated Rank: 260

Dutchess County, NY
Daily Commute: 52.8 minutes
Public Transit: *LOOP*
28 city buses
28 commuter rail
Interstate Highways: I–87, I–97
AMTRAK Weekly Departures:
25 N Albany
7 N Montreal
44 S New York
7 S Washington
Domestic Airline Service
Nearest is Newburgh (SWF) 15 miles SW
Places Rated Score: 80.57 Places Rated Rank: 77

Eau Claire, WI
Daily Commute: 33.5 minutes
Public Transit: *ECT*
12 city buses

Interstate Highway: I–94
Domestic Airline Service (Nonhub)
Eau Claire County (EAU) 5 miles NE
1 nonstop commuter destination:
Minneapolis (MSP)
Places Rated Score: 15.84 Places Rated Rank: 301

Edmonton, AB
Daily Commute: 45.6 minutes
Public Transit: *ETS*
457 city buses
48 trolly coaches
27 light rail coaches
National Highways: AB–2, TC–16
VIA Weekly Departures:
3 E Toronto
3 W Vancouver
Domestic Airline Service (Large hub)
Edmonton International (YEG) 19 miles S
38 nonstop destinations:
Calgary (YYC)
Vancouver (YVR)
Toronto (YYZ)
Places Rated Score: 80.30 Places Rated Rank: 78

El Paso, TX
Daily Commute: 43.1 minutes
Public Transit: *Sun Metro*
119 city buses
Interstate Highway: I–10
AMTRAK Weekly Departures:
3 E Miami
3 E Chicago
6 W Los Angeles
Domestic Airline Service (Medium hub)
El Paso International (ELP) 8 miles E
20 nonstop jet destinations:
Dallas (DFW)
Phoenix (PHX)
Dallas (DAL)
Places Rated Score: 64.19 Places Rated Rank: 137

Elkhart–Goshen, IN
Daily Commute: 35.4 minutes
Interstate Highway: I–80
AMTRAK Weekly Departures:
7 E New York
7 E Washington
14 W Chicago
Domestic Airline Service
Nearest is South Bend (SBN) 22 miles W
Places Rated Score: 29.75 Places Rated Rank: 242

Elmira, NY
Daily Commute: 36.3 minutes
Public Transit: *CCTS*
25 city buses
Domestic Airline Service (Nonhub)
Elmira/Corning Regional (ELM) 11 miles NW
2 nonstop jet destinations:
Pittsburgh (PIT)
Philadelphia (PHL)
2 nonstop commuter destinations:
Philadelphia (PHL)
New York (LGA)
Places Rated Score: 26.71 Places Rated Rank: 253

Enid, OK
Daily Commute: 30.8 minutes
Domestic Airline Service
Nearest is Oklahoma City (OKC) 95 miles S
Places Rated Score: 6.52 Places Rated Rank: 317

Erie, PA
Daily Commute: 35.6 minutes
Public Transit: *MTA*
52 city buses
Interstate Highways: I–79, I–90
AMTRAK Weekly Departures:
7 E New York
7 W Chicago
Domestic Airline Service (Nonhub)
Erie International (ERI) 6 miles SW
3 nonstop commuter destinations:
Pittsburgh (PIT)
Detroit (DTW)
Philadelphia (PHL)
Places Rated Score: 49.37 Places Rated Rank: 186

Eugene–Springfield, OR
Daily Commute: 38.1 minutes
Public Transit: *LTD*
73 city buses
Interstate Highway: I–5
AMTRAK Weekly Departures:
14 N Seattle
7 S Los Angeles
Domestic Airline Service (Small hub)
Mahlon Sweet Field (EUG) 8 miles NW
4 nonstop jet destinations:
San Francisco (SFO)
Denver (DIA)
Portland (PDX)
2 nonstop commuter destinations:
Salt Lake City (SLC)
Seattle (SEA)
Places Rated Score: 47.12 Places Rated Rank: 197

Evansville–Henderson, IN–KY
Daily Commute: 39.1 minutes
Public Transit: *METS*
21 city buses
Interstate Highway: I–64
Domestic Airline Service (Nonhub)
Evansville-Dress Regional (EVV) 6 miles NE
5 nonstop jet destinations:
Chicago (ORD)
St. Louis (STL)
Atlanta (ATL)
7 nonstop commuter destinations:
Cincinnati (CVG)
Indianapolis (IND)
Memphis (MEM)
Places Rated Score: 38.44 Places Rated Rank: 217

Fargo–Moorhead, ND–MN
Daily Commute: 30.7 minutes
Public Transit: *MAT*
18 city buses
Interstate Highway: I–29
AMTRAK Weekly Departures:
4 E Chicago
4 W Seattle
Domestic Airline Service (Nonhub)
Hector International (FAR) 3 miles NW
2 nonstop commuter destinations:
Minneapolis (MSP)
Denver (DIA)
Places Rated Score: 57.11 Places Rated Rank: 165

Fayetteville, NC
Daily Commute: 38.3 minutes
Public Transit: *FAST*
12 city buses
Interstate Highway: I–95
AMTRAK Weekly Departures:
7 N New York
7 S Miami
Domestic Airline Service (Nonhub)
Fayetteville Municipal (FAY) 3 miles S
2 nonstop jet destinations:
Charlotte (CLT)
Atlanta (ATL)
Places Rated Score: 27.80 Places Rated Rank: 247

Fayetteville–Springdale–Rogers, AR
Daily Commute: 36.5 minutes

Public Transit: *ATA*
13 city buses
Domestic Airline Service (Nonhub)
Drake Field (FYV) 3 miles S
3 nonstop jet destinations:
Dallas (DFW)
St. Louis (STL)
Nashville (BNA)
4 nonstop commuter destinations:
Memphis (MEM)
Kansas City (MCI)
Little Rock (LIT)
Places Rated Score: 25.71 Places Rated Rank: 255

Fitchburg–Leominster, MA

Daily Commute: 46.2 minutes
Public Transit: *MART*
21 city buses
35 commuter rail
Domestic Airline Service
Nearest is Worcester (ORH) 29 miles S

Places Rated Score: 20.57 Places Rated Rank: 276

Flint, MI

Daily Commute: 44.9 minutes
Public Transit: *MTA*
139 city buses
Interstate Highways: I–69, I–75
AMTRAK Weekly Departures:
6 E Toronto
7 W Chicago
Domestic Airline Service (Part of Detroit hub)
Bishop International (FNT) 5 miles SW
3 nonstop commuter destinations:
Detroit (DTW)
Pittsburgh (PIT)
Milwaukee (MKE)
Places Rated Score: 84.94 Places Rated Rank: 52

Florence, AL

Daily Commute: 44.5 minutes
Domestic Airline Service
Nearest is Huntsville (HSV) 46 miles E
Places Rated Score: 0.35 Places Rated Rank: 350

Florence, SC

Daily Commute: 40.9 minutes
Public Transit: *Pee Dee RTA*
3 city buses
Interstate Highways: I–20, I–95
AMTRAK Weekly Departures:
7 N New York
7 S Miami
Domestic Airline Service (Nonhub)
Florence Regional (FLO) 2 miles E
1 nonstop jet destination:
Atlanta (ATL)
1 nonstop commuter destination:
Charlotte (CLT)
Places Rated Score: 11.44 Places Rated Rank: 308

Fort Collins–Loveland, CO

Daily Commute: 39.6 minutes
Public Transit: *TRANSFORT*
15 city buses
Interstate Highway: I–25
Domestic Airline Service (Part of Denver hub)
Fort Collins Municipal (FNL) 9 miles SE
1 nonstop commuter destination:
Denver (DIA)
Places Rated Score: 81.16 Places Rated Rank: 72

Fort Lauderdale, FL

Daily Commute: 49.5 minutes
Public Transit: *BCT/TCRA*
191 city buses
25 commuter rail
Interstate Highway: I–95
AMTRAK Weekly Departures:
14 N New York
17 S Miami
Domestic Airline Service (Part of Miami hub)
Ft. Lauderdale/Hollywood (FLL) 3 miles SW
39 nonstop jet destinations:
Atlanta (ATL)
Newark (EWR)
New York (LGA)

Southwest Florida Regional (RSW) 10 miles SE
27 nonstop jet destinations:
Atlanta (ATL)
Detroit (DTW)
Charlotte (CLT)
2 nonstop commuter destinations:
Miami (MIA)
Orlando (MCO)
Places Rated Score: 50.91 Places Rated Rank: 178

Fort Pierce–Port St. Lucie, FL

Daily Commute: 44.8 minutes
Interstate Highway: I–95
Domestic Airline Service
Nearest is Melbourne (MLB) 57 miles NW
Places Rated Score: 17.61 Places Rated Rank: 292

Fort Smith, AR–OK

Daily Commute: 41.3 minutes
Interstate Highway: I–40
Domestic Airline Service (Nonhub)
Fort Smith Regional (FSM) 4 miles SE
2 nonstop commuter destinations:
Dallas (DFW)
Memphis (MEM)
Places Rated Score: 2.88 Places Rated Rank: 340

Fort Walton Beach, FL

Daily Commute: 38.7 minutes
AMTRAK Weekly Departures:
3 E Miami
3 W Los Angeles
Domestic Airline Service
Nearest is Pensacola (PNS) 80 miles W
Places Rated Score: 23.17 Places Rated Rank: 267

Fort Wayne, IN

Daily Commute: 40.9 minutes
Public Transit: *PTC*
20 city buses
Interstate Highway: I–69
AMTRAK Weekly Departures:
7 E New York
7 E Washington
14 W Chicago
Domestic Airline Service (Nonhub)

Fort Wayne/Baer Field (FWA) 9 miles SW
6 nonstop jet destinations:
Chicago (ORD)
Detroit (DTW)
Pittsburgh (PIT)
4 nonstop commuter destinations:
Cincinnati (CVG)
Detroit (DTW)
Indianapolis (IND)
Places Rated Score: 45.15 Places Rated Rank: 200

Fort Worth–Arlington, TX
Daily Commute: 49.7 minutes
Public Transit: *The T*
110 city buses
Interstate Highways: I–20, I–35W
AMTRAK Weekly Departures:
3 N Chicago
3 W Los Angeles
Domestic Airline Service
Nearest is Dallas (DFW) 20 miles NE
Places Rated Score: 45.39 Places Rated Rank: 199

Fresno, CA
Daily Commute: 41.2 minutes
Public Transit: *FAX*
124 city buses
AMTRAK Weekly Departures:
21 N San Francisco
21 S Bakersfield
Domestic Airline Service (Small hub)
Fresno Air Terminal (FAT) 5 miles NE
7 nonstop jet destinations:
Dallas (DFW)
Salt Lake City (SLC)
Los Angeles (LAX)
8 nonstop commuter destinations:
San Francisco (SFO)
Los Angeles (LAX)
Santa Ana (SNA)
Places Rated Score: 63.80 Places Rated Rank: 138

Gadsden, AL
Daily Commute: 42.5 minutes
Interstate Highway: I–59
Domestic Airline Service
Nearest is Anniston (ANB) 25 miles S
Places Rated Score: 17.81 Places Rated Rank: 291

Gainesville, FL
Daily Commute: 39.8 minutes
Public Transit: *RTS*
30 city buses
Interstate Highway: I–75
AMTRAK Weekly Departures:
7 N New York
7 S Miami
Domestic Airline Service (Nonhub)
J.R. Alison Municipal (GNV) 3 miles NE
3 nonstop jet destinations:
Atlanta (ATL)
Charlotte (CLT)
Miami (MIA)
3 nonstop commuter destinations:
Charlotte (CLT)
Miami (MIA)
Orlando (MCO)
Places Rated Score: 36.54 Places Rated Rank: 225

Galveston–Texas City, TX
Daily Commute: 51.3 minutes
Public Transit: *Island Transit*
14 city buses
4 light rail cars
Interstate Highway: I–45
Domestic Airline Service
Nearest is Houston (HOU) 35 miles NW
Places Rated Score: 59.78 Places Rated Rank: 154

✓ Gary, IN
Daily Commute: 51.2 minutes
Public Transit: *GPTC/NICTD*
50 city buses
45 commuter rail
Interstate Highways: I–65, I–80, I–90, I–94
AMTRAK Weekly Departures:
7 E New York
21 E Pontiac
6 E Toronto
7 E Washington
42 W Chicago
Domestic Airline Service
Nearest is Chicago (MDW) 38 miles NW
Places Rated Score: 92.72 Places Rated Rank: 24

Glens Falls, NY
Daily Commute: 41.3 minutes
Public Transit: *GGFT*
6 city buses
Interstate Highway: I–87
AMTRAK Weekly Departures:
7 N Montreal
7 S Washington
Domestic Airline Service
Nearest is Albany (ALB) 50 miles SW
Places Rated Score: 37.13 Places Rated Rank: 222

Goldsboro, NC
Daily Commute: 37.4 minutes
Domestic Airline Service
Nearest is Raleigh–Durham (RDU) 60 miles NW
Places Rated Score: 43.26 Places Rated Rank: 204

Grand Forks, ND–MN
Daily Commute: 27.4 minutes
Public Transit: *City Bus*
12 city buses
Interstate Highway: I–29
AMTRAK Weekly Departures:
4 E Chicago
4 W Seattle
Domestic Airline Service (Nonhub)
Grand Forks International (GFK) 10 miles NW
1 nonstop commuter destination:
Minneapolis (MSP)
Places Rated Score: 61.21 Places Rated Rank: 148

Grand Junction, CO
Daily Commute: 33.0 minutes
Interstate Highway: I–70
AMTRAK Weekly Departures:
7 E Chicago
3 W Los Angeles
4 W Oakland
Domestic Airline Service (Nonhub)
Walker Field (GJT) 3 miles NE
3 nonstop commuter destinations:
Denver (DIA)
Salt Lake City (SLC)
Phoenix (PHX)
Places Rated Score: 25.35 Places Rated Rank: 259

Grand Rapids–Muskegon–Holland, MI
Daily Commute: 39.2 minutes
Public Transit: *GRATA*
68 city buses
Interstate Highway: I–96
Domestic Airline Service (Small hub)
Kent County International (GRR) 6 miles SE
10 nonstop jet destinations:
Chicago (ORD)
Detroit (DTW)
Minneapolis (MSP)
6 nonstop commuter destinations:
Indianapolis (IND)
Milwaukee (MKE)
Chicago (MDW)
Places Rated Score: 54.94 Places Rated Rank: 167

Great Falls, MT
Daily Commute: 30.8 minutes
Public Transit: *GFT*
15 city buses
Interstate Highway: I–15
Domestic Airline Service (Small hub)
Great Falls International (GTF) 4 miles SW
5 nonstop jet destinations:
Salt Lake City (SLC)
Minneapolis (MSP)
Spokane (GEG)
1 nonstop commuter destination:
Billings (BIL)
Places Rated Score: 45.79 Places Rated Rank: 198

Greeley, CO
Daily Commute: 39.2 minutes
Public Transit: *The Bus*
10 city buses
Interstate Highway: I–25
AMTRAK Weekly Departures:

Domestic Airline Service (Nonhub)
Austin Straubel International (GRB) 8 miles SW
3 nonstop jet destinations:
Detroit (DTW)
Chicago (ORD)
Minneapolis (MSP)
2 nonstop commuter destinations:
Milwaukee (MKE)
Chicago (MDW)
Places Rated Score: 53.56 Places Rated Rank: 172

Greensboro–Winston-Salem–High Point, NC
Daily Commute: 40.6 minutes
Public Transit: *WSTA/GTA*
74 city buses
Interstate Highways: I–40, I–85
AMTRAK Weekly Departures:
14 N New York
14 S Charlotte
7 S New Orleans
7 W Raleigh
Domestic Airline Service (Nonhub)
Piedmont Triad International (GSO) 8 miles W
28 nonstop jet destinations:
Atlanta (ATL)
Charlotte (CLT)
Newark (EWR)
12 nonstop commuter destinations:
Nashville (BMA)
Washington (IAD)
Cincinnati (CVG)
Smith Reynolds (INT) 25 miles NE
1 nonstop commuter destination:
Charlotte (CLT)
Places Rated Score: 81.36 Places Rated Rank: 69

Greenville, NC
Daily Commute: 38.1 minutes
Public Transit: *GATD*
6 city buses
Domestic Airline Service (Nonhub)
Pitt/Greenville (PGV) 2 miles N
1 nonstop commuter destination:
Charlotte (CLT)
Places Rated Score: 1.85 Places Rated Rank: 346

Greenville–Spartanburg–Anderson, SC
Daily Commute: 40.2 minutes
Public Transit: *GTA*
18 city buses
Interstate Highways: I–26, I–85
AMTRAK Weekly Departures:
7 N New York
7 S New Orleans
Domestic Airline Service (Small hub)
Greenville–Spartanburg (GSP) 3 miles S
7 nonstop jet destinations:
Atlanta (ATL)
Charlotte (CLT)
Detroit (DTW)
5 commuter airlines, 5 markets:
Cincinnati (CVG)
Nashville (BNA)
Memphis (MEM)
Places Rated Score: 48.29 Places Rated Rank: 191

Hagerstown, MD
Daily Commute 47.1 minutes

Daily Commute: 35.0 minutes
Public Transit: *METRO*
170 city buses
VIA Weekly Departures:
6 W Montreal
Domestic Airline Service (Small hub)
Halifax International (YHZ) 26 miles NE
11 nonstop destinations:
Toronto (YYZ)
Ottawa (YOW)
Montreal (YUL)
Places Rated Score: 77.25 Places Rated Rank: 89

✓ Hamilton, ON
Daily Commute: 41.7 minutes
Public Transit: *HSR*
158 city buses
National Highway: QEW
VIA Weekly Departures:
7 E Toronto
7 S New York
Domestic Airline Service
Nearest is Toronto (YYZ) 35 miles NE
Places Rated Score: 93.41 Places Rated Rank: 22

Hamilton–Middletown, OH
Daily Commute: 44.9 minutes
Public Transit: *MTS*
4 city buses
Interstate Highway: I–75
AMTRAK Weekly Departures:
3 E Washington
3 W Chicago
Domestic Airline Service
Nearest is Cincinnati (CVG) 34 miles SW
Places Rated Score: 61.88 Places Rated Rank: 144

Harrisburg–Lebanon–Carlisle, PA
Daily Commute: 41.7 minutes
Public Transit: *CAT*
50 city buses
Interstate Highways: I–76, I–81, I–93
AMTRAK Weekly Departures:
38 E New York
5 E Philadelphia
14 W Pittsburgh

Domestic Airline Service (Small hub)
Harrisburg International (MDT) 8 miles SE
7 nonstop jet destinations:
Chicago (ORD)
Pittsburgh (PIT)
Charlotte (CLT)
8 nonstop commuter destinations:
Philadelphia (PHL)
Baltimore (BWI)
Boston (BOS)
Places Rated Score: 64.81 Places Rated Rank: 136

Hartford, CT
Daily Commute: 44.4 minutes
Public Transit: *CT Transit*
217 city buses
13 commuter rail
2 ferries
Interstate Highways: I–84, I–91
AMTRAK Weekly Departures:
7 N Montreal
42 N Springfield
33 S New Haven
5 S New York
20 S Washington
Domestic Airline Service (Medium hub)
Bradley International (BDL) 14 miles W
27 nonstop jet destinations:
Chicago (ORD)
Atlanta (ATL)
Pittsburgh (PIT)
7 nonstop commuter destinations:
New York (JFK)
Washington (IAD)
Buffalo (BUF)
Places Rated Score: 83.19 Places Rated Rank: 61

Hattiesburg, MS
Daily Commute: 40.4 minutes
Interstate Highway: I–59
AMTRAK Weekly Departures:
7 N New York
7 S New Orleans
Domestic Airline Service
Hattiesburg–Laurel Regional (PIB) 8 miles NW
1 nonstop commuter destination:
Memphis (MEM)
Places Rated Score: 5.14 Places Rated Rank: 327

Hickory–Morganton–Lenoir, NC
Daily Commute: 38.9 minutes
Public Transit: *Piedmont Wagon*
3 city buses
Interstate Highway: I–40
Domestic Airline Service
Nearest is Charlotte (CLT) 50 miles SE
Places Rated Score: 74.11 Places Rated Rank: 100

Honolulu, HI
Daily Commute: 52.8 minutes
Public Transit: *DTS*
439 city buses
Domestic Airline Service (Large hub)
Honolulu International (HNL) 3 miles N
23 nonstop jet destinations:
Kahului (OGG)
Los Angeles (LAX)
Lihue (LIH)
7 nonstop commuter destinations:
Kahului (OGG)
Kapalua (JHM)
Molokai–Kaunakak (MKK)
Places Rated Score: 28.92 Places Rated Rank: 244

Houma, LA
Daily Commute: 51.0 minutes
Domestic Airline Service
Nearest is New Orleans (MSY) 40 miles NE
Places Rated Score: 0.10 Places Rated Rank: 351

Houston, TX
Daily Commute: 56.8 minutes
Public Transit: *METRO*
991 city buses
Interstate Highways: I–10, I–45
AMTRAK Weekly Departures:
3 E Miami
3 W Los Angeles
Domestic Airline Service (Large hub)
Houston Intercontinental (IAH) 20 miles N
81 nonstop jet destinations:
Dallas (DFW)
Chicago (ORD)
Los Angeles (LAX)
William P. Hobby (HOU) 10 miles SE
38 nonstop jet destinations:
Dallas (DAL)
New Orleans (MSY)
Dallas (DFW)
Places Rated Score: 87.74 Places Rated Rank: 38

Huntington–Ashland, WV–KY–OH
Daily Commute: 41.7 minutes
Public Transit: *TTA*
22 city buses
Interstate Highway: I–64
AMTRAK Weekly Departures:
3 E Washington
3 W Chicago
Domestic Airline Service (Part of Charleston hub)
Tri-State/Ferguson Field (HTS) 7 miles SW
1 nonstop jet destination:
Pittsburgh (PIT)
3 nonstop commuter destinations:
Cincinnati (CVG)
Pittsburgh (PIT)
Charlotte (CLT)
Places Rated Score: 27.88 Places Rated Rank: 246

Huntsville, AL
Daily Commute: 43.4 minutes
Public Transit: *HTA*
9 city buses
Interstate Highway: I–65
Domestic Airline Service (Small hub)
Huntsville International (HSV) 9 miles SW
4 nonstop jet destinations:
Atlanta (ATL)
Dallas (DFW)
Charlotte (CLT)
2 nonstop commuter destinations:
Memphis (MEM)
Nashville (BNA)
Places Rated Score: 13.96 Places Rated Rank: 305

Indianapolis, IN
Daily Commute: 46.8 minutes
Public Transit: *METRO*
138 city buses
Interstate Highways: I–65, I–69, I–70, I–74
AMTRAK Weekly Departures:
3 E Washington
3 N Chicago
Domestic Airline Service (Medium hub)
Indianapolis International (IND) 7 miles SW
36 nonstop jet destinations:
Chicago (ORD)
St. Louis (STL)
Atlanta (ATL)
14 nonstop commuter destinations:
Cincinnati (CVG)
Milwaukee (MKE)
Nashville (BNA)
Places Rated Score: 81.97 Places Rated Rank: 68

Iowa City, IA
Daily Commute: 34.5 minutes
Public Transit: *ICT/CAMBUS*
37 city buses

Interstate Highway: I–80
Domestic Airline Service
Nearest is Cedar Rapids (CID) 22 miles NW
Places Rated Score: 42.30 Places Rated Rank: 207

Jackson, MI
Daily Commute: 43.8 minutes
Public Transit: *JTA*
8 city buses
Interstate Highway: I–94
AMTRAK Weekly Departures:
21 E Pontiac
21 W Chicago
Domestic Airline Service
Nearest is Lansing (LAN) 38 miles N
Places Rated Score: 21.48 Places Rated Rank: 272

Jackson, MS
Daily Commute: 43.8 minutes
Public Transit: *JATRAN*
32 city buses

Memphis (MEM)
Nashville (BNA)
Dallas (DFW)
Places Rated Score: 35.61 Places Rated Rank: 228

Jackson, TN
Daily Commute: 37.8 minutes
Public Transit: *JTA*
9 city buses
Interstate Highway: I–40
Domestic Airline Service
McKellor Field (MKL) 7 miles W
1 nonstop commuter destination:
Memphis (MEM)
Places Rated Score: 5.27 Places Rated Rank: 325

Jacksonville, FL
Daily Commute: 48.4 minutes
Public Transit: *JTA*
137 city buses
Interstate Highways: I–10, I–95
AMTRAK Weekly Departures:
14 N New York
17 S Miami
7 S Tampa
3 W Los Angeles
Domestic Airline Service (Medium hub)
Jacksonville International (JAX) 9 miles N
25 nonstop jet destinations:
Atlanta (ATL)
Charlotte (CLT)
Dallas (DFW)
5 nonstop commuter destinations:
Miami (MIA)
Tampa (TPA)
Orlando (MCO)
Places Rated Score: 70.71 Places Rated Rank: 112

Jacksonville, NC
Daily Commute: 40.9 minutes
Domestic Airline Service (Nonhub)
Albert J. Ellis (OAJ) 10 miles NE
2 nonstop jet destinations:
Atlanta (ATL)
Charlotte (CLT)
1 nonstop commuter destination:
Charlotte (CLT)
Places Rated Score: 3.26 Places Rated Rank: 338

Jamestown, NY
Daily Commute: 32.3 minutes
Domestic Airline Service (Part of Buffalo hub)
Chautauqua County/Jamestown (JHW) 5 miles N
1 nonstop commuter destination:
Pittsburgh (PIT)
Places Rated Score: 50.23 Places Rated Rank: 182

Janesville–Beloit, WI
Daily Commute: 38.3 minutes
Public Transit: *JTS*
25 city buses
Interstate Highway: I–90
Domestic Airline Service
Nearest is Madison (MSN) 35 miles NW
Places Rated Score: 27.50 Places Rated Rank: 249

Jersey City, NJ

7 city buses
Interstate Highway: I–81
Domestic Airline Service (Nonhub)
Tri-City Regional (TRI) 12 miles SW
2 nonstop jet destinations:
Atlanta (ATL)
Charlotte (CLT)
4 nonstop commuter destinations:
Cincinnati (CVG)
Nashville (BNA)
Pittsburgh (PIT)
Places Rated Score: 12.46 Places Rated Rank: 307

Johnstown, PA
Daily Commute: 39.2 minutes
Public Transit: *CCTA*
25 city buses
2 cable inclines
AMTRAK Weekly Departures:
14 E New York
14 W Pittsburgh
Domestic Airline Service (Nonhub)
Johnstown/Cambria County (JST) 5 miles E
1 nonstop commuter destination:
Pittsburgh (PIT)
Places Rated Score: 31.99 Places Rated Rank: 237

Joplin, MO
Daily Commute: 36.6 minutes
Interstate Highway: I–44
Domestic Airline Service (Nonhub)
Joplin Municipal (JLN) 5 miles E
1 nonstop jet destination:
St. Louis (STL)
1 nonstop commuter destination:
Memphis (MEM)
Places Rated Score: 5.32 Places Rated Rank: 324

Kalamazoo–Battle Creek, MI
Daily Commute: 38.4 minutes
Public Transit: *METRO*
47 city buses
Interstate Highway: I–94
AMTRAK Weekly Departures:
21 E Pontiac

6 E Toronto
28 W Chicago
Domestic Airline Service (Nonhub)
Kalamazoo/Battle Creek International (AZO) 4 miles SE
4 nonstop jet destinations:
Chicago (ORD)
Detroit (DTW)
Minneapolis (MSP)
3 nonstop commuter destinations:
Cincinnati (CVG)
Detroit (DTW)
Pittsburgh (PIT)
Places Rated Score: 61.06 Places Rated Rank: 149

Kankakee, IL
Daily Commute: 42.7 minutes
Interstate Highway: I–57
AMTRAK Weekly Departures:
12 N Chicago
7 S Carbondale
5 S New Orleans
Domestic Airline Service
Nearest is Chicago (MDW) 46 miles NE
Places Rated Score: 70.30 Places Rated Rank: 115

Kansas City, MO–KS
Daily Commute: 46.0 minutes
Public Transit: *KCATA*
220 city buses
Interstate Highways: I–29, I–35, I–70
AMTRAK Weekly Departures:
14 E Chicago
7 E St. Louis
7 W Los Angeles
Domestic Airline Service (Medium hub)
Kansas City International (MCI) 15 miles NW
44 nonstop jet destinations:
St. Louis (STL)
Dallas (DFW)
Denver (DIA)
13 nonstop commuter destinations:
Omaha (OMA)
Wichita (ICT)
Des Moines (DES)
Places Rated Score: 85.98 Places Rated Rank: 46

Kenosha, WI
Daily Commute: 46.6 minutes
Public Transit: *KTC*
34 city buses
Interstate Highway: I–94
Domestic Airline Service
Nearest is Chicago (ORD) 35 miles SW
Places Rated Score: 81.36 Places Rated Rank: 70

Killeen–Temple, TX
Daily Commute: 35.1 minutes
Interstate Highway: I–35
AMTRAK Weekly Departures:
3 N Chicago
3 W Los Angeles
Domestic Airline Service (Part of Waco hub)
Killeen Municipal (ILE) 3 miles E
2 nonstop jet destinations:
Dallas (DFW)
Houston (IAH)
Places Rated Score: 17.46 Places Rated Rank: 294

✓ Kitchener, ON
Daily Commute: 39.0 minutes
Public Transit: *K Transit*
95 city buses
National Highway: ON–40
VIA Weekly Departures:
14 E Toronto
7 W Chicago
7 W Sarnia
Domestic Airline Service
Nearest is Toronto (YYZ) 40 miles E
Places Rated Score: 93.89 Places Rated Rank: 20

Knoxville, TN
Daily Commute: 45.8 minutes
Public Transit: *KTRANS*
45 city buses
Interstate Highways: I–40, I–75
Domestic Airline Service (Small hub)
McGhee Tyson (TYS) 13 miles S
10 nonstop jet destinations:
Atlanta (ATL)
Chicago (ORD)
Memphis (MEM)
6 commuter airlines, 6 markets:
Cincinnati (CVG)
Charlotte (CLT)
Nashville (BNA)
Places Rated Score: 35.80 Places Rated Rank: 227

Kokomo, IN
Daily Commute: 36.3 minutes
Domestic Airline Service
Nearest is Indianapolis (IND) 47 miles S
Places Rated Score: 50.91 Places Rated Rank: 177

La Crosse, WI–MN
Daily Commute: 32.8 minutes
Public Transit: *LCMTU*
13 city buses
Interstate Highway: I–90
AMTRAK Weekly Departures:
7 N Seattle
7 S Chicago
Domestic Airline Service (Nonhub)
La Crosse Municipal (LSE) 4 miles NW
2 nonstop jet destinations:
Minneapolis (MSP)
Chicago (ORD)
1 nonstop commuter destination:
Milwaukee (MKE)
Places Rated Score: 50.73 Places Rated Rank: 179

Lafayette, IN
Daily Commute: 35.1 minutes
Public Transit: *GLPTC*
33 city buses
Interstate Highway: I–65
AMTRAK Weekly Departures:
3 E Washington
3 N Chicago
Domestic Airline Service (Nonhub)
Purdue University (LAF) 2 miles SW
2 nonstop commuter destinations
Detroit (DTW)
Chicago (ORD)
Places Rated Score: 27.32 Places Rated Rank: 250

Lafayette, LA
Daily Commute: 44.7 minutes
Public Transit: *COLT*
12 city buses
Interstate Highways: I–10, I–49
AMTRAK Weekly Departures:
3 E Miami
3 W Los Angeles
Domestic Airline Service (Nonhub)
Lafayette Municipal (LFT) 2 miles SE
2 nonstop jet destinations:
Houston (IAH)
Dallas (DFW)
2 nonstop commuter destinations:
Dallas (DFW)
Memphis (MEM)
Places Rated Score: 14.76 Places Rated Rank: 303

Lake Charles, LA
Daily Commute: 40.9 minutes

Public Transit: *LCTA*
8 city buses
Interstate Highway: I–10
AMTRAK Weekly Departures:
3 E Miami
3 W Los Angeles
Domestic Airline Service (Nonhub)
Lake Charles Regional (LCH) 5 miles S
1 nonstop jet destination:
Houston (IAH)
1 nonstop commuter destination:
Dallas (DFW)
Places Rated Score: 11.10 Places Rated Rank: 310

Lakeland–Winter Haven, FL
Daily Commute: 44.4 minutes
Public Transit: *Citrus Connect*
16 city buses
Interstate Highway: I–4
AMTRAK Weekly Departures:
7 N New York

29 W Harrisburg
14 W Pittsburgh
Domestic Airline Service (Part of Harrisburg hub)
Lancaster Muncipal (LNS) 4 miles N
2 nonstop commuter destinations:
Pittsburgh (PIT)
Philadelphia (PHL)
Places Rated Score: 70.12 Places Rated Rank: 117

Lansing–East Lansing, MI
Daily Commute: 40.6 minutes
Public Transit: *CATA*
48 city buses
Interstate Highways: I–69, I–96
AMTRAK Weekly Departures:
6 E Toronto
7 W Chicago
Domestic Airline Service (Nonhub)
Capital City (LAN) 4 miles NW
5 nonstop jet destinations:
Detroit (DTW)
Chicago (ORD)
Pittsburgh (PIT)
4 nonstop commuter destinations:
Chicago (ORD)
Cincinnati (CVG)
Detroit (DTW)
Places Rated Score: 48.39 Places Rated Rank: 190

Laredo, TX
Daily Commute: 37.6 minutes
Public Transit: *El Metro*
27 city buses
Interstate Highway: I–35
Domestic Airline Service (Nonhub)
Laredo International (LRD) 5 miles NE
1 nonstop jet destination:
Houston (IAH)
1 nonstop commuter destination:
Dallas (DFW)
Places Rated Score: 16.17 Places Rated Rank: 300

Las Cruces, NM
Daily Commute: 40.7 minutes
Public Transit: *RoadRUNNER*
8 city buses

Interstate Highways: I–10, I–25
Domestic Airline Service
Nearest is El Paso (ELP) 50 miles SE
Places Rated Score: 43.47 Places Rated Rank: 203

Las Vegas, NV–AZ
Daily Commute: 44.1 minutes
Public Transit: *ATC*
119 city buses
Interstate Highway: I–15
AMTRAK Weekly Departures:
3 E Chicago
3 W Los Angeles
Domestic Airline Service (Large hub)
McCarran International (LAS) 7 miles S
59 nonstop jet destinations:
Los Angeles (LAX)
Phoenix (PHX)
Dallas (DFW)
7 nonstop commuter destinations:
Grand Canyon (GCN)
Los Angeles (LAX)

Places Rated Score: 57.98

Lawrence, MA–NH
Daily Commute: 49.1 minutes
Public Transit: *MVRTA*
36 city buses
35 commuter rail
Interstate Highway: I–95
Domestic Airline Service
Nearest is Boston (BOS) 35 miles S
Places Rated Score: 57.40 Places Rated Rank: 164

Lawton, OK
Daily Commute: 32.8 minutes
Interstate Highway: I–44
Domestic Airline Service (Nonhub)
Lawton Municipal (LAW) 2 miles S
1 nonstop commuter destination:
Dallas (DFW)
Places Rated Score: 9.89 Places Rated Rank: 313

Lewiston–Auburn, ME
Daily Commute: 33.9 minutes
Public Transit: *Lewiston–Hudson Bus*
10 city buses
Interstate Highway: I–95
Domestic Airline Service
Nearest is Portland (PWM) 35 miles S
Places Rated Score: 5.62 Places Rated Rank: 321

Lexington, KY
Daily Commute: 39.8 minutes
Public Transit: *LEXTRAN*
33 city buses
Interstate Highways: I–64, I–75
Domestic Airline Service (Small hub)
Blue Grass Field (LEX) 4 miles W
6 nonstop jet destinations:
Atlanta (ATL)
Pittsburgh (PIT)
Cincinnati (CVG)
4 nonstop commuter destinations:
Cincinnati (CVG)
Detroit (DTW)
Nashville (BNA)
Places Rated Score: 37.74 Places Rated Rank: 219

Lima, OH
Daily Commute: 35.5 minutes
Public Transit: *ACRTA*
7 city buses
Interstate Highway: I–75
Domestic Airline Service
Nearest is Dayton (DAY) 60 miles S
Places Rated Score: 5.97 Places Rated Rank: 320

Lincoln, NE
Daily Commute: 34.5 minutes
Public Transit: *StarTRAN*
48 city buses
Interstate Highway: I–80
AMTRAK Weekly Departures:
16 E Chicago
14 S St. Louis
3 W Los Angeles
4 W Oakland
2 W Seattle
Domestic Airline Service (Part of Omaha hub)
Lincoln Municipal (LNK) 4 miles NW
3 nonstop jet destinations:
Chicago (ORD)
Denver (DIA)
St. Louis (STL)
2 nonstop commuter destinations:
Minneapolis (MSP)
Kansas City (MCI)
Places Rated Score: 84.60 Places Rated Rank: 53

Little Rock–North Little Rock, AR
Daily Commute: 42.7 minutes
Public Transit: *CAT*
50 city buses
Interstate Highways: I–30, I–40
AMTRAK Weekly Departures:
3 N Chicago
3 S Los Angeles
Domestic Airline Service (Small hub)
Adams Field (LIT) 2 miles E
16 nonstop jet destinations:
Dallas (DFW)
St. Louis (STL)
Dallas (DAL)
4 nonstop commuter destinations:
Dallas (DFW)
Nashville (BNA)
New Orleans (MSY)
Places Rated Score: 59.38 Places Rated Rank: 157

✓ **London, ON**
Daily Commute: 38.0 minutes
Public Transit: *Transit*
128 city buses
National Highway: ON–40
VIA Weekly Departures:
46 E Toronto
12 E Ottawa
14 W Chicago
14 W Sarnia
56 W Windsor
Domestic Airline Service (Nonhub)
London Municipal (YXU) 7 miles NE
9 nonstop destinations:
Toronto (YYZ)
Ottawa (YOW)
Detroit (DTW)
Places Rated Score: 88.91 Places Rated Rank: 34

Long Island, NY
Daily Commute: 64.6 minutes
Public Transit: *Suffolk Transit*
152 city buses
365 commuter rail
Domestic Airline Service (Large hub)
Long Island MacArthur (ISP)
9 nonstop jet destinations:
Orlando (MCO)
Pittsburgh (PIT)
Fort Lauderdale (FLL)
6 nonstop commuter destinations:
Baltimore (BWI)
Washington (DCA)
Philadelphia (PHL)
Places Rated Score: 71.01 Places Rated Rank: 109

Longview–Marshall, TX
Daily Commute: 40.8 minutes
Interstate Highway: I–20
AMTRAK Weekly Departures:
3 N Chicago
3 S Los Angeles
Domestic Airline Service (Nonhub)
Gregg County (GGG) 3 miles S
1 nonstop commuter destination:
Dallas (DFW)
Places Rated Score: 4.57 Places Rated Rank: 333

✓ **Los Angeles–Long Beach, CA**
Daily Commute: 56.8 minutes
Public Transit: *LACMTA/SCRTD*
2,694 city buses
130 commuter rail
36 light rail cars
16 heavy rail cars
Interstate Highways: I–10, I–5
AMTRAK Weekly Departures:
10 E Chicago
3 E Miami
23 N Santa Barbara
7 N Seattle
55 S San Diego
Domestic Airline Service (Large hub)
Los Angeles International (LAX) 10 miles SW
73 nonstop jet destinations:
Las Vegas (LAS)
San Francisco (SFO)
Honolulu (HNL)
34 nonstop commuter destinations:
San Diego (SAN)
Palm Springs (PSP)
Fresno (FAT)
Daugherty Field (LGB) 22 miles SE
1 nonstop jet destination:
Phoenix (PHX)
Burbank (BUR) 16 miles NW
12 nonstop jet destinations:
Oakland (OAK)
Las Vegas (LAS)
Sacramento (SMF)
3 nonstop commuter destinations:
Salt Lake City (SLC)
San Diego (SAN)
Fresno (FAT)
Places Rated Score: 94.30 Places Rated Rank: 18

Louisville, KY–IN
Daily Commute: 46.0 minutes
Public Transit: *TARC*
250 city buses
Interstate Highways: I–64, I–65, I–71
Domestic Airline Service (Small hub)
Standiford Field (SDF) 4 miles S
22 nonstop jet destinations:
Atlanta (ATL)
St. Louis (STL)
Chicago (MDW)
4 nonstop commuter destinations:
Cincinnati (CVG)
Nashville (BNA)
Memphis (MEM)
Places Rated Score: 69.42 Places Rated Rank: 121

Lowell, MA–NH
Daily Commute: 49.5 minutes
Public Transit: *LRTA*
28 city buses
35 commuter rail
Interstate Highway: I–95
Domestic Airline Service
Nearest is Boston (BOS) 36 miles SE
Places Rated Score: 49.16 Places Rated Rank: 188

Lubbock, TX
Daily Commute: 35.0 minutes
Public Transit: *Citibus*
31 city buses
Interstate Highway: I–27
Domestic Airline Service (Small hub)
Lubbock International (LBB) 4 miles N
8 nonstop jet destinations:
Dallas (DAL)
Dallas (DFW)
Austin (AUS)

1 nonstop jet destination:
Atlanta (ATL)
4 nonstop commuter destinations:
Charlotte (CLT)
Pittsburgh (PIT)
Washington (DCA)
Places Rated Score: 25.67 Places Rated Rank: 257

Macon, GA
Daily Commute: 40.6 minutes
Public Transit: *BCTA*
20 city buses
Interstate Highways: I–16, I–75
Domestic Airline Service (Nonhub)
Middle Georgia Regional (MCN) 9 miles S
1 nonstop jet destination:
Atlanta (ATL)
Places Rated Score: 2.22 Places Rated Rank: 345

Madison, WI
Daily Commute: 38.5 minutes
Public Transit: *MMT*
140 city buses
Interstate Highways: I–90, I–94
Domestic Airline Service (Small hub)
Dane County/Truax Field (MSN) 5 miles NE
5 nonstop jet destinations:
Chicago (ORD)
Detroit (DTW)
Minneapolis (MSP)
2 nonstop commuter destinations:
Cincinnati (CVG)
Milwaukee (MKE)
Places Rated Score: 49.29 Places Rated Rank: 187

Manchester, NH
Daily Commute: 48.8 minutes
Public Transit: *MTA*
20 city buses
Interstate Highway: I–93
Domestic Airline Service (Small hub)
Manchester Municipal (MHT) 3 miles S
8 nonstop jet destinations:
Chicago (ORD)
Philadelphia (PHL)
Pittsburgh (PIT)

3 nonstop commuter destinations:
New York (LGA)
Cincinnati (CVG)
Washington (IAD)
Places Rated Score: 27.96 Places Rated Rank: 245

Mansfield, OH
Daily Commute: 36.8 minutes
Public Transit: *RCT*
8 city buses
Interstate Highway: I–70
Domestic Airline Service
Nearest is Columbus (CMH) 67 miles SW
Places Rated Score: 4.64 Places Rated Rank: 332

McAllen–Edinburg–Mission, TX
Daily Commute: 38.5 minutes
Domestic Airline Service (Small hub)
McAllen International (MFE) 2 miles S
2 nonstop jet destinations:
Houston (IAH)
Dallas (DFW)

Seattle (SEA)
Places Rated Score: 22.23 Places Rated Rank: 269

Melbourne–Titusville–Palm Bay, FL
Daily Commute: 44.4 minutes
Public Transit: *SCAT*
14 city buses
Interstate Highway: I–95
Domestic Airline Service (Part of Orlando hub)
Melbourne Regional (MLB) 2 miles NW
3 nonstop jet destinations:
Atlanta (ATL)
Charlotte (CLT)
Newark (EWR)
2 nonstop commuter destinations:
Orlando (MCO)
Miami (MIA)
Places Rated Score: 57.96 Places Rated Rank: 162

Memphis, TN–AR–MS
Daily Commute: 47.2 minutes
Public Transit: *MATA*
160 city buses
Interstate Highways: I–40, I–55
AMTRAK Weekly Departures:
5 N Chicago
5 S New Orleans
Domestic Airline Service (Medium hub)
Memphis International (MEM) 10 miles SE
46 nonstop jet destinations:
Atlanta (ATL)
Minneapolis (MSP)
Detroit (DTW)
28 nonstop commuter destinations:
Huntsville (HSV)
Gulfport (GPT)
Jackson (JAN)
Places Rated Score: 82.19 Places Rated Rank: 66

Merced, CA
Daily Commute: 35.9 minutes
Public Transit: *MTS*
3 city buses
AMTRAK Weekly Departures:
21 N San Francisco

21 S Bakersfield
Domestic Airline Service (Part of Fresno hub)
Merced Municipal (MCE) 3 miles SW
1 nonstop commuter destination:
San Francisco (SFO)
Places Rated Score: 24.06 Places Rated Rank: 264

Miami, FL
Daily Commute: 53.5 minutes
Public Transit: *MDTA*
517 city buses
76 heavy rail cars
35 commuter rail
Interstate Highway: I–95
AMTRAK Weekly Departures:
14 N New York
3 W Los Angeles
Domestic Airline Service (Large hub)
Miami International (MIA) 8 miles NW
50 nonstop jet destinations:
New York (JFK)
Atlanta (ATL)
San Juan (SJU)
19 nonstop commuter destinations:
Nassau (NAS)
Orlando (MCO)
Tampa (TPA)
Places Rated Score: 84.56 Places Rated Rank: 54

✓ **Middlesex-Somerset-Hunterdon, NJ**
Daily Commute: 56.6 minutes
Public Transit: *NJTC*
559 city buses
Interstate Highways: I–78, I–80
AMTRAK Weekly Departures:
30 N New York
7 S Charlotte
7 W Pittsburgh
Domestic Airline Service
Nearest is Newark (EWR) 23 miles NE
Places Rated Score: 91.41 Places Rated Rank: 29

✓ **Milwaukee-Waukesha, WI**
Daily Commute: 43.3 minutes
Public Transit: *MCTS*
474 city buses
Interstate Highways: I–43, I–94
AMTRAK Weekly Departures:
41 S Chicago
7 W Seattle
Domestic Airline Service (Medium hub)
General Mitchell International (MKE) 5 miles S
34 nonstop jet destinations:
Chicago (ORD)
Minneapolis (MSP)
Detroit (DTW)
14 nonstop commuter destinations:
Indianapolis (IND)
Cincinnati (CVG)
Grand Rapids (GRR)
Places Rated Score: 90.33 Places Rated Rank: 32

✓ **Minneapolis-St. Paul, MN-WI**
Daily Commute: 45.0 minutes
Public Transit: *MCTO*
860 city buses
Interstate Highways: I–35, I–94
AMTRAK Weekly Departures:
7 S Chicago
7 W Seattle
Domestic Airline Service (Large hub)
Minneapolis-St. Paul International (MSP) 6 miles SW
87 nonstop jet destinations:
Chicago (ORD)
Detroit (DTW)
Denver (DIA)
37 nonstop commuter destinations:
Appleton (ATW)
Wausau (CWA)
Sioux City (SUX)
Places Rated Score: 95.22 Places Rated Rank: 14

Mobile, AL
Daily Commute: 47.3 minutes
Public Transit: *MTA*
33 city buses
Interstate Highways: I–10, I–65
AMTRAK Weekly Departures:
3 E Miami
3 W Los Angeles
Domestic Airline Service (Small hub)
Mobile Regional (MOB) 11 miles W
3 nonstop jet destinations:
Atlanta (ATL)
Dallas (DFW)
Charlotte (CLT)
2 nonstop commuter destinations:
Memphis (MEM)
Nashville (BNA)
Places Rated Score: 38.23 Places Rated Rank: 218

Modesto, CA
Daily Commute: 47.7 minutes
Public Transit: *MAX*
26 city buses
AMTRAK Weekly Departures:
21 N San Francisco
21 S Bakersfield
Domestic Airline Service (Nonhub)
Modesto Municipal (MOD) 3 miles E
1 nonstop commuter destination:
San Francisco (SFO)
Places Rated Score: 22.76 Places Rated Rank: 268

Monmouth-Ocean, NJ
Daily Commute: 58.3 minutes
Public Transit: *NJTC*
357 city buses
Domestic Airline Service
Nearest is Newark (EWR) 47 miles NW
Places Rated Score: 83.41 Places Rated Rank: 59

Monroe, LA
Daily Commute: 39.8 minutes
Public Transit: *MTS*
14 city buses
Interstate Highway: I–20
Domestic Airline Service (Nonhub)
Monroe Regional (MLU) 3 miles E
3 nonstop jet destinations:
Dallas (DFW)
Atlanta (ATL)
Houston (IAH)
2 nonstop commuter destinations:
Memphis (MEM)
Dallas (DFW)
Places Rated Score: 20.09 Places Rated Rank: 278

Montgomery, AL
Daily Commute: 42.1 minutes
Public Transit: *MAT*
29 city buses
Interstate Highways: I–65, I–85
Domestic Airline Service (Nonhub)
Dannelly Field (MGM) 6 miles SW
2 nonstop jet destinations:
Atlanta (ATL)
Dallas (DFW)
3 nonstop commuter destinations:
Memphis (MEM)
Charlotte (CLT)
Nashville (BNA)
Places Rated Score: 18.62 Places Rated Rank: 287

✓ Montreal, PQ
Daily Commute: 48.7 minutes
Public Transit: *STCUM*
2,292 city buses
594 heavy rail coaches
National Highways: (I–87), (I–89), PQ–20, TC–1
VIA Weekly Departures:
6 E Halifax
3 N Jonquiere
31 N Quebec
3 N Sanmaur
7 S Washington
26 W Ottawa
38 W Toronto
14 W Windsor
Domestic Airline Service (Large hub)
Dorval International (YUL) 14 miles W
82 nonstop destinations:
Toronto (YYZ)
Vancouver (YVR)
New York (JFK)

Public Transit: *MTA*
100 city buses
Interstate Highways: I–24, I–40, I–65
Domestic Airline Service (Medium hub)
Nashville International (BNA) 5 miles SE
37 nonstop jet destinations:
Dallas (DFW)
Atlanta (ATL)
Chicago (ORD)
37 nonstop commuter destinations:
Cincinnati (CVG)
Birmingham (BHM)
Indianapolis (IND)
Places Rated Score: 74.36 — Places Rated Rank: 99

New Bedford, MA
Daily Commute: 45.1 minutes
Public Transit: *SERTA*
64 city buses
Interstate Highway: I–195
Domestic Airline Service (Part of Boston hub)
New Bedford Municipal (EWB) 3 miles NW

Interstate Highway: I–69
Domestic Airline Service
Nearest is Indianapolis (IND) 69 miles SW
Places Rated Score: 71.13 — Places Rated Rank: 108

Myrtle Beach, SC
Daily Commute: 40.3 minutes
Public Transit: *CRPTA*
7 city buses
Domestic Airline Service (Small hub)
Myrtle Beach Jetport (MYR) 2 miles S
4 nonstop jet destinations:
Charlotte (CLT)
Atlanta (ATL)
Philadelphia (PHL)
3 nonstop commuter destinations:
Charlotte (CLT)
Cincinnati (CVG)
Greensboro (GSO)
Places Rated Score: 19.88 — Places Rated Rank: 281

Naples, FL
Daily Commute: 40.0 minutes
Interstate Highway: I–75
Domestic Airline Service (Part of Fort Myers hub)
Naples Municipal (APF) 2 miles NE
2 nonstop jet destinations:
Miami (MIA)
Tampa (TPA)
4 nonstop commuter destinations:
Orlando (MCO)
Miami (MIA)
Key West (EYW)
Places Rated Score: 31.86 — Places Rated Rank: 238

Nashua, NH
Daily Commute: 48.8 minutes
Public Transit: *City Bus*
4 city buses
Interstate Highway: I–93
Domestic Airline Service
Nearest is Manchester (MHT) 12 miles N
Places Rated Score: 42.45 — Places Rated Rank: 206

Nashville, TN
Daily Commute: 48.6 minutes

64 N Boston
28 N Springfield
7 N St. Albans
6 S New York
8 S Newport News
6 S Richmond
64 S Washington
Domestic Airline Service (Part of New York–Tri-State hub)
Tweed–New Haven (HVN) 3 miles SE
3 nonstop jet destinations:
Chicago (ORD)
Newark (EWR)
Philadelphia (PHL)
4 nonstop commuter destinations:
Baltimore (BWI)
Washington (DCA)
Washington (IAD)
Places Rated Score: 96.72 — Places Rated Rank: 7

New London–Norwich, CT–RI
Daily Commute: 40.3 minutes
Interstate Highway: I–95
AMTRAK Weekly Departures:
57 N Boston
42 S Washington
Domestic Airline Service (Nonhub)
Groton/New London (GON) 4 miles SE
1 nonstop commuter destination:
Philadelphia (PHL)
Places Rated Score: 27.53 — Places Rated Rank: 248

New Orleans, LA
Daily Commute: 52.5 minutes
Public Transit: *RTA*
430 city buses
22 light rail cars
5 ferries
Interstate Highways: I–10, I–59
AMTRAK Weekly Departures:
3 E Miami
5 N Chicago
7 N New York
3 W Los Angeles
Domestic Airline Service (Medium hub)

New Orleans International (MSY) 10 miles W
47 nonstop jet destinations:
Los Angeles (LAX)
Atlanta (ATL)
Dallas (DFW)
3 nonstop commuter destinations:
Orlando (MCO)
Little Rock (LIT)
Shreveport (SHV)
Places Rated Score: 77.56 Places Rated Rank: 87

✓ New York, NY
Daily Commute: 75.8 minutes
Public Transit: *NYCTA*
5,266 heavy rail cars
4,784 city buses
1,672 commuter rail
8 ferries
Interstate Highways: I–78, I–87, I–95
AMTRAK Weekly Departures:
25 N Albany
64 N Boston
14 N Montreal
14 N Springfield
7 S Miami
7 S New Orleans
8 S Newport News
21 S Philadelphia
13 S Richmond
7 S Tampa
186 S Washington
7 W Chicago
14 W Pittsburgh
7 W Toronto
Domestic Airline Service (Large hub)
Kennedy International (JFK) 15 miles SE
43 nonstop jet destinations:
Los Angeles (LAX)
Miami (MIA)
San Juan (SJU)
18 nonstop commuter destinations:
Boston (BOS)
Washington (DCA)
Washington (IAD)
La Guardia (LGA) 8 miles NE
61 nonstop jet destinations:
Chicago (ORD)
Boston (BOS)
Washington (DCA)
17 nonstop commuter destinations:
Washington (IAD)
Burlington (BTV)
Providence (PVD)
Westchester County (HPN) 25 miles NE
7 nonstop jet destinations:
Chicago (ORD)
Detroit (DTW)
Pittsburgh (PIT)
6 nonstop commuter destinations:
Washington (DCA)
Baltimore (BWI)
Philadelphia (PHL)
Places Rated Score: 98.34 Places Rated Rank: 3

✓ Newark, NJ
Daily Commute: 56.2 minutes
Public Transit: *NJTC*
691 commuter rail
492 city buses
16 light rail cars
Interstate Highways: I–78, I–80, I–95
AMTRAK Weekly Departures:
195 E New York
64 N Boston
7 N Montreal
14 N Springfield
7 S Charlotte
7 S Miami
7 S New Orleans
11 S Philadelphia
13 S Richmond
176 S Washington
14 W Pittsburgh
Domestic Airline Service (Large hub)
Newark International (EWR) 3 miles S
77 nonstop jet destinations:
Chicago (ORD)
Atlanta (ATL)
Orlando (MCO)
8 nonstop commuter destinations:
Washington (IAD)
Baltimore (BWI)
Cincinnati (CVG)
Places Rated Score: 96.59 Places Rated Rank: 8

Newburgh, NY–PA
Daily Commute: 58.5 minutes
Interstate Highways: I–84, I–87
Domestic Airline Service (Small hub)
Stewart International (SWF) 4 miles NW
8 nonstop jet destinations:
Chicago (ORD)
Pittsburgh (PIT)
Atlanta (ATL)
3 nonstop commuter destinations:
Philadelphia (PHL)
Washington (IAD)
Boston (BOS)
Places Rated Score: 38.48 Places Rated Rank: 216

Norfolk–Virginia Beach–Newport News, VA–NC
Daily Commute: 45.6 minutes
Public Transit: *TRT/PENTRAN*
231 city buses
2 ferries
Interstate Highway: I–64
AMTRAK Weekly Departures:
7 N Boston
2 N New York
Domestic Airline Service (Nonhub)
Norfolk International (ORF) 0.5 miles NE
20 nonstop jet destinations:
Atlanta (ATL)
Charlotte (CLT)
Chicago (ORD)
6 nonstop commuter destinations:
Washington (DCA)
Washington (IAD)
New York (JFK)
Newport News–Patrick Henry International (PHF) 10 miles NW
3 nonstop jet destinations:
Atlanta (ATL)
Pittsburgh (PIT)
Charlotte (CLT)
6 nonstop commuter destinations:
Charlotte (CLT)
Baltimore (BWI)
Washington (DCA)
Places Rated Score: 67.87 Places Rated Rank: 127

Oakland, CA
Daily Commute: 57.5 minutes
Public Transit: *ACT*
745 city buses
4 ferries
Interstate Highway: I–80
AMTRAK Weekly Departures:
4 E Chicago
21 E Sacramento
7 N Seattle
7 S Los Angeles
Domestic Airline Service (Part of San Francisco hub)
Metropolitan Oakland International (OAK) 4 miles SE
21 nonstop jet destinations:

Los Angeles (LAX)
Burbank (BUR)
Seattle (SEA)
Places Rated Score: 80.86 Places Rated Rank: 74

Ocala, FL
Daily Commute: 44.7 minutes
Interstate Highway: I–75
AMTRAK Weekly Departures:
7 N New York
7 S Miami
Domestic Airline Service
Nearest is Gainesville (GNV) 40 miles N
Places Rated Score: 2.34 Places Rated Rank: 344

Odessa–Midland, TX
Daily Commute: 36.5 minutes
Interstate Highway: I–20
Domestic Airline Service (Small hub)
Midland International (MAF) 15 miles NE

62 city buses
Interstate Highways: I–35, I–40, I–44
Domestic Airline Service (Medium hub)
Will Rogers World (OKC) 10 miles SW
20 nonstop jet destinations:
Dallas (DFW)
St. Louis (STL)
Dallas (DAL)
1 nonstop commuter destination:
Cincinnati (CVG)
Places Rated Score: 60.89 Places Rated Rank: 150

Olympia, WA
Daily Commute: 44.0 minutes
Public Transit: *IT*
70 city buses
Interstate Highway: I–5
AMTRAK Weekly Departures:
3 E Chicago
24 N Seattle
7 S Eugene
7 S Los Angeles
7 S Portland
Domestic Airline Service
Nearest is Seattle (SEA) 45 miles NE
Places Rated Score: 75.79 Places Rated Rank: 93

Omaha, NE–IA
Daily Commute: 38.8 minutes
Public Transit: *OTA*
126 city buses
Interstate Highway: I–80
AMTRAK Weekly Departures:
9 E Chicago
3 W Los Angeles
4 W Oakland
2 W Seattle
Domestic Airline Service (Small hub)
Omaha Eppley (OMA) 4 miles NE
18 nonstop jet destinations:
Denver (DIA)
Chicago (ORD)
St. Louis (STL)
3 nonstop commuter destinations:
Kansas City (MCI)
Cincinnati (CVG)

Minneapolis (MSP)
Places Rated Score: 77.26 Places Rated Rank: 88

Orange County, CA
Daily Commute: 54.6 minutes
Public Transit: *OCTA*
382 city buses
Interstate Highway: I–5
AMTRAK Weekly Departures:
27 N Los Angeles
23 N Santa Barbara
50 S San Diego
Domestic Airline Service (Large hub)
John Wayne International (SNA) 0.3 miles
26 nonstop jet destinations:
Dallas (DFW)
San Jose (SJC)
Oakland (OAK)
3 nonstop commuter destinations:
Los Angeles (LAX)
Fresno (FAT)

7 S Tampa
3 W Los Angeles
Domestic Airline Service (Large hub)
Orlando International (MCO) 6 miles SE
56 nonstop jet destinations:
Atlanta (ATL)
Dallas (DFW)
Newark (EWR)
19 nonstop commuter destinations:
Birmingham (BHM)
Naples (APF)
Nashville (BNA)
Places Rated Score: 80.72 Places Rated Rank: 75

✓ Oshawa, ON
Daily Commute: 35.1 minutes
Public Transit: *OT*
39 city buses
National Highway: ON–40
VIA Weekly Departures:
13 E Montreal
14 E Ottawa
20 W Toronto
Domestic Airline Service
Nearest is Toronto (YYZ) 50 miles W
Places Rated Score: 95.60 Places Rated Rank: 10

✓ Ottawa–Hull, ON–PQ
Daily Commute: 44.3 minutes
Public Transit: *OC Transpo*
671 city buses
Interstate Highways: ON–41, TC–17
VIA Weekly Departures:
26 E Montreal
25 W Toronto
14 W Windsor
Domestic Airline Service (Medium hub)
MacDonald–Cartier International (YOW) 11 miles S
52 nonstop destinations:
Toronto (YYZ)
Vancouver (YVR)
Halifax (YHZ)
Places Rated Score: 92.70 Places Rated Rank: 25

Owensboro, KY
Daily Commute: 37.0 minutes

Public Transit: *OTS*
6 city buses
Domestic Airline Service (Nonhub)
Owensboro/Daviess County (OWB) 3 miles S
1 nonstop commuter destination:
Nashville (BNA)
Places Rated Score: 7.49 Places Rated Rank: 316

Panama City, FL

Daily Commute: 37.8 minutes
Domestic Airline Service (Nonhub)
Panama City/Bay County (PFN) 5 miles NW
1 nonstop jet destination:
Atlanta (ATL)
2 nonstop commuter destinations:
Memphis (MEM)
Tampa (TPA)
Places Rated Score: 4.76 Places Rated Rank: 330

Parkersburg–Marietta, WV–OH

Daily Commute: 38.8 minutes
Public Transit: *Easy Rider*
7 city buses
Interstate Highway: I–77
Domestic Airline Service (Nonhub)
Wood County/Wilson Field (PKB) 6 miles NE
1 nonstop commuter destination:
Pittsburgh (PIT)
Places Rated Score: 9.01 Places Rated Rank: 315

Pensacola, FL

Daily Commute: 42.8 minutes
Public Transit: *ECTS*
23 city buses
Interstate Highway: I–10
AMTRAK Weekly Departures:
3 E Miami
3 W Los Angeles
Domestic Airline Service (Small hub)
Pensacola Regional (PNS) 3 miles NE
9 nonstop jet destinations:
Atlanta (ATL)
Charlotte (CLT)
Houston (IAH)
5 nonstop commuter destinations:
Orlando (MCO)
Memphis (MEM)
Nashville (BNA)
Places Rated Score: 43.02 Places Rated Rank: 205

Peoria–Pekin, IL

Daily Commute: 38.9 minutes
Public Transit: *GP Transit*
41 city buses
Interstate Highway: I–74
AMTRAK Weekly Departures:
7 E Chicago
7 W Los Angeles
Domestic Airline Service (Small hub)
Greater Peoria Regional (PIA) 4 miles W
3 nonstop jet destinations:
St. Louis (STL)
Chicago (ORD)
Denver (DIA)
2 nonstop commuter destinations:
Chicago (ORD)
Minneapolis (MSP)
Places Rated Score: 48.10 Places Rated Rank: 193

✓ Philadelphia, PA–NJ

Daily Commute: 53.2 minutes
Public Transit: *SEPTA*
1,120 city buses
394 heavy rail cars
279 commuter rail
100 light rail cars
35 trolly coaches
Interstate Highways: I–76, I–95
AMTRAK Weekly Departures:
64 N Boston
7 N Montreal
200 N New York
14 N Springfield
14 S Charlotte
7 S Miami
7 S New Orleans
8 S Newport News
13 S Richmond
7 S Tampa
187 S Washington
29 W Harrisburg
14 W Pittsburgh
Domestic Airline Service (Large hub)
Philadelphia International (PHL) 7 miles SW
71 nonstop jet destinations:
Atlanta (ATL)
Chicago (ORD)
Boston (BOS)
30 nonstop commuter destinations
Washington (DCA)
Baltimore (BWI)
New York (JFK)
Places Rated Score: 98.40 Places Rated Rank: 2

Phoenix–Mesa, AZ

Daily Commute: 49.0 minutes
Public Transit: *PTD*
358 city buses
Interstate Highways: I–10, I–17
AMTRAK Weekly Departures:
3 E Miami
3 N Chicago
6 W Los Angeles
Domestic Airline Service (Large hub)
Sky Harbor International (PHX) 3 miles SE
78 nonstop jet destinations:
Los Angeles (LAX)
Las Vegas (LAS)
Chicago (ORD)
10 nonstop commuter destinations:
Yuma (YUM)
Palm Springs (PSP)
Flagstaff (FLG)
Places Rated Score: 85.03 Places Rated Rank: 51

Pine Bluff, AR

Daily Commute: 40.0 minutes
Public Transit: *PBT*
8 city buses
Domestic Airline Service
Nearest is Little Rock (LIT) 45 miles N
Places Rated Score: 39.54 Places Rated Rank: 213

✓ Pittsburgh, PA

Daily Commute: 48.4 minutes
Public Transit: *PAT*
787 city buses
44 light rail cars
4 cable inclines
Interstate Highways: I–70, I–76, I–79
AMTRAK Weekly Departures:
14 E New York
7 E Washington
7 W Chicago
Domestic Airline Service (Large hub)
Greater Pittsburgh International (PIT) 12 miles NW
99 nonstop jet destinations:
Philadelphia (PHL)
Chicago (ORD)
Charlotte (CLT)
36 nonstop commuter destinations:
State College (SCE)
New York (JFK)
Akron (CAK)
Places Rated Score: 95.10 Places Rated Rank: 15

Pittsfield, MA
Daily Commute: 33.2 minutes
Public Transit: *BRTA*
14 city buses
AMTRAK Weekly Departures:
7 E Boston
7 W Albany
Domestic Airline Service
Nearest is Albany (ALB) 45 miles NW
Places Rated Score: 37.42 Places Rated Rank: 221

Portland, ME
Daily Commute: 37.6 minutes
Public Transit: *METRO*
20 city buses
3 ferries
Interstate Highway: I–95
Domestic Airline Service (Small hub)
Portland International Jetport (PWM) 2 miles W
9 nonstop jet destinations:
Chicago (ORD)

564 city buses
23 light rail cars
Interstate Highways: I–5, I–80
AMTRAK Weekly Departures:
3 E Chicago
11 E Spokane
24 N Seattle
7 S Eugene
7 S Los Angeles
Domestic Airline Service (Medium hub)
Portland International (PDX) 9 miles NE
46 nonstop jet destinations:
San Francisco (SFO)
Los Angeles (LAX)
Seattle (SEA)
3 nonstop commuter destinations:
Seattle (SEA)
Redmond (RDM)
Eugene (EUG)
Places Rated Score: 85.09 Places Rated Rank: 50

Portsmouth–Rochester, NH–ME
Daily Commute: 51.7 minutes
Public Transit: *COAST*
10 city buses
Interstate Highway: I–95
Domestic Airline Service
Nearest is Boston (BOS) 52 miles SW
Places Rated Score: 43.65 Places Rated Rank: 202

Providence–Fall River–Warwick, RI–MA
Daily Commute: 41.9 minutes
Public Transit: *RIPTA*
219 city buses
Interstate Highway: I–95
AMTRAK Weekly Departures:
64 N Boston
1 S New York
8 S Newport News
5 S Richmond
42 S Washington
Domestic Airline Service (Small hub)
Green State (PVD) 6 miles S
14 nonstop jet destinations:
Chicago (ORD)
Atlanta (ATL)

Pittsburgh (PIT)
5 nonstop commuter destinations:
Washington (IAD)
Cincinnati (CVG)
Newark (EWR)
Places Rated Score: 82.07 Places Rated Rank: 67

Provo–Orem, UT
Daily Commute: 35.9 minutes
Interstate Highway: I–15
AMTRAK Weekly Departures:
7 E Chicago
3 W Los Angeles
4 W Oakland
Domestic Airline Service
Nearest is Salt Lake City (SLC) 50 miles N
Places Rated Score: 61.76 Places Rated Rank: 145

Pueblo, CO
Daily Commute: 36.7 minutes
Public Transit: *CityBus*

Domestic Airline Service
Nearest is Fort Myers (RSW) 29 miles SE
Places Rated Score: 27.16 Places Rated Rank: 251

Quebec City, PQ
Daily Commute: 37.2 minutes
Public Transit: *CTCUQ*
393 city buses
National Highway: PQ–20
Domestic Airline Service (Small hub)
Jean Lesage International (YQB) 12 miles NW
18 nonstop destinations:
Toronto (YYZ)
Montreal (YMX)
Ottawa (YOW)
Places Rated Score: 86.06 Places Rated Rank: 45

Racine, WI
Daily Commute: 39.8 minutes
Public Transit: *Belle Urban*
44 city buses
Interstate Highway: I–94
AMTRAK Weekly Departures:
41 N Milwaukee
34 S Chicago
Domestic Airline Service
Nearest is Milwaukee (MKE) 30 miles N
Places Rated Score: 50.64 Places Rated Rank: 180

Raleigh–Durham–Chapel Hill, NC
Daily Commute: 43.3 minutes
Public Transit: *CAT*
106 city buses
Interstate Highways: I–40, I–85
AMTRAK Weekly Departures:
14 N New York
14 S Charlotte
7 S Tampa
Domestic Airline Service (Large hub)
Raleigh–Durham International (RDU) 9 miles NW
34 nonstop jet destinations:
Atlanta (ATL)
Chicago (ORD)
Dallas (DFW)
5 nonstop commuter destinations:
Washington (IAD)

Cincinnati (CVG)
Baltimore (BWI)
Places Rated Score: 79.27 Places Rated Rank: 79

Rapid City, SD
Daily Commute: 35.0 minutes
Public Transit: *RCTS*
5 city buses
Interstate Highway: I–90
Domestic Airline Service (Nonhub)
Rapid City Regional (RAP) 9 miles SE
2 nonstop jet destinations:
Minneapolis (MSP)
Denver (DIA)
3 nonstop commuter destinations:
Salt Lake City (SLC)
Denver (DIA)
Sioux Falls (FSD)
Places Rated Score: 20.82 Places Rated Rank: 275

Reading, PA
Daily Commute: 40.0 minutes
Public Transit: *BARTA*
44 city buses
Interstate Highway: I–76
Domestic Airline Service (Part of Allentown hub)
Reading Regional/Spaatz Field (RDG) 3 miles NW
2 nonstop commuter destinations:
Pittsburgh (PIT)
Philadelphia (PHL)
Places Rated Score: 69.37 Places Rated Rank: 122

Redding, CA
Daily Commute: 36.5 minutes
Public Transit: *RABA*
11 city buses
Interstate Highway: I–5
AMTRAK Weekly Departures:
7 N Seattle
7 S Los Angeles
Domestic Airline Service (Nonhub)
Redding Municipal (RDD) 6 miles SE
1 nonstop jet destination:
Portland (PDX)
1 nonstop commuter destination:
San Francisco (SFO)
Places Rated Score: 24.31 Places Rated Rank: 262

Regina, SK
Daily Commute: 34.8 minutes
Public Transit: *RTA*
80 city buses
National Highways: SK–11, TC–1
Domestic Airline Service (Small hub)
Regina Municipal (YQR) 4 miles SW
8 nonstop destinations:
Toronto (YYZ)
Vancouver (YVR)
Winnipeg (YWG)
Places Rated Score: 75.59 Places Rated Rank: 94

Reno, NV
Daily Commute: 37.0 minutes
Public Transit: *CITIFARE*
52 city buses
Interstate Highway: I–80
AMTRAK Weekly Departures:
4 E Chicago
4 W Oakland
Domestic Airline Service (Medium hub)
Reno Cannon International (RNO) 3 miles SE
22 nonstop jet destinations:
Las Vegas (LAS)
Seattle (SEA)
Los Angeles (LAX)
3 nonstop commuter destinations:
San Francisco (SFO)
Salt Lake City (SLC)
Elko (EKO)
Places Rated Score: 74.73 Places Rated Rank: 97

Richland–Kennewick–Pasco, WA
Daily Commute: 41.0 minutes
Public Transit: *Ben Franklin Transit*
51 city buses
Interstate Highway: I–82
AMTRAK Weekly Departures:
4 E Spokane
4 W Portland
Domestic Airline Service (Small hub)
Tri-Cities (PSC) 12 miles E
3 nonstop jet destinations:
Salt Lake City (SLC)
Seattle (SEA)
Portland (PDX)
Places Rated Score: 24.48 Places Rated Rank: 261

Richmond–Petersburg, VA
Daily Commute: 46.9 minutes
Public Transit: *GRTC*
138 city buses
Interstate Highways: I–64, I–85, I–95
AMTRAK Weekly Departures:
14 N Boston
29 N New York
7 S Charlotte
7 S Miami
7 S Tampa
Domestic Airline Service (Small hub)
Richmond International (RIC) 6 miles E
14 nonstop jet destinations:
Atlanta (ATL)
Charlotte (CLT)
Pittsburgh (PIT)
3 nonstop commuter destinations:
Washington (IAD)
Washington (DCA)
Baltimore (BWI)
Places Rated Score: 68.51 Places Rated Rank: 125

Riverside–San Bernardino, CA
Daily Commute: 59.3 minutes
Public Transit: *OMNITRANS*
200 city buses
Interstate Highways: I–10, I–15
AMTRAK Weekly Departures:
10 E Chicago
10 W Los Angeles
Domestic Airline Service (Part of Los Angeles hub)
Ontario International (ONT)
22 nonstop jet destinations:
Phoenix (PHX)
Oakland (OAK)
Sacramento (SMF)
2 nonstop commuter destinations:
Los Angeles (LAX)
Fresno (FAT)
Palm Springs Regional (PSP) 2 miles E
10 nonstop jet destinations:
Dallas (DFW)
Chicago (ORD)
Denver (DIA)
4 nonstop commuter destinations:
Los Angeles (LAX)
Phoenix (PHX)
Las Vegas (LAS)
Places Rated Score: 76.80 Places Rated Rank: 90

Roanoke, VA
Daily Commute: 39.3 minutes
Public Transit: *Valley Metro*
29 city buses
Interstate Highway: I–81
Domestic Airline Service (Nonhub)
Roanoke/Woodrum Regional (ROA) 3 miles NW
4 nonstop jet destinations:
Charlotte (CLT)

Atlanta (ATL)
Pittsburgh (PIT)
6 nonstop commuter destinations:
Pittsburgh (PIT)
Detroit (DTW)
Washington (DCA)
Places Rated Score: 33.20 Places Rated Rank: 233

Rochester, MN
Daily Commute: 31.5 minutes
Public Transit: *RTS*
18 city buses
Interstate Highway: I–90
Domestic Airline Service (Small hub)
Rochester Municipal (RST) 7 miles SW
2 nonstop jet destinations:
Minneapolis (MSP)
Chicago (ORD)
Places Rated Score: 35.87 Places Rated Rank: 226

Rochester, NY

Chicago (ORD)
Pittsburgh (PIT)
New York (LGA)
7 nonstop commuter destinations:
New York (JFK)
Baltimore (BWI)
Newark (EWR)
Places Rated Score: 73.88 Places Rated Rank: 103

Rockford, IL
Daily Commute: 39.4 minutes
Public Transit: *RMTD*
31 city buses
Interstate Highways: I–39, I–90
Domestic Airline Service (Nonhub)
Greater Rockford (RFD) 4 miles S
3 nonstop commuter destinations:
Detroit (DTW)
Minneapolis (MSP)
Chicago (ORD)
Places Rated Score: 21.50 Places Rated Rank: 271

Rocky Mount, NC
Daily Commute: 38.7 minutes
Public Transit: *RMT*
5 city buses
Interstate Highway: I–95
AMTRAK Weekly Departures:
21 N New York
7 S Charlotte
7 S Miami
7 S Tampa
Domestic Airline Service (Part of Raleigh hub)
Rocky Mount/Wilson (RWI) 7 miles SW
1 nonstop commuter destination:
Charlotte (CLT)
Places Rated Score: 48.18 Places Rated Rank: 192

Sacramento, CA
Daily Commute: 47.3 minutes
Public Transit: *SACRT*
162 city buses
32 light rail cars
Interstate Highways: I–5, I–80
AMTRAK Weekly Departures:
4 E Chicago
7 N Seattle
7 S Los Angeles
4 W Oakland
21 W San Jose
Domestic Airline Service (Medium hub)
Sacramento Metropolitan (SMF) 10 miles NW
20 nonstop jet destinations:
Los Angeles (LAX)
San Diego (SAN)
Burbank (BUR)
7 nonstop commuter destinations:
San Francisco (SFO)
Santa Barbara (SBA)
San Luis Obispo (SBP)
Places Rated Score: 70.09 Places Rated Rank: 118

Saginaw-Bay City-Midland, MI
Daily Commute: 40.7 minutes
Public Transit: *STS/Metro*
57 city buses
Interstate Highway: I–75

Public Transit: *SCT*
41 city buses
National Highway: QEW
VIA Weekly Departures:
7 S New York
14 E Toronto
7 W Niagara Falls
Domestic Airline Service
Nearest is Buffalo (BUF) 50 miles S
Places Rated Score: 73.91 Places Rated Rank: 102

✓ St. Cloud, MN
Daily Commute: 33.4 minutes
Public Transit: *Metro Bus*
18 city buses
Interstate Highway: I–94
AMTRAK Weekly Departures:
4 E Chicago
4 W Seattle
Domestic Airline Service
Nearest is Minneapolis–St. Paul (MSP) 68 miles SE
Places Rated Score: 94.42 Places Rated Rank: 17

Saint John, NB
Daily Commute: 32.0 minutes
Public Transit: *SJT*
35 city buses
Domestic Airline Service (Small hub)
Saint John Municipal (YSJ) 10 miles NE
6 nonstop destinations:
Toronto (YYZ)
Halifax (YHZ)
Montreal (YUL)
Places Rated Score: 32.82 Places Rated Rank: 235

St. John's, NF
Daily Commute: 36.0 minutes
Public Transit: *SJTC*
60 city buses
Domestic Airline Service (Small hub)
St. John's Municipal (YYT) 5 miles NW
8 nonstop destinations:
Toronto (YYZ)
Halifax (YHZ)
Montreal (YUL)
Places Rated Score: 70.22 Places Rated Rank: 116

St. Joseph, MO
Daily Commute: 38.1 minutes
Public Transit: *Express*
10 city buses
Interstate Highway: I–29
Domestic Airline Service
Nearest is Kansas City (MCI) 30 miles SE
Places Rated Score: 71.48 Places Rated Rank: 107

✓ **St. Louis, MO–IL**
Daily Commute: 49.9 minutes
Public Transit: *Bi-State*
589 city buses
26 light rail cars
Interstate Highways: I–44, I–55, I–64, I–70
AMTRAK Weekly Departures:
24 N Chicago
14 W Kansas City
3 W Los Angeles
Domestic Airline Service (Large hub)
Lambert–St. Louis International (STL) 10 miles NW
98 nonstop jet destinations:
Chicago (ORD)
Detroit (DTW)
Kansas City (MCI)
3 nonstop commuter destinations:
Cincinnati (CVG)
Nashville (BNA)
Milwaukee (MKE)
Places Rated Score: 95.25 Places Rated Rank: 13

Salem, OR
Daily Commute: 41.4 minutes
Public Transit: *Cherriots*
44 city buses
Interstate Highway: I–5
AMTRAK Weekly Departures:
14 N Seattle
7 S Eugene
7 S Los Angeles
Domestic Airline Service
Nearest is Portland (PDX) 55 miles N
Places Rated Score: 70.08 Places Rated Rank: 119

Salinas, CA
Daily Commute: 38.3 minutes
Public Transit: *MST*
50 city buses
AMTRAK Weekly Departures:
7 N Seattle
7 S Los Angeles
Domestic Airline Service (Nonhub)
Monterey Peninsula (MRY) 21 miles SW
3 nonstop commuter destinations:
San Francisco (SFO)
Los Angeles (LAX)
Santa Ana (SNA)
Places Rated Score: 36.77 Places Rated Rank: 223

✓ **Salt Lake City–Ogden, UT**
Daily Commute: 42.2 minutes
Public Transit: *UTA*
399 city buses
Interstate Highways: I–15, I–80, I–84
AMTRAK Weekly Departures:
7 E Chicago
3 W Los Angeles
4 W Oakland
Domestic Airline Service (Large hub)
Salt Lake City International (SLC) 3 miles W
56 nonstop jet destinations:
Los Angeles (LAX)
Denver (DIA)
Phoenix (PHX)
24 nonstop commuter destinations:
Boise (BOI)
Sun Valley (SUN)
Rapid City (RAP)
Places Rated Score: 93.17 Places Rated Rank: 23

San Angelo, TX
Daily Commute: 33.9 minutes
Public Transit: *ANTRAN*
5 city buses
Domestic Airline Service (Nonhub)
Mathis Field (SJT) 7 miles SW
1 nonstop commuter destination:
Dallas (DFW)
Places Rated Score: 16.59 Places Rated Rank: 298

San Antonio, TX
Daily Commute: 47.2 minutes
Public Transit: *VIA*
488 city buses
Interstate Highways: I–10, I–35, I–37
AMTRAK Weekly Departures:
3 E Miami
6 N Chicago
6 W Los Angeles
Domestic Airline Service (Medium hub)
San Antonio International (SAT) 7 miles N
32 nonstop jet destinations:
Dallas (DFW)
Dallas (DAL)
Houston (IAH)
2 nonstop commuter destinations:
McAllen (MFE)
Austin (AUS)
Places Rated Score: 81.14 Places Rated Rank: 73

San Diego, CA
Daily Commute: 46.4 minutes
Public Transit: *SDT*
498 city buses
59 light rail cars
Interstate Highways: I–15, I–5, I–8
AMTRAK Weekly Departures:
32 N Los Angeles
23 N Santa Barbara
Domestic Airline Service (Large hub)
San Diego/Lindbergh International (SAN) 2 miles W
42 nonstop jet destinations:
San Francisco (SFO)
Phoenix (PHX)
Las Vegas (LAS)
4 nonstop commuter destinations:
Los Angeles (LAX)
Burbank (BUR)
Santa Barbara (SBA)
Places Rated Score: 87.26 Places Rated Rank: 41

San Francisco, CA
Daily Commute: 54.9 minutes
Public Transit: *Muni/BART*
913 city buses
406 heavy rail cars
270 trolly coaches
101 light rail cars
90 commuter rail
26 cable cars
4 ferries
Interstate Highway: I–80
Domestic Airline Service (Large hub)
San Francisco International (SFO) 8 miles SE
58 nonstop jet destinations:
Los Angeles (LAX)
Chicago (ORD)
Seattle (SEA)
16 nonstop commuter destinations:
Reno (RNO)
Sacramento (SMF)
Fresno (FAT)
Places Rated Score: 86.33 Places Rated Rank: 44

San Jose, CA
Daily Commute: 49.9 minutes
Public Transit: *SCCTD*
393 city buses
32 light rail cars

28 commuter rail
Interstate Highway: I–80
AMTRAK Weekly Departures:
15 N Sacramento
7 N Seattle
7 S Los Angeles
Domestic Airline Service (Part of San Francisco hub)
San Jose International (SJC) 2 miles NW
24 nonstop jet destinations:
Los Angeles (LAX)
Santa Ana (SNA)
San Diego (SAN)
3 nonstop commuter destinations:
San Francisco (SFO)
Santa Barbara (SBA)
Los Angeles (LAX)
Places Rated Score: 85.28 Places Rated Rank: 49

San Luis Obispo–Atascadero–Paso Robles, CA
Daily Commute: 38.7 minutes

Places Rated Score: 16.83 Places Rated Rank: 296

Santa Barbara–Santa Maria–Lompoc, CA
Daily Commute: 37.4 minutes
Public Transit: *MTD*
65 city buses
AMTRAK Weekly Departures:
7 N Seattle
7 S Los Angeles
28 S San Diego
Domestic Airline Service (Nonhub)
Santa Barbara Municipal (SBA) 7 miles W
3 nonstop jet destinations:
San Francisco (SFO)
Denver (DIA)
Los Angeles (LAX)
6 nonstop commuter destinations:
Los Angeles (LAX)
San Jose (SJC)
San Francisco (SFO)
Places Rated Score: 58.54 Places Rated Rank: 160

Santa Cruz–Watsonville, CA
Daily Commute: 51.0 minutes
Public Transit: *METRO*
66 city buses
Domestic Airline Service
Nearest is San Jose (SJC) 23 miles NE
Places Rated Score: 66.96 Places Rated Rank: 131

Santa Fe, NM
Daily Commute: 38.2 minutes
Public Transit: *Santa Fe Trails*
23 city buses
Interstate Highway: I–25
Domestic Airline Service (Part of Albuquerque hub)
Santa Fe Municipal (SAF) 10 miles SW
1 nonstop commuter destination:
Denver (DIA)
Places Rated Score: 65.15 Places Rated Rank: 134

Santa Rosa, CA
Daily Commute: 50.4 minutes
Public Transit: *SCTA*
51 city buses
Domestic Airline Service (Part of San Francisco hub)
Sonoma County (STS) 6 miles NW
1 nonstop commuter destination:
San Francisco (SFO)
Places Rated Score: 65.34 Places Rated Rank: 133

Sarasota–Bradenton, FL
Daily Commute: 40.0 minutes
Public Transit: *SCTA*
29 city buses
Interstate Highway: I–75
Domestic Airline Service (Part of Tampa hub)
Sarasota–Bradenton (SRQ) 3 miles N
15 nonstop jet destinations:
Atlanta (ATL)
Charlotte (CLT)
Detroit (DTW)
3 nonstop commuter destinations:
Miami (MIA)
Orlando (MCO)
Fort Lauderdale (FLL)

7 nonstop destinations:
Toronto (YYZ)
Vancouver (YVR)
Winnipeg (YWG)
Places Rated Score: 67.03 Places Rated Rank: 129

Savannah, GA
Daily Commute: 45.1 minutes
Public Transit: *CAT*
47 city buses
Interstate Highways: I–16, I–95
AMTRAK Weekly Departures:
14 N New York
7 S Miami
7 S Tampa
Domestic Airline Service (Small hub)
Savannah International (SAV) 7 miles NW
4 nonstop jet destinations:
Atlanta (ATL)
Charlotte (CLT)
Cincinnati (CVG)
1 nonstop commuter destination:
Greensboro (GSO)
Places Rated Score: 37.61 Places Rated Rank: 220

Scranton–Wilkes-Barre–Hazleton, PA
Daily Commute: 38.3 minutes
Public Transit: *SCTA*
64 city buses
Interstate Highways: I–81, I–84
Domestic Airline Service (Nonhub)
Wilkes-Barre/Scranton International (AVP) 5 miles SW
3 nonstop jet destinations:
Pittsburgh (PIT)
Atlanta (ATL)
Philadelphia (PHL)
3 nonstop commuter destinations:
Philadelphia (PHL)
Baltimore (BWI)
Washington (IAD)
Places Rated Score: 35.51 Places Rated Rank: 229

Seattle–Bellevue–Everett, WA
Daily Commute: 51.6 minutes
Public Transit: *METRO*

1,066 city buses
118 trolly coaches
25 ferries
8 monorail cars
3 light rail cars
Interstate Highways: I–5, I–90
AMTRAK Weekly Departures:
4 E Chicago
7 N Vancouver
7 S Eugene
7 S Los Angeles
10 S Portland
Domestic Airline Service (Large hub)
Seattle–Tacoma International (SEA) 10 miles S
63 nonstop jet destinations:
San Francisco (SFO)
Los Angeles (LAX)
Anchorage (ANC)
7 nonstop commuter destinations:
Portland (PDX)
Pasco (PSC)
Eugene (EUG)
Places Rated Score: 83.40 Places Rated Rank: 60

Sharon, PA
Daily Commute: 36.1 minutes
Public Transit: *SVT*
6 city buses
Interstate Highway: I–80
Domestic Airline Service
Nearest is Youngstown (YNG) 10 miles E
Places Rated Score: 6.47 Places Rated Rank: 318

✓ Sheboygan, WI
Daily Commute: 31.5 minutes
Public Transit: *STA*
30 city buses
Interstate Highway: I–43
Domestic Airline Service
Nearest is Milwaukee (MKE) 63 miles S
Places Rated Score: 87.81 Places Rated Rank: 35

Sherbrooke, PQ
Daily Commute: 31.7 minutes
Public Transit: *CMTS*
55 city buses
National Highways: I–91, PQ–10
Domestic Airline Service
Nearest is Montreal (YUL) 100 miles W
Places Rated Score: 25.67 Places Rated Rank: 256

Sherman–Denison, TX
Daily Commute: 44.0 minutes
Domestic Airline Service
Nearest is Dallas (DFW) 65 miles SW
Places Rated Score: 0.36 Places Rated Rank: 349

Shreveport–Bossier City, LA
Daily Commute: 42.1 minutes
Public Transit: *SparTran*
37 city buses
Interstate Highways: I–20, I–49
Domestic Airline Service (Small hub)
Shreveport Regional (SHV) 4 miles SW
5 nonstop jet destinations:
Dallas (DFW)
Atlanta (ATL)
St. Louis (STL)
3 nonstop commuter destinations:
Memphis (MEM)
Dallas (DFW)
New Orleans (MSY)
Places Rated Score: 33.51 Places Rated Rank: 232

Sioux City, IA–NE
Daily Commute: 32.3 minutes
Public Transit: *STC*
21 city buses
Interstate Highway: I–29
Domestic Airline Service (Nonhub)
Sioux Gateway (SUX) 6 miles S
2 nonstop jet destinations:
Minneapolis (MSP)
St. Louis (STL)
3 nonstop commuter destinations:
Minneapolis (MSP)
Denver (DIA)
Chicago (ORD)
Places Rated Score: 39.27 Places Rated Rank: 214

Sioux Falls, SD
Daily Commute: 32.5 minutes
Public Transit: *The Bus*
21 city buses
Interstate Highways: I–29, I–90
Domestic Airline Service (Small hub)
Joe Foss Field (FSD) 3 miles NW
4 nonstop jet destinations:
Minneapolis (MSP)
Denver (DIA)
Chicago (ORD)
3 nonstop commuter destinations:
Salt Lake City (SLC)
Minneapolis (MSP)
Rapid City (RAP)
Places Rated Score: 50.30 Places Rated Rank: 181

South Bend, IN
Daily Commute: 38.9 minutes
Public Transit: *Transpo*
45 city buses
Interstate Highway: I–80
AMTRAK Weekly Departures:
7 E New York
7 E Washington
14 W Chicago
Domestic Airline Service (Small hub)
Michiana Regional (SBN) 3 miles NW
5 nonstop jet destinations:
Chicago (ORD)
Pittsburgh (PIT)
Cincinnati (CVG)
3 nonstop commuter destinations:
Cincinnati (CVG)
Indianapolis (IND)
Detroit (DTW)
Places Rated Score: 54.17 Places Rated Rank: 171

Spokane, WA
Daily Commute: 39.6 minutes
Public Transit: *STA*
119 city buses
Interstate Highway: I–90
AMTRAK Weekly Departures:
4 E Chicago
4 W Portland
4 W Seattle
Domestic Airline Service (Small hub)
Spokane International (GEG) 5 miles SW
20 nonstop jet destinations:
Seattle (SEA)
Portland (PDX)
Salt Lake City (SLC)
Places Rated Score: 66.97 Places Rated Rank: 130

Springfield, IL
Daily Commute: 38.2 minutes
Public Transit: *SMTD*
37 city buses
Interstate Highways: I–55, I–72
AMTRAK Weekly Departures:
29 N Chicago
7 S Kansas City
14 S St. Louis
3 W Los Angeles
Domestic Airline Service (Nonhub)

Springfield Capital (SPI) 3 miles NW
2 nonstop jet destinations:
St. Louis (STL)
Chicago (ORD)
Places Rated Score: 61.47 Places Rated Rank: 146

Springfield, MA
Daily Commute: 39.8 minutes
Public Transit: *PVTA*
145 city buses
Interstate Highways: I–90, I–91
AMTRAK Weekly Departures:
7 E Boston
7 N Montreal
33 S New Haven
5 S New York
20 S Washington
7 W Albany
Domestic Airline Service (Medium hub)
Bradley International (BDL) 24 miles S
27 nonstop jet destinations:

Public Transit: *City Utility*
19 city buses
Interstate Highway: I–44
Domestic Airline Service (Small hub)
Springfield Regional (SGF) 5 miles NW
4 nonstop jet destinations:
St. Louis (STL)
Dallas (DFW)
Denver (DIA)
4 nonstop commuter destinations:
Dallas (DFW)
Memphis (MEM)
Kansas City (MCI)
Places Rated Score: 26.67 Places Rated Rank: 254

Stamford–Norwalk, CT
Daily Commute: 53.2 minutes
Public Transit: *CT Transit*
44 city buses
Interstate Highway: I–95
AMTRAK Weekly Departures:
57 N Boston
14 N Springfield
7 N Montreal
6 S New York
6 S Richmond
71 S Washington
Domestic Airline Service
Nearest is White Plains (HPM) 15 miles W
Places Rated Score: 82.70 Places Rated Rank: 63

State College, PA
Daily Commute: 36.3 minutes
Public Transit: *Centre Line*
26 city buses
Domestic Airline Service (Nonhub)
University Park (SCE) 4 miles N
4 nonstop commuter destinations:
Pittsburgh (PIT)
Philadelphia (PHL)
Detroit (DTW)
Places Rated Score: 18.80 Places Rated Rank: 286

Steubenville–Weirton, OH–WV
Daily Commute: 41.5 minutes
Public Transit: *SVTC*
4 city buses

Domestic Airline Service
Nearest is Pittsburgh (PIT) 33 miles NE
Places Rated Score: 1.53 Places Rated Rank: 347

Stockton–Lodi, CA
Daily Commute: 46.6 minutes
Public Transit: *Metro Rapid Transit*
42 city buses
Interstate Highway: I–5
AMTRAK Weekly Departures:
21 W Bakersfield
21 W San Francisco
Domestic Airline Service
Nearest is Modesto (MOD) 30 miles SE
Places Rated Score: 6.03 Places Rated Rank: 319

Sudbury, ON
Daily Commute: 30.7 minutes
Public Transit: *Sudbury Transit*
39 city buses
National Highway: TC–17

Domestic Airline Service
Nearest is Columbia (CAE) 40 miles W
Places Rated Score: 5.18 Places Rated Rank: 326

Syracuse, NY
Daily Commute: 41.0 minutes
Public Transit: *RTA–Centro*
169 city buses
Interstate Highways: I–81, I–90
AMTRAK Weekly Departures:
25 S New York
7 W Chicago
10 W Niagara Falls
7 W Toronto
Domestic Airline Service (Small hub)
Syracuse–Hancock International (SYR) 4 miles NE
16 nonstop jet destinations:
Chicago (ORD)
Pittsburgh (PIT)
Detroit (DTW)
7 nonstop commuter destinations:
Boston (BOS)
New York (JFK)
Baltimore (BWI)
Places Rated Score: 78.93 Places Rated Rank: 83

Tacoma, WA
Daily Commute: 51.0 minutes
Public Transit: *Pierce Transit*
171 city buses
1 ferry
Interstate Highway: I–5
AMTRAK Weekly Departures:
3 E Chicago
24 N Seattle
7 S Eugene
7 S Los Angeles
7 S Portland
Domestic Airline Service
Nearest is Seattle (SEA) 18 miles NE
Places Rated Score: 67.37 Places Rated Rank: 128

Tallahassee, FL
Daily Commute: 41.1 minutes
Public Transit: *TALTRAN*
42 city buses

Interstate Highway: I–10
AMTRAK Weekly Departures:
3 E Miami
3 W Los Angeles
Domestic Airline Service (Small hub)
Tallahassee Regional (TLH) 4 miles SW
6 nonstop jet destinations:
Atlanta (ATL)
Charlotte (CLT)
Miami (MIA)
4 nonstop commuter destinations:
Orlando (MCO)
Tampa (TPA)
Miami (MIA)
Places Rated Score: 38.68 Places Rated Rank: 215

Tampa–St. Petersburg–Clearwater, FL
Daily Commute: 46.8 minutes
Public Transit: *Hartline/PSTA*
239 city buses
Interstate Highways: I–4, I–75
AMTRAK Weekly Departures:
7 N New York
Domestic Airline Service (Large hub)
Tampa International (TPA) 4 miles W
49 nonstop jet destinations:
Atlanta (ATL)
Dallas (DFW)
Newark (EWR)
11 nonstop commuter destinations:
Miami (MIA)
West Palm Beach (PBI)
Fort Lauderdale (FLL)
St. Petersburg/Clearwater International (PIE) 17 miles SW
11 nonstop jet destinations:
Chicago (MDW)
Miami (MIA)
Indianapolis (IND)
3 nonstop commuter destinations:
Naples (APF)
Miami (MIA)
Fort Lauderdale (FLL)
Places Rated Score: 87.05 Places Rated Rank: 42

Terre Haute, IN
Daily Commute: 40.5 minutes
Public Transit: *Transit Utility*
11 city buses
Interstate Highway: I–70
Domestic Airline Service (Nonhub)
Hulman Regional (HUF) 5 miles E
1 nonstop commuter destination:
Chicago (ORD)
Places Rated Score: 3.14 Places Rated Rank: 339

Texarkana, TX–Texarkana, AR
Daily Commute: 40.8 minutes
Interstate Highway: I–30
AMTRAK Weekly Departures:
3 N Chicago
3 W Los Angeles
Domestic Airline Service (Nonhub)
Texarkana Municipal (TXK) 4 miles NE
1 nonstop commuter destination:
Dallas (DFW)
Places Rated Score: 4.65 Places Rated Rank: 331

Thunder Bay, ON
Daily Commute: 31.5 minutes
Public Transit: *TB Transit*
39 city buses
National Highway: TC–17
Domestic Airline Service (Nonhub)
Thunder Bay (YQT) 5 miles W
2 nonstop destinations:
Toronto (YYZ)
Ottawa (YOW)
Places Rated Score: 59.27 Places Rated Rank: 158

Toledo, OH
Daily Commute: 40.0 minutes
Public Transit: *TARTA*
149 city buses
Interstate Highways: I–75, I–80
AMTRAK Weekly Departures:
7 E New York
7 E Washington
14 W Chicago
Domestic Airline Service (Nonhub)
Toledo Express (TOL) 10 miles W
4 nonstop jet destinations:
Pittsburgh (PIT)
Chicago (ORD)
Atlanta (ATL)
2 nonstop commuter destinations:
Cincinnati (CVG)
Detroit (DTW)
Places Rated Score: 60.08 Places Rated Rank: 152

Topeka, KS
Daily Commute: 36.5 minutes
Public Transit: *TMTA*
23 city buses
Interstate Highways: I–35, I–70
AMTRAK Weekly Departures:
7 E Chicago
7 W Los Angeles
Domestic Airline Service
Part of Kansas City hub
Forbes Field (FOE) 6 miles S
1 nonstop commuter destination:
Kansas City (MCI)
Places Rated Score: 85.69 Places Rated Rank: 47

✓ Toronto, ON
Daily Commute: 50.0 minutes
Public Transit: *TTC/GO Transit*
1,723 city buses
953 heavy rail coaches
295 light rail coaches
National Highways: ON–2, ON–40
VIA Weekly Departures:
38 E Montreal
25 E Ottawa
6 N Cochrane
7 S New York
7 W Chicago
4 W London
14 W Niagara Falls
7 W Sarnia
3 W Vancouver
28 W Windsor
Domestic Airline Service (Large hub)
Pearson International (YYZ) 18 miles NW
102 nonstop destinations:
Montreal (YUL)
Ottawa (YOW)
Vancouver (YVR)
Places Rated Score: 98.29 Places Rated Rank: 4

✓ Trenton, NJ
Daily Commute: 47.3 minutes
Public Transit: *NJTC*
234 city buses
Interstate Highway: I–95
AMTRAK Weekly Departures:
50 N Boston
7 N Montreal
101 N New York
14 N Springfield
7 S Charlotte
7 S Miami
7 S New Orleans
8 S Newport News
21 S Philadelphia
13 S Richmond
7 S Tampa
82 S Washington

Domestic Airline Service (Small hub)
Mercer County (TTN) 4 miles NW
2 nonstop jet destinations:
Boston (BOS)
Greensboro (GSO)
Places Rated Score: 96.53 Places Rated Rank: 9

Trois-Rivieres, PQ
Daily Commute: 32.3 minutes
National Highway: PQ-40
Domestic Airline Service
Nearest is Quebec (YQB) 80 miles NE
Places Rated Score: 3.68 Places Rated Rank: 335

Tucson, AZ
Daily Commute: 45.3 minutes
Public Transit: *Sun Tran*
161 city buses
Interstate Highways: I-10, I-19
AMTRAK Weekly Departures:

Places Rated Score: 62.53 Places Rated Rank: 141

Tulsa, OK
Daily Commute: 42.3 minutes
Public Transit: *MTA*
66 city buses
Interstate Highway: I-44
Domestic Airline Service (Medium hub)
Tulsa International (TUL) 5 miles NE
15 nonstop jet destinations:
Dallas (DFW)
Dallas (DAL)
St. Louis (STL)
2 nonstop commuter destinations:
Cincinnati (CVG)
Memphis (MEM)
Places Rated Score: 51.72 Places Rated Rank: 175

Tuscaloosa, AL
Daily Commute: 39.8 minutes
Public Transit: *CP&TA*
4 city buses
Interstate Highways: I-20, I-59
AMTRAK Weekly Departures:
7 N New York
7 S New Orleans
Domestic Airline Service (Part of Birmingham hub)
Van De Graaf (TCL) 5 miles W
1 nonstop commuter destination:
Nashville (BNA)
Places Rated Score: 49.86 Places Rated Rank: 183

Tyler, TX
Daily Commute: 42.2 minutes
Public Transit: *Tyler Transit*
6 city buses
Interstate Highway: I-20
Domestic Airline Service (Nonhub)
Tyler/Pounds Field (TYR) 3 miles W
2 nonstop jet destinations:
Dallas (DFW)
Houston (IAH)
2 nonstop commuter destinations:
Dallas (DFW)
Austin (AUS)
Places Rated Score: 3.39 Places Rated Rank: 337

Utica-Rome, NY
Daily Commute: 37.4 minutes
Public Transit: *UTA*
32 city buses
Interstate Highway: I-90
AMTRAK Weekly Departures:
10 N Niagara Falls
18 S New York
7 W Toronto
Domestic Airline Service (Part of Syracuse hub)
Oneida County (UCA) 7 miles NW
1 nonstop commuter destination:
Philadelphia (PHL)
Places Rated Score: 68.62 Places Rated Rank: 124

Vallejo-Fairfield-Napa, CA
Daily Commute: 56.8 minutes
Public Transit: *The VINE*
31 city buses
Interstate Highway: I-80
AMTRAK Weekly Departures:

120 light rail coaches
National Highways: (I-5), TC-1
VIA Weekly Departures:
7 S Seattle
3 E Toronto
Domestic Airline Service (Large hub)
Vancouver International (YVR) 11 miles SW
32 nonstop destinations:
Toronto (YYZ)
Calgary (YYC)
Los Angeles (LAX)
Places Rated Score: 74.93 Places Rated Rank: 95

Ventura, CA
Daily Commute: 52.8 minutes
Public Transit: *SCAT*
33 city buses
AMTRAK Weekly Departures:
23 N Santa Barbara
7 N Seattle
12 S Los Angeles
28 S San Diego
Domestic Airline Service (Part of Los Angeles hub)
Oxnard Municipal (OXR) 11 miles SE
1 nonstop commuter destination:
Los Angeles (LAX)
Places Rated Score: 70.04 Places Rated Rank: 120

Victoria, BC
Daily Commute: 35.0 minutes
Public Transit: *BC Transit*
151 city buses
VIA Weekly Departures:
7 N Courtenay
Domestic Airline Service (Large hub)
Victoria International (YYJ) 19 miles N
8 nonstop destinations:
Vancouver (YVR)
Toronto (YYZ)
Calgary (YYC)
Places Rated Score: 68.28 Places Rated Rank: 126

Victoria, TX
Daily Commute: 41.4 minutes
Domestic Airline Service (Large hub)
Victoria Regional (VCT) 6 miles NE

1 nonstop jet destination:
Houston (IAH)
Places Rated Score: 1.42 Places Rated Rank: 348

Vineland–Millville–Bridgeton, NJ
Daily Commute: 42.2 minutes
Public Transit: *NJTC*
38 city buses
Domestic Airline Service
Nearest is Atlantic City (ACY) 35 miles E
Places Rated Score: 78.51 Places Rated Rank: 85

Visalia–Tulare–Porterville, CA
Daily Commute: 37.8 minutes
Public Transit: *City Coach*
10 city buses
Domestic Airline Service (Part of Fresno hub)
Visalia Municipal (VIS) 6 miles W
1 nonstop commuter destination:
San Francisco (SFO)
Places Rated Score: 27.12 Places Rated Rank: 252

Waco, TX
Daily Commute: 37.2 minutes
Public Transit: *WTS*
12 city buses
Interstate Highway: I–35
AMTRAK Weekly Departures:
3 N Chicago
3 W Los Angeles
Domestic Airline Service (Nonhub)
Waco Regional (ACT) 5 miles NW
2 nonstop jet destinations:
Dallas (DFW)
Houston (IAH)
Places Rated Score: 31.01 Places Rated Rank: 239

✓ **Washington, DC–MD–VA–WV**
Daily Commute: 63.0 minutes
Public Transit: *WMATA*
1,429 city buses
588 heavy rail cars
54 commuter rail
Interstate Highways: I–66, I–95
AMTRAK Weekly Departures:
62 N Boston
7 N Montreal
141 N New York
14 N Springfield
7 S Charlotte
7 S Miami
7 S New Orleans
3 S Newport News
13 S Richmond
7 S Tampa
17 W Chicago
14 W Kansas City
7 W St. Louis
Domestic Airline Service (Large hub)
Dulles International (IAD) 26 miles W
35 nonstop jet destinations:
Atlanta (ATL)
Denver (DIA)
Los Angeles (LAX)
41 nonstop commuter destinations:
Newark (EWR)
New York (JFK)
Raleigh (RDU)
Washington National (DCA) 3 miles S
52 nonstop jet destinations:
New York (LGA)
Chicago (ORD)
Boston (BOS)
16 nonstop commuter destinations:
New York (JFK)
Philadelphia (PHL)
Norfolk (ORF)
Places Rated Score: 95.49 Places Rated Rank: 12

Waterbury, CT
Daily Commute: 41.3 minutes
Public Transit: *NETC*
12 city buses
35 commuter rail
Interstate Highway: I–84
Domestic Airline Service
Nearest is New Haven (HVN) 30 miles SE
Places Rated Score: 70.68 Places Rated Rank: 113

Waterloo–Cedar Falls, IA
Daily Commute: 31.5 minutes
Public Transit: *MET*
14 city buses
Interstate Highway: I–380
Domestic Airline Service (Nonhub)
Waterloo Municipal (ALO) 4 miles NW
2 nonstop jet destinations:
St. Louis (STL)
Chicago (ORD)
2 nonstop commuter destinations:
Minneapolis (MSP)
Chicago (ORD)
Places Rated Score: 41.39 Places Rated Rank: 210

Wausau, WI
Daily Commute: 33.4 minutes
Public Transit:
20 city buses
Domestic Airline Service (Nonhub)
Central Wisconsin Regional (CWA) 11 miles S
1 nonstop jet destination:
Chicago (ORD)
3 nonstop commuter destinations:
Minneapolis (MSP)
Detroit (DTW)
Milwaukee (MKE)
Places Rated Score: 30.57 Places Rated Rank: 240

West Palm Beach–Boca Raton, FL
Daily Commute: 44.7 minutes
Public Transit: *CoTran*
57 city buses
Interstate Highway: I–95
AMTRAK Weekly Departures:
14 N New York
17 S Miami
3 W Los Angeles
Domestic Airline Service (Medium hub)
Palm Beach International (PBI) 3 miles W
25 nonstop jet destinations:
Atlanta (ATL)
Newark (EWR)
New York (LGA)
4 nonstop commuter destinations:
Tampa (TPA)
Orlando (MCO)
Nassau (PID)
Places Rated Score: 65.70 Places Rated Rank: 132

Wheeling, WV–OH
Daily Commute: 42.4 minutes
Public Transit: *OVRTA*
16 city buses
Interstate Highway: I–70
Domestic Airline Service
Nearest is Pittsburgh (PIT) 50 miles NE
Places Rated Score: 2.87 Places Rated Rank: 341

Wichita, KS
Daily Commute: 38.7 minutes
Public Transit: *MTA*
43 city buses
Interstate Highway: I–35
AMTRAK Weekly Departures:
7 E Chicago
7 W Los Angeles
Domestic Airline Service (Small hub)

Wichita Mid-Continent (ICT) 5 miles SW
10 nonstop jet destinations:
Dallas (DFW)
St. Louis (STL)
Denver (DIA)
3 nonstop commuter destinations:
Kansas City (MCI)
Cincinnati (CVG)
Dallas (DFW)
Places Rated Score: 59.45 Places Rated Rank: 156

Wichita Falls, TX
Daily Commute: 33.2 minutes
Public Transit: *WFTS*
9 city buses
Interstate Highway: I–44
Domestic Airline Service (Nonhub)
Wichita Falls Municipal (SPS) 6 miles N
1 nonstop commuter destination:
Dallas (DFW)
Places Rated Score: 21.10 Places Rated Rank: 273

Wilmington, NC
Daily Commute: 39.2 minutes
Public Transit: *WTA*
9 city buses
Interstate Highway: I–40
Domestic Airline Service (Nonhub)
New Hanover International (ILM) 3 miles NE
2 nonstop jet destinations:
Charlotte (CLT)
Atlanta (ATL)
Places Rated Score: 12.66 Places Rated Rank: 306

✓ Wilmington–Newark, DE–MD
Daily Commute: 44.8 minutes
Public Transit: *DART*
126 city buses
Interstate Highway: I–95
AMTRAK Weekly Departures:
64 N Boston
7 N Montreal
131 N New York
14 N Springfield
7 S Charlotte
7 S Miami
7 S New Orleans
8 S Newport News
13 S Richmond
7 S Tampa
182 S Washington
Domestic Airline Service
Nearest is Philadelphia (PHL) 20 miles NE
Places Rated Score: 94.11 Places Rated Rank: 19

✓ Windsor, ON
Daily Commute: 36.5 minutes
Public Transit: *Transit Windsor*
71 city buses
National Highways: (I–75), (I–94), ON–40
VIA Weekly Departures:
27 E Toronto
Domestic Airline Service (Large hub)
Windsor International (YQG) 6 miles SE
2 nonstop destinations:
Ottawa (YOW)
Toronto (YYZ)
Places Rated Score: 95.58 Places Rated Rank: 11

Winnipeg, MB
Daily Commute: 41.2 minutes
Public Transit: *WTS*
423 city buses
National Highways: (I–29), TC–1
VIA Weekly Departures:
3 E Toronto
3 W Vancouver
Domestic Airline Service (Medium hub)
Winnipeg International (YWG) 4 miles W
25 nonstop destinations:
Toronto (YYZ)
Vancouver (YVR)
Calgary (YYC)
Places Rated Score: 85.57 Places Rated Rank: 48

Worcester, MA–CT
Daily Commute: 46.2 minutes
Public Transit: *RTA*
42 city buses
52 commuter rail

Yakima, WA
Daily Commute: 34.8 minutes
Public Transit: *YTS*
19 city buses
Interstate Highway: I–82
Domestic Airline Service (Nonhub)
Yakima Air Terminal (YKM) 3 miles S
2 nonstop jet destinations:
Seattle (SEA)
Portland (PDX)
Places Rated Score: 19.88 Places Rated Rank: 282

Yolo, CA
Daily Commute: 38.1 minutes
Public Transit: *UNITRANS/YoloBus*
42 city buses
Interstate Highways: I–5, I–80
AMTRAK Weekly Departures:
4 E Chicago
21 E Sacramento
7 N Seattle
7 S Los Angeles
4 W Oakland
21 W San Jose
Domestic Airline Service
Nearest is Sacramento (SMF) 12 miles NE
Places Rated Score: 74.60 Places Rated Rank: 98

York, PA
Daily Commute: 43.3 minutes
Public Transit: *YCTA*
18 city buses
Interstate Highway: I–83
Domestic Airline Service
Nearest is Harrisburg (MDT) 20 miles NW
Places Rated Score: 22.00 Places Rated Rank: 270

Youngstown–Warren, OH
Daily Commute: 41.2 minutes
Public Transit: *WRTA*
28 city buses
Interstate Highways: I–76, I–80
Domestic Airline Service (Nonhub)
Youngstown–Warren Regional (YNG) 10 miles N
2 nonstop jet destinations:
Akron (CAK)

Pittsburgh (PIT)
Places Rated Score: 16.20 Places Rated Rank: 299

Yuba City, CA
Daily Commute: 43.4 minutes
Public Transit: *Sutter Transit*
7 city buses
AMTRAK Weekly Departures:
7 N Seattle
7 S Los Angeles
Domestic Airline Service
Nearest is Sacramento (SMF) 40 miles S
Places Rated Score: 32.61 Places Rated Rank: 236

Yuma, AZ
Daily Commute: 34.5 minutes
Interstate Highway: I-8
AMTRAK Weekly Departures:
3 E Miami
3 N Chicago
6 W Los Angeles
Domestic Airline Service (Nonhub)
Yuma International (YUM) 3 miles SE
2 nonstop jet destinations:
Phoenix (PHX)
Los Angeles (LAX)
Places Rated Score: 17.17 Places Rated Rank: 295

Et Cetera

FERRYBOATS, CABLE CARS, MONORAILS, AERIAL TRAMS, AND INCLINES

Besides the ubiquitous bus and the different rail systems in larger cities, North American transit systems operate other types of vehicles. Although these modes have little impact on total mass transit, they are by far the most fun to watch and ride, undeniably adding to a city's flavor.

San Francisco has the nation's only **cable car** system. In operation since the nineteenth century, the MUNI's 41 cars and the 26 cars in New Orleans's **trolly** system are the only transit properties in the National Register of Historic Places. New York operates the only public aerial tram, between Roosevelt Island and Manhattan. **Automated guideways**, the newest public transit mode, are electric vehicles running over fixed guideways without operators or other crewpersons. You can catch one in Detroit, MI; Jacksonville, Miami, and Tampa, FL; and in Morgantown, WV.

The largest transit vehicles are **ferryboats**, which range in size up to 380 feet and can carry as many as 2,500 commuters per trip. Public ferryboat systems, which provide frequent "bridge" service over a fixed route and on a published schedule between two or more points, are part of the mass-transit mix in 13 metro areas:

Boston, MA	Massachusetts Bay Transit Authority
Erie, PA	Erie Metropolitan Transit Authority
Galveston, TX	Texas Department of Transportation
Halifax, NS	METRO
New Orleans, LA	Mississippi River Bridge Authority
New York, NY	City of New York–Staten Island Ferry
Norfolk, VA	Tidewater Transportation District
Portland, ME	Casco Bay Transit District
San Francisco, CA	Golden Gate Bridge Transportation
Seattle, WA	Washington State Ferries
Tacoma, WA	Pierce County Ferry
Vallejo, CA	Vallejo TS
Vancouver, BC	BC Transit

Four metro areas operate cog or cable incline cars that traverse steep hills:

Chattanooga, TN–GA	Lookout Mountain
Dubuque, IA	Fourth Street Elevator
Johnstown, PA	Johnstown–Westmont Incline
Pittsburgh, PA	Monongahela and Duquesne Heights

CONTRADICTORY RULES OF THE ROAD

Driving across political boundaries can mean a brush with contradictory traffic codes. Here are examples, with one caveat. The information comes from the American Automobile Association's latest *Digest of Motor Laws*, but it may not reflect recent changes in the law.

Speed Limits. There are two kinds of speed limits—absolute and *prima facie*, a legal phrase meaning "at first view." If the speed limit of 55 is absolute, going 56 means breaking the law. If the speed limit of 55 is prima facie, however, going 56 or even 60 is merely apparent evidence of unreasonable and imprudent speed. Drivers may escape a fine if they can convince the traffic court that their speed was reasonable and safe in light of the highway's condition, traffic, and visibility. In all Canadian provinces but Newfoundland and Nova Scotia, speed limits are absolute. States where all or some speed limits are prima facie are:

Arizona
Connecticut
District of Columbia
Hawaii
Idaho
Louisiana
Massachusetts
New Hampshire
New Jersey
Oregon
Rhode Island
South Dakota
Utah

Right and Left Turn on Red. In 1947, California became the first state to permit drivers to turn right on a red signal after a complete stop. The last was Massachusetts, in 1980. New York City now is the only major jurisdiction that prohibits the turn. According to the Federal Highway Administration, fewer accidents occur when drivers turn right on a red light than when they turn right on a green light. Furthermore, the rule saves each driver an average of 14 seconds at a turn, cuts gasoline consumption and exhaust emissions, and allows intersections to handle more traffic.

In the past 15 years, most states have enacted statutes permitting left turns on a red signal, but only after a complete stop and only from a one-way street into another one-way street. The practice remains prohibited everywhere in Canada except Alberta, British Columbia, and Ontario. Seven states and DC also prohibit turning left on red:

Connecticut
District of Columbia
Missouri
North Carolina
Rhode Island
Vermont

dictions prohibit their use:

Alabama
Hawaii
Illinois
Louisiana
Maryland (except western counties)
Michigan
Minnesota
Mississippi
New Mexico
Wisconsin

Glass Tinting. Tinted automobile window glass is a frequently chosen factory option. Over the past 10 years, however, aftermarket application of black and gunmetal-gray plastic sheeting to the inside of the windshield has become extremely popular. Because it interferes with night vision, it is restricted in varying degrees everywhere except Newfoundland.

Audio Headsets. The issue here is whether the ears are as necessary for safe driving as the eyes. When you don't hear an ambulance siren, a ticket for failing to yield the right-of-way to an emergency vehicle is the likely consequence. But when you can't hear a train whistle or the air horn of an oncoming 18-wheeler, the result could be far more serious. Accordingly, these jurisdictions prohibit the driver from wearing an audio headset:

Alaska
California
Colorado
Florida
Georgia
Illinois
Maryland
Massachusetts
Minnesota
Ohio
Pennsylvania
Quebec
Rhode Island
Virginia
Washington

Motorcycle Helmets. The mileage fatality rate (deaths per 100 million miles) for motorcycle travel is five times that for auto travel, and the major cause is head injuries. Consequently, many states and all Canadian provinces require motorcycle riders to wear helmets. Motorcyclists have challenged the law, but state courts have generally upheld it because it affects the biker's right to receive insurance compensation for injuries. Only Colorado, Illinois and Iowa do not require protective headgear of any kind for motorcyclists and passengers.

Mandatory Annual Safety Inspections. Many states and provinces require regular safety inspection and/or emissions testing of automobiles to rid the highways of dangerous vehicles with bald tires, wobbly suspensions, smoky exhausts, and defective brakes and lights. In many of those states where inspections are not mandatory, state troopers are authorized to stop and inspect vehicles which they believe are a danger to other motorists or lack required equipment. The following

Manitoba
Massachusetts
Mississippi
Missouri
New Brunswick
Newfoundland
New Hampshire
New Jersey
New York
Rhode Island
Saskatchewan
South Carolina
Texas
Utah
Vermont
Virginia
West Virginia

Some states only require emissions tests in certain "high traffic" cities and counties. The following jurisdictions have a required emission inspection of some sort, either statewide or in extended counties or metro areas:

British Columbia
California
Colorado
Connecticut
Delaware
District of Columbia
Florida
Georgia
Illinois
Indiana
Louisiana
Maryland
Massachusetts
Michigan
Missouri
Nevada
New Jersey
New York
North Carolina
Ohio
Oklahoma
Ontario
Oregon
Pennsylvania
Rhode Island
Texas
Utah
West Virginia
Wisconsin

Mandatory Seat Belt Use. Because automobile accidents are the leading cause of death among young children, all states and provinces now require the use of special vehicle restraints for children who are less than preschool age. Most jurisdictions also require the use of seat belts by the driver and all front-seat passengers. Only Kentucky and New Hampshire do not.

Radar Detectors. All states and provinces use radar in their speed enforcement programs, and all but seven—Manitoba, Newfoundland, Ontario, Prince Edward Island, Quebec, and Virginia—plus the District of Columbia permit drivers to install radar detectors for advance warning.

DRIVER LICENSING

When you settle in a new state or province, you have to surrender your old driver's license and get a new one. The time permitted to do this ranges from "immediately" in 9 states and New Brunswick, to 30 days in 21 jurisdictions, and up to 6 months in British Columbia and Vermont. New Hampshire allows you as much time as your former state gives newcomers. Hawaii lets you keep your license until it expires.

Required Tests

For a new resident with a valid driver's license from a former state, the requirement for getting a license from the new jurisdiction varies considerably. A vision test is required almost everywhere, but in 13 states and provinces all other tests may be waived. Washington requires you to get behind the wheel with a license examiner for a road test; in 33 other jurisdictions a road test may be waived or required at the discretion of the examiner.

Problem Drivers

If your license has been revoked, you won't get a new one simply by moving to another state. Every license application is checked with the National Driver Registry, a federal data file of persons whose license to drive has been denied or withdrawn. Moreover, most states belong to the National Driver License Compact, an agreement among states to share information on drivers who accumulate tickets in one jurisdiction and try to escape control in another. All provinces are members of the Canadian Driver License Compact; traffic offense information covering eight categories is exchanged among the jurisdictions.

Driver's License and Car Registration after Moving

A Guide for Persons with Current Paperwork from a Former Jurisdiction

	DRIVER'S LICENSING					VEHICLE REGISTRATION	
	Time Limit	Written Test	Vision Test	Road Test	NDL Compact	Time Limit	Inspection Required
Alabama	30 days	•	•		✓	30 days	
Alaska	90 days	•	•		✓	10 days	
Alberta	90 days				✓	3 months	s
Arizona	immediately	○	•	○	✓	immediately	
Arkansas	30 days		•		✓	10 days	s
British Columbia	6 months	○	•	○	✓	30 days	e
California	10 days	•	•	○	✓	20 days	e
Colorado	30 days	•	•	○	✓	immediately	e
Connecticut	30 days	○	•	○	✓	60 days	e
Delaware	60 days	•	•	○	✓	60 days	s/e
District of Columbia	30 days	•	•	○	✓	*	s/e
Florida	30 days	○	•	○	✓	10 days	e
Georgia	30 days	•	•			30 days	e
Hawaii	*	•	•	○	✓	10 days	s
Idaho	90 days	•	•		✓	90 days	
Illinois	90 days	•	•		✓	30 days	e
Indiana	60 days	•	•		✓	60 days	e
Iowa	immediately	•	•		✓	90 days	
Kansas	90 days	•	•		✓	*	
Kentucky	immediately	•	•			15 days	
Louisiana	90 days		•		✓	immediately	s/e
Maine	30 days	•	•	○	✓	30 days	s
Manitoba	90 days		•		✓	3 months	s
Maryland	30 days	○	•	○	✓	30 days	e
Massachusetts	immediately		•			immediately	s/e
Michigan	immediately	•	•			immediately	e
Minnesota	60 days	•	•	○	✓	60 days	
Mississippi	60 days	•	•	○	✓	30 days	s
Missouri	immediately	•	•	○	✓	30 days	s/e
Montana	90 days	○	•	○	✓	immediately	

DRIVER'S LICENSING						VEHICLE REGISTRATION	
	Time Limit	Written Test	Vision Test	Road Test	NDL Compact	Time Limit	Inspection Required
Nebraska	30 days	•	•	○	✓	*	
Nevada	30 days	○	•	○	✓	45 days	e
New Brunswick	immediately				✓	6 months	s
New Hampshire	60 days	○	•	○	✓	60 days	s
New Jersey	60 days	•	•	○	✓	60 days	s/e
New Mexico	30 days	•	•		✓	30 days	
New York	30 days	•	•		✓	30 days	s/e
Newfoundland	90 days	○	○		✓	30 days	s
North Carolina	30 days	•	•	○	✓	immediately	s/e
North Dakota	60 days	•	•	○	✓	immediately	
Nova Scotia	90 days	•	•	○	✓	30 days	s
South Carolina	90 days		•	○	✓	45 days	s
South Dakota	90 days	○	•	○	✓	90 days	
Tennessee	30 days	○	•	○	✓	immediately	
Texas	30 days	○	•	○	✓	30 days	s/e
Utah	60 days	•	•		✓	60 days	s/e
Vermont	6 months	○	•	○	✓	6 months	s
Virginia	30 days	○	•		✓	30 days	s
Washington	30 days	•	•	•	✓	30 days	
West Virginia	30 days	•	•		✓	30 days	s/e
Wisconsin	immediately	•	•	○		immediately	e
Wyoming	120 days	•	•	○	✓	immediately	

• Required, ○ May be waived, * License of registration valid until expiration

s Safety inspection, e Emissions test, s/e Both

Source: American Automobile Association, *Digest of Motor Laws*, 1996; U.S. Federal Highway Administration, *Driver License Administration Requirements and Fees*, 1996.

FINDING YOUR WAY ON THE INTERSTATE

By staying with a combination of interstate routes, it is possible for you to drive from one metro area in the United States to almost any other without stopping for a traffic light.

Five of the routes are more than 2,000 miles long. the longest, I-90, stretches 3,082 miles between downtown Boston and Seattle's waterfront. The next longest routes are I-80 (2,907 miles, from San Francisco, CA, to Hackensack, NJ), I-10 (2,460 miles along the nation's southern border, from Los Angeles to Jacksonville, FL), I-40 (2,461 miles, from Barstow, CA, to Smithfield, NC), and I-70 (2,175 miles from Cove Fort, UT, to Baltimore, MD). Three of these routes, I-10, I-80, and I-90, cross the country from coast to coast, and I-40 nearly makes it.

Six interstate routes span the nation in a north-south direction: I-5 (1,382 miles, from San Diego to Bellingham, WA), I-15 (1,437 miles, from San Diego to the Montana–Canada border), I-35 (1,568 miles, from suburban New Orleans to Chicago), I-65 (888 miles, from Mobile, AL, to Gary–Hammond, IN), I-75 (1,787 miles, from Naples, FL, to the Michigan–Canada border), and 1-95 (1,894 miles, from the city of Miami to the Maine–Canada border).

The Interstate System: A Route Log and Finder List

Route	Total Mileage	Mileage by State		Selected Cities Served
4	132.06	Florida	132.06	Daytona Beach, Lakeland, Orlando, Tampa, Winter Haven
5	1,382.05	California	797.01	Anaheim, Los Angeles, Redding, Sacramento, San Diego, Santa Ana, Stockton
		Oregon	308.41	Eugene, Medford, Portland, Salem
		Washington	276.63	Bellingham, Olympia, Seattle, Tacoma, Vancouver
8	348.32	California	170.00	El Centro, San Diego
		Arizona	178.32	Casa Grande, Yuma
10	2,459.96	California	242.50	Los Angeles, Riverside, San Bernardino
		Arizona	391.94	Phoenix, Tucson
		New Mexico	164.28	Deming, Las Cruces
		Texas	880.60	Beaumont, El Paso, Houston, San Antonio
		Louisiana	274.42	Baton Rouge, Lafayette, Lake Charles, New Orleans
		Mississippi	77.10	Biloxi, Gulfport, Pascagoula
		Alabama	66.30	Mobile
		Florida	362.82	Jacksonville, Pensacola, Tallahassee
12	85.59	Louisiana	85.59	Baton Rouge
15	1,436.85	California	287.30	Riverside, San Bernardino, San Diego
		Nevada	123.77	Las Vegas
		Arizona	29.37	—
		Utah	405.49	Brigham City, Ogden, Orem, Provo, St. George, Salt Lake City
		Idaho	195.87	Blackfoot, Idaho Falls, Pocatello
		Montana	395.05	Butte, Great Falls, Helena, Sweetgrass
16	165.41	Georgia	165.41	Macon, Savannah
17	145.24	Arizona	145.24	Flagstaff, Phoenix
19	63.35	Arizona	63.35	Nogales, Tucson
20	1,538.31	Texas	635.98	Abilene, Arlington, Dallas, Fort Worth, Longview, Marshall, Midland, Odessa, Tyler
		Louisiana	189.87	Monroe, Shreveport
		Mississippi	154.50	Jackson, Meridian, Vicksburg
		Alabama	214.70	Anniston, Birmingham, Tuscaloosa
		Georgia	201.75	Atlanta, Augusta
		South Carolina	141.51	Columbia, Florence
24	316.52	Illinois	38.73	Metropolis
		Kentucky	93.37	Hopkinsville, Paducah
		Tennessee	180.30	Chattanooga, Clarksville, Nashville
		Georgia	4.12	—
25	1,062.52	New Mexico	462.68	Albuquerque, Las Cruces, Santa Fe
		Colorado	298.94	Colorado Springs, Denver, Fort Collins, Longmont, Pueblo
		Wyoming	300.90	Casper, Cheyenne
26	260.90	North Carolina	39.95	Asheville, Hendersonville
		South Carolina	220.95	Charleston, Columbia, Spartanburg
27	124.38	Texas	124.38	Amarillo, Lubbock
29	752.26	Missouri	130.30	Kansas City, St. Joseph
		Iowa	151.81	Council Bluffs, Sioux City
		South Dakota	252.65	Sioux Falls
		North Dakota	217.50	Fargo, Grand Forks
30	366.71	Texas	223.63	Dallas, Fort Worth, Texarkana
		Arkansas	143.08	Little Rock, Texarkana

Route	Total Mileage	Mileage by State		Selected Cities Served
35	1,568.27	Texas	503.83	Arlington, Austin, Dallas, Fort Worth, Laredo, San Antonio, Temple, Waco
		Oklahoma	235.96	Norman, Oklahoma City
		Kansas	235.52	Kansas City, Lawrence, Topeka, Wichita
		Missouri	114.80	Kansas City
		Iowa	218.47	Ames, Des Moines
		Minnesota	259.69	Albert Lea, Duluth, Minneapolis, St. Paul
37	143.06	Texas	143.06	Corpus Christi, San Antonio
39	131.03	Illinois	131.03	Bloomington, Rockford
40	2,460.68	California	154.60	Barstow, Needles
		Arizona	359.23	Flagstaff, Kingman
		New Mexico	371.37	Albuquerque, Gallup, Tucumcari
		Texas	177.00	Amarillo
		Oklahoma	331.03	Clinton, Oklahoma City
		[illegible]	284.80	Fort Smith, Little Rock
45	284.99	Texas	284.99	Dallas, Galveston, Houston, Texas City
49	206.57	Louisiana	206.57	Alexandria, Lafayette, Nachitoches, Opelousas, Shreveport
55	943.69	Louisiana	65.81	Hammond, La Place
		Mississippi	289.70	Grenada, Jackson, McComb
		Tennessee	12.20	Memphis
		Arkansas	72.22	Blytheville, West Memphis
		Missouri	209.40	Cape Girardeau, St. Louis
		Illinois	294.36	Bloomington, Chicago, East St. Louis, Joliet, Springfield
57	380.57	Missouri	22.00	Charleston, Sikeston
		Illinois	358.57	Champaign, Chicago, Kankakee, Rantoul, Urbana
59	444.02	Louisiana	11.48	New Orleans, Slidell
		Mississippi	171.20	Hattiesburg, Laurel, Meridian
		Alabama	241.40	Birmingham, Gadsden, Tuscaloosa
		Georgia	19.94	—
64	944.19	Missouri	14.70	St. Louis
		Illinois	128.12	Belleville, East St. Louis
		Indiana	124.04	Evansville, New Albany
		Kentucky	191.55	Frankfort, Lexington, Louisville
		West Virginia	186.86	Charleston, Huntington, White Sulphur Springs
		Virginia	298.92	Charlottesville, Newport News, Norfolk, Richmond
65	888.08	Alabama	367.00	Birmingham, Decatur, Mobile, Montgomery
		Tennessee	121.40	Nashville
		Kentucky	137.60	Bowling Green, Elizabethtown, Louisville
		Indiana	262.08	Gary, Indianapolis, Lafayette
66	76.37	Virginia	75.26	Arlington, Fairfax, Falls Church, Front Royal, Vienna
		District of Columbia	1.11	Washington, DC
68	72.00	West Virginia	72.00	Morgantown
69	356.19	Indiana	157.79	Anderson, Fort Wayne, Indianapolis, Muncie
		Michigan	198.40	Battle Creek, Flint, Lansing

Edmonton
Jasper
Calgary
Saskatoon
Vancouver
Victoria
Seattle
Regina
Winnipeg
Portland
St. Paul
Salt Lake City
Cheyenne
Des Moines
San Francisco
Denver
Kansas City
Las Vegas
Los Angeles
Oklahoma City
Phoenix
Albuquerque
Ft. Worth
Houston
HI
OAHU
Pearl City
Honolulu

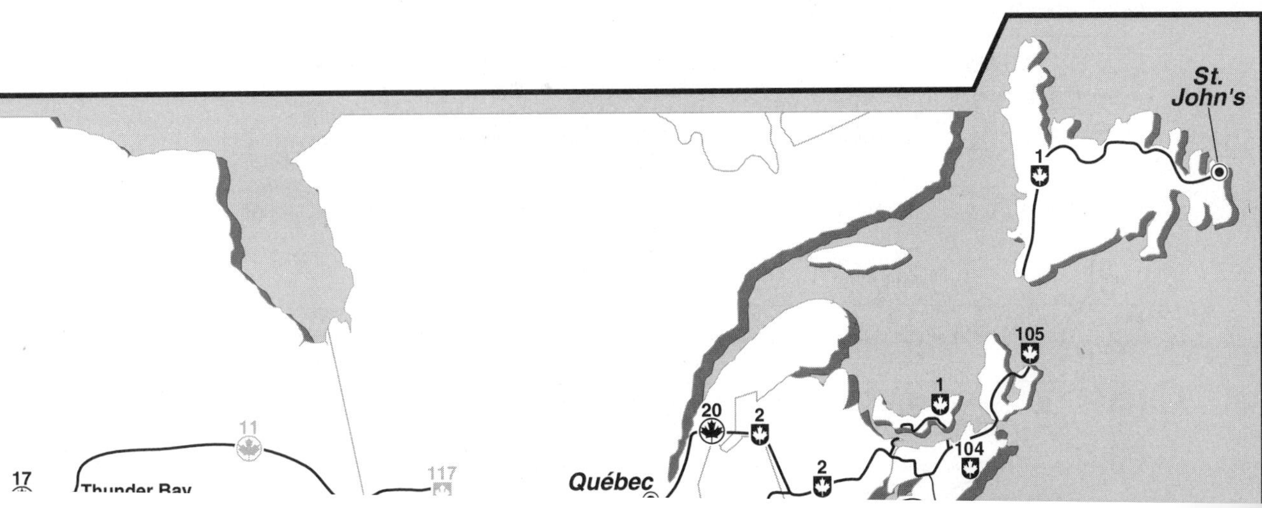

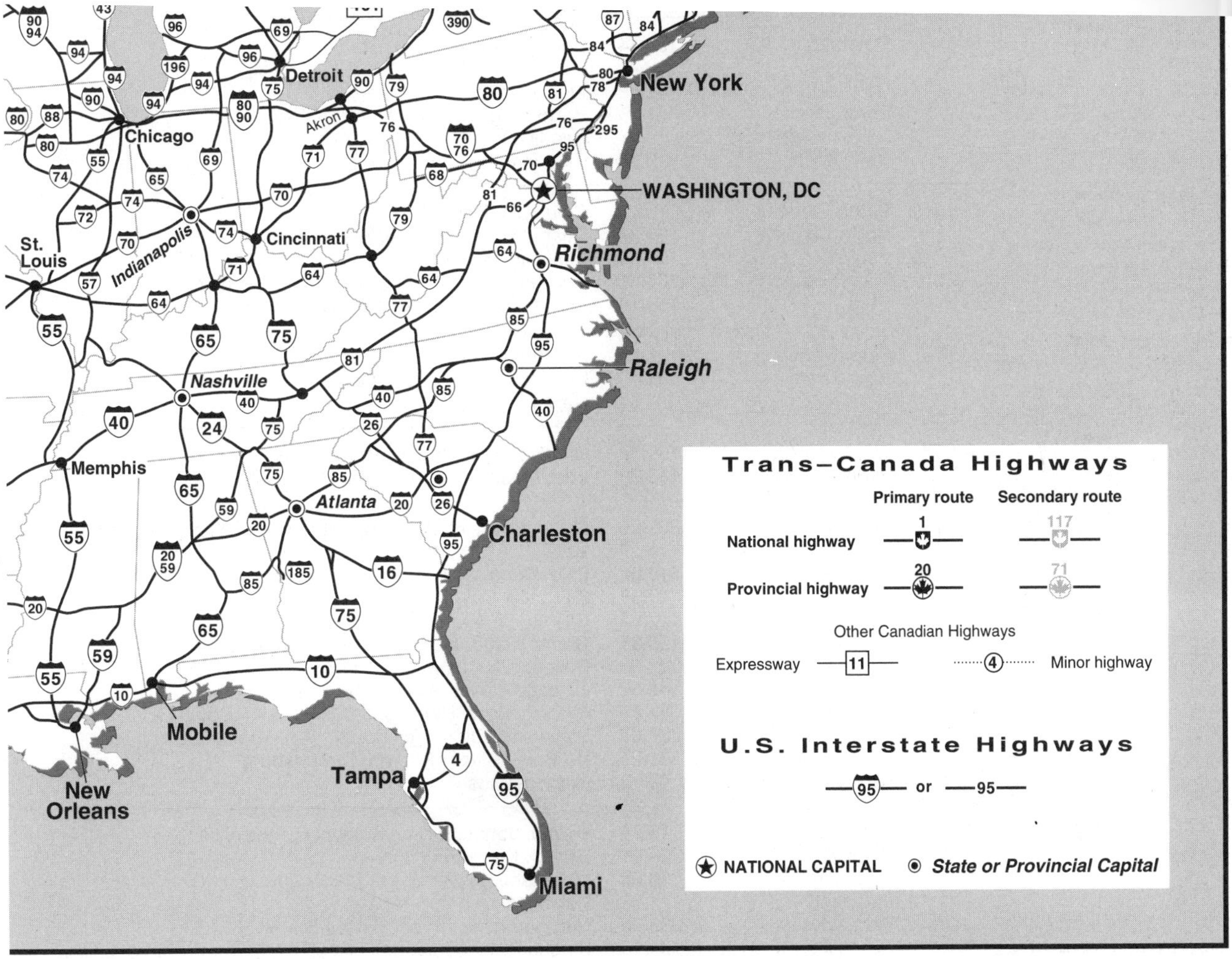

New York
WASHINGTON, DC
Detroit
Akron
Chicago
Cincinnati
St. Louis
Indianapolis
Richmond
Raleigh
Nashville
Memphis
Atlanta
Charleston
Mobile
New Orleans
Tampa
Miami

Trans–Canada Highways

	Primary route	Secondary route
National highway	1	117
Provincial highway	20	71

Other Canadian Highways

Expressway 11 ········ 4 ········ Minor highway

U.S. Interstate Highways

95 or —95—

NATIONAL CAPITAL · *State or Provincial Capital*

Thomas Nast, Cartographer

Route	Total Mileage	Mileage by State		Selected Cities Served
70	2,175.46	Utah	230.77	Cove Fort, Green River, Richfield
		Colorado	450.30	Denver, Grand Junction
		Kansas	424.17	Kansas City, Lawrence, Topeka
		Missouri	251.60	Columbia, Kansas City, St. Louis
		Illinois	160.25	East St. Louis, Effingham, Vandalia
		Indiana	156.27	Indianapolis, Richmond, Terre Haute
		Ohio	225.69	Columbus, Dayton, Springfield, Zanesville
		West Virginia	14.45	Wheeling
		Pennsylvania	168.73	Pittsburgh
		Maryland	93.23	Baltimore, Hagerstown
71	345.58	Kentucky	97.92	Covington, Louisville
		Ohio	247.66	Cincinnati, Cleveland, Columbus, Mansfield
72	78.66	Illinois	78.66	Champaign, Decatur, Springfield
74	416.89	Iowa	5.39	Davenport
		Illinois	220.18	Bloomington, Champaign, Moline, Peoria, Rock Island, Urbana
		Indiana	171.87	Crawfordsville, Indianapolis, Shelbyville
		Ohio	19.45	Cincinnati
75	1,786.99	Florida	472.06	Bradenton, Fort Myers, Gainesville, Lakeland, Naples, Ocala, St. Petersburg, Sarasota, Tampa
		Georgia	355.00	Atlanta, Macon, Valdosta
		Tennessee	161.60	Chattanooga, Knoxville
		Kentucky	191.60	Covington, Lexington, Richmond
		Ohio	211.53	Cincinnati, Dayton, Lima, Middletown, Toledo
		Michigan	395.20	Bay City, Detroit, Flint, Saginaw
76	618.49	Colorado	184.14	Denver, Fort Morgan, Sterling
		Nebraska	2.48	—
		Ohio	77.82	Akron, Youngstown
		Pennsylvania	351.25	Harrisburg, Lancaster, Philadelphia, Pittsburgh, Reading
		New Jersey	2.80	Camden
77	598.25	South Carolina	75.17	Columbia, Rock Hill
		North Carolina	105.37	Charlotte, Mooresville, Statesville
		Virginia	67.40	Bluefield, Wytheville
		West Virginia	187.21	Beckley, Bluefield, Charleston, Parkersburg
		Ohio	163.10	Akron, Canton, Cleveland, Marietta
78	145.34	Pennsylvania	76.69	Allentown, Bethlehem, Easton
		New Jersey	68.15	Irvington, Jersey City, Newark, Plainfield
		New York	0.50	New York City
79	344.25	West Virginia	160.52	Charleston, Fairmont, Morgantown
		Pennsylvania	183.73	Erie, Meadville, Pittsburgh, Washington
80	2,906.75	California	202.20	Davis, Fairfield, Oakland, Sacramento, San Francisco, Vallejo,
		Nevada	410.67	Elko, Reno, Sparks, Winnemucca
		Utah	197.58	Salt Lake City
		Wyoming	402.86	Cheyenne, Evanston, Laramie, Rawlings, Rock Springs
		Nebraska	455.31	Grand Island, Kearney, Lincoln, Omaha
		Iowa	306.55	Davenport, Des Moines, Iowa City
		Illinois	163.52	Chicago, Joliet, Moline, Rock Island
		Indiana	151.65	Elkhart, Gary, Hammond, Mishawaka, South Bend
		Ohio	237.07	Cleveland, Elyria, Toledo, Warren, Youngstown
		Pennsylvania	311.24	Du Bois, Milton, Sharon, Stroudsburg
		New Jersey	68.10	Bergen–Passaic
81	855.07	Tennessee	75.30	Bristol, Johnson City, Kingsport, Knoxville
		Virginia	324.01	Bristol, Roanoke
		West Virginia	26.00	Martinsburg
		Maryland	11.96	Hagerstown
		Pennsylvania	233.70	Harrisburg, Scranton, Wilkes-Barre
		New York	184.10	Binghamton, Syracuse

Route	Total Mileage	Mileage by State		Selected Cities Served
82	142.99	Washington	132.20	Kennewick, Pasco, Richland, Yakima
		Oregon	10.79	Hermiston
83	84.11	Maryland	34.05	Baltimore
		Pennsylvania	50.06	Harrisburg, York
84	995.62	Oregon	375.15	Baker, Pendleton, Portland
		Idaho	275.36	Boise, Twin Falls
		Utah	117.18	Ogden
		Pennsylvania	49.75	Scranton
		New York	71.60	Orange County
		Connecticut	98.52	Bristol, Danbury, Hartford, New Britain, Waterbury
		Massachusetts	8.06	—
85	667.11	Alabama	80.00	Auburn, Montgomery, Opelika
		Georgia	178.94	Atlanta
		South Carolina	106.13	Anderson, Greenville, Spartanburg
		North Carolina	233.40	Burlington, Charlotte, Durham, Gastonia, Greensboro,
89	191.32	New Hampshire	60.93	Concord, Lebanon
		Vermont	130.39	Burlington, Montpelier
90	3,081.87	Washington	297.01	Seattle, Spokane
		Idaho	73.73	Coeur d'Alene, Kellogg
		Montana	549.98	Billings, Bozeman, Butte, Missoula
		Wyoming	208.79	Buffalo, Sheridan
		South Dakota	412.84	Rapid City, Sioux Falls
		Minnesota	275.70	Albert Lea, Austin, Rochester
		Wisconsin	187.17	Beloit, Janesville, La Crosse, Madison
		Illinois	108.05	Chicago, Elgin, Rockford
		Indiana	156.90	Elkhart, Gary, Hammond, Mishawaka, South Bend
		Ohio	244.13	Cleveland, Elyria, Lorain, Toledo
		Pennsylvania	46.60	Erie
		New York	386.77	Albany, Buffalo, Rochester, Rome, Schenectady, Syracuse, Troy, Utica
		Massachusetts	134.20	Boston, Pittsfield, Springfield, Worcester
91	290.52	Connecticut	57.98	Hartford, Meriden, New Haven
		Massachusetts	54.92	Springfield
		Vermont	177.62	Brattleboro, St. Johnsbury
93	188.91	Massachusetts	46.00	Boston, Lawrence, Lowell
		New Hampshire	131.85	Concord, Manchester
		Vermont	11.06	St. Johnsbury
94	1,606.71	Montana	247.91	Billings, Glendive, Miles City
		North Dakota	352.50	Bismarck, Fargo
		Minnesota	259.49	Minneapolis, Moorhead, St. Cloud, St. Paul
		Wisconsin	348.11	Eau Claire, Kenosha, Madison, Milwaukee, Racine
		Illinois	77.37	Chicago, Lake County
		Indiana	45.73	Gary, Hammond, Michigan City, Portage
		Michigan	275.60	Ann Arbor, Battle Creek, Benton Harbor, Detroit, Jackson, Kalamazoo

Route	Total Mileage	Mileage by State		Selected Cities Served
95	1,894.02	Florida	382.40	Boca Raton, Daytona Beach, Fort Lauderdale, Fort Pierce, Hialeah, Hollywood, Jacksonville, Melbourne, Miami, Palm Beach, Pompano Beach
		Georgia	111.69	Brunswick, Savannah
		South Carolina	198.76	Florence
		North Carolina	181.39	Fayetteville
		Virginia	174.52	Arlington, Petersburg, Richmond
		District of Columbia	0.12	Washington, DC
		Maryland	108.83	Baltimore
		Delaware	23.43	Wilmington
		Pennsylvania	51.95	Philadelphia
		New Jersey	79.08	Elizabeth, Newark, Trenton
		New York	23.35	New York City
		Connecticut	111.57	Bridgeport, Milford, New Haven, New London, Norwalk, Stamford
		Rhode Island	43.31	Cranston, Pawtucket, Providence, Warwick
		Massachusetts	89.60	Attleboro, Boston
		New Hampshire	16.13	Portsmouth
		Maine	297.89	Augusta, Bangor, Portland
96	192.70	Michigan	192.70	Detroit, Grand Rapids, Lansing, Muskegon
97	17.88	Maryland	17.88	Annapolis, Baltimore

Source: U.S. Department of Transportation, *Interstate System Route Log and Finder List*, undated.

In March of 1996, the *New York Times* began a seven-part "Downsizing of America" series. "On the Battlefields of Business, Millions of Casualties," said the opening article's headline. Just as the massive series reached its fifth installment, the federal government announced 700,000 new jobs were created in February, the largest one-month increase in 12 years. With mixed messages like these, are you comfortable or scared?

Jobs will be a pervasive issue for the rest of the century. Among all the mobility factors in *Places Rated*, it is the most important. For some, it is the *only* factor. While we may never see any overheated boom towns this century, many metro areas are expected to recover jobs lost during the recessions of the early 1990s and gain a good many more besides.

FORECASTING WHERE THE JOBS WILL BE

Economists who follow employment trends have an old joke: If you take each local planner's numbers for job growth in his or her area and add them all together, the total jobs forecasted would require that every man, woman, and child hold down one day job and moonlight two others.

Fortunately, economists with a macro view have a better perspective. Although no one can predict the future with certainty, forecasting where jobs will be plentiful over the next few years isn't merely a matter of gazing into a crystal ball.

Let's ask the perennial question: Do people move to where the jobs are, or do jobs come to where the people are? Economists argue about this quite a bit, but most believe that jobs come to where the peop[illegible] words, any growing place that has a concentration of workers with a variety of skills is by definition a job Mecca.

But there's more to it than that. Some metro areas are saddled with sunset industries—shipbuilding, textiles, sawmills, and steel, for example—while others have sunrise industries, such as health care, higher education, and software. Most metro areas have varying mixes of both. Forecasting which ones will gain the jobs is as much a matter of determining the prospects for certain industries as it is predicting population shifts.

The great American job machine has churned out record numbers of jobs for decades and, depending on which expert is talking, the machine is either showing significant wear and tear or has shifted into a new and different gear. Still, by the year 2000, no longer just a year in which science fiction stories are set, more than 4 million new jobs could be added to the U.S. economy. Although projected employment increases are expected to occur at half the pace of the past, the growth in certain occupations will be quite healthy.

The biggest continuing trend is massive growth in service-oriented sectors and marked decline in goods-producing industries. In other words, opportunities for highly trained white-collar workers are growing rapidly, while the number of blue-collar jobs is declining.

BLUE-COLLAR BLUES . . .

Shortly after World War II, the number of white-collar jobs surpassed the number of blue-collar jobs for the first time in the history of North America. White-collar workers as a group earn somewhat less than blue-collar workers because so many white-collar jobs are low-pay clerical and retail positions and so many blue-collar jobs are skilled occupations protected by union contracts. But white-collar jobs, though paying less, provide a ladder of opportunity that blue-collar jobs don't. And the work is steadier. One of the biggest union issues now is security against layoffs and plant closings rather than higher wages. Blue-collar workers are beginning to want the security of the white-collar world, and they are willing to sacrifice higher wage demands.

The shrinking world of blue-collar work is divided into five basic industries. For the most part, job opportunities in four are expected to drop or merely hold steady to the year 2000.

Farming, Forestry, and Fishing

From Mississippi to Saskatchewan, the family farm is disappearing as mechanized agribusiness rounds up more acreage and concentrates on fewer crops. Despite some modest recovery from the agricultural production slump of the mid-1980s, exports will probably not regain the world dominance they once enjoyed. Still, some metro areas—those in California's Central Valley (Stockton, Merced, Bakersfield, Fresno) and in Canada's prairie provinces (Regina, Saskatoon, Winnipeg)—have large numbers of farming jobs.

One portion of the agricultural sector, agricultural services (such as landscaping and lawn services), has been growing rapidly, and the growth is expected to continue—yet another indication of the shift toward a service economy.

Mining: A Hard Place

Jobs in mining, once a stable employer in the West, are in a deep hole and likely to remain there. Half of these jobs are in hard-hatted oil and natural gas production and high-tech oil field services, disaster industries for the Southwest and Rockies since 1986. The simple reason is that foreign oil is cheaper.

Metal mining isn't expected to recover from any of the deep cuts experienced over the past decade, either. Exports of raw ores are expected to rise, but slow growth in basic steel as well as iron and steel foundries will limit increases in demand. And while coal is becoming more important as an alternative energy source, the number of jobs in coal mines won't grow. Instead, new production methods will mean continued shrinking of employment.

Construction: Rebuilding Rather than Building

Here's a footloose industry if there ever was one. Building contracts run out? Move on to another location. Why else do you think many itinerant general contractors have Southwestern drawls? This industry is expected to provide most of the blue-collar jobs to 1998 and beyond. Whenever you see a place forecasted to gain a large number of blue-collar jobs, you'll be seeing hammers, bulldozers, bricks, and lumber.

Slow population growth and household formation, however, will slow home building in the 1990s; while little growth is likely for new single-family homes or house alterations and additions, this trend will be offset by declines in new apartment and condo construction. Nonresidential construction may recover from the oversupply of office and commercial space, but getting rid of the excess stock may take years in certain parts of the continent.

Manufacturing: Anything but Durable

Here is a job sector that's predicted to grow glacially or not at all. Smokestacks, low-rise buildings near rail tracks, even high-tech assembly work—we can kiss it good-bye over time. Much of it is moving offshore or to developing countries.

Although manufacturing will lose hundreds of thousands of jobs by the year 2000, output is expected almost to keep pace with total GNP growth. At the same time, the occupational composition of the remaining manufacturing jobs will change. In general, following the trend of the disappearing blue-collar job, manufacturing employment will shift from production and assembly line jobs toward professional, managerial, and technical occupations. The shift is more pronounced in industries in which imports play a significant role. In some of those cases, design and engineering are done domestically, but much of the actual assembly is performed overseas.

Computer manufacturing has been one of the fastest-growing industries during the past 25 years. The nature of work in this industry, however, is uncharacteristic of most manufacturing industries. It employs a high concentration of scientific personnel and a relatively low concentration of production workers. Employment in computer manufacturing is expected to expand beyond the year 2000, with even more of a shift at that time from production to research and development occupations.

The printing and publishing business is one of the manufacturing sectors that has registered consistent job gains in the past few years. Even during the recession, both output and employment increased steadily. And the introduction of electronic composition systems and other new technologies has not put a damper on this trend. As elsewhere, however, occupational shifts are occurring within the printing trades, from fewer typesetters and other craftspeople to more front-office personnel such as writers, editors, managers, and salesworkers. Growth is expected to continue with vigor throughout the rest of the 1990s.

Fastest Disappearing Jobs

Jobs that are declining are the ones hit by technological advances and organizational change. Bank tellers will lose out to more ATM machines, for instance, and typists and word processors will drop out of sight because office automation is getting so simple that professionals and managers will do their own typing and word processing.

Occupation	Jobs Gone
Farmers	−273,000
Typists and word processors	−212,000
Bookkeeping and accounting clerks	−178,000
Bank tellers	−152,000
Sewing machine operators	−140,000
Private household servants	−108,000
Computer operators	−98,000
Billing, posting machine operators	−64,000
Office machine operators	−56,000

Seventeen Occupations: Half the Growth

Occupations that will see the most new openings tend to be (1) large in size rather than fast growing; and, with exceptions in health care and in education, (2) require the least education and training, and (3) offer the lowest pay.

Occupation	New Openings
Cashiers	562,000
Janitors	559,000
Retail salespersons	532,000
Waiters and waitresses	479,000
Registered nurses	473,000
General managers and top executives	466,000
Systems analysts	445,000
Home health aides	428,000
Guards	415,000
Nursing aides and orderlies	387,000
High School teachers	386,000
Marketing and sales managers	380,000

Transportation, Communications, and Public Utilities

This catchall industry classification embraces electric power generation, 18-wheel trucking, airline food and baggage handlers, cable television, and much more. In recent years, deregulation has boosted employment in the air transportation industry, as many smaller firms entered the market and price competition stimulated demand. But, in the long run, consolidation and takeovers are expected to dampen the rate of job growth.

Overall, employment in this group is expected to decrease over the rest of the decade due to declining industry employment and technological changes. The railroad industry, for example, is expected to lose tens of thousands of jobs; likewise, the number of water transportation workers is expected to decline. Greater efficiency in scheduling, marketing, and cost control in the trucking industry is expected to produce greater gains in output than in employment.

... AND A WHITE-COLLAR CHORUS

White-collar work, which corresponds roughly with service-oriented occupations, is divided into four basic industry categories. With some variations within categories, this is where the real action is expected to occur in the remaining years of the 20th century.

Trade

Retail jobs outnumber wholesale positions by five to one and are expected to increase in number by nearly a million by the end of the decade. Unfortunately, retail trade jobs (hamburger flipping, counter help, damage estimating, aisle sweeping, cashiering) aren't worth having if your cash needs are immediate and above average. These jobs do, however, provide rapid advancement to managerial slots, which are still lower-paid despite the title. Retail trade stores are the most ubiquitous establishments in North America, and heavy opportunity in this sector goes hand in hand with a local area that is swelling with people.

Finance, Insurance, and Real Estate

Referred to in regional developers' shorthand as FIRE, this is the purest of the white-collar industrial classifications. Here the compensation is greater than that in the retail trade, and potentially greater by far than in any other industry. It is a briefcase and tie industry—an office-with-a-capital-O environment. It has both heavier government regulation than other industries and more unreported crime.

Banking, credit agencies, and investment offices—a big part of the FIRE industries—should enjoy substantial rates of business growth in the next decade, but not necessarily growth in numbers of jobs. Consolidation and technological advances in automatic banking and other financial transactions will actually slow rates of employment gain. This doesn't mean no new jobs in these fields; there will be some growth—for example, thousands more in credit agencies and investment offices by the year 2000. But the rate of employment growth will be slower than in the past and will not match the growth in business output.

Metro Area Winners and Losers

Of the metro areas forecasted to gain over 50,000 jobs between now and the year 2000, four are in regions that many analysts predicted would wither throughout the rest of the century.

Job Winners, 1997–2000

Washington, DC–MD–VA–WV	101,194
Atlanta, GA	91,642
Orange County, CA	90,493
San Diego, CA	89,682
Orlando, FL	83,014
Chicago, IL	82,568
Dallas, TX	81,873
Houston, TX	78,210
Phoenix–Mesa, AZ	76,175
Tampa–St. Petersburg–Clearwater, FL	73,911
Minneapolis–St. Paul, MN–WI	71,837
Detroit, MI	67,545
Riverside–San Bernardino, CA	61,901
Seattle–Bellevue–Everett, WA	54,314
Sacramento, CA	51,494
Philadelphia, PA–NJ	51,451
Denver, CO	50,065

Job Losers, 1997–2000

Steubenville–Weirton, OH–WV	−190
Decatur, IL	−1,240
Newark, NJ	−3,833
New York, NY	−42,762

Source: Woods & Poole Economics, Inc., employment forecasts

Similarly, greater efficiency in the insurance industry—computerized underwriting, for example—will mean that job gains will be limited for insurance carriers and for independent agents and brokers. Not zero growth, but slower growth. Rapid projected growth in the real estate industry is expected to have a favorable impact on employment for brokers (increasing by 44 percent) and appraisers (increasing by 41 percent).

Service

Think of high-rise copper and glass office buildings and medical centers with piped-in music. Think of white smocks and clipboards and shaded college campuses. These are the most desirable kinds of developments—the kinds city fathers and mothers dream of. If the landscape is full of these buildings, you've got a well-educated work force, higher incomes, and a stable, service-oriented economy.

The service division includes careers in business, health, recreation, the professions, and education—an increasing proportion of which will require formal education and certification. Health and education, typically underwritten by government or third-party payers, lead the way in this division. It makes sense if you think about it; the numbers of educational staff are rising with the numbers of children of the baby-boom generation, and the health-care industry is growing as the population ages and needs more medical attention. Overall, this category has been and is projected to be the fastest-growing for new jobs, adding 10 million by the year 2000, for a total of more than 32 million payroll jobs.

The big story in services is computer and data processing, systems design, programming, and software development. Another big story in business services, with a very large projected increase unemployment, is the personnel supply business, especially the temporary help industry. No longer limited to placing office workers, temporary personnel service businesses are beginning to place workers from industrial, medical, managerial, engineering, and technical occupations as well. The employers like the lower fringe benefits and the access to added help during peak times, and the temporary workers like the flexibility, variety, and experience.

With the trend toward development of new service businesses, the demand is growing for research, management, and consulting services. Independent laboratories for research and development, market researchers, personnel training or management consultants, economic researchers, efficiency experts, lobbyists, and other business consultants will be in increasing demand.

In the professions, the legal services industry has been growing, taking a place among the top 10 fastest growing employment industries. If you thought the legal profession was filled to capacity, think again. Increasing liability litigation, corporate mergers and acquisitions, high divorce levels, geographic expansion of law firms, a greater degree of legal specialization within firms, and an increase in litigation in general keep things moving.

In health care, too, important shifts are taking place. Cost-containment policies have halted the expansion of hospitals and hospital employment, with health-care delivery moving from the hospital to outpatient-care centers. Look for employment growth in the emergency care clinics, surgicenters, and walk-in treatment centers that are popping up all around us.

Government

If you're considering a job in government, especially the federal government, you might reconsider. The federal government will definitely be shrinking because of military base closings and budgetary reductions. Total public employment is, however, projected to rise over the next decade, with most of the increase occurring among municipal workers such as teachers, firefighters, and police. On the other hand, count on a decline of jobs among clerical and administrative support workers.

For government jobs, though, some places—Austin, TX; Columbus, OH; Madison, WI; Toronto, ON; and Atlanta, GA—are in enviable positions. They are state or provincial capitals with large bureaucracies that face little unemployment threat. That they are all higher-education centers doesn't hurt, either.

SCORING: JOBS

If you're out of work or looking for better employment, would the raw odds of tracking down a job be better in Dallas, Denver, or Duluth? What about Honolulu, Houston, or Huntsville? To help you answer these questions, *Places Rated* compares the number of new jobs forecasted between now and the year 2000, as well as the percent rate of job growth during this three-year period.

Which of those two factors is more important? A rosy three-year growth forecast—such as Punta Gorda, FL's 9.1 percent—always looks good at first view. But that works out to only 1,400 new jobs a year. In contrast, St. Louis's more modest 2.0 percent forecast results in over 10,000 new jobs a year.

Back to the question: Which gets more weight? Number of new jobs or percent growth? *Factor analysis,* a mathematical procedure that sorts and groups many pieces of information into fewer "factors," can also determine the relative importance of each factor. In the case of jobs, factor analysis assigns a weight of 74 percent to number of new jobs and 26 percent to percent growth.

A metro area's final score is it percentile on a scale of 0 to 100 corresponding to its weighted average scores for new jobs and for percent growth. Atlanta's score is 100; Johnson City–Kingsport–Bristol's is 50.09; and New York's is 0.00. They are respectively the best, average, and worst North American metro areas for jobs between now and the new millenium.

In ranking the 351 metro areas for near-term job growth, *Places Rated Almanac* factors two criteria: (1) the percent increase in new jobs by the year 2000, and (2) the total number of new jobs created between now and that date. Scores are given as percentiles where 0 is worst, 50 average, and 100 best. The higher the score, then, the more promising the metro area's job outlook. Places that are tied get the same rank and are listed in alphabetical order.

Metro Areas from Best to Worst

Places Rated Rank		Places Rated Score
1.	Atlanta, GA	100.00
2.	Dallas, TX	99.99
3.	Houston, TX	99.98
4.	Orange County, CA	99.97
5.	San Diego, CA	99.96
6.	Minneapolis–St. Paul, MN–WI	99.95
7.	Phoenix–Mesa, AZ	99.93
8.	Orlando, FL	99.90
9.	Riverside–San Bernardino, CA	99.81
10.	Seattle–Bellevue–Everett, WA	99.72
10.	Washington, DC–MD–VA–WV	99.72
12.	Raleigh–Durham–Chapel Hill, NC	99.49
13.	Fort Worth–Arlington, TX	99.39
14.	Tampa–St. Petersburg–Clearwater, FL	99.36
15.	Denver, CO	98.93
16.	Sacramento, CA	98.91
17.	Portland–Vancouver, OR–WA	98.87
18.	Salt Lake City–Ogden, UT	98.82
19.	Austin–San Marcos, TX	98.62
20.	Las Vegas, NV–AZ	98.20
21.	Nashville, TN	96.19
22.	Charlotte–Gastonia–Rock Hill, NC–SC	94.92
23.	Detroit, MI	94.63
24.	Oakland, CA	94.29
25.	San Antonio, TX	94.25
26.	Chicago, IL	91.47
27.	Fort Lauderdale, FL	90.74
28.	San Jose, CA	90.02
29.	West Palm Beach–Boca Raton, FL	89.21
30.	Grand Rapids–Muskegon–Holland, MI	89.17
31.	Middlesex–Somerset–Hunterdon, NJ	88.41
32.	Columbus, OH	88.18
33.	Tucson, AZ	87.55
34.	El Paso, TX	86.56
35.	Greensboro–Winston-Salem–High Point, NC	85.44
36.	Cincinnati, OH–KY–IN	85.36
37.	Indianapolis, IN	84.56
38.	Toronto, ON	82.89
39.	Memphis, TN–AR–MS	82.28
40.	Jacksonville, FL	80.67
41.	Richmond–Petersburg, VA	79.75
42.	Ventura, CA	78.72
43.	Boise City, ID	78.09
44.	Greenville–Spartanburg–Anderson, SC	77.95
45.	Columbia, SC	77.94
46.	Sarasota–Bradenton, FL	77.46
47.	Laredo, TX	77.35
48.	Albuquerque, NM	75.96
49.	Augusta–Aiken, GA–SC	75.52
50.	Knoxville, TN	75.02
51.	Tacoma, WA	73.95
52.	Santa Rosa, CA	73.75
53.	Miami, FL	73.35
54.	Montreal, PQ	71.89
55.	Vancouver, BC	71.76
56.	Norfolk–Virginia Beach–Newport News, VA–NC	70.98
57.	St. Louis, MO–IL	70.93
58.	Portsmouth–Rochester, NH–ME	70.92

Places Rated Rank		Places Rated Score
59.	Fort Myers–Cape Coral, FL	69.79
60.	Louisville, KY–IN	68.43
61.	Fayetteville–Springdale–Rogers, AR	68.26
62.	Springfield, MO	67.96
63.	Philadelphia, PA–NJ	67.79
64.	McAllen–Edinburg–Mission, TX	67.35
65.	Madison, WI	67.23
66.	Boulder–Longmont, CO	66.42
67.	Milwaukee–Waukesha, WI	66.34
68.	Colorado Springs, CO	66.14
69.	Long Island, NY	65.36
70.	Tulsa, OK	65.31
71.	Little Rock–North Little Rock, AR	65.21
72.	Kansas City, MO–KS	65.02
73.	Appleton–Oshkosh–Neenah, WI	64.68
74.	Baton Rouge, LA	64.34
75.	Fresno, CA	64.08
76.	Birmingham, AL	64.06
77.	Myrtle Beach, SC	63.23
77.	Ocala, FL	63.23
79.	Harrisburg–Lebanon–Carlisle, PA	63.12
80.	Huntsville, AL	62.99
81.	Baltimore, MD	62.80
82.	Naples, FL	62.59
83.	Hickory–Morganton–Lenoir, NC	62.28
84.	Lexington, KY	61.66
85.	Fort Wayne, IN	61.58
86.	Provo–Orem, UT	61.32
87.	Ann Arbor, MI	61.25
88.	Monmouth–Ocean, NJ	60.54
89.	Fort Collins–Loveland, CO	60.43
90.	Oklahoma City, OK	60.23
91.	Rochester, NY	60.13
92.	Charleston–North Charleston, SC	59.83
93.	Greenville, NC	59.59
94.	Salinas, CA	58.58
95.	Biloxi–Gulfport–Pascagoula, MS	58.16
96.	Punta Gorda, FL	57.70
97.	Anchorage, AK	57.13
98.	Green Bay, WI	56.40
99.	Yolo, CA	56.39
100.	Melbourne–Titusville–Palm Bay, FL	56.32
101.	Des Moines, IA	56.06
102.	Daytona Beach, FL	55.69
103.	San Francisco, CA	55.61
104.	Vallejo–Fairfield–Napa, CA	55.48
105.	St. Cloud, MN	55.40
106.	Champaign–Urbana, IL	55.35
107.	Fort Smith, AR–OK	54.31
108.	Bryan–College Station, TX	53.86
109.	Tallahassee, FL	53.83
110.	Brazoria, TX	53.70
111.	Jackson, MS	53.65
112.	Elkhart–Goshen, IN	53.56
113.	Kalamazoo–Battle Creek, MI	53.26
114.	Wichita, KS	53.12
115.	Fort Pierce–Port St. Lucie, FL	53.06
116.	Mobile, AL	52.95
117.	Albany–Schenectady–Troy, NY	52.43
118.	Lafayette, LA	51.52
119.	Galveston–Texas City, TX	51.37
120.	Santa Barbara–Santa Maria–Lompoc, CA	51.12
121.	Ottawa–Hull, ON–PQ	50.79
122.	Wilmington–Newark, DE–MD	50.26
123.	Johnson City–Kingsport–Bristol, TN–VA	50.09
124.	Brownsville–Harlingen–San Benito, TX	49.82
124.	Wilmington, NC	49.82
126.	Lansing–East Lansing, MI	49.51
127.	Portland, ME	49.49
128.	Bakersfield, CA	49.08
129.	Lincoln, NE	48.83
130.	Modesto, CA	48.77
131.	Gainesville, FL	48.73
132.	Olympia, WA	48.29
133.	Pensacola, FL	47.74
134.	Omaha, NE–IA	47.38
135.	San Luis Obispo–Atascadero–Paso Robles, CA	46.90
136.	Lafayette, IN	46.82
137.	Santa Cruz–Watsonville, CA	46.13
138.	Santa Fe, NM	45.98
139.	Las Cruces, NM	45.84
140.	Akron, OH	45.67
141.	Edmonton, AB	45.55
142.	Salem, OR	45.36
143.	Tuscaloosa, AL	45.31
144.	Pittsburgh, PA	45.04
145.	Bloomington–Normal, IL	44.84
146.	Greeley, CO	44.70
147.	Sioux Falls, SD	44.65
148.	Spokane, WA	44.42
149.	Bellingham, WA	44.39
150.	Joplin, MO	44.38
151.	York, PA	44.10
152.	Odessa–Midland, TX	44.05
153.	Victoria, BC	43.94
154.	Medford–Ashland, OR	43.49
155.	Fort Walton Beach, FL	43.45
156.	Burlington, VT	43.32
157.	Bloomington, IN	43.31
158.	Florence, AL	43.30
159.	New Orleans, LA	42.86
160.	Honolulu, HI	42.73
160.	Stockton–Lodi, CA	42.73
162.	Calgary, AB	42.62
163.	Chattanooga, TN–GA	42.55
164.	Wausau, WI	42.47
165.	Asheville, NC	42.15
166.	Killeen–Temple, TX	41.90
167.	Rocky Mount, NC	41.77
168.	Montgomery, AL	41.38
169.	Lubbock, TX	40.82
170.	Corpus Christi, TX	40.64
171.	Dothan, AL	40.57
172.	Yuma, AZ	40.48
173.	Columbia, MO	40.40
174.	Reno, NV	40.26
175.	London, ON	40.24
176.	Tyler, TX	40.15
177.	Atlantic City–Cape May, NJ	40.07
178.	Longview–Marshall, TX	39.94
179.	Chico–Paradise, CA	39.86
179.	Dayton–Springfield, OH	39.86
181.	Kitchener, ON	39.73
182.	Charlottesville, VA	39.72
183.	Visalia–Tulare–Porterville, CA	38.86
184.	Cleveland–Lorain–Elyria, OH	38.76
185.	Hamilton–Middletown, OH	38.55
186.	Fayetteville, NC	38.43
187.	State College, PA	38.42
188.	Clarksville–Hopkinsville, TN–KY	38.32
189.	Evansville–Henderson, IN–KY	38.27
189.	La Crosse, WI–MN	38.27
191.	Richland–Kennewick–Pasco, WA	38.25
192.	Eau Claire, WI	37.43
193.	Grand Junction, CO	37.42
194.	Flagstaff, AZ–UT	37.32
195.	Merced, CA	37.26
196.	Iowa City, IA	37.14
197.	Jackson, TN	37.03
198.	Duluth–Superior, MN–WI	36.99
199.	Newburgh, NY–PA	36.85
200.	Dover, DE	36.76
201.	Rochester, MN	36.67
202.	Trenton, NJ	36.66
203.	Savannah, GA	36.55
204.	Quebec City, PQ	36.49
205.	Lynchburg, VA	36.45
206.	Lakeland–Winter Haven, FL	36.41
207.	Hartford, CT	36.38
208.	Saskatoon, SK	36.27
209.	Fargo–Moorhead, ND–MN	36.26
210.	Cedar Rapids, IA	36.24
211.	Redding, CA	36.08
212.	Barnstable–Yarmouth, MA	35.94
213.	Panama City, FL	35.51
214.	Buffalo–Niagara Falls, NY	35.22
215.	Fitchburg–Leominster, MA	35.16
215.	Worcester, MA–CT	35.16
217.	Allentown–Bethlehem–Easton, PA	34.52
217.	Amarillo, TX	34.52
219.	Wichita Falls, TX	34.48
220.	Oshawa, ON	34.31
221.	Hattiesburg, MS	34.18
222.	Columbus, GA–AL	34.10
223.	Sheboygan, WI	33.91
224.	Decatur, AL	33.87
225.	Bridgeport, CT	33.77
225.	Danbury, CT	33.77
225.	Stamford–Norwalk, CT	33.77
228.	Eugene–Springfield, OR	33.72

Places Rated Rank		Places Rated Score
229.	Victoria, TX	33.47
230.	Waterloo–Cedar Falls, IA	33.36
231.	Waco, TX	33.21
231.	Yuba City, CA	33.21
233.	Dubuque, IA	33.19
234.	Manchester, NH	33.08
234.	Nashua, NH	33.08
236.	Hamilton, ON	32.74
237.	Terre Haute, IN	32.66
238.	Providence–Fall River–Warwick, RI–MA	32.65
239.	South Bend, IN	32.63
240.	Davenport–Moline–Rock Island, IA–IL	32.50
251.	Lawton, OK	31.79
252.	Lawrence, KS	31.77
253.	Lancaster, PA	31.59
254.	New London–Norwich, CT–RI	31.48
255.	Jacksonville, NC	31.42
256.	Hagerstown, MD	31.25
257.	Muncie, IN	30.98
258.	Athens, GA	30.96
259.	Anniston, AL	30.94
260.	Rockford, IL	30.84
261.	Yakima, WA	30.75
262.	Rapid City, SD	30.73
263.	Topeka, KS	30.67
264.	Benton Harbor, MI	30.66
265.	Roanoke, VA	30.62
266.	Bremerton, WA	30.35
267.	Canton–Massillon, OH	30.30
268.	Regina, SK	30.27
269.	Saginaw–Bay City–Midland, MI	30.06
270.	Billings, MT	30.04
271.	Beaumont–Port Arthur, TX	29.84
272.	Peoria–Pekin, IL	29.83
273.	Syracuse, NY	29.62
274.	Sioux City, IA–NE	29.60
275.	Lake Charles, LA	29.57
276.	Bergen–Passaic, NJ	29.36
277.	Owensboro, KY	29.34
278.	Sherman–Denison, TX	29.25
279.	Halifax, NS	29.12
280.	Monroe, LA	29.04
281.	Bangor, ME	28.96
282.	San Angelo, TX	28.85
283.	Texarkana, TX–Texarkana, AR	28.77
284.	Houma, LA	28.66
294.	Gary, IN	27.72
295.	Racine, WI	27.71
296.	Lewiston–Auburn, ME	27.41
297.	St. John's, NF	27.34
298.	Glens Falls, NY	26.95
299.	Kenosha, WI	26.87
300.	Toledo, OH	26.64
301.	Springfield, IL	26.53
302.	Charleston, WV	26.49
303.	Windsor, ON	26.46
304.	Huntington–Ashland, WV–KY–OH	26.40
305.	New Bedford, MA	25.98
306.	Altoona, PA	25.93
307.	Elmira, NY	25.84
308.	Jersey City, NJ	25.60
309.	Reading, PA	25.44
310.	Trois–Rivieres, PQ	25.29
311.	Albany, GA	25.22
312.	Pine Bluff, AR	25.09
313.	Janesville–Beloit, WI	24.93
314.	Sharon, PA	24.50
315.	St. Catharines–Niagara, ON	24.44
316.	Scranton–Wilkes-Barre–Hazleton, PA	24.35
317.	Jackson, MI	24.14
318.	Sherbrooke, PQ	23.48
319.	Thunder Bay, ON	23.38
320.	Parkersburg–Marietta, WV–OH	23.35
321.	Shreveport–Bossier City, LA	23.30
322.	Casper, WY	22.99
323.	Grand Forks, ND–MN	22.96
324.	Enid, OK	22.79
333.	Flint, MI	22.22
334.	Jamestown, NY	22.15
335.	Dutchess County, NY	22.02
336.	Cumberland, MD–WV	21.85
337.	New Haven–Meriden, CT	21.85
338.	Waterbury, CT	21.85
339.	Danville, VA	21.59
340.	St. Joseph, MO	20.82
341.	Binghamton, NY	20.63
342.	Utica–Rome, NY	19.61
343.	Pittsfield, MA	18.59
344.	Springfield, MA	17.99
345.	Steubenville–Weirton, OH–WV	17.74
346.	Chicoutimi–Jonquiere, PQ	15.25
347.	Decatur, IL	13.27
348.	Boston, MA–NH	10.33
349.	Los Angeles–Long Beach, CA	8.48
350.	Newark, NJ	8.40
351.	New York, NY	0.00

PLACE PROFILES: Jobs

The following table details job statistics for each metro area. Under **Growth Rate** are the percent increase in jobs since 1990 and the forecasted percent increase in jobs to the year 2000.

Under **New Jobs** are the forecasted number of new jobs in predominantly blue-collar industries (farming, forestry, fishing, mining, construction, manufacturing, transportation, and public utilities) and in predominantly white-collar industries (trade, finance, insurance, real estate, services, and government other than military). In addition, the numbers of new jobs in industries where earnings per worker are higher than usual are called *good* while those in industries where earnings are typical are called *average*. Minus figures indicate forecasted losses in any of these categories.

Included in the charts under **Unemployment**

Threat is an arrow symbol indicating the metro area's vulnerability to recession based on too many blue-collar and military jobs. An arrow pointing downward (⇓) indicates the unemployment threat is lower than average. An upward-pointing arrow (⇑) indicates it's higher, while an arrow pointing neither up nor down (⇔) indicates an average unemployment threat.

Growth forecasts for U.S. metro areas are from July 1, 1997, to July 1, 2000; those for Canadian metro areas are from December 31, 1997, to December 31, 2000. U.S. figures are derived from employment forecasts from Woods & Poole Economics, Inc., of Washington, DC, and are used here with permission. Canadian figures are derived by Places Rated Partnership from Statistics Canada's *Labour Force Annual Averages*, 1989–1996.

A check mark (✓) in front of a metro area's name highlights it as one of the top 35 places for job growth between now and the year 2000.

	Growth Rates		NEW JOBS						
	1990–1997	1997–2000	Blue Collar	White Collar	Good Earnings	Average Earnings	Unemployment Threat	Score	Rank
Metro Area Average	8.1	2.9	1,355	9,682	1,454	1,933	⇔		
Abilene, TX	6.1	0.6	0	436	43	−31	⇔	22.42	327
Akron, OH	11.6	2.6	−134	9,923	294	1,462	⇔	45.67	140
Albany, GA	6.6	1.3	103	751	225	36	⇔	25.22	311
Albany-Schenectady-Troy, NY	5.2	2.8	300	14,504	−333	2,475	⇓	52.43	117
Albuquerque, NM	21.4	4.5	3,013	16,098	3,664	2,280	⇔	75.96	48
Alexandria, LA	6.1	3.0	325	1,628	424	305	⇓	32.40	244
Allentown-Bethlehem-Easton, PA	4.7	1.8	−1,104	6,900	−1,172	1,727	⇑	34.52	217
Altoona, PA	9.2	1.6	−316	1,453	−94	100	⇔	25.93	306
Amarillo, TX	16.6	2.3	526	2,246	583	311	⇓	34.52	217
Anchorage, AK	14.5	5.5	0	7,480	2,818	1,290	⇓	57.13	97
Ann Arbor, MI	11.6	3.8	861	11,533	1,285	2,958	⇔	61.25	87
Anniston, AL	6.6	2.7	404	1,359	421	182	⇑	30.94	259
Appleton-Oshkosh-Neenah, WI	18.1	4.1	3,516	5,688	3,539	1,532	⇑	64.68	73
Asheville, NC	14.6	3.3	980	3,410	837	712	⇑	42.15	165
Athens, GA	10.3	2.4	184	1,764	295	210	⇔	30.96	258
✓ **Atlanta, GA**	16.9	4.1	16,617	75,025	21,784	14,507	⇔	100.00	1
Atlantic City-Cape May, NJ	4.0	3.9	170	8,412	273	268	⇓	40.07	177
Augusta-Aiken, GA-SC	8.0	5.8	3,498	11,339	2,738	3,352	⇑	75.52	49
✓ **Austin-San Marcos, TX**	29.9	6.2	8,253	33,170	8,665	9,246	⇔	98.62	19
Bakersfield, CA	6.3	3.0	1,050	7,223	1,045	1,674	⇓	49.08	128
Baltimore, MD	4.1	2.9	−3,653	46,039	−3,726	7,065	⇔	62.80	81
Bangor, ME	−0.3	2.7	200	2,050	150	140	⇔	28.96	281
Barnstable-Yarmouth, MA	7.4	3.3	290	3,240	380	460	⇓	35.94	212
Baton Rouge, LA	18.1	3.4	2,497	8,923	2,249	2,491	⇔	64.34	74
Beaumont-Port Arthur, TX	10.2	1.6	−143	3,160	−626	586	⇑	29.84	271
Bellingham, WA	17.3	4.5	922	2,954	753	635	⇔	44.39	149
Benton Harbor, MI	7.7	2.2	253	1,659	359	324	⇑	30.66	264
Bergen-Passaic, NJ	−2.9	0.7	−3,877	8,832	−2,361	3,914	⇔	29.36	276
Billings, MT	20.4	1.8	101	1,395	260	87	⇓	30.04	270
Biloxi-Gulfport-Pascagoula, MS	24.5	4.5	2,118	6,668	1,998	972	⇑	58.16	95
Binghamton, NY	−1.5	1.3	−722	2,525	−705	−186	⇑	20.63	341
Birmingham, AL	14.4	2.7	1,826	12,631	1,995	2,956	⇔	64.06	76
Bismarck, ND	19.1	2.5	337	1,188	365	118	⇓	32.16	246
Bloomington, IN	18.7	4.3	697	2,594	400	831	⇔	43.31	157
Bloomington-Normal, IL	16.0	4.2	628	3,269	666	1,029	⇓	44.84	145
Boise City, ID	30.7	5.4	4,369	8,436	3,735	2,598	⇑	78.09	43

	Growth Rates 1990–1997	Growth Rates 1997–2000	NEW JOBS Blue Collar	NEW JOBS White Collar	NEW JOBS Good Earnings	NEW JOBS Average Earnings	Unemployment Threat	Score	Rank
Metro Area Average	8.1	2.9	1,355	9,682	1,454	1,933	⇔		
Boston, MA-NH	−0.4	0.9	−8,040	20,530	−9,470	1,300	⇔	10.33	348
Boulder-Longmont, CO	26.5	5.0	2,593	7,612	2,673	1,620	⇔	66.42	66
Brazoria, TX	6.7	5.4	1,921	3,184	1,616	1,433	⇑	53.70	110
Bremerton, WA	9.5	2.1	478	1,797	97	199	⇔	30.35	266
Bridgeport, CT	−3.2	0.9	−2,260	6,940	−1,730	3,960	⇔	33.77	225
Brockton, MA	3.8	2.1	230	3,920	550	320	⇓	32.46	242
Brownsville-Harlingen-San Benito, TX	24.0	4.4	896	4,478	950	1,036	⇔	49.82	124
Bryan-College Station, TX	18.4	6.0	647	4,136	648	1,604	⇓	53.86	108
Buffalo-Niagara Falls, NY	1.8	1.9	−1,952	14,554	−1,766	1,349	⇔	35.22	214
[illegible]	[illegible]	[illegible]	[illegible]	[illegible]	1,210	830	⇔	43.32	156
[illegible]	[illegible]	[illegible]	[illegible]	[illegible]	[illegible]	[illegible]	[illegible]	[illegible]	162
Charleston-North Charleston, SC	−9.5	[illegible]	[illegible]	[illegible]	[illegible]	[illegible]	[illegible]	[illegible]	[illegible]
✓ **Charlotte-Gastonia-Rock Hill, NC-SC**	13.7	3.8	6,785	25,752	8,711	6,462	⇑	94.92	22
Charlottesville, VA	11.1	3.4	289	3,045	256	1,027	⇔	39.72	182
Chattanooga, TN-GA	13.6	2.7	511	6,932	730	707	⇑	42.55	163
Cheyenne, WY	11.6	0.2	−50	131	−3	4	⇔	22.26	332
✓ **Chicago, IL**	5.3	1.8	1,057	81,511	−1,592	17,814	⇔	91.47	26
Chico-Paradise, CA	12.9	3.7	750	2,839	504	552	⇓	39.86	179
Chicoutimi-Jonquiere, PQ	−7.5	−2.7	−180	780	−160	50	⇑	15.25	346
Cincinnati, OH-KY-IN	9.8	3.1	4,013	26,520	5,202	4,371	⇔	85.36	36
Clarksville-Hopkinsville, TN-KY	19.7	2.7	629	2,081	777	585	⇑	38.32	188
Cleveland-Lorain-Elyria, OH	3.4	1.3	−3,556	20,755	−3,213	3,528	⇔	38.76	184
Colorado Springs, CO	19.7	4.2	3,086	8,716	3,109	1,545	⇑	66.14	68
Columbia, MO	18.3	3.6	677	2,589	859	450	⇓	40.40	173
Columbia, SC	10.9	5.0	2,174	14,737	2,543	5,392	⇔	77.94	45
Columbus, GA-AL	6.4	2.2	689	2,626	700	449	⇑	34.10	222
✓ **Columbus, OH**	13.0	3.9	2,294	35,396	3,428	7,198	⇔	88.18	32
Corpus Christi, TX	6.5	2.8	835	4,294	769	951	⇔	40.64	170
Cumberland, MD-WV	2.5	0.8	−391	766	−402	141	⇔	21.85	336
✓ **Dallas, TX**	13.7	4.0	16,363	65,510	20,135	14,382	⇔	99.99	2
Danbury, CT	−3.2	0.9	−2,260	6,940	−1,730	3,960	⇔	33.77	225
Danville, VA	4.6	0.2	0	136	110	24	⇑	21.59	339
Davenport-Moline-Rock Island, IA-IL	7.6	2.1	−197	4,607	187	415	⇔	32.50	240
Dayton-Springfield, OH	4.9	2.0	213	11,431	709	354	⇑	39.86	179
Daytona Beach, FL	21.4	4.4	1,819	6,856	1,510	1,026	⇓	55.69	102
Decatur, AL	10.3	2.6	630	1,220	591	451	⇑	33.87	224
Decatur, IL	3.8	−1.8	−413	−827	−357	−438	⇑	13.27	347
✓ **Denver, CO**	18.0	3.9	10,078	39,987	10,989	8,430	⇓	98.93	15
Des Moines, IA	11.4	4.0	486	11,938	1,027	1,818	⇓	56.06	101
✓ **Detroit, MI**	6.5	2.8	2,621	64,924	6,094	8,761	⇑	94.63	23
Dothan, AL	10.7	3.9	802	2,302	1,117	553	⇑	40.57	171

	Growth Rates 1990–1997	Growth Rates 1997–2000	NEW JOBS Blue Collar	NEW JOBS White Collar	NEW JOBS Good Earnings	NEW JOBS Average Earnings	Unemployment Threat	Score	Rank
Metro Area Average	8.1	2.9	1,355	9,682	1,454	1,933	⇔		
Dover, DE	17.4	3.6	152	2,353	92	436	⇑	36.76	200
Dubuque, IA	11.6	3.0	506	1,330	630	157	⇑	33.19	233
Duluth-Superior, MN-WI	12.8	3.0	264	3,852	273	494	⇓	36.99	198
Dutchess County, NY	−10.0	1.3	−536	2,254	−854	415	⇔	22.02	335
Eau Claire, WI	15.1	3.2	727	2,119	886	284	⇔	37.43	192
Edmonton, AB	7.8	3.4	1,110	6,200	850	990	⇔	45.55	141
✓ **El Paso, TX**	18.2	5.8	4,905	13,634	5,335	4,087	⇑	86.56	34
Elkhart-Goshen, IN	17.1	3.9	3,287	2,084	3,371	469	⇑	53.56	112
Elmira, NY	2.6	2.4	−38	1,218	−5	−64	⇔	25.84	307
Enid, OK	8.4	0.7	−47	287	−18	−15	⇓	22.79	324
Erie, PA	7.1	2.1	501	2,795	601	168	⇑	31.85	249
Eugene-Springfield, OR	11.8	2.4	303	3,833	395	179	⇔	33.72	228
Evansville-Henderson, IN-KY	14.3	2.4	778	3,644	895	483	⇑	38.27	189
Fargo-Moorhead, ND-MN	18.0	2.4	551	2,153	769	457	⇓	36.26	209
Fayetteville, NC	14.8	2.4	663	3,281	1,213	504	⇑	38.43	186
Fayetteville-Springdale-Rogers, AR	28.2	5.7	3,711	5,701	3,559	974	⇑	68.26	61
Fitchburg-Leominster, MA	−0.7	1.9	−970	7,920	−730	1,610	⇔	35.16	215
Flagstaff, AZ-UT	13.1	4.3	284	1,813	317	373	⇔	37.32	194
Flint, MI	5.9	1.3	−1,453	4,230	−1,793	209	⇑	22.22	333
Florence, AL	17.2	4.1	1,214	1,873	1,315	486	⇑	43.30	158
Florence, SC	8.8	2.0	−23	1,472	93	866	⇑	31.90	248
Fort Collins-Loveland, CO	27.1	5.8	2,224	5,577	2,007	859	⇔	60.43	89
✓ **Fort Lauderdale, FL**	18.1	4.8	3,564	32,113	6,626	4,211	⇓	90.74	27
Fort Myers-Cape Coral, FL	20.5	6.7	1,033	12,526	1,018	2,730	⇓	69.79	59
Fort Pierce-Port St. Lucie, FL	13.1	6.0	1,212	6,363	789	857	⇓	53.06	115
Fort Smith, AR-OK	20.5	5.2	2,320	3,972	2,291	449	⇑	54.31	107
Fort Walton Beach, FL	18.8	4.5	515	3,966	542	486	⇑	43.45	155
Fort Wayne, IN	14.2	3.2	3,218	7,345	3,391	1,374	⇑	61.58	85
✓ **Fort Worth-Arlington, TX**	15.2	5.6	11,708	37,120	12,199	7,601	⇔	99.39	13
Fresno, CA	10.5	3.2	4,247	9,255	3,464	1,129	⇓	64.08	75
Gadsden, AL	14.7	2.9	292	1,166	328	175	⇑	32.46	242
Gainesville, FL	16.7	4.8	667	5,699	743	904	⇓	48.73	131
Galveston-Texas City, TX	8.8	5.0	686	4,605	397	2,124	⇔	51.37	119
Gary, IN	8.3	2.2	−935	7,901	−197	−458	⇑	27.72	294
Glens Falls, NY	6.4	1.9	82	1,131	−42	157	⇔	26.95	298
Goldsboro, NC	3.3	2.5	102	1,275	367	−5	⇑	27.75	293
Grand Forks, ND-MN	−5.1	1.2	48	649	178	130	⇓	22.96	323
Grand Junction, CO	19.8	3.6	494	1,646	455	338	⇓	37.42	193
✓ **Grand Rapids-Muskegon-Holland, MI**	14.4	3.8	6,929	16,886	8,654	2,612	⇑	89.17	30
Great Falls, MT	11.1	0.6	−40	306	−133	−97	⇔	22.35	330
Greeley, CO	21.5	4.2	1,355	2,067	1,455	367	⇔	44.70	146
Green Bay, WI	23.2	4.2	2,101	4,305	2,085	1,298	⇑	56.40	98
✓ **Greensboro-Winston-Salem-High Point, NC**	11.0	3.6	4,541	23,094	5,900	3,504	⇑	85.44	35
Greenville, NC	13.2	7.1	1,067	3,933	1,097	2,101	⇔	59.59	93
Greenville-Spartanburg-Anderson, SC	11.5	3.7	3,651	16,671	4,067	3,300	⇑	77.95	44
Hagerstown, MD	11.5	2.8	−354	2,436	−300	387	⇔	31.25	256

	Growth Rates 1990–1997	Growth Rates 1997–2000	NEW JOBS Blue Collar	NEW JOBS White Collar	NEW JOBS Good Earnings	NEW JOBS Average Earnings	Unemployment Threat	Score	Rank
Metro Area Average	8.1	2.9	1,355	9,682	1,454	1,933	⇔		
Halifax, NS	3.0	1.3	330	2,510	260	420	⇓	29.12	279
Hamilton, ON	1.8	0.8	890	4,150	710	620	⇑	32.74	236
Hamilton-Middletown, OH	15.6	3.3	141	4,294	516	429	⇑	38.55	185
Harrisburg-Lebanon-Carlisle, PA	6.9	3.2	2,061	10,829	2,335	2,806	⇔	63.12	79
Hartford, CT	−6.4	1.0	−2,200	9,360	−2,080	4,590	⇔	36.38	207
Hattiesburg, MS	15.7	2.8	172	1,434	335	472	⇔	34.18	221
Hickory-Morganton-Lenoir, NC	12.4	4.1	3,924	4,925	4,120	913	⇑	62.28	83
Honolulu, HI	1.2	1.4	2,032	6,109	1,751	833	⇔	42.73	160
Houma, LA	11.5	1.2	487	480	184	436	⇓	28.66	284
[illegible]	[illegible]	[illegible]	[illegible]	[illegible]	[illegible]	[illegible]	⇔	99.98	3
Jackson, TN	21.9	3.2	544	[illegible]	[illegible]	[illegible]	[illegible]	[illegible]	[illegible]
Jacksonville, FL	5.8	3.9	3,693	18,845	3,193	5,083	⇔	80.67	40
Jacksonville, NC	13.2	2.1	214	1,507	46	452	⇑	31.42	255
Jamestown, NY	4.2	0.8	−148	723	−151	−16	⇑	22.15	334
Janesville-Beloit, WI	11.5	1.0	−91	924	190	−24	⇑	24.93	313
Jersey City, NJ	−1.0	0.0	0	3,002	−2,350	1,721	⇓	25.60	308
Johnson City-Kingsport-Bristol, TN-VA	14.5	3.0	1,929	5,781	2,071	847	⇑	50.09	123
Johnstown, PA	6.0	2.7	77	2,941	63	337	⇔	31.93	247
Joplin, MO	18.8	4.1	1,754	2,085	1,748	163	⇑	44.38	150
Kalamazoo-Battle Creek, MI	13.5	3.4	1,490	7,236	1,850	1,349	⇑	53.26	113
Kankakee, IL	14.4	2.8	138	1,354	260	170	⇔	31.82	250
Kansas City, MO-KS	10.1	1.7	2,155	15,731	3,245	2,488	⇔	65.02	72
Kenosha, WI	14.7	1.6	−328	1,296	−216	149	⇑	26.87	299
Killeen-Temple, TX	14.5	2.5	732	3,149	932	1,200	⇑	41.90	166
Kitchener, ON	10.3	4.4	630	2,540	530	440	⇑	39.73	181
Knoxville, TN	20.3	4.6	3,425	15,217	2,577	2,525	⇔	75.02	50
Kokomo, IN	12.9	1.7	50	1,011	88	170	⇑	27.95	289
La Crosse, WI-MN	17.0	3.3	523	2,307	786	399	⇔	38.27	189
Lafayette, IN	16.5	4.2	1,332	3,294	1,227	742	⇑	46.82	136
Lafayette, LA	14.4	3.8	2,000	5,148	2,441	653	⇔	51.52	118
Lake Charles, LA	13.5	2.0	310	1,524	502	−19	⇑	29.57	275
Lakeland-Winter Haven, FL	15.1	2.4	809	4,581	931	0	⇔	36.41	206
Lancaster, PA	4.0	1.3	206	3,189	857	529	⇑	31.59	253
Lansing-East Lansing, MI	10.1	3.6	400	9,295	537	1,492	⇔	49.51	126
Laredo, TX	45.5	9.7	2,388	5,333	2,498	1,863	⇓	77.35	47
Las Cruces, NM	14.4	5.2	586	2,942	83	1,147	⇓	45.84	139
✓ **Las Vegas, NV-AZ**	28.7	7.5	7,611	41,174	4,696	9,405	⇓	98.20	20
Lawrence, KS	15.5	2.6	224	1,100	373	207	⇔	31.77	252
Lawrence, MA-NH	1.1	0.9	−1,080	4,000	−810	140	⇑	22.42	327
Lawton, OK	7.1	2.6	363	1,287	317	431	⇑	31.79	251

	Growth Rates 1990–1997	Growth Rates 1997–2000	NEW JOBS Blue Collar	NEW JOBS White Collar	NEW JOBS Good Earnings	NEW JOBS Average Earnings	Unemployment Threat	Score	Rank
Metro Area Average	8.1	2.9	1,355	9,682	1,454	1,933	⇔		
Lewiston–Auburn, ME	3.4	2.1	−110	1,270	−80	320	⇑	27.41	296
Lexington, KY	14.4	3.4	3,014	7,217	2,642	1,845	⇔	61.66	84
Lima, OH	6.2	1.7	239	1,330	395	145	⇑	27.90	291
Lincoln, NE	13.2	3.9	1,418	5,035	1,397	925	⇔	48.83	129
Little Rock–North Little Rock, AR	17.5	3.4	1,968	10,762	2,693	2,418	⇔	65.21	71
London, ON	10.6	4.5	560	2,970	450	460	⇔	40.24	175
Long Island, NY	−1.1	1.4	−600	19,190	2,710	6,050	⇓	65.36	69
Longview–Marshall, TX	14.4	3.1	1,089	2,547	1,092	450	⇔	39.94	178
Los Angeles–Long Beach, CA	−6.5	0.7	−14,955	47,693	−18,336	12,052	⇔	8.48	349
Louisville, KY–IN	13.8	3.0	2,670	16,709	2,512	2,220	⇔	68.43	60
Lowell, MA–NH	−1.4	0.8	−2,870	10,410	−3,190	1,050	⇔	22.70	325
Lubbock, TX	10.2	3.1	516	3,935	645	956	⇓	40.82	169
Lynchburg, VA	9.1	2.8	606	2,746	702	514	⇑	36.45	205
Macon, GA	−9.0	1.9	508	2,257	685	273	⇔	27.94	290
Madison, WI	17.1	3.6	2,296	8,955	2,978	2,960	⇓	67.23	65
Manchester, NH	4.1	2.2	−370	5,210	−370	780	⇑	33.08	234
Mansfield, OH	4.1	1.0	−420	1,343	−264	−13	⇑	22.36	329
McAllen–Edinburg–Mission, TX	24.1	5.9	1,618	8,539	1,680	2,405	⇔	67.35	64
Medford–Ashland, OR	19.0	4.3	891	2,981	719	521	⇔	43.49	154
Melbourne–Titusville–Palm Bay, FL	13.9	4.0	2,538	6,846	2,210	952	⇔	56.32	100
Memphis, TN–AR–MS	6.5	2.9	7,452	11,328	7,624	1,935	⇔	82.28	39
Merced, CA	−5.2	3.8	1,095	1,659	1,017	717	⇔	37.26	195
Miami, FL	7.9	2.4	358	27,578	2,265	4,984	⇓	73.35	53
✓ **Middlesex–Somerset–Hunterdon, NJ**	10.5	4.6	1,487	30,699	4,699	7,696	⇔	88.41	31
Milwaukee–Waukesha, WI	9.0	2.1	1,705	18,548	2,694	2,781	⇑	66.34	67
✓ **Minneapolis–St. Paul, MN–WI**	16.0	3.7	15,468	56,369	16,991	12,680	⇔	99.95	6
Mobile, AL	18.8	2.7	1,798	5,481	1,624	1,691	⇔	52.95	116
Modesto, CA	9.9	3.3	2,180	4,198	2,153	775	⇔	48.77	130
Monmouth–Ocean, NJ	8.8	2.8	854	12,171	1,006	3,765	⇓	60.54	88
Monroe, LA	9.9	1.9	276	1,170	348	174	⇔	29.04	280
Montgomery, AL	15.7	2.5	916	3,890	1,177	707	⇔	41.38	168
Montreal, PQ	1.7	0.7	4,370	20,880	3,760	2,870	⇑	71.89	54
Muncie, IN	16.0	2.2	201	1,369	158	244	⇔	30.98	257
Myrtle Beach, SC	18.2	7.8	653	7,483	322	2,166	⇓	63.23	77
Naples, FL	20.9	7.3	1,850	6,410	611	1,522	⇓	62.59	82
Nashua, NH	4.1	2.2	−370	5,210	−370	780	⇑	33.08	234
✓ **Nashville, TN**	21.3	4.6	8,718	26,596	9,261	4,332	⇔	96.19	21
New Bedford, MA	3.9	1.4	−1,110	4,530	−890	460	⇑	25.98	305
New Haven–Meriden, CT	−4.9	0.3	−2,090	3,290	−2,120	1,790	⇔	21.85	336
New London–Norwich, CT–RI	1.9	2.5	−110	3,920	−430	580	⇑	31.48	254
New Orleans, LA	7.2	1.5	742	10,380	1,112	741	⇓	42.86	159
New York, NY	−5.7	−0.9	−24,796	−17,966	−33,626	−2,662	⇓	0.00	351
Newark, NJ	−3.0	−0.4	−6,331	2,498	−6,286	1,824	⇔	8.40	350
Newburgh, NY–PA	4.9	2.9	147	4,370	355	764	⇔	36.85	199

	Growth Rates 1990–1997	Growth Rates 1997–2000	NEW JOBS Blue Collar	NEW JOBS White Collar	NEW JOBS Good Earnings	NEW JOBS Average Earnings	Unemployment Threat	Score	Rank
Metro Area Average	8.1	2.9	1,355	9,682	1,454	1,933	⇔		
Norfolk–Virginia Beach–Newport News, VA–NC	3.0	3.1	2,834	23,840	3,207	1,882	⇑	70.98	56
✓ Oakland, CA	0.2	3.8	6,220	38,385	7,194	6,293	⇔	94.29	24
Ocala, FL	24.5	6.9	2,034	5,004	1,985	1,235	⇔	63.23	77
Odessa–Midland, TX	8.1	3.2	1,282	3,093	1,357	1,073	⇓	44.05	152
Oklahoma City, OK	2.7	2.4	3,235	10,831	3,204	1,512	⇔	60.23	90
Olympia, WA	19.5	4.8	772	4,043	609	1,025	⇓	48.29	132
Omaha, NE–IA	9.8	2.0	1,098	8,098	1,537	1,258	⇔	47.38	134
✓ Orange County, CA	2.4	5.6	10,124	80,369	19,503	17,156	⇔	99.97	4
✓ Orlando, FL	18.3	9.3	11,118	71,896	11,526	10,226	⇓	99.90	8
Oshawa, ON	8.6	3.7	420	1,540	350	260	⇑	34.31	220
✓ Phoenix–Mesa, AZ	17.8	5.1	12,020	64,155	13,086	19,984	⇔	[illegible]	7
Pine Bluff, AR	5.2	1.0	163	298	190	232	⇑	25.09	312
Pittsburgh, PA	4.2	1.5	−2,270	21,457	−1,664	2,933	⇔	45.04	144
Pittsfield, MA	−4.3	0.2	−480	660	−620	80	⇔	18.59	343
Portland, ME	2.7	4.4	350	7,860	380	1,810	⇔	49.49	127
✓ Portland–Vancouver, OR–WA	18.3	4.1	10,731	33,466	11,692	7,466	⇔	98.87	17
Portsmouth–Rochester, NH–ME	14.1	8.5	1,360	11,170	1,650	1,990	⇔	70.92	58
Providence–Fall River–Warwick, RI–MA	−1.0	1.7	−1,630	9,800	−2,110	1,900	⇔	32.65	238
Provo–Orem, UT	28.6	6.2	1,512	8,155	1,493	906	⇔	61.32	86
Pueblo, CO	11.6	2.1	76	1,220	20	143	⇓	28.64	285
Punta Gorda, FL	22.6	9.1	745	3,649	308	876	⇓	57.70	96
Quebec City, PQ	4.4	1.9	550	4,880	400	870	⇓	36.49	204
Racine, WI	7.0	1.8	108	1,590	110	157	⇑	27.71	295
✓ Raleigh–Durham–Chapel Hill, NC	24.8	6.7	10,918	37,826	10,617	9,391	⇔	99.49	12
Rapid City, SD	14.9	2.2	428	972	518	73	⇑	30.73	262
Reading, PA	2.0	1.2	−122	2,376	51	139	⇑	25.44	309
Redding, CA	9.8	3.7	538	2,419	488	233	⇓	36.08	211
Regina, SK	6.0	2.6	230	1,460	190	260	⇓	30.27	268
Reno, NV	13.7	2.9	970	4,791	1,411	164	⇓	40.26	174
Richland–Kennewick–Pasco, WA	20.9	3.3	317	3,059	163	471	⇓	38.25	191
Richmond–Petersburg, VA	9.5	3.2	3,355	17,108	4,105	4,881	⇔	79.75	41
✓ Riverside–San Bernardino, CA	13.3	5.4	12,583	49,318	11,890	14,297	⇔	99.81	9
Roanoke, VA	8.5	1.6	203	2,378	585	329	⇔	30.62	265
Rochester, MN	13.7	3.3	717	2,243	731	225	⇔	36.67	201
Rochester, NY	5.8	2.8	1,851	16,668	2,160	1,449	⇑	60.13	91
Rockford, IL	10.1	1.9	−114	4,000	−111	290	⇑	30.84	260
Rocky Mount, NC	8.4	4.1	850	2,502	1,042	731	⇑	41.77	167

	Growth Rates		NEW JOBS						
	1990–1997	1997–2000	Blue Collar	White Collar	Good Earnings	Average Earnings	Unemployment Threat	Score	Rank
Metro Area Average	8.1	2.9	1,355	9,682	1,454	1,933	⇔		
✓ Sacramento, CA	6.0	6.3	8,552	42,942	6,008	16,648	⇓	98.91	16
Saginaw–Bay City–Midland, MI	9.1	2.1	−287	4,692	−111	72	⇑	30.06	269
St. Catharines–Niagara, ON	1.2	0.5	250	1,530	200	180	⇑	24.44	315
St. Cloud, MN	22.6	5.7	1,378	5,025	1,683	797	⇔	55.40	105
Saint John, NB	3.4	1.5	450	1,970	380	250	⇔	28.59	286
St. John's, NF	5.1	2.2	130	1,020	120	100	⇓	27.34	297
St. Joseph, MO	3.3	0.2	225	−137	198	−107	⇑	20.82	340
St. Louis, MO–IL	7.4	2.0	2,611	27,775	1,774	2,770	⇔	70.93	57
Salem, OR	17.0	3.1	1,593	3,645	1,342	741	⇔	45.36	142
Salinas, CA	−5.5	5.3	2,749	7,296	1,124	2,112	⇓	58.58	94
✓ Salt Lake City–Ogden, UT	23.8	5.7	10,105	34,093	8,525	9,079	⇔	98.82	18
San Angelo, TX	10.3	1.9	319	807	386	157	⇔	28.85	282
✓ San Antonio, TX	12.4	4.9	5,712	32,565	5,438	7,535	⇔	94.25	25
✓ San Diego, CA	4.0	6.0	13,823	75,859	15,331	14,655	⇔	99.96	5
San Francisco, CA	−1.9	2.1	874	24,535	−2,917	3,882	⇓	5.61	103
✓ San Jose, CA	2.3	2.9	7,998	23,177	11,749	991	⇑	90.02	28
San Luis Obispo–Atascadero–Paso Robles, CA	8.5	4.7	848	4,618	767	1,055	⇓	46.90	135
Santa Barbara–Santa Maria–Lompoc, CA	7.6	3.4	1,907	6,128	1,087	1,527	⇔	51.12	120
Santa Cruz–Watsonville, CA	12.2	3.9	1,926	3,551	1,385	560	⇔	46.13	137
Santa Fe, NM	23.9	4.7	497	4,067	474	684	⇓	45.98	138
Santa Rosa, CA	17.2	5.6	3,994	9,612	3,127	2,107	⇔	73.75	52
Sarasota–Bradenton, FL	25.7	7.0	2,478	19,468	2,117	1,689	⇓	77.46	46
Saskatoon, SK	11.8	5.1	180	1,230	140	170	⇓	36.27	208
Savannah, GA	10.7	2.5	857	3,172	852	337	⇔	36.55	203
Scranton–Wilkes-Barre–Hazleton, PA	3.3	0.7	−1,062	3,488	−720	540	⇑	24.35	316
✓ Seattle–Bellevue–Everett, WA	9.3	3.5	14,645	39,669	15,141	8,335	⇔	99.72	10
Sharon, PA	3.0	1.8	−393	1,429	−329	99	⇔	24.50	314
Sheboygan, WI	14.7	2.5	911	872	991	132	⇑	33.91	223
Sherbrooke, PQ	1.5	0.6	200	810	160	120	⇔	23.48	318
Sherman–Denison, TX	8.6	2.3	233	1,018	168	193	⇑	29.25	278
Shreveport–Bossier City, LA	9.3	0.7	−402	1,872	−128	−66	⇔	23.30	321
Sioux City, IA–NE	7.0	2.5	280	1,625	323	71	⇔	29.60	274
Sioux Falls, SD	23.2	3.4	793	3,297	843	916	⇔	44.65	147
South Bend, IN	13.4	1.8	−38	2,835	−140	728	⇔	32.63	239
Spokane, WA	5.8	2.9	1,313	4,788	1,320	1,040	⇔	44.42	148
Springfield, IL	4.6	1.5	43	1,907	117	119	⇓	26.53	301
Springfield, MA	−2.8	0.4	−1,450	2,560	−1,630	240	⇔	17.99	344
Springfield, MO	23.3	6.0	2,022	10,119	2,413	1,554	⇔	67.96	62
Stamford–Norwalk, CT	−3.2	0.9	−2,260	6,940	−1,730	3,960	⇔	33.77	225
State College, PA	10.3	3.7	660	2,366	539	550	⇔	38.42	187
Steubenville–Weirton, OH–WV	−0.4	−0.3	−554	364	−463	−4	⇑	17.74	345
Stockton–Lodi, CA	9.8	2.3	1,400	3,994	1,073	1,088	⇔	42.73	160
Sudbury, ON	5.5	2.3	190	1,030	140	180	⇓	28.44	287
Sumter, SC	9.3	2.6	537	853	548	308	⇑	32.19	245
Syracuse, NY	0.1	1.4	−10	5,661	−459	467	⇔	29.62	273
Tacoma, WA	15.2	5.1	2,077	14,344	1,849	3,884	⇔	73.95	51

	Growth Rates 1990–1997	Growth Rates 1997–2000	NEW JOBS Blue Collar	NEW JOBS White Collar	NEW JOBS Good Earnings	NEW JOBS Average Earnings	Unemployment Threat	Score	Rank
Metro Area Average	8.1	2.9	1,355	9,682	1,454	1,933	⇔		
Tallahassee, FL	16.0	4.2	614	6,701	372	2,337	⇓	53.83	109
✓ **Tampa–St. Petersburg–Clearwater, FL**	16.0	5.8	9,083	64,828	9,244	8,862	⇓	99.36	14
Terre Haute, IN	16.0	2.5	325	1,837	274	226	⇔	32.66	237
Texarkana, TX–Texarkana, AR	4.9	2.4	225	1,304	101	174	⇔	28.77	283
Thunder Bay, ON	1.6	0.7	170	860	160	80	⇔	23.38	319
Toledo, OH	8.9	1.1	−1,070	5,168	−1,102	471	⇔	26.64	300
Topeka, KS	6.3	1.9	89	2,173	150	525	⇓	30.67	263
Toronto, ON	0.3	0.1	5,710	28,350	4,630	5,020	⇔	82.89	38
Trenton, NJ	4.5	1.7	−546	4,422	−343	2,131	⇓	36.66	202
			[illegible]	[illegible]	[illegible]	[illegible]	⇔	25.29	310
Ventura, CA	13.1	5.3	3,603	16,237	3,947	[illegible]	[illegible]	[illegible]	[illegible]
Victoria, BC	15.6	6.7	240	2,290	150	390	⇓	43.94	153
Victoria, TX	9.8	3.2	289	1,078	317	447	⇓	33.47	229
Vineland–Millville–Bridgeton, NJ	−0.1	0.8	−304	848	−137	233	⇑	22.51	326
Visalia–Tulare–Porterville, CA	13.7	2.6	886	3,257	946	543	⇓	38.86	183
Waco, TX	15.4	2.0	551	1,754	626	306	⇔	33.21	231
✓ **Washington, DC–MD–VA–WV**	6.3	3.2	9,322	91,872	10,828	14,993	⇓	99.72	10
Waterbury, CT	−4.9	0.3	−2,090	3,290	−2,120	1,790	⇔	21.85	336
Waterloo–Cedar Falls, IA	8.3	3.3	−172	2,853	−114	433	⇑	33.36	230
Wausau, WI	16.9	3.8	1,285	1,629	1,561	427	⇑	42.47	164
✓ **West Palm Beach–Boca Raton, FL**	18.1	6.1	3,943	29,876	3,693	4,329	⇓	89.21	29
Wheeling, WV–OH	5.6	2.2	−253	1,923	−70	210	⇓	27.78	292
Wichita, KS	7.6	3.1	1,962	8,182	2,009	1,226	⇑	53.12	114
Wichita Falls, TX	7.4	3.1	612	2,003	505	338	⇔	34.48	219
Williamsport, PA	4.8	0.6	−129	512	−146	83	⇑	22.27	331
Wilmington, NC	18.6	4.7	824	4,552	362	1,385	⇔	49.82	124
Wilmington–Newark, DE–MD	5.5	2.2	77	7,319	246	3,893	⇔	50.26	122
Windsor, ON	2.4	1.0	410	1,590	340	190	⇑	26.46	303
Winnipeg, MB	0.6	0.3	940	4,490	780	750	⇔	32.48	241
Worcester, MA–CT	−0.7	1.9	−970	7,920	−730	1,610	⇔	35.16	215
Yakima, WA	7.7	1.8	867	1,169	895	119	⇔	30.75	261
Yolo, CA	28.4	5.4	1,259	4,269	1,983	1,017	⇓	56.39	99
York, PA	6.2	3.4	1,081	5,730	1,184	743	⇑	44.10	151
Youngstown–Warren, OH	5.0	1.5	−1,238	5,789	−940	643	⇑	28.17	288
Yuba City, CA	11.2	3.1	383	1,500	247	291	⇔	33.21	231
Yuma, AZ	22.7	3.7	1,038	1,570	407	473	⇓	40.48	172

Et Cetera

LIFE IN A BOOM TOWN

If you could live anywhere you choose, would you choose a boom town? There are practically none in North America at this writing. But if there were, the advantages would include rising personal incomes ensuring real estate appreciation; expanding personal employment opportunities; improved infrastructures; somewhat lower violent crime; increasing amenities; and high-quality health care and education.

The disadvantages of living in a boom town include rising costs of living; increased property crime rates; environmental pollution; and, maybe worst of all, noticeable loss of personal discretionary time.

But if you stay in a no-growth area, you face possible job loss, depreciating value of real estate, boarded-up businesses, and backwater schools and health care. Any advantages? Try declining living costs, increased personal time, and lower crime rates.

Employment opportunities are the single most important factor behind geographic mobility. Joblessness or underemployment can push a settled person to become a mobile one. Consider, for example, that in 1980 you moved from withering Chicago or Detroit to booming Los Angeles. Now it's 1997 and you're thinking about your next move. Who would have guessed during the 1980 job boom that California would be grabbing the ropes a decade later, or that the Great Lakes states would be well into their own comeback?

The past decade has seen some surprising shifts in regional economic growth. So the big question remains: Will a move to Anaheim or San Jose or Raleigh really solve your jobless or underemployment problem? If there is any trend to be spotted from the past, it is that boom times and slumps aren't permanent in any metro area.

A JOBS MENU

Using the terms "white collar" or "blue collar" to distinguish between jobs that deal with information or things, are mental or physical, clean or messy, salaried or hourly, high-paying or low-paying, year-round or seasonal, skilled or unskilled, professional or unionized, isn't always precise.

According to Standard Occupational Classification definitions, white-collar jobs take in professional and technical workers, managers and administrators, sales workers, and clerical workers. Blue-collar occupations include craftsworkers, mechanics and installers, production operatives, drivers, and nonfarm laborers.

But a quick look at some white-collar clerical job titles in the following chart shows that many can be as unskilled, non-salaried, and seasonal as jobs in the laboring category, while many blue-collar craftsworker jobs can be as skilled, salaried, and highly paid as those in the professional and technical category.

Job Prospects

The numbers next to each job title are thousands of new job openings forecasted for the ten-year period ending in 2005 due to expansion and replacing workers who've left the labor force. An up arrow (⇑) indicates a rate of growth higher than 25 percent, while a down arrow (⇓) indicates that jobs in this area will be found only by taking the place of workers who've changed careers, retired, died, or otherwise moved on.

Education

Jobs requiring a high school diploma are indicated by **(HS)**. Jobs needing postsecondary training **(PS)** require education beyond high school but short of a bachelor's degree, including on-the-job training, vocational school, or community college. College and above **(C)** demands at least a bachelor's degree. If no education is indicated, as in the case for actors and musicians, the job may be entered with less than a high school education.

For some jobs a range of education levels is shown. For example, some high school graduates become administrative services managers by advancing through the ranks of an organization. Even though a higher degree is not always required for administrative services managers, a college degree boosts their chance of advancing to top-level management. Education requirements also vary within an occupation. For instance, nursing can be entered by earning a diploma, associate degree, or bachelor's degree.

Working Conditions

Repetitious means a job in which the same duties are performed continuously in a short period of time. Sometimes a machine sets the pace of work. Examples include workers on automotive assembly lines as well as cashiers and bank tellers.

Geographically concentrated means the job is localized in a particular region. Most textile jobs are concentrated in a handful of states. Advertising and public relations jobs are found mainly in large cities. Most petroleum and mining engineers are found along the Gulf of Mexico and in the Southwest.

Mobile means different work settings for workers who don't stay in a single office, factory, or laboratory. For example, in addition to working in an office, property and real estate managers frequently visit properties they oversee; manufacturing sales representatives travel to different cities to visit customers; and messengers deliver packages to various locations.

Physical stamina means physically demanding. Workers must endure physical stress and strain, including lifting heavy objects. Construction work is often strenuous, and workers spend most of the day on their feet—bending, kneeling, lifting, and maneuvering heavy objects. On the other hand, teachers spend much of their day on their feet, which is physically tiring. However, the table does not indicate physical stamina as a key characteristic of teachers because they can teach while sitting at a desk.

Part-time indicates opportunities for part-time work are favorable. Most waiters and waitresses work part-time, as do retail salesworkers and security guards. Many medical assistants, cooks, librarians, and teacher assistants also work part-time.

Irregular hours means working under a schedule that's not the standard 8-hour day. This can include night or weekend shifts, rotating schedules, or working for several days and then having several days off. Many nurses and security guards work nights or weekends. Other occupations that work on shifts include firefighters, pilots, real estate agents, and flight attendants.

OCCUPATIONS	Jobs in Thousands	Growth Rate %	Education	us	ally ted	ile	ina	me	urs
EXECUTIVE, ADMINISTRATIVE, AND MANAGERIAL									
Accountants and auditors	312		C						
Administrative services managers	87		HS, PS, C						
Budget analysts	19		C						
Construction and building inspectors	28		HS, PS			•	•		
Construction contractors and managers	97	⇑	PS, C			•			
Cost estimators	48		PS, C						
Education administrators	176		C						
Employment interviewers	43		PS						
Engineering, science, and data processing managers	165	⇑	C						
Financial managers	324		C						
Food services and lodging managers, restaurant and hotel	313	⇑	C						•
General managers and top executives	1,104		C						
Government chief executives and legislators	26		C			•		•	•
Health services managers			C						
Industrial production managers	43	⇓	C						
Inspectors and compliance officers except construction	50		C			•			
Management analysts and consultants	109		C						
Marketing, advertising, and public relations managers	211	⇑	C						
Personnel, training, and labor relations specialists and managers	104		C		•				
Property and real estate managers	81		C			•			
Purchasing agents and managers	55		PS, C						
Underwriters	25		PS, C						
Wholesale and retail buyers and merchandise managers	50		PS, C						
PROFESSIONAL SPECIALTY									
Engineers									
Aerospace engineers	16		C						
Chemical engineers	21		C						

OCCUPATIONS	New Jobs in Thousands	Growth Rate %	Education	Job Characteristics					
				repetitious	geographically concentrated	mobile	physical stamina	part-time	irregular hours
Civil engineers	90		C						
Electrical and electronics engineers	157		C						
Industrial engineers	47		C						
Mechanical engineers	98		C						
Metallurgical, ceramic, and materials engineers	6		C						
Mining engineers	1	⇓	C		•				
Nuclear engineers	5		C		•				
Petroleum engineers	4	⇓	C		•				
Architects and surveyors									
Architects	35		C						
Landscape architects	5		C		•				
Surveyors	30	⇓	PS, C			•			
Computer, mathematical, and operations research occupations									
Actuaries	4		C						
Computer systems analysts	819	⇑	C						
Mathematicians	3		C						
Operations research analysts	35	⇑	C						
Statisticians	3		C						
Lawyers and judicial workers									
Judges and magistrates	11		C						
Lawyers	268	⇑	C						
Life scientists									
Agricultural scientists	12		C						
Biological scientists	43	⇑	C						
Foresters and conservation scientists	18		C		•	•	•		
Physical scientists									
Chemists	45		C						
Geologists and geophysicists	24		C						
Meteorologists	2		C						
Physicists and astronomers	5	⇓	C						
Social scientists and urban planners									
Economists and marketing research analysts	30	⇑	C						
Psychologists	45		C						
Sociologists	15		C						
Urban and regional planners	13		C						
Social and recreation workers									
Human services workers	170	⇑	PS, C			•			•
Social workers	288	⇑	C			•			
Recreation workers	86		HS, PS, C			•	•	•	•
Religious workers									
Protestant ministers	22		PS, C			•			•
Rabbis	5		PS, C			•			•
Roman Catholic priests	15		PS, C			•			•
Teachers, librarians, and counselors									
Adult education teachers	211		C					•	•
Archivists and curators	9		C					•	•
College and university faculty	395		C						

OCCUPATIONS	New Jobs in Thousands	Growth Rate %	Education	repetitious	geographically concentrated	mobile	physical stamina	part-time	irregular hours
				Job Characteristics					
Counselors	93		C						
Kindergarten and elementary school teachers	726	⇑	C						
Librarians	47		C					•	•
Secondary school teachers	782	⇑	C						
Health diagnosing occupations									
Chiropractors	20	⇑	C						•
Dentists	54		C						•
Optometrists	12		C						•
Physical therapists	[illegible]	[illegible]	[illegible]						
Physician assistants	22		C						•
Recreational therapists	11		C			•	•	•	
Registered nurses	740	⇑	PS, C				•	•	•
Respiratory therapists	37	⇑	PS, C						
Speech-language pathologists and audiologists	52		C						
Communications occupations									
Public relations specialists	44		C		•				
Radio and television announcers and newscasters	21	⇓	HS, PS, C						•
Reporters and correspondents	13	⇓	C			•			•
Writers and editors	111		PS, C						
Visual arts occupations									
Designers	130	⇑	HS, PS, C						
Photographers and camera operators	61	⇑	PS			•			
Visual artists	117		HS, PS, C						
Performing arts occupations									
Actors, directors, producers	47	⇑				•	•	•	•
Dancers, choreographers	11					•			•
Musicians, conductors	105								
TECHNICIANS AND RELATED SUPPORT									
Health technologists and technicians									
Clinical laboratory technologists	86		PS, C	•					
Dental hygienists	74	⇑	PS					•	
Dispensing opticians	28		HS, PS						
EEG technologists	3	⇑	PS	•					
EKG technicians	3	⇓	HS	•					
Emergency medical technicians	72	⇑	PS			•		•	•
Licensed practical nurses	341	⇑	PS				•	•	•
Medical record technicians	59	⇑	PS						•

OCCUPATIONS	New Jobs in Thousands	Growth Rate %	Education	Job Characteristics: repetitious	geographically concentrated	mobile	physical stamina	part-time	irregular hours
Nuclear medicine technologists	5	⇑	PS						
Radiologic technologists	82	⇑	PS	•					
Surgical technologists	27	⇑	PS						
Technicians except health									
Aircraft pilots	32		C			•			•
Air traffic controllers	6	⇓	HS, PS, C						•
Broadcast technicians	9	⇓	PS						•
Computer programmers	228		C						
Drafters	70		PS						
Engineering technicians	207		PS						
Library technicians	9		HS					•	•
Paralegals	74	⇑	PS						
Science technicians	79		PS						
Tool programmers, numerical control	34	⇓	PS, C						
MARKETING AND SALES									
Cashiers	1,772			•				•	•
Counter and rental clerks	203	⇑		•				•	•
Insurance agents and brokers	88		PS, C						
Real estate agents, brokers, and appraisers	113		HS, PS			•		•	•
Retail sales workers	1,821							•	•
Securities and financial services sales representatives	126	⇑	C						
Travel agents	55		HS					•	•
ADMINISTRATIVE SUPPORT INCLUDING CLERICAL									
Adjusters, investigators, and collectors	399	⇑	HS, PS, C						
Bank tellers	244	⇓	HS, PS	•				•	
Clerical supervisors and managers	613		HS, PS, C						
Computer and peripheral equipment operators	62	⇓	PS						•
Credit clerks and authorizers	49		HS	•					
General office clerks	908		HS					•	
Information clerks									
Hotel and motel desk clerks	84		HS	•					
Interviewing and new accounts clerks	36		HS	•					
Mail clerks and messengers	70	⇓	HS	•		•	•	•	
Receptionists and information clerks	508	⇑	HS	•					
Reservation and transportation ticket agents and travel clerks	31	⇓	HS	•					
Material recording, scheduling, dispatching, and distributing									
Dispatchers	65		HS	•					•
Postal clerks and mail carriers	126		HS	•		•	•	•	
Stock clerks	443		HS	•					
Traffic, shipping, and receiving clerks	150		HS	•					
Record clerks									
Billing clerks	98		HS	•					
Bookkeeping, accounting, and auditing clerks	400	⇓	HS	•					
Brokerage clerks and statement clerks	9		HS	•					
File clerks	102	⇓	HS	•					

OCCUPATIONS	New Jobs in Thousands	Growth Rate %	Education	Job Characteristics: repetitious	geographically concentrated	mobile	physical stamina	part-time	irregular hours
Order clerks	95		HS	•					
Payroll and timekeeping clerks	35	↓	HS	•					
Personnel clerks	27	↓	HS	•					
Secretaries	1,102		HS						
Stenographers and court reporters	22		PS	•				•	
Teacher aides	480	↑	HS, PS					•	
[illegible]	81		HS	•					•
[illegible]	[illegible]	[illegible]	HS	•					
Guards									
Police, dectectives, and special agents	416		HS	•					
Food and beverage preparation and service occupations									
Chefs, cooks, and other kitchen workers	1,102		HS, PS	•				•	•
Food and beverage service workers	2,263		HS	•				•	•
Health service occupations									
Dental assistants	137	↑	HS					•	
Medical assistants	155	↑	HS					•	
Nursing aids and psychiatric aides	594	↑	HS, PS					•	•
Personal service and cleaning occupations									
Animal caretakers except farm	62	↑	HS			•	•		•
Barbers and cosmetologists	253	↓	PS	•				•	•
Flight attendants	49	↑	HS, PS			•			•
Gardeners and groundskeepers	128			•		•	•	•	•
Homemaker-home health aides	488	↑				•		•	
Janitors and cleaners	1,140			•			•	•	•
Private household workers	245	↓				•	•	•	•
AGRICULTURE, FORESTRY, FISHING									
Farm operators and managers	221				•	•	•		•
Fishers, hunters, and trappers	11	↓			•	•	•	•	•
Timber cutting and logging workers	22				•	•	•		•
MECHANICS, INSTALLERS, AND REPAIRERS									
Aircraft mechanics and engine specialists	49								
Automotive body repairers	92		PS				•		
Automotive mechanics	347		PS				•		
Electronic equipment repairers									
Commercial and industrial electronic equipment repairers	20		PS			•	•		
Communications equipment mechanics	26		PS			•	•		
Computer and office machine repairers	66		PS			•	•		
Electronic home entertainment equipment repairers	9	↓	PS			•	•		

OCCUPATIONS	New Jobs in Thousands	Growth Rate %	Education	Job Characteristics: repetitious	geographically concentrated	mobile	physical stamina	part-time	irregular hours
Elevator installers and repairers	10		HS			•	•		
Farm equipment repairers	17		PS				•		
General maintenance mechanics	508		PS				•		
Heating, air-conditioning, and refrigeration technicians	125	⇑	HS, PS			•	•		
Home appliance and power tool repairers	19	⇓				•	•		
Industrial machinery repairers	173		PS			•	•		•
Millwrights	20	⇓							
Mobile heavy equipment mechanics	37		PS				•		
Motorcycle, boat, and small engine mechanics	14		PS				•		
Musical instrument repairers and tuners	4					•	•		
Telephone installers and repairers	43	⇓	PS			•	•		
Vending machine servicers and repairers	4		HS			•	•		
CONSTRUCTION TRADES									
Bricklayers and stonemasons	43		HS, PS	•		•	•		
Carpenters	290		HS, PS			•	•		
Carpet installers	28		HS, PS	•		•	•		
Concrete masons and terrazzo workers	41		HS, PS			•	•		
Drywall workers and lathers	50		HS, PS			•	•		
Electricians	152		HS, PS			•	•		
Glaziers	9		HS, PS			•	•		
Insulation workers	34		HS, PS	•		•	•		
Numerical-control machine-tool operators	175		HS	•					•
Painters and paperhangers	174		HS, PS	•		•	•	•	
Plasterers	11		HS, PS	•		•	•		
Plumbers and pipefitters	92		PS			•	•		
Roofers	42		HS, PS	•		•	•		
Roustabouts	5				•	•	•		•
Sheet-metal workers	45		PS			•	•		
Structural and reinforcing ironworkers	19		HS, PS		•	•	•		
Tilesetters	7		HS, PS	•		•	•		
PRODUCTION									
Assemblers									
Blue-collar worker supervisors	480		HS						•
Precision assemblers	91	⇓	HS	•					
Food processing occupations									
Butchers and meat, poultry, and fish cutters	58	⇓	HS	•					
Inspectors, testers, and graders	138	⇓	HS	•					•
Metalworking and plastics-working occupations									
Boilermakers	4	⇓	HS			•	•		
Jewelers	8		PS						
Machinists	79	⇓							
Metalworking and plastics-working machine operators	152		HS	•					•
Tool and die makers	34	⇓	PS						•
Welders, cutters, and welding machine operators	28		PS	•			•		•

OCCUPATIONS	New Jobs in Thousands	Growth Rate %	Education	repetitious	geographically concentrated	mobile	physical stamina	part-time	irregular hours
Plant and systems operators									
Electric power-generating plant operators and power distributors	10	⇓	HS						•
Stationary engineers	7	⇓	HS						•
Water and wastewater treatment plant operators	30		HS						•
Printing occupations									
Prepress workers	43		HS						•
Printing press operators	62		HS	•					•
[illegible]	18		HS	•					
Dental laboratory technicians	11		PS, C						
Ophthalmic laboratory technicians	7		PS, C	•					
Painting and coating machine operators	47			•					
Photographic process workers	17		HS	•				•	•
TRANSPORTATION AND MATERIAL MOVING									
Busdrivers	193		HS	•		•		•	•
Material moving equipment operators	298		HS, PS	•		•			
Truckdrivers	823		HS	•		•	•		•
Water transportation occupations	10	⇓	HS, C			•	•		•

LEGAL HOLIDAYS

Properly speaking, the United States has no national holidays. A day off on Independence Day, Thanksgiving, or Christmas comes by the grace of local state legislatures rather than presidential proclamations or acts of Congress.

The only thing *national* about the U.S. holiday calendar is the 10 days off given to everyone who works for the federal government: Christmas, Independence Day, Labor Day, New Year's Day, Thanksgiving, and five Mondays—Columbus Day, Memorial Day, Veterans Day, Washington's Birthday, and Martin Luther King Day. The first four holiday Mondays were approved in 1968 to create predictable long weekends. The fifth, approved in 1986, honors Martin Luther King, Jr., on the third Monday of January.

Most states observe federal legal holidays, and, depending on where you are, they commemorate 72 local ones as well. The Civil War era produced more events and heroes to honor with days off than any other period in American history. However, they aren't all celebrated nationwide. Just as no former secessionist state takes notice of Lincoln's birthday, so none of the Union states honor Robert E. Lee's birthday. Memorial Day, a date originally created to mourn those who died for the Union cause, isn't observed in Alabama, Mississippi, or South Carolina. Those states, as well as Florida, Georgia, Kentucky, and Louisiana, celebrate Confederate Memorial Day instead.

In contrast, the Canadian provinces celebrate 10 national holidays in harmony with the terms of Canada's Holidays Act. Four days—Christmas, Labour Day, New Year's Day, and Remembrance Day (formerly Armistice Day, as was the U.S.'s Veterans Day)— may be said to be North American holidays since they are celebrated on the same date for the same reason throughout the United States. Again, depending on where you are in Canada, some 15 local holidays are observed as well.

A North American List of Days

JANUARY

Fixed Dates

January 1, *New Year's Day*: All states and Canadian provinces
January 8, *Battle of New Orleans Day*: Louisiana
January 15, *Martin Luther King Day*: All states
January 19, *Robert E. Lee's Birthday*: Arkansas, Florida, Kentucky, Louisiana, and South Carolina; *Confederate Heroes Day*: Texas
January 30, *Franklin D. Roosevelt's Birthday*: Kentucky

Movable Feasts

Third Monday, *Robert E. Lee's Birthday*: Alabama and Mississippi; *Lee-Jackson-King Day*: Virginia

FEBRUARY

Fixed Dates

February 12, *Lincoln's Birthday*: Alaska, California, Colorado, Connecticut, Florida, Illinois, Indiana, Iowa, Kansas, Kentucky, Maryland, Missouri, Montana, New Jersey, New Mexico, New York, Utah, Vermont, Washington, and West Virginia
February 15, *Susan B. Anthony's Birthday*: Florida and Minnesota
February 19, *Robert E. Lee Day*: Kentucky

Movable Feasts

First Monday, *Lincoln's Birthday*: Delaware and Oregon
Second Monday, *Lincoln Day*: Arizona
Third Monday, *Washington's Birthday*: All states; *Alberta Family Day*: Alberta
Tuesday before Ash Wednesday, *Mardi Gras*: Alabama, Florida (some counties), and Louisiana (some parishes)

MARCH

Fixed Dates

March 2, *Texas Independence Day*: Texas
March 17, *Evacuation Day*: Massachusetts (Suffolk County only)
March 20, *Youth Day*: Oklahoma
March 25, *Maryland Day*: Maryland
March 26, *Prince Jonah Kuhio Kalanianaole Day*: Hawaii

Movable Feasts

First Monday, *Casimir Pulaski's Birthday*: Illinois
First Tuesday, *Town Meeting Day*: Vermont
Second Monday, *Commonwealth Day*: Newfoundland
Nearest Monday to March 17, *St. Patrick's Day*: Newfoundland
Last Monday, *Seward's Day*: Alaska

APRIL

Fixed Dates

April 2, *Pascua Florida Day*: Florida
April 3, *Arbor Day*: Arizona
April 13, *Thomas Jefferson's Birthday*: Alabama and Oklahoma
April 21, *San Jacinto Day*: Texas
April 22, *Arbor Day*: Nebraska; *Oklahoma Day*: Oklahoma
April 26, *Confederate Memorial Day*: Florida and Georgia

Movable Feasts

Two days before Easter, *Good Friday*: Delaware, Florida, Hawaii, Indiana, Louisiana, Maryland, New Jersey, North Dakota, Pennsylvania, Tennessee, Wisconsin, and all Canadian provinces
One day after Easter, *Easter Monday*: North Carolina and all Canadian provinces
Third Monday, *Patriots' Day*: Maine and Massachusetts
Nearest Monday to April 23, *St. George's Day*: Newfoundland
Fourth Monday, *Fast Day*: New Hampshire
Last Monday, *Confederate Memorial Day*: Alabama and Mississippi

MAY

Fixed Dates

May 1, *Bird Day*: Oklahoma
May 4, *Rhode Island Independence Day*: Rhode Island
May 8, *Truman Day*: Missouri
May 10, *Confederate Memorial Day*: South Carolina
May 11, *Minnesota Day*: Minnesota
May 20, *Mecklenburg Independence Day*: North Carolina
May 25, *Memorial Day*: New Mexico, South Dakota, and Vermont
May 30, *Memorial Day*: Delaware, Illinois, Maryland, and New Hampshire

Movable Feasts

First Tuesday after first Monday, *Primary Election Day*: Indiana
First Monday before May 25, *Victoria Day and the Sovereign's Birthday*: All Canadian provinces
Last Monday, *Memorial Day*: All states except Alabama, Mississippi, and South Carolina, and those celebrating on May 25 or 30

JUNE

Fixed Dates

June 3, *Confederate Memorial Day*: Kentucky and Louisiana; *Jefferson Davis's Birthday*: Florida and South Carolina
June 9, *Senior Citizens Day*: Oklahoma
June 11, *King Kamehameha I Day*: Hawaii
June 14, *Flag Day*: Pennsylvania
June 15, *Separation Day*: Delaware
June 17, *Bunker Hill Day*: Massachusetts (Suffolk County only)
June 19, *Emancipation Day*: Texas
June 20, *West Virginia Day*: West Virginia
June 24, *Quebec Day*: Quebec

Movable Feasts

First Monday, *Jefferson Davis's Birthday*: Alabama and Mississippi
Nearest Monday to June 24, *Discovery Day*: Newfoundland

JULY

Fixed Dates

July 1, *Canada Day*: All Canadian provinces
July 4, *Independence Day*: All states
July 24, *Pioneer Day*: Utah

Movable Feasts

Nearest Monday to July 12, *Orangemen's Day*: Newfoundland

AUGUST

Fixed Dates

August 16, *Bennington Battle Day*: Vermont
August 27, *Lyndon Johnson's Birthday*: Texas
August 30, *Huey Long Day*: Louisiana

Movable Feasts

First Monday, *British Columbia Day*: British Columbia; *Civic Holiday*: Manitoba, Ontario, and Saskatchewan; *Colorado Day*: Colorado; *Heritage Day*: Alberta; *New Brunswick Day*: New Brunswick
Second Monday, *Victory Day*: Rhode Island
Third Friday, *Admission Day*: Hawaii

SEPTEMBER

Fixed Dates

September 9, *Admission Day*: California
September 12, *Defenders' Day*: Maryland
September 16, *Cherokee Strip Day*: Oklahoma

Movable Feasts

First Monday, *Labor Day*: All states and Canadian provinces
First Tuesday, *Primary Election Day*: Wisconsin
Second Tuesday, *Primary Election Day*: Wyoming
First Saturday after full moon, *Indian Day*: Oklahoma

OCTOBER

Fixed Dates

October 10, *Leif Erickson Day*: Minnesota; *Oklahoma Historical Day*: Oklahoma
October 12, *Columbus Day*: Maryland
October 18, *Alaska Day*: Alaska
October 31, *Nevada Day*: Nevada

Movable Feasts

Second Monday, *Columbus Day*: All states except Alaska, Iowa, Maryland, Michigan, Mississippi, Nevada, North Carolina, North Dakota, Oregon, South Carolina, and Washington
Thanksgiving Day: All Canadian provinces
Fourth Monday, *Veterans Day*: Arkansas, Montana, North Carolina, and Utah

NOVEMBER

Fixed Dates

November 1, *All Saints' Day*: Louisiana

ginia, Wisconsin, and Wyoming

DECEMBER

Fixed Dates

December 7, *Delaware Day*: Delaware
December 10, *Wyoming Day*: Wyoming
December 25, *Christmas Day*: All states and Canadian provinces
December 26, *Boxing Day*: All Canadian provinces

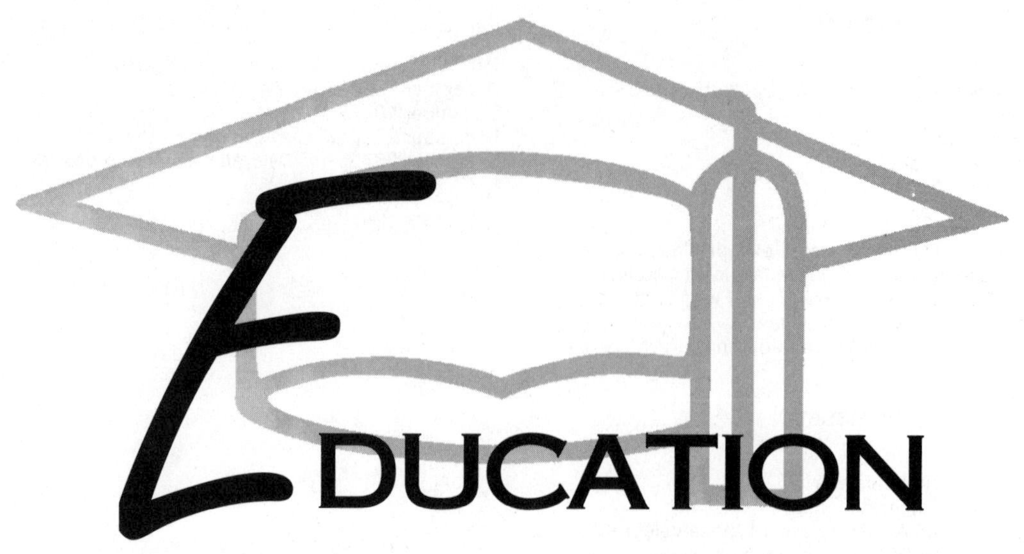

Nine months of the year, 3 people out of every 10 are either working in an educational institution or attending one as a student. Keeping the enterprise going is the biggest item on city budgets. Whether the results are worth all the money spent is sometimes an excuse for teachers, administrators, parents, politicians, and taxpayers to shout at each other.

Education is no longer the sacred cow it once was. The scores of high school students on most standardized tests aren't much better today than they were 30 years ago. A surprising number of high school seniors can't draw inferences from written material, write a persuasive essay, or solve a math problem requiring several steps.

Parents and teachers blame each other. Although the public trusts teachers more than they do politicians, journalists, or business eople, teachers don't get high marks. For their part, teachers are even stingier graders; most parents, they say, are too tired and uninterested to get involved in their child's schooling.

PUBLIC K-12

The quality of the public schools usually tips the balance when a relocating family weighs a neighborhood's good and bad points. But often their choice is influenced by a real estate agent's hearsay that the schools are great—or ought to be because the local tax rate is high. Are there ways to compare districts and schools more objectively? Definitely.

Shopping for a District

A sign of the times: In some of Long Island's 130 school districts, local cops check the addresses of children and discover interlopers who live beyond the district's boundaries taking up seats in local schools. Parents had registered their kids under the addresses of relatives or friends to meet residency requirements.

Moving into an unfamiliar area means tepping into a thicket of school districts, each with its own politics, funding, philosophy, standards, curricula, and results. Since your taxes support the district, you'll want to find out their differences with a consumer's eye. Visit the district principal or superintendent's office and consider several factors:

A good district can give you a written philosophy or a statement of educational objectives approved within the last five years by the state board of education. If educational philosophy and objectives are explicit and under constant examination and review, then a district takes its mission seriously.

The classroom teachers in the district should have not only a standard certificate but also (in 50 percent of the cases or better) at least a master's degree or equivalent in the subject they teach.

A district's holding power—that is, the percentage of its ninth-grade pupils who stay in school and finish—should be at least 90 percet. If 95 percent of a district's enrollment is in average daily attendance, that's a good indication of how closely parents and schools keep tabs on children.

Beware of the professional revolving door. A high number of eligible teachers not getting tenure might mean that the district has tough standards, but it could also be a sign that the district cuts costs by hiring beginners and then refusing them tenure at the end of their probationary period. Under this scheme, it is possible for a child to progress from kindergarten through high school and have inexperienced, unfamiliar teachers each year.

Shopping for a School

Outside Washington, DC, parents bring lawn chairs,

North America's Forty Largest School Districts

In the 1930s, America was fragmented into 128,000 school districts. After decades of consolidation, there are fewer than 15,000 (1,000 in Canada). They range in size from several hundred that don't operate schools (but bus children to other districts) to the giant ones listed below.

School System	Enrollment
New York City Public Schools	973,407
Los Angeles Unified District	680,848
City of Chicago Schools	405,102
Dade County (Miami)	300,107
Philadelphia City Schools	201,218
Houston Independent School District	198,190
Memphis City School District	110,271
Orange County (Orlando)	105,970
Montgomery County (MD) Schools	104,426
Metropolitan (Toronto) Separate Board	104,244
Peel Board of Education (Mississauga, ON)	96,345
Jefferson County (Louisville)	95,838
Pinellas County (St. Petersburg)	95,390
Milwaukee School District	92,475
Albuquerque Public Schools	91,768
Baltimore County Public Schools	88,932
Commission des Écoles Catholiques (Montréal)	87,659
Orleans Parish (New Orleans)	84,444
Jefferson County (CO) Schools	81,501
Scarborough (ON) Board of Education	79,703
Granite (Salt Lake City) District	77,998
Charlotte/Mecklenburg County (NC) Schools	77,332
Long Beach (CA) Unified District	75,825
Distric of Columbia Schools	75,794
De Kalb County (Decatur, GA) Schools	75,464
Cobb County (Marietta, GA) Schools	74,564
Fresno Unified District	74,105
Fort Worth Independent School District	71,012

Source: CMG Information Services.

paperbacks, and blankets days before the Prince George's County school district throws open a window to register children in choice magnet schools on a first-come, first-served basis.

Moving into a good school district won't necessarily mean that you'll find quality education in all of its schools. Get a district map of neighborhood boundaries for the schools as well as a list of Parent-Teacher Association (PTA) contacts. Talking with a local parent will save you time. Then make an appointment with the school's principal or the head guidance counselor to obtain specific information.

A good high school should have one guidance counselor for every 200 students, and it should have at least one full-time career counselor.

Classroom size in high school should average no more than 30 students. The size of the senior class shouldn't be less than 300 students. If the enrollment is much smaller than that, many worthwhile specialized courses won't be offered.

A quality high school should offer four years of English, three years of mathematics, three years of science, three years of social studies, two years of foreign languages; second-year courses in biology, astronomy, chemistry, and physics; college-preparatory courses in the humanities; at least one year of computer literacy; and Advanced Placement (AP) courses for college credit.

Don't cross a high school off your list if it doesn't measure up on all of these points. A school can have all but one or two and still be a good one. Relocation experts advise clients that the stability of a town is reflected best in its schools. If the high school is good, chances are that the schools at the lower levels will also be good.

In choosing an elementary school or a junior high, again ask questions of principals and other parents.

Class size in elementary schools should average no more than 20 pupils. Reading should be emphasized over all other subjects, but writing, problem solving in math, hands-on work in science, and the social studies curriculum should get their due.

In elementary schools, there should be a full-time librarian and a classroom-size library. There should also be one large room or auditorium for school meetings, arts performances, and special guest presentations.

In junior high or middle schools (grades 7, 8, and 9), there should be special provision for both bright students and slow learners.

PRIVATE K–12

One statistic about elementary and secondary education in the United States since 1930 is the nearly 100-percent growth in the number of private schools, in contrast to the 75-percent decline in the number of public schools. This isn't to say that the public schools are collapsing; most of the schools that have closed are rural, one-room buildings. But it does show that private schools are a thriving alternative.

Today, one out of nine school-age children attends a

Catholic Private Schools

Whatever the reason—religious content, cultural tradition, dress codes, discipline, a more rigorous education—at least one out of eight children attends a Catholic private school in these metro areas.

Dubuque, IA	34.9%
New Orleans, LA	19.9
Jersey City, NJ	19.8
Erie, PA	16.1
Owensboro, KY	15.8
Philadelphia, PA–NJ	15.2
Waterloo–Cedar Falls, IA	15.0
Cincinnati, OH–KY–IN	15.0
Toledo, OH	14.2
Bergen–Passaic, NJ	14.1
Cleveland–Lorain–Elyria, OH	13.9
St. Louis, MO–IL	13.8
Scranton–Wilkes-Barre–Hazleton, PA	13.1
Green Bay, WI	13.1
Wilmington–Newark, DE–MD	13.0
South Bend, IN	12.7
Louisville, KY–IN	12.6

Source: CMG Information Services.

The percentage of children attending Catholic schools in several Canadian metro areas is much higher than the list above. These are *public* schools, however, operating under separate Catholic school boards.

Non-Catholic Private Schools

While more than half of all private school pupils in the United States are in Catholic parochial systems, two out of three private schools are non-Catholic. Many are operated as religious schools by groups such as the Evangelical Lutheran Church, the Seventh-Day Adventist Board of Education, and the National Society for Hebrew Day Schools. Many others are nonsectarian. Below are metro areas where at least one child in 10 attends a non-Catholic private school.

Charlottesville, VA	15.5%
Clarksville–Hopkinsville, TN–KY	13.7
Tallahassee, FL	12.5
West Palm Beach–Boca Raton, FL	12.4
Lancaster, PA	11.7
Fort Lauderdale, FL	11.5
Chattanooga, TN–GA	11.3
Jackson, MS	10.9
Montgomery, AL	10.6
Wilmington–Newark, DE–MD	10.6
Trenton, NJ	10.3
Columbus, GA–AL	10.2
Benton Harbor, MI	10.2
Grand Rapids–Muskegon–Holland, MI	9.9
Savannah, GA	9.9
Jackson, TN	9.6
Baltimore, MD	9.3
Florence, SC	9.3
Dothan, AL	9.2
Tampa–St. Petersburg–Clearwater, FL	9.2
New York, NY	9.1
Honolulu, HI	9.0

Source: CMG Information Services.

private or parochial school. In spite of the decline in school enrollments during the 1980s, private schools held on to more of their enrollment than did public schools, losing only 6 percent as compared with 11 percent for public schools. Today, enrollment is on the rise in both sectors.

Recent research from the Department of Education shows that students in private high schools take more courses than their public school counterparts and that they take these courses in smaller classes. Critics of public education point out that because private institutions forgo the smorgasbord of electives that public schools offer their students, graduates of private high schools have tougher basic courses on their transcripts and are better prepared for college study. In fact, private school pupils generally score higher on the Scholastic Aptitude Tests (SATs) than students in public schools.

In most Canadian provinces, Catholic schools are publicly funded and run by separate school boards. In the United States, they are the private school alternative with the biggest enrollment (2.5 million pupils). Next (1.7 million pupils) comes what might be called "Other Religious," since this category takes in schools run by Protestant denominations, plus Jewish academies and day schools and non-denominational Christian academies. Non-sectarian schools enroll another 768,000 pupils, most of whom attend institutions belonging to the National Association of Independent Schools (NAIS).

COLLEGES AND UNIVERSITIES

Educators like to say that schooling leads to just three outcomes: more schooling, employment, or unemployment. When high school graduates go on to college or find jobs, the public education system is successful; if they do neither, the system is considered a flop.

In fact, nearly half of metro-area high school graduates eventually go to college, and 7 out of 10 of these begin their freshman year at an institution within 50 miles of home.

More than an Education

Everywhere from Abilene to Yuma, chamber of commerce promotional brochures tout local colleges and universities as frequently as other urban assets. And with good reason. Among the 20 million students taking college courses in North America, 15 million are studying in metro areas. For 21 million other people, the typical location for their evening or weekend continuing education course is a local college classroom.

Colleges and universities contribute other things besides education. In smaller metro areas, a worthy theater where a touring group of professional players can stage *Playboy of the Western World* or an auditorium where an orchestra and choral group can perform *The Messiah* can only be found at the local college campus.

Colleges and universities are stable white-collar em-

Grand Campuses: North America's Twenty Largest Universities

Some 15 million persons attend baccalaureate and graduate-level institutions in the United States and Canada. In both countries, slightly more men than women enroll, and in both countries, slightly more women than men graduate. Below are the continent's largest universities.

University	Students
University of Minnesota, Minneapolis	54,672
Ohio State University, Columbus	52,183
University of Toronto, Toronto	50,150
The University of Texas, Austin	49,253
University of Wisconsin, Madison	41,824
Texas A & M University, College Station	41,710
University of California, Los Angeles	35,407
University of Arizona, Tucson	35,129

Source: Statistics Canada, *Universities: Enrollment and Degrees*; U.S Department of Education, *Directory of Postsecondary Institutions.*

North America's Twenty Largest Community Colleges

About one in four people going on to college after high school attends a community college. Almost all institutions are publicly supported. Many of the largest ones below have several campuses.

College	Students
Miami–Dade (FL) Community College	53,683
Northern Virginia Community College	38,343
Houston Community College System	37,410
College of Du Page (Glen Ellyn, IL)	31,625
Central Piedmont Community College (Charlotte)	30,391
Pima Community College (Tucson)	30,175
City College of San Francisco	29,707
Oakland Community College (Bloomfield, MI)	29,363
Macomb Community College (Warren, MI)	28,943

Source: Statistics Canada, *Universities: Enrollment and Degrees*, U.S Department of Education, *Directory of Postsecondary Institutions.*

ployers, too. In Iowa City, IA, Lawrence, KS, and Bryan–College Station, TX, they are *the* major employers.

Finally, there is the connection between research-oriented universities and healthy economies. Two historic examples are Stanford University's impetus to the growth of Silicon Valley high-tech enterprises in San Jose and Bay Area environs, and MIT's faculty and alumni who started electronics firms along Route 128 outside of Boston.

Among nearly 4,000 higher education institutions in North America, the most common is the *Associate of Arts* college. Otherwise known as Community or Junior Colleges, these institutions offer associate of arts certificates or degree programs but no baccalaureate degrees to the 6 million full- and part-time students enrolled.

The 672 *Baccalaureate* institutions enroll 830,000 full- and part-time students. These colleges are undergraduate-level institutions exclusively; their highest offering is the bachelor's degree. They are typically private, though the largest baccalaureate college is public (Denver's Metropolitan State College, with 23,000 students).

Comprehensive institutions enroll another 3 million full- and part-time students. Of 953 in North America, the largest by far are branches of the California State University system. Comprehensive universities and colleges are mainly undergraduate institutions, though their highest offering is the master's degree.

Doctoral universities award the Ph.D as their highest degree. These institutions tend to be public and large. With 598 campuses, they enroll well over 5 million full- and part-time students.

SCORING: EDUCATION

To profile a metro area's academic features, *Places Rated* details the local mix of public and private schools and public and private colleges and universities.

Places Rated's tack for scoring, however, is based only on the variety of higher education options that meet the needs of residents: low-cost night and weekend continuing education courses for people who work, full-time graduate courses in the professions, courses leading to occupational certification in two-year colleges, and the traditional bachelor's degree curriculum offered in a college or university.

Counting colleges and universities reveals which metro areas are enriched and which aren't. But a clearer picture can be made by totaling up the number of students in the area's two-year schools and in its baccalaureate and graduate-level institutions.

Like ratings in the arts and transportation, ratings in education get better with population size. There are exceptions, though. One hundred and two metro areas are larger than Ann Arbor, MI, but only 12 are ranked higher in education. Likewise, Lincoln, NE, Bangor, ME, and Saskatoon, SK, are ranked much higher than their population size indicates.

To derive the higher education score, two major

criteria are used. The first is "College Town," which is enrollment weighted by number of years of typical attendance to get the highest degree offered (i.e., *Associate of Arts* enrollment is weighted by 2, *Baccalaureate* enrollment by 4, *Comprehensive* enrollment by 6, and *Doctoral* enrollment by 9). This large number is then divided by the metro area's population. On this criterion, places like Bryan–College Station, TX, or Lawrence, KS, come out very high.

But there's only one game in town in Bryan–College Station (Texas A&M) and in Lawrence (University of Kansas). Something else is needed to reward higher education variety. The second criterion, then, is total number of "available institutions." Here, the top-ranking places are New York, Chicago, and Los Angeles.

Combining these factors—"College Town" and "available institutions"—by weighting one-third for the first and two-thirds for the latter, produces the score. Scores are then normalized such that the 50th percentile is the average. Higher scores indicate more education options after high school; lower scores indicate fewer.

RANKINGS: Higher Education

The following criteria are used to rate a metro area for higher education opportunities available to residents: (1) enrollment in community or two-year colleges, (2) enrollment in baccalaureate-level institutions, (3) enrollment in comprehensive institutions, and (4) enrollment in doctoral-level institutions. Each factor is weighted progressively heavier, and no distinction is made between publicly and privately run institutions. Places with tie scores get the same rank and are listed alphabetically.

Metro Areas from Best to Worst

Places Rated Rank		Places Rated Score
1.	Boston, MA–NH	99.75
2.	New York, NY	99.65
3.	Chicago, IL	98.19
4.	Los Angeles–Long Beach, CA	97.91
5.	Oakland, CA	97.20
6.	San Francisco, CA	96.62
7.	Orange County, CA	95.80
8.	Long Island, NY	95.34
9.	Washington, DC–MD–VA–WV	95.26
10.	Baltimore, MD	94.95
11.	Philadelphia, PA–NJ	94.87
12.	San Jose, CA	94.48
13.	Ann Arbor, MI	94.34
14.	Springfield, MA	93.67
15.	Manchester, NH	93.09
16.	Newark, NJ	93.01
17.	Worcester, MA–CT	92.80
18.	Lawrence, KS	92.27
19.	Denver, CO	92.18
20.	Kansas City, MO–KS	91.68
21.	Detroit, MI	91.67
22.	New Haven–Meriden, CT	91.04
23.	Minneapolis–St. Paul, MN–WI	90.03
24.	St. Louis, MO–IL	90.00
25.	Dallas, TX	89.98
26.	Bangor, ME	89.80
27.	Seattle–Bellevue–Everett, WA	88.86
28.	Cleveland–Lorain–Elyria, OH	88.72
29.	Providence–Fall River–Warwick, RI–MA	87.96
30.	Portland–Vancouver, OR–WA	87.80
31.	Saskatoon, SK	87.80
32.	Phoenix–Mesa, AZ	87.45
33.	Burlington, VT	87.37
34.	Trenton, NJ	87.01
35.	San Diego, CA	86.92
36.	Riverside–San Bernardino, CA	86.86
37.	Omaha, NE–IA	86.58
38.	Atlanta, GA	86.09
39.	Lincoln, NE	85.98
40.	Pittsburgh, PA	85.83
41.	Raleigh–Durham–Chapel Hill, NC	85.70
42.	Lexington, KY	85.66
43.	Columbia, MO	85.04
44.	Dayton–Springfield, OH	84.94
45.	Portsmouth–Rochester, NH–ME	84.23
46.	Syracuse, NY	83.76
47.	Oklahoma City, OK	83.58
48.	Tuscaloosa, AL	83.36
49.	Milwaukee–Waukesha, WI	83.18
50.	Nashville, TN	83.10
51.	Portland, ME	82.99
52.	Columbus, OH	82.66
53.	Austin–San Marcos, TX	82.20
53.	Buffalo–Niagara Falls, NY	82.20
55.	Lansing–East Lansing, MI	81.49
56.	Miami, FL	81.33
57.	Albany–Schenectady–Troy, NY	81.01
58.	Charlotte–Gastonia–Rock Hill, NC–SC	80.96
59.	Sherbrooke, PQ	80.74
60.	Hartford, CT	80.31
61.	Scranton–Wilkes-Barre–Hazleton, PA	80.30
62.	Tampa–St. Petersburg–Clearwater, FL	80.24
63.	Huntsville, AL	80.16
64.	Bloomington–Normal, IL	79.19
65.	Springfield, MO	79.10
66.	Madison, WI	79.00
67.	Salem, OR	78.95
68.	Utica–Rome, NY	78.59
69.	Harrisburg–Lebanon–Carlisle, PA	78.55
70.	Grand Rapids–Muskegon–Holland, MI	78.35
71.	Cincinnati, OH–KY–IN	77.75
72.	Kalamazoo–Battle Creek, MI	77.65
73.	Des Moines, IA	77.52
74.	Greensboro–Winston-Salem–High Point, NC	77.47
75.	South Bend, IN	77.16
76.	Fort Worth–Arlington, TX	77.08
77.	Columbia, SC	76.19
78.	Daytona Beach, FL	76.02
79.	La Crosse, WI–MN	75.66
80.	Indianapolis, IN	75.53
81.	Cedar Rapids, IA	75.37
81.	Montreal, PQ	75.37
83.	Brockton, MA	74.75
84.	Rochester, NY	74.69
85.	Peoria–Pekin, IL	74.40
86.	St. Cloud, MN	74.23
87.	Akron, OH	73.61
88.	Birmingham, AL	73.40
89.	Lakeland–Winter Haven, FL	73.32
90.	Honolulu, HI	73.15
90.	Vancouver, BC	73.15
92.	Allentown–Bethlehem–Easton, PA	72.91
93.	Sacramento, CA	72.66

Places Rated Rank		Places Rated Score
94.	Orlando, FL	72.21
95.	Santa Barbara–Santa Maria–Lompoc, CA	72.11
96.	Flint, MI	71.56
97.	Provo–Orem, UT	71.50
98.	Toronto, ON	71.41
99.	Santa Fe, NM	71.34
100.	Houston, TX	71.20
101.	New Orleans, LA	71.11
102.	Colorado Springs, CO	70.97
103.	Salt Lake City–Ogden, UT	70.86
104.	London, ON	70.72
105.	Regina, SK	70.62
106.	Ventura, CA	70.27
107.	Norfolk–Virginia Beach–Newport News, VA–NC	69.94
108.	Halifax, NS	69.90
119.	Athens, GA	67.98
120.	Albuquerque, NM	67.51
121.	Bergen–Passaic, NJ	66.72
122.	Richmond–Petersburg, VA	66.62
123.	Santa Cruz–Watsonville, CA	66.14
124.	Greenville–Spartanburg–Anderson, SC	65.88
125.	Greeley, CO	65.69
126.	Kenosha, WI	65.66
127.	Lynchburg, VA	65.49
128.	Gary, IN	65.43
129.	Fargo–Moorhead, ND–MN	65.42
130.	Lawrence, MA–NH	65.19
131.	Montgomery, AL	64.73
132.	Spokane, WA	64.57
133.	Louisville, KY–IN	64.42
134.	Champaign–Urbana, IL	64.30
135.	Middlesex–Somerset–Hunterdon, NJ	64.22
136.	Nashua, NH	63.91
137.	Muncie, IN	63.88
138.	State College, PA	63.23
139.	Toledo, OH	62.84
140.	Fort Wayne, IN	62.76
141.	Iowa City, IA	62.67
142.	Knoxville, TN	62.01
143.	Davenport–Moline–Rock Island, IA–IL	61.67
144.	Green Bay, WI	61.36
145.	Grand Forks, ND–MN	61.22
146.	Reading, PA	60.60
147.	Winnipeg, MB	60.33
148.	Hattiesburg, MS	60.04
149.	Lancaster, PA	59.91
150.	Gainesville, FL	59.55
151.	Huntington–Ashland, WV–KY–OH	59.40
152.	Fitchburg–Leominster, MA	59.19
153.	Jackson, TN	58.89
154.	Springfield, IL	58.58
155.	Bloomington, IN	58.46
156.	Quebec City, PQ	58.40
157.	Fresno, CA	58.29
158.	Memphis, TN–AR–MS	58.04
159.	Terre Haute, IN	57.68

Places Rated Rank		Places Rated Score
160.	Wheeling, WV–OH	57.55
161.	San Antonio, TX	57.32
162.	Lafayette, IN	57.23
163.	Hamilton–Middletown, OH	57.22
164.	Reno, NV	57.07
165.	Vallejo–Fairfield–Napa, CA	56.25
166.	Ottawa–Hull, ON–PQ	56.15
167.	Macon, GA	55.70
168.	Mobile, AL	55.41
169.	Charleston–North Charleston, SC	54.83
170.	Johnson City–Kingsport–Bristol, TN–VA	54.77
171.	Charleston, WV	54.72
172.	Santa Rosa, CA	54.67
173.	Eugene–Springfield, OR	53.57
174.	Waco, TX	53.29
185.	Edmonton, AB	51.21
186.	Greenville, NC	50.95
187.	Galveston–Texas City, TX	50.66
188.	Fort Collins–Loveland, CO	50.54
189.	Wichita, KS	50.11
190.	Killeen–Temple, TX	49.98
191.	Sumter, SC	49.95
192.	Boise City, ID	49.82
193.	Clarksville–Hopkinsville, TN–KY	49.56
194.	Yolo, CA	49.38
195.	Chattanooga, TN–GA	48.68
196.	Youngstown–Warren, OH	47.61
197.	Lubbock, TX	47.57
198.	Redding, CA	47.32
199.	Kitchener, ON	47.13
200.	Asheville, NC	47.07
201.	Janesville–Beloit, WI	47.00
202.	Canton–Massillon, OH	46.83
203.	Bellingham, WA	46.78
204.	Sarasota–Bradenton, FL	45.87
205.	Tyler, TX	45.66
206.	Longview–Marshall, TX	45.00
207.	Tucson, AZ	44.85
208.	Augusta–Aiken, GA–SC	44.18
209.	Decatur, AL	44.16
210.	Anchorage, AK	44.14
211.	Rocky Mount, NC	44.10
212.	Jamestown, NY	42.57
213.	Las Cruces, NM	42.50
214.	St. Joseph, MO	42.21
215.	Fayetteville–Springdale–Rogers, AR	42.16
216.	El Paso, TX	42.06
217.	Parkersburg–Marietta, WV–OH	42.05
218.	Owensboro, KY	41.90
219.	Chico–Paradise, CA	41.80
220.	Trois–Rivieres, PQ	41.78
221.	Steubenville–Weirton, OH–WV	41.22
222.	West Palm Beach–Boca Raton, FL	41.17
223.	Hickory–Morganton–Lenoir, NC	40.78
224.	Cumberland, MD–WV	40.65

Places Rated Rank		Places Rated Score
225.	Kankakee, IL	40.52
226.	Joplin, MO	40.49
227.	Fort Pierce–Port St. Lucie, FL	40.41
228.	Jacksonville, FL	40.36
229.	Sharon, PA	40.10
230.	Savannah, GA	40.06
231.	Johnstown, PA	39.93
232.	Florence, AL	39.43
233.	Evansville–Henderson, IN–KY	39.13
234.	Olympia, WA	38.53
235.	Jersey City, NJ	37.90
236.	Waterloo–Cedar Falls, IA	37.76
237.	Stockton–Lodi, CA	36.75
238.	Dover, DE	36.19
239.	Bismarck, ND	35.91
240.	Bryan–College Station, TX	35.63
241.	Tulsa, OK	35.58
242.	Pueblo, CO	35.38
254.	Jackson, MI	[illegible]
255.	Waterbury, CT	32.51
256.	Goldsboro, NC	32.05
257.	New London–Norwich, CT–RI	31.90
258.	Sioux City, IA–NE	31.65
259.	Windsor, ON	31.45
260.	Barnstable–Yarmouth, MA	31.28
261.	Columbus, GA–AL	31.01
262.	Fayetteville, NC	30.87
263.	San Luis Obispo–Atascadero–Paso Robles, CA	30.59
264.	Williamsport, PA	30.57
265.	Atlantic City–Cape May, NJ	29.93
266.	Decatur, IL	29.43
267.	Dothan, AL	28.37
268.	Wilmington, NC	28.21
269.	Lima, OH	28.19
270.	Albany, GA	27.74
271.	Florence, SC	27.37
272.	Sioux Falls, SD	27.34
273.	Bremerton, WA	27.31
274.	St. Catharines–Niagara, ON	26.19
275.	Baton Rouge, LA	26.18
276.	Brownsville–Harlingen–San Benito, TX	25.92
277.	Lafayette, LA	25.90
278.	Lowell, MA–NH	25.54
279.	Bakersfield, CA	25.22
280.	York, PA	25.13
281.	Odessa–Midland, TX	24.97
282.	Victoria, BC	24.96
283.	Modesto, CA	24.77
284.	Anniston, AL	23.96
285.	Thunder Bay, ON	23.24
286.	Flagstaff, AZ–UT	23.12
287.	Visalia–Tulare–Porterville, CA	22.48
288.	Las Vegas, NV–AZ	22.40
289.	Grand Junction, CO	22.00
290.	Elkhart–Goshen, IN	21.33
291.	Gadsden, AL	21.32
292.	Binghamton, NY	21.29
293.	Sudbury, ON	20.34
294.	Beaumont–Port Arthur, TX	20.16
295.	Yuba City, CA	19.98
296.	Victoria, TX	19.78

Places Rated Rank		Places Rated Score
297.	Danville, VA	19.27
298.	Shreveport–Bossier City, LA	19.11
299.	Texarkana, TX–Texarkana, AR	18.98
300.	Billings, MT	18.89
301.	Brazoria, TX	18.83
302.	Laredo, TX	18.34
303.	New Bedford, MA	17.98
304.	Fort Walton Beach, FL	17.66
305.	Rapid City, SD	16.88
306.	St. John's, NF	15.93
307.	Oshawa, ON	15.37
308.	Danbury, CT	15.34
309.	Corpus Christi, TX	14.68
310.	Sherman–Denison, TX	14.04
311.	Pine Bluff, AR	13.87
312.	Alexandria, LA	13.65
313.	Hagerstown, MD	13.28
314.	Topeka, KS	12.67
315.	Panama City, FL	12.19
316.	Myrtle Beach, SC	10.60
317.	Rockford, IL	10.59
318.	Wausau, WI	10.35
319.	Monroe, LA	9.10
320.	Glens Falls, NY	8.87
321.	McAllen–Edinburg–Mission, TX	8.71
322.	Merced, CA	8.65
323.	Altoona, PA	7.21
323.	Fort Myers–Cape Coral, FL	7.21
325.	Naples, FL	6.75
326.	Cheyenne, WY	6.73
327.	Yakima, WA	6.21
328.	Mansfield, OH	6.20
329.	Sheboygan, WI	6.08
330.	San Angelo, TX	5.97
331.	Elmira, NY	5.81
332.	Lawton, OK	5.36
333.	Yuma, AZ	5.04
334.	Casper, WY	4.92
335.	Lake Charles, LA	3.93
336.	Vineland–Millville–Bridgeton, NJ	3.72
337.	Wichita Falls, TX	3.67
338.	Houma, LA	3.18
339.	Medford–Ashland, OR	2.50
340.	Stamford–Norwalk, CT	2.44
341.	Richland–Kennewick–Pasco, WA	2.26
342.	Fort Smith, AR–OK	1.74
343.	Pittsfield, MA	1.66
344.	Ocala, FL	1.46
345.	Jacksonville, NC	1.45
346.	Biloxi–Gulfport–Pascagoula, MS	1.25
347.	Great Falls, MT	0.54
348.	Punta Gorda, FL	0.50
349.	Enid, OK	0.28
350.	Saint John, NB	0.00
350.	Racine, WI	0.00

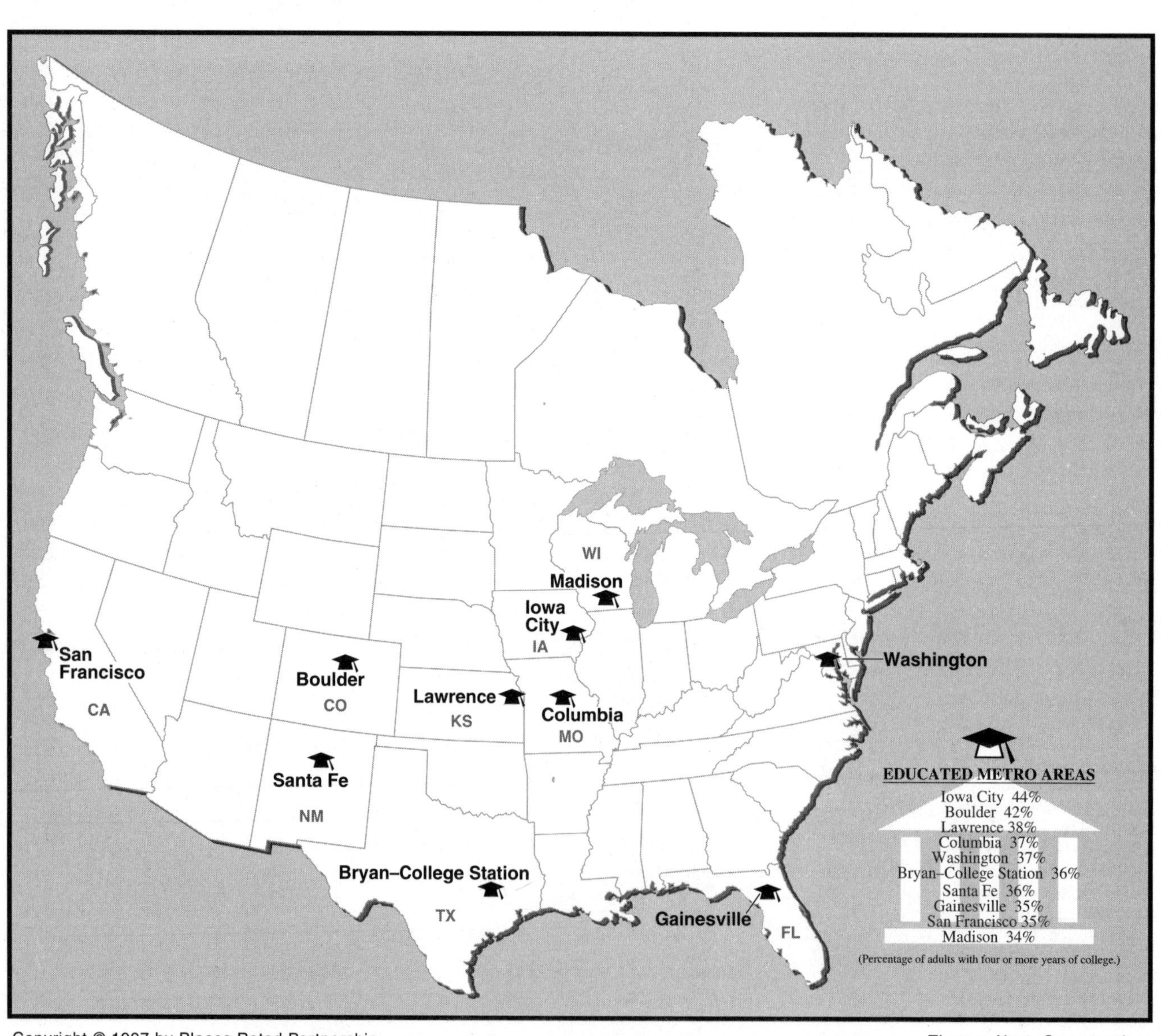

Thomas Nast, Cartographer

PLACE PROFILES: Education

The following pages show six sides of education in metropolitan areas: (1) public schools, (2) private schools, (3) two-year colleges, (4) baccalaureate-level colleges, (5) comprehensive-level colleges and universities, and (6) doctoral-level universities.

Finding a good public school system isn't easy. A typical metro area has thirty or more, each with varying indicators of school quality. Still, information on how much local public education is fragmented into different

the sum of full and part-time students. For Comprehensive and Doctoral institutions the first enrollment figure is undergraduate students, the second is graduate students; if there is only one figure, the institution's entire enrollment is graduate students. Public-controlled institutions in the United States are *italicized*. In Canada, degree-granting institutions get their charters from the province, or are affiliated with institutions that do. They essentially are publicly supported.

Figures for American and Canadian public and pri-

local schools that belong to the National Association of Independent Schools (NAIS) and their total enrollment, and the number of Other private schools and pupils.

Under "Associate of Arts," below **Colleges and Universities,** are the number of community, junior, or two-year colleges. Under the "Baccalaureate" subheading are the names of colleges where the highest degree granted is the bachelor's. Under the "Comprehensive" subheading are institutions where the master's is the highest degree granted. Under the "Doctoral" subheading are universities where the highest degree granted is the doctorate. Enrollment figures (in parentheses) are

Similar data for Canadian higher education institutions come from the Association of Canadian Community Colleges, *ACCC Directory of Canadian Colleges and Institutes,* 1996; the Association of Universities and Colleges of Canada, *Directory of Canadian Universities,* 1996; and Statistics Canada's Universities: *Enrollment and Degrees,* 1996, and *Community Colleges and Related Institutions,* 1996.

A check mark (✓) preceding the metro area's name identifies it as one of *Places Rated Almanac's* top 35 places for higher education.

Abilene, TX
Public K–12 (98.05%)
5 districts, 62 schools
24,093 students
Private K–12 (1.95%)
3 Other, 464 students
Colleges and Universities
Baccalaureate
McMurry University (2,041)
Comprehensive
Hardin-Simmons University (2,184/185)
Doctoral
Abilene Christian University (3,422/702)
Places Rated Score: 34.69
Places Rated Rank: 245

Akron, OH
Public K–12 (89.10%)
30 districts, 205 schools
106,815 students
Private K–12 (10.90%)
28 Catholic, 9,695 students
2 NAIS, 875 students
15 Other, 2,472 students
Colleges and Universities
Associate of Arts
2 campuses (977)
Baccalaureate
Hiram College (1,417)
Doctoral
Kent State University (23,909/8,253)
University of Akron (28,973/5,475)
Places Rated Score: 73.61
Places Rated Rank: 87

Albany, GA
Public K–12 (91.93%)
2 districts, 38 schools
20,507 students
Private K–12 (8.07%)
1 Catholic, 446 students
5 Other, 1,354 students
Colleges and Universities
Associate of Arts
2 campuses (6,069)
Comprehensive
Albany State College (2,782/324)
Places Rated Score: 27.74
Places Rated Rank: 270

Albany–Schenectady–Troy, NY
Public K–12 (88.90%)
58 districts, 242 schools
129,048 students
Private K–12 (11.10%)
42 Catholic, 10,863 students
6 NAIS, 1,695 students
28 Other, 3,551 students
Colleges and Universities
Associate of Arts
6 campuses (22,953)
Baccalaureate
Siena College (3,624)
Skidmore College (2,747)
SUNY College at Cobleskill (3,092)
Comprehensive
College of Saint Rose (2,250/2,291)
Russell Sage College (4,190/1,523)
SUNY Empire State College (9,025/393)
Union College (2,187/877)
Doctoral
Albany College of Pharmacy (647/24)
Albany Medical College (654)
Rensselaer Polytechnic (4,358/3,112)
SUNY at Albany (15,904/6,612)
Places Rated Score: 81.01
Places Rated Rank: 57

Albuquerque, NM
Public K–12 (90.54%)

8 districts, 175 schools
108,393 students
Private K–12 (9.46%)
18 Catholic, 6,206 students
3 NAIS, 1,822 students
57 Other, 3,303 students
Colleges and Universities
Associate of Arts
4 campuses (24,730)
Doctoral
University of New Mexico (20,703/11,157)
Places Rated Score: 67.51
Places Rated Rank: 120

Alexandria, LA
Public K–12 (91.33%)
2 districts, 54 schools
24,500 students
Private K–12 (8.67%)
4 Catholic, 1,546 students
3 Other, 779 students
Colleges and Universities
Associate of Arts
1 campus (4,046)
Baccalaureate
Louisiana College (1,280)
Places Rated Score: 13.65
Places Rated Rank: 312

Allentown–Bethlehem–Easton, PA
Public K–12 (85.87%)
26 districts, 153 schools
84,595 students
Private K–12 (14.13%)
38 Catholic, 10,817 students
5 NAIS, 1,713 students
18 Other, 1,388 students
Colleges and Universities
Associate of Arts
4 campuses (18,043)
Baccalaureate
Cedar Crest College (1,576)
Lafayette College (2,352)
Muhlenberg College (2,317)
Comprehensive
College of St. Francis De Sales (3,340/480)
Moravian College (2,018/206)
Penn State University (875/64)
Doctoral
Lehigh University (4,577/2,230)
Places Rated Score: 72.91
Places Rated Rank: 92

Altoona, PA
Public K–12 (89.33%)
8 districts, 37 schools
20,068 students
Private K–12 (10.67%)
10 Catholic, 1,668 students
1 NAIS, 135 students
7 Other, 595 students
Colleges and Universities
Comprehensive
Penn State University (2,724/16)
Places Rated Score: 7.21
Places Rated Rank: 323

Amarillo, TX
Public K–12 (95.43%)
5 districts, 68 schools
37,072 students
Private K–12 (4.57%)
7 Catholic, 846 students
8 Other, 930 students
Colleges and Universities
Associate of Arts
2 campuses (10,680)
Comprehensive
West Texas State University (6,043/1,915)
Places Rated Score: 33.20
Places Rated Rank: 251

Anchorage, AK
Public K–12 (95.57%)
1 district, 82 schools
46,103 students
Private K–12 (4.43%)
15 Other, 2,135 students
Colleges and Universities
Associate of Arts
1 campus (376)
Comprehensive
Alaska Pacific University (689/2,556)
University of Alaska (28,374/823)
Places Rated Score: 44.14
Places Rated Rank: 210

✓ Ann Arbor, MI
Public K–12 (92.88%)
27 districts, 157 schools
77,024 students
Private K–12 (7.12%)
10 Catholic, 2,205 students
1 NAIS, 442 students
31 Other, 3,257 students
Colleges and Universities
Associate of Arts
1 campus (16,707)
Baccalaureate
Adrian College (1,229)
Cleary College (1,441)
Concordia College (774)
Comprehensive
Siena Heights College (2,094/240)
Doctoral
Eastern Michigan University (22,925/9,338)
University of Michigan (26,298/15,067)
Places Rated Score: 94.34
Places Rated Rank: 13

Anniston, AL
Public K–12 (92.68%)
5 districts, 37 schools
20,479 students
Private K–12 (7.32%)
1 Catholic, 182 students
5 Other, 1,436 students
Colleges and Universities
Associate of Arts
1 campus (1,028)
Comprehensive
Jacksonville State University (8,120/1,618)
Places Rated Score: 23.96
Places Rated Rank: 284

Appleton–Oshkosh–Neenah, WI
Public K–12 (82.86%)
18 districts, 113 schools
52,638 students
Private K–12 (17.14%)
35 Catholic, 7,202 students
25 Other, 3,689 students
Colleges and Universities
Associate of Arts
1 campus (13,060)
Baccalaureate
Lawrence University (1,264)
Comprehensive
University of Wisconsin (10,406/2,429)
Places Rated Score: 51.71
Places Rated Rank: 183

Asheville, NC
Public K–12 (92.78%)
3 districts, 53 schools
27,766 students
Private K–12 (7.22%)
1 Catholic, 218 students
3 NAIS, 798 students
16 Other, 1,144 students
Colleges and Universities
Associate of Arts
2 campuses (6,521)
Baccalaureate
Mars Hill College (1,586)
Comprehensive
University of North Carolina (4,042/73)
Warren Wilson College (527/85)
Places Rated Score: 47.07
Places Rated Rank: 200

Athens, GA
Public K–12 (89.32%)
3 districts, 30 schools
17,702 students
Private K–12 (10.68%)
1 Catholic, 376 students
1 NAIS, 707 students
5 Other, 1,034 students
Colleges and Universities
Associate of Arts
1 campus (2,141)
Doctoral
University of Georgia (25,919/8,216)
Places Rated Score: 67.98
Places Rated Rank: 119

Atlanta, GA
Public K–12 (91.10%)
27 districts, 784 schools
520,095 students
Private K–12 (8.90%)
12 Catholic, 5,105 students
10 NAIS, 8,555 students
170 Other, 36,870 students
Colleges and Universities
Associate of Arts
14 campuses (52,353)
Baccalaureate
American College/Applied Arts (886)
Clayton State College (7,304)
Devry Institute of Technology (4,066)
Morehouse College (3,223)
Morris Brown College (2,534)
Reinhardt College (1,050)
Spelman College (2,111)
Comprehensive
Agnes Scott College (638/15)
Kennesaw State College (15,292/2,002)
Life College (1,249/2,752)
Oglethorpe University (1,401/272)
Southern College of Technology (4,477/471)
West Georgia College (6,089/2,574)
Doctoral
Clark Atlanta University (3,538/1,385)
Columbia Theological Seminary (816)
Emory University (6,053/5,138)
Georgia Institute of Technology (10,936/4,352)
Georgia State University (24,722/9,763)
Places Rated Score: 86.09
Places Rated Rank: 38

Atlantic City–Cape May, NJ
Public K–12 (86.92%)
41 districts, 111 schools
45,466 students

Private K-12 (13.08%)
18 Catholic, 5,058 students
10 Other, 1,785 students
Colleges and Universities
Associate of Arts
1 campus (9,392)
Baccalaureate
Stockton State College (6,100)
Places Rated Score: 29.93
Places Rated Rank: 265

Augusta-Aiken, GA-SC
Public K-12 (94.15%)
5 districts, 129 schools
81,472 students
Private K-12 (5.85%)
4 Catholic, 1,280 students
2 NAIS, 432 students
35 Other, 3,351 students
Colleges and Universities

Places Rated Rank: [illegible]

Austin-San Marcos, TX
Public K-12 (94.83%)
29 districts, 294 schools
159,167 students
Private K-12 (5.17%)
10 Catholic, 2,096 students
2 NAIS, 690 students
29 Other, 5,898 students
Colleges and Universities
Associate of Arts
3 campuses (44,527)
Baccalaureate
Concordia Lutheran College (848)
Huston-Tillotson College (659)
Southwestern University (1,258)
Comprehensive
SW Texas State University (21,249/4,150)
St. Edwards University (2,631/416)
Doctoral
University of Texas (35,911/13,342)
Places Rated Score: 82.20
Places Rated Rank: 53

Bakersfield, CA
Public K-12 (95.77%)
52 districts, 228 schools
133,941 students
Private K-12 (4.23%)
7 Catholic, 2,016 students
44 Other, 3,906 students
Colleges and Universities
Associate of Arts
3 campuses (27,828)
Comprehensive
Cal State University (4,680/2,272)
Places Rated Score: 25.22
Places Rated Rank: 279

✓ Baltimore, MD
Public K-12 (83.99%)
7 districts, 609 schools
358,132 students
Private K-12 (16.01%)
80 Catholic, 28,490 students
22 NAIS, 9,946 students
187 Other, 29,850 students
Colleges and Universities
Associate of Arts
10 campuses (89,475)
Baccalaureate
United States Naval Academy (4,344)
Villa Julie College (1,989)
Comprehensive
College of Notre Dame (3,300/579)
Coppin State College (3,180/637)
Goucher College (986/87)
Maryland Institute College of Art (1,678/129)
Towson State University (16,497/2,589)
University of Baltimore (3,837/3,259)
Western Maryland College (1,333/2,222)
Doctoral

11 districts, 44 schools
14,623 students
Private K-12 (5.65%)
1 Catholic, 80 students
6 Other, 796 students
Colleges and Universities
Associate of Arts
2 campuses (3,986)
Comprehensive
Husson College (2,491/337)
Doctoral
University of Maine (11,919/3,169)
Places Rated Score: 89.80
Places Rated Rank: 26

Barnstable-Yarmouth, MA
Public K-12 (96.53%)
12 districts, 38 schools
20,486 students
Private K-12 (3.47%)
2 NAIS, 329 students
8 Other, 407 students
Colleges and Universities
Associate of Arts
1 campus (5,993)
Baccalaureate
Massachusetts Maritime Academy (771)
Places Rated Score: 31.28
Places Rated Rank: 260

Baton Rouge, LA
Public K-12 (82.80%)
7 districts, 181 schools
98,694 students
Private K-12 (17.20%)
21 Catholic, 12,049 students
1 NAIS, 762 students
37 Other, 7,674 students
Colleges and Universities
Doctoral
Louisiana State University (24,537/7,759)
Southern University (20,474/3,082)
Places Rated Score: 26.18
Places Rated Rank: 275

Beaumont-Port Arthur, TX
Public K-12 (92.37%)
16 districts, 145 schools
72,420 students
Private K-12 (7.63%)
9 Catholic, 3,282 students
13 Other, 2,701 students
Colleges and Universities
Associate of Arts
2 campuses (5,885)
Doctoral
Lamar University (13,134/1,307)
Places Rated Score: 20.16
Places Rated Rank: 294

Bellingham, WA
Public K-12 (90.70%)
7 districts, 49 schools
23,656 students
Private K-12 (9.30%)
1 Catholic, 300 students

Public K-12 ([illegible])
16 districts, 76 schools
30,174 students
Private K-12 (13.64%)
6 Catholic, 1,203 students
23 Other, 3,562 students
Colleges and Universities
Associate of Arts
1 campus (5,391)
Doctoral
Andrews University (2,636/2,437)
Places Rated Score: 34.72
Places Rated Rank: 244

Bergen-Passaic, NJ
Public K-12 (83.95%)
97 districts, 388 schools
167,411 students
Private K-12 (16.05%)
92 Catholic, 28,167 students
3 NAIS, 1,381 students
11 Other, 2,456 students
Colleges and Universities
Associate of Arts
3 campuses (26,519)
Baccalaureate
Felician College (1,156)
Ramapo College (5,433)
Comprehensive
William Paterson College (9,669/2,276)
Doctoral
Fairleigh Dickinson University (8,454/5,369)
Places Rated Score: 66.72
Places Rated Rank: 121

Billings, MT
Public K-12 (94.18%)
20 districts, 61 schools
21,889 students
Private K-12 (5.82%)
3 Catholic, 784 students
5 Other, 569 students
Colleges and Universities
Baccalaureate

Rocky Mountain College (923)
Comprehensive
Eastern Montana College (4,263/836)
Places Rated Score: 18.89
Places Rated Rank: 300

Biloxi–Gulfport–Pascagoula, MS

Public K–12 (91.71%)
11 districts, 112 schools
59,540 students
Private K–12 (8.29%)
17 Catholic, 4,355 students
10 Other, 1,025 students
Colleges and Universities
Associate of Arts
1 campus (550)
Places Rated Score: 1.25
Places Rated Rank: 346

Binghamton, NY

Public K–12 (92.02%)
19 districts, 78 schools
43,730 students
Private K–12 (7.98%)
13 Catholic, 2,668 students
10 Other, 1,123 students
Colleges and Universities
Associate of Arts
1 campus (8,866)
Doctoral
SUNY at Binghamton (9,928/3,360)
Places Rated Score: 21.29
Places Rated Rank: 292

Birmingham, AL

Public K–12 (93.12%)
15 districts, 270 schools
142,949 students
Private K–12 (6.88%)
15 Catholic, 3,794 students
4 NAIS, 1,204 students
42 Other, 5,569 students
Colleges and Universities
Associate of Arts
6 campuses (19,553)
Baccalaureate
Miles College (1,385)
Comprehensive
Birmingham Southern College (1,809/111)
University of Montevallo (3,096/854)
Doctoral
Samford University (3,739/1,129)
University of Alabama (16,047/6,106)
Places Rated Score: 73.40
Places Rated Rank: 88

Bismarck, ND

Public K–12 (90.19%)
26 districts, 62 schools
16,971 students
Private K–12 (9.81%)
6 Catholic, 1,481 students
5 Other, 364 students
Colleges and Universities
Associate of Arts
2 campuses (3,555)
Comprehensive
University of Mary (1,921/287)
Places Rated Score: 35.91
Places Rated Rank: 239

Bloomington, IN

Public K–12 (90.95%)
2 districts, 25 schools
13,323 students
Private K–12 (9.05%)
1 Catholic, 427 students
16 Other, 898 students
Colleges and Universities
Doctoral
Indiana University (34,846/10,340)
Places Rated Score: 58.46
Places Rated Rank: 155

Bloomington–Normal, IL

Public K–12 (91.92%)
13 districts, 56 schools
21,619 students
Private K–12 (8.08%)
4 Catholic, 1,248 students
4 Other, 652 students
Colleges and Universities
Baccalaureate
Illinois Wesleyan University (1,845)
Doctoral
Illinois State University (21,006/4,924)
Places Rated Score: 79.19
Places Rated Rank: 64

Boise City, ID

Public K–12 (95.00%)
11 districts, 117 schools
63,380 students
Private K–12 (5.00%)
6 Catholic, 1,652 students
16 Other, 1,687 students
Colleges and Universities
Associate of Arts
1 campus (712)
Comprehensive
Albertson College of Idaho (768/1,079)
Boise State University (18,044/5,019)
Northwest Nazarene College (1,170/1,910)
Places Rated Score: 49.82
Places Rated Rank: 192

✓ Boston, MA–NH

Public K–12 (87.03%)
141 districts, 888 schools
429,699 students
Private K–12 (12.97%)
118 Catholic, 36,666 students
50 NAIS, 13,157 students
115 Other, 14,201 students
Colleges and Universities
Associate of Arts
18 campuses (63,039)
Baccalaureate
Berklee College of Music (3,075)
Boston Architectural Center (1,983)
Endicott College (1,467)
Gordon College (1,264)
Mount Ida College (1,604)
Pine Manor College (875)
Radcliffe College (2,692)
Wellesley College (2,482)
Wentworth Inst. of Technology (3,299)
Wheaton College (1,329)
Comprehensive
Atlantic Union College (2,322/72)
Babson College (1,770/1,762)
Bentley College (5,290/2,187)
Cambridge College (554/1,767)
Curry College (1,435/31)
Eastern Nazarene College (1,435/253)
Emmanuel College (1,504/298)
Framingham State College (7,118/842)
Massachusetts College of Art (3,009/84)
Regis College (1,384/38)
Salem State College (12,453/2,708)
Museum of Fine Arts School (1,184/58)
Suffolk University (3,484/3,406)
Wheelock College (1,092/1,652)
Doctoral
Andover Newton Theological School (710)
Boston College (11,808/4,646)
Boston University (20,851/13,754)
Brandeis University (3,140/1,156)
Emerson College (2,947/848)
Gordon–Conwell Theological Seminary (1,144)
Harvard University (10,856/14,162)
Lesley College (1,930/6,989)
Massachusetts College of Pharmacy (1,267/55)
Massachusetts Inst. of Technology (5,007/6,279)
New England Conservatory of Music (380/396)
Northeastern University (29,484/6,564)
Simmons College (1,379/2,137)
Tufts University (5,766/4,265)
University of Massachusetts Boston (15,856/3,485)
Places Rated Score: 99.75
Places Rated Rank: 1

Boulder–Longmont, CO

Public K–12 (92.50%)
2 districts, 79 schools
39,653 students
Private K–12 (7.50%)
4 Catholic, 1,015 students
30 Other, 2,201 students
Colleges and Universities
Doctoral
University of Colorado (26,710/7,281)
Places Rated Score: 51.31
Places Rated Rank: 184

Brazoria, TX

Public K–12 (97.74%)
8 districts, 67 schools
43,124 students
Private K–12 (2.26%)
1 Catholic, 283 students
3 Other, 715 students
Colleges and Universities
Associate of Arts
2 campuses (11,442)
Places Rated Score: 18.83
Places Rated Rank: 301

Bremerton, WA

Public K–12 (96.46%)
5 districts, 66 schools
40,258 students
Private K–12 (3.54%)
1 Catholic, 200 students
16 Other, 1,277 students
Colleges and Universities
Associate of Arts
1 campus (10,046)
Places Rated Score: 27.31
Places Rated Rank: 273

Bridgeport, CT

Public K–12 (85.51%)
17 districts, 142 schools
66,911 students
Private K–12 (14.49%)
29 Catholic, 9,372 students
3 NAIS, 840 students
12 Other, 1,123 students
Colleges and Universities
Associate of Arts
1 campus (3,863)
Comprehensive
Fairfield University (4,262/923)
Sacred Heart University (4,996/2,420)

Doctoral
University of Bridgeport (1,117/1,380)
Places Rated Score: 68.10
Places Rated Rank: 116

Brockton, MA
Public K–12 (94.80%)
10 districts, 69 schools
36,820 students
Private K–12 (5.20%)
4 Catholic, 1,215 students
12 Other, 804 students
Colleges and Universities
Associate of Arts
1 campus (10,107)
Baccalaureate
Stonehill College (3,040)
Comprehensive
Bridgewater State College
(8,472/2,367)

Colleges and Universities
Associate of Arts
2 campuses (13,731)
Comprehensive
University of Texas (2,259/476)
Places Rated Score: 25.92
Places Rated Rank: 276

Bryan–College Station, TX
Public K–12 (93.39%)
2 districts, 30 schools
18,271 students
Private K–12 (6.61%)
1 Catholic, 397 students
7 Other, 896 students
Colleges and Universities
Doctoral
Texas A & M University (36,298/9,367)
Places Rated Score: 35.63
Places Rated Rank: 240

Buffalo–Niagara Falls, NY
Public K–12 (83.69%)
41 districts, 287 schools
175,305 students
Private K–12 (16.31%)
91 Catholic, 26,171 students
5 NAIS, 1,466 students
39 Other, 6,525 students
Colleges and Universities
Associate of Arts
10 campuses (32,195)
Baccalaureate
Hilbert College (890)
Medaille College (1,670)
Comprehensive
Canisius College (3,947/1,667)
D'Youville College (1,501/420)
Daemen College (1,980/135)
Niagara University (2,556/665)
SUNY College at Buffalo
(11,982/2,602)
Doctoral
SUNY at Buffalo (19,778/9,726)
Places Rated Score: 82.20
Places Rated Rank: 54

✓Burlington, VT
Public K–12 (92.43%)
10 districts, 53 schools
23,004 students
Private K–12 (7.57%)
5 Catholic, 1,342 students
1 NAIS, 91 students
13 Other, 451 students
Colleges and Universities
Baccalaureate
Champlain College (2,683)
Comprehensive
St. Michaels College (2,003/1,689)
Trinity College (1,296/263)
Doctoral
University of Vermont (13,250/1,861)
Places Rated Score: 87.37
Places Rated Rank: 33

Calgary, AB
Public Instruction (96.85%)

Canton–Massillon, OH
Public K–12 (91.45%)
20 districts, 134 schools
68,432 students
Private K–12 (8.55%)
16 Catholic, 5,080 students
9 Other, 1,317 students
Colleges and Universities
Associate of Arts
2 campuses (8,620)
Baccalaureate
Mount Union College (1,558)
Comprehensive
Malone College (2,317/155)
Walsh University (1,509/497)
Places Rated Score: 46.83
Places Rated Rank: 202

Casper, WY
Public K–12 (98.80%)
1 district, 40 schools
12,899 students
Private K–12 (1.20%)
3 Other, 157 students
Colleges and Universities
Associate of Arts
1 campus (5,160)
Places Rated Score: 4.92
Places Rated Rank: 334

Cedar Rapids, IA
Public K–12 (88.97%)
10 districts, 67 schools
28,274 students
Private K–12 (11.03%)
9 Catholic, 2,845 students
7 Other, 659 students
Colleges and Universities
Associate of Arts
1 campus (13,529)
Baccalaureate
Coe College (1,349)
Cornell College (1,162)
Mount Mercy College (1,526)
Places Rated Score: 75.37
Places Rated Rank: 82

Champaign–Urbana, IL
Public K–12 (94.53%)
17 districts, 59 schools
24,380 students
Private K–12 (5.47%)
3 Catholic, 699 students
7 Other, 712 students
Colleges and Universities
Associate of Arts
1 campus (15,761)
Doctoral
University of Illinois (29,040/12,897)
Places Rated Score: 64.30
Places Rated Rank: 134

Charleston, WV
Public K–12 (94.51%)
2 districts, 112 schools
41,922 students
Private K–12 (5.49%)
5 Catholic, 1,250 students

Places Rated Rank: 171

Charleston–North Charleston, SC
Public K–12 (90.55%)
4 districts, 133 schools
90,433 students
Private K–12 (9.45%)
8 Catholic, 2,932 students
3 NAIS, 1,306 students
54 Other, 5,197 students
Colleges and Universities
Associate of Arts
2 campuses (15,268)
Baccalaureate
Johnson & Wales University (1,533)
Comprehensive
Charleston Southern University
(2,521/543)
Citadel Military College (2,600/3,048)
College of Charleston (9,645/3,503)
Doctoral
Medical University of South Carolina
(1,147/1,347)
Places Rated Score: 54.83
Places Rated Rank: 169

Charlotte–Gastonia–Rock Hill, NC–SC
Public K–12 (92.13%)
11 districts, 320 schools
187,542 students
Private K–12 (7.87%)
10 Catholic, 3,408 students
3 NAIS, 3,552 students
74 Other, 9,050 students
Colleges and Universities
Associate of Arts
5 campuses (83,704)
Baccalaureate
Barber–Scotia College (706)
Davidson College (1,592)
Johnson C. Smith University (1,568)
Comprehensive
Belmont Abbey College (1,184/102)
Catawba College (1,017/11)
Livingstone College (545/70)

Queens College (1,513/469)
University of North Carolina **(16,448/3,635)**
Wingate College (1,551/64)
Winthrop University (4,726/2,306)
Places Rated Score: 80.96
Places Rated Rank: 58

Charlottesville, VA
Public K–12 (84.53%)
6 districts, 45 schools
18,098 students
Private K–12 (15.47%)
5 NAIS, 1,782 students
15 Other, 1,529 students
Colleges and Universities
Associate of Arts
1 campus (6,993)
Doctoral
University of Virginia (14,814/15,090)
Places Rated Score: 68.23
Places Rated Rank: 115

Chattanooga, TN–GA
Public K–12 (87.02%)
8 districts, 130 schools
68,557 students
Private K–12 (12.98%)
3 Catholic, 1,302 students
5 NAIS, 2,649 students
34 Other, 6,277 students
Colleges and Universities
Associate of Arts
3 campuses (15,829)
Baccalaureate
Southern College of SDA (2,004)
Comprehensive
Covenant College (774/25)
University of Tennessee (8,658/1,667)
Doctoral
Tennessee Temple University (898/50)
Places Rated Score: 48.68
Places Rated Rank: 195

Cheyenne, WY
Public K–12 (94.98%)
2 districts, 42 schools
14,673 students
Private K–12 (5.02%)
2 Catholic, 510 students
5 Other, 265 students
Colleges and Universities
Associate of Arts
1 campus (7,600)
Places Rated Score: 6.73
Places Rated Rank: 326

✓Chicago, IL
Public K–12 (84.45%)
340 districts, 2,059 schools
1,147,900 students
Private K–12 (15.55%)
422 Catholic, 161,716 students
13 NAIS, 6,329 students
307 Other, 43,251 students
Colleges and Universities
Associate of Arts
30 campuses (491,708)
Baccalaureate
Barat College (882)
Devry Institute of Technology (8,432)
Interrnational Academy of Merchandising (947)
Judson College (661)
Robert Morris College (3,125)
Trinity Christian College (608)
Trinity College (984)
Comprehensive
Aurora University (1,841/588)
College of Osteopathic Medicine (126/546)
Chicago State University **(8,114/3,356)**
College of St. Francis (4,070/1,277)
Columbia College (7,901/472)
Concordia University (1,671/732)
Elmhurst College (3,427/708)
Governors State University **(3,777/4,436)**
Illinois Benedictine College (2,122/1,204)
John Marshall Law School (1,488)
Keller Graduate School of Management (2,155)
Lake Forest College (1,061/25)
Lake Forest Graduate School of Management (775)
Lewis University (4,212/895)
Moody Bible Institute (1,422/73)
National College of Chiropractic (12/818)
North Central College (2,573/590)
North Park College/Seminary (1,309/430)
Northeastern Illinois University **(10,036/5,333)**
Rosary College (1,047/1,671)
School of Art Institute of Chicago (1,737/382)
St. Xavier University (2,518/1,982)
Doctoral
DePaul University (10,870/7,978)
Illinois Inst. of Technology (2,906/5,180)
Illinois School of Professional Psychology (657)
Loyola University of Chicago (11,709/7,011)
National-Louis University (4,849/10,026)
Northern Illinois University **(19,451/11,190)**
Northwestern University (11,368/8,739)
Roosevelt University (6,281/2,937)
Rush University (191/1,256)
Trinity Evangelical Divinity School (2,238)
University of Chicago (3,365/7,921)
University of Health Sciences (97/973)
University of Illinois **(18,693/11,116)**
Wheaton College (2,407/430)
Places Rated Score: 98.19
Places Rated Rank: 3

Chico–Paradise, CA
Public K–12 (95.19%)
17 districts, 67 schools
32,968 students
Private K–12 (4.81%)
3 Catholic, 641 students
14 Other, 1,026 students
Colleges and Universities
Associate of Arts
1 campus (18,995)
Comprehensive
Cal State University (14,736/2,120)
Places Rated Score: 41.80
Places Rated Rank: 219

Chicoutimi–Jonquiere, PQ
Public Instruction
3 districts, 64 schools
7,703 students
Colleges and Universities
Associate of Arts
2 campuses (7,213)
Doctoral
Universite du Quebec (7,157/604)
Places Rated Score: 33.39
Places Rated Rank: 250

Cincinnati, OH–KY–IN
Public K–12 (82.30%)
70 districts, 433 schools
248,535 students
Private K–12 (17.70%)
123 Catholic, 45,254 students
3 NAIS, 1,979 students
54 Other, 6,215 students
Colleges and Universities
Associate of Arts
8 campuses (18,289)
Baccalaureate
Thomas More College (1,591)
Comprehensive
Cincinnati Bible College (683/481)
College of Mount Saint Joseph (2,718/238)
Northern Kentucky University **(13,223/1,481)**
Xavier University (4,926/3,007)
Doctoral
Union Institute (729/1,355)
University of Cincinnati **(27,828/10,460)**
Places Rated Score: 77.75
Places Rated Rank: 71

Clarksville–Hopkinsville, TN–KY
Public K–12 (84.82%)
2 districts, 42 schools
28,452 students
Private K–12 (15.18%)
3 Catholic, 500 students
12 Other, 4,593 students
Colleges and Universities
Associate of Arts
2 campuses (5,470)
Comprehensive
Austin Peay State University (10,169/722)
Places Rated Score: 49.56
Places Rated Rank: 193

✓ Cleveland–Lorain–Elyria, OH
Public K–12 (82.81%)
81 districts, 619 schools
332,135 students
Private K–12 (17.19%)
147 Catholic, 55,681 students
7 NAIS, 2,443 students
71 Other, 10,839 students
Colleges and Universities
Associate of Arts
11 campuses (86,297)
Baccalaureate
Dyke College (1,701)
Comprehensive
Baldwin-Wallace College (5,126/662)
John Carroll University (3,991/2,404)
Lake Erie College (658/168)
Notre Dame College (992/44)
Oberlin College (3,044/23)
Ursuline College (1,681/223)
Doctoral
Case Western Reserve University (3,759/6,432)
Cleveland State University (17,078/8,185)
Places Rated Score: 88.72
Places Rated Rank: 28

Colorado Springs, CO
Public K–12 (94.51%)
16 districts, 157 schools
76,887 students
Private K–12 (5.49%)
5 Catholic, 1,330 students
2 NAIS, 468 students
29 Other, 2,665 students

Colleges and Universities
Associate of Arts
3 campuses (18,226)
Baccalaureate
United States Air Force Academy (4,301)
Comprehensive
Colorado College (2,248/237)
Colorado Technical College (1,903/408)
Doctoral
University of Colorado (5,402/2,421)
Places Rated Score: 70.97
Places Rated Rank: 102

Columbia, MO
Public K–12 (93.83%)
6 districts, 38 schools
17,758 students
Private K–12 (6.17%)
1 Catholic, 386 students
10 Other, 782 students

9 districts, 141 schools
82,989 students
Private K–12 (8.15%)
5 Catholic, 1,047 students
2 NAIS, 891 students
54 Other, 5,430 students
Colleges and Universities
Associate of Arts
2 campuses (26,217)
Baccalaureate
Benedict College (2,832)
Comprehensive
Columbia College (1,312/129)
Doctoral
Columbia Bible College/Seminary (532/661)
University of South Carolina (18,891/17,295)
Places Rated Score: 76.19
Places Rated Rank: 77

Columbus, GA–AL
Public K–12 (87.39%)
5 districts, 77 schools
43,292 students
Private K–12 (12.61%)
5 Catholic, 1,182 students
1 NAIS, 693 students
24 Other, 4,371 students
Colleges and Universities
Associate of Arts
3 campuses (5,607)
Comprehensive
Columbus College (6,352/1,091)
Troy State University (520/1,036)
Places Rated Score: 31.01
Places Rated Rank: 261

Columbus, OH
Public K–12 (90.94%)
50 districts, 457 schools
230,860 students
Private K–12 (9.06%)
40 Catholic, 14,074 students
4 NAIS, 2,005 students
51 Other, 6,913 students

Colleges and Universities
Associate of Arts
3 campuses (30,317)
Baccalaureate
College of Art and Design (1,921)
Denison University (2,027)
Devry Institute of Technology (3,780)
Ohio Dominican College (1,900)
Ohio Wesleyan University (1,999)
Comprehensive
Capital University (3,014/1,277)
Franklin University (5,898/437)
Ohio State University–Newark (2,037/147)
Ohio University (2,989/263)
Otterbein College (2,877/159)
Doctoral
Ohio State University (45,841/18,096)
Places Rated Score: 82.66
Places Rated Rank: 52

Texas A & M University (3,911/3,512)
Places Rated Score: 14.68
Places Rated Rank: 309

Cumberland, MD–WV
Public K–12 (90.18%)
2 districts, 38 schools
15,255 students
Private K–12 (9.82%)
5 Catholic, 966 students
6 Other, 696 students
Colleges and Universities
Associate of Arts
2 campuses (5,233)
Comprehensive
Frostburg State University (5,074/1,248)
Places Rated Score: 40.65
Places Rated Rank: 224

✓ Dallas, TX
Public K–12 (91.98%)
77 districts, 879 schools
503,451 students
Private K–12 (8.02%)
31 Catholic, 11,196 students
9 NAIS, 4,804 students
118 Other, 27,896 students
Colleges and Universities
Associate of Arts
13 campuses (117,599)
Baccalaureate
Devry Institute of Technology (3,124)
Northwood University (687)
Paul Quinn College (934)
SW Assemblies of God College (941)
Comprehensive
Amber University (1,837/1,383)
Dallas Baptist University (3,289/556)
Doctoral
Dallas Theological Seminary (2,133)
East Texas State University (5,896/6,373)
Southern Methodist University (6,106/4,495)

Texas Woman's University (6,320/6,215)
University of Dallas (1,293/2,608)
University of North Texas (23,327/9,909)
University of Texas (5,991/5,823)
University of Texas SW Medical Center (546/1,300)
Places Rated Score: 89.98
Places Rated Rank: 25

Danbury, CT
Public K–12 (89.57%)
8 districts, 48 schools
28,321 students
Private K–12 (10.43%)
8 Catholic, 1,969 students
2 NAIS, 531 students
6 Other, 799 students
Colleges and Universities
Comprehensive
Western Connecticut State University

6 Other, 1,147 students
Colleges and Universities
Associate of Arts
1 campus (6,355)
Comprehensive
Averett College (1,615/954)
Places Rated Score: 19.27
Places Rated Rank: 297

Davenport–Moline–Rock Island, IA–IL
Public K–12 (88.99%)
24 districts, 141 schools
62,986 students
Private K–12 (11.01%)
18 Catholic, 5,808 students
12 Other, 1,988 students
Colleges and Universities
Associate of Arts
4 campuses (18,543)
Baccalaureate
Augustana College (2,194)
Hamilton Technical College (638)
Comprehensive
Palmer College of Chiropractic (98/2,111)
St. Ambrose University (1,996/908)
Teikyo Marycrest University (1,410/178)
Places Rated Score: 61.67
Places Rated Rank: 143

Dayton–Springfield, OH
Public K–12 (88.47%)
43 districts, 281 schools
157,086 students
Private K–12 (11.53%)
35 Catholic, 13,733 students
1 NAIS, 385 students
27 Other, 6,352 students
Colleges and Universities
Associate of Arts
8 campuses (46,319)
Baccalaureate
Antioch College (808)
Cedarville College (2,351)
Central State University (3,261)

Wilberforce University (882)
Wittenberg University (2,213)
Comprehensive
McGregor School of Antioch University (478/452)
Doctoral
Air Force Institute of Technology (912)
United Theological Seminary (686)
University of Dayton (7,392/9,702)
Wright State University (16,450/6,776)
Places Rated Score: 84.94
Places Rated Rank: 44

Daytona Beach, FL
Public K–12 (93.00%)
2 districts, 71 schools
55,281 students
Private K–12 (7.00%)
7 Catholic, 1,596 students
35 Other, 2,566 students
Colleges and Universities
Associate of Arts
2 campuses (38,869)
Baccalaureate
Bethune Cookman College (2,470)
Comprehensive
Embry-Riddle University (13,757/4,272)
Stetson University (2,236/1,306)
Places Rated Score: 76.02
Places Rated Rank: 78

Decatur, AL
Public K–12 (95.60%)
4 districts, 54 schools
24,602 students
Private K–12 (4.40%)
1 Catholic, 243 students
9 Other, 890 students
Colleges and Universities
Associate of Arts
1 campus (28,590)
Places Rated Score: 44.16
Places Rated Rank: 209

Decatur, IL
Public K–12 (89.35%)
10 districts, 57 schools
20,745 students
Private K–12 (10.65%)
5 Catholic, 1,197 students
7 Other, 1,275 students
Colleges and Universities
Associate of Arts
1 campus (7,803)
Baccalaureate
Millikin University (2,022)
Places Rated Score: 29.43
Places Rated Rank: 266

✓Denver, CO
Public K–12 (91.73%)
18 districts, 523 schools
293,587 students
Private K–12 (8.27%)
35 Catholic, 10,958 students
6 NAIS, 2,650 students
144 Other, 12,850 students
Colleges and Universities
Associate of Arts
11 campuses (68,454)
Baccalaureate
Denver Technical College (1,034)
Metropolitan State College (23,347)
Comprehensive
Colorado Christian University (1,359/163)
Regis University (7,711/1,826)
Doctoral
Colorado School of Mines (2,090/1,256)
Denver Conservative Baptist Seminary (808)
University of Colorado (8,042/6,943)
University of Colorado Health Sciences Center (672/1,542)
University of Denver (4,143/7,396)
Places Rated Score: 92.18
Places Rated Rank: 19

Des Moines, IA
Public K–12 (92.47%)
21 districts, 159 schools
68,673 students
Private K–12 (7.53%)
13 Catholic, 4,132 students
8 Other, 1,457 students
Colleges and Universities
Associate of Arts
5 campuses (20,649)
Baccalaureate
Grand View College (1,759)
Simpson College (2,102)
Comprehensive
University of Osteopathic Medicine (78/1,236)
Doctoral
Drake University (5,944/18,693)
Places Rated Score: 77.52
Places Rated Rank: 73

✓Detroit, MI
Public K–12 (88.30%)
104 districts, 1,254 schools
701,934 students
Private K–12 (11.70%)
174 Catholic, 52,990 students
7 NAIS, 4,351 students
252 Other, 35,699 students
Colleges and Universities
Associate of Arts
9 campuses (163,762)
Baccalaureate
Baker College of Port Huron (755)
Center for Creative Studies (1,118)
Detroit College of Business (6,897)
Lawrence Institute of Technology (5,985/492)
Comprehensive
Madonna University (5,219/857)
University of Michigan (8,751/1,467)
Walsh College of Accounting (2,706/2,134)
Doctoral
Oakland University (12,890/3,416)
University of Detroit Mercy (5,463/3,711)
Wayne State University (23,904/16,159)
Places Rated Score: 91.67
Places Rated Rank: 21

Dothan, AL
Public K–12 (90.84%)
5 districts, 43 schools
22,898 students
Private K–12 (9.16%)
1 NAIS, 435 students
8 Other, 1,874 students
Colleges and Universities
Associate of Arts
2 campuses (7,229)
Comprehensive
Troy State University (2,636/1,207)
Places Rated Score: 28.37
Places Rated Rank: 267

Dover, DE
Public K–12 (91.01%)
6 districts, 49 schools
23,087 students
Private K–12 (8.99%)
1 Catholic, 448 students
31 Other, 1,833 students
Colleges and Universities
Associate of Arts
1 campus (3,346)
Baccalaureate
Wesley College (3,328)
Comprehensive
Delaware State University (2,704/231)
Places Rated Score: 36.19
Places Rated Rank: 238

Dubuque, IA
Public K–12 (65.06%)
2 districts, 25 schools
12,097 students
Private K–12 (34.94%)
20 Catholic, 6,497 students
Colleges and Universities
Comprehensive
Clarke College (980/144)
Loras College (1,863/171)
Doctoral
University of Dubuque (1,043/603)
Places Rated Score: 51.75
Places Rated Rank: 182

Duluth-Superior, MN-WI
Public K–12 (92.58%)
16 districts, 94 schools
29,934 students
Private K–12 (7.42%)
9 Catholic, 1,696 students
1 NAIS, 408 students
7 Other, 295 students
Colleges and Universities
Associate of Arts
5 campuses (9,317)
Comprehensive
College of Saint Scholastica (2,317/424)
University of Wisconsin (2,966/1,368)
Doctoral
University of Minnesota (12,890/672)
Places Rated Score: 69.03
Places Rated Rank: 111

Dutchess County, NY
Public K–12 (88.75%)
15 districts, 73 schools
40,965 students
Private K–12 (11.25%)
13 Catholic, 2,911 students
7 NAIS, 1,525 students
15 Other, 756 students
Colleges and Universities
Associate of Arts
1 campus (10,491)
Baccalaureate
Culinary Institute of America (3,117)
Comprehensive
Bard College (1,153/113)
Marist College (5,395/756)
Vassar College (2,474)
Places Rated Score: 68.50
Places Rated Rank: 114

Eau Claire, WI
Public K–12 (87.78%)
11 districts, 54 schools
22,626 students
Private K–12 (12.22%)
16 Catholic, 2,370 students

11 Other, 779 students
Colleges and Universities
Associate of Arts
1 campus (5,148)
Comprehensive
University of Wisconsin (11,128/2,498)
Places Rated Score: 32.85
Places Rated Rank: 252

Edmonton, AB
Public Instruction (95.55%)
355 schools, 146,723 students
Private Instruction (4.45%)
28 Catholic and other, 6,824 students
Colleges and Universities
Associate of Arts
2 campuses (26,200)
Baccalaureate
Concordia College (1,383)
The King's University College (504)

16 Catholic, 4,624 students
9 Other, 2,341 students
Colleges and Universities
Associate of Arts
2 campuses (28,540)
Doctoral
University of Texas (17,596/3,972)
Places Rated Score: 42.06
Places Rated Rank: 216

Elkhart–Goshen, IN
Public K–12 (92.77%)
7 districts, 54 schools
27,922 students
Private K–12 (7.23%)
3 Catholic, 631 students
20 Other, 1,544 students
Colleges and Universities
Baccalaureate
Goshen College (1,382)
Places Rated Score: 21.33
Places Rated Rank: 290

Elmira, NY
Public K–12 (89.58%)
4 districts, 23 schools
15,489 students
Private K–12 (10.42%)
5 Catholic, 1,060 students
6 Other, 742 students
Colleges and Universities
Associate of Arts
1 campus (123)
Comprehensive
Elmira College (1,982/698)
Places Rated Score: 5.81
Places Rated Rank: 331

Enid, OK
Public K–12 (93.18%)
8 districts, 32 schools
10,136 students
Private K–12 (6.82%)
7 Other, 742 students
Colleges and Universities
Comprehensive
Phillips University (780/122)
Places Rated Score: 0.28
Places Rated Rank: 349

Erie, PA
Public K–12 (80.54%)
14 districts, 79 schools
40,996 students
Private K–12 (19.46%)
24 Catholic, 8,193 students
1 NAIS, 166 students
14 Other, 1,546 students
Colleges and Universities
Associate of Arts
3 campuses (807)
Comprehensive
Edinboro University of Pennsylvania (8,652/998)
Gannon University (3,930/887)
Mercyhurst College (2,768/87)
Penn State University (3,376/255)

1 campus (15,978)
Doctoral
University of Oregon (14,019/3,423)
Places Rated Score: 53.57
Places Rated Rank: 173

Evansville–Henderson, IN–KY
Public K–12 (87.14%)
6 districts, 82 schools
45,092 students
Private K–12 (12.86%)
17 Catholic, 4,789 students
15 Other, 1,863 students
Colleges and Universities
Associate of Arts
3 campuses (7,982)
Comprehensive
University of Evansville (3,163/198)
University of Southern Indiana (8,812/432)
Places Rated Score: 39.13
Places Rated Rank: 233

Fargo–Moorhead, ND–MN
Public K–12 (93.83%)
17 districts, 71 schools
27,680 students
Private K–12 (6.17%)
5 Catholic, 1,144 students
5 Other, 676 students
Colleges and Universities
Associate of Arts
1 campus (1,604)
Baccalaureate
Concordia College at Moorhead (3,081)
Comprehensive
Moorhead State University (9,347/992)
Doctoral
North Dakota State University (8,870/1,728)
Places Rated Score: 65.42
Places Rated Rank: 129

Fayetteville, NC
Public K–12 (95.58%)
1 district, 70 schools
46,081 students
Private K–12 (4.42%)
2 Catholic, 436 students
19 Other, 1,696 students
Colleges and Universities
Associate of Arts
1 campus (11,928)
Baccalaureate
Methodist College (2,196)
Comprehensive
Fayetteville State University (3,970/1,165)
Places Rated Score: 30.87
Places Rated Rank: 262

Fayetteville–Springdale–Rogers, AR
Public K–12 (95.71%)
16 districts, 78 schools
38,972 students
Private K–12 (4.29%)
2 Catholic, 421 students
10 Other, 1,325 students

7 districts, 35 schools
19,734 students
Private K–12 (15.86%)
6 Catholic, 1,735 students
3 NAIS, 724 students
7 Other, 1,260 students
Colleges and Universities
Associate of Arts
1 campus (6,794)
Comprehensive
Fitchburg State College (5,733/3,619)
Places Rated Score: 59.19
Places Rated Rank: 152

Flagstaff, AZ–UT
Public K–12 (97.18%)
8 districts, 43 schools
20,923 students
Private K–12 (2.82%)
1 Catholic, 234 students
5 Other, 374 students
Colleges and Universities
Doctoral
Northern Arizona University (16,448/7,643)
Places Rated Score: 23.12
Places Rated Rank: 286

Flint, MI
Public K–12 (92.79%)
21 districts, 151 schools
83,273 students
Private K–12 (7.21%)
11 Catholic, 3,762 students
1 NAIS, 147 students
24 Other, 2,566 students
Colleges and Universities
Associate of Arts
1 campus (18,883)
Baccalaureate
Baker College (5,269)
Detroit College of Business (1,169)
Comprehensive
GMI Engineering and Management Institute (2,386/832)
University of Michigan (7,403/581)

Places Rated Score: 71.56
Places Rated Rank: 96

Florence, AL
Public K–12 (97.18%)
6 districts, 49 schools
21,536 students
Private K–12 (2.82%)
1 Catholic, 259 students
3 Other, 366 students
Colleges and Universities
Associate of Arts
1 campus (4,764)
Comprehensive
University of North Alabama (6,230/805)
Places Rated Score: 39.43
Places Rated Rank: 232

Florence, SC
Public K–12 (90.07%)
5 districts, 38 schools
23,556 students
Private K–12 (9.93%)
1 Catholic, 176 students
17 Other, 2,422 students
Colleges and Universities
Associate of Arts
1 campus (8,212)
Comprehensive
Francis Marion University (4,700/957)
Places Rated Score: 27.37
Places Rated Rank: 271

Fort Collins–Loveland, CO
Public K–12 (94.64%)
3 districts, 73 schools
34,645 students
Private K–12 (5.36%)
2 Catholic, 480 students
12 Other, 1,484 students
Colleges and Universities
Comprehensive
National Technological University (4,866)
Doctoral
Colorado State University (20,146/4,378)
Places Rated Score: 50.54
Places Rated Rank: 188

Fort Lauderdale, FL
Public K–12 (83.81%)
1 district, 186 schools
173,628 students
Private K–12 (16.19%)
20 Catholic, 9,813 students
4 NAIS, 5,265 students
112 Other, 18,455 students
Colleges and Universities
Associate of Arts
4 campuses (54,817)
Baccalaureate
Art Institute of Fort Lauderdale (2,858)
National Education Center (1,143)
Comprehensive
Fort Lauderdale College (1,544/59)
Doctoral
Nova University (4,910/12,476)
Places Rated Score: 68.53
Places Rated Rank: 112

Fort Myers–Cape Coral, FL
Public K–12 (91.06%)
1 district, 65 schools
44,230 students
Private K–12 (8.94%)
2 Catholic, 1,017 students
22 Other, 3,323 students
Colleges and Universities
Associate of Arts
1 campus (14,379)
Places Rated Score: 7.21
Places Rated Rank: 324

Fort Pierce–Port St. Lucie, FL
Public K–12 (89.92%)
2 districts, 46 schools
33,419 students
Private K–12 (10.08%)
4 Catholic, 1,498 students
1 NAIS, 243 students
16 Other, 2,005 students
Colleges and Universities
Associate of Arts
1 campus (25,439)
Places Rated Score: 40.41
Places Rated Rank: 227

Fort Smith, AR–OK
Public K–12 (95.93%)
25 districts, 88 schools
33,848 students
Private K–12 (4.07%)
4 Catholic, 926 students
8 Other, 510 students
Colleges and Universities
Associate of Arts
1 campus (8,748)
Places Rated Score: 1.74
Places Rated Rank: 342

Fort Walton Beach, FL
Public K–12 (96.62%)
1 district, 36 schools
28,177 students
Private K–12 (3.38%)
8 Other, 986 students
Colleges and Universities
Associate of Arts
1 campus (15,641)
Places Rated Score: 17.66
Places Rated Rank: 304

Fort Wayne, IN
Public K–12 (84.21%)
16 districts, 142 schools
79,346 students
Private K–12 (15.79%)
20 Catholic, 6,400 students
1 NAIS, 581 students
56 Other, 7,892 students
Colleges and Universities
Associate of Arts
2 campuses (7,272)
Baccalaureate
Indiana Institute of Technology (1,366)
ITT Technical Institute (2,242)
Lutheran College of Health Professions (738)
Comprehensive
Huntington College (606/41)
Indiana University–Purdue University (14,531/1,374)
St. Francis College (848/358)
Places Rated Score: 62.76
Places Rated Rank: 140

Fort Worth–Arlington, TX
Public K–12 (95.26%)
37 districts, 444 schools
257,024 students
Private K–12 (4.74%)
12 Catholic, 3,939 students
4 NAIS, 2,403 students
33 Other, 6,437 students
Colleges and Universities
Associate of Arts
4 campuses (50,325)
Comprehensive
Southwestern Adventist College (1,121/24)
Texas Wesleyan University (1,687/504)
Doctoral
SW Baptist Theological Seminary (363/3,677)
Texas Christian University (6,739/1,390)
University of Texas (20,406/4,323)
Places Rated Score: 77.08
Places Rated Rank: 76

Fresno, CA
Public K–12 (96.61%)
50 districts, 320 schools
185,950 students
Private K–12 (3.39%)
7 Catholic, 2,314 students
46 Other, 4,207 students
Colleges and Universities
Associate of Arts
4 campuses (43,024)
Comprehensive
Cal State University (16,377/4,302)
Fresno Pacific College (886/1,396)
San Joaquin College of Law (73/393)
Places Rated Score: 58.29
Places Rated Rank: 157

Gadsden, AL
Public K–12 (94.80%)
3 districts, 41 schools
16,871 students
Private K–12 (5.20%)
1 Catholic, 191 students
6 Other, 735 students
Colleges and Universities
Associate of Arts
1 campus (11,432)
Places Rated Score: 21.32
Places Rated Rank: 291

Gainesville, FL
Public K–12 (90.34%)
1 district, 39 schools
24,923 students
Private K–12 (9.66%)
1 Catholic, 435 students
1 NAIS, 275 students
23 Other, 1,956 students
Colleges and Universities
Associate of Arts
1 campus (17,331)
Doctoral
University of Florida (31,814/10,689)
Places Rated Score: 59.55
Places Rated Rank: 150

Galveston–Texas City, TX
Public K–12 (95.85%)
9 districts, 88 schools
59,106 students
Private K–12 (4.15%)
6 Catholic, 1,456 students
3 Other, 1,100 students
Colleges and Universities
Associate of Arts
2 campuses (9,240)
Baccalaureate
Texas A & M University (3,320)
Doctoral
University of Texas Medical Branch (1,213/1,274)
Places Rated Score: 50.66
Places Rated Rank: 187

Gary, IN
Public K–12 (89.65%)

23 districts, 193 schools
110,212 students
Private K-12 (10.35%)
27 Catholic, 8,160 students
31 Other, 4,564 students
Colleges and Universities
Associate of Arts
3 campuses (4,975)
Baccalaureate
Calumet College of St. Joseph (1,503)
Comprehensive
Indiana University Northwest (7,006/1,181)
Purdue University Calumet (11,100/1,371)
Valparaiso University (3,299/877)
Places Rated Score: 65.43
Places Rated Rank: 128

Glens Falls, NY

Grand Rapids–Muskegon–Holland, MI
Public K-12 (85.16%)
50 districts, 378 schools
171,570 students
Private K-12 (14.84%)
40 Catholic, 9,870 students
83 Other, 20,020 students
Colleges and Universities
Associate of Arts
3 campuses (32,377)
Baccalaureate
Baker College of Muskegon (2,359)
Davenport College (12,957)
Hope College (3,308)
Jordan College (2,961)
Kendall College of Art and Design (718)
Comprehensive
Aquinas College (2,461/1,083)
Calvin College (3,925/429)

6 NAIS, 2,601 students
62 Other, 6,682 students
Colleges and Universities
Associate of Arts
5 campuses (37,680)
Baccalaureate
Bennett College (673)
Greensboro College (1,140)
Guilford College (2,057)
***Winston-Salem State University* (3,511)**
Comprehensive
Elon College (3,288/208)
High Point University (3,161)
***North Carolina A & T University* (8,076/1,338)**
Salem College (841/132)
Doctoral
***University of North Carolina* (12,331/3,976)**
Wake Forest University (3,768/1,883)

Goldsboro, NC
Public K-12 (93.64%)
1 district, 27 schools
14,009 students
Private K-12 (6.36%)
1 Catholic, 254 students
5 Other, 698 students
Colleges and Universities
Associate of Arts
1 campus (4,198)
Baccalaureate
Mount Olive College (1,285)
Places Rated Score: 32.05
Places Rated Rank: 256

Grand Forks, ND–MN
Public K-12 (93.38%)
15 districts, 51 schools
18,181 students
Private K-12 (6.62%)
6 Catholic, 964 students
8 Other, 324 students
Colleges and Universities
Associate of Arts
1 campus (1,381)
Baccalaureate
University of Minnesota (2,427)
Doctoral
University of North Dakota (10,538/2,504)
Places Rated Score: 61.22
Places Rated Rank: 145

Grand Junction, CO
Public K-12 (94.36%)
4 districts, 43 schools
18,514 students
Private K-12 (5.64%)
1 Catholic, 446 students
8 Other, 661 students
Colleges and Universities
Associate of Arts
1 campus (385)
Baccalaureate
Mesa State College (5,643)
Places Rated Score: 22.00
Places Rated Rank: 289

Private K-12 (5.23%)
2 Catholic, 568 students
5 Other, 245 students
Colleges and Universities
Comprehensive
College of Great Falls (1,567/193)
Places Rated Score: 0.54
Places Rated Rank: 347

Greeley, CO
Public K-12 (96.07%)
13 districts, 63 schools
24,484 students
Private K-12 (3.93%)
6 Other, 1,001 students
Colleges and Universities
Associate of Arts
1 campus (18,130)
Doctoral
University of Northern Colorado (12,616/5,940)
Places Rated Score: 65.69
Places Rated Rank: 125

Green Bay, WI
Public K-12 (83.22%)
9 districts, 66 schools
32,945 students
Private K-12 (16.78%)
20 Catholic, 5,187 students
15 Other, 1,456 students
Colleges and Universities
Associate of Arts
1 campus (13,705)
Comprehensive
St. Norbert College (2,225/213)
University of Wisconsin (5,961/843)
Places Rated Score: 61.36
Places Rated Rank: 144

Greensboro–Winston-Salem–High Point, NC
Public K-12 (92.38%)
12 districts, 286 schools
135,016 students
Private K-12 (7.62%)
7 Catholic, 1,847 students

1 campus (6,554)
Doctoral
East Carolina University (17,600/4,295)
Places Rated Score: 50.95
Places Rated Rank: 186

Greenville–Spartanburg–Anderson, SC
Public K-12 (94.77%)
16 districts, 260 schools
137,657 students
Private K-12 (5.23%)
5 Catholic, 919 students
2 NAIS, 1,192 students
80 Other, 5,486 students
Colleges and Universities
Associate of Arts
4 campuses (17,975)
Baccalaureate
Anderson College (1,539)
Limestone College (2,168)
University of South Carolina (4,349)
Wofford College (1,276)
Comprehensive
Central Wesleyan College (1,583/159)
Converse College (1,023/906)
Furman University (2,488/932)
Doctoral
Clemson University (14,234/4,504)
Places Rated Score: 65.88
Places Rated Rank: 124

Hagerstown, MD
Public K-12 (90.24%)
1 district, 43 schools
18,564 students
Private K-12 (9.76%)
1 Catholic, 277 students
1 NAIS, 130 students
14 Other, 1,601 students
Colleges and Universities
Associate of Arts
2 campuses (4,775)
Places Rated Score: 13.28
Places Rated Rank: 313

Halifax, NS
Public K–12 (98.3%)
3 school boards, 148 schools
57,076 students
Private K–12 (1.7%)
4 Catholic and Other
1,009 students
Colleges and Universities
Associate of Arts
4 campuses (6,756)
Baccalaureate
University of King's College (694)
Comprehensive
Mount St. Vincent University (3,359/243)
Nova Scotia College of Art and Design (556/20)
St. Mary's University (6,928/677)
Doctoral
Dalhousie University (8,697/2,193)
Technical University of Nova Scotia (1,070/379)
Places Rated Score: 69.90
Places Rated Rank: 108

Hamilton, ON
Public K–13 (64.30%)
91 schools, 40,615 students
Catholic Separate K–13 (32.03%)
40 schools, 20,233 students
Private K–13 (3.65%)
11 schools, 2,310 students
Colleges and Universities
Associate of Arts
1 campus (14,000)
Baccalaureate
Redeemer College (472)
Doctoral
McMaster University (14,453/2,632)
Places Rated Score: 52.79
Places Rated Rank: 177

Hamilton–Middletown, OH
Public K–12 (91.83%)
10 districts, 78 schools
52,949 students
Private K–12 (8.17%)
9 Catholic, 3,367 students
8 Other, 1,345 students
Colleges and Universities
Associate of Arts
3 campuses (8,493)
Doctoral
Miami University (15,286/3,757)
Places Rated Score: 57.22
Places Rated Rank: 163

Harrisburg–Lebanon–Carlisle, PA
Public K–12 (89.08%)
35 districts, 218 schools
95,280 students
Private K–12 (10.92%)
15 Catholic, 5,541 students
3 NAIS, 1,610 students
26 Other, 4,532 students
Colleges and Universities
Associate of Arts
5 campuses (17,204)
Baccalaureate
Dickinson College (2,312)
Messiah College (2,350)
Comprehensive
Lebanon Valley College (1,655/225)
Shippensburg University (6,311/1,596)
Widener University (1,118)
Doctoral
Penn State University (2,860/2,727)
Places Rated Score: 78.55
Places Rated Rank: 69

Hartford, CT
Public K–12 (91.40%)
58 districts, 385 schools
187,469 students
Private K–12 (8.60%)
43 Catholic, 12,468 students
9 NAIS, 3,071 students
31 Other, 2,103 students
Colleges and Universities
Associate of Arts
9 campuses (31,009)
Baccalaureate
Charter Oak State College (1,184)
Comprehensive
Central Connecticut State (12,769/3,184)
Hartford Graduate Center (2,327)
St. Joseph College (1,424/1,125)
Trinity College (2,015/207)
Doctoral
University of Hartford (5,697/2,587)
Wesleyan University (2,873/994)
Places Rated Score: 80.31
Places Rated Rank: 60

Hattiesburg, MS
Public K–12 (97.12%)
6 districts, 27 schools
18,597 students
Private K–12 (2.88%)
1 Catholic, 178 students
5 Other, 374 students
Colleges and Universities
Comprehensive
William Carey College (2,515/406)
Doctoral
University of Southern Mississippi (13,809/4,205)
Places Rated Score: 60.04
Places Rated Rank: 148

Hickory–Morganton–Lenoir, NC
Public K–12 (97.25%)
6 districts, 93 schools
46,855 students
Private K–12 (2.75%)
1 NAIS, 41 students
20 Other, 1,284 students
Colleges and Universities
Associate of Arts
3 campuses (14,556)
Comprehensive
Lenoir-Rhyne College (1,723/143)
Places Rated Score: 40.78
Places Rated Rank: 223

Honolulu, HI
Public K–12 (86.42%)
1 district, 241 schools
179,915 students
Private K–12 (13.58%)
27 Catholic, 9,523 students
9 NAIS, 8,434 students
62 Other, 10,311 students
Colleges and Universities
Associate of Arts
4 campuses (24,835)
Baccalaureate
Brigham Young University (2,510)
University of Hawaii (918)
Comprehensive
Chaminade University (3,877/532)
Hawaii Pacific University (9,775/1,240)
Doctoral
University of Hawaii (19,472/15,753)
Places Rated Score: 73.15
Places Rated Rank: 91

Houma, LA
Public K–12 (87.19%)
3 districts, 76 schools
38,305 students
Private K–12 (12.81%)
12 Catholic, 5,352 students
3 Other, 277 students
Colleges and Universities
Comprehensive
Nicholls State University (8,425/1,487)
Places Rated Score: 3.18
Places Rated Rank: 338

Houston, TX
Public K–12 (94.10%)
44 districts, 924 schools
685,093 students
Private K–12 (5.90%)
49 Catholic, 14,722 students
4 NAIS, 3,563 students
135 Other, 24,652 students
Colleges and Universities
Associate of Arts
9 campuses (137,502)
Baccalaureate
University of Houston (12,127)
Comprehensive
Houston Baptist University (1,755/447)
Prairie View A & M University (11,073/2,152)
University of Houston (4,612/5,055)
Doctoral
Baylor College of Medicine (42/1,034)
Rice University (2,913/1,641)
Texas Southern University (10,956/2,594)
University of Saint Thomas (1,760/3,025)
University of Texas Health Science Center (711/2,976)
Places Rated Score: 71.20
Places Rated Rank: 100

Huntington–Ashland, WV–KY–OH
Public K–12 (97.06%)
17 districts, 137 schools
52,058 students
Private K–12 (2.94%)
6 Catholic, 933 students
7 Other, 644 students
Colleges and Universities
Associate of Arts
2 campuses (5,259)
Comprehensive
Ohio University (2,706/366)
Doctoral
Marshall University (11,927/4,293)
Places Rated Score: 59.40
Places Rated Rank: 151

Huntsville, AL
Public K–12 (92.37%)
4 districts, 85 schools
49,271 students
Private K–12 (7.63%)
2 Catholic, 523 students
1 NAIS, 522 students
18 Other, 3,023 students
Colleges and Universities
Associate of Arts
4 campuses (31,202)
Baccalaureate
Athens State College (4,292)
Oakwood College (1,527)
Doctoral
Alabama A & M University (4,174/1,598)
University of Alabama (9,078/2,911)

Places Rated Score: 80.16
Places Rated Rank: 63

Indianapolis, IN
Public K–12 (89.16%)
55 districts, 426 schools
238,057 students
Private K–12 (10.84%)
44 Catholic, 15,031 students
2 NAIS, 1,348 students
120 Other, 12,560 students
Colleges and Universities
Associate of Arts
2 campuses (10,522)
Baccalaureate
Franklin College of Indiana (917)
ITT Technical Institute (1,691)
Marian College (1,539)
Comprehensive

Public K–12 (
5 districts, 28 schools
11,687 students
Private K–12 (8.83%)
2 Catholic, 846 students
4 Other, 286 students
Colleges and Universities
Doctoral
University of Iowa (23,692/13,627)
Places Rated Score: 62.67
Places Rated Rank: 141

Jackson, MI
Public K–12 (88.40%)
12 districts, 54 schools
24,151 students
Private K–12 (11.60%)
8 Catholic, 2,412 students
7 Other, 757 students
Colleges and Universities
Associate of Arts
1 campus (12,050)
Baccalaureate
Spring Arbor College (2,595)
Places Rated Score: 32.65
Places Rated Rank: 254

Jackson, MS
Public K–12 (86.01%)
8 districts, 120 schools
70,912 students
Private K–12 (13.99%)
8 Catholic, 2,538 students
1 NAIS, 343 students
25 Other, 8,656 students
Colleges and Universities
Associate of Arts
5 campuses (12,016)
Baccalaureate
Belhaven College (1,263)
Tougaloo College (1,286)
Comprehensive
Millsaps College (1,355/134)
Mississippi College (3,068/2,013)
Doctoral
Jackson State University (5,456/747)
Reformed Theological Seminary (615)
University of Mississippi Medical Center (643/1,027)

Places Rated Score: 69.65
Places Rated Rank: 109

Jackson, TN
Public K–12 (88.86%)
1 district, 22 schools
13,817 students
Private K–12 (11.14%)
1 Catholic, 234 students
1 NAIS, 757 students
5 Other, 742 students
Colleges and Universities
Associate of Arts
1 campus (4,896)
Baccalaureate
Lambuth University (1,387)
Comprehensive
Union University (2,784/223)
Places Rated Score: 58.89
Places Rated Rank: 153

2 campuses (
Baccalaureate
Flagler College (1,496)
Jones College (1,243)
Comprehensive
Edward Waters College (759/882)
Jacksonville University (2,522/680)
Doctoral
University of North Florida (10,464/1,874)
Places Rated Score: 40.36
Places Rated Rank: 228

Jacksonville, NC
Public K–12 (96.78%)
2 districts, 36 schools
19,372 students
Private K–12 (3.22%)
1 Catholic, 271 students
5 Other, 373 students
Colleges and Universities
Associate of Arts
1 campus (6,043)
Places Rated Score: 1.45
Places Rated Rank: 345

Jamestown, NY
Public K–12 (95.84%)
19 districts, 58 schools
25,911 students
Private K–12 (4.16%)
3 Catholic, 599 students
8 Other, 525 students
Colleges and Universities
Associate of Arts
2 campuses (5,019)
Comprehensive
SUNY College at Fredonia (4,771/836)
Places Rated Score: 42.57
Places Rated Rank: 212

Janesville–Beloit, WI
Public K–12 (91.93%)
8 districts, 57 schools
25,876 students
Private K–12 (8.07%)
8 Catholic, 1,315 students
12 Other, 958 students

Colleges and Universities
Associate of Arts
1 campus (16,367)
Comprehensive
Beloit College (1,216/10)
Places Rated Score: 47.00
Places Rated Rank: 201

Jersey City, NJ
Public K–12 (79.09%)
13 districts, 101 schools
67,974 students
Private K–12 (20.91%)
52 Catholic, 16,991 students
1 NAIS, 111 students
8 Other, 873 students
Colleges and Universities
Associate of Arts
1 campus (4,660)
Comprehensive
Jersey City State College

70,253 students
Private K–12 (2.28%)
2 Catholic, 382 students
13 Other, 1,255 students
Colleges and Universities
Associate of Arts
2 campuses (8,118)
Baccalaureate
Emory and Henry College (826)
King College (635)
Comprehensive
Milligan College (786/86)
Doctoral
East Tennessee State University (11,384/2,992)
Places Rated Score: 54.77
Places Rated Rank: 170

Johnstown, PA
Public K–12 (86.78%)
26 districts, 79 schools
34,797 students
Private K–12 (13.22%)
23 Catholic, 4,543 students
12 Other, 756 students
Colleges and Universities
Associate of Arts
1 campus (1,208)
Baccalaureate
Mount Aloysius College (4,799)
University of Pittsburgh (3,824)
Comprehensive
St. Francis College (1,994/632)
Places Rated Score: 39.93
Places Rated Rank: 231

Joplin, MO
Public K–12 (96.23%)
12 districts, 68 schools
24,555 students
Private K–12 (3.77%)
4 Catholic, 442 students
8 Other, 519 students
Colleges and Universities
Associate of Arts
1 campus (3,033)

Baccalaureate
Missouri Southern State College (7,239)
Ozark Christian College (611)
Places Rated Score: 40.49
Places Rated Rank: 226

Kalamazoo–Battle Creek, MI
Public K–12 (91.52%)
32 districts, 185 schools
75,673 students
Private K–12 (8.48%)
12 Catholic, 3,443 students
29 Other, 3,565 students
Colleges and Universities
Associate of Arts
2 campuses (31,824)
Baccalaureate
Albion College (1,690)
Davenport College (2,649)
Kalamazoo College (1,250)
Doctoral
Western Michigan University (22,974/10,394)
Places Rated Score: 77.65
Places Rated Rank: 72

Kankakee, IL
Public K–12 (88.05%)
14 districts, 46 schools
17,757 students
Private K–12 (11.95%)
6 Catholic, 1,540 students
5 Other, 870 students
Colleges and Universities
Associate of Arts
1 campus (9,902)
Comprehensive
Olivet Nazarene University (2,140/351)
Places Rated Score: 40.52
Places Rated Rank: 225

✓ Kansas City, MO–KS
Public K–12 (90.47%)
65 districts, 610 schools
271,699 students
Private K–12 (9.53%)
52 Catholic, 15,066 students
2 NAIS, 1,309 students
73 Other, 12,252 students
Colleges and Universities
Associate of Arts
7 campuses (65,880)
Baccalaureate
Devry Institute of Technology (2,546)
Kansas City Art Institute (626)
William Jewell College (2,464)
Comprehensive
Avila College (1,196/254)
Mid-America Nazarene College (1,418/218)
Ottawa University (531/94)
Park College (15,434/152)
Rockhurst College (2,331/1,121)
St. Mary College (1,023)
Doctoral
University of Kansas Medical Center (661/2,577)
University of Missouri (9,530/8,400)
Places Rated Score: 91.68
Places Rated Rank: 20

Kenosha, WI
Public K–12 (86.40%)
13 districts, 45 schools
22,349 students
Private K–12 (13.60%)
9 Catholic, 2,288 students
8 Other, 1,229 students
Colleges and Universities
Associate of Arts
1 campus (15,297)
Comprehensive
Carthage College (2,473/175)
University of Wisconsin (6,421/341)
Places Rated Score: 65.66
Places Rated Rank: 126

Killeen–Temple, TX
Public K–12 (98.27%)
14 districts, 120 schools
52,125 students
Private K–12 (1.73%)
2 Catholic, 322 students
6 Other, 598 students
Colleges and Universities
Associate of Arts
2 campuses (19,846)
Comprehensive
Baylor University (2,222/338)
University of Central Texas (722/588)
Places Rated Score: 49.98
Places Rated Rank: 190

Kitchener, ON
Public K–13 (63.60%)
113 schools, 56,128 students
Catholic Separate K–13 (26.40%)
52 schools, 23,303 students
Private K–13 (9.99%)
42 schools, 8,820 students
Colleges and Universities
Associate of Arts
1 campus (4,500)
Doctoral
University of Waterloo (20,508/2,107)
Wilfrid Laurier University (7,387/773)
Places Rated Score: 47.13
Places Rated Rank: 199

Knoxville, TN
Public K–12 (94.82%)
11 districts, 177 schools
98,091 students
Private K–12 (5.18%)
4 Catholic, 1,393 students
1 NAIS, 741 students
10 Other, 3,229 students
Colleges and Universities
Associate of Arts
5 campuses (12,486)
Baccalaureate
Knoxville College (2,118)
Maryville College (929)
Doctoral
University of Tennessee (22,572/9,597)
Places Rated Score: 62.01
Places Rated Rank: 142

Kokomo, IN
Public K–12 (92.48%)
7 districts, 34 schools
17,587 students
Private K–12 (7.52%)
2 Catholic, 460 students
11 Other, 970 students
Colleges and Universities
Associate of Arts
1 campus (3,408)
Comprehensive
Indiana University (5,262/364)
Places Rated Score: 35.06
Places Rated Rank: 243

La Crosse, WI–MN
Public K–12 (82.38%)
9 districts, 40 schools
17,258 students
Private K–12 (17.62%)
11 Catholic, 2,259 students
13 Other, 1,433 students
Colleges and Universities
Associate of Arts
2 campuses (19,407)
Comprehensive
University of Wisconsin (8,924/2,095)
Viterbo College (1,407/3,467)
Places Rated Score: 75.66
Places Rated Rank: 79

Lafayette, IN
Public K–12 (92.63%)
7 districts, 46 schools
23,850 students
Private K–12 (7.37%)
4 Catholic, 877 students
10 Other, 1,021 students
Colleges and Universities
Associate of Arts
1 campus (3,739)
Doctoral
Purdue University (34,716/8,496)
Places Rated Score: 57.23
Places Rated Rank: 162

Lafayette, LA
Public K–12 (85.92%)
5 districts, 125 schools
68,430 students
Private K–12 (14.08%)
27 Catholic, 9,782 students
13 Other, 1,429 students
Colleges and Universities
Associate of Arts
2 campuses (4,739)
Doctoral
University of SW Louisiana (18,337/2,091)
Places Rated Score: 25.90
Places Rated Rank: 277

Lake Charles, LA
Public K–12 (92.00%)
2 districts, 62 schools
33,967 students
Private K–12 (8.00%)
8 Catholic, 2,296 students
7 Other, 659 students
Colleges and Universities
Comprehensive
McNeese State University (8,634/1,820)
Places Rated Score: 3.93
Places Rated Rank: 335

Lakeland–Winter Haven, FL
Public K–12 (93.48%)
1 district, 104 schools
64,505 students
Private K–12 (6.52%)
4 Catholic, 1,079 students
25 Other, 3,421 students
Colleges and Universities
Associate of Arts
1 campus (16,679)
Baccalaureate
SE College Assemblies of God (1,345)
Tampa College Lakeland (1,472)
Comprehensive
Florida Southern College (4,010/112)
Places Rated Score: 73.32
Places Rated Rank: 89

Lancaster, PA
Public K–12 (84.74%)
17 districts, 129 schools

62,938 students
Private K-12 (15.26%)
9 Catholic, 2,655 students
2 NAIS, 553 students
92 Other, 8,129 students
Colleges and Universities
Associate of Arts
1 campus (494)
Baccalaureate
Elizabethtown College (2,021)
Franklin and Marshall College (1,894)
Comprehensive
Millersville University of Pennsylvania (8,163/3,442)
Places Rated Score: 59.91
Places Rated Rank: 149

Lansing-East Lansing, MI
Public K-12 (92.92%)
27 districts, 169 schools

Michigan State University (33,124/11,731)
Places Rated Score: 81.49
Places Rated Rank: 55

Laredo, TX
Public K-12 (94.69%)
4 districts, 57 schools
38,646 students
Private K-12 (5.31%)
6 Catholic, 1,978 students
2 Other, 188 students
Colleges and Universities
Associate of Arts
1 campus (12,337)
Comprehensive
Texas A & M International University (1,128/1,097)
Places Rated Score: 18.34
Places Rated Rank: 302

Las Cruces, NM
Public K-12 (97.10%)
3 districts, 53 schools
33,257 students
Private K-12 (2.90%)
2 Catholic, 339 students
7 Other, 653 students
Colleges and Universities
Associate of Arts
1 campus (3,615)
Doctoral
New Mexico State University (15,690/3,079)
Places Rated Score: 42.50
Places Rated Rank: 213

Las Vegas, NV-AZ
Public K-12 (96.01%)
17 districts, 251 schools
166,627 students
Private K-12 (3.99%)
9 Catholic, 2,926 students
2 NAIS, 832 students
38 Other, 3,161 students
Colleges and Universities
Associate of Arts
2 campuses (44,246)
Doctoral
University of Nevada (22,561/5,688)
Places Rated Score: 22.40
Places Rated Rank: 288

✓ Lawrence, KS
Public K-12 (96.81%)
3 districts, 32 schools
11,805 students
Private K-12 (3.19%)
1 Catholic, 307 students
1 Other, 82 students
Colleges and Universities
Baccalaureate
Haskell Indian Junior College (1,257)
Comprehensive
Baker University (1,424/413)
Doctoral
University of Kansas (26,090/9,623)
Places Rated Score: 92.27

Associate of Arts
3 campuses (12,572)
Baccalaureate
Bradford College (510)
Merrimack College (3,849)
Places Rated Score: 65.19
Places Rated Rank: 130

Lawton, OK
Public K-12 (98.14%)
12 districts, 65 schools
22,749 students
Private K-12 (1.86%)
1 Catholic, 216 students
2 Other, 216 students
Colleges and Universities
Comprehensive
Cameron University (8,073/498)
Places Rated Score: 5.36
Places Rated Rank: 332

Lewiston-Auburn, ME
Public K-12 (93.24%)
7 districts, 42 schools
16,507 students
Private K-12 (6.76%)
4 Catholic, 1,068 students
4 Other, 128 students
Colleges and Universities
Associate of Arts
3 campuses (2,291)
Baccalaureate
Bates College (1,618)
Places Rated Score: 34.37
Places Rated Rank: 247

Lexington, KY
Public K-12 (93.68%)
9 districts, 120 schools
65,531 students
Private K-12 (6.32%)
9 Catholic, 2,423 students
4 NAIS, 795 students
17 Other, 1,203 students
Colleges and Universities
Associate of Arts
3 campuses (8,258)
Baccalaureate
Asbury College (1,179)
Berea College (1,681)
Midway College (941)
Transylvania University (1,028)
Comprehensive
Eastern Kentucky University (16,252/2,940)
Georgetown College (1,279/573)
Doctoral
Asbury Theological Seminary (901)
University of Kentucky (19,660/7,288)
Places Rated Score: 85.66
Places Rated Rank: 42

Lima, OH
Public K-12 (89.81%)
16 districts, 66 schools
29,648 students
Private K-12 (10.19%)
8 Catholic, 2,830 students

Lincoln, NE
Public K-12 (86.99%)
8 districts, 65 schools
32,750 students
Private K-12 (13.01%)
11 Catholic, 3,377 students
19 Other, 1,522 students
Colleges and Universities
Associate of Arts
2 campuses (9,288)
Baccalaureate
Nebraska Wesleyan University (1,856)
Union College (624)
Doctoral
University of Nebraska (22,244/6,837)
Places Rated Score: 85.98
Places Rated Rank: 39

Little Rock-North Little Rock, AR
Public K-12 (86.48%)
21 districts, 178 schools
83,095 students
Private K-12 (13.52%)
12 Catholic, 4,368 students
1 NAIS, 1,199 students
35 Other, 7,422 students
Colleges and Universities
Associate of Arts
3 campuses (1,619)
Baccalaureate
Arkansas Baptist College (674)
Hendrix College (1,030)
Philander Smith College (940)
Comprehensive
University of Central Arkansas (9,799/1,958)
Doctoral
University of Arkansas (14,522/2,756)
University of Arkansas for Medical Sciences (734/1,266)
Places Rated Score: 68.00
Places Rated Rank: 118

London, ON
Public K-13 (74.70%)
114 schools, 60,161 students

Catholic Separate K-13 (20.85%)
41 schools, 16,798 students
Private K-13 (4.43%)
17 schools, 3,570 students
Colleges and Universities
Associate of Arts
2 campuses (23,000)
Baccalaureate
Brescia College (847)
Huron College (842)
King's College (2,278)
Doctoral
University of Western Ontario (21,355/3,171)
Places Rated Score: 70.72
Places Rated Rank: 104

✓ Long Island, NY
Public K-12 (87.80%)
130 districts, 635 schools
397,698 students
Private K-12 (12.20%)
75 Catholic, 35,008 students
10 NAIS, 3,262 students
95 Other, 17,005 students
Colleges and Universities
Associate of Arts
6 campuses (69,185)
Baccalaureate
Five Towns College (763)
St. Josephs College (2,338)
SUNY College at Old Westbury (5,316)
SUNY College of Technology (12,327)
U.S. Merchant Marine Academy (1,027)
Comprehensive
Dowling College (4,582/2,527)
Long Island University (1,682/793)
Molloy College (4,059/115)
New York Institute of Technology (6,583/3,758)
Doctoral
Adelphi University (4,965/6,060)
Hofstra University (9,960/4,747)
Long Island University (5,150/4,730)
SUNY at Stony Brook (13,606/7,467)
Places Rated Score: 95.34
Places Rated Rank: 8

Longview-Marshall, TX
Public K-12 (97.12%)
20 districts, 109 schools
42,352 students
Private K-12 (2.88%)
2 Catholic, 302 students
7 Other, 956 students
Colleges and Universities
Associate of Arts
1 campus (14,162)
Baccalaureate
Wiley College (614)
Comprehensive
East Texas Baptist University (1,564/22)
Letourneau University (2,126/77)
Places Rated Score: 45.00
Places Rated Rank: 206

✓ Los Angeles-Long Beach, CA
Public K-12 (88.29%)
97 districts, 1,761 schools
1,589,355 students
Private K-12 (11.71%)
265 Catholic, 94,821 students
30 NAIS, 12,782 students
917 Other, 103,220 students
Colleges and Universities
Associate of Arts
31 campuses (465,008)
Baccalaureate
Claremont McKenna College (909)
Devry Institute of Technology (3,013)
ITT Technical Institute (1,092)
Pitzer College (788)
Pomona College (1,517)
Scripps College (624)
Comprehensive
Antioch University (330/562)
Art Center College of Design (1,650/61)
Azusa Pacific University (1,975/1,676)
Cal State University Dominguez Hills (8,316/4,246)
Cal State University Long Beach (25,669/7,618)
Cal State University Northridge (24,869/7,242)
California Institute of the Arts (676/336)
California State Polytechnic University (18,389/2,937)
Cleveland Chiropractic College (602)
College of Osteopathic Medicine (72/645)
Harvey Mudd College (636/13)
Loyola Marymount University (5,439/2,834)
Masters College (1,035/252)
Mount Saint Marys College (1,558/592)
Occidental College (1,692/39)
Otis College of Art and Design (718/17)
Pacific Oaks College (343/585)
University of West Los Angeles (363/889)
West Coast University (763/865)
Whittier College (1,224/903)
Woodbury University (1,116/220)
Doctoral
Biola University (2,267/1,032)
Cal State University Los Angeles (18,361/7,222)
California Institute of Technology (932/1,215)
California School of Professional Psychology (617)
Claremont Graduate School (2,037)
Fuller Theological Seminary (3,659)
Pepperdine University (3,563/5,042)
University of California Los Angeles (33,303/12,986)
University of Laverne (3,130/2,831)
University of Southern California (16,577/15,091)
Places Rated Score: 97.91
Places Rated Rank: 4

Louisville, KY-IN
Public K-12 (84.16%)
13 districts, 264 schools
149,470 students
Private K-12 (15.84%)
74 Catholic, 22,334 students
6 NAIS, 1,361 students
60 Other, 4,432 students
Colleges and Universities
Associate of Arts
6 campuses (22,282)
Baccalaureate
Sullivan College (2,179)
Comprehensive
Bellarmine College (3,431/732)
Indiana University SE (7,374/665)
Doctoral
Southern Baptist Theological Seminary (105/1,924)
Spalding University (874/468)
University of Louisville (20,159/6,527)
Places Rated Score: 64.42
Places Rated Rank: 133

Lowell, MA-NH
Public K-12 (89.45%)
11 districts, 76 schools
43,451 students
Private K-12 (10.55%)
15 Catholic, 3,947 students
2 NAIS, 642 students
5 Other, 538 students
Colleges and Universities
Doctoral
University of Massachusetts (12,234/3,223)
Places Rated Score: 25.54
Places Rated Rank: 278

Lubbock, TX
Public K-12 (95.26%)
8 districts, 96 schools
42,669 students
Private K-12 (4.74%)
2 Catholic, 383 students
7 Other, 1,740 students
Colleges and Universities
Comprehensive
Lubbock Christian University (1,450/26)
Doctoral
Texas Tech University (22,055/6,230)
Texas Tech University Health Sciences Center (766/497)
Places Rated Score: 47.57
Places Rated Rank: 197

Lynchburg, VA
Public K-12 (92.83%)
5 districts, 69 schools
30,448 students
Private K-12 (7.17%)
1 Catholic, 319 students
2 NAIS, 289 students
5 Other, 1,745 students
Colleges and Universities
Associate of Arts
1 campus (5,953)
Baccalaureate
Randolph-Macon Woman's College (768)
Sweet Briar College (618)
Comprehensive
Lynchburg College (2,210/915)
Doctoral
Liberty University (10,791/3,410)
Places Rated Score: 65.49
Places Rated Rank: 127

Macon, GA
Public K-12 (88.80%)
5 districts, 83 schools
51,418 students
Private K-12 (11.20%)
4 Catholic, 1,369 students
29 Other, 5,113 students
Colleges and Universities
Associate of Arts
4 campuses (12,284)
Comprehensive
Fort Valley State College (3,418/467)
Doctoral
Mercer University (5,229/3,151)
Places Rated Score: 55.70
Places Rated Rank: 167

Madison, WI
Public K-12 (92.19%)
16 districts, 124 schools
52,611 students
Private K-12 (7.81%)
12 Catholic, 2,837 students
18 Other, 1,621 students

Colleges and Universities
Associate of Arts
4 campuses (34,399)
Comprehensive
Edgewood College (1,469/595)
Doctoral
University of Wisconsin (34,246/13,611)
Places Rated Score: 79.00
Places Rated Rank: 66

✓ Manchester, NH
Public K–12 (89.43%)
5 districts, 40 schools
26,660 students
Private K–12 (10.57%)
14 Catholic, 2,288 students
1 NAIS, 295 students
7 Other, 569 students
Colleges and Universities

Mansfield, OH
Public K–12 (91.22%)
16 districts, 74 schools
31,838 students
Private K–12 (8.78%)
9 Catholic, 1,689 students
9 Other, 1,377 students
Colleges and Universities
Associate of Arts
1 campus (4,121)
Comprehensive
Ohio State University (1,725/268)
Places Rated Score: 6.20
Places Rated Rank: 328

McAllen–Edinburg–Mission, TX
Public K–12 (98.73%)
15 districts, 185 schools
120,576 students
Private K–12 (1.27%)
3 Catholic, 1,050 students
5 Other, 495 students
Colleges and Universities
Comprehensive
University of Texas Pan American (16,295/1,416)
Places Rated Score: 8.71
Places Rated Rank: 321

Medford–Ashland, OR
Public K–12 (95.82%)
9 districts, 54 schools
26,590 students
Private K–12 (4.18%)
1 Catholic, 196 students
1 NAIS, 301 students
8 Other, 664 students
Colleges and Universities
Comprehensive
Southern Oregon State College (5,711/1,982)
Places Rated Score: 2.50
Places Rated Rank: 339

Melbourne–Titusville–Palm Bay, FL
Public K–12 (91.11%)
1 district, 76 schools
59,112 students
Private K–12 (8.89%)
9 Catholic, 3,112 students
22 Other, 2,656 students
Colleges and Universities
Associate of Arts
3 campuses (24,248)
Baccalaureate
Rollins College Brevard (727)
Doctoral
Florida Institute of Technology (2,592/4,375)
Places Rated Score: 68.05
Places Rated Rank: 117

Memphis, TN–AR–MS
Public K–12 (89.54%)
12 districts, 280 schools
192,804 students
Private K–12 (10.46%)
17 Catholic, 5,013 students

Memphis State University (17,231/5,513)
University of Tennessee (523/1,639)
Places Rated Score: 58.04
Places Rated Rank: 158

Merced, CA
Public K–12 (95.52%)
21 districts, 77 schools
43,517 students
Private K–12 (4.48%)
4 Catholic, 1,167 students
14 Other, 876 students
Colleges and Universities
Associate of Arts
1 campus (10,781)
Places Rated Score: 8.65
Places Rated Rank: 322

Miami, FL
Public K–12 (85.60%)
1 district, 319 schools
300,107 students
Private K–12 (14.40%)
37 Catholic, 19,303 students
4 NAIS, 2,288 students
169 Other, 28,891 students
Colleges and Universities
Associate of Arts
5 campuses (82,823)
Baccalaureate
Florida Memorial College (1,719)
Comprehensive
SE University of the Health Science (1,116)
St. Thomas University (2,507/1,382)
Doctoral
Barry University (6,471/3,788)
Florida International University (24,251/8,416)
University of Miami (10,186/6,605)
Places Rated Score: 81.33
Places Rated Rank: 56

Middlesex–Somerset–Hunterdon, NJ
Public K–12 (86.29%)
74 districts, 294 schools
137,911 students
Private K–12 (13.71%)
44 Catholic, 14,643 students
6 NAIS, 2,746 students
24 Other, 4,522 students
Colleges and Universities
Associate of Arts
3 campuses (26,343)
Doctoral
Rutgers University (25,963/8,821)
Places Rated Score: 64.22
Places Rated Rank: 135

Milwaukee–Waukesha, WI
Public K–12 (80.90%)
50 districts, 415 schools
221,990 students
Private K–12 (19.10%)
102 Catholic, 28,267 students
3 NAIS, 1,675 students
130 Other, 22,452 students

Mount Mary College [illegible]
Doctoral
Marquette University (8,876/3,359)
Medical College of Wisconsin (1,341)
University of Wisconsin (25,553/6,538)
Places Rated Score: 83.18
Places Rated Rank: 49

✓ Minneapolis–St. Paul, MN–WI
Public K–12 (88.67%)
97 districts, 696 schools
406,364 students
Private K–12 (11.33%)
88 Catholic, 24,039 students
4 NAIS, 3,354 students
178 Other, 24,545 students
Colleges and Universities
Associate of Arts
18 campuses (90,880)
Baccalaureate
Crown College (606)
Macalester College (1,915)
North Central Bible College (1,180)
Northwestern College (1,307)
Comprehensive
Augsburg College (3,561/217)
Bethel College (2,282/77)
College of Saint Catherine (2,932/707)
Concordia College (1,658/25)
Hamline University (1,546/1,389)
Metropolitan State University (6,792/420)
Minneapolis College of Art and Design (646)
University of Wisconsin (5,830/1,692)
Doctoral
Luther NW Theological Seminary (783)
University of Minnesota (46,827/18,021)
University of St. Thomas (5,856/7,419)
Places Rated Score: 90.03
Places Rated Rank: 23

Mobile, AL
Public K–12 (86.64%)
2 districts, 137 schools
83,740 students

Private K–12 (13.36%)
15 Catholic, 5,704 students
2 NAIS, 1,585 students
25 Other, 5,620 students
Colleges and Universities
Associate of Arts
3 campuses (13,597)
Comprehensive
Spring Hill College (1,352/272)
University of Mobile (1,833/209)
Doctoral
University of South Alabama (12,535/2,470)
Places Rated Score: 55.41
Places Rated Rank: 168

Modesto, CA
Public K–12 (95.01%)
31 districts, 131 schools
85,454 students
Private K–12 (4.99%)
5 Catholic, 1,505 students
40 Other, 2,983 students
Colleges and Universities
Associate of Arts
1 campus (21,908)
Comprehensive
Cal State University Modesto (5,068/1,828)
Places Rated Score: 24.77
Places Rated Rank: 283

Monmouth–Ocean, NJ
Public K–12 (87.05%)
81 districts, 261 schools
145,896 students
Private K–12 (12.95%)
29 Catholic, 15,134 students
3 NAIS, 940 students
26 Other, 5,622 students
Colleges and Universities
Associate of Arts
2 campuses (30,222)
Comprehensive
Beth Medrash Govoha (436/1,228)
Georgian Court College (2,320/1,002)
Monmouth College (3,262/1,886)
Places Rated Score: 52.95
Places Rated Rank: 176

Monroe, LA
Public K–12 (91.93%)
2 districts, 52 schools
28,927 students
Private K–12 (8.07%)
5 Catholic, 1,043 students
8 Other, 1,497 students
Colleges and Universities
Doctoral
NE Louisiana University (13,038/1,993)
Places Rated Score: 9.10
Places Rated Rank: 319

Montgomery, AL
Public K–12 (86.93%)
5 districts, 90 schools
52,396 students
Private K–12 (13.07%)
6 Catholic, 1,468 students
1 NAIS, 786 students
23 Other, 5,624 students
Colleges and Universities
Associate of Arts
3 campuses (3,382)
Baccalaureate
Huntingdon College (941)
Comprehensive
Alabama State University (5,768/694)
Auburn University Montgomery (7,698/1,171)
Faulkner University (1,543/366)
Troy State University (5,169/899)
Places Rated Score: 64.73
Places Rated Rank: 131

Montreal, PQ
Public Instruction
27 districts, 903 schools
305,199 students
Colleges and Universities
Associate of Arts
15 campuses (75,338)
Comprehensive
Ecole de technologie superieure (2,478/63)
Doctoral
Concordia University (22,126/3,703)
Ecole des Hautes Etudes Commerciales (7,601/1,740)
Ecole Polytechnique (4,298/1,546)
McGill University (20,276/8,203)
Universite de Montreal (31,581/8,570)
Universite du Quebec (36,680/4,377)
Places Rated Score: 75.37
Places Rated Rank: 81

Muncie, IN
Public K–12 (95.01%)
8 districts, 41 schools
18,159 students
Private K–12 (4.99%)
2 Catholic, 453 students
6 Other, 500 students
Colleges and Universities
Associate of Arts
1 campus (4,251)
Doctoral
Ball State University (20,016/3,671)
Places Rated Score: 63.88
Places Rated Rank: 137

Myrtle Beach, SC
Public K–12 (96.65%)
1 district, 37 schools
24,662 students
Private K–12 (3.35%)
1 Catholic, 264 students
9 Other, 590 students
Colleges and Universities
Associate of Arts
1 campus (3,489)
Comprehensive
Coastal Carolina University (4,123/647)
Places Rated Score: 10.60
Places Rated Rank: 316

Naples, FL
Public K–12 (92.82%)
1 district, 31 schools
22,565 students
Private K–12 (7.18%)
3 Catholic, 775 students
1 NAIS, 250 students
10 Other, 720 students
Colleges and Universities
Associate of Arts
1 campus (1,433)
Comprehensive
International College (836/32)
Doctoral
Walden University (992)
Places Rated Score: 6.75
Places Rated Rank: 325

Nashua, NH
Public K–12 (91.92%)
7 districts, 49 schools
28,401 students
Private K–12 (8.08%)
6 Catholic, 1,815 students
1 NAIS, 100 students
7 Other, 582 students
Colleges and Universities
Associate of Arts
1 campus (1,734)
Baccalaureate
Daniel Webster College (1,268)
Comprehensive
Rivier College (2,299/1,393)
Places Rated Score: 63.91
Places Rated Rank: 136

Nashville, TN
Public K–12 (89.46%)
13 districts, 302 schools
167,886 students
Private K–12 (10.54%)
10 Catholic, 3,674 students
10 NAIS, 4,863 students
42 Other, 11,233 students
Colleges and Universities
Associate of Arts
6 campuses (19,419)
Comprehensive
Belmont University (3,267/348)
Cumberland University (976/30)
David Lipscomb University (2,386/108)
Fisk University (906/28)
Trevecca Nazarene College (1,067/319)
Doctoral
Meharry Medical College (668)
Middle Tennessee State University (40,292/6,134)
Tennessee State University (8,254/1,752)
Vanderbilt University (5,652/4,201)
Places Rated Score: 83.10
Places Rated Rank: 50

New Bedford, MA
Public K–12 (90.47%)
13 districts, 54 schools
29,065 students
Private K–12 (9.53%)
8 Catholic, 2,203 students
2 NAIS, 742 students
3 Other, 115 students
Colleges and Universities
Comprehensive
University of Massachusetts Dartmouth (6,645/591)
Places Rated Score: 17.98
Places Rated Rank: 303

✓ New Haven–Meriden, CT
Public K–12 (88.33%)
17 districts, 149 schools
72,935 students
Private K–12 (11.67%)
22 Catholic, 5,981 students
7 NAIS, 3,074 students
8 Other, 584 students
Colleges and Universities
Associate of Arts
1 campus (7,126)
Comprehensive
Albertus Magnus College (744/12)
Quinnipiac College (3,835/1,289)
Southern Connecticut State University (11,654/7,267)
Doctoral
University of New Haven (3,871/3,027)
Yale University (5,287/5,663)
Places Rated Score: 91.04
Places Rated Rank: 22

New London–Norwich, CT–RI

Public K–12 (90.48%)
14 districts, 78 schools
30,088 students
Private K–12 (9.52%)
12 Catholic, 2,533 students
2 NAIS, 480 students
3 Other, 154 students
Colleges and Universities
Associate of Arts
3 campuses (7,729)
Baccalaureate
United States Coast Guard Academy (946)
Comprehensive
Connecticut College (1,897/154)
Places Rated Score: 31.90
Places Rated Rank: 257

St. Francis College (2,535)
St. Josephs College (1,154)
Comprehensive
Audrey Cohen College (1,428/61)
Bank Street College of Education (1,469)
College of Insurance (763/191)
College of Mount Saint Vincent (1,190/46)
College of New Rochelle (7,172/2,282)
Cooper Union (983/67)
CUNY Bernard Baruch College (15,809/3,140)
CUNY Brooklyn College (13,273/5,555)
CUNY City College (14,216/4,501)
CUNY College of Staten Island (13,949/1,499)
CUNY Hunter College (17,545/5,600)
CUNY Lehman College (10,696/2,264)

42 Other, 8,956 students
Colleges and Universities
Associate of Arts
8 campuses (46,034)
Baccalaureate
Bloomfield College (2,518)
Centenary College (1,248)
Comprehensive
Caldwell College (1,875/22)
College of Saint Elizabeth (1,654/17)
Kean College of New Jersey (12,922/2,357)
Montclair State College (12,693/4,423)
Upsala College (1,520/46)
Doctoral
Drew University (1,553/920)
New Jersey Inst. of Technology (6,999/3,114)
Rutgers University (6,540/3,794)
Seton Hall University (6,899/5,181)

Baccalaureate
Dillard University (1,728)
Comprehensive
Loyola University In New Orleans (4,235/2,194)
Our Lady of Holy Cross College (1,016/126)
Southern University New Orleans (7,148/260)
Xavier University (3,354/526)
Doctoral
LSU Medical Center (2,817/2,717)
New Orleans Baptist Theological Seminary (670/1,481)
Tulane University of Louisiana (7,631/4,813)
University of New Orleans (16,049/5,964)
Places Rated Score: 71.11
Places Rated Rank: 101

✓ New York, NY

Public K–12 (79.15%)
66 districts, 1,422 schools
1,137,953 students
Private K–12 (20.85%)
433 Catholic, 169,412 students
54 NAIS, 22,588 students
382 Other, 107,800 students
Colleges and Universities
Associate of Arts
32 campuses (143,356)
Baccalaureate
Barnard College (2,262)
Boricua College (2,821)
College of Aeronautics (1,813)
Concordia College (898)
CUNY Medgar Evers College (5,976)
CUNY New York City Technical College (13,181)
Cuny York College (8,278)
Derech Ayson Rabbinical Seminary (750)
Dominican College of Blauvelt (1,572)
Marymount College (1,275)
Marymount Manhattan College (1,842)
New York School of Interior Design (853)

(1,325/2,913)
Pratt Institute (2,014/1,231)
Queens College (17,924/4,270)
Sarah Lawrence College (1,104/203)
School of Visual Arts (7,630/283)
St. Thomas Aquinas College (2,015/103)
SUNY College at Purchase (5,882/45)
SUNY Maritime College (785/223)
Touro College (10,557/1,314)
United Talmudical Academy (1,319/150)
Wagner College (1,572/381)
Doctoral
Beth Medrash Eeyun Hatalmud (1,080/20)
Columbia University New York City (6,701/15,272)
Columbia University Teachers College (5,709)
CUNY Graduate School and University Center (4,662)
CUNY John Jay College Criminal Justice (10,056/849)
Fordham University (6,321/8,217)
Juilliard School (511/602)
Long Island University–Brooklyn Campus (6,493/2,491)
Manhattan School of Music (458/427)
New School for Social Research (5,600/2,800)
New York University (15,303/18,670)
Pace University (6,813/2,638)
Polytechnic University (1,858/2,533)
St. Johns University (14,463/6,079)
SUNY Health Science Center Brooklyn (693/1,077)
Yeshiva University (2,020/3,072)
Places Rated Score: 99.65
Places Rated Rank: 2

✓ Newark, NJ

Public K–12 (85.13%)
135 districts, 594 schools
280,787 students
Private K–12 (14.87%)
116 Catholic, 33,943 students
14 NAIS, 6,165 students

3 NAIS, 454 students
10 Other, 3,121 students
Colleges and Universities
Associate of Arts
1 campus (8,636)
Baccalaureate
United States Military Academy (4,351)
Comprehensive
Mount Saint Mary College (1,745/320)
Places Rated Score: 34.65
Places Rated Rank: 246

Norfolk–Virginia Beach–Newport News, VA–NC

Public K–12 (91.47%)
19 districts, 368 schools
249,348 students
Private K–12 (8.53%)
14 Catholic, 4,843 students
6 NAIS, 3,201 students
56 Other, 15,203 students
Colleges and Universities
Associate of Arts
9 campuses (45,917)
Baccalaureate
Virginia Wesleyan College (1,781)
Comprehensive
Christopher Newport University (6,329/164)
Norfolk State University (9,261/1,712)
Doctoral
College of William and Mary (5,957/3,183)
Hampton University (5,308/501)
Old Dominion University (14,856/8,928)
Regent University (1,747)
Places Rated Score: 69.94
Places Rated Rank: 107

✓ Oakland, CA

Public K–12 (89.10%)
45 districts, 557 schools
324,235 students
Private K–12 (10.90%)
65 Catholic, 20,985 students

7 NAIS, 2,245 students
174 Other, 16,418 students
Colleges and Universities
Associate of Arts
15 campuses (184,652)
Baccalaureate
Patten College (1,247)
Comprehensive
Cal State University (12,496/4,449)
California College Arts and Crafts (1,250/80)
Holy Names College (736/445)
John F Kennedy University (442/1,895)
Mills College (774/309)
St. Marys College of California (2,863/1,136)
Doctoral
School of Professional Psychology (643)
University of California Berkeley (21,710/8,912)
Places Rated Score: 97.20
Places Rated Rank: 5

Ocala, FL
Public K–12 (91.82%)
1 district, 40 schools
28,990 students
Private K–12 (8.18%)
1 Catholic, 528 students
18 Other, 2,054 students
Colleges and Universities
Associate of Arts
1 campus (9,684)
Places Rated Score: 1.46
Places Rated Rank: 344

Odessa-Midland, TX
Public K–12 (94.89%)
3 districts, 83 schools
51,505 students
Private K–12 (5.11%)
2 Catholic, 499 students
1 NAIS, 490 students
9 Other, 1,782 students
Colleges and Universities
Associate of Arts
2 campuses (14,051)
Comprehensive
University of Texas Permian Basin (1,962/1,173)
Places Rated Score: 24.97
Places Rated Rank: 281

Oklahoma City, OK
Public K–12 (94.01%)
67 districts, 379 schools
168,031 students
Private K–12 (5.99%)
16 Catholic, 3,894 students
3 NAIS, 2,219 students
25 Other, 4,588 students
Colleges and Universities
Associate of Arts
6 campuses (51,516)
Comprehensive
Langston University (5,594/62)
Oklahoma Baptist University (2,818)
Oklahoma Christian University (1,737/47)
Oklahoma City University (2,496/3,352)
Southern Nazarene University (1,393/216)
University of Central Oklahoma (14,796/6,068)
Doctoral
University of Oklahoma (16,908/6,294)
University of Oklahoma Health Sciences Center (1,498/2,251)
Places Rated Score: 83.58
Places Rated Rank: 47

Olympia, WA
Public K–12 (96.62%)
8 districts, 71 schools
37,519 students
Private K–12 (3.38%)
1 Catholic, 245 students
14 Other, 1,067 students
Colleges and Universities
Associate of Arts
1 campus (6,825)
Comprehensive
Evergreen State College (4,132/370)
St. Martins College (1,541/514)
Places Rated Score: 38.53
Places Rated Rank: 234

Omaha, NE–IA
Public K–12 (86.14%)
28 districts, 250 schools
111,459 students
Private K–12 (13.86%)
49 Catholic, 15,491 students
3 NAIS, 328 students
38 Other, 2,112 students
Colleges and Universities
Associate of Arts
3 campuses (29,753)
Baccalaureate
College of Saint Mary (1,607)
Dana College (659)
Comprehensive
Bellevue College (3,514/167)
Doctoral
Creighton University (4,698/2,390)
University of Nebraska (13,535/2,692)
University of Nebraska Medical Center (1,142/1,694)
Places Rated Score: 86.58
Places Rated Rank: 37

✓ Orange County, CA
Public K–12 (90.22%)
32 districts, 525 schools
415,064 students
Private K–12 (9.78%)
44 Catholic, 18,149 students
3 NAIS, 1,288 students
224 Other, 25,562 students
Colleges and Universities
Associate of Arts
9 campuses (240,473)
Baccalaureate
ITT Technical Institute (962)
Comprehensive
Cal State University Fullerton (22,372/4,876)
Chapman University (6,126/6,190)
Christ College Irvine (673/225)
Southern California College (1,071/95)
Western State University College of Law (446/1,590)
Doctoral
University of California Irvine (13,888/2,646)
Places Rated Score: 95.80
Places Rated Rank: 7

Orlando, FL
Public K–12 (91.12%)
4 districts, 266 schools
197,599 students
Private K–12 (8.88%)
12 Catholic, 5,710 students
1 NAIS, 1,092 students
74 Other, 12,455 students
Colleges and Universities
Associate of Arts
3 campuses (58,642)
Baccalaureate
ITT Technical Institute (830)
Comprehensive
Orlando College (1,746/163)
Rollins College (3,295/702)
Doctoral
University of Central Florida (19,319/5,606)
Places Rated Score: 72.21
Places Rated Rank: 94

Oshawa, ON
Public K–13 (67.06%)
110 schools, 59,494 students
Catholic Separate K–13 (27.48%)
46 schools, 24,381 students
Private K–13 (5.44%)
23 schools, 4,830 students
Colleges and Universities
Associate of Arts
1 campus (25,000)
Places Rated Score: 15.37
Places Rated Rank: 307

Ottawa-Hull, ON–PQ
Public K–13 (70.90%)
201 schools, 100,898 students
Catholic Separate K–13 (23.49%)
84 schools, 33,439 students
Private K–13 (5.60%)
38 schools, 7,980 students
Colleges and Universities
Associate of Arts
4 campuses (22,000)
Doctoral
Carleton University (19,121/2,642)
College Dominicain de Philosophe (466/27)
Saint Paul University (432/283)
Universite du Quebec (5,485/326)
University of Ottawa (20,162/4,110)
Places Rated Score: 56.15
Places Rated Rank: 166

Owensboro, KY
Public K–12 (83.35%)
2 districts, 31 schools
14,657 students
Private K–12 (16.65%)
10 Catholic, 2,777 students
5 Other, 151 students
Colleges and Universities
Associate of Arts
2 campuses (4,525)
Baccalaureate
Brescia College (1,025)
Kentucky Wesleyan College (870)
Places Rated Score: 41.90
Places Rated Rank: 218

Panama City, FL
Public K–12 (93.66%)
1 district, 33 schools
22,505 students
Private K–12 (6.34%)
2 Catholic, 291 students
7 Other, 1,233 students
Colleges and Universities
Associate of Arts
1 campus (21,477)
Places Rated Score: 12.19
Places Rated Rank: 315

Parkersburg-Marietta, WV–OH
Public K–12 (96.29%)

9 districts, 59 schools
26,073 students
Private K–12 (3.71%)
4 Catholic, 826 students
3 Other, 179 students
Colleges and Universities
Associate of Arts
1 campus (3,039)
Baccalaureate
West Virginia University Parkersburg (5,120)
Comprehensive
Marietta College (1,590/56)
Places Rated Score: 42.05
Places Rated Rank: 217

Pensacola, FL
Public K–12 (90.96%)
2 districts, 94 schools
59,952 students

Peoria–Pekin, IL
Public K–12 (87.44%)
46 districts, 160 schools
56,467 students
Private K–12 (12.56%)
14 Catholic, 4,458 students
39 Other, 3,656 students
Colleges and Universities
Associate of Arts
2 campuses (21,754)
Baccalaureate
Eureka College (528/90)
Comprehensive
Bradley University (5,607/1,258)
Places Rated Score: 74.40
Places Rated Rank: 85

✓ Philadelphia, PA–NJ
Public K–12 (78.67%)
194 districts, 1,138 schools
673,901 students
Private K–12 (21.33%)
322 Catholic, 129,923 students
41 NAIS, 17,100 students
275 Other, 35,652 students
Colleges and Universities
Associate of Arts
26 campuses (127,012)
Baccalaureate
Delaware Valley College of Science (2,492)
Haverford College (1,165)
Ursinus College (2,982)
Comprehensive
American College (734)
Beaver College (1,534/1,603)
Cabrini College (1,698/532)
Chestnut Hill College (1,017/589)
Cheyney University (1,444/468)
Eastern College (1,712/511)
Gwynedd-Mercy College (2,351/257)
Holy Family College (3,050/337)
La Salle University (5,299/1,921)
Lincoln University (1,278/198)
Neumann College (1,376/64)
Penn State University Delaware (1,946/57)
Penn State University Ogontz (4,353/322)
Philadelphia College of Bible (886/133)
Philadelphia College of Osteopathic Medicine (846)
Philadelphia College of Textiles and Science (3,328/787)
Rosemont College (675/110)
Rowan College of New Jersey (9,511/1,919)
Rutgers University Camden (4,216/1,219)
St. Charles Borromeo Seminary (287/430)
St. Josephs University (4,467/4,828)
Swarthmore College (1,385)
University of the Arts (1,472/125)
West Chester University of Pennsylvania (11,766/3,438)
Doctoral

(1,671/1,383)
University of Pennsylvania (12,581/12,816)
Villanova University (8,568/4,930)
Westminster Theological Seminary (601)
Widener University (4,774/2,469)
Places Rated Score: 94.87
Places Rated Rank: 11

✓ Phoenix–Mesa, AZ
Public K–12 (93.06%)
77 districts, 559 schools
399,131 students
Private K–12 (6.94%)
26 Catholic, 9,895 students
3 NAIS, 1,313 students
84 Other, 18,562 students
Colleges and Universities
Associate of Arts
12 campuses (172,484)
Baccalaureate
Al Collins Graphic Design School (974)
Devry Institute of Technology (3,598)
Comprehensive
American School of International Management (1,662)
Grand Canyon University (1,812/442)
Ottawa University (1,367/2,503)
University of Phoenix (5,100/3,396)
Western International University (945/393)
Doctoral
Arizona State University (36,637/14,725)
Places Rated Score: 87.45
Places Rated Rank: 32

Pine Bluff, AR
Public K–12 (98.71%)
6 districts, 38 schools
16,554 students
Private K–12 (1.29%)
1 Catholic, 164 students
1 Other, 52 students
Colleges and Universities
Comprehensive
University of Arkansas (4,806/97)
Places Rated Score: 13.87
Places Rated Rank: 311

Pittsburgh, PA
Public K–12 (85.41%)
117 districts, 640 schools
318,828 students
Private K–12 (14.59%)
156 Catholic, 39,354 students
9 NAIS, 3,076 students
110 Other, 12,054 students
Colleges and Universities
Associate of Arts
18 campuses (61,691)
Baccalaureate
Chatham College (780)
Penn State University Fayette (1,248)
St. Vincent College (1,439)
Seton Hill College (1,024)
University of Pittsburgh (1,679)

Point Park College (3,454/136)
Robert Morris College (5,315/1,178)
Slippery Rock University of Pennsylvania (8,398/1,048)
Washington and Jefferson College (1,385)
Doctoral
Carnegie Mellon University (4,475/2,664)
Duquesne University (5,580/4,727)
University of Pittsburgh (22,300/11,834)
Places Rated Score: 85.83
Places Rated Rank: 40

Pittsfield, MA
Public K–12 (86.84%)
9 districts, 39 schools
15,013 students
Private K–12 (13.16%)
7 Catholic, 1,925 students
1 NAIS, 168 students
7 Other, 182 students
Colleges and Universities
Associate of Arts
1 campus (3,703)
Places Rated Score: 1.66
Places Rated Rank: 343

Portland, ME
Public K–12 (91.64%)
15 districts, 84 schools
30,403 students
Private K–12 (8.36%)
6 Catholic, 1,261 students
2 NAIS, 764 students
14 Other, 747 students
Colleges and Universities
Associate of Arts
3 campuses (4,377)
Comprehensive
St. Josephs College (3,359/1,111)
University of Southern Maine (11,214/2,952)
Places Rated Score: 82.99
Places Rated Rank: 51

✓ Portland–Vancouver, OR–WA
Public K–12 (93.96%)
59 districts, 532 schools
276,372 students
Private K–12 (6.04%)
36 Catholic, 9,683 students
2 NAIS, 1,323 students
147 Other, 6,752 students
Colleges and Universities
Associate of Arts
5 campuses (106,886)
Baccalaureate
Concordia College (1,511)
Comprehensive
Lewis and Clark College (1,833/2,098)
Linfield College (3,119/80)
Marylhurst College (1,636/233)
Reed College (1,210/20)
University of Portland (2,537/1,566)
Warner Pacific College (615/17)
Doctoral
George Fox College (1,355/220)
Oregon Graduate Institute (849)
Oregon Health Science University **(314/1,062)**
Pacific University (1,011/691)
Portland State University (18,968/17,870)
Places Rated Score: 87.80
Places Rated Rank: 30

Portsmouth–Rochester, NH–ME
Public K–12 (88.85%)
15 districts, 75 schools
31,404 students
Private K–12 (11.15%)
7 Catholic, 1,667 students
2 NAIS, 1,394 students
10 Other, 878 students
Colleges and Universities
Associate of Arts
2 campuses (3,182)
Doctoral
University of New Hampshire (12,864/3,213)
Places Rated Score: 84.23
Places Rated Rank: 45

✓ Providence–Fall River–Warwick, RI–MA
Public K–12 (86.93%)
33 districts, 324 schools
139,724 students
Private K–12 (13.07%)
68 Catholic, 17,782 students
7 NAIS, 2,659 students
21 Other, 570 students
Colleges and Universities
Associate of Arts
3 campuses (37,034)
Baccalaureate
Roger Williams University (4,289)
Comprehensive
Bryant College (4,068/803)
Johnson & Wales University (8,264/659)
Rhode Island College **(9,263/3,360)**
Rhode Island School of Design (1,844/142)
Doctoral
Brown University (5,875/1,718)
Providence College (5,271/480)
University of Rhode Island (13,986/5,032)
Places Rated Score: 87.96
Places Rated Rank: 29

Provo–Orem, UT
Public K–12 (98.28%)
3 districts, 104 schools
71,193 students
Private K–12 (1.72%)
10 Other, 1,245 students
Colleges and Universities
Associate of Arts
1 campus (203)
Baccalaureate
Utah Valley State College **(11,884)**
Doctoral
Brigham Young University (33,709/4,152)
Places Rated Score: 71.50
Places Rated Rank: 97

Pueblo, CO
Public K–12 (96.22%)
2 districts, 50 schools
22,165 students
Private K–12 (3.78%)
2 Catholic, 444 students
1 NAIS, 125 students
5 Other, 302 students
Colleges and Universities
Associate of Arts
1 campus (5,104)
Comprehensive
University of Southern Colorado (5,112/348)
Places Rated Score: 35.38
Places Rated Rank: 242

Punta Gorda, FL
Public K–12 (94.49%)
1 district, 20 schools
14,067 students
Private K–12 (5.51%)
1 Catholic, 248 students
3 Other, 572 students
Colleges and Universities
Associate of Arts
1 campus (956)
Places Rated Score: 0.50
Places Rated Rank: 348

Quebec City, PQ
Public Instruction
3 districts, 247 schools
45,634 students
Colleges and Universities
Associate of Arts
5 campuses (19,500)
Comprehensive
Ecole Nationale d'Administration Publique (963)
Doctoral
Universite Laval (31,251/7,262)
Places Rated Score: 58.40
Places Rated Rank: 156

Racine, WI
Public K–12 (83.00%)
12 districts, 57 schools
29,731 students
Private K–12 (17.00%)
17 Catholic, 3,862 students
1 NAIS, 477 students
15 Other, 1,752 students
Places Rated Score: 0.00
Places Rated Rank: 351

Raleigh–Durham–Chapel Hill, NC
Public K–12 (92.65%)
9 districts, 215 schools
121,869 students
Private K–12 (7.35%)
10 Catholic, 1,989 students
3 NAIS, 1,945 students
35 Other, 5,739 students
Colleges and Universities
Associate of Arts
6 campuses (25,922)
Baccalaureate
St. Augustines College (2,160)
Shaw University (2,652)
Comprehensive
Meredith College (2,771/217)
North Carolina Central University **(5,065/1,814)**
Doctoral
Duke University (6,425/6,059)
North Carolina State University **(28,118/5,351)**
SE Baptist Theological Seminary (72/601)
University of North Carolina (17,333/10,493)
Places Rated Score: 85.70
Places Rated Rank: 41

Rapid City, SD
Public K–12 (92.74%)
5 districts, 48 schools
19,938 students
Private K–12 (7.26%)
2 Catholic, 794 students
10 Other, 766 students
Colleges and Universities
Baccalaureate
National College (859)
Doctoral
South Dakota School of Mines and Technology (2,654/353)
Places Rated Score: 16.88
Places Rated Rank: 305

Reading, PA
Public K–12 (91.19%)
21 districts, 108 schools
55,577 students
Private K–12 (8.81%)
13 Catholic, 3,446 students
31 Other, 1,925 students
Colleges and Universities
Associate of Arts
1 campus (4,989)
Baccalaureate
Albright College (1,683)
Alvernia College (1,386)
Comprehensive
Kutztown University (7,824/1,616)
Penn State University (1,958/379)
Places Rated Score: 60.60
Places Rated Rank: 146

Redding, CA
Public K–12 (93.03%)
27 districts, 70 schools
29,693 students
Private K–12 (6.97%)
2 Catholic, 612 students
18 Other, 1,613 students
Colleges and Universities
Associate of Arts
1 campus (19,335)
Comprehensive
Simpson College (616/164)
Places Rated Score: 47.32
Places Rated Rank: 198

Regina, SK
Public K–12 (69.71%)
3 divisions, 70 schools
27,341 students
Catholic Separate K–12 (27.34%)
29 schools, 10,724 students

Private K-12 (2.93%)
6 schools, 1,156 students
Colleges and Universities
Associate of Arts
1 campus (9,000)
Baccalaureate
Campion College (1,265)
Canadian Bible College (333)
Luther College (902)
Saskatchewan Indian College (756)
Doctoral
University of Regina (7,502/904)
Places Rated Score: 70.62
Places Rated Rank: 105

Reno, NV
Public K-12 (94.20%)
1 district, 78 schools
42,505 students
Private K-12 (5.80%)

California State University (10,707/4,447)
University of Redlands (4,086/1,340)
Doctoral
La Sierra University (1,906/806)
Loma Linda University (1,374/2,442)
University of California (7,639/1,732)
Places Rated Score: 86.86
Places Rated Rank: 36

Roanoke, VA
Public K-12 (94.10%)
5 districts, 75 schools
34,279 students
Private K-12 (5.90%)
1 Catholic, 376 students
1 NAIS, 490 students
5 Other, 1,284 students
Colleges and Universities
Associate of Arts

20 Other, 4,212 students
Colleges and Universities
Associate of Arts
1 campus (16,425)
Comprehensive
Rockford College (1,352/558)
Places Rated Score: 10.59
Places Rated Rank: 317

Rocky Mount, NC
Public K-12 (91.18%)
2 districts, 41 schools
16,172 students
Private K-12 (8.82%)
1 Catholic, 100 students
10 Other, 1,464 students
Colleges and Universities
Associate of Arts
2 campuses (6,193)
Baccalaureate

Public K-12 ([illegible])
9 districts, 68 schools
36,975 students
Private K-12 (4.65%)
3 Catholic, 905 students
10 Other, 900 students
Colleges and Universities
Associate of Arts
1 campus (9,129)
Places Rated Score: 2.26
Places Rated Rank: 341

Richmond-Petersburg, VA
Public K-12 (92.93%)
17 districts, 244 schools
143,943 students
Private K-12 (7.07%)
10 Catholic, 2,515 students
8 NAIS, 3,894 students
18 Other, 4,550 students
Colleges and Universities
Associate of Arts
5 campuses (33,422)
Baccalaureate
Randolph-Macon College (1,272)
Comprehensive
University of Richmond (4,315/1,178)
Virginia State University (4,261/546)
Doctoral
Virginia Commonwealth University (19,292/8,177)
Virginia Union University (1,548/173)
Places Rated Score: 66.62
Places Rated Rank: 122

Riverside-San Bernardino, CA
Public K-12 (94.23%)
62 districts, 741 schools
570,809 students
Private K-12 (5.77%)
34 Catholic, 9,175 students
2 NAIS, 424 students
276 Other, 25,341 students
Colleges and Universities
Associate of Arts
12 campuses (142,728)
Comprehensive
California Baptist College (836/44)

19,753 students
Private K-12 (10.62%)
4 Catholic, 1,665 students
9 Other, 682 students
Colleges and Universities
Associate of Arts
1 campus (5,374)
Doctoral
Mayo Graduate School (1,365)
Places Rated Score: 32.78
Places Rated Rank: 253

Rochester, NY
Public K-12 (90.22%)
64 districts, 297 schools
181,123 students
Private K-12 (9.78%)
51 Catholic, 14,417 students
3 NAIS, 996 students
40 Other, 4,212 students
Colleges and Universities
Associate of Arts
5 campuses (36,744)
Baccalaureate
Hobart William Smith Colleges (1,982)
Comprehensive
Nazareth College of Rochester (2,333/1,445)
Roberts Wesleyan College (1,074/105)
St. John Fisher College (2,981/372)
SUNY College at Brockport (8,372/3,114)
SUNY College at Geneseo (5,486/822)
Doctoral
Rochester Inst. of Technology (13,207/2,581)
University of Rochester (6,244/5,580)
Places Rated Score: 74.69
Places Rated Rank: 84

Rockford, IL
Public K-12 (87.37%)
25 districts, 124 schools
55,661 students
Private K-12 (12.63%)
10 Catholic, 3,524 students
1 NAIS, 312 students

145 Other, 11,017 students
Colleges and Universities
Associate of Arts
10 campuses (92,365)
Comprehensive
Cal State University (21,811/6,080)
Places Rated Score: 72.66
Places Rated Rank: 93

Saginaw-Bay City-Midland, MI
Public K-12 (85.84%)
22 districts, 152 schools
69,934 students
Private K-12 (14.16%)
25 Catholic, 5,407 students
41 Other, 6,125 students
Colleges and Universities
Associate of Arts
4 campuses (18,287)
Comprehensive
Northwood University (1,504/80)
Saginaw Valley State University (14,080/3,144)
Places Rated Score: 52.12
Places Rated Rank: 180

St. Catharines-Niagara, ON
Public K-13 (64.54%)
67 schools, 27,122 students
Catholic Separate K-13 (23.46%)
31 schools, 9,859 students
Private K-13 (11.97%)
24 schools, 5,040 students
Colleges and Universities
Associate of Arts
1 campus (5,600)
Comprehensive
Brock University (10,443/617)
Places Rated Score: 26.19
Places Rated Rank: 274

St. Cloud, MN
Public K-12 (86.12%)
14 districts, 54 schools
29,617 students
Private K-12 (13.88%)
19 Catholic, 4,124 students

10 Other, 650 students
Colleges and Universities
Baccalaureate
College of Saint Benedict (2,034)
Comprehensive
St. Cloud State University (18,315/3,674)
St. Johns University (2,169/439)
Places Rated Score: 74.23
Places Rated Rank: 86

Saint John, NB
Public K-12 (99%)
2 districts, 67 schools
23,939 students
Private K-12 (1%)
1 Other, 129 students
Colleges and Universities
Comprehensive
Mount Allison University (2,361/3)
Places Rated Score: 0.00
Places Rated Rank: 350

St. John's, NF
Public K-12 (45.09%)
2 Integrated Boards, 41 schools
14,564 students
Catholic Separate K-12 (54.55%)
45 schools, 17,730 students
Private K-12 (1%)
2 schools, 19,441 students
Colleges and Universities
Associate of Arts
2 campuses (9,000)
Doctoral
Memorial University of Newfoundland (15,750/1,419)
Places Rated Score: 15.93
Places Rated Rank: 306

St. Joseph, MO
Public K-12 (92.80%)
7 districts, 46 schools
17,197 students
Private K-12 (7.20%)
5 Catholic, 1,060 students
3 Other, 275 students
Colleges and Universities
Associate of Arts
1 campus (865)
Baccalaureate
Missouri Western State College (6,139)
Places Rated Score: 42.21
Places Rated Rank: 214

✓ St. Louis, MO-IL
Public K-12 (82.26%)
117 districts, 768 schools
380,163 students
Private K-12 (17.74%)
208 Catholic, 63,934 students
12 NAIS, 3,940 students
92 Other, 14,106 students
Colleges and Universities
Associate of Arts
14 campuses (112,739)
Baccalaureate
Harris-Stowe State College (2,885)
ITT Technical Institute (1,002)
McKendree College (2,203)
Missouri Baptist College (1,797)
Principia College (673)
Comprehensive
Fontbonne College (1,974/681)
Lindenwood College (2,479/1,524)
Logan College of Chiropractic (816)
Maryville University, Saint Louis (4,501/1,369)
Parks College of Saint Louis University (1,284)
St. Louis College of Pharmacy (732/74)
Doctoral
Concordia Seminary (606)
Southern Illinois University (10,713/4,821)
St. Louis University (9,881/5,243)
University of Missouri (16,394/4,351)
Washington University (6,583/6,109)
Webster University (4,300/12,388)
Places Rated Score: 90.00
Places Rated Rank: 24

Salem, OR
Public K-12 (92.78%)
26 districts, 121 schools
51,113 students
Private K-12 (7.22%)
8 Catholic, 1,527 students
40 Other, 2,450 students
Colleges and Universities
Associate of Arts
1 campus (38,893)
Comprehensive
Western Oregon State College (4,069/1,430)
Willamette University (1,923/693)
Places Rated Score: 78.95
Places Rated Rank: 67

Salinas, CA
Public K-12 (93.67%)
27 districts, 110 schools
65,565 students
Private K-12 (6.33%)
9 Catholic, 2,632 students
3 NAIS, 863 students
13 Other, 938 students
Colleges and Universities
Associate of Arts
2 campuses (40,373)
Comprehensive
Monterey Institute of International Studies (372/672)
Doctoral
Naval Postgraduate School (2,027)
Places Rated Score: 52.79
Places Rated Rank: 178

Salt Lake City-Ogden, UT
Public K-12 (97.68%)
7 districts, 378 schools
279,853 students
Private K-12 (2.32%)
10 Catholic, 3,651 students
3 NAIS, 1,750 students
21 Other, 1,238 students
Colleges and Universities
Associate of Arts
3 campuses (31,471)
Baccalaureate
ITT Technical Institute (610)
Comprehensive
Weber State University (20,984/234)
Westminster College (2,223/599)
Doctoral
University of Utah (26,292/4,975)
Places Rated Score: 70.86
Places Rated Rank: 103

San Angelo, TX
Public K-12 (97.64%)
6 districts, 56 schools
19,417 students
Private K-12 (2.36%)
1 Catholic, 232 students
3 Other, 237 students
Colleges and Universities
Comprehensive
Angelo State University (7,297/617)
Places Rated Score: 5.97
Places Rated Rank: 330

San Antonio, TX
Public K-12 (92.57%)
25 districts, 443 schools
266,815 students
Private K-12 (7.43%)
47 Catholic, 13,977 students
1 NAIS, 735 students
37 Other, 6,700 students
Colleges and Universities
Associate of Arts
3 campuses (53,151)
Baccalaureate
Texas Lutheran College (1,631)
Comprehensive
Incarnate Word College (2,527/687)
Trinity University (2,298/246)
Doctoral
Our Lady of the Lake University (2,606/1,155)
St. Marys University (2,867/1,838)
University of Texas Health Science (1,151/1,794)
University of Texas San Antonio (18,993/3,212)
Places Rated Score: 57.32
Places Rated Rank: 161

✓ San Diego, CA
Public K-12 (92.71%)
45 districts, 544 schools
413,598 students
Private K-12 (7.29%)
41 Catholic, 13,361 students
7 NAIS, 2,959 students
190 Other, 16,193 students
Colleges and Universities
Associate of Arts
13 campuses (183,382)
Baccalaureate
Cal State University San Marcos (2,042/493)
Comprehensive
Coleman College (1,436/23)
National University (5,888/9,539)
Point Loma Nazarene College (2,219/729)
Doctoral
California School of Professional Psychology (642)
California Western School of Law (841)
San Diego State University (26,851/7,518)
University of California San Diego (15,420/2,993)
University of San Diego (4,057/2,452)
U.S. International University (533/1,917)
Places Rated Score: 86.92
Places Rated Rank: 35

✓ San Francisco, CA
Public K-12 (80.80%)
50 districts, 353 schools
184,454 students
Private K-12 (19.20%)
74 Catholic, 25,856 students
22 NAIS, 6,866 students
141 Other, 11,104 students
Colleges and Universities
Associate of Arts
8 campuses (119,492)
Comprehensive
College of Notre Dame (927/1,107)

Dominican College of San Rafael (753/345)
New College of California (577/348)
San Francisco Art Institute (644/152)
Doctoral
California Inst. of Integral Studies (960)
Golden Gate Baptist Seminary (59/606)
Golden Gate University (2,790/7,433)
San Francisco State University (22,404/8,686)
San Francisco Theological Seminary (692)
University of California San Francisco (43/2,469)
University of San Francisco (5,723/4,093)
Places Rated Score: 96.62
Places Rated Rank: 6

✓ San Jose, CA

Cogswell College (917)
Comprehensive
San Jose State University (23,275/7,346)
Doctoral
Santa Clara University (4,530/4,639)
Stanford University (7,050/9,165)
Places Rated Score: 94.48
Places Rated Rank: 12

San Luis Obispo–Atascadero–Paso Robles, CA

Public K–12 (92.98%)
14 districts, 73 schools
33,646 students
Private K–12 (7.02%)
5 Catholic, 1,274 students
22 Other, 1,266 students
Colleges and Universities
Associate of Arts
1 campus (11,052)
Comprehensive
California Polytechnic State University (16,412/1,622)
Places Rated Score: 30.59
Places Rated Rank: 263

Santa Barbara–Santa Maria–Lompoc, CA

Public K–12 (89.79%)
25 districts, 104 schools
55,668 students
Private K–12 (10.21%)
9 Catholic, 2,777 students
6 NAIS, 1,215 students
27 Other, 2,337 students
Colleges and Universities
Associate of Arts
2 campuses (33,896)
Baccalaureate
Westmont College (1,366)
Doctoral
Fielding Institute (891)
University of California Santa Barbara (17,087/2,520)
Places Rated Score: 72.11
Places Rated Rank: 95

Santa Cruz–Watsonville, CA

Public K–12 (90.35%)
13 districts, 64 schools
36,763 students
Private K–12 (9.65%)
3 Catholic, 725 students
25 Other, 3,203 students
Colleges and Universities
Associate of Arts
1 campus (20,364)
Baccalaureate
Bethany College of the Assemblies of God (681)
Doctoral
University of California Santa Cruz (9,841/1,012)
Places Rated Score: 66.14
Places Rated Rank: 123

Santa Fe, NM

Places Rated Score: 71.34
Places Rated Rank: 99

Santa Rosa, CA

Public K–12 (91.62%)
43 districts, 140 schools
68,261 students
Private K–12 (8.38%)
9 Catholic, 3,002 students
1 NAIS, 179 students
45 Other, 3,062 students
Colleges and Universities
Associate of Arts
2 campuses (44,075)
Comprehensive
Sonoma State University (6,323/1,425)
Places Rated Score: 54.67
Places Rated Rank: 172

Sarasota–Bradenton, FL

Public K–12 (89.51%)
2 districts, 77 schools
54,371 students
Private K–12 (10.49%)
5 Catholic, 1,897 students
2 NAIS, 816 students
37 Other, 3,656 students
Colleges and Universities
Associate of Arts
2 campuses (25,759)
Baccalaureate
Ringling School of Art and Design (698)
Places Rated Score: 45.87
Places Rated Rank: 204

✓ Saskatoon, SK

Public K–12 (66.98%)
4 divisions, 79 schools
31,021 students
Catholic Separate K–13 (29.82%)
37 schools, 13,810 students
Private K–12 (3.19%)
8 Other, 1,482 students
Colleges and Universities
Associate of Arts
5 campuses (18,450)
Baccalaureate
St. Thomas More College (1,229)
Doctoral
University of Saskatchewan (15,758/2,115)
Places Rated Score: 87.80
Places Rated Rank: 31

Savannah, GA

Public K–12 (86.12%)
3 districts, 67 schools
43,529 students
Private K–12 (13.88%)
6 Catholic, 2,039 students
2 NAIS, 1,275 students
21 Other, 3,704 students
Colleges and Universities
Associate of Arts
2 campuses (4,992)
Baccalaureate

81,663 students
Private K–12 (17.61%)
46 Catholic, 13,018 students
3 NAIS, 1,637 students
23 Other, 2,796 students
Colleges and Universities
Associate of Arts
5 campuses (39,753)
Comprehensive
Bloomsburg University of Pennsylvania (8,380/1,099)
College Misericordia (1,882/179)
King's College (2,615/20)
Marywood College (2,065/1,435)
Penn State University Hazleton (1,343/46)
Penn State University Wilkes-Barre (970/206)
Penn State University Worthington-Scranton (1,478/308)
University of Scranton (4,706/1,033)
Wilkes University (2,835/2,045)
Doctoral
Baptist Bible College and Seminary (592/227)
Places Rated Score: 80.30
Places Rated Rank: 61

✓ Seattle–Bellevue–Everett, WA

Public K–12 (89.60%)
36 districts, 604 schools
330,410 students
Private K–12 (10.40%)
43 Catholic, 14,110 students
11 NAIS, 3,168 students
149 Other, 21,082 students
Colleges and Universities
Associate of Arts
11 campuses (116,337)
Baccalaureate
ITT Technical Institute (1,008)
NW College Assemblies of God (765)
Comprehensive
Antioch University Seattle (222/721)
City University (3,542/7,189)

University of Washington Bothell (608/37)
Doctoral
Seattle Pacific University (2,971/809)
Seattle University (3,340/1,720)
University of Washington (31,318/10,408)
Places Rated Score: 88.86
Places Rated Rank: 27

Sharon, PA
Public K–12 (91.50%)
13 districts, 43 schools
18,953 students
Private K–12 (8.50%)
5 Catholic, 1,309 students
7 Other, 452 students
Colleges and Universities
Baccalaureate
Grove City College (2,255)
Thiel College (998)
Comprehensive
Penn State University Shenango (1,411/85)
Places Rated Score: 40.10
Places Rated Rank: 229

Sheboygan, WI
Public K–12 (86.78%)
9 districts, 49 schools
18,368 students
Private K–12 (13.22%)
6 Catholic, 1,255 students
14 Other, 1,544 students
Colleges and Universities
Comprehensive
Lakeland College (3,605/93)
Places Rated Score: 6.08
Places Rated Rank: 329

Sherbrooke, PQ
Public Instruction
2 districts, 62 schools
15,396 students
Colleges and Universities
Associate of Arts
2 campuses (10,243)
Baccalaureate
Thomas More Institute for Adult Education (240)
Comprehensive
Bishop's University (2,554/24)
Doctoral
Universite de Sherbrooke (15,172/3,826)
Places Rated Score: 80.74
Places Rated Rank: 59

Sherman–Denison, TX
Public K–12 (95.43%)
13 districts, 54 schools
18,078 students
Private K–12 (4.57%)
1 Catholic, 186 students
6 Other, 680 students
Colleges and Universities
Associate of Arts
1 campus (5,145)
Comprehensive
Austin College (1,173/35)
Places Rated Score: 14.04
Places Rated Rank: 310

Shreveport–Bossier City, LA
Public K–12 (94.72%)
4 districts, 138 schools
78,605 students
Private K–12 (5.28%)
6 Catholic, 1,845 students
1 NAIS, 244 students
12 Other, 2,294 students
Colleges and Universities
Associate of Arts
2 campuses (7,752)
Comprehensive
Centenary College of Louisiana (904/462)
Louisiana State University Shreveport (5,294/1,001)
Places Rated Score: 19.11
Places Rated Rank: 298

Sioux City, IA–NE
Public K–12 (87.83%)
9 districts, 56 schools
21,169 students
Private K–12 (12.17%)
9 Catholic, 2,626 students
3 Other, 307 students
Colleges and Universities
Associate of Arts
1 campus (4,232)
Baccalaureate
Briar Cliff College (1,464)
Comprehensive
Morningside College (1,647/748)
Places Rated Score: 31.65
Places Rated Rank: 258

Sioux Falls, SD
Public K–12 (82.90%)
11 districts, 77 schools
26,371 students
Private K–12 (17.10%)
7 Catholic, 3,658 students
14 Other, 1,781 students
Colleges and Universities
Associate of Arts
1 campus (433)
Comprehensive
Augustana College (2,109/103)
Sioux Falls College (1,184/60)
Places Rated Score: 27.34
Places Rated Rank: 272

South Bend, IN
Public K–12 (82.73%)
5 districts, 65 schools
38,480 students
Private K–12 (17.27%)
18 Catholic, 5,886 students
1 NAIS, 359 students
13 Other, 1,788 students
Colleges and Universities
Associate of Arts
3 campuses (7,559)
Baccalaureate
St. Marys College (1,595)
Comprehensive
Bethel College (1,086/27)
Indiana University South Bend (8,945/2,498)
Doctoral
University of Notre Dame (8,118/3,142)
Places Rated Score: 77.16
Places Rated Rank: 75

Spokane, WA
Public K–12 (91.67%)
14 districts, 144 schools
68,535 students
Private K–12 (8.33%)
11 Catholic, 2,783 students
1 NAIS, 290 students
23 Other, 3,153 students
Colleges and Universities
Associate of Arts
4 campuses (26,758)
Comprehensive
Eastern Washington University (11,896/2,205)
Whitworth College (1,564/442)
Doctoral
Gonzaga University (3,168/2,349)
Places Rated Score: 64.57
Places Rated Rank: 132

Springfield, IL
Public K–12 (86.85%)
19 districts, 119 schools
41,413 students
Private K–12 (13.15%)
12 Catholic, 4,158 students
17 Other, 2,115 students
Colleges and Universities
Associate of Arts
3 campuses (16,554)
Comprehensive
Sangamon State University (3,512/2,712)
Places Rated Score: 58.58
Places Rated Rank: 154

✓ Springfield, MA
Public K–12 (87.85%)
28 districts, 188 schools
91,457 students
Private K–12 (12.15%)
24 Catholic, 8,661 students
5 NAIS, 1,355 students
28 Other, 2,636 students
Colleges and Universities
Associate of Arts
2 campuses (15,979)
Baccalaureate
Amherst College (1,674)
Bay Path College (736)
Hampshire College (1,271)
Comprehensive
College of Our Lady of the Elms (1,297/237)
Mount Holyoke College (2,080/208)
Western New England College (3,245/1,982)
Westfield State College (5,468/1,368)
Doctoral
American International College (1,449/827)
Smith College (2,788/306)
Springfield College (3,210/968)
University of Massachusetts Amherst (22,200/5,801)
Places Rated Score: 93.67
Places Rated Rank: 14

Springfield, MO
Public K–12 (95.44%)
19 districts, 112 schools
45,354 students
Private K–12 (4.56%)
5 Catholic, 1,157 students
9 Other, 1,012 students
Colleges and Universities
Associate of Arts
4 campuses (4,522)
Baccalaureate
Central Bible College (1,060)
Evangel College (1,724)
Comprehensive
Baptist Bible College (1,983/67)
Drury College (3,599/542)
SW Missouri State University (20,409/2,598)

Places Rated Score: 79.10
Places Rated Rank: 65

Stamford–Norwalk, CT
Public K–12 (85.33%)
8 districts, 87 schools
42,740 students
Private K–12 (14.67%)
13 Catholic, 3,471 students
9 NAIS, 3,717 students
3 Other, 157 students
Colleges and Universities
Associate of Arts
1 campus (7,233)
Places Rated Score: 2.44
Places Rated Rank: 340

State College, PA
Public K–12 (92.07%)
5 districts, 29 schools

Comprehensive
Laurentian University (7,472/285)
Places Rated Score: 20.34
Places Rated Rank: 293

Sumter, SC
Public K–12 (92.86%)
2 districts, 28 schools
20,171 students
Private K–12 (7.14%)
2 Catholic, 370 students
8 Other, 1,182 students
Colleges and Universities
Associate of Arts
2 campuses (13,270)
Baccalaureate
Morris College (989)
Places Rated Score: 49.95
Places Rated Rank: 191

Doctoral
Florida A & M (9,544/686)
Florida State University (25,282/6,471)
Places Rated Score: 68.52
Places Rated Rank: 113

Tampa–St. Petersburg–Clearwater, FL
Public K–12 (87.03%)
4 districts, 377 schools
264,200 students
Private K–12 (12.97%)
44 Catholic, 11,561 students
6 NAIS, 2,149 students
173 Other, 25,651 students
Colleges and Universities
Associate of Arts
5 campuses (78,314)
Baccalaureate
Eckerd College (1,525)
ITT Technical Institute (642)

Places Rated Rank: [illegible]

Steubenville–Weirton, OH–WV
Public K–12 (90.22%)
8 districts, 60 schools
23,116 students
Private K–12 (9.78%)
13 Catholic, 2,293 students
3 Other, 213 students
Colleges and Universities
Associate of Arts
2 campuses (2,629)
Baccalaureate
Bethany College (751)
Comprehensive
Franciscan University of Steubenville (1,803/443)
Places Rated Score: 41.22
Places Rated Rank: 221

Stockton–Lodi, CA
Public K–12 (92.87%)
19 districts, 158 schools
98,407 students
Private K–12 (7.13%)
10 Catholic, 3,258 students
30 Other, 4,300 students
Colleges and Universities
Associate of Arts
2 campuses (26,754)
Comprehensive
Humphreys College (789/108)
Doctoral
University of the Pacific (3,785/3,508)
Places Rated Score: 36.75
Places Rated Rank: 237

Sudbury, ON
Public K–13 (51.50%)
55 schools, 19,388 students
Catholic Separate K–13 (47.37%)
68 schools, 17,834 students
Private K–13 (1.10%)
2 schools, 420 students
Colleges and Universities
Associate of Arts
1 campus (6,000)

Baccalaureate
Cazenovia College (1,201)
Comprehensive
Colgate University (2,801/26)
Le Moyne College (2,608)
SUNY College at Oswego (8,588/1,701)
Doctoral
SUNY College of Environmental Science and Forestry (1,134/663)
SUNY Health Science Center at Syracuse (467/742)
Syracuse University (14,470/8,349)
Places Rated Score: 83.76
Places Rated Rank: 46

Tacoma, WA
Public K–12 (92.57%)
15 districts, 207 schools
111,753 students
Private K–12 (7.43%)
7 Catholic, 2,883 students
2 NAIS, 1,060 students
28 Other, 5,024 students
Colleges and Universities
Associate of Arts
2 campuses (26,588)
Comprehensive
Pacific Lutheran University (3,595/1,159)
University of Puget Sound (2,964/1,351)
University of Washington (653/67)
Places Rated Score: 51.76
Places Rated Rank: 181

Tallahassee, FL
Public K–12 (86.11%)
2 districts, 62 schools
37,485 students
Private K–12 (13.89%)
1 Catholic, 591 students
1 NAIS, 941 students
29 Other, 4,512 students
Colleges and Universities
Associate of Arts
2 campuses (13,778)

Places Rated Rank: 62

Terre Haute, IN
Public K–12 (95.25%)
5 districts, 48 schools
24,611 students
Private K–12 (4.75%)
4 Catholic, 516 students
15 Other, 712 students
Colleges and Universities
Associate of Arts
1 campus (4,009)
Comprehensive
Rose-Hulman Institute of Technology (1,287/112)
St. Mary-of-the-Woods College (1,181/92)
Doctoral
Indiana State University (12,901/2,593)
Places Rated Score: 57.68
Places Rated Rank: 159

Texarkana, TX–Texarkana, AR
Public K–12 (97.61%)
16 districts, 46 schools
18,212 students
Private K–12 (2.39%)
3 Other, 445 students
Colleges and Universities
Associate of Arts
1 campus (7,685)
Comprehensive
East Texas State University (1,011/1,301)
Places Rated Score: 18.98
Places Rated Rank: 299

Thunder Bay, ON
Public K–13 (65.42%)
47 schools, 16,732 students
Catholic Separate K–13 (26.36%)
23 schools, 6,744 students
Private K–13 (8.21%)
10 schools, 2,100 students
Colleges and Universities

Associate of Arts
1 campus (3,700)
Comprehensive
Lakehead University (7,495/356)
Places Rated Score: 23.24
Places Rated Rank: 285

Toledo, OH
Public K–12 (84.02%)
25 districts, 188 schools
98,180 students
Private K–12 (15.98%)
47 Catholic, 16,540 students
1 NAIS, 430 students
12 Other, 1,700 students
Colleges and Universities
Associate of Arts
2 campuses (10,802)
Baccalaureate
Lourdes College (1,868)
Doctoral
Bowling Green State University (16,751/4,761)
Medical College of Ohio (964)
University of Toledo (25,649/5,568)
Places Rated Score: 62.84
Places Rated Rank: 139

Topeka, KS
Public K–12 (91.42%)
5 districts, 71 schools
26,894 students
Private K–12 (8.58%)
7 Catholic, 2,122 students
4 Other, 401 students
Colleges and Universities
Comprehensive
Washburn University of Topeka (7,932/1,283)
Places Rated Score: 12.67
Places Rated Rank: 314

Toronto, ON
Public K–13 (64.91%)
672 schools, 345,464 students
Catholic Separate K–13 (28.05%)
301 schools, 149,321 students
Private K–13 (7.02%)
178 schools, 37,380 students
Colleges and Universities
Associate of Arts
7 campuses (49,000)
Baccalaureate
Ontario Bible College (551)
Ryerson Polytechnical Institute (21,791)
Comprehensive
Ontario Theological Seminary (314/232)
Doctoral
Ontario Institute for Studies in Education (37/2,518)
University of Toronto (40,639/9,511)
York University (35,481/3,305)
Places Rated Score: 71.41
Places Rated Rank: 98

✓ Trenton, NJ
Public K–12 (77.91%)
11 districts, 92 schools
46,396 students
Private K–12 (22.09%)
23 Catholic, 7,023 students
9 NAIS, 3,721 students
23 Other, 2,411 students
Colleges and Universities
Associate of Arts
2 campuses (12,821)
Baccalaureate
Thomas Edison State College (8,768)
Comprehensive
Rider College (4,839/1,477)
Trenton State College (6,186/976)
Doctoral
Princeton Theological Seminary (934)
Princeton University (4,651/1,913)
Places Rated Score: 87.01
Places Rated Rank: 34

Trois-Rivieres, PQ
Public Instruction
2 districts, 60 schools
14,640 students
Colleges and Universities
Associate of Arts
2 campuses (5,003)
Doctoral
Universite du Quebec (11,030/957)
Places Rated Score: 41.78
Places Rated Rank: 220

Tucson, AZ
Public K–12 (91.31%)
17 districts, 196 schools
111,017 students
Private K–12 (8.69%)
11 Catholic, 4,397 students
3 NAIS, 552 students
28 Other, 5,622 students
Colleges and Universities
Associate of Arts
2 campuses (40,101)
Comprehensive
University of Phoenix Tucson (1,084/1,042)
Doctoral
University of Arizona (28,347/9,974)
Places Rated Score: 44.85
Places Rated Rank: 207

Tulsa, OK
Public K–12 (92.92%)
61 districts, 280 schools
127,279 students
Private K–12 (7.08%)
13 Catholic, 6,514 students
1 NAIS, 964 students
15 Other, 2,215 students
Colleges and Universities
Associate of Arts
3 campuses (40,755)
Doctoral
Oral Roberts University (3,374/652)
University of Tulsa (3,810/1,805)
Places Rated Score: 35.58
Places Rated Rank: 241

Tuscaloosa, AL
Public K–12 (94.79%)
2 districts, 49 schools
23,334 students
Private K–12 (5.21%)
1 Catholic, 255 students
1 NAIS, 462 students
5 Other, 565 students
Colleges and Universities
Associate of Arts
2 campuses (12,969)
Baccalaureate
Stillman College (958)
Doctoral
University of Alabama (17,254/5,133)
Places Rated Score: 83.36
Places Rated Rank: 48

Tyler, TX
Public K–12 (95.53%)
8 districts, 60 schools
29,007 students
Private K–12 (4.47%)
2 Catholic, 513 students
5 Other, 843 students
Colleges and Universities
Associate of Arts
1 campus (11,393)
Comprehensive
University of Texas (2,914/2,736)
Places Rated Score: 45.66
Places Rated Rank: 205

Utica–Rome, NY
Public K–12 (94.15%)
28 districts, 102 schools
50,262 students
Private K–12 (5.85%)
13 Catholic, 2,610 students
8 Other, 512 students
Colleges and Universities
Associate of Arts
5 campuses (13,332)
Baccalaureate
Hamilton College (1,761)
Utica College of Syracuse University (2,995)
Comprehensive
SUNY Inst. of Technology (2,891/362)
Places Rated Score: 78.59
Places Rated Rank: 68

Vallejo–Fairfield–Napa, CA
Public K–12 (90.97%)
15 districts, 139 schools
85,198 students
Private K–12 (9.03%)
11 Catholic, 3,944 students
28 Other, 4,512 students
Colleges and Universities
Associate of Arts
2 campuses (33,011)
Comprehensive
Pacific Union College (1,945/77)
Places Rated Score: 56.25
Places Rated Rank: 165

Vancouver, BC
Public K–12 (90.65%)
11 districts, 576 schools
256,320 students
Private K–12 (9.35%)
126 Catholic and Other, 26,460 students
Colleges and Universities
Associate of Arts
11 campuses (71,716)
Comprehensive
Northwest Baptist Theological College (252/30)
Regent College (416/190)
Trinity Western University (2,082/89)
Doctoral
Simon Fraser University (15,890/2,321)
University of British Columbia (23,784/6,947)
Places Rated Score: 73.15
Places Rated Rank: 90

Ventura, CA
Public K–12 (90.54%)
22 districts, 185 schools
125,451 students
Private K–12 (9.46%)
13 Catholic, 4,656 students
5 NAIS, 772 students
75 Other, 7,677 students
Colleges and Universities

Associate of Arts
3 campuses (42,935)
Comprehensive
California Lutheran University (2,219/1,539)
Places Rated Score: 70.27
Places Rated Rank: 106

Victoria, BC
Public K–12 (89.73%)
3 districts, 114 schools
42,058 students
Private K–12 (10.27%)
30 Catholic and Other, 4,816 students
Colleges and Universities
Associate of Arts
1 campus (4,842)
Doctoral
University of Victoria (13,602/1,973)
Places Rated Score: 24.96

[illegible]

1 campus (3,678)
Comprehensive
University of Houston Victoria (865/905)
Places Rated Score: 19.78
Places Rated Rank: 296

Vineland–Millville–Bridgeton, NJ
Public K–12 (88.24%)
16 districts, 53 schools
23,433 students
Private K–12 (11.76%)
5 Catholic, 1,478 students
1 NAIS, 193 students
6 Other, 1,451 students
Colleges and Universities
Associate of Arts
1 campus (4,145)
Places Rated Score: 3.72
Places Rated Rank: 336

Visalia–Tulare–Porterville, CA
Public K–12 (97.09%)
51 districts, 145 schools
80,151 students
Private K–12 (2.91%)
3 Catholic, 675 students
22 Other, 1,725 students
Colleges and Universities
Associate of Arts
2 campuses (17,847)
Places Rated Score: 22.48
Places Rated Rank: 287

Waco, TX
Public K–12 (94.92%)
18 districts, 95 schools
35,606 students
Private K–12 (5.08%)
4 Catholic, 885 students
1 NAIS, 190 students
6 Other, 831 students
Colleges and Universities
Associate of Arts
2 campuses (14,387)
Doctoral
Baylor University (11,218/2,306)

Places Rated Score: 53.29
Places Rated Rank: 174

✓ Washington, DC–MD–VA–WV
Public K–12 (88.91%)
28 districts, 1,170 schools
639,104 students
Private K–12 (11.09%)
118 Catholic, 36,237 students
40 NAIS, 15,571 students
257 Other, 27,880 students
Colleges and Universities
Associate of Arts
8 campuses (134,758)
Baccalaureate
Columbia Union College (1,454)
Corcoran School of Art (645)
Shepherd College (4,335)
Comprehensive
Bowie State University (3,197/2,126)
[illegible]

American University (6,916/7,100)
Catholic University of America (2,561/3,903)
Gallaudet University (1,709/495)
George Mason University (19,897/7,415)
George Washington University (7,936/13,488)
Georgetown University (7,881/6,788)
Howard University (8,973/3,372)
University of Maryland College Park (28,398/11,076)
Places Rated Score: 95.26
Places Rated Rank: 9

Waterbury, CT
Public K–12 (84.77%)
8 districts, 68 schools
32,923 students
Private K–12 (15.23%)
15 Catholic, 4,601 students
4 NAIS, 1,137 students
2 Other, 177 students
Colleges and Universities
Associate of Arts
1 campus (6,878)
Baccalaureate
Teikyo Post University (2,701)
Places Rated Score: 32.51
Places Rated Rank: 255

Waterloo–Cedar Falls, IA
Public K–12 (81.95%)
6 districts, 41 schools
18,092 students
Private K–12 (18.05%)
9 Catholic, 3,316 students
3 Other, 668 students
Colleges and Universities
Associate of Arts
1 campus (3,544)
Doctoral
University of Northern Iowa (13,059/2,224)
Places Rated Score: 37.76
Places Rated Rank: 236

Wausau, WI
Public K–12 (85.30%)
9 districts, 46 schools
18,987 students
Private K–12 (14.70%)
13 Catholic, 2,320 students
10 Other, 951 students
Colleges and Universities
Associate of Arts
1 campus (16,061)
Places Rated Score: 10.35
Places Rated Rank: 318

West Palm Beach–Boca Raton, FL
Public K–12 (83.84%)
1 district, 143 schools
113,661 students
Private K–12 (16.16%)
15 Catholic, 5,158 students
5 NAIS, 2,751 students
78 Other, 14,004 students

Places Rated Rank: 222

Wheeling, WV–OH
Public K–12 (84.75%)
10 districts, 64 schools
23,552 students
Private K–12 (15.25%)
15 Catholic, 3,264 students
3 NAIS, 605 students
7 Other, 369 students
Colleges and Universities
Associate of Arts
2 campuses (6,539)
Baccalaureate
West Liberty State College (2,761)
Comprehensive
Ohio University Eastern Campus (1,263/412)
Wheeling Jesuit College (1,525/257)
Places Rated Score: 57.55
Places Rated Rank: 160

Wichita, KS
Public K–12 (90.07%)
24 districts, 218 schools
87,601 students
Private K–12 (9.93%)
21 Catholic, 7,058 students
1 NAIS, 883 students
16 Other, 1,721 students
Colleges and Universities
Associate of Arts
2 campuses (12,596)
Baccalaureate
Bethel College (804)
Comprehensive
Friends University (1,749/626)
Kansas Newman College (2,342/11)
Doctoral
Wichita State University (15,785/4,404)
Places Rated Score: 50.11
Places Rated Rank: 189

Wichita Falls, TX
Public K–12 (96.35%)

9 districts, 55 schools
24,186 students
Private K–12 (3.65%)
1 Catholic, 385 students
5 Other, 530 students
Colleges and Universities
Comprehensive
Midwestern State University (6,411/1,104)
Places Rated Score: 3.67
Places Rated Rank: 337

Williamsport, PA
Public K–12 (93.88%)
8 districts, 40 schools
20,227 students
Private K–12 (6.12%)
5 Catholic, 993 students
5 Other, 326 students
Colleges and Universities
Baccalaureate
Lycoming College (1,584)
Pennsylvania College of Technology (5,849)
Places Rated Score: 30.57
Places Rated Rank: 264

Wilmington, NC
Public K–12 (93.46%)
2 districts, 43 schools
27,577 students
Private K–12 (6.54%)
2 Catholic, 232 students
1 NAIS, 328 students
19 Other, 1,371 students
Colleges and Universities
Associate of Arts
2 campuses (6,369)
Comprehensive
University of North Carolina Wilmington (8,933/561)
Places Rated Score: 28.21
Places Rated Rank: 268

Wilmington-Newark, DE–MD
Public K–12 (76.39%)
7 districts, 135 schools
74,521 students
Private K–12 (23.61%)
30 Catholic, 12,689 students
9 NAIS, 3,788 students
64 Other, 6,552 students
Colleges and Universities
Associate of Arts
2 campuses (12,568)
Baccalaureate
Goldey-Beacom College (2,120)
Comprehensive
Widener University (568/1,465)
Doctoral
University of Delaware (22,040/3,367)
Wilmington College (2,386/1,127)
Places Rated Score: 69.28
Places Rated Rank: 110

Windsor, ON
Public K–13 (51.52%)
41 schools, 19,901 students
Catholic Separate K–13 (42.49%)
41 schools, 16,415 students
Private K–13 (5.90%)
11 schools, 2,310 students
Colleges and Universities
Associate of Arts
1 campus (4,800)
Doctoral
University of Windsor (14,678/910)
Places Rated Score: 31.45
Places Rated Rank: 259

Winnipeg, MB
Public K–12 (92.15%)
10 divisions, 254 schools
107,012 students
Private K–12 (7.85%)
41 Catholic and other, 9,120 students
Colleges and Universities
Associate of Arts
2 campuses (14,000)
Comprehensive
University of Winnipeg (7,085/190)
Doctoral
University of Manitoba (20,343/3,574)
Places Rated Score: 60.33
Places Rated Rank: 147

✓ Worcester, MA–CT
Public K–12 (89.32%)
34 districts, 162 schools
72,223 students
Private K–12 (10.68%)
18 Catholic, 6,123 students
4 NAIS, 1,297 students
12 Other, 1,214 students
Colleges and Universities
Associate of Arts
3 campuses (9,596)
Baccalaureate
College of the Holy Cross (2,711)
Comprehensive
Anna Maria College (788/1,038)
Assumption College (2,481/415)
Nichols College (1,749/517)
Worcester State College (6,979/1,276)
Doctoral
Clark University (2,747/1,163)
University of Massachusetts Medical School (462)
Worcester Polytechnic Institute (2,912/1,249)
Places Rated Score: 92.80
Places Rated Rank: 17

Yakima, WA
Public K–12 (95.34%)
15 districts, 79 schools
43,715 students
Private K–12 (4.66%)
3 Catholic, 797 students
11 Other, 1,339 students
Colleges and Universities
Associate of Arts
1 campus (6,486)
Comprehensive
Heritage College (544/421)
Places Rated Score: 6.21
Places Rated Rank: 327

Yolo, CA
Public K–12 (91.97%)
6 districts, 49 schools
23,418 students
Private K–12 (8.03%)
4 Catholic, 1,124 students
10 Other, 922 students
Colleges and Universities
Associate of Arts
1 campus (669)
Doctoral
University of California, Davis (18,200/4,798)
Places Rated Score: 49.38
Places Rated Rank: 194

York, PA
Public K–12 (91.90%)
16 districts, 97 schools
49,863 students
Private K–12 (8.10%)
8 Catholic, 1,985 students
1 NAIS, 264 students
23 Other, 2,145 students
Colleges and Universities
Associate of Arts
1 campus (237)
Comprehensive
Penn State University York (2,305/548)
York College Pennsylvania (5,523/112)
Places Rated Score: 25.13
Places Rated Rank: 280

Youngstown-Warren, OH
Public K–12 (90.25%)
48 districts, 223 schools
99,374 students
Private K–12 (9.75%)
34 Catholic, 8,936 students
12 Other, 1,799 students
Colleges and Universities
Associate of Arts
7 campuses (4,891)
Doctoral
Youngstown State University (16,691/2,257)
Places Rated Score: 47.61
Places Rated Rank: 196

Yuba City, CA
Public K–12 (95.81%)
20 districts, 70 schools
29,012 students
Private K–12 (4.19%)
2 Catholic, 481 students
11 Other, 789 students
Colleges and Universities
Associate of Arts
1 campus (15,797)
Places Rated Score: 19.98
Places Rated Rank: 295

Yuma, AZ
Public K–12 (96.66%)
9 districts, 35 schools
22,976 students
Private K–12 (3.34%)
2 Catholic, 483 students
3 Other, 312 students
Colleges and Universities
Associate of Arts
1 campus (11,994)
Places Rated Score: 5.04
Places Rated Rank: 333

Et Cetera

CONTINUING EDUCATION: A GROWING TREND

More and more, education is seen as a lifelong experience rather than one that ends abruptly upon graduation from high school or college. There are reasons for this: Workers in technical industries need retraining, professionals need state of the art courses for recertification, and others pursue personal and vocational interests. Today, there are more than twice as many adults enrolled in part-time education as there are full-time

SAT Scores by State

State	Raw Score Verbal	Raw Score Math	% Graduates Taking Test
Alabama	491	538	8
Alaska	445	489	47
Arizona	448	496	27
Arkansas	482	523	6
California	417	485	45
Colorado	462	518	29
Connecticut	431	477	81
Delaware	429	468	68
District of Columbia	412	445	53
Florida	420	469	48
Massachusetts	[illegible]	[illegible]	[illegible]
Michigan	484	549	11
Minnesota	506	579	9
Mississippi	498	540	4
Missouri	495	550	9
Montana	473	536	21
Nebraska	494	556	9
Nevada	434	483	30
New Hampshire	444	491	70
New Jersey	420	478	70
New Mexico	485	530	11
New York	419	473	74
North Carolina	411	454	60
North Dakota	515	592	5
Ohio	460	515	23
Oklahoma	491	536	9
Oregon	448	499	51
Pennsylvania	419	461	70
Rhode Island	425	463	70
South Carolina	401	443	58
South Dakota	505	563	5
Tennessee	497	543	12
Texas	419	474	47
Utah	513	563	4
Vermont	429	472	68
Virginia	428	468	65
Washington	443	494	48
West Virginia	448	484	17
Wisconsin	501	572	9
Wyoming	476	525	10

Source: College Entrance Examination Board, 1996.

SOLVING THE SAT PUZZLE . . . OR TRYING

After 17 years of unbroken decline, the average scores of students on the Scholastic Aptitude Tests (SAT), given by the College Entrance Examination Board, bottomed out in 1980 and started slowly upward in 1982. At the current rate of recovery, however, math scores won't match their 1963 high until the year 2000 and verbal scores not until well into the next century.

Two researchers pointed out that SAT scores started declining 18 years after the 1945 atomic bomb tests and began rising 18 years after the United States suspended all but underground atomic testing in 1963. The steepest drops in scores occurred in states nearest the bomb detonations, especially Nevada and Utah; smaller declines occurred in the northeastern and southeastern states that were far from the proving grounds. According to these researchers, those who blame the drop in SAT scores on television viewing, the Vietnam War, the child-spacing effect, changes in the number and mix of students taking the test, and poorer performance of schools are overlooking the effects of atomic fallout on the cognitive abilities of children.

But in Texas two other scholars of SAT trends have a different theory. The states that have the records of the highest scores, they claim, are not those that spend the most money for education, nor those with a long tradition of quality public education, but those with the coldest winters: Average scores from cold-weather states are consistently higher than scores from warm-weather states. They offer two explanations for the link between cold weather and high SAT scores: (1) research on thermal conditions and human behavior suggests that cool room temperatures reduce mistakes on tests, and 2) long winters force children to remain inside after school and on weekends, thereby favoring family interaction, which is critical for pupil achievement.

Nonsense, another researcher points out. If one were to rank the states by their average total SATs, one would be ranking the states by the percent of college-bound seniors who actually took the test. When the percentage is low, students taking the test are among the highest

Mandatory Continuing Education for Selected Professions

	Dentists	Lawyers	Nurses	Psychologists	Physicians	Social Workers
Alabama	•	•	•	•	•	•
Alaska	•		•	•	•	•
Alberta	•				•	
Arizona		•	•	•	•	•
Arkansas		•		•	E	•
British Columbia	•				•	
California	•	•	•	•	•	
Colorado		•	•			
Connecticut						
Delaware	•	•	•	•	•	•
District of Columbia			•		•	•
Florida	•	•	•	•	•	•
Georgia	•	•		•	•	•
Hawaii					•	
Idaho		•		•		•
Illinois	•				•	•
Indiana	•	•				
Iowa	•	•	•	•	•	•
Kansas	•	•	•	•	•	•
Kentucky	•	•	•	•	•	
Louisiana		•	•	•		•
Maine	•	•		•	•	•
Manitoba	•			•		
Maryland	•	•		•	•	•
Massachusetts	•		•	•	•	•
Michigan	•		E		•	
Minnesota	•	•	•	•	•	•
Mississippi		•	•	•		•
Missouri		•			•	•
Montana		•		•		•
Nebraska	•		•	•		•
Nevada	•	•	•	•	•	•
New Brunswick	•				•	
New Hampshire	•	•	•	•	•	
New Jersey	•					
New Mexico	•	•	•	•	•	•
New York		•				
Newfoundland	•					
North Carolina		•		•		•
North Dakota	•	•		•		•
Nova Scotia						
Ohio	•	•	•	•	•	•
Oklahoma	•	•		•		•
Ontario					•	
Oregon	•	•	•	•		•
Pennsylvania		•		•	•	E
Quebec	•					
Rhode Island	•	•		•	•	
Saskatchewan	•				•	
South Carolina		•		•		•
South Dakota	•					•
Tennessee	•	•				•
Texas		•	•	•	•	•
Utah		•		•		
Vermont		•		•		
Virginia		•				
Washington		•		•	•	•
West Virginia	E	•		•	•	•
Wisconsin		•		•	•	•
Wyoming	•	•				•

Source: Louis Phillips and Associates; Places Rated Partnership Survey, 1996.
• - continuing education required
E - enabling legislation passed but not implemented

achievers; more students in the test-taking pool usually means more students of average ability.

OUTSTANDING SECONDARY SCHOOLS

The U.S. Department of Education periodically polls the chief education officer in each of the states and the Council for American Private Education for the names of the best secondary schools in the country.

Of the thousands nominated since 1990, just 715 have received official recognition for excellence in education. The schools must withstand a tough screening, which includes a careful look at curricula and academic achievement; inspection of buildings, classrooms, and facilities; informal observations of classes, lunch periods and assemblies; and interviews with pupils, parents, teachers, and administrators. The people who do the screening are specialists in school improvement and accreditation and none work for the federal government.

Of these outstanding secondary schools, 648 are located in metro areas. The schools include 350 junior high schools (JHS), middle schools (MS), and intermediate schools (IS), as well as 298 high schools (HS). 143 of these schools are private and are indicated by an (*) asterisk.

McKinley MS,
Roosevelt MS, Tijeras
Taylor MS, Albuquerque
Van Buren MS, Albuquerque

Allentown–Bethlehem–Easton, PA
*Central Catholic HS, Allentown

Amarillo, TX
Crockett MS, Amarillo

Anchorage, AK
East Anchorage HS, Anchorage
West Anchorage HS, Anchorage

Ann Arbor, MI
Pinkney MS, Pinckney

Appleton–Oshkosh–Neenah, WI
Hortonville MS, Hortonville

Athens, GA
Cedar Shoals HS, Athens

Atlanta, GA
Banneker HS, College Park
Chamblee HS, Chamblee
Duluth HS, Duluth
McCleskey MS, Marietta
Mundy's Mill MS, Jonesboro
Otwell MS, Cumming
Pickneyville MS, Norcross
Ralph Bunche MS, Atlanta
South Cobb HS, Austell
Sprayberry HS, Marietta
Trickum MS, Lilburn

Austin–San Marcos, TX
Canyon Vista MS, Austin
Chilholm Trail MS, Round Rock
Georgetown HS, Georgetown
Hill Country MS, Austin
James Bowie HS, Austin
Noel Grisham MS, Austin
West Ridge MS, Austin
Westwood HS, Austin

Bakersfield, CA
Fruitvale JHS, Bakersfield
Highland HS, Bakersfield

Baltimore, MD
... HS, Severn

*Episcopal HS, Baton Rouge
*St. Joseph's Academy, Baton Rouge

Beaumont–Port Arthur, TX
*Monsignor Kelly HS, Beaumont

Bergen–Passaic, NJ
Fair Lawn HS, Fair Lawn
*Immaculate Heart Academy, Washington Township
Northern Valley Regional HS, Old Tappan
*Queen of Peace HS, North Arlington

Birmingham, AL
Grantswood Community School, Irondale
Hewitt–Trussville HS, Trussville
Louis Pizitz MS, Birmingham
Mountain Brook HS, Mountain Brook
Vestavia Hills HS, Vestavia Hills

Bismarck, ND
Century HS, Bismarck

Boston, MA–NH
Broad Meadows MS, Quincy
Clarke MS, Lexington
James Timilty MS, Boston
Mansfield HS, Mansfield
Marblehead MS, Marblehead
Simonds MS, Burlington

Buffalo–Niagara Falls, NY
Kenmore East HS, Tonawanda

Cedar Rapids, IA
Harding MS, Cedar Rapids
Metro HS, Cedar Rapids
Washington HS, Cedar Rapids

Champaign–Urbana, IL
Champaign Central HS, Champaign

Charleston, WV
Andrew Jackson MS, Cross Lanes
Capital HS, Charleston
DuPont JHS, Belle
Winfield HS, Winfield

Charleston–North Charleston, SC
Williams MS, Charleston

Alonzo Stagg HS, Palos Hills
Barrington HS, Barrington
*Carmel HS, Mundelein
Community HS, West Chicago
Deer Path JHS, Lake Forest
Deerfield HS, Deerfield
Elk Grove HS, Elk Grove Village
Highland Upper Grades, Libertyville
Homewood–Flossmoor HS, Flossmoor
*Immaculate Heart of Mary HS, Westchester
Lake Bluff JHS, Lake Bluff
Libertyville HS, Libertyville
*Madonna HS, Chicago
Maine Township HS West, Des Plaines
Margaret Mead JHS, Elk Grove Village
*Marian Catholic HS, Chicago Heights
*Mother McAuley HS, Chicago
Mundelein HS, Mundelein
New Trier Township HS, Winnetka
Niles North HS, Skokie
Niles West HS, Skokie
Northbrook JHS, Northbrook
Northwood MS, Woodstock
Palatine HS, Palatine
Prospect HS, Mount Prospect
*Regina Domican HS, Wilmette
Rolling Meadows HS, Rolling Meadows
Schaumburg HS, Schaumburg
St. Charles HS, St. Charles
Stevenson HS, Prairie View
Sundling JHS, Palatine
Wilmette JHS, Wilmette

Cincinnati, OH–KY–IN
Anderson HS, Cincinnati
Harrison HS, Harrison
Hoffman School, Cincinnati
Madeira HS, Cincinnati
Mason MS, Mason
*Notre Dame Academy, Covington
Princeton HS, Cincinnati
Princeton JHS, Cincinnati

Clarksville–Hopkinsville, TN–KY
Fort Campbell HS, Fort Campbell North
Mahaffey MS, Fort Campbell North

Cleveland–Lorain–Elyria, OH
Beachwood MS, Beachwood
*Beaumont Catholic HS, Cleveland Heights
*Elyria Catholic HS, Elyria
Kenston HS, Chagrin Falls
Mentor Shore JHS, Mentor
Orange HS, Pepper Pike
Perry HS, Perry
*Regina HS, South Euclid
Solon HS, Solon
*St. Edward HS, Lakewood
*St. Joseph Academy, Cleveland
Willoughby South HS, Willoughby

Colorado Springs, CO
Rampart HS, Colorado Springs

Columbia, MO
Hickman HS, Columbia
Jefferson JH, Columbia

Columbia, SC
Irmo MS, Columbia
Chapin HS, Chapin
*Heathwood Hall Episcopal School, Columbia
Irmo HS, Columbia
Lexington MS, Lexington
Richland Northeast HS, Columbia
Spring Valley HS, Columbia
Summit Parkway MS, Columbia

Columbus, OH
*Columbus School for Girls, Columbus
*Our Lady of Perpetual Help, Grove City
*St. Francis de Sales HS, Columbus

Dallas, TX
Anna MS, Anna
Armstrong MS, Plano
*Bishop Lynch HS, Dallas
Blalack JH, Carrollton
Booker T. Washington HS, Dallas
Carpenter MS, Plano
Clark HS, Plano
Coppell MS West, Coppell
Edward Marcus HS, Flower Mound
Forest Meadow JHS, Dallas
*Jesuit College Prep, Dallas
Lyles MS, Garland
McCulloch MS, Dallas
Milliken MS, Lewisville
Park Hill JH, Dallas
Plano East HS, Plano
Plano Senior HS, Plano
Renner MS, Plano
Richardson JHS, Richardson
Strickland MS, Denton
Turner HS, Carrollton
*Ursuline Academy, Dallas
Vivian Field JHS, Farmers Branch

Danbury, CT
Barlow HS, West Redding

Dayton–Springfield, OH
Centerville HS, Centerville
Mad River MS, Dayton
Oakwood HS, Dayton

Daytona Beach, FL
Mainland HS, Daytona Beach
Spruce Creek HS, Port Orange

Denver, CO
Cherry Creek HS, Englewood
Cherry Creek West MS, Littleton
Heritage HS, Littleton
Horizon HS, Brighton
*Lutheran HS, Denver
Smoky Hill HS, Aurora
*St. Mary's Academy, Englewood

Detroit, MI
Cass Technical HS, Detroit
Covington MS, Birmingham
*De La Salle Collegiate HS, Warren
East Hills MS, Bloomfield Hills
North Farmington HS, Farmington Hills
Orchard Lake MS, West Bloomfield
Rochester Adams HS, Rochester Hills
Southfield–Lathrup HS, Lathrup Village
Troy Athens HS, Troy
Van Hoosen MS, Rochester
West Bloomfield HS, West Bloomfield

El Paso, TX
Socorro HS, El Paso

Erie, PA
*Mercyhurst Prep, Erie

Evansville–Henderson, IN–KY
North HS, Evansville

Fayetteville–Springdale–Rogers, AR
Old High MS, Bentonville

Florence, AL
Mars Hill Bible School, Florence
Muscle Shoals HS, Muscle Shoals

Fort Lauderdale, FL
*Chaminade–Madonna Prep, Hollywood
Cooper City HS, Cooper City
Coral Springs MS, Coral Springs
Forest Glen MS, Coral Springs
Ramblewood MS, Coral Springs
Rogers MS, Fort Lauderdale
*St. Thomas Aquinas HS, Fort Lauderdale
Tequesta Trace MS, Fort Lauderdale
*University School, Fort Lauderdale

Fort Myers–Cape Coral, FL
Bonita Springs MS, Bonita Springs
Caloosa MS, Cape Coral
Fort Myers MS, Fort Myers

Fort Smith, AR–OK
Northside HS, Fort Smith

Fort Walton Beach, FL
Niceville HS, Niceville

Fort Worth–Arlington, TX
Carroll HS, Southlake
Carroll MS, Southlake
Grapevine MS, Grapevine
Lawrence Bell HS, Hurst

Fresno, CA
Clark IS, Clovis
Clovis HS, Clovis
Edison Computech 7–8, Fresno
Kastner IS, Fresno

Gary, IN
Munster HS, Munster
Wilbur Wright MS, Munster

Grand Rapids–Muskegon–Holland, MI
Caledonia HS, Caledonia
East Grand Rapids HS, Grand Rapids
East Grand Rapids MS, Grand Rapids
Rockford HS, Rockford
Rockford MS, Rockford

Greensboro–Winston-Salem–High Point, NC
Williams HS, Burlington

Greenville–Spartanburg–Anderson, SC
Spartanburg HS, Spartanburg

Hamilton–Middletown, OH
Lakota HS, West Chester

Harrisburg–Lebanon–Carlisle, PA
Feaser MS, Middletown
*Harrisburg Academy, Wormleysburg
Hershey HS, Hershey
Trinity HS, Camp Hill

Hartford, CT
Deane MS, Wethersfield
Granby Memorial MS, Granby
RHAM HS, Hebron
Southington HS, Southington
Wallace MS, Newington
Wethersfield HS, Wethersfield

Honolulu, HI
*ASSETS School, Honolulu
Castle HS, Kaneohe
Dole IS, Honolulu
Kailua IS, Kailua
Kalaheo HS, Kailua
Leilehua HS, Wahiawa

Houston, TX
Arnold JH, Houston
Bleyl JH, Houston
*Duchesne Academy, Houston
James Taylor HS, Katy
Klein Oak HS, Spring
Labay JH, Houston
Langham Creek HS, Houston
Mayde Creek HS, Houston
Northbrook MS, Houston
Olle MS, Houston
*River Oaks Academy, Houston
Spring Forest MS, Houston
Spring HS, Spring
Spring Oaks MS, Houston
Stovall JHS, Houston
Strack IS, Klein
Washington JH, Conroe

Huntsville, AL
Bob Jones HS, Madison

Indianapolis, IN
Craig MS, Indianapolis
*Lutheran HS, Indianapolis
*Roncalli HS, Indianapolis

Jacksonville, FL
Landrum MS, Ponte Vedra Beach

Johnson City–Kingsport–Bristol, TN–VA
Science Hill HS, Johnson City

Kansas City, MO–KS
Blue Valley North HS, Overland Park
Mission Valley MS, Shawnee Mission
Olathe South HS, Olathe
Oregon Trail JHS, Olathe
Oxford MS, Overland Park
*Rogers Academy, Kansas City
Truman HS, Independence

Knoxville, TN
Maryville MS, Maryville

Lafayette, IN
Jefferson HS, Lafayette

Lafayette, LA
*St. Thomas More HS, Lafayette

Lansing–East Lansing, MI
Everett HS, Lansing
Holt HS, Holt

Las Vegas, NV–AZ
Mike O'Callaghan MS, Las Vegas

Long Island, NY
Baldwin HS, Baldwin
Elmont Memorial HS, Elmont
Floral Park HS, Floral Park
Jericho HS, Jericho
Lynbrook HS, Lynbrook
New Hyde Park HS, New Hyde Park
North Shore HS, Glen Head
*Sacred Heart Academy, Hempstead

Memphis, TN–AR–MS
Craigmont HS, Memphis
Germantown HS, Germantown
*St. Mary's Episcopal School, Memphis

Miami, FL
Design and Architecture HS, Miami
George Washington Carver MS, Miami
*Gulliver Prep, Miami
Jefferson MS, Miami
MAST Academy, Miami
New World School of the Arts, Miami
North Dade Center for Modern Languages, Miami
*Our Lady of Lourdes Academy, Miami

Middlesex–Somerset–Hunterdon, NJ
Churchill JHS, East Brunswick
East Brunswick HS, East Brunswick
Hammarskjold MS, East Brunswick

New Orleans, LA
*Archbishop Blenk HS, Gretna
*Archbishop Chapelle HS, Metairie
*De La Salle HS, New Orleans
McDonough HS, New Orleans
McMain HS, New Orleans
*Mount Carmel Academy, New Orleans
*St. Mary's Dominican HS, New Orleans
*Ursuline Academy, New Orleans
Warren Easton Fundamental HS, New Orleans
*Xavier University Prep, New Orleans

New York, NY
Bowne HS, Flushing
Bronxville HS, Bronxville
*Convent of the Sacred Heart School, New York
*Dominican Academy, New York
Eastchester HS, Eastchester

Carmenita JHS, Cerritos
Center for Enriched Studies, Los Angeles
Culver City HS, Culver City
El Monte HS, El Monte
*Sacred Heart Academy, La Canada Flintridge
Gretchen Whitney HS, Cerritos
Huntington MS, San Marino
La Canada HS, La Canada Flintridge
Louisville HS, Woodland Hills
Manhattan Beach IS, Manhattan Beach
Medea Creek MS, Agoura Hills
Mira Costa HS, Manhattan Beach
*Notre Dame Academy, Los Angeles
Oak Park HS, Agoura Hills
Parrias MS, Redondo Beach
*Ramona Convent HS, Alhambra
Rosemont MS, La Crescenta
South Pasadena MS, South Pasadena
Walnut HS, Walnut

Louisville, KY–IN
*Assumption HS, Louisville
duPont Manual HS, Louisville
Floyd Central HS, Floyds Knobs
*St. Xavier HS, Louisville
*Trinity HS, Louisville

Lubbock, TX
Lubbock HS, Lubbock

Lynchburg, VA
Glass HS, Lynchburg
Heritage HS, Lynchburg

Macon, GA
Houston County HS, Warner Robins
*Mount De Sales HS, Macon
Warner Robins HS, Warner Robins

Madison, WI
James Madison HS, Madison

McAllen–Edinburg–Mission, TX
Travis MS, McAllen

Melbourne–Titusville–Palm Bay, FL
*Central Catholic HS, Melbourne

Custer HS, Milwaukee
Fritsche MS, Milwaukee
*Milwaukee Lutheran HS, Milwaukee
Milwaukee Trade HS, Milwaukee
Nicolet HS, Glendale
Oconomowoc HS, Oconomowoc
*Pius XI HS, Milwaukee
Rufus King HS, Milwaukee

Minneapolis–St. Paul, MN–WI
Apple Valley HS, Apple Valley
Breck School, Minneapolis
Dassel–Cokato HS, Cokato
Eagan HS, Eagan
Eden Prairie HS, Eden Prairie
Hastings MS, Hastings
Hosterman MS, New Hope
Irondale HS, New Brighton
Lindgren IS, St. Louis Park
St. Anthony MS, Minneapolis
Stillwater JHS, Stillwater
*Trinity School, Bloomington
Valley MS, Apple Valley
Wayzata HS, Plymouth

Mobile, AL
Davidson HS, Mobile
*Phillips Preparatory School, Mobile

Myrtle Beach, SC
Conway MS, Conway
Socastee HS, Myrtle Beach
St. James MS, Surfside Beach

Nashua, NH
Amherst MS, Amherst

Nashville, TN
Glendale MS, Nashville
*St. Cecilia Academy, Nashville
Wright MS, Nashville

New Bedford, MA
*Bishop Stang HS, North Dartmouth
Coyle and Cassidy HS, Taunton

New Haven–Meriden, CT
*Sacred Heart Academy, Hamden

*St. Raymond HS for Boys, Bronx
*Shulamith HS for Girls, Brooklyn
*The Berkeley Carroll School, Brooklyn
*The Ursuline School, New Rochelle
*Xavier HS, New York

Newark, NJ
Columbia HS, Maplewood
*Kimberley Academy, Montclair

Norfolk–Virginia Beach–Newport News, VA–NC
*Cape Henry Collegiate, Virginia Beach
Gildersleeve MS, Newport News
*Hampton Roads Academy, Newport News
Hines MS, Newport News
Northside MS, Norfolk
Syms MS, Hampton

Oakland, CA
Alameda HS, Alameda
Alvarado MS, Union City
*Bishop O'Dowd HS, Oakland
Charlotte Wood MS, Danville
*Holy Names HS, Oakland
Irvington HS, Fremont
Miramonte HS, Orinda
San Lorenzo HS, San Lorenzo
Stone Valley MS, Alamo

Oklahoma City, OK
Sequoyah MS, Edmond

Olympia, WA
Capital HS, Olympia
New Century HS, Lacey

Omaha, NE–IA
*Duchesne Academy, Omaha
*Marian HS, Omaha
Millard Central MS, Omaha
Ralston HS, Ralston
Valley HS, Valley
Westside HS, Omaha

Orange County, CA
Brea Olinda HS, Brea
*Fairmont JHS, Anaheim
Foothill HS, Santa Ana
Hewes MS, Santa Ana
La Habra HS, La Habra
La Paz IS, Mission Viejo
Laguna Beach HS, Laguna Beach
Laguna Hills HS, Laguna Hills
Lakeside MS, Irvine
Los Alamitos HS, Los Alamitos
Los Alisos IS, Mission Viejo
Mission Viejo HS, Mission Viejo
Venado MS, Irvine
Westminster HS, Westminster

Orlando, FL
Apopka HS, Apopka
Neptune MS, Kissimmee

Pensacola, FL
*Pensacola Catholic HS, Pensacola

Philadelphia, PA–NJ
Arcola IS, Norristown
East HS, West Chester
Fugett MS, West Chester
Gordon MS, Coatesville
*Gwynedd Mercy HS, Gwynedd Valley
Hatboro-Horsham HS, Horsham
*Holy Ghost Prep, Bensalem
Indian Valley MS, Harleysville
Keith Valley MS, Horsham
*Merion Mercy Academy, Merion Station
*Moorestown Friends School, Moorestown
*Mount St. Joseph Academy, Flourtown
North Penn HS, Lansdale
Radnor HS, Radnor
South Brandywine MS, Coatesville
Upper Dublin HS, Fort Washington
Upper Moreland MS, Hatboro
Upper Perkiomen HS, Pennsburg
Upper Perkiomen MS, East Greenville
*Villa Joseph Marie HS, Holland
Wayne MS, Malvern
*West Philadelphia Catholic HS, Philadelphia

Phoenix–Mesa, AZ
Desert Sky MS, Glendale
Greenway HS, Phoenix
Mohave MS, Scottsdale
Red Mountain HS, Mesa
Western Sky MS, Phoenix
*Xavier Prep, Phoenix

Pittsburgh, PA
Boyce MS, Upper St. Clair
Dorseyville MS, Pittsburgh
Fort Couch MS, Upper St. Clair
Fox Chapel Area HS, Pittsburgh
Hampton HS, Allison Park
Independence MS, Bethel Park
Mt. Lebanon HS, Pittsburgh
Mt. Lebanon JHS, Pittsburgh
North Allegheny HS, Wexford
Quaker Valley HS, Leetsdale
*Sewickley Academy, Sewickley
Shaler Area MS, Glenshaw
Taylor Allderdice HS, Pittsburgh

Portland, ME
Old Orchard Beach HS, Old Orchard Beach

Providence–Fall River–Warwick, RI–MA
*Bishop Hendricken HS, Warwick
Davisville MS, North Kingstown
*La Salle Academy, Providence
*Mount St. Charles Academy, Woonsocket
*St. Mary Academy, Providence

Punta Gorda, FL
Murdock MS, Port Charlotte

Reading, PA
Wyomissing Area HS, Wyomissing

Richmond–Petersburg, VA
Freeman HS, Henrico County
Liberty MS, Ashland
*St. Gertrude HS, Richmond
Tuckahoe MS, Richmond

Riverside–San Bernardino, CA
Eisenhower HS, Rialto
University Heights MS, Riverside
Vineyard JHS, Alta Loma

Rochester, NY
*Canandaigua Academy, Canandaigua
*The Harley School, Rochester

Rockford, IL
*Boylan Central Catholic HS, Rockford

Sacramento, CA
Rio Americano HS, Sacramento

St. Louis, MO–IL
Conant HS, Hoffman
*Cor Jesu Academy, St. Louis
Crestview MS, Ellisville
Green MS, St. Louis
LaSalle Springs MS, Glencoe
*Lutheran HS South, St. Louis
Nerinx Hall HS, Webster Groves
North Kirkwood MS, Kirkwood
Parkway South HS, Manchester
Pattonville HS, Maryland Heights
Rockwood Eureka HS, Eureka
*St. Joseph's Academy, St. Louis
*Villa Duchesne, St. Louis
*Westminster Christian Academy, St. Louis
Wydown MS, Clayton

Salinas, CA
*The York School, Monterey

Salt Lake City–Ogden, UT
Bryant IS, Salt Lake City
Granger HS, West Valley City

San Antonio, TX
Cole HS, San Antonio
John Marshall HS, San Antonio
Lackland HS, San Antonio
Northside Health Careers HS, San Antonio
Stevenson MS, San Antonio

San Diego, CA
*Our Lady of Peace Academy, San Diego
Black Mountain MS, San Diego
Cajon Park School, Santee
Diegueno JHS, Encinitas
Earl Warren JHS, Solana Beach
La Mesa MS, La Mesa
Oak Grove MS, Jamul
Peirce MS, Ramona
Poway HS, Poway
Rancho Buena Vista HS, Vista
*The Bishop's School, La Jolla
Torrey Pines HS, San Diego
Twin Peaks MS, Poway
Vista HS, Vista

San Francisco, CA
*Covenant of the Sacred Heart HS, San Francisco
Crocker MS, Hillsborough
Davidson MS, San Rafael
Hillsdale HS, San Mateo
Lowell HS, San Francisco
Nathaniel Bowditch MS, Foster City
San Mateo HS, San Mateo
Taylor MS, Millbrae

San Jose, CA
*Bullis Purissima School, Los Altos Hills
Cupertino HS, Cupertino
Davis IS, San Jose
Kennedy JHS, Cupertino
Los Gatos HS, Los Gatos
Rogers MS, San Jose
Rolling Hills MS, Los Gatos
*St. Francis HS, Mountain View

San Luis Obispo–Atascadero–Paso Robles, CA
Paulding MS, Arroyo Grande

Santa Barbara–Santa Maria–Lompoc, CA
*Midland School, Santa Barbara
*St. Joseph HS, Santa Maria

Santa Rosa, CA
Montgomery HS, Santa Rosa

Savannah, GA
Myers MS, Savannah
*Savannah Country Day School, Savannah

Seattle–Bellevue–Everett, WA
Cedarcrest HS, Duvall
*Holy Names Academy, Seattle
Inglewood JHS, Redmond
Kent-Meridian HS, Kent
*The Northwest School, Seattle

Sheboygan, WI
Horace Mann MS, Sheboygan

Shreveport–Bossier City, LA
Byrd HS, Shreveport

South Bend, IN
Penn HS, Mishawaka
*Trinity School, South Bend
Young MS, Mishawaka

Spokane, WA
*Ganzaga Prep, Spokane

Springfield, MA
*Williston Northampton HS, Easthampton

Stamford–Norwalk, CT
Weston HS, Weston

State College, PA
State College Area HS, State College

Sumter, SC
Sumter HS, Sumter

Syracuse, NY
Skaneateles HS, Skaneateles
Westhill HS, Syracuse

Tampa–St. Petersburg–Clearwater, FL
*Berkeley Prep, Tampa
Plant HS, Tampa
Woodrow Wilson MS, Tampa

Toledo, OH
*Central Catholic HS, Toledo

Trenton, NJ
West Windsor–Plainsboro HS, Princeton Junction

Tucson, AZ
Flowing Wells HS, Tucson
Safford Technology MS, Tucson

Utica–Rome, NY
Mount Markham MS, West Winfield

Ventura, CA
Anacapa MS, Ventura
Blackstock JHS, Oxnard
Green JHS, Oxnard
*The Thacher School, Ojai

Washington, DC–MD–VA–WV
Banneker Academic HS, Washington
*Bishop O'Connell HS, Arlington
Churchill HS, Potomac
*De Matha Catholic HS, Hyattsville
Duke Ellington School of the Arts, Washington
Dunbar HS, Washington
Frederick HS, Frederick
*Good Counsel HS, Wheaton–Glenmont
*Hebrew Academy, Silver Spring
Herbert Hoover MS, Rockville
Hine JHS, Washington
Martin Luther King MS, Beltsville
Montgomery HS, Rockville
Redland MS, Rockville
Roosevelt HS, Greenbelt
*The Lab School of Washington, Washington
Thomas Johnson HS, Frederick
Walter Johnson HS, Bethesda
Westland IS, Bethesda

Waterbury, CT
Alcott MS, Wolcott
Rochambeau MS, Southbury

West Palm Beach–Boca Raton, FL
Loggers Run MS, Boca Raton

Wilmington, NC
Hoggard HS, Wilmington

Wilmington–Newark, DE–MD
*Padua Academy, Wilmington

CLIMATE

"The fortunate people of the planet," John Kenneth Galbraith wrote years ago in *Harper's,* "are those who live by the seasons. There is far more difference between a Vermont farm in the summer and that farm in the winter than there is between San Diego and Sao Paulo. This means that people who live where the seasons are good and strong have no need to travel; they can stay at home and let change come to them. This simple truth will one day be recognized and then we will see a great reverse migration from Florida to Maine and on into Québec."

Galbraith's forecast may be too optimistic. Pathways to seasonal sun are well worn; a quick count of Maine and Québecois license plates in Florida and Texas Gulf parking lots in February proves that. Americans and Canadians say they prefer mild, sunny climates, and when asked where in the continent these climates are, they point to the fast-growing lower half of the Pacific Coast, Florida, and anywhere along the South Atlantic and Gulf Coast Shore. Certainly this area, between 25 degrees and 35 degrees latitude, has been drawing migrants for decades.

But other places north of the Mason-Dixon line and hundreds of miles from ocean beaches benefit from population growth, and many of these enjoy mild climates, too. Some of these places might surprise you.

There's an enormous variety of global climates found right here at home. Northern maritime, mild Mediterranean, southerly mountain, lowland desert, tropical "paradise," desert highland, rugged northern continental, windward slope, leeward slope, humid subtropical—you name it, and you'll meet up with it somewhere in North America.

Climate is a part of your circumstances that can't be bought, built, remodeled, or relocated. A place's climate is there for keeps, and the weather events that go along with it—rain, snow, heat, cold, drought, wind—will have a profound effect on your life.

SIX FACTORS TO KEEP IN MIND

If you can live anywhere you wish and are open to all the variety the continent offers, know that a combination of water, latitude, elevation, prevailing winds, mountain ranges, and urban development lies behind any metro area's climate.

Water

Oceans and other large bodies of water take the edge off temperature. Water warms up slowly, holds much more heat than does land, and cools more slowly. Places near or surrounded by water tend to be cooler in summer and warmer in winter than others far from water.

In July it only heats up to 75°F on the Santa Monica Pier in Los Angeles; meanwhile, 15 miles north in the San Fernando Valley, it's 95°. If Toronto were to be gathered up and then set down at the same latitude, but

North American Geographical Extremes

Coterminous United States

Geographic center: near Lebanon, Smith County, Kansas
Northernmost point: Lake of the Woods Projection, Minnesota
Southernmost point: Cape Sable, Florida
Easternmost point: West Quoddy Head, Maine
Westernmost point: Cape Alava, Washington
Highest point: Mount Whitney, California: 14,494 feet

United States and Outlying Areas

Geographic center (50 states): Castle Rock, Butte County, South Dakota
Northernmost point: Point Barrow, Alaska
Southernmost point: Orote Point, Guam
Easternmost point: East Point, St. Croix, Virgin Islands
Westernmost point: Kure Island, Hawaii

hundreds of miles west of its Lake Ontario shore, winter would arrive a month sooner and spring a month later.

While bodies of water soften hot and cold temperatures, they also influence the local micro-climate. Utah's ancient Great Salt Lake is the big reason why there is much more snow in Salt Lake City than in other nearby areas. Face Lake Michigan in a Chicago winter and you may have to grab a rail, so strong is the easterly wind that comes in unobstructed from miles offshore.

Latitude

The continent's heartland, away from the moderating effects of water, experiences wide swings of temperature. These continental climates tend to be even more rigorous in the higher latitudes. The closer to the poles you get, the more exaggerated the seasonal shifts, because extreme northerly locations see the greatest seasonal variation in the amount and intensity of sunlight.

In Edmonton, AB (53.55 N), 800,000 residents see 8:00 am sunrises and 3:30 pm sunsets in late December with daylight savings time. By July, the day lengthens to 17 hours and the Alberta capitol becomes an intensely sunlit spot.

Far to the southwest, the solar energy pouring over Honolulu (21.20 N) in June is twice what it is in December, but in Anchorage (61.10 N) it is 20 times as great. Places in the far north experience not only Siberian winters but short, sunbaked summers as well.

Inheriting Climates

In less than 25 years, greenhouse warming will cause these Canadian metro areas to have the same climates that American metro areas farther south have now.

Toronto, ON	Indianapolis, IN
Sudbury, ON	Cleveland–Lorain–Elyria, OH
Winnipeg, MB	Minneapolis–St. Paul, MN–WI
Edmonton, AB	Cheyenne, WY
Vancouver, BC	San Francisco, CA

Source: Environment Canada, *Climates of Canada.*

Elevation

stations just 15 miles apart, but differing in elevation by 4,700 feet, the average annual temperatures differ by 16°F.

In the United States, places that combine high altitudes with southerly latitudes get the mild, short winters of the South and the cooler nights and crisp falls of the North. Asheville, NC, in the southern Appalachians, and Santa Fe, NM, in the southern Rockies, have long been known for their mild, four-season climates.

Wind

Consider a pair of metro areas 3,200 miles apart: Bellingham, WA, and Portland, ME. Both sit high in

Windy Metro Areas

	Average Wind Speed
St. John's, NF	15.1 mph
Amarillo, TX	13.5
Rochester, MN	13.1
Cheyenne, WY	12.9
Regina, SK	12.9
Casper, WY	12.9
Great Falls, MT	12.7
Portsmouth–Rochester, NH–ME	12.5
Barnstable–Yarmouth, MA	12.5
Boston, MA–NH	12.5
Manchester, NH	12.5
Lubbock, TX	12.4
Oklahoma City, OK	12.3
Fargo–Moorhead, ND–MN	12.3
Wichita, KS	12.3
New Haven–Meriden, CT	12.0
Corpus Christi, TX	12.0

Listed above are metro areas described in the Place Profiles with average annual wind speeds of 12 mph or more.

Wet Metro Areas

Precipitation days detailed in the Place Profiles are days on which at least one-tenth of an inch of precipitation falls.

	Precipitation Days
St. John's, NF	144
Saint John, NB	138
Halifax, NS	138
Montreal, PQ	120
Quebec City, PQ	117
Vancouver, BC	114
Victoria, BC	100
Portland–Vancouver, OR–WA	100
Seattle–Bellevue–Everett, WA	95
Charleston, WV	93
Bellingham, WA	93
Eugene–Springfield, OR	90
Washington, DC–MD–VA–WV	87
Binghamton, NY	87
Olympia, WA	84

Listed above are weather stations described in the Place Profiles with the equivalent of 12 or more weeks of precipitation throughout the year.

northern latitudes on their respective coasts. Both peek through some of the foggiest mornings on the continent. You'd naturally suppose the two have similar climates.

But Bellingham is much milder because of the winds that blow from west to east across the continent. The West Coast is a landfall for air that has moved thousands of miles over water; cities even hundreds of miles inland still feel some of the beneficial effects of the Pacific winds. Interior cities in the East feel few consequences of the Atlantic save on those rare occasions when the prevailing wind direction doesn't prevail. Sad to say, this reversal of wind direction often portends a storm.

Snowy Metro Areas

Canada and the U.S. are among the few countries that keep meteorological records of snow depth. Most others measure snow in terms of water content.

St. John's, NF	141.4 inches
Quebec City, PQ	135.1
Saint John, NB	115.1
Syracuse, NY	114.0
Flagstaff, AZ–UT	100.8
Montreal, PQ	92.5
Buffalo–Niagara Falls, NY	91.1
Rochester, NY	89.9
Ottawa–Hull, ON–PQ	89.6
Bangor, ME	85.6
Thunder Bay, ON	84.0
Binghamton, NY	82.4
Casper, WY	78.8
Halifax, NS	78.2
Duluth–Superior, MN–WI	78.0
Burlington, VT	76.9

Listed above are weather stations described in the Place Profiles with average annual snowfalls of 75 inches or more.

Mountain Ranges

The only barriers big enough to deflect and channel winds, rain, and snow are mountains. Mountain people aren't relating folk tales when they tell visitors that the weather on one side of a mountain range is often radically different from that on the other.

The windward side of British Columbia's Coast Mountains is a lush coastal rain forest; the leeward side, a dry grass and sagebrush steppe. In winter, the Great Divide shields Colorado Springs from much of the Arctic air the moves down the continent. In summer, the hidden, windward side of the city's mountain vista is a lush, evergreen parkland at lower elevations; the leeward side where the city sits is a semi-arid steppe descending to dry, shortgrass prairie.

Urban Development

Finally, urban development makes heat islands within the surrounding countryside. Office buildings, factories, and cars produce enormous amounts of waste heat. Brick, concrete, and asphalt surfaces absorb and store heat during the day; at night the stored heat drifts up into the air, keeping the city from cooling off. At night in winter, Montréal's core can be 30 degrees warmer than the environs. In general, wind speed, visibility, sunshine, and heating needs are less in the center of the city than in nearby country, but temperature, cloudiness, thunderstorm frequency, and air pollution levels are higher.

SCORING: CLIMATE

Name many important aspects in life that aren't influenced in some way by climate. It decides what we'll wear, when we vacation, whether we'll work outside—

Cold Metro Areas

It gets so frigid for so long in some Canadian areas that radio weather reports commonly give out Celsius temperatures without bothering to say "minus."

	0°F Days	32°F Days
Anchorage, AK	34	194
Bismarck, ND	51	186
Calgary, AB	33	201
Duluth–Superior, MN–WI	51	186
Edmonton, AB	35	185
Fargo–Moorhead, ND–MN	54	180
Minneapolis–St. Paul, MN–WI	34	158
Regina, SK	55	204
Rochester, MN	35	165
Saskatoon, SK	59	202
Sioux Falls, SD	33	171
Thunder Bay, ON	49	204
Waterloo–Cedar Falls, IA	31	159
Winnipeg, MB	62	195

Listed above are weather stations described in the Place Profiles where more than 30 zero-degree days per year are combined with more than 150 freezing days.

Stormy Metro Areas

A storm day is one on which at least one thunderstorm cell is observed. Florida metro areas can experience four or five thunderstorms a day. They hit on summer afternoons and reduce the heat dramatically.

	Storm Days
Punta Gorda, FL	89
Naples, FL	89
Fort Myers–Cape Coral, FL	89
Tampa–St. Petersburg–Clearwater, FL	87
Sarasota–Bradenton, FL	87
Lakeland–Winter Haven, FL	87
Tallahassee, FL	83
Ocala, FL	83
Gainesville, FL	81

even how much we pay to keep the indoors comfortable. It affects travel safety and mobility. Certainly, it affects how we feel and behave.

Rating places by their climates isn't new. Canada has a "severity index" for hundreds of locations. There's one for New Zealand rating human comfort in various cities, using rainfall, sunshine, temperature, humidity,

Hot Metro Areas

Areas in Florida and Texas are stricken by summer combinations of days over 90°F and high humidities. Three desert metro areas have more than 130 ninety-degree days per year—Phoenix (167), Tucson (140), and Las Vegas (134)—but all have an annual average relative humidity of less than 40 percent.

	90°F Days	Humidity
Ocala, FL	120	77%
Punta Gorda, FL	120	73
Brownsville–Harlingen–San Benito, TX	116	75
Fort Myers–Cape Coral, FL	114	73
Waco, TX	111	71
San Antonio, TX	111	70
San Angelo, TX	109	64
Lakeland–Winter Haven, FL	108	73
Austin–San Marcos, TX	107	70
Corpus Christi, TX	106	76
Wichita Falls, TX	106	67
Victoria, TX	105	75
McAllen–Edinburg–Mission, TX	104	75
Abilene, TX	102	63
Naples, FL	101	73
Bryan–College Station, TX	101	71

Listed above are weather stations described in the Place Profiles that combine 100 or more 90-degree days with an average annual relative humidity of 60 percent or higher.

and wind. In the United States, the "weather stress index" from the National Oceanic and Atmospheric Administration (NOAA) uses temperature, humidity, and wind speed to calculate discomfort based on variation of those three elements from the normal.

To rate the climates in 351 metro areas, *Places Rated* considers twelve data elements, including such elements as monthly high and low temperatures, wind speeds, humidity, darkness, clear days, and precipitation in the form of rain and snow. You might wonder whether all these data elements are more than needed. Many go hand in hand with one another. In the language of statistics, they are correlated.

Take two: winter temperatures and snow. Places like Boston, Calgary, and Minneapolis–St. Paul have cold

[illegible] know whether to pack a raincoat.

So the several pieces of climate data we started with—winter temperatures and snowfalls, or cloudiness and precipitation—can be reduced to fewer pieces.

Which ones can be cut and which kept? Which ones, at minimum, are sufficient to do the job? Factor analysis, a mathematical procedure that systematically transforms many pieces of information about a set of items into fewer pieces of information—called "factors"—is useful here. Each factor takes in one or more of the original pieces of information.

For climate, factor analysis uncovered three critical things. First is *mildness* (weight: 72 percent), which takes in everything from winter temperatures influenced by

Clear Metro Areas

Clear days are recorded when the cloud cover is observed to be less than 30 percent.

	Clear Days
Yuma, AZ	242
Las Vegas, NV–AZ	211
Phoenix-Mesa, AZ	211
Fresno, CA	196
Tucson, AZ	194
El Paso, TX	193
Laredo, TX	193
Las Cruces, NM	193
Bakersfield, CA	192
Riverside–San Bernardino, CA	192
Sacramento, CA	189
Modesto, CA	185

Listed above are weather stations described in the Place Profiles where more than half the year are clear days.

Life at the Top

Metro areas in the Rockies are high indeed. East of the Mississippi, the highest is Asheville, NC, at 2,140 feet. In Canada, at 3,501 feet, it's Calgary, AB.

MA	Elevation
Santa Fe, NM	7,360
Flagstaff, AZ–UT	7,000
Cheyenne, WY	6,120
Colorado Springs, CO	6,090
Boulder–Longmont, CO	5,480
Casper, WY	5,340
Albuquerque, NM	5,310
Denver, CO	5,290
Fort Collins–Loveland, CO	5,000
Grand Junction, CO	4,840
Greeley, CO	4,720
Provo–Orem, UT	4,720
Pueblo, CO	4,680
Reno, NV	4,400
Las Cruces, NM	4,270
Salt Lake City–Ogden, UT	4,220

Source: U.S. Geological Survey, *National Gazeteer of the United States.*

wind chill to summer temperatures influenced by humidity. Winners in this factor include Honolulu and San Francisco. Losers include Winnipeg, MB, Regina, SK, and Grand Forks, ND.

Call the second factor *brightness* (weight: 16 percent), which embraces the number of clear days and wet days, plus latitude—an indicator of potential sunlight. Winners here are locations in the desert Southwest: Las Vegas, Phoenix, and Tucson. Among the losers are Halifax and St. Johns in Atlantic Canada and Seattle, Bremerton, and Bellingham in Washington's Puget Sound area.

The third factor is *stability* (weight: 12 percent), which takes in thunderstorms, snow, and the difference between January's mean low temperature and July's mean high. The Puget Sound area has winners in this factor. Florida's storminess is the main reason why locations like Punta Gorda, Naples, and Tallahassee are among the losers.

To get a final score, each metro area's scores for mildness, brightness, and stability are weighted by their relative importance. A metro area's final score is its percentile on a scale of 0 to 100 corresponding to its weighted average. San Francisco's final score is 98.12; Charleston, WV's is 50.28; and Winnipeg's is 3.40. They are, respectively, the best, average, and worst North American metro areas for climate.

SCORING EXAMPLES

A location near the center of California's Pacific coast, another in the western foothills of the Allegheny Mountains, and still another on the prairie illustrate the best, average, and worst metro areas by *Places Rated*'s scoring method for climate.

Best: San Francisco, CA

Beware of chamber of commerce blandishments about a place's annual average temperature. San Francisco's is 57°F. So is St. Louis's. But San Francisco enjoys both a diurnal (24-hour) temperature range of 12 degrees and an annual range (the difference between January's and July's average temperatures) of 12 degrees. St. Louis has a diurnal range of 17 degrees and an annual range of 47.

The temperature swings in these two cities highlight the difference between a marine climate and a hot continental climate. San Francisco's climate is somewhat cool and remarkably stable year-round. St. Louis's is neither.

In spite of sea fogs and the low stratus associated with them (which appeals to many San Franciscans), this metro area's percent of possible sunshine is greater than that of New York and Boston. Thunderstorms here are rare. On none of the year's 365 days do temperatures hit zero; on just a handful do they fall to freezing or exceed 90°F. More than any other factor, it is San Francisco's infrequent extremes of heat and cold, coupled with a temperature range ideal for human activity and comfort, that produces the top *Places Rated* climate rating.

Average: Charleston, WV

West Virginia's capital sits in the midst of the largest North American climate zone, the Hot Continental. The climate here is marked by sharp temperature contrasts between the days and nights and between the seasons as well. For all that, winters are short and only moderately cold compared with cities in the Northeast and around the Great Lakes. Thanks somewhat to its elevation and surrounding topography, summers are cooler than locations farther south.

On a mildness scale from 0 to 100, Charleston earns a respectable 59. Its brightness score of 21, however, is among the worst on the Continent and the stormy months of June and July are the biggest reasons behind a stability score of just 41. When all factors are weighted by their importance in *Places Rated*'s scoring method, they produce a final score of 50.28.

Worst: Winnipeg, MB

Sometimes called Winterpeg, Manisnowba, this city, an hour and a half's drive over the North Dakota border, endures many humorous jabs about its infamous winters. When it comes to extremes of cold and snow, though, there are many other weather stations in the Canadian and American Arctic that regularly record worse winters than here.

Still, January at the corner of Portage and Main in the center of Manitoba's capital may be the coldest spot of any major city in North America. The Pacific is 1,200 miles west and the Atlantic 1,800 miles east; any moderating effect from either ocean has dissipated long before getting here. Moreover, cold arctic air moves unobstructed across Manitoba and isn't altered in the slightest when it hits Winnipeg.

Daily and seasonal temperatures swing wildly, producing a great variation in climate from month to month in a single winter or from year to year depending on the character and origin of air masse… its favor, Winnipeg is relatively dry… stormy weather than locations farthe… mildness factor, however, the city gets…

RANKINGS: Climate

Three factors are used to determine a score for climate: (1) *mildness,* (2) *brightness,* (3) and *stability.* Scores are rounded to two decimal places. Locations with tie scores get the same rank and are listed alphabetically. Metro areas described in the Place Profiles later on in this chapter are shown in boldface type in the list below.

CA 97.0[illegible]
4. Ventura, CA 97.52
5. **San Luis Obispo–Atascadero–Paso Robles, CA** 96.93

6. **San Diego, CA** 96.92
7. Orange County, CA 96.84
8. Oakland, CA 96.83
9. **Santa Barbara–Santa Maria–Lompoc, CA** 96.68
10. **Salinas, CA** 96.50

11. Santa Cruz–Watsonville, CA 96.34
12. **Riverside–San Bernardino, CA** 94.01
13. San Jose, CA 93.79
14. **Santa Rosa, CA** 93.74
15. Vallejo–Fairfield–Napa, CA 90.38

16. **Yuma, AZ** 89.29
17. **Seattle-Bellevue-Everett, WA** 89.03
18. **Brownsville–Harlingen–San Benito, TX** 88.82
19. Stockton–Lodi, CA 88.57
20. **Sacramento, CA** 88.05

21. **McAllen–Edinburg–Mission, TX** 87.91
22. Yolo, CA 87.61
23. **Miami, FL** 87.53
24. Fort Lauderdale, FL 87.35
25. Yuba City, CA 86.17

26. **Modesto, CA** 85.81
27. **Bakersfield, CA** 85.68
28. **Corpus Christi, TX** 85.62
29. Visalia–Tulare–Porterville, CA 85.54
30. **Chico–Paradise, CA** 85.07

31. **Victoria, BC** 84.86
32. **West Palm Beach–Boca Raton, FL** 84.67
33. Fort Pierce–Port St. Lucie, FL 84.65
34. **Laredo, TX** 84.63
35. Merced, CA 84.41

39. **Eugene–Springfield, OR** [illegible]
40. Bremerton, WA 82.49

41. Melbourne–Titusville–Palm Bay, FL 82.30
42. **Naples, FL** 82.00
43. **Phoenix–Mesa, AZ** 81.91
44. **Fort Myers–Cape Coral, FL** 81.51
45. **Vancouver, BC** 81.49

46. Salem, OR 81.48
47. **Redding, CA** 81.06
48. Tacoma, WA 80.79
49. Punta Gorda, FL 80.31
50. **Olympia, WA** 80.01

51. **Portland–Vancouver, OR–WA** 79.99
52. **Daytona Beach, FL** 79.91
53. **Tucson, AZ** 79.62
54. **Orlando, FL** 79.22
55. **Lakeland–Winter Haven, FL** 79.17

56. **Tampa–St. Petersburg–Clearwater, FL** 78.84
57. **Ocala, FL** 77.09
58. **Galveston–Texas City, TX** 76.66
59. **Victoria, TX** 76.29
60. **Jacksonville, FL** 75.67

61. **Savannah, GA** 74.90
62. **San Antonio, TX** 74.88
63. Brazoria, TX 74.77
64. Houma, LA 74.65
65. **Gainesville, FL** 74.61

66. **Houston, TX** 74.44
67. **Las Vegas, NV–AZ** 74.33
68. **Panama City, FL** 74.18
69. **Bryan–College Station, TX** 73.99
70. **Austin–San Marcos, TX** 73.75

71. **Medford–Ashland, OR** 73.73
72. **New Orleans, LA** 73.28
73. **Pensacola, FL** 73.26
74. **Biloxi–Gulfport–Pascagoula, MS** 72.80

Charleston, SC [illegible]
77. Beaumont–Port Arthur, TX 70.73
78. Sumter, SC 70.40
79. **Wilmington, NC** 69.59
80. Jacksonville, NC 69.43

81. Fort Walton Beach, FL 69.36
82. Lake Charles, LA 69.03
83. Albany, GA 68.93
84. Alexandria, LA 68.92
85. Tyler, TX 68.86

86. **Tallahassee, FL** 68.71
87. Lafayette, LA 68.69
88. **Odessa–Midland, TX** 68.59
89. Richland–Kennewick–Pasco, WA 68.47
90. **Baton Rouge, LA** 68.24

91. **Mobile, AL** 67.23
92. **Greenville–Spartanburg–Anderson, SC** 66.93
93. **Columbus, GA–AL** 66.91
94. **Reno, NV** 66.79
95. Florence, SC 66.76

96. Killeen–Temple, TX 66.52
97. **Greenville, NC** 66.21
98. Macon, GA 66.12
99. **San Angelo, TX** 66.03
100. Goldsboro, NC 65.89

101. **Columbia, SC** 65.84
102. **Las Cruces, NM** 65.71
103. Rocky Mount, NC 65.66
104. Fayetteville, NC 65.43
105. **Montgomery, AL** 65.34

106. **Atlanta, GA** 65.20
107. **Charlotte–Gastonia–Rock Hill, NC–SC** 64.94
108. **Augusta–Aiken, GA–SC** 64.93
109. **Athens, GA** 64.87
110. **Norfolk–Virginia Beach–Newport News, VA–NC** 64.85

Places Rated Rank		Places Rated Score
111.	**Raleigh-Durham-Chapel Hill, NC**	64.82
112.	**Myrtle Beach, SC**	64.11
113.	**Waco, TX**	64.07
114.	**Abilene, TX**	64.01
115.	Texarkana, TX-Texarkana, AR	63.27
116.	**Hattiesburg, MS**	62.99
117.	**Dallas, TX**	62.87
117.	Fort Worth-Arlington, TX	62.87
119.	Longview-Marshall, TX	62.60
120.	Anniston, AL	62.05
121.	Tuscaloosa, AL	61.67
122.	Hickory-Morganton-Lenoir, NC	61.65
123.	**Birmingham, AL**	61.31
124.	**Lubbock, TX**	61.27
125.	**Asheville, NC**	60.62
126.	Dothan, AL	59.93
127.	**Greensboro-Winston-Salem-High Point, NC**	59.83
128.	Lynchburg, VA	59.71
129.	**Shreveport-Bossier City, LA**	59.62
130.	**Barnstable-Yarmouth, MA**	59.45
131.	**Jackson, MS**	59.40
132.	**Johnson City-Kingsport-Bristol, TN-VA**	58.66
133.	**Huntsville, AL**	58.24
134.	**Roanoke, VA**	58.20
135.	Gadsden, AL	58.15
136.	Danville, VA	58.12
137.	**Albuquerque, NM**	57.94
138.	**Yakima, WA**	57.72
139.	**Chattanooga, TN-GA**	57.26
140.	**Charlottesville, VA**	56.94
141.	Dover, DE	56.83
142.	**Baltimore, MD**	56.80
143.	Decatur, AL	56.77
143.	Florence, AL	56.77
143.	Pine Bluff, AR	56.77
146.	**Memphis, TN-AR-MS**	56.53
147.	**Knoxville, TN**	56.15
148.	**Washington, DC-MD-VA-WV**	55.45
149.	**Richmond-Petersburg, VA**	55.39
150.	Monroe, LA	55.30
151.	**Little Rock-North Little Rock, AR**	54.80
152.	**Long Island, NY**	54.47
153.	Sherman-Denison, TX	54.38
154.	**Monmouth-Ocean, NJ**	53.91
155.	**Wichita Falls, TX**	53.71
156.	**New York, NY**	53.09
156.	**Santa Fe, NM**	53.09
158.	Lawton, OK	52.43
159.	Vineland-Millville-Bridgeton, NJ	52.07
160.	Jackson, TN	52.02
161.	New Bedford, MA	51.80
162.	**Amarillo, TX**	51.66
163.	**Nashville, TN**	51.65
164.	**Atlantic City-Cape May, NJ**	51.62
165.	**Fort Smith, AR-OK**	51.52
166.	**Wilmington-Newark, DE-MD**	51.28
167.	**Charleston, WV**	50.28
168.	Boulder-Longmont, CO	50.00
169.	**Spokane, WA**	49.98
170.	**Fayetteville-Springdale-Rogers, AR**	49.56
171.	**Oklahoma City, OK**	49.51
172.	**Philadelphia, PA-NJ**	49.39
173.	**Boise City, ID**	49.12
174.	Newark, NJ	48.55
175.	Owensboro, KY	48.29
176.	Huntington-Ashland, WV-KY-OH	48.18
177.	Jersey City, NJ	47.24
178.	Clarksville-Hopkinsville, TN-KY	47.13
179.	Bridgeport, CT	47.11
179.	**New Haven-Meriden, CT**	47.11
181.	**Tulsa, OK**	47.04
182.	**Providence-Fall River-Warwick, RI-MA**	46.96
183.	**Boston, MA-NH**	46.46
184.	New London-Norwich, CT-RI	45.88
185.	Parkersburg-Marietta, WV-OH	44.98
186.	**Lancaster, PA**	44.72
187.	Trenton, NJ	44.45
188.	York, PA	44.33
189.	**Flagstaff, AZ-UT**	44.31
190.	Enid, OK	44.29
191.	**Lexington, KY**	44.24
192.	**Louisville, KY-IN**	43.86
193.	Stamford-Norwalk, CT	43.64
194.	Cumberland, MD-WV	42.56
195.	**Harrisburg-Lebanon-Carlisle, PA**	42.44
196.	**Halifax, NS**	42.25
196.	**St. John's, NF**	42.25
198.	Joplin, MO	41.75
199.	**Evansville-Henderson, IN-KY**	41.34
200.	**Scranton-Wilkes-Barre-Hazleton, PA**	41.17
201.	Middlesex-Somerset-Hunterdon, NJ	41.05
202.	**Denver, CO**	40.33
203.	Brockton, MA	39.96
204.	Newburgh, NY-PA	39.20
205.	Bergen-Passaic, NJ	39.17
206.	Hagerstown, MD	38.92
207.	**Cincinnati, OH-KY-IN**	38.07
208.	**Springfield, MO**	38.02
209.	**Wheeling, WV-OH**	37.39
210.	**Colorado Springs, CO**	37.21
211.	Johnstown, PA	36.90
212.	Pueblo, CO	36.73
213.	Steubenville-Weirton, OH-WV	36.71
214.	Danbury, CT	36.59
214.	Waterbury, CT	36.59
216.	**Fort Collins-Loveland, CO**	36.57
217.	Lawrence, MA-NH	36.14
218.	Lowell, MA-NH	36.10
219.	Hamilton-Middletown, OH	35.99
220.	**Allentown-Bethlehem-Easton, PA**	35.89
221.	Springfield, MA	35.62
222.	Reading, PA	35.56
223.	Dutchess County, NY	35.55
224.	**Hartford, CT**	35.49
225.	**St. Louis, MO-IL**	35.03
226.	Bloomington, IN	34.80
227.	**Portland, ME**	34.75
228.	**Portsmouth-Rochester, NH-ME**	34.63
229.	**Grand Junction, CO**	34.36
230.	**Wichita, KS**	34.20
231.	Altoona, PA	34.06
232.	Worcester, MA-CT	33.95
233.	Fitchburg-Leominster, MA	33.94
234.	**Columbus, OH**	33.85
235.	Provo-Orem, UT	33.71
236.	Sharon, PA	33.70
237.	Lawrence, KS	33.31
238.	**Pittsburgh, PA**	33.20
239.	Greeley, CO	32.99
240.	Williamsport, PA	32.90
241.	**Anchorage, AK**	32.69
242.	Nashua, NH	32.45
243.	Oshawa, ON	32.42
244.	Muncie, IN	31.69
245.	**Dayton-Springfield, OH**	31.08
246.	Terre Haute, IN	30.92
247.	**State College, PA**	30.89
248.	**Cheyenne, WY**	30.88
249.	**Columbia, MO**	30.80
250.	**Manchester, NH**	30.43
251.	Lewiston-Auburn, ME	30.42
252.	St. Catharines-Niagara, ON	30.35
253.	**Cleveland-Lorain-Elyria, OH**	29.88
254.	Jamestown, NY	29.73
255.	Elmira, NY	29.69
256.	**Indianapolis, IN**	29.65
256.	Mansfield, OH	29.65
258.	**Akron, OH**	29.64
258.	Canton-Massillon, OH	29.64
260.	Youngstown-Warren, OH	29.55
261.	**Rochester, NY**	29.35
262.	Erie, PA	29.21
263.	Kokomo, IN	29.08
264.	**Salt Lake City-Ogden, UT**	29.07
265.	**Topeka, KS**	28.93
266.	Pittsfield, MA	28.66
267.	Ann Arbor, MI	28.45
268.	Sheboygan, WI	28.42
269.	Windsor, ON	28.34
270.	**Detroit, MI**	28.30
271.	**Great Falls, MT**	27.94
272.	South Bend, IN	27.88
273.	Lima, OH	27.60
274.	**Billings, MT**	27.35
275.	Kenosha, WI	27.12
276.	**Saint John, NB**	26.98
277.	**Binghamton, NY**	26.95
278.	Benton Harbor, MI	26.78
278.	**Toledo, OH**	26.78
280.	**Albany-Schenectady-Troy, NY**	26.72
281.	Flint, MI	26.66

Places Rated Rank		Places Rated Score
282.	**Buffalo–Niagara Falls, NY**	26.45
283.	Lafayette, IN	26.35
284.	**Springfield, IL**	26.34
285.	**Kansas City, MO–KS**	26.21
286.	**Bangor, ME**	26.15
287.	St. Joseph, MO	26.12
288.	**Syracuse, NY**	25.88
289.	Gary, IN	25.60
289.	Jackson, MI	25.60
291.	Saginaw–Bay City–Midland, MI	25.57
292.	Decatur, IL	25.56
293.	Champaign–Urbana, IL	25.41
294.	**Toronto, ON**	25.40
305.	Kankakee, IL	23.31
306.	Kitchener, ON	23.05
307.	**Casper, WY**	22.81
308.	**Grand Rapids–Muskegon–Holland, MI**	22.61
309.	Elkhart–Goshen, IN	22.56
310.	**Davenport–Moline–Rock Island, IA–IL**	21.89
311.	**Peoria–Pekin, IL**	21.68
312.	**Omaha, NE–IA**	21.45
313.	**Iowa City, IA**	21.03
314.	London, ON	20.68
315.	**Lincoln, NE**	20.57
316.	Rockford, IL	19.44
317.	**Des Moines, IA**	18.89
317.	Janesville–Beloit, WI	18.89
328.	Dubuque, IA	[illegible]
329.	Sherbrooke, PQ	15.94
330.	**Green Bay, WI**	15.82
331.	**Waterloo–Cedar Falls, IA**	15.25
332.	Appleton–Oshkosh–Neenah, WI	14.59
333.	**Edmonton, AB**	12.90
334.	Wausau, WI	12.89
335.	Trois-Rivieres, PQ	12.02
336.	**Quebec City, PQ**	11.62
337.	**Minneapolis–St. Paul, MN–WI**	10.76
338.	Eau Claire, WI	10.40
339.	**Rochester, MN**	9.37
340.	**Sioux Falls, SD**	9.22
341.	**Bismarck, ND**	8.69

PLACE PROFILES: Climate

The following pages are brief profiles of 202 weather stations across the continent. The narrative summaries describing climate and landscape at United States and Canadian points are condensed from those that appear in the NOAA's *Local Climatological Data* and in Environment Canada's *Canadian Climate Program* series, respectively. Canadian climate data have been converted from Celsius and metric measurements to Fahrenheit and English measurements.

These summaries describe each metro area's location and its distinctive climate and landscape features. *Location* details the place's elevation and its latitude north of the equator and longitude west of Greenwich, England. With these coordinates, you can roughly determine whether one place is farther north, south, east, or west from another.

When *landscape* is described, it is usually how the terrain influences the local climate and what varieties of vegetation grow there naturally. Few people would deny that landscape is an important element on its own; for many, it is as important as climate. Some prefer mountains or seacoast, others rolling hills or flatwoods forests, while still others favor stark desert vistas. Rather than rating landscapes, they are described briefly here and the decision is left up to you.

The descriptions for *climate* are capsule summaries of each location's type and general features. To help you visualize the annual temperature and precipitation patterns for each place, look at the graphic boxes to the right.

In the TEMPERATURE box (see example) the white band shows the normal high and low air temperatures as they rise and fall over the year. The darkened area underneath shows the apparent temperature, which is air temperature influenced by winter wind chill and summer humidity.

In each PRECIPITATION box (see example) is a graph showing the amount of rain and snow for each

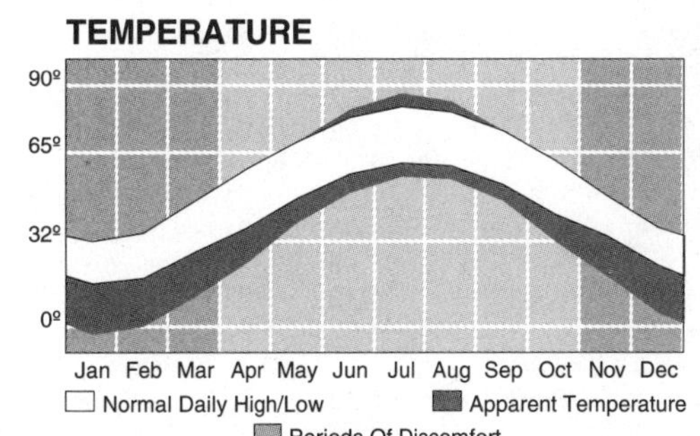

PRECIPITATION

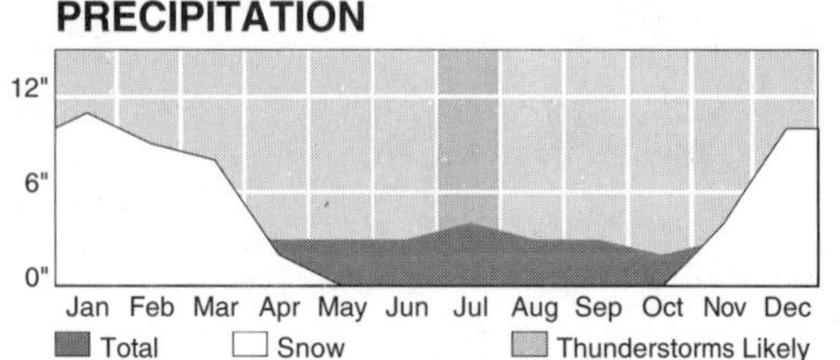

ANNUAL
Precipitation: 36.8"
Snow: 47.5"
DAYS
Precipitation: 76
Thunderstorm: 38

month of the year. The white lumps that occur in many places during the winter months indicate snow. Rainfall is shown by the dark wave. A vertical band shows thunderstorms in the months they occur most frequently.

Rounding out each place's climate picture are annual summaries for relative humidity, wind speed, snowfalls and rainfalls, clear and cloudy days, very hot and very cold days, thunderstorm days and precipitation days (days on which there is at least 0.1 inch of precipitation).

A check mark (✓) preceding a metro area's name highlights it as one of the top 35 metro areas in the continent for a combination of climate mildness, brightness, and stability.

Abilene, TX

Location: 32.25 N, 99.41 W, at 1,780 feet, in west-central Texas, 216 miles NW of Austin.
Landscape: Rolling plains, treeless except for mesquite, are broken by low hills to the south and west. There is a continual gentle rise to the east. Except for some dry-land cotton and feed farming, cattle grazing dominates the surrounding terrain.
Climate: Roughly midway between the humid climate of East Texas and the semiarid desert that is west and north. Most rain occurs in thunderstorms from April through June, in September and October. Severe storms or tornadoes are rare. Summer brings hot days and cool nights, with temperatures dropping to the 60s or 70s most nights. High summer temperatures are associated with clear skies, southwesterly winds, and dry air. Low relative humidity makes the climate comfortable. The region receives almost 70 percent of possible sunshine over the year. Rapid temperature changes occur in winter, as polar air replaces warm, moist tropical air. Temperatures may fall 30° in one hour. Strongest winds come from the north and often bring cold and severe weather.

Mildness: 62 Brightness: 93 Stability: 23

Places Rated Score: 64.01 **Places Rated Rank: 114**

TEMPERATURE

90º
65º
32º
0º
Jan Feb Mar Apr May Jun Jul Aug Sep Oct Nov Dec
Normal Daily High/Low
Apparent Temperature
Periods Of Discomfort

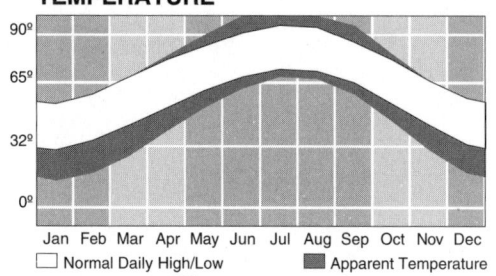

ANNUAL
Humidity: 62%
Wind Speed: 11.9 mph
DAYS
0º or below: 0
32º or below: 52
90º or above: 102
Clear: 150
Cloudy: 121

PRECIPITATION

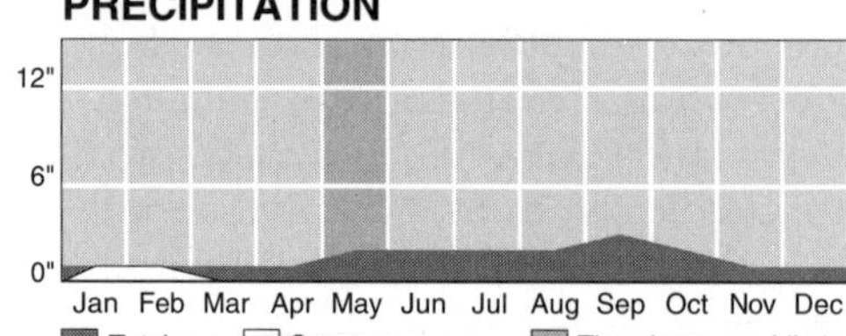

ANNUAL
Precipitation: 24.4"
Snow: 4.7"
DAYS
Precipitation: 38
Thunderstorm: 43

Akron, OH

Location: 40.55 N, 81.26 W, at 1,210 feet, on the Little Cuyahoga River in the northeastern part of the state. Cleveland is 37 miles north.
Landscape: Rolling, with highest elevations almost 1,300 feet above sea level. The city spreads over the watershed dividing the drainage of northern Ohio into the St. Lawrence and Mississippi River systems. Many small lakes provide water for local industry as well as recreation for the densely populated region. The area is mainly industrial, the number of farms having fallen dramatically in recent years.
Climate: Lake Erie has a considerable effect on area weather, tempering cold air masses during the winter and contributing to brief but heavy snow squalls until the lake freezes over. Snowfall is much heavier north of the weather station near the lake, in the area commonly referred to as the Snow Belt. Spring comes late here. Summers are moderately warm, though humid. September, October, and November are pleasant, but there is considerable morning fog. Average date of last freeze: April 30. First freeze: October 22.

Mildness: 29 Brightness: 20 Stability: 49

Places Rated Score: 29.64 **Places Rated Rank: 258**

TEMPERATURE

90º
65º
32º
0º
Jan Feb Mar Apr May Jun Jul Aug Sep Oct Nov Dec
Normal Daily High/Low
Apparent Temperature
Periods Of Discomfort

ANNUAL
Humidity: 70%
Wind Speed: 9.7 mph
DAYS
0º or below: 5
32º or below: 128
90º or above: 8
Clear: 68
Cloudy: 198

PRECIPITATION

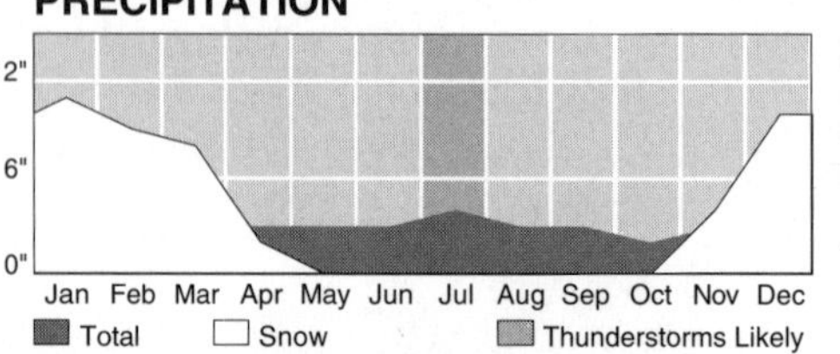

ANNUAL
Precipitation: 36.8"
Snow: 47.5"
DAYS
Precipitation: 76
Thunderstorm: 38

Albany–Schenectady–Troy, NY

Location: 42.45 N, 73.48 W, at 270 feet, on the west bank of the Hudson River 150 miles north of New York City and 8 miles south of the confluence of the Hudson and Mohawk rivers.
Landscape: The point at which the city meets the river is only a few feet above sea level. Eleven miles west, the Helderberg escarpment rises to between 1,400 and 1,800 feet. East is a rugged valley floor rising to hills 1,600 to 2,000 feet high. The valley floor on which the city sits is gently rolling.
Climate: Harsh Continental subject to some moderating influences from the Atlantic Ocean to the south. Winters are cold and occasionally severe. Maximum temperatures during cold months often do not rise above 32°F. In the warmer months, temperatures rise quickly during the day to moderate levels, then plunge at night to cool. Occasional hot spells of a week or more occur during the summer.

Mildness: 21 Brightness: 31 Stability: 61

Places Rated Score: 26.72 **Places Rated Rank: 280**

TEMPERATURE

90° 65° 32° 0°
Jan Feb Mar Apr May Jun Jul Aug Sep Oct Nov Dec
Normal Daily High/Low Apparent Temperature
Periods Of Discomfort

ANNUAL
Humidity: 68%
Wind Speed: 8.9 mph
DAYS
0° or below: 17
32° or below: 155
90° or above: 8
Clear: 69
Cloudy: 185

PRECIPITATION

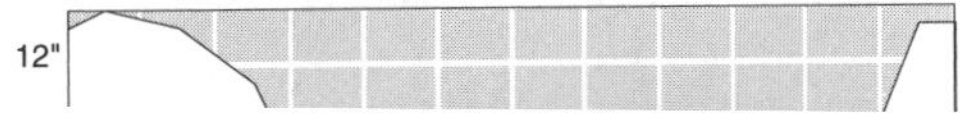

ANNUAL
Precipitation: 36.2"

lies NW 55 miles.
Landscape: High plateau encircled by sections of the Cibola National Forest. Typical steppe or shortgrass prairie with scattered shrubs and low trees cover the area. Common vegetation includes sagebrush or shadscale, and a mixture of short grasses. There may be willows and sedges along streams in the area. The area is a center for mining, timber, and ranching operations.
Climate: Arid Continental. The low humidity and cool nights make the heat feel much less intense; there are no muggy days. Half the 9 inches of annual precipitation falls between July and September in the form of brief but severe thunderstorms. Long drizzles are unknown. These storms have a moderating effect on the heat and do not greatly interfere with outdoor activities. The low rainfall and mild temperatures—91°F in July, 46°F in January—make the city a health resort.

Mildness: 47 Brightness: 97 Stability: 38

Places Rated Score: 57.94 **Places Rated Rank: 137**

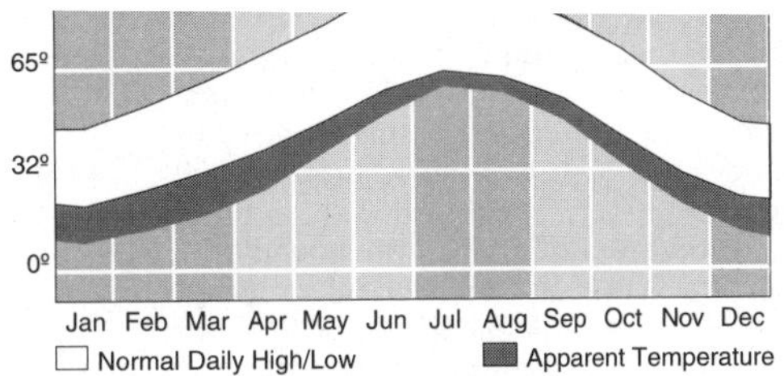

Wind Speed: 9.0 mph
DAYS
0° or below: 1
32° or below: 114
90° or above: 66
Clear: 168
Cloudy: 87

PRECIPITATION

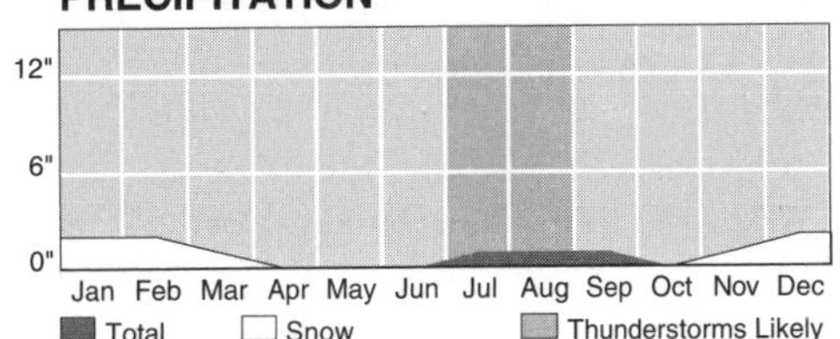

ANNUAL
Precipitation: 8.9"
Snow: 11.1"
DAYS
Precipitation: 33
Thunderstorm: 38

Allentown–Bethlehem–Easton, PA

Location: 40.39 N, 75.26 W, at 390 feet, the tri-city area is in eastern Pennsylvania, in the Lehigh River valley. Allentown is 82 miles NE of Harrisburg, the state capital. Easton lies on the Delaware River, across from New Jersey. Bethlehem is along the Lehigh River between the other two.
Landscape: The Blue Mountain is 12 miles north; the South Mountain fringes the southern edge. Other than these rises of up to 2,000 feet, the country is gently rolling with numerous small streams. Wooded lots of eastern deciduous forest alternate with open hills or fields.
Climate: A four-season Continental climate with long, pleasant autumns and a fairly early spring. Temperatures are modified by the mountain ranges; at times there may be 10° to 15° difference between Allentown and Philadelphia, only 50 miles to the south. Summer maximum temperatures are not excessive; however, humidity is quite high and can cause much discomfort. Winters are comparatively mild, being only infrequently below zero. Rain falls as spring showers. Stormy days occur from mid-June through August.

Mildness: 32 Brightness: 42 Stability: 55

Places Rated Score: 35.89 **Places Rated Rank: 220**

TEMPERATURE

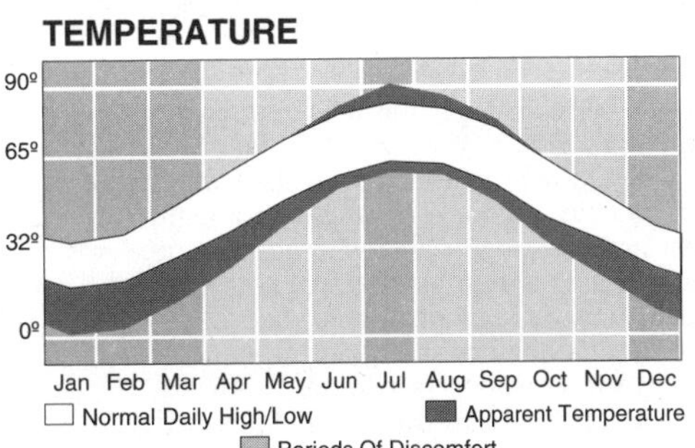

ANNUAL
Humidity: 68%
Wind Speed: 9.2 mph
DAYS
0° or below: 1
32° or below: 123
90° or above: 15
Clear: 93
Cloudy: 161

PRECIPITATION

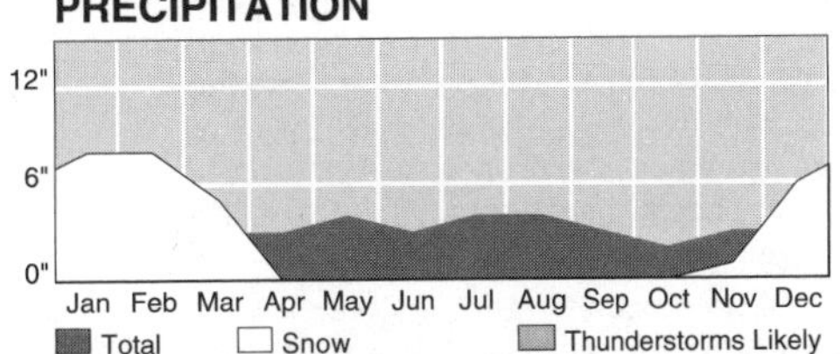

ANNUAL
Precipitation: 43.5"
Snow: 31.3"
DAYS
Precipitation: 70
Thunderstorm: 31

Amarillo, TX

Location: 35.14 N, 101.42 W, at 3,600 feet, between the Canadian and Red rivers, in the heart of the Texas Panhandle. Nearer the capitals of four other states, the city is 500 miles NW of Austin.
Landscape: The city sits atop the cap rock, or High Plains, of the Southwest. There is little relief from the low flat prairie and scrubby vegetation. Spanish for "yellow," Amarillo refers to the color of the clay soil in the area. Cotton and sorghum are primary crops.
Climate: Semiarid Continental. The area is generally dry, but thunderstorms occur between April and September. This varies greatly from year to year, and droughts are fairly frequent. The area is subject to rapid and great temperature changes, especially in winter, when fast-moving cold air comes down from the Plains and the Rocky Mountains. Nearness to paths of moving pressure systems causes strong winds, especially in March and April. Though summer days are hot, the low humidity lessens the felt heat and makes for pleasant mornings and nights.

Mildness: 44 Brightness: 93 Stability: 26

Places Rated Score: 51.66 **Places Rated Rank: 162**

TEMPERATURE

90º 65º 32º 0º
Jan Feb Mar Apr May Jun Jul Aug Sep Oct Nov Dec
Normal Daily High/Low Apparent Temperature Periods Of Discomfort

ANNUAL
Humidity: 59%
Wind Speed: 13.6 mph
DAYS
0º or below: 2
32º or below: 111
90º or above: 66
Clear: 157
Cloudy: 104

PRECIPITATION

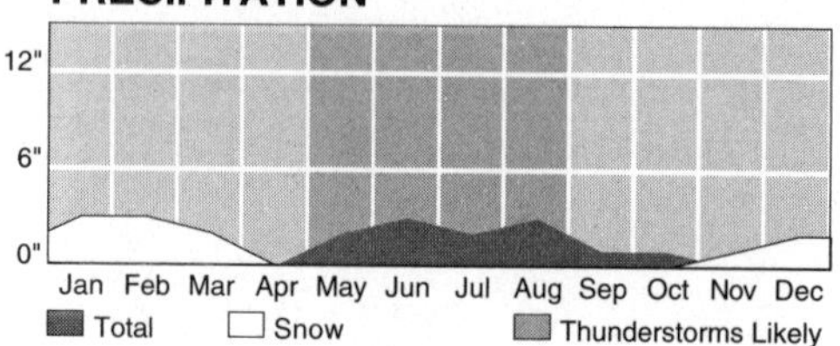

ANNUAL
Precipitation: 19.6"
Snow: 15.4"
DAYS
Precipitation: 38
Thunderstorm: 49

Anchorage, AK

Location: 61.10 N, 150.01 W, at 110 feet, in a broad valley on Alaska's south coast. Cook Inlet is to the west, north, and south and the Chugach Mountains are to the NNE and SSW.
Landscape: Terrain rises gradually to the east with marshes interspersed with glacial moraines, depressions, streams, and knolls. Beyond, the Chugach Mountains rise sharply to between 4,000 feet and 5,000 feet, with some peaks 8,000 feet to 10,000 feet high.
Climate: The four seasons are well marked in Anchorage, though in length and other characteristics they differ considerably from the standards of the middle latitudes. The rivers and lakes thaw in mid-April to early May. Snow arrives in early October and departs in mid-April. The mountains block the warm air and moisture from the Gulf of Alaska. One hundred miles north, the Alaska Range blocks much of the cold air from the interior. Consequently, when temperatures in the interior are −50°F or −60°F, they will be −15°F to −30°F in Anchorage.

Mildness: 17 Brightness: 20 Stability: 100

Places Rated Score: 32.69 **Places Rated Rank: 241**

TEMPERATURE

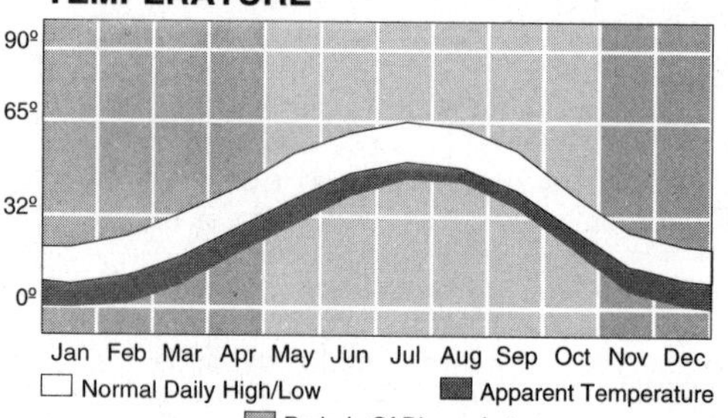

ANNUAL
Humidity: 68%
Wind Speed: 7.0 mph
DAYS
0º or below: 34
32º or below: 194
90º or above: 12
Clear: 61
Cloudy: 240

PRECIPITATION

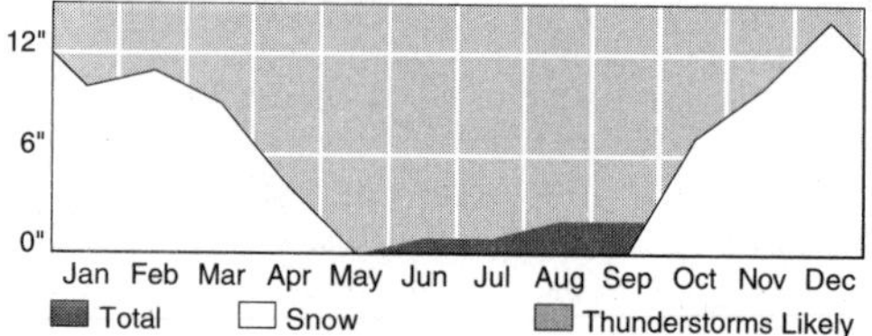

ANNUAL
Precipitation: 15.9"
Snow: 69.5"
DAYS
Precipitation: 57
Thunderstorm: 0

Asheville, NC

Location: 35.26 N, 82.33 W, at 2,140 feet, on the French Broad River in western North Carolina, at eastern gateway to the Great Smoky mountains.
Landscape: Two miles upstream from the city, the Swannanoa River joins the French Broad River from the east. The entire valley is called the Asheville Plateau and is flanked on the east and west by mountain ranges. Thirty miles south, the Blue Ridge Mountains form an escarpment, with an average elevation of 2,700 feet. Forests are dominated by tall, broadleaf trees such as oak, hickory, walnut, maple, and basswood, providing a continuous and dense canopy in summer but shedding their leaves completely in winter. There are lower layers of small trees and shrubs: dogwood, blueberry, haw and the like.
Climate: Temperate but invigorating. Considerable variation in temperature occurs from day to day throughout the year. Frost-free spring arrives early and is a long season with warm, clear days. The valley has a pronounced effect on wind direction, which is mostly from the northwest. Destructive weather events are rare. However, the French Broad Valley is subject to flooding, with especially high water occurring in 12-year cycles.

Mildness: 69 Brightness: 28 Stability: 49

Places Rated Score: 60.62 **Places Rated Rank: 125**

TEMPERATURE

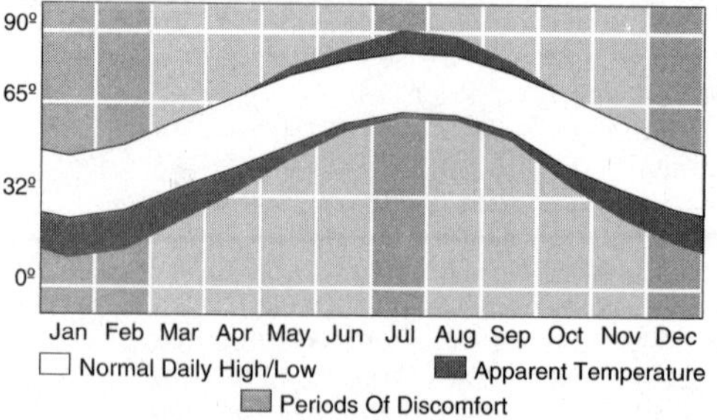

ANNUAL
Humidity: 74%
Wind Speed: 7.6 mph
DAYS
0º or below: 1
32º or below: 99
90º or above: 11
Clear: 101
Cloudy: 151

PRECIPITATION

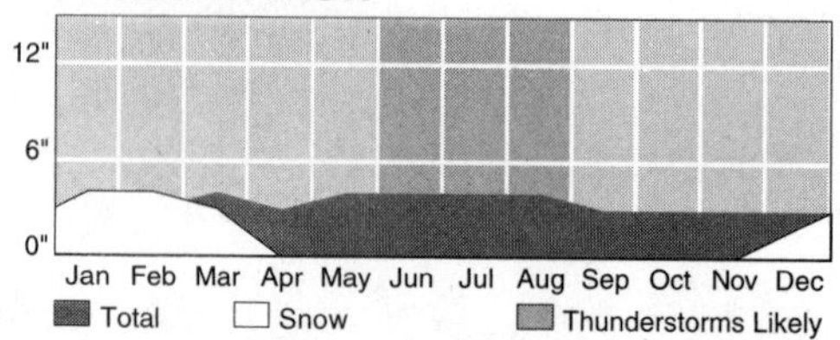

ANNUAL
Precipitation: 47.6"
Snow: 15.6"
DAYS
Precipitation: 75
Thunderstorm: 45

Athens, GA

Location: 33.57 N, 83.19 W, at 800 feet, on the Oconee River in the Piedmont Plateau section of northeast Georgia, 60 miles east of Atlanta.
Landscape: Elevations here range between 600 and 800 feet, the topography rolling to hilly. The streams drain southeast to the Savannah River. In the midst of stands of southern yellow pine are varieties of oak, elm, hickory, and walnut.
Climate: Continental, moderated by the Atlantic Ocean, 200 miles to the southeast, the Gulf of Mexico, 275 miles to the south, and the southern Appalachian Mountains to the north and northwest, which all exert some influence on the city's climate. Summers are hot and humid, but long stretches of extreme heat are noticeably absent. Precipitation is evenly distributed throughout the year, usually as rain, though snow is possible. The mountains to the north are a partial barrier to extremely cold airflows. As a result, the city's winters aren't severe. Cold spells are short-lived and are broken up by periods of warm southerly airflow.

TEMPERATURE

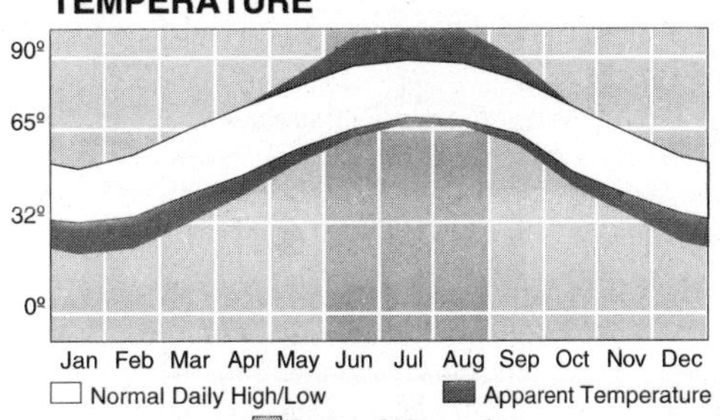

ANNUAL
Humidity: 70%
Wind Speed: 7.4 mph
DAYS
0º or below: 1
32º or below: 54
90º or above: 50
Clear: 112
Cloudy: 147

PRECIPITATION

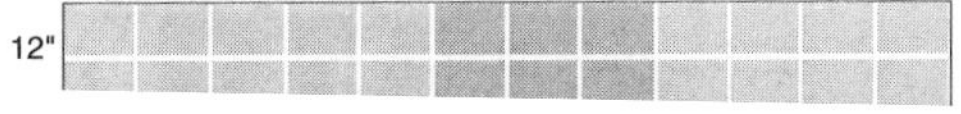

ANNUAL
Precipitation: 49.7"

toward the east, west, and south. Because Atlanta has a mean elevation of 1,000 feet and a location on a plateau with mountains to the north, its exposure to the cold north air is blocked, and its elevation retards the moist hot air from the Gulf of Mexico.
Climate: The city's relatively high elevation creates moderate summer weather and four distinct seasons. Abundant rainfall fosters natural vegetation and growth of crops. In summer, afternoon high temperatures equal or exceed 90°F one day in five, but a temperature of 100°F is rare. Atlanta's winters are mild. Cold spells are not unusual, but they rarely disrupt outdoor activities for long. Snow is light and stays on the ground only briefly. Ice storms, however, occur about one year in ten and cause heavy damage. Atlanta averages 50 thunderstorms a year, which occur mostly in the spring, sometimes spinning off destructive tornadoes. The average date of the last freeze is March 24; the first freeze is around mid-November, with an average growing period of over 230 days.

Mildness: 76 Brightness: 38 Stability: 30

Places Rated Score: 65.20 **Places Rated Rank: 106**

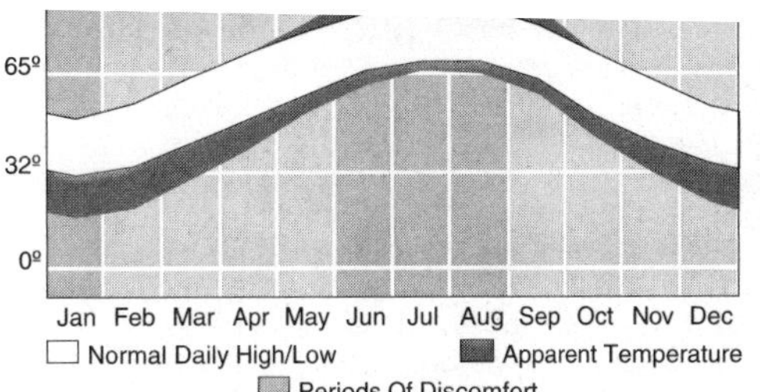

Wind Speed: 9.1 mph
DAYS
0º or below: 0
32º or below: 49
90º or above: 38
Clear: 111
Cloudy: 148

PRECIPITATION

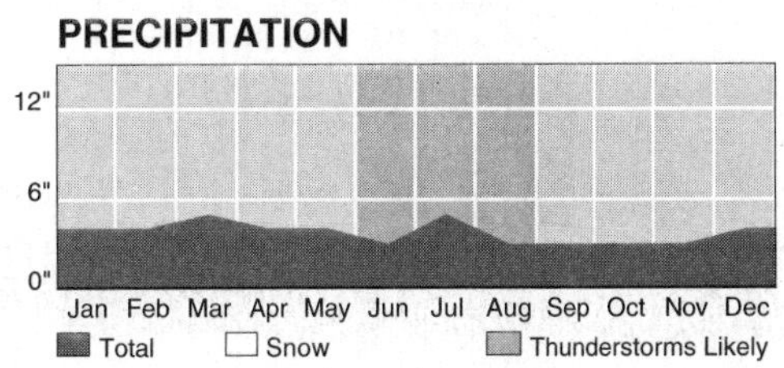

ANNUAL
Precipitation: 50.8"
Snow: 2.0"
DAYS
Precipitation: 76
Thunderstorm: 48

Atlantic City–Cape May, NJ

Location: 39.27 N, 74.34 W, at 60 feet, the weather station is on a sand island south of Absecon Inlet on New Jersey's Atlantic shore, some 60 miles SE of Philadelphia.
Landscape: The surrounding terrain is flat and sandy. Immense tidal marshes are crossed over by highways and rail track that hide deep channels separating the island from the mainland. The natural vegetation is a scrubby evergreen and laurel forest typical of the temperate rainforest. Stands of pine are common.
Climate: Continental, but the moderating influence of the Atlantic Ocean is apparent throughout the year. Summers are relatively cooler, winters warmer than those of other places at the same latitude. During the warm season, sea breezes in the late morning and afternoon prevent excessive heat. Fall is long, lasting until almost mid-November. On the other hand, warming is somewhat delayed in the spring. Ocean temperatures range from an average near 37°F in winter to 72°F in August. Precipitation is moderate and well distributed throughout the year.

Mildness: 50 Brightness: 48 Stability: 65

Places Rated Score: 51.62 **Places Rated Rank: 164**

TEMPERATURE

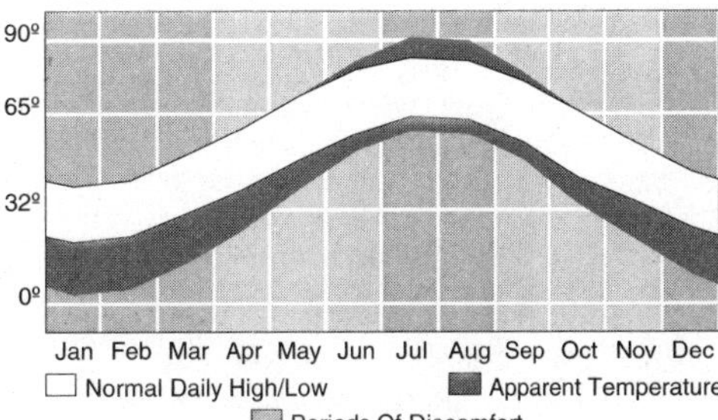

ANNUAL
Humidity: 69%
Wind Speed: 10.0 mph
DAYS
0º or below: 3
32º or below: 108
90º or above: 17
Clear: 94
Cloudy: 160

PRECIPITATION

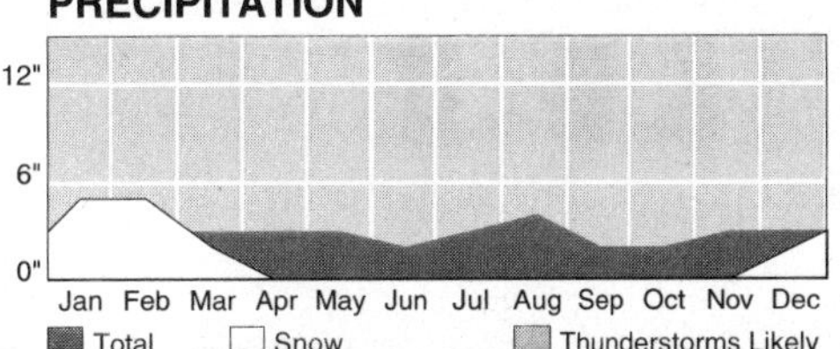

ANNUAL
Precipitation: 40.3"
Snow: 16.1"
DAYS
Precipitation: 64
Thunderstorm: 26

Augusta-Aiken, GA-SC

Location: 33.22 N, 81.58 W, at 150 feet, on the Savannah River, which forms part of the boundary between Georgia and South Carolina.
Landscape: Generally flat, with gentle slopes and local relief of less than 200 feet. Nearby is the fall line that divides the upcountry Piedmont Plateau and the Coastal Plain low country. To the west are low-rise sandhills. The trees are a mixed forest of southern yellow pines, oak, and hickory.
Climate: Warm and mild, with occasional hot spells. In the winter, measurable snow is a rarity and remains on the ground only a short time. While frosts are typical in late spring or early fall, in 100 years of weather records a temperature of zero or colder has never been reached. The growing season averages 241 days, from March 16 to November 16, although frosts have been reported as late as April 21 and as early as October 17. In some low-lying areas, Savannah River flooding is still a threat.

Mildness: 76 Brightness: 46 Stability: 18

Places Rated Score: 64.93 **Places Rated Rank: 108**

TEMPERATURE

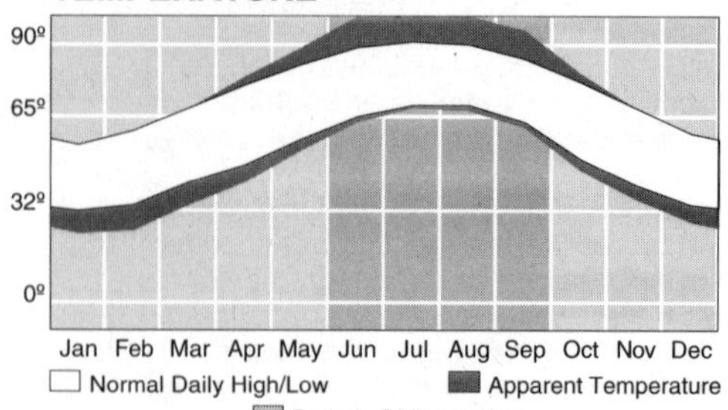

ANNUAL
Humidity: 69%
Wind Speed: 6.5 mph
DAYS
0º or below: 0
32º or below: 55
90º or above: 76
Clear: 111
Cloudy: 148

PRECIPITATION

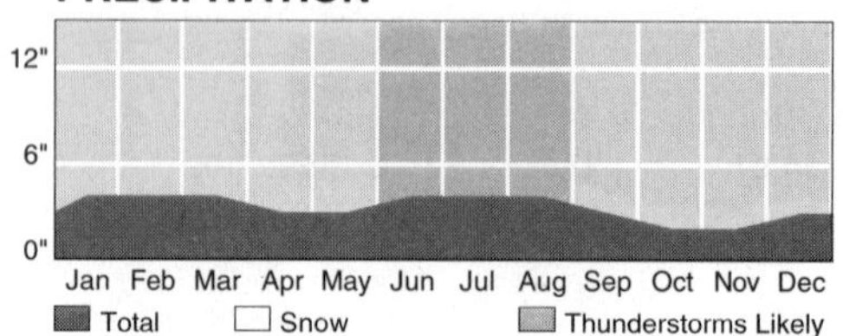

ANNUAL
Precipitation: 44.7"
Snow: 1.2"
DAYS
Precipitation: 71
Thunderstorm: 56

Austin-San Marcos, TX

Location: 30.17 N, 97.42 W, at 590 feet, on the Colorado River where it crosses the Balcones Escarpment.
Landscape: Elevations within the city limits vary from 400 to 900 feet above sea level as it spreads over a sequence of low hills and wide terraces. Native trees include cedar, oak, walnut, mesquite, and pecan. The nearby Highland Lakes have been formed by a series of dams on the Colorado River, which curves through the city and separates the Texas Hill Country from the Blackland Prairies of East Texas.
Climate: Humid Subtropical. Although summers are hot, night temperatures usually drop into the 70s. Winters are mild, with below-freezing temperatures on fewer than 25 days. Prevailing winds are southerly, though strong northers bring cold spells which rarely last more than a few days. Precipitation is well distributed, but heaviest in late spring, with a secondary rainfall peak in September. Summer brings heavy thunderstorms; winter rains are slow and steady. Snowfall is inconsequential and destructive weather infrequent.

Mildness: 80 Brightness: 77 Stability: 23

Places Rated Score: 73.75 **Places Rated Rank: 70**

TEMPERATURE

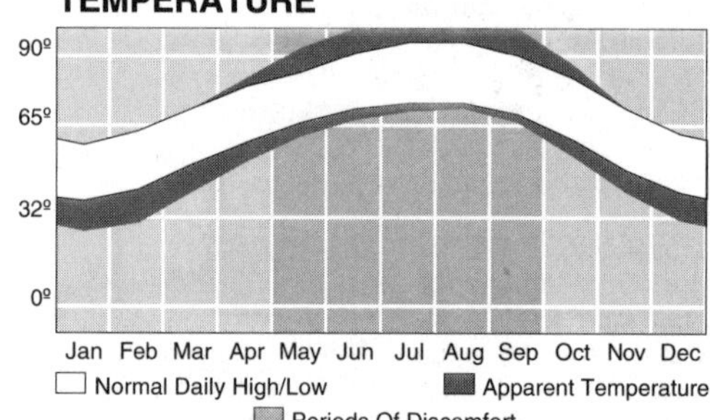

ANNUAL
Humidity: 70%
Wind Speed: 9.2 mph
DAYS
0º or below: 0
32º or below: 21
90º or above: 107
Clear: 116
Cloudy: 135

PRECIPITATION

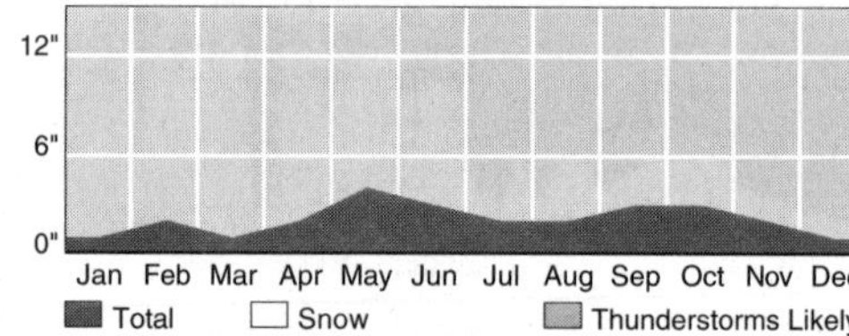

ANNUAL
Precipitation: 31.9"
Snow: 0.9"
DAYS
Precipitation: 47
Thunderstorm: 41

✓ Bakersfield, CA

Location: 35.25 N, 119.03 W, at 490 feet, in the extreme southern end of the great San Joaquin Valley in south-central California. The city is partially surrounded by a horseshoe-shaped rim of mountains with an opening at the northwest.
Landscape: The Sierra Nevada to the northeast blocks much of the cold air that flows southward over the country in the winter. This range also catches and stores snow, which is used for irrigation in the valley below. The valley is suited for Mediterranean and specialized forms of agriculture.
Climate: Because of the surrounding topography, there are three different climates within short distances of each other: valley, mountain, and desert. The overall climate, however, is warm and semiarid. Ninety percent of the precipitation falls between October and April, typical of the southern half of California. Thunderstorms and snow are rare in the valley. Summers are hot, cloudless, and dry but occasionally relieved by ocean breezes from the west. Winters are mild. Average growing season: 265 days.

Mildness: 76 Brightness: 100 Stability: 79

Places Rated Score: 85.68 **Places Rated Rank: 27**

TEMPERATURE

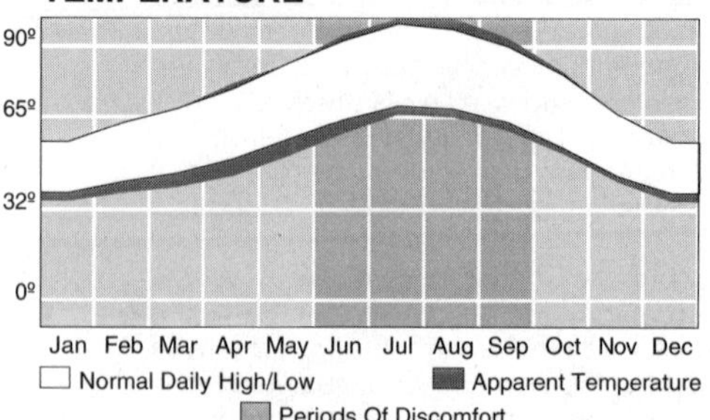

ANNUAL
Humidity: 51%
Wind Speed: 6.4 mph
DAYS
0º or below: 0
32º or below: 14
90º or above: 108
Clear: 192
Cloudy: 92

PRECIPITATION

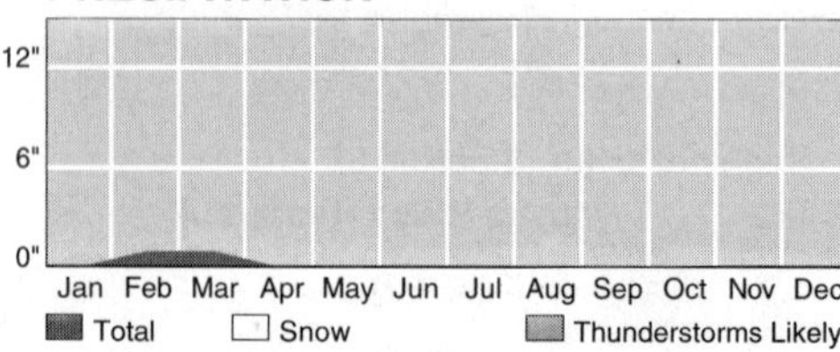

ANNUAL
Precipitation: 5.7"
Snow: 0.0"
DAYS
Precipitation: 18
Thunderstorm: 2

Baltimore, MD

Location: 39.17 N, 76.37 W, at 10 feet, on the western shore of the Chesapeake Bay, midway between the rigorous climates of the North and the milder ones of the South.
Landscape: The wide Severn River drains low, long rolling forested hills into the upper Bay. Typical southeastern mixed forest has broadleaf deciduous and needleleaf evergreen trees.
Climate: Subtropical with a definite Marine influence. Summers are hot and humid though often lifted by a bay breeze. Winters are chilly and rainy. Snow is minimal and doesn't last long. Rain falls throughout the year but is greatest in late summer and early fall. This is also the time of hurricanes and severe thunderstorms. In summer, Baltimore is influenced by the great high-pressure system known as the Bermuda High, which brings a constant flow of warm, humid air masses from the Deep South. The Appalachian Mountains to the west and the ocean to the east produce an equable climate compared with other locations farther inland at the same latitude.

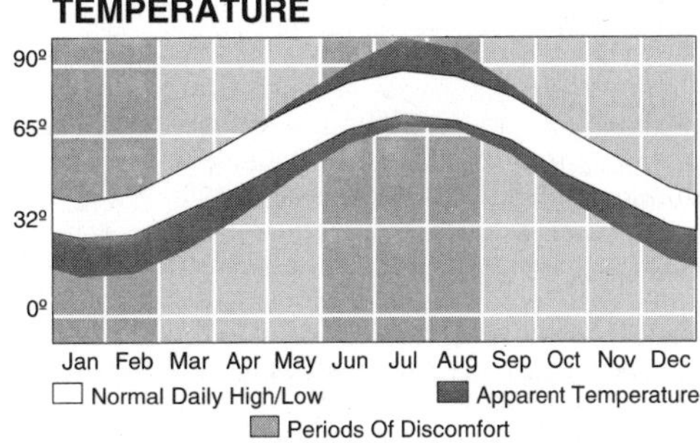

ANNUAL
Humidity: 65%
Wind Speed: 9.2 mph
DAYS
0º or below: 0
32º or below: 97
90º or above: 31
Clear: 105
Cloudy: 151

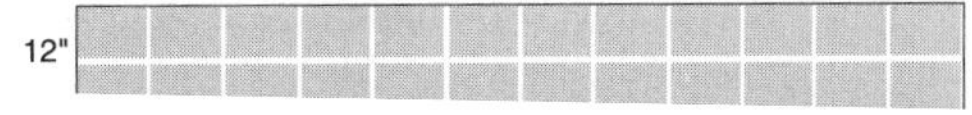

ANNUAL
Precipitation: 42.4"

Landscape: Rolling hills, low mountains, some high relief predominate. Much of the local topography is the result of glacial activity. The soil is generally acid, not highly productive for crop farming, but well suited to growing conifers. The city is surrounded by vast timber stands of spruce-fir, mixed hardwoods and white pine that cover nearly 90 percent of Maine's total land area.
Climate: Alternating air masses create strong seasonal contrasts in temperature. Winters are moderately long and somewhat severe. Snow cover tends to stay on the ground all winter. Though daily highs top 50°F one-third of the year, springs and summers are mild but all too short. The frost-free growing season here is just 140 days.

Mildness: 17 Brightness: 32 Stability: 87

Places Rated Score: 26.15 **Places Rated Rank: 286**

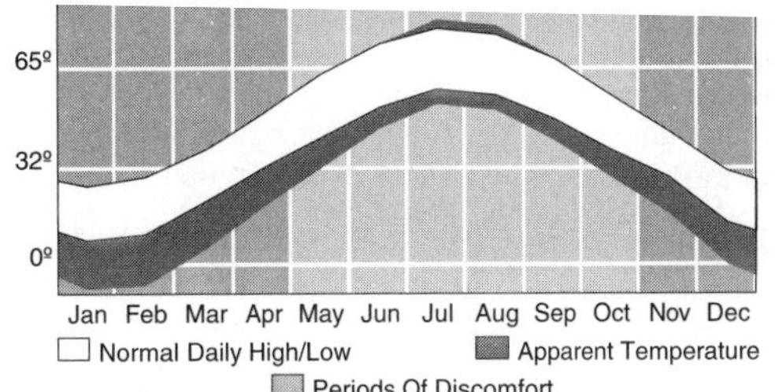

Wind Speed: 8.8 mph
DAYS
0º or below: 20
32º or below: 166
90º or above: 8
Clear: 101
Cloudy: 165

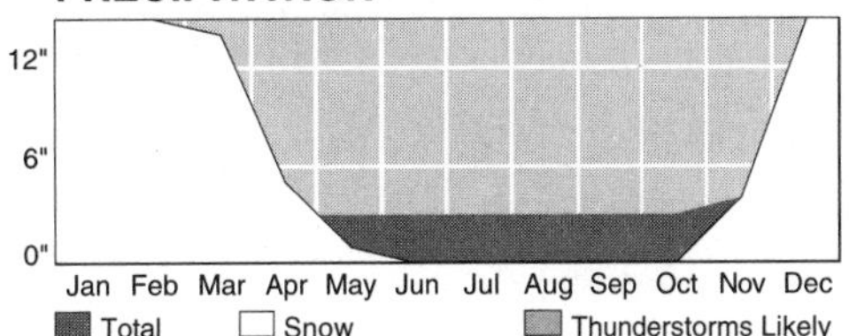

ANNUAL
Precipitation: 41.2"
Snow: 85.6"
DAYS
Precipitation: 80
Thunderstorm: 16

Barnstable–Yarmouth, MA

Location: 41.40 N, 69.58 W, at 50 feet, 60 miles SE of Boston on a hooked peninsula jutting out 65 miles into the Atlantic Ocean.
Landscape: The western end of the Cape is higher and hillier than the eastern, or "outer Cape," which is almost flat and treeless. The Cape is only 1 to 20 miles wide, bounded by Cape Cod Bay to the north and west, Buzzards Bay to the west, and Vineyard and Nantucket Sounds in the south. The sandy soil of glacial origin is arranged in rolling hills and dunes. The northern hook, designated a national seashore, embraces an area of dunes, marshes, lakes, and pinewoods.
Climate: Mild Maritime, with cool summers and cold, wet winters that are seldom severe. In summer, temperatures are ideal for outdoor recreation. Both subzero and days when the air temperature exceeds 90°F are rare. Because the Cape extends into the warm Gulf Stream, its warmer winters and cooler summers contrast favorably with the rest of the southern New England mainland.

Mildness: 60 Brightness: 22 Stability: 93

Places Rated Score: 59.45 **Places Rated Rank: 130**

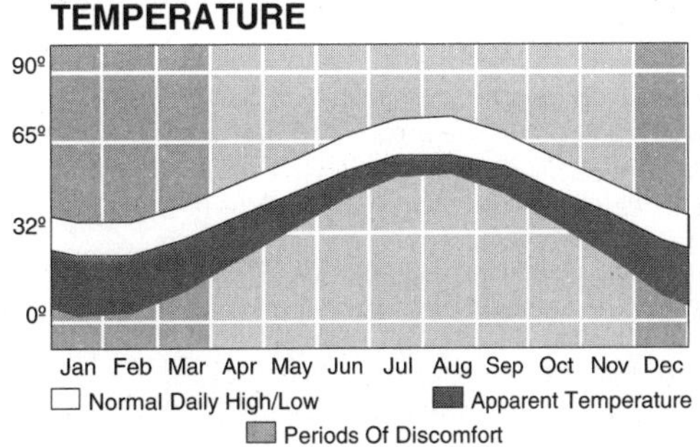

ANNUAL
Humidity: 68%
Wind Speed: 12.5 mph
DAYS
0º or below: 1
32º or below: 118
90º or above: 3
Clear: 98
Cloudy: 163

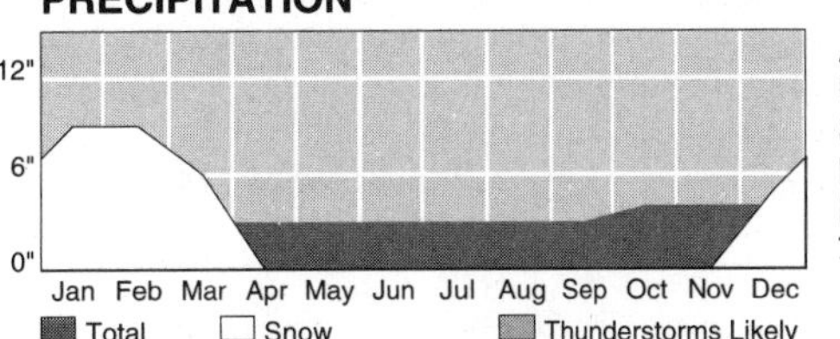

ANNUAL
Precipitation: 45.1"
Snow: 30.0"
DAYS
Precipitation: 76
Thunderstorm: 19

Baton Rouge, LA

Location: 30.32 N, 91.08 W, at 60 feet, at the head of deepwater navigation on the Mississippi River, 80 miles west of New Orleans in the southeastern part of the state.
Landscape: Terrain is related to the Mississippi River. Land is flat, irregular, gently sloping southern Gulf Coastal Plain. The many streams are sluggish. Marshes, swamps, and lakes are numerous. Organic marsh soils are naturally fertile, but poorly drained and subject to flooding. The vegetation is a typical temperate rainforest of evergreen, live oak, laurel, and magnolia.
Climate: Humid Subtropical, having an annual range of temperature that is small to moderate. Rainfall is an abundant 40–60 inches and well distributed throughout the year, though February and March tend to be slightly wetter. Early summer mornings may be as much as twenty degrees cooler than the afternoons. There are tropical storms in summer, hurricanes in summer and fall, occasionally accompanied by tornadoes. Winter temperatures can fall below freezing.

Mildness: 84 Brightness: 30 Stability: 8

Places Rated Score: 68.24 **Places Rated Rank: 90**

TEMPERATURE

90º 65º 32º 0º
Jan Feb Mar Apr May Jun Jul Aug Sep Oct Nov Dec
Normal Daily High/Low | Apparent Temperature | Periods Of Discomfort

ANNUAL
Humidity: 74%
Wind Speed: 7.6 mph
DAYS
0º or below: 0
32º or below: 22
90º or above: 86
Clear: 99
Cloudy: 147

PRECIPITATION

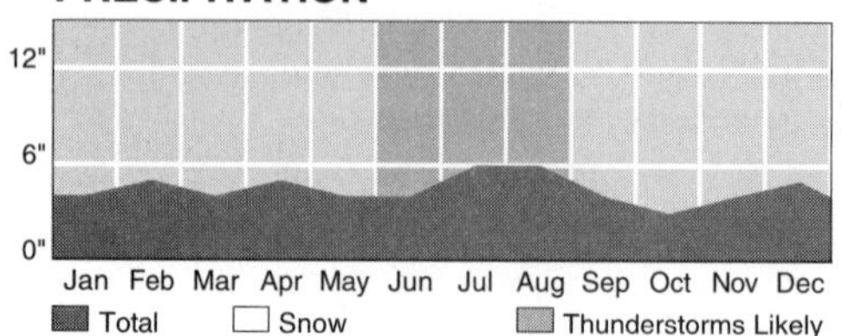

ANNUAL
Precipitation: 60.9"
Snow: 0.2"
DAYS
Precipitation: 71
Thunderstorm: 72

Bellingham, WA

Location: 48.48 N, 122.32 W, at 150 feet, on Bellingham Bay at lower Whatcom Falls, 40 miles south of Vancouver, British Columbia.
Landscape: Dominated by the broad, glacier-carved Skagit River Valley with fjords and deep undersea troughs. East of Bellingham are the North Cascade Mountains and 10,775-foot-high Mt. Baker. The archipelago San Juan Islands are in nearby Puget Sound. The humid needleleaf forests are dominated by Douglas fir and hemlock, western red cedar, spruce and other conifers. Deciduous trees include alder, birch and maple.
Climate: Marine, moist temperate zone. Winter days are mild, but the nights are chilly. Summers are cool and drier. The cooler air temperatures reduce evaporation and produce a damp, humid climate with heavy cloud cover. There are few clear days. Snow is likely from mid-November through March, even occasionally in April. Winter temperatures will fall to freezing but there are no records of zero.

Mildness: 90 Brightness: 4 Stability: 100

Places Rated Score: 83.13 **Places Rated Rank: 38**

TEMPERATURE

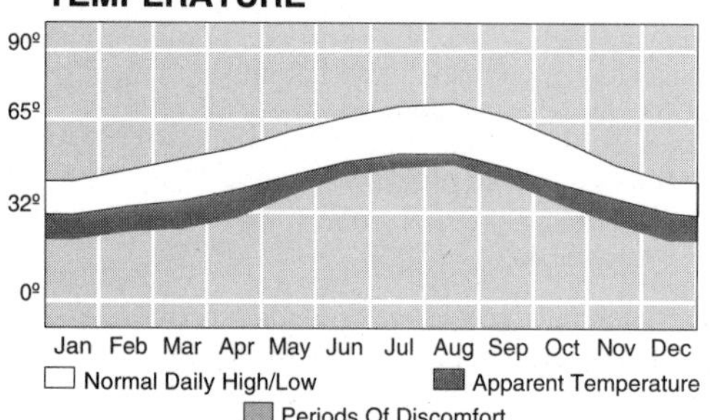

ANNUAL
Humidity: 80%
Wind Speed: 7.5 mph
DAYS
0º or below: 0
32º or below: 68
90º or above: 0
Clear: 64
Cloudy: 216

PRECIPITATION

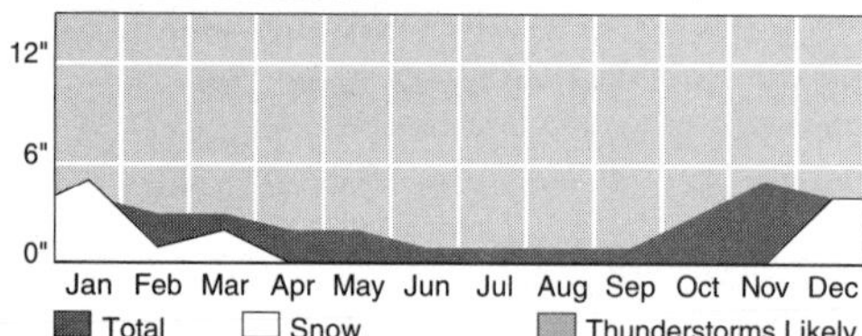

ANNUAL
Precipitation: 36.2"
Snow: 14.3"
DAYS
Precipitation: 93
Thunderstorm: 6

Billings, MT

Location: 45.48 N, 108.32 W, at 3,570 feet, on the west bank of the Yellowstone River, in south-central Montana, near the border between the Great Plains and the Rocky Mountains.
Landscape: The natural vegetation is northern floodplain forest of mixed hardwood and pine. The area is the center of a vast, rich agricultural belt; irrigation and sufficient rain during early spring and fall make it possible to raise a variety of crops here, including sugar beets.
Climate: Best classified as Semiarid Continental. About a third of the yearly total of 15 inches of rain falls during May and June. The winter months are usually dry and cold, although heavy snows can occur anytime. The heaviest snows come either in spring or fall, when the temperature may take an unexpected drop. Blizzard conditions are expected. Severe cold spells are sometimes relieved by the Chinook winds moving down the Yellowstone Valley bringing warm Pacific air. Springs are changeable, cloudy, and cool. Summers are mild, dry, sunny, with cool to cold nights.

Mildness: 14 Brightness: 80 Stability: 63

Places Rated Score: 27.35 **Places Rated Rank: 274**

TEMPERATURE

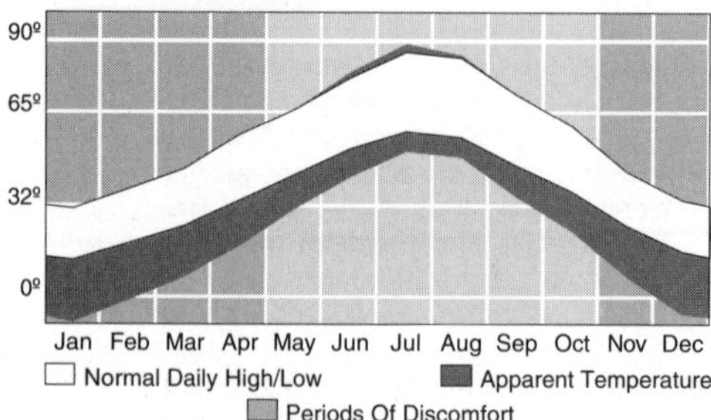

ANNUAL
Humidity: 54%
Wind Speed: 11.2 mph
DAYS
0º or below: 18
32º or below: 150
90º or above: 29
Clear: 89
Cloudy: 164

PRECIPITATION

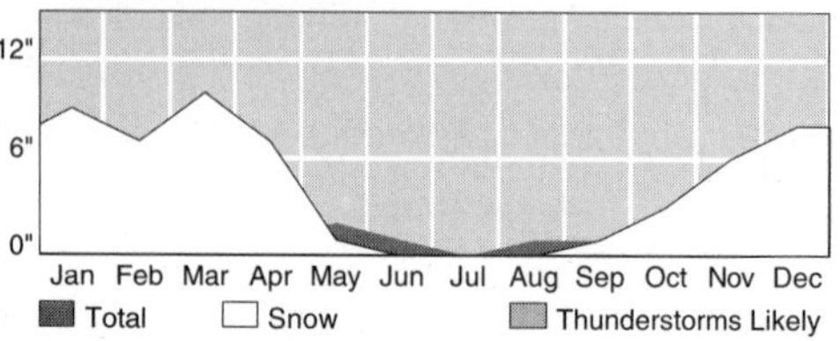

ANNUAL
Precipitation: 15.1"
Snow: 56.5"
DAYS
Precipitation: 29
Thunderstorm: 27

Biloxi–Gulfport–Pascagoula, MS

Location: 30.23 N, 88.59 W, at 10 feet, along the thickly settled stretch of Gulf of Mexico coast 60 miles east of New Orleans.
Landscape: Flat, consisting of low-lying delta floodplains sloping down to sand beaches and rather shallow harbors and bays. Gulf Islands National Seashore lies offshore in the Mississippi Sound and the Intracoastal Waterway passes between New Orleans and Biloxi or Mobile. Common trees here are evergreen oaks, laurel and magnolia, though there are large areas of loblolly and slash pine in the sandy upland areas. Tree ferns, small palms, and shrubs make up the lower growth.
Climate: The Gulf modifies local climate, an effect not felt farther inland. Temperatures of 90°F or higher occur only half as often here as they do in Hattiesburg, 60 miles north. However, there is no such reverse effect on cold air moving down from the north in winter. Rainfall is plentiful and is

TEMPERATURE

90º 65º 32º 0º
Jan Feb Mar Apr May Jun Jul Aug Sep Oct Nov Dec
Normal Daily High/Low — Apparent Temperature — Periods Of Discomfort

ANNUAL
Humidity: 75%
Wind Speed: 8.2 mph
DAYS
0º or below: 0
32º or below: 15
90º or above: 55
Clear: 101
Cloudy: 146

PRECIPITATION

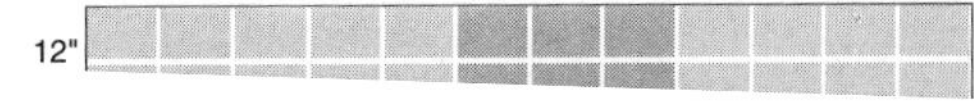

ANNUAL
Precipitation: 61.8"

south-central New York state.
Landscape: Within a radius of approximately 5 miles around the city, hills rise to some 1,400 feet to 1,600 feet. In the spring, melting snow and rains sometimes cause flooding along the riverbanks. Remnants of an extensive northern hardwood forest, cleared in the last century, can still be seen on the tops of hills. In the valleys, dairy, poultry, and other livestock are raised.
Climate: Representative of the humid area of the northeastern United States and decidedly Continental in character. Since the area is next to the St. Lawrence Valley storm track and subject to intruding arctic air masses that approach from the west and north, the local weather undergoes frequent and rapid changes. Winters are cold but usually not severe. However, moisture-laden winds from the Great Lakes bring much snow. Summers are pleasantly cool and invigorating.

Mildness: 27 Brightness: 7 Stability: 70

Places Rated Score: 26.95 **Places Rated Rank: 277**

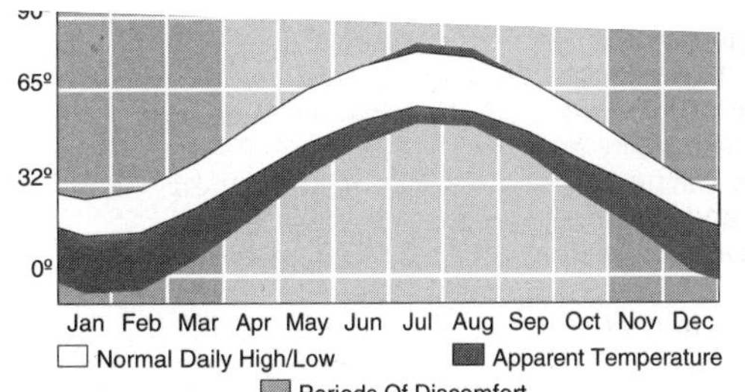

Wind Speed: 10.2 mph
DAYS
0º or below: 8
32º or below: 145
90º or above: 3
Clear: 51
Cloudy: 212

PRECIPITATION

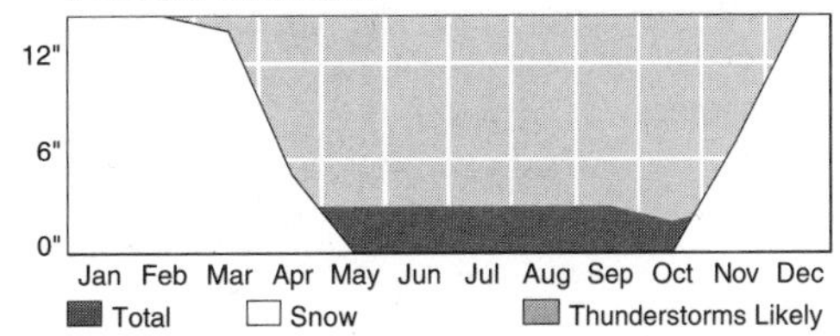

ANNUAL
Precipitation: 37.0"
Snow: 82.4"
DAYS
Precipitation: 87
Thunderstorm: 29

Birmingham, AL

Location: 33.34 N, 86.45 W, at 620 feet, in north-central Alabama in the Appalachian foothills, 300 miles inland from the Gulf of Mexico.
Landscape: Hilly and located in a valley between a ridge of hills, extending from the northeast to the west, and the Red Mountain ridge, covering the east to the southwest. This valley is 8 miles long and 2 miles to 4 miles wide. The Red Mountain ridge approaches a height of 600 feet above the valley floor. Rolling terrain extends to the southwest and west.
Climate: Ideal solar radiation and cold-air drainage produce extreme temperature inversions and low minimum temperatures. Location 300 miles from the Gulf of Mexico provides a safe distance from the direct effects of tropical hurricanes, although it does receive heavy rains from these storms. Occasionally temperatures can drop to freezing. The average growing season is 239 days.

Mildness: 74 Brightness: 34 Stability: 18

Places Rated Score: 61.31 **Places Rated Rank: 123**

TEMPERATURE

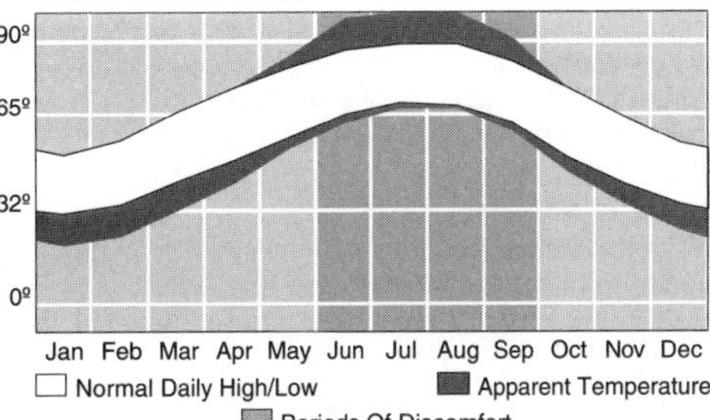

ANNUAL
Humidity: 70%
Wind Speed: 7.2 mph
DAYS
0º or below: 0
32º or below: 57
90º or above: 39
Clear: 99
Cloudy: 155

PRECIPITATION

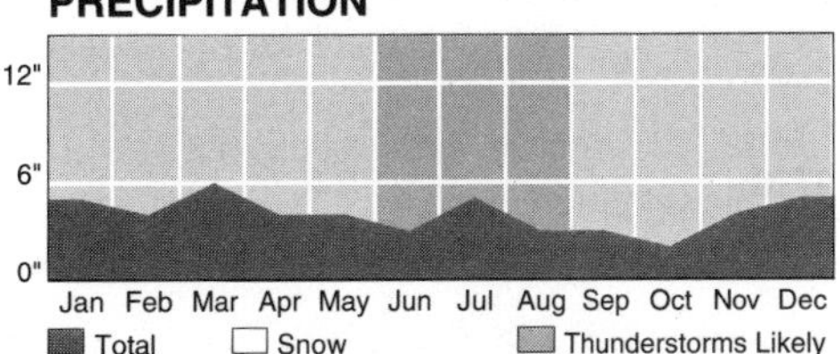

ANNUAL
Precipitation: 54.6"
Snow: 2.0"
DAYS
Precipitation: 75
Thunderstorm: 57

Bismarck, ND

Location: 46.46 N, 100.45 W, at 1,650 feet, in south-central North Dakota, near the center of the North American landmass, on the east bank of the Missouri River.
Landscape: The capital city sits in a shallow basin 7 miles wide and 11 miles long. The closest hills, about 3 miles away, are 200 feet or 300 feet high. West, across the river, the land is hilly and considerably higher.
Climate: Semiarid, Continental in character, and invigorating. The temperature range from summer's hottest to winter's coldest is 135 degrees, typical of the northern Great Plains. In summer, readings of 100°F or more may be expected 6 years out of 10. Readings of −30°F in winter are experienced 7 years out of 10. On many days of the year, the temperature does not rise above zero. Average January temperature is 8°F; average July temperature is 71°F.

Mildness: 2 Brightness: 83 Stability: 42

Places Rated Score: 8.69 **Places Rated Rank: 341**

TEMPERATURE

90º 65º 32º 0º
Jan Feb Mar Apr May Jun Jul Aug Sep Oct Nov Dec
Normal Daily High/Low | Apparent Temperature | Periods Of Discomfort

ANNUAL
Humidity: 68%
Wind Speed: 10.2 mph
DAYS
0º or below: 51
32º or below: 186
90º or above: 23
Clear: 93
Cloudy: 165

PRECIPITATION

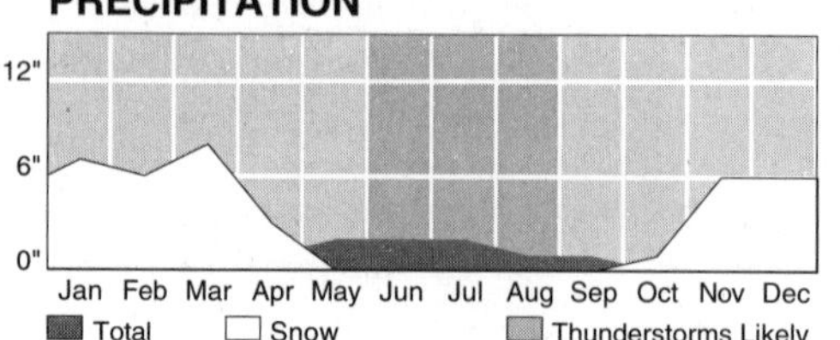

ANNUAL
Precipitation: 15.5"
Snow: 41.9"
DAYS
Precipitation: 34
Thunderstorm: 34

Boise City, ID

Location: 43.34 N, 116.13 W, at 2,840 feet, cradled in the valley of the Boise River about 8 miles below the mouth of a mountain canyon, where this valley widens.
Landscape: The Boise Mountains rise to a height of 5,000 feet to 6,000 feet within 8 miles. Their slopes are partially mantled with sagebrush and chaparral, changing to stands of fir, spruce, and pine trees higher up.
Climate: An Upland Continental climate in summer tempered by periods of cloudy or stormy and mild weather during almost every winter. The cause of this modification in the winter months is the flow of warm, moist Pacific air, called Chinook winds. While this air is considerably moderated by the time it reaches Boise, its effect is nonetheless felt. Summer hot spells rarely last longer than a few days, but temperatures may reach 100°F each year. However, due to the low humidity, the average July evening temperature of 62°F is comfortable. In general, the climate is dry and temperate, with enough variation to be stimulating.

Mildness: 33 Brightness: 91 Stability: 74

Places Rated Score: 49.12 **Places Rated Rank: 173**

TEMPERATURE

90º 65º 32º 0º
Jan Feb Mar Apr May Jun Jul Aug Sep Oct Nov Dec
Normal Daily High/Low | Apparent Temperature | Periods Of Discomfort

ANNUAL
Humidity: 56%
Wind Speed: 8.7 mph
DAYS
0º or below: 2
32º or below: 124
90º or above: 44
Clear: 120
Cloudy: 155

PRECIPITATION

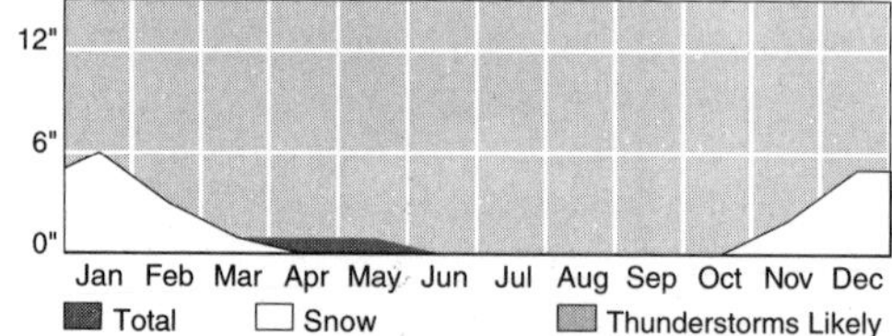

ANNUAL
Precipitation: 12.1"
Snow: 20.9"
DAYS
Precipitation: 34
Thunderstorm: 15

Boston, MA–NH

Location: 42.22 N, 71.02 W, at 20 feet, at the mouths of the Mystic and Charles rivers, on Massachusetts Bay.
Landscape: The western section of Massachusetts Bay is called Boston Bay, and its innermost part is called Boston Harbor, a large, sheltered body of water studded with many small islands, known as the Harbor Islands. Sections of Boston are rolling; two of the more famous hills are Beacon Hill in Boston and Bunker Hill in Charlestown.
Climate: The Atlantic greatly influences the climate, which can be roughly described as damp, changeable, and relatively mild considering its northern location. Sea breezes moderate the temperature in both summer and winter. Rain is plentiful and well distributed throughout the year. Greater Boston receives a great amount of snow, though in the city and south it often becomes sleet with little accumulation. But don't count on it. Snowfall accumulation records were broken in 1994 and 1996.

Mildness: 43 Brightness: 37 Stability: 79

Places Rated Score: 46.46 **Places Rated Rank: 183**

TEMPERATURE

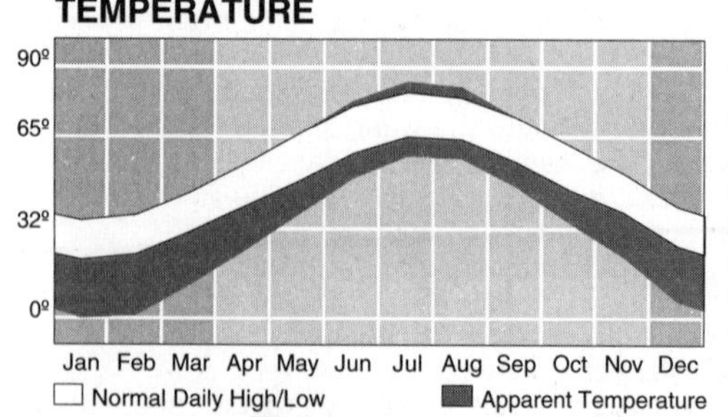

ANNUAL
Humidity: 65%
Wind Speed: 12.5 mph
DAYS
0º or below: 1
32º or below: 99
90º or above: 12
Clear: 98
Cloudy: 163

PRECIPITATION

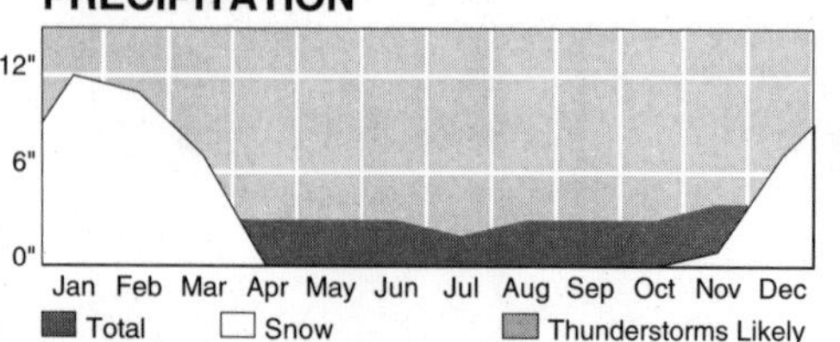

ANNUAL
Precipitation: 41.5"
Snow: 40.9"
DAYS
Precipitation: 75
Thunderstorm: 21

✓Brownsville–Harlingen–San Benito, TX

Location: 25.54 N, 97.26 W, at 20 feet, at the extreme southern tip of Texas, on the Mexican border and the alluvial soils of the Rio Grande. After Honolulu and Miami, this is the southernmost metro area in America.

Landscape: The Gulf of Mexico is 18 miles to the east, and more than half the land toward the coast consists of tidal marshlands, which have the net effect of "moving" the coast 10 miles nearer to the city. Winding between muddy banks at the city's southern boundary is the Rio Grande, making Brownsville a port city with a deepwater channel to the Gulf of Mexico. This fertile valley between the coastal prairie and the western deserts flourishes with palm trees and bougainvillea as well as citrus groves.

Climate: Humid Subtropical. It's always summer here, accounting for the area's agricultural importance in growing citrus fruits, cotton, and warm-weather vegetables. Part of the climate is man-made; irrigation, used for all the crops, ... to the humidity. Summer temperatures

TEMPERATURE

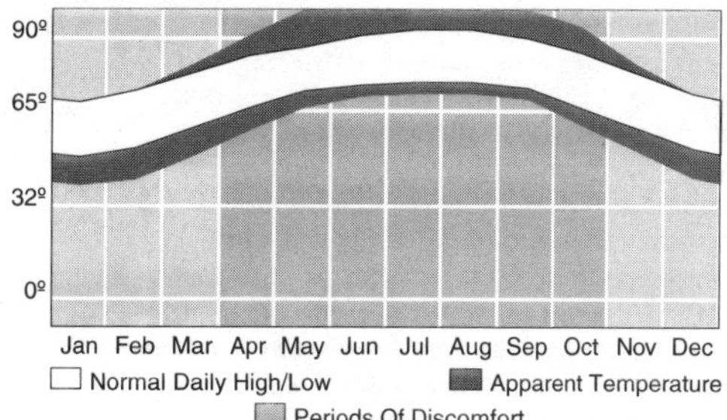

ANNUAL
Humidity: 74%
Wind Speed: 11.4 mph
DAYS
0º or below: 0
32º or below: 2
90º or above: 116
Clear: 96
Cloudy: 138

PRECIPITATION

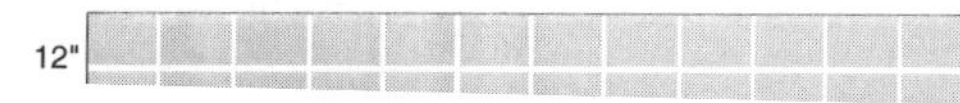

ANNUAL
Precipitation: 26.6"

capital.

Landscape: Part of the Blacklands area of the Coastal Plains. Streams wind through oak and hickory woods. Elm, sycamore, and cottonwood are also common. Once a center of large plantations, the soil allows a broad range of agricultural efforts, including vineyards.

Climate: Spring arrives early with temperatures in March in the 70s during the day. Thunderstorms occur in every month, peaking in May and June. Summers are long and hot, unrelieved by moderate temperatures at night. Winters are comparatively mild, with an occasional freezing day and a rare trace of snow. The area can be frost-free up to 300 days in a mild year. The annual precipitation of 20 to 30 inches falls mostly during the growing season.

Mildness: 80 Brightness: 76 Stability: 24

Places Rated Score: 73.99 **Places Rated Rank: 69**

65º
32º
0º
Jan Feb Mar Apr May Jun Jul Aug Sep Oct Nov Dec
Normal Daily High/Low
Apparent Temperature
Periods Of Discomfort

Humidity: 70%
Wind Speed: 11.2 mph
DAYS
0º or below: 0
32º or below: 23
90º or above: 101
Clear: 131
Cloudy: 136

PRECIPITATION

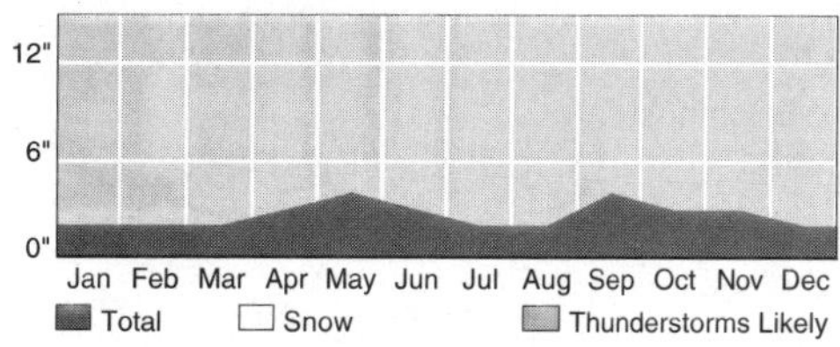

ANNUAL
Precipitation: 39.1"
Snow: 0.3"
DAYS
Precipitation: 54
Thunderstorm: 43

Buffalo–Niagara Falls, NY

Location: 42.56 N, 78.44 W, at 710 feet, at the eastern end of Lake Erie, which is 9 miles WSW. Lake Ontario is 25 miles north. The two lakes are connected by the Niagara River and the famous falls of the same name.

Landscape: The surrounding country is comparatively low and level to the west, and gently rolling towards east and south, rising to pronounced hills within 12 miles to 18 miles, and to 1,000 feet above Lake Erie at a point 35 miles south–southeast of the city.

Climate: The weather here is varied and changeable. Wide seasonal swings of temperature are tempered somewhat by the surrounding lakes. Spring comes late, primarily because of the ice buildup and cold water on Lake Erie. Summers are mild, with more sun here than anywhere else in the state. Thunderstorms are infrequent. Autumn has long, dry periods and is frost-free until mid-October. Winters are famous for snow: 90 inches are expected each year.

Mildness: 23 Brightness: 18 Stability: 68

Places Rated Score: 26.45 **Places Rated Rank: 282**

TEMPERATURE

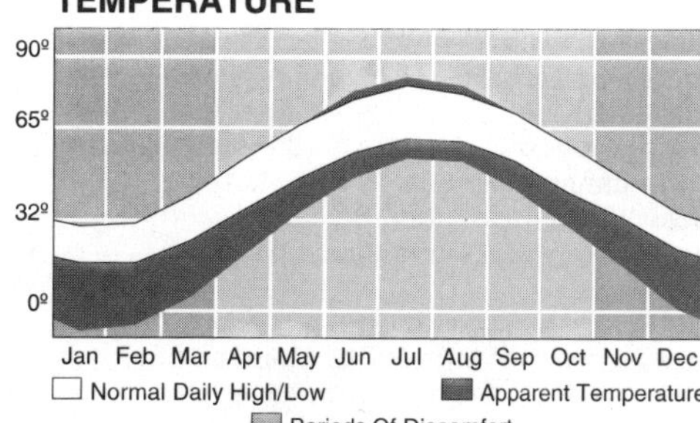

ANNUAL
Humidity: 71%
Wind Speed: 11.9 mph
DAYS
0º or below: 5
32º or below: 131
90º or above: 4
Clear: 54
Cloudy: 208

PRECIPITATION

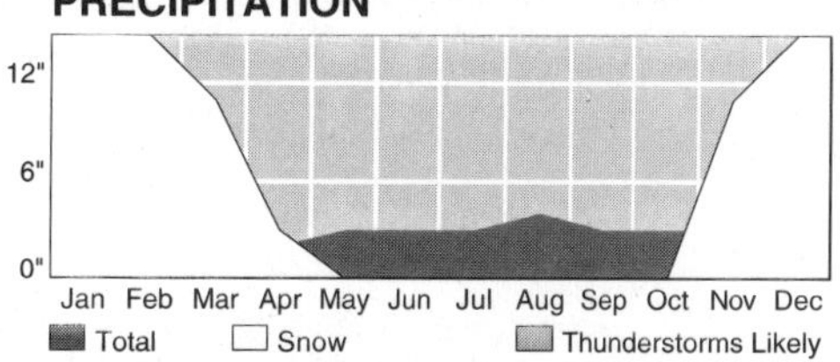

ANNUAL
Precipitation: 38.6"
Snow: 91.1"
DAYS
Precipitation: 65
Thunderstorm: 30

Burlington, VT

Location: 44.28 N, 73.09 W, at 330 feet, on the eastern shore of Lake Champlain 75 miles south of Montréal, Québec.
Landscape: The highest peaks of the Adirondacks in New York State are visible 35 miles west across the lake. Vermont's Green Mountains foothills begin 10 miles to the east and southeast. Northern white pine, eastern hemlock, maple, oak and beech are common trees in the surrounding forest.
Climate: Northerly latitude assures the variety and vigor of a true New England climate. The summer, while not long, is pleasant. Fall is cool, extending through October. Winters are cold, with brief, intense cold snaps formed by high pressure systems moving down from central Canada and Hudson Bay. Lake Champlain's tempering effect produces temperatures along the lakeshore from 5 degrees to 10 degrees warmer than those at the airport 3.5 miles inland. Because of its location in the path of the St. Lawrence Valley storm track and the effects of the lake, this is one of the cloudiest cities in the United States.

Mildness: 13 Brightness: 22 Stability: 68

Places Rated Score: 18.53 **Places Rated Rank: 319**

TEMPERATURE

90º 65º 32º 0º

Jan Feb Mar Apr May Jun Jul Aug Sep Oct Nov Dec

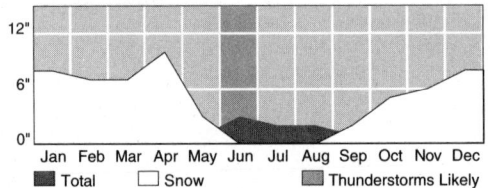

Normal Daily High/Low Apparent Temperature Periods Of Discomfort

ANNUAL
Humidity: 68%
Wind Speed: 9.0 mph
DAYS
0º or below: 28
32º or below: 157
90º or above: 6
Clear: 58
Cloudy: 206

PRECIPITATION

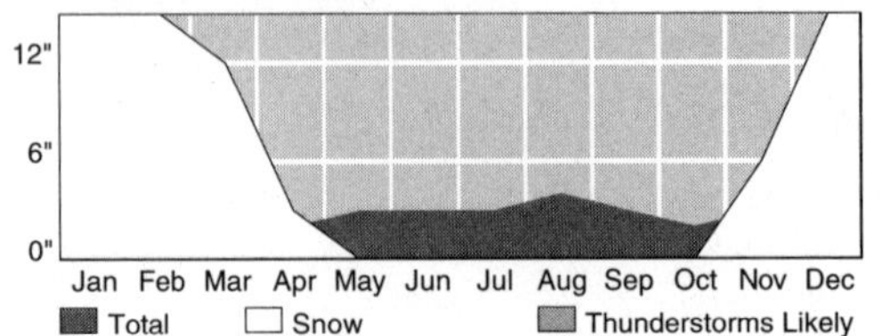

ANNUAL
Precipitation: 34.5"
Snow: 76.9"
DAYS
Precipitation: 75
Thunderstorm: 22

Calgary, AB

Location: 51.06 N, 114.01 W, at 3,501 feet, less than 50 miles east of the Continental Divide in southern Alberta.
Landscape: The Elbow and Bow rivers provide strong relief in an otherwise large, treeless tract of undulating prairie grassland. Foothills of the Rocky Mountains begin rising west of the city. In the east, gently rolling ground meets flat prairie land.
Climate: Continental, with strong temperature contrasts between day and night as well as summer and winter. Situated on the eastern side of the Rockies, the area rarely enjoys the moderating effects of the Pacific. Embedded in the zone of westerly winds, changing seasons are marked by northerly air circulations in winter and occasional instances of moist, tropical air from the Gulf of Mexico bringing heavy rainfall in the summer. The higher elevation of the city contributes to longer winters and shorter summers. Temperatures are influenced by the northerly latitude as well as the location on a valley floor, especially during the winter when the sun is low on the horizon.

Mildness: 5 Brightness: 71 Stability: 90

Places Rated Score: 17.74 **Places Rated Rank: 322**

TEMPERATURE

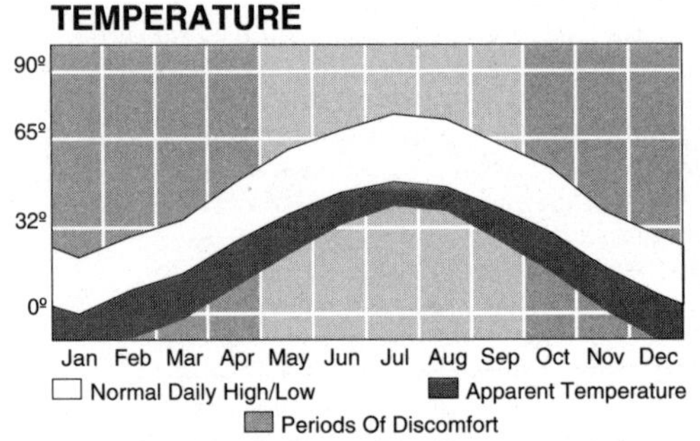

ANNUAL
Humidity: 64%
Wind Speed: 10.1 mph
DAYS
0º or below: 33
32º or below: 201
90º or above: 5
Clear: 118
Cloudy: 100

PRECIPITATION

12" 6" 0"

Jan Feb Mar Apr May Jun Jul Aug Sep Oct Nov Dec

Total Snow Thunderstorms Likely

ANNUAL
Precipitation: 16.7"
Snow: 59.9"
DAYS
Precipitation: 36
Thunderstorm: 25

Casper, WY

Location: 42.55 N, 106.28 W, at 5,340 feet, in east central Wyoming in the North Platte River valley, some 170 miles north of the state capital at Cheyenne.
Landscape: Surrounding countryside is rolling and hilly with considerable flat prairie land. Chief vegetation is sagebrush or shadscale, with a mixture of short grasses. To the south, the Casper Range of the Laramie Mountains and Medicine Bow NF rise 3,500 feet above the valley floor. Badlands, wind and water-carved chasms are typical along this edge of the Wyoming Basin.
Climate: Rather dry due to the effective moisture barrier of the Cascades, the Sierra Nevada, and the Rocky Mountains, which block most of the moist Pacific winds. Summertime precipitation is almost all in the form of thunderstorms, which generally provide ample moisture for grasslands. Annual snowfall averages 77 inches, but the winter season is not severe, contrary to common belief. The dryness of the air prevents discomfort during both the warm summer months and winter cold snaps. Summer highs average 84°F, winter lows 15°F.

Mildness: 11 Brightness: 78 Stability: 52

Places Rated Score: 22.81 **Places Rated Rank: 307**

TEMPERATURE

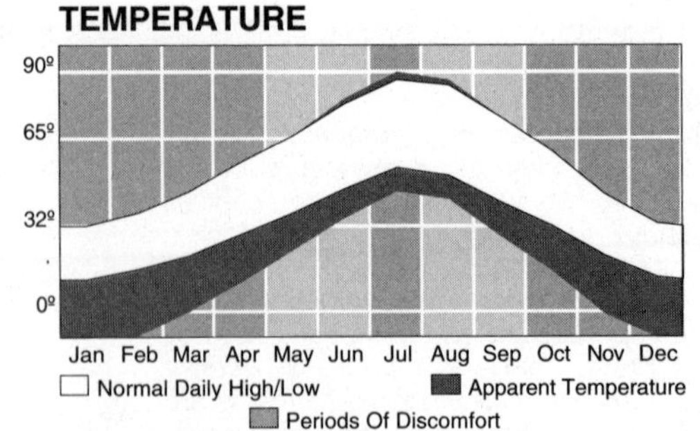

ANNUAL
Humidity: 57%
Wind Speed: 12.9 mph
DAYS
0º or below: 21
32º or below: 180
90º or above: 28
Clear: 107
Cloudy: 147

PRECIPITATION

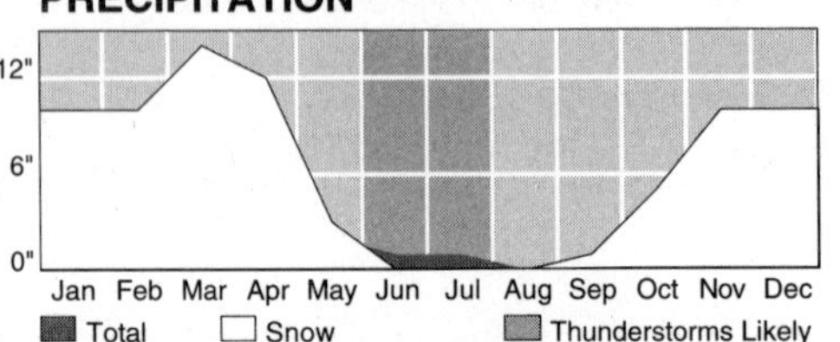

ANNUAL
Precipitation: 12.5"
Snow: 78.8"
DAYS
Precipitation: 38
Thunderstorm: 34

Charleston, WV

Location: 38.22 N, 81.36 W, at 1,020 feet, in the western foothills of the Allegheny Mountains at the junction of the Kanawha and Elk rivers.
Landscape: The surrounding hilltops are around 1,100 feet above sea level, about 500 feet higher than the valleys. Common trees are oak, beech, maple, sweet chestnut and birch. In spite of extensive clear-cutting to make room for coal production and petrochemical plants, remnants of the ancient Appalachian oak forest can still be seen here.
Climate: Hot Continental, characterized by sharp temperature contrasts, both seasonal and day-to-day. May through September is generally warm; November through March moderately cold. April and October are months of rapid transition. Cold spells occur on the average of two or three times each winter, but they seldom last longer than several days. Ample precipitation is well distributed throughout the year, with a maximum in July and a minimum in October. Because of the conditions of terrain and airflow, Charleston

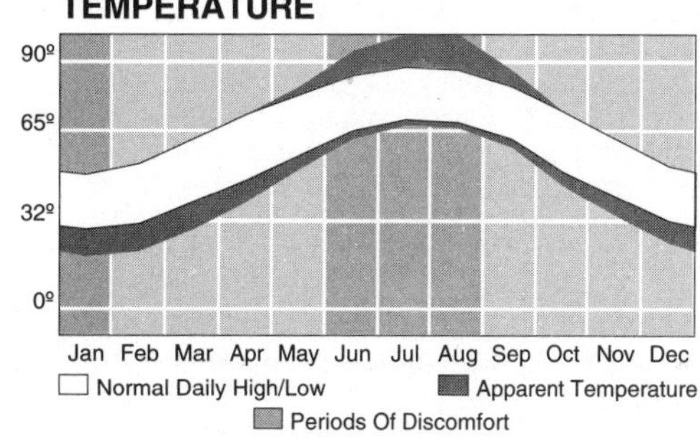

ANNUAL
Humidity: 68%
Wind Speed: 7.4 mph
DAYS
0º or below: 0
32º or below: 65
90º or above: 44
Clear: 111
Cloudy: 151

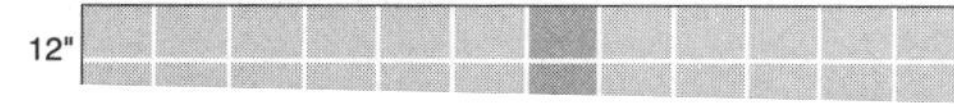

ANNUAL
Precipitation: 43.1"

Landscape: Charleston is the place where the ... Cooper rivers meet to form the Atlantic Ocean" is the traditional geography lesson of Charleston schoolchildren. Before expansion began in 1960, Charleston was limited to a narrow peninsula extending into a broad bay, with the Atlantic Ocean three miles away. The terrain is generally level and the soil sandy to sandy loam. Because of the low elevation, a portion of the city and nearby coastal islands are vulnerable to tidal flooding.
Climate: Generally temperate, modified considerably by the ocean. Summer is warm and humid, but temperatures over 100°F are infrequent. Forty percent of the annual rainfall occurs then. The fall passes from an Indian summer to the pre-winter cold spells that begin in November. From late September to early November the weather is pleasantly cool and sunny. Winters are mild; temperatures of 20°F or less are unusual. Spring is warm, windy, and changeable. Most storms occur then.

Mildness: 88 Brightness: 15 Stability: 20

Places Rated Score: 71.55 **Places Rated Rank: 76**

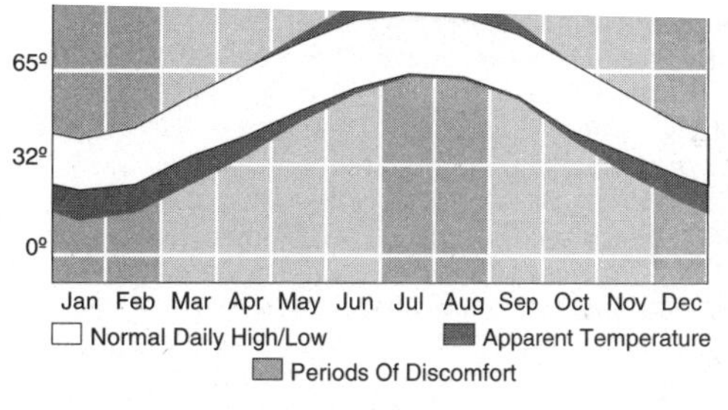

Humidity: 69%
Wind Speed: 6.2 mph
DAYS
0º or below: 5
32º or below: 100
90º or above: 22
Clear: 64
Cloudy: 189

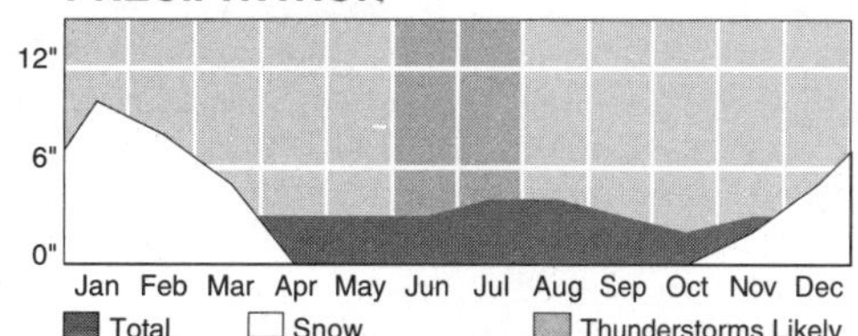

ANNUAL
Precipitation: 42.5"
Snow: 32.3"
DAYS
Precipitation: 93
Thunderstorm: 45

Charlotte–Gastonia–Rock Hill, NC–SC

Location: 35.13 N, 80.56 W, at 720 feet, in the southern Piedmont, 137 miles SW of Raleigh, NC, and 92 miles north of Columbia, SC.
Landscape: The Piedmont is an area of rolling country between the mountains to the west and the Coastal Plain to the east. Once covered by the eastern hardwood forest, there are many wooded areas. Common trees are oak, hickory, birch, beech, and maple.
Climate: Moderate, characterized by cool winters and summers that are quite warm. The mountains have a moderating effect on winter temperatures, causing appreciable warming of cold air coming from the west and northwest. Winter weather is changeable, alternating between mild and cool spells, with occasional cold periods. Extreme cold is rare. Snow is infrequent, occurring, on the average, once a month from December through March. Summers are long and warm, with afternoon temperatures frequently in the 90s. Nights are cooler, with temperatures dropping into the low 70s even in the warmest months.

Mildness: 73 Brightness: 44 Stability: 37

Places Rated Score: 64.94 **Places Rated Rank: 107**

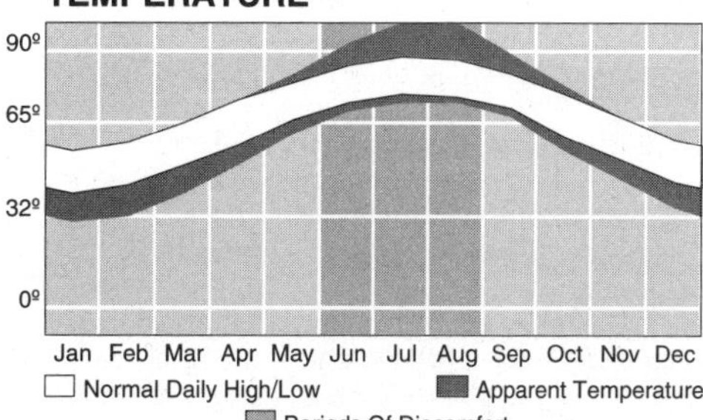

ANNUAL
Humidity: 70%
Wind Speed: 8.6 mph
DAYS
0º or below: 0
32º or below: 34
90º or above: 52
Clear: 102
Cloudy: 154

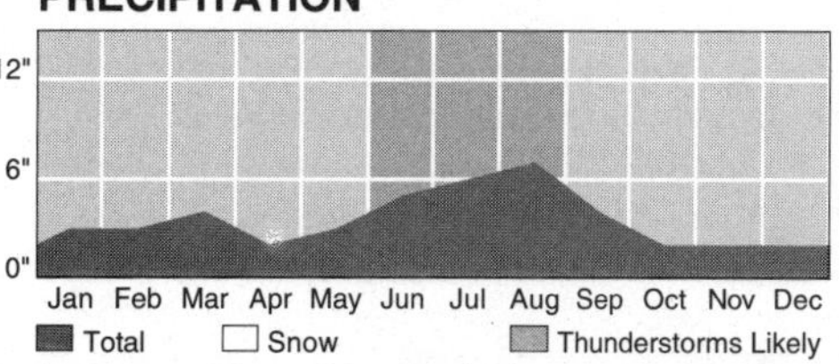

ANNUAL
Precipitation: 48.5"
Snow: 0.7"
DAYS
Precipitation: 74
Thunderstorm: 58

Charlottesville, VA

Location: 38.02 N, 78.31 W, at 870 feet, in the center of Virginia's Albemarle County on the central Piedmont Plateau, 110 miles SW of Washington, DC.

Landscape: Among the red clay foothills of the Blue Ridge Mountains, which lie to the west. These ranges make the topography rolling to quite steep. Elevations range from 300 feet to 800 feet, with some points in the Blue Ridge as high as 3,200 feet. The Rivana River marks the east border. Approaches to the natural bowl are through wooded hills, by orchards and fertile pastures. The surrounding mixed forest has tall broadleaf deciduous oak, hickory, sweetgum, red maple, and winged elm, together with loblolly, and shortleaf pine.

Climate: Modified Continental, with mild winters and warm, humid summers. The mountains produce various steering and blocking effects on storms and air masses. Chesapeake Bay to the east further modifies the climate, making it warmer in winter, cooler in summer. Precipitation is well distributed throughout the year, with the maximum in July, the minimum in January. Tornadoes and violent storms are rare, but severe thunderstorms occur each year.

Mildness: 61 Brightness: 46 Stability: 49

Places Rated Score: 56.94 **Places Rated Rank: 140**

TEMPERATURE

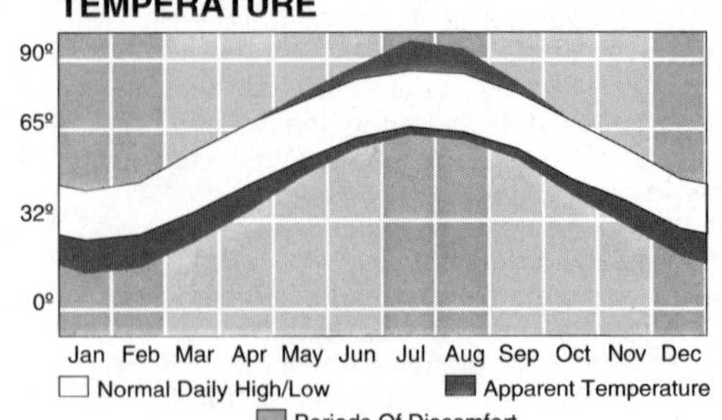

ANNUAL
Humidity: 66%
Wind Speed: 7.7 mph
DAYS
0º or below: 0
32º or below: 87
90º or above: 31
Clear: 111
Cloudy: 147

PRECIPITATION

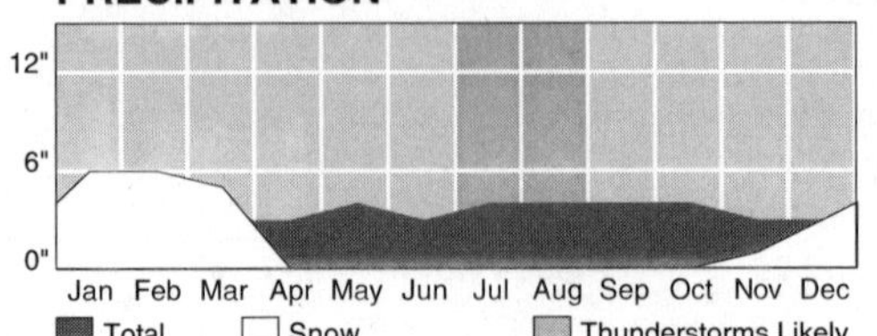

ANNUAL
Precipitation: 47.3"
Snow: 24.2"
DAYS
Precipitation: 72
Thunderstorm: 39

Chattanooga, TN–GA

Location: 35.02 N, 85.12 W, at 690 feet, in the southern portion of the Great Valley of the Tennessee River, an area between the Cumberland Mountains to the west and the Appalachian Mountains to the east.

Landscape: Local topography is complex, with the difference in elevation between minor valleys and ridges being as much as 500 feet. The city is almost completely surrounded by steep mountains. Lookout Mountain at 2,126 feet has a view of seven states. Nearby Signal Mountain overlooks the "Grand Canyon of the Tennessee," where the Tennessee River cuts a gorge 1,000 feet deep. Forests of mixed hardwood and second-growth pine prevail throughout the region.

Climate: Moderate Continental with cool winters and summers that are quite warm. In winter the Cumberlands have a moderating influence on the local climate, retarding the flow of cold air from the north and west. Winter weather is changeable and alternates between cool spells and an occasional cold period. Extreme or prolonged cold is rare. Summer temperatures average in the high 80s or low 90s. Most afternoon summer temperatures are modified by brief thundershowers, which cause the mercury to drop 10° to 15°.

Mildness: 69 Brightness: 32 Stability: 20

Places Rated Score: 57.26 **Places Rated Rank: 139**

TEMPERATURE

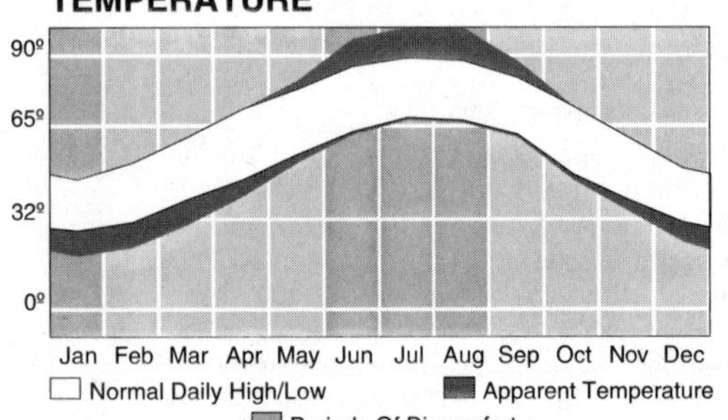

ANNUAL
Humidity: 70%
Wind Speed: 6.0 mph
DAYS
0º or below: 0
32º or below: 73
90º or above: 48
Clear: 104
Cloudy: 155

PRECIPITATION

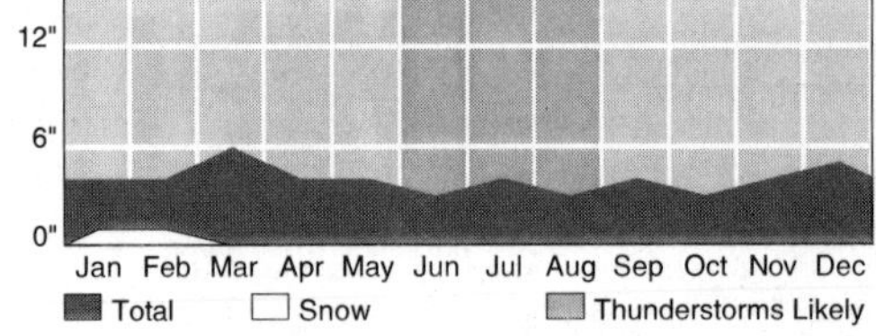

ANNUAL
Precipitation: 53.5"
Snow: 4.4"
DAYS
Precipitation: 83
Thunderstorm: 55

Cheyenne, WY

Location: 41.09 N, 104.49 W, at 6,120 feet, on a broad plateau between the North and South Platte rivers in extreme southeastern Wyoming.

Landscape: The surrounding country is mostly rolling prairie which rises rapidly to a ridge 9,000 feet high 30 miles west. This ridge is known as the Laramie Mountains, one of the ranges of the Rockies. It extends in a north-south direction. Prairie grasses in the highlands of the Wyoming Basin are a mixture of short-stem varieties. Greasewood and sagebrush grow in the highly alkaline soil.

Climate: Continental characteristics of large daily and annual temperature ranges. Cheyenne lies in the wind shadow of the ridge which spares it from some of the cold air masses blowing down from Canada. While wind is a noticeable weather element, the strong winds are from a westerly direction and tend to raise the temperature. Lying in the lee of the mountain prevents moisture from reaching the area, causing a semiarid climate. Showers, thunderstorms, and hail are not infrequent. There may be heavy snows through early May; freezes have occurred as late as mid-June.

Mildness: 21 Brightness: 72 Stability: 50

Places Rated Score: 30.88 **Places Rated Rank: 248**

TEMPERATURE

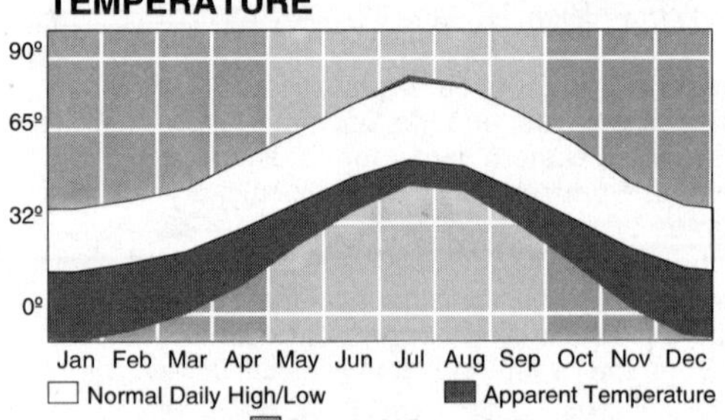

ANNUAL
Humidity: 55%
Wind Speed: 12.9 mph
DAYS
0º or below: 12
32º or below: 173
90º or above: 9
Clear: 105
Cloudy: 133

PRECIPITATION

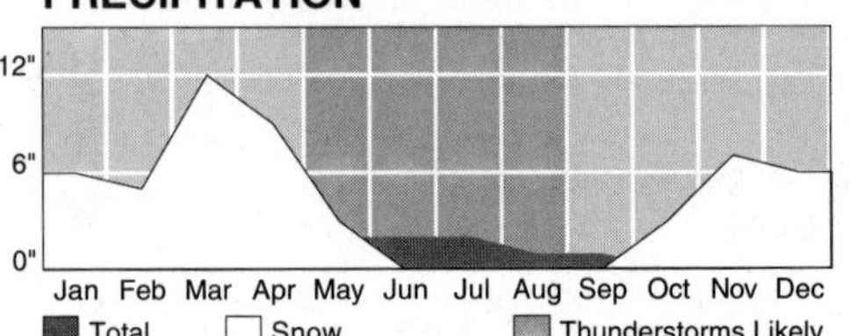

ANNUAL
Precipitation: 14.4"
Snow: 55.2"
DAYS
Precipitation: 28
Thunderstorm: 50

Chicago, IL

Location: 41.44 N, 87.46 W, at 620 feet, on a plain along the southwest shore of Lake Michigan that, for the most part, is only some tens of feet above the lake.
Landscape: Because the surrounding land is flat, topography does not significantly affect airflow in or near the city. Lower frictional drag over Lake Michigan permits winds to be frequently stronger along the lakeshore. Trees are deciduous hardwoods including maple, oak, and hickory.
Climate: Predominantly Continental, with warm to hot summers and cold winters. Chicago has been appropriately nicknamed the Windy City. The climate of the city proper is modified by the lake, with summer temperatures near the shore often 10° cooler than elsewhere. Summer hot spells bring an uncomfortable combination of high temperature and high humidity and may last for several days, then end abruptly with a shift of winds to the north or northwest. They are often accompanied by thunderstorms.

TEMPERATURE

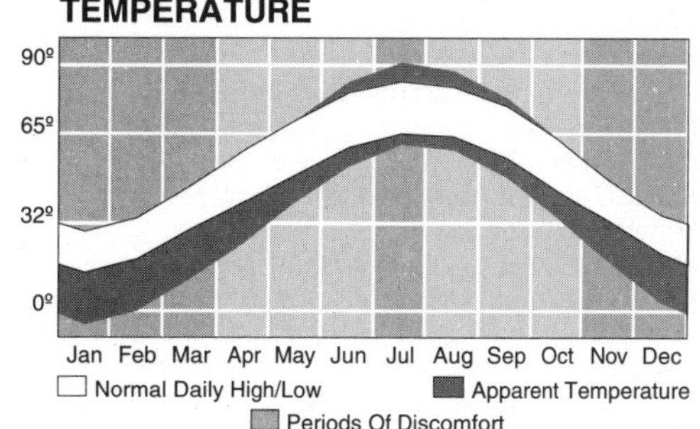

ANNUAL
Humidity: 70%
Wind Speed: 10.4 mph
DAYS
0º or below: 7
32º or below: 132
90º or above: 17
Clear: 84
Cloudy: 176

PRECIPITATION

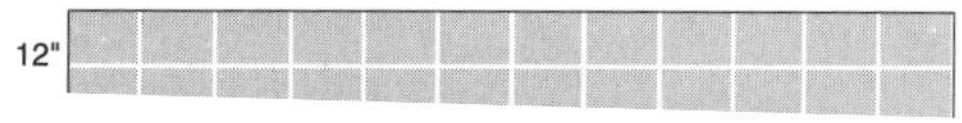

ANNUAL
Precipitation: 37.4"

Landscape: Chaparral Province, where steep slopes climb steadily to high mountains. Stream-cut canyons drain to the Sacramento River. Tall digger pine and blue oak dominate the forest. Between valley and mountain, there is a transitional mix of chaparral-covered rounded hills, pine forests, and open grassy fields. Paradise is 1,010 feet higher than Chico. Lassen Volcanic National Park is northeast.
Climate: Temperate Continental that is high enough to feel the bite of four seasons. Protected from ocean influences, summers are longer, winters colder, and there is a greater range of daily and seasonal temperatures. Winter winds tend to blow from the northwest bringing isotherms in a north-south parallel with the contours of the mountains. This is the rainy season. With the northward migration of the Pacific high, deflecting storms far to the north, summer is long and dry.

Mildness: 79 Brightness: 98 Stability: 89
Places Rated Score: 85.07 **Places Rated Rank: 30**

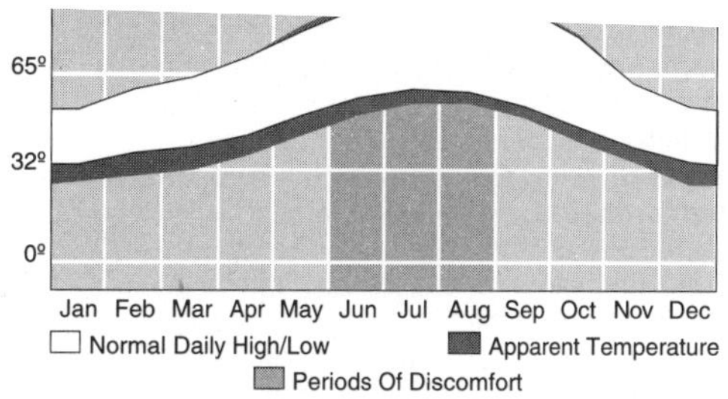

Wind Speed: 7.1 mph
DAYS
0º or below: 0
32º or below: 36
90º or above: 88
Clear: 174
Cloudy: 113

PRECIPITATION

ANNUAL
Precipitation: 26.3"
Snow: 0.2"
DAYS
Precipitation: 39
Thunderstorm: 2

Cincinnati, OH–KY–IN

Location: 39.06 N, 84.31 W, at 683 feet, on the north bank of the Ohio River, 103 miles SW of the state capital, Columbus.
Landscape: The city extends over two ranges of hills bisected by the Mill Creek Valley, with hills extending some 400 feet above the valley floor. Metro Cincinnati incorporates the lower portion of the Little Miami Valley to the east and extends to within 5 or 6 miles of the Great Miami Valley to the west.
Climate: Basically moderate Continental, with a 20° range in daily temperatures. December is the coldest month with the average high at 37°F. In July the average temperature is 85°F. Changes in regional weather are frequent due to the passage of numerous cyclonic storms in winter and spring, and thunderstorms during the summer. Fall is pleasant, with the least rainfall of any season, an abundance of sunshine and comfortable temperatures.

Mildness: 39 Brightness: 33 Stability: 39
Places Rated Score: 38.07 **Places Rated Rank: 207**

TEMPERATURE

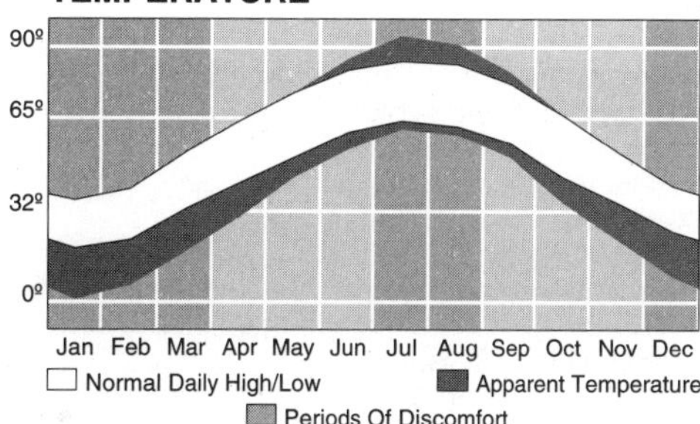

ANNUAL
Humidity: 70%
Wind Speed: 9.1 mph
DAYS
0º or below: 2
32º or below: 107
90º or above: 23
Clear: 81
Cloudy: 186

PRECIPITATION

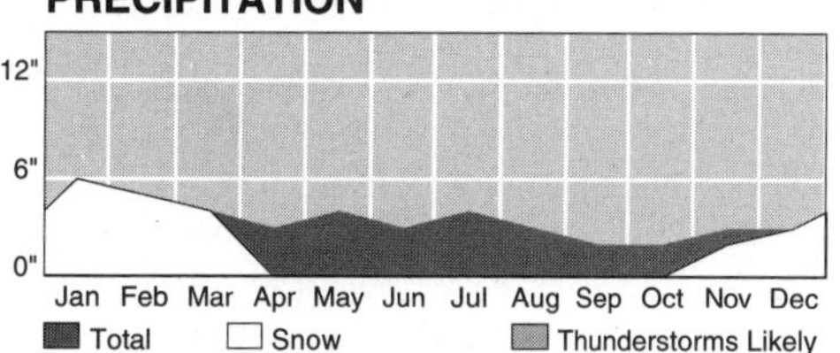

ANNUAL
Precipitation: 41.3"
Snow: 23.2"
DAYS
Precipitation: 73
Thunderstorm: 39

Cleveland–Lorain–Elyria, OH

Location: 41.25 N, 81.52 W, at 770 feet, situated on the south shore of Lake Erie, with a lake frontage of 31 miles.
Landscape: The fourth largest of the Great Lakes is a major feature of local topography as the surrounding terrain is mostly level. The Cuyahoga River flows in a north-south valley bisecting the city. A ridge at the southeastern edge of the city rises some 500 feet above shore level. Cleveland is a major port on the St. Lawrence Seaway.
Climate: In the winter, Cleveland lies in the path of many cold air masses advancing south and east out of Canada. Extreme low temperatures are modified as the air passes over the comparatively warm water of the lake. But this also means considerable winter cloudiness and frequent snows. There are 146 foggy days throughout the year. Spring is generally a brief transition period. Summer heat is also moderated by the lake, since breezes are felt a considerable distance inland. Fall is the most pleasant season, with mild, sunny weather often extending into November or even early December.

Mildness: 29 Brightness: 17 Stability: 55

Places Rated Score: 29.88 **Places Rated Rank: 253**

TEMPERATURE

90º 65º 32º 0º

Jan Feb Mar Apr May Jun Jul Aug Sep Oct Nov Dec

Normal Daily High/Low ■ Apparent Temperature ■ Periods Of Discomfort

ANNUAL
Humidity: 70%
Wind Speed: 10.6 mph
DAYS
0º or below: 5
32º or below: 123
90º or above: 12
Clear: 66
Cloudy: 202

PRECIPITATION

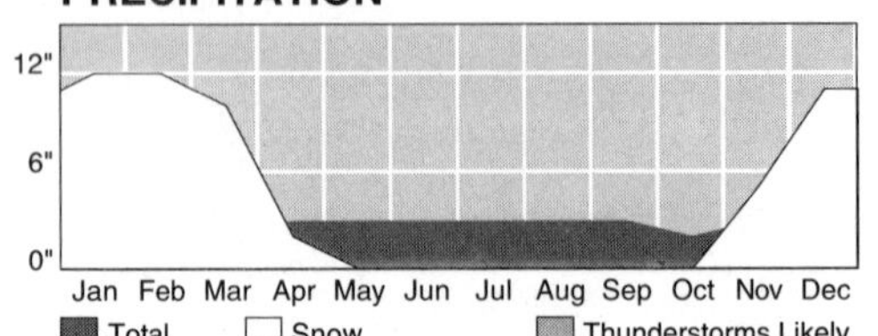

ANNUAL
Precipitation: 36.6"
Snow: 55.4"
DAYS
Precipitation: 80
Thunderstorm: 34

Colorado Springs, CO

Location: 38.49 N, 104.43 W, at 6,090 feet, on the eastern slope of Colorado's Rocky Mountains, 75 miles south of Denver.
Landscape: Relatively flat and gently undulating semiarid prairie land of eastern Colorado. High plains prairie meet the foothills of the Rockies with the typical prairie short grasses and woody shrubs. There are stands of mixed spruce-fir forests, especially over the lower foothills. Immediately to the west, the mountains rise abruptly to heights ranging from 10,000 feet to 14,000 feet. The land slopes upward to the north, reaching an average height of 8,000 feet within 20 miles at the top of Palmer Lake Divide.
Climate: Continental moderated by outlying elevations gives this area the pleasant plains-and-mountain mixture of climate that has established it as a resort. Precipitation is generally light, with 80 percent falling as rain from April to October. Temperatures are on the mild side for a city in this latitude and at this elevation.

Mildness: 26 Brightness: 83 Stability: 45

Places Rated Score: 37.21 **Places Rated Rank: 210**

TEMPERATURE

90º 65º 32º 0º

Jan Feb Mar Apr May Jun Jul Aug Sep Oct Nov Dec

Normal Daily High/Low ■ Apparent Temperature ■ Periods Of Discomfort

ANNUAL
Humidity: 51%
Wind Speed: 10.0 mph
DAYS
0º or below: 7
32º or below: 160
90º or above: 19
Clear: 127
Cloudy: 118

PRECIPITATION

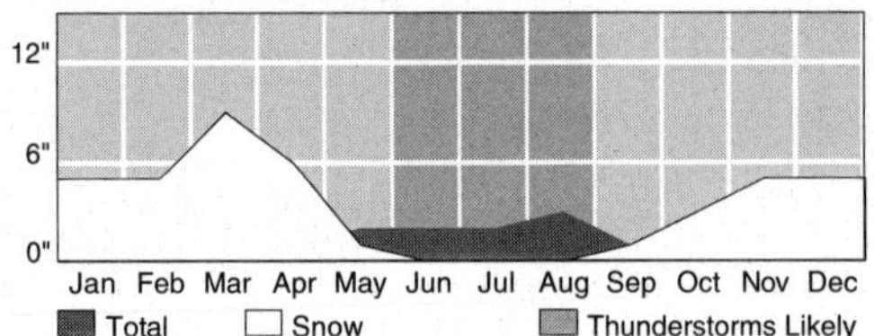

ANNUAL
Precipitation: 16.2"
Snow: 42.6"
DAYS
Precipitation: 27
Thunderstorm: 50

Columbia, MO

Location: 38.49 N, 92.13 W, at 890 feet, in north central Missouri in the valley of the Missouri River. Kansas City is 120 miles west; St. Louis 100 miles east.
Landscape: Gently rolling plains of the broad river valley. Just at the division between prairie and eastern forest ecologies with features of both. Vegetation is forest-steppe, an intermingling of prairie, groves and woodlands. Columbia's elevation is almost 900 feet, as the land slopes gradually to the western high prairie.
Climate: The interior location and wide temperature ranges indicate a Continental climate. Winters are moderately cold and summers warm, often humid. Each summer brings some temperatures over 100°F. Yet summer hot spells are relieved by thunderstorms, and winter cold snaps are often interrupted by days that are almost balmy, with temperatures as high as the 50s and 60s. The late spring and early summer months are the rainiest, but by late summer the rain diminishes so that by middle or late August, the moisture in the top 2 feet of soil is often depleted.

Mildness: 27 Brightness: 59 Stability: 19

Places Rated Score: 30.80 **Places Rated Rank: 249**

TEMPERATURE

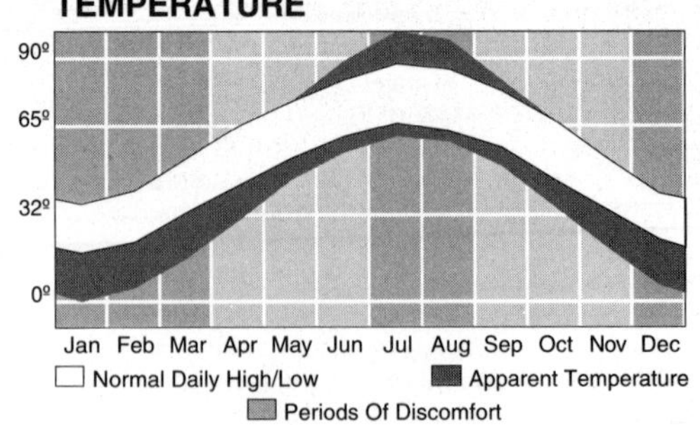

ANNUAL
Humidity: 72%
Wind Speed: 9.9 mph
DAYS
0º or below: 2
32º or below: 108
90º or above: 37
Clear: 104
Cloudy: 170

PRECIPITATION

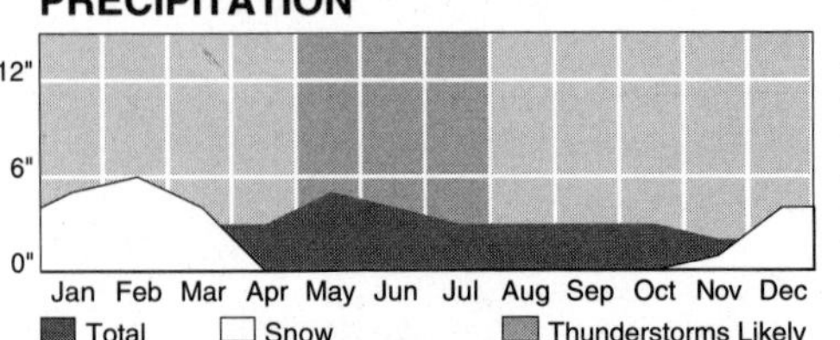

ANNUAL
Precipitation: 39.1"
Snow: 23.1"
DAYS
Precipitation: 60
Thunderstorm: 52

Columbia, SC

Location: 33.57 N, 81.07 W, at 210 feet, on the Congaree River in the center of the state, near the confluence of the Broad and Saluda rivers.
Landscape: The fall line, or division between the Piedmont and the Coastal Plain, is near Columbia. The soil ranges from sand to clay loam. Terrain is rolling, sloping from about 350 feet above sea level in the northern part of the city to about 200 feet at the city's southeastern edge. Trees common to the eastern deciduous forest are prevalent.
Climate: Although the Appalachians to the north shield the city from northern cold fronts in the winter, the surrounding gently rolling terrain offers little moderating effect on summer heat. Summers are long and hot, with high temperatures from May to September. Temperatures will surpass 100°F an average of six times a year. Winters are mild; only about a third of the days have freezing temperatures. Snow accumu- ... and may bring some

TEMPERATURE

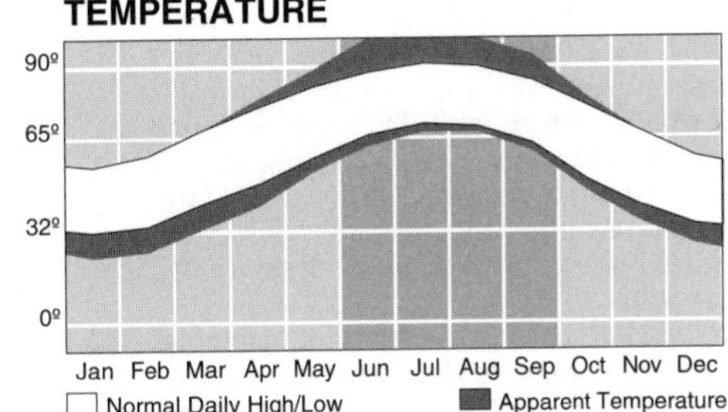

Normal Daily High/Low ■ Apparent Temperature ■ Periods Of Discomfort

ANNUAL
Humidity: 69%
Wind Speed: 6.9 mph
DAYS
0º or below: 0
32º or below: 58
90º or above: 77
Clear: 115
Cloudy: 147

PRECIPITATION

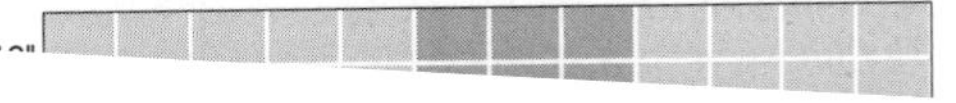

ANNUAL
Precipitation: 49.9"

Location: ... chee River at the western boundary of Georgia, ... miles west of the Atlantic and 170 miles north of the Gulf of Mexico.
Landscape: This is an area between the Coastal Plain and the Piedmont. Elevation ranges from between 200 feet and 500 feet. The terrain is basically level, and effects of terrain on climate are therefore negligible. Surrounding wooded areas include oak, hickory, and pine of the Southeastern Forest.
Climate: Subtropical with periods of Maritime and Continental effects. Rainfall averages 50 inches a year; the stormiest and wettest month is July, the driest October. Snow is rare but by no means unknown, with each winter bringing at least a few flakes. Most days from June through August will see temperatures of 90°F or higher, with uncomfortable humidity. The unpleasant effects of this heat are balanced by the mild winters, during which temperatures seldom drop below 20°F.

Mildness: 78 Brightness: 45 Stability: 19

Places Rated Score: 66.91 **Places Rated Rank: 93**

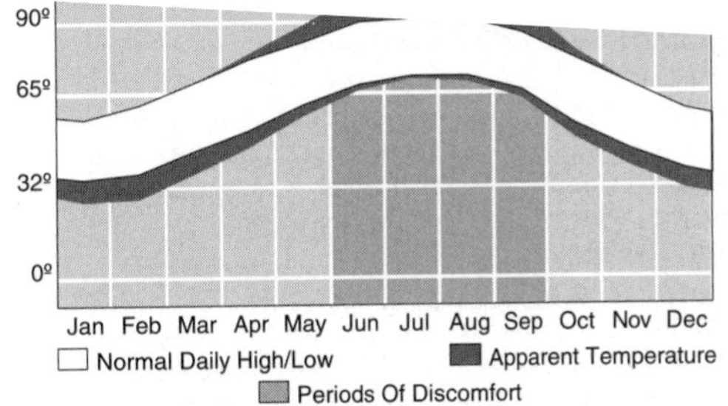

Normal Daily High/Low ■ Apparent Temperature ■ Periods Of Discomfort

Humidity: ...
Wind Speed: 6.8 mph
DAYS
0º or below: 0
32º or below: 43
90º or above: 77
Clear: 110
Cloudy: 151

PRECIPITATION

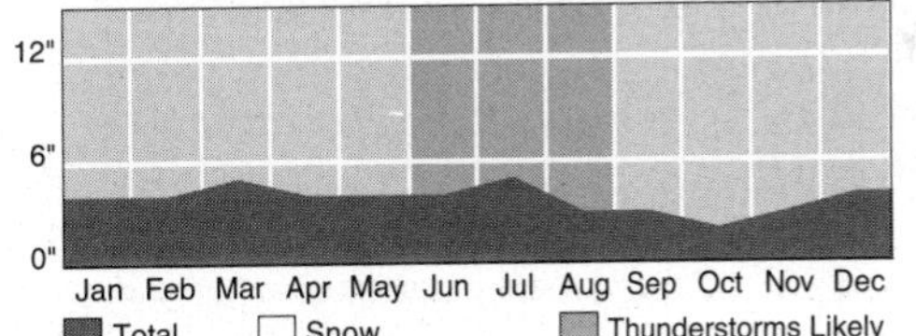

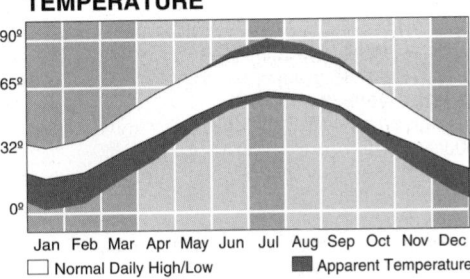

■ Total □ Snow ■ Thunderstorms Likely

ANNUAL
Precipitation: 51.0"
Snow: 0.5"
DAYS
Precipitation: 70
Thunderstorm: 55

Columbus, OH

Location: 40.00 N, 82.53 W, at 810 feet, in the center of the Ohio and in the drainage area of the Ohio River.
Landscape: Four small rivers—the Scioto, Alum, Big Walnut, and Olentangy—flow through and near the city. These are gorge-like in character with little floodplain. Tall, broadleafed trees are in wooded areas. Ash, elm, hickory, oak and maple are common.
Climate: The city is located in an area of changeable weather. Cold air masses from central and northwest Canada frequently invade the region. Tropical Gulf masses often reach central Ohio during the summer but to a much lesser extent in fall and winter. Temperatures in July are in the mid- to high 80s. There are more than 100 freezing days through the winter. Columbus's four rivers provide variations in the microclimate of the area, contributing to the formation of shallow ground fog at daybreak in the summer and fall.

Mildness: 36 Brightness: 20 Stability: 41

Places Rated Score: 33.85 **Places Rated Rank: 234**

TEMPERATURE

90º
65º
32º
0º
Jan Feb Mar Apr May Jun Jul Aug Sep Oct Nov Dec

□ Normal Daily High/Low ■ Apparent Temperature ■ Periods Of Discomfort

ANNUAL
Humidity: 69%
Wind Speed: 8.4 mph
DAYS
0º or below: 4
32º or below: 118
90º or above: 19
Clear: 72
Cloudy: 190

PRECIPITATION

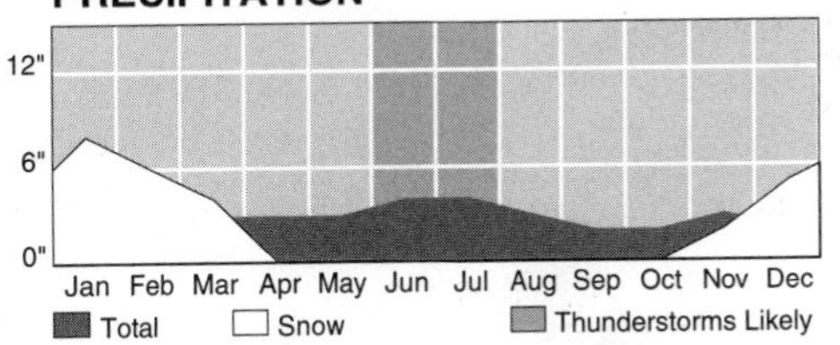

■ Total □ Snow ■ Thunderstorms Likely

ANNUAL
Precipitation: 38.1"
Snow: 27.6"
DAYS
Precipitation: 82
Thunderstorm: 40

✓Corpus Christi, TX

Location: 27.46 N, 97.30 W, at 40 feet, on Corpus Christi Bay in the southern part of the Texas Gulf coastline, roughly halfway between Galveston to the north and Brownsville to the south.
Landscape: Coastal prairie. Padre and Mustang Islands shelter the harbor from the Gulf. Long sand beaches and occasional salt marshes are common along the bay. Inland to the west are level black lands important in agriculture. The Bay is a landlocked harbor connected by a deep-water channel to the Gulf of Mexico.
Climate: Although on the Gulf, Corpus Christi has a climate midway between humid Subtropical conditions of the northeast Gulf Coast and the semiarid Desert ones to the west and southwest. Tropical storms, usual from June through November, add to the total rainfall. Peak rainfall months are May and September. Winter months are the driest. There is little variation in the summer temperature from day to day, which averages in the high 80s or low 90s. Nights are cooler, even pleasant, with temperatures dropping into the low 70s because of sea breezes.

Mildness: 91 Brightness: 74 Stability: 45

Places Rated Score: 85.62 **Places Rated Rank: 28**

TEMPERATURE

90º 65º 32º 0º
Jan Feb Mar Apr May Jun Jul Aug Sep Oct Nov Dec
Normal Daily High/Low Apparent Temperature
Periods Of Discomfort

ANNUAL
Humidity: 76%
Wind Speed: 12.0 mph
DAYS
0º or below: 0
32º or below: 7
90º or above: 106
Clear: 102
Cloudy: 142

PRECIPITATION

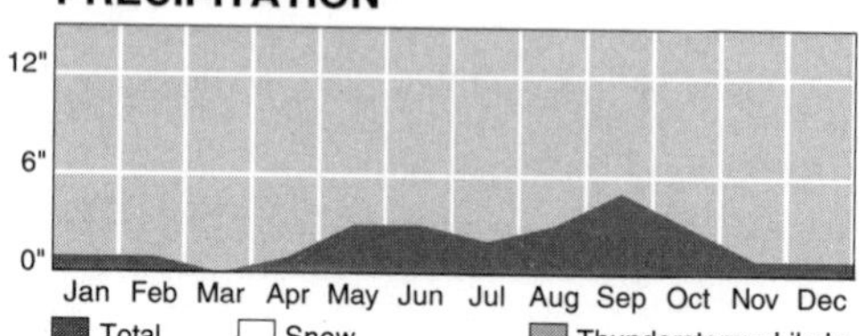

ANNUAL
Precipitation: 30.1"
Snow: 0.1"
DAYS
Precipitation: 38
Thunderstorm: 27

Dallas, TX

Location: 32.51 N, 96.51 W, at 440 feet, in north-central Texas, 190 miles NE of Austin, near the headwaters of the Trinity River.
Landscape: Located on flat prairies of the Coastal Plain on both sides of the Trinity River. The area is gently rolling river valley with ridge and bluff relief to the west. Forest-steppe vegetation is characterized by the intermingling of prairie, groves, and strips of deciduous trees. The upland forest is dominated by post oak, blackjack oak and Texas hickory.
Climate: Subtropical, with hot, humid summers. It is also Continental, characterized by a wide range in annual temperature. Winters tend to be mild, but northers occur, bringing cold air masses down from the Great Plains and the Rocky Mountains. These cold snaps are not prolonged, however. Much of the rain falls at night; downpours may accompany thunderstorms during April and May. July and August are relatively dry. Snowfall is slight and doesn't accumulate.

Mildness: 65 Brightness: 85 Stability: 18

Places Rated Score: 62.87 **Places Rated Rank: 117**

TEMPERATURE

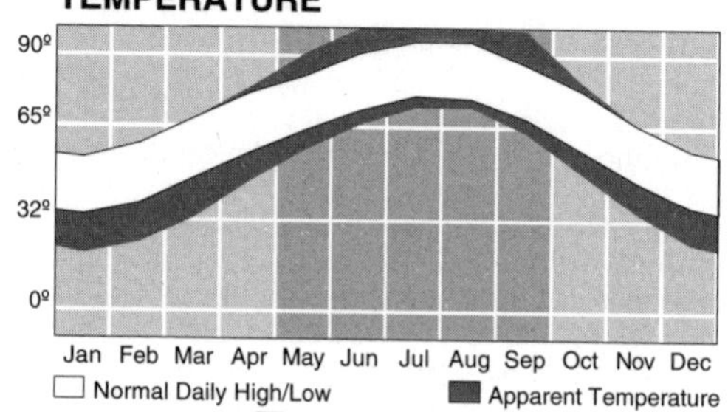

ANNUAL
Humidity: 69%
Wind Speed: 10.7 mph
DAYS
0º or below: 0
32º or below: 40
90º or above: 100
Clear: 135
Cloudy: 133

PRECIPITATION

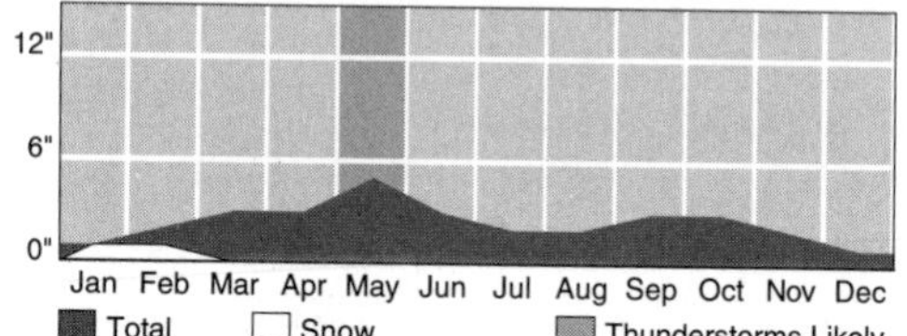

ANNUAL
Precipitation: 36.1"
Snow: 2.7"
DAYS
Precipitation: 49
Thunderstorm: 47

Davenport–Moline–Rock Island, IA–IL

Location: 41.35 N, 90.25 W, at 580 feet, on the banks of the Mississippi River in east central Iowa.
Landscape: The topography is characterized by rolling prairie. Close to the river there is considerable truck gardening and dairying. Field production of grains and livestock is greater away from the large streams.
Climate: Temperate Continental, with a wide temperature range throughout the year. There are some intensely hot, humid periods in summer and severely cold periods in winter. Nearness to major storm tracks brings substantial weather changes, frequently occurring at three- or four-day intervals. Maxima of 90°F or higher have occurred as frequently as 55 days a year (1936), but in 1882 there were none. Readings of zero or below have been made during every winter, ranging from 37 times in 1874–75 to one time during four other winters. The city experienced heavy flooding in 1993.

Mildness: 15 Brightness: 57 Stability: 29

Places Rated Score: 21.89 **Places Rated Rank: 310**

TEMPERATURE

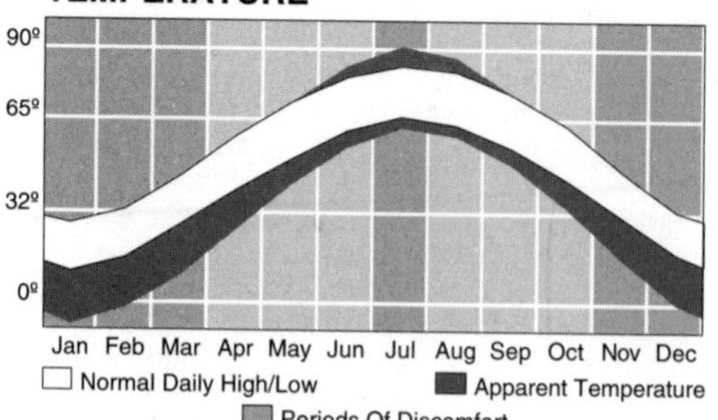

ANNUAL
Humidity: 70%
Wind Speed: 9.9 mph
DAYS
0º or below: 15
32º or below: 129
90º or above: 14
Clear: 101
Cloudy: 163

PRECIPITATION

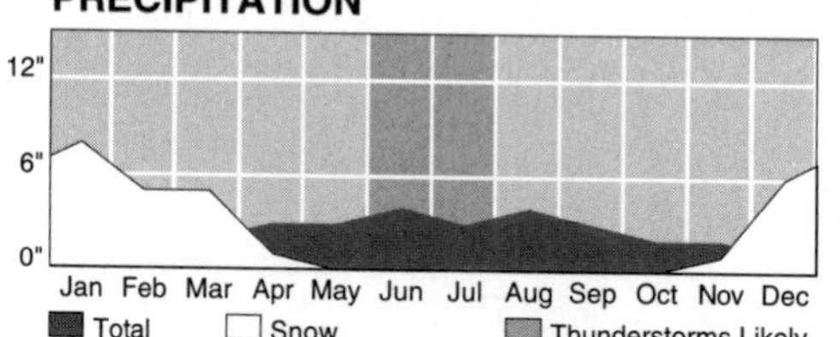

ANNUAL
Precipitation: 33.8"
Snow: 29.2"
DAYS
Precipitation: 61
Thunderstorm: 46

Dayton–Springfield, OH

Location: 39.53 N, 84.53 W, at 1,020 feet, near the center of the Miami River Valley, 50 miles north of Cincinnati at the forks of the Great Miami River.

Landscape: Dayton is 50 to 200 feet below the adjacent rolling country and spreads over the floodplain and into the surrounding hills. Three rivers converge from the north and join within the city limits flowing south to the Ohio River. Natural vegetation is pitch pine, large-leaf magnolia, and sourwood, as well as a hardwood forest of oak, hickory, yellow poplar, ash, and maple.

Climate: A moderating influence is brought by the downward slope of the Miami River. Cold, polar air flowing across the Great Lakes causes cloudiness during the winter, accompanied by frequent snow flurries, which add little to the total snowfall. Extreme temperatures are usually of short duration in either the summer or winter. High relative humidity during ... discomfort.

TEMPERATURE

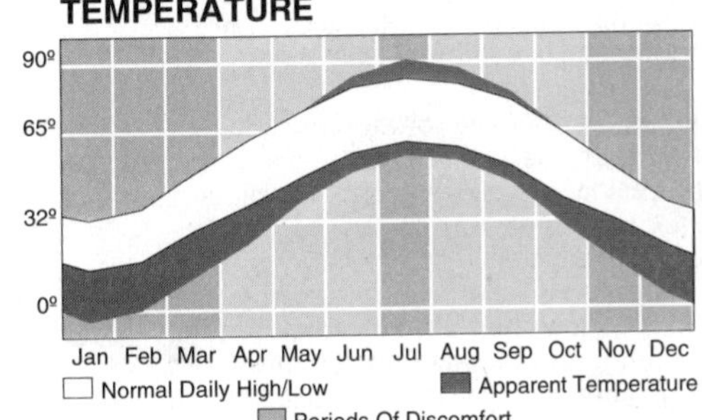

ANNUAL
Humidity: 70%
Wind Speed: 9.9 mph
DAYS
0º or below: 9
32º or below: 134
90º or above: 13
Clear: 76
Cloudy: 189

PRECIPITATION

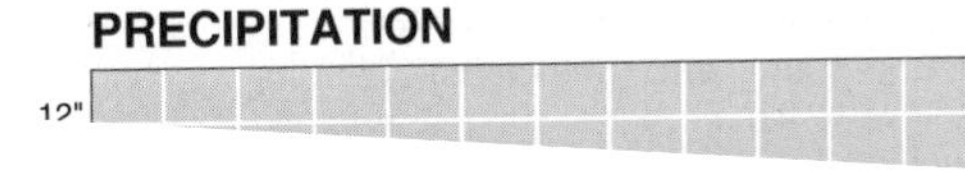

ANNUAL
Precipitation: 40.0"
Snow: 27.7"

...and Intracoastal Waterway along the state's ... tic coast, 60 miles north of Cape Canaveral.

Landscape: The surrounding land is flat, mainly the sandy soil of a tidewater lagoon, with no elevations above 35 feet. Coastal Plain vegetation in this region is palm and sea grape. The climax forest is evergreen-oak and magnolia. The hard white sand beach is 25 miles long and 500 feet wide at low tide.

Climate: Nearness to the ocean results in a climate tempered by land and sea breezes. Daytime June through September can be humid and hot. A sea breeze starts at midday, and afternoon thundershowers lower temperatures to comfortable levels. Winters can have cold airflows from the north, but usually are mild because of the city's ocean setting and southerly latitude.

Mildness: 94 Brightness: 16 Stability: 12

Places Rated Score: 79.91 **Places Rated Rank: 52**

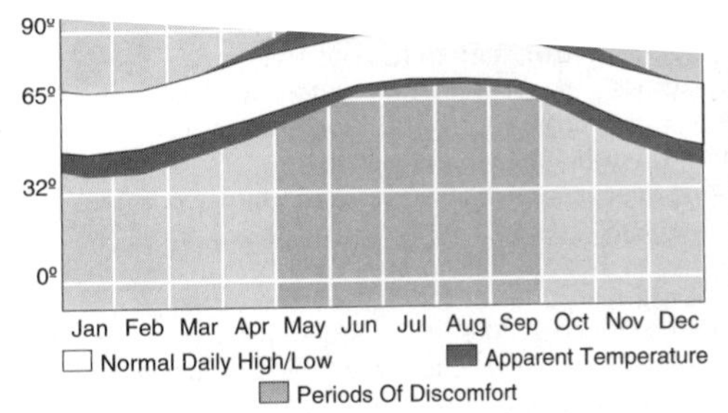

Wind Speed: 8.7 mph
DAYS
0º or below: 0
32º or below: 6
90º or above: 54
Clear: 97
Cloudy: 135

PRECIPITATION

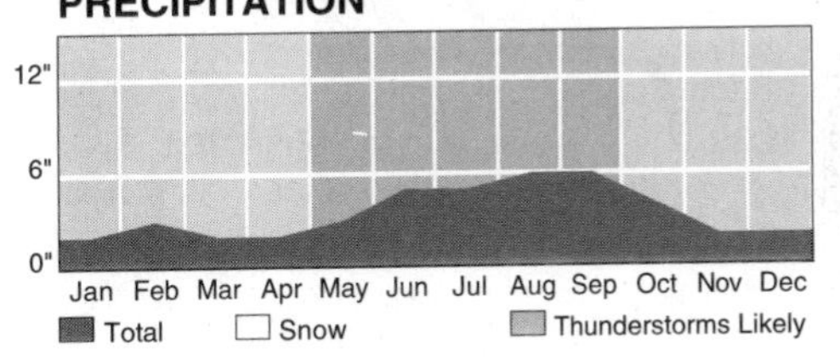

ANNUAL
Precipitation: 47.9"
Snow: 0.0"
DAYS
Precipitation: 80
Thunderstorm: 75

Denver, CO

Location: 39.46 N, 104.52 W, at 5,290 feet, the Mile-High City rests on the eastern slope of the Rocky Mountains in north central Colorado.

Landscape: Denver is far from any significant source of moisture and is isolated from the Pacific Ocean by three mountain ranges: the Coastal Ranges, the Sierra Nevada, and the Rockies. The Front Range of the Southern Rockies rises abruptly to 14,000 feet nearby, but the landscape of Denver proper is unimpressive prairie.

Climate: A mild, sunny, semiarid climate, reaching over much of the central Rocky Mountain region. There is little humidity or precipitation and lots of sunshine. During the cold months, invasion of cold air from the north can be abrupt and severe. Yet many of these air masses from Canada are too low to reach Denver and so are deflected off to the east by the mountains. For this reason, Denver often has milder winters than cities of comparable latitude on the Great Plains. Spring is wet, cloudy, and windy. Summers are cool. Fall is the most pleasant season.

Mildness: 30 Brightness: 80 Stability: 49

Places Rated Score: 40.33 **Places Rated Rank: 202**

TEMPERATURE

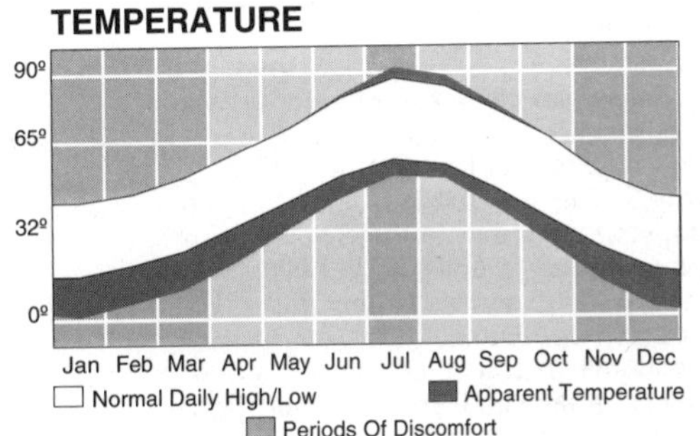

ANNUAL
Humidity: 54%
Wind Speed: 8.7 mph
DAYS
0º or below: 10
32º or below: 155
90º or above: 33
Clear: 115
Cloudy: 120

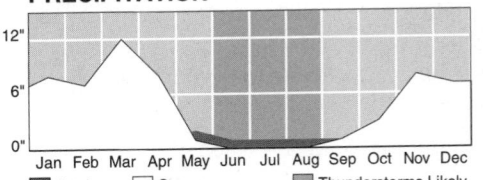

PRECIPITATION

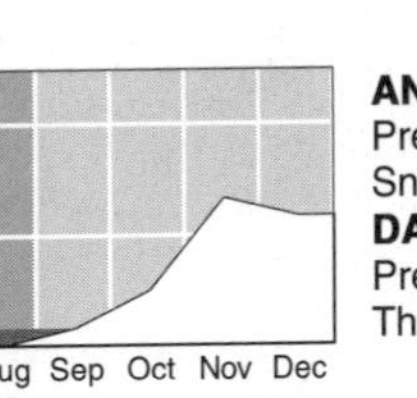

ANNUAL
Precipitation: 15.4"
Snow: 60.4"
DAYS
Precipitation: 34
Thunderstorm: 39

Des Moines, IA

Location: 41.32 N, 93.39 W, at 940 feet, close to the center of Iowa at the confluence of the Des Moines and Raccoon rivers and roughly in the geographic center of the continental United States.

Landscape: The terrain is flat to gently rolling prairie, ideally suited to agriculture. Most of the soil in Iowa is dark, rich, sandy loam with good drainage. The state has the highest rate of agricultural production per acre in the nation. Des Moines is the heart of the Corn Belt.

Climate: Situated in the center of the country, far from any large body of water, Des Moines has a Continental climate, characterized by rather long, cold winters, hot summers, and short springs and falls. Winter cold is often intensified by the winds that sweep over the flat land though bitterly cold days are rare. Prevailing winds are southerly and precipitation falls in showers or occasional thunderstorms from late April through October. Autumn is sunny with diminishing precipitation. The city suffered extensive damage from flooding in 1993.

Mildness: 11 Brightness: 69 Stability: 23

Places Rated Score: 18.89 **Places Rated Rank: 317**

TEMPERATURE

90º 65º 32º 0º

Jan Feb Mar Apr May Jun Jul Aug Sep Oct Nov Dec

Normal Daily High/Low · Apparent Temperature · Periods Of Discomfort

ANNUAL
Humidity: 70%
Wind Speed: 10.8 mph
DAYS
0º or below: 16
32º or below: 137
90º or above: 26
Clear: 104
Cloudy: 164

PRECIPITATION

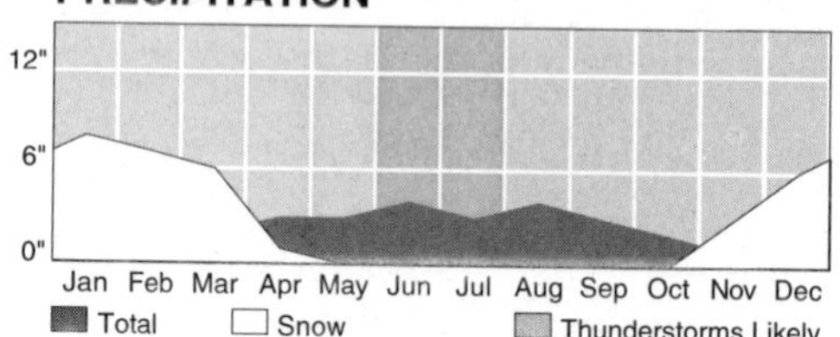

ANNUAL
Precipitation: 33.1"
Snow: 33.2"
DAYS
Precipitation: 54
Thunderstorm: 46

Detroit, MI

Location: 42.14 N, 83.20 W, at 630 feet, in the southeastern corner of the state, across the St. Clair River from Windsor, Ontario.

Landscape: One of the few metro areas that crosses international boundaries. Detroit lies on an important waterway that connects Lake Huron to Lake Erie. Nearly flat land slopes up gently from the water's edge northwestward for about 10 miles, then gives way to increasingly rolling terrain. The Irish Hills, about 40 miles northwest, are more than 1,000 feet high.

Climate: The winters, while cold, are modified by the Great Lakes, which warm and moisten the cold arctic air that passes over the northern Plains. As a result, the area is quite cloudy, especially in the winter. Summers in the city are warm and sunny. Brief showers can occur every few days but often fall on only part of the city. Winter storms may bring rain, snow, or both. Freezing rain and sleet are common.

Mildness: 23 Brightness: 37 Stability: 54

Places Rated Score: 28.30 **Places Rated Rank: 270**

TEMPERATURE

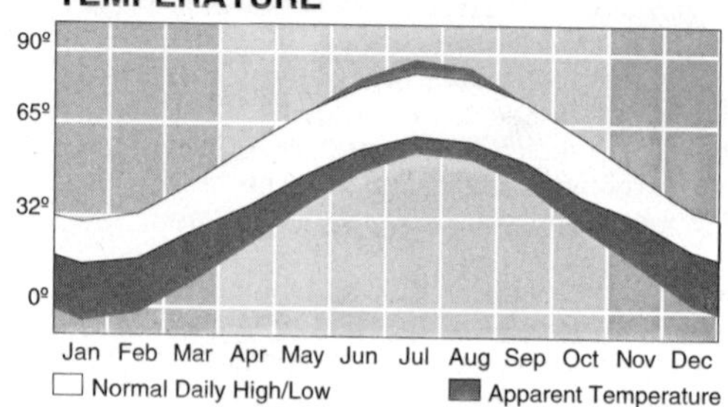

ANNUAL
Humidity: 70%
Wind Speed: 10.4 mph
DAYS
0º or below: 7
32º or below: 136
90º or above: 12
Clear: 75
Cloudy: 185

PRECIPITATION

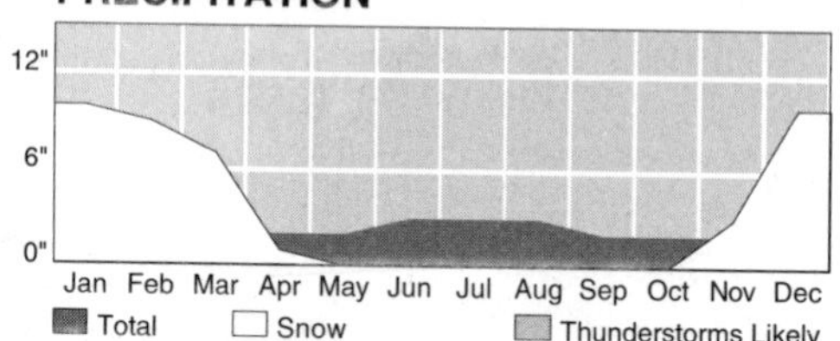

ANNUAL
Precipitation: 32.6"
Snow: 41.4"
DAYS
Precipitation: 65
Thunderstorm: 32

Duluth–Superior, MN–WI

Location: 46.50 N, 92.11 W, at 1,430 feet, Duluth is located at Lake Superior's western tip. Directly opposite, on the flats occupying the east banks of St. Louis Bay, lies the city of Superior, Wisconsin. These two cities are referred to as the Twin Ports.

Landscape: Duluth lies at the base of a range of hills that rise abruptly to between 600 feet and 800 feet above the lake level. Two or 3 miles back from the waterfront, however, the country assumes the character of a slightly rolling plateau. The Duluth–Superior harbor, the second largest of the Great Lakes ports, is ice-bound four months of the year.

Climate: Rugged Continental in character. Winters are long and quite cold. Snow comes early and remains on the ground until springtime. While the airport area to the north receives more than 75 inches of snow a year, the city proper receives only about 55 inches. Summers are seldom hot due to the northerly latitude and proximity of Lake Superior.

Mildness: 3 Brightness: 39 Stability: 60

Places Rated Score: 7.68 **Places Rated Rank: 345**

TEMPERATURE

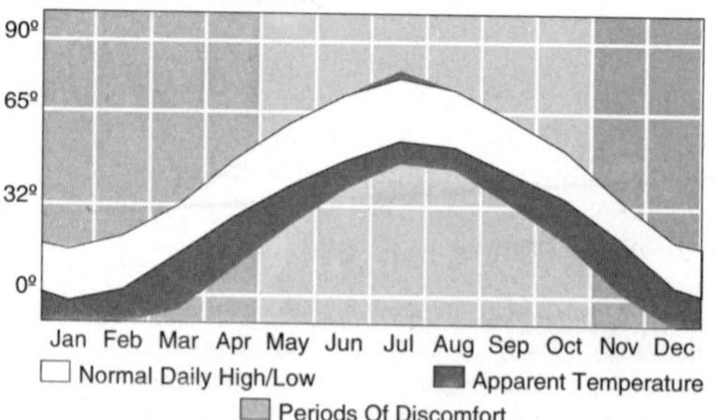

ANNUAL
Humidity: 72%
Wind Speed: 11.0 mph
DAYS
0º or below: 51
32º or below: 186
90º or above: 7
Clear: 77
Cloudy: 186

PRECIPITATION

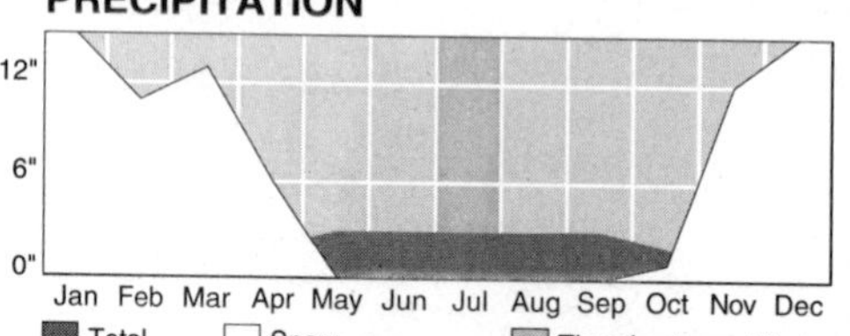

ANNUAL
Precipitation: 30.0"
Snow: 78.0"
DAYS
Precipitation: 60
Thunderstorm: 34

Edmonton, AB

Location: 53.34 N, 113.31 W, at 2,201 feet, occupies a rolling plain on both banks of the North Saskatchewan River in central Alberta.

Landscape: Elevation ranges are plus or minus 100 feet within a 10-mile radius. The land slopes off to the northeast and southeast, except for ridges 20 miles southeast and 20 miles west, which rise 350 feet above the airport elevation. The North Saskatchewan River flows northeast; the Sturgeon, a secondary river, lies 7 miles to the northwest.

Climate: Continental, characterized by two major seasons of summer and winter, with short, rarely orderly transitions of spring and autumn. The occurrence of snow divides the year. The warmer five months rarely have measurable snowfalls. The cooler five receive nearly all their precipitation as snow. The remaining two months, April and October, average half their totals as snow. Winter is characterized by a persistent snow cover that normally begins November 16 and stays through the season until around March 17.

TEMPERATURE

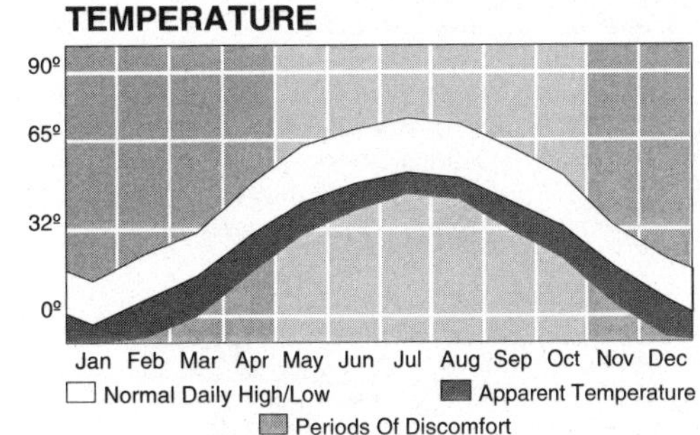

ANNUAL
Humidity: 68%
Wind Speed: 8.8 mph
DAYS
0º or below: 35
32º or below: 185
90º or above: 3
Clear: 99
Cloudy: 114

PRECIPITATION

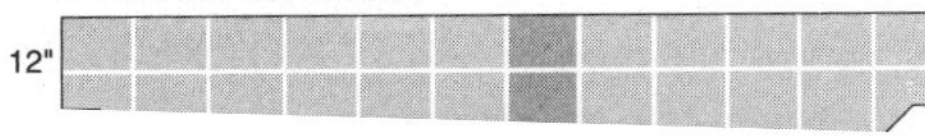

ANNUAL
Precipitation: 18.4"
Snow: 53.6"

Juarez, Mexico.

Landscape: High desert with typical sparse vegetation. Shrubs and cacti predominate. However, there is an underground lake that supplies abundant water. Mountains and mesas characterize the terrain. The Franklin Mountains begin within the city limits and extend northward some 16 miles. Some of these peaks reach as high as 4,500 feet to 5,000 feet above sea level. This is a region of cattle ranches and irrigated farms that produce cotton, fruits, and vegetables.

Climate: Semiarid Desert, dry and sunny. Summer temperatures are high but not extreme. The low relative humidity lessens the felt heat. The winter is mild, typical of arid areas at low altitudes. Rainfall is scarce year-round and fosters only scrublike desert vegetation. Irrigation is necessary for crops, gardens, and lawns. Winter nights can be cold, but the days are warm, averaging in the 50s. Similarly, summer days are hot but the nights cool, averaging in the 60s. Days can be windy, with annoying dust and sandstorms.

Mildness: 62 Brightness: 99 Stability: 37

Places Rated Score: 71.95 **Places Rated Rank: 75**

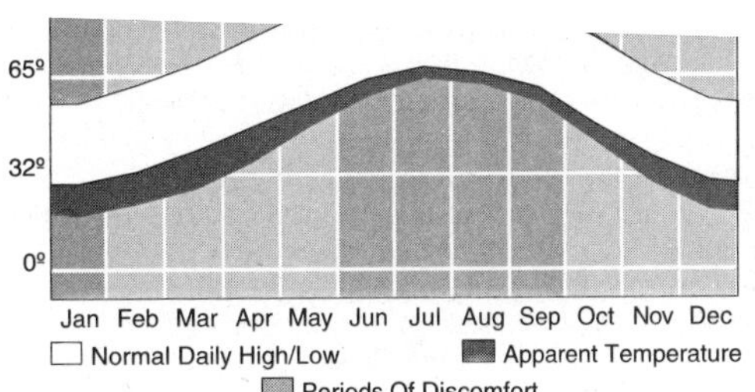

Wind Speed: 8.8 mph
DAYS
0º or below: 0
32º or below: 61
90º or above: 105
Clear: 192
Cloudy: 73

PRECIPITATION

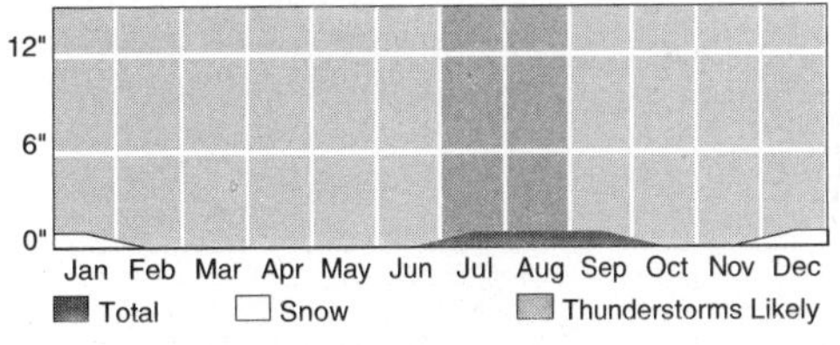

ANNUAL
Precipitation: 8.8"
Snow: 5.5"
DAYS
Precipitation: 22
Thunderstorm: 34

Eugene–Springfield, OR

Location: 44.07 N, 123.13 W, at 360 feet, at the southern end of the fertile Willamette Valley and bounded on both sides by mountain ranges. The Cascades lie east and the Coast Ranges west.

Landscape: To the north, the valley widens and levels out. Hills of the rolling, wooded Coast Ranges begin about 5 miles west of the airport and rise to between 1,500 feet and 2,000 feet midway between the city and the Pacific, 50 miles to the west. The Cascades, 75 miles east, reach heights of 10,000 feet. These sheltering ranges and the proximity of the ocean contribute to the extremely mild climate. This is one of the nation's most important agricultural and lumbering areas.

Climate: Mild Maritime climate. Temperature minima below 20°F occur only five times a year. The temperature rarely reaches the mid-90s. Seasonal change is gradual, with intermediate seasons being as long as summer and winter.

Mildness: 89 Brightness: 14 Stability: 97

Places Rated Score: 83.09 **Places Rated Rank: 39**

TEMPERATURE

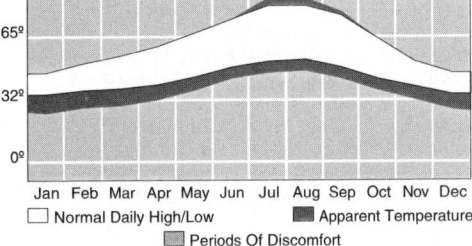

90º
65º
32º
0º
Jan Feb Mar Apr May Jun Jul Aug Sep Oct Nov Dec
Normal Daily High/Low Apparent Temperature
Periods Of Discomfort

ANNUAL
Humidity: 75%
Wind Speed: 7.6 mph
DAYS
0º or below: 0
32º or below: 54
90º or above: 15
Clear: 74
Cloudy: 209

PRECIPITATION

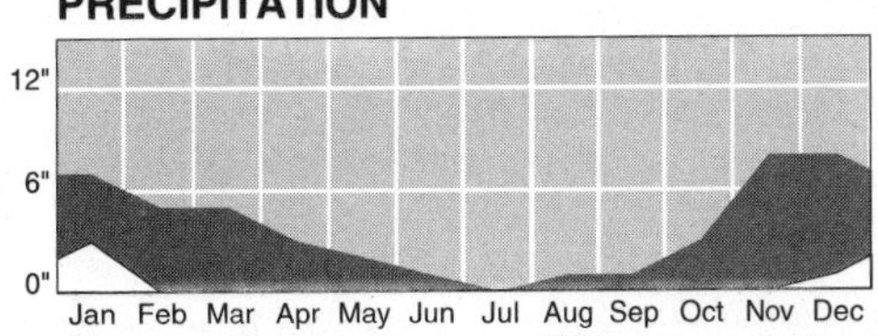

ANNUAL
Precipitation: 49.4"
Snow: 6.6"
DAYS
Precipitation: 90
Thunderstorm: 3

Evansville-Henderson, IN-KY

Location: 38.03 N, 87.32 W, at 380 feet, on the Ohio River near the juncture of Indiana, Illinois, and Kentucky.
Landscape: The country around Evansville ranges from level to rolling. Dress Regional Airport, where weather observations have been made since 1940, is in a shallow valley with low hills to the east and west that run parallel to the valley but slope downward to the south. The open end of this valley slopes down to the southwest toward Evansville and the Ohio River.
Climate: Prevailing wind here is from the south, and, although Evansville is 550 miles from the Gulf of Mexico, its weather generally resembles that of its neighbors to the south. Strong cold winds sometimes blow from the north and northwest following cold fronts. As soon as the high-pressure ridge moves by, the wind backs around again from the south. Snowfall varies a great deal from year to year; accumulation is rare. Average growing season: 199 days. Average date of last freeze: April 7. First freeze: October 23.

Mildness: 42 Brightness: 49 Stability: 28

Places Rated Score: 41.34 **Places Rated Rank: 199**

TEMPERATURE

90º 65º 32º 0º
Jan Feb Mar Apr May Jun Jul Aug Sep Oct Nov Dec
Normal Daily High/Low Apparent Temperature
Periods Of Discomfort

ANNUAL
Humidity: 70%
Wind Speed: 8.0 mph
DAYS
0º or below: 3
32º or below: 119
90º or above: 19
Clear: 102
Cloudy: 163

PRECIPITATION

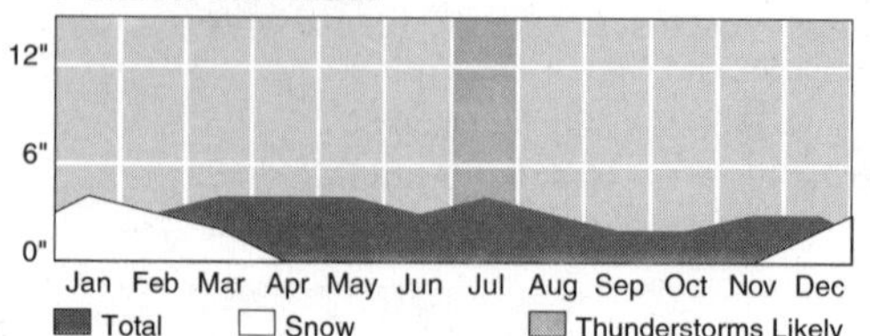

ANNUAL
Precipitation: 43.1"
Snow: 13.7"
DAYS
Precipitation: 73
Thunderstorm: 43

Fargo-Moorhead, ND-MN

Location: 46.54 N, 96.48 W, at 900 feet, these twin cities lie in the Red River Valley of the north.
Landscape: The river flows between the two cities and is part of the Hudson Bay drainage area. The river has no effect on the climate but does cause occasional, severe spring flooding. Surrounding terrain is flat, open, and fertile, suitable for crop and dairy farming.
Climate: Summers are generally comfortable, with a few days of hot and humid weather; nights are cool. Winter months are cold and dry, with maximum temperatures rising above freezing only six times per month. At night, the temperature drops below zero half the time. With the flat terrain, surface friction has little slowing effect on the wind, contributing to the legendary Dakota blizzards. Strong winds with even, light snowfall cause heavy snowdrifts. Surprisingly, the area averages less than 40 inches of snow per year.

Mildness: 1 Brightness: 74 Stability: 39

Places Rated Score: 6.06 **Places Rated Rank: 347**

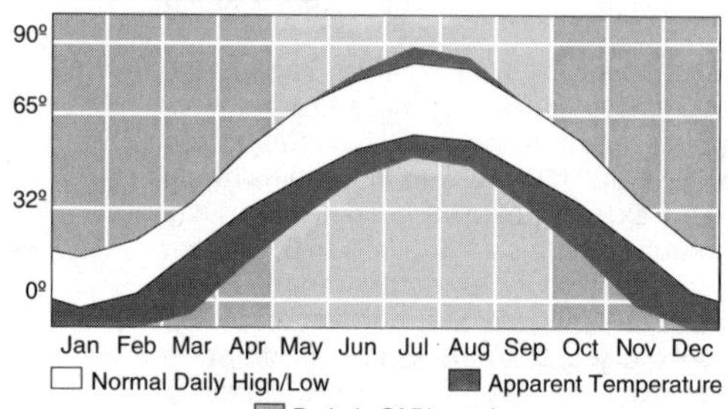

ANNUAL
Humidity: 71%
Wind Speed: 12.3 mph
DAYS
0º or below: 54
32º or below: 180
90º or above: 15
Clear: 88
Cloudy: 168

PRECIPITATION

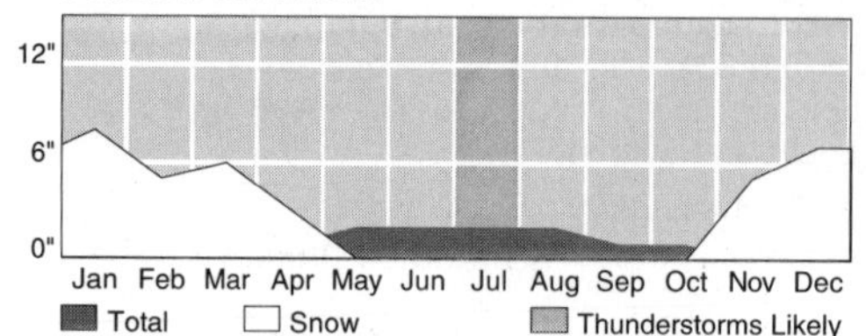

ANNUAL
Precipitation: 19.5"
Snow: 38.0"
DAYS
Precipitation: 48
Thunderstorm: 31

Fayetteville-Springdale-Rogers, AR

Location: 36.06 N, 94.10 W, at 1,270 feet, in northwestern Arkansas 50 miles north of Fort Smith.
Landscape: Situated on the White River in the Boston Mountains where elevations can reach over 2,000 feet. This is the highest part of the Ozark Plateau. Rugged, wooded mountain country of broadleaf deciduous oak and hickory with lower layers of weakly developed small trees and shrubs, redbud and dogwood.
Climate: Modified Continental, with hot, humid summers and briefer winters than other locations at this latitude. Winter to winter can vary from warm and humid Maritime to cold and dry Continental, but each winter is relatively free from climatic extremes. Snowfalls are minimal; precipitation in January and February falls as icy rain. Temperatures can be freezing or below from late November through February, but seldom are zero or below. Spring is likely to be a wet transition period from late February through April.

Mildness: 50 Brightness: 66 Stability: 26

Places Rated Score: 49.56 **Places Rated Rank: 170**

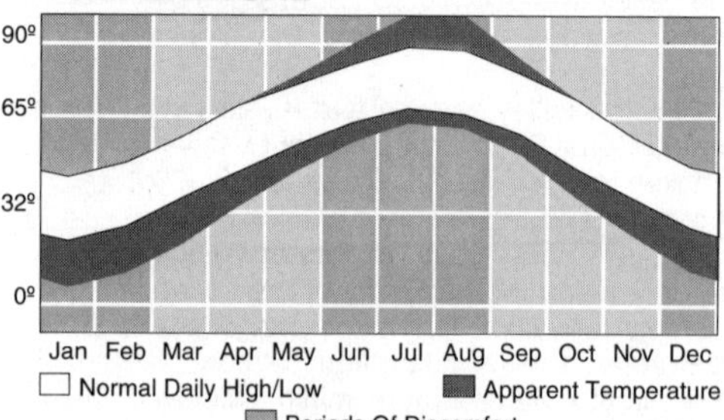

ANNUAL
Humidity: 69%
Wind Speed: 10.3 mph
DAYS
0º or below: 1
32º or below: 105
90º or above: 56
Clear: 126
Cloudy: 136

PRECIPITATION

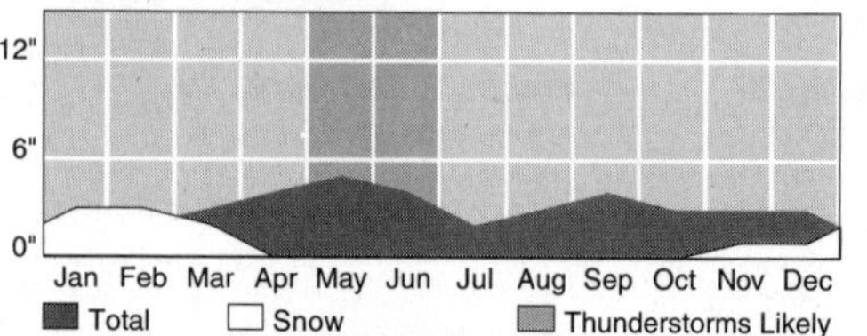

ANNUAL
Precipitation: 44.0"
Snow: 11.3"
DAYS
Precipitation: 62
Thunderstorm: 50

Flagstaff, AZ–UT

Location: 35.08 N, 111.40 W, at 7,000 feet, in Coconino County, 80 miles south of the Grand Canyon and 125 miles NE of Phoenix.

Landscape: Part of a geographic region known as the Colorado Plateau, a series of generally level plateaus, mostly separated by steep-sided chasms. There is little arable land. The highest point in Arizona is Humphreys Peak in the San Francisco Mountains, near Flagstaff. The city sits on the northern border of the Prescott National Forest. Lumbering is an important economic base for the area.

Climate: Vigorous, cool to cold winters, warm summers. In Flagstaff the mean January temperature is 28°F, and the mean July temperature is 66°F. Flagstaff proper gets about 13 inches of precipitation yearly, though surrounding mountains and plateaus receive somewhat more moisture, 20 to 40 inches, with up to 5 feet of snow falling in peak areas. Accumulations vary from year to year.

TEMPERATURE

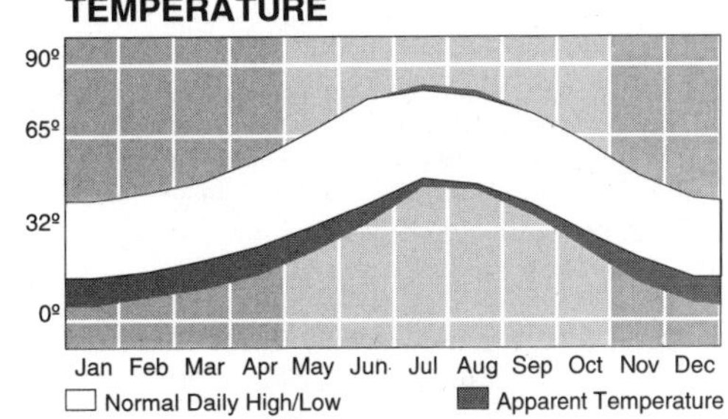

ANNUAL
Humidity: 54%
Wind Speed: 6.5 mph
DAYS
0º or below: 8
32º or below: 210
90º or above: 1
Clear: 162
Cloudy: 101

PRECIPITATION

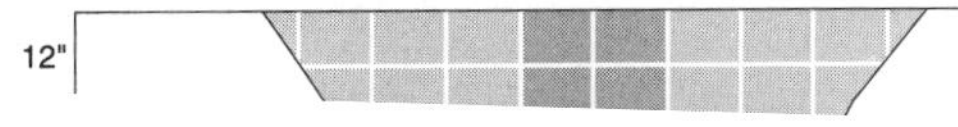

ANNUAL
Precipitation: 22.8"

Range, 55 miles north of Denver.

Landscape: Lies in some of the most spectacular mountain terrain in the country. Steep, nearly vertical, cliffs, high waterfalls, and forested mountain slopes cut by swift rivers are all found to the west. Within 30 miles to the east, the landscape settles into grassland prairies of the Great Plains. Semiarid steppe prairie has scattered shrubs and low trees.

Climate: Near the center of the continent, Fort Collins and Loveland are removed from any major source of airborne moisture and are further shielded from rainfall by the high Rockies to the west. The four seasons are well defined. There are sunny days year-round. In wintertime, cold airmasses from Canada may bring temperatures well below zero at night. In summer, hot, dry air from the desert to the southwest brings with it daytime temperatures of 90°F. However, low humidity makes it comfortable.

Mildness: 26 Brightness: 81 Stability: 44

Places Rated Score: 36.57 **Places Rated Rank: 216**

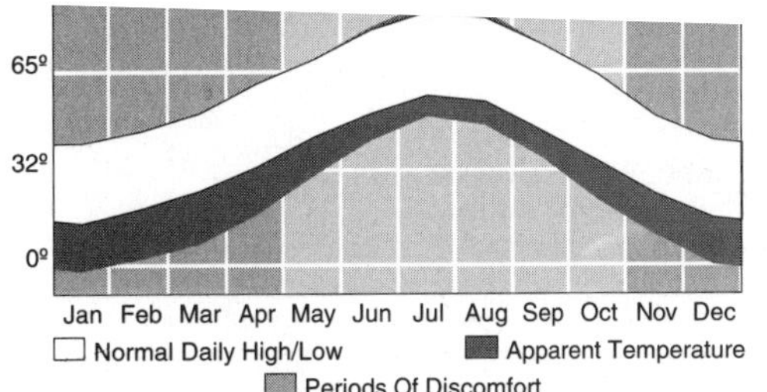

Wind Speed: 10.0 mph
DAYS
0º or below: 11
32º or below: 167
90º or above: 22
Clear: 127
Cloudy: 118

PRECIPITATION

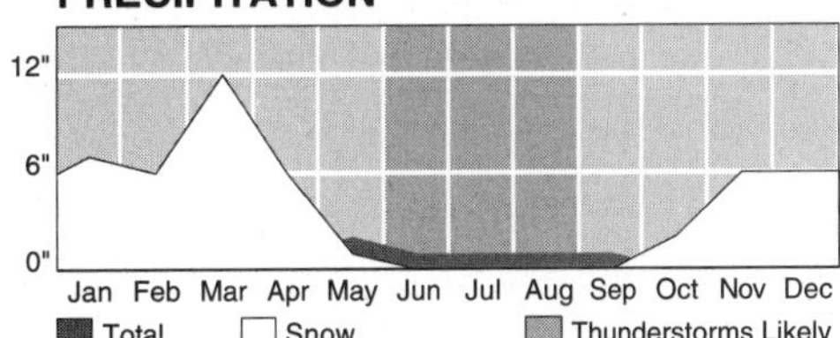

ANNUAL
Precipitation: 15.1"
Snow: 50.5"
DAYS
Precipitation: 33
Thunderstorm: 50

Fort Myers–Cape Coral, FL

Location: 26.35 N, 81.52 W, at 20 feet, on the broad Caloosahatchee River in southwestern Florida, 120 miles SSE of Tampa.

Landscape: The city is the western terminus of the cross-state Okeechobee Waterway, linking the Atlantic Ocean and the Gulf of Mexico. The land is level and low. The climax growth of the coastal plain in this area north of the Everglades is evergreen-oak and magnolia. Spanish moss trails from live oak and bald cypress. Tree ferns, small palms and shrubs make up the lower layer.

Climate: Subtropical as summer and winter temperature extremes are checked by the influence of the Gulf. Mild winters have many bright, warm days. Nights are moderately cool. Rainfall averages more than 50 inches annually, with two-thirds of this total coming daily between June and September. Most rain falls as late afternoon or early evening thunderstorms, bringing welcome relief from the heat.

Mildness: 96 Brightness: 17 Stability: 5

Places Rated Score: 81.51 **Places Rated Rank: 44**

TEMPERATURE

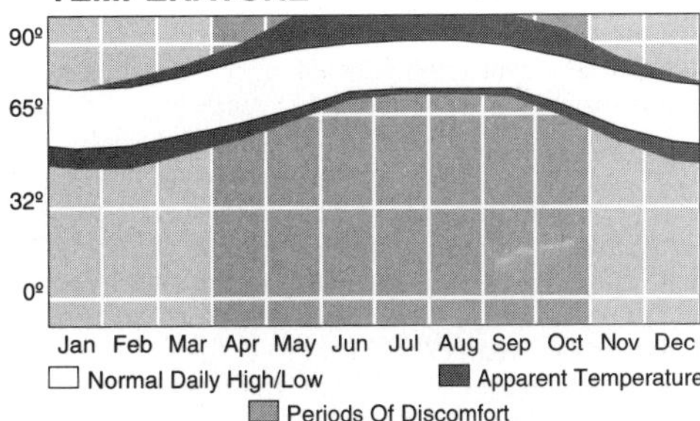

ANNUAL
Humidity: 72%
Wind Speed: 8.0 mph
DAYS
0º or below: 0
32º or below: 1
90º or above: 114
Clear: 98
Cloudy: 99

PRECIPITATION

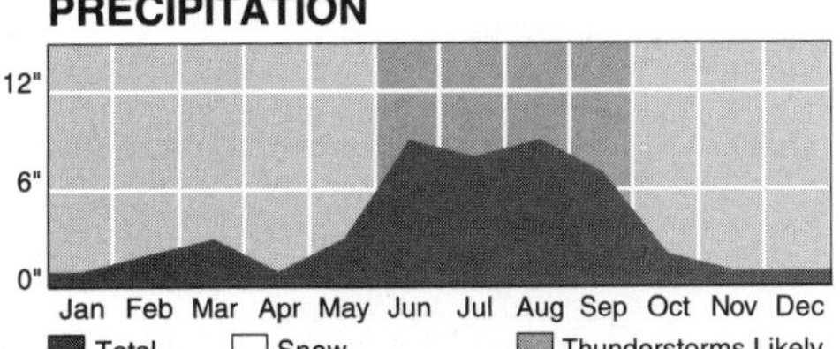

ANNUAL
Precipitation: 53.4"
Snow: 0.0"
DAYS
Precipitation: 71
Thunderstorm: 89

Fort Smith, AR–OK

Location: 35.20 N, 94.22 W, at 450 feet, at the confluence of the Poteau and Arkansas rivers in the western part of the state.
Landscape: About 20 miles to the northwest are the Cookson Hills, which have an elevation of 1,500 feet. To the northeast, the Boston Mountains of the Ozark region of Arkansas rise 2,700 feet. West, south, and east, the terrain is broken hills separated by creek and river-bottom land. The bottomlands are fertile and produce large yields of hay, beans, and spinach. Small wild game is plentiful; lakes and streams have an abundance of fish. The economy is based on the deposits of coal and natural gas, timber, and fertile farmlands of the surrounding region.
Climate: Hot Continental. Well suited to raising fruits and berries. This is Arkansas wine country. The climate is generally mild, except during the summer, which can be hot. Precipitation is markedly greater in the summer months.

Mildness: 56 Brightness: 67 Stability: 13

Places Rated Score: 51.52 **Places Rated Rank: 165**

TEMPERATURE

90º 65º 32º 0º
Jan Feb Mar Apr May Jun Jul Aug Sep Oct Nov Dec
Normal Daily High/Low ■ Apparent Temperature ■ Periods Of Discomfort

ANNUAL
Humidity: 70%
Wind Speed: 7.6 mph
DAYS
0º or below: 0
32º or below: 77
90º or above: 77
Clear: 123
Cloudy: 147

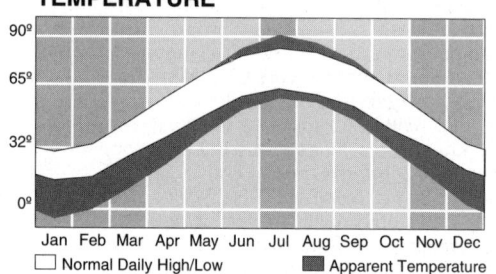

PRECIPITATION

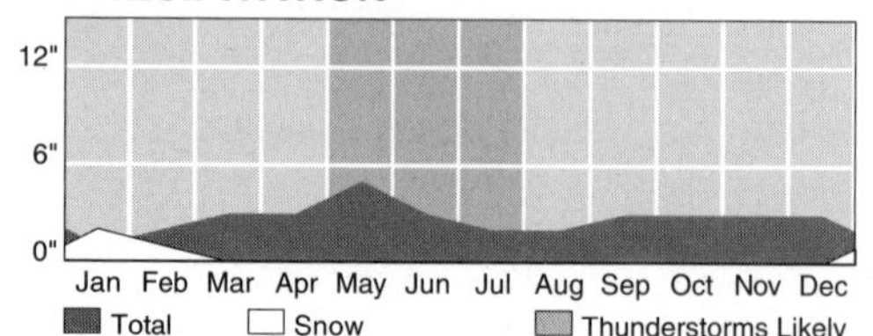

ANNUAL
Precipitation: 40.9"
Snow: 6.3"
DAYS
Precipitation: 62
Thunderstorm: 57

Fort Wayne, IN

Location: 41.00 N, 85.12 W, at 790 feet, at the junction of the St. Mary's, St. Joseph, and Maumee rivers in northeast Indiana.
Landscape: Terrain is generally level south and east of the city. Southwest and west, the land is somewhat rolling, while to the northwest and north it becomes hilly. The highest point in the area is 40 miles north, near the town of Angola, where the elevation is 1,060 feet above sea level.
Climate: Similar to that of other midwestern cities at the same latitude. Precipitation is well distributed throughout the year, varying from a monthly rate of 2 inches in February to 4 inches in May. Damaging hailstorms may be expected twice a year. Snow usually covers the ground for 30 days each winter, but heavy snowstorms are rare. Average date of last freeze is in late April and the first freeze in mid-October.

Mildness: 22 Brightness: 35 Stability: 38

Places Rated Score: 25.27 **Places Rated Rank: 296**

TEMPERATURE

90º 65º 32º 0º
Jan Feb Mar Apr May Jun Jul Aug Sep Oct Nov Dec
Normal Daily High/Low ■ Apparent Temperature ■ Periods Of Discomfort

ANNUAL
Humidity: 72%
Wind Speed: 10.0 mph
DAYS
0º or below: 10
32º or below: 131
90º or above: 16
Clear: 78
Cloudy: 185

PRECIPITATION

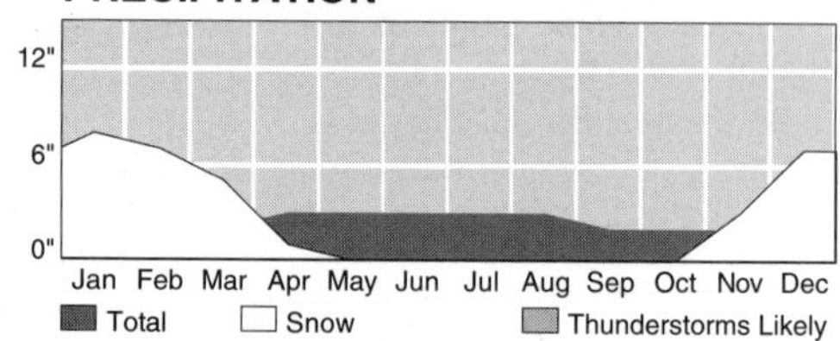

ANNUAL
Precipitation: 34.8"
Snow: 32.9"
DAYS
Precipitation: 71
Thunderstorm: 39

Fresno, CA

Location: 36.47 N, 119.43 W, at 340 feet, in the middle of the long San Joaquin Valley near its eastern edge.
Landscape: The valley runs northwest to southeast and is about 225 miles long, with an average width of about 50 miles. The terrain around Fresno is generally level, with an abrupt upward slope 15 miles eastward to the foothills of the Sierra Nevada. This mountain range lies 50 miles to the east and has elevations from 12,000 feet to 14,000 feet. Forty-five miles to the west lie the foothills of the Coast Ranges.
Climate: Dry and sunny. Winters are mild with 90 percent of the city's precipitation falling between November and April. Summers are hot and there is less humidity. They are virtually rainless. Because of the great amount of sunshine the valley receives, and the blockage of cooler moist air from the Pacific, daily maximum temperatures in July climb to the upper 90s.

Mildness: 74 Brightness: 100 Stability: 77

Places Rated Score: 84.07 **Places Rated Rank: 36**

TEMPERATURE

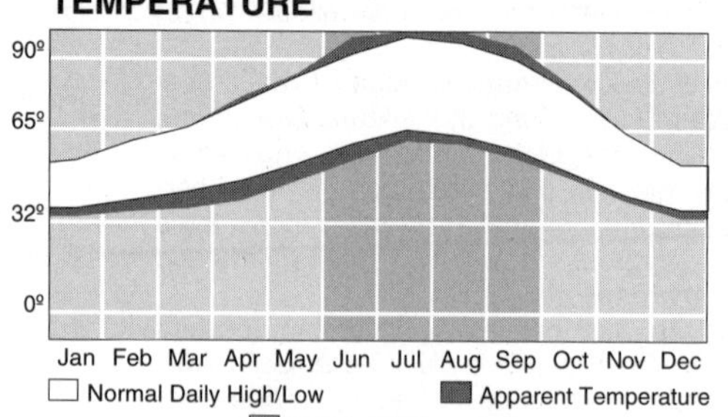

ANNUAL
Humidity: 59%
Wind Speed: 6.4 mph
DAYS
0º or below: 0
32º or below: 26
90º or above: 105
Clear: 195
Cloudy: 97

PRECIPITATION

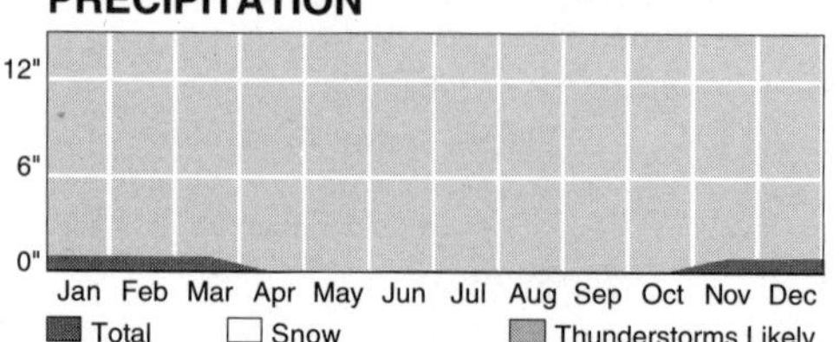

ANNUAL
Precipitation: 10.6"
Snow: 0.1"
DAYS
Precipitation: 26
Thunderstorm: 5

Gainesville, FL

Location: 29.41 N, 82.16 W, at 140 feet, in north-central Florida, 66 miles SW of Jacksonville and midway between the Atlantic Coast and the Gulf of Mexico.

Landscape: The terrain is rolling ranch and farm country with several lakes to the east and south. Geological relief includes sinkholes and caverns in this area of Florida's underlying limestone. There are swamps, flatwoods forest with longleaf and slash pines. Gallberry, saw palmetto, and fetterbush are the undergrowth. Plants and animals normally found in ravines of the Appalachian Mountains are at home here.

Climate: Subtropical in character, with a small annual range of temperature changes. Humid, hot summers are cooled by frequent, heavy afternoon thunderstorms. While winters are mild there can be freezing temperatures a dozen times a year; October through mid-April, it is mostly dry and clear with warm days and cool nights.

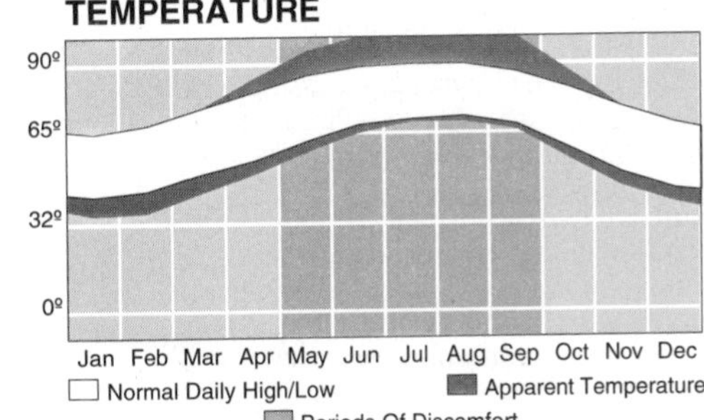

ANNUAL
Humidity: 76%
Wind Speed: 6.7 mph
DAYS
0º or below: 0
32º or below: 12
90º or above: 78
Clear: 102
Cloudy: 134

PRECIPITATION

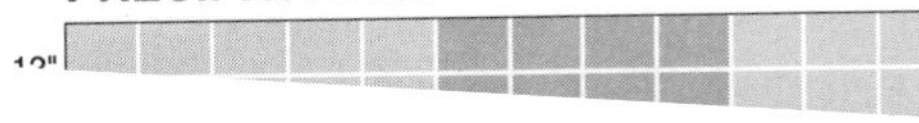

ANNUAL
Precipitation: 51.8"

off the southeast coast of Texas, 49 miles

Landscape: The island is nearly 3 miles across at its widest point and 29 miles long. It is typical of barrier islands with wide, sandy beaches and salt marshes. Palms, oleander, bougainvillea, and other subtropical plants flourish. The island's low-lying terrain makes it especially vulnerable to tidal surges.

Climate: Predominantly mild Marine. Though cold fronts from the northwest can sometimes reach the coast, winters tend to be mild. Temperatures go below freezing perhaps four times a year. Normal daily maximum temperatures range from 60°F in January to 88°F in August, while minimums range from 48°F in January to the upper 70s in the summer. Hurricanes are possible and tropical rains with high winds likely.

Mildness: 90 Brightness: 28 Stability: 19

Places Rated Score: 76.66 **Places Rated Rank: 58**

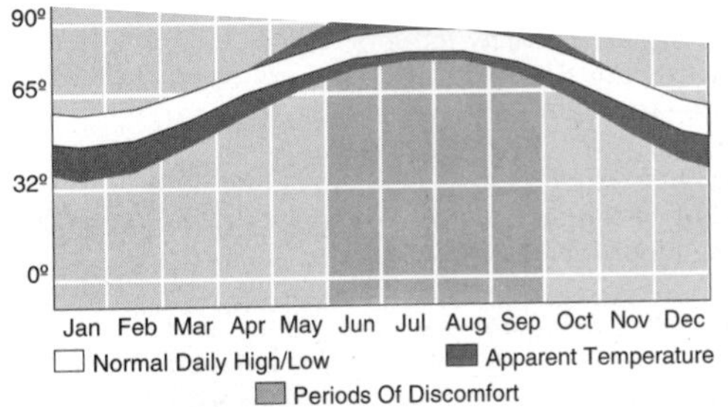

Wind Speed: 11.0 mph
DAYS
0º or below: 0
32º or below: 24
90º or above: 96
Clear: 96
Cloudy: 155

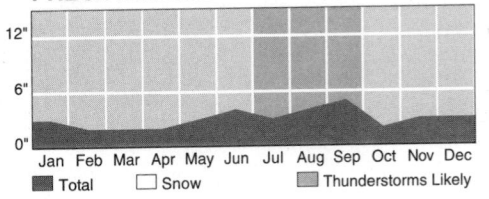

PRECIPITATION

ANNUAL
Precipitation: 42.3"
Snow: 0.2"
DAYS
Precipitation: 67
Thunderstorm: 62

Grand Junction, CO

Location: 39.06 N, 108.33 W, at 4,840 feet, in the Grand Valley of western Colorado, at the junction of the Colorado and Gunnison rivers, 20 miles east of the Utah border.

Landscape: Nearby is the lake-studded Grand Mesa, the Colorado National Monument, and the Grand Mesa and Uncompahgre National Forests. Sagebrush and cactus can be found in the canyons. Pine, spruce, and aspen forests cover the subalpine areas. Shortgrass prairie, bunched and sparsely distributed, scattered trees and shrubs are the growth in the desert plateau.

Climate: The interior location, coupled with the ring of high mountains, results in low rainfall. Agriculture depends heavily on irrigation, derived from mountain streams and runoff. Winter snows are frequent but light and do not remain long. In the summer, relative humidity is low, making the region as dry as parts of Arizona. Sunny days predominate in all seasons. The city's climate is marked by wide seasonal temperature changes, but thanks to the protection of the surrounding mountains, sudden and severe weather changes are infrequent.

Mildness: 20 Brightness: 96 Stability: 28

Places Rated Score: 34.36 **Places Rated Rank: 229**

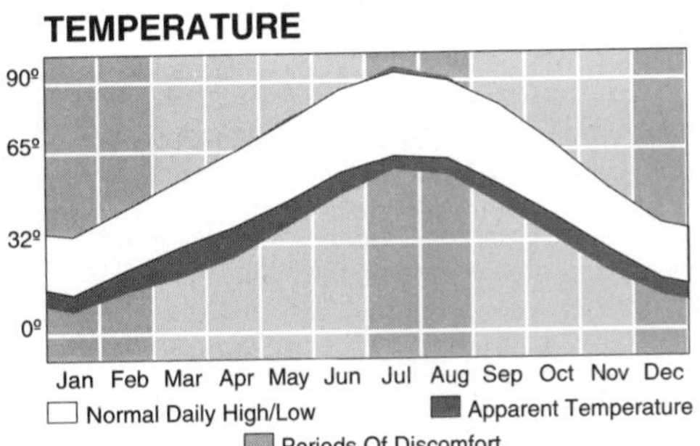

ANNUAL
Humidity: 48%
Wind Speed: 8.1 mph
DAYS
0º or below: 5
32º or below: 134
90º or above: 62
Clear: 136
Cloudy: 122

PRECIPITATION

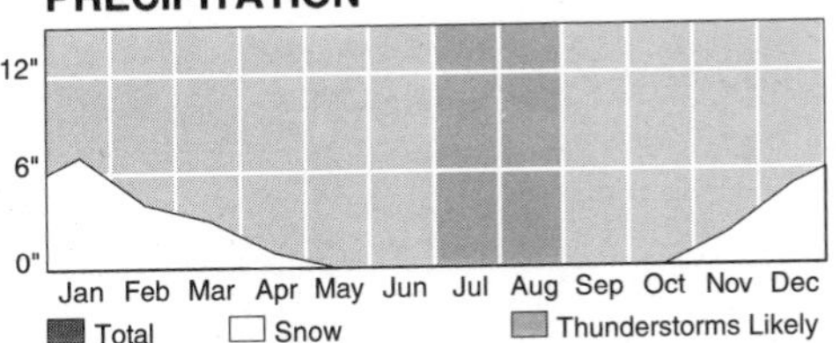

ANNUAL
Precipitation: 8.6"
Snow: 25.1"
DAYS
Precipitation: 27
Thunderstorm: 36

Grand Rapids–Muskegon–Holland, MI

Location: 42.53 N, 85.31 W, at 780 feet, in the Grand River valley 30 miles east of Lake Michigan.
Landscape: The Grand River, Michigan's largest stream, bisects the city. The valley has tall hills and bluffs rising on all sides, ranging in elevation from 600 feet to 1,000 feet. The area is known for fruit growing, especially peaches and cherries.
Climate: Largely determined by the proximity of Lake Michigan. In spring, the cooling effect of the lake retards the growth of vegetation until the danger of frost is past. In the fall, the warming effect holds off frost until the crops have matured. Summer days are warm and pleasant, with cooler nights. Winters are snowy and cold, but extremely cold temperatures or prolonged cold spells are rare because of the warm lake breeze. Average growing season: 170 days. Average date of last freeze: April 25. First freeze: October 12.

Mildness: 19 Brightness: 20 Stability: 55

Places Rated Score: 22.61 **Places Rated Rank: 308**

TEMPERATURE

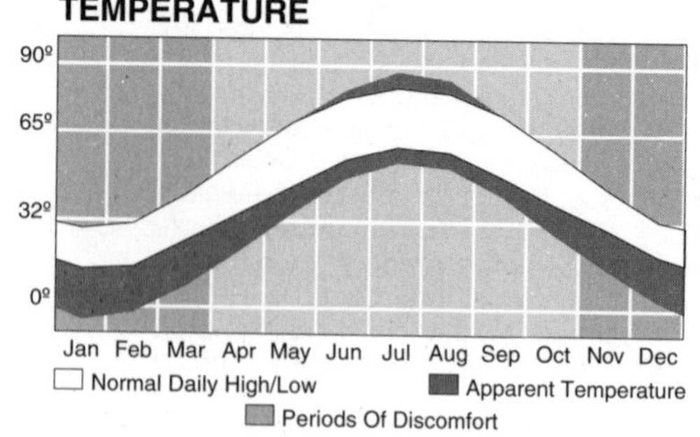

ANNUAL
Humidity: 72%
Wind Speed: 9.8 mph
DAYS
0º or below: 8
32º or below: 146
90º or above: 11
Clear: 64
Cloudy: 206

PRECIPITATION

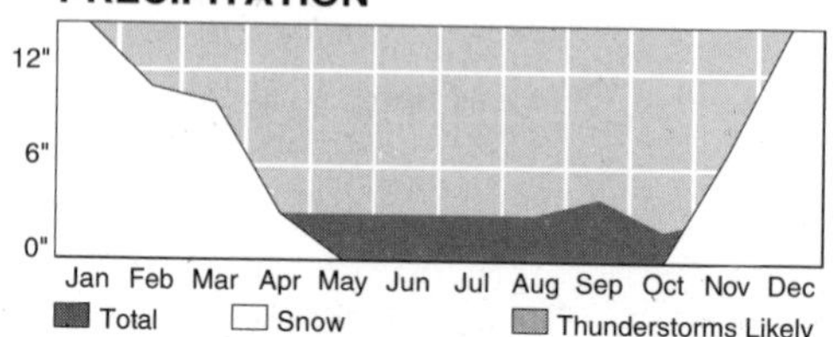

ANNUAL
Precipitation: 36.0"
Snow: 71.6"
DAYS
Precipitation: 75
Thunderstorm: 34

Great Falls, MT

Location: 47.29 N, 111.22 W, at 3,660 feet, astride the main stem of the Missouri River at its confluence with the Sun River in west-central Montana.
Landscape: The valley is bordered by mountain ranges that lie about 30 miles away from east to south, 40 miles to the southwest, and 60 miles to 100 miles from west to northwest. Terrain plays an important part in the climate here; the Continental Divide to the west and the Big Belt and Little Belt mountains to the south are major factors in producing the frequent wintertime Chinook winds blowing through this part of the state.
Climate: Semiarid Steppe. Summers are cool, sunny, and pleasant. Seventy percent of the annual rainfall occurs between April and September, the growing season. Winters are cold but continually modified by Chinook winds, which bear warm air from the Pacific, causing rapid warming and preventing accumulation of snow.

Mildness: 15 Brightness: 69 Stability: 75

Places Rated Score: 27.94 **Places Rated Rank: 271**

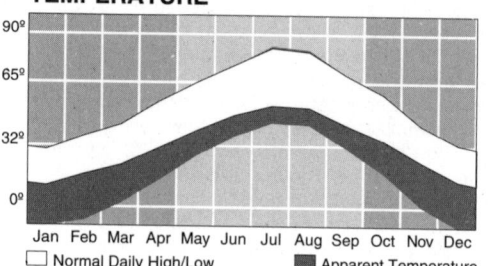

TEMPERATURE

90º
65º
32º
0º
Jan Feb Mar Apr May Jun Jul Aug Sep Oct Nov Dec
Normal Daily High/Low
Apparent Temperature
Periods Of Discomfort

ANNUAL
Humidity: 56%
Wind Speed: 12.7 mph
DAYS
0º or below: 28
32º or below: 155
90º or above: 18
Clear: 79
Cloudy: 180

PRECIPITATION

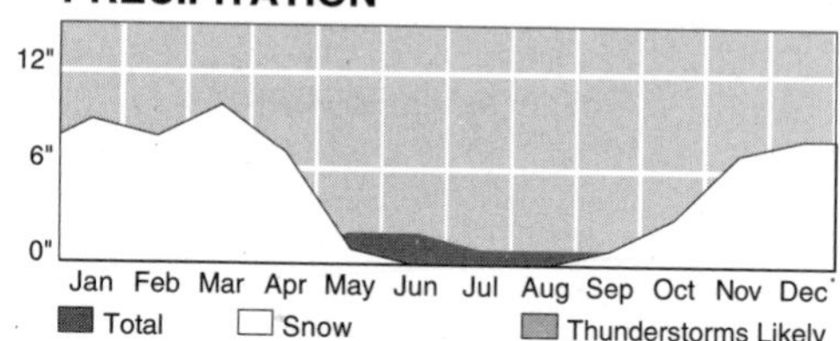

ANNUAL
Precipitation: 15.2"
Snow: 59.1"
DAYS
Precipitation: 32
Thunderstorm: 25

Green Bay, WI

Location: 44.29 N, 88.08 W, at 700 feet, at the mouth of the Fox River, which empties into the southmost end of Green Bay, a long and narrow bay off Lake Michigan in northeast Wisconsin.
Landscape: The comparatively small temperature variation and the fact that the majority of precipitation falls during the growing periods contribute to successful dairy farming, as well as large acreages of vegetables, grown mostly for canning. Apple and cherry orchards predominate locally, with potatoes grown widely farther west.
Climate: Continental, modified somewhat by the proximity of Lake Superior to the northwest and Lake Michigan and Green Bay to the east. Summers are pleasant, with cool evenings and nights. Thunderstorms and heavy rains can be expected in late summer and fall. Winters tend to be long and cold. The area experiences a moderate amount of snow for a city in this region and latitude.

Mildness: 8 Brightness: 45 Stability: 55

Places Rated Score: 15.82 **Places Rated Rank: 330**

TEMPERATURE

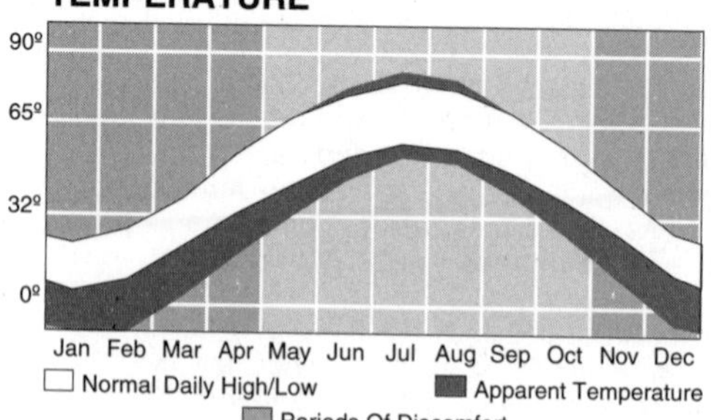

ANNUAL
Humidity: 73%
Wind Speed: 9.9 mph
DAYS
0º or below: 29
32º or below: 163
90º or above: 7
Clear: 86
Cloudy: 177

PRECIPITATION

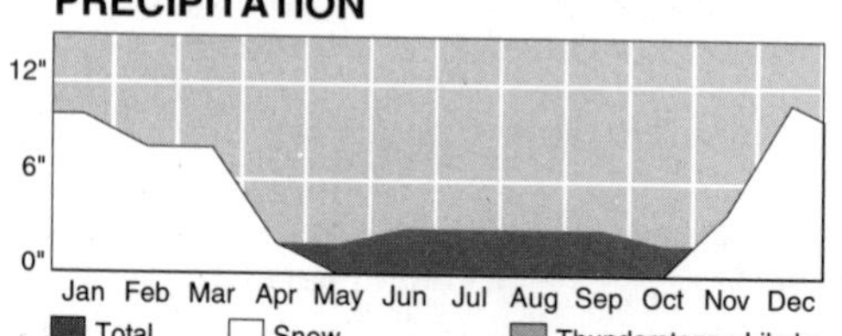

ANNUAL
Precipitation: 28.8"
Snow: 46.1"
DAYS
Precipitation: 63
Thunderstorm: 33

Greensboro–Winston-Salem–High Point, NC

Location: 36.05 N, 79.57 W, at 900 feet, in the northern Piedmont section of north-central North Carolina at the headwaters of the Haw and Deep rivers.
Landscape: Bounded to the west and north by ridges beyond which lie the Brushy and Blue Ridge mountains, respectively. Gently rolling hills merging to higher elevations. Red clay soil dominates and heavy applications of lime and fertilizers are necessary for good crop yields. There are no major rivers but a dense network of streams keeps the area well-drained.
Climate: Winter temperatures and rainfall are both modified by the mountain barrier. Freezing temperatures occur on more than half the winter days, but zero weather is almost unknown. Light snow may fall, perhaps two snows of an inch or more per year; ice-glazing is more common here than in most of North Carolina—an average of four times a year—but it is seldom severe or long-lasting.

Mildness: 64 Brightness: 56 Stability: 42

TEMPERATURE

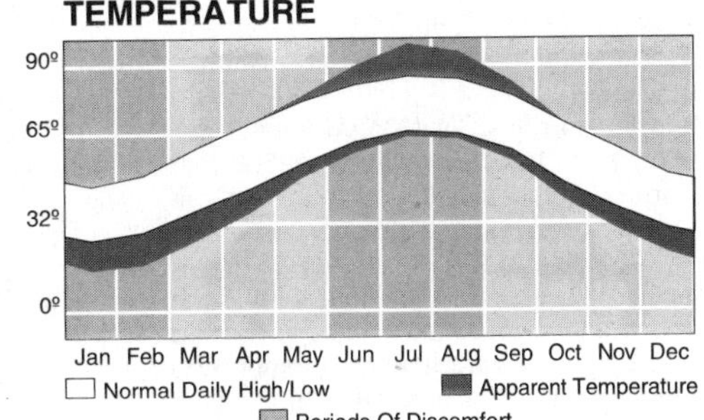

ANNUAL
Humidity: 69%
Wind Speed: 7.5 mph
DAYS
0º or below: 0
32º or below: 85
90º or above: 32
Clear: 109
Cloudy: 149

PRECIPITATION

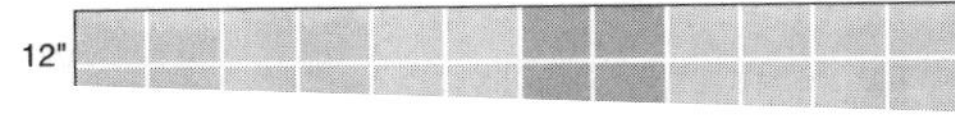

ANNUAL
Precipitation: 42.6"

Landscape: The inner Coastal Plain is higher and better drained than the Tidewater. The Coastal Plain is fronted with pines. Sandy soils dominate the plain; red clay dominates in the Piedmont. The area is an overlapping ecological zone, and vegetation is both mid-latitude and subtropical.
Climate: Subtropical, with humid hot summers and winters that are generally mild. There are no zero degree days. Mountains to the north and northwest protect the area from cold fronts. Rain falls throughout the year with thunderstorms peaking in July and August. Occasional storms from the Atlantic may strike this location.

Mildness: 75 Brightness: 42 Stability: 37

Places Rated Score: 66.21 **Places Rated Rank: 97**

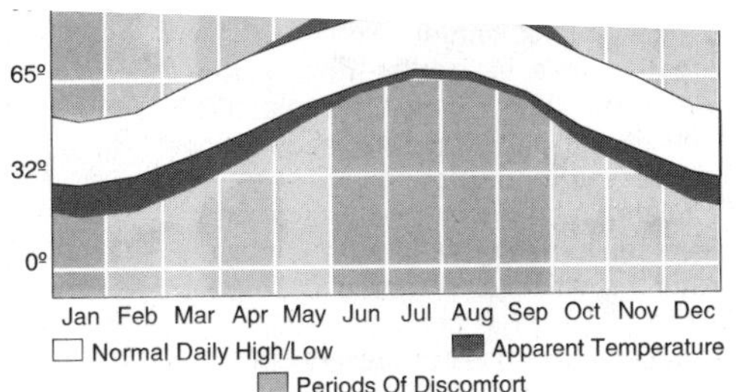

Wind Speed: 7.8 mph
DAYS
0º or below: 0
32º or below: 77
90º or above: 39
Clear: 110
Cloudy: 149

PRECIPITATION

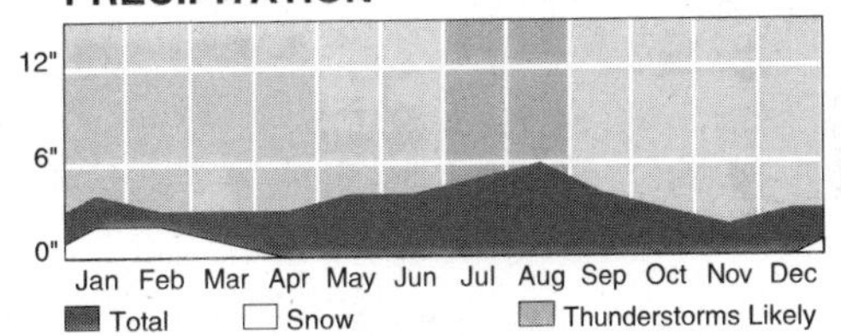

ANNUAL
Precipitation: 49.0"
Snow: 7.0"
DAYS
Precipitation: 77
Thunderstorm: 42

Greenville–Spartanburg–Anderson, SC

Location: 34.54 N, 82.13 W, at 860 feet, on the Piedmont Plateau, on the eastern slope of the southern Appalachian Mountains.
Landscape: Rolling country with the first ridge of mountains about 20 miles to the northwest. These mountains protect the area from the full force of the cold air masses that move southeastward from central Canada during the winter.
Climate: The area's elevation is conducive to cool nights, even during the summer. The temperature rises to 90°F or above on almost half of the days during the summer but then falls to 70°F or lower at night. Winters are mild and pleasant, with the temperature falling below freezing during daylight hours only several times annually, though the nights are colder. There are usually two freezing rainstorms and two or three small snowstorms each winter. Rainfall is abundant and well distributed throughout the year. The region is fairly stormy, but tornadoes are infrequent. Average growing season: 225 days.

Mildness: 76 Brightness: 41 Stability: 38

Places Rated Score: 66.93 **Places Rated Rank: 92**

TEMPERATURE

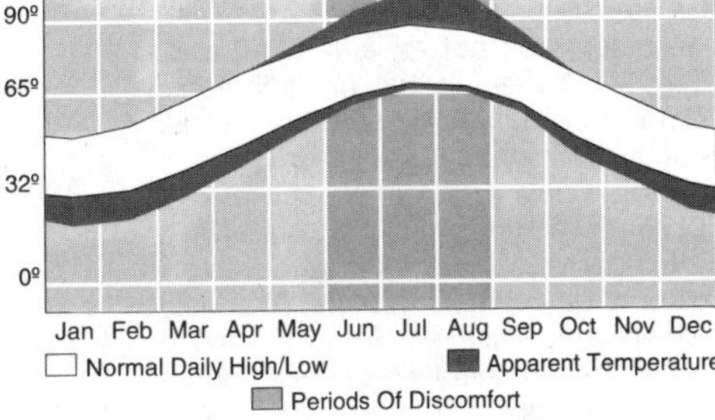

ANNUAL
Humidity: 68%
Wind Speed: 7.0 mph
DAYS
0º or below: 0
32º or below: 68
90º or above: 29
Clear: 121
Cloudy: 144

PRECIPITATION

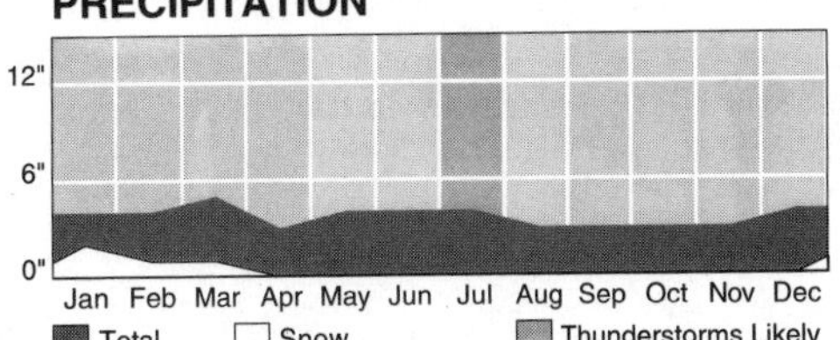

ANNUAL
Precipitation: 51.3"
Snow: 6.3"
DAYS
Precipitation: 81
Thunderstorm: 44

Halifax, NS

Location: 44.38 N, 63.30 W, at 476 feet, lies on the west side of the harbor on a peninsula with the Gulf of St. Lawrence to the north, the Bay of Fundy to the west, and the Atlantic Ocean to the south and east.
Landscape: The area is flat to rolling, with numerous small lakes, especially to the north and east. Elevations of 500 feet are reached in three areas in the vicinity: 11 miles to the north, 21 miles to the north-northwest in the Devon area, and in the Mt. Uniacke area, 25 miles to the northwest.
Climate: Each year there is an average of 122 days with fog at the International Airport. Atlantic and Fundy waters help to keep the air temperature cool in spring and summer and moderate the harshness of winter. The presence of the Gulf Stream is credited with prolonging fall—the season Nova Scotians consider to be the finest of the year. Atlantic storms produce highly changeable weather; winter storms are especially devastating.

Mildness: 48 Brightness: 1 Stability: 95

Places Rated Score: 42.25 **Places Rated Rank: 196**

TEMPERATURE

90º 65º 32º 0º
Jan Feb Mar Apr May Jun Jul Aug Sep Oct Nov Dec
Normal Daily High/Low Apparent Temperature Periods Of Discomfort

ANNUAL
Humidity: 80%
Wind Speed: 11.2 mph
DAYS
0º or below: 2
32º or below: 146
90º or above: 0
Clear: 88
Cloudy: 163

PRECIPITATION

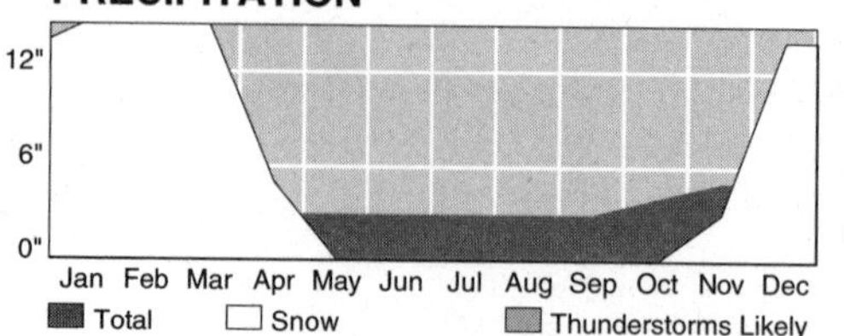

ANNUAL
Precipitation: 53.7"
Snow: 78.2"
DAYS
Precipitation: 138
Thunderstorm: 10

Harrisburg–Lebanon–Carlisle, PA

Location: 40.13 N, 76.51 W, at 340 feet, on the east bank of the Susquehanna River in the Great Valley formed by the eastern foothills of the Appalachian chain and about 60 miles southeast of the state's geographic center.
Landscape: Area is nestled in a saucerlike depression 8 miles to 10 miles south of the Blue Ridge Mountains. This serves as a barrier to the severe winter weather experienced 50 miles to 100 miles to the north and west. Although Harrisburg is too far inland to derive full benefits of the coastal climate, it does receive precipitation produced when warm, maritime air from the Atlantic is forced upslope to cross the mountains.
Climate: Although the saucer-shaped valley protects the area from generally severe winter weather, it often traps cool air, which causes the accumulation of heavy fog and industrial smoke. Fortunately, the weather is changeable enough so that this trapped air does not remain for long. Average growing season: 201 days.

Mildness: 43 Brightness: 34 Stability: 52

Places Rated Score: 42.44 **Places Rated Rank: 195**

TEMPERATURE

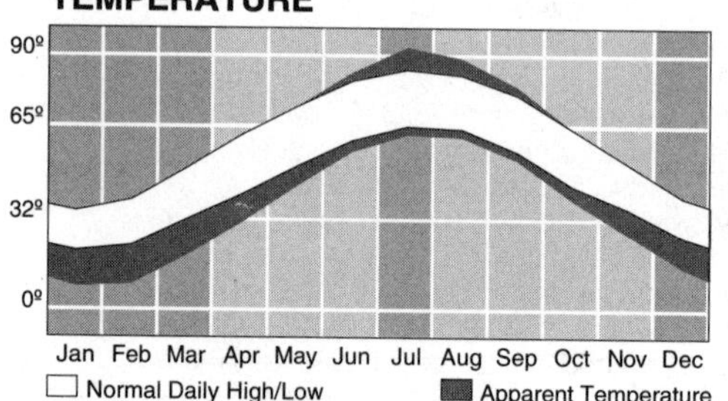

ANNUAL
Humidity: 65%
Wind Speed: 7.6 mph
DAYS
0º or below: 3
32º or below: 106
90º or above: 21
Clear: 87
Cloudy: 169

PRECIPITATION

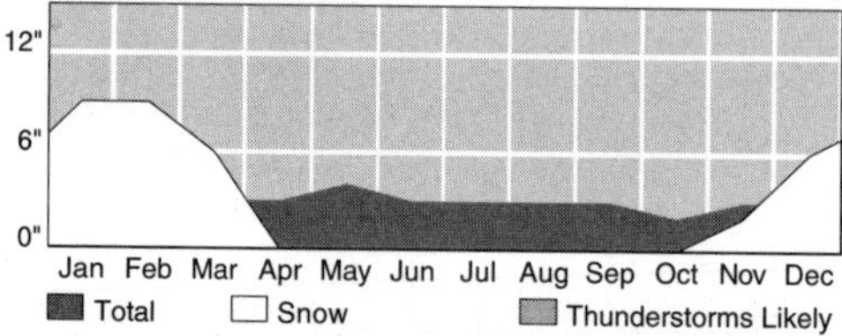

ANNUAL
Precipitation: 40.5"
Snow: 34.3"
DAYS
Precipitation: 76
Thunderstorm: 31

Hartford, CT

Location: 41.56 N, 72.41 W, at 160 feet, on the Connecticut River about 30 miles due north of Long Island Sound.
Landscape: Slight rise of ground between north-south mountain ranges whose heights do not exceed 1,200 feet. Near the state's geographic center, in the physiographic region known as the Central Lowlands. Cleared land areas are fertile. The Connecticut River maintains land drainage.
Climate: Varies from the cold Continental climate in winter to the warm maritime air of summer. Hartford's latitude places it well within the northern temperate climate zone, with westerly winds bearing the majority of weather systems. Proximity to the ocean is also significant, since many storms move upward along the Atlantic Coast, frequently producing strong and persistent northeast winds. Hartford has a mean January temperature of 25°F and an average July temperature of 78°F; it receives more than 40 inches of precipitation yearly.

Mildness: 31 Brightness: 35 Stability: 66

Places Rated Score: 35.49 **Places Rated Rank: 224**

TEMPERATURE

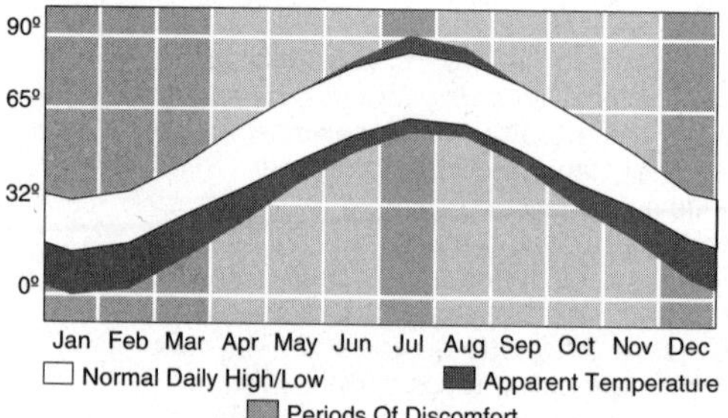

ANNUAL
Humidity: 64%
Wind Speed: 8.5 mph
DAYS
0º or below: 6
32º or below: 135
90º or above: 18
Clear: 81
Cloudy: 175

PRECIPITATION

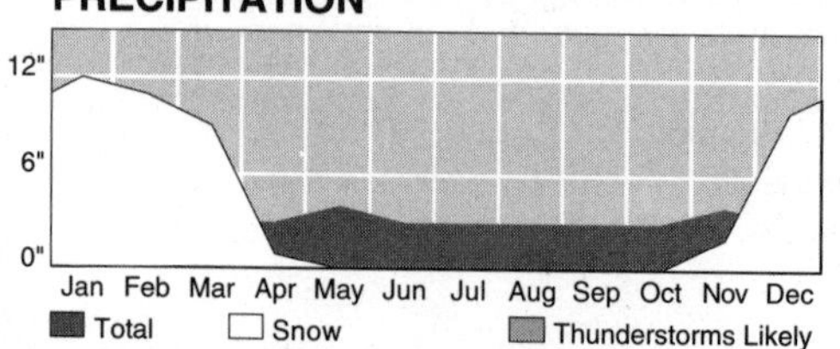

ANNUAL
Precipitation: 44.1"
Snow: 47.3"
DAYS
Precipitation: 76
Thunderstorm: 20

Hattiesburg, MS

Location: 31.19 N, 89.18 W, at 160 feet, in the southern part of Mississippi some 70 miles north of Gulfport and the Gulf of Mexico.
Landscape: In the Piney Woods section of the Gulf Coastal Plain—a long-leaf pine belt that has slash and loblolly pine. Mississippi, as a whole, has large forest resources, and Hattiesburg was founded by pioneer lumbermen in the 1880s. Topographical features include alluvial soils, gentle sloping plains, and extensive ground water resources. However, most of the numerous streams are sluggish; there are many marshes, lakes, and swamps.
Climate: Subtropical with local average precipitation of 60 to 70 inches each year falling as rain. The area is subject to thunderstorms in midsummer and hurricanes in the late summer and early autumn. Winter minimums average 44°F; and sleet are rare. Summer maximums exceed 95°F

TEMPERATURE

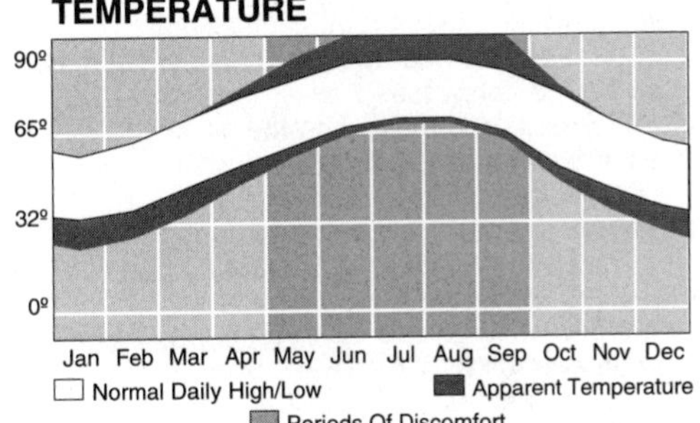

ANNUAL
Humidity: 74%
Wind Speed: 7.4 mph
DAYS
0º or below: 0
32º or below: 44
90º or above: 95
Clear: 111
Cloudy: 150

PRECIPITATION

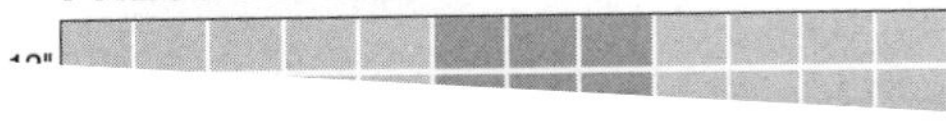

ANNUAL
Precipitation: 60.6"

Tropic of Cancer in the Pacific Ocean,
mild temperatures.
Landscape: Oahu, the island on which Honolulu is located, is the third largest of the Hawaiian Islands. The Koolau Range, at an average height of 2,000 feet, parallels the northeast coast. The Waianae Mountains, somewhat higher in elevation, parallel the west coast. Much of the city lies along the coastal plain, leeward of the Koolaus.
Climate: Mild Marine Tropical having the least seasonal temperature change of any American city; the difference between the mean January minimum temperature and the August maximum mean temperature is only about 22 degrees. There are no heating-degree days here. Although it can be uncomfortably warm occasionally, the persistent tradewinds give relief.

Mildness: 100 Brightness: 39 Stability: 84
Places Rated Score: 97.74 **Places Rated Rank: 2**

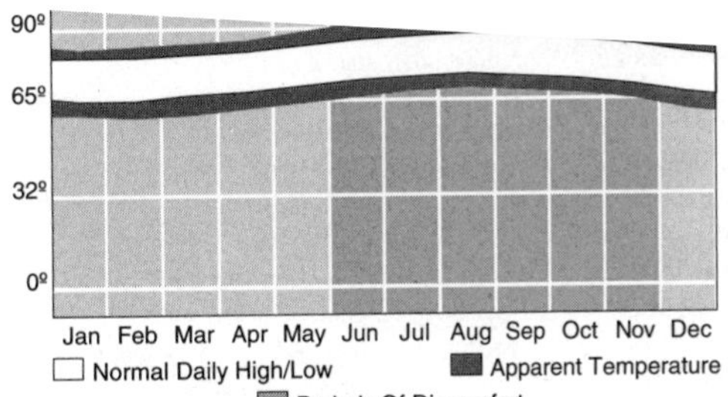

Wind Speed: 11.3 mph
DAYS
0º or below: 0
32º or below: 0
90º or above: 23
Clear: 90
Cloudy: 95

PRECIPITATION

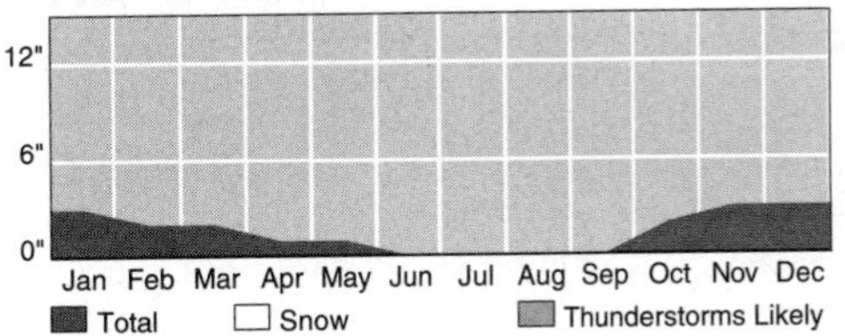

ANNUAL
Precipitation: 22.0"
Snow: 0.0"
DAYS
Precipitation: 47
Thunderstorm: 14

Houston, TX

Location: 29.39 N, 95.17 W, at 50 feet, in the flat Coastal Plain of Texas, about 50 miles inland from the Gulf of Mexico and 25 miles from Galveston Bay.
Landscape: Coastal Prairie includes low, flat lands suitable for agriculture, bayous bordered by magnolias, and wooded heights. The numerous small streams and bayous, together with the bay, favor the development of fog. Meandering Buffalo Bayou, the original city site, has become the famed Houston Ship Channel. Marshy areas are still evident in the reeds and cattails.
Climate: Predominantly mild Marine. Temperatures are modified by winds from the Gulf but these breezes also assure high humidity year round. Summer days are hot and humid, though the evenings are relatively cool. Winters are mild. Polar air penetrates the area frequently enough to provide some stimulating variety. Although temperatures dip below freezing occasionally, they never remain there long, accounting for a year-round growing season. Destructive windstorms are infrequent, but thunderstorms and hurricanes do occur.

Mildness: 88 Brightness: 35 Stability: 12
Places Rated Score: 74.44 **Places Rated Rank: 66**

TEMPERATURE

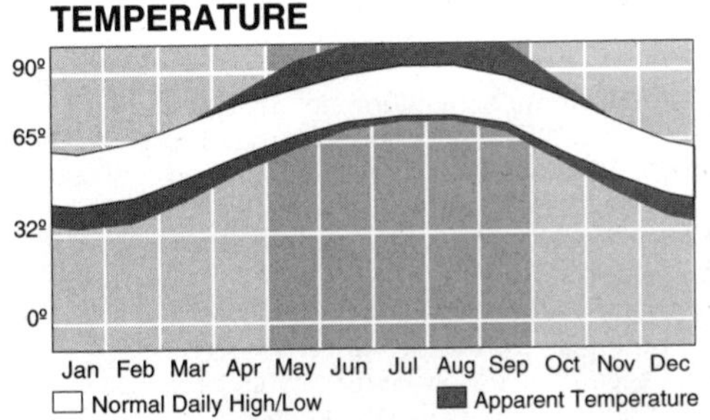

ANNUAL
Humidity: 74%
Wind Speed: 7.9 mph
DAYS
0º or below: 0
32º or below: 24
90º or above: 96
Clear: 91
Cloudy: 160

PRECIPITATION

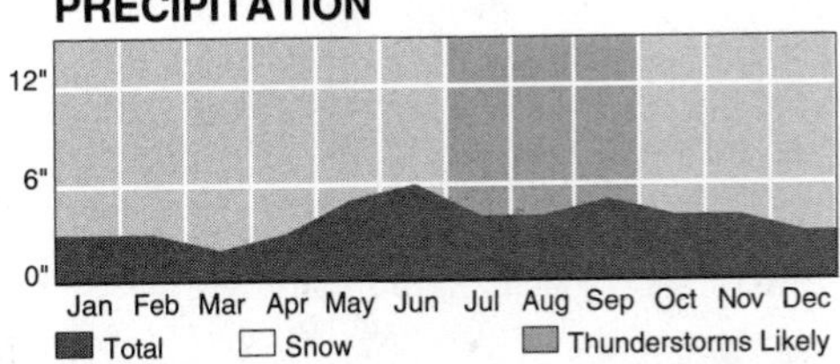

ANNUAL
Precipitation: 50.8"
Snow: 0.4"
DAYS
Precipitation: 64
Thunderstorm: 62

Huntsville, AL

Location: 34.39 N, 86.46 W, at 620 feet, just north of the Tennessee River, 20 miles from the border with Tennessee.
Landscape: The city is almost surrounded by the foothills of the Appalachian Mountains. The Tennessee River winds its way westward about 7 miles south of the city, and the broad and fertile Tennessee Valley, with flat to gently rolling terrain, extends to the west.
Climate: Cold air masses from the north predominate during the winter, but at times mild air from the Gulf of Mexico, spreading northward to Huntsville and beyond, may persist for several days. There are few severely cold days. Temperatures drop below zero on an average of once a year. Springs are variable and can be stormy as cold polar air and warm Gulf air meet. Summers are hot and humid, relieved only by the showers that come about every three days. Falls are dry, cooler, and pleasant. The length of the growing season, 241 days, and high rainfall make the area suitable for truck farming.

Mildness: 70 Brightness: 32 Stability: 20

Places Rated Score: 58.24 **Places Rated Rank: 133**

TEMPERATURE

90º 65º 32º 0º
Jan Feb Mar Apr May Jun Jul Aug Sep Oct Nov Dec
Normal Daily High/Low Apparent Temperature
Periods Of Discomfort

ANNUAL
Humidity: 71%
Wind Speed: 8.2 mph
DAYS
0º or below: 0
32º or below: 67
90º or above: 50
Clear: 100
Cloudy: 164

PRECIPITATION

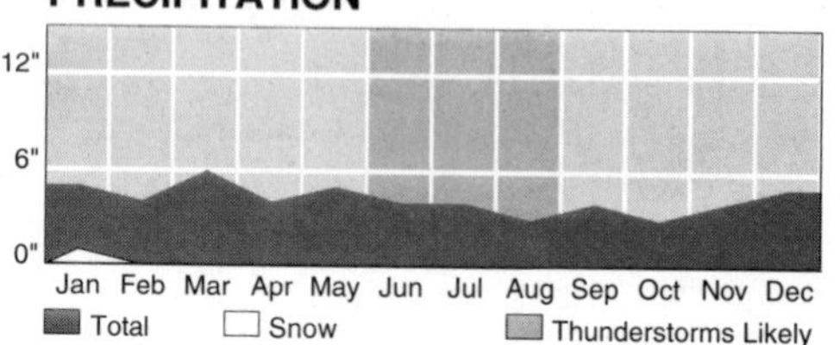

ANNUAL
Precipitation: 57.2"
Snow: 2.8"
DAYS
Precipitation: 79
Thunderstorm: 54

Indianapolis, IN

Location: 39.44 N, 86.16 W, at 790 feet, in the central part of Indiana, the greater part of the city lies east of the White River.
Landscape: Mostly level or slightly rolling terrain. White River flows approximately from north to south. From the airport, 7 miles southwest of the city, the terrain slopes gradually downward to the city, then upward again past the city to the east.
Climate: Continental with rather warm summers, moderately cold winters, and occasional wide variations in temperatures, especially during the cold season. Snowfalls of 3 inches or more occur about three times annually. Periods of muggy weather can occur in summer although these air masses from the Gulf of Mexico are soon replaced by cooler air from the northern Plains and Great Lakes. Occasionally, hot dry winds from the Southwest prevail. Late spring and fall are the most pleasant seasons. Precipitation, well distributed throughout the year, is normally adequate for good crops. Several flood-control reservoirs protect most formerly flood-prone areas.

Mildness: 27 Brightness: 39 Stability: 31

Places Rated Score: 29.65 **Places Rated Rank: 256**

TEMPERATURE

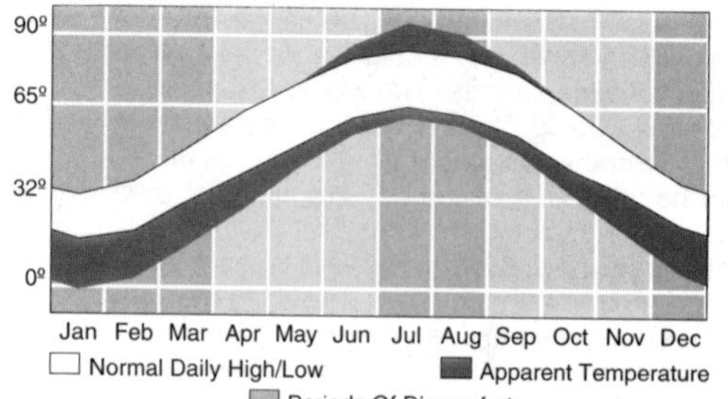

ANNUAL
Humidity: 73%
Wind Speed: 9.6 mph
DAYS
0º or below: 7
32º or below: 119
90º or above: 19
Clear: 87
Cloudy: 179

PRECIPITATION

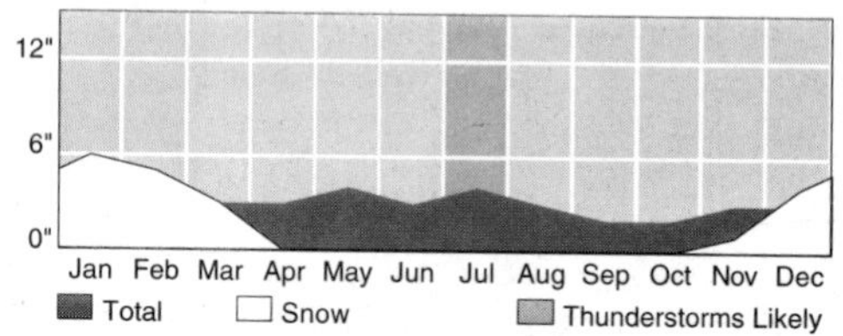

ANNUAL
Precipitation: 39.9"
Snow: 22.7"
DAYS
Precipitation: 71
Thunderstorm: 43

Iowa City, IA

Location: 41.39 N, 91.32 W, at 640 feet, lies along both banks of the Iowa River in eastern Iowa, 25 miles south of Cedar Rapids.
Landscape: Iowa has more prime agricultural soil than any other state. Iowa City is the center of a region dominated by cattle, grain, hogs and poultry production. The area is characterized by rolling to fairly steep hills. Soil is prairie, high in organic content. The Iowa River provides an extensive drainage basin.
Climate: Continental climate with extremes in both temperature and precipitation; potential for violent storms. Summer highs can reach 100°F accompanied by high humidity. Extended periods of such heat can stress livestock, crops and people. Average winter temperatures range from 15°F to 25°F, but can get much colder. Average frost-free season is 150 days. Precipitation can be highly variable, with large amounts falling all at once and then long periods of nothing at all. The area is typical of the state as a whole, susceptible to droughts and floods, and receiving blizzards and tornadoes.

Mildness: 14 Brightness: 60 Stability: 26

Places Rated Score: 21.03 **Places Rated Rank: 313**

TEMPERATURE

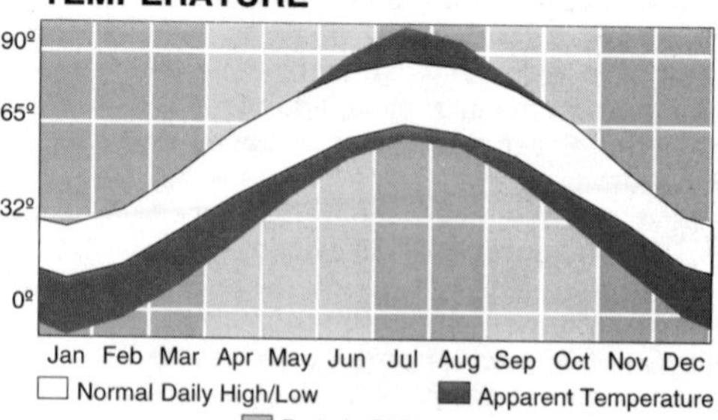

ANNUAL
Humidity: 72%
Wind Speed: 10.7 mph
DAYS
0º or below: 15
32º or below: 139
90º or above: 26
Clear: 90
Cloudy: 175

PRECIPITATION

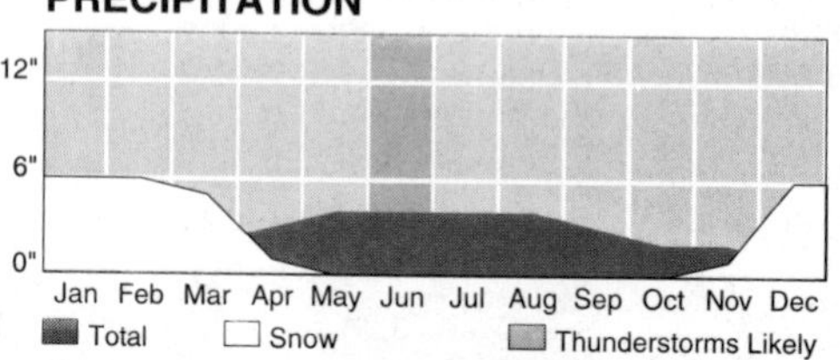

ANNUAL
Precipitation: 36.3"
Snow: 28.6"
DAYS
Precipitation: 59
Thunderstorm: 41

Jackson, MS

Location: 32.19 N, 90.05 W, at 310 feet, about 45 miles east of the Mississippi River on the west bank of the Pearl River and about 150 miles north of the Gulf of Mexico.
Landscape: Alluvial plains up to 3 miles wide extend along the river near Jackson, and some levees have been built on both sides of the river. Rolling hills of the central coastal plain are predominant but there are bluffs along the river. Forests are mixed broadleafed deciduous and southern yellow pine.
Climate: Significantly humid during most of the year, with one short cold season and one long warm one. In summer, the southerly winds and accompanying warm Gulf air masses predominate, resulting in a warm, humid Maritime climate. Summer days are hot and humid, and often so are the nights. In winter, colder northern air occasionally invades the area, causing rapid and sometimes dramatic temperature shifts. Average freeze-free period: 235 days.

Mildness: 73 Brightness: 42 Stability: 9

TEMPERATURE

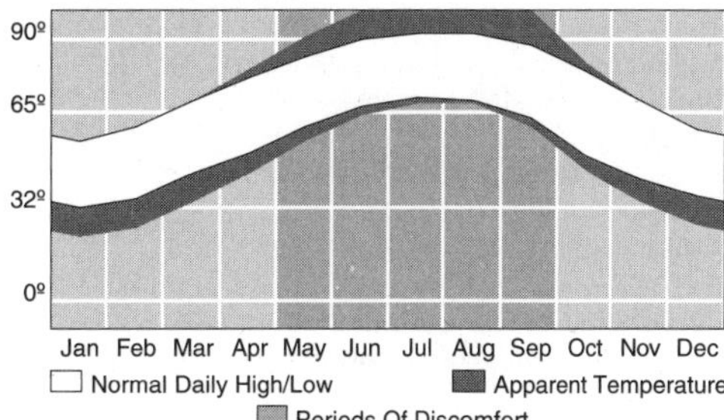

ANNUAL
Humidity: 74%
Wind Speed: 7.4 mph
DAYS
0º or below: 0
32º or below: 50
90º or above: 84
Clear: 111
Cloudy: 150

PRECIPITATION

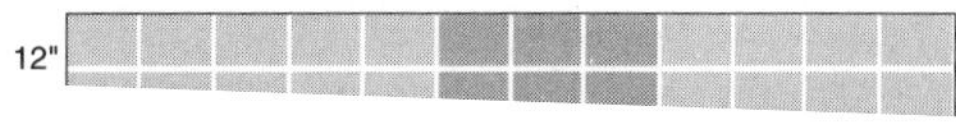

ANNUAL
Precipitation: 55.4"

Ocean.
Landscape: Near the northern boundary of the trade winds. The surrounding terrain is irregular and level. Jacksonville is the leading deepwater port on the southern United States Atlantic coast. The St. Johns River is the state's longest. Forest areas are typical southern mixed; pine predominates.
Climate: Subtropical atmosphere is heavy with humidity. The average daily sunshine ranges from five and one-half hours in December to nine hours in May. The greatest amount of rain, mostly in the form of local thundershowers, falls during the last summer months, when a measurable amount can be expected every other day. It rains over 50 inches annually. Temperatures average 55°F in January and 82°F in July.

Mildness: 90 Brightness: 29 Stability: 13

Places Rated Score: 75.67 **Places Rated Rank: 60**

65º
32º
0º
Jan Feb Mar Apr May Jun Jul Aug Sep Oct Nov Dec
Normal Daily High/Low
Apparent Temperature
Periods Of Discomfort

Wind Speed: 8.0 mph
DAYS
0º or below: 0
32º or below: 12
90º or above: 82
Clear: 95
Cloudy: 143

PRECIPITATION

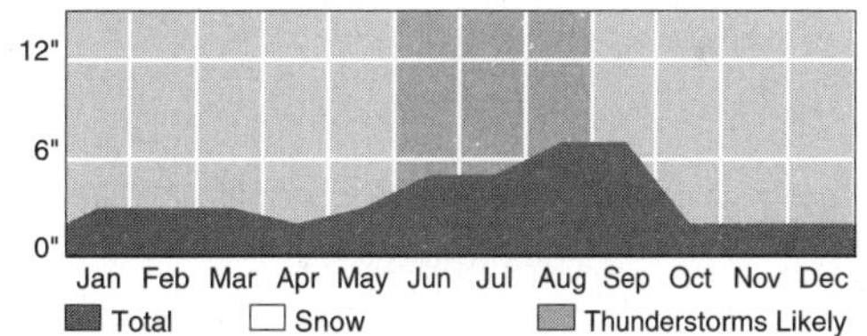

ANNUAL
Precipitation: 51.3"
Snow: 0.0"
DAYS
Precipitation: 70
Thunderstorm: 65

Johnson City–Kingsport–Bristol, TN–VA

Location: 36.31 N, 82.32 W, at 1,280 feet, tri-city area is located in the extreme upper east Tennessee Valley.
Landscape: Terrain ranges from gently rolling on the east and south to hilly on the west and north. Mountain ranges begin about 10 miles to the southeast and 15 miles to the west and north, with many peaks and ridges rising to 4,000 feet, and some to 6,000 feet in the southeast.
Climate: The topography has considerable influence on the weather changes peculiar to this area. The moist, easterly airflow in the lower levels of the atmosphere affects primarily the eastern slopes of the mountains where it produces an abundance of precipitation in these higher ridges. The air masses reach the tri-city area drier and slightly warmer. Although average annual rainfall is 41 inches in the vicinity, annual amounts of 80 inches have been recorded in mountainous sections to the east and south. Snowfall seldom begins before November and rarely remains on the ground more than a few days. Mountainous regions to the southeast, however, are frequently blanketed for long periods.

Mildness: 69 Brightness: 24 Stability: 41

Places Rated Score: 58.66 **Places Rated Rank: 132**

TEMPERATURE

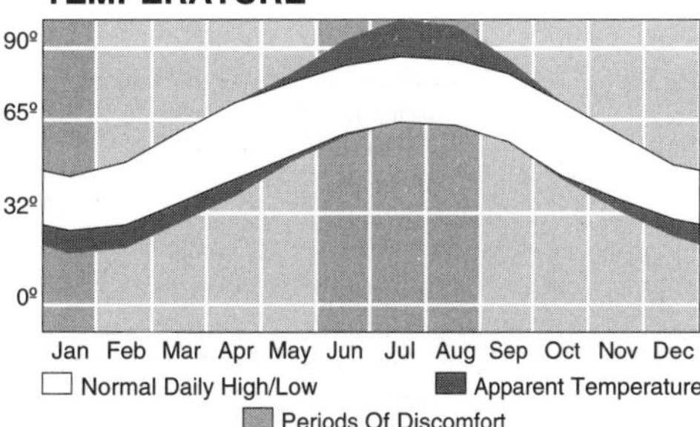

ANNUAL
Humidity: 71%
Wind Speed: 5.5 mph
DAYS
0º or below: 0
32º or below: 88
90º or above: 27
Clear: 88
Cloudy: 165

PRECIPITATION

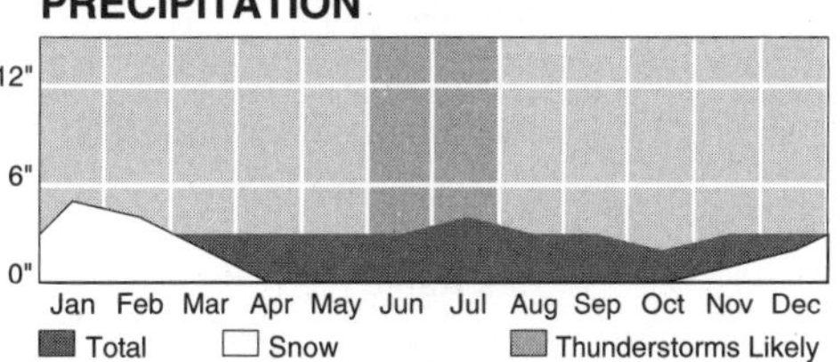

ANNUAL
Precipitation: 43.8"
Snow: 16.9"
DAYS
Precipitation: 83
Thunderstorm: 42

Kansas City, MO–KS

Location: 39.19 N, 94.43 W, at 970 feet, near the geographic center of the United States. Kansas City, Kansas, located in the northeastern part of its state, and Kansas City, Missouri, on the western side of its state, are on opposite banks of the Kansas River where it meets the Missouri River.
Landscape: The surrounding terrain is gently rolling. Its Continental climate is modified by a lack of natural obstructions to the free sweep of air currents from all directions.
Climate: Early spring brings a period of frequent and rapid fluctuations of weather, tapering off as spring progresses. Summer days are warm, sometimes hot, but nights are mild with moderate humidity. As with so many locations in America's heartland, fall is the most pleasant season, characterized by many mild sunny days and cool nights. Average date of last freeze: April 7. First freeze: October 26.

Mildness: 20 Brightness: 71 Stability: 19

Places Rated Score: 26.21 **Places Rated Rank: 285**

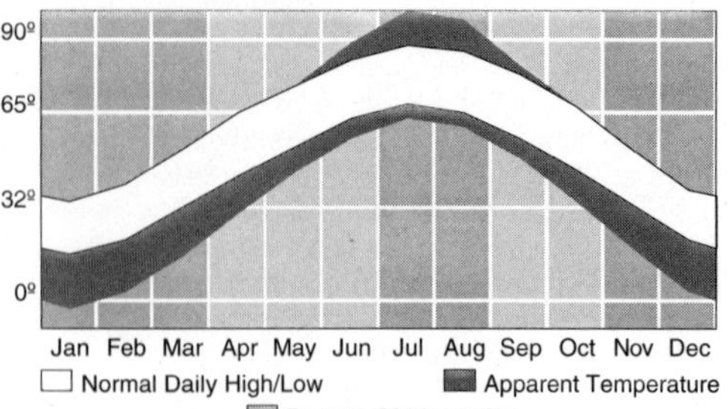

ANNUAL
Humidity: 70%
Wind Speed: 10.8 mph
DAYS
0º or below: 5
32º or below: 105
90º or above: 40
Clear: 120
Cloudy: 149

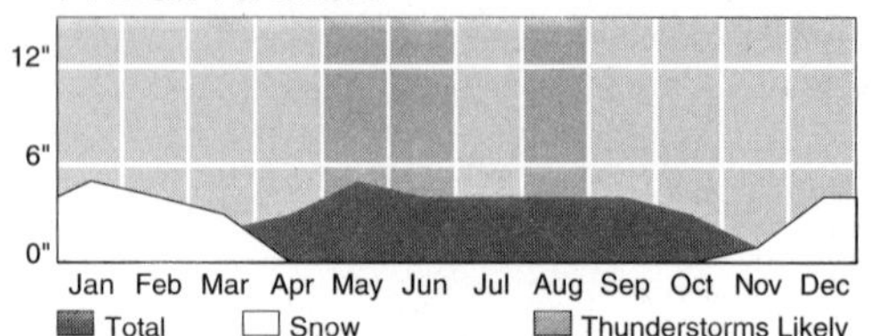

ANNUAL
Precipitation: 37.6"
Snow: 20.2"
DAYS
Precipitation: 59
Thunderstorm: 51

Knoxville, TN

Location: 35.49 N, 83.59 W, at 880 feet, on the Tennessee River in a broad valley between the Cumberland Mountains and the Great Smoky Mountains. Nashville is 175 miles west.
Landscape: The Cumberlands serve to retard and weaken the force of the cold winter air moving down from the northern Plains during the colder months, and the Smokies shelter Knoxville from much of the hot, humid tropical air that moves northward during the summertime.
Climate: Moderate Continental, thanks to the sheltering effects of the two mountain ranges. Though summers are long, the nights are almost always cool, with the average diurnal variation being about 20 degrees. The mean daytime temperature for July is 81°F, but nighttime temperatures are in the mid-70s. Freezing temperatures are common from December to March but seldom fall to zero or below.

Mildness: 66 Brightness: 27 Stability: 33

Places Rated Score: 56.15 **Places Rated Rank: 147**

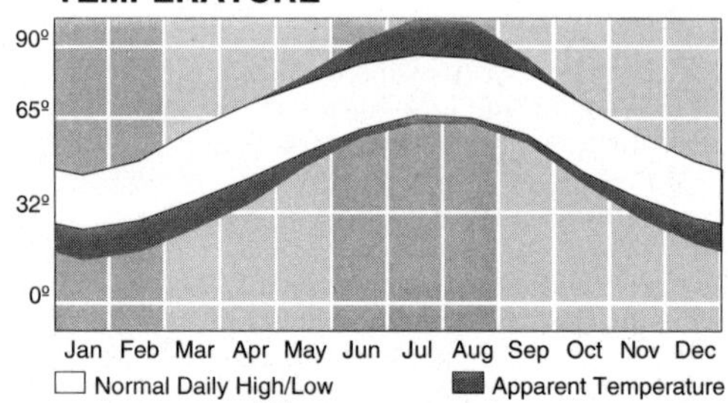

ANNUAL
Humidity: 72%
Wind Speed: 6.9 mph
DAYS
0º or below: 1
32º or below: 73
90º or above: 33
Clear: 96
Cloudy: 162

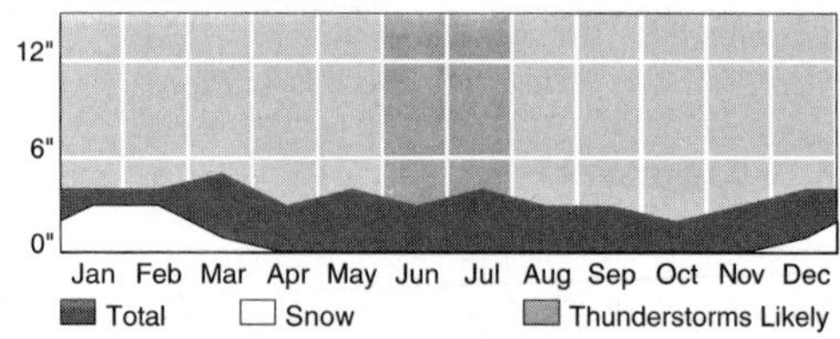

ANNUAL
Precipitation: 47.1"
Snow: 11.9"
DAYS
Precipitation: 83
Thunderstorm: 47

La Crosse, WI–MN

Location: 43.52 N, 91.15 W, at 650 feet, the city is on the east bank of the Mississippi River at the confluence with the Black and La Crosse rivers.
Landscape: Situated on a level, sandy plain, but steep-sided hills with narrow valleys are characteristic of most of the surrounding area. The leading field crops are corn, hay, and oats. Dairying is the principal farm activity.
Climate: The location of the city in a natural bowl between the hills results in colder temperatures at night due to air drainage and in valley fogs that often persist through forenoon. The Continental climate means frequent variations in temperature. Winters are cold and humid; snows are frequent. Summers are warm and moderately humid. Most of the annual precipitation falls during the main growing season extending from May to September.

Mildness: 8 Brightness: 63 Stability: 38

Places Rated Score: 16.46 **Places Rated Rank: 323**

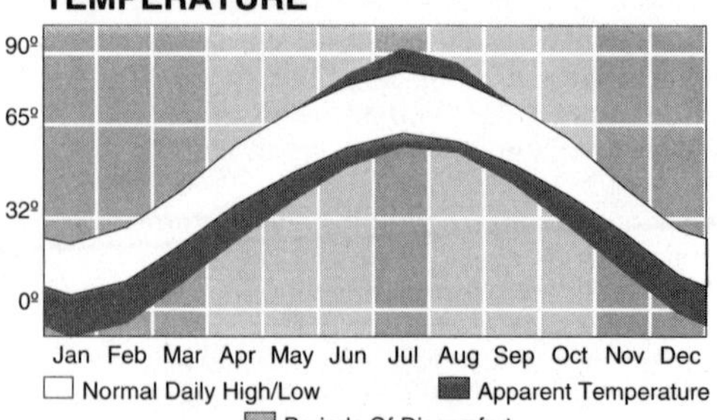

ANNUAL
Humidity: 71%
Wind Speed: 8.8 mph
DAYS
0º or below: 24
32º or below: 154
90º or above: 13
Clear: 95
Cloudy: 173

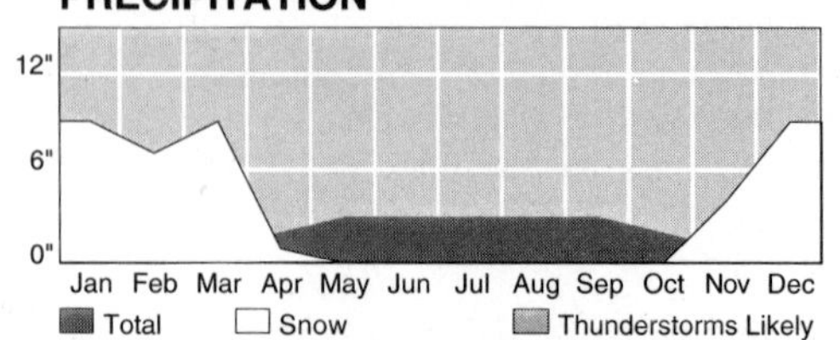

ANNUAL
Precipitation: 30.6"
Snow: 42.3"
DAYS
Precipitation: 56
Thunderstorm: 37

Lakeland–Winter Haven, FL

Location: 28.01 N, 81.55 W, at 150 feet, in central Florida 32 miles east of Tampa, 50 miles from the Gulf of Mexico and 70 miles from the Atlantic.

Landscape: This rolling lake-ridge section has the highest elevation in the Florida peninsula. Floodplain prairies and pine flatwoods mix with live oak hammocks. Forests are a mix of hardwood, longleaf and slash pine found in coastal areas. Aromatic and evergreen bayberry and sweet bay are scattered throughout.

Climate: The subtropical latitude and the proximity of the Gulf of Mexico and the Atlantic cause winters to be pleasant. Days are bright and warm; nights are cool. Rainfall is light to moderate. Occasionally, major cold waves overspread the area, bringing temperatures down below freezing. High temperatures of the long summers are moderated in the afternoon by thundershowers.

Mildness: 94 Brightness: 18 Stability: 5

Places Rated Rank: 55

TEMPERATURE

90º 65º 32º 0º
Jan Feb Mar Apr May Jun Jul Aug Sep Oct Nov Dec
Normal Daily High/Low — Apparent Temperature — Periods Of Discomfort

ANNUAL
Humidity: 72%
Wind Speed: 8.3 mph
DAYS
0º or below: 0
32º or below: 3
90º or above: 108
Clear: 101
Cloudy: 121

PRECIPITATION

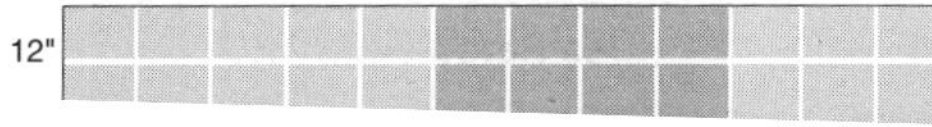

ANNUAL
Precipitation: 47.5"
Snow: 0.0"

try.

Landscape: In the center of the fertile Piedmont plateau, where grain and dairy products are produced. The relief is gently sloping upward as hill rises above valley. The soil is fine and fertile. The area is drained by the Susquehanna River system which flows 20 miles to the west. The forest is mixed deciduous hardwoods, including oak, maple, ash, and elm.

Climate: Pennsylvania, as a whole, has a humid Continental climate, but topographic differences result in local eccentricities. Lancaster, in the southeast, has long, hot summers and comparatively mild winters. The growing season is 170 to 200 days. Precipitation is more than adequate, averaging 35 to 50 inches. Average annual snowfall is 20 inches. The seasons are distinct but not harsh.

Mildness: 43 Brightness: 40 Stability: 59

Places Rated Score: 44.72 **Places Rated Rank: 186**

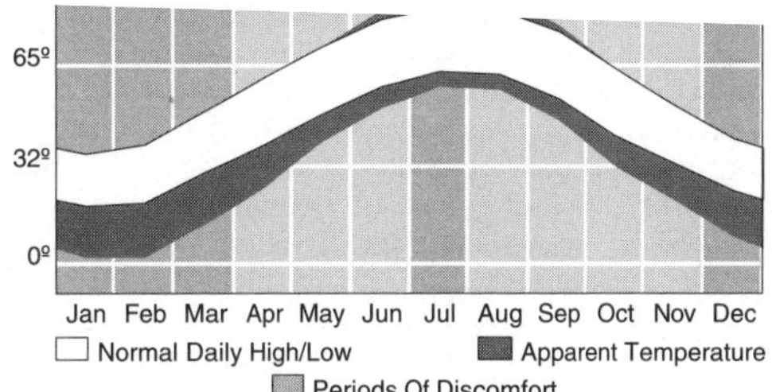

Wind Speed: 9.6 mph
DAYS
0º or below: 1
32º or below: 122
90º or above: 18
Clear: 93
Cloudy: 160

PRECIPITATION

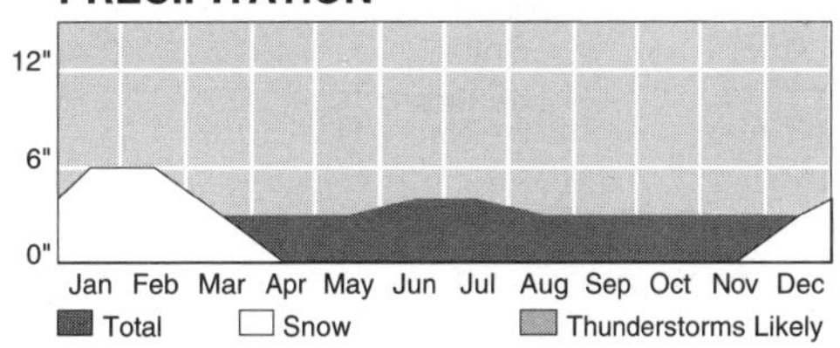

ANNUAL
Precipitation: 41.2"
Snow: 20.8"
DAYS
Precipitation: 74
Thunderstorm: 27

Lansing–East Lansing, MI

Location: 42.46 N, 84.36 W, at 840 feet, at the junction of the Grand, Red Cedar, and Sycamore rivers in the southern part of the state, 84 miles west of Detroit.

Landscape: Large agricultural area. Landscape is lowland, punctuated with glacial uplands. Soil is productive mixed organic bog, created when prehistoric inland lakes filled in with rich nutrients. Bog soils are well adapted for vegetable production. Throughout southern Michigan, hardwood tree species are regenerating in the original forests.

Climate: Humid Continental. However, the presence of the Great Lakes influences temperature, the number of frost-free days, and the ratio of sunshine to cloudy days. Average annual temperature is 50°F. Frost-free periods average 170 to 180 days. Average precipitation is 31 inches annually. Snow, sleet, hail, and ice storms are common, and tornadoes and blizzards sometimes occur. Snowfall averages 30 inches annually. Heavy cloud cover in the fall and early winter is common.

Mildness: 18 Brightness: 35 Stability: 56

Places Rated Score: 23.89 **Places Rated Rank: 302**

TEMPERATURE

90º 65º 32º 0º
Jan Feb Mar Apr May Jun Jul Aug Sep Oct Nov Dec
Normal Daily High/Low — Apparent Temperature — Periods Of Discomfort

ANNUAL
Humidity: 74%
Wind Speed: 9.9 mph
DAYS
0º or below: 14
32º or below: 149
90º or above: 11
Clear: 71
Cloudy: 190

PRECIPITATION

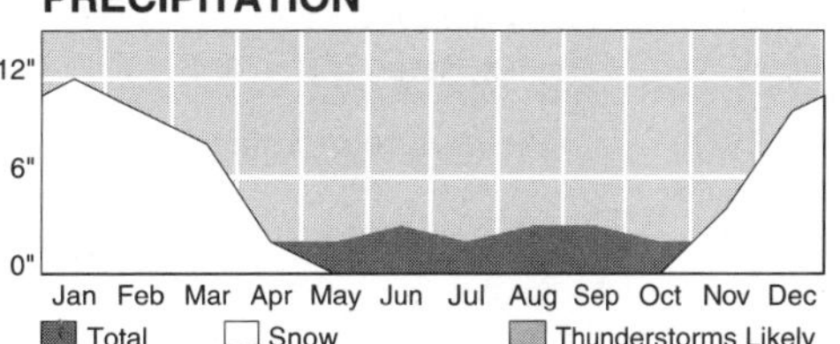

ANNUAL
Precipitation: 30.6"
Snow: 48.9"
DAYS
Precipitation: 64
Thunderstorm: 32

✓Laredo, TX

Location: 27.34 N, 99.30 W, at 430 feet, in south Texas on the Rio Grande River, opposite Nuevo Laredo, Mexico, and 230 miles SW of Austin.
Landscape: Prairie; rolling hills and undulating plains, with western shrub vegetation. On the slopes leading down to the Rio Grande, the ceniza shrub dominates. The Rio Grande valley is mostly covered by brush, mesquite, cedar, pot oak, and an occasional dense growth of prickly pear. Extensive irrigation has brought once arid land into fertile agricultural farms. Level land toward the east is suitable for grazing.
Climate: Semiarid Desert. The climate is distinctly dry, though rainfall as showers is fairly evenly distributed throughout the year. Rainfall is about 20 inches annually. Summers are long and hot; temperatures are in the mid-90s over 150 days. Typical of the desert, night temperatures fall about 20 degrees. Winters are short. December and January, the driest months, record minimum temperatures in the 40s. There is seldom freezing and no temperatures of zero.

Mildness: 84 Brightness: 99 Stability: 33

Places Rated Score: 84.63 **Places Rated Rank: 34**

TEMPERATURE

90º 65º 32º 0º
Jan Feb Mar Apr May Jun Jul Aug Sep Oct Nov Dec
Normal Daily High/Low Apparent Temperature
Periods Of Discomfort

ANNUAL
Humidity: 42%
Wind Speed: 8.8 mph
DAYS
0º or below: 0
32º or below: 8
90º or above: 167
Clear: 192
Cloudy: 73

PRECIPITATION

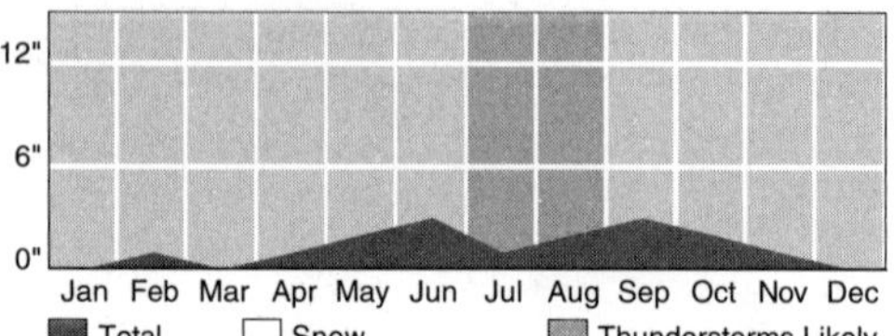

ANNUAL
Precipitation: 21.4"
Snow: 0.2"
DAYS
Precipitation: 29
Thunderstorm: 34

Las Cruces, NM

Location: 32.37 N, 106.44 W, at 4,270 feet, on the Rio Grande River near the southern edge of the state, 40 miles NW of El Paso, TX.
Landscape: The wide, level Mesilla Valley runs northwest to southeast through this area. Rolling desert borders the southwest and west. About 12 miles east the Organ Mountains, with peaks above 8,500 feet, form a rugged backdrop. The northwest portion of the valley narrows to low hills and buttes. Only plants adapted to the highly alkaline conditions survive. These include thorn scrub, savanna, or steppe grassland, pricklypear and saguaro cactus. In this higher altitude there are belts of oak and juniper woodland.
Climate: Desert characterized by low rainfall, moderately warm summers, and mild, pleasant winters. The rainfall is light, but since almost all of it falls during the summer growing months, considerable forage is available on nearby grazing lands. The rain falls in brief showers; drizzles are unknown.

Mildness: 52 Brightness: 99 Stability: 40

Places Rated Score: 65.71 **Places Rated Rank: 102**

TEMPERATURE

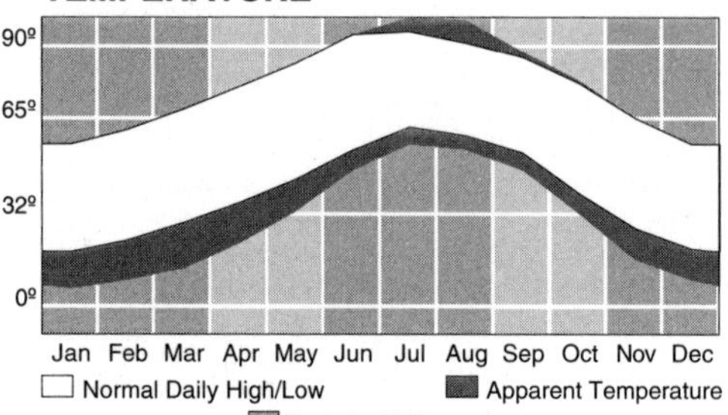

ANNUAL
Humidity: 42%
Wind Speed: 8.8 mph
DAYS
0º or below: 0
32º or below: 38
90º or above: 86
Clear: 192
Cloudy: 73

PRECIPITATION

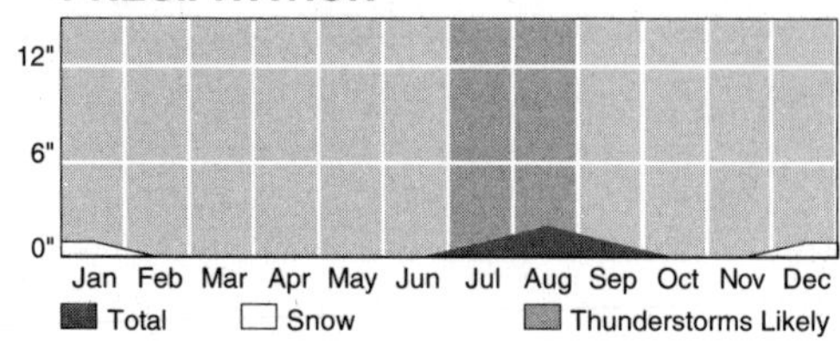

ANNUAL
Precipitation: 10.5"
Snow: 5.5"
DAYS
Precipitation: 22
Thunderstorm: 34

Las Vegas, NV–AZ

Location: 36.05 N, 115.10 W, at 2,160 feet, at the tip of southern Nevada just west of the Colorado River valley. Los Angeles is SW nearly 300 miles.
Landscape: Near the center of a broad desert valley surrounded by mountains from 2,000 to 10,000 feet higher than the valley's floor. These mountains act as effective barriers to moisture laden storms moving in from the Pacific Ocean. The thick-branched Joshua tree grows among creosote bushes and jumbled boulders in the Mojave Desert region. Las Vegas is the center of a large mining and ranching area.
Climate: Summers are typical of a desert climate. Humidity is low with maximum temperatures in the 100 degree levels. Nearby mountains contribute to relatively cool nights. Spring and fall are ideal, rarely interrupted by adverse weather conditions. Winters, too, are mild, with daytime averages of 60°F, clear skies, and warm sunshine. There are few overcast or rainy days.

Mildness: 56 Brightness: 100 Stability: 43

Places Rated Score: 74.33 **Places Rated Rank: 67**

TEMPERATURE

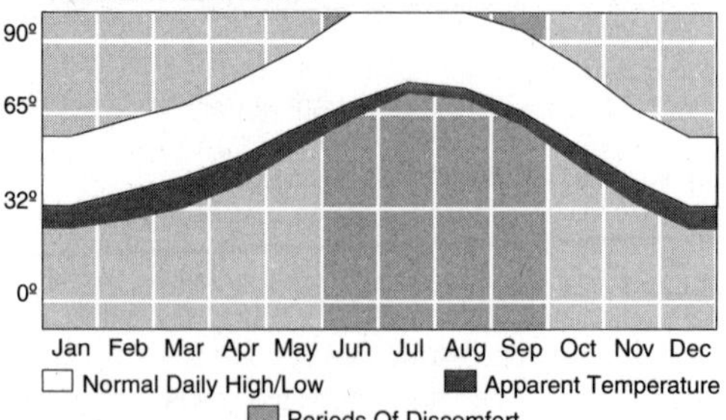

ANNUAL
Humidity: 30%
Wind Speed: 9.3 mph
DAYS
0º or below: 0
32º or below: 37
90º or above: 134
Clear: 211
Cloudy: 72

PRECIPITATION

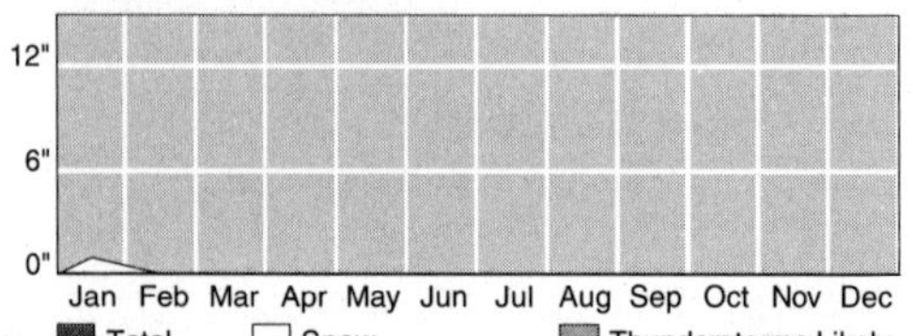

ANNUAL
Precipitation: 4.1"
Snow: 1.3"
DAYS
Precipitation: 13
Thunderstorm: 13

Lexington, KY

Location: 38.02 N, 84.36 W, at 970 feet, in the heart of Kentucky Bluegrass country 23 miles east of the capital at Frankfort.

Landscape: Gently rolling plateau with varying elevations of 900 feet to 1,050 feet. The surrounding country is noted for its beauty, fertile soil, excellent grass, stock farms, and burley tobacco. There are no bodies of water nearby that are large enough to have an effect on climate.

Climate: Decidedly Continental, temperate, yet subject to sudden large but brief changes in temperature. Precipitation is evenly distributed throughout the winter, spring, and summer, with an average of 12 inches falling in each of these seasons. Snowfall is variable, but the ground does not retain snow for more than a few days at a time. The months of September and October are the most pleasant of the year; they have the least precipitation, the most clear days, and generally comfortable temperatures.

Mildness: 49 Brightness: 32 Stability: 35

TEMPERATURE

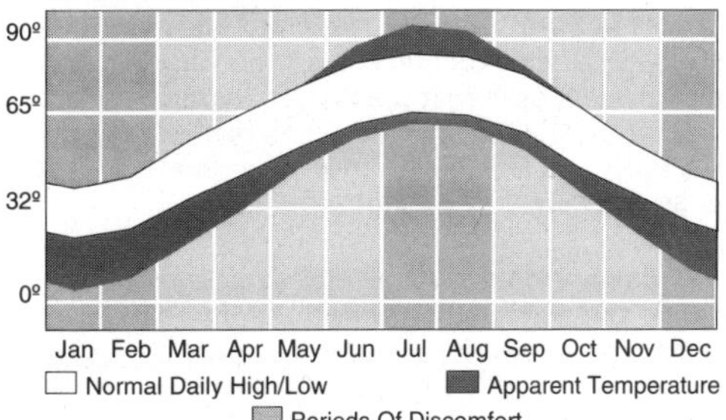

ANNUAL
Humidity: 71%
Wind Speed: 9.2 mph
DAYS
0º or below: 2
32º or below: 97
90º or above: 22
Clear: 90
Cloudy: 174

PRECIPITATION

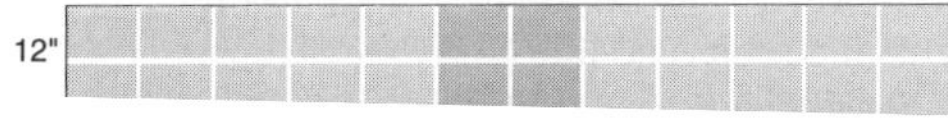

ANNUAL
Precipitation: 44.6"
Snow: 15.7"

Landscape: ... lowlands of the state. Surrounded by grain- and livestock-producing region. Soil is deep, rich silt loam and sandy loam, noted for fertility in growing corn, grain, and wheat. The Missouri River provides drainage, except in times of heavy rainfall, when severe flooding can occur.

Climate: The majority of winter outbreaks of severely cold air from Canada move over the Lincoln area. However, the centers of some cold air masses move so far to the east that their full effect is not felt here. The Chinook effect often produces rapid rises in temperature during the winter, with a shift of the wind to the west. An average winter brings 26 inches of snow, most of which doesn't melt until spring. The crop season, April through September, receives three-fourths of the yearly precipitation. Humidity remains at a comfortable level, except for short periods during the summer and there is an average of 64 percent of possible sunlight. Destructive weather is rare because of the location beyond the edge of the tornado and hail belt.

Mildness: 12 Brightness: 82 Stability: 19

Places Rated Score: 20.57 **Places Rated Rank: 315**

65º
32º
0º
Jan Feb Mar Apr May Jun Jul Aug Sep Oct Nov Dec
Normal Daily High/Low
Apparent Temperature
Periods Of Discomfort

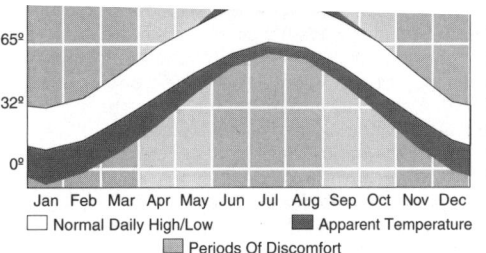

Wind Speed: 10.3 mph
DAYS
0º or below: 17
32º or below: 146
90º or above: 43
Clear: 117
Cloudy: 149

PRECIPITATION

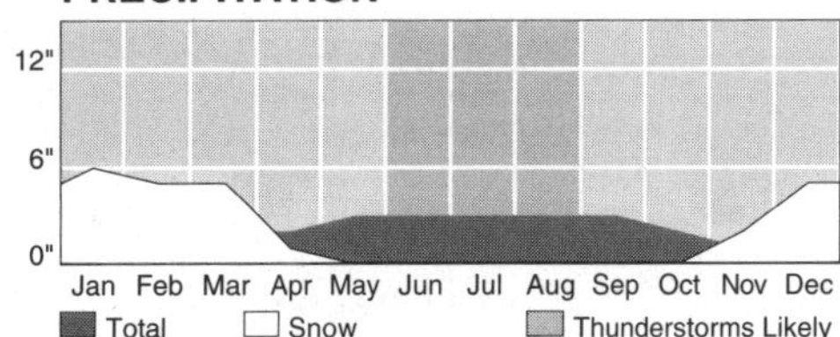

ANNUAL
Precipitation: 28.3"
Snow: 27.1"
DAYS
Precipitation: 49
Thunderstorm: 46

Little Rock–North Little Rock, AR

Location: 34.44 N, 92.14 W, at 260 feet, on the Arkansas River near the geographic center of the state.

Landscape: To the west lie the Ouachita Mountains and to the east the flat lowlands of the Mississippi River valley. Little Rock is surrounded by farmland. Poultry, cattle, and a variety of agricultural products are processed in the city. Bauxite is mined nearby. Lumber also contributes to the economic base.

Climate: Modified four-season Continental climate. The area is exposed to all North American air-mass types, but the Gulf of Mexico gives the summer season prolonged periods of warmer and more humid weather. Sixty-two percent of the normal annual precipitation occurs during the growing season of 233 days. Winters are mild, but polar and arctic outbreaks are not uncommon. Glaze and ice storms, though infrequent, can be severe.

Mildness: 63 Brightness: 54 Stability: 13

Places Rated Score: 54.80 **Places Rated Rank: 151**

TEMPERATURE

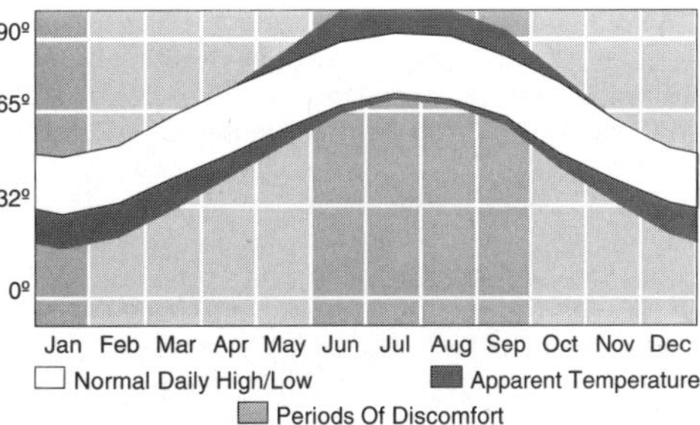

ANNUAL
Humidity: 71%
Wind Speed: 7.8 mph
DAYS
0º or below: 0
32º or below: 57
90º or above: 73
Clear: 118
Cloudy: 147

PRECIPITATION

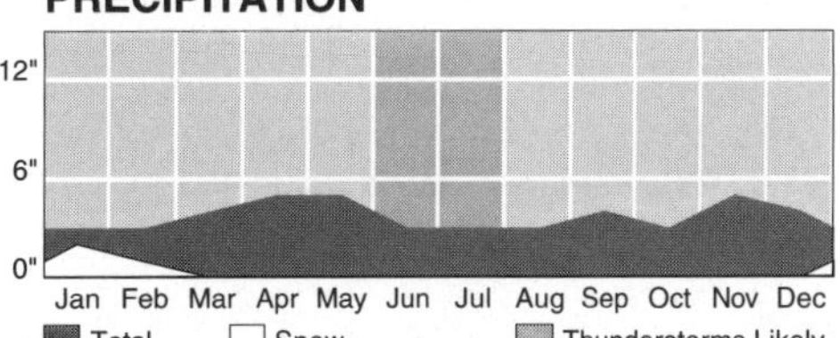

ANNUAL
Precipitation: 50.9"
Snow: 5.1"
DAYS
Precipitation: 72
Thunderstorm: 57

Long Island, NY

Location: 40.44 N, 73.37 W, at 100 feet, station is at the extreme tip of Long Island 120 miles east of New York City.
Landscape: This peninsula is from 12 to 23 miles wide and 118 miles long. Terrain is generally flat, with only a gradual rise in elevation. Eastern deciduous forest dominated by tall, broadleaf trees such as oak, beech, hickory, and sweet chestnut that provide a dense canopy in summer and shed their leaves entirely in winter. Small trees and shrubs make up the undergrowth.
Climate: Seasonal and daily temperature fluctuations are tempered by the effects of the surrounding water. Summers tend to be hot and humid with afternoon showers. In coastal areas, there are an average of 7 days between June and September when afternoon temperature exceeds 90°F. Inland, there are 10 to 15 such days. Winters can be cold with icy rain. Snowfall is light, averaging about 29 inches seasonally, and lasts but a little while. Occasionally tropical weather systems produce storms of strong wind and heavy rain in the late summer or fall, and coastal low pressure systems will produce a heavy snowfall in winter.

Mildness: 53 Brightness: 44 Stability: 76

Places Rated Score: 54.47 **Places Rated Rank: 152**

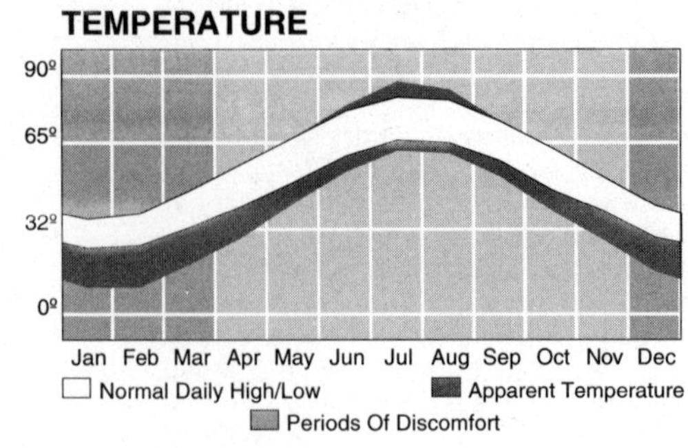

ANNUAL
Humidity: 69%
Wind Speed: 8.9 mph
DAYS
0º or below: 0
32º or below: 85
90º or above: 10
Clear: 106
Cloudy: 132

PRECIPITATION

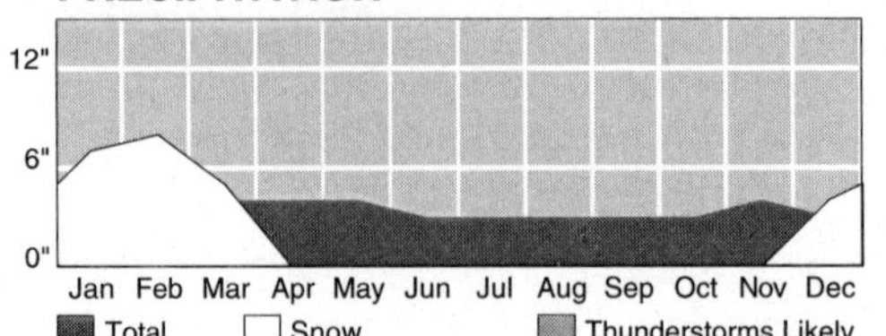

ANNUAL
Precipitation: 44.7"
Snow: 26.7"
DAYS
Precipitation: 71
Thunderstorm: 24

✓ Los Angeles–Long Beach, CA

Location: 33.56 N, 118.24 W, at 100 feet, on the Pacific Coast of Southern California.
Landscape: Major features are the Pacific Ocean, 3 miles to the west, and the southern California coastal mountain ranges, a buffer on the inland side of the coastal plain to the more extreme conditions of the interior. Coastal plain vegetation includes chaparral, varieties of oak, laurel, and Pacific bayberry. Numerous geologic faults cause periodic tremors, and the strong dry Santa Ana winds pose the threat of fires spreading into the brush hills around the city.
Climate: Semiarid Mediterranean is pleasant and mild throughout the year. Characteristic features of the two-season climate are low clouds at night and morning, and sunny afternoons that prevail during spring and summer and often during the remainder of the year. Combined with a sea breeze, the coastal cloudiness causes mild temperatures throughout the year. There can be great differences in temperature, humidity, fog, sunshine, and rain over fairly short distances. Temperature ranges are least and humidity is higher close to the coast; precipitation increases with elevation.

Mildness: 98 Brightness: 81 Stability: 99

Places Rated Score: 97.68 **Places Rated Rank: 3**

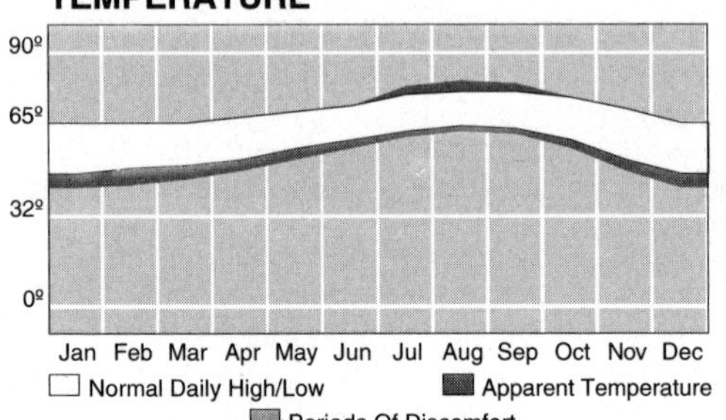

ANNUAL
Humidity: 71%
Wind Speed: 6.2 mph
DAYS
0º or below: 0
32º or below: 0
90º or above: 5
Clear: 143
Cloudy: 107

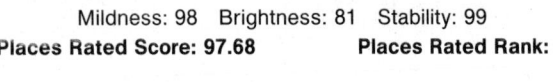

PRECIPITATION

12"
6"
0"
Jan Feb Mar Apr May Jun Jul Aug Sep Oct Nov Dec
Total Snow Thunderstorms Likely

ANNUAL
Precipitation: 12.0"
Snow: 0.0"
DAYS
Precipitation: 21
Thunderstorm: 1

Louisville, KY–IN

Location: 38.11 N, 85.44 W, at 480 feet, on the south bank of the Ohio River, across from Indiana, 54 miles west of Frankfort, the state capital.
Landscape: The eastern part of the city is residential and consists of rolling hills and plateaus. Kentucky bluegrass grows on rich limestone soil. The western, industrial part of the city lies on the river's floodplain. A low range of hills on the Indiana bank provides a partial barrier to icy blasts of winter.
Climate: Continental, but more variable because of its position in mid-latitudes; in the belt of westerly winds and not completely shut off from influences of the Gulf of Mexico. Winters are moderately cold. Snows, although seldom heavy, are a regular occurrence from November through March. Spring arrives in early April. Summers are quite warm, with notable temperatures in June. High relative humidity and high intensity rainstorms are common during both spring and summer.

Mildness: 48 Brightness: 35 Stability: 32

Places Rated Score: 43.86 **Places Rated Rank: 192**

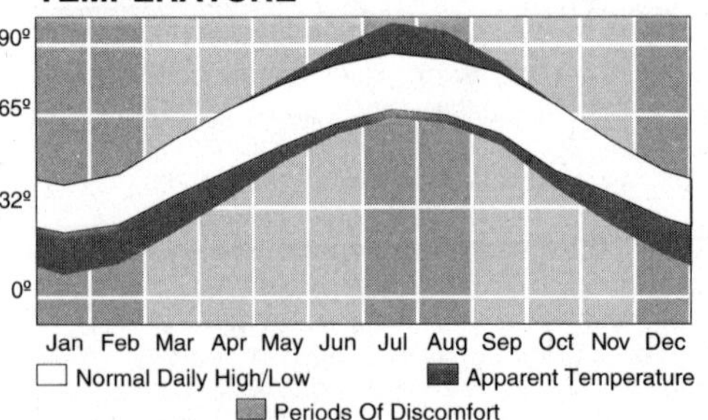

ANNUAL
Humidity: 70%
Wind Speed: 8.3 mph
DAYS
0º or below: 2
32º or below: 90
90º or above: 35
Clear: 92
Cloudy: 171

PRECIPITATION

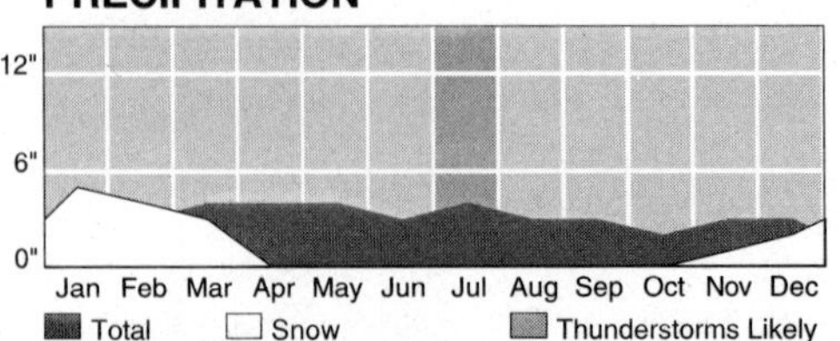

ANNUAL
Precipitation: 44.4"
Snow: 16.2"
DAYS
Precipitation: 76
Thunderstorm: 45

Lubbock, TX

Location: 33.39 N, 101.49 W, at 3,250 feet, over 380 miles NW of Austin, in the high plateau area called the South Plains region.
Landscape: The *LLano Estacado* or High Plains form a great table land; essentially level with numerous small playas, small stream valleys, and low hummocks. Steppe vegetation is generally short grasses that are bunched and sparsely distributed. Gently sloping and generally treeless, there are no appreciable terrain features that affect wind flow across the plateau. Land is suitable for growing cotton and grains, and vineyards have recently been established.
Climate: Semiarid Continental; transition between desert conditions to the west and humid climates to the east. Normal precipitation is 18 inches per year, with maximum precipitation occurring May through September, when warm tropical air is carried inland from the Gulf of Mexico. This air mass produces moderate to heavy afternoon and evening convective thunderstorms, sometimes with hail. Dry westerly winds

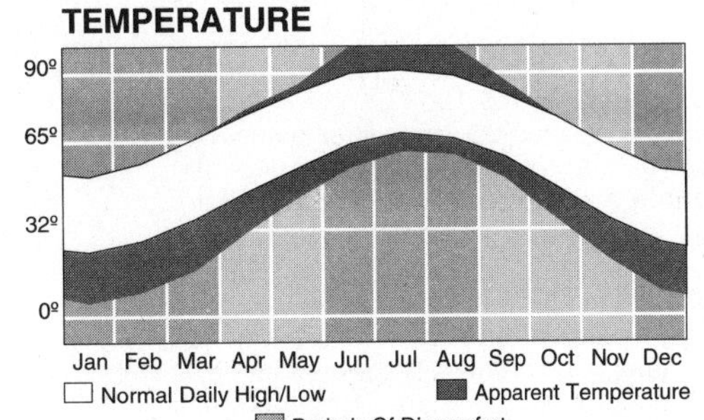

ANNUAL
Humidity: 60%
Wind Speed: 12.4 m
DAYS
0º or below: 1
32º or below: 93
90º or above: 80
Clear: 160
Cloudy: 103

PRECIPITATION

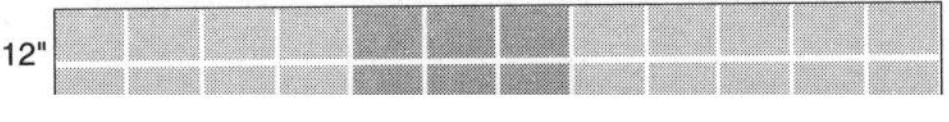

ANNUAL
Precipitation: 18.7"

Landscape: There are 18,000 acres of lake surface within or just outside the city limits. However, lakes are frozen from December 17 to April 5. Most farming is dairying, with field crops mainly of corn, oats, and alfalfa. The majority of fruits grown are apples, strawberries, and raspberries.
Climate: Continental, typical of interior North America, with a large annual temperature range and frequent short periods of temperature changes. The absolute temperature range is from 107°F to −37°F. Winter temperatures average 20°F and summer ones 68°F. The most common air masses are of polar origin, with occasional outbreaks of arctic air during the winter. Much of the precipitation falls between May and September. Lighter winter precipitation falls over a longer period of time. Average growing season: 175 days.

Mildness: 10 Brightness: 47 Stability: 42

Places Rated Score: 16.33 **Places Rated Rank: 324**

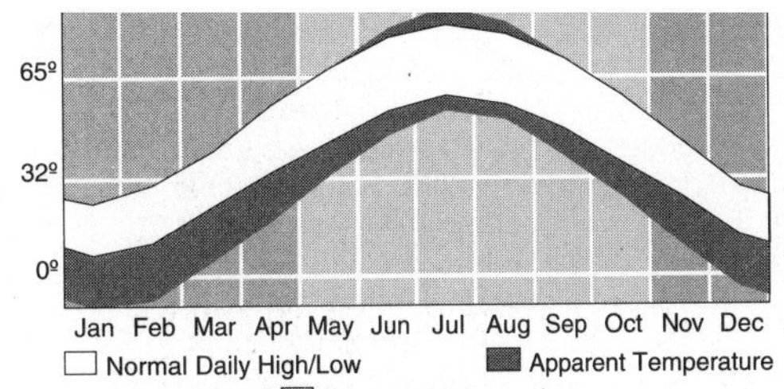

Humidity: 72%
Wind Speed: 9.9 mph
DAYS
0º or below: 25
32º or below: 161
90º or above: 14
Clear: 90
Cloudy: 179

PRECIPITATION

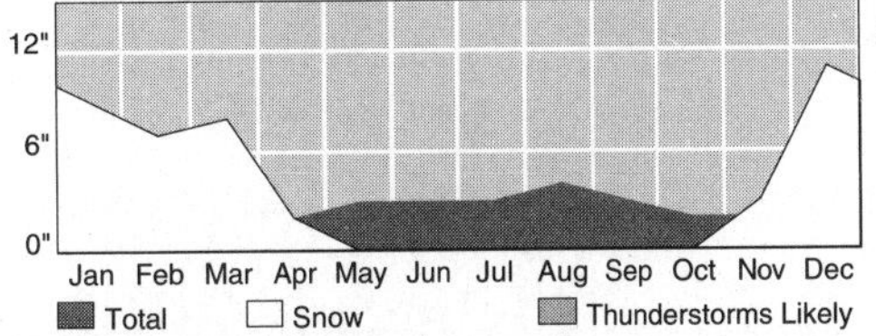

ANNUAL
Precipitation: 30.9"
Snow: 42.6"
DAYS
Precipitation: 64
Thunderstorm: 40

Manchester, NH

Location: 42.59 N, 71.24 W, at 250 feet, rises from both banks of the Merrimack River in southeast New Hampshire, 53 miles north of Boston.
Landscape: Loosely encircled by the New Hampshire hills, the area relief consists of low rolling hills and low mountains. Rural farmlands have fertile soils. There are a few somewhat poorly drained lakes and basin areas. Evergreen forests alternate with deciduous wooded areas and marshy terrain.
Climate: This is a four-season Continental climate. The air is cold and dry in winter, cool and dry in summer. Hot summer weather is infrequent. The winter windchill factor is low as the area is protected from strong winds by the hilly terrain. The annual precipitation is 39 inches with annual snowfall averaging 53 inches. Average frost-free days number 150.

Mildness: 22 Brightness: 39 Stability: 76

Places Rated Score: 30.43 **Places Rated Rank: 250**

TEMPERATURE

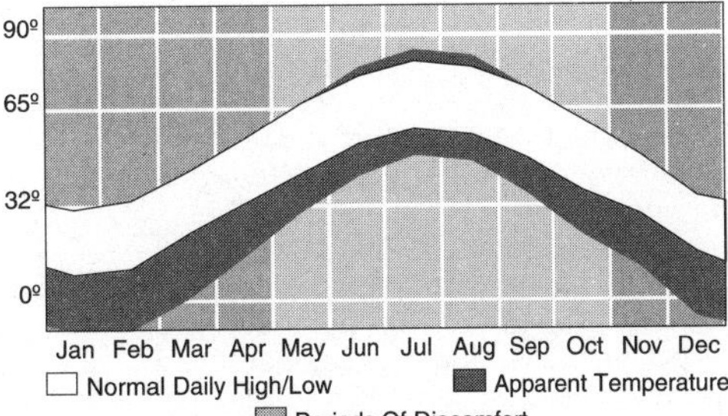

ANNUAL
Humidity: 67%
Wind Speed: 12.5 mph
DAYS
0º or below: 14
32º or below: 170
90º or above: 11
Clear: 98
Cloudy: 163

PRECIPITATION

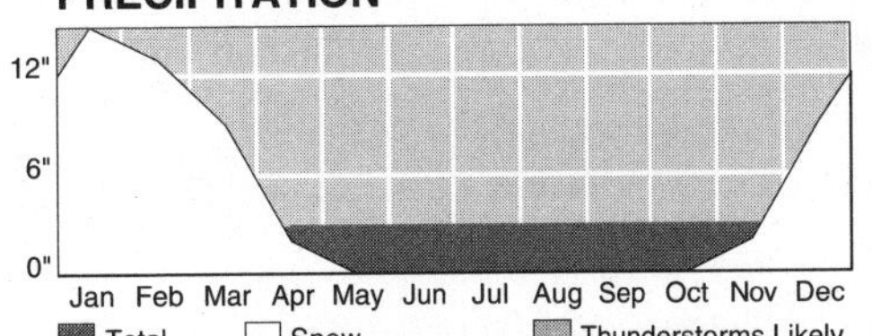

ANNUAL
Precipitation: 39.3"
Snow: 51.6"
DAYS
Precipitation: 77
Thunderstorm: 19

mate 217 ph

...ission, TX

... at 100 feet, in the lower Rio ... 75 miles west of the Gulf of ...

...phy of the Rio Grande Plain with ...s, bougainvillea and winter poinsettias ... towns, but the native upland sage and ...as lost out to development, both agricultural and ... Citrus groves and winter gardens are the result of ...tensive irrigation.

Climate: Subtropical influenced by the Gulf of Mexico. Winters are mild. Average minimum temperatures are mid-40s. Summers can be hot, humid and stormy. There are more than 100 days over 90°F. High humidity is constant throughout the year. During the months of May through August it feels oppressive. While the Sierra Madre Oriental Mountains in Mexico block the westerly air from the Chihuahuan Desert, both affect the climate of this river plain.

Mildness: 94 Brightness: 76 Stability: 40

Places Rated Score: 87.91 **Places Rated Rank: 21**

TEMPERATURE

90º 65º 32º 0º

Jan Feb Mar Apr May Jun Jul Aug Sep Oct Nov Dec

Normal Daily High/Low · Apparent Temperature · Periods Of Discomfort

ANNUAL
Humidity: 74%
Wind Speed: 11.4 mph
DAYS
0º or below: 0
32º or below: 7
90º or above: 104
Clear: 96
Cloudy: 138

PRECIPITATION

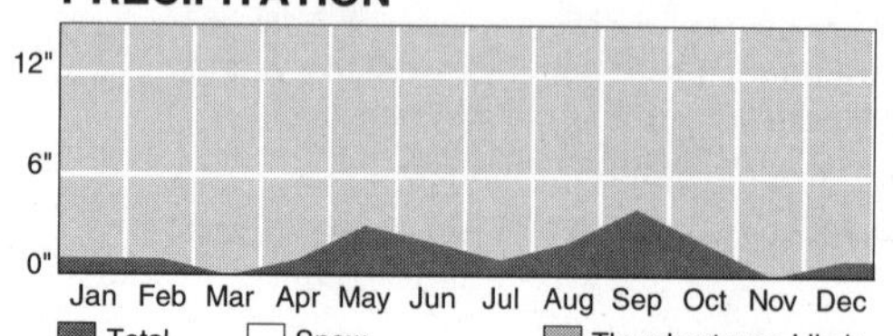

ANNUAL
Precipitation: 22.8"
Snow: 0.0"
DAYS
Precipitation: 34
Thunderstorm: 27

Medford–Ashland, OR

Location: 42.23 N, 122.53 W, at 1,300 feet, in extreme southwest Oregon 25 miles north of the California border. Crater Lake National Park is nearby.

Landscape: In a mountain valley formed by the Rogue River and one of its tributaries, Bear Creek. Most of the valley ranges in elevation from 1,300 to 1,400 feet above sea level. The valley's outlet to the ocean 80 miles west is the narrow canyon of the Rogue. Principal trees of the dense Pacific conifer forest are Douglas fir, western red cedar, western hemlock, silver fir, and Sitka spruce.

Climate: Moderate, with marked seasonal characteristics. Late fall, winter, and early spring are cloudy, damp, and cool. The remainder of the year is warm, dry, and sunny. The rain shadow afforded by the Siskiyous and the Coast Range results in relatively light rainfall, most of which falls in the wintertime. Snowfalls are light and seldom remain on the ground more than 24 hours. Winters are mild, with the temperatures just dipping below freezing during December and January. Summer days can reach 90°F, but nights are cool.

Mildness: 69 Brightness: 81 Stability: 87

Places Rated Score: 73.73 **Places Rated Rank: 71**

TEMPERATURE

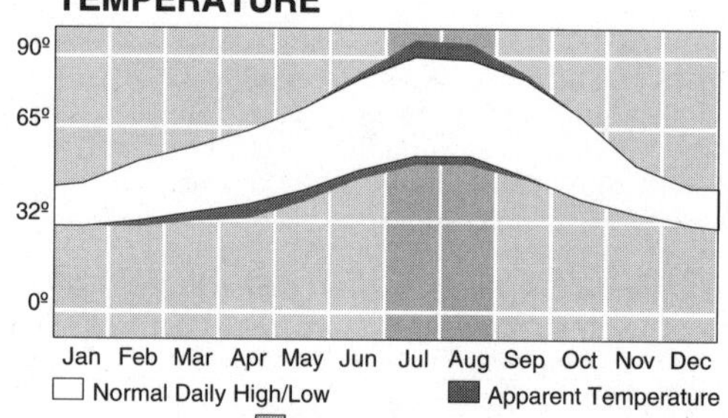

ANNUAL
Humidity: 65%
Wind Speed: 4.8 mph
DAYS
0º or below: 0
32º or below: 86
90º or above: 54
Clear: 117
Cloudy: 169

PRECIPITATION

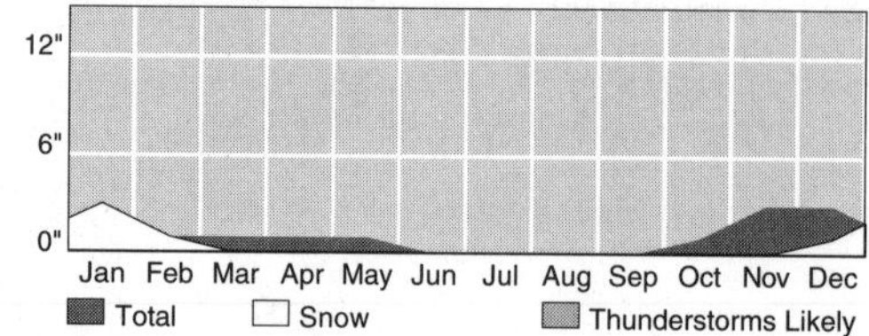

ANNUAL
Precipitation: 18.9"
Snow: 7.3"
DAYS
Precipitation: 49
Thunderstorm: 7

Memphis, TN–AR–MS

Location: 35.03 N, 90.00 W, at 270 feet, on the Mississippi River in the southwest corner of the state, covering the tri-state borders.

Landscape: Slightly rolling delta topography, across from the level alluvial area on the Arkansas side. Major crops are cotton, corn and other vegetables, as well as orchards of peaches and apples. The favorable terrain supports dairying and raising cattle and hogs.

Climate: Moderate, blending features of Continental with Subtropical. Though not in the normal paths of storms coming either from the Gulf of Mexico or from Canada, Memphis is affected by both and therefore has comparatively frequent changes in weather. Freezing days are not uncommon during winter. Hot steamy weather can be expected during summer. The average annual temperature is in the low 60s and varies from the low 40s in January to the low 80s in July. Average growing season is 230 days with annual rainfall of more than 50 inches.

Mildness: 66 Brightness: 51 Stability: 13

Places Rated Score: 56.53 **Places Rated Rank: 146**

TEMPERATURE

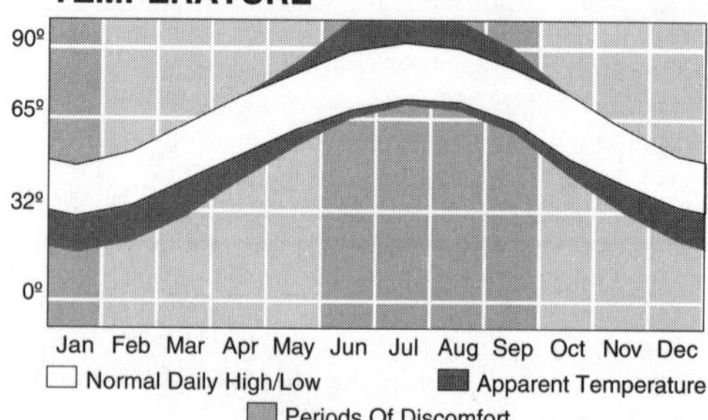

ANNUAL
Humidity: 69%
Wind Speed: 8.9 mph
DAYS
0º or below: 0
32º or below: 59
90º or above: 86
Clear: 118
Cloudy: 151

PRECIPITATION

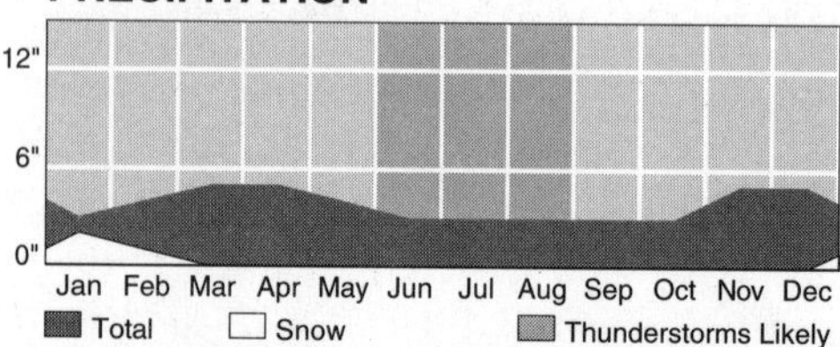

ANNUAL
Precipitation: 52.1"
Snow: 5.1"
DAYS
Precipitation: 73
Thunderstorm: 59

✓Miami, FL

Location: 25.48 N, 80.18 W, at 10 feet, on the lower southeast coast of Florida, 90 miles from Cuba.
Landscape: To the south lies Biscayne Bay, and east of it Miami Beach. The surrounding countryside is level and sparsely wooded.
Climate: Essentially Subtropical Marine characterized by a long, warm summer with abundant rainfall and a mild, dry winter. The Atlantic Ocean greatly influences the city's small range of daily temperatures and aids the rapid warming of colder air masses that pass to the east of the state. During the early-morning hours, more rainfall occurs at Miami Beach than at the airport 9 miles inland, while during the afternoon the reverse is true. Even more striking is the difference in the annual number of days over 90°F: at Miami Beach, 15 days; at the airport, 60. Freezing temperatures occur occasionally in surrounding farming districts but almost never near the ocean. In 1977, for the first time in Miami's history, traces of

TEMPERATURE

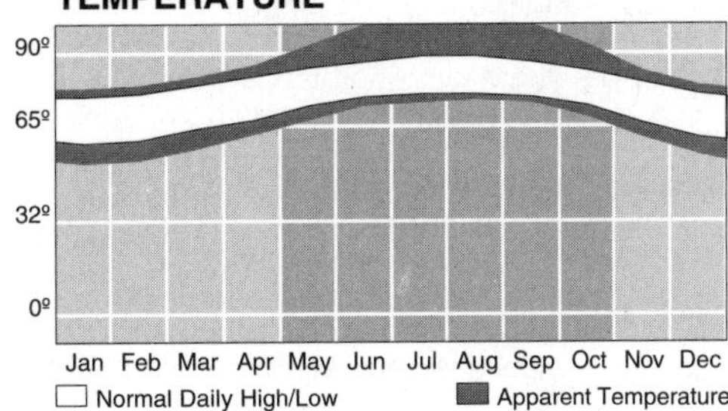

ANNUAL
Humidity: 72%
Wind Speed: 9.3 mph
DAYS
0° or below: 0
32° or below: 0
90° or above: 55
Clear: 75
Cloudy: 115

PRECIPITATION

ANNUAL
Precipitation: 55.9"

Landscape: Rolling prairie. The St. Lawrence Seaway and the Milwaukee, Menomonee, and Kinnickinnic rivers are integral parts of the landscape, forming a natural harbor as they enter Lake Michigan.
Climate: Influenced by storms that move eastward across the upper Ohio River valley and the Great Lakes region. Large high-pressure systems moving southeastward out of Canada also have an effect, and it is seldom that two or three days will pass without a distinct change in the weather, particularly during winter and spring. The major influence on the climate is Lake Michigan. Generally, the lake cools the shoreline in summer and warms it in winter. Thunderstorms occur less frequently in Milwaukee than in areas to the south and west. Winter days can be cold and severe winter storms can produce 10 or more inches of snow. Annual snowfall of nearly 50 inches. Winters are cloudy. And summers are clear, receiving an average of 70 percent of possible sunshine.

Mildness: 18 Brightness: 40 Stability: 58

Places Rated Score: 24.57 **Places Rated Rank: 299**

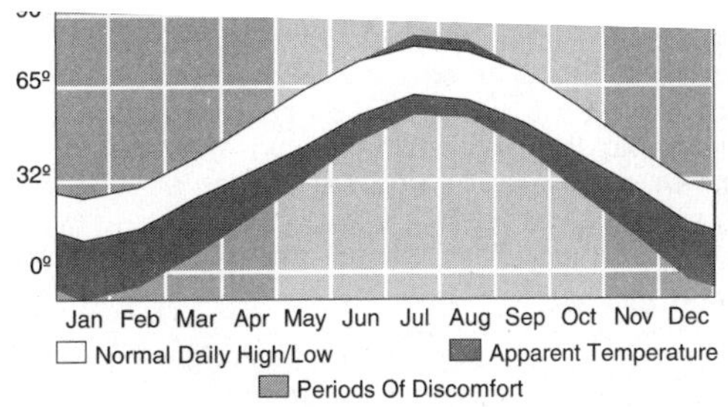

Humidity: 72%
Wind Speed: 11.5 mph
DAYS
0° or below: 16
32° or below: 141
90° or above: 10
Clear: 90
Cloudy: 175

PRECIPITATION

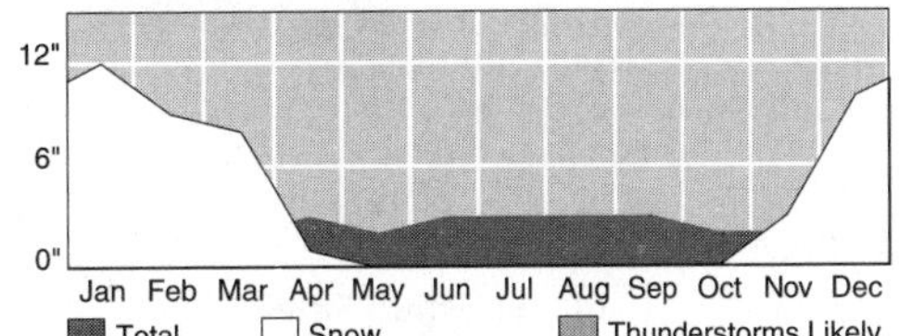

ANNUAL
Precipitation: 32.9"
Snow: 46.5"
DAYS
Precipitation: 65
Thunderstorm: 35

Minneapolis–St. Paul, MN–WI

Location: 44.53 N, 93.13 W, at 830 feet, the Twin Cities are located at the confluence of the Mississippi and Minnesota rivers over the heart of an artesian water basin in the southeast section of the state. Minneapolis is on the west bank of the Mississippi; St. Paul is on the east bank.
Landscape: The topography is flat or gently rolling grasslands with numerous lakes that are small, shallow, and ice-covered in winter. Gallery forests line the waterways. Structurally the area is part of the Canadian Shield, underlain with granite, gneiss, and schist. Glacier activity extended to this point.
Climate: Predominantly Continental in climate, the two cities are near the geographic center of North America. There are wide variations in temperature, ample summer rainfall, and scanty winter precipitation. In general, there exists a tendency toward extremes in almost all climatic features. Severe storms of all types—blizzards, freezing rain, tornadoes, wind, and hail—occur.

Mildness: 4 Brightness: 66 Stability: 37

Places Rated Score: 10.76 **Places Rated Rank: 337**

TEMPERATURE

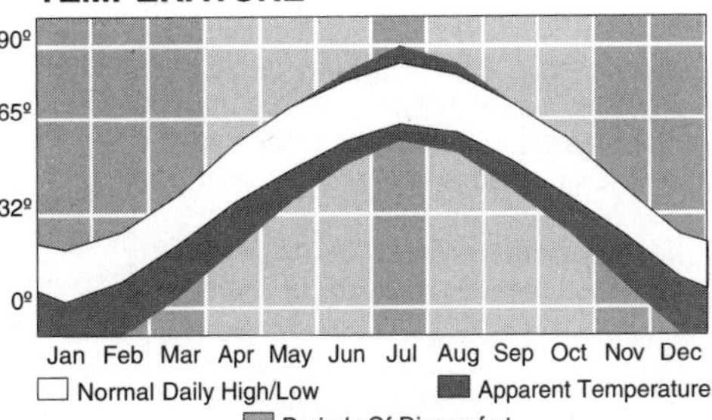

ANNUAL
Humidity: 69%
Wind Speed: 10.5 mph
DAYS
0° or below: 34
32° or below: 158
90° or above: 15
Clear: 96
Cloudy: 168

PRECIPITATION

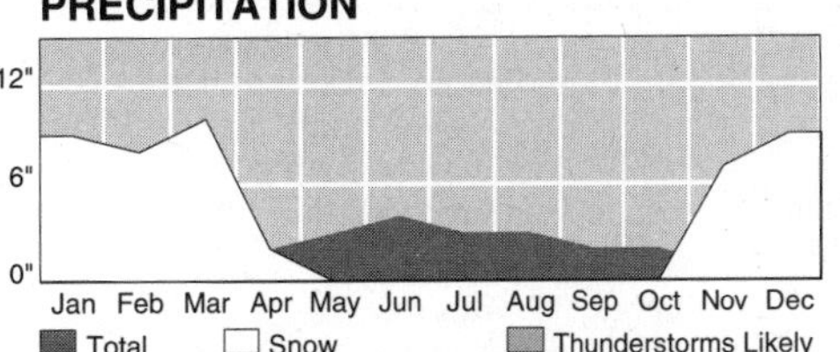

ANNUAL
Precipitation: 28.3"
Snow: 49.5"
DAYS
Precipitation: 55
Thunderstorm: 37

Mobile, AL

Location: 30.41 N, 88.15 W, at 210 feet, station is 35 miles south of Mobile on the Gulf of Mexico near the entrance to Mobile Bay.
Landscape: Gulf coastal plain where ecologies range from sea level sandy beaches and saltmarshes to typical southern pine forests.
Climate: Subtropical in character as the normal annual rainfall amount here is one of the highest in the continental United States. It is evenly distributed throughout the year, with a slight maximum at the height of the summer thunderstorm season. Although destructive hurricanes are extremely infrequent, this seems due more to chance than to location. The area is subject to hurricanes from the West Indies and the Gulf of Mexico. The growing season averages 274 days, enough for citrus fruits to be grown in the area. Summers are consistently warm; winters are mild.

Mildness: 85 Brightness: 23 Stability: 6

Places Rated Score: 67.23 **Places Rated Rank: 91**

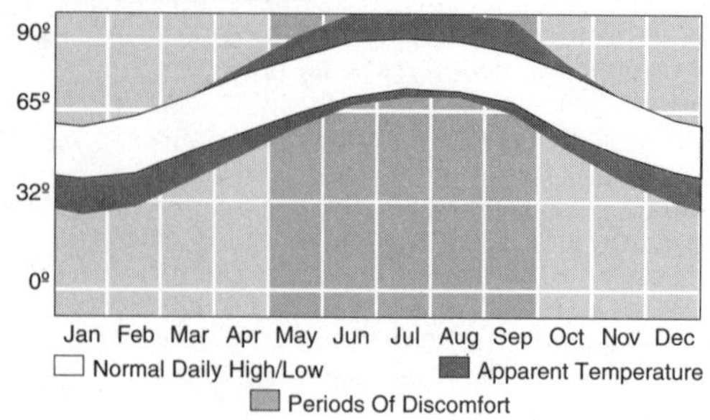

ANNUAL
Humidity: 72%
Wind Speed: 9.0 mph
DAYS
0º or below: 0
32º or below: 21
90º or above: 76
Clear: 102
Cloudy: 147

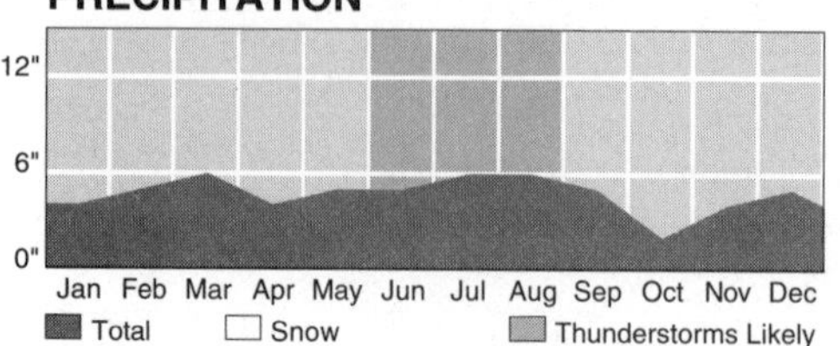

ANNUAL
Precipitation: 64.0"
Snow: 0.5"
DAYS
Precipitation: 80
Thunderstorm: 79

✓ Modesto, CA

Location: 37.39 N, 121.00 W, at 90 feet, south of Sacramento, east of San Francisco, at the northern end of the San Joaquin Valley.
Landscape: The rich farmlands and grasslands of the valley are drained and irrigated by snow-fed streams flowing from the high slopes of the Sierra Nevada. Stream flow continues well into the dry summer months. Many of the streams have been dammed to hold water supplies for irrigation, industrial and domestic use throughout this part of the year. Modesto is the gateway to Yosemite National Park to the east and Gold Country to the north.
Climate: The San Joaquin Valley lies between the Coast Range and the Sierra Nevada. The area, well-protected from the Pacific Ocean, displays Continental climate characteristics of warmer summers, colder winters, greater daily and seasonal temperature ranges, and generally lower relative humidities. Annual precipitation averages 12 inches. The valley has a freeze-free season of 225 to 300 days. In winter the area is subject to northers, rather mild temperatures accompanied by dry, persistent winds that many people find unpleasant.

Mildness: 78 Brightness: 99 Stability: 86

Places Rated Score: 85.81 **Places Rated Rank: 26**

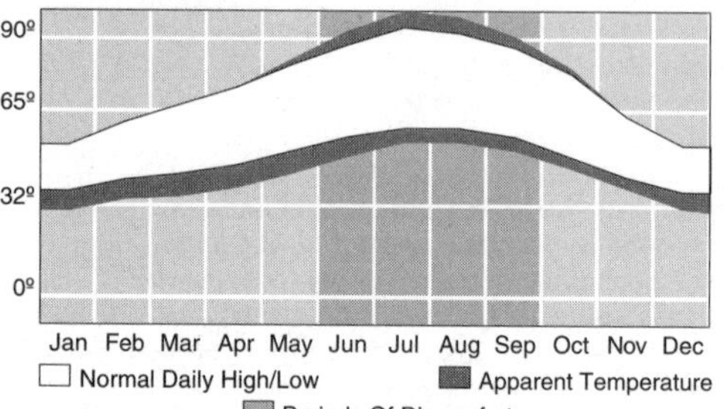

ANNUAL
Humidity: 61%
Wind Speed: 7.5 mph
DAYS
0º or below: 0
32º or below: 21
90º or above: 81
Clear: 184
Cloudy: 104

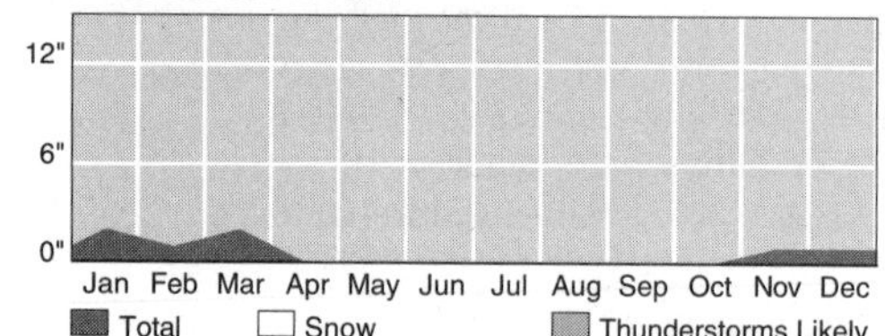

ANNUAL
Precipitation: 12.1"
Snow: 0.1"
DAYS
Precipitation: 26
Thunderstorm: 5

Monmouth–Ocean, NJ

Location: 39.57 N, 74.12 W, at 40 feet, two counties in the center of New Jersey's Atlantic coast, 95 miles south of New York City.
Landscape: Generally flat Coastal Plain is composed of tidal marshes and beach sand. The dunes provide vantage points for observing bird migrations along the Atlantic flyway. More than half of Ocean County is covered by unbroken forests of pine, oak and cedar. The famous Pine Barrens of southern New Jersey are hundreds of square miles of second growth pine, scrub growth and swamps. Protection is given to recovering American holly and wild black cherry, vegetation that once was abundant.
Climate: Continental, moderated by the Atlantic Ocean. Summers are cooler, winters warmer than those of other places at the same latitude. During summer sea breezes in the late morning and afternoon prevent excessive heat. On occasion, sea breezes may lower the temperature 20 degrees within a half hour. Fall is long, lasting until almost mid-November. On the other hand, warming is somewhat delayed in the spring. Precipitation is moderate and distributed throughout the year. Variation exists from year to year in amount of rainfall during late summer and early fall.

Mildness: 54 Brightness: 35 Stability: 74

Places Rated Score: 53.91 **Places Rated Rank: 154**

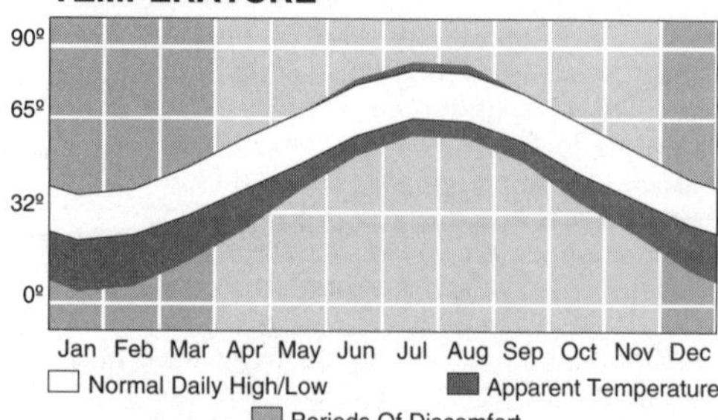

ANNUAL
Humidity: 63%
Wind Speed: 10.2 mph
DAYS
0º or below: 0
32º or below: 98
90º or above: 12
Clear: 93
Cloudy: 160

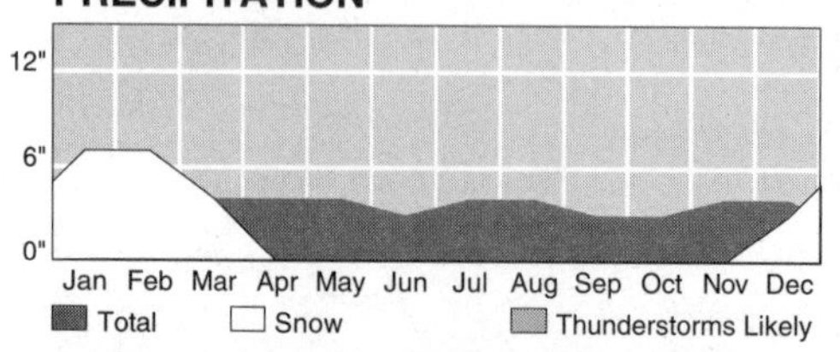

ANNUAL
Precipitation: 47.1"
Snow: 23.3"
DAYS
Precipitation: 73
Thunderstorm: 24

Montgomery, AL

Location: 32.18 N, 86.24 W, at 220 feet, the capital is on the Alabama River in the south-central part of the state.
Landscape: Located in a gently rolling area of southern Alabama. Fertile soil. About two-thirds of Alabama is covered by forests, largely made up of southern yellow pine, red cedar and other conifers. No local topographic features appreciably influence climate.
Climate: From June through September, humidity and temperature conditions show little daily change. During summer, 100-degree readings are infrequent. From April through September, all precipitation is from local heat thundershowers in the afternoon. Rain is abundant and includes all types and intensities from December through March. During the coldest months from December through February there are frequent shifts between mild, moist air from the Gulf of Mexico and dry, cool continental air. Hard freezes are infrequent during winter; snow is rare enough to be a curiosity.

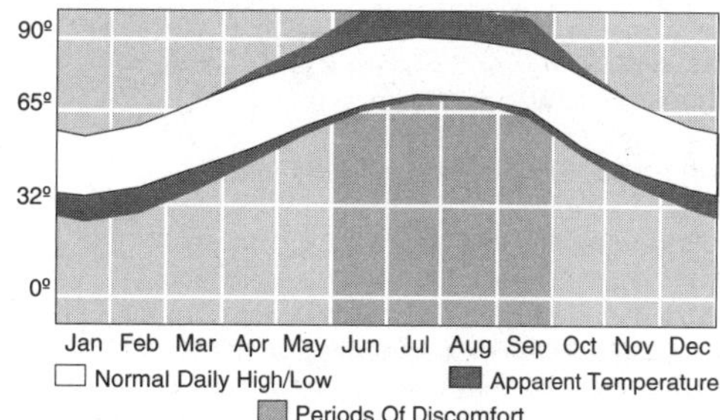

ANNUAL
Humidity: 71%
Wind Speed: 6.6 mph
DAYS
0º or below: 0
32º or below: 39
90º or above: 81
Clear: 108
Cloudy: 150

PRECIPITATION

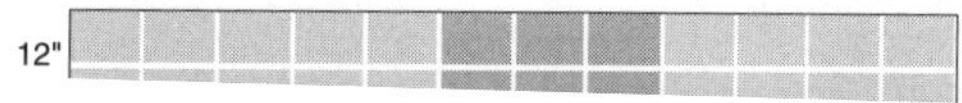

ANNUAL
Precipitation: 53.4"

rivers.
Landscape: The Laurentians lie to the north, the Appalachians to the south and southeast. Most of Montreal Island is situated between 100 feet and 150 feet above sea level with the exception of Mount Royal, which rises to 750 feet.
Climate: Halfway between the equator and the North Pole, the city has climate influenced by aspects of Continental and Maritime regimes. There can be severe temperature differences between summer and winter, but because of the Maritime influence, it is wet more or less uniformly throughout the year. Every Montrealer is familiar with the cold waves of winter, the mild spells of spring, the sultry days of summer, and the gray periods of fall. On average, the first snowflakes appear in mid-November and the first winter broadside of 5 inches hits a month later.

Mildness: 12 Brightness: 10 Stability: 73

Places Rated Score: 16.16 **Places Rated Rank: 326**

65º
32º
0º
Jan Feb Mar Apr May Jun Jul Aug Sep Oct Nov Dec
Normal Daily High/Low
Apparent Temperature
Periods Of Discomfort

Humidity: 72%
Wind Speed: 9.7 mph
DAYS
0º or below: 15
32º or below: 155
90º or above: 10
Clear: 108
Cloudy: 137

PRECIPITATION

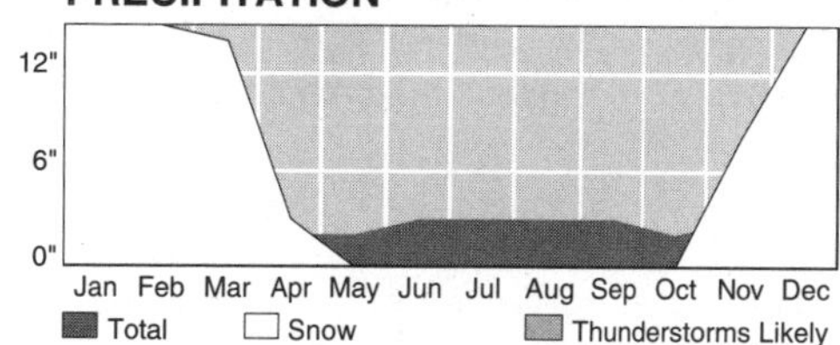

ANNUAL
Precipitation: 37.3"
Snow: 92.5"
DAYS
Precipitation: 120
Thunderstorm: 25

Myrtle Beach, SC

Location: 34.03 N, 78.53 W, at 90 feet, 100 miles NE of Charleston in the center of the Atlantic coast area known as the Grand Strand, which extends 43 miles and has a populated area only a few blocks wide.
Landscape: Low and swampy inland; the entire area is quite flat. Elevations are no greater than 50 feet above sea level. There are many more trees and wooded areas than are often found in a beach area. The beaches themselves are white sand. The water is quite clean, as there are no harbors, shipping, or major industries nearby. Also, no rivers or streams empty into the sea for a distance of almost 30 miles. Inland are stands of southern yellow pine, often mixed with hickory, sweetgum, and other deciduous trees.
Climate: Subtropical, having mild winters and warm summers, as a rule. Sunny days are common. The ocean has a pronounced modifying effect on temperatures, and the Blue Ridge Mountains inland block the cold air from the interior. Some tropical storms reach the area every few years.

Mildness: 76 Brightness: 39 Stability: 20

Places Rated Score: 64.11 **Places Rated Rank: 112**

TEMPERATURE

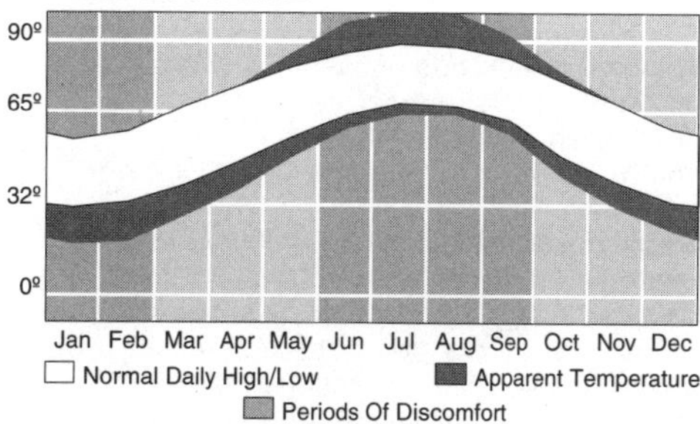

ANNUAL
Humidity: 70%
Wind Speed: 8.6 mph
DAYS
0º or below: 0
32º or below: 63
90º or above: 56
Clear: 102
Cloudy: 154

PRECIPITATION

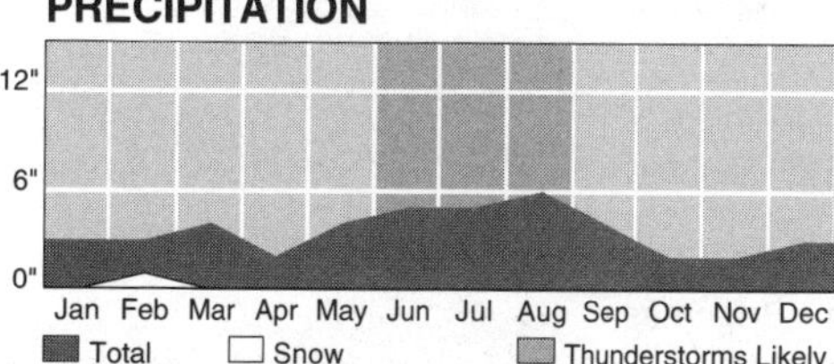

ANNUAL
Precipitation: 49.2"
Snow: 1.8"
DAYS
Precipitation: 69
Thunderstorm: 58

Naples, FL

Location: 26.10 N, 81.47 W, at 0 feet, on Florida's southern Gulf coast 25 miles south of Ft. Myers.
Landscape: On a 7-mile mainland beach at the edge of the Everglades; inland is a waste of mangrove islands and stands of Cypress, evergreen oaks, laurel, small palms, and shrubs. Much of the surrounding flat, sandy land is less than 15 feet in elevation and vulnerable to hurricane-borne tidal surges.
Climate: Subtropical, with summer and winter temperature extremes checked by the influence of the Gulf. Mild winters have many bright, warm days. Traces of snow have occurred only a few times this century. Nights are moderately cool. Rainfall averages more than 50 inches annually, with two-thirds of this total coming daily between June and September. Most rain falls as late afternoon or early evening thunderstorms, bringing relief from the heat.

Mildness: 96 Brightness: 16 Stability: 5
Places Rated Score: 82.00 **Places Rated Rank: 42**

TEMPERATURE

90º 65º 32º 0º
Jan Feb Mar Apr May Jun Jul Aug Sep Oct Nov Dec
Normal Daily High/Low — Apparent Temperature — Periods Of Discomfort

ANNUAL
Humidity: 72%
Wind Speed: 8.0 mph
DAYS
0º or below: 0
32º or below: 0
90º or above: 101
Clear: 98
Cloudy: 99

PRECIPITATION

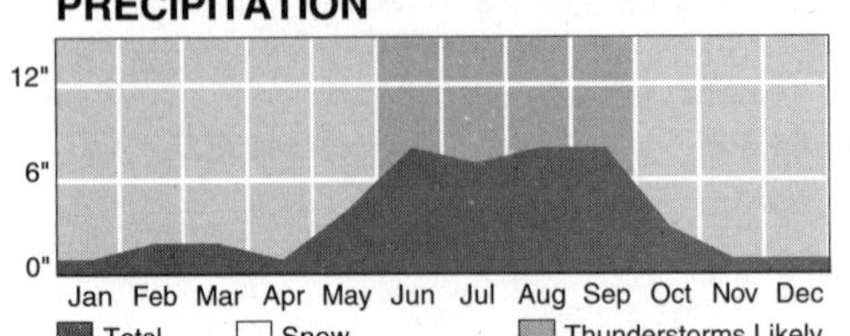

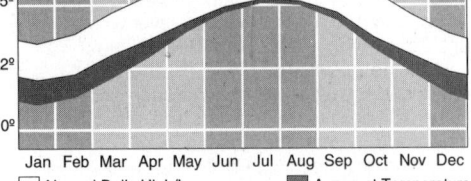

ANNUAL
Precipitation: 51.1"
Snow: 0.0"
DAYS
Precipitation: 72
Thunderstorm: 89

Nashville, TN

Location: 36.07 N, 86.41 W, at 590 feet, on the Cumberland River in the northwestern corner of the Nashville Basin.
Landscape: The escarpment of the Highland Rim rises 400 feet above the mean elevation of the basin, forming an amphitheater around the city from the southwest to the southeast.
Climate: Temperate Continental characteristic temperatures where extremes of heat or cold are rare, yet fairly frequent changes give variety. In July, the mean temperature is 80°F, and that of January is 37°F. The humidity is moderate when compared with other locations east of the Mississippi and south of the Ohio River. The city is not in the most highly traveled path of general storm systems that cross the country. However it is in a zone that experiences thunderstorms fairly often and snow falls each winter. The growing season is some 211 days with rainfall averaging 47 inches each year.

Mildness: 61 Brightness: 34 Stability: 20
Places Rated Score: 51.65 **Places Rated Rank: 163**

TEMPERATURE

90º 65º 32º 0º
Jan Feb Mar Apr May Jun Jul Aug Sep Oct Nov Dec
Normal Daily High/Low — Apparent Temperature — Periods Of Discomfort

ANNUAL
Humidity: 70%
Wind Speed: 8.0 mph
DAYS
0º or below: 1
32º or below: 76
90º or above: 51
Clear: 103
Cloudy: 156

PRECIPITATION

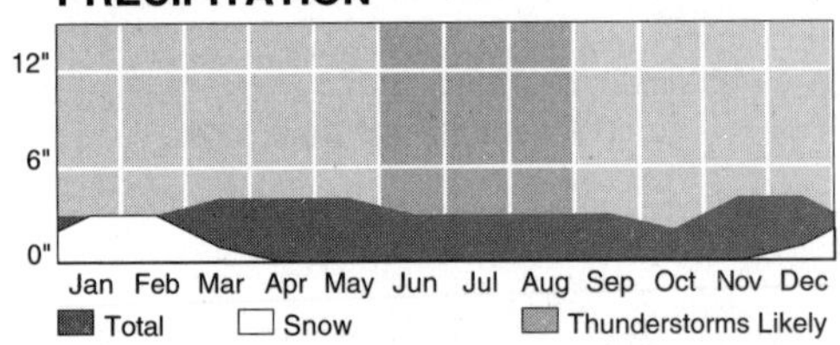

ANNUAL
Precipitation: 47.3"
Snow: 10.2"
DAYS
Precipitation: 81
Thunderstorm: 54

New Haven–Meriden, CT

Location: 41.10 N, 73.08 W, at 10 feet, a port city in south central Connecticut, on Long Island Sound at the mouth of the Quinnipiac River.
Landscape: Lying in the central lowlands of the state, where the surrounding land is wide and fertile. A narrow strip along Long Island Sound includes an indented shoreline with low, rocky headlands, smooth, sandy beaches, and broad, flat tidal marshes.
Climate: Moderate Continental climate, with four well-defined seasons and considerable diversity of weather over short time periods. Nearness to the Atlantic moderates the temperatures, often through cloud cover. Precipitation falls as snow in winter; thunderstorms may bring heavy rains in summer. Annual precipitation is 42 inches. Hurricanes occasionally strike along the shore during August or September. There is a January mean temperature of 30°F, and July averages 74°F.

Mildness: 45 Brightness: 37 Stability: 74
Places Rated Score: 47.11 **Places Rated Rank: 179**

TEMPERATURE

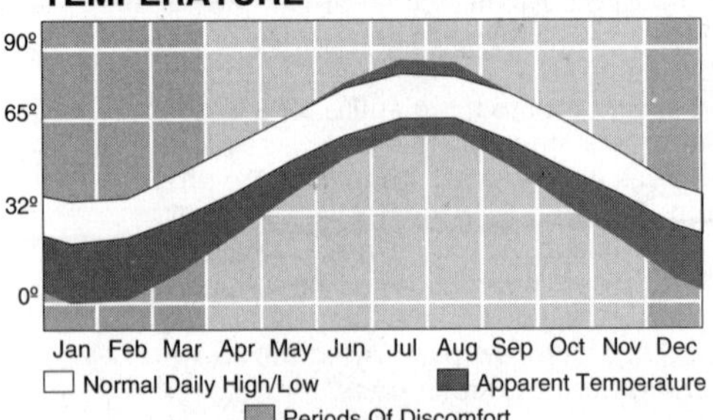

ANNUAL
Humidity: 67%
Wind Speed: 12.0 mph
DAYS
0º or below: 1
32º or below: 101
90º or above: 7
Clear: 99
Cloudy: 159

PRECIPITATION

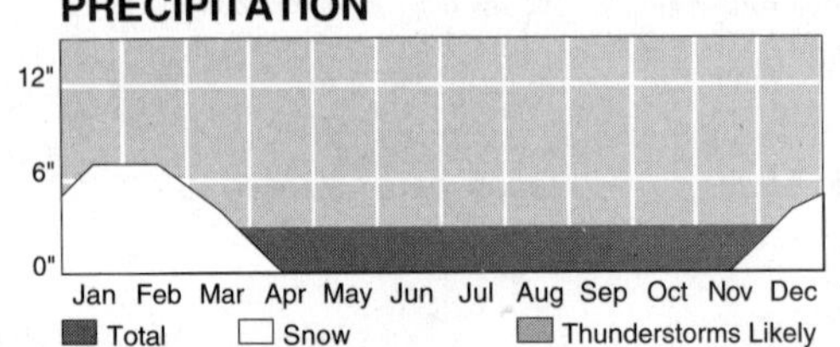

ANNUAL
Precipitation: 41.7"
Snow: 24.9"
DAYS
Precipitation: 76
Thunderstorm: 24

New Orleans, LA

Location: 29.59 N, 90.15 W, at 0 feet, in southern Louisiana, mostly on the east bank of the Mississippi.

Landscape: The metropolitan area is surrounded by water; Lake Pontchartrain to the north, the Mississippi River to the west and south, and bayous, lakes, and marshy delta land to the west and south. Elevations in the city vary from a few feet above mean sea level to a few feet below. A massive levee system offers protection from river flooding and tidal surges.

Climate: Best described as humid with surrounding water modifying the temperature and decreasing the range of temperatures. Heavy and frequent rains are typical, and there are daily afternoon thunderstorms from mid-June through September. From December to March, precipitation is likely to be steady rain of two or three days' duration, instead of showers. During winter and spring, cold rain forms fog that inhibits air and river transportation. The city has been hard hit

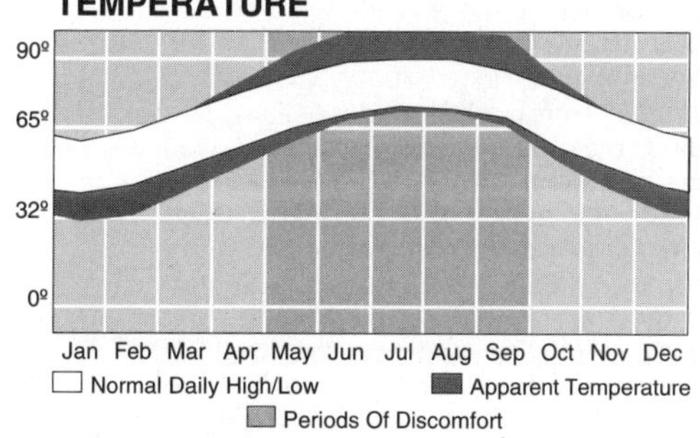

ANNUAL
Humidity: 75%
Wind Speed: 8.2 mph
DAYS
0º or below: 0
32º or below: 13
90º or above: 67
Clear: 101
Cloudy: 146

PRECIPITATION

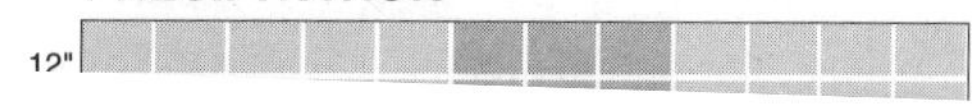

ANNUAL
Precipitation: 61.9"

southernmost tip of New York State.

Landscape: Topography is diversified by numerous waterways. The city's physical setting is an assortment of islands and parts of islands. Only the Bronx is on the mainland. The heart of the city proper is Manhattan, which is totally urban except for Central Park and other smaller parks.

Climate: Close to the path of most storm and frontal systems that move across the continent. Therefore, weather conditions affecting the city approach from a westerly direction. New York City can thus expect higher temperatures in summer and lower ones in winter than would otherwise be expected in a coastal area. However, the frequent passage of weather systems often helps reduce the length of warm and cold spells and also keeps periods of air stagnation brief. Although Continental characteristics are dominant, ocean influence is by no means absent. Sea breezes moderate the afternoon heat of summer and delay the advent of winter snows.

Mildness: 53 Brightness: 42 Stability: 68

Places Rated Score: 53.09 **Places Rated Rank: 156**

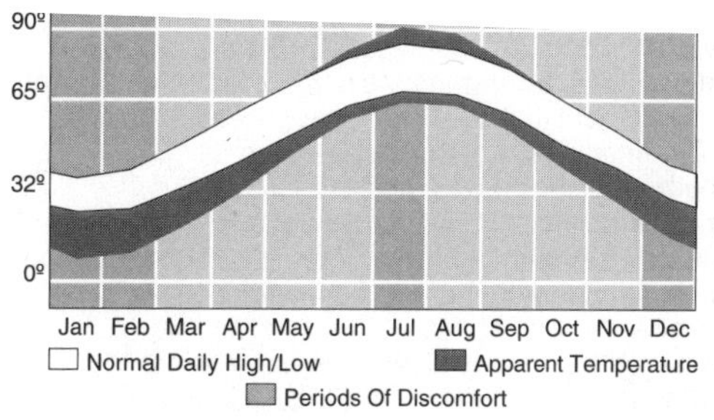

Humidity: 64%
Wind Speed: 9.4 mph
DAYS
0º or below: 0
32º or below: 81
90º or above: 16
Clear: 106
Cloudy: 132

PRECIPITATION

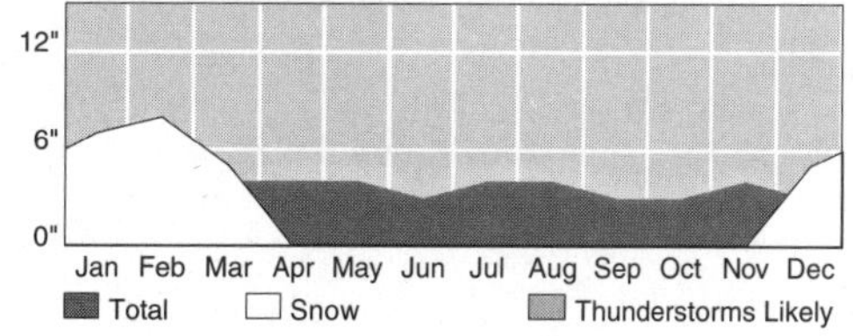

ANNUAL
Precipitation: 47.3"
Snow: 28.1"
DAYS
Precipitation: 79
Thunderstorm: 24

Norfolk–Virginia Beach–Newport News, VA–NC

Location: 36.54 N, 76.12 W, at 20 feet, on low level land, with Chesapeake Bay immediately to the north, Hampton Roads to the west, and the Atlantic Ocean to the east.

Landscape: Tidewater lowlands near the coast and the southern border of Virginia, the area is almost surrounded by water. Crossed by numerous rivers and waterways, arable land is flat and descends gently to sea level with no nearby hilly areas. Norfolk and its sister cities compose the Port of Hampton Roads, one of the world's finest natural harbors.

Climate: Subtropical characteristics with mild winters and especially pleasant springs and falls. Summers, though, are warm, humid, and long. A temperature of zero has never been recorded here, although there is occasional snow. The metro area is in a favorable geographic position, being north of the track of hurricanes and tropical storms and south of high-latitude storm systems.

Mildness: 72 Brightness: 39 Stability: 51

Places Rated Score: 64.85 **Places Rated Rank: 110**

TEMPERATURE

90º
65º
32º
0º
Jan Feb Mar Apr May Jun Jul Aug Sep Oct Nov Dec
Normal Daily High/Low
Apparent Temperature
Periods Of Discomfort

ANNUAL
Humidity: 67%
Wind Speed: 10.6 mph
DAYS
0º or below: 0
32º or below: 54
90º or above: 30
Clear: 105
Cloudy: 153

PRECIPITATION

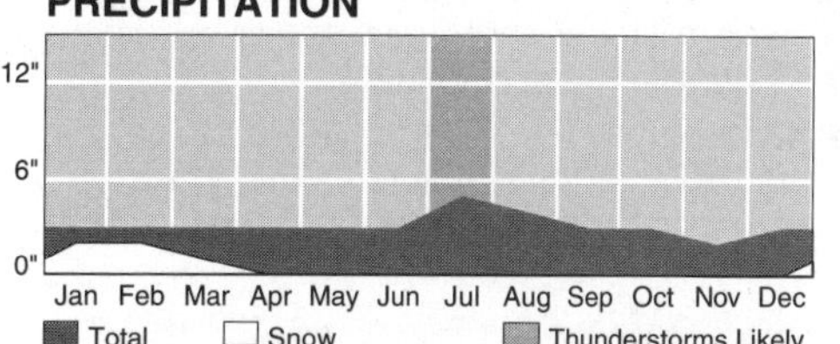

ANNUAL
Precipitation: 44.6"
Snow: 7.4"
DAYS
Precipitation: 75
Thunderstorm: 37

Ocala, FL

Location: 29.12 N, 82.05 W, at 80 feet, in north central Florida, 20 miles south of Gainesville and 90 miles west of Daytona Beach and the Atlantic.

Landscape: This is hilly and rural ridge country, just west of Ocala National Forest where there are local deposits of pure limestone, the geological basis for the peninsula. The terrain and climate has proved perfect for breeding horses and cattle. Artesian springs and outlets form the Silver River. Stands of sand pine, longleaf, slash and other yellow southern pine, and cypress mix with hardwoods of the Eastern deciduous forest. Old live oaks outnumber palm trees.

Climate: Subtropical in character with summers that are hotter and more humid than coastal locations but that are cooled by afternoon thunderstorms. Winters are mild and there is no snow. The annual range of temperature changes is small but there is a subtle though definite four-season climate.

Mildness: 93 Brightness: 20 Stability: 6

Places Rated Score: 77.09 **Places Rated Rank: 57**

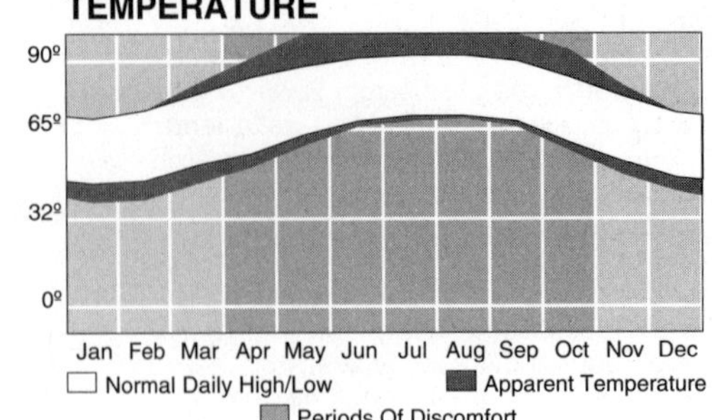

ANNUAL
Humidity: 76%
Wind Speed: 6.7 mph
DAYS
0º or below: 0
32º or below: 12
90º or above: 120
Clear: 102
Cloudy: 134

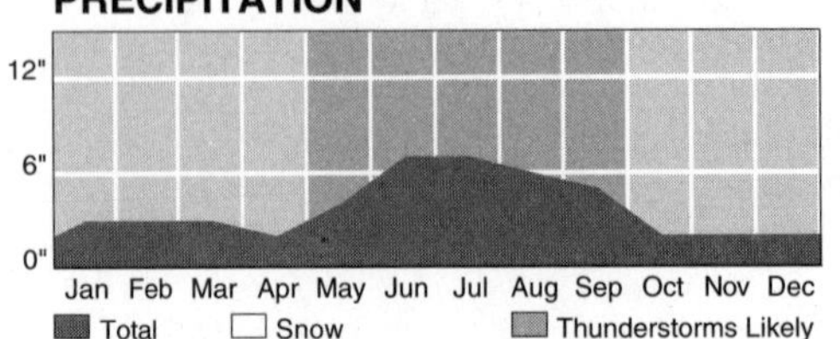

ANNUAL
Precipitation: 51.6"
Snow: 0.0"
DAYS
Precipitation: 77
Thunderstorm: 83

Odessa–Midland, TX

Location: 31.57 N, 102.11 W, at 2,860 feet, on the southern edge of the High Plains panhandle, 336 miles NW of Austin.

Landscape: Grassy High Plains cover consists mainly of shortgrasses with few trees in the area, most of them mesquite. Flat tableland, with only slight and infrequent breaks. This is the petroleum-rich Permian Basin. A large crater remains from a meteorite shower, and the Guadalupe Mountains are a dim blue bulk on the western horizon.

Climate: Semiarid Desert-Steppe. Droughts occur with monotonous frequency, resulting in dust storms so severe that suspended dust remains in the air several days after the storm has passed. Though summer afternoon temperatures are frequently above 90°F, low humidity and rapid evaporation have a cooling effect. The climate is generally pleasant, with the most disagreeable weather concentrated in late winter and spring. Most precipitation is the result of violent thunderstorms in spring and early summer.

Mildness: 62 Brightness: 98 Stability: 32

Places Rated Score: 68.59 **Places Rated Rank: 88**

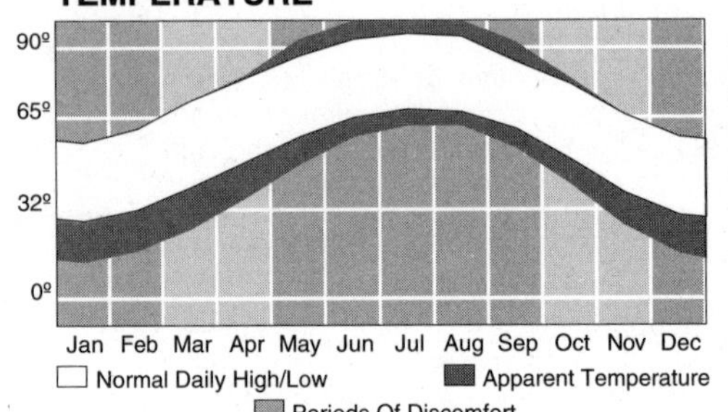

ANNUAL
Humidity: 58%
Wind Speed: 11.1 mph
DAYS
0º or below: 0
32º or below: 63
90º or above: 103
Clear: 165
Cloudy: 104

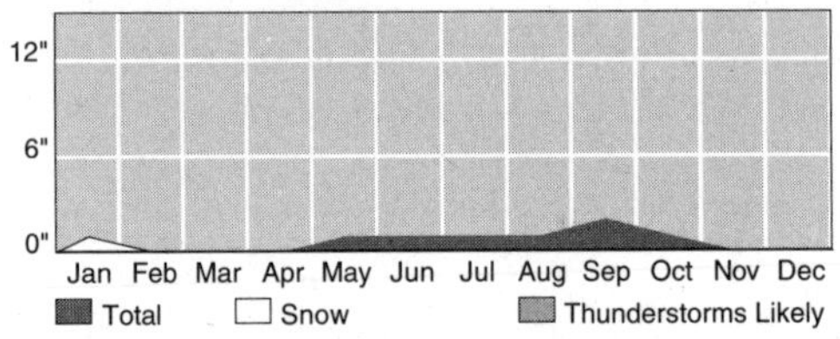

ANNUAL
Precipitation: 15.0"
Snow: 4.3"
DAYS
Precipitation: 23
Thunderstorm: 37

Oklahoma City, OK

Location: 35.24 N, 97.36 W, at 1,280 feet, along the North Canadian River near Oklahoma's geographic center, some 1,000 miles south of Canada and 500 miles north of the Gulf of Mexico.

Landscape: The surrounding countryside is a plain or gently rolling grassland. The nearest hills or low-rise mountains are the Arbuckles, 80 miles south. A major oil field is beneath the city, and rows of derricks mark the skyline.

Climate: Although some influence is exerted at times by warm, moist air from the Gulf of Mexico, the Continental climate of the city falls mainly under controls characteristic of the Great Plains. This produces pronounced daily and seasonal temperature changes and considerable variation in seasonal and annual precipitation. Summers are long and hot, broken by rain falling both as showers and thunderstorms. Occasionally there will be hail and destructive winds. Winters are comparatively mild and short. Moisture in the form of sleet arrives on frontal passages from the north.

Mildness: 46 Brightness: 86 Stability: 18

Places Rated Score: 49.51 **Places Rated Rank: 171**

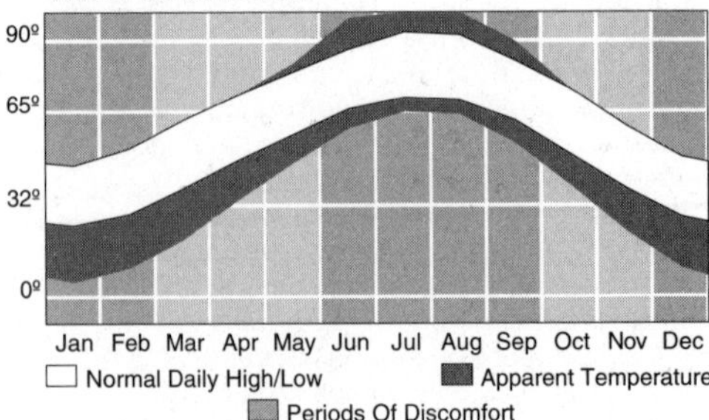

ANNUAL
Humidity: 67%
Wind Speed: 12.3 mph
DAYS
0º or below: 0
32º or below: 79
90º or above: 70
Clear: 139
Cloudy: 130

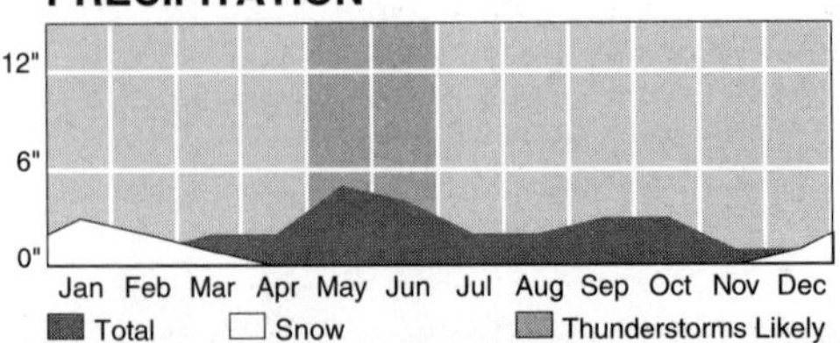

ANNUAL
Precipitation: 33.4"
Snow: 9.1"
DAYS
Precipitation: 48
Thunderstorm: 50

Olympia, WA

Location: 46.58 N, 122.54 W, at 190 feet, the capital lies at the southernmost end of Puget Sound, some 60 miles south-southwest of Seattle.
Landscape: The Olympic Peninsula, with its fine remnants of Pacific Northwest rainforests, active glaciers, and alpine meadows, lies to the northwest. The city and vicinity are well protected by the Coast Ranges from the strong south and southwest winds accompanying many Pacific storms.
Climate: Characterized by warm, generally dry summers and wet, mild winters. Fall rains begin in October and continue with few interruptions until spring. During the rainy season there is little variation in temperature, with days in the 40s and 50s and nights in the 30s, and constant cloud cover. The summer highs are between 60°F and 80°F, with up to 20 days without rain. The summer is marked by clear skies at night and frequent morning fog.

Stability: 99

TEMPERATURE

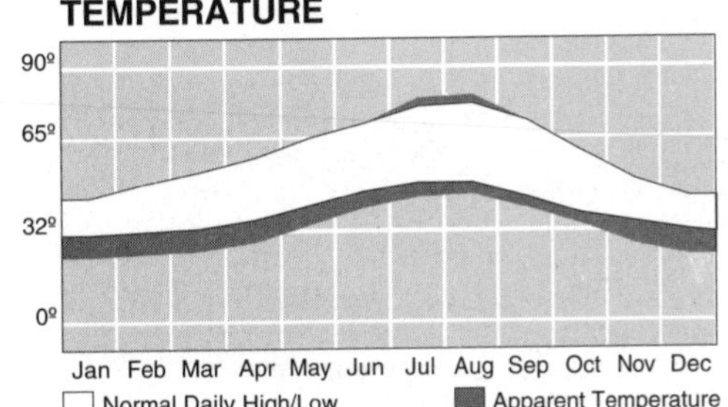

ANNUAL
Humidity: 78%
Wind Speed: 6.7 mph
DAYS
0º or below: 0
32º or below: 85
90º or above: 6
Clear: 52
Cloudy: 229

PRECIPITATION

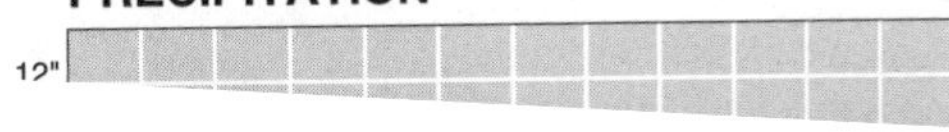

ANNUAL
Precipitation: 50.6"
Snow: 17.3"

ka, on the west bank of the Missouri River, opp
Bluffs, Iowa.
Landscape: Among rolling hills that rise 300 feet above the riverbank, this is a fertile agricultural region, part of a glacial plain with a well-developed drainage system. Soil is silt loam and sandy loam, highly suitable for growing corn, grain sorghums and wheat.
Climate: Typically Continental, with relatively warm summers and cold, dry winters. It is situated midway between two climates, those of the humid East and the dry West, and is affected by weather conditions characteristic of either. Omaha is also affected by most storms that cross the country. This causes periodic and rapid changes in weather, especially during the winter. Snowfall is not significant but the days do get cold and these cold spells may linger. Sunshine is well distributed throughout the year.

Mildness: 13 Brightness: 77 Stability: 24

Places Rated Score: 21.45 **Places Rated Rank: 312**

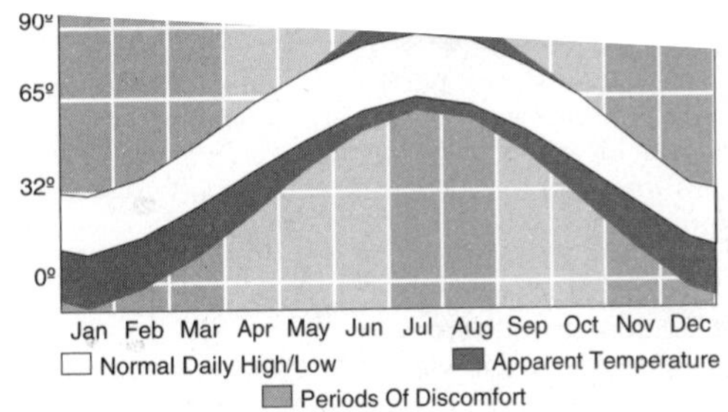

Wind Speed: 10.5 mph
DAYS
0º or below: 13
32º or below: 138
90º or above: 38
Clear: 111
Cloudy: 149

PRECIPITATION

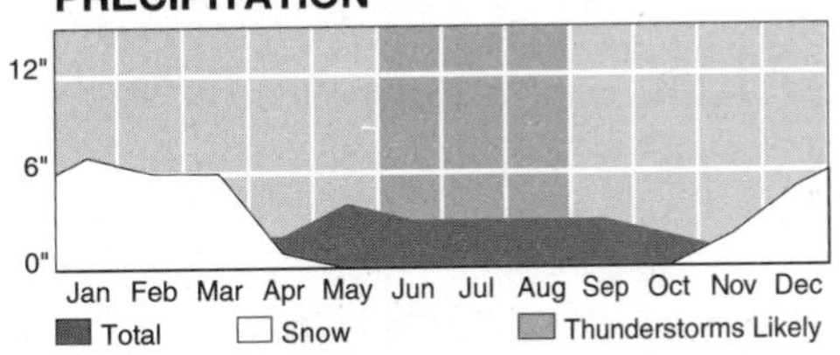

ANNUAL
Precipitation: 29.9"
Snow: 29.9"
DAYS
Precipitation: 49
Thunderstorm: 45

Orlando, FL

Location: 28.27 N, 81.19 W, at 100 feet, in the east central ridge section of the Florida peninsula.
Landscape: The countryside is flat, almost surrounded by lakes, with no natural barriers to exterior weather systems. More than 50 lakes lie within the city limits, and Orange County's thousand lakes, many of them spring fed, moderate the climate throughout the year. Sinkholes are also part of the terrain. Land is fertile, highly suitable for citrus, bulb flowers, and winter vegetable growth. Both deciduous hardwoods like maple and oak flourish along with palms. Azaleas are a winter treat as they bloom January through March.
Climate: Typical Subtropical with high year-round relative humidity because of the surrounding water, hovering near 90 percent at night and dipping to 50 percent in the afternoon. The rainy season extends from June through September; afternoon thundershowers occur daily. Rain is light during the winter, and snow and sleet are rare. Winter temperatures may drop to freezing at night, but days are clear and dry, with brilliant sunshine.

Mildness: 94 Brightness: 22 Stability: 8

Places Rated Score: 79.22 **Places Rated Rank: 54**

TEMPERATURE

90º
65º
32º
0º
Jan Feb Mar Apr May Jun Jul Aug Sep Oct Nov Dec
Normal Daily High/Low
Apparent Temperature
Periods Of Discomfort

ANNUAL
Humidity: 72%
Wind Speed: 8.6 mph
DAYS
0º or below: 0
32º or below: 3
90º or above: 90
Clear: 90
Cloudy: 128

PRECIPITATION

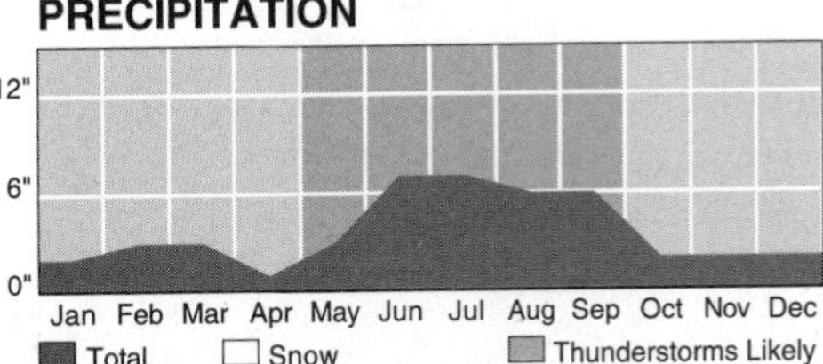

ANNUAL
Precipitation: 48.1"
Snow: 0.0"
DAYS
Precipitation: 65
Thunderstorm: 80

Ottawa-Hull, ON–PQ

Location: 45.19 N, 75.40 W, at 374 feet, the capital of Canada is in the southeastern part of the province at the confluence of the Ottawa, Gatineau, and Rideau rivers.
Landscape: The Ottawa River winds through the city, separating Quebec (Hull) to the north from Ontario and the city of Ottawa to the south, and separating farmland from the Gatineau Hills. The Rideau River flows northward through the city to the Ottawa River. South from the city there is a general rise in elevation from the river valley to an area of rolling farmland. On the north side of the Ottawa River the terrain rises sharply in a wooded section of the Gatineau Hills to an elevation of 1,300 feet in the Eardley Escarpment.
Climate: Best described as both stimulating and variable; cold and snowy in winter, warm in summer. There is no pronounced dry season. This is a Continental climate with a Maritime air from both the Atlantic Ocean and Gulf of Mexico. There are two main seasons with shorter transitional periods of spring and autumn. Good or bad periods commonly do not last for more than a few days.

Mildness: 8 Brightness: 38 Stability: 75

Places Rated Score: 16.11 **Places Rated Rank: 327**

TEMPERATURE

90º
65º
32º
0º
Jan Feb Mar Apr May Jun Jul Aug Sep Oct Nov Dec
Normal Daily High/Low
Apparent Temperature
Periods Of Discomfort

ANNUAL
Humidity: 70%
Wind Speed: 9.1 mph
DAYS
0º or below: 18
32º or below: 165
90º or above: 10
Clear: 109
Cloudy: 142

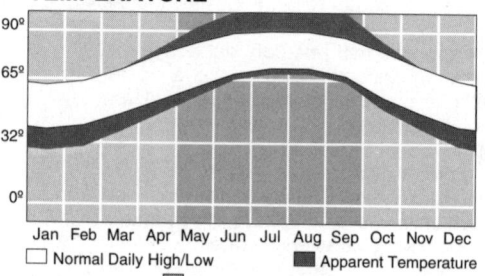

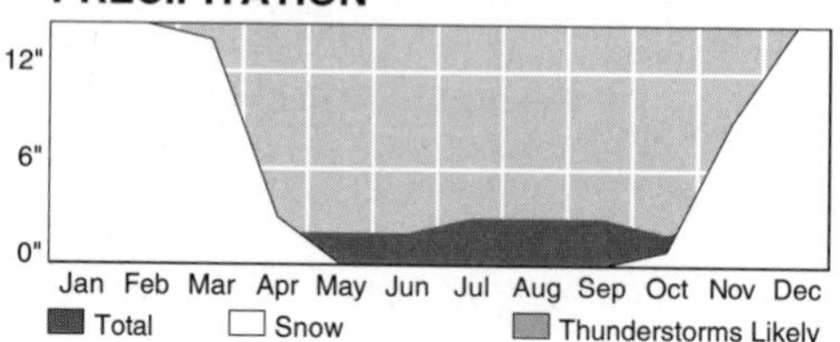

ANNUAL
Precipitation: 34.6"
Snow: 89.6"
DAYS
Precipitation: 81
Thunderstorm: 24

Panama City, FL

Location: 30.13 N, 85.36 W, at 30 feet, on the Gulf of Mexico in Florida's Panhandle, 120 miles west of Tallahassee, the state capital.
Landscape: This landlocked, deep-water harbor is on the Atlantic Intracoastal Waterway with the port of entry on St. Andrew Bay. A sandy coastal region of shallow bays, white beaches, and dunes where elevations range from a few feet above sea level to more than 100 feet. The interior forested swamp includes evergreen oaks and members of the laurel and magnolia families. There is a lower stratum of tree ferns, shrubs, and herbaceous plants. The longleaf, loblolly, and slash pines represent second-growth forest.
Climate: Subtropical in temperature and rainfall. The Panhandle of Florida is cooler in summer and still pleasant in winter. The Yucatán Current runs near here, bringing its moderating influence.

Mildness: 88 Brightness: 35 Stability: 13

Places Rated Score: 74.18 **Places Rated Rank: 68**

TEMPERATURE

90º
65º
32º
0º
Jan Feb Mar Apr May Jun Jul Aug Sep Oct Nov Dec
Normal Daily High/Low
Apparent Temperature
Periods Of Discomfort

ANNUAL
Humidity: 72%
Wind Speed: 8.4 mph
DAYS
0º or below: 0
32º or below: 6
90º or above: 37
Clear: 106
Cloudy: 136

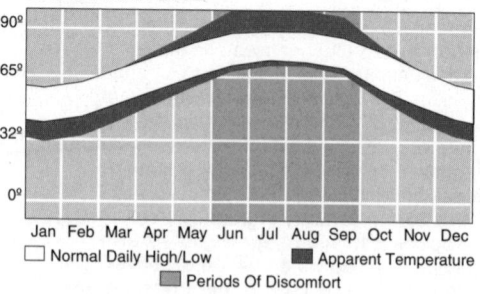

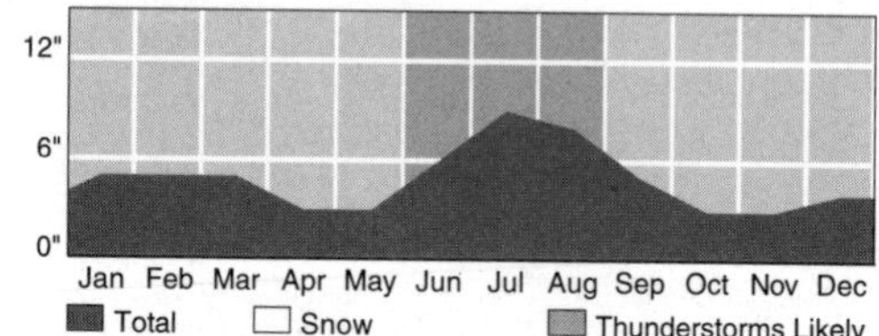

ANNUAL
Precipitation: 65.1"
Snow: 0.3"
DAYS
Precipitation: 66
Thunderstorm: 68

Pensacola, FL

Location: 30.28 N, 87.12 W, at 110 feet, in the Panhandle of Florida on Pensacola Bay, 6 miles from the Gulf of Mexico.
Landscape: On a somewhat hilly, sandy slope separated from the Gulf of Mexico by a long, narrow island that forms a natural breakwater for the harbor. The sand is a glistening white that is nearly pure quartz. Salt marshes are common features. Evidence of Southern Mixed Forest include a variety of hardwoods among the loblollys and shortleaf pine. Elevations range from a few feet above sea level to more than 100 feet; most of the city is well above storm tides. Pensacola's deep, natural harbor has made it a shipping and commercial fishing center.
Climate: The Gulf of Mexico, about 6 miles away, moderates the weather throughout the year, tempering the cold northers of winter, and causing cool and refreshing sea breezes during summer days. Average summer temperature is 80°F; average winter temperature is 55°F.

Mildness: 87 Brightness: 36 Stability: 12

Places Rated Score: 73.26 **Places Rated Rank: 73**

TEMPERATURE

90º
65º
32º
0º
Jan Feb Mar Apr May Jun Jul Aug Sep Oct Nov Dec
Normal Daily High/Low
Apparent Temperature
Periods Of Discomfort

ANNUAL
Humidity: 72%
Wind Speed: 8.4 mph
DAYS
0º or below: 0
32º or below: 19
90º or above: 47
Clear: 106
Cloudy: 136

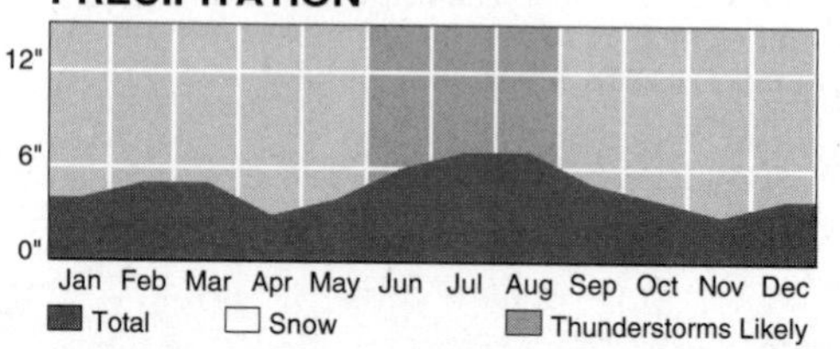

ANNUAL
Precipitation: 62.3"
Snow: 0.3"
DAYS
Precipitation: 66
Thunderstorm: 68

Peoria–Pekin, IL

Location: 40.40 N, 89.41 W, at 650 feet, in north central Illinois, 150 miles SW of Chicago.
Landscape: The Illinois River widens into Lake Peoria with gently rising topography extending to level tableland. This is the heart of Illinois' central farm country. All soil is rich and arable. Once forested with eastern deciduous oak, maple and other hardwoods, now these serve as windbreaks for wide fields.
Climate: Typically Continental, characterized by changeable weather and a wide range of temperatures. For example, 1936 had 17 days with temperatures of 100°F or higher in July, whereas the early part of that same year had 26 days within a 31-day period when the temperature was zero. The same year had the absolute maximum record of 113°F, set on July 15. June and September are usually the most pleasant months of the year. During October and early November, residents enjoy Indian summer, with its extended period of

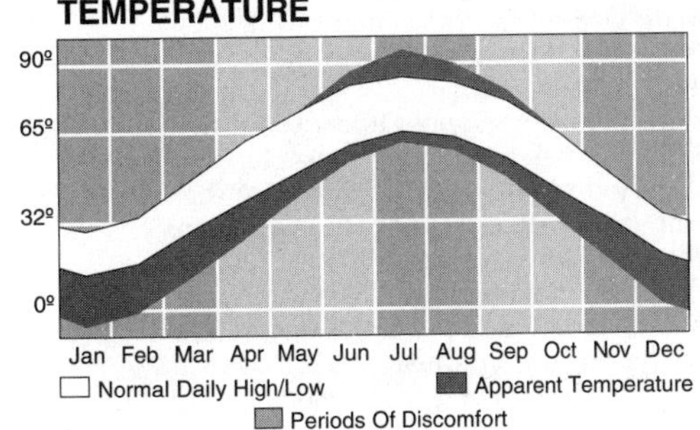

ANNUAL
Humidity: 72%
Wind Speed: 10.0 mph
DAYS
0º or below: 12
32º or below: 127
90º or above: 27
Clear: 94
Cloudy: 173

PRECIPITATION

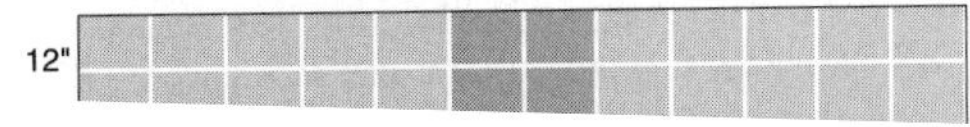

ANNUAL
Precipitation: 36.3"
Snow: 25.1"

Landscape: The Appalachian [illegible] Atlantic Ocean to the east have a moderating effect on the city's climate. Surrounding land is low and fertile.
Climate: Sustained periods of either extreme highs or lows seldom last for more than three or four days. Occasionally during the summer, the area becomes engulfed in marine air, so that high humidity adds to the discomfort of warm temperatures. Precipitation is evenly distributed throughout the year, with maximum amounts during late summer. Snowfall often is considerably higher in the northern suburbs than in the city, where sometimes rain will fall instead. Winters often bring high winds, accompanying cold air after the passage of a deep low-pressure system. Average annual precipitation totals 41 inches. Daily temperature averages range from 24°F in January to 76°F in July.

Mildness: 50 Brightness: 41 Stability: 57

Places Rated Score: 49.39 **Places Rated Rank: 172**

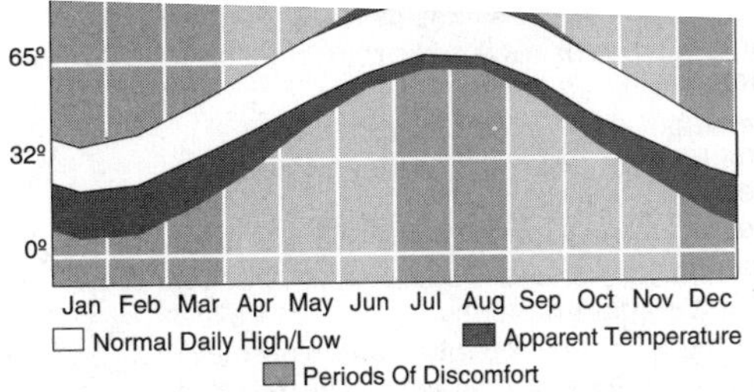

Wind Speed: 9.6 mph
DAYS
0º or below: 0
32º or below: 94
90º or above: 23
Clear: 93
Cloudy: 160

PRECIPITATION

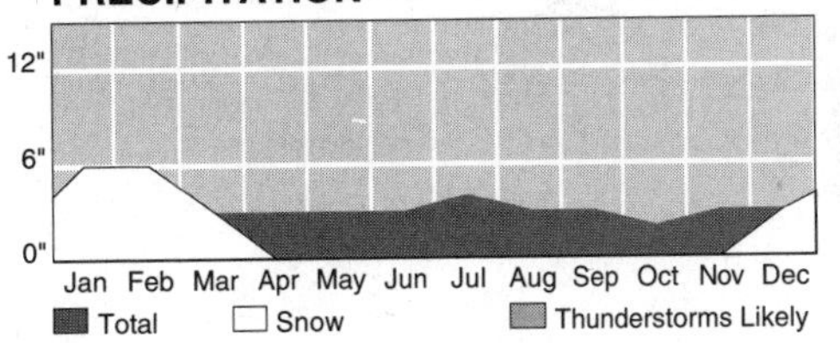

ANNUAL
Precipitation: 41.4"
Snow: 20.8"
DAYS
Precipitation: 74
Thunderstorm: 27

Phoenix–Mesa, AZ

Location: 33.26 N, 112.01 W, at 1,110 feet, in the center of the Salt River Valley.
Landscape: The valley is oval and flat. To the south, west, and north are mountain ranges. The famous Superstition Mountains, which rise to an elevation of 5,000 feet, are 35 miles east. Though desert, the valley supports large cotton and citrus growth. The Sonoran Desert itself can bloom with saguaro, cholla, cereus, but creosote bush is common. The water supply is partly from reservoirs on the Salt and Verde rivers and partly from an underground water table.
Climate: Typical arid desert, with low annual rainfall and low humidity. Daytime temperatures are high throughout the summer. Many days exceed 100°F in the afternoon and remain above 85°F all night. Winters are mild, but nighttime temperatures frequently drop below freezing December through February. The majority of days are clear and sunny and the valley floor is generally free of wind except during the thunderstorm season in July and August. Annual precipitation is only about 7 inches.

Mildness: 72 Brightness: 100 Stability: 35

Places Rated Score: 81.91 **Places Rated Rank: 43**

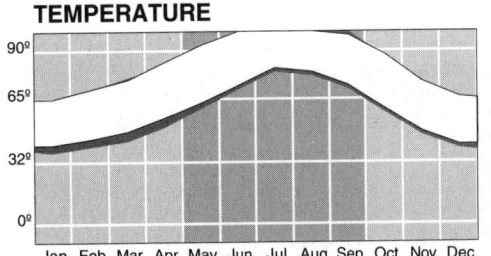

TEMPERATURE

90º
65º
32º
0º
Jan Feb Mar Apr May Jun Jul Aug Sep Oct Nov Dec
Normal Daily High/Low
Apparent Temperature
Periods Of Discomfort

ANNUAL
Humidity: 37%
Wind Speed: 6.2 mph
DAYS
0º or below: 0
32º or below: 10
90º or above: 167
Clear: 210
Cloudy: 70

PRECIPITATION

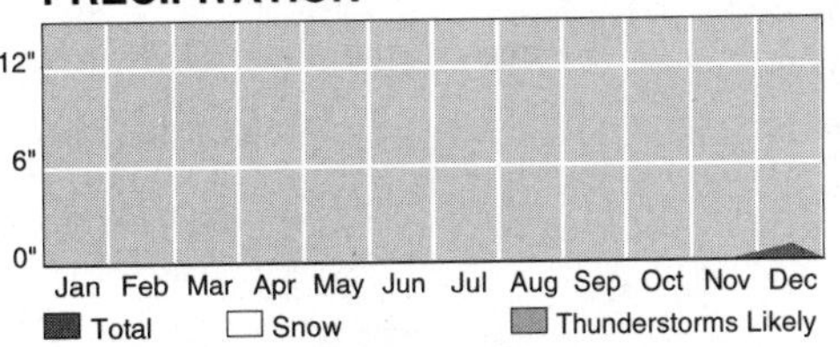

ANNUAL
Precipitation: 7.7"
Snow: 0.0"
DAYS
Precipitation: 14
Thunderstorm: 23

Pittsburgh, PA

Location: 40.30 N, 80.13 W, at 1,140 feet, in the foothills of the Allegheny Mountains where the confluence of the Allegheny and Monongahela rivers form the Ohio River. The city is about 100 miles south of Lake Erie.
Landscape: Pittsburgh was built over what once was a rich bituminous coal seam. Terrain has been highly dissected and is now rugged hill country. Steep slopes predominate, but some gently sloping or level plateau remnants are found. Forests are categorized as Appalachian oak.
Climate: Humid Continental, modified only slightly by its nearness to the Atlantic Seaboard and the Great Lakes. The predominant air is of polar origin from Canada and moves in by way of storm tracks, which vary in origin from Hudson Bay to the Rockies. There are frequent inversions of air from the Gulf of Mexico during the summer, resulting in spells of warm, humid weather. Precipitation is well distributed and there is a 50 percent chance of measurable precipitation on any given day; during the winter, one-fourth of it is snow.

Mildness: 34 Brightness: 20 Stability: 52

Places Rated Score: 33.20 **Places Rated Rank: 238**

TEMPERATURE

90º 65º 32º 0º
Jan Feb Mar Apr May Jun Jul Aug Sep Oct Nov Dec
Normal Daily High/Low ■ Apparent Temperature
Periods Of Discomfort

ANNUAL
Humidity: 67%
Wind Speed: 9.1 mph
DAYS
0º or below: 5
32º or below: 124
90º or above: 7
Clear: 58
Cloudy: 204

PRECIPITATION

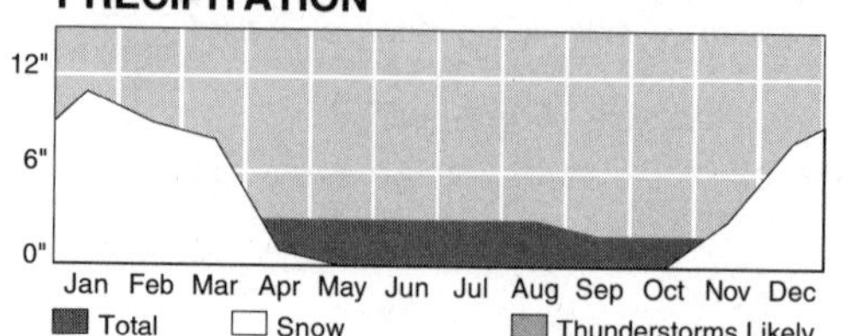

ANNUAL
Precipitation: 36.9"
Snow: 43.1"
DAYS
Precipitation: 71
Thunderstorm: 35

Portland, ME

Location: 43.39 N, 70.19 W, at 40 feet, on a hilly section of the southern coast of Maine, some 45 miles SE of the White Mountains.
Landscape: The position on two peninsulas that jut into Casco Bay give the city a large deepwater harbor, making it the economic center of the state. Terrain is rolling, coastal lowland, penetrated extensively by ocean inlets. The forest is primarily evergreen with oak, maple and other hardwoods throughout.
Climate: As a rule, the city has pleasant summers and falls, cold winters with frequent thaws, and disagreeable springs. Autumn has the greatest number of sunny days. Winters are severe; they begin late but extend deep into what is normally considered springtime, and temperatures well below zero are recorded frequently. Normal monthly precipitation is uniform throughout the year, but heavy snowfalls, sometimes totaling more than 100 inches per year, do occur.

Mildness: 27 Brightness: 30 Stability: 87

Places Rated Score: 34.75 **Places Rated Rank: 227**

TEMPERATURE

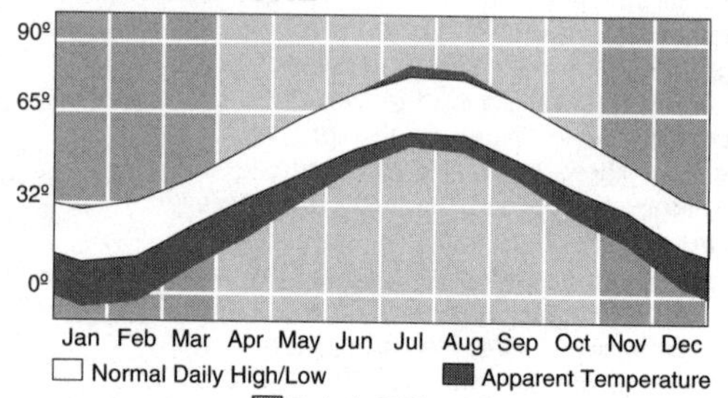

ANNUAL
Humidity: 69%
Wind Speed: 8.8 mph
DAYS
0º or below: 15
32º or below: 156
90º or above: 5
Clear: 101
Cloudy: 165

PRECIPITATION

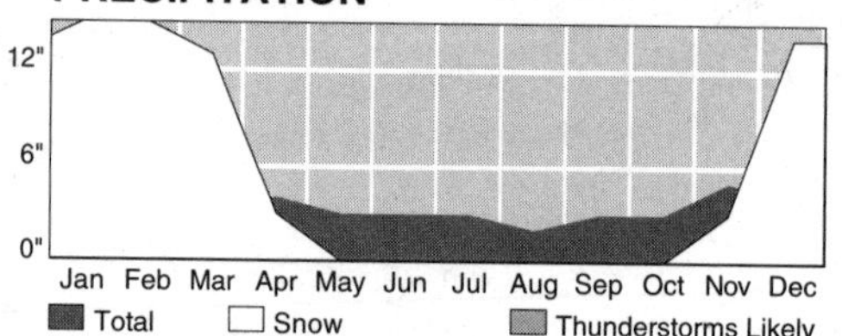

ANNUAL
Precipitation: 44.3"
Snow: 70.5"
DAYS
Precipitation: 81
Thunderstorm: 16

Portland-Vancouver, OR-WA

Location: 45.36 N, 122.36 W, at 20 feet, on the Columbia River, 65 miles inland from the Pacific Ocean.
Landscape: Midway between the northerly oriented low Coast Ranges on the west and the higher Cascade Range on the east, each 30 miles distant. The long growing season, with its mild temperatures and ample moisture, favors local nursery and seed industries.
Climate: A rainy climate in winter, marked by relatively mild temperatures and cloudy skies. Summers are pleasantly mild with northwesterly winds and little precipitation. Fall and spring are transitional in nature. Fog occurs frequently in fall and winter. At all times, incursions of marine air are a moderating influence. Extremes in winter and summer come from the continental interior. Destructive winds are infrequent.

Mildness: 88 Brightness: 7 Stability: 97

Places Rated Score: 79.99 **Places Rated Rank: 51**

TEMPERATURE

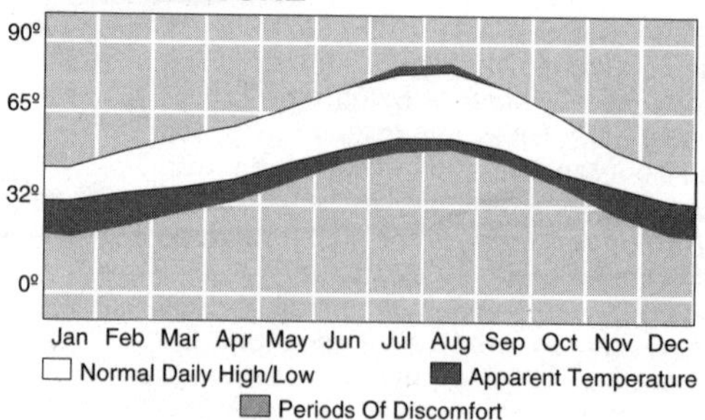

ANNUAL
Humidity: 72%
Wind Speed: 7.9 mph
DAYS
0º or below: 0
32º or below: 44
90º or above: 10
Clear: 68
Cloudy: 223

PRECIPITATION

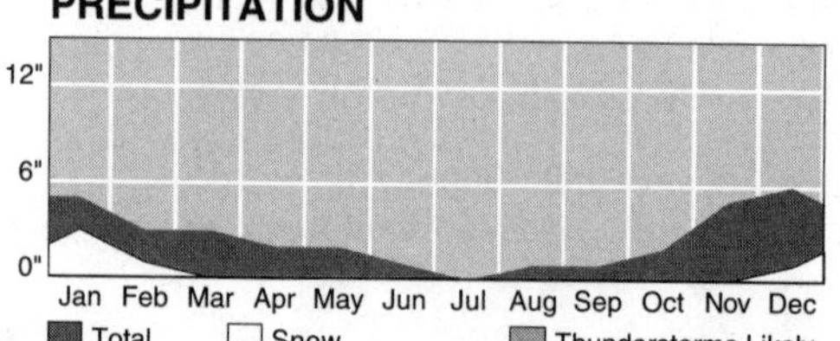

ANNUAL
Precipitation: 36.3"
Snow: 6.5"
DAYS
Precipitation: 100
Thunderstorm: 7

Portsmouth–Rochester, NH–ME

Location: 43.01 N, 70.50 W, at 80 feet, on the Atlantic coast of southeastern New Hampshire, at the mouth of the Piscataqua River, opposite Kittery, Maine. Rochester is on the east bank of the Cocheco River. The Salmon Falls River flows through East Rochester.

Landscape: New Hampshire's Eastern Slope descends gradually to the sea. Part of the state's brief seacoast consists of sandy beaches and Portsmouth Harbor. Fine timber growth around the bay and an excellent harbor contributed to a profitable ship-building industry. The Eastern Slope itself is covered with a moderately fertile soil produced from disintegrating slate.

Climate: Definitely Continental in temperature range and precipitation. January's average high is just over freezing and the monthly mean is 21°F. There are four zero-degree days and more than 100 freezing days each year. The maximum for July is 82°F, cooling at night to less than 60°F. Much of the yearly precipitation falls as snow from December through

TEMPERATURE

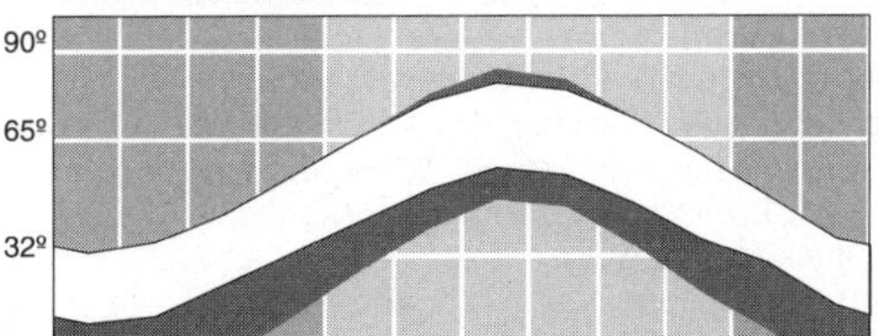

ANNUAL
Humidity: 65%
Wind Speed: 12.5 mph
DAYS
0º or below: 4
32º or below: 130
90º or above: 7
Clear: 98
Cloudy: 163

PRECIPITATION

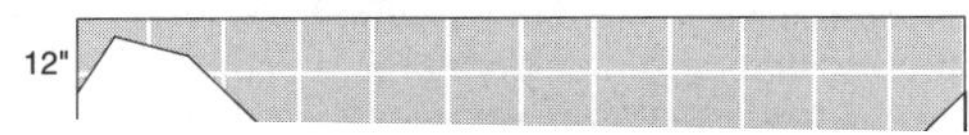

ANNUAL
Precipitation: 46.0"

of Long Island Sound and the Atlantic Ocean. The Providence River flows through Providence and empties into the bay. This is an area protected from severe climatic changes by both the oceans and land forms. Terrain is typical eastern lowland, gently rolling, including the bay shores and islands. Soil is sandy and gravelly.

Climate: A moderate Marine climate. Many major snowstorms change to rain before reaching the area; snow is not uncommon but does not remain for long periods of time. In summer, the area is cooled by refreshing breezes. Fog may be dense at times but is not frequent. Severe coastal storms in the fall can bring destructive winds.

Mildness: 43 Brightness: 41 Stability: 77

Places Rated Score: 46.96 **Places Rated Rank: 182**

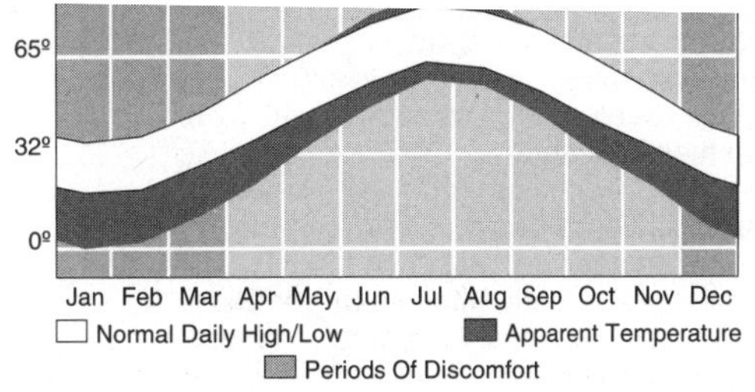

Wind Speed: 10.5 mph
DAYS
0º or below: 2
32º or below: 117
90º or above: 8
Clear: 98
Cloudy: 164

PRECIPITATION

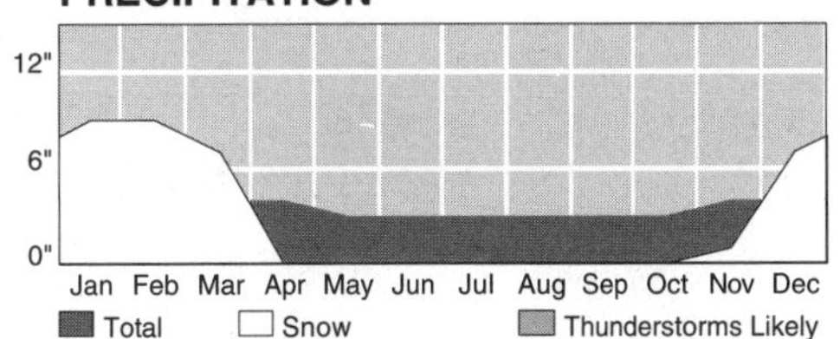

ANNUAL
Precipitation: 45.5"
Snow: 35.6"
DAYS
Precipitation: 72
Thunderstorm: 21

Québec City, PQ

Location: 46.48 N, 71.23 W, at 239 feet, at the confluence of the St. Lawrence and St. Charles rivers in southeastern Canada, 150 miles NE of Montréal.

Landscape: In the vicinity of Québec City, the relatively narrow St. Lawrence River valley is oriented in a southwest to northeast direction. From the south shore of the St. Lawrence River, the terrain gradually rises to reach elevations of 900 to 1,800 feet in the Appalachians, 25 miles southeast of the airport. The Laurentians rise abruptly to elevations between 900 and 1,800 feet; elevations over 3,000 feet occur some 30 miles northeast.

Climate: The snow season is long, lasting four to five months. Spring arrives suddenly and sometimes not at all. Fall may be as fleeting as spring but almost always is pleasant. Winter's first significant snowfall arrives in early November. Foul weather of any kind seldom lasts for long; most storms leave the area within two days.

Mildness: 7 Brightness: 7 Stability: 80

Places Rated Score: 11.62 **Places Rated Rank: 336**

TEMPERATURE

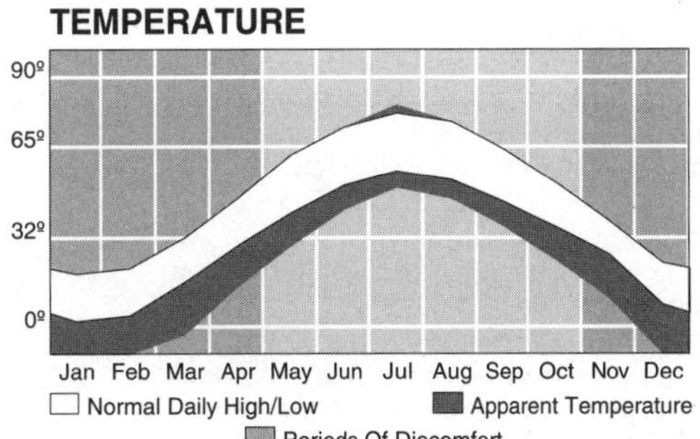

ANNUAL
Humidity: 72%
Wind Speed: 9.9 mph
DAYS
0º or below: 26
32º or below: 180
90º or above: 5
Clear: 100
Cloudy: 150

PRECIPITATION

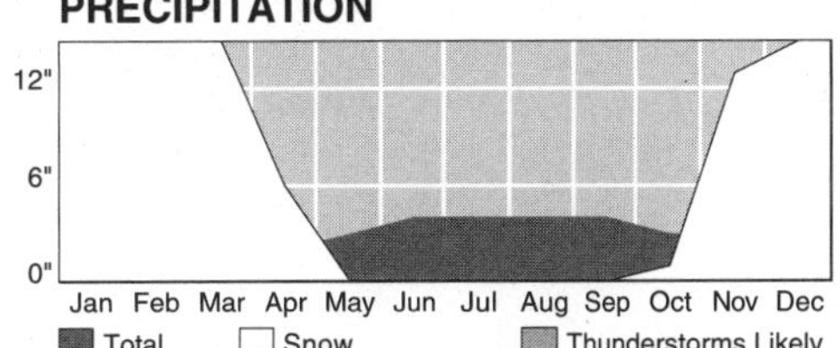

ANNUAL
Precipitation: 46.3"
Snow: 135.1"
DAYS
Precipitation: 117
Thunderstorm: 24

Raleigh-Durham-Chapel Hill, NC

Location: 35.52 N, 78.47 W, at 420 feet, the station is centrally located between the Coastal Plain and the Piedmont Plateau.

Landscape: The topography is rolling, with elevations from 200 feet to 500 feet within a 10-mile radius. Broadleaf deciduous and needleleaf evergreen trees make up the medium tall to tall forests. Loblolly pine and other southern yellow pine mix with hickory, sweetgum, red maple, and winged elm. Low shrubs of dogwood, viburnum, and blueberry are common.

Climate: Located between mountains to the west and the Atlantic Coast to the east and south, the metro area enjoys a favorable climate. The western mountains form a partial barrier to cold air masses moving eastward from the nation's interior. There are few days in the heart of the winter when the temperature falls below 20°F. Tropical air is present during much of the summer, bringing warm temperatures and high humidity. In midsummer, afternoon temperatures reach 90°F or higher every fourth day. Rainfall is well distributed throughout the year. July has the greatest amount of rainfall, and November the least.

Mildness: 73 Brightness: 44 Stability: 40

Places Rated Score: 64.82 **Places Rated Rank: 111**

TEMPERATURE

90º 65º 32º 0º

Jan Feb Mar Apr May Jun Jul Aug Sep Oct Nov Dec

Normal Daily High/Low — Apparent Temperature — Periods Of Discomfort

ANNUAL
Humidity: 69%
Wind Speed: 7.8 mph
DAYS
0º or below: 0
32º or below: 77
90º or above: 39
Clear: 110
Cloudy: 149

PRECIPITATION

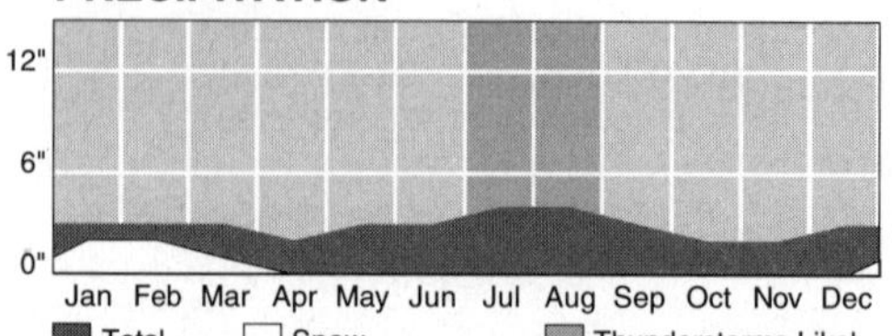

ANNUAL
Precipitation: 41.4"
Snow: 7.0"
DAYS
Precipitation: 74
Thunderstorm: 42

Rapid City, SD

Location: 44.03 N, 103.04 W, at 3,160 feet, in southwest South Dakota on Rapid Creek at the eastern edge of the Black Hills, not far from the geographical center of North America.

Landscape: The city is surrounded by contrasting landforms, including the forested Black Hills to the west and rolling prairie to the east. Rapid Creek rushes through the heart of town on its way east to the Missouri River, 200 miles away. To the southeast lie the eroded Badlands and the White River. Prairie soils are fertile. Coniferous forests cover the Black Hills.

Climate: Semiarid Continental, greatly affected by the Black Hills. There are large daily and seasonal temperature ranges. In the lee of the Black Hills storms are deflected from the city, making winters here among the warmest in South Dakota. Snowfall is light, averaging 40 inches annually. Spring temperatures vary widely; summer days are warm, nights are cool.

Mildness: 16 Brightness: 63 Stability: 46

Places Rated Score: 24.94 **Places Rated Rank: 297**

TEMPERATURE

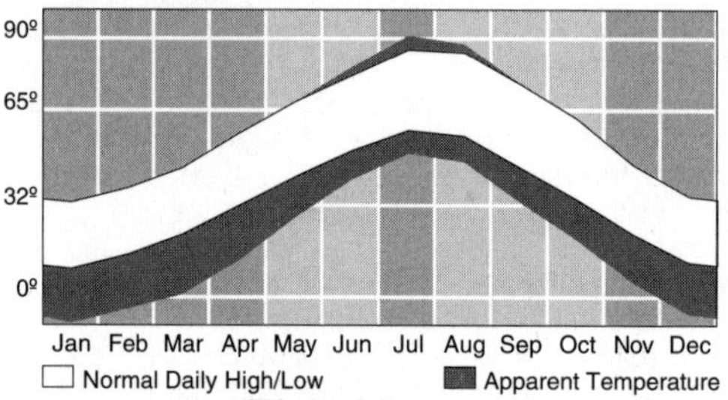

ANNUAL
Humidity: 61%
Wind Speed: 11.3 mph
DAYS
0º or below: 25
32º or below: 169
90º or above: 32
Clear: 111
Cloudy: 139

PRECIPITATION

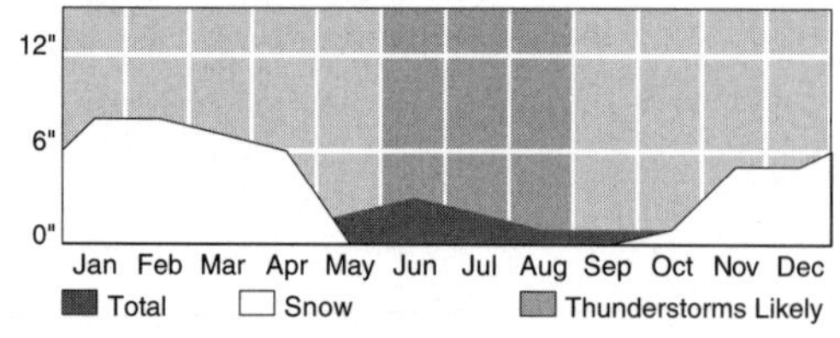

ANNUAL
Precipitation: 16.6"
Snow: 42.7"
DAYS
Precipitation: 60
Thunderstorm: 40

Redding, CA

Location: 40.30 N, 122.18 W, at 500 feet, in the Sacramento Valley some 150 miles north of Sacramento and 100 miles south of the Oregon border.

Landscape: Mountains surround the city on three sides, forming a huge horseshoe. The Coast Ranges are located 30 miles west, the Sierra Nevada system 40 miles east, and the Cascade Range about 50 miles north-northeast. The western part of the valley floor is mostly rolling hills with scrub oak trees. The Sacramento River flows in a north-south direction through the eastern portion of the valley.

Climate: Precipitation is confined mostly to rain during the winter and spring months. Snowfall is infrequent and light. June through September are hot months and temperatures often exceed 100°F. Temperatures almost always drop into comfortable ranges at night. The summer and fall are nearly cloudless.

Mildness: 73 Brightness: 99 Stability: 74

Places Rated Score: 81.06 **Places Rated Rank: 47**

TEMPERATURE

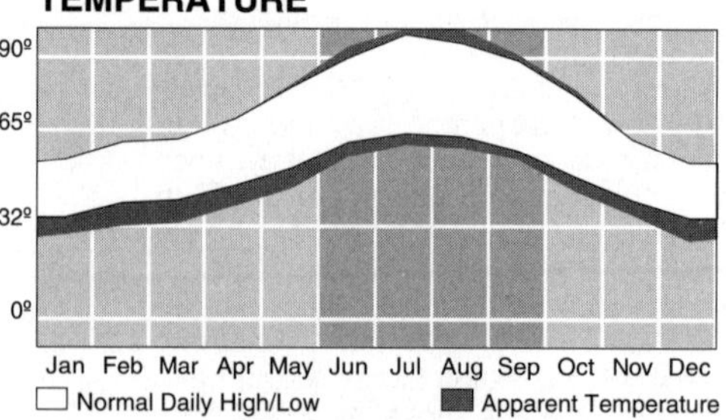

ANNUAL
Humidity: 54%
Wind Speed: 7.1 mph
DAYS
0º or below: 0
32º or below: 20
90º or above: 99
Clear: 174
Cloudy: 113

PRECIPITATION

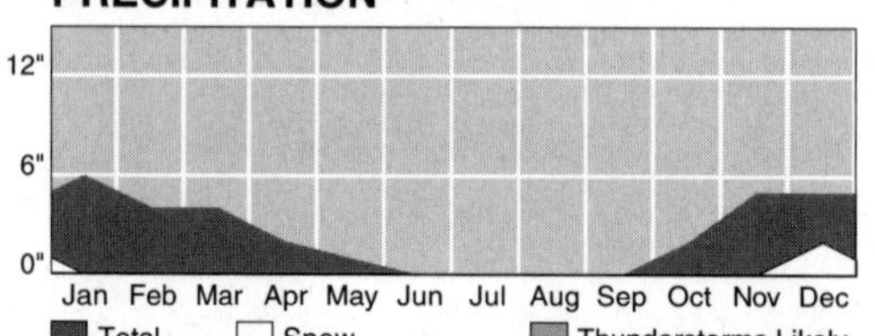

ANNUAL
Precipitation: 33.3"
Snow: 3.4"
DAYS
Precipitation: 30
Thunderstorm: 11

Regina, SK

Location: 50.27 N, 104.37 W, at 1,893 feet, on the banks of Wascana Creek, which lies in a shallow basin running southeast to northwest.
Landscape: The surrounding area is a level plain. The land rises slowly to the northeast and peaks at an elevation of about 2,500 feet some 20 miles away. The Ou'Appelle River to the north meanders in an easterly direction in a deep narrow valley. Draining into the Ou'Appelle, Last Mountain Lake, 50 miles long and 2 to 3 miles wide, lies northwest. Southwest is the Missouri Coteau, a broken escarpment with an average elevation of 2,400 feet. The Dirt Hills, part of the escarpment, rise over 2,700 feet and can be seen to the southwest.
Climate: Regina is Canada's sunniest provincial capital. Being far from influences of oceans or mountains, it has large daily, and extremely large annual, ranges of temperature. High temperature, low humidity, strong winds, and clear skies cause moisture deficits in summer. Winter cold is not only

TEMPERATURE

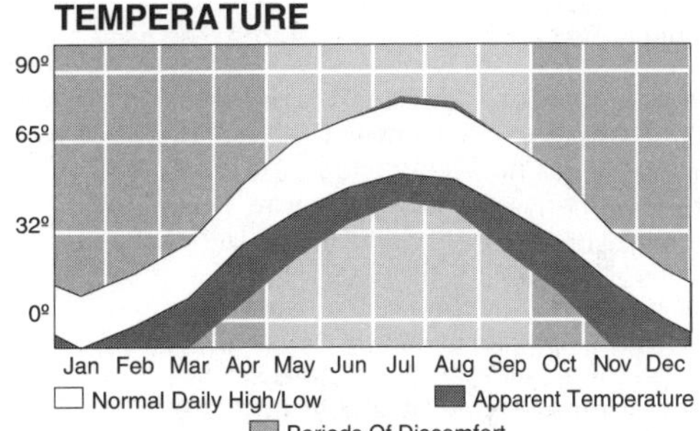

ANNUAL
Humidity: 71%
Wind Speed: 12.9 mph
DAYS
0º or below: 55
32º or below: 204
90º or above: 14
Clear: 128
Cloudy: 114

PRECIPITATION

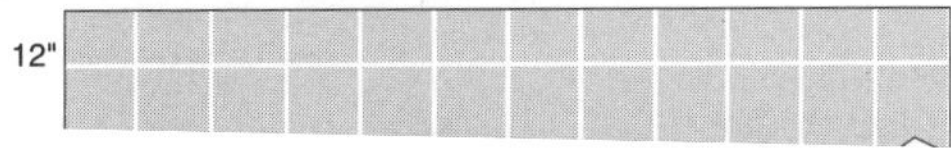

ANNUAL
Precipitation: 15.1"
Snow: 45.6"

Landscape: At the west edge of Truckee Meadows. The Sierra Nevadas rise to elevations of 9,000 to 10,000 feet. Hills to the east reach 6,000 to 7,000 feet. The Truckee River, flowing from the Sierra Nevada east through Reno, drains into Pyramid Lake to the northeast. The rivers here flow into landlocked lakes or simply evaporate in the desert. Sagebrush and saltbrush are common in this high country desert.
Climate: Desert with sunshine abundant throughout the year. Temperatures are mild, but the daily range may exceed 45°F. Even when afternoons reach the upper 90s, a light jacket is needed shortly after sunset. Nights with a minimum temperature over 60°F are rare. Afternoon temperatures are moderate, and only about ten days a year fail to reach a level above freezing. Humidity is low during the summer months and moderately low during winter.

Mildness: 51 Brightness: 98 Stability: 80

Places Rated Score: 66.79 **Places Rated Rank: 94**

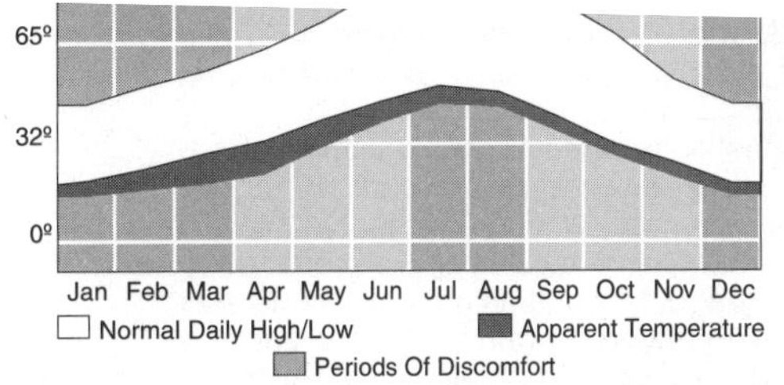

Wind Speed: 6.6 mph
DAYS
0º or below: 3
32º or below: 189
90º or above: 52
Clear: 159
Cloudy: 113

PRECIPITATION

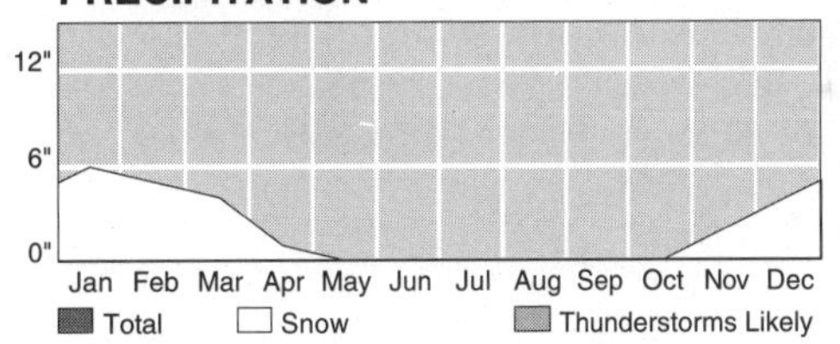

ANNUAL
Precipitation: 7.5"
Snow: 24.6"
DAYS
Precipitation: 23
Thunderstorm: 14

Richmond–Petersburg, VA

Location: 37.30 N, 77.20 W, at 160 feet, in east-central Virginia at the head of navigation on the James River between Tidewater Virginia and the Piedmont.
Landscape: This is a hilly region rising to the Blue Ridge Mountains about 90 miles to the west. Elevations range from a few feet above sea level along the rocky course of the James River to a little over 300 feet in parts of the western section of the city.
Climate: Subtropical in many respects, or a water- and mountain-modified Continental, with warm, humid summers and generally mild winters. The mountains to the west act as a barrier to cold air in winter; the open waters of the Chesapeake Bay 60 miles to the east and the Atlantic also contribute to mild winters and to humid summers. Coldest weather occurs in late December and in January, with a normal temperature range from 20°F to 50°F. Precipitation is uniformly distributed throughout the year, though dry periods do occur in the autumn, when long periods of pleasant, mild weather are most common.

Mildness: 62 Brightness: 40 Stability: 37

Places Rated Score: 55.39 **Places Rated Rank: 149**

TEMPERATURE

90º
65º
32º
0º
Jan Feb Mar Apr May Jun Jul Aug Sep Oct Nov Dec
Normal Daily High/Low
Apparent Temperature
Periods Of Discomfort

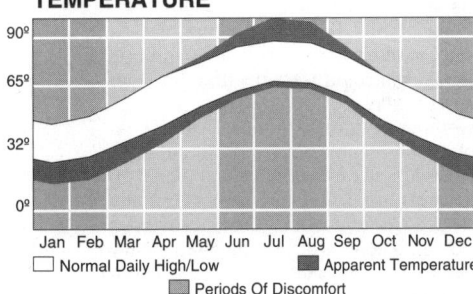

ANNUAL
Humidity: 68%
Wind Speed: 7.7 mph
DAYS
0º or below: 0
32º or below: 85
90º or above: 41
Clear: 99
Cloudy: 160

PRECIPITATION

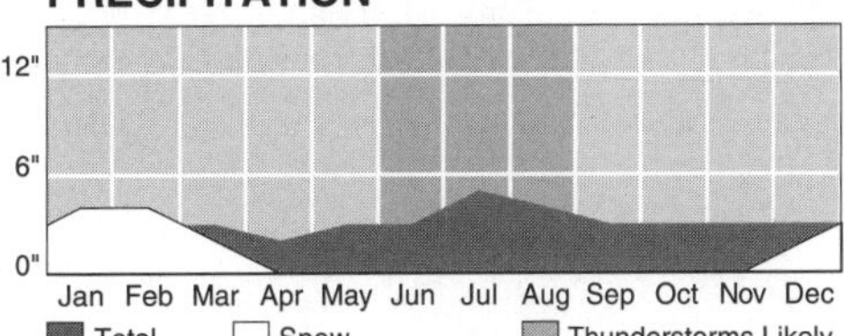

ANNUAL
Precipitation: 43.2"
Snow: 13.9"
DAYS
Precipitation: 74
Thunderstorm: 43

✓ Riverside–San Bernardino, CA

Location: 33.57 N, 117.23 W, at 840 feet, the station at Riverside is in California's desert country, 60 miles east of Los Angeles.
Landscape: At the edge of the Sonoran Desert, sometimes known as the upper Colorado Desert. Transition vegetation of mountain, valley, and desert includes cactus, and evergreen scrub pine. California fan palm trees also grow here. Joshua Tree National Monument is to the southeast. Under cultivation, this region is famous for its citrus groves.
Climate: Arid high desert effects show in the warm, dry summers. Nights are always noticeably cooler. Most of the annual precipitation falls in the winter as rain. There are few cloudy days, and thunderstorms or other destructive weather events are rare.

Mildness: 92 Brightness: 99 Stability: 91

Places Rated Score: 94.01 **Places Rated Rank: 12**

TEMPERATURE

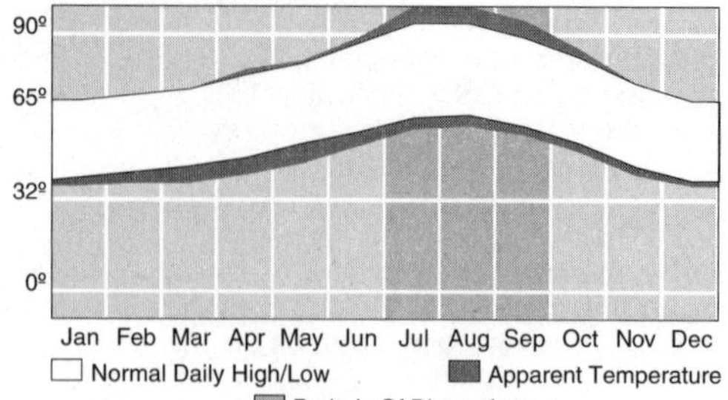

ANNUAL
Humidity: 59%
Wind Speed: 6.4 mph
DAYS
0º or below: 0
32º or below: 14
90º or above: 92
Clear: 192
Cloudy: 92

PRECIPITATION

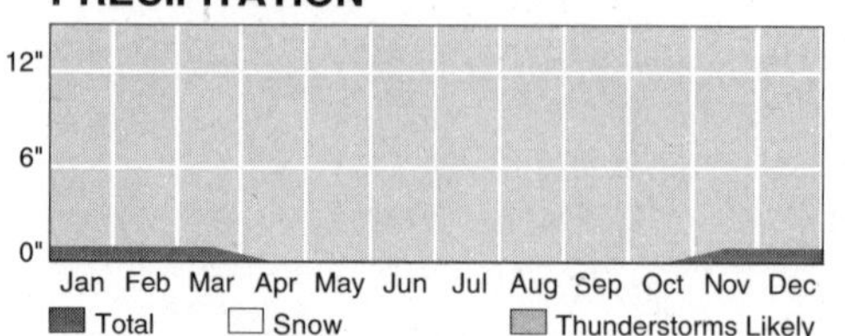

ANNUAL
Precipitation: 9.6"
Snow: 0.0"
DAYS
Precipitation: 18
Thunderstorm: 2

Roanoke, VA

Location: 37.19 N, 79.58 W, at 1,150 feet, in the southern part of the Great Valley, near the headwaters of the Roanoke River, 223 miles SE of Washington, DC.
Landscape: In a natural bowl with the Blue Ridge Mountains to the west and the Allegheny Mountains to the north. Within the city, Mill Mountain rises detached from surrounding ranges. Numerous creeks and small streams from nearby mountains intersect the landscape and empty into the winding Roanoke River. Great Valley soils are dark and fertile while mountain soils are thin. Wooded areas are typical, mixing broadleaf deciduous and needleleaf evergreens.
Climate: Mild Continental as the mountain barrier moderates cold air from the north before it reaches the area. The elevation of the city produces cool summer nights. Rainfall is well distributed throughout the year, with an average of 23 inches in the warm season. Snow falls each winter, with extremes ranging from a trace to 60 inches.

Mildness: 62 Brightness: 44 Stability: 53

Places Rated Score: 58.20 **Places Rated Rank: 134**

TEMPERATURE

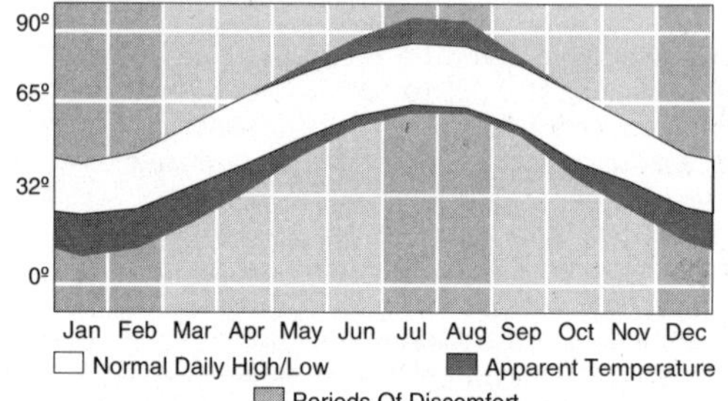

ANNUAL
Humidity: 65%
Wind Speed: 8.0 mph
DAYS
0º or below: 0
32º or below: 92
90º or above: 31
Clear: 101
Cloudy: 151

PRECIPITATION

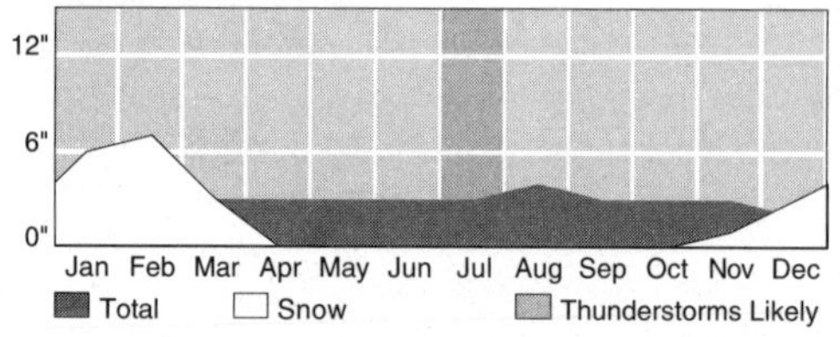

ANNUAL
Precipitation: 41.1"
Snow: 22.8"
DAYS
Precipitation: 69
Thunderstorm: 35

Rochester, MN

Location: 43.55 N, 92.30 W, at 1,300 feet, in the Zumbro River valley in southeastern Minnesota.
Landscape: Farmland surrounds this city on the upland plateau. The south branch of the Zumbro River flows through the city. The country is flat glaciated terrain with little relief except for gentle rolling contours.
Climate: Continental weather pattern with four definite seasons. Winters are cold, but summers are pleasant, with temperatures reaching as high as 90°F on only ten days in an average summer. On the average, heavy fog occurs 35 times a year, and thunderstorms occur about once every three days during the growing season. These storms are often heavy downpours with high winds bringing occasional flash flooding. About four times each year, hail will fall. Tornadoes are rare but do occur.

Mildness: 4 Brightness: 51 Stability: 35

Places Rated Score: 9.37 **Places Rated Rank: 339**

TEMPERATURE

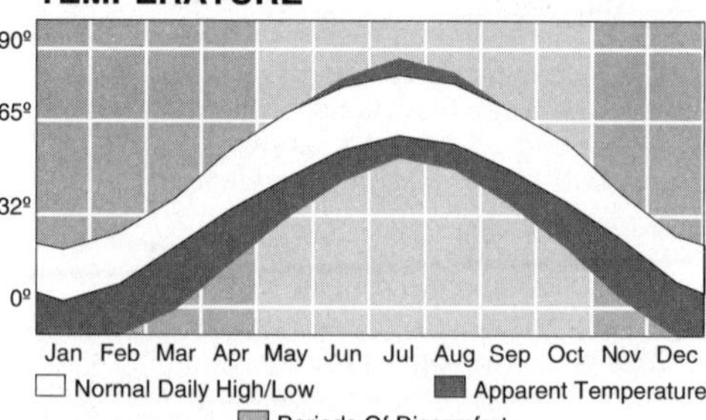

ANNUAL
Humidity: 74%
Wind Speed: 13.1 mph
DAYS
0º or below: 35
32º or below: 165
90º or above: 10
Clear: 87
Cloudy: 181

PRECIPITATION

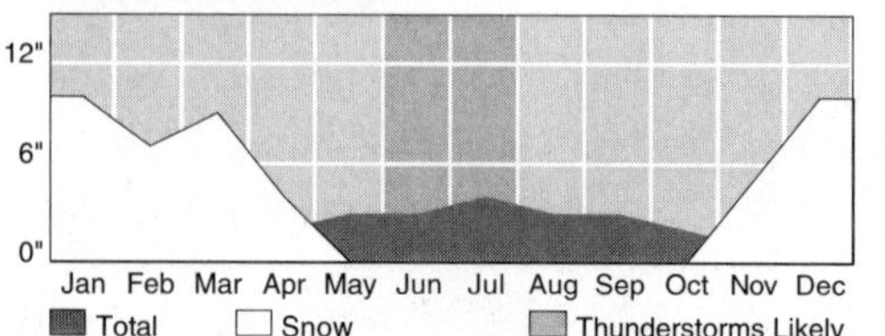

ANNUAL
Precipitation: 29.7"
Snow: 48.8"
DAYS
Precipitation: 61
Thunderstorm: 41

Rochester, NY

Location: 43.08 N, 77.40 W, at 600 feet, at the mouth of the Genesee River at about the midpoint of the south shore of Lake Ontario.
Landscape: Sloping terrain with lime-rich soils. The land rises from a lakeshore elevation of 246 feet to over 1000 feet 20 miles south. Moisture in the air from the lake enhances conditions for fruit growing.
Climate: Lake Ontario plays a major role in the weather, moderating temperatures but often increasing precipitation by the Lake Effect. Summer temperatures rarely rise above 90°F. Winter temperatures seldom fall below −15°F. The area is prone to heavy snowstorms and blizzards. These storms are even heavier near the lake. Snow cover is continuous from December to May. The average growing season is 150 to 180 days.

Mildness: 26 Brightness: 17 Stability: 73

Places Rated Score: 29.35 **Places Rated Rank: 261**

TEMPERATURE

90º
65º
32º
0º
Jan Feb Mar Apr May Jun Jul Aug Sep Oct Nov Dec
Normal Daily High/Low Apparent Temperature
Periods Of Discomfort

ANNUAL
Humidity: 71%
Wind Speed: 9.7 mph
DAYS
0º or below: 10
32º or below: 135
90º or above: 11
Clear: 61
Cloudy: 199

PRECIPITATION

ANNUAL
Precipitation: 32.0"
Snow: 89.9"

Landscape: Connected by a deep-water ship channel, this inland port is the geographical center of one of the great interior low-lying, broad valleys between California's Coast Ranges and the Sierra Nevada. The land is tabletop-flat and, when irrigated, perfect for growing fruits and vegetables.
Climate: Mediterranean. The two mountain ranges shelter the area from many storms and violent weather, adding to the mildness of the climate. Occasionally, however, northerly winds reach the valley over the Siskiyou Mountains, bringing tulmultuous weather. These winds may bring heavy rains in winter or increased heat in summer. Summers are sunny and hot, but low humidity lessens the felt heat. Winters are short and mild; snow is rare, though the Sierra Nevada snow fields, 70 miles east, usually provide an adequate water supply. The average last occurrence of frost is in mid-February.

Mildness: 82 Brightness: 99 Stability: 91

Places Rated Score: 88.05 **Places Rated Rank: 20**

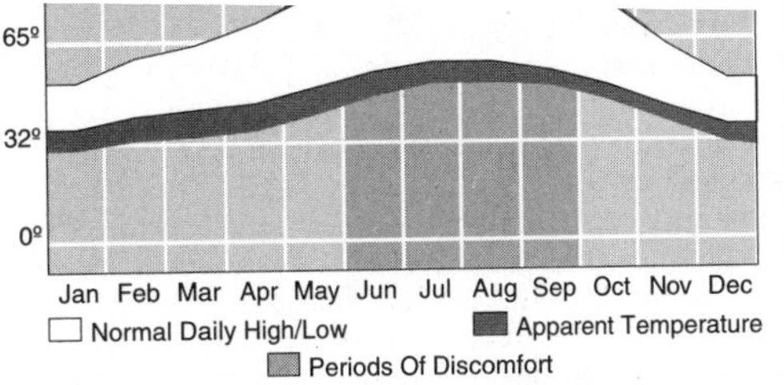

Wind Speed: 7.9 mph
DAYS
0º or below: 0
32º or below: 21
90º or above: 73
Clear: 188
Cloudy: 101

PRECIPITATION

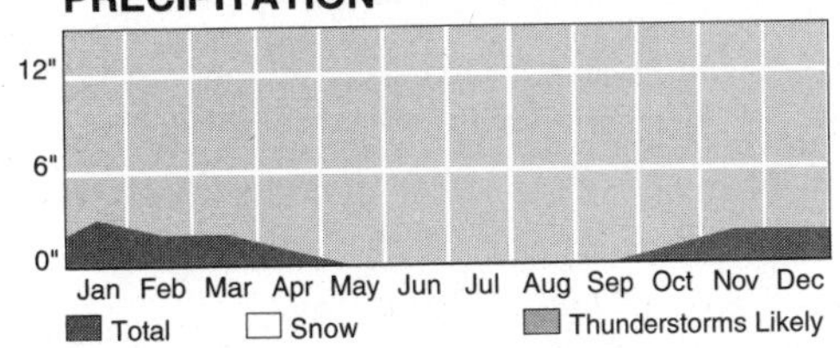

ANNUAL
Precipitation: 17.5"
Snow: 0.0"
DAYS
Precipitation: 32
Thunderstorm: 2

Saint John, NB

Location: 45.19 N, 65.53 W, at 358 feet, on New Brunswick's southern Atlantic coast 90 miles east of Fredericton, the provincial capital. The airport station is about 10 miles ENE of downtown.
Landscape: The surrounding countryside is rolling and wooded, with hills that slope down to tidal marshes at the Bay of Fundy. The Saint John River is greatly affected by the high tides of the Bay at this deep-sea port.
Climate: Qualifies as Marine climate though there is a definite Continental flavor. During the winter, cold air flows from the center of North America. Most storms originate either over the North Pacific or the Gulf of Mexico. In summer, the predominant air mass is warmed by passage over the North American landmass. Off-shore winds modify the air masses, producing mild periods during the winter and cool weather the rest of the year. Winter storms frequently bring rain to the Fundy coast.

Mildness: 26 Brightness: 1 Stability: 96

Places Rated Score: 26.98 **Places Rated Rank: 276**

TEMPERATURE

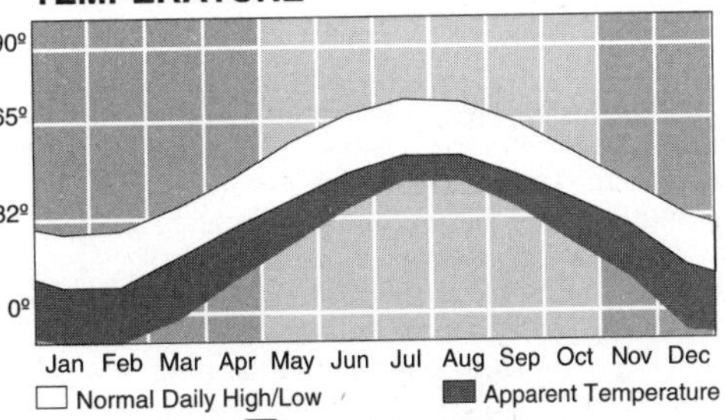

ANNUAL
Humidity: 78%
Wind Speed: 11.5 mph
DAYS
0º or below: 14
32º or below: 173
90º or above: 0
Clear: 105
Cloudy: 166

PRECIPITATION

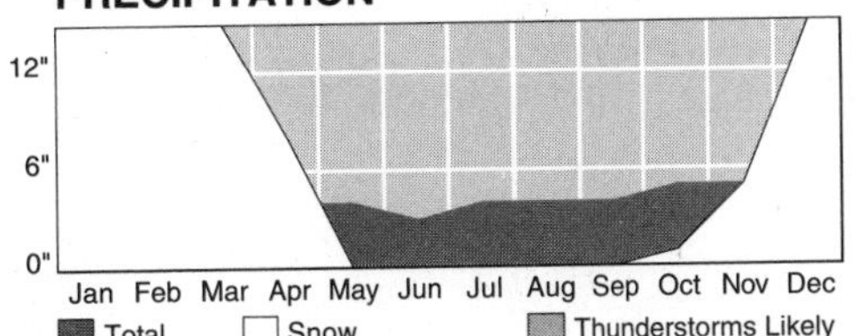

ANNUAL
Precipitation: 56.9"
Snow: 115.1"
DAYS
Precipitation: 138
Thunderstorm: 11

St. John's, NF

Location: 47.37 N, 52.45 W, at 459 feet, at the eastern end of the Avalon Peninsula on the Atlantic coast.
Landscape: Rugged, with many small lakes and rivers dominating the surrounding landscape. The Atlantic Ocean lies to the east, Conception Bay is to the west, and Windsor Lake is located to the southwest. The land slopes east to the ocean and, to the west, the terrain plunges in sheer cliffs at Conception Bay. In all but the eastern quadrant, there are many hills within a short distance.
Climate: The Marine climate brings changeable weather—ample precipitation in a variety of forms, high humidity, low visibility, more clouds, less sunshine, and strong winds. The open sea keeps winter air temperatures a little higher and summer temperatures slightly lower on the coast than at places inland. Spring comes rather late and is short; summer is also short and keeps its cool character. Hardly a winter goes by without three or four east coast gales. The seasons are called character-building and invigorating by proud natives. Freezing rainstorms, called silver thaws, are a major winter hazard and can be severe at times. St. John's is the snowiest major city in Canada.

Mildness: 43 Brightness: 0 Stability: 100

Places Rated Score: 42.25 **Places Rated Rank: 196**

TEMPERATURE

90º 65º 32º 0º
Jan Feb Mar Apr May Jun Jul Aug Sep Oct Nov Dec
Normal Daily High/Low Apparent Temperature
Periods Of Discomfort

ANNUAL
Humidity: 83%
Wind Speed: 15.1 mph
DAYS
0º or below: 0
32º or below: 176
90º or above: 0
Clear: 60
Cloudy: 195

PRECIPITATION

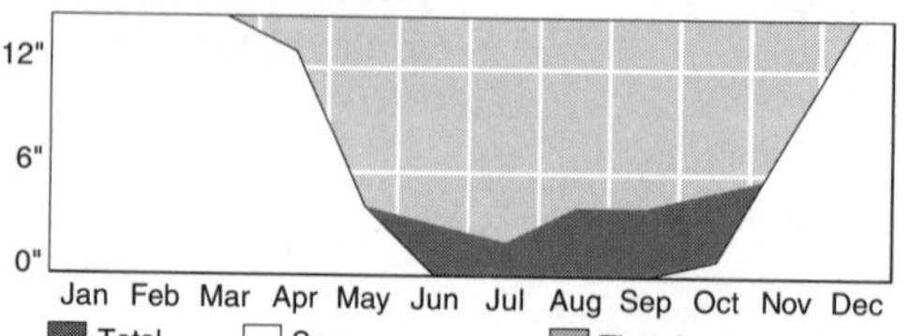

ANNUAL
Precipitation: 59.6"
Snow: 141.4"
DAYS
Precipitation: 144
Thunderstorm: 3

St. Louis, MO–IL

Location: 38.45 N, 90.22 W, at 570 feet, at the central eastern edge of the state, slightly east of the geographic center of the United States and 126 miles east of Jefferson City, the state capital.
Landscape: On the west bank of the Mighty Mississippi River where it meets with the Missouri. The surrounding terrain is gently rolling hills and undulating plains, with occasional high bluffs characteristic of parts of the Mississippi Valley.
Climate: Modified Continental. St. Louis is in the enviable position of having a changeable, four-season climate without prolonged periods of extreme cold, heat, or humidity. To the south is the warm, moist air of the Gulf of Mexico and to the north the region of cold polar air masses. Alternating invasions by these influences, and the conflict along the frontal zones where they meet, produce a great variety of weather conditions, but none lasting long enough to become monotonous. Winters are brisk but seldom severe. Snowfall averages less than 20 inches per season. Summers are quite warm, often uncomfortably so when coupled with high humidity. These oppressive spells are often relieved by storms.

Mildness: 36 Brightness: 45 Stability: 21

Places Rated Score: 35.03 **Places Rated Rank: 225**

TEMPERATURE

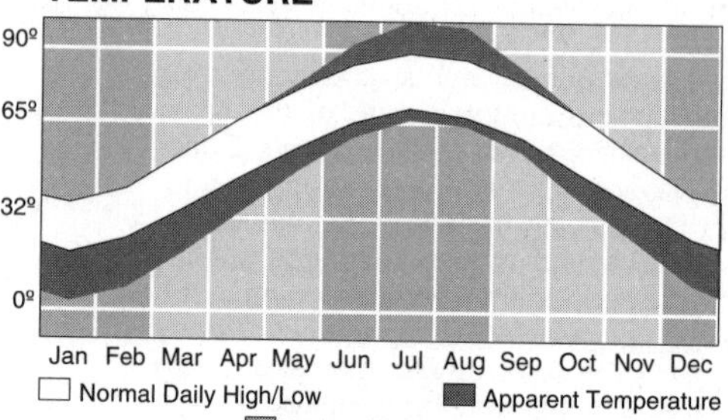

ANNUAL
Humidity: 71%
Wind Speed: 9.6 mph
DAYS
0º or below: 3
32º or below: 107
90º or above: 37
Clear: 101
Cloudy: 163

PRECIPITATION

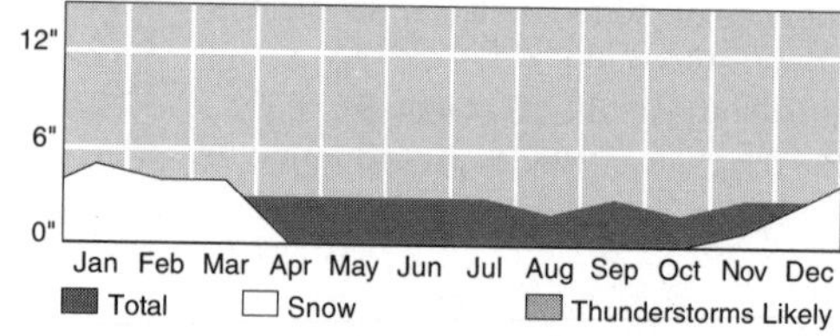

ANNUAL
Precipitation: 37.5"
Snow: 19.8"
DAYS
Precipitation: 71
Thunderstorm: 46

✓ Salinas, CA

Location: 36.36 N, 121.54 W, at 380 feet, on the Salinas River some 85 miles south of San Francisco.
Landscape: Monterey Bay to the west is a great sweeping indentation on the Pacific coast. Sandy and rocky beaches verge on tidepools along the shore. High, grassy bluffs of the Diablo and Santa Lucia mountains of the Coast Range provide added relief. Inland, the natural vegetation is a mixed evergreen forest dominated by cypress and pine groves.
Climate: Marine, with year-round mild temperatures moving through gradual transitions. The ocean is the biggest climate factor. Under the influence of the Pacific High, cooling produces nightly low-stratus clouds, known as California stratus, and early morning fog. Both are dissipated before noon leaving most afternoons clear and sunny. Most precipitation falls from December through March. Winter fog is common. Summers are dry and thunderstorms rare.

Mildness: 99 Brightness: 23 Stability: 100

Places Rated Score: 96.50 **Places Rated Rank: 10**

TEMPERATURE

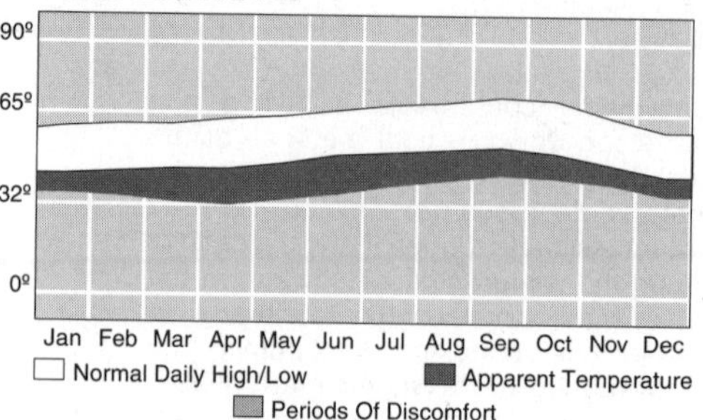

ANNUAL
Humidity: 73%
Wind Speed: 10.6 mph
DAYS
0º or below: 0
32º or below: 1
90º or above: 2
Clear: 160
Cloudy: 104

PRECIPITATION

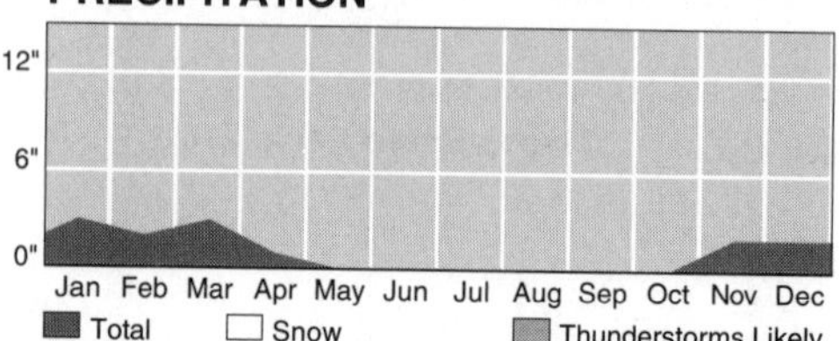

ANNUAL
Precipitation: 18.7"
Snow: 0.1"
DAYS
Precipitation: 35
Thunderstorm: 0

Salt Lake City–Ogden, UT

Location: 40.47 N, 111.57 W, at 4,220 feet, in north central Utah on the Jordan River, about 100 miles from borders with Idaho and Nevada to the north and west, and 70 miles SW of Wyoming.
Landscape: A vast, high desert valley surrounded by imposing peaks. To the east, the rugged Wasatch Mountains rise from heights of 8,000 feet to 12,000 feet; to the southwest, the Oguirrh Mountains climb to 10,000 feet. Nearby, the Great Salt Lake stretches 48 miles west and 90 miles north.
Climate: Though by no means mild, it is modified by the surrounding mountains, which deflect stormy weather elsewhere. There are four well-defined seasons, including a long winter. Summers are hot, but the dry air lessens felt heat, and nights are cool. Winters are cold but not severe. Most of the precipitation is snow, with accumulations staying on the ground for most of the winter. Fall is short, with spring longer and sometimes stormy. Nearby Great Salt Lake also helps

TEMPERATURE

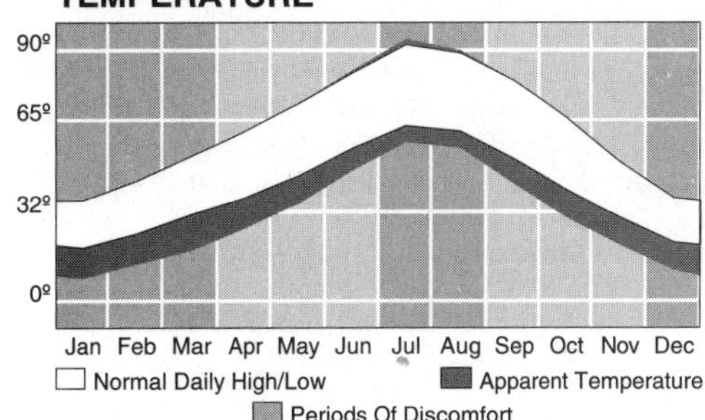

ANNUAL
Humidity: 55%
Wind Speed: 8.8 mph
DAYS
0º or below: 3
32º or below: 134
90º or above: 58
Clear: 125
Cloudy: 139

PRECIPITATION

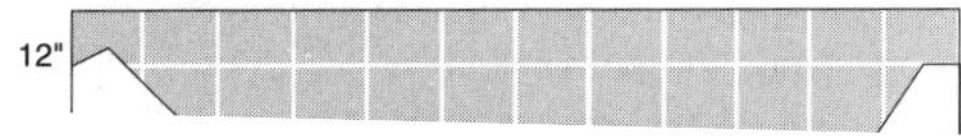

ANNUAL
Precipitation: 16.2"
Snow: 57.9"

plateaus; broken hills and grassy slopes are excellent for grazing livestock. Semiarid, or Steppe, but with sufficient water from the Concho River and deep wells for extensive irrigation. Natural vegetation includes a variety of grasses and oakes mixed with juniper and mesquite.
Climate: Desert characteristics prevail between the humid climate of eastern Texas and the dry High Plains of west Texas. There is a long summer that is hot. Rapid temperature drops occur after sunset, truly desert-like, and certainly welcome. Rainfall is typical of the Great Plains most often occurring from thunderstorm activity. Heaviest rains are in spring and fall. The prevailing south to southwest winds are brisk and modify summer heat. Occasional uncomfortable hot spells with humid air permeate the area. Winters are short and mild. Rapid temperature drops of 20 to 30 degrees may occur when cold polar air invades the region.

Mildness: 66 Brightness: 89 Stability: 24
Places Rated Score: 66.03 **Places Rated Rank: 99**

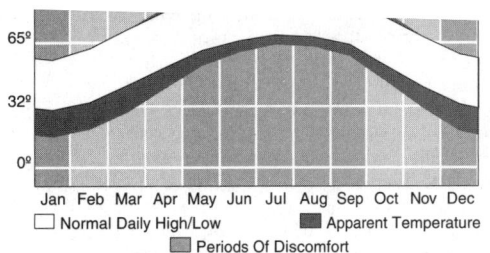

65º
32º
0º
Jan Feb Mar Apr May Jun Jul Aug Sep Oct Nov Dec
Normal Daily High/Low
Apparent Temperature
Periods Of Discomfort

Wind Speed: 10.4 mph
DAYS
0º or below: 0
32º or below: 52
90º or above: 109
Clear: 154
Cloudy: 114

PRECIPITATION

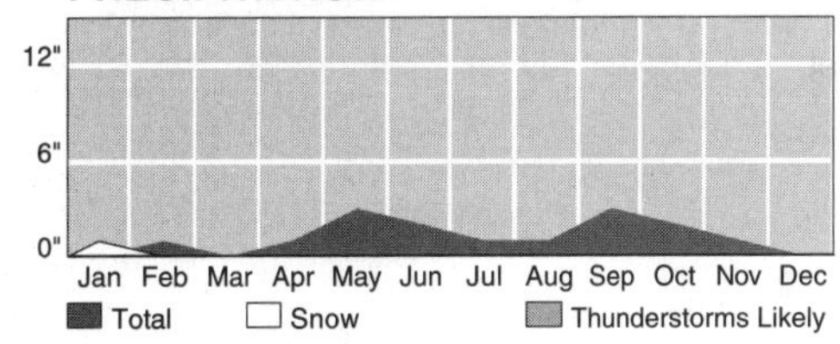

ANNUAL
Precipitation: 20.5"
Snow: 3.1"
DAYS
Precipitation: 33
Thunderstorm: 38

San Antonio, TX

Location: 29.32 N, 98.28 W, at 790 feet, in the south central Texas Blacklands, 150 miles north of Mexico.
Landscape: Near the edge of the Balcones Escarpment this is typical Prairie. Rolling hill country yields to gently sloping open acres between the Edwards Plateau and the Gulf Coastal Plain. The headwaters of the San Antonio River, fed by artesian wells, is here. Soils are blackland clay and silty loam. Vegetation consists of grasses and live oak trees, along with mesquite and cacti.
Climate: Subtropical, with only two seasons. There is mild weather during normal winter months and a long, hot summer. Though 140 miles from the Gulf of Mexico, the city frequently feels the influence of its hot, moist air. Thunderstorms and rains have occurred in every month of the year. They are common during the summer, with most rain falling in May and September. The winds during the winter are from the north and from the south in the summer.

Mildness: 82 Brightness: 71 Stability: 26
Places Rated Score: 74.88 **Places Rated Rank: 62**

TEMPERATURE

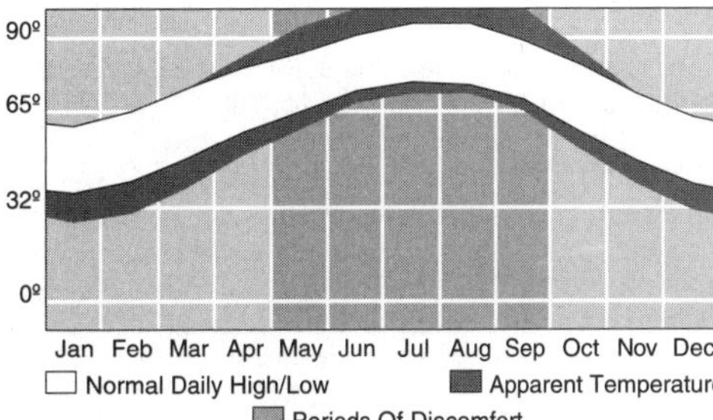

ANNUAL
Humidity: 69%
Wind Speed: 9.1 mph
DAYS
0º or below: 0
32º or below: 22
90º or above: 111
Clear: 106
Cloudy: 141

PRECIPITATION

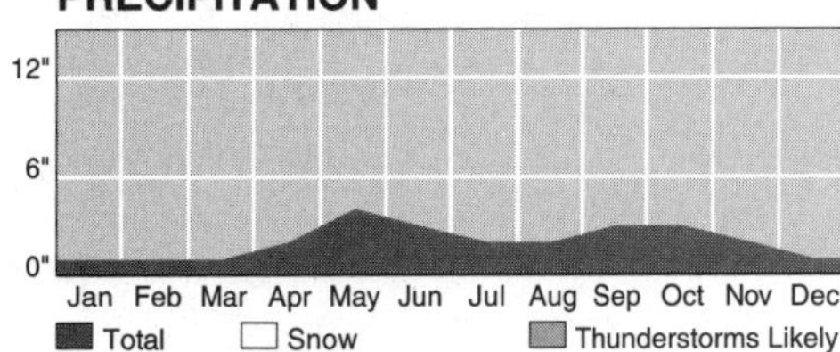

ANNUAL
Precipitation: 31.0"
Snow: 0.7"
DAYS
Precipitation: 46
Thunderstorm: 36

✓San Diego, CA

Location: 32.44 N, 117.10 W, at 10 feet, just above the Mexican border on San Diego Bay and the Pacific Ocean.
Landscape: Backed by coastal foothills and mountains to the east. Topographical relief is further provided by cliffs that rise from the bay. Stream valleys are narrow where they drain the hills. Evergreens with thick, hard leaves like eucalyptus are prevalent. California live oak, tan oak and California laurel are also common. Chaparral is a low-growing shrub.
Climate: Typically Marine, sometimes called Mediterranean. There are no freezing days and an average of only three 90-degree days each year. Dry easterly winds sometimes blow in the vicinity for several days at a time, bringing temperatures in the 90s and even in the 100s in eastern sections of the city. Summers tend to be dry and mild; springs are cooler, and there is rain from November through March. Storms are practically unknown. Sunshine is abundant though there is considerable fog along the coast, and many low clouds in early morning and evening during the summer.

Mildness: 99 Brightness: 54 Stability: 99

Places Rated Score: 96.92 **Places Rated Rank: 6**

TEMPERATURE

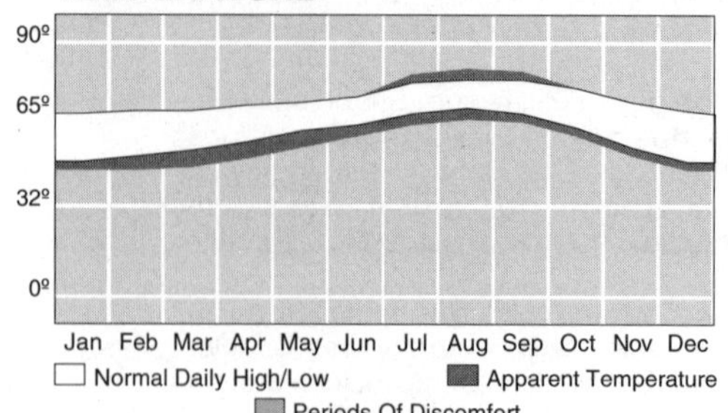

ANNUAL
Humidity: 69%
Wind Speed: 7.0 mph
DAYS
0º or below: 0
32º or below: 0
90º or above: 3
Clear: 146
Cloudy: 102

PRECIPITATION

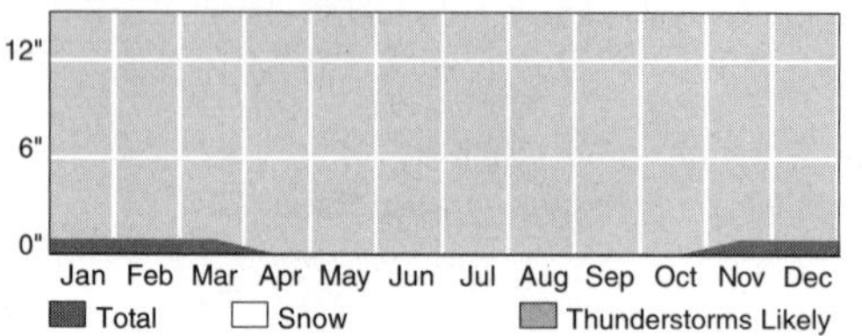

ANNUAL
Precipitation: 9.9"
Snow: 0.0"
DAYS
Precipitation: 19
Thunderstorm: 0

✓San Francisco, CA

Location: 37.46 N, 122.26 W, at 80 feet, on a narrow peninsula of 43 hills on California's northern coast, 90 miles SW of Sacramento.
Landscape: These 49 square miles separate the natural harbor of San Francisco Bay from the Pacific Ocean. A range of hills with elevations of nearly 1,000 feet runs from north to south. The complex topography causes great climatic variability in patterns of fog, sun, and temperature. Now highly urbanized, the natural forest includes fir, spruce, and hemlock found in Golden Gate Park or the Army's Presidio. Flowers bloom throughout the year, and warm clothing is needed every month.
Climate: Two-season Mediterranean climate with a cool, pleasant summer and a mild spring. Unique location causes San Francisco to be known as the air-conditioned city because of the sea-breezes. Sea fogs and associated low stratus clouds are a striking characteristic of the city's climate. On the average, though, the sun shines during 66% of the daylight hours.

Mildness: 99 Brightness: 63 Stability: 100

Places Rated Score: 98.12 **Places Rated Rank: 1**

TEMPERATURE

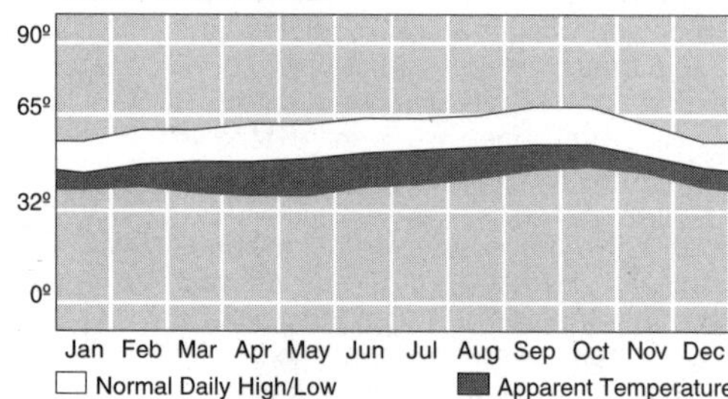

ANNUAL
Humidity: 73%
Wind Speed: 10.6 mph
DAYS
0º or below: 0
32º or below: 6
90º or above: 4
Clear: 160
Cloudy: 104

PRECIPITATION

ANNUAL
Precipitation: 19.7"
Snow: 0.0"
DAYS
Precipitation: 42
Thunderstorm: 0

✓San Luis Obispo-Atascadero-Paso Robles, CA

Location: 35.18 N, 120.40 W, at 310 feet, in the foothills of the Santa Lucia Mountains about 90 miles NW of Santa Barbara.
Landscape: Wooded San Luis Obispo Creek has stretches of fast-falling water. The Santa Lucia Mountains rise to clifftop, ocean views. Cypress and pine groves predominate in the mixed evergreen forest. Almond trees are a fruitful cultivation. Orchards of walnuts, apples, and vineyards also grow well.
Climate: Mediterranean with generally two seasons. The ocean is the biggest climate factor. The Coast Ranges and higher altitude also serve to keep the weather mild most of the year. Cool temperatures and sea breezes are common. Daily and seasonal temperature shifts are slight. Thunderstorms are rare but fog and cloudy mornings are typical.

Mildness: 98 Brightness: 85 Stability: 99

Places Rated Score: 96.93 **Places Rated Rank: 5**

TEMPERATURE

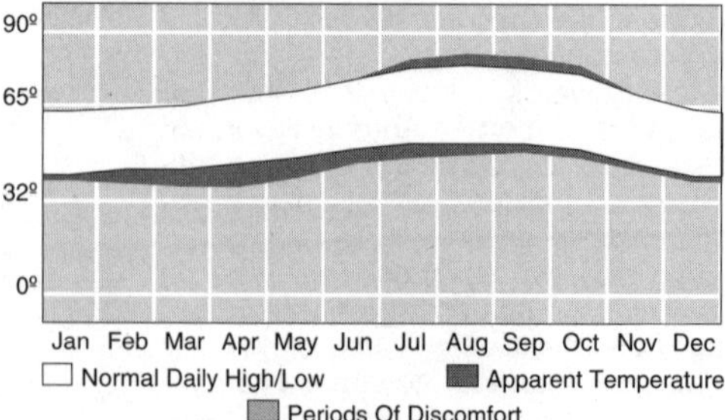

ANNUAL
Humidity: 70%
Wind Speed: 6.1 mph
DAYS
0º or below: 0
32º or below: 3
90º or above: 12
Clear: 170
Cloudy: 85

PRECIPITATION

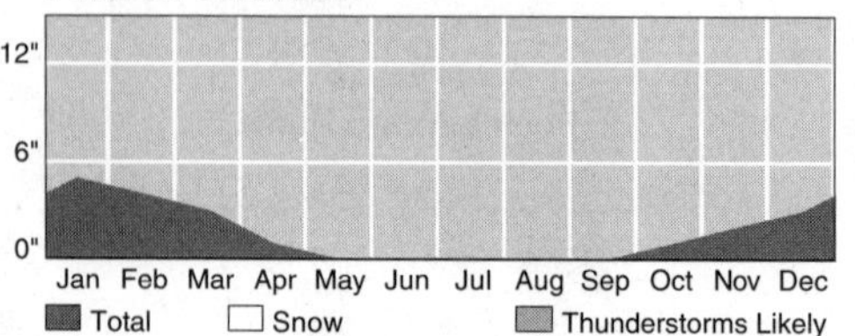

ANNUAL
Precipitation: 23.5"
Snow: 0.0"
DAYS
Precipitation: 28
Thunderstorm: 1

✓Santa Barbara-Santa Maria-Lompoc, CA

Location: 34.26 N, 119.50 W, at 10 feet, on the Pacific Ocean in the Santa Maria Valley, 90 miles NW of Los Angeles.
Landscape: Bounded by the foothills of the San Rafael Mountains, the Solomon Hills, and the Casmalia Hills, the valley is flat and fertile. These three cities lie along the Pacific coast at the base of the Santa Ynez Mountains. The Los Padres National Forest encompasses many of the ranges in the area. Vegetation ranges from chaparral to oak woodlands and pine groves. Cypress and palm trees complete the variety.
Climate: Mediterranean, which includes a winter rainy season, typical of the California coast. During the rest of the year, particularly from June to October, there is little or no precipitation. Clear, sunny afternoons prevail on most days. At night and in the morning, however, the California stratus and fog appear.

Mildness: 98 Brightness: 65 Stability: 99

TEMPERATURE

ANNUAL
Humidity: 70%
Wind Speed: 6.1 mph
DAYS
0º or below: 0
32º or below: 6
90º or above: 3
Clear: 175
Cloudy: 78

PRECIPITATION

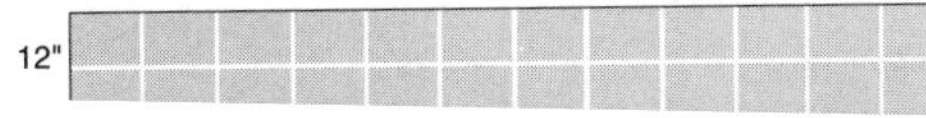

ANNUAL
Precipitation: 16.3"

Santa Fe River in the rolling foothills of the Sangre de Cristo Mountains, which rise to peaks of 10,000 feet. Westward the terrain slopes downward to the Rio Grande River, some 20 miles away. The high mountains to the east protect the city from much of winter's cold. Engelmann spruce, subalpine fir and aspen cover the intermediate slopes, and ponderosa pine is on the lower, drier, more exposed slopes.
Climate: Semiarid Steppe with cool and pleasant summers. Dry and invigorating. Days are in the 80s, with nights in the 50s. Long cloudy periods are unknown. Winters are crisp, clear, and sunny, with considerable daytime warming. Snowfall averages 35 inches a year in the city while driving just a half-hour east brings 250 inches for alpine skiing.

Mildness: 41 Brightness: 88 Stability: 70

Places Rated Score: 53.09 **Places Rated Rank: 156**

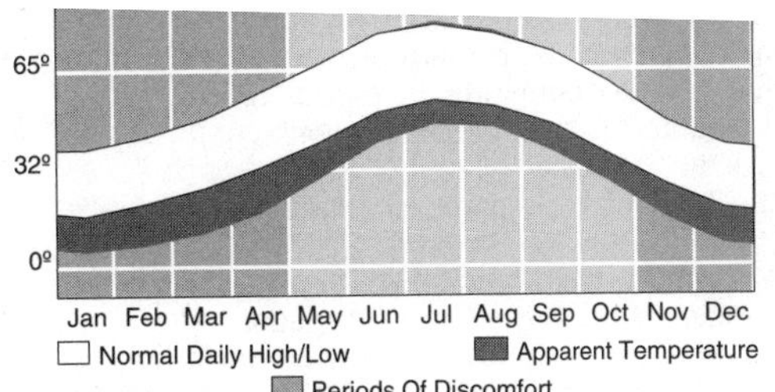

Wind Speed: 9.0 mph
DAYS
0º or below: 2
32º or below: 157
90º or above: 23
Clear: 168
Cloudy: 87

PRECIPITATION

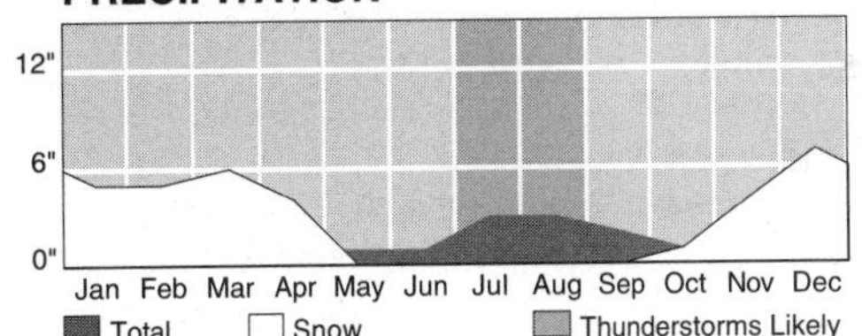

ANNUAL
Precipitation: 18.7"
Snow: 33.7"
DAYS
Precipitation: 33
Thunderstorm: 38

✓Santa Rosa, CA

Location: 38.27 N, 122.42 W, at 170 feet, in the Russian River Valley 50 miles north of San Francisco.
Landscape: This valley runs parallel to the Pacific Coast, with only low hills, 300 feet to 500 feet, between it and the ocean 25 miles southwest. Higher hills rise 10 miles to the east leading into the foothills of the Coast Ranges. Principal trees of the conifer forest are Douglas fir, western red cedar, western hemlock, and Sitka spruce.
Climate: The nearness of the ocean and the surrounding topography join with the prevailing westerly circulation to produce a predominantly southerly air flow year-round. However, the area is sufficiently far inland to assure it a varied climate. Summers are warm, winters cool, and there is a daily temperature shift. There is less fog and drizzle here than at other points along the coast.

Mildness: 94 Brightness: 85 Stability: 98

Places Rated Score: 93.74 **Places Rated Rank: 14**

TEMPERATURE

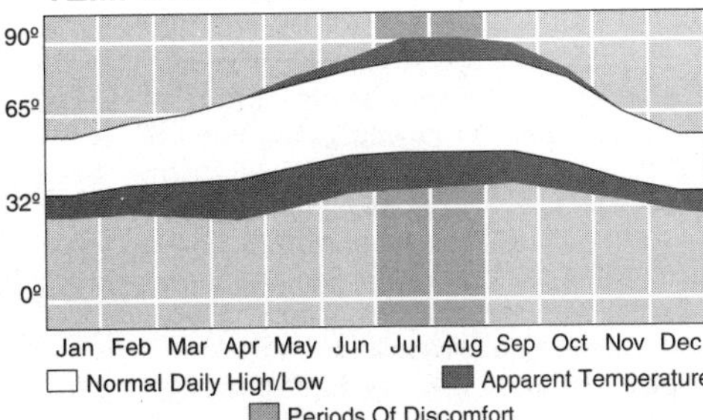

ANNUAL
Humidity: 73%
Wind Speed: 10.6 mph
DAYS
0º or below: 0
32º or below: 37
90º or above: 34
Clear: 160
Cloudy: 104

PRECIPITATION

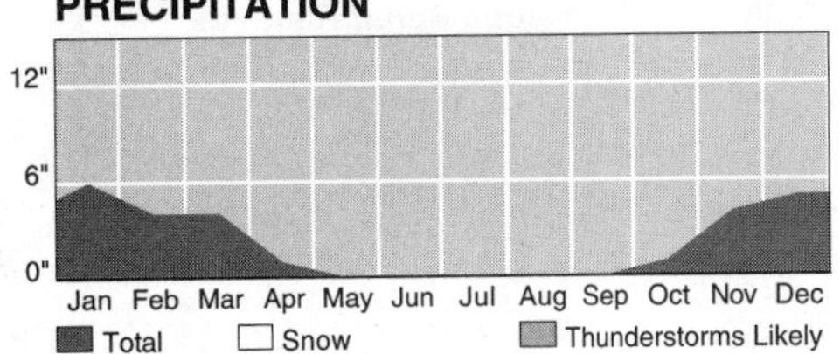

ANNUAL
Precipitation: 30.3"
Snow: 0.2"
DAYS
Precipitation: 46
Thunderstorm: 0

Sarasota–Bradenton, FL

Location: 27.27 N, 82.28 W, at 20 feet, on the south bank of the Manatee River near its mouth at Tampa Bay, midway on Florida's west coast, 50 miles south of Tampa.
Landscape: The area includes numerous islands, separating Sarasota Bay from the Gulf of Mexico, and miles of white-sand beaches. The southern Gulf Coastal Plains are flat and irregular. There is less than 300 feet variation in altitude over the gently rolling areas. Most of the numerous streams are sluggish; marshes, swamps, and lakes are numerous. Evergreen oaks, laurel, and magnolia are common. Trees are not tall and the leaf canopy is not dense.
Climate: Subtropical. Humidity is relatively high year-round. Winters are not cold but are inclined to be rainy. Summers are hot with frequent thunderstorms. Cloudiness is also a factor. The Gulf of Mexico moderates temperature extremes of both summer and winter. August is to Sarasota what February is to New England: time to vacation elsewhere.

Mildness: 94 Brightness: 54 Stability: 9

Places Rated Score: 83.27 **Places Rated Rank: 37**

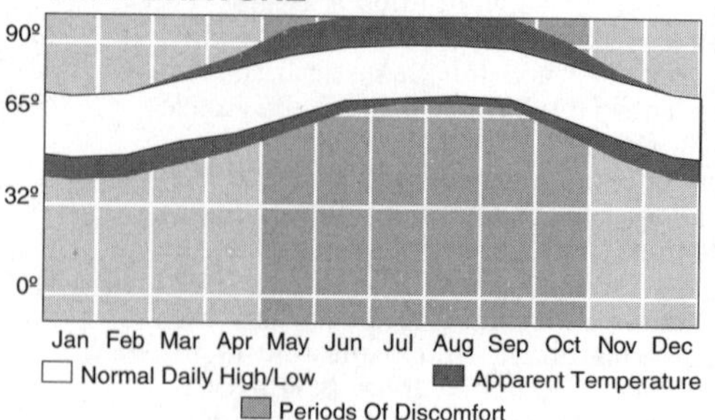

ANNUAL
Humidity: 72%
Wind Speed: 8.3 mph
DAYS
0º or below: 0
32º or below: 0
90º or above: 78
Clear: 101
Cloudy: 121

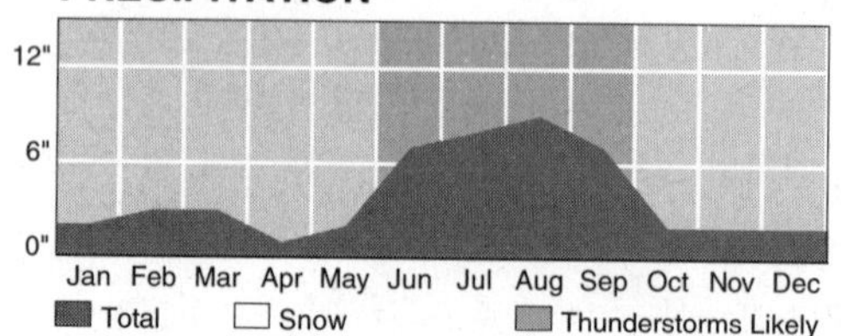

ANNUAL
Precipitation: 53.7"
Snow: 0.0"
DAYS
Precipitation: 69
Thunderstorm: 87

Saskatoon, SK

Location: 52.14 N, 106.37 W, at 1,644 feet, on the South Saskatchewan River in the central south region of the Province.
Landscape: Mixed forest of white and black spruce, jack pine, tamarack, and birch covers the northern reaches of the Province. Prairie grasses and woodlands cover the southwest. The plain is flat, undulating, and hummocky, with deep, fertile soils left by glacial deposition. The horizon is vast, without any landscape barriers to impede air mass movements.
Climate: The Prairies are the sunniest region in Canada, and Saskatoon is the sunniest major city. July is the sunniest month; December is the dullest. In June, the wettest month, frequent storms reduce the number of hours of sun, in spite of 17-hour days. Though winters are long, 8 hours of sunshine are possible. The area is also dry with most precipitation concentrated during the growing season, from May to August. Blizzards are a notorious feature of Prairie winters. Snowfall during such storms may be negligible but strong winds and intense cold can be lethal.

Mildness: 0 Brightness: 99 Stability: 83

Places Rated Score: 8.14 **Places Rated Rank: 343**

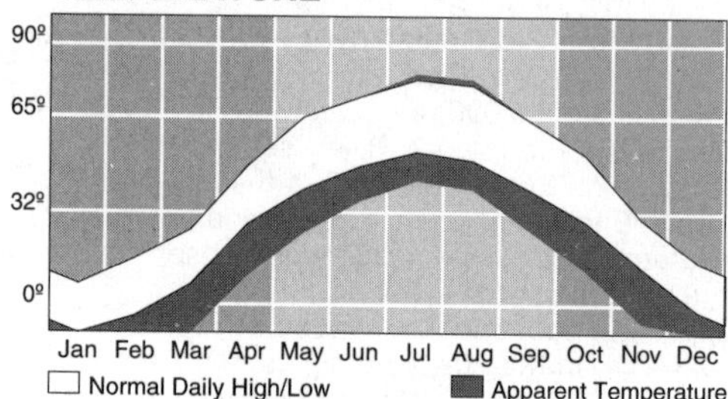

ANNUAL
Humidity: 69%
Wind Speed: 10.9 mph
DAYS
0º or below: 59
32º or below: 202
90º or above: 12
Clear: 119
Cloudy: 115

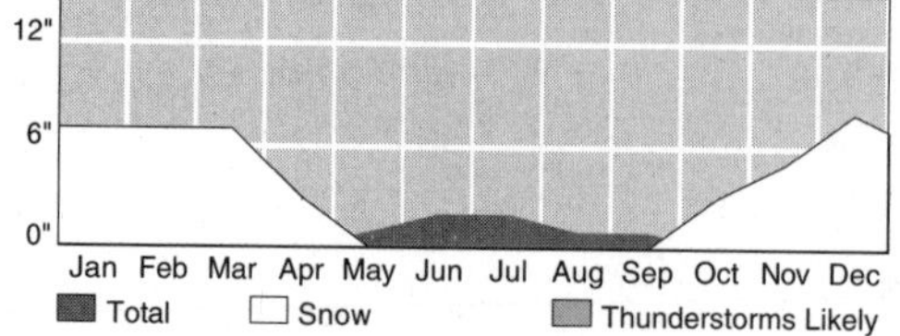

ANNUAL
Precipitation: 13.7"
Snow: 44.4"
DAYS
Precipitation: 24
Thunderstorm: 19

Savannah, GA

Location: 32.08 N, 81.12 W, at 50 feet, on Georgia's north coastal border at the mouth of the Savannah River, 18 miles from the Atlantic Ocean.
Landscape: Surrounded by flat land, low and marshy to the north and east, rising to several feet above sea level to the west and south. About half the land to the west and south is clear of trees and the other half is woods, much of which lie in swamp. The outer coastal plain is a temperate rainforest that includes live oak, loblolly pine, laurel, and magnolia.
Climate: Temperate Subtropical with summer temperatures moderated by thundershowers almost every afternoon. Sunshine is adequate in all seasons; seldom are there more than two or three days in succession without it. The long growing season is accompanied by abundant rain.

Mildness: 83 Brightness: 67 Stability: 21

Places Rated Score: 74.90 **Places Rated Rank: 61**

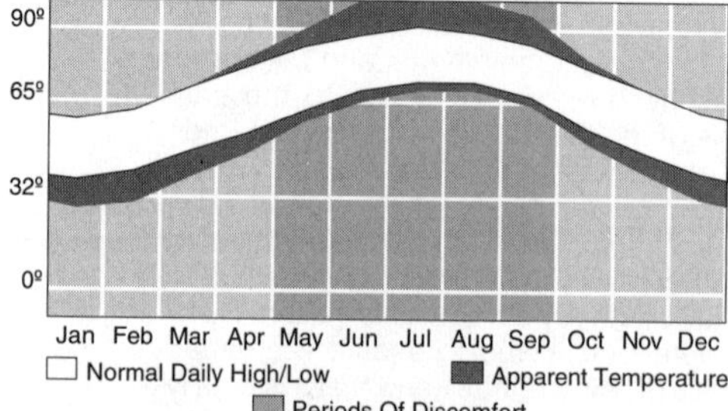

ANNUAL
Humidity: 69%
Wind Speed: 7.9 mph
DAYS
0º or below: 0
32º or below: 31
90º or above: 69
Clear: 104
Cloudy: 151

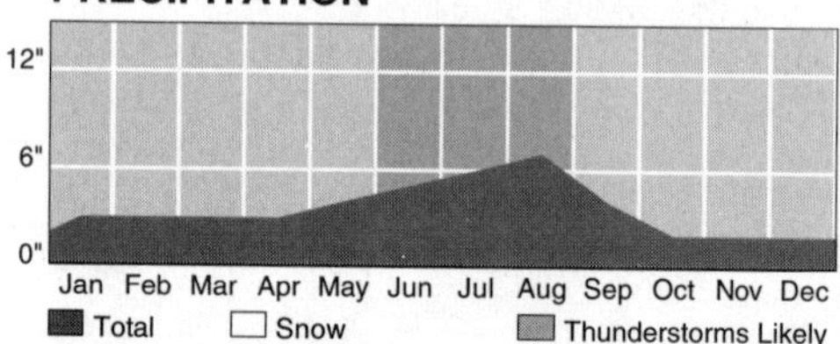

ANNUAL
Precipitation: 49.2"
Snow: 0.4"
DAYS
Precipitation: 68
Thunderstorm: 62

Scranton–Wilkes-Barre–Hazleton, PA

Location: 41.20 N, 75.44 W, at 930 feet, the weather station is located at the airport, between the cities of Scranton and Wilkes-Barre in the Wyoming Valley, 100 miles NE of Philadelphia.
Landscape: The Lackawanna River flows through Scranton and into the Susquehanna River. Wilkes-Barre is also on the Susquehanna. The surrounding Pocono Mountains protect the Wyoming Valley from high winds and adverse precipitation. This valley land is rich, fertile, and well-drained. Mountains, which once yielded iron, and later coal, are again covered with forests. There are many lakes and streams in the area.
Climate: Continental, though cool in summer with frequent, brief showers. Winter temperatures in the valley are not severe. Annual snowfall is 47 inches. Severe snowstorms are infrequent. Annual precipitation is 36 inches. Some tropical

TEMPERATURE

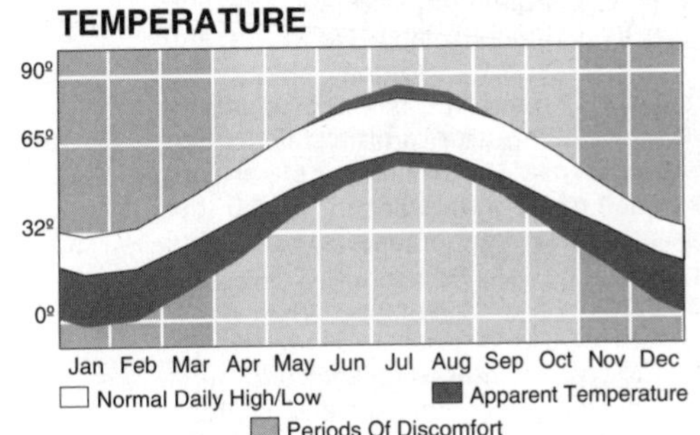

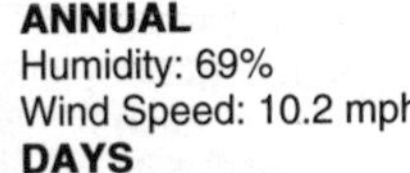

ANNUAL
Humidity: 69%
Wind Speed: 10.2 mph
DAYS
0º or below: 6
32º or below: 127
90º or above: 8
Clear: 70
Cloudy: 190

PRECIPITATION

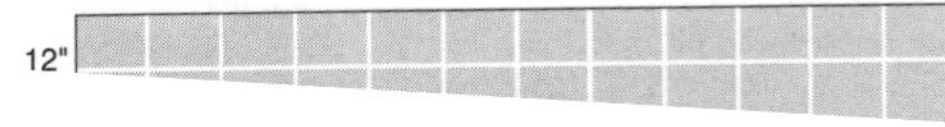

ANNUAL
Precipitation: 36.2"
Snow: 46.9"

the NW Pacific coast of Washington.
Landscape: On a narrow, hilly isthmus between Puget Sound on the west and Lake Washington on the east. The Cascade Range and the Olympic Mountains dominate the horizon and serve as barriers to easterly and northerly weather systems. The metro area landscape is highly urbanized, fronting the eastern shore of Puget Sound.
Climate: Midlatitude coast climate, characterized by moderate temperatures, a pronounced though not sharply defined rainy season, and considerable cloudiness, particularly during the winter. Occasionally, severe winter storms come in from the north. Summers are pleasant, and winters are relatively mild, with prevailing temperatures in the 40s. Summer heat and winter cold are modified by the nearness of the ocean. Although the city receives an average of 38 inches of precipitation annually, mostly in winter, there is measurable rainfall on an average of 150 days a year.

Mildness: 91 Brightness: 32 Stability: 100

Places Rated Score: 89.03 **Places Rated Rank: 17**

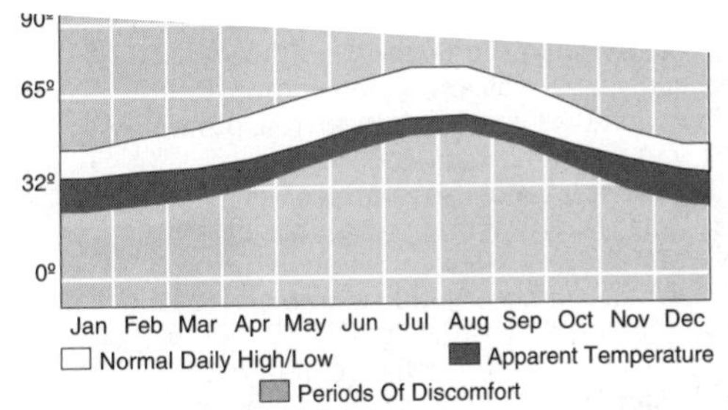

Wind Speed: 9.0 mph
DAYS
0º or below: 0
32º or below: 32
90º or above: 3
Clear: 58
Cloudy: 226

PRECIPITATION

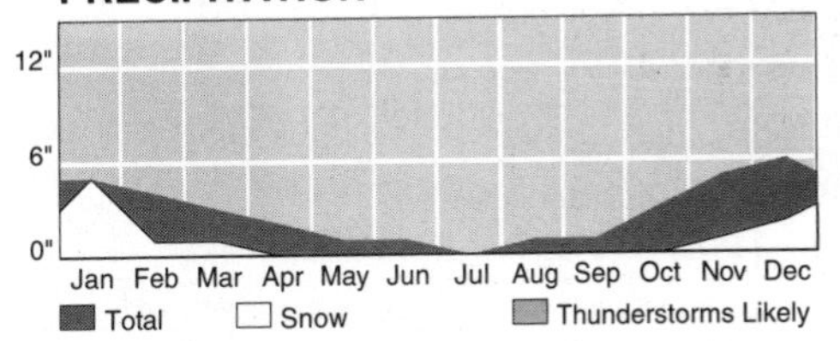

ANNUAL
Precipitation: 38.0"
Snow: 11.8"
DAYS
Precipitation: 95
Thunderstorm: 8

Shreveport–Bossier City, LA

Location: 32.28 N, 93.49 W, at 250 feet, on the banks of the Red River, in northwest Louisiana, some 30 miles south of Arkansas and 15 miles east of Texas.
Landscape: Part of the city is situated in the Red River bottomlands and the remainder in the gently rolling hills that begin a mile west of the river. Land area resources include petroleum, natural gas, cotton, and lumber.
Climate: Transitional between the humid Subtropical climate prevalent to the south and the Continental climates of the Great Plains and Middle West to the north. Winter months are normally mild, with cold spells generally of short duration. The typical pattern is a drop in temperature the first day, minimum temperatures the second day, and gradual warming on the third. Summers are hot and humid, relieved only by the thunderstorms that come about eight times per month during that season. April and May are pleasant. Fall, which lasts from late September to December, is delightful for outdoor activities.

Mildness: 75 Brightness: 27 Stability: 11

Places Rated Score: 59.62 **Places Rated Rank: 129**

TEMPERATURE

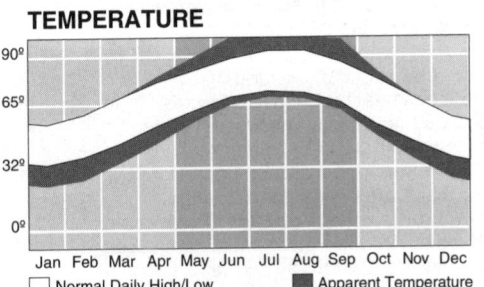

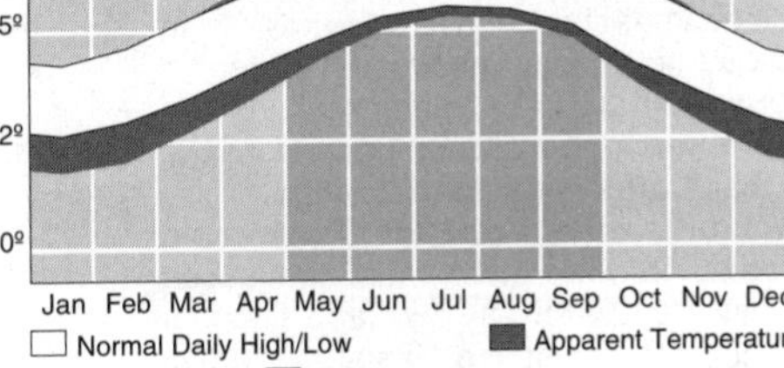

ANNUAL
Humidity: 73%
Wind Speed: 8.4 mph
DAYS
0º or below: 0
32º or below: 36
90º or above: 90
Clear: 114
Cloudy: 151

PRECIPITATION

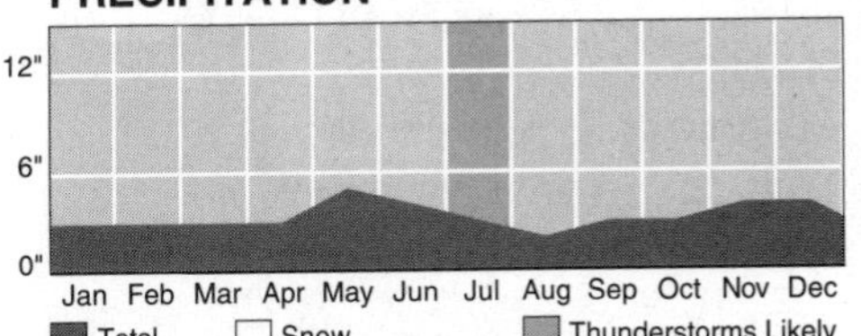

ANNUAL
Precipitation: 46.1"
Snow: 1.7"
DAYS
Precipitation: 64
Thunderstorm: 57

Sioux City, IA–NE

Location: 42.24 N, 96.23 W, at 1,090 feet, along the Missouri River at a point where Iowa touches both Nebraska and South Dakota.

Landscape: The terrain is rolling, except for the river valleys and bottomlands. The Sioux City business district lies in the river valley, and the residential sections, for the most part, are spread over the hills, which range from 100 feet to 200 feet higher. Corn, small grains, and grazing grasses are products of abundant rainfall here.

Climate: Typically Continental and largely determined by the movement and interaction of the large-scale weather systems. Under normal conditions, winters are cold and summers warm, with most rain falling between April and September. Except for an occasional dry year, rain is plentiful. There is considerable fluctuation in temperature and precipitation from season to season and year to year, as elsewhere in the Northern Plains.

Mildness: 10 Brightness: 53 Stability: 22

Places Rated Score: 16.17 **Places Rated Rank: 325**

TEMPERATURE

90º 65º 32º 0º

Jan Feb Mar Apr May Jun Jul Aug Sep Oct Nov Dec

Normal Daily High/Low Apparent Temperature Periods Of Discomfort

ANNUAL
Humidity: 71%
Wind Speed: 11.0 mph
DAYS
0º or below: 22
32º or below: 150
90º or above: 24
Clear: 104
Cloudy: 157

PRECIPITATION

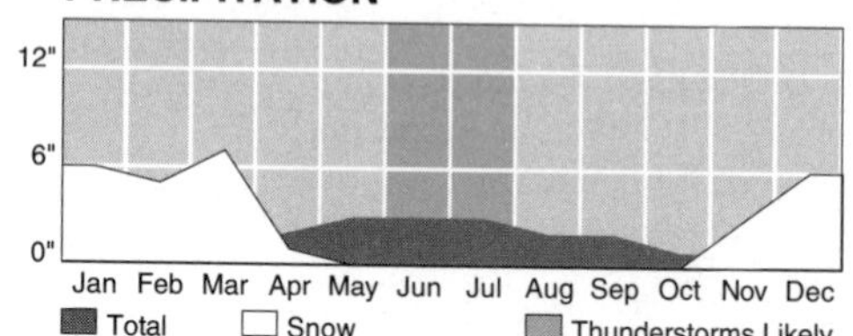

ANNUAL
Precipitation: 25.9"
Snow: 31.8"
DAYS
Precipitation: 47
Thunderstorm: 43

Sioux Falls, SD

Location: 43.34 N, 96.44 W, at 1,420 feet, in the Big Sioux River valley in southeastern South Dakota.

Landscape: Surrounding terrain is gently rolling. Within a 100-mile radius of the city, the land slopes upward 300 feet to 400 feet in the north and northwest and downward in the southeast. There is little change in elevation in the other directions.

Climate: Invigorating Continental. Cold air masses from the north often move in rapidly, causing strong, gusty winds for several hours. During late fall and winter, these cold fronts sometimes bring temperature drops of 20 degrees to 30 degrees in a day. Severe cold spells rarely last more than a few days. During a cold winter, frost may penetrate the ground to a depth of 3 feet to 4 feet unless there is heavy snow cover. There are usually one or two heavy snowstorms each winter. Summer temperatures may climb over 100°F once or twice a year.

Mildness: 4 Brightness: 68 Stability: 14

Places Rated Score: 9.22 **Places Rated Rank: 340**

TEMPERATURE

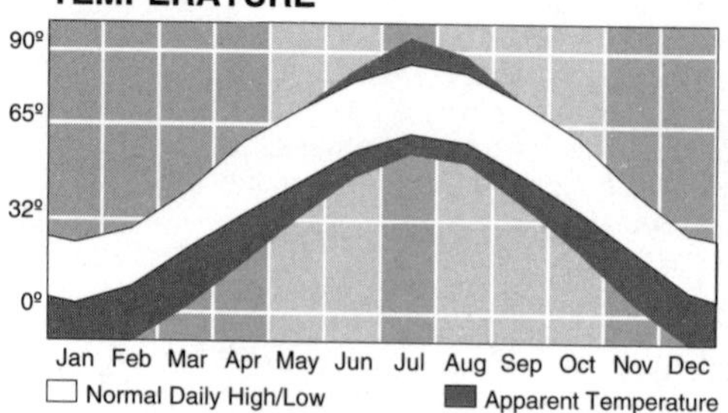

ANNUAL
Humidity: 71%
Wind Speed: 11.1 mph
DAYS
0º or below: 33
32º or below: 171
90º or above: 28
Clear: 106
Cloudy: 156

PRECIPITATION

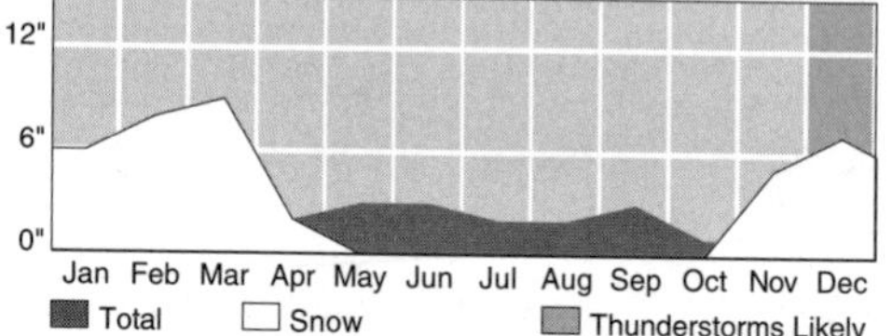

ANNUAL
Precipitation: 23.9"
Snow: 39.6"
DAYS
Precipitation: 43
Thunderstorm: 57

Spokane, WA

Location: 47.38 N, 117.32 W, at 2,360 feet, is on the eastern edge of the broad Columbia Basin area of Washington, bounded by the Cascade Range on the west and the Rocky Mountains to the east.

Landscape: The elevations in eastern Washington vary from less than 400 feet above sea level near Pasco to 5,000 feet in the extreme eastern edge of the state. Spokane is in the upper plateau area, where the long, gradual slope from the Columbia River meets the sharp rise of the Rockies.

Climate: Combines some of the characteristics of the damp coastal climate with the arid interior climate. Most air masses are brought from the west or southwest and lose most of their moisture passing over the Coast and Cascade ranges. Sometimes dry, continental air masses from the east invade the area, bringing high temperatures with low humidity in the summer and subzero temperatures in the winter. Generally, Spokane has a mild climate during summer and a cold, coastal climate during winter.

Mildness: 32 Brightness: 81 Stability: 94

Places Rated Score: 49.98 **Places Rated Rank: 169**

TEMPERATURE

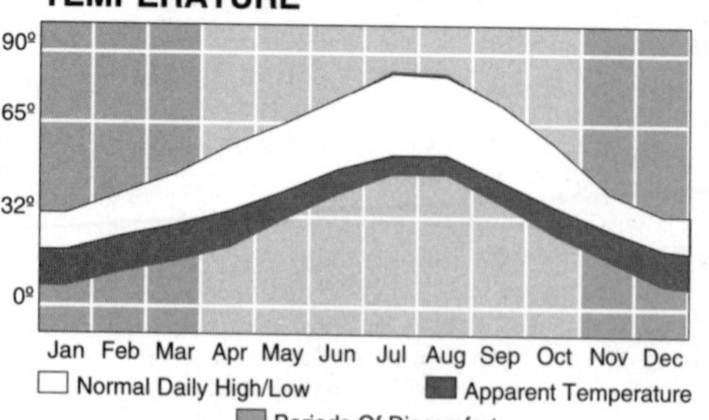

ANNUAL
Humidity: 65%
Wind Speed: 8.9 mph
DAYS
0º or below: 5
32º or below: 141
90º or above: 21
Clear: 86
Cloudy: 192

PRECIPITATION

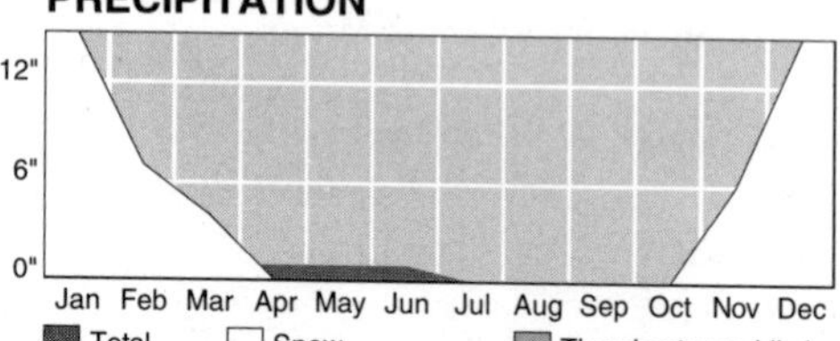

ANNUAL
Precipitation: 16.5"
Snow: 50.4"
DAYS
Precipitation: 57
Thunderstorm: 11

Springfield, IL

Location: 39.51 N, 89.41 W, at 590 feet, in the central part of the state on the Sangamon River.
Landscape: Surrounding country is nearly level. There are no large hills in the area, but rolling terrain is found near the Sangamon River and Spring Creek. The city is in the midst of a rich agricultural and coal region.
Climate: Typically Continental in character, with warm to hot summers and cold winters. There are sharp seasonal changes, but no extended periods of severely cold weather. Monthly average temperatures range from the upper 20s in January to the upper 70s in July. Considerable variation takes place frequently within each season. Summer weather is often uncomfortably warm and humid. While winters are less severe than those farther to the north, prairie winds may accentuate the cold. The prevailing wind direction is souther-

TEMPERATURE

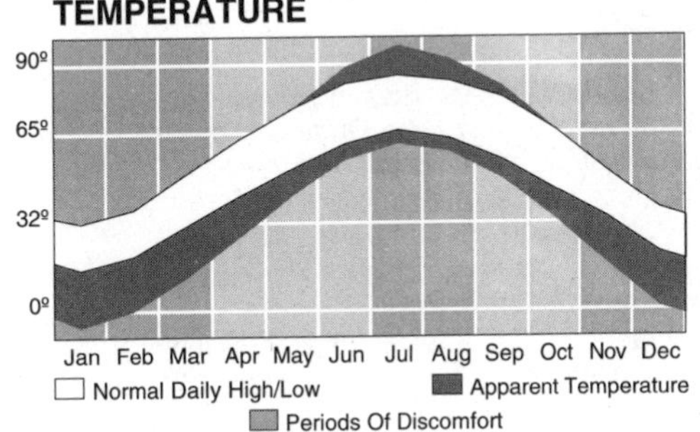

ANNUAL
Humidity: 72%
Wind Speed: 11.1 mph
DAYS
0º or below: 8
32º or below: 119
90º or above: 28
Clear: 103
Cloudy: 168

PRECIPITATION

ANNUAL
Precipitation: 35.3"

Location: 37.14 N, 93.23 W, at …
Ozark Plateau 135 miles SW of Jefferson City, the state capital.
Landscape: This is flat or gently rolling tableland, practically atop the crest of the Ozark Plateau. Located in the state's poultry and dairy region, the economy is based on agriculture and lumber products. Trees are in scattered wood lots and include oak, maple, cottonwood and walnut.
Climate: The mild and changeable climate is often associated with high places in southerly latitudes, with warmer winters and cooler summers than other parts of the state at lower elevations. As a result the city and surrounding countryside enjoy what is described as a Plateau climate. The city sits astride two major drainage systems: the Missouri River system to the north and the White-Mississippi system to the south.

Mildness: 38 Brightness: 56 Stability: 17

Places Rated Score: 38.02 **Places Rated Rank: 208**

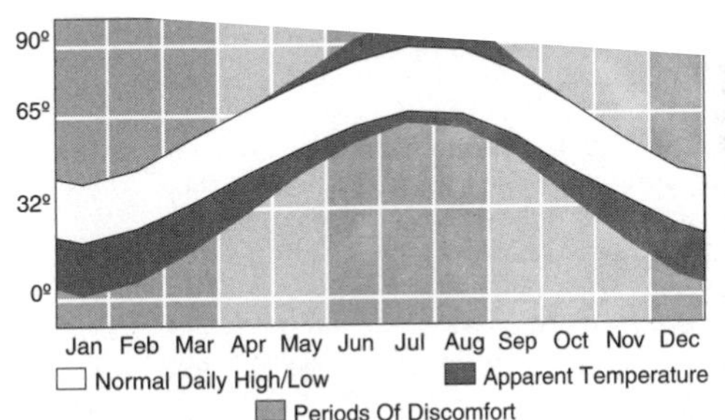

Wind Speed: 10.6 mph
DAYS
0º or below: 3
32º or below: 105
90º or above: 40
Clear: 115
Cloudy: 154

PRECIPITATION

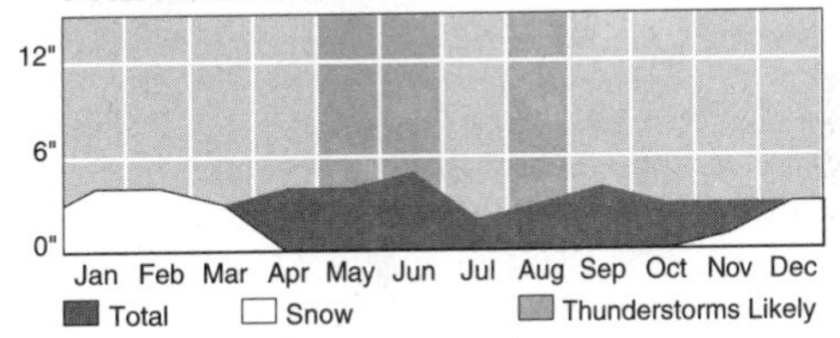

ANNUAL
Precipitation: 43.0"
Snow: 17.1"
DAYS
Precipitation: 62
Thunderstorm: 55

State College, PA

Location: 40.48 N, 77.52 W, at 1,170 feet, in Centre County, the geographic center of Pennsylvania.
Landscape: The orientation of the ridges and valleys of the Appalachian Mountains is northeast to southwest. Elevations within Centre County vary from 977 feet to 2,400 feet. The rolling meadows of the Nittany Valley and foothills of the Allegheny Plateau rise to the west. Forests of pine, hemlock, and hardwoods of beech, maple, oak, ash, and cherry were once more common before the clear-cut harvests. The surrounding higher elevations are now covered with second-growth forests.
Climate: The weather is moderated by the surrounding mountain elevations and protected by its eastern slope location. This translates to drier, somewhat less humid seasons. Winters are cold and relatively dry, with thick cloud cover. Summer and fall are the most pleasant seasons of the year.

Mildness: 31 Brightness: 16 Stability: 53

Places Rated Score: 30.89 **Places Rated Rank: 247**

TEMPERATURE

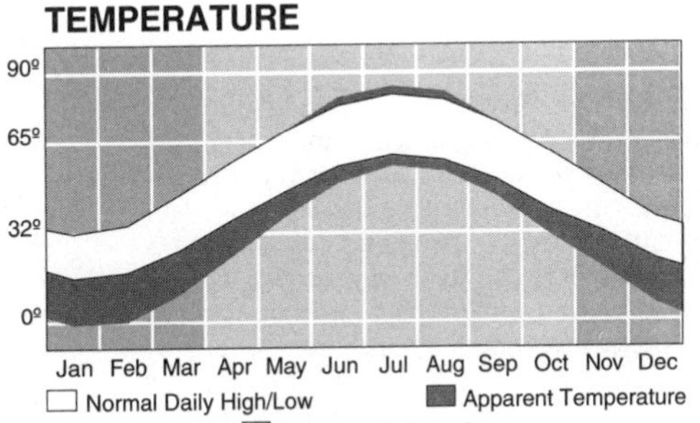

ANNUAL
Humidity: 67%
Wind Speed: 9.1 mph
DAYS
0º or below: 5
32º or below: 131
90º or above: 8
Clear: 58
Cloudy: 204

PRECIPITATION

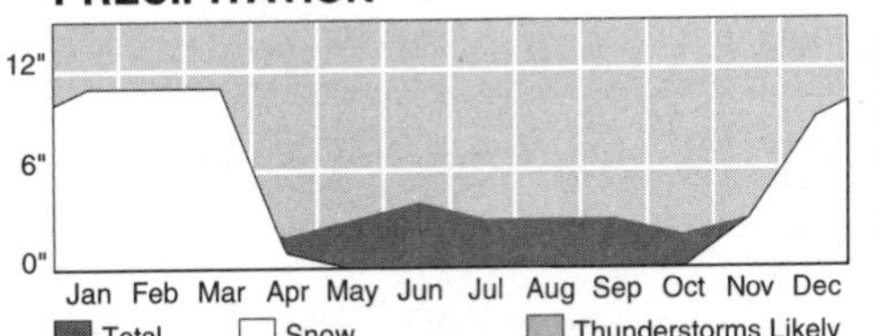

ANNUAL
Precipitation: 37.5"
Snow: 49.7"
DAYS
Precipitation: 76
Thunderstorm: 35

Syracuse, NY

Location: 43.07 N, 76.07 W, at 410 feet, at approximately the geographic center of New York State, 135 miles NW of Albany.

Landscape: Gently rolling terrain stretches northward for about 30 miles to the eastern end of Lake Ontario. Oneida Lake lies about 8 miles NE of the city. Five miles to the south, hills rise to about 1,500 feet. Immediately to the west, terrain is gently rolling, with elevations 500 feet to 800 feet above sea level.

Climate: Continental and comparatively humid. Nearly all cyclonic systems moving from the interior of the country and passing through the St. Lawrence Valley will affect Syracuse. Seasonal and daily changes are marked and produce an invigorating climate. Winters can be cold and severe. Autumn, winter, and spring show great changeability. Summer nights generally are cool, but days can be uncomfortable because of the humidity. The area is overcast, and the cloudiest months are December, January, and February.

Mildness: 22 Brightness: 16 Stability: 71

Places Rated Score: 25.88 **Places Rated Rank: 288**

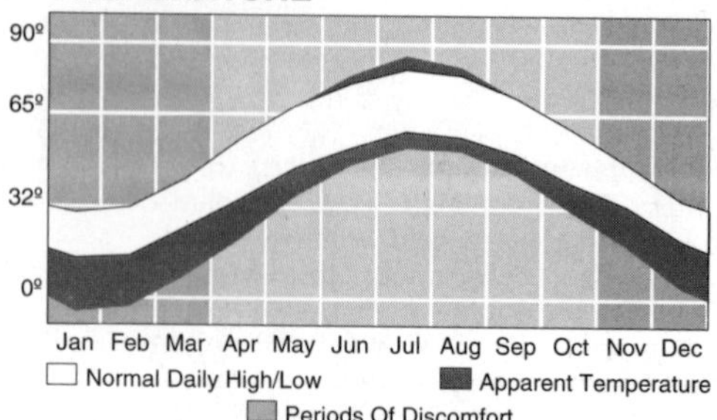

ANNUAL
Humidity: 71%
Wind Speed: 9.5 mph
DAYS
0º or below: 9
32º or below: 136
90º or above: 9
Clear: 62
Cloudy: 205

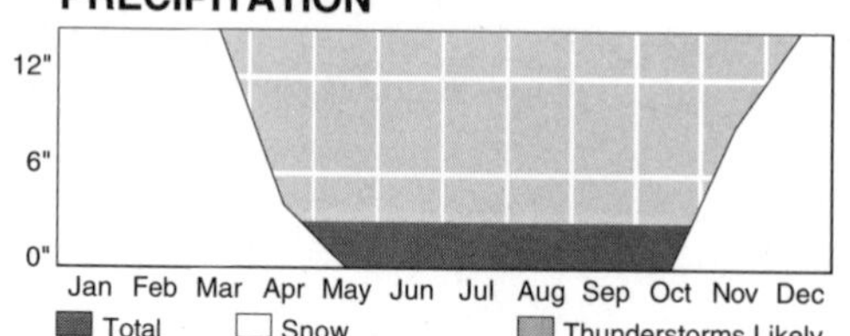

ANNUAL
Precipitation: 38.9"
Snow: 114.0"
DAYS
Precipitation: 75
Thunderstorm: 27

Tallahassee, FL

Location: 30.23 N, 84.22 W, at 60 feet, midway between Pensacola and Jacksonville, 30 miles north of the Gulf of Mexico and 20 miles south of Georgia.

Landscape: Hilly capital of a lowland state with natural forests of oak and magnolia. Rolling red clay hills are covered with varied hardwoods. The larger plant growth in north Florida is longleaf and other pines, cypresses, magnolias, bays, gums, and oaks, both the scrubby black-jack and imposing live oak. The many artesian wells, springs, and small lakes in the area support varieties of water plants.

Climate: Average year-round temperatures compare with those of southern portions of California, Brazil, China, and Australia. The yearly average of 68°F has varied from 64°F to 71°F. In contrast to the southern part of Florida, there is a more definite march of the four seasons here, with considerable winter rainfall and much less winter sunshine. Summer is the least pleasant time of the year; thunderstorms occur on the average of every other day. High humidities and high temperatures cause discomfort.

Mildness: 87 Brightness: 25 Stability: 5

Places Rated Score: 68.71 **Places Rated Rank: 86**

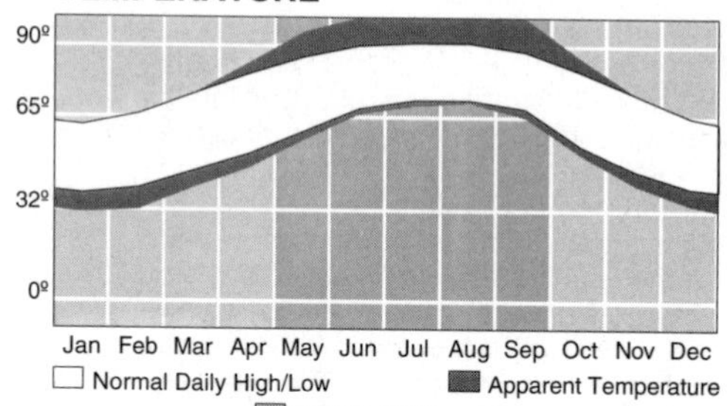

ANNUAL
Humidity: 73%
Wind Speed: 6.3 mph
DAYS
0º or below: 0
32º or below: 31
90º or above: 87
Clear: 102
Cloudy: 134

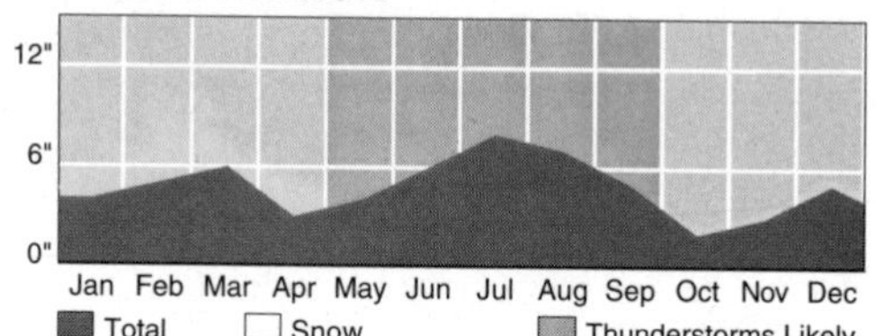

ANNUAL
Precipitation: 65.7"
Snow: 0.0"
DAYS
Precipitation: 74
Thunderstorm: 83

Tampa–St. Petersburg–Clearwater, FL

Location: 27.58 N, 82.32 W, at 20 feet, on Florida's central Gulf coast near the tip of Pinellas Peninsula, adjacent to Tampa Bay.

Landscape: The Hillsborough River and an estuary form a marine horseshoe around Tampa proper. This is flat country connected on the east and south by bridges. A string of sand-reef island resorts lie to the west. The outer coastal plain forest consists of southern yellow pine and laurel. Citrus groves and other agriculture abound in the fertile, rolling country to the east. Clearwater occupies a high coastal elevation along the Pinellas Peninsula. St. Petersburg lies at the southern tip of the peninsula.

Climate: Temperature throughout the year is modified by the waters of the Gulf of Mexico and surrounding bays. Thunderstorms are frequent during late summer afternoons. The resulting temperature drop feels good. Snowfall is negligible, and freezing temperatures are rare. During the cool season night ground fogs occur frequently because of the flat terrain.

Mildness: 94 Brightness: 20 Stability: 6

Places Rated Score: 78.84 **Places Rated Rank: 56**

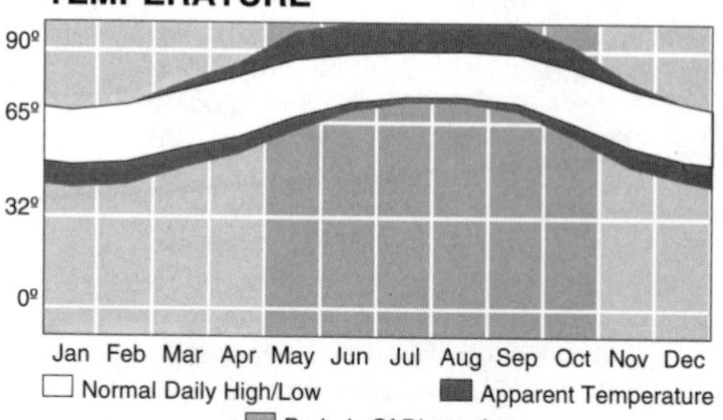

ANNUAL
Humidity: 72%
Wind Speed: 8.3 mph
DAYS
0º or below: 0
32º or below: 3
90º or above: 85
Clear: 101
Cloudy: 121

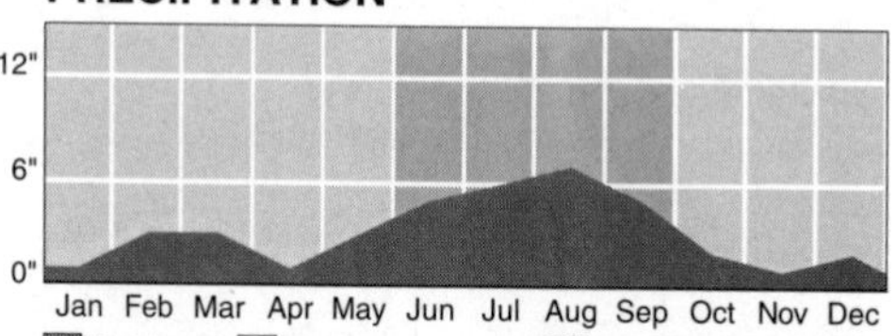

ANNUAL
Precipitation: 43.9"
Snow: 0.0"
DAYS
Precipitation: 69
Thunderstorm: 87

Toledo, OH

Location: 41.36 N, 83.48 W, at 670 feet, on the western end of Lake Erie at the mouth of the Maumee River.
Landscape: The city has excellent harbor facilities, making it a large transportation center for rail, water, and motor freight. With only a slight slope toward the river and Lake Erie, the land is generally flat. Rich agricultural land is found in the surrounding area, especially up the Maumee River toward the Indiana state line. The terrain is level and drainage rather poor, conducive to flooding.
Climate: Nearness to Lake Erie has a moderating effect on temperature, and extremes are seldom recorded. Humidity is high, and there is an excessive amount of cloudiness. In the winter months, the sun shines during only 30 percent of the daylight hours; December and January, the cloudiest months, sometimes receive as little as 16 percent of the possible amount of sunshine. Snowfall is generally light and distributed evenly from November to March. Severe windstorms are ... days a year having sus-

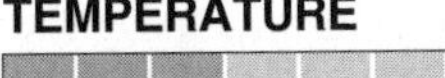

TEMPERATURE

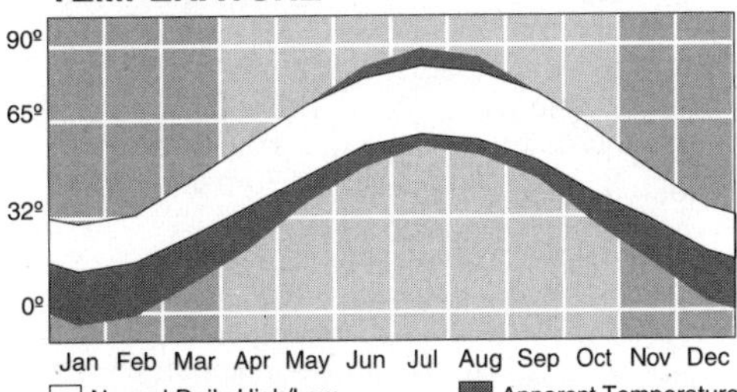

ANNUAL
Humidity: 72%
Wind Speed: 9.4 mph
DAYS
0º or below: 8
32º or below: 145
90º or above: 13
Clear: 72
Cloudy: 185

PRECIPITATION

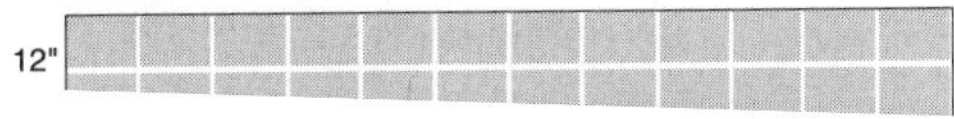

ANNUAL
Precipitation: 33.0"

River about 60 miles above the junction with the Missouri River.
Landscape: The Kansas River valley ranges from 2 to 4 miles wide, and is bordered on both sides by rolling prairie uplands of 200 to 300 feet. Flooding is always a threat from the Kansas River and two tributaries.
Climate: Temperate with sharp Continental features from year to year. April through September brings 70 percent of the annual precipitation. These rains arrive as thunderstorms, which are of short duration and occur most often at night and in the early morning hours. Oppressively warm periods with high humidity in summer and bitter cold spells of winter are brief events. Spring and fall are transitional seasons having numerous days of fair weather interspersed with short bouts of stormy weather or cold air invasions that gradually increase in intensity.

Mildness: 24 Brightness: 67 Stability: 16

Places Rated Score: 28.93 **Places Rated Rank: 265**

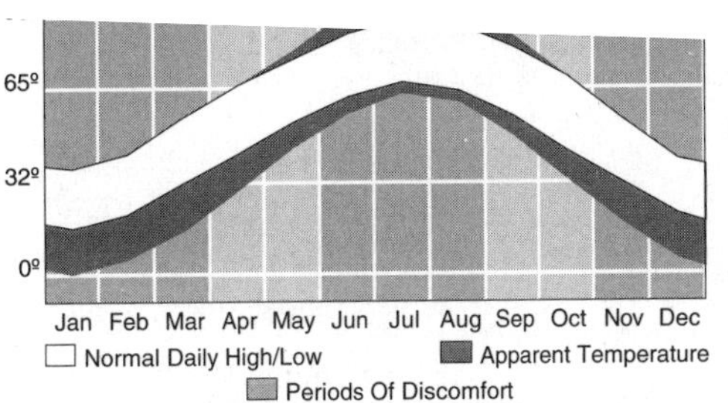

Wind Speed: 9.9 mph
DAYS
0º or below: 6
32º or below: 123
90º or above: 45
Clear: 114
Cloudy: 154

PRECIPITATION

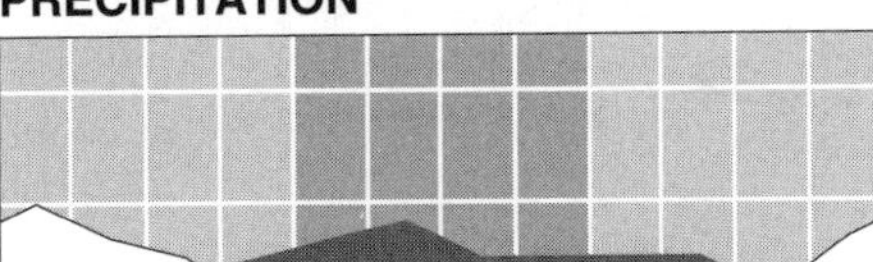

ANNUAL
Precipitation: 35.2"
Snow: 21.2"
DAYS
Precipitation: 59
Thunderstorm: 54

Toronto, ON

Location: 43.40 N, 79.38 W, at 568 feet, on the northwest shore of Lake Ontario, 135 highway miles from Buffalo, NY.
Landscape: Nestled in a shallow basin with a gentle rise in land to the Niagara escarpment west to northwest. Toronto benefits from its Great Lakes location and its role as an inland port on the St. Lawrence Seaway.
Climate: One of the most reliable precipitation regimes in the world, with markedly dry or wet spells both uncommon. The four well-marked seasons include cold-to-cool winters with periods of snow, or rain and snow, alternating with bright sunshine. There is a slow return to warmth in spring along with showery weather. Summer brings periods of heat and humidity with occasional thunderstorms. Increasing cloudiness, more frequent rains and rapidly dropping temperatures are characteristic of autumn's precipitation pattern.

Mildness: 16 Brightness: 48 Stability: 73

Places Rated Score: 25.40 **Places Rated Rank: 294**

TEMPERATURE

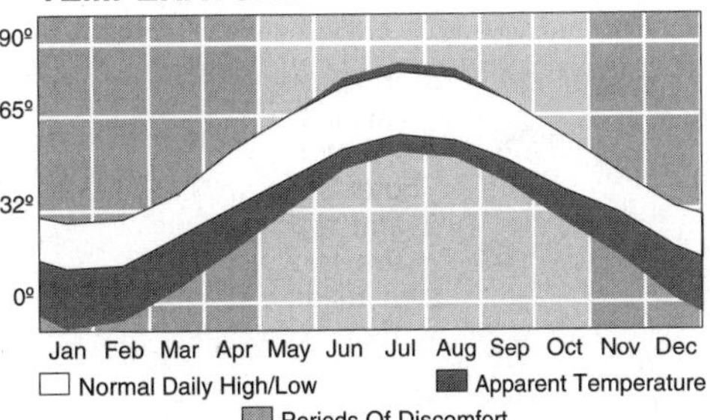

ANNUAL
Humidity: 75%
Wind Speed: 9.6 mph
DAYS
0º or below: 5
32º or below: 155
90º or above: 15
Clear: 110
Cloudy: 134

PRECIPITATION

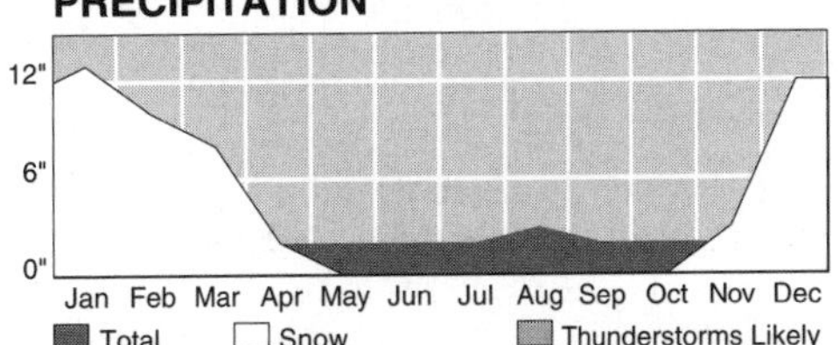

ANNUAL
Precipitation: 30.0"
Snow: 51.6"
DAYS
Precipitation: 69
Thunderstorm: 27

Tucson, AZ

Location: 32.08 N, 110.56 W, at 2,580 feet, on the Santa Cruz River, 120 miles SE of Phoenix and 60 miles above the Mexican border.
Landscape: High desert at the foot of the Catalina Mountains in a broad, flat to gently rolling valley floor rimmed by mountains. Saguaro, spiny cholla and prickly pear cactus are prevalent. To the northeast, the Coronado National Forest is typical of pine, spruce, fir forests of the higher elevations. The city is in the midst of a citrus fruit, vegetable, cotton, livestock and dairy producing area.
Climate: Desert. A sunny, dry climate and a unique desert-mountain location. There is a long, hot season beginning in April that ends in October. High temperatures are modified by low humidity, reducing discomfort. July and August can be unpleasant. Tucson lies in the zone receiving more sunshine than any other in the United States. Clear skies or thin, high clouds permit intense surface heating during the day and active radiational cooling at night. Temperatures below freezing are rare as is snowfall. Summer is the rainy season with active thunderstorms.

Mildness: 74 Brightness: 100 Stability: 28

Places Rated Score: 79.62 **Places Rated Rank: 53**

TEMPERATURE

90º 65º 32º 0º
Jan Feb Mar Apr May Jun Jul Aug Sep Oct Nov Dec
Normal Daily High/Low
Apparent Temperature
Periods Of Discomfort

ANNUAL
Humidity: 39%
Wind Speed: 8.3 mph
DAYS
0º or below: 0
32º or below: 18
90º or above: 140
Clear: 194
Cloudy: 81

PRECIPITATION

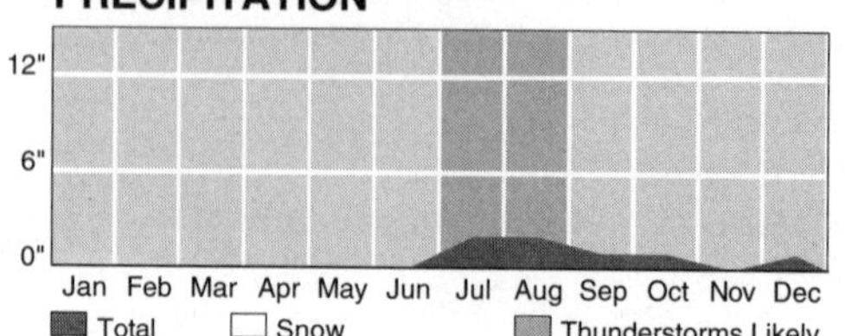

ANNUAL
Precipitation: 12.0"
Snow: 1.3"
DAYS
Precipitation: 12
Thunderstorm: 42

Tulsa, OK

Location: 36.12 N, 95.54 W, at 650 feet, lies along the Arkansas River in NE Oklahoma at an elevation of almost 700 feet above sea level.
Landscape: The surrounding terrain is gently rolling. There are no natural formations such as mountains or large water surfaces that influence its climate.
Climate: Tulsa is far enough north to escape long periods of heat in summer, yet far enough south to miss the extreme cold of winter. The influence of warm moist air from the Gulf of Mexico is often felt in the high humidity, but the climate is essentially Continental, characterized by rapid temperature changes. Generally, the winter months are mild. Temperatures of 100°F or higher are frequently experienced from the latter part of July to early September but are accompanied by low humidity and a good southerly breeze. Fall is long, with a great number of sunny days and cool, bracing nights.

Mildness: 45 Brightness: 80 Stability: 16

Places Rated Score: 47.04 **Places Rated Rank: 181**

TEMPERATURE

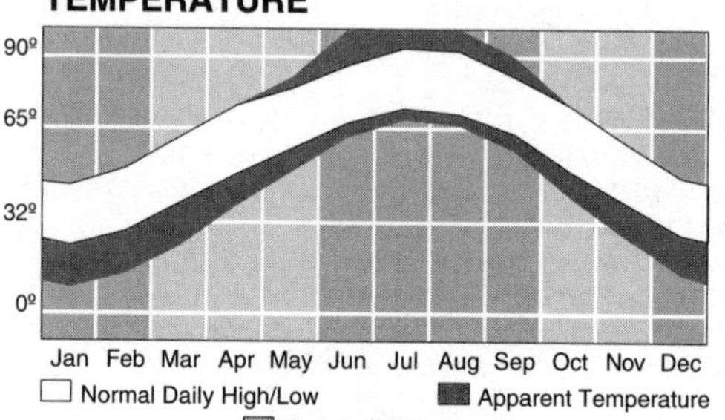

ANNUAL
Humidity: 69%
Wind Speed: 10.3 mph
DAYS
0º or below: 1
32º or below: 78
90º or above: 74
Clear: 126
Cloudy: 136

PRECIPITATION

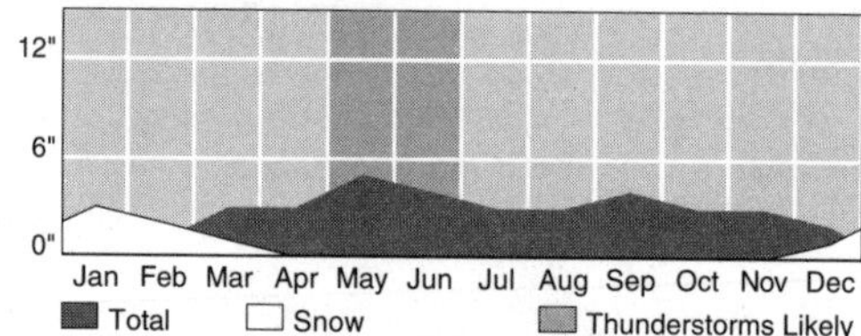

ANNUAL
Precipitation: 40.6"
Snow: 9.1"
DAYS
Precipitation: 54
Thunderstorm: 50

Vancouver, BC

Location: 49.11 N, 123.10 W, at 10 feet, on a narrow peninsula between an arm of the Fraser River on the south, the Strait of Georgia on the west, and Burrard Inlet on the north. The Coast Range mountain peaks are to the immediate west.
Landscape: A gradual slope in the land runs from south to north. The city is sheltered from the Pacific Ocean by the mass of Vancouver Island, but the ocean's proximity keeps climate moderate throughout the year.
Climate: The infinite variety of Canada's climate is most striking in British Columbia. Within the Greater Vancouver area it is possible to play golf and ski on the same midwinter day. January is normally the most severe month in Vancouver. Spring arrives by March. July is the most pleasant month of the year with moderate temperatures, long periods of sunshine, and only a little rain. The transition to winter occurs from mid-August through September with cooler and longer nights and more moisture in the air, making fog more prevalent. Then the rainy season returns in October.

Mildness: 89 Brightness: 3 Stability: 100

Places Rated Score: 81.49 **Places Rated Rank: 45**

TEMPERATURE

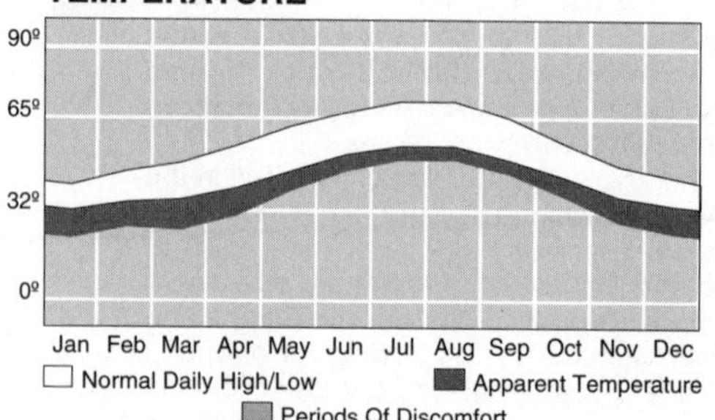

ANNUAL
Humidity: 80%
Wind Speed: 7.5 mph
DAYS
0º or below: 0
32º or below: 55
90º or above: 0
Clear: 87
Cloudy: 156

PRECIPITATION

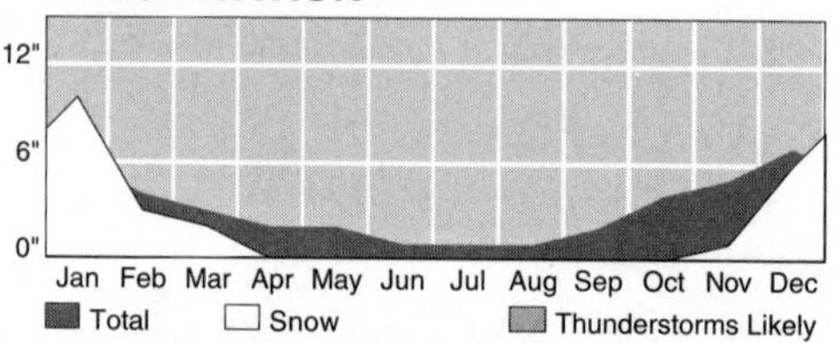

ANNUAL
Precipitation: 43.8"
Snow: 23.8"
DAYS
Precipitation: 114
Thunderstorm: 6

✓ Victoria, BC

Location: 48.39 N, 123.26 W, at 62 feet, the capital of British Columbia, Victoria is located on the southeast tip of Vancouver Island, 66 miles across the bay from the city of Vancouver, BC.

Landscape: Victoria is a major port with two harbors—the outer for ocean shipping, the inner for coastal shipping to the Canadian and US mainlands. Surrounding countryside is rolling farmland, hedgerows and gardens, resembling rural Great Britain.

Climate: Climate is Marine mild, nurtured by the California Current, and protected from the open sea by mainland British Columbia on the southeast and Washington state on the southwest. The Pacific air stream allows for mild winters, mild but not hot summers, and small seasonal temperature differences. Rain is more common than snow in the winter, and there have been some winters when there is no snowfall. Victoria's summers are typically dry, warm and sunny. Resi

TEMPERATURE

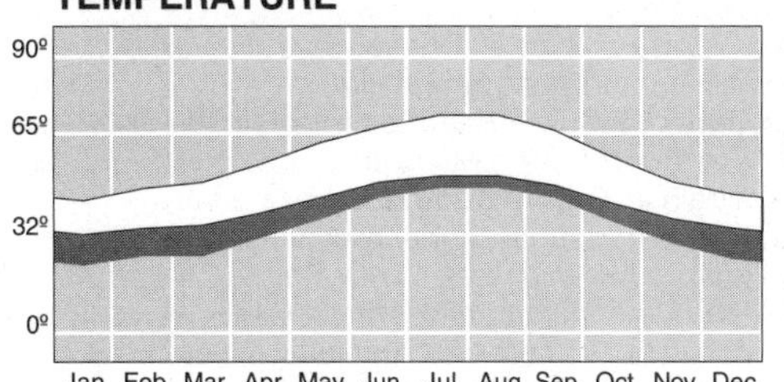

ANNUAL
Humidity: 80%
Wind Speed: 6.9 mph
DAYS
0º or below: 0
32º or below: 60
90º or above: 1
Clear: 97
Cloudy: 139

PRECIPITATION

..., 125 miles SE of Austin.

Landscape: Low, rolling prairie and plateau, with occasional forested areas. Areas of wide salt meadows provide for cattle grazing. The Guadalupe River runs nearby, its mile-wide valley well forested with oaks, pecans, and cypress.

Climate: Humid Subtropical. Rain is the principal weather feature and is well distributed throughout the year. Often cloudy and stormy, thunderstorms reach a peak in August. Summer temperatures over 90°F more than 100 days are bearable due to sea breezes from the Gulf of Mexico, 30 miles or so south. Moderately humid year-round, nights can be oppressive from late June to early August. Destructive storms with tornadoes are rare. Winter weather conditions alternate between clear, cold, dry periods and cloudy, mild, drizzly days as fronts move down from the north.

Mildness: 88 Brightness: 46 Stability: 16

Places Rated Score: 76.29 **Places Rated Rank: 59**

TEMPERATURE

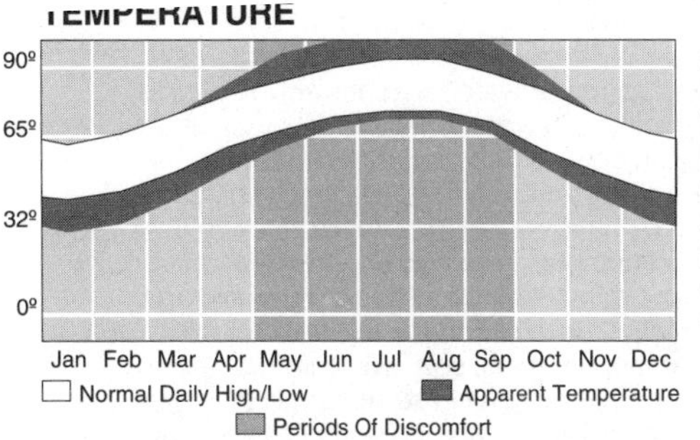

ANNUAL
Humidity: 74%
Wind Speed: 10.0 mph
DAYS
0º or below: 0
32º or below: 11
90º or above: 105
Clear: 85
Cloudy: 162

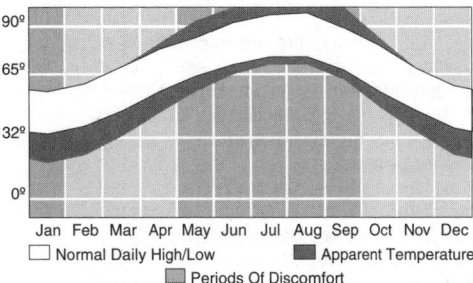

PRECIPITATION

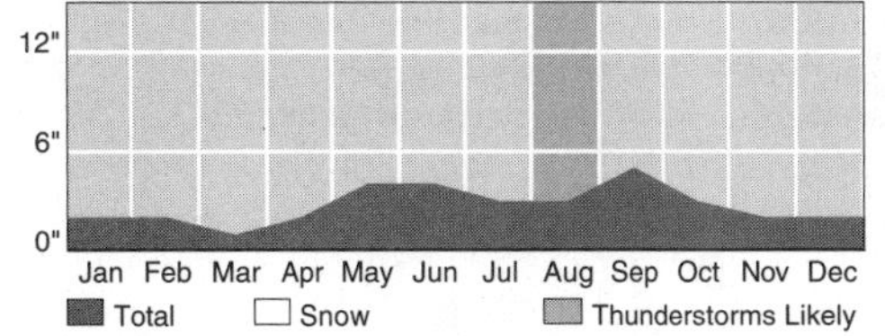

ANNUAL
Precipitation: 37.4"
Snow: 0.1"
DAYS
Precipitation: 55
Thunderstorm: 51

Waco, TX

Location: 31.37 N, 97.13 W, at 500 feet, on the Brazos River in north central Texas, 100 miles NE of Austin.

Landscape: In the wide, rich valley of the Brazos River on the edge of the gently rolling Blackland Prairie and rimmed by the low hills of the Balcones Escarpment. Soils are rich bottomland, black, waxy, loam and sandy types. Wooded areas of pecan, elm, live oak, burr oak, cottonwood, and mesquite are common. Lake Waco, a reservoir of 7,260 surface acres, lies inside the city limits.

Climate: Humid Subtropical though a Continental element is captured in the extreme variations of temperature. Tropical Maritime air masses predominate throughout the late spring, summer and early fall. Summers are hot. Though winters are mild, polar air comes in as cold fronts move down from the High Plains with strong, gusty winds. The cold lasts only a few days before a rapid warming occurs. Spring and fall are pleasant.

Mildness: 66 Brightness: 86 Stability: 18

Places Rated Score: 64.07 **Places Rated Rank: 113**

TEMPERATURE

90º
65º
32º
0º
Jan Feb Mar Apr May Jun Jul Aug Sep Oct Nov Dec
Normal Daily High/Low
Apparent Temperature
Periods Of Discomfort

ANNUAL
Humidity: 70%
Wind Speed: 11.2 mph
DAYS
0º or below: 0
32º or below: 33
90º or above: 111
Clear: 131
Cloudy: 136

PRECIPITATION

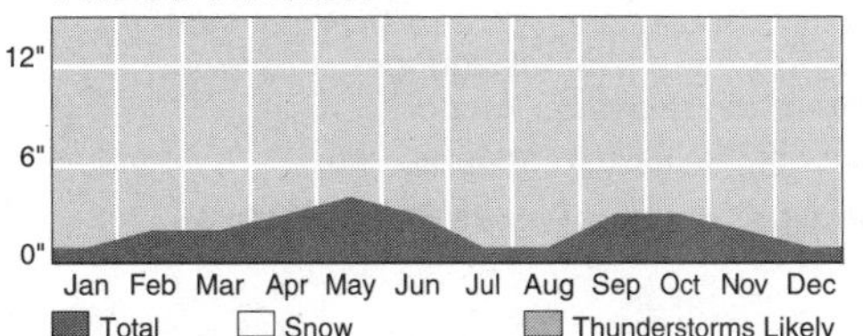

ANNUAL
Precipitation: 32.0"
Snow: 1.4"
DAYS
Precipitation: 46
Thunderstorm: 43

Washington, DC–MD–VA–WV

Location: 38.51 N, 77.02 W, at 10 feet, at the western edge of the Middle Atlantic Coastal Plain, 50 miles east of the Blue Ridge Mountains and 35 miles west of Chesapeake Bay at the junction of the Potomac and Anacostia rivers.
Landscape: The national capital is surrounded on three sides by Maryland and across the Potomac River from Arlington and Fairfax counties, Virginia. The area's landscape is urban and suburban residential. The city itself is divided along a north-south axis by Rock Creek and Rock Creek Park.
Climate: The area has a temperate mid-latitude climate. Summers are warm and humid, winters mild; generally pleasant weather prevails in the spring and autumn. The coldest weather occurs in late January and early February (average temperature 37°F) and the warmest month is July (average 79°F). There are no pronounced wet and dry seasons. Thunderstorms during the summer often bring sudden heavy showers and damaging winds, hail, or lightning. In winter, snow accumulations of more than 10 inches are rare.

Mildness: 61 Brightness: 33 Stability: 49

Places Rated Score: 55.45 **Places Rated Rank: 148**

TEMPERATURE

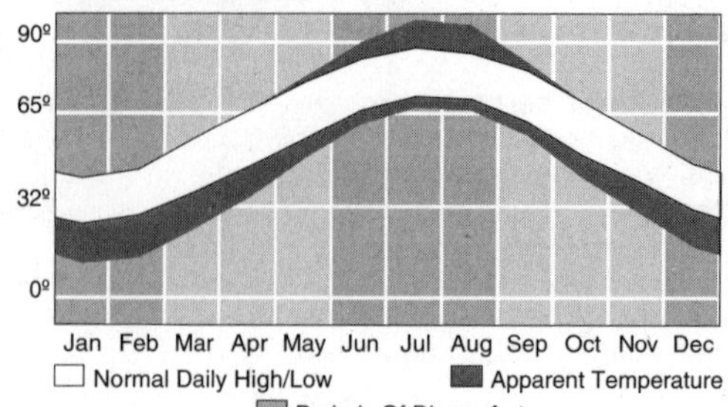

ANNUAL
Humidity: 64%
Wind Speed: 9.4 mph
DAYS
0º or below: 0
32º or below: 71
90º or above: 34
Clear: 97
Cloudy: 163

PRECIPITATION

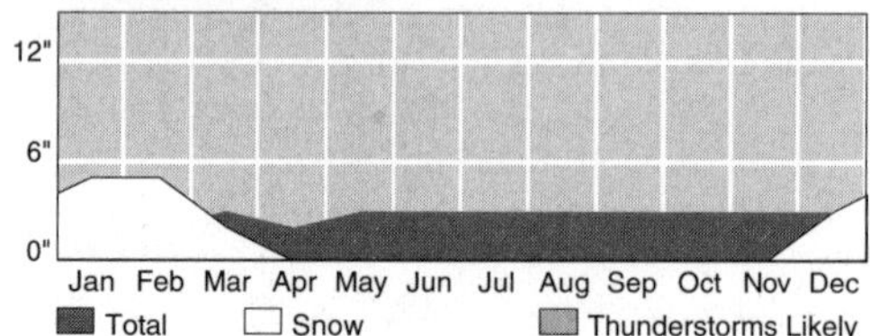

ANNUAL
Precipitation: 38.6"
Snow: 16.6"
DAYS
Precipitation: 87
Thunderstorm: 30

Waterloo–Cedar Falls, IA

Location: 42.33 N, 92.24 W, at 870 feet, on the banks of the Cedar River in northeastern Iowa.
Landscape: This area is far removed from the moderating influences of any large body of water. The terrain is level to gently rolling and is ideally suited to agriculture. The flat, open topography has no influence on climate other than offering little resistance to winds, which in winter can greatly increase felt cold.
Climate: Definitely Continental in character, with hot summers, cold winters, and short springs and falls. The average annual rainfall is 34 inches, with two-thirds of this total falling in the April-to-September crop season. As befits its landlocked, northerly location, the temperature range is large: January's mean temperature is 16°F, July's 73°F. In a year, there are more than 30 days of zero or below, and 15 days when the mercury hits 90°F or above, including two 100° days.

Mildness: 8 Brightness: 60 Stability: 31

Places Rated Score: 15.25 **Places Rated Rank: 331**

TEMPERATURE

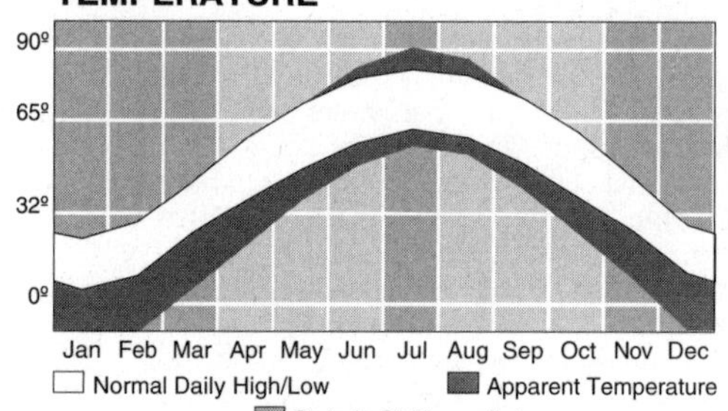

ANNUAL
Humidity: 72%
Wind Speed: 10.7 mph
DAYS
0º or below: 31
32º or below: 159
90º or above: 15
Clear: 90
Cloudy: 175

PRECIPITATION

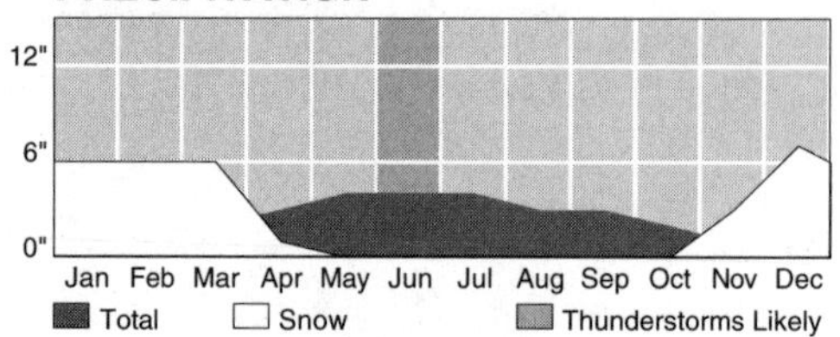

ANNUAL
Precipitation: 33.7"
Snow: 32.1"
DAYS
Precipitation: 56
Thunderstorm: 41

✓West Palm Beach–Boca Raton, FL

Location: 26.41 N, 80.07 W, at 20 feet, along the densely-settled Atlantic coast in the southeastern part of the state, above Fort Lauderdale.
Landscape: Originally a barren sand key transformed by a shipwreck, when a cargo of coconuts washed ashore and took root. The Boca Raton Inlet and its lakes harbor hidden, sharp-pointed rocks. The Atlantic Ocean forms the eastern edge of the coastal ridge, and the Gulf Stream flows northward 2 miles offshore, its nearest approach to the Florida coast. The coastal plain growth at the eastern edge of the Everglades is primarily sawgrass and mangrove. Most of the swampland has now been drained for development.
Climate: Because of its southerly location near the ocean, the area has an equable climate. Winters are pleasantly warm. Summer daytime temperatures are high but are tempered by the ocean breeze. Cumulus clouds often shade the land without completely obscuring the sun. The thermometer rarely climbs beyond 95°F. The moist unstable air in this area results in frequent short rain showers.

Mildness: 97 Brightness: 7 Stability: 10

Places Rated Score: 84.67 **Places Rated Rank: 32**

TEMPERATURE

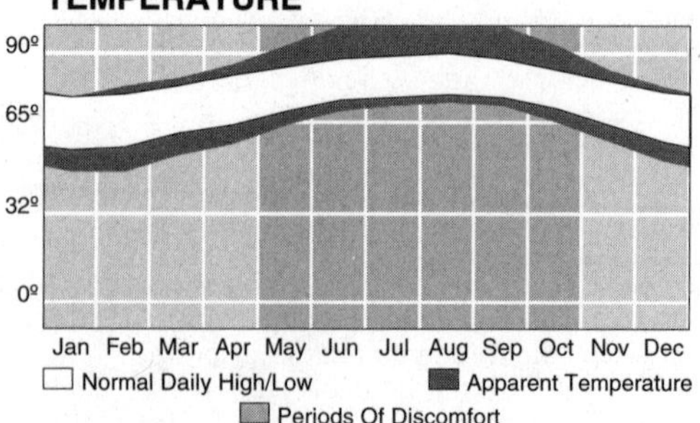

ANNUAL
Humidity: 71%
Wind Speed: 9.7 mph
DAYS
0º or below: 0
32º or below: 1
90º or above: 76
Clear: 75
Cloudy: 131

PRECIPITATION

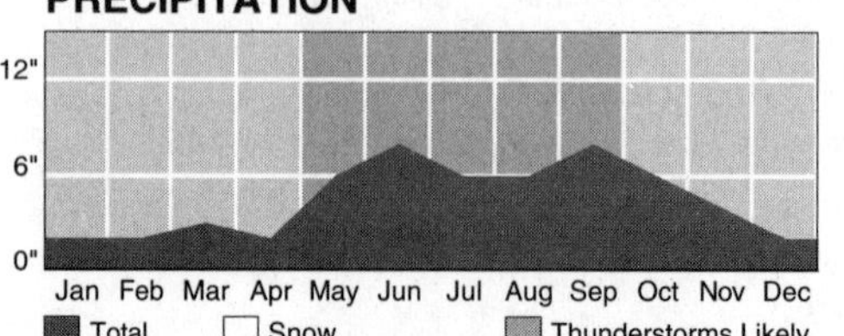

ANNUAL
Precipitation: 60.8"
Snow: 0.0"
DAYS
Precipitation: 80
Thunderstorm: 79

Wheeling, WV–OH

Location: 39.54 N, 80.45 W, at 620 feet, on the Ohio River in the northern part of West Virginia's western Panhandle. Pittsburgh is NE some 60 miles.
Landscape: The dominating features are the Ohio River and the Appalachians. The topography consists of steep slopes following the irregular boundary of the river. The upland soil is shallow, clay, acidic, favoring forest growth. Near the river, soil is blacker and more fertile. Coal mining continues to be an economic mainstay, as does harvesting hardwood.
Climate: Mid-latitude Continental climate, featuring cyclonic storms in winter and thunderstorms in summer. Steep narrow valleys make flash flooding a feared weather phenomenon. Precipitation averages 4 inches each month, and greater amounts occur at higher elevations. Temperatures range from an average 28°F in January to 72°F in July.

Mildness: 41 Brightness: 18 Stability: 45

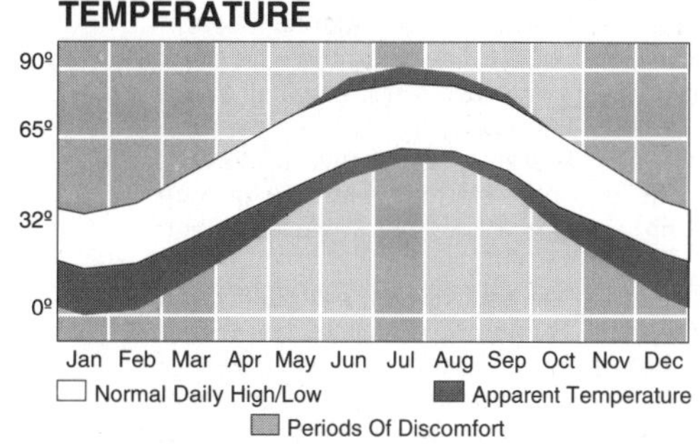

ANNUAL
Humidity: 67%
Wind Speed: 9.1 mph
DAYS
0º or below: 2
32º or below: 115
90º or above: 16
Clear: 58
Cloudy: 204

PRECIPITATION

Topeka and 45 miles north of the Oklahoma border.
Landscape: Located in gentle sloping topography along the Arkansas River in the basically flat terrain of the Central Great Plains. There are no large bodies of water nearby to affect the city's climate. Natural tree areas occur along the river and its tributaries.
Climate: Continental, lying in the path of alternate masses of warm, moist air moving northward from the Gulf of Mexico and cold, dry air from the polar regions. The city is subject to frequent and often abrupt weather changes. Winds are generally from the south. Summers can be hot, with more than 60 days over 90°F during that time. Winters are mild, and snowfalls are light, averaging 16 inches a year. Thunderstorms occur mainly during the spring and early summer. They can be severe and cause damage from heavy rain, large hail, strong winds and tornadoes.

Mildness: 25 Brightness: 91 Stability: 14

Places Rated Score: 34.20 **Places Rated Rank: 230**

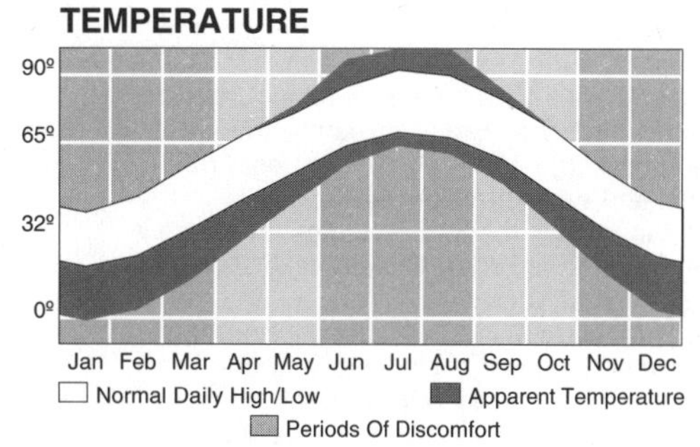

ANNUAL
Humidity: 67%
Wind Speed: 12.3 mph
DAYS
0º or below: 2
32º or below: 114
90º or above: 62
Clear: 128
Cloudy: 140

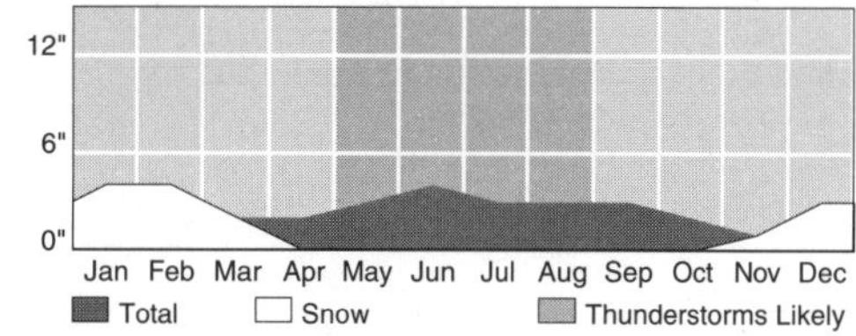

ANNUAL
Precipitation: 29.3"
Snow: 16.1"
DAYS
Precipitation: 48
Thunderstorm: 54

Wichita Falls, TX

Location: 33.58 N, 98.29 W, at 990 feet, on the Wichita River in the North Central Plains, 10 miles south of the Red River and Oklahoma border. Austin lies SE 284 miles.
Landscape: Gently rolling mesquite plain and buffalo grass prairie. The big river valley is also an important feature with high bluffs. Good, rich soil has long been used for agricultural production.
Climate: Continental with Subtropical features. Characterized by rapid changes in temperature, large daily and annual temperature extremes, and by rather erratic rainfall. While Blue Northers may drop the temperature 20 to 30 degrees within an hour, winters are relatively mild. Snow over an inch occurs only two days a year. The average temperature in the coldest month of January is around 40°F. Summers average in the mid-80s, but 100° days are frequent in periods of hot weather. Prolonged dry periods are common. Winds are southerly and are strong in all months.

Mildness: 51 Brightness: 90 Stability: 13

Places Rated Score: 53.71 **Places Rated Rank: 155**

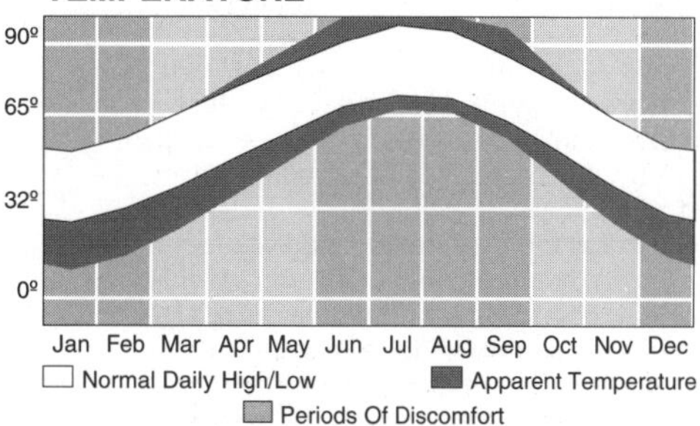

ANNUAL
Humidity: 67%
Wind Speed: 11.6 mph
DAYS
0º or below: 0
32º or below: 66
90º or above: 106
Clear: 152
Cloudy: 120

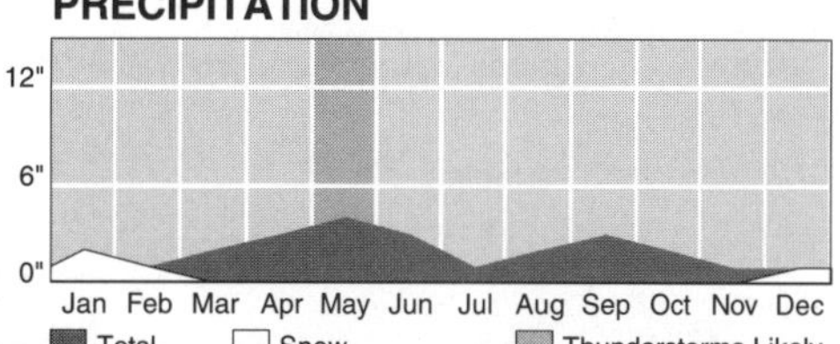

ANNUAL
Precipitation: 28.9"
Snow: 5.8"
DAYS
Precipitation: 39
Thunderstorm: 47

Wilmington, NC

Location: 34.16 N, 77.54 W, at 30 feet, in the Tidewater section of southeast North Carolina, on the Atlantic Ocean.
Landscape: The city proper is built adjacent to the east bank of the Cape Fear River. The surrounding terrain, typical of the state's Coastal Plain, is level and low-lying, with the average elevation less than 40 feet. There are many rivers, creeks, and lakes nearby, most with considerable swampy growth surrounding them. Large tracts of woods alternate with cultivated fields.
Climate: A strong Maritime influence from the Atlantic Ocean moderates all four seasons. Summers are quite warm and humid, but excessive heat is rare. During the colder part of the year, polar air masses reach the coastal areas, causing sharp drops in temperature. However, much of the bite of these air masses has diminished by the time they reach the Wilmington area. Snowfall is slight. Rainfall is ample and well distributed, with most occurring in summer thundershowers. In winter, rain may fall steadily for several days. Hurricanes are likely to affect the region with strong tides, and high winds with heavy rains.

Mildness: 81 Brightness: 30 Stability: 34

Places Rated Score: 69.59 **Places Rated Rank: 79**

TEMPERATURE

90º 65º 32º 0º
Jan Feb Mar Apr May Jun Jul Aug Sep Oct Nov Dec
Normal Daily High/Low — Apparent Temperature — Periods Of Discomfort

ANNUAL
Humidity: 70%
Wind Speed: 8.7 mph
DAYS
0º or below: 0
32º or below: 43
90º or above: 46
Clear: 111
Cloudy: 150

PRECIPITATION

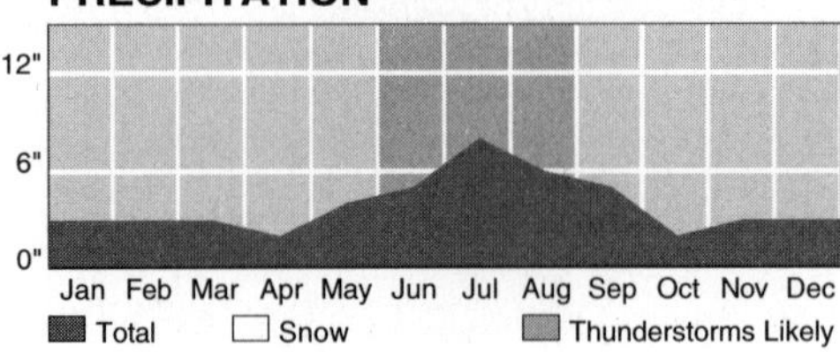

ANNUAL
Precipitation: 54.3"
Snow: 1.9"
DAYS
Precipitation: 77
Thunderstorm: 47

Wilmington–Newark, DE–MD

Location: 39.40 N, 75.36 W, at 80 feet, 29 miles south of Philadelphia, on the Delaware River above Delaware Bay and the Atlantic Ocean.
Landscape: Part of the Atlantic Coastal Plain which is mainly flat lowland with many marshes. Small streams and tidal estuaries make up the drainage. Low rolling hills begin near here and extend north and west into Pennsylvania.
Climate: Greatly influenced by the large bodies of water mentioned above as well as the broad Chesapeake Bay 35 miles west. Humidity is high all year. Fog is frequent and may occur in any month. Rain distribution is uniform throughout the year, though summer brings the greatest amounts as thunderstorms. Southeast winds may bring storms up from the South Atlantic; hurricanes may bring heavy rains but high winds are seldom a problem. Snowfall is generally light and seldom remains long on the ground.

Mildness: 50 Brightness: 52 Stability: 59

Places Rated Score: 51.28 **Places Rated Rank: 166**

TEMPERATURE

90º 65º 32º 0º
Jan Feb Mar Apr May Jun Jul Aug Sep Oct Nov Dec
Normal Daily High/Low — Apparent Temperature — Periods Of Discomfort

ANNUAL
Humidity: 66%
Wind Speed: 9.1 mph
DAYS
0º or below: 1
32º or below: 100
90º or above: 19
Clear: 97
Cloudy: 164

PRECIPITATION

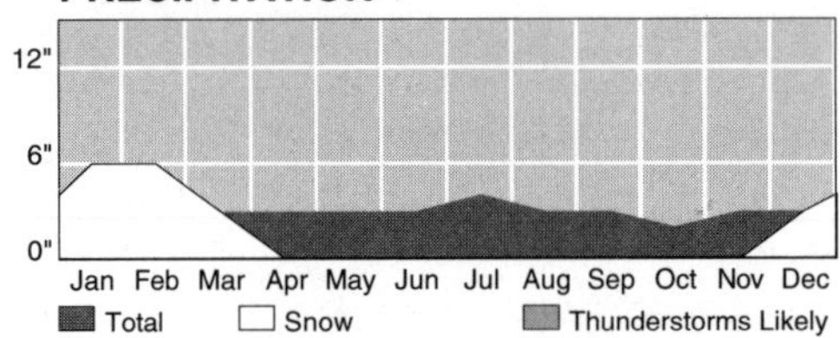

ANNUAL
Precipitation: 40.8"
Snow: 20.4"
DAYS
Precipitation: 71
Thunderstorm: 29

Winnipeg, MB

Location: 49.54 N, 97.14 W, at 784 feet, situated in the broad flat valley of the Red River which flows northeast through the city.
Landscape: The east side of the valley is a nearly level plain comprised of extensive swamplands. The west side terminates with an abrupt rise known as the Manitoba escarpment, which is pierced by the broad flat Assiniboine Valley extending to the west.
Climate: Typically Continental, the main features are a precipitation regime with an early summer maximum and a wide range of annual, seasonal, day-to-day, and diurnal temperatures. Snowfall, which has fallen in Manitoba in every month but July, is not heavy—it just seems that way. Once the snow arrives in mid-November, it normally stays until the middle of April, making winter seem long.

Mildness: 0 Brightness: 86 Stability: 57

Places Rated Score: 3.40 **Places Rated Rank: 351**

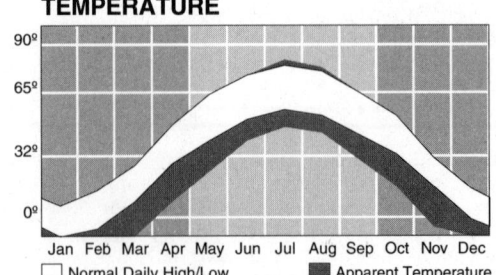

TEMPERATURE

90º 65º 32º 0º
Jan Feb Mar Apr May Jun Jul Aug Sep Oct Nov Dec
Normal Daily High/Low — Apparent Temperature — Periods Of Discomfort

ANNUAL
Humidity: 73%
Wind Speed: 11.6 mph
DAYS
0º or below: 62
32º or below: 195
90º or above: 12
Clear: 123
Cloudy: 125

PRECIPITATION

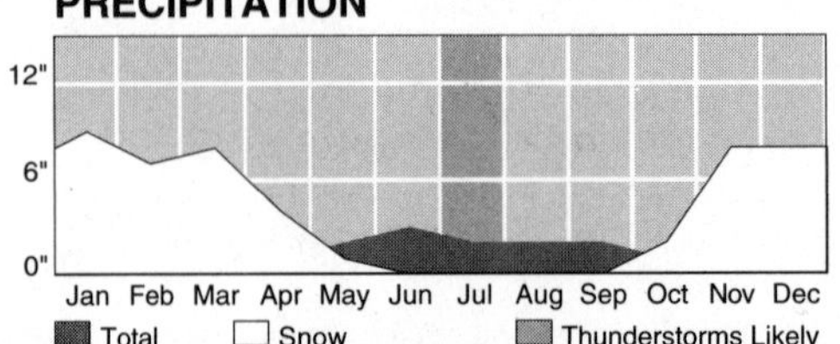

ANNUAL
Precipitation: 20.7"
Snow: 49.2"
DAYS
Precipitation: 48
Thunderstorm: 27

Yakima, WA

Location: 46.34 N, 120.32 W, at 1,060 feet, in a small valley 173 miles SE of Olympia, the state capital.
Landscape: The local topography is complex, with a number of minor valleys and ridges giving a local elevation as high as 1,000 feet in this irrigated upper part of the east-west Yakima Valley east of the Cascade Range. There are marked variations in air drainage, winds and temperatures within short distances.
Climate: Relatively mild and dry, with characteristics of both Maritime and Continental climates, modified by the Cascade and the Rocky Mountain ranges. Yakima lies in the rain shadow of the Cascades; precipitation is generally light. Summers are dry and hot. There is a rapid temperature fall after sunset, making the nights pleasantly cool. Shielded from most of the cold air masses from Canada, winters are cool with only light snowfall of 20 inches to 25 inches per

TEMPERATURE

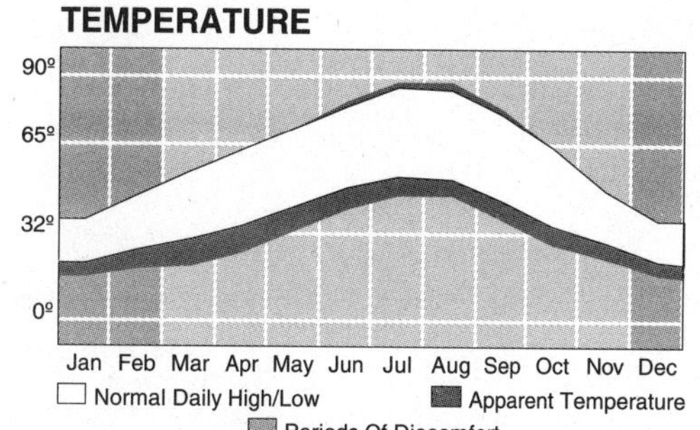

ANNUAL
Humidity: 60%
Wind Speed: 7.1 mph
DAYS
0º or below: 4
32º or below: 149
90º or above: 33
Clear: 109
Cloudy: 164

PRECIPITATION

southwest corner of Arizona near the California and Mexican borders, about 6 miles west of the confluence of the Gila and Colorado Rivers.
Landscape: The land is typical desert steppe, with dry, sandy, and dusty soil. There is scant vegetation. Sagebrush and prairie shortgrass are common. Craggy buttes and mountains take their characteristic texture from wind erosion rather than water erosion. Surrounding mountain ranges are the dominant geologic feature. They include the Trigo, Chocolate, Castle Dome, Mohawk, and Gila ranges.
Climate: Definitely a desert product. Home heating is necessary from late October to mid-April as the evenings and nights cool dramatically. It is dry, with many places in the world receiving more rain in a year than has fallen in Yuma in the past 90 years. Yuma is officially the sunniest place in America.

Mildness: 78 Brightness: 100 Stability: 66
Places Rated Score: 89.29 **Places Rated Rank: 16**

TEMPERATURE

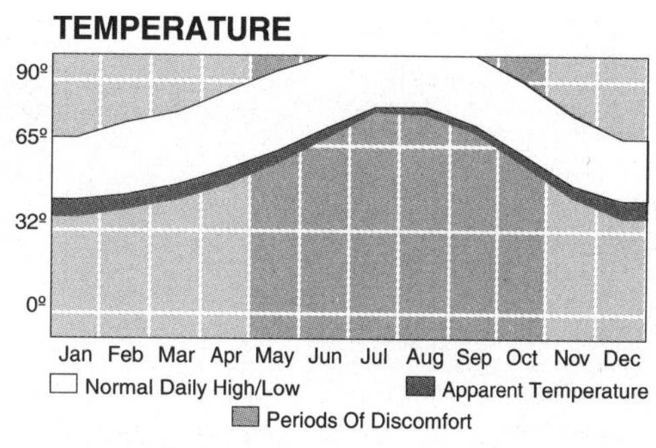

ANNUAL
Humidity: 37%
Wind Speed: 7.8 mph
DAYS
0º or below: 0
32º or below: 117
90º or above: 5
Clear: 242
Cloudy: 52

PRECIPITATION

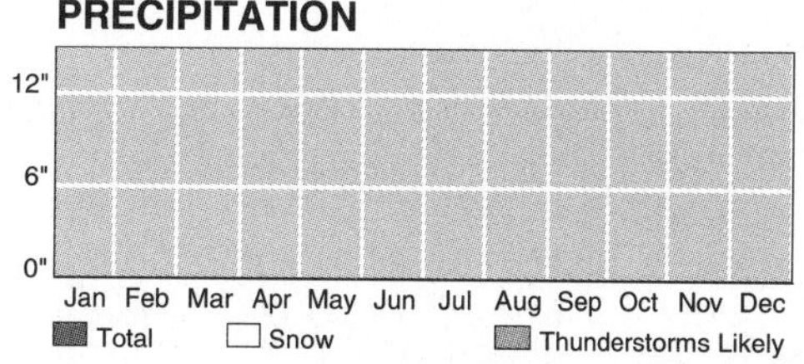

ANNUAL
Precipitation: 3.2"
Snow: 0.0"
DAYS
Precipitation: 8
Thunderstorm: 1

Et Cetera

IT'S NOT THE HEAT, IT'S THE HUMIDITY

Humidity, or the amount of moisture in the air, is a big factor in climatic comfort. It intensifies heat. Hot days that are also humid aren't comfortable when the body's natural evaporative cooling becomes overloaded.

Moreover, just as warm air is able to hold more moisture, so damp air is able to hold heat better and longer. In hot, humid climates, heat is retained in the damp air even after sundown, producing nights almost as hot as the days. In contrast, drier climates offer greater comfort not only during hot summer days but also at night, which can be cool and sometimes even chilly.

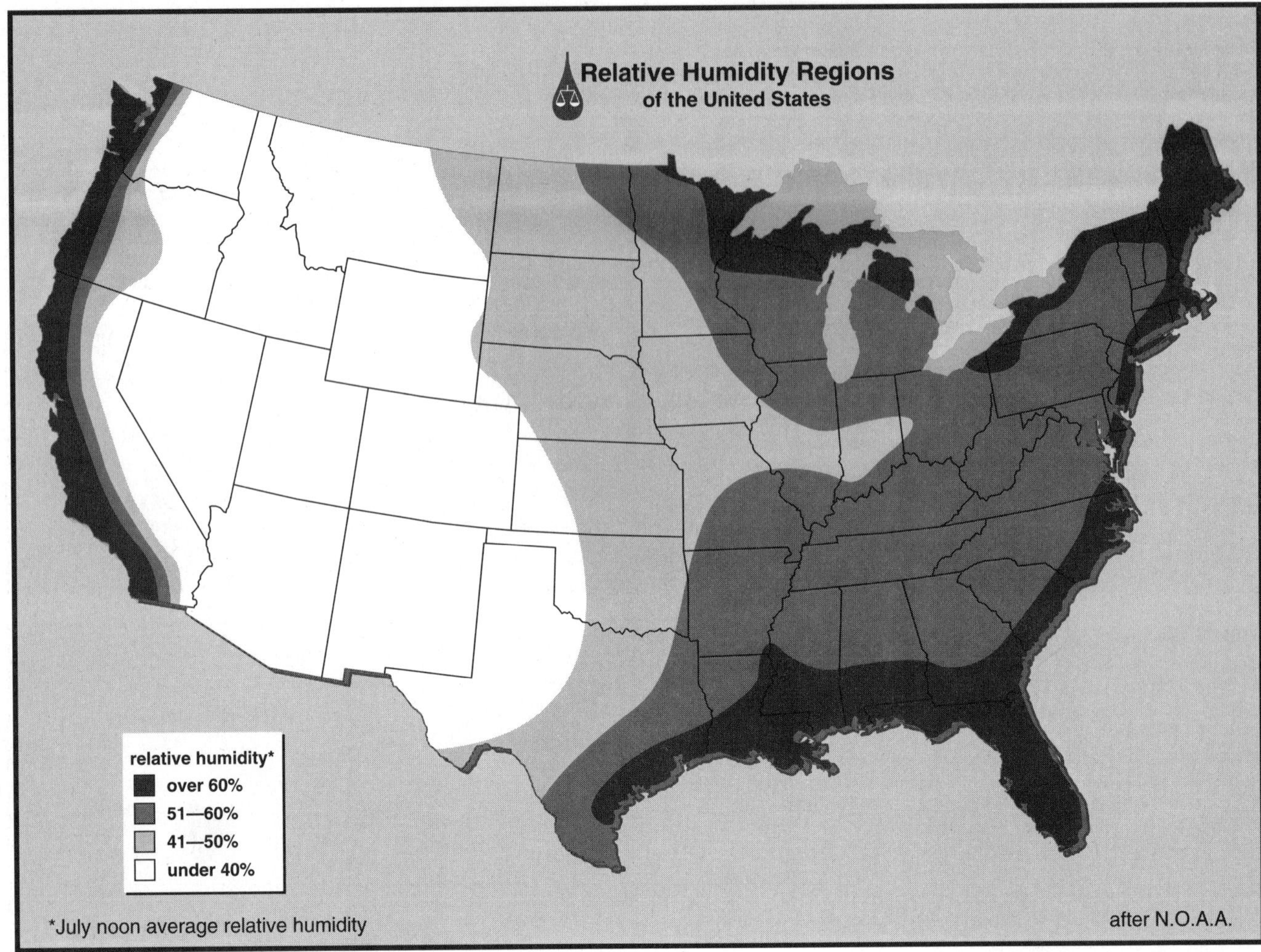

Thomas Nast, Cartographer

Excessive humidity can aggravate certain types of arthritis and rheumatism and, combined with low temperatures, can have a harmful effect on those suffering from pulmonary diseases. Very moist air also encourages the growth of a wide variety of bacteria and molds, thus increasing the chances of infection.

Low humidity has its own undesirable consequences. When it drops below 50 percent, most people experience dry nasal passages and perhaps a dry, tickling throat. In the Southwest where relative humidity can drop to 20 percent, many people suffer from nosebleeds, flaking skin, and a chronic sore throat.

Humidity affects hair, too. The range between dry and saturated air produces a three percent difference in hair length. In moist air, people with naturally curly hair have the frizzies as hair length increases, while others with long straight hair find it going limp. Hair is such a reliable indicator of humidity that it is the primary element of the hair hygrometer, a meteorological instrument in use from the late 1700s through the 1960s.

The table "Apparent Temperature" shows the relationship between relative humidity and temperature. To find the apparent temperature, locate air temperature at the top and relative humidity along the left. The intersection of the horizontal row and figures opposite

Apparent Temperature

Rel Humid %	Air Temperature (Degrees Fahrenheit)					
	85	90	95	100	105	110
20	82	87	93	99	105	112
30	84	90	96	104	113	123
40	86	93	101	110	123	137
50	88	96	107	120	135	150
60	90	100	114	132	149	
70	93	106	124	144		
80	97	113	130			
90	102	122				
100	108					

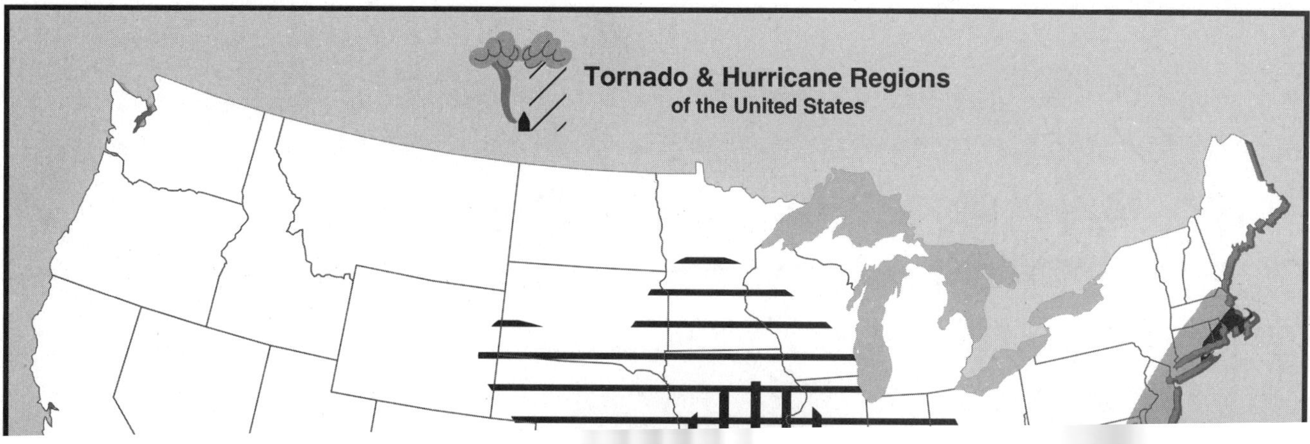

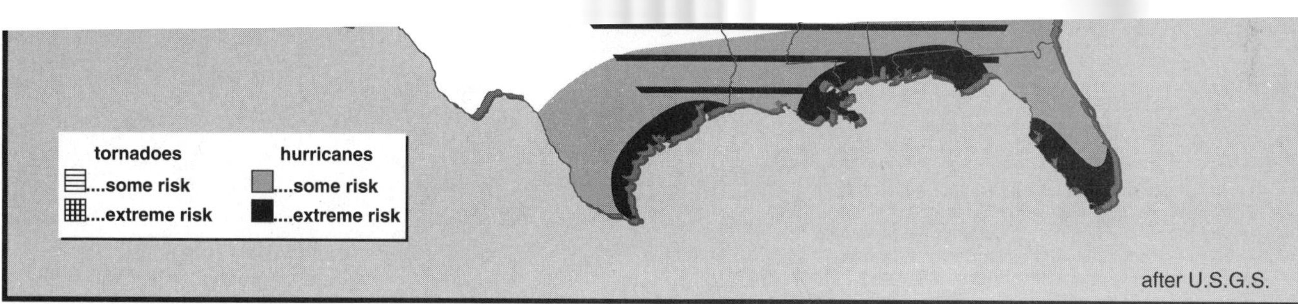

Thomas Nast, Cartographer

humidity with the vertical row below temperature is the apparent temperature. For example, air temperature of 85°F feels like 88° at 50 percent humidity and 102° when the humidity is 90 percent.

WHEN THE WIND BLOWS

As long as air temperature is lower than skin temperature, when the wind blows your body loses heat more quickly than if the wind is calm. Each molecule of air that touches exposed skin carries off some body heat. The faster the wind, the more molecules of air come in contact with skin, which in turn gives up heat to each molecule by conduction.

Wind chill is a centuries-old concept, but it was first experimentally measured in Antarctica during World War II when two explorers, Charles Passel and Paul Siple, exposed a plastic container of water to varying combinations of wind speed and air temperature and timed how long the water turned to ice. It is now a popular index heard on local weather reports.

The idea remains controversial. After all, sunshine

Wind Chill Factor

Wind Speed (mph)	45	40	35	30	25	20	15	10	5	0	−5	−10	−15	−20	−25	−30	−35	−40	−45
4	45	40	35	30	25	20	15	10	5	0	−5	−10	−15	−20	−25	−30	−35	−40	−45
5	43	37	32	27	22	16	11	6	0	−5	−10	−15	−21	−26	−31	−36	−42	−47	−52
10	34	26	22	16	10	3	−3	−9	−15	−22	−27	−34	−40	−46	−52	−58	−64	−71	−77
15	29	23	16	9	2	−5	−11	−18	−25	−31	−38	−45	−51	−58	−65	−72	−78	−85	−92
20	26	19	12	4	−3	−10	−17	−24	−31	−39	−46	−53	−60	−67	−74	−81	−88	−95	−103
25	23	16	8	1	−7	−15	−22	−29	−36	−44	−51	−59	−66	−74	−81	−88	−96	−103	−110
30	21	13	6	−2	−10	−18	−25	−33	−41	−49	−56	−64	−71	−79	−86	−93	−101	−109	−116
35	20	12	4	−4	−12	−20	−27	−35	−43	−52	−58	−67	−74	−82	−89	−97	−105	−113	−120
40	19	11	3	−5	−13	−21	−29	−37	−45	−53	−60	−69	−76	−84	−92	−100	−107	−115	−123
45	18	10	2	−6	−14	−22	−30	−38	−46	−54	−62	−70	−78	−85	−93	−102	−109	−117	−125

Air Temperature (°F)

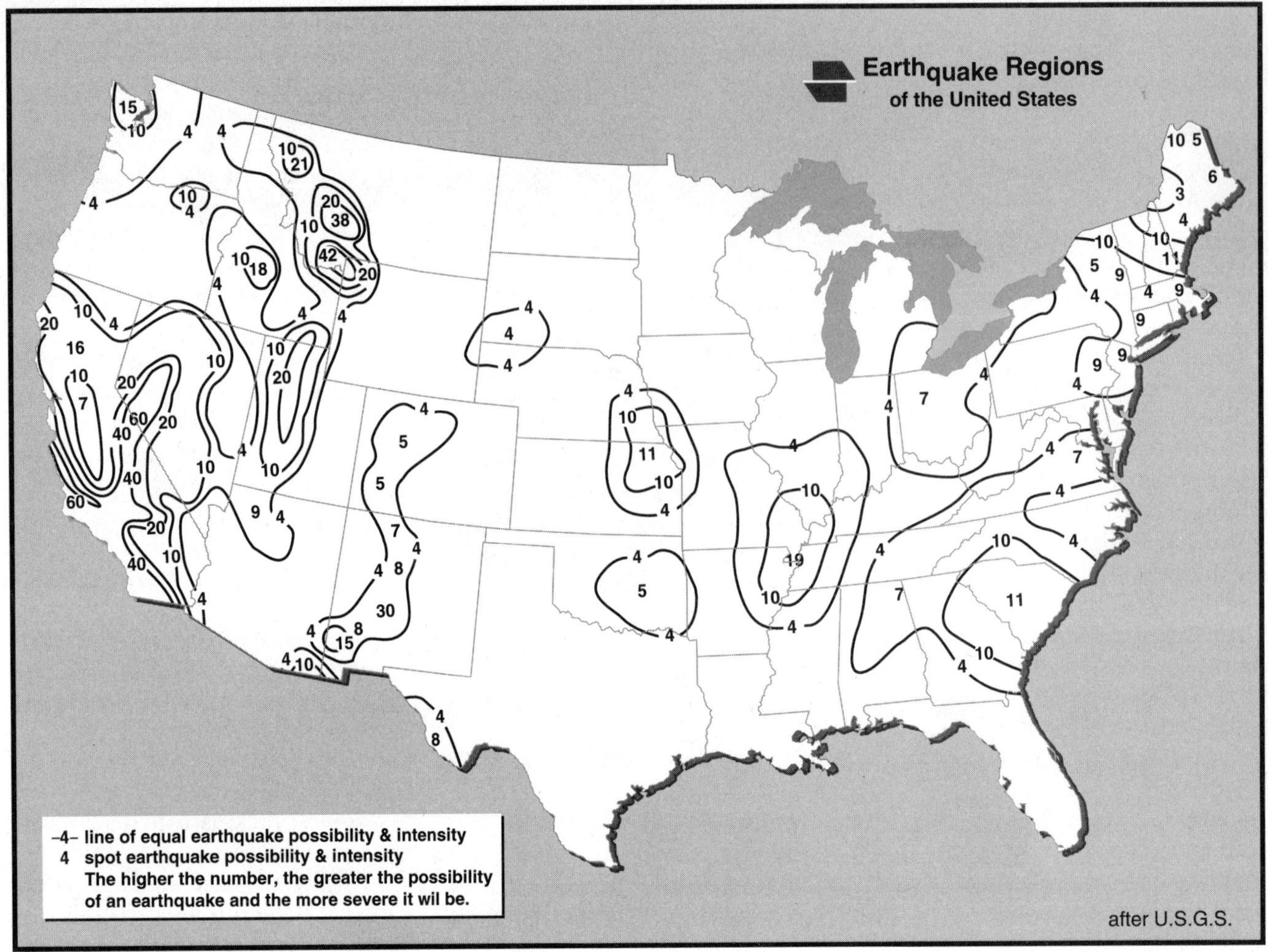

Thomas Nast, Cartographer

and exercise warm the body even as it gives up heat from wind chill. Moreover, the index assumes the skin is bare, which is unlikely if people dress properly.

The table "Wind Chill" gives the wind-chill temperature as a relationship between air temperature and the wind's speed. First locate the air temperature across the bottom, then the wind speed in the left column. At 0°F, for example, the wind chill index in a wind of 20 miles per hour is −39°F.

NATURAL HAZARDS

Perhaps no natural sight was more dramatic on live TV than the eruption of Mount St. Helens in 1980. An internal blast equal to 10 million tons of TNT blew off the topmost 1,300 feet of the mountain. Fortunately, volcanoes usually give warning. Even more fortunately, the places where volcanic activity is a potential hazard are very few.

Other violent natural events are more common and, although less cataclysmic than a volcanic eruption, can cause great damage and threaten lives. Many of these natural hazards follow definite geographic patterns in North America, and some metro areas are at much greater risk than others.

The Sun Belt Is Also a Storm Belt

Most severe storms occur in the southern half of the United States. For this reason, you might say that the Sun Belt is also a storm belt.

Thunderstorms and Lightning. Thunderstorms are common and don't usually cause death. But lightning kills 250 North Americans a year. It remains the most common and frequent natural danger. At any given moment there are about 2,000 thunderstorms in progress around the globe. In the time it takes to read this paragraph, lightning will have struck the earth 700 times.

Florida, the Sunshine State, is actually the country's stormiest state, with three times as much thunder and lightning as any other. California, along with Oregon and Washington, is one of the most storm-free states. In a typical year, coastal California towns will average between two and five thunderstorm episodes. Most

American places average between 35 and 50. Fort Myers–Cape Coral, Florida, averages 128. (A thunderstorm episode represents the presence of a single storm cell; a metro area like Fort Myers–Cape Coral can register four or five episodes in a single day.)

The Place Profiles earlier in this chapter tell how many thunderstorm days each place can expect in an average year. The southeastern quadrant of the country generally receives more rain and thunderstorms than the rest, although the thunderstorms of the Great Plains are awesome spectacles.

Tornadoes. They're not nearly as large or long-lived as hurricanes and they release far less total force, but

and sucks them up hundreds of feet into a whirling vortex. Wind speeds close to 300 miles per hour have been recorded.

Although no one can tell for certain just where tornadoes might touch down, their season, origin, and direction of travel are predictable. Tornadoes peak in late spring and early summer, and most originate in the central and southern American Great Plains, in Oklahoma, Texas, Arkansas, Kansas, and Missouri.

After forming in intense heat and rising air, the storms proceed northeastward at 25 to 40 miles per hour. Most do not last very long or travel very far. Half travel less than 5 miles, although several have been tracked over 200 miles.

In season, one tornado every five days is reported in Canada, compared to five tornadoes every day in the United States. One third of all tornadoes reported in North America occur in Kansas, Oklahoma, and Texas. Metro areas in Oklahoma, eastern Texas, Arkansas, northern Louisiana and Mississippi, eastern Tennessee, Kansas, Missouri, and parts of Nebraska, Iowa, and Illinois have a high potential for tornado danger. About 70 or 80 hit Canada's populated places in a typical year, mainly in Ontario. Most are too weak to cause serious damage.

Hurricanes. Giant tropical cyclonic storms starting up at sea, hurricanes are unmatched for sheer power over a very large area. They last for days, measure hundreds of miles across, and release tremendous energy in the form of high winds, torrential rains, lightning, and tidal surges. They usually occur from June through November and strike the Gulf and southern Atlantic Coast, though they will also strike locations farther north. Like thunderstorms, hurricanes are much less frequent and less severe on the Pacific Coast.

Hurricanes usually originate in the tropical waters of the Atlantic Ocean. Most occur toward summer's end because it takes that long for the water temperature and evaporation rate to rise sufficiently to begin the spiraling, counterclockwise rotation of wind around a low pressure system. When the winds are less than 39 miles per hour, the cyclone is a tropical depression; when winds speed up to between 39 and 74 miles per hour, the cyclone becomes a tropical storm. And when the winds reach 74 miles per hour, the storm becomes a hurricane.

Often the greatest danger and destruction from hurricanes aren't winds but tidal surges that sweep

other in slightly different directions. When the pressure becomes too great for the rock substance to hold, it shears suddenly. This shearing, along with the consequent shuddering, swaying, and even shifting of immense masses of underground rock, is experienced on the earth's surface as an earthquake.

Those conditions necessary to cause an earthquake exist only in certain areas. The entire area ringing the Pacific Ocean is earthquake-prone, from western South America to Central America, North America's Pacific states and provinces, through Alaska's Aleutian Island chain across to Japan, down through China, and ending in New Zealand. This last area has more earthquakes than any other place in the world.

According to the map "Earthquake Hazard Zones," much of North America is free from the threat of earthquakes, but some areas appear to be resting on powder kegs. (U.S. Geological Survey seismologists warn that the map is experimental and that its predictions cannot be guaranteed.)

Northeast. There is much disagreement among geologists concerning earthquake risk in the Northeast. A number of theories about seismic trends have been advanced, and attempts have been made to relate these trends to various fault systems. The best known of these systems is the Boston–Ottawa trend, shown on the map as a continuous area from the Atlantic coast of Massachusetts to the St. Lawrence River valley, encompassing the two cities for which it is named. Most people are unaware that Boston suffered a severe earthquake in the 1700s and that it remains earthquake-prone today.

Southeast. One theory about earthquake risk is that possible earthquake epicenters (the points of origin of ground tremors) are not randomly distributed but occur in zones. In the Southeast, these zones run both parallel to and across the Appalachians. Historically, the greatest shock recorded east of the Mississippi occurred in Charleston, South Carolina, in 1886. The present hazard in South Carolina and eastern Georgia is as high as in the Boston–Ottawa trend.

Midwest and Rocky Mountains. The zone of greatest hazard in the Mississippi Valley lies around the side of the cataclysmic series of quakes that occurred near New Madrid, Missouri. The biggest city in this zone is Memphis. The risk of seismic activity is greater in the Rocky Mountains region. The three biggest mountain cities—Denver, Albuquerque, and Salt Lake City—all lie within risk zones.

Pacific Northwest. The Puget Sound area near Seattle has experienced three major shocks within the past 40 years, causing considerable damage. In 1964, an earthquake in Anchorage registered 8.4 on the Richter scale (a 9-point span on a seismograph used to express the relative magnitude of an earthquake).

California and Nevada. Much more seismic activity (and, therefore, more research and data) is present in California and Nevada than anywhere else in North America. The greatest hazards are found in the San Andreas, Owens Valley, and Garlock fault systems, shown on the map as zones numbered as high as 60. All the metro areas in California are affected by these faults, particularly Bakersfield, Los Angeles–Long Beach, Oakland, San Francisco, San Jose, and Santa-Cruz–Watsonville. These places, most of which have mild climates and pleasant terrain, are in real danger.

NORTH AMERICAN WEATHER EXTREMES

No organization validates world records for climate. Data from Environment Canada and from the U.S. Environmental Data Service are current and reliable for North America. These agencies also recognize several world records for temperature, differing forms of precipitation, and other phenomena.

Temperature records are reported by more than 10,000 stations around the world. The theoretical hottest it can ever get has been put at slightly under 140°F, because hot air is lighter and quickly rises above overlying, cooler layers. More than 70 years ago, the highest point a thermometer ever reached in ambient air in the shade was 136°F at El Azizia, Libya, in the northern Sahara.

The current North American heat record, 134°F, was set more than eight decades ago at Greenland Ranch station in California's Death Valley. Canada's record high temperature, a modest 113°F, hit Midale and Yellow Grass, Saskatchewan, in 1937.

The theoretical coldest it can get on the earth's surface has been estimated at −130°F, in still air, at 14,000 feet in the middle of polar night. The new world record is −129°F, measured at 11,000 feet at Vostok, Antarctica, in 1983. The North American record is −81°F, measured at 2,000 feet at Snag, in Canada's Yukon Territory.

World *snowfall* records are entirely North American for a single reason: Among countries that keep meteorological records, Canada and the United States record snow depth while others measure snow in terms of water content. Thus, the world's greatest 24-hour snowfall, 76 inches, occurred at Silver Lake, Colorado, in mid-April of 1921. The greatest annual snowfall, more than 93 feet total, fell on Ranier Paradise Ranger Station, Washington, during the 1971–72 season. The greatest depth of snow on the ground, nearly 38 feet, was measured at Tamarack, California, on March, 11, 1911. Canadian snowfall records, all set in British Columbia, are nowhere near these amounts.

Records for *rainfall* were generally set at U.S. points and on La Reunion Island east of Madagascar. The gauges set 5,000 feet up on Mt. Waialeale, Kauai Island, Hawaii, record the world's heaviest annual average rains: 460 inches. The North American record outside of Hawaii, 256 inches, was established at Henderson Lake, on Vancouver Island, British Columbia.

The world's heaviest one-hour rainfall, 12 inches, hit Holt, Missouri, on June 22, 1947. Nine years later, in 1956, an identical amount fell on Kilauea Sugar Plantation, Kauai Island, Hawaii. La Reunion Island, in the path of Indian Ocean tropical storms, regularly gets the world's heaviest short-term rains: 12-hour rain, 53 inches; 24-hour rain, 74 inches; 5-day rain, 152 inches.

Wind is climate's most variable element. The values include peak wind, or the greatest 5-second average wind speed during the previous hour, and fastest mile, the fastest speed in miles per hour of any wind over a 24-hour observation day. Canada's highest average annual wind (22 mph) is measured at Cape Warwick, on Resolution Island, Northwest Territories. The North American record is 35 mph, measured on top of New Hampshire's Mt. Washington. Here, too, the world's fastest peak wind (231 mph) and fastest mile (188 mph) were both recorded in the spring of 1934.

Fog, simply put, is a cloud that touches the ground. As a cloud, it is composed of uncountable millions of visible water droplets formed when air is cooled to the saturation point. Cooling occurs when strong nighttime surface radiation cools the air near the ground; when humid and warm air moves across colder land; and when moist air moves up and over higher terrain. Thick fog is reported when visibility is less than half a mile; a day of fog is defined as one on which thick fog occurred once during the day.

The foggiest area in Canada and one of the world's foggiest is Newfoundland's Avalon Peninsula, socked in more than half the year. The two foggiest points in United States, at opposite ends of the country, are Cape Disappointment at the mouth of the Columbia River in Washington, and Moose Peak Lighthouse, off Maine's northern coast.

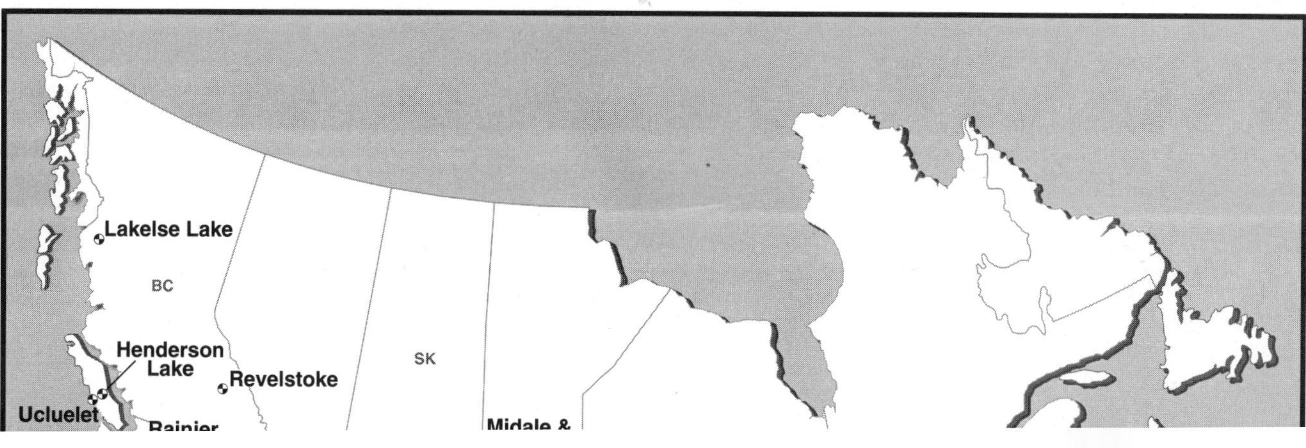

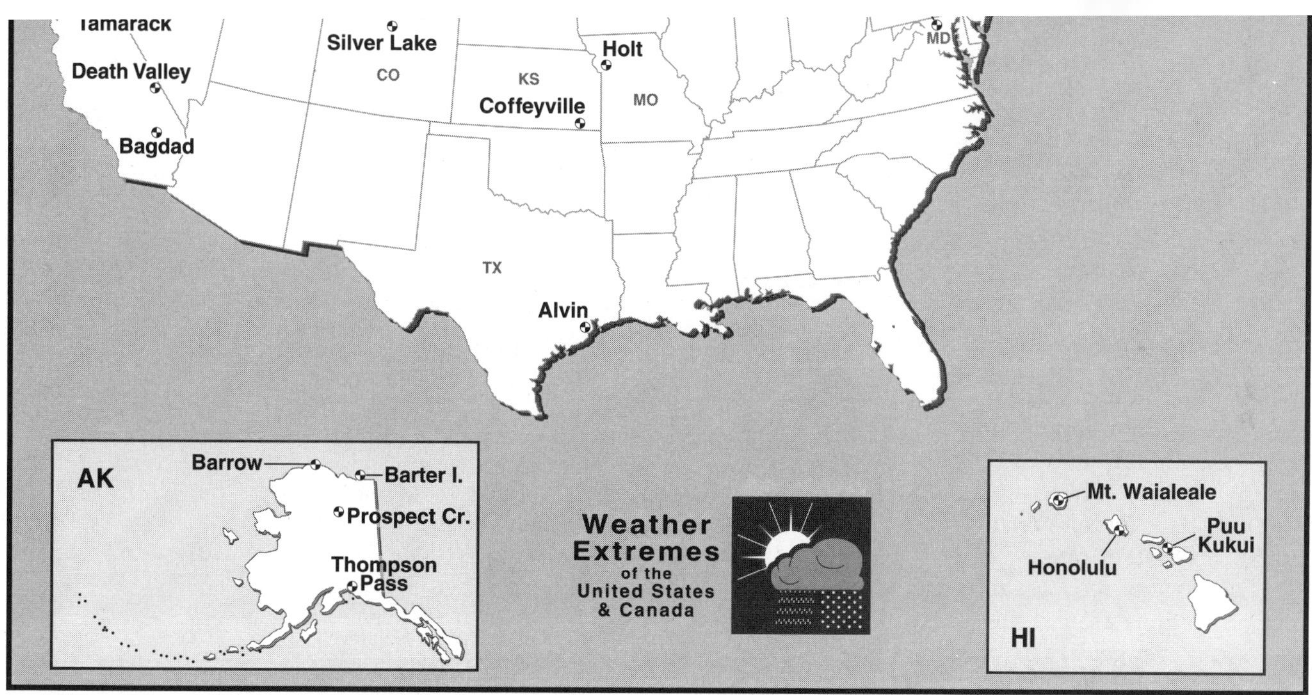

Thomas Nast, Cartographer

Hail is rain collecting into ice lumps as it falls to earth from a convective cloud during a thunderstorm. In North America, the area along the eastern slope of the Rocky Mountains from New Mexico on up to Alberta gets more hail days, more hailstorms, and more and bigger hailstones than any other area on the continent. The heaviest authenticated hailstone (1.67 pounds) fell east of here at Coffeyville, Kansas, in 1970. Canada's heaviest hailstone (10.23 ounces) fell near Cedoux, Saskatchewan, in 1973.

Going to Extremes

Air temperature decreases with increasing elevation. The usual rate of increase—called the *lapse rate*—is 3.3°F per 1,000 feet. In general, the mean temperature of a high location is 3.3° lower per 1,000 of elevation than that of nearby lower-altitude stations.

	Highest Place (Elevation)	Lowest Place (Elevation)
Alabama	Cheaha Mountain, 2,407′	Gulf of Mexico (sea level)
Alaska	Mount McKinley, 20,320′	Pacific Ocean (sea level)
Alberta	Mount Columbia, 12,293′	Slave River, 557′
Arizona	Humphreys Peak, 12,633′	Colorado River, 70′
Arkansas	Magazine Mountain, 2,753′	Ouachita River, 55′
British Columbia	Fairweather Mountain, 15,298′	Pacific Ocean (sea level)
California	Mount Whitney, 14,494′	Death Valley, −282′
Colorado	Mount Elbert, 14,433′	Arkansas River, 3,350′
Connecticut	Mount Frissell, 2,380′	Long Island Sound (sea level)
Delaware	On Ebright Road, 442′	Atlantic Ocean (sea level)
Florida	Sec. 30, T. 6N., R. 20W, 345′	Atlantic Ocean (sea level)
Georgia	Brasstown Bald, 4,784′	Atlantic Ocean (sea level)
Hawaii	Mauna Kea, 13,796′	Pacific Ocean (sea level)
Idaho	Borah Peak, 12,662′	Snake River, 710′
Illinois	Charles Mound, 1,235′	Ohio River, 320′
Indiana	Franklin Township, 1,257′	Ohio River, 320′
Iowa	Sec. 29, T. 100N, R. 41W, 1,670′	Mississippi River, 480′
Kansas	Mount Sunflower, 4,039′	Verdigris River, 680′
Kentucky	Black Mountain, 4,145′	Mississippi River, 257′
Louisiana	Driskill Mountain, 535′	New Orleans, −5′
Maine	Mount Katahdin, 5,268′	Atlantic Ocean (sea level)
Manitoba	Baldy Mountain, 2,730′	Hudson Bay (sea level)
Maryland	Backbone Mountain, 3,360′	Atlantic Ocean (sea level)
Massachusetts	Mount Greylock, 3,491′	Atlantic Ocean (sea level)
Michigan	Mount Curwood, 1,980′	Lake Erie, 572′
Minnesota	Eagle Mountain, 2,301′	Lake Superior, 602′
Mississippi	Woodall Mountain, 806′	Gulf of Mexico (sea level)
Missouri	Taum Sauk Mountain, 1,772′	St. Francis River, 230′
Montana	Granite Peak, 12,799′	Kootenai River, 1,800′
Nebraska	Johnson Township, 5,426′	SE corner of State, 840′
Nevada	Boundary Peak, 13,145′	Colorado River, 470′
New Brunswick	Mount Carleton, 2,690′	Gulf of St. Lawrence (sea level)
New Hampshire	Mount Washington, 6,288′	Atlantic Ocean (sea level)
New Jersey	High Point, 1,803′	Atlantic Ocean (sea level)
New Mexico	Wheeler Peak, 13,161′	Red Bluff Reservoir, 2,817′
New York	Mount Marcy, 5,344′	Atlantic Ocean (sea level)
Newfoundland	Mount Caubvick, 5,321′	Atlantic Ocean (sea level)
North Carolina	Mount Mitchell, 6,684′	Atlantic Ocean (sea level)
North Dakota	White Butte, 3,506′	Red River, 750′
Nova Scotia	Cape Breton Highlands, 1,745′	Atlantic Ocean (sea level)
Ohio	Campbell Hill, 1,550′	Ohio River, 433′
Oklahoma	Black Mesa, 4,978′	Little River, 287′
Ontario	Ishpatina Ridge, 2,274′	Hudson Bay (sea level)
Oregon	Mount Hood, 11,239′	Pacific Ocean (sea level)
Pennsylvania	Mount Davis, 3,213′	Delaware River (sea level)
Quebec	Mount d'Iberville, 5,321′	Hudson Bay (sea level)
Rhode Island	Jerimoth Hill, 812′	Atlantic Ocean (sea level)
Saskatchewan	Cypress Hills, 4,816′	Lake Athabasca, 700′
South Carolina	Sassafras Mountain, 3,560′	Atlantic Ocean (sea level)
South Dakota	Harney Peak, 7,242′	Big Stone Lake, 962′
Tennessee	Clingmans Dome, 6,643′	Mississippi River, 182′
Texas	Guadalupe Peak, 8,749′	Gulf of Mexico (sea level)
Utah	Kings Peak, 13,528′	Beaverdam Creek, 2,000′
Vermont	Mount Mansfield, 4,393′	Lake Champlain, 95′
Virginia	Mount Rogers, 5,729′	Atlantic Ocean (sea level)
Washington	Mount Rainer, 14,410′	Pacific Ocean (sea level)
West Virginia	Spruce Knob, 4,862′	Potomac River, 240′
Wisconsin	Timms Hill, 1,951′	Lake Michigan, 581′
Wyoming	Gannett Peak, 13,804′	Belle Fourche River, 3,100′

Source: U.S. Geological Survey, *Elevations and Distances*; Canadian National Atlas Information Service.

Domestic violence on the farm and pushers developing a base for their illegal pharmaceutical trade aren't uncommon items in the *Duluth News-Tribune*. Down I-35 in the Twin Cities, stories of convenience store stickups and drug-related drive-by killings aren't uncommon in the Minneapolis *Star Tribune* either. If you were passing through either metro area and heard of these crimes, you might wonder whether you were any safer on the northern prairie than you'd be in East Los Angeles or the Bronx.

In fact, neither Duluth nor Minneapolis–St. Paul have crime rates anywhere near the metro-area average. The odds of your being a crime victim in either place are much below what they would be elsewhere. Among the metro areas profiled in *Places Rated Almanac,* reporters working the police beat in some have so few violent crime stories to write up that a reader of the paper may wonder whether anything interesting goes on there at all. In other metro areas, day-to-day existence seems just plain dangerous.

If you decide to live in greater Johnstown, PA, for instance, the odds of your being a violent crime victim in a year's residence are 555 to 1. On the other hand, should you choose Miami the odds increase to 50 to 1. One could say that life in rapidly growing southern Florida is more than 11 times as dangerous as it is in Pennsylvania's lagging, post-industrial Conemaugh River Valley.

But quoting odds distorts the local crime picture. Violence doesn't lurk in every metro area neighborhood. Veteran cops tell you that most murders occur within the same few square miles or even blocks. Sailors going ashore in an unfamiliar port get the word from commanders on which streets to avoid because of high risk for robberies and aggravated assaults.

Moreover, if you're young, white, female, and earn enough money, your chances of meeting up with crime are much less than those of an older, poor male. Why then a chapter on crime if a combination of factors such as age, sex, race, income, and a wise selection of neighborhood can statistically remove you from danger?

The simple answer is that you are a different kind of crime victim whenever you have to trim back shrubbery along your home's foundation to restrict a crook's potential hiding places, or get rid of the mailbox and install a mail slot in your front door, or press down your car's door locks when driving down a darkened avenue, or keep feeling for your wallet at street festivals, or use only empty elevators, or stay indoors evenings more than you really care to. In some metro areas such tactics are advised, in others they are merely prudent, and in still others they may not be necessary at all.

CRIME RISK: SEVERAL CONNECTIONS

Why some metro areas are safer than others provokes arguments among citizens, politicians, police, and social scientists. For all of the debate, experts recognize several factors.

Population size is closely tied to crime rates. Metro areas with lower crime rates—Grand Forks, ND, or Wausau, WI, for example—have smaller populations. Metro areas with the highest rates—Los Angeles–Long Beach or New York are two extreme examples—have large, overcrowded populations. There are exceptions,

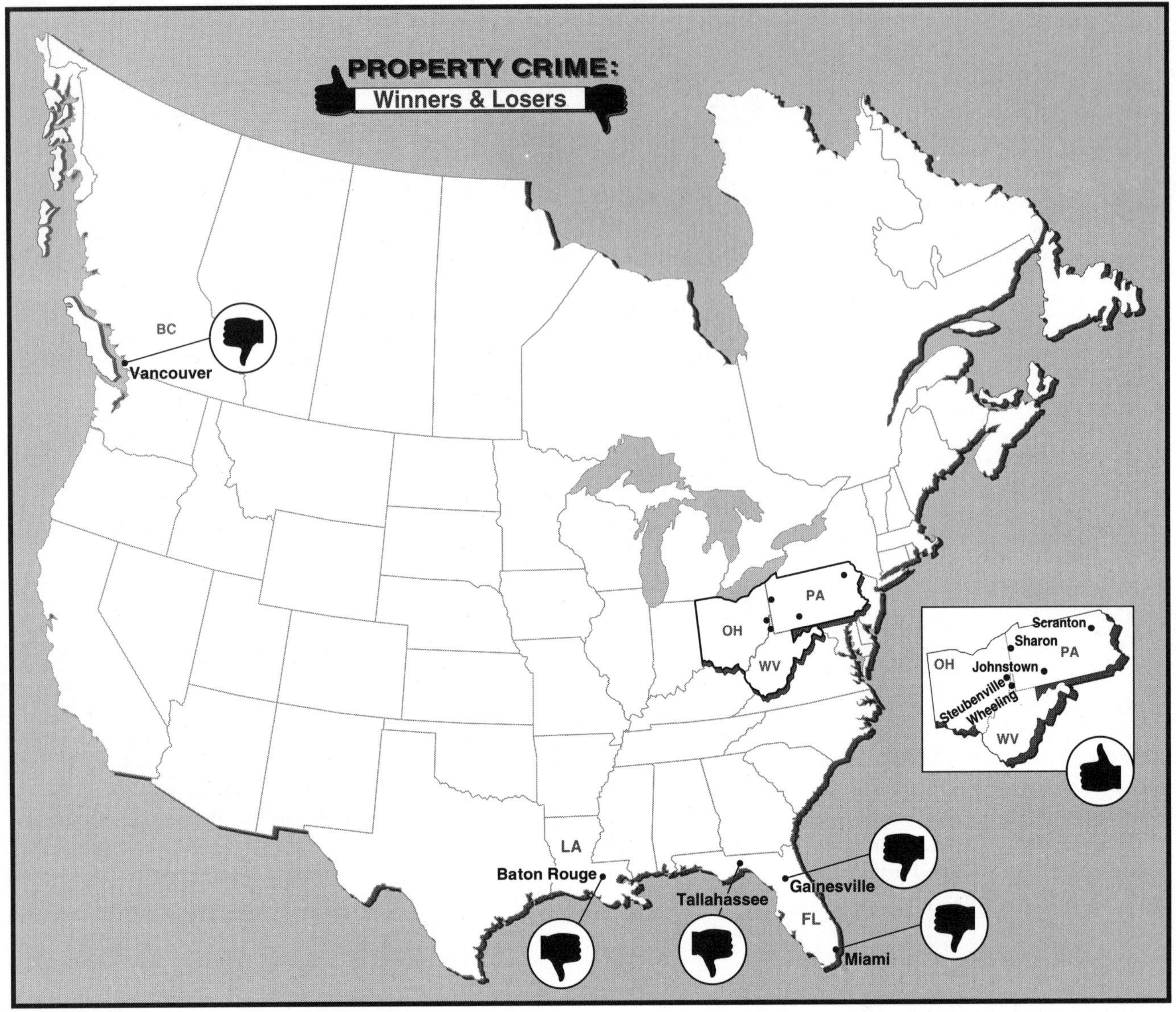

 Thomas Nast, Cartographer

to be sure. Toronto's crime rate is as low as that of Ann Arbor, Gainesville's, Jacksonville's, and Tallahassee's crime rates resemble that of New York.

Climate, too, has a striking connection with lawbreaking. Police respond to more disturbance calls on days immediately after summer temperatures are highest than on any other days of the year. Burglary, vandalism, and rape increase with ambient temperature up to 85°F.

Indeed, in the Sun Belt and in the Frost Belt, cops and criminals are busiest throughout July and August when all crimes except robbery are the likeliest to happen. Since people spend more time outdoors during these months, they are more exposed. Homes, too, are more unprotected during this time of year because they are left with open windows and unlocked doors. Robbery is the cold-weather exception. It is highest in December when shoppers and retail stores doing brisk holiday business make tempting targets.

Time of day and the *photoperiod*, or length of the day, are two other factors. After sundown is the time most cars are stolen, most persons and businesses are robbed, most persons are assaulted, and most thefts are committed. Burglaries, purse-snatchings and pocket-pickings, on the other hand, happen more often during daylight hours. Indeed, some police dispatchers contend that the number of daylight minutes is a predictor of the kind of 911 calls they handle.

Even local *traffic* plays a role. The ease with which a criminal can drive off down the street, escape onto an arterial road and disappear among commuters on the Interstate is an encouragement. Neighborhoods near Houston's I–610 Beltway urged the city to turn their streets into cul-de-sacs, and in Elizabeth City, NJ, cops stationed barricades at the corner of Madison Avenue and Fanny Street to stop neighboring Newark lawbreakers from fleeing into their jurisdiction.

Age and sex figure into the equation, too. Some 4 million persons in North America have arrest records for misdeeds other than traffic violations. The proportion of

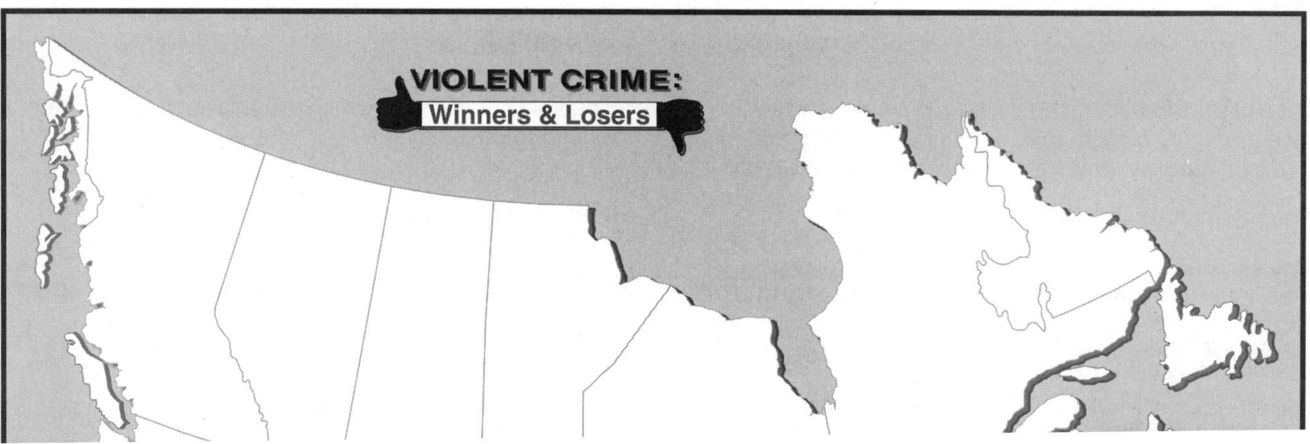

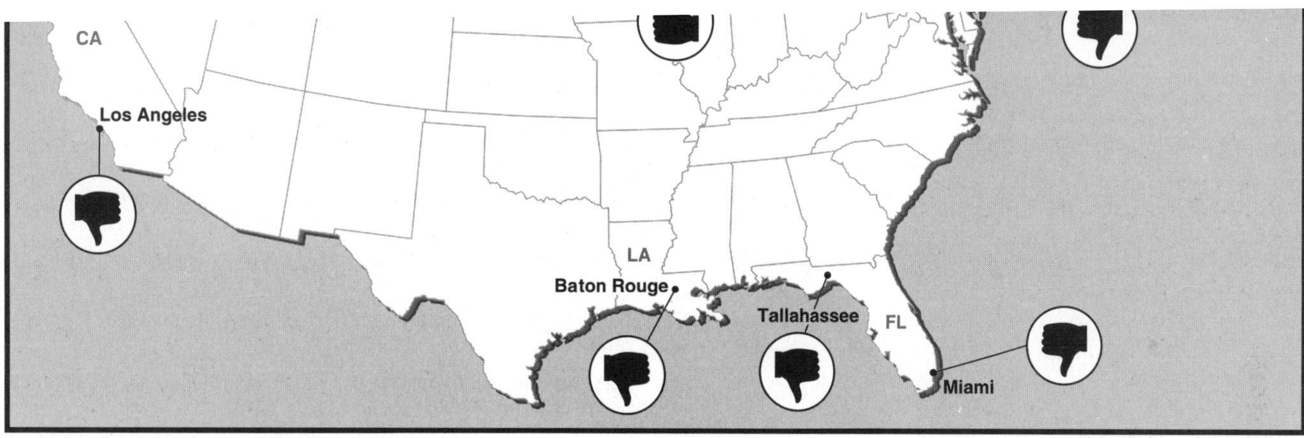

Thomas Nast, Cartographer

suspects who are male is much higher than their proportion in the general population. Half the persons picked up by police for violent and property crimes are under 20 years of age and four-fifths are male.

None of this should be taken to mean that persons hold up convenience stores, boost Chevrolet Camaros, or duke it out in disco parking lots because they are young and male, but these characteristics are associated with other factors in crime. Some criminologists warn that falling crime rates may well be short-lived once a huge group of pre-teen males grows up and takes to the streets.

The *economy* also plays a role, too. In most metro areas, each time the unemployment rate goes up the police make more arrests. But joblessness and loss of income won't automatically make a place unsafe. Metro areas in the Ohio Valley, in the Northern Plains and in Atlantic Canada suffer job losses during business slumps but continue to experience low crime rates.

More affluent areas, given similar sets of circumstances, aren't nearly as safe as they seem: Rich offenders are arrested less often than poor ones, especially on suspicion. Once arrested, they are convicted with less frequency. This is especially true in juvenile cases involving thefts and break-ins.

Transience affects crime rates. A warning sign for crooks is a stable neighborhood where people know one another and look out for one another's safety and property no matter how many cops cruise the area. High neighborhood turnover leading to more and more strangers living next to each other leads to higher crime rates. Moreover, resort areas that draw transients—Las Vegas, Miami, or Orlando, for instance—also have serious crime problems. When visitors are added to the year-round residents, the higher population betters the odds that victim and crook will meet.

Police strength, too, is linked to the local crime rate. Most metro areas have between one and three sworn uniformed officers for every 1,000 residents. In Manhattan, there are 1,300 police officers per square mile. In sparsely populated parts of Alaska and the Canadian Yukon and Northwest Territories, there aren't any.

Neighborhood Crime Watches

It is not uncommon to see a crime in progress without recognizing it as such. Here are some situations that might be observed in any neighborhood. These are situations a trained police officer would investigate if he or she were making the observation.

Situtations Involving Vehicles

Situation	Possible Significance
Moving vehicles, especially if moving slowly without lights, following an aimless or repetitive course.	Casing for a place to rob or burglarize; drug pusher, sex offender, or vandal
Parked, occupied vehicle, especially at an unusual hour	Lookout for burglary in progress (sometimes two people masquerading as lovers)
Vehicle parked in neighbor's drive being loaded with valuables, even if the vehicle looks legitimate, i.e., moving van or commercial van	Burglary or larceny in progress
Abandoned vehicle with or without license plate	Stolen or abandoned after being used in a crime
Persons loitering around parked cars	Burglary of vehicle contents, theft of accessories, vandalism
Persons detatching accessories and mechanical parts	Theft or vandalism
Apparent business transaction from a vehicle near school, park, or quiet residential neighborhood	Drug sales
Persons being forced into vehicle	Kidnapping, rape, robbery
Objects thrown from a moving vehicle	Disposal of contraband

Situations Involving Property

Situation	Possible Significance
Property in homes, garages, or storage areas, especially if several items of the same kind such as TVs and bicycles	Storage of stolen property

Situations Involving Property

Situation	Possible Significance
Property in vehicles, especially meaningful at night or if property is household goods, appliances, unmounted tape decks, stereo equipment	Stolen property, burglary in progress
Property being removed from a house or building; meaningful if residents are at work, on vacation, or are known to be absent	Burglary or larceny in progress
Open doors, broken doors or windows, or other signs of forced entry	Burglary in progress or the scene of a recent burglary

Situations Involving Persons

Situation	Possible Significance
Door-to-door solicitors—especially if one goes to the back of the house and one stays in front. Can be men or women, clean-cut and well dressed	Casing for burglary, burglary in progress, soliciting violation
Waiting in front of a house	Lookout for burglary in progress
Forced entry or entry through a window	Burglary, vandalism, theft
Persons shortcutting through yards	Fleeing the scene of a crime
Persons running, especially if carrying items of value	Fleeing the scene of a crime
Persons carrying property, especially if property isn't boxed or wrapped	Offender leaving the scene of a burglary, robbery, or larceny
High volume of human traffic in and out of residence	Drug sales, vice activities, "fence" operation

It's natural to think personal safety in a metro area rises or falls in proportion to the size of the local police force, but it just isn't so. Police enforce traffic codes, investigate accidents, find lost children and calm down fighting spouses. They battle crime, too, but most of what they do is after the fact. They respond to complaints; they interview victims and fill out reports; they follow up on tips; and they collar suspects and bring them to book. A large number of police per capita, however, is usually an indication of a high-crime area rather than an area where crime is being foiled.

Other factors related to criminal activity include the practices of local prosecutors, judges, juries, and parole boards; the attitudes of the community toward crime; and the willingness of ordinary citizens to report crime.

CRIME INDEXES

Each year, the Federal Bureau of Investigation in Washington and the Canadian Centre for Justice Statistics in Ottawa report crime figures from police departments in their respective countries. Eight crimes make up a Crime Index for measuring local wrongdoing. Four are violent crimes; the other four are property crimes.

Violent Crime

Murder is the most reported of all crimes and has the highest rate of charges being laid. In spite of press conferences announcing dramatic drops in homicide rates, they are at a historic high in both the United States and Canada, though Canada's rate is less than a fourth that of its more violent southern neighbor.

Half of all victims knew their killers, perhaps even sat across from them at the breakfast table the morning of the crime or loaned them money the week before. Victims and killers are becoming less connected, however. One murder in eight involves a victim and a stranger, one in twenty a juvenile gang killing. Based on the number of unsolved homicides each year and an increase in slayings involving strangers, the FBI estimates at least 25 serial killers are on the loose in the United States.

Rape, too, frequently involves acquainted victims and aggressors. It is the most under-reported violent crime and has the highest proportion of "unfounded" complaints. Except in Illinois, Michigan, Minnesota, and

Assault is simply an attempt, successful or not, to severely injure another person. Assault is usually accompanied by the use of a weapon. Its rate is highest in August, lowest in February, higher in Canada's West and America's West than in other parts of these countries and higher in areas with resort or military economies.

Property Crime

Burglary is either forcible entry, unlawful entry where no force is used, or attempted forcible entry, all to commit a felony or theft. Most burglaries, jailed pros say, take hours to plan and minutes to pull off. The typical target is the home or apartment. Nearly half of the incidents involve walking in rather than breaking in. The usual time is between 9:00 and 11:00 A.M. or between 1:00 and 3:00 P.M. when you're least likely to be inside.

Larceny-theft, after drunk driving, is the most common crime in North America. Skipping out of a self-serve gas station is one example. Shoplifting a Russian sable coat is another. In almost all of the cases, the victim never sees the offender.

Auto theft, it's been said, is a victimless crime because you get over your loss with a check from the insurance company. About one in ten stolen luxury vehicles shows up in third world showrooms where a market for used Mercedes, Lexuses, Ford Explorers and even Harley-Davidson motorcycles flourishes. The North American auto-theft capitals—Miami, FL, and Vancouver, BC—are ports at opposite ends of the continent. Each area has seen an increase in persons arrested who had recently arrived from California and New York where auto insurance fraud and packing ship containers with automobiles is an underground art.

Arson was added to the Crime Index in 1979 following a Congressional mandate. It includes any willful or malicious burning or attempt to burn, with or without the intent to defraud, a house, building, car, airplane or personal property of someone else. It doesn't include fires of suspicious or unknown origin.

CAVEATS

Metro areas are rated for personal safety based on the number of crimes actually reported to local police. Yet more than 60 percent of all crime goes unreported according to national victim surveys, and that percentage can vary from one metro area to another.

In the past, too, some police departments have either padded the figures to oust a judge considered soft on crime or to persuade the city council to increase the department's budget, or they fudged the number of crimes to create an image of effective law enforcement.

It's important to distinguish between the *incidence* of crime and the crime *rate*. Incidence is simply how many crimes are reported in a given place. The more people living in a place, the greater the crime incidence will be. In Quebec City, police investigate some 600 aggravated assaults a year. South of Chicago, police in Kankakee handle a similar number. From these figures, you might think that Quebec's capital is as dangerous as Kankakee. But 687,000 people live in Quebec City and its environs, while just 101,000 live in greater Kankakee.

A truer measure of safety is the crime rate—the number of crimes per 100,000 people. Quebec City's assault rate is 91. Kankakee's rate is 512, or more than five times that of Quebec City.

SCORING: CRIME

The single offense most often reported to local cops is larceny-theft: a stolen bike, a necklace missing from a jewelry retailer's display case, hubcaps gone from a used-car lot, a customer bolting from a fast-food restaurant. Yet these heists are counted as heavily as homicides to determine an area's crime rate. When it comes to comparing places, this method doesn't realistically show relative danger.

The realistic way to judge metro areas for personal safety is simple: For each place, *Places Rated* averages the rates for violent and property crimes for the latest five-year period, but since property crimes are much less serious than crimes against people, they are given one-tenth the weight of violent crimes. [Note, (1) although forcible rape is a violent crime, figures for forcible rape aren't included in the scoring because comparable data aren't reported for Canada and for Illinois, Michigan, and Minnesota, and (2) although arson has been considered a property crime since 1979, arson figures aren't included in the scoring because they are unavailable for many metro areas.] Each metro area's standard score begins with the addition of two factors:

1. *Violent crime rate.* The rates for murder, robbery, and aggravated assault are added together.
2. *Property crime rate.* The rates for burglary, larceny-theft, and motor vehicle theft are totaled, and the result is divided by 10.

This sum is then scaled against a standard where the average sum for all metro areas is set at 50. Places with *lower* crime rates than the metro area average earn standard scores *better* than 50. On the other hand, places with *higher* crime rates than the average get standard scores *worse* than 50.

SCORING EXAMPLES

A small location in southwest Pennsylvania, a larger one on the upper Mississippi, and an even larger one in southeast Florida are the best, average, and worst metro areas by *Places Rated's* scoring method for crime.

Best: Johnstown, PA

The one connection people make with this metro area is a famous flood that took 2,100 lives over a century ago, in 1889. Some 60 miles east of Pittsburgh, Johnstown's main industries are coal, chemicals, and concrete.

The area has another distinction: Violent and property crime rates here are well below the average for all metro areas. When scaled on a normal distribution from 0 to 100 against this average of 50, Johnstown earns a score of 95.69—not perfect (there is some crime here, after all), but the best score for all metro areas in North America.

Average: Davenport–Rock Island–Moline, IA–IL

Is there an area with a score of 50, exactly at the middle on the scale of 0 to 100? No there isn't. The one coming closest to this mythical mean, however, is in America's heartland.

Davenport–Rock Island–Moline is a group of cities on both banks of the Mississippi River separating western Illinois from eastern Iowa. When you include East Moline, the three-county area is known far and wide as the "Quad Cities."

Property crime here is slightly below the metro area average; violent crime, a shade above. When its violent crime rate is added to one-tenth its property crime rate and the sum scaled against the average for all metro areas, the Quad Cities earns a score of 49.96. You can't get much closer to 50 than that.

Worst: Miami, FL

Most metro areas in Florida rank near the bottom in personal safety. Of all the states, Florida has the highest rate for both violent crime and property crime. Miami, the state's best-known city, was the tropical backdrop for a bloody Friday-night television series in the early 1980s and continues to be the setting for Edna Buchanan's, Carl Hiaasen's, and Elmore Leonard's best-selling crime fiction.

Beset by rapid population growth and caught in the crosscurrents of the drug trade, Miami is truly a North American crime capital. Lawbreaking is so startlingly high in this vacation area that a standard item in hotel and rental car packets is a bulletin on guerrilla tactics for staying out of harm's way.

Metro Miami's violent crime rate is nearly four times the metro area average, and its property crime is more than twice that average. How dangerous is that? On a normal distribution of 0 to 100 where the metro area average is 50, Miami earns a 0.

RANKINGS: Crime

In ranking each metro area for relative safety, *Places Rated* adds two numbers: (1) its violent crime rate and (2) its property crime rate divided by 10. The result is then scaled against the average sum for all metro areas to produce a standard score. The higher the standard score, the safer the metro area. Places with tie scores get the same rank and are listed in alphabetical order.

Metro Areas from Best to Worst

Places Rated Rank		Places Rated Score
1.	Johnstown, PA	95.69
2.	Nashua, NH	95.58
3.	Portsmouth–Rochester, NH–ME	95.11
4.	Wheeling, WV–OH	95.09
5.	Altoona, PA	94.70
6.	Wausau, WI	94.43
7.	State College, PA	93.56
8.	Scranton–Wilkes-Barre–Hazleton, PA	93.46
9.	Parkersburg–Marietta, WV–OH	93.37
19.	Bismarck, ND	91.62
19.	Fargo–Moorhead, ND–MN	91.62
21.	Rochester, MN	91.43
22.	Utica–Rome, NY	91.40
23.	York, PA	91.37
23.	Danville, VA	91.37
25.	Bloomington–Normal, IL	91.17
26.	Binghamton, NY	91.13
27.	Sheboygan, WI	91.00
28.	Provo–Orem, UT	90.71
29.	Hagerstown, MD	90.29
30.	Allentown–Bethlehem–Easton, PA	90.10
31.	Grand Forks, ND–MN	90.06
32.	Lewiston–Auburn, ME	89.96
33.	Johnson City–Kingsport–Bristol, TN	89.72
34.	Fayetteville–Springdale–Rogers, AR	89.58
35.	Punta Gorda, FL	89.29
36.	Steubenville–Weirton, OH–WV	89.18
37.	Owensboro, KY	88.67
38.	Huntington–Ashland, WV–KY–OH	88.61
39.	Duluth–Superior, MN–WI	88.45
40.	Fort Collins–Loveland, CO	88.28
41.	Florence, AL	88.18
42.	Saint John, NB	88.12
43.	Jamestown, NY	88.06
44.	St. John's, NF	87.51
45.	Cumberland, MD–WV	86.89
46.	New London–Norwich, CT–RI	86.82
47.	Dubuque, IA	86.61
48.	St. Cloud, MN	86.48
49.	Middlesex–Somerset–Hunterdon, NJ	86.41
50.	Green Bay, WI	86.39
51.	Muncie, IN	86.28
52.	Sioux Falls, SD	86.21
53.	Monmouth–Ocean, NJ	86.10
54.	Chicoutimi–Jonquiere, PQ	86.04
55.	Manchester, NH	85.79
56.	Long Island, NY	85.41
57.	Cheyenne, WY	85.38
58.	Syracuse, NY	85.22
59.	Hattiesburg, MS	84.94
60.	Decatur, AL	84.73
61.	Erie, PA	84.42
62.	Olympia, WA	84.04
63.	Bremerton, WA	84.01
73.	Joplin, MO	82.56
74.	Kitchener, ON	82.54
75.	Harrisburg–Lebanon–Carlisle, PA	82.48
76.	Lynchburg, VA	82.46
77.	Reading, PA	82.17
78.	Fort Walton Beach, FL	82.15
79.	Newburgh, NY–PA	81.27
80.	Jacksonville, NC	81.25
81.	Glens Falls, NY	80.87
82.	Youngstown–Warren, OH	80.07
83.	Stamford–Norwalk, CT	79.98
84.	Billings, MT	79.64
85.	Trois–Rivieres, PQ	79.56
86.	Kokomo, IN	79.13
87.	St. Catharines–Niagara, ON	78.99
88.	Janesville–Beloit, WI	78.93
88.	Portland, ME	78.93
90.	Boise City, ID	78.84
91.	Kenosha, WI	78.79
92.	Charleston, WV	78.64
93.	Bellingham, WA	78.29
93.	Madison, WI	78.29
95.	Bergen–Passaic, NJ	78.20
96.	Cedar Rapids, IA	78.11
97.	Bloomington, IN	78.08
98.	Sherbrooke, PQ	77.88
99.	Albany–Schenectady–Troy, NY	77.82
100.	Boulder–Longmont, CO	77.46
101.	Roanoke, VA	77.22
102.	Burlington, VT	75.99
103.	Windsor, ON	75.96
104.	Fort Wayne, IN	75.90
105.	Iowa City, IA	75.87
106.	Hickory–Morganton–Lenoir, NC	75.77
107.	Springfield, MO	75.62
108.	Rochester, NY	74.89
109.	Grand Junction, CO	74.63
110.	San Luis Obispo–Atascadero–Paso Robles, CA	74.44
111.	Quebec City, PQ	74.31
112.	Fort Smith, AR–OK	74.22
113.	Waterloo–Cedar Falls, IA	73.89
114.	Asheville, NC	73.86
115.	Ann Arbor, MI	72.04
116.	Toronto, ON	71.63
117.	Ventura, CA	71.46
118.	Eugene–Springfield, OR	71.29
119.	Providence–Fall River–	
128.	Rapid City, SD	68.19
129.	Biloxi–Gulfport–Pascagoula, MS	67.40
130.	Redding, CA	66.97
131.	Chico–Paradise, CA	66.86
131.	Santa Barbara–Santa Maria–Lompoc, CA	66.86
133.	Salem, OR	66.13
134.	Hamilton, ON	66.09
135.	Cleveland–Lorain–Elyria, OH	65.95
136.	Columbia, MO	65.28
137.	San Jose, CA	65.10
137.	Sudbury, ON	65.10
139.	London, ON	65.06
140.	Colorado Springs, CO	65.03
140.	St. Joseph, MO	65.03
142.	Canton–Massillon, OH	64.65
143.	Killeen–Temple, TX	64.32
144.	Minneapolis–St. Paul, MN–WI	64.10
145.	Hamilton–Middletown, OH	63.68
146.	Flagstaff, AZ–UT	63.31
147.	Des Moines, IA	62.85
148.	Akron, OH	62.59
149.	Ottawa–Hull, ON–PQ	62.55
150.	Evansville–Henderson, IN–KY	62.13
151.	Merced, CA	61.83
152.	Salt Lake City–Ogden, UT	61.79
153.	Great Falls, MT	60.95
154.	Lafayette, LA	60.37
155.	Waterbury, CT	59.33
156.	Louisville, KY–IN	59.13
157.	Racine, WI	58.82
158.	Sherman–Denison, TX	58.75
159.	Lawrence, KS	58.67
160.	Cincinnati, OH–KY–IN	58.43
161.	Dover, DE	58.24
162.	Hartford, CT	57.89
163.	Columbus, GA–AL	57.26
164.	Grand Rapids–Muskegon–Holland, MI	56.99

Places Rated Rank		Places Rated Score
165.	Milwaukee–Waukesha, WI	56.91
166.	Lansing–East Lansing, MI	55.41
167.	Casper, WY	54.82
168.	Spokane, WA	54.46
169.	Saskatoon, SK	54.34
170.	Orange County, CA	54.02
171.	Dayton–Springfield, OH	52.23
172.	Fort Myers–Cape Coral, FL	51.68
173.	Omaha, NE–IA	51.44
174.	Philadelphia, PA–NJ	51.12
175.	Champaign–Urbana, IL	50.88
176.	South Bend, IN	50.76
177.	Bryan–College Station, TX	50.52
178.	Davenport–Moline–Rock Island, IA–IL	49.96
179.	Calgary, AB	49.84
180.	Richmond–Petersburg, VA	49.72
181.	Abilene, TX	49.56
182.	Las Cruces, NM	49.40
183.	Peoria–Pekin, IL	49.20
184.	Montreal, PQ	48.44
185.	Lawrence, MA–NH	48.40
186.	San Angelo, TX	47.73
186.	Trenton, NJ	47.73
188.	Salinas, CA	47.41
189.	Victoria, BC	46.26
190.	Macon, GA	46.22
191.	Huntsville, AL	45.66
192.	Lubbock, TX	45.42
193.	Raleigh–Durham–Chapel Hill, NC	45.30
193.	Reno, NV	45.30
195.	Decatur, IL	44.87
196.	Norfolk–Virginia Beach–Newport News, VA	44.67
197.	Seattle–Bellevue–Everett, WA	44.35
197.	Santa Cruz–Watsonville, CA	44.35
199.	Barnstable–Yarmouth, MA	44.12
199.	Lowell, MA–NH	44.12
201.	Dothan, AL	43.72
202.	Augusta–Aiken, GA–SC	42.66
203.	Lincoln, NE	42.00
204.	Goldsboro, NC	41.22
205.	Bridgeport, CT	40.90
206.	Yolo, CA	40.63
207.	Lawton, OK	40.52
208.	Toledo, OH	40.40
209.	Indianapolis, IN	40.05
210.	Thunder Bay, ON	39.24
211.	Buffalo–Niagara Falls, NY	39.05
212.	Columbus, OH	38.90
213.	Greensboro–Winston-Salem–High Point, NC	38.86
214.	Brockton, MA	38.78
215.	Washington, DC–MD–VA–WV	38.44
216.	Visalia–Tulare–Porterville, CA	38.29
217.	Austin–San Marcos, TX	37.87
218.	Edmonton, AB	37.75
219.	Rockford, IL	37.71
220.	Santa Fe, NM	37.64
221.	Longview–Marshall, TX	37.15
222.	Portland–Vancouver, OR–WA	36.88
223.	Denver, CO	36.58
224.	Athens, GA	36.28
225.	Saginaw–Bay City–Midland, MI	36.24
226.	Rocky Mount, NC	36.20
227.	Lexington, KY	36.05
228.	Naples, FL	35.94
229.	Amarillo, TX	35.64
229.	McAllen–Edinburg–Mission, TX	35.64
231.	Fort Pierce–Port St. Lucie, FL	35.49
232.	Mansfield, OH	35.38
232.	Texarkana, TX–Texarkana, AR	35.38
234.	Yuma, AZ	35.16
235.	Vallejo–Fairfield–Napa, CA	35.01
236.	Montgomery, AL	34.75
237.	Brownsville–Harlingen–San Benito, TX	34.72
238.	Fitchburg–Leominster, MA	34.64
239.	Enid, OK	34.49
240.	New Haven–Meriden, CT	34.31
241.	Tulsa, OK	32.85
242.	Wichita, KS	32.28
243.	Boston, MA–NH	32.13
244.	Winnipeg, MB	31.88
245.	Kalamazoo–Battle Creek, MI	31.67
246.	Odessa–Midland, TX	31.21
247.	Anchorage, AK	30.68
248.	Clarksville–Hopkinsville, TN–KY	30.26
249.	Yakima, WA	29.91
250.	Panama City, FL	29.87
251.	Jackson, MI	29.32
252.	Sioux City, IA–NE	28.94
253.	Greenville, NC	28.84
254.	Halifax, NS	28.37
255.	Chattanooga, TN–GA	28.20
256.	Daytona Beach, FL	28.06
257.	Mobile, AL	27.93
258.	Yuba City, CA	27.76
259.	Melbourne–Titusville–Palm Bay, FL	27.23
260.	Springfield, IL	26.99
261.	Gary, IN	26.01
262.	Tyler, TX	25.85
263.	Houston, TX	25.69
264.	St. Louis, MO–IL	25.62
265.	Knoxville, TN	25.49
266.	Anniston, AL	25.37
267.	Laredo, TX	25.27
268.	Regina, SK	24.92
269.	Savannah, GA	24.42
270.	Kankakee, IL	24.32
271.	Phoenix–Mesa, AZ	24.29
272.	Lima, OH	24.17
273.	Springfield, MA	24.04
274.	Sacramento, CA	23.61
275.	Las Vegas, NV–AZ	22.60
276.	New Bedford, MA	21.86
277.	Vineland–Millville–Bridgeton, NJ	21.33
278.	Wichita Falls, TX	21.07
279.	Jackson, MS	20.98
280.	Tacoma, WA	20.87
281.	Corpus Christi, TX	20.73
282.	Oklahoma City, OK	20.38
283.	San Antonio, TX	20.16
284.	San Diego, CA	19.96
285.	Greenville–Spartanburg–Anderson, SC	19.82
286.	Bakersfield, CA	19.52
287.	Vancouver, BC	19.46
288.	Charleston–North Charleston, SC	19.19
289.	Galveston–Texas City, TX	19.13
290.	Modesto, CA	19.02
291.	Newark, NJ	18.49
292.	Wilmington, NC	18.38
293.	Sarasota–Bradenton, FL	18.19
295.	Lake Charles, LA	17.57
295.	Victoria, TX	17.57
296.	Monroe, LA	17.36
297.	Gadsden, AL	16.53
298.	Beaumont–Port Arthur, TX	16.23
299.	Detroit, MI	15.87
300.	Tucson, AZ	15.13
301.	Waco, TX	14.48
302.	Nashville, TN	14.37
303.	San Francisco, CA	13.37
303.	Pensacola, FL	13.37
305.	Fort Worth–Arlington, TX	13.26
306.	Birmingham, AL	12.53
307.	Atlanta, GA	11.96
308.	Florence, SC	11.88
309.	Benton Harbor, MI	11.64
310.	Alexandria, LA	11.37
311.	Pine Bluff, AR	10.77
312.	Atlantic City–Cape May, NJ	10.66
313.	Ocala, FL	10.56
314.	Oakland, CA	10.49
315.	Tuscaloosa, AL	10.19
316.	Columbia, SC	10.06
317.	Shreveport–Bossier City, LA	9.99
318.	Memphis, TN–AR–MS	9.63
319.	Albany, GA	9.36
320.	Myrtle Beach, SC	9.11
321.	Sumter, SC	8.90
322.	Stockton–Lodi, CA	8.71
323.	El Paso, TX	8.26
324.	Riverside–San Bernardino, CA	8.05
325.	Fayetteville, NC	7.96
326.	Orlando, FL	7.54
327.	Jersey City, NJ	7.16
328.	Kansas City, MO–KS	6.97
329.	Flint, MI	6.88
330.	Fort Lauderdale, FL	6.60
331.	Topeka, KS	6.24
332.	Fresno, CA	5.96
333.	Lakeland–Winter Haven, FL	5.93
334.	Charlotte–Gastonia–Rock Hill, NC–SC	5.34
335.	Pueblo, CO	5.26
336.	Dallas, TX	5.00
337.	Chicago, IL	4.98
338.	Albuquerque, NM	4.48
339.	Baltimore, MD	3.91
340.	Tampa–St. Petersburg–Clearwater, FL	3.14

Places Rated Rank	Places Rated Score
341. West Palm Beach–Boca Raton, FL	2.99
342. Jackson, TN	2.38
343. New Orleans, LA	1.55
344. Little Rock–North Little Rock, AR	1.48
345. Jacksonville, FL	1.03
346. Gainesville, FL	0.89
347. Los Angeles–Long Beach, CA	0.42
348. Tallahassee, FL	0.09
349. New York, NY	0.06
350. Baton Rouge, LA	0.02
351. Miami, FL	0.00

grouped into violent and property categories, and a total rate for each of these categories is also given.

Note: Although figures for rape are shown for most metro areas, they aren't included in the scoring because comparable data are unavailable for jurisdictions in Illinois, Michigan, and Minnesota, and all of Canada.

Figures for the United States are derived from the FBI's *Crime in the United States* for the latest five years for which data are available and from the Bureau's unpublished "Crime by County" reports for each of these years. For American metro areas not included in either

The next to the last column indicates the crime trend over the previous five years: 164 metro areas have an arrow pointing upward (⇑), meaning their *Places Rated* crime rates during this period are up; 125 metro areas have an arrow pointing downward (⇓), meaning their crime rates have dropped; and 62 metro areas have an arrow pointing neither up nor down (⇔), meaning their crime rates are essentially unchanged. A check mark (✓) next to a metro area's name highlights it as one of the top 35 places for safety from crime.

Metro Area	Murder	Rape	Robbery	Assault	VIOLENT	Burglary	Theft	Auto Theft	PROPERTY	SCORE	TREND	RANK
Metro Area Average	6.9	40.0	161.2	390.3	558.3	1,241	3,405	460	5,106	50.00	⇓	
Abilene, TX	7.2	69.8	131.4	506.8	645.3	1,257	2,842	186	4,285	49.56	⇑	181
Akron, OH	4.1	48.2	184.9	309.6	498.6	888	2,978	448	4,315	62.59	⇑	148
Albany, GA	16.5	58.3	385.5	445.3	847.4	2,795	4,710	417	7,922	9.36	⇔	319
Albany–Schenectady–Troy, NY	5.2	25.1	106.9	253.1	365.1	880	2,673	173	3,726	77.82	⇔	99
Albuquerque, NM	9.3	58.3	246.1	890.0	1,145.4	1,873	4,143	563	6,579	4.48	⇔	338
Alexandria, LA	10.8	49.1	96.5	958.5	1,065.8	1,314	3,623	312	5,249	11.37	⇓	310
✓ Allentown–Bethlehem–Easton, PA	3.5	18.6	65.8	135.2	204.5	595	2,263	222	3,080	90.10	⇓	30
✓ Altoona, PA	.9	29.7	36.0	113.1	150.1	625	1,419	154	2,199	94.70	⇔	5
Amarillo, TX	10.2	51.6	129.9	403.2	543.3	1,481	5,043	321	6,845	35.64	⇓	229
Anchorage, AK	8.0	93.9	220.0	473.0	701.0	943	4,234	685	5,862	30.68	⇓	247
Ann Arbor, MI	2.8	42.4	87.3	297.4	387.4	848	3,186	257	4,291	72.04	⇑	115
Anniston, AL	10.9	46.1	134.1	783.4	928.4	1,297	2,745	230	4,272	25.37	⇓	266
✓ Appleton–Oshkosh–Neenah, WI	1.5	10.4	11.6	73.6	86.7	527	2,883	100	3,510	92.77	⇑	11
Asheville, NC	7.6	29.0	108.6	239.3	355.5	1,309	2,757	304	4,370	73.86	⇑	114
Athens, GA	10.1	44.7	199.6	352.6	562.3	1,670	4,414	502	6,586	36.28	⇔	224
Atlanta, GA	12.4	52.0	370.4	498.5	881.4	1,599	4,449	919	6,967	11.96	⇑	307

Metro Area	Murder	Rape	Robbery	Assault	VIOLENT	Burglary	Theft	Auto Theft	PROPERTY	SCORE	TREND	RANK
Metro Area Average	6.9	40.0	161.2	390.3	558.3	1,241	3,405	460	5,106	50.00	⇓	
Atlantic City-Cape May, NJ	6.9	57.9	299.2	471.2	777.3	1,583	6,341	377	8,300	10.66	⇑	312
Augusta-Aiken, GA-SC	15.0	46.6	216.2	401.2	632.4	1,616	2,982	567	5,165	42.66	⇑	202
Austin-San Marcos, TX	6.5	54.9	191.1	282.3	479.9	1,612	5,025	590	7,226	37.87	⇑	217
Bakersfield, CA	11.8	40.5	200.0	664.4	876.2	1,641	3,418	582	5,641	19.52	⇔	286
Baltimore, MD	15.9	50.6	586.3	637.8	1,240.0	1,332	3,729	844	5,904	3.91	⇓	339
✓ Bangor, ME	3.5	24.2	31.9	57.9	93.3	564	3,042	144	3,750	91.76	⇑	16
Barnstable-Yarmouth, MA	1.6	30.2	41.4	678.3	721.2	1,367	2,495	254	4,116	44.12	⇔	199
Baton Rouge, LA	20.1	54.0	485.1	1175.7	1,680.9	2,441	5,652	855	8,947	0.02	⇑	350
Beaumont-Port Arthur, TX	10.8	71.6	288.1	564.1	862.9	1,843	3,824	650	6,318	16.23	⇑	298
Bellingham, WA	2.6	63.9	39.5	174.5	216.6	964	3,924	252	5,139	78.29	⇔	93
Benton Harbor, MI	9.0	88.6	169.2	805.0	983.2	1,496	4,163	359	6,018	11.64	⇑	309
Bergen-Passaic, NJ	3.1	15.9	168.6	195.3	367.0	722	2,308	620	3,650	78.20	⇑	95
Billings, MT	2.8	18.0	71.3	72.4	146.5	964	4,362	313	5,639	79.64	⇓	84
Biloxi-Gulfport-Pascagoula, MS	4.2	101.8	100.9	311.1	416.2	1,818	2,420	337	4,575	67.40	⇑	129
✓ Binghamton, NY	2.9	22.0	32.1	145.0	180.1	553	2,400	98	3,052	91.13	⇔	26
Birmingham, AL	20.4	53.2	297.9	701.8	1,020.1	1,437	3,315	708	5,459	12.53	⇓	306
✓ Bismarck, ND	3.1	22.4	8.7	91.7	103.5	505	3,012	166	3,684	91.62	⇓	19
Bloomington, IN	5.4	23.2	20.6	377.7	403.7	542	2,553	206	3,300	78.08	⇓	97
✓ Bloomington-Normal, IL	4.5	n.a.	42.1	147.4	194.0	676	2,140	91	2,907	91.17	⇑	25
Boise City, ID	2.5	38.5	29.0	247.8	279.3	871	3,344	215	4,429	78.84	⇓	90
Boston, MA-NH	4.6	34.3	212.5	616.0	833.2	1,008	2,356	998	4,362	32.13	⇑	243
Boulder-Longmont, CO	2.2	40.4	33.0	171.8	207.0	974	4,163	220	5,357	77.46	⇑	100
Brazoria, TX	5.2	37.3	45.8	253.6	304.5	799	2,313	316	3,427	83.52	⇑	66
Bremerton, WA	3.4	61.4	56.6	182.7	242.7	838	2,883	239	3,960	84.01	⇑	63
Bridgeport, CT	13.6	23.8	391.6	251.0	656.2	1,317	2,450	1,354	5,121	40.90	⇑	205
Brockton, MA	4.0	32.2	185.0	518.4	707.3	1,519	2,001	1,327	4,847	38.78	⇑	214
Brownsville-Harlingen-San Benito, TX	11.5	22.3	117.8	467.2	596.5	1,784	4,093	546	6,423	34.72	⇓	237
Bryan-College Station, TX	4.1	56.2	98.0	388.2	490.3	1,269	4,144	316	5,728	50.52	⇔	177
Buffalo-Niagara Falls, NY	6.7	39.8	284.5	436.3	727.6	1,165	2,788	663	4,616	39.05	⇓	211
Burlington, VT	2.1	46.8	24.3	72.3	98.8	1,341	4,984	322	6,647	75.99	⇑	102
Calgary, AB	2.5	n.a.	146.5	231.7	380.7	1,695	4,311	896	6,902	49.84	⇑	179
Canton-Massillon, OH	4.3	39.7	202.5	250.4	457.3	1,088	2,737	665	4,489	64.65	⇓	142
Casper, WY	3.1	30.0	34.6	399.4	437.0	1,310	4,186	300	5,796	54.82	⇔	167
Cedar Rapids, IA	1.2	11.3	46.2	179.5	226.9	1,020	3,821	223	5,064	78.11	⇔	96
Champaign-Urbana, IL	5.7	n.a.	153.9	358.3	517.9	1,382	3,811	221	5,413	50.88	⇔	175
Charleston, WV	7.9	29.3	116.1	208.1	332.2	926	2,688	322	3,935	78.64	⇓	92
Charleston-North Charleston, SC	9.0	59.6	194.4	665.8	869.2	1,344	3,913	509	5,766	19.19	⇑	288
Charlotte-Gastonia-Rock Hill, NC-SC	14.3	48.5	327.9	784.1	1,126.2	1,864	4,158	381	6,403	5.34	⇑	334
Charlottesville, VA	5.2	35.0	71.1	188.5	264.8	584	2,971	180	3,736	84.01	⇔	63
Chattanooga, TN-GA	11.3	46.0	207.5	599.4	818.1	1,312	3,050	643	5,004	28.20	⇑	255
Cheyenne, WY	3.2	42.4	25.0	150.0	178.2	460	3,763	131	4,354	85.38	⇑	57
Chicago, IL	14.6	n.a.	577.4	653.7	1,245.7	1,129	3,384	844	5,357	4.98	⇔	337
Chico-Paradise, CA	5.5	46.0	67.8	348.6	421.9	1,342	2,904	337	4,584	66.86	⇓	131
Chicoutimi-Jonquiere, PQ	1.2	n.a.	66.6	125.9	193.7	1,555	2,168	350	4,073	86.04	⇔	54
Cincinnati, OH-KY-IN	4.4	52.7	191.4	336.3	532.1	949	3,227	270	4,446	58.43	⇔	160
Clarksville-Hopkinsville, TN-KY	7.3	55.7	85.4	819.9	912.6	1,021	2,594	185	3,800	30.26	⇑	248

Metro Area	Murder	Rape	Robbery	Assault	VIOLENT	Burglary	Theft	Auto Theft	PROPERTY	SCORE	TREND	RANK
Metro Area Average	6.9	40.0	161.2	390.3	558.3	1,241	3,405	460	5,106	50.00	⇓	
Cleveland-Lorain-Elyria, OH	9.4	59.2	273.3	224.6	507.2	881	2,187	772	3,840	65.95	⇑	135
Colorado Springs, CO	4.9	60.9	96.2	262.9	364.1	1,095	3,983	303	5,380	65.03	⇑	140
Columbia, MO	3.4	33.3	89.5	325.3	418.3	794	3,849	164	4,806	65.28	⇑	136
Columbia, SC	11.1	74.8	294.6	725.7	1,031.5	1,386	3,967	550	5,902	10.06	⇑	316
Columbus, GA-AL	10.8	33.8	167.5	320.0	498.3	1,157	3,391	364	4,912	57.26	⇑	163
Columbus, OH	8.9	65.4	312.3	292.6	613.8	1,435	3,668	667	5,770	38.90	⇑	212
Corpus Christi, TX	9.0	59.9	148.6	480.7	638.3	1,774	5,596	464	7,834	20.73	⇓	281
Cumberland, MD-WV	1.6	18.5	19.8	308.3	329.7	551	1,893	98	2,542	86.89	⇓	45
Dallas, TX	17.9	63.9	404.6	618.6	1,041.1	1,734	4,585	1,074	7,393	5.00	⇑	336
✓ Danbury, CT	[illegible]	[illegible]	[illegible]	[illegible]								
[illegible]	[illegible]	[illegible]	[illegible]	[illegible]	[illegible]	1,232	3,713	664	5,608	36.58	⇑	223
Des Moines, IA	3.6	29.4	83.8	275.8	363.3	892	4,468	278	5,637	62.85	⇑	147
Detroit, MI	16.2	52.8	381.3	537.9	935.3	1,119	3,448	1,096	5,663	15.87	⇑	299
Dothan, AL	7.5	34.2	89.4	608.3	705.2	921	3,209	191	4,321	43.72	⇑	201
Dover, DE	4.5	99.6	105.6	431.0	541.1	847	3,332	198	4,377	58.24	⇓	161
Dubuque, IA	.5	26.6	17.3	249.9	267.7	648	2,420	151	3,219	86.61	⇑	47
Duluth-Superior, MN-WI	2.8	34.6	33.7	135.3	171.8	842	2,715	232	3,789	88.45	⇔	39
Dutchess County, NY	4.4	16.2	104.8	249.0	358.2	645	2,113	148	2,905	83.45	⇑	68
✓ Eau Claire, WI	1.0	8.5	11.1	78.9	90.9	673	2,960	139	3,773	91.76	⇔	16
Edmonton, AB	3.4	n.a.	185.7	241.9	431.0	1,932	4,923	875	7,731	37.75	⇑	218
El Paso, TX	8.4	49.1	239.1	676.4	923.9	1,312	5,266	877	7,454	8.26	⇑	323
Elkhart-Goshen, IN	2.8	48.4	82.2	341.2	426.2	836	3,209	169	4,214	69.57	⇓	123
Elmira, NY	2.8	33.5	49.3	210.6	262.7	676	3,204	98	3,978	82.74	⇑	71
Enid, OK	4.6	58.0	75.5	556.3	636.3	1,535	4,249	268	6,051	34.49	⇓	239
Erie, PA	2.7	42.3	141.2	176.9	320.8	702	2,191	213	3,106	84.42	⇔	61
Eugene-Springfield, OR	2.1	46.9	100.6	174.3	277.1	1,150	4,025	314	5,489	71.29	⇓	118
Evansville-Henderson, IN-KY	4.5	31.8	71.1	456.1	531.7	917	2,881	236	4,034	62.13	⇑	150
✓ Fargo-Moorhead, ND-MN	1.6	31.4	15.5	60.6	77.7	510	3,231	203	3,944	91.62	⇔	19
Fayetteville, NC	15.8	69.1	311.6	592.7	920.2	2,301	4,679	596	7,576	7.96	⇓	325
✓ Fayetteville-Springdale-Rogers, AR	5.1	26.9	22.7	127.1	154.9	767	2,724	210	3,701	89.58	⇑	34
Fitchburg-Leominster, MA	7.3	63.7	77.2	761.9	846.4	1,105	2,409	422	3,935	34.64	⇑	238
Flagstaff, AZ-UT	6.3	42.9	56.5	283.4	346.2	861	4,706	190	5,758	63.31	⇑	146
Flint, MI	14.5	64.0	297.5	761.5	1,073.5	1,660	3,904	814	6,378	6.88	⇔	329
Florence, AL	5.5	12.8	36.1	231.8	273.4	612	2,106	116	2,834	88.18	⇑	41
Florence, SC	12.9	73.2	196.5	789.3	998.7	1,757	3,660	394	5,811	11.88	⇔	308
Fort Collins-Loveland, CO	1.6	43.3	16.5	193.3	211.5	584	2,725	123	3,432	88.28	⇑	40
Fort Lauderdale, FL	7.8	38.8	361.5	566.8	936.2	1,828	5,049	965	7,842	6.60	⇓	330
Fort Myers-Cape Coral, FL	7.2	40.3	204.1	329.7	541.1	1,492	2,952	655	5,099	51.68	⇓	172
Fort Pierce-Port St. Lucie, FL	8.7	43.4	168.5	514.9	692.2	1,697	3,197	481	5,374	35.49	⇑	231
Fort Smith, AR-OK	5.7	41.6	50.5	303.0	359.2	996	3,007	285	4,287	74.22	⇔	112
Fort Walton Beach, FL	2.8	18.5	62.0	269.4	334.2	783	2,401	179	3,363	82.15	⇓	78
Fort Wayne, IN	7.2	33.1	134.2	172.4	313.8	795	3,237	478	4,510	75.90	⇑	104

Metro Area	Murder	Rape	Robbery	Assault	VIOLENT	Burglary	Theft	Auto Theft	PROPERTY	SCORE	TREND	RANK
Metro Area Average	6.9	40.0	161.2	390.3	558.3	1,241	3,405	460	5,106	50.00	⇓	
Fort Worth–Arlington, TX	13.2	62.0	285.9	523.5	822.6	1,694	4,581	1,007	7,281	13.26	⇑	305
Fresno, CA	15.3	54.9	388.2	606.1	1,009.6	1,812	3,646	1,873	7,331	5.96	⇓	332
Gadsden, AL	12.7	41.9	157.9	797.4	968.0	1,307	3,468	441	5,216	16.53	⇓	297
Gainesville, FL	8.1	72.9	294.2	902.2	1,204.5	2,394	5,898	592	8,884	0.89	⇓	346
Galveston–Texas City, TX	16.0	63.8	251.1	506.1	773.2	1,581	4,461	692	6,734	19.13	⇓	289
Gary, IN	16.8	46.0	225.7	614.9	857.4	984	2,783	1,129	4,896	26.01	⇑	261
Glens Falls, NY	2.0	25.2	14.0	380.7	396.7	607	2,259	80	2,945	80.87	⇔	81
Goldsboro, NC	12.6	29.4	189.2	486.5	688.3	1,477	2,992	296	4,765	41.22	⇓	204
✓ Grand Forks, ND–MN	.8	24.9	15.0	105.3	121.2	484	3,207	231	3,922	90.06	⇔	31
Grand Junction, CO	8.9	23.4	42.2	215.2	266.3	1,050	3,856	251	5,158	74.63	⇓	109
Grand Rapids–Muskegon–Holland, MI	4.2	67.8	130.0	396.7	530.9	1,050	3,273	296	4,619	56.99	⇑	164
Great Falls, MT	7.6	66.2	26.7	132.4	166.8	1,023	6,370	425	7,818	60.95	⇓	153
Greeley, CO	4.2	45.0	44.2	254.4	302.7	1,102	4,059	242	5,403	69.92	⇑	121
Green Bay, WI	1.4	27.4	24.4	202.9	228.7	503	2,994	156	3,653	86.39	⇓	50
Greensboro–Winston-Salem–High Point, NC	10.0	39.2	206.8	436.3	653.1	1,637	3,441	306	5,384	38.86	⇓	213
Greenville, NC	13.7	41.0	191.9	497.2	702.8	2,059	3,699	315	6,072	28.84	⇓	253
Greenville–Spartanburg–Anderson, SC	9.3	49.8	169.0	767.1	945.3	1,312	3,262	328	4,902	19.82	⇓	285
✓ Hagerstown, MD	3.3	21.8	53.8	218.2	275.3	550	1,636	135	2,321	90.29	⇔	29
Halifax, NS	2.6	n.a.	152.0	339.4	494.0	1,954	5,878	391	8,224	28.37	⇑	254
Hamilton, ON	2.1	n.a.	96.5	219.2	317.8	1,326	3,684	707	5,717	66.09	⇔	134
Hamilton–Middletown, OH	4.4	39.5	116.6	333.4	454.4	1,044	3,306	279	4,629	63.68	⇔	145
Harrisburg–Lebanon–Carlisle, PA	4.6	27.5	130.2	224.6	359.4	603	2,226	227	3,056	82.48	⇔	75
Hartford, CT	4.4	30.1	220.6	291.9	516.9	1,093	2,932	634	4,659	57.89	⇑	162
Hattiesburg, MS	5.0	31.2	57.3	241.3	303.7	938	2,121	121	3,179	84.94	⇔	59
Hickory–Morganton–Lenoir, NC	8.9	27.7	84.1	290.7	383.6	1,142	2,492	196	3,829	75.77	⇑	106
Honolulu, HI	3.7	33.1	113.3	124.6	241.6	1,113	4,455	463	6,031	69.78	⇓	122
Houma, LA	7.9	31.2	101.9	433.3	543.1	926	2,101	183	3,210	68.23	⇓	127
Houston, TX	18.2	58.2	339.3	380.7	738.2	1,569	3,220	1,342	6,131	25.69	⇑	263
Huntington–Ashland, WV–KY–OH	5.0	41.5	68.7	174.2	247.9	763	2,071	160	2,994	88.61	⇔	38
Huntsville, AL	8.1	33.3	122.3	443.4	573.9	1,042	4,073	307	5,422	45.66	⇓	191
Indianapolis, IN	9.0	64.4	217.9	421.7	648.6	1,273	3,383	639	5,295	40.05	⇓	209
Iowa City, IA	1.0	37.3	21.4	356.7	379.1	760	2,934	167	3,861	75.87	⇑	105
Jackson, MI	5.7	92.1	84.0	821.8	911.5	820	2,891	217	3,929	29.32	⇑	251
Jackson, MS	21.9	60.4	365.0	305.7	692.6	2,376	3,900	978	7,253	20.98	⇓	279
Jackson, TN	14.9	68.1	294.8	923.7	1,233.4	1,796	4,733	392	6,921	2.38	⇔	342
Jacksonville, FL	16.0	87.2	432.5	878.8	1,327.3	2,055	4,518	859	7,432	1.03	⇑	345
Jacksonville, NC	5.4	30.9	94.0	181.0	280.4	1,160	2,696	192	4,048	81.25	⇑	80
Jamestown, NY	1.3	16.1	37.5	162.7	201.6	713	2,770	96	3,578	88.06	⇓	43
Janesville–Beloit, WI	1.8	27.3	60.5	158.4	220.8	855	3,935	214	5,003	78.93	⇔	88
Jersey City, NJ	7.0	25.5	592.1	518.2	1,117.3	1,496	2,835	1,516	5,846	7.16	⇑	327
✓ Johnson City–Kingsport–Bristol, TN	4.1	22.2	30.6	199.9	234.6	720	1,958	189	2,867	89.72	⇑	33
✓ Johnstown, PA	1.6	17.9	27.5	151.2	180.3	431	919	113	1,464	95.69	⇔	1
Joplin, MO	4.5	28.3	50.7	149.4	204.6	1,057	3,248	283	4,589	82.56	⇔	73
Kalamazoo–Battle Creek, MI	6.1	49.5	150.4	577.9	734.4	1,334	3,772	302	5,408	31.67	⇑	245
Kankakee, IL	11.6	n.a.	282.3	512.1	806.0	1,549	3,557	532	5,638	24.32	⇑	270

Metro Area	Murder	Rape	Robbery	Assault	VIOLENT	Burglary	Theft	Auto Theft	PROPERTY	SCORE	TREND	RANK
Metro Area Average	6.9	40.0	161.2	390.3	558.3	1,241	3,405	460	5,106	50.00	⇓	
Kansas City, MO–KS	14.3	61.2	389.2	710.3	1,113.8	1,655	3,471	819	5,944	6.97	⇓	328
Kenosha, WI	3.6	41.9	98.4	157.0	258.9	925	3,429	289	4,643	78.79	⇓	91
Killeen–Temple, TX	9.8	80.3	97.2	377.7	484.7	1,118	2,892	245	4,255	64.32	⇓	143
Kitchener, ON	1.6	n.a.	56.8	116.8	175.2	1,271	3,316	302	4,889	82.54	⇑	74
Knoxville, TN	13.8	46.7	171.0	630.9	815.7	1,798	2,891	694	5,383	25.49	⇓	265
Kokomo, IN	1.6	29.1	49.2	314.3	365.1	691	2,655	183	3,529	79.13	⇓	86
✓ La Crosse, WI–MN	1.3	16.4	12.0	72.4	85.8	326	3,383	113	3,823	91.76	⇑	16
Lafayette, IN	1.8	27.9	28.1	208.6	238.5	631	3,354	177	4,161	83.10	⇓	70
Lafayette, LA	9.5	33.5	108.4	413.4	531.4	944	2,976	318	4,237	60.37	⇓	154
Lake Charles, LA	10.1	63.0	154.1	710.0	874.3	1,455	4,167	356	5,978	17.57	⇓	294
Lawton, OK	7.8	55.7	128.8	578.8	715.5	1,230	3,049	294	4,574	40.52	⇓	207
✓ Lewiston–Auburn, ME	1.5	25.9	47.6	89.8	138.9	922	2,695	153	3,770	89.96	⇔	32
Lexington, KY	7.7	48.1	154.6	569.3	731.7	1,076	3,586	256	4,918	36.05	⇓	227
Lima, OH	4.4	46.6	134.5	792.2	931.2	1,124	3,045	238	4,407	24.17	⇓	272
Lincoln, NE	2.6	47.3	63.0	424.4	490.1	1,077	5,365	219	6,660	42.00	⇓	203
Little Rock–North Little Rock, AR	17.3	79.2	317.4	924.9	1,259.6	1,862	4,969	671	7,501	1.48	⇓	344
London, ON	1.5	n.a.	63.9	218.4	283.9	1,358	4,416	404	6,178	65.06	⇑	139
Long Island, NY	3.2	8.7	128.9	137.6	269.7	727	2,091	616	3,434	85.41	⇑	56
Longview–Marshall, TX	11.4	66.9	129.6	527.4	668.3	1,472	3,544	407	5,424	37.15	⇑	221
Los Angeles–Long Beach, CA	20.1	42.0	708.6	932.0	1,660.7	1,324	2,778	1,390	5,492	0.42	⇑	347
Louisville, KY–IN	6.9	32.2	181.0	367.8	555.7	1,017	2,717	399	4,133	59.13	⇓	156
Lowell, MA–NH	3.9	37.3	136.9	613.4	754.2	964	1,937	885	3,786	44.12	⇔	199
Lubbock, TX	8.8	71.0	138.5	392.2	539.5	1,394	4,057	341	5,793	45.42	⇓	192
Lynchburg, VA	6.8	30.9	69.8	305.5	382.1	575	2,117	142	2,833	82.46	⇔	76
Macon, GA	13.8	44.2	160.5	338.9	513.2	1,347	4,197	424	5,968	46.22	⇑	190
Madison, WI	1.2	29.2	89.7	184.1	275.1	761	3,518	276	4,555	78.29	⇑	93
Manchester, NH	7.2	28.4	96.8	40.7	144.7	1,074	3,175	361	4,609	85.79	⇑	55
Mansfield, OH	2.2	42.8	101.3	685.3	788.8	1,187	3,015	219	4,422	35.38	⇓	232
McAllen–Edinburg–Mission, TX	8.3	24.0	90.1	471.7	570.1	1,911	3,956	714	6,581	35.64	⇓	229
Medford–Ashland, OR	3.0	49.4	49.0	299.8	351.8	901	3,850	263	5,013	69.11	⇓	125
Melbourne–Titusville–Palm Bay, FL	4.0	36.1	140.9	580.8	725.7	1,521	4,138	396	6,054	27.23	⇑	259
Memphis, TN–AR–MS	20.5	88.9	511.1	458.9	990.5	1,940	3,080	1,397	6,417	9.63	⇓	318
Merced, CA	7.5	38.3	96.5	370.0	474.0	1,409	2,772	464	4,645	61.83	⇓	151
Miami, FL	17.7	58.6	943.9	1095.9	2,057.5	2,538	6,399	1,922	10,859	0.00	⇑	351
Middlesex–Somerset–Hunterdon, NJ	1.8	14.5	92.5	155.8	250.1	685	2,349	401	3,435	86.41	⇑	49
Milwaukee–Waukesha, WI	11.1	39.1	311.3	150.5	472.9	884	3,343	982	5,209	56.91	⇑	165
Minneapolis–St. Paul, MN–WI	4.1	45.1	175.7	238.5	418.3	995	3,480	471	4,945	64.10	⇔	144
Mobile, AL	11.5	36.0	305.0	521.4	837.8	1,794	2,616	432	4,843	27.93	⇓	257
Modesto, CA	7.0	46.7	159.4	670.7	837.1	1,634	3,799	679	6,111	19.02	⇓	290

Metro Area	Murder	Rape	Robbery	Assault	VIOLENT	Burglary	Theft	Auto Theft	PROPERTY	SCORE	TREND	RANK
Metro Area Average	**6.9**	**40.0**	**161.2**	**390.3**	**558.3**	**1,241**	**3,405**	**460**	**5,106**	**50.00**	⇓	
Monmouth-Ocean, NJ	2.2	21.9	72.1	177.0	251.3	751	2,539	193	3,482	86.10	⇑	53
Monroe, LA	11.2	38.6	97.5	755.9	864.7	1,488	4,347	272	6,107	17.36	⇓	296
Montgomery, AL	14.2	46.4	208.1	502.8	725.1	1,554	3,171	409	5,134	34.75	⇓	236
Montreal, PQ	3.1	n.a.	294.3	177.4	474.8	1,910	3,198	1,000	6,108	48.44	⇑	184
Muncie, IN	6.6	33.8	75.8	159.7	242.1	1,122	2,160	261	3,542	86.28	⇔	51
Myrtle Beach, SC	11.7	61.3	182.6	652.5	846.7	2,128	5,380	485	7,993	9.11	⇓	320
Naples, FL	6.6	79.3	159.5	553.8	719.9	1,561	3,091	397	5,048	35.94	⇑	228
✓ Nashua, NH	2.3	43.9	25.7	41.8	69.8	474	1,933	216	2,623	95.58	⇑	2
Nashville, TN	10.4	70.7	278.3	676.4	965.1	1,350	3,730	561	5,640	14.37	⇓	302
New Bedford, MA	1.0	46.0	254.5	601.2	856.7	1,942	2,734	805	5,481	21.86	⇑	276
New Haven-Meriden, CT	6.6	33.5	296.8	375.4	678.8	1,305	3,464	880	5,648	34.31	⇑	240
New London-Norwich, CT-RI	8.3	29.8	84.3	199.3	291.9	739	2,026	171	2,936	86.82	⇑	46
New Orleans, LA	33.9	53.7	580.1	661.1	1,275.1	1,748	4,303	1,211	7,262	1.55	⇑	343
New York, NY	23.6	35.5	1072.5	780.6	1,876.8	1,314	3,151	1,515	5,979	0.06	⇑	349
Newark, NJ	8.6	39.7	531.9	417.3	957.8	1,076	2,444	1,469	4,989	18.49	⇔	291
Newburgh, NY-PA	4.3	22.2	97.7	284.0	386.1	717	2,122	149	2,988	81.27	⇑	79
Norfolk-Virginia Beach-Newport News, VA	13.1	48.6	269.8	285.8	568.7	1,052	4,029	500	5,580	44.67	⇑	196
Oakland, CA	13.8	46.0	407.8	571.4	993.0	1,375	3,918	889	6,182	10.49	⇓	314
Ocala, FL	8.5	65.4	233.8	804.6	1,046.9	1,708	3,595	322	5,625	10.56	⇑	313
Odessa-Midland, TX	9.9	64.7	118.2	428.3	556.4	1,777	5,098	372	7,246	31.21	⇑	246
Oklahoma City, OK	8.8	69.3	204.1	500.4	713.3	1,754	4,625	758	7,138	20.38	⇓	282
Olympia, WA	2.3	66.9	38.2	159.4	199.8	900	3,253	233	4,385	84.04	⇔	62
Omaha, NE-IA	5.2	39.4	128.5	455.1	588.9	900	3,252	494	4,646	51.44	⇓	173
Orange County, CA	6.8	24.7	227.0	287.6	521.5	1,139	3,058	839	5,037	54.02	⇑	170
Orlando, FL	5.5	49.3	255.2	764.0	1,024.7	1,922	4,114	620	6,656	7.54	⇓	326
Oshawa, ON	1.5	n.a.	62.3	171.5	235.3	1,091	2,635	366	4,093	83.67	⇑	65
Ottawa-Hull, ON-PQ	1.7	n.a.	146.3	149.5	297.5	1,525	4,097	707	6,329	62.55	⇓	149
Owensboro, KY	2.5	29.3	50.3	138.7	191.4	815	2,586	147	3,548	88.67	⇓	37
Panama City, FL	6.4	54.0	90.2	569.1	665.8	1,432	4,552	328	6,313	29.87	⇓	250
✓ Parkersburg-Marietta, WV-OH	3.6	30.8	22.1	132.3	158.1	548	1,923	134	2,604	93.37	⇓	9
Pensacola, FL	6.6	54.2	200.3	741.2	948.1	1,781	3,874	347	6,002	13.37	⇓	303
Peoria-Pekin, IL	5.3	n.a.	187.6	432.6	625.6	1,243	3,045	230	4,517	49.20	⇓	183
Philadelphia, PA-NJ	11.6	32.3	347.4	311.3	670.3	826	2,238	802	3,866	51.12	⇑	174
Phoenix-Mesa, AZ	9.8	39.3	200.6	514.5	724.8	1,729	3,590	1,135	6,453	24.29	⇑	271
Pine Bluff, AR	18.2	87.6	288.8	745.0	1,052.0	2,248	2,746	533	5,527	10.77	⇑	311
Pittsburgh, PA	4.1	28.8	159.4	204.2	367.6	601	1,617	579	2,797	83.52	⇑	66
Pittsfield, MA	1.8	16.3	42.7	347.5	392.0	895	1,593	224	2,712	82.59	⇑	72
Portland, ME	2.1	35.3	57.2	168.2	227.6	1,114	3,554	268	4,936	78.93	⇑	88
Portland-Vancouver, OR-WA	5.1	55.5	213.6	434.1	652.8	1,173	3,664	772	5,610	36.88	⇓	222
✓ Portsmouth-Rochester, NH-ME	2.6	31.7	22.7	46.1	71.4	557	1,972	284	2,813	95.11	⇑	3
Providence-Fall River-Warwick, RI-MA	3.9	30.3	110.7	281.0	395.6	1,081	2,466	770	4,316	71.19	⇑	119
✓ Provo-Orem, UT	.8	34.7	14.8	87.8	103.4	537	3,247	148	3,932	90.71	⇔	28
Pueblo, CO	7.7	75.5	124.9	1116.4	1,249.1	1,337	3,577	290	5,204	5.26	⇑	335
✓ Punta Gorda, FL	3.9	15.7	61.3	171.3	236.6	813	1,945	194	2,952	89.29	⇓	35
Quebec City, PQ	1.6	n.a.	155.6	91.0	248.1	1,782	3,082	521	5,385	74.31	⇑	111
Racine, WI	6.8	20.3	210.5	250.1	467.4	1,105	3,501	443	5,049	58.82	⇑	157

Metro Area	Murder	Rape	Robbery	Assault	VIOLENT	Burglary	Theft	Auto Theft	PROPERTY	SCORE	TREND	RANK
Metro Area Average	6.9	40.0	161.2	390.3	558.3	1,241	3,405	460	5,106	50.00	⇓	
Raleigh-Durham-Chapel Hill, NC	9.7	36.0	210.0	345.8	565.6	1,680	3,534	331	5,544	45.30	⇓	193
Rapid City, SD	2.8	104.1	50.6	294.0	347.4	825	4,115	230	5,170	68.19	⇓	128
Reading, PA	3.3	22.5	155.7	196.2	355.2	750	2,117	280	3,148	82.17	⇑	77
Redding, CA	6.3	64.0	85.8	329.4	421.5	1,274	2,927	373	4,574	66.97	⇓	130
Regina, SK	2.6	n.a.	129.5	348.0	480.0	2,926	5,331	562	8,819	24.92	⇑	268
Reno, NV	7.5	79.8	197.5	322.1	527.1	1,198	4,346	385	5,930	45.30	⇑	193
Richland-Kennewick-Pasco, WA	5.2	65.9	56.6	269.7	331.5	999	3,772	232	5,003	70.82	⇑	120
Richmond-Petersburg, VA	18.7	40.3	238.3	288.1	545.1	1,113	3,715	441	5,269	49.72	⇑	180
MI	8.6	58.0	169.5	596.4	774.5	1,013	3,227	225	4,466	36.24	⇑	225
St. Catharines-Niagara, ON	2.2	n.a.	47.6	160.7	210.5	1,540	3,158	399	5,096	78.99	⇑	87
St. Cloud, MN	2.0	27.2	14.1	77.1	93.2	2,424	2,382	185	4,991	86.48	⇑	48
Saint John, NB	2.3	n.a.	26.2	129.0	157.4	1,056	2,688	263	4,006	88.12	⇑	42
St. John's, NF	1.8	n.a.	36.7	132.6	171.1	1,000	2,747	255	4,002	87.51	⇑	44
St. Joseph, MO	3.0	31.0	48.1	369.8	421.0	990	3,572	249	4,811	65.03	⇑	140
St. Louis, MO-IL	16.4	149.3	290.0	539.5	845.9	1,282	3,156	624	5,062	25.62	⇓	264
Salem, OR	5.1	51.2	115.7	171.5	292.3	1,116	4,396	454	5,966	66.13	⇔	133
Salinas, CA	8.6	36.0	184.7	468.1	661.4	1,014	2,996	347	4,356	47.41	⇓	188
Salt Lake City-Ogden, UT	3.8	50.8	85.5	235.8	325.1	998	4,829	313	6,140	61.79	⇑	152
San Angelo, TX	6.5	56.2	45.3	517.4	569.2	1,230	3,814	199	5,243	47.73	⇑	186
San Antonio, TX	17.6	50.4	250.5	303.0	571.1	1,930	5,585	1,079	8,594	20.16	⇑	283
San Diego, CA	9.2	34.9	294.6	570.3	874.2	1,281	2,998	1,314	5,593	19.96	⇑	284
San Francisco, CA	9.4	35.2	531.7	441.9	982.9	1,029	3,672	953	5,654	13.37	⇑	303
San Jose, CA	4.2	40.9	118.5	361.5	484.2	770	2,961	437	4,168	65.10	⇔	137
San Luis Obispo-Atascadero-Paso Robles, CA	2.8	38.9	43.9	402.2	448.9	837	2,344	177	3,358	74.44	⇓	110
Santa Barbara-Santa Maria-Lompoc, CA	3.6	37.4	103.0	353.2	459.8	1,125	2,866	216	4,207	66.86	⇔	131
Santa Cruz-Watsonville, CA	3.9	33.5	121.1	466.6	591.6	1,163	3,895	329	5,387	44.35	⇓	197
Santa Fe, NM	5.5	18.5	79.8	791.9	877.2	1,253	1,765	262	3,280	37.64	⇓	220
Santa Rosa, CA	4.1	44.6	81.2	346.0	431.4	1,122	2,875	316	4,312	68.33	⇓	126
Sarasota-Bradenton, FL	5.3	42.5	207.0	615.0	827.3	1,835	4,111	396	6,342	18.19	⇔	293
Saskatoon, SK	3.5	n.a.	98.1	295.0	396.7	1,879	3,971	401	6,250	54.34	⇑	169
Savannah, GA	15.6	49.2	373.9	318.3	707.8	1,587	4,372	650	6,609	24.42	⇑	269
✓ Scranton-Wilkes-Barre-Hazleton, PA	2.5	45.4	40.4	165.1	207.9	462	1,441	170	2,073	93.46	⇔	8
Seattle-Bellevue-Everett, WA	4.9	68.2	193.1	309.7	507.8	1,149	4,436	641	6,226	44.35	⇑	197
✓ Sharon, PA	1.6	18.0	40.2	186.1	227.9	427	1,573	161	2,160	92.58	⇓	12
✓ Sheboygan, WI	.9	16.8	19.7	86.4	107.0	548	3,161	112	3,821	91.00	⇑	27
Sherbrooke, PQ	.5	n.a.	72.2	101.1	173.7	2,329	2,706	594	5,629	77.88	⇑	98
Sherman-Denison, TX	6.4	52.7	113.4	292.1	411.9	1,444	3,863	306	5,612	58.75	⇑	158
Shreveport-Bossier City, LA	21.0	49.7	267.1	620.6	908.7	1,749	4,893	503	7,145	9.99	⇓	317

Metro Area	Murder	Rape	Robbery	Assault	VIOLENT	Burglary	Theft	Auto Theft	PROPERTY	SCORE	TREND	RANK
Metro Area Average	6.9	40.0	161.2	390.3	558.3	1,241	3,405	460	5,106	50.00	⇓	
Sioux City, IA–NE	2.6	51.1	87.1	650.0	739.7	1,308	4,135	250	5,693	28.94	⇓	252
Sioux Falls, SD	2.0	65.6	28.9	221.1	251.9	618	2,710	127	3,454	86.21	⇓	52
South Bend, IN	8.7	55.7	192.6	253.1	454.4	1,564	4,121	379	6,064	50.76	⇓	176
Spokane, WA	3.8	42.2	121.0	301.7	426.5	1,320	4,298	324	5,941	54.46	⇓	168
Springfield, IL	5.9	n.a.	255.4	502.6	763.8	1,723	3,684	294	5,701	26.99	⇓	260
Springfield, MA	4.3	47.2	205.0	673.8	883.1	1,282	2,603	1,023	4,908	24.04	⇑	273
Springfield, MO	2.8	30.3	65.0	196.5	264.3	1,098	3,722	224	5,043	75.62	⇔	107
Stamford–Norwalk, CT	4.5	11.6	150.4	135.6	290.5	947	2,640	558	4,146	79.98	⇑	83
✓ State College, PA	.8	23.2	18.1	91.4	110.3	493	2,440	82	3,016	93.56	⇑	7
Steubenville–Weirton, OH–WV	2.9	8.6	31.8	328.0	362.6	482	1,112	125	1,719	89.18	⇓	36
Stockton–Lodi, CA	13.8	54.8	363.9	545.3	922.9	1,850	4,360	1,127	7,337	8.71	⇓	322
Sudbury, ON	3.2	n.a.	74.3	213.7	291.1	2,062	3,104	935	6,101	65.10	⇑	137
Sumter, SC	11.4	57.7	215.9	895.8	1,123.2	1,739	3,158	388	5,285	8.90	⇑	321
Syracuse, NY	3.1	25.0	96.2	161.9	261.3	829	2,569	155	3,554	85.22	⇑	58
Tacoma, WA	8.9	86.2	239.8	567.5	816.2	1,314	4,123	596	6,034	20.87	⇓	280
Tallahassee, FL	8.7	82.1	386.5	1094.4	1,489.6	2,642	5,730	867	9,238	0.09	⇑	348
Tampa–St. Petersburg–Clearwater, FL	7.3	54.0	327.4	863.1	1,197.8	1,722	4,217	819	6,758	3.14	⇑	340
✓ Terre Haute, IN	3.5	32.1	37.4	115.6	156.4	669	2,002	271	2,942	92.36	⇔	13
Texarkana, TX–Texarkana, AR	10.8	55.2	182.1	477.3	670.2	1,300	4,010	300	5,610	35.38	⇑	232
Thunder Bay, ON	2.8	n.a.	101.7	403.6	508.0	1,773	4,558	460	6,790	39.24	⇓	210
Toledo, OH	7.2	73.2	293.2	269.4	569.8	1,251	3,977	814	6,042	40.40	⇑	208
Topeka, KS	8.5	54.2	231.8	758.3	998.6	2,542	4,496	304	7,342	6.24	⇓	331
Toronto, ON	2.2	n.a.	140.3	208.2	350.7	986	3,313	411	4,710	71.63	⇑	116
Trenton, NJ	5.1	42.9	259.3	345.1	609.5	1,002	2,712	1,127	4,841	47.73	⇑	186
Trois–Rivieres, PQ	1.3	n.a.	89.3	126.4	217.1	1,615	2,811	518	4,944	79.56	⇑	85
Tucson, AZ	7.9	60.9	161.8	509.0	678.8	1,440	6,119	801	8,359	15.13	⇓	300
Tulsa, OK	7.9	61.4	198.7	541.0	747.6	1,497	2,743	892	5,132	32.85	⇑	241
Tuscaloosa, AL	8.2	51.4	192.9	712.9	914.0	1,381	5,309	356	7,047	10.19	⇔	315
Tyler, TX	11.0	81.0	154.0	499.3	664.3	1,695	4,629	524	6,848	25.85	⇓	262
✓ Utica–Rome, NY	4.0	22.9	61.8	120.4	186.2	693	2,094	133	2,920	91.40	⇓	22
Vallejo–Fairfield–Napa, CA	7.0	43.1	214.8	512.4	734.1	1,126	3,370	518	5,014	35.01	⇓	235
Vancouver, BC	3.5	n.a.	237.4	249.5	490.4	2,428	6,091	988	9,507	19.46	⇔	287
Ventura, CA	4.4	27.8	133.2	329.7	467.3	956	2,207	399	3,562	71.46	⇔	117
Victoria, BC	2.1	n.a.	131.5	237.2	370.7	1,554	5,417	419	7,389	46.26	⇔	189
Victoria, TX	7.8	42.1	133.5	696.2	837.5	1,766	4,243	337	6,346	17.57	⇔	294
Vineland–Millville–Bridgeton, NJ	8.6	62.7	278.2	576.6	863.4	1,516	3,575	404	5,494	21.33	⇓	277
Visalia–Tulare–Porterville, CA	10.1	40.7	125.2	544.9	680.1	1,384	3,236	557	5,177	38.29	⇔	216
Waco, TX	14.9	76.5	229.9	615.1	859.8	1,853	4,208	607	6,669	14.48	⇓	301
Washington, DC–MD–VA–WV	15.9	31.8	324.0	378.3	718.2	859	3,272	646	4,777	38.44	⇔	215
Waterbury, CT	6.6	29.9	179.3	204.1	389.9	1,468	3,423	877	5,767	59.33	⇑	155
Waterloo–Cedar Falls, IA	4.6	35.1	87.3	234.3	326.2	1,264	3,200	194	4,658	73.89	⇔	113
✓ Wausau, WI	.6	8.6	9.8	78.0	88.4	414	2,402	104	2,920	94.43	⇑	6
West Palm Beach–Boca Raton, FL	9.8	44.3	359.1	690.4	1,059.3	2,348	5,026	864	8,237	2.99	⇑	341
✓ Wheeling, WV–OH	2.9	19.3	40.0	119.4	162.3	540	1,213	161	1,914	95.09	⇓	4
Wichita, KS	8.3	63.7	293.2	313.0	614.5	1,711	4,172	650	6,533	32.28	⇓	242
Wichita Falls, TX	9.6	65.3	212.8	492.9	715.3	1,634	4,982	396	7,012	21.07	⇑	278

Metro Area	Murder	Rape	Robbery	Assault	VIOLENT	Burglary	Theft	Auto Theft	PROPERTY	SCORE	TREND	RANK
Metro Area Average	6.9	40.0	161.2	390.3	558.3	1,241	3,405	460	5,106	50.00	⇓	
✓ Williamsport, PA	1.6	19.2	55.1	105.9	162.6	633	1,975	129	2,737	92.83	⇓	10
Wilmington, NC	7.6	46.7	202.5	498.1	708.1	2,078	5,028	401	7,506	18.38	⇑	292
Wilmington-Newark, DE-MD	3.2	59.9	149.9	304.9	458.1	859	2,732	340	3,931	69.25	⇑	124
Windsor, ON	2.5	n.a.	76.9	161.6	241.0	1,274	3,629	325	5,228	75.96	⇑	103
Winnipeg, MB	2.6	n.a.	228.0	340.4	571.0	1,954	4,367	695	7,015	31.88	⇓	244
Worcester, MA-CT	2.6	36.4	143.1	129.5	275.2	1,142	1,990	641	3,773	83.22	⇓	69
Yakima, WA	5.7	80.2	118.5	435.9	560.1	1,929	4,998	438	7,365	29.91	⇑	249
Yolo, CA	5.9	49.3	109.8	396.9	512.7	1,378	4,581	627	6,586	40.63	⇓	206
✓ York, PA	3.2	22.8	75.6	99.9	178.7	516	2,339	147	3,002	91.37	⇔	23

Et Cetera

CAPITAL PUNISHMENT

In 1972, the U.S. Supreme Court struck down on Eighth Amendment grounds (forbidding cruel and unusual punishment) laws that permitted wide discretion in the application of the death penalty. In 1976, the court also struck down mandatory use of the death penalty for specified crimes but upheld laws that permitted executions after consideration of aggravating and mitigating circumstances. That same year, Canada abolished the death penalty entirely.

While the justice of capital punishment continues to be debated in state houses, courts, and in political campaigns throughout the United States, one thing is clear: Execution doesn't follow soon after a guilty verdict. In the 38 states with death penalty laws, half of the 3,000 convicted inmates have been on Death Row more than 3 years. Several recent executions have taken place 15 years after sentencing.

Supporters of capital punishment cite the huge financial burden the delays cost and point to the demographics of Death Row: All inmates are convicted murderers, two out of three have at least one prior felony conviction, nearly 10 percent have a prior murder conviction, and 40 percent were on bail, probation, or parole at the time of the murder.

The most compelling arguments against capital punishment are that it is barbaric and irreversible, that mistakes have and will be made, and that in many areas adequate legal defenses aren't provided. Moreover, a life sentence would cost a state one-third of the millions it spends seeing a typical death conviction through the extensive appeals process.

Death Penalty Differences

Twelve states and Canada have abandoned or avoided the death penalty in the modern age. Implementation in the 38 states that have it on their statutes is far from consistent.

Twenty-six states have executed convicted murderers in the years since capital punishment was reinstated. Among some 3,000 persons sentenced, fewer than 300 have been executed. Three out of five executions have taken place in Georgia, Florida, Louisiana, and Texas. New Hampshire and South Dakota have capital punishment statutes but have never imposed the sentence.

Methods of execution vary. Idaho and Utah offer the choice of receiving a lethal injection or facing a firing squad, the latter method a relic of nineteenth-century Mormonism requiring murderers to atone for their crime by having their blood spilled on the ground. Lethal injections and electrocution are the most common execution methods. Montana prescribes hanging as one of two acceptable methods.

NATIONAL AND REGIONAL CRIME RATES

With one-fourth the murder rate, one-third the robbery rate, and less than half the aggravated assault rate of the United States, Canada is a much less violent country

States with Death Penalties and Their Methods of Execution

Lethal Injection	Electrocution	Lethal Gas	Firing Squad	Hanging
Arizona *	Alabama	Arizona *	Idaho *	Montana *
Arkansas *	Arkansas *	California *	Utah *	
California *	Florida	Maryland		
Colorado	Georgia	Mississippi *		
Delaware	Indiana	North Carolina *		
Idaho *	Kentucky	Wyoming *		
Illinois	Nebraska			
Kansas	Ohio *			
Louisiana	South Carolina			
Mississippi *	Tennessee			
Missouri	Virginia *			
Montana *				
Nevada				
New Hampshire				
New Jersey				
New Mexico				
North Carolina *				
Ohio *				
Oklahoma				
Oregon				
Pennsylvania				
South Dakota				
Texas				
Utah *				
Virginia *				
Washington				
Wyoming *				

Source: NAACP Legal Defense and Educational Fund.
* Authorizes two methods of execution. New York recently reinstated the death penalty, but the method of execution is not specified.

than its southern neighbor. For all that, there are more burglaries in Canada per capita and a nearly identical rate for theft.

Although criminal activity varies from place to place and from year to year, regional patterns haven't changed much in decades. The murder rate in the West South Central states, where the frequency of people killing one another has traditionally been the country's highest, is nearly nine times that of Canada's Atlantic provinces. Armed robbery, a big-city crime, is highest in the Mid-Atlantic states, lowest again in the Atlantic provinces.

Criminologists recognize the geographic pattern of crime-ridden places immediately. The continent's more dangerous places are located on the East Coast south of Delaware Bay. This area is growing, and the resulting conditions of strangers living close together are strongly associated with crime.

There are other reasons for high crime in this area. Professional crooks travel to where the living is easy and the pickings bountiful; they don't stay in the industrial towns of the North but head South to warm weather and popular resorts. This is one factor behind Miami's decades-old crime image.

Finally, most of the more dangerous places are hot much of the year. Knowing what we do about climate's influence on crime, it isn't surprising that large southern cities going through a steamy summer are America's most violent. Persons bidding farewell to Cedar Rapids, Milwaukee, Pittsburgh, or Syracuse to make their new homes in Palm Beach, Orlando, Phoenix, or Las Vegas may need time not only for acclimatizing to warm weather, but also for getting used to crime's share in the local evening news.

DRUNK DRIVING

In a typical year, 1.6 million people are arrested for DUI/DWI. Drunk driving, as it's otherwise called, is the most common single cause of arrest in the United States and the penalties for the crime have gotten more severe. Most states and all provinces in Canada mandate license suspensions for first offenses, and license revocations and jail terms for repeat offenses. Three other ways of controlling the drunk driver come by means of legislation.

Blood-Alcohol Exceptions. The American Medical Association (AMA) says that anyone with a blood-alcohol (BAC) level of 0.05 percent is too drunk to drive. Above that threshold, the probability of a crash rises dramatically. For all that, most state law uses the 0.10 percent baseline, or twice the AMA standard. Fifteen states, including California with the highest number of drunk-driving arrests on the continent, have lowered the illegal *per se* BAC level to 0.08 percent. Canadian federal law

Regional Crime Rates

Region	Murder	Rape	Robbery	Assault	Burglary	Larceny-Theft	Motor Vehicle Theft
U.S. Average	**9.0**	**39.2**	**237.7**	**430.2**	**1,041.8**	**3,025.4**	**591.2**
New England: Connecticut, Maine, Massachusetts, New Hampshire, Rhode Island, Vermont	3.9	28.6	134.4	322.3	828.6	2,271.2	547.4
Mid-Atlantic: New Jersey, New York, Pennsylvania	8.2	25.7	345.9	342.5	795.3	2,282.5	616.9
Great Lakes: Illinois, Indiana, Michigan, Ohio, Wisconsin	8.4	44.2	230.6	373.4	898.2	2,888.7	507.8
Plains: Iowa, Kansas, Minnesota, Missouri, Nebraska, North Dakota, South Dakota	5.3	39.8	128.3	294.9	857.8	2,822.4	347.2
South Atlantic: Delaware, District of Columbia, Florida, Georgia, Maryland, North Carolina, South Carolina	10.1	41.2	254.4	524.4	1,271.4	3,569.9	585.2
Canadian Average	**2.3**	**n.a.**	**98.1**	**186.2**	**1,331.7**	**3,226.1**	**382.7**
Atlantic: New Brunswick, Newfoundland, Nova Scotia, Prince Edward Island	1.5	n.a.	20.7	107.0	814.2	1,121.7	173.1
East: Ontario, Quebec	2.4	n.a.	112.9	155.8	1,255.1	2,773.3	384.1
West: Alberta, British Columbia, Manitoba, Saskatchewan	2.9	n.a.	90.2	257.1	1,636.8	3,265.4	437.3

Source: FBI, *Crime in the United States,* 1995; Statistics Canada, *Canadian Crime Statistics,* 1995.

sets the threshold at 0.08 percent, but most of the provinces have gone further, lowering it to 0.05 percent.

Dram Shop Laws allow the last person and establishment to serve a drink to an intoxicated patron to be held responsible for the patron's actions immediately afterward. Victims of drunk drivers may sue not just the driver but also the bar owner, bartender, or party host who served the driver.

Happy Hour Prohibitions, a new form of server responsibility law, mean that drinking establishments cannot encourage excessive or immoderate consumption. Prohibitions against bars advertising a Happy Hour, selling two drinks for the price of one, or changing their prices at any time during the day is the law in Ontario and fifteen states.

Arizona
Illinois
Indiana
Kansas
Massachusetts
Missouri
Nebraska
New Jersey
New Mexico
Pennsylvania
Rhode Island
Tennessee
Texas
Utah
Vermont

HANDGUNS

Handgun control isn't a subject to be lightly entered into in conversation unless you have the time and are ready for a prolonged discussion.

Canada's 1992 gun control law, C-17, passed after the mass-murder of 14 young women on a Montreal campus, requires would-be buyers of rifles and shotguns to obtain a Firearms Acquisition Certificate (FAC), wait 28 days for background checks, and then undergo mandatory training in firearms use. All handguns are restricted weapons, available only to collectors and gun-club members after rigorous background checks.

In the United States, the controversy continues. Changes in regulations occur frequently from state to state and even within municipalities. The National Rifle Association, the fiercest defender of gun enthusiasts, attempts to keep its members informed of regulation changes with a regular publication of state-by-state gun purchase and carrying laws, but even this comes with a disclaimer warning of the constant changes. The variations in different states' restrictions can be immense, reflecting how well those who vehemently defend their weapons and those who would take them away have done their jobs in state legislatures.

DUI Laws
(Driving Under the Influence)

STATE	Blood Alcohol	Open Container	Anti-Consumption
Alabama	0.08		
Alaska	0.10	•	•
Alberta	0.05		
Arizona	0.10		•
Arkansas	0.10		•
British Columbia	0.05		
California	0.08	•	•
Colorado	0.10		•
Connecticut	0.10		
Delaware	0.10		•
District of Columbia	0.05	•	•
Florida	0.08	•	
Georgia	0.08	•	
Hawaii	0.08	•	•
Idaho	0.10	•	•
Illinois	0.10	•	
Indiana	0.10	•	•
Iowa	0.10	•	•
Kansas	0.08	•	•
Kentucky			•
Louisiana	0.10		
Maine	0.08	•	•
Manitoba	0.08		
Maryland	0.10		•
Massachusetts	0.08		•
Michigan	0.10	•	•
Minnesota	0.10	•	•
Mississippi	0.10		
Missouri	0.10		•
Montana	0.10		•
Nebraska	0.10		•
Nevada	0.10	•	•
New Brunswick	0.05		
New Hampshire	0.08	•	
New Jersey	0.10		•
New Mexico	0.08	•	•
New York	0.10		•
Newfoundland	0.05		
North Carolina	0.08	•	•
North Dakota	0.10	•	•
Nova Scotia	0.08		
Ohio	0.10	•	•
Oklahoma	0.10	•	•
Ontario	0.05		
Oregon	0.08	•	•
Pennsylvania	0.10		•
Prince Edward Island	0.05		
Quebec	0.08		
Rhode Island	0.10		
Saskatchewan	0.06		
South Carolina	0.10	•	•
South Dakota	0.10	•	
Tennessee	0.10	•	•
Texas	0.10		•
Utah	0.08	•	•
Vermont	0.08		•
Virginia	0.08		•
Washington	0.10	•	•
West Virginia	0.10		•
Wisconsin	0.10	•	
Wyoming	0.10		•

Source: Transport Canada, 1996; U.S. Department of Transportation, 1996.

State Restrictions on Purchase and Carrying of Handguns

	PURCHASE OF HANDGUNS				PROHIBITED		
	Instant Check	Federal Waiting Period	Permit to Purchase	Owner ID Card	Open Carry	Assault Weapons	Concealed Carry
Alabama		●			●		
Alaska		●					○
Arizona		●					
Arkansas		●			●		
California					●	●	●
Colorado	●						●
Connecticut					●	●	
Delaware	●						○
District of Columbia	●		●	●	●	●	●
Florida	●				●		
Maryland					●	●	●
Massachusetts			●	●	●		●
Michigan			●		●		●
Minnesota			●		●		●
Mississippi		●					
Missouri			●				●
Montana		●					
Nebraska	●						○
Nevada	●		●				○
New Hampshire	●						
New Jersey			●	●	●	●	●
New Mexico		●					○
New York			●	●	●	*	●
North Carolina			●				●
North Dakota		●			●		
Ohio		●	●	●		*	●
Oklahoma		●			●		○
Oregon							
Pennsylvania		●			●		
Rhode Island					●		●
South Carolina	●		●		●		●
South Dakota		●					
Tennessee					●		
Texas		●			●		●
Utah	●				●		
Vermont		●			●		
Virginia	●		●			●	
Washington		●					
West Virginia		●					○
Wisconsin	●						●
Wyoming		●					

Source: National Rifle Association.
A bullet ● indicates state law. Under the prohibited concealed carry column, a bullet indicates extremely restrictive state laws and a hollow bullet ○ indicates moderately restrictive state laws. *Many cities ban assault weapons in the absence of similar state legislation. Since state laws are subject to frequent change, this chart is not to be considered legal advice or a restatement of the law.

Most people would exchange any worn-out city for a serene place that's safer, cheaper, and less crowded. The escape to a smaller place is a sustaining dream for big-city residents, according to opinion polls.

You might even pack up and make your own break if the chance arrives in the form of a job transfer, a mid-life change, or retirement. You may be pleased to discover that towns with courthouse squares, angle parking, and kids riding two-wheelers on streets actually named Main still exist. You might write home that you'd finally found a sense of cohesion, of continuity and tradition, of community spirit and neighborliness that you thought had vanished. You're happier than you've been in years.

For about four months.

Because in your headlong rush to abandon the aggravations of big-city life, you abandoned the classic marble art museum you barely glanced at in passing twice each day in the crush of commuter traffic. You left behind a library system with a generous budget not just for books, but for software, videos, compact-disc recordings, and fascinating lectures and exhibits. You also turned your back on the local newspaper's arts section, the local public television station's earnest fundraising auctions, and your annual subscription to the repertory theater's season.

Of all the factors that coalesce into quality of life, the one called the arts inevitably improves with the size of the city. The likelihood of professional sports teams, zoological gardens, and amusement parks being found improves with population size, too. Many of the most valuable recreation assets—lakes, hiking trails, forests, campgrounds—are found far from cities; indeed, they *must* be far from cities. The arts alone are big-city phenomena.

Places Rated's top two metro areas for the arts are New York and Washington. This isn't to say that culture cannot be found in smaller metro areas. Although it is safe to assume that the larger a metro area is, the more artistic and cultural amenities it will possess, there are exceptions.

TUNING IN TO CONCERT RADIO

While album rock, oldies, and country dominate FM radio formats, nearly 8 of every 100 hours of FM listening in New York and Toronto is classical music. Metropolitan audiences can tune in to music aired around the clock by 447 concert format (classical) radio stations. Forty-six of these stations with the biggest share of the fine-arts audience (CFMX-FM in Toronto or WCRB-FM in Boston, for example) are commercial operations, but most belong to National Public Radio or the CBC in Canada. The cities of license for nearly all are within 238 metro areas; 35 metro areas have two stations, and 19 have three or more.

THE LIVELY ARTS CALENDAR

The cultural side of urban life might be divided into two categories: possessions and performances. Collected art on museum walls and books on a public library's shelves belong in the first group. The lively arts—symphony, opera, dance, and theater—belong in the second.

Despite the competition, the audience's increasingly precious leisure time, rolling economic recessions, and the drop in government arts funding, the lively arts continue to endure. This isn't the case everywhere, however.

In recent years, the Nashville Symphony filed for bankruptcy, the Oklahoma and New Orleans symphonies closed for good, and Montreal's, Toronto's, and Vancouver's orchestras went on life-support. Most professional theaters are operating in the red. The Joffrey Ballet, going broke in New York, moved to less expensive Chicago. Other major ballet companies have merged or formed partnerships—Cleveland's with San Jose's, Tulsa's with Knoxville's—to cut costs, ensure a

Operatic Chestnuts

Ten operas accounted for nearly one-third of all performances during the latest season. By number of productions, they were:

Barber of Seville, 17
Tosca, 15
La Traviata, 15
Le Boheme, 14
The Marriage of Figaro, 13
Carmen, 13
The Magic Flute, 13
Lucia di Lammermoor, 12

are endangered.

Touring Artists Bookings

Long before the Brassissimo Vienna, Harlem Spiritual Ensemble, or Borealis Wind Quintet comes to town for a date at the local performing arts center, they are booked by a college or nonprofit community concert association.

Filling the concert halls with classical artists, big business for agents and presenters in former times, is getting tougher and less fun. In spite of 1990s marketing twists like rush-hour recitals, sound clips on the Internet, park concerts, tie-ins with art exhibits, celebrity narrators, and free kids' admission, younger audiences are demanding more popular entertainment.

Opera

Opera fans boast that their passion embraces the greatest of the performing arts, since it combines a love for orchestral music, vocal music, theater, and dance. The first grand opera performed in this country was Rossini's *The Barber of Seville,* at New York's Park Theater in 1825. To this day, New York remains America's operatic capital, though the art form has been diffused throughout the continent. From 650 performing groups in the late 1970s, opera has expanded to nearly 1,000 professional and amateur groups, reaching an audience of 20 million during the 1995-1996 season.

Some of these performing groups are college and university workshops, others local clubs and choruses. But 152 are companies with annual budgets topping $250,000. Full-scale opera productions using professional orchestras and bringing the world's leading singers to the stage aren't cheap tickets, and most metro areas haven't the resources or audiences to support this singular form of the lively arts.

is the center for great dance. America's top companies are here, including the New York City Ballet, the American Ballet Theater, the Alvin Ailey American Dance Theater, the Martha Graham Company, the Merce Cunningham Dance Company, the Paul Tayler Dance Company, and the Dance Theater of Harlem.

In the 1960s, Rudolf Nureyev heralded a boom in ballet when he jumped the fence from Russia to the West. He showed how athletic dance could be, and suddenly it was socially acceptable for teenage boys to join dance classes. The growth decade for dance was the 1970s, when touring New York dance troupes spread the gospel to new audiences. The charisma of another Russian émigré—Mikhail Baryshnikov, later the artistic director of the American Ballet Theater—helped consolidate the popularity of dance.

North America has a number of well-established dance companies. The New York City Ballet and Toronto's National Ballet of Canada are pushing fifty, and Seattle's Pacific Northwest Ballet is twenty-five. Unlikely as it may seem, the ballet company of Dayton, OH, is older than all three, at well over half a century.

Symphony Orchestras

"The greatest instrument ever invented," Andre Previn once called the symphony. Of course, it is really a collection of many different instruments and musicians. The original definition—"to sound together," from the Greek—is just vague enough to embrace all the ensembles playing some type of symphonic music today in America.

In all, there are some 1,500 groups, ranging in size and experience from youths playing before captive audiences of parents to accomplished and well-paid professionals working under the baton of Kurt Masur at the New York Philharmonic. Orchestras are far from uncommon in metro areas: 276 metro areas claim at least one. Thirty-six of these places support four or more orchestras, and fourteen metro areas support eight or more.

Professional Theater

Long known as the "fabulous invalid," theater continues to hold its own despite perennial predictions of its demise. In *Huckleberry Finn,* Mark Twain described two scamsters who arrive in a small Arkansas town and tout a theatrical production pompously titled the "Royal Nonesuch." The performance consisted of an actor, wearing bright body paint but nothing else, streaking across the stage to the delight and outrage of the audience.

The history of American theater is a blend of the grand and comic. Its many forms have encompassed Shakespeare, vaudeville, and Broadway musicals, and its first challenge came with silent movies at the century's turn, when the number of legitimate theaters fell from 1,500 to 500. In the 1920s, a resurgence took place on Broadway, which opened more than 400 new theaters in less than a decade. In the 1950s, off-Broadway grew in response to overcommercialized mainstream theater.

Broadway was once the center of American theater. It alone established what was successful and then sent its hits on the road to the provinces. New York still has the greatest concentration of theaters, yet a number of regional theaters are now recognized for their vigor and innovation, including the Arena Stage in Washington, DC, the Guthrie in Minneapolis, MN, and the Trinity Rep in Providence, RI.

Theatrical Chestnuts

North American Professional theater plays to an audience of 18 million people. Some 2,300 unique plays—fringe to avant garde to Shakespeare—see nearly 50,000 performances. The following 13 plays were the most produced in the latest season.

A Christmas Carol, 43
Lend Me a Tenor, 24
Shirley Valentine, 17
Other People's Money, 16
Love Letters, 15
A Midsummer Night's Dream, 14
Twelfth Night, 13
Prelude to a Kiss, 13
Lips Together, Teeth Apart, 13
The Cocktail Hour, 12
I Hate Hamlet, 12
My Children! My Africa!, 12
The Mystery of Irma Vep, 12

Source: Theatre Communications Group.

On another level are the fringe theater groups across the continent, surviving on a shoestring, or disappearing only to be replaced by others. Some of the productions undoubtedly make Twain's "Royal Nonesuch" seem like great theater. Yet the appeal of small theater is that you may be happily surprised by its spunk and sense of craft. It's worth quoting the self-description of Germinal Stage Denver, a group that calls itself "the runt stepchild of regional theaters, a mom-and-pop store of Thespis, a vestige of the little theater movement masquerading as an institution. In 13 years, we've gone through several periods of artistic coherence, but these days we're just trying to do the best plays we can, as well as we can, without talking too much about it."

ART MUSEUMS AND GALLERIES

In ancient Greece, it wasn't just the devoutly religious who visited temples; uninvited tourists also stole in to admire the statues and paintings. In revolutionary France, artists had their daily exclusive run of the Louvre in order to copy the great works of the past. But on infrequent public days, the peasants, prostitutes, soldiers, and common laborers came in great numbers. To this day, going to an art museum has something of the democratic, the sacred, and the carnival to it.

The first great North American art museums were founded in Montreal in 1860, and in Boston and New York 10 years later. New York now has more art museums than any other city on the continent, and the Metropolitan Museum, with almost five million visitors a year, is its most popular tourist attraction.

To qualify for inclusion in *Places Rated,* the American Association of Museums' requirements are as solid as any: "an organized and permanent nonprofit institution, essentially educational or aesthetic in purpose, with professional staff, which owns and utilizes tangible objects, cares for them, and exhibits them to the public on some regular schedule."

THE PUBLIC LIBRARY: SOMETHING FOR EVERYONE

Every metro area, no matter how small, poor, or isolated, has a network of public libraries. More than any of the different arts institutions mentioned above, libraries are vital centers and ultimate cultural resources for everyone.

Again, New York. Within the five boroughs and suburban Putnam, Rockland, and Westchester counties are five library systems acquiring 2 million books each year to add to the 36 million already housed in 276 libraries. Immense as these amenities are, that's one new book for every five people. Other metro areas do better; small ones in the inner South and in Texas do a lot worse.

What Are the Arts, Anyway?

"We know what culture is," says a Sharon, PA, newspaper editor. "We find it in our refrigerators every week." Although people can't get together on a single definition, or even on one element that culture shares, it's possible to name certain things about art that seem to ring true. For example, the following two lists draw a distinction that most would recognize:

Definitely Art	Possibly Art
anything by Shakespeare	comic books
ballet	folk music, blues, jazz

The Most Popular Art Museums

Twenty-four North American art museums are visited by at least one-half million people each year.

Museum	Attendance
National Gallery of Art Washington, DC	6,500,000
Metropolitan Museum of Art New York, NY	4,700,000
Art Institute of Chicago Chicago, IL	1,300,000
Los Angeles County Museum of Art Los Angeles, CA	1,000,000
Hirshhorn Museum & Sculpture Garden Washington, DC	908,000
New York State Museum	900,000
Saint Louis Art Museum St. Louis, MO	650,000
Walker Art Center Minneapolis, MN	650,000
Philadelphia Museum of Art Philadelphia, PA	600,000
Arthur M. Sackler Gallery Washington, DC	500,000
Cleveland Museum of Art Cleveland, OH	500,000
High Museum of Art Atlanta, GA	500,000
The Huntington Los Angeles–Long Beach, CA	500,000
Indianapolis Museum of Art Indianapolis, IN	500,000
National Gallery of Canada Ottawa, ON	500,000
National Museum of African Art Washington, DC	500,000
National Museum of American Art Washington, DC	500,000
Oakland Museum Oakland, CA	500,000
Whitney Museum of American Art New York, NY	500,000

Source: American Art Directory, 1996; Places Rated research.

SCORING: THE ARTS

Let's admit the point that it isn't possible to rank metro areas in the arts with total fairness. But let's also point out that some areas seem shortchanged while others have riches and all can be compared using arts-related data elements. *Places Rated* considers fourteen.

For **Art Museums and Galleries** these are: (1) number of art museums, (2) annual museum attendance, and (3) per capita museum attendance. For **The Lively Arts Calendar** they include: (4) annual ballet performances, (5) touring artist bookings, (6) opera performances, (7) professional theater performances, and (8) symphony performances. For **Public Libraries** add: (9) number of people served by libraries, (10) percent of total population served by libraries, (11) total library books, (12), number of library books per capita, (13) annual library circulation, and (14) library circulation per capita.

This embraces a lot of information. Off the bat, you might wonder whether they are more than needed because many go hand in hand with one another. In the language of statistics, they are correlated.

Take two: number of art museums on the one hand and museum attendance on the other. Big places like New York and Toronto tend to have many art museums and big crowds of people visiting them. Smaller places like Rapid City, SD, or Yakima, WA, tend to have fewer art museums, and fewer people buying tickets as well. In other words, if you know something about the number of art museums in a city, you also know something about how many visitors stand behind velvet cordons looking at the exhibits.

So the two pieces of information we started with—number of art museums and museum attendance—could actually be reduced to just one piece of information. To go a step further, we don't really need all fourteen data elements that we've collected about each metro area to rate their relative strength in the arts: fewer pieces of information will do.

How much can be eliminated? How many pieces of information are enough? Enter *factor analysis,* a mathematical procedure that systematically reduces many pieces of information about a set of items (here, pieces of arts information about a set of metro areas) to fewer pieces of information, called "factors." Each factor embodies one or more of the original pieces of information.

For the arts, factor analysis uncovered three critical things. In decreasing order of importance, they are (1) what might be called "bigness," which takes in number of art museums; total museum attendance; number of ballet, touring artist, opera, and symphony performances; number of people served by libraries; total library books; and total library circulation.

Call the second factor "reading popularity." This embodies the percent of total population served by libraries, number of library books per capita, and library circulation per capita. Call the final factor "museum popularity," which takes in per capita museum attendance.

Factor analysis produces a score for each metro area on each factor. New York, Los Angeles, and Chicago ought to be the best in bigness, and they are. Las Vegas with one million people and Daytona Beach with almost a half million people should do well in bigness, but they don't. Small places like Washington's state capital, Olympia, or St. Cloud near the Minnesota twin cities, or Stamford–Norwalk outside New York, are tops in reading popularity while places in the sun belt touch the bottom. For the highest museum popularity score, Santa Fe edges out Washington, DC.

To arrive at a final score, each metro area's scores for *bigness, reading popularity,* and *museum popularity* are weighted by their relative importance. A metro area's final score is its percentile on a scale of 0 to 100 corresponding to its weighted average. New York's score is 100; Lexington–Fayette, KY's is 50.01; and Las Vegas's is 0.00. They are respectively the best, average, and worst North American metro areas in the arts.

RANKINGS: The Arts

Fourteen data elements are used to derive a metro area's score for the arts. Using a factor analysis technique, these are grouped into three broad factors: (1) *bigness,* (2) *reading popularity,* and (3) *museum popularity.* Places that are tied get the same rank and are listed in alphabetical order.

Metro Areas from Best to Worst

Places Rated Rank		Places Rated Score
1.	New York, NY	99.99
2.	Washington, DC–MD–VA–WV	99.87
3.	Los Angeles–Long Beach, CA	99.84
4.	Chicago, IL	99.81
5.	Toronto, ON	99.72
6.	Boston, MA–NH	99.42
7.	Philadelphia, PA–NJ	99.15
8.	Baltimore, MD	98.89
9.	Long Island, NY	98.85
10.	San Francisco, CA	98.59
11.	Cleveland–Lorain–Elyria, OH	98.25
12.	Montreal, PQ	98.21
13.	Minneapolis–St. Paul, MN–WI	97.96
14.	Newark, NJ	97.54
15.	Oakland, CA	97.50
16.	Seattle–Bellevue–Everett, WA	96.87
17.	Detroit, MI	96.60
18.	St. Louis, MO–IL	96.04
19.	Atlanta, GA	95.97
20.	San Jose, CA	95.76
21.	Hartford, CT	95.67
22.	Orange County, CA	95.01
23.	Vancouver, BC	94.58
24.	Buffalo–Niagara Falls, NY	94.01
25.	Dallas, TX	93.32
26.	Houston, TX	93.19
27.	Milwaukee–Waukesha, WI	92.98
28.	Pittsburgh, PA	92.68
29.	Cincinnati, OH–KY–IN	92.35
30.	Columbus, OH	91.71
31.	Miami, FL	91.69
32.	Riverside–San Bernardino, CA	91.25
33.	Indianapolis, IN	91.03
34.	Phoenix–Mesa, AZ	90.95
35.	Denver, CO	90.70
36.	San Diego, CA	90.59
37.	Middlesex–Somerset–Hunterdon, NJ	90.28
38.	Honolulu, HI	89.98
39.	Bergen–Passaic, NJ	89.76
40.	Tampa–St. Petersburg–Clearwater, FL	88.77
41.	Salt Lake City–Ogden, UT	88.40
42.	Kansas City, MO–KS	86.98
43.	Olympia, WA	86.56
44.	Stamford–Norwalk, CT	85.90
45.	Portland–Vancouver, OR–WA	85.47
46.	Calgary, AB	84.44
47.	Fort Lauderdale, FL	84.32
48.	Dayton–Springfield, OH	83.56
49.	Monmouth–Ocean, NJ	82.89
50.	Charlotte–Gastonia–Rock Hill, NC–SC	82.43
51.	Richmond–Petersburg, VA	81.77
52.	New Haven–Meriden, CT	81.11
53.	Raleigh–Durham–Chapel Hill, NC	80.99
54.	Toledo, OH	80.77
55.	Fort Worth–Arlington, TX	80.16
56.	Barnstable–Yarmouth, MA	79.68
57.	St. Cloud, MN	79.53
58.	Tacoma, WA	79.49
59.	Norfolk–Virginia Beach–Newport News, VA–NC	79.35
60.	Winnipeg, MB	79.22
61.	Orlando, FL	79.03
62.	Fort Wayne, IN	78.75
63.	Rochester, NY	78.10
64.	Hamilton, ON	77.85
65.	Edmonton, AB	77.14
66.	Omaha, NE–IA	75.57
67.	Fargo–Moorhead, ND–MN	75.21
68.	Canton–Massillon, OH	75.15
69.	Akron, OH	74.33
70.	Syracuse, NY	74.09
71.	Ottawa–Hull, ON–PQ	73.97
72.	Trenton, NJ	73.68
73.	New Orleans, LA	73.28
74.	Gary, IN	73.07
75.	Saskatoon, SK	72.34
76.	Albany–Schenectady–Troy, NY	72.06
77.	Benton Harbor, MI	71.82
78.	Madison, WI	71.65
79.	Louisville, KY–IN	71.06
80.	Nashville, TN	70.93

Places Rated Rank		Places Rated Score
81.	Jacksonville, FL	70.86
82.	Bridgeport, CT	70.83
83.	Providence–Fall River–Warwick, RI–MA	70.75
84.	Grand Rapids–Muskegon–Holland, MI	70.57
85.	St. Catharines–Niagara, ON	69.98
86.	West Palm Beach–Boca Raton, FL	69.92
87.	Oklahoma City, OK	69.77
88.	Jamestown, NY	69.60
89.	Bismarck, ND	69.54
90.	Albuquerque, NM	69.31
101.	London, ON	63.77
102.	Spokane, WA	63.02
103.	Jersey City, NJ	62.44
104.	Wilmington–Newark, DE–MD	59.82
105.	Memphis, TN–AR–MS	59.70
106.	Lawrence, MA–NH	59.48
107.	Boulder–Longmont, CO	59.13
108.	Victoria, BC	58.85
109.	Pittsfield, MA	58.46
110.	Lincoln, NE	58.42
111.	New London–Norwich, CT–RI	58.39
112.	Grand Forks, ND–MN	58.26
113.	Jackson, TN	58.20
114.	Ann Arbor, MI	57.84
115.	Scranton–Wilkes-Barre–Hazleton, PA	57.21
116.	Greenville–Spartanburg–Anderson, SC	57.09
117.	Bellingham, WA	57.05
118.	Peoria–Pekin, IL	57.00
119.	Quebec City, PQ	56.61
120.	Tucson, AZ	56.59
121.	Knoxville, TN	56.25
122.	Halifax, NS	56.10
123.	Santa Rosa, CA	56.09
124.	Kalamazoo–Battle Creek, MI	55.95
125.	Vallejo–Fairfield–Napa, CA	55.93
126.	Greenville, NC	55.81
127.	Columbia, SC	55.78
128.	Youngstown–Warren, OH	55.76
129.	Ventura, CA	55.65
130.	Bangor, ME	55.40
131.	Tulsa, OK	55.32
132.	Birmingham, AL	55.07
133.	South Bend, IN	54.76
134.	Clarksville–Hopkinsville, TN–KY	54.71
135.	Colorado Springs, CO	54.69
136.	Sheboygan, WI	54.21
137.	Macon, GA	54.20

Places Rated Rank		Places Rated Score
138.	Charleston–North Charleston, SC	54.10
139.	San Antonio, TX	54.07
140.	Danbury, CT	54.01
141.	Des Moines, IA	53.96
142.	Columbia, MO	53.59
143.	Charlottesville, VA	53.55
144.	Janesville–Beloit, WI	52.78
145.	Davenport–Moline–Rock Island, IA–IL	52.52
146.	Portland, ME	52.51
147.	Gainesville, FL	52.35
148.	Melbourne–Titusville–Palm	
156.	Champaign–Urbana, IL	50.68
157.	Lexington, KY	50.65
158.	Mansfield, OH	50.48
159.	St. Joseph, MO	50.24
160.	Parkersburg–Marietta, WV–OH	50.23
161.	Salinas, CA	50.12
162.	Provo–Orem, UT	50.00
163.	Fitchburg–Leominster, MA	49.44
164.	Trois-Rivieres, PQ	49.35
165.	Windsor, ON	49.30
166.	Santa Barbara–Santa Maria–Lompoc, CA	49.24
167.	Rochester, MN	49.22
168.	Kokomo, IN	49.04
169.	Charleston, WV	48.02
170.	Wichita, KS	47.81
171.	Hamilton–Middletown, OH	47.56
172.	Roanoke, VA	47.53
173.	Nashua, NH	47.38
174.	Eugene–Springfield, OR	47.31
175.	Appleton–Oshkosh–Neenah, WI	47.06
176.	Augusta–Aiken, GA–SC	46.61
177.	Las Vegas, NV–AZ	46.05
178.	Lima, OH	46.03
179.	Jackson, MS	45.17
180.	Wheeling, WV–OH	44.92
181.	Lansing–East Lansing, MI	44.83
182.	Topeka, KS	44.78
183.	Elmira, NY	44.64
184.	Dutchess County, NY	44.62
185.	Bloomington, IN	44.53
186.	Mobile, AL	44.28
187.	Binghamton, NY	43.87
188.	Daytona Beach, FL	43.68
189.	Dubuque, IA	43.67
190.	Lafayette, IN	43.63
191.	Harrisburg–Lebanon–Carlisle, PA	43.47

Places Rated Rank		Places Rated Score
192.	Baton Rouge, LA	43.22
193.	Sioux Falls, SD	42.45
194.	Fort Myers–Cape Coral, FL	42.42
195.	Savannah, GA	42.37
196.	Asheville, NC	42.23
197.	Rockford, IL	42.15
198.	Manchester, NH	42.07
199.	Decatur, IL	42.04
200.	Flint, MI	41.94
201.	Little Rock–North Little Rock, AR	41.81
202.	Greeley, CO	41.62
203.	Eau Claire, WI	[illegible]
212.	Elkhart–Goshen, IN	40.22
213.	Medford–Ashland, OR	40.10
214.	Fort Collins–Loveland, CO	40.07
215.	Shreveport–Bossier City, LA	39.93
216.	Green Bay, WI	39.52
217.	Erie, PA	39.44
218.	Racine, WI	39.29
219.	Atlantic City–Cape May, NJ	39.18
220.	Boise City, ID	38.95
221.	Springfield, IL	38.69
222.	Athens, GA	38.57
223.	Bloomington–Normal, IL	38.53
224.	Stockton–Lodi, CA	38.50
225.	Brockton, MA	37.88
226.	Bremerton, WA	37.32
226.	Sioux City, IA–NE	37.32
228.	Huntington–Ashland, WV–KY–OH	37.30
229.	Hagerstown, MD	36.59
230.	Amarillo, TX	36.58
231.	Vineland–Millville–Bridgeton, NJ	36.36
232.	Kenosha, WI	36.15
233.	Springfield, MO	35.99
234.	New Bedford, MA	35.97
235.	Anniston, AL	35.95
236.	Fresno, CA	35.82
237.	Albany, GA	35.53
238.	Pueblo, CO	35.05
239.	Waterbury, CT	35.02
240.	Hickory–Morganton–Lenoir, NC	34.99
241.	Glens Falls, NY	34.72
242.	Steubenville–Weirton, OH–WV	34.10
243.	Fayetteville, NC	33.69
244.	Biloxi–Gulfport–Pascagoula, MS	33.55
245.	Utica–Rome, NY	33.48
246.	Gadsden, AL	33.45
247.	Newburgh, NY–PA	33.39
248.	Fort Pierce–Port St. Lucie, FL	32.85

Places Rated Rank		Places Rated Score
249.	San Luis Obispo–Atascadero–Paso Robles, CA	32.22
250.	Anchorage, AK	32.12
251.	Naples, FL	32.09
252.	Oshawa, ON	31.99
253.	San Angelo, TX	31.45
254.	Yakima, WA	31.26
255.	Terre Haute, IN	31.03
256.	Reading, PA	31.00
257.	Lancaster, PA	30.98
258.	Abilene, TX	30.71
258.	St. John's, NF	30.71
260.	Grand Junction, CO	30.58
261.	Jackson, MI	30.57
262.	Monroe, LA	29.85
263.	Cheyenne, WY	29.75
264.	State College, PA	29.33
265.	Lawrence, KS	29.24
266.	Beaumont–Port Arthur, TX	28.66
267.	Williamsport, PA	28.37
268.	Flagstaff, AZ–UT	28.34
269.	Lafayette, LA	28.13
270.	Reno, NV	28.04
271.	Huntsville, AL	27.73
272.	Galveston–Texas City, TX	27.61
273.	Rocky Mount, NC	27.48
274.	Modesto, CA	27.40
275.	Columbus, GA–AL	27.39
276.	Tallahassee, FL	27.20
277.	Decatur, AL	27.07
278.	Saint John, NB	26.71
279.	Cumberland, MD–WV	26.45
280.	Lynchburg, VA	25.93
281.	Wausau, WI	25.64
282.	Richland–Kennewick–Pasco, WA	25.28
283.	Johnstown, PA	25.19
283.	Sherman–Denison, TX	25.19
285.	Yolo, CA	24.67
286.	Bakersfield, CA	24.54
287.	Corpus Christi, TX	23.89
288.	Brazoria, TX	23.80
289.	Wilmington, NC	23.45
290.	El Paso, TX	23.43
291.	Pensacola, FL	23.22
292.	Billings, MT	23.17
293.	Myrtle Beach, SC	23.07
294.	Sherbrooke, PQ	22.79
295.	Visalia–Tulare–Porterville, CA	22.26
296.	Lubbock, TX	21.82
297.	Montgomery, AL	21.65
297.	Odessa–Midland, TX	21.65
299.	Altoona, PA	21.27
300.	Great Falls, MT	20.85
301.	Longview–Marshall, TX	20.41
302.	Sudbury, ON	20.19
303.	Danville, VA	20.01
304.	Waco, TX	19.44
305.	Owensboro, KY	19.20
306.	Tuscaloosa, AL	18.90
307.	Burlington, VT	18.44
308.	McAllen–Edinburg–Mission, TX	18.21
309.	York, PA	18.09
310.	Muncie, IN	17.99
311.	Lake Charles, LA	17.67
312.	Merced, CA	17.32
313.	Pine Bluff, AR	17.29
314.	Wichita Falls, TX	17.10
315.	Chico–Paradise, CA	16.89
316.	Houma, LA	16.38
317.	Lewiston–Auburn, ME	16.31
318.	Panama City, FL	15.70
319.	Yuba City, CA	15.24
320.	Rapid City, SD	15.10
321.	Chattanooga, TN–GA	15.02
322.	Victoria, TX	14.98
323.	Florence, AL	14.21
324.	Ocala, FL	14.02
325.	Punta Gorda, FL	13.93
326.	Goldsboro, NC	13.83
327.	Chicoutimi–Jonquiere, PQ	13.78
328.	Enid, OK	13.69
329.	Fayetteville–Springdale–Rogers, AR	13.57
330.	Florence, SC	12.98
331.	Redding, CA	12.49
332.	Sumter, SC	11.66
333.	Dothan, AL	11.14
334.	Joplin, MO	10.19
335.	Bryan–College Station, TX	9.56
336.	Jacksonville, NC	9.30
337.	Kankakee, IL	9.09
338.	Yuma, AZ	8.04
339.	Brownsville–Harlingen–San Benito, TX	6.54
340.	Dover, DE	4.11
341.	Fort Smith, AR–OK	3.86
342.	Sharon, PA	1.67
343.	Lakeland–Winter Haven, FL	1.63
344.	Laredo, TX	1.60
345.	Killeen–Temple, TX	1.35
346.	Lawton, OK	1.00
347.	Texarkana, TX–Texarkana, AR	0.65
348.	Hattiesburg, MS	0.13
349.	Las Cruces, NM	0.02
350.	Tyler, TX	0.01
351.	Fort Walton Beach, FL	0.00

PLACE PROFILES: The Arts

The profiles that follow are divided into four headings and show cultural and artistic features in each metro area.

Under the first heading, **Concert Radio,** are concert radio stations whose city of license is within the metro area. Concert radio stations are stations with all or a significant part of their programming dedicated to a classical music format. For powerful radio stations, programming may also be received in nearby metro areas. In these instances, the media market defined by A. C. Nielsen Ratings Service in the U.S. or the Bureau of Broadcast Measurement in Canada is listed for the metro area that receives fine arts broadcasting from another area.

The **Lively Arts Calendar** heading encompasses the total number of touring artist bookings at local campus and civic auditoriums and the names of resident symphony orchestras, opera companies, professional theaters, and ballet companies.

Under the heading **Art Museums and Galleries** are nonprofit institutions whose main function is exhibiting art to the public. Museums listed are either accredited by the American Association of Museums, or are institutions with three or more curators, a publication program, and a research library, or record more than 15,000 annual visitors.

The **Public Libraries** heading shows the total number of public library systems within the metro area and their central-city, suburban, and rural branches along with figures on the size of their book collections and their annual circulation, or the number of book checkouts.

The information is derived from these sources: American Association of Museums, *Official Museum Directory,* 1996; American Library Association, *American Library Directory, 1996–1997,* 1996; American Symphony Orchestra League, *Symphony* magazine, January-February 1996, and *Orchestra and Business Directory,* 1996; Association of Canadian Orchestras, *Directory of Canadian Orchestras,* 1996; Canadian Museums Association, *Official Directory of Canadian Museums,* 1996; Con-

Quebec, 1996; Corporation for Public Broadcasting, *Public Broadcasting Directory,* 1996; Musical America, *International Directory of the Performing Arts,* 1996; Opera America, *Profile,* 1996; Opera Canada Publications, *Opera Canada* magazine, 1996; Professional Association of Canadian Theaters, *The Theater Listing,* 1996; R. R. Bowker Publishing, *American Art Directory,* 1996, and *Broadcasting and Cable Yearbook,* 1996; Statistics Canada, Performing Arts, 1993, and Public Libraries, 1992; Theater Communications Group, *Profile 21,* 1996; and U.S Department of Education, National Center for Education Statistics, unpublished public library statistics, 1996.

Resident Ensembles: 11 dates
Abilene Opera Association
Abilene Philharmonic
Public Libraries
1 system, 2 branches
251,157 books; circulation: 475,436
Places Rated Score: 30.71
Places Rated Rank: 258

Akron, OH
Concert Radio
In Cleveland media market
WKSU-FM
Lively Arts Calendar
Touring Artists Bookings: 58 dates
Resident Ensembles: 98 dates
Akron Symphony
Ohio Ballet
Art Museums and Galleries
Akron Art Museum
Kent State University Art Galleries
University of Akron Galleries
Public Libraries
11 systems, 21 branches
2,055,211 books; circulation: 7,234,532
Places Rated Score: 74.33
Places Rated Rank: 69

Albany, GA
Concert Radio
WUNV-FM
Lively Arts Calendar
Touring Artists Bookings: 19 dates
Resident Ensemble: 18 dates
Albany Symphony
Art Museums and Galleries
Albany Museum of Art
Public Libraries
1 system, 4 branches
260,659 books; circulation: 632,149
Places Rated Score: 35.53
Places Rated Rank: 237

Albany–Schenectady–Troy, NY
Concert Radio
WAMC-FM, WCAN-FM, WMHT-FM
Lively Arts Calendar
Touring Artists Bookings: 204 dates

Schenectady Symphony
St. Cecilia Orchestra
Art Museums and Galleries
Albany Institute of History & Art
Canajoharie Art Gallery
New York State Museum
State University of New York Galleries
Public Libraries
49 systems, 15 branches
2,431,001 books; circulation: 5,120,842
Places Rated Score: 72.06
Places Rated Rank: 76

Albuquerque, NM
Concert Radio
KHFM-FM
Lively Arts Calendar
Touring Artists Bookings: 30 dates
Resident Ensembles: 310 dates
Albuquerque Civic Light Opera
Chamber Orchestra of Albuquerque
New Mexico Repertory Theater
New Mexico Symphony
Opera Southwest
Art Museums and Galleries
Albuquerque Museum
Indian Pueblo Cultural Center
University of New Mexico Art Galleries
Public Libraries
11 systems, 12 branches
1,397,563 books; circulation: 3,172,953
Places Rated Score: 69.31
Places Rated Rank: 90

Alexandria, LA
Concert Radio
KLSA-FM
Lively Arts Calendar
Resident Ensemble: 5 dates
Rapides Symphony
Art Museums and Galleries
Alexandria Museum of Art
Public Libraries
1 system, 9 branches
325,219 books; circulation: 582,892
Places Rated Score: 40.36
Places Rated Rank: 210

Touring Artists Bookings: 113 dates
Resident Ensembles: 138 dates
Allentown Symphony
Ballet Guild of Lehigh Valley
Pennsylvania Sinfonia Orchestra
Pennsylvania Stage Company
Touchstone Theater
Art Museums and Galleries
Allentown Art Museum
Kemerer Museum of Decorative Arts
Lafayette College Williams Gallery
Lehigh University Art Galleries
Public Libraries
18 systems, 6 branches
1,074,120 books; circulation: 3,036,078
Places Rated Score: 51.65
Places Rated Rank: 149

Altoona, PA
Lively Arts Calendar
Touring Artists Bookings: 5 dates
Resident Ensemble: 7 dates
Altoona Symphony
Public Libraries
8 systems, 1 branch
402,665 books; circulation: 622,251
Places Rated Score: 21.27
Places Rated Rank: 299

Amarillo, TX
Lively Arts Calendar
Resident Ensembles: 28 dates
Amarillo Symphony
Lone Star Ballet
Art Museums and Galleries
Amarillo Art Center
Public Libraries
3 systems, 3 branches
588,142 books; circulation: 1,622,236
Places Rated Score: 36.58
Places Rated Rank: 230

Anchorage, AK
Concert Radio
KLEF-FM
Lively Arts Calendar
Touring Artists Bookings: 39 dates
Resident Ensembles: 38 dates

Anchorage Civic Orchestra
Anchorage Opera
Anchorage Symphony
Art Museums and Galleries
Anchorage Museum of History & Art
Visual Arts Center of Alaska
Public Libraries
1 system, 4 branches
415,192 books; circulation: 1,314,783
Places Rated Score: 32.12
Places Rated Rank: 250

Ann Arbor, MI
Concert Radio
In Detroit media market
WUOM-FM
Lively Arts Calendar
Touring Artists Bookings: 447 dates
Resident Ensembles: 87 dates
Adrian Symphony
Ann Arbor Chamber Orchestra
Ann Arbor Symphony
Comic Opera Guild
Opera Lenawee
Purple Rose Theater
Art Museums and Galleries
University of Michigan Museum of Art
Artrain
Public Libraries
20 systems, 13 branches
1,181,910 books; circulation: 2,907,886
Places Rated Score: 57.84
Places Rated Rank: 114

Anniston, AL
Lively Arts Calendar
Touring Artists Bookings: 6 dates
Public Libraries
4 systems, 1 branch
246,920 books; circulation: 345,526
Places Rated Score: 35.95
Places Rated Rank: 235

Appleton–Oshkosh–Neenah, WI
Concert Radio
In Green Bay media market
Lively Arts Calendar
Touring Artists Bookings: 85 dates
Resident Ensembles: 10 dates
Fox Valley Symphony
Oshkosh Opera House Foundation
Oshkosh Symphony
Art Museums and Galleries
Bergstrom-Mahler Museum
Paine Art Center & Arboretum
Public Libraries
14 systems, 3 branches
1,087,068 books; circulation: 3,551,434
Places Rated Score: 47.06
Places Rated Rank: 175

Asheville, NC
Concert Radio
In Greenville–Spartanburg media market
WCQS-FM
Lively Arts Calendar
Touring Artists Bookings: 29 dates
Resident Ensemble: 17 dates
Asheville Symphony
Art Museums and Galleries
Asheville Art Museum
Public Libraries
2 systems, 11 branches
366,183 books; circulation: 1,179,300
Places Rated Score: 42.23
Places Rated Rank: 196

Athens, GA
Concert Radio
In Atlanta media market
WUGA-FM
Lively Arts Calendar
Touring Artists Bookings: 6 dates
Resident Ensemble: 25 dates
University of Georgia Theater
Art Museums and Galleries
Georgia Museum of Art
Public Libraries
1 system, 12 branches
265,938 books; circulation: 900,563
Places Rated Score: 38.57
Places Rated Rank: 222

✓ Atlanta, GA
Concert Radio
WABE-FM, WGKA-AM
Lively Arts Calendar
Touring Artists Bookings: 380 dates
Resident Ensembles: 697 dates
Symphony Orchestras
Atlanta Community Symphony
Atlanta Pops Orchestra
Atlanta Symphony
Cobb Symphony
Orchestra Atlanta
Opera Company
Atlanta Opera
Ballet Company
Atlanta Ballet
Professional Theaters
Academy Theater
Actor's Express
Alliance Theater Company
Horizon Theater Company
Jomandi Productions
Seven Stages
Shakespeare Tavern
Theater Emory
Theater in the Square
Theatrical Outfit
Art Museums and Galleries
Agnes Scott College Dalton Gallery
Callanwolde Fine Arts Center
Emory University Museum of Art
Georgia State University Art Gallery
High Museum of Art
Nexus Contemporary Art Center
Public Libraries
12 systems, 117 branches
5,445,765 books; circulation: 16,818,141
Places Rated Score: 95.97
Places Rated Rank: 19

Atlantic City–Cape May, NJ
Concert Radio
In Philadelphia media market
Lively Arts Calendar
Touring Artists Bookings: 195 dates
Resident Ensembles: 30 dates
Atlantic Contemporary Ballet Theater
Atlantic Symphony
Art Museums and Galleries
Noyes Museum
Public Libraries
9 systems, 15 branches
1,148,853 books; circulation: 1,662,633
Places Rated Score: 39.18
Places Rated Rank: 219

Augusta–Aiken, GA–SC
Concert Radio
WACG-FM
Lively Arts Calendar
Touring Artists Bookings: 14 dates
Resident Ensembles: 59 dates
Augusta Ballet Company
Augusta Opera Company
Augusta Symphony
Art Museums and Galleries
Gertrude Herbert Institute of Art
Public Libraries
2 systems, 26 branches
663,399 books; circulation: 1,551,887
Places Rated Score: 46.61
Places Rated Rank: 176

Austin–San Marcos, TX
Concert Radio
KMFA-FM
Lively Arts Calendar
Touring Artists Bookings: 101 dates
Resident Ensembles: 212 dates
Austin Civic Orchestra Society
Austin Lyric Opera
Austin Symphony
Ballet Austin
Live Oak Theater
Texas Chamber Symphony
University of Texas Theater
Zachary Scott Theater Center
Art Museums and Galleries
Elisabet Ney Museum
Laguna Gloria Art Museum
UT Huntington Art Gallery
Public Libraries
20 systems, 18 branches
1,966,806 books; circulation: 4,838,181
Places Rated Score: 64.11
Places Rated Rank: 100

Bakersfield, CA
Concert Radio
KPRX-FM
Lively Arts Calendar
Touring Artists Bookings: 5 dates
Resident Ensemble: 50 dates
Bakersfield Symphony
Art Museums and Galleries
Bakersfield Museum of Art
Public Libraries
1 system, 25 branches
990,698 books; circulation: 2,163,759
Places Rated Score: 24.54
Places Rated Rank: 286

✓ Baltimore, MD
Concert Radio
WBJC-FM, WHFC-FM, WJHU-FM
Lively Arts Calendar
Touring Artists Bookings: 403 dates
Resident Ensembles: 463 dates
Symphony Orchestras
Annapolis Chamber Orchestra
Annapolis Symphony
Baltimore Chamber Orchestra
Baltimore Concert Artists
Baltimore Symphony
Hopkins Symphony
Women Composers Orchestra
Opera Companies
Annapolis Opera
Baltimore Opera Company
Baltimore Opera Touring Theater
Ballet Companies
Ballet Theater of Annapolis
Maryland Ballet
Professional Theater
Center Stage
Art Museums and Galleries
Baltimore Museum of Art
James Lewis Museum of Art

Maryland Institute
Mitchell Art Gallery St. John's College
Museum for Contemporary Art
Walters Art Gallery
Public Libraries
3 systems, 76 branches
6,638,001 books; circulation: 25,116,920
Places Rated Score: 98.89
Places Rated Rank: 8

Bangor, ME
Concert Radio
WMEH-FM
Lively Arts Calendar
Touring Artists Bookings: 50 dates
Resident Ensemble: 20 dates
Bangor Symphony

Lively Arts Calendar
Touring Artists Bookings: 6 dates
Resident Ensemble: 20 dates
Cape Cod Symphony Orchestra
Public Libraries
10 independent systems
874,369 books; circulation: 1,986,794
Places Rated Score: 79.68
Places Rated Rank: 56

Baton Rouge, LA
Concert Radio
WRKF-FM
Lively Arts Calendar
Touring Artists Bookings: 10 dates
Resident Ensembles: 61 dates
Baton Rouge Ballet Theater
Baton Rouge Opera
Baton Rouge Symphony
Art Museums and Galleries
Louisiana Arts & Science Center
LSU Galleries
Public Libraries
3 systems, 13 branches
1,267,807 books; circulation: 2,780,787
Places Rated Score: 43.22
Places Rated Rank: 192

Beaumont–Port Arthur, TX
Concert Radio
KVLU-FM
Lively Arts Calendar
Touring Artists Bookings: 23 dates
Resident Ensembles: 16 dates
Beaumont Civic Opera
Symphony of Southeast Texas
Art Museums and Galleries
Art Museum of Southeast Texas
Public Libraries
13 systems, 4 branches
807,183 books; circulation: 1,377,465
Places Rated Score: 28.66
Places Rated Rank: 266

Bellingham, WA
Concert Radio
In Seattle–Tacoma media market
KZAZ-FM
Lively Arts Calendar
Touring Artists Bookings: 27 dates
Resident Ensemble: 5 dates
Whatcom Symphony
Art Museums and Galleries
Whatcom Museum of History & Art
Public Libraries
1 system, 11 branches
452,404 books; circulation: 1,773,442
Places Rated Score: 57.05
Places Rated Rank: 117

Benton Harbor, MI
Concert Radio
In South Bend–Elkhart media market
WAUS-FM
Lively Arts Calendar

Bergen–Passaic, NJ
Concert Radio
In New York media market
Lively Arts Calendar
Touring Artists Bookings: 169 dates
Resident Ensembles: 30 dates
Ars Musica Chorale & Orchestra
Bergen Philharmonic Orchestra
Irine Fokine Ballet Company
New Jersey Philharmonic
Ridgewood Symphony
Wayne Chamber Orchestra
Art Museums and Galleries
Bergen Museum of Art & Science
Public Libraries
76 systems, 12 branches
5,301,878 books; circulation: 8,034,897
Places Rated Score: 89.76
Places Rated Rank: 39

Billings, MT
Concert Radio
KEMC-FM
Lively Arts Calendar
Touring Artists Bookings: 40 dates
Resident Ensemble: 12 dates
Billings Symphony & Chorale
Art Museums and Galleries
Yellowstone Art Center
Public Libraries
2 independent systems
282,048 books; circulation: 519,348
Places Rated Score: 23.17
Places Rated Rank: 292

Biloxi–Gulfport–Pascagoula, MS
Concert Radio
WMAH-FM
Lively Arts Calendar
Touring Artists Bookings: 5 dates
Resident Ensembles: 8 dates
Gulf Coast Opera Theater
Gulf Coast Symphony
Public Libraries
4 systems, 16 branches
576,576 books; circulation: 1,539,305
Places Rated Score: 33.55
Places Rated Rank: 244

Binghamton, NY
Concert Radio
WSKG-FM
Lively Arts Calendar
Touring Artists Bookings: 12 dates
Resident Ensembles: 45 dates
BC Pops
Binghamton Symphony & Choral Society
Tri-Cities Opera
Art Museums and Galleries
Roberson Museum
Public Libraries
16 systems, 4 branches
673,487 books; circulation: 1,633,677

Birmingham Opera Theater
Art Museums and Galleries
Birmingham Museum of Art
Public Libraries
40 systems, 21 branches
1,873,534 books; circulation: 4,476,647
Places Rated Score: 55.07
Places Rated Rank: 132

Bismarck, ND
Concert Radio
In Minot–Dickinson media market
KCND-FM
Lively Arts Calendar
Touring Artists Bookings: 4 dates
Resident Ensemble: 15 dates
Bismarck-Mandan Symphony
Public Libraries
5 independent systems
239,150 books; circulation: 510,243
Places Rated Score: 69.54
Places Rated Rank: 89

Bloomington, IN
Concert Radio
In Indianapolis media market
WFIU-FM
Lively Arts Calendar
Touring Artists Bookings: 30 dates
Resident Ensembles: 66 dates
Bloomington Symphony
Indiana University Theater
Art Museums and Galleries
IU Art Museum
Public Libraries
1 system, 1 branch
225,048 books; circulation: 1,144,315
Places Rated Score: 44.53
Places Rated Rank: 185

Bloomington–Normal, IL
Concert Radio
In Peoria media market
Lively Arts Calendar
Touring Artists Bookings: 15 dates
Resident Ensemble: 20 dates
ISU Theater
Art Museums and Galleries
Illinois Wesleyan Galleries

Public Libraries
14 independent systems
411,021 books; circulation: 1,176,077
Places Rated Score: 38.53
Places Rated Rank: 223

Boise City, ID
Concert Radio
KBSU-FM
Lively Arts Calendar
Touring Artists Bookings: 204 dates
Resident Ensembles: 51 dates
Ballet Idaho
Boise Opera
Art Museums and Galleries
Boise Art Museum
Rosenthal Gallery of Art
Public Libraries
12 systems, 6 branches
692,382 books; circulation: 1,945,338
Places Rated Score: 38.95
Places Rated Rank: 220

✓ Boston, MA–NH
Concert Radio
WBOQ-FM, WCRB-FM, WGBH-FM, WHRB-FM
Lively Arts Calendar
Touring Artists Bookings: 561 dates
Resident Ensembles: 903 dates
Symphony Orchestras
Boston Baroque
Boston Classical Orchestra
Boston Festival Opera Ltd.
Boston Modern Orchestra Project
Boston Philharmonic
Boston Symphony
Boston Symphony Chamber Players
Cape Ann Symphony
Civic Symphony Orchestra of Boston
Concord Orchestra
French Symphony of Boston
Handel & Haydn Society
Indian Hill Symphony
Jamaica Plain Symphony
Melrose Symphony
New Arts Symphony
New England Philharmonic
New England String Ensemble
North Shore Philharmonic Orchestra
Plymouth Philharmonic Orchestra
Pro Arte Chamber Orchestra of Boston
Symphony by the Sea
Symphony Pro Musica
Waltham Philharmonic Orchestra
Opera Companies
Boston Lyric Opera Company
Boston Opera Association
Longwood Opera
Opera Company of Boston
Ballet Companies
Boston Ballet
Boston Ballet II
Boston Flamenco Ballet
Professional Theaters
American Repertory Theater
Huntington Theater Company
New Repertory Theater
Art Museums and Galleries
Art Complex Museum
Boston College Museum of Art
Boston University Art Gallery
Boston Athenaeum
Danforth Museum of Art
De Cordova Museum & Sculpture Park
Harvard University Art Museums
Institute of Contemporary Art
Isabella S. Gardner Museum
Museum of Fine Arts
Rose Art Museum Brandeis University
Wellesley College Museum
Public Libraries
126 systems, 68 branches
16,563,249 books; circulation: 22,346,100
Places Rated Score: 99.42
Places Rated Rank: 6

Boulder–Longmont, CO
Concert Radio
In Denver media market
Lively Arts Calendar
Touring Artists Bookings: 25 dates
Resident Ensembles: 66 dates
Boulder Philharmonic Orchestra
Colorado Music Festival Orchestra
Longmont Symphony
Art Museums and Galleries
CU Art Galleries
Leanin' Tree Museum of Western Art
Public Libraries
6 systems, 3 branches
648,425 books; circulation: 2,940,916
Places Rated Score: 59.13
Places Rated Rank: 107

Brazoria, TX
Concert Radio
In Houston media market
Lively Arts Calendar
Resident Ensemble: 6 dates
Brazosport Symphony
Public Libraries
1 system, 10 branches
370,989 books; circulation: 1,176,507
Places Rated Score: 23.80
Places Rated Rank: 288

Bremerton, WA
Concert Radio
In Seattle–Tacoma media market
Lively Arts Calendar
Touring Artists Bookings: 2 dates
Resident Ensemble: 7 dates
Bremerton Symphony
Public Libraries
1 system, 8 branches
353,676 books; circulation: 1,814,801
Places Rated Score: 37.82
Places Rated Rank: 226

Bridgeport, CT
Concert Radio
In Hartford–New Haven media market
WMNR-FM, WRXC-FM, WSHU-FM
Lively Arts Calendar
Touring Artists Bookings: 45 dates
Resident Ensemble: 8 dates
Greater Bridgeport Symphony
Art Museums and Galleries
Housatonic Museum of Art
Public Libraries
18 systems, 7 branches
1,909,790 books; circulation: 2,822,203
Places Rated Score: 70.83
Places Rated Rank: 82

Brockton, MA
Concert Radio
In Boston media market
Lively Arts Calendar
Touring Artists Bookings: 10 dates
Resident Ensemble: 5 dates
Brockton Symphony
Art Museums and Galleries
Fuller Museum of Art
Public Libraries
13 systems, 4 branches
695,200 books; circulation: 871,877
Places Rated Score: 37.88
Places Rated Rank: 225

Brownsville–Harlingen–San Benito, TX
Concert Radio
KMBH-FM
Lively Arts Calendar
Touring Artists Bookings: 2 dates
Art Museums and Galleries
Brownsville Art League Museum
Public Libraries
8 independent systems
237,665 books; circulation: 342,829
Places Rated Score: 6.54
Places Rated Rank: 339

Bryan–College Station, TX
Concert Radio
In Waco–Temple–Bryan media market
KAMU-FM
Lively Arts Calendar
Touring Artists Bookings: 19 dates
Resident Ensemble: 5 dates
Brazos Valley Symphony
Public Libraries
1 system, 1 branch
168,450 books; circulation: 418,560
Places Rated Score: 9.56
Places Rated Rank: 335

✓ Buffalo–Niagara Falls, NY
Concert Radio
WNED-FM
Lively Arts Calendar
Touring Artists Bookings: 62 dates
Resident Ensembles: 367 dates
Ars Nova Musicians Chamber Orchestra
Buffalo Philharmonic Orchestra
Empire State Ballet
Greater Buffalo Opera Company
Orchard Park Symphony
Studio Arena Theater
Art Museums and Galleries
Albright-Knox Art Gallery
Burchfield-Penney Art Center
Hallwall's Contemporary Art Center
Public Libraries
35 systems, 30 branches
3,462,793 books; circulation: 9,788,142
Places Rated Score: 94.01
Places Rated Rank: 24

Burlington, VT
Concert Radio
In Burlington–Plattsburgh media market
WVPS-FM
Lively Arts Calendar
Touring Artists Bookings: 94 dates
Resident Ensembles: 39 dates
Burklyn Ballet Theater
Vermont Symphony
Art Museums and Galleries
Francis Colburn Gallery
Robert H. Fleming Museum
Public Libraries
15 systems, 1 branch
298,756 books; circulation: 622,167
Places Rated Score: 18.44
Places Rated Rank: 307

Calgary, AB
Concert Radio
CBR-AM, CBR-FM
Lively Arts Calendar
Touring Artists Bookings: 244 dates
Resident Ensembles: 478 dates
Alberta Ballet
Alberta Theater Projects
Calgary Opera
Calgary Philharmonic Orchestra
Garry Theater
Loose Mose Theater
Lunchbox Theater
Maenad Theater
One Yellow Rabbit Theater
Pleiades Mystery Theater
Pumphouse Theaters Society
Quest Theater

1,281,439 books; circulation: 8,359,175
Places Rated Score: 84.44
Places Rated Rank: 46

Canton–Massillon, OH
Concert Radio
In Cleveland media market
WRMU-FM
Lively Arts Calendar
Touring Artists Bookings: 1 date
Resident Ensembles: 65 dates
Canton Ballet Company
Canton Symphony
Art Museums and Galleries
Canton Museum of Art
Public Libraries
8 systems, 15 branches
1,564,625 books; circulation: 5,098,848
Places Rated Score: 75.15
Places Rated Rank: 68

Casper, WY
Lively Arts Calendar
Touring Artists Bookings: 17 dates
Resident Ensemble: 6 dates
Wyoming Symphony
Art Museums and Galleries
Nicolaysen Art Museum
Public Libraries
1 system, 1 branch
264,042 books; circulation: 409,666
Places Rated Score: 41.48
Places Rated Rank: 204

Cedar Rapids, IA
Lively Arts Calendar
Touring Artists Bookings: 40 dates
Resident Ensemble: 32 dates
Cedar Rapids Symphony
Art Museums and Galleries
Cedar Rapids Museum of Art
Cornell College Armstrong Gallery
Public Libraries
10 systems, 2 branches
490,613 books; circulation: 1,833,220
Places Rated Score: 51.07
Places Rated Rank: 155

Champaign–Urbana, IL
Concert Radio
WILL-FM
Lively Arts Calendar
Touring Artists Bookings: 72 dates
Resident Ensembles: 33 dates
Champaign-Urbana Symphony
Sinfonia Da Camera
University of Illinois Theater
Art Museums and Galleries
UI Krannert Art Museum
Public Libraries
10 systems, 1 branch
591,333 books; circulation: 1,900,489
Places Rated Score: 50.68
Places Rated Rank: 155

Charleston–North Charleston, SC

Places Rated Score: 54.10
Places Rated Rank: 138

Charleston, WV
Concert Radio
WVPN-FM
Lively Arts Calendar
Touring Artists Bookings: 53 dates
Resident Ensembles: 47 dates
Charleston Ballet
Lilliput Orchestra
Lilliput Orchestra Opera
West Virginia Symphony
Art Museums and Galleries
Sunrise Art Museum
Public Libraries
4 systems, 12 branches
779,291 books; circulation: 1,398,015
Places Rated Score: 48.02
Places Rated Rank: 169

Charlotte–Gastonia–Rock Hill, NC–SC
Concert Radio
WDAV-FM, WNSC-FM, WSGE-FM
Lively Arts Calendar
Touring Artists Bookings: 159 dates
Resident Ensembles: 356 dates
Charlotte City Ballet
Charlotte Philharmonic Orchestra
Charlotte Repertory Orchestra
Charlotte Symphony Orchestra Society
North Carolina Dance Theater
Opera Carolina
Salisbury Symphony
Art Museums and Galleries
Davidson College Art Gallery
Gaston County Museum of Art & History
Mint Museum of Art
Public Libraries
5 systems, 42 branches
2,550,835 books; circulation: 8,570,266
Places Rated Score: 82.43
Places Rated Rank: 50

Charlottesville, VA
Concert Radio
WTJU-FM
Lively Arts Calendar
Touring Artists Bookings: 56 dates
Resident Ensemble: 27 dates
Ash Lawn–Highland Opera Company
Art Museums and Galleries
Bayly Art Museum
Public Libraries
2 systems, 7 branches
398,371 books; circulation: 1,431,432
Places Rated Score: 53.55
Places Rated Rank: 143

Chattanooga, TN–GA
Concert Radio
WSMC-FM
Lively Arts Calendar
Touring Artists Bookings: 19 dates

Places Rated Rank: 321

Cheyenne, WY
Concert Radio
In Scottsbluff–Sterling media market
Lively Arts Calendar
Touring Artists Bookings: 10 dates
Resident Ensemble: 7 dates
Cheyenne Symphony
Art Museums and Galleries
State Museum Art Gallery
Public Libraries
1 system, 2 branches
152,741 books; circulation: 573,243
Places Rated Score: 29.75
Places Rated Rank: 263

✓ Chicago, IL
Concert Radio
WFMT-FM, WMWA-FM, WNIB-FM, WNIU-FM, WNIZ-FM
Lively Arts Calendar
Touring Artists Bookings: 855 dates
Resident Ensembles: 1,274 dates
Symphony Orchestras
American Festival Orchestra/Chicago Chamber Players
Baroque Music Chorus & Orchestra
Chicago Bar Association Symphony
Chicago Chamber Orchestra
Chicago Philharmonia
Chicago Sinfonietta
Chicago String Ensemble
Chicago Symphonic Wind Ensemble
Chicago Symphony
Chinese Classical Orchestra
Concerts Symphoniques
Downers Grove Choral Society & Orchestra
DuPage Symphony
Elgin Symphony
Elmhurst Symphony
Fox Valley Symphony
Grant Park Symphony & Chorus
Illinois Philharmonic Orchestra
Lake Forest Symphony
Lake Shore Symphony
Lincolnwood Chamber Orchestra

Loop Chamber Orchestra
New Philharmonic
Northbrook Symphony
Northwest Symphony
Sinfonetta Americana
Skokie Valley Symphony
Southwest Symphony
Symphony II
Symphony of Oak Park & River Forest
Symphony of the Shores
Waukegan Symphony & Concert Chorus
Wheaton Symphony
Zion Chamber Orchestra
Opera Companies
Chicago Opera Repertory Theater
Chicago Opera Theater
Du Page Opera Theater
Hungarian Opera Workshop
Light Opera Works
Lyric Opera of Chicago
Opera Factory
Ballet Companies
Ballet Chicago
Joffrey Ballet of Chicago
Von Heidecke's Chicago Festival Ballet
Professional Theaters
Bailiwick Repertory
Center Theater
Child's Play Touring Theater
Court Theater
Free Street Theater
Goodman Theater
Illinois Theater Center
National Jewish Theater
NIU Stage Company
Organic Theater Company
Remains Theater
Shakespeare Repertory
Steppenwolf Theater Company
Victory Gardens Theater
Wisdom Bridge Theater
Art Museums and Galleries
Art Institute of Chicago
Hyde Park Art Center
Illinois State Museum Art Gallery
Museum of Contemporary Art
Northwestern University Block Gallery
Spertus Museum of Judaica
Terra Museum of American Art
UI, Chicago, Gallery
University of Chicago Galleries
Public Libraries
192 systems, 99 branches
23,164,903 books; circulation: 52,936,789
Places Rated Score: 99.81
Places Rated Rank: 4

Chico–Paradise, CA
Concert Radio
KCHO-FM
Lively Arts Calendar
Touring Artists Bookings: 51 dates
Resident Ensembles: 17 dates
Chico Symphony
Paradise Symphony
Art Museums and Galleries
CSU Art Gallery
Public Libraries
1 system, 3 branches
259,187 books; circulation: 509,103
Places Rated Score: 16.89
Places Rated Rank: 315

Chicoutimi–Jonquiere, PQ
Lively Arts Calendar
Touring Artists Bookings: 18 dates
Resident Ensembles: 26 dates
La Rubrique
Orchestre Symphonique du Saguenay-Lac-St-Jean
Art Museums and Galleries
Centre National d'Exposition
Espace Virtuel
Public Libraries
2 systems, 6 branches
107,159 books; circulation: 436,694
Places Rated Score: 13.78
Places Rated Rank: 327

✓ Cincinnati, OH–KY–IN
Concert Radio
WGUC-FM
Lively Arts Calendar
Touring Artists Bookings: 51 dates
Resident Ensembles: 386 dates
Symphony Orchestras
Blue Ash Symphony
Cincinnati Chamber Orchestra
Cincinnati Symphony
Northern Kentucky Symphony
Opera Companies
CCM Opera/Musical Theater
Cincinnati Opera Association
Ballet Company
Cincinnati Ballet
Professional Theaters
ArtReach Touring Theater
Ensemble Theater
Playhouse in the Park
Art Museums and Galleries
Cincinnati Art Museum
Cincinnati Institute of Fine Arts
Contemporary Arts Center
UC Tangeman Gallery
Public Libraries
17 systems, 56 branches
6,273,819 books; circulation: 16,185,829
Places Rated Score: 92.35
Places Rated Rank: 29

Clarksville–Hopkinsville, TN–KY
Concert Radio
In Nashville media market
Lively Arts Calendar
Touring Artists Bookings: 4 dates
Art Museums and Galleries
Trahern Gallery
Public Libraries
3 independent systems
198,670 books; circulation: 514,300
Places Rated Score: 54.71
Places Rated Rank: 134

✓ Cleveland–Lorain–Elyria, OH
Concert Radio
WCLV-FM
Lively Arts Calendar
Touring Artists Bookings: 567 dates
Resident Ensembles: 543 dates
Symphony Orchestras
Cleveland Chamber Symphony
Cleveland Orchestra
Cleveland Women's Orchestra
Lakeland Civic Orchestra
Ohio Chamber Orchestra
Shaker Symphony
Suburban Symphony
Trinity Chamber Orchestra
Opera Companies
Cleveland Opera
Lyric Opera Cleveland
Ballet Companies
Cleveland San Jose Ballet
North Coast Ballet Theater
Professional Theaters
Cleveland Play House
Cleveland Public Theater
Great Lakes Theater Festival
Art Museums and Galleries
Cleveland Center for Contemporary Art
Cleveland Museum of Art
CSU Art Gallery
Oberlin College Allen Art Museum
Reinberger Galleries
Public Libraries
34 systems, 86 branches
8,961,063 books; circulation: 31,669,355
Places Rated Score: 98.25
Places Rated Rank: 11

Colorado Springs, CO
Concert Radio
KCME-FM
Lively Arts Calendar
Touring Artists Bookings: 22 dates
Resident Ensembles: 84 dates
Colorado Opera Festival
Colorado Springs Symphony
Pikes Peak Symphony
Art Museums and Galleries
Colorado Springs Fine Arts Center
CU Gallery of Contemporary Art
Public Libraries
3 systems, 11 branches
1,022,367 books; circulation: 3,367,562
Places Rated Score: 54.69
Places Rated Rank: 135

Columbia, MO
Concert Radio
KBIA-FM
Lively Arts Calendar
Touring Artists Bookings: 20 dates
Resident Ensemble: 23 dates
Missouri Symphony Society
Art Museums and Galleries
Museum of Art & Archaeology
Public Libraries
2 systems, 2 branches
338,299 books; circulation: 1,069,165
Places Rated Score: 53.59
Places Rated Rank: 142

Columbia, SC
Lively Arts Calendar
Touring Artists Bookings: 16 dates
Resident Ensembles: 126 dates
Carolina Ballet
Columbia City Ballet
South Carolina Philharmonic & Chamber Orchestra
Southeastern Regional Opera
USC Theater
Art Museums and Galleries
Columbia Museum of Art
USC McKissick Museum
Public Libraries
2 systems, 17 branches
968,524 books; circulation: 3,512,630
Places Rated Score: 55.78
Places Rated Rank: 127

Columbus, GA–AL
Concert Radio
WTJB-FM
Lively Arts Calendar
Touring Artists Bookings: 2 dates
Resident Ensemble: 26 dates
Columbus Symphony
Art Museums and Galleries

Columbus College Gallery
Columbus Museum
Public Libraries
2 systems, 9 branches
579,257 books; circulation: 719,704
Places Rated Score: 27.39
Places Rated Rank: 275

✓ Columbus, OH
Concert Radio
WOSU-FM
Lively Arts Calendar
Touring Artists Bookings: 276 dates
Resident Ensembles: 234 dates
Symphony Orchestras
Central Ohio Symphony
Columbus Pro Musica Chamber Orchestra

Columbus Cultural Arts Center
Columbus Museum of Art
Denison University Gallery
OSU Wexner Center for the Arts
Schumacher Gallery
Public Libraries
21 systems, 34 branches
4,812,716 books; circulation: 20,839,431
Places Rated Score: 91.71
Places Rated Rank: 30

Corpus Christi, TX
Concert Radio
KEDT-FM
Lively Arts Calendar
Touring Artists Bookings: 23 dates
Resident Ensembles: 26 dates
Corpus Christi Ballet
Corpus Christi Symphony
Art Museums and Galleries
Art Museum of South Texas
Public Libraries
9 systems, 4 branches
499,237 books; circulation: 1,672,505
Places Rated Score: 23.89
Places Rated Rank: 287

Cumberland, MD–WV
Concert Radio
In Washington media market
WFWM-FM
Lively Arts Calendar
Touring Artists Bookings: 4 dates
Resident Ensemble: 6 dates
Western Maryland Symphony
Public Libraries
3 systems, 6 branches
217,848 books; circulation: 570,622
Places Rated Score: 26.45
Places Rated Rank: 279

✓ Dallas, TX
Concert Radio
WRR-FM
Lively Arts Calendar
Touring Artists Bookings: 60 dates
Resident Ensembles: 500 dates
Symphony Orchestras

Chamber Symphony Metrocrest
Dallas Bach Orchestra & Choir
Dallas Chamber Orchestra
Dallas Symphony
Dallas Wind Symphony
Garland Symphony
Irving Symphony
Las Colinas Symphony
Lewisville Lake Symphony
New Philharmonic Orchestra Irving
Northeast Texas Symphony
Orchestra of New Spain
Plano Chamber Orchestra
Richardson Symphony
Texas Symphony
Opera Company
Dallas Opera
Ballet Companies

54 systems, 33 branches
5,520,895 books; circulation: 13,374,731
Places Rated Score: 93.32
Places Rated Rank: 25

Danbury, CT
Concert Radio
In Hartford–New Haven media market
Lively Arts Calendar
Touring Artists Bookings: 5 dates
Resident Ensemble: 5 dates
Ridgefield Symphony
Art Museums and Galleries
Aldrich Museum of Contemporary Art
Public Libraries
13 systems, 1 branch
704,579 books; circulation: 1,549,677
Places Rated Score: 54.01
Places Rated Rank: 140

Danville, VA
Concert Radio
In Roanoke–Lynchburg media market
Lively Arts Calendar
Touring Artists Bookings: 10 dates
Art Museums and Galleries
Museum of Fine Arts & History
Public Libraries
2 systems, 4 branches
203,119 books; circulation: 414,658
Places Rated Score: 20.01
Places Rated Rank: 303

Davenport–Moline–Rock Island, IA–IL
Concert Radio
WVIK-FM
Lively Arts Calendar
Touring Artists Bookings: 27 dates
Resident Ensembles: 25 dates
Augustana Symphony
Quad City Symphony
Art Museums and Galleries
Augustana College Gallery of Art
Davenport Museum of Art
Public Libraries
21 systems, 13 branches
1,183,959 books; circulation: 2,886,284

Places Rated Score: 52.52
Places Rated Rank: 145

Dayton–Springfield, OH
Concert Radio
WDPR-FM
Lively Arts Calendar
Touring Artists Bookings: 99 dates
Resident Ensembles: 119 dates
Dayton Ballet
Dayton Opera Association
Dayton Philharmonic Orchestra
Ohio Lyric Theater of Springfield
Springfield Symphony
Art Museums and Galleries
Dayton Art Institute
Springfield Museum of Art
Public Libraries

Stetson University Duncan Gallery
Public Libraries
1 independent system, 13 branches
728,644 books; circulation: 2,564,303
Places Rated Score: 43.68
Places Rated Rank: 188

Decatur, AL
Lively Arts Calendar
Touring Artists Bookings: 20 dates
Art Museums and Galleries
CSCC Art Gallery
Public Libraries
7 independent systems
157,220 books; circulation: 414,076
Places Rated Score: 27.07
Places Rated Rank: 277

Decatur, IL
Lively Arts Calendar
Touring Artists Bookings: 20 dates
Resident Ensemble: 18 dates
Millikin-Decatur Symphony
Art Museums and Galleries
Kirkland Fine Arts Center
Public Libraries
8 systems, 1 branch
347,973 books; circulation: 1,028,071
Places Rated Score: 42.04
Places Rated Rank: 199

Denver, CO
Concert Radio
KCFR-FM, KPOF-AM, KVOD-FM
Lively Arts Calendar
Touring Artists Bookings: 168 dates
Resident Ensembles: 364 dates
Arapahoe Philharmonic
Ballet Denver
Central City Opera House Association
Colorado Ballet
Colorado Symphony
Denver Center Theater Company
Germinal Stage
Jefferson Symphony
Opera Colorado
Art Museums and Galleries
Denver Art Museum

Museum of Western Art
Public Libraries
8 systems, 56 branches
4,587,694 books; circulation: 14,208,799
Places Rated Score: 90.70
Places Rated Rank: 35

Des Moines, IA
Lively Arts Calendar
Touring Artists Bookings: 25 dates
Resident Ensembles: 67 dates
Ballet Iowa
Des Moines Community Orchestra
Des Moines Metro Opera
Des Moines Symphony
Drake Symphony
Art Museums and Galleries
Des Moines Art Center
Salisbury House
Public Libraries
28 systems, 5 branches
1,197,236 books; circulation: 3,009,803
Places Rated Score: 53.96
Places Rated Rank: 141

✓ Detroit, MI
Concert Radio
WQRS-FM
Lively Arts Calendar
Touring Artists Bookings: 314 dates
Resident Ensembles: 385 dates
Birmingham-Bloomfield Symphony
Dearborn Orchestral Society
Detroit Repertory Theater
Detroit Symphony
Detroit Symphony Civic Orchestra
Farmington Area Philharmonic
Grosse Pointe Symphony
Lake St. Clair Symphony
Livonia Symphony
Michigan Chamber Orchestra
Michigan Opera Theater
National Sinfonietta
Pontiac-Oakland Symphony
Southern Great Lakes Symphony
Warren Symphony, The Michigan Orchestra
Wayne State Repertory Theater
Art Museums and Galleries
Cranbrook Academy of Art Museum
Creative Arts Center
Detroit Institute of Arts
Meadow Brook Art Gallery
WSU Community Arts Gallery
Public Libraries
76 systems, 93 branches
10,932,018 books; circulation: 19,470,988
Places Rated Score: 96.60
Places Rated Rank: 17

Dothan, AL
Concert Radio
WRWA-FM
Art Museums and Galleries
Wiregrass Museum of Art
Public Libraries
6 systems, 2 branches
304,726 books; circulation: 404,454
Places Rated Score: 11.14
Places Rated Rank: 333

Dover, DE
Concert Radio
In Philadelphia media market
Lively Arts Calendar
Touring Artists Bookings: 5 dates
Public Libraries
3 independent systems
116,790 books; circulation: 260,168
Places Rated Score: 4.11
Places Rated Rank: 340

Dubuque, IA
Lively Arts Calendar
Touring Artists Bookings: 25 dates
Resident Ensemble: 28 dates
Dubuque Symphony
Art Museums and Galleries
Dubuque Association of Art
Public Libraries
4 systems, 1 branch
315,102 books; circulation: 608,679
Places Rated Score: 43.67
Places Rated Rank: 189

Duluth–Superior, MN–WI
Concert Radio
WHSA-FM, WHSA-FM, WSCD-FM
Lively Arts Calendar
Touring Artists Bookings: 14 dates
Resident Ensembles: 65 dates
Duluth-Superior Symphony
Minnesota Ballet
Art Museums and Galleries
UM Tweed Museum of Art
Public Libraries
16 systems, 3 branches
960,120 books; circulation: 2,347,641
Places Rated Score: 68.31
Places Rated Rank: 94

Dutchess County, NY
Concert Radio
In New York media market
WRHV-FM
Lively Arts Calendar
Touring Artists Bookings: 192 dates
Resident Ensemble: 40 dates
Hudson Valley Philharmonic Socity
Art Museums and Galleries
Vassar College Art Gallery
Public Libraries
21 systems, 2 branches
588,903 books; circulation: 1,201,835
Places Rated Score: 44.62
Places Rated Rank: 184

Eau Claire, WI
Concert Radio
WUEC-FM
Lively Arts Calendar
Touring Artists Bookings: 17 dates
Resident Ensemble: 4 dates
Chippewa Valley Symphony
Public Libraries
10 independent systems
434,495 books; circulation: 1,355,282
Places Rated Score: 41.51
Places Rated Rank: 203

Edmonton, AB
Concert Radio
CBX-FM, CKUA-FM
Lively Arts Calendar
Touring Artists Bookings: 136 dates
Resident Ensembles: 352 dates
Azimuth Theater Associaton
Catalyst Theater
Chinook Theater Society
Citadel Theater
Edmonton Fringe Theater Event
Edmonton Opera Association
Edmonton Philarmonic Society
Edmonton Symphony
Leave It To Jane Theater
Northern Light Theater
Phoenix Theater
Stage Polaris
Theater Network Society
Workshop West Theater
Art Museums and Galleries
Latitude 53 Gallery
The Edmonton Art Gallery
University of Alberta Collections
Public Libraries
5 systems, 17 branches
1,215,281 books; circulation: 9,109,433
Places Rated Score: 77.14
Places Rated Rank: 65

El Paso, TX
Concert Radio
KTEP-FM
Lively Arts Calendar
Touring Artists Bookings: 71 dates
Resident Ensembles: 65 dates
Ballet El Paso
El Paso Philharmonic Strings
El Paso Symphony
Art Museums and Galleries
El Paso Museum of Art
Public Libraries
1 system, 10 branches
612,916 books; circulation: 1,731,820
Places Rated Score: 23.43
Places Rated Rank: 290

Elkhart–Goshen, IN
Concert Radio
WGCS-FM
Lively Arts Calendar
Touring Artists Bookings: 4 dates
Resident Ensemble: 7 dates
Elkhart County Symphony
Art Museums and Galleries
Midwest Museum of American Art
Public Libraries
6 systems, 3 branches
471,842 books; circulation: 1,629,164
Places Rated Score: 40.22
Places Rated Rank: 212

Elmira, NY
Lively Arts Calendar
Touring Artists Bookings: 56 dates
Resident Ensemble: 5 dates
Elmira Symphony & Choral Society
Art Museums and Galleries
Arnot Art Museum
Public Libraries
2 systems, 4 branches
377,107 books; circulation: 631,106
Places Rated Score: 44.64
Places Rated Rank: 183

Enid, OK
Concert Radio
In Oklahoma City media market
Lively Arts Calendar
Touring Artists Bookings: 5 dates
Resident Ensemble: 15 dates
Enid-Phillips Symphony
Public Libraries
1 independent system
81,880 books; circulation: 183,942
Places Rated Score: 13.69
Places Rated Rank: 328

Erie, PA
Concert Radio
WMCE-FM, WQLN-FM
Lively Arts Calendar
Touring Artists Bookings: 47 dates
Resident Ensemble: 22 dates

Erie Philharmonic
Art Museums and Galleries
Erie Art Museum
Public Libraries
8 systems, 6 branches
647,443 books; circulation: 1,887,622
Places Rated Score: 39.44
Places Rated Rank: 217

Eugene–Springfield, OR
Concert Radio
KWAX-FM
Lively Arts Calendar
Touring Artists Bookings: 236 dates
Resident Ensembles: 152 dates
Eugene Ballet Company
Eugene Opera
Eugene Symphony

WKPB-FM, WNIN-FM
Lively Arts Calendar
Touring Artists Bookings: 30 dates
Resident Ensemble: 29 dates
Evansville Philharmonic Orchestra
Art Museums and Galleries
Museum of Art & Science
Public Libraries
8 systems, 12 branches
1,114,553 books; circulation: 2,638,364
Places Rated Score: 68.97
Places Rated Rank: 91

Fargo–Moorhead, ND–MN
Concert Radio
KCCM-FM
Lively Arts Calendar
Touring Artists Bookings: 31 dates
Resident Ensembles: 26 dates
Fargo-Moorhead Civic Opera Company
Fargo-Moorhead Symphony
Art Museums and Galleries
NDSU Art Gallery
Plains Art Museum
Public Libraries
5 systems, 12 branches
517,603 books; circulation: 1,400,124
Places Rated Score: 75.21
Places Rated Rank: 67

Fayetteville, NC
Concert Radio
In Raleigh–Durham media market
Lively Arts Calendar
Resident Ensemble: 7 dates
Fayetteville Symphony
Art Museums and Galleries
Fayetteville Museum of Art
Public Libraries
1 system, 6 branches
440,612 books; circulation: 1,851,502
Places Rated Score: 33.69
Places Rated Rank: 243

Fayetteville–Springdale–Rogers, AR
Concert Radio
In Fort Smith media market
KUAF-FM

Lively Arts Calendar
Touring Artists Bookings: 61 dates
Resident Ensemble: 20 dates
North Arkansas Symphony
Art Museums and Galleries
Arts Center for the Ozarks
Public Libraries
2 systems, 14 branches
363,930 books; circulation: 1,062,903
Places Rated Score: 13.57
Places Rated Rank: 329

Fitchburg–Leominster, MA
Concert Radio
In Boston media market
Lively Arts Calendar
Touring Artists Bookings: 2 dates
Art Museums and Galleries

Lively Arts Calendar
Touring Artists Bookings: 25 dates
Resident Ensembles: 28 dates
Flagstaff Festival of the Arts
Flagstaff Symphony
Art Museums and Galleries
Museum of Northern Arizona
Public Libraries
8 systems, 1 branch
284,992 books; circulation: 644,681
Places Rated Score: 28.34
Places Rated Rank: 268

Flint, MI
Concert Radio
WFBE-FM, WFUM-FM
Lively Arts Calendar
Resident Ensemble: 6 dates
Flint Symphony
Art Museums and Galleries
Flint Institute of Arts
Public Libraries
2 systems, 19 branches
1,005,541 books; circulation: 1,779,462
Places Rated Score: 41.94
Places Rated Rank: 200

Florence, AL
Concert Radio
In Huntsville–Decatur media market
WQPR-FM
Lively Arts Calendar
Touring Artists Bookings: 7 dates
Public Libraries
9 independent systems
226,737 books; circulation: 398,635
Places Rated Score: 14.21
Places Rated Rank: 323

Florence, SC
Lively Arts Calendar
Touring Artists Bookings: 8 dates
Resident Ensemble: 5 dates
Florence Symphony
Art Museums and Galleries
Florence Museum
Public Libraries
1 system, 5 branches
156,835 books; circulation: 329,029

Places Rated Score: 12.98
Places Rated Rank: 330

Fort Collins–Loveland, CO
Concert Radio
In Denver media market
Lively Arts Calendar
Touring Artists Bookings: 108 dates
Resident Ensemble: 10 dates
Fort Collins Symphony
Art Museums and Galleries
CSU Gallery
Public Libraries
5 independent systems
403,148 books; circulation: 1,677,183
Places Rated Score: 40.07
Places Rated Rank: 214

2,100,438 books; circulation: 6,457,040
Places Rated Score: 84.32
Places Rated Rank: 47

Fort Myers–Cape Coral, FL
Concert Radio
WSFP-FM
Lively Arts Calendar
Touring Artists Bookings: 87 dates
Resident Ensemble: 17 dates
Southwest Florida Symphony & Chorus
Art Museums and Galleries
ECC Gallery of Fine Art
Public Libraries
3 systems, 10 branches
703,947 books; circulation: 2,317,475
Places Rated Score: 42.42
Places Rated Rank: 194

Fort Pierce–Port St. Lucie, FL
Concert Radio
WQCS-FM
Lively Arts Calendar
Touring Artists Bookings: 4 dates
Resident Ensembles: 13 dates
Atlantic Classical Orchestra
Treasure Coast Symphony
Public Libraries
2 systems, 9 branches
440,516 books; circulation: 1,325,376
Places Rated Score: 32.85
Places Rated Rank: 248

Fort Smith, AR–OK
Lively Arts Calendar
Touring Artists Bookings: 5 dates
Resident Ensemble: 8 dates
Fort Smith Symphony
Art Museums and Galleries
Fort Smith Art Center
Public Libraries
2 systems, 5 branches
213,848 books; circulation: 979,878
Places Rated Score: 3.86
Places Rated Rank: 341

Fort Walton Beach, FL
Concert Radio
In Mobile–Pensacola media market

Lively Arts Calendar
Touring Artists Bookings: 10 dates
Resident Ensembles: 24 dates
Northwest Florida Ballet
Okaloosa Symphony
Public Libraries
1 system, 6 branches
128,787 books; circulation: 123,194
Places Rated Score: 0.00
Places Rated Rank: 351

Fort Wayne, IN
Concert Radio
WBNI-FM
Lively Arts Calendar
Touring Artists Bookings: 44 dates
Resident Ensembles: 100 dates
Fort Wayne Ballet
Fort Wayne Philharmonic Orchestra
Art Museums and Galleries
Fort Wayne Museum of Art
Public Libraries
17 systems, 15 branches
3,090,909 books; circulation: 5,277,619
Places Rated Score: 78.75
Places Rated Rank: 62

Fort Worth–Arlington, TX
Concert Radio
KTCU-FM
Lively Arts Calendar
Touring Artists Bookings: 19 dates
Resident Ensembles: 286 dates
Fort Worth Ballet
Fort Worth Civic Orchestra
Fort Worth Opera
Fort Worth Symphony & Chamber Orchestra
Stage West
Art Museums and Galleries
Amon Carter Museum
Kimbell Art Museum
Modern Art Museum
Public Libraries
29 systems, 13 branches
2,355,542 books; circulation: 6,926,843
Places Rated Score: 80.16
Places Rated Rank: 55

Fresno, CA
Concert Radio
KVPR-FM
Lively Arts Calendar
Touring Artists Bookings: 40 dates
Resident Ensembles: 24 dates
Fresno Ballet
Fresno Philharmonic Orchestra
Art Museums and Galleries
Fresno Art Center & Museum
Public Libraries
3 systems, 36 branches
1,107,477 books; circulation: 2,057,067
Places Rated Score: 35.82
Places Rated Rank: 236

Gadsden, AL
Concert Radio
In Birmingham media market
WSGN-FM
Lively Arts Calendar
Touring Artists Bookings: 5 dates
Resident Ensemble: 3 dates
Gadsden Symphony
Art Museums and Galleries
Gadsden Museum of Fine Arts
Public Libraries
5 systems, 3 branches
254,372 books; circulation: 440,225
Places Rated Score: 33.45
Places Rated Rank: 246

Gainesville, FL
Concert Radio
WUFT-FM
Lively Arts Calendar
Touring Artists Bookings: 4 dates
Resident Ensembles: 97 dates
Gainesville Chamber Orchestra
Gainesville Symphony
Hippodrome State Theater
University of Florida Theater
Art Museums and Galleries
Samuel P. Harn Museum of Art
University of Florida Gallery
Public Libraries
1 system, 9 branches
575,729 books; circulation: 1,784,349
Places Rated Score: 52.35
Places Rated Rank: 147

Galveston–Texas City, TX
Concert Radio
In Houston media market
Lively Arts Calendar
Touring Artists Bookings: 25 dates
Resident Ensemble: 6 dates
Galveston Symphony
Public Libraries
7 independent systems
624,965 books; circulation: 1,004,744
Places Rated Score: 27.61
Places Rated Rank: 272

Gary, IN
Concert Radio
In Chicago media market
Lively Arts Calendar
Touring Artists Bookings: 204 dates
Resident Ensemble: 25 dates
Northwest Indiana Symphony
Art Museums and Galleries
Valparaiso Museum of Art
Public Libraries
9 systems, 35 branches
2,470,667 books; circulation: 5,036,413
Places Rated Score: 73.07
Places Rated Rank: 74

Glens Falls, NY
Concert Radio
In Albany–Schenectady–Troy media market
Lively Arts Calendar
Resident Ensembles: 19 dates
Glens Falls Symphony
Lake George Opera Festival
Art Museums and Galleries
Hyde Collection
Public Libraries
18 independent systems
367,182 books; circulation: 958,778
Places Rated Score: 34.72
Places Rated Rank: 241

Goldsboro, NC
Concert Radio
In Raleigh–Durham media market
Public Libraries
1 system, 6 branches
96,115 books; circulation: 366,193
Places Rated Score: 13.83
Places Rated Rank: 326

Grand Forks, ND–MN
Concert Radio
In Fargo–Valley City media market
KFJM-FM
Lively Arts Calendar
Touring Artists Bookings: 15 dates
Art Museums and Galleries
North Dakota Museum of Art
Public Libraries
3 independent systems
255,276 books; circulation: 686,616
Places Rated Score: 58.26
Places Rated Rank: 112

Grand Junction, CO
Concert Radio
KPRN-FM
Lively Arts Calendar
Touring Artists Bookings: 5 dates
Resident Ensemble: 9 dates
Grand Junction Symphony
Art Museums and Galleries
Western Colorado Center for the Arts
Public Libraries
2 systems, 6 branches
228,643 books; circulation: 657,672
Places Rated Score: 30.58
Places Rated Rank: 260

Grand Rapids–Muskegon–Holland, MI
Concert Radio
WBLU-FM, WFGR-FM, WVGR-FM
Lively Arts Calendar
Touring Artists Bookings: 86 dates
Resident Ensembles: 125 dates
Grand Rapids Ballet Company
Grand Rapids Symphony
Holland Chamber Orchestra
Opera Grand Rapids
West Shore Symphony
Art Museums and Galleries
Calvin College Art Gallery
Grand Rapids Art Museum
Hope College Gallery
Muskegon Museum of Art
Public Libraries
24 systems, 36 branches
2,863,191 books; circulation: 6,232,658
Places Rated Score: 70.57
Places Rated Rank: 84

Great Falls, MT
Concert Radio
KGPR-FM
Lively Arts Calendar
Resident Ensemble: 10 dates
Great Falls Symphony
Art Museums and Galleries
C.M. Russell Museum
Public Libraries
3 independent systems
143,245 books; circulation: 436,792
Places Rated Score: 20.85
Places Rated Rank: 300

Greeley, CO
Concert Radio
In Denver media market
Lively Arts Calendar
Touring Artists Bookings: 27 dates
Resident Ensemble: 12 dates
Greeley Philharmonic Orchestra
Public Libraries
9 systems, 2 branches
373,487 books; circulation: 815,198
Places Rated Score: 41.62
Places Rated Rank: 202

Green Bay, WI
Concert Radio
WPNE-FM
Lively Arts Calendar
Touring Artists Bookings: 49 dates
Resident Ensembles: 21 dates
Green Bay Symphony
Pamiro Opera Company
Art Museums and Galleries
Neville Public Museum
Public Libraries
2 systems, 9 branches
391,137 books; circulation: 1,690,143
Places Rated Score: 39.52
Places Rated Rank: 216

Greensboro–Winston-Salem–High Point, NC

Art Museums and Galleries
Green Hill Center for North Carolina Art
Reynolda House Museum of American Art
Scales Fine Arts Center
Southeastern Center for Contemporary Art
UNC Weatherspoon Art Gallery
Public Libraries
6 systems, 36 branches
2,114,559 books; circulation: 5,592,322
Places Rated Score: 65.62
Places Rated Rank: 97

Greenville, NC
Lively Arts Calendar
Touring Artists Bookings: 29 dates
Art Museums and Galleries
ECU Gray Gallery
Greenville Museum of Art
Public Libraries
4 systems, 12 branches
378,221 books; circulation: 796,418
Places Rated Score: 55.81
Places Rated Rank: 126

Greenville–Spartanburg–Anderson, SC
Lively Arts Calendar
Touring Artists Bookings: 120 dates
Resident Ensembles: 48 dates
Anderson Symphony
Greenville Symphony
Spartanburg Symphony
Art Museums and Galleries
Anderson County Arts Center
BJU Collection of Sacred Art
Clemson University Lee Gallery
Greenville County Museum of Art
Sandor Teszler Library Gallery
Public Libraries
5 systems, 31 branches
1,734,466 books; circulation: 3,863,141
Places Rated Score: 57.09
Places Rated Rank: 116

Hagerstown, MD
Concert Radio
In Washington media market
WETH-FM
Lively Arts Calendar
Touring Artists Bookings: 90 dates
Resident Ensemble: 16 dates
Maryland Symphony
Art Museums and Galleries
Washington County Museum of Fine Arts
Public Libraries
1 system, 6 branches
239,435 books; circulation: 858,639
Places Rated Score: 36.59
Places Rated Rank: 229

Halifax, NS
Concert Radio
CBH-FM
Lively Arts Calendar

5 systems, 16 branches
779,426 books; circulation: 2,574,298
Places Rated Score: 56.10
Places Rated Rank: 122

Hamilton, ON
Concert Radio
In Toronto media market
Lively Arts Calendar
Touring Artists Bookings: 29 dates
Resident Ensembles: 191 dates
Hamilton Philharmonic
Opera Hamilton
Symphony Hamilton
Te Deum Orchestra
Theater Aquarius
Theater Erebus
Art Museums and Galleries
Art Gallery of Hamilton
Dundas Valley School of Art Gallery
Grimsby Public Art Gallery
Hamilton Place Gallery
McMaster University Art Gallery
Public Libraries
4 systems, 31 branches
1,296,426 books; circulation: 4,978,756
Places Rated Score: 77.85
Places Rated Rank: 64

Hamilton–Middletown, OH
Concert Radio
In Cincinnati media market
Lively Arts Calendar
Touring Artists Bookings: 15 dates
Resident Ensembles: 10 dates
Hamilton-Fairfield Symphony
Middletown Symphony
Sorg Opera Company
Art Museums and Galleries
Miami University Art Gallery
Public Libraries
2 systems, 5 branches
673,450 books; circulation: 2,556,011
Places Rated Score: 47.56
Places Rated Rank: 171

Harrisburg–Lebanon–Carlisle, PA
Concert Radio
WITF-FM
Lively Arts Calendar
Touring Artists Bookings: 115 dates
Resident Ensembles: 37 dates
Harrisburg Civic Opera Association
Harrisburg Symphony
Public Libraries
19 systems, 12 branches
844,456 books; circulation: 3,537,216
Places Rated Score: 43.47
Places Rated Rank: 191

✓ Hartford, CT
Concert Radio
WJMJ-FM
Lively Arts Calendar
Touring Artists Bookings: 1,285 dates

Ezra & Cecile Zilkha Gallery
Hill-Stead Museum
New Britain Museum of American Art
Wadsworth Atheneum
Public Libraries
69 systems, 23 branches
4,816,238 books; circulation: 9,095,661
Places Rated Score: 95.67
Places Rated Rank: 21

Hattiesburg, MS
Concert Radio
WUSM-FM
Lively Arts Calendar
Touring Artists Bookings: 20 dates
Public Libraries
1 system, 1 branch
85,101 books; circulation: 186,187
Places Rated Score: 0.13
Places Rated Rank: 348

Hickory–Morganton–Lenoir, NC
Concert Radio
In Charlotte media market
Lively Arts Calendar
Touring Artists Bookings: 12 dates
Resident Ensemble: 8 dates
Western Piedmont Symphony
Art Museums and Galleries
Hickory Museum of Art
Public Libraries
5 systems, 7 branches
506,453 books; circulation: 1,361,284
Places Rated Score: 34.99
Places Rated Rank: 240

Honolulu, HI
Concert Radio
KHPR-FM
Lively Arts Calendar
Touring Artists Bookings: 80 dates
Resident Ensembles: 495 dates
Hawaii Opera Theater
Hawaii State Ballet
Honolulu Theater for Youth
Art Museums and Galleries
Contemporary Museum

Honolulu Academy of Arts
University of Hawaii Gallery
Public Libraries
1 system, 48 branches
2,874,796 books; circulation: 7,250,318
Places Rated Score: 89.98
Places Rated Rank: 38

Houma, LA
Concert Radio
In New Orleans media market
KTLN-FM
Lively Arts Calendar
Touring Artists Bookings: 4 dates
Public Libraries
2 systems, 13 branches
313,028 books; circulation: 545,574
Places Rated Score: 16.38
Places Rated Rank: 316

✓ Houston, TX
Concert Radio
KUHF-FM
Lively Arts Calendar
Touring Artists Bookings: 403 dates
Resident Ensembles: 432 dates
Alley Theater
Clear Lake Symphony
Houston Ballet
Houston Grand Opera Association
Houston Symphony
Southwest Jazz Ballet Company
Symphony North of Houston
Art Museums and Galleries
Contemporary Arts Museum
Museum of Fine Arts
Public Libraries
14 systems, 74 branches
6,543,865 books; circulation: 15,193,500
Places Rated Score: 93.19
Places Rated Rank: 26

Huntington–Ashland, WV–KY–OH
Concert Radio
WOUL-FM, WVWV-FM
Lively Arts Calendar
Touring Artists Bookings: 89 dates
Resident Ensemble: 10 dates
Huntington Chamber Orchestra
Art Museums and Galleries
Huntington Museum of Art
Public Libraries
5 systems, 15 branches
660,248 books; circulation: 1,566,771
Places Rated Score: 37.30
Places Rated Rank: 228

Huntsville, AL
Concert Radio
WLRH-FM
Lively Arts Calendar
Touring Artists Bookings: 31 dates
Resident Ensembles: 29 dates
Huntsville Opera Theater
Huntsville Symphony
Art Museums and Galleries
Huntsville Museum of Art
UAH Gallery of Art
Public Libraries
2 systems, 7 branches
445,579 books; circulation: 2,015,148
Places Rated Score: 27.73
Places Rated Rank: 271

✓ Indianapolis, IN
Concert Radio
WFYI-FM, WICR-FM, WSYW-FM
Lively Arts Calendar
Touring Artists Bookings: 33 dates
Resident Ensembles: 435 dates
Anderson Symphony
Carmel Symphony
Indiana Opera Theater
Indiana Repertory Theater
Indianapolis Ballet Theater
Indianapolis Chamber Orchestra
Indianapolis Opera
Indianapolis Symphony
Philharmonic Orchestra of Indianapolis
Art Museums and Galleries
Anderson Fine Arts Center
Indianapolis Center for Contemporary Art
Indianapolis Museum of Art
Public Libraries
30 systems, 33 branches
3,727,327 books; circulation: 13,321,621
Places Rated Score: 91.03
Places Rated Rank: 33

Iowa City, IA
Concert Radio
In Cedar Rapids–Waterloo–Dubuque media market
KSUI-FM
Lively Arts Calendar
Touring Artists Bookings: 68 dates
Resident Ensemble: 25 dates
University of Iowa Theater
Art Museums and Galleries
University of Iowa Museum of Art
Public Libraries
5 independent systems
268,572 books; circulation: 1,335,166
Places Rated Score: 51.36
Places Rated Rank: 152

Jackson, MI
Concert Radio
In Lansing media market
Lively Arts Calendar
Touring Artists Bookings: 20 dates
Resident Ensemble: 12 dates
Jackson Symphony
Art Museums and Galleries
Ella Sharp Museum
Public Libraries
1 system, 12 branches
331,850 books; circulation: 795,750
Places Rated Score: 30.57
Places Rated Rank: 261

Jackson, MS
Concert Radio
WMPN-FM
Lively Arts Calendar
Touring Artists Bookings: 4 dates
Resident Ensembles: 107 dates
Ballet Mississippi
Mississippi Opera
Mississippi Symphony
New Stage Theater
Art Museums and Galleries
Mississippi Museum of Art
Public Libraries
3 systems, 36 branches
917,098 books; circulation: 1,412,247
Places Rated Score: 45.17
Places Rated Rank: 179

Jackson, TN
Concert Radio
WKNP-FM
Lively Arts Calendar
Resident Ensemble: 14 dates
Jackson Symphony
Public Libraries
2 systems, 3 branches
155,231 books; circulation: 278,992
Places Rated Score: 58.20
Places Rated Rank: 113

Jacksonville, FL
Concert Radio
WFCF-FM, WJCT-FM
Lively Arts Calendar
Touring Artists Bookings: 86 dates
Resident Ensembles: 201 dates
Florida Ballet
Jacksonville Symphony
Art Museums and Galleries
Cummer Gallery of Art
Jacksonville Art Museum
Public Libraries
3 systems, 21 branches
2,427,800 books; circulation: 4,319,853
Places Rated Score: 70.86
Places Rated Rank: 81

Jacksonville, NC
Concert Radio
In Greenville–New Bern–Washington media market
Lively Arts Calendar
Touring Artists Bookings: 9 dates
Public Libraries
1 system, 3 branches
117,652 books; circulation: 374,284
Places Rated Score: 9.30
Places Rated Rank: 336

Jamestown, NY
Concert Radio
In Buffalo media market
Lively Arts Calendar
Touring Artists Bookings: 952 dates
Resident Ensembles: 47 dates
Chautauqua Opera
Chautuqua Ballet Company
Fredonia Chamber Players
Public Libraries
22 systems, 1 branch
654,455 books; circulation: 1,450,710
Places Rated Score: 69.60
Places Rated Rank: 88

Janesville–Beloit, WI
Concert Radio
In Madison media market
Lively Arts Calendar
Touring Artists Bookings: 8 dates
Resident Ensemble: 14 dates
Beloit Janesville Symphony
Art Museums and Galleries
Wright Museum of Art
Public Libraries
7 independent systems
436,989 books; circulation: 1,545,958
Places Rated Score: 52.78
Places Rated Rank: 144

Jersey City, NJ
Concert Radio
In New York media market
Lively Arts Calendar
Touring Artists Bookings: 19 dates
Art Museums and Galleries
JCSC Courtney Art Gallery
Jersey City Museum
Public Libraries
11 systems, 15 branches
2,053,508 books; circulation: 1,030,664
Places Rated Score: 62.44

Places Rated Rank: 103

Johnson City–Kingsport–Bristol, TN–VA
Concert Radio
WCSK-FM, WETS-FM
Lively Arts Calendar
Touring Artists Bookings: 12 dates
Resident Ensembles: 39 dates
Johnson City Symphony
Kingsport Symphony
Road Company
Art Museums and Galleries
ETSU Carroll Reece Museum
Public Libraries
11 systems, 18 branches
775,312 books; circulation: 2,034,855
Places Rated Score: 41.17

Places Rated Rank: 283

Joplin, MO
Concert Radio
KXMS-FM
Lively Arts Calendar
Touring Artists Bookings: 7 dates
Art Museums and Galleries
Spiva Center for the Arts
Public Libraries
5 systems, 1 branch
234,126 books; circulation: 585,345
Places Rated Score: 10.19
Places Rated Rank: 334

Kalamazoo–Battle Creek, MI
Concert Radio
WMUK-FM
Lively Arts Calendar
Touring Artists Bookings: 39 dates
Resident Ensembles: 37 dates
Battle Creek Symphony
Kalamazoo Symphony
Art Museums and Galleries
Art Center of Battle Creek
Kalamazoo Institute of Arts
Western Michigan University Gallery
Public Libraries
23 systems, 11 branches
1,350,772 books; circulation: 2,728,279
Places Rated Score: 55.95
Places Rated Rank: 124

Kankakee, IL
Concert Radio
In Chicago media market
Lively Arts Calendar
Touring Artists Bookings: 5 dates
Resident Ensemble: 7 dates
Kankakee Valley Symphony
Public Libraries
6 independent systems
206,845 books; circulation: 402,010
Places Rated Score: 9.09
Places Rated Rank: 337

Kansas City, MO–KS
Concert Radio
KXTR-FM
Lively Arts Calendar
Touring Artists Bookings: 101 dates
Resident Ensembles: 285 dates
Coterie
Independence Symphony
Kansas City Camerata
Kansas City Chamber Orchestra
Kansas City Symphony
Liberty Symphony
Lyric Opera of Kansas City
Missouri Repertory Theater
Northland Symphony
Philharmonia of Greater Kansas City
State Ballet of Missouri
Unicorn Theater
Art Museums and Galleries

Lively Arts Calendar
Touring Artists Bookings: 17 dates
Resident Ensemble: 4 dates
Kenosha Symphony
Art Museums and Galleries
Kenosha Public Museum
Public Libraries
6 branches
286,847 books; circulation: 1,048,296
Places Rated Score: 36.15
Places Rated Rank: 232

Killeen–Temple, TX
Concert Radio
KNCT-FM
Lively Arts Calendar
Touring Artists Bookings: 29 dates
Public Libraries
9 independent systems
276,271 books; circulation: 723,301
Places Rated Score: 1.35
Places Rated Rank: 345

Kitchener, ON
Lively Arts Calendar
Touring Artists Bookings: 267 dates
Resident Ensembles: 174 dates
Kitchener-Waterloo Chamber Orchestra
Kitchener-Waterloo Community Orchestra
Kitchener-Waterloo Symphony
Theater & Company
Wilfrid Laurier University Symphony
Art Museums and Galleries
Kitchener-Waterloo Art Gallery
University of Waterloo Gallery
Public Libraries
4 systems, 19 branches
780,363 books; circulation: 2,708,443
Places Rated Score: 64.86
Places Rated Rank: 99

Knoxville, TN
Concert Radio
WUOT-FM
Lively Arts Calendar
Touring Artists Bookings: 90 dates
Resident Ensembles: 268 dates
Appalachian Ballet Company
Clarence Brown Theater Company
Knoxville City Ballet
Knoxville Opera Company
Knoxville Symphony
Oak Ridge Orchestra
Art Museums and Galleries
Ewing Gallery of Art & Architecture
Knoxville Museum of Art
UT McClung Museum
Public Libraries
10 systems, 29 branches
1,161,988 books; circulation: 3,002,934
Places Rated Score: 56.25
Places Rated Rank: 121

Kokomo, IN

Concert Radio
WHLA-FM
Lively Arts Calendar
Touring Artists Bookings: 25 dates
Resident Ensemble: 6 dates
La Crosse Symphony
Art Museums and Galleries
Pump House Center for the Arts
Public Libraries
4 systems, 7 branches
384,879 books; circulation: 1,191,122
Places Rated Score: 41.11
Places Rated Rank: 206

Lafayette, IN
Concert Radio
WBAA-AM
Lively Arts Calendar
Touring Artists Bookings: 20 dates
Resident Ensembles: 44 dates
Lafayette Symphony
Purdue University Theater
Art Museums and Galleries
Greater Lafayette Museum of Art
Purdue University Galleries
Public Libraries
5 systems, 3 branches
463,488 books; circulation: 1,425,511
Places Rated Score: 43.63
Places Rated Rank: 190

Lafayette, LA
Concert Radio
KRVS-FM
Lively Arts Calendar
Touring Artists Bookings: 21 dates
Resident Ensemble: 9 dates
Arcadiana Symphony
Art Museums and Galleries
University Art Museum
Public Libraries
5 systems, 20 branches
663,927 books; circulation: 1,592,133
Places Rated Score: 28.13
Places Rated Rank: 269

Lake Charles, LA

Lively Arts Calendar
Resident Ensemble: 8 dates
Lake Charles Symphony
Art Museums and Galleries
Imperial Calcasieu Museum
Public Libraries
1 system, 13 branches
274,487 books; circulation: 661,016
Places Rated Score: 17.67
Places Rated Rank: 311

Lakeland–Winter Haven, FL
Concert Radio
In Tampa–St. Petersburg media market
Lively Arts Calendar
Touring Artists Bookings: 51 dates
Resident Ensemble: 7 dates
Imperial Symphony
Art Museums and Galleries
Polk Museum of Art
Public Libraries
11 systems, 1 branch
322,038 books; circulation: 753,872
Places Rated Score: 1.63
Places Rated Rank: 343

Lancaster, PA
Concert Radio
WIXQ-FM
Lively Arts Calendar
Touring Artists Bookings: 22 dates
Resident Ensembles: 77 dates
Fulton Opera House
Independent Eye
Lancaster Opera Company
Lancaster Symphony
Art Museums and Galleries
Community Gallery of Lancaster
Heritage Center of Lancaster County
Public Libraries
10 systems, 7 branches
440,879 books; circulation: 1,567,989
Places Rated Score: 30.98
Places Rated Rank: 257

Lansing–East Lansing, MI
Concert Radio
WKAR-FM
Lively Arts Calendar
Touring Artists Bookings: 55 dates
Resident Ensembles: 112 dates
BoarsHead: Michigan Public Theater
MSU Theater
Opera Company of Mid Michigan
Art Museums and Galleries
Kresge Art Museum
Lansing Art Gallery
Public Libraries
17 systems, 13 branches
733,498 books; circulation: 2,263,832
Places Rated Score: 44.83
Places Rated Rank: 181

Laredo, TX
Lively Arts Calendar
Resident Ensembles: 23 dates
Chamber Orchestra of the Two Laredos
Laredo Philharmonic Orchestra
Public Libraries
1 system, 2 branches
86,965 books; circulation: 233,678
Places Rated Score: 1.60
Places Rated Rank: 344

Las Cruces, NM
Concert Radio
In El Paso media market
KRWG-FM
Lively Arts Calendar
Touring Artists Bookings: 6 dates
Resident Ensemble: 12 dates
Las Cruces Symphony
Art Museums and Galleries
NMSU Art Gallery
Public Libraries
3 independent systems
165,018 books; circulation: 334,362
Places Rated Score: 0.02
Places Rated Rank: 349

Las Vegas, NV–AZ
Concert Radio
KNPR-FM
Lively Arts Calendar
Touring Artists Bookings: 119 dates
Resident Ensembles: 46 dates
Las Vegas Civic Symphony
Nevada Opera Theater
Nevada Symphony
Art Museums and Galleries
Las Vegas Art Museum
UNLV Beam Fine Art Gallery
Public Libraries
1 system, 8 branches
1,668,842 books; circulation: 4,538,753
Places Rated Score: 46.05
Places Rated Rank: 177

Lawrence, KS
Concert Radio
In Kansas City media market
KANU-FM
Lively Arts Calendar
Touring Artists Bookings: 33 dates
Resident Ensemble: 4 dates
Lawrence Chamber Players
Art Museums and Galleries
KU Spencer Museum of Art
Public Libraries
3 independent systems
227,922 books; circulation: 638,789
Places Rated Score: 29.24
Places Rated Rank: 265

Lawrence, MA–NH
Concert Radio
In Boston media market
Art Museums and Galleries
Addison Gallery of American Art
Public Libraries
23 systems, 2 branches
1,446,479 books; circulation: 2,302,616
Places Rated Score: 59.48
Places Rated Rank: 106

Lawton, OK
Concert Radio
In Wichita Falls media market
KCCU-FM
Lively Arts Calendar
Touring Artists Bookings: 4 dates
Resident Ensemble: 12 dates
Lawton Philharmonic Orchestra
Public Libraries
2 systems, 1 branch
118,099 books; circulation: 231,356
Places Rated Score: 1.00
Places Rated Rank: 346

Lewiston–Auburn, ME
Concert Radio
In Portland media market
Lively Arts Calendar
Touring Artists Bookings: 19 dates
Public Libraries
5 independent systems
219,296 books; circulation: 478,608
Places Rated Score: 16.31
Places Rated Rank: 317

Lexington, KY
Concert Radio
WEKU-FM, WUKY-FM
Lively Arts Calendar
Touring Artists Bookings: 65 dates
Resident Ensemble: 104 dates
Lexington Ballet
Art Museums and Galleries
Berea College Museums
Headley-Whitney Museum
UK Art Museum
Public Libraries
7 systems, 5 branches
861,069 books; circulation: 2,698,201
Places Rated Score: 50.65
Places Rated Rank: 157

Lima, OH
Concert Radio
In Dayton media market
WGLE-FM
Lively Arts Calendar
Touring Artists Bookings: 9 dates
Resident Ensemble: 14 dates
Lima Symphony
Public Libraries
5 systems, 10 branches
537,646 books; circulation: 1,399,015
Places Rated Score: 46.03
Places Rated Rank: 178

Lincoln, NE
Concert Radio
KUCV-FM
Lively Arts Calendar
Touring Artists Bookings: 79 dates
Resident Ensembles: 77 dates
Lincoln Orchestra
Nebraska Jazz Orchestra
Nebraska Repertory Theater
University of Nebraska Theater
Art Museums and Galleries
Nebraska Wesleyan Elder Art Gallery
UN Sheldon Art Gallery
Public Libraries
1 system, 6 branches
559,420 books; circulation: 1,796,793
Places Rated Score: 58.42
Places Rated Rank: 110

Little Rock–North Little Rock, AR
Concert Radio
KLRE-FM, KUAR-FM
Lively Arts Calendar
Touring Artists Bookings: 18 dates
Resident Ensembles: 143 dates
Arkansas Repertory Theater
Arkansas Symphony
Arts Center Children's Theater
Ballet Arakansas
Opera Theater at Wildwood
Art Museums and Galleries
Arkansas Arts Center
Public Libraries
4 systems, 16 branches
1,010,777 books; circulation: 1,564,329
Places Rated Score: 41.81
Places Rated Rank: 201

London, ON
Concert Radio
In Toronto media market
CBBL-FM, CIXX-FM
Lively Arts Calendar

Touring Artists Bookings: 6 dates
Resident Ensembles: 286 dates
Grand Theater
London Communty Orchestra
Orchestra London Canada

Art Museums and Galleries
Art Gallery St. Thomas-Elgin
London Regional Art Gallery
McIntosh Gallery

Public Libraries
4 systems, 36 branches
1,154,426 books; circulation: 3,127,566

Places Rated Score: 63.77
Places Rated Rank: 101

✓ Long Island, NY

Concert Radio
In New York media market

Heckscher Museum
Hofstra Museum
Institute for Contemporary Art
Parrish Art Museum

Public Libraries
108 systems, 20 branches
13,705,027 books; circulation: 27,624,421

Places Rated Score: 98.85
Places Rated Rank: 9

Longview–Marshall, TX

Concert Radio
In Shreveport media market

Lively Arts Calendar
Touring Artists Bookings: 7 dates
Resident Ensembles: 12 dates
Longview Opera Repertory Company
Longview Symphony
Marshall Symphony

Art Museums and Galleries
Longview Museum & Arts Center

Public Libraries
5 independent systems
383,820 books; circulation: 536,091

Places Rated Score: 20.41
Places Rated Rank: 301

✓ Los Angeles–Long Beach, CA

Concert Radio
KCSN-FM, KKGO-FM, KUSC-FM

Lively Arts Calendar
Touring Artists Bookings: 1,737 dates
Resident Ensembles: 886 dates

Symphony Orchestras
American Jazz Philharmonic
Antelope Valley Symphony
Beverly Hills Symphony
Brentwood Westwood Symphony
Carson Dominguez Hills Symphony
Claremont Symphony
Glendale Symphony
Japan America Symphony
Long Beach Symphony
Los Angeles Chamber Orchestra
Los Angeles Doctors Symphony
Los Angeles Mozart Orchestra
Los Angeles Performing Arts Orchestra
Los Angeles Philharmonic Orchestra
Pasadena Symphony
Santa Monica Symphony
West Coast Ensemble

Opera Companies
Casa Itallana Opera Company
Guild Opera Company
Long Beach Civic Light Opera
Long Beach Opera
Los Angeles Concert Opera
Los Angeles Music Center Opera
Opera a la Carte (Gilbert & Sullivan)
Santa Cecilia Opera

Ballet Companies
Ballet Folklorico de Mexico
Los Angeles Ballet
Mainstage International Chamber Ballet

Professional Theaters
Colony Studio Theater
Cornerstone Theater Company

Lang Galleries of Claremont Colleges
Long Beach Museum of Art
Los Angeles County Museum of Art
Loyola Marymount Laband Art Gallery
Norton Simon Museum
Otis-Parsons Art Gallery
Pacific-Asia Museum
Palos Verdes Art Center
Plaza De La Raza
Skirball Museum, Hebrew Union College
Southwest Museum
UCLA Wight Art Gallery
USC Fisher Gallery

Public Libraries
32 systems, 195 branches
18,275,339 books; circulation: 36,524,026

Places Rated Score: 99.84
Places Rated Rank: 3

Louisville, KY–IN

Concert Radio
WFPK-FM, WUOL-FM

Lively Arts Calendar
Touring Artists Bookings: 311 dates
Resident Ensembles: 279 dates
Actors Theater
Kentucky Opera
Louisville Ballet
Stage One: Children's Theater
The Louisville Orchestra

Art Museums and Galleries
Allen Hite Art Institute Gallery
J.B. Speed Art Museum

Public Libraries
8 systems, 26 branches
1,539,771 books; circulation: 4,285,467

Places Rated Score: 71.06
Places Rated Rank: 79

Lowell, MA–NH

Concert Radio
In Boston media market

Lively Arts Calendar
Touring Artists Bookings: 30 dates
Resident Ensemble: 45 dates
Merrimack Repertory Theater

Art Museums and Galleries
Whistler House Museum of Art

Public Libraries
11 systems, 1 branch
822,140 books; circulation: 1,497,424

Places Rated Score: 51.23
Places Rated Rank: 153

Lubbock, TX

Concert Radio
KOHM-FM

Lively Arts Calendar
Touring Artists Bookings: 220 dates
Resident Ensemble: 10 dates
Lubbock Symphony

Art Museums and Galleries
Municipal Garden & Art Center

Public Libraries
4 systems, 1 branch
298,041 books; circulation: 621,996

Places Rated Score: 21.82

399,069 books; circulation: 1,196,031

Places Rated Score: 25.93
Places Rated Rank: 280

Macon, GA

Lively Arts Calendar
Touring Artists Bookings: 10 dates
Resident Ensemble: 13 dates
Macon Symphony

Art Museums and Galleries
Museum of Arts & Sciences
Tubman African American Museum

Public Libraries
2 systems, 17 branches
632,680 books; circulation: 2,747,857

Places Rated Score: 54.20
Places Rated Rank: 137

Madison, WI

Concert Radio
WERN-FM, WORT-FM

Lively Arts Calendar
Touring Artists Bookings: 97 dates
Resident Ensembles: 149 dates
Ballet Colbert
Madison Opera
Madison Repertory Theater
Madison Symphony
University of Wisconsin Theater
Wisconsin Chamber Orchestra

Art Museums and Galleries
Madison Art Center
UW Elvehjem Museum of Art

Public Libraries
17 systems, 7 branches
1,201,403 books; circulation: 4,500,564

Places Rated Score: 71.65
Places Rated Rank: 78

Manchester, NH

Concert Radio
In Boston media market

Lively Arts Calendar
Touring Artists Bookings: 54 dates
Resident Ensembles: 34 dates
New Hampshire Philharmonic Orchestra
New Hampshire Symphony

Art Museums and Galleries
Chapel Art Center

Currier Gallery of Art
Public Libraries
8 systems, 2 branches
505,906 books; circulation: 955,650
Places Rated Score: 42.07
Places Rated Rank: 198

Mansfield, OH
Concert Radio
In Cleveland media market
WOSV-FM
Lively Arts Calendar
Touring Artists Bookings: 4 dates
Resident Ensemble: 28 dates
Mansfield Symphony
Art Museums and Galleries
Mansfield Art Center
Public Libraries
5 systems, 8 branches
503,551 books; circulation: 2,080,551
Places Rated Score: 50.48
Places Rated Rank: 158

McAllen–Edinburg–Mission, TX
Concert Radio
KHID-FM
Lively Arts Calendar
Touring Artists Bookings: 4 dates
Resident Ensembles: 40 dates
Rio Grande Valley Ballet
Valley Symphony & Chorale
Public Libraries
10 independent systems
544,318 books; circulation: 1,104,120
Places Rated Score: 18.21
Places Rated Rank: 308

Medford–Ashland, OR
Concert Radio
KSOR-FM, KSRG-FM
Lively Arts Calendar
Touring Artists Bookings: 8 dates
Resident Ensembles: 107 dates
Britt Festival Orchestra
Oregon Shakespeare Festival
Rogue Opera
Rogue Valley Symphony
Art Museums and Galleries
Rogue Gallery
Stevenson Union Gallery
Public Libraries
1 system, 14 branches
354,690 books; circulation: 1,229,579
Places Rated Score: 40.10
Places Rated Rank: 213

Melbourne–Titusville–Palm Bay, FL
Lively Arts Calendar
Touring Artists Bookings: 113 dates
Resident Ensembles: 29 dates
Brevard Symphony
Florida Space Coast Philharmonic
Art Museums and Galleries
Brevard Art Center & Museum
Public Libraries
15 branches
988,456 books; circulation: 3,117,179
Places Rated Score: 51.81
Places Rated Rank: 148

Memphis, TN–AR–MS
Concert Radio
WKNO-FM
Lively Arts Calendar
Touring Artists Bookings: 29 dates
Resident Ensembles: 168 dates
Germantown Symphony
Memphis Concert Ballet
Memphis Symphony
Opera Memphis
Playhouse on the Square
Art Museums and Galleries
Dixon Gallery & Gardens
Memphis Brooks Museum of Art
MSU Art Museum
Public Libraries
6 systems, 33 branches
2,162,872 books; circulation: 5,392,782
Places Rated Score: 59.70
Places Rated Rank: 105

Merced, CA
Concert Radio
In Fresno–Visalia media market
Lively Arts Calendar
Resident Ensemble: 7 dates
Merced Symphony
Public Libraries
1 system, 16 branches
372,112 books; circulation: 302,381
Places Rated Score: 17.32
Places Rated Rank: 312

✓ Miami, FL
Concert Radio
WTMI-FM
Lively Arts Calendar
Touring Artists Bookings: 360 dates
Resident Ensembles: 287 dates
Ballet Spectacular
Coconut Grove Playhouse
Florida Grand Opera
Miami Chamber Symphony
Miami City Ballet
Miami Symphony
New World Symphony
North Miami Beach Opera
North Miami Beach Symphony
Art Museums and Galleries
Bass Museum of Art
Center For Fine Arts
FIU Art Museum
North Miami Center of Contemporary Art
UM Lowe Art Museum
Public Libraries
7 systems, 32 branches
3,770,213 books; circulation: 9,465,491
Places Rated Score: 91.69
Places Rated Rank: 31

Middlesex–Somerset–Hunterdon, NJ
Concert Radio
In New York media market
Lively Arts Calendar
Touring Artists Bookings: 183 dates
Resident Ensembles: 184 dates
American Repertory Ballet
Crossroads Theater Company
George Street Playhouse
Philharmonic Orchestra of New Jersey
Riverside Symphonia
Rutgers University Theater
Art Museums and Galleries
Hunterdon Art Center
Jane V. Zimmerli Art Museum
Public Libraries
42 systems, 17 branches
3,964,967 books; circulation: 7,311,688
Places Rated Score: 90.28
Places Rated Rank: 37

✓ Milwaukee–Waukesha, WI
Concert Radio
WFMR-FM
Lively Arts Calendar
Touring Artists Bookings: 179 dates
Resident Ensembles: 567 dates
American Inside Theater
First Stage Milwaukee
Florentine Opera Company
Milwaukee Ballet
Milwaukee Catholic Symphony
Milwaukee Chamber Orchestra
Milwaukee Chamber Theater
Milwaukee Repertory Theater
Milwaukee Symphony
Skylight Opera Theater
Theater X
Waukesha Symphony
Art Museums and Galleries
Charles Allis Art Museum
Haggerty Museum of Art
Milwaukee Art Museum
Ozaukee Art Center
UWM Art Museum
West Bend Gallery of Fine Arts
Public Libraries
41 systems, 12 branches
5,011,457 books; circulation: 12,019,031
Places Rated Score: 92.98
Places Rated Rank: 27

✓ Minneapolis–St. Paul, MN–WI
Concert Radio
KSJN-FM
Lively Arts Calendar
Touring Artists Bookings: 879 dates
Resident Ensembles: 836 dates
Andahazy Ballet Company
Bloomington Symphony
Children's Theater Company
Civic Orchestra of Minneapolis
Great American History Theater
Guthrie Theater
Illusion Theater
James Sewell Ballet
Lakewood Symphony
Metropolitan Symphony
Minneapolis Pops Orchestra
Minnesota Opera
Minnesota Orchestra
Minnetonka Symphony
Mixed Blood Theater Company
North Star Opera
Penumbra Theater Company
Playright's Center
Saint Paul Chamber Orchestra
Theater de la Jeune Lune
University of Minnesota Theater
Art Museums and Galleries
Bloomington Art Center
Gallery 101
Hamline University Galleries
Minneapolis Institute of Art
Minnesota Museum of American Art
UM Weisman Art Museum
Walker Art Center
Public Libraries
27 systems, 106 branches
7,115,921 books; circulation: 27,651,759
Places Rated Score: 97.96
Places Rated Rank: 13

Mobile, AL
Concert Radio
WHIL-FM
Lively Arts Calendar
Touring Artists Bookings: 264 dates
Resident Ensemble: 5 dates
Mobile Opera
Art Museums and Galleries
Eastern Shore Art Center

Mobile Museum of Art
Public Libraries
16 systems, 7 branches
753,086 books; circulation: 2,166,980
Places Rated Score: 44.28
Places Rated Rank: 186

Modesto, CA
Lively Arts Calendar
Touring Artists Bookings: 12 dates
Resident Ensembles: 62 dates
Modesto Civic Ballet Company
Modesto Symphony
Townsend Opera Players
Art Museums and Galleries
University Art Gallery
Public Libraries
1 system, 12 branches

Metro Lyric Opera
Monmouth Symphony
Paradise Chamber Orchestra
Public Libraries
29 systems, 30 branches
3,040,087 books; circulation: 7,246,676
Places Rated Score: 82.89
Places Rated Rank: 49

Monroe, LA
Concert Radio
KEDM-FM
Lively Arts Calendar
Touring Artists Bookings: 11 dates
Resident Ensemble: 10 dates
Monroe Symphony
Art Museums and Galleries
Masur Museum of Art
Public Libraries
1 system, 4 branches
291,303 books; circulation: 836,973
Places Rated Score: 29.85
Places Rated Rank: 262

Montgomery, AL
Lively Arts Calendar
Touring Artists Bookings: 5 dates
Resident Ensembles: 80 dates
Alabama Shakespeare Festival
Montgomery Ballet
Montgomery Symphony
Art Museums and Galleries
Montgomery Museum of Fine Arts
Public Libraries
5 systems, 16 branches
488,581 books; circulation: 633,639
Places Rated Score: 21.65
Places Rated Rank: 297

✓ Montreal, PQ
Lively Arts Calendar
Touring Artists Bookings: 1,994 dates
Resident Ensembles: 808 dates
Symphony Orchestras
McGill Chamber Orchestra
Montreal Chamber Orchestra
Orchestre Symphonique de la Monteregie

Orchestre Symphonique de Montreal
Opera Companies
Karoussos Opera Productions
L'Opera de Montreal
Ballet Companies
Les Ballets Jazz de Montreal
Les Grands Ballets Canadiens
Professional Theaters
Beton Blues
Black Theater Workshop
Carbone 14
Centaur Theater Company
Clowns Gone Bad Productions
DynamO Theater
Festival Theater des Ameriques
Geordie Productions
Groupe de la Veilee
Imago Theater

Theater de Campagnie Carrousel
Theater de la Ligue Nationale Di
Theater de la Manufacture
Theater de Quat'sous
Theater du Cafe De La Place
Theater du Nouveau Monde
Theater du Rideau Vert
Theater du Vieux-Terrebonne
Theater Experimental des Femmes
Theater Sans Fils
Theater Ubu
Theater Zoopsie
Art Museums and Galleries
Bronfman Centre Art Gallery
Centre Canadien d'Architecture
Centre International d'Art Contemporain
Concordia Art Gallery
Dorval Cultural Centre
Galerie l'Industrielle-Alliance
Galerie Powerhouse
Maison Louis-Hippolyte Lafontaine
Musee d'Art Contemporain
Musee de la Ville de Lachine
Musee des Arts Decoratifs
Musee des Beaux-Arts de Montreal
Musee Itinerant d'Art Byzantin
Musee Marc-Aurele Fortin
Visual Arts Centre
Public Libraries
55 systems, 196 branches
6,481,409 books; circulation: 14,386,819
Places Rated Score: 98.21
Places Rated Rank: 12

Muncie, IN
Concert Radio
In Indianapolis media market
WBST-FM
Lively Arts Calendar
Touring Artists Bookings: 13 dates
Resident Ensemble: 6 dates
Muncie Symphony
Art Museums and Galleries
Ball State University Museum of Art
Public Libraries
1 system, 5 branches
264,020 books; circulation: 689,961
Places Rated Score: 17.99
Places Rated Rank: 310

Myrtle Beach, SC
Concert Radio
WHMC-FM
Lively Arts Calendar
Touring Artists Bookings: 5 dates
Resident Ensembles: 5 dates
Long Bay Symphony
Myrtle Beach Philharmonic
Public Libraries
2 systems, 5 branches
249,591 books; circulation: 647,456
Places Rated Score: 23.07
Places Rated Rank: 293

Naples, FL
Lively Arts Calendar

Nashua, NH
Concert Radio
In Boston media market
Lively Arts Calendar
Touring Artists Bookings: 6 dates
Resident Ensembles: 77 dates
American Stage Festival
Nashua Symphony & Choral
Public Libraries
13 systems, 1 branch
535,575 books; circulation: 1,383,697
Places Rated Score: 47.38
Places Rated Rank: 173

Nashville, TN
Concert Radio
WPLN-FM
Lively Arts Calendar
Touring Artists Bookings: 97 dates
Resident Ensembles: 132 dates
Nashville Ballet
Nashville Opera
Tennessee Opera Theater
Tennessee Repertory Theater
Art Museums and Galleries
Botanical Gardens & Museum of Art
Fisk University Galleries
Vanderbilt Fine Arts Gallery
Public Libraries
16 systems, 26 branches
2,136,314 books; circulation: 5,362,074
Places Rated Score: 70.93
Places Rated Rank: 80

New Bedford, MA
Concert Radio
In Providence media market
Lively Arts Calendar
Touring Artists Bookings: 86 dates
Resident Ensemble: 7 dates
New Bedford Symphony
Public Libraries
6 systems, 4 branches
587,401 books; circulation: 662,907
Places Rated Score: 35.97
Places Rated Rank: 234

New Haven–Meriden, CT

Concert Radio
WGRS-FM, WPKT-FM
Lively Arts Calendar
Touring Artists Bookings: 143 dates
Resident Ensembles: 283 dates
Connecticut Chamber Orchestra
Long Wharf Theater
Meriden Symphony
New Haven Symphony
Orchestra New England
Wallingford Symphony
Yale Repertory Theater
Art Museums and Galleries
Yale Center for British Art
Yale University Art Gallery
Public Libraries
18 systems, 9 branches
2,113,007 books; circulation: 3,437,815
Places Rated Score: 81.11
Places Rated Rank: 52

New London–Norwich, CT–RI
Concert Radio
In Hartford–New Haven media market
WNPR-FM
Lively Arts Calendar
Touring Artists Bookings: 69 dates
Resident Ensembles: 81 dates
Eastern Connecticut Symphony
O'Neill Theater Center
Art Museums and Galleries
Florence Griswold Museum
Lyman Allyn Art Museum
Public Libraries
23 systems, 1 branch
885,076 books; circulation: 1,844,391
Places Rated Score: 58.39
Places Rated Rank: 111

New Orleans, LA
Concert Radio
WTUL-FM, WWNO-FM
Lively Arts Calendar
Touring Artists Bookings: 60 dates
Resident Ensembles: 169 dates
Delta Festival Ballet
Louisiana Philharmonic Orchestra
New Orleans Ballet Association
New Orleans Opera Association
Art Museums and Galleries
Louisiana State Museum
New Orleans Museum of Art
Tulane University Galleries
UNO Fine Arts Gallery
Public Libraries
8 systems, 48 branches
2,686,674 books; circulation: 4,399,968
Places Rated Score: 73.28
Places Rated Rank: 73

✓ New York, NY
Concert Radio
WKCR-FM, WNYC-FM, WQXR-AM, WQXR-FM, WVIP-AM
Lively Arts Calendar
Touring Artists Bookings: 2,915 dates
Resident Ensembles: 3,544 dates
Symphony Orchestras
American Composers Orchestra
American Symphony
Bachanalia Festival Orchestra
Bel Canto Society
Clarion Concerts
Cosmopolitan Symphony
Empire State Pops Orchestra
Fine Arts Symphony
Greenwich Village Orchestra
Hunter Symphony
International Chamber Orchestra
Little Orchestra Society of New York
Manhattan Philharmonic
Mozart Festival Orchestra
New American Chamber Orchestra
New York Chamber Symphony
New York City Symphony
New York Orchestral Society
New York Philharmonic
New York Pops Orchestra
New York Pro Arte Chamber Orchestra
New York Scandia Symphony
New York Sinfonia Orchestra
Orchestra of St. Luke's
Orpheus Chamber Orchestra
Philharmonia Virtuosi
Symphony for United Nations
Tchaikovsky Chamber Orchestra
The Boston Group
The Concordia Orchestra
The Riverside Symphony
West End Symphony
Westchester Symphony
Opera Companies
After Dinner Opera Company
Amato Opera Theater
American Chamber Opera
American Opera Projects
Dicapo Opera Theater
Empire State Opera
Il Piccolo Teatro Dell' Opera
Juilliard Opera Center
l'Opera Francais de New York
La Gran Scena Opera Company
Liederkranz Opera Theater
Magic Circle Opera Repertory Ensemble
Manhattan Opera Association
Marcel Achille Opera
Metropolitan Opera Association
National Company New York City Opera
New Rochelle Opera
New York City Opera
New York Gilbert & Sullivan Players
New York Grand Opera
New York Opera Project
Opera Northeast
Opera on the Go
Opera Orchestra of New York
PALA Opera Association
Queens Opera Association
Regina Opera Company
Rockland Opera
Village Light Opera Group
Ballet Companies
American Ballet Theater
Anglo-American Ballet
Ballet Hispanico of New York
Ballet Manhattan
Bronx Opera Company
Center for Contemporary Opera
Children's Free Opera & Dance
Feld Ballets/NY
Les Ballets Trockadero de Monte Carlo
New York City Ballet
New York Theater Ballet
Rebecca Kelly Ballet
The Joffrey Ballet
Professional Theaters
Acting Company
American International Lyric Theater
Circle Repertory Company
Classic Stage Company
Encompass Music Theater
Jean Cocteau Repertory Theater
Lincoln Center Theater
Mabou Mines
Manhattan Theater Club
Measured Breaths Theater Company
Music Theater Group
New Dramatists
New Federal Theater
New York Shakespeare Festival
New York Theater Workshop
Ontological-Hysteric Theater
Open Eye: New Stagings
Pan Asian Repertory Theater
Playwrights Horizons
Roundabout Theater Company
Second Stage Theater
Theater for a New Audience
Theater for the New City
Theater Rococo
Theaterworks-USA
Vineyard Theater
Vivaldi Traveling Circus
Women's Project & Productions
Wooster Group
Young Playwrights Festival
Art Museums and Galleries
American Craft Museum
Americas Society
Asia Society Galleries
Bronx Museum of the Arts
Bronx River Art Center
Brooklyn Museum
Cloisters
Frick Collection
Hammond Museum
Hispanic Society of America
International Center of Photography
International Museum of African Art
Jamaica Arts Center
Jewish Museum
Katonah Museum of Art
Metropolitan Museum of Art
Museum of Modern Art
National Academy of Design Museum
NYU Grey Art Gallery
Pelham Art Center
Pierpont Morgan Library & Art Museum
Solomon Guggenheim Museum
Whitney Museum of American Art
Yeshiva University Museum
Public Libraries
66 systems, 210 branches
35,966,244 books; circulation: 44,041,619
Places Rated Score: 99.99
Places Rated Rank: 1

✓ Newark, NJ
Concert Radio
In New York media market
Lively Arts Calendar
Touring Artists Bookings: 249 dates
Resident Ensembles: 332 dates
Colonial Symphony
Community Opera of New York
Livingston Symphony
Metropolitan Orchestra
New Jersey Ballet Company
New Jersey Shakespeare Festival
New Jersey State Opera
New Jersey Symphony
New Philharmonic of New Jersey
New Sussex Symphony
Opera at Florham
Plainfield Symphony
Summit Symphony
Westfield Symphony
Art Museums and Galleries
Kean College Gallery
Montclair Art Museum
Morris Museum
Newark Museum

Public Libraries
80 systems, 36 branches
8,584,648 books; circulation: 11,343,017
Places Rated Score: 97.54
Places Rated Rank: 14

Newburgh, NY–PA
Concert Radio
In New York media market
WOSR-FM
Lively Arts Calendar
Touring Artists Bookings: 135 dates
Public Libraries
18 systems, 7 branches
706,169 books; circulation: 1,511,181
Places Rated Score: 33.39
Places Rated Rank: 247

Norfolk–Virginia Beach–Newport

Virginia Symphony
Williamsburg Symphonia
Art Museums and Galleries
Abby Rockefeller Folk Art Center
Charles H. Taylor Arts Center
Chrysler Museum
Hampton University Museum
Heritage Foundation Museum
Muscarelle Museum of Art
Peninsula Fine Arts Center
Portsmouth Fine Arts Gallery
Virginia Beach Center for the Arts
Public Libraries
11 systems, 38 branches
3,391,071 books; circulation: 8,897,648
Places Rated Score: 79.35
Places Rated Rank: 59

✓ Oakland, CA
Concert Radio
KSMC-FM
Lively Arts Calendar
Touring Artists Bookings: 984 dates
Resident Ensembles: 306 dates
Berkeley Ballet Theater
Berkeley Opera
Berkeley Repertory Theater
Berkeley Symphony
California Chamber Orchestra & Chamber Opera Company
California Opera
California Symphony
CitiArts Theater
Classical Philharmonic/Northern California
Fremont Symphony
Livermore Amador Symphony
Oakland Ballet
Oakland East Bay Symphony
Oakland Ensemble Theater
Oakland Lyric Opera
Prometheus Symphony
San Francisco Bay Philharmonic
San Francisco Chamber Orchestra
Art Museums and Galleries
Bedford Gallery
Berkeley Art Center
Judah Magnes Memorial Museum
Oakland Museum
Richmond Art Center
University of California Art Museum
Public Libraries
9 systems, 60 branches
4,283,578 books; circulation: 12,477,566
Places Rated Score: 97.50
Places Rated Rank: 15

Ocala, FL
Concert Radio
In Orlando–Daytona Beach–Melbourne media market
Lively Arts Calendar
Resident Ensemble: 6 dates
Central Florida Smyphony
Art Museums and Galleries
Appleton Museum of Art

Midland-Odessa Symphony & Chorale
Art Museums and Galleries
Art Institute for the Permian Basin
Public Libraries
2 systems, 1 branch
359,936 books; circulation: 810,672
Places Rated Score: 21.65
Places Rated Rank: 297

Oklahoma City, OK
Concert Radio
KCSC-FM, KGOU-FM, KROU-FM
Lively Arts Calendar
Touring Artists Bookings: 28 dates
Resident Ensembles: 237 dates
Ballet Oklahoma
Cimarron Circuit Opera Company
Lyric Theater of Oklahoma
Oklahoma City Philharmonic Orchestra
Oklahoma Festival Ballet
Art Museums and Galleries
Mabee-Gerrer Museum of Art
Oklahoma City Art Museum
OU Jones Museum of Art
Public Libraries
7 systems, 19 branches
1,311,272 books; circulation: 6,118,623
Places Rated Score: 69.77
Places Rated Rank: 87

Olympia, WA
Concert Radio
In Seattle–Tacoma media market
Lively Arts Calendar
Touring Artists Bookings: 38 dates
Resident Ensemble: 10 dates
Olympia Symphony
Art Museums and Galleries
Evergreen Galleries
Washington State Capital Museum
Public Libraries
1 system, 9 branches
412,967 books; circulation: 1,779,466
Places Rated Score: 86.56
Places Rated Rank: 43

Omaha, NE–IA
Concert Radio
KIOS-FM, KIWR-FM, KVNO-FM
Lively Arts Calendar
Touring Artists Bookings: 38 dates
Resident Ensembles: 539 dates
Ballet Omaha
Emmy Gifford Children's Theater
Nebraska Theater Caravan
Nebraska Wind Symphony
Omaha Magic Theater
Omaha Symphony
Omaha Symphony Chamber Orchestra
Opera/Omaha
Art Museums and Galleries
Joslyn Art Museum
Public Libraries
23 systems, 9 branches
1,362,049 books; circulation: 3,163,582
Places Rated Score: 75.57
Places Rated Rank: 66

Cypress Pops Orchestra
Fullerton Civic Light Opera
Mozart Camerata
Opera Pacific
Pacific Symphony
Saddleback Chamber Players
South Coast Repertory Theater
University of California Theater
Art Museums and Galleries
Art Institute of Southern California
Brea Civic & Cultural Center Gallery
Charles W. Bowers Museum
Irvine Fine Arts Center
Laguna Art Museum
Newport Harbor Art Museum
Public Libraries
9 systems, 43 branches
4,597,164 books; circulation: 13,421,644
Places Rated Score: 95.01
Places Rated Rank: 22

Orlando, FL
Concert Radio
WMFE-FM, WPRK-FM
Lively Arts Calendar
Touring Artists Bookings: 26 dates
Resident Ensembles: 128 dates
Orlando Opera Company
Orlando Philharmonic
Southern Ballet Theater
Art Museums and Galleries
Maitland Art Center
Morse Museum of American Art
Orlando Museum of Art
Rollins College Cornell Museum
Public Libraries
13 systems, 23 branches
2,585,215 books; circulation: 8,703,298
Places Rated Score: 79.03
Places Rated Rank: 61

Oshawa, ON
Lively Arts Calendar
Resident Ensemble: 4 dates
Oshawa-Durham Symphony
Art Museums and Galleries
Robert McLaughlin Gallery
The Station Gallery
Public Libraries

2 systems, 23 branches
466,205 books; circulation: 1,513,099
Places Rated Score: 31.99
Places Rated Rank: 252

Ottawa–Hull, ON–PQ
Lively Arts Calendar
Touring Artists Bookings: 271 dates
Resident Ensembles: 285 dates
Great Canadian Theater Company
Groupe Derives Urbaines
National Arts Centre
National Arts Centre Orchestra
Odyssey Theater
Opera Lyra Ottawa
Ottawa Symphony
Passionate Balance
Rag & Bone Puppet Theater
Theater de l'Ille
Art Museums and Galleries
Algonquin College Museum
Axe Neo-7 Art Contemporain
Centre Culturel l'Imagier
Galerie Montcalm
Gallery 101
Museum of Contemporary Photography
National Gallery of Canada
Saw Gallery
Wildlife & Wilderness Art Museum
Public Libraries
15 systems, 84 branches
1,964,514 books; circulation: 6,110,024
Places Rated Score: 73.97
Places Rated Rank: 71

Owensboro, KY
Concert Radio
In Evansville media market
WKWC-FM
Lively Arts Calendar
Touring Artists Bookings: 105 dates
Resident Ensemble: 15 dates
Owensboro Symphony
Art Museums and Galleries
Owensboro Museum of Fine Art
Public Libraries
1 independent system
134,292 books; circulation: 341,332
Places Rated Score: 19.20
Places Rated Rank: 305

Panama City, FL
Concert Radio
WKGC-FM
Lively Arts Calendar
Touring Artists Bookings: 10 dates
Art Museums and Galleries
Visual Arts Center of Northwest Florida
Public Libraries
1 system, 6 branches
150,428 books; circulation: 418,801
Places Rated Score: 15.70
Places Rated Rank: 318

Parkersburg–Marietta, WV–OH
Concert Radio
WMRT-FM, WVPG-FM
Lively Arts Calendar
Touring Artists Bookings: 4 dates
Resident Ensemble: 100 dates
Mid Ohio Valley Ballet Company
Art Museums and Galleries
Parkersburg Art Center
Public Libraries
3 systems, 5 branches
336,833 books; circulation: 981,675
Places Rated Score: 50.23
Places Rated Rank: 160

Pensacola, FL
Concert Radio
WUWF-FM
Lively Arts Calendar
Touring Artists Bookings: 153 dates
Resident Ensemble: 9 dates
Greater Pensacola Symphony
Art Museums and Galleries
Pensacola Museum of Art
Visual Arts Gallery Pensacola
Public Libraries
1 system, 6 branches
206,234 books; circulation: 891,467
Places Rated Score: 23.22
Places Rated Rank: 291

Peoria–Pekin, IL
Concert Radio
WCBU-FM
Lively Arts Calendar
Touring Artists Bookings: 96 dates
Resident Ensembles: 15 dates
Peoria Civic Opera
Peoria Symphony
Art Museums and Galleries
Lakeview Museum of Arts & Sciences
Public Libraries
24 systems, 10 branches
1,545,580 books; circulation: 2,389,340
Places Rated Score: 57.00
Places Rated Rank: 118

✓ Philadelphia, PA–NJ
Concert Radio
WFLN-FM
Lively Arts Calendar
Touring Artists Bookings: 522 dates
Resident Ensembles: 972 dates
Symphony Orchestras
Burlington Civic Orchestra
Concerto Soloists Chamber Orchestra
Haddonfield Symphony
Kennett Symphony
Lansdowne Symphony
North Penn Symphony
Orchestra Society of Philadelphia
Pennsylvania Ballet Orchestra
Pennsy Pops
Philadelphia Doctors' Symphony
Philadelphia Orchestra
Philharmonic of Southern New Jersey
Pottstown Symphony
South Jersey Symphony
West Jersey Chamber Symphony
Opera Companies
AVA Opera Theater
Lyric Opera Theater
Opera Company of Philadelphia
Ballet Companies
National Ballet of New Jersey
Peninsula Ballet
Professional Theaters
Arden Theater Company
Festival Theater for New Plays
Novel Stages
People's Theater Company
Philadelphia Drama Guild
Philadelphia Theater Company
Society Hill Playhouse
Temple University Theater
Walnut Street Theater Company
Wilma Theater
Art Museums and Galleries
Brandywine River Museum
Institute for Contemporary Art
La Salle University Art Museum
Paley Gallery
Pennsylvania Academy of the Fine Arts
Perkins Center for the Arts
Philadelphia Museum of Art
Philadelphia Art Alliance
Please Touch Museum
Rutgers University Stedman Art Gallery
University of Pennsylvania Galleries
Widner University Art Museum
Woodmere Art Museum
Public Libraries
124 systems, 92 branches
12,220,670 books; circulation: 23,561,726
Places Rated Score: 99.15
Places Rated Rank: 7

✓ Phoenix–Mesa, AZ
Concert Radio
KBAQ-FM
Lively Arts Calendar
Touring Artists Bookings: 622 dates
Resident Ensembles: 325 dates
Arizona Opera Company
Arizona Theater Company
Ballet Arizona
Childsplay
Fine Arts Orchestra
Mesa Symphony
Metro Pops Orchestra
Scottsdale Symphony
The Phoenix Symphony
Art Museums and Galleries
Arizona State University Gallery
Fleischer Museum
Heard Museum
Phoenix Art Museum
Plotkin Judaica Museum
Scottsdale Center for the Arts
Public Libraries
29 systems, 26 branches
4,646,763 books; circulation: 16,195,049
Places Rated Score: 90.95
Places Rated Rank: 34

Pine Bluff, AR
Lively Arts Calendar
Touring Artists Bookings: 3 dates
Resident Ensemble: 4 dates
Pine Bluff Symphony
Art Museums and Galleries
Southeast Arkansas Arts & Science Center
Public Libraries
1 system, 2 branches
115,561 books; circulation: 211,868
Places Rated Score: 17.29
Places Rated Rank: 313

✓ Pittsburgh, PA
Concert Radio
WQED-FM
Lively Arts Calendar
Touring Artists Bookings: 176 dates
Resident Ensembles: 595 dates
American Wind Symphony
Carnegie-Mellon Philharmonic
City Theater Company
Civic Light Opera
Edgewood Symphony
McKeesport Symphony
Opera Theater of Pittsburgh
Pittsburgh Ballet Theater
Pittsburgh Civic Orchestra
Pittsburgh Opera
Pittsburgh Public Theater
Pittsburgh Symphony
River City Brass Band
Westmoreland Symphony
Art Museums and Galleries
Associated Artists of Pittsburgh Gallery

Carnegie Museum of Art
Frick Art Museum
Pittsburgh Center for the Arts
Westmoreland Museum of Art
Public Libraries
97 systems, 29 branches
5,522,761 books; circulation: 10,361,699
Places Rated Score: 92.68
Places Rated Rank: 28

Pittsfield, MA
Concert Radio
In Albany–Schenectady–Troy media market
Lively Arts Calendar
Touring Artists Bookings: 27 dates
Resident Ensembles: 45 dates
Berkshire Opera Company

Concert Radio
WMEA-FM, WPKM-FM
Lively Arts Calendar
Touring Artists Bookings: 29 dates
Resident Ensembles: 88 dates
Portland Stage Company
Portland Symphony
Art Museums and Galleries
Portland Museum of Art
Public Libraries
19 systems, 5 branches
721,599 books; circulation: 1,535,414
Places Rated Score: 52.51
Places Rated Rank: 146

Portland–Vancouver, OR–WA
Concert Radio
KBPS-AM, KBPS-FM, KOPB-FM
Lively Arts Calendar
Touring Artists Bookings: 327 dates
Resident Ensembles: 232 dates
Mt. Hood Pops Orchestra
Oregon Ballet Theater
Oregon Symphony
Portland Baroque Orchestra
Portland Opera Association
Portland Repertory Theater
Sinphonia Concertante Orchestra
Vancouver Symphony
Art Museums and Galleries
Portland Art Museum
North View Gallery
Public Libraries
33 systems, 26 branches
2,075,753 books; circulation: 17,210,964
Places Rated Score: 85.47
Places Rated Rank: 45

Portsmouth–Rochester, NH–ME
Concert Radio
In Boston media market
Lively Arts Calendar
Touring Artists Bookings: 42 dates
Art Museums and Galleries
Lamont Gallery
UNH Art Gallery
Public Libraries
28 independent systems
790,612 books; circulation: 1,754,294
Places Rated Score: 51.53
Places Rated Rank: 150

Providence–Fall River–Warwick, RI–MA
Concert Radio
WLKW-AM
Lively Arts Calendar
Touring Artists Bookings: 41 dates
Resident Ensembles: 76 dates
Rhode Island Civic Chorale & Orchestra
Rhode Island Philharmonic Orchestra
State Ballet of Rhode Island
Trinity Repertory Theater
Art Museums and Galleries
Brown University Art Galleries
Rhode Island School of Design Gallery
Public Libraries

Resident Ensemble: 10 dates
Utah Valley Symphony
Art Museums and Galleries
BYU Larsen Gallery
Museum of Art
Public Libraries
9 independent systems
554,342 books; circulation: 2,564,810
Places Rated Score: 50.00
Places Rated Rank: 162

Pueblo, CO
Concert Radio
In Colorado Springs media market
Lively Arts Calendar
Touring Artists Bookings: 38 dates
Resident Ensemble: 6 dates
Pueblo Symphony
Art Museums and Galleries
Sangre De Cristo Arts Center
Public Libraries
1 system, 2 branches
287,586 books; circulation: 832,337
Places Rated Score: 35.05
Places Rated Rank: 238

Punta Gorda, FL
Concert Radio
In Fort Myers–Naples media market
Lively Arts Calendar
Touring Artists Bookings: 21 dates
Resident Ensembles: 31 dates
Charlotte County Memorial Celebrity Series
Friends of Music of Charlotte County
Performing Arts Society of South Florida
Public Libraries
1 system, 4 branches
141,886 books; circulation: 517,381
Places Rated Score: 13.93
Places Rated Rank: 325

Quebec City, PQ
Concert Radio
CBV-FM
Lively Arts Calendar
Touring Artists Bookings: 405 dates
Resident Ensembles: 123 dates
Opera de Quebec
Orchestre Symphonique de Quebec
Theater de la Bordee
Theater de la Commune
Theater du Bois de Coulonge
Theater Niveau Parking
Theater Repere
Art Museums and Galleries
Centre d'Animation Photographie
Musee du Quebec
Musee du Seminaire de Quebec
Public Libraries
11 systems, 125 branches
1,061,416 books; circulation: 3,563,422
Places Rated Score: 56.61
Places Rated Rank: 119

[illegible] books; circulation: 1,193,197
Places Rated Score: 39.29
Places Rated Rank: 218

Raleigh–Durham–Chapel Hill, NC
Concert Radio
WCPE-FM, WUNC-FM
Lively Arts Calendar
Touring Artists Bookings: 255 dates
Resident Ensembles: 341 dates
Durham Symphony
National Opera Company
North Carolina Symphony
PlayMakers Repertory Company
Raleigh Symphony
Triangle Opera Theater Associates
Art Museums and Galleries
City Gallery of Contemporary Art
Duke University Museum of Art
North Carolina Museum of Art
UNC Ackland Art Museum
Public Libraries
4 systems, 36 branches
1,929,528 books; circulation: 7,702,395
Places Rated Score: 80.99
Places Rated Rank: 53

Rapid City, SD
Lively Arts Calendar
Touring Artists Bookings: 30 dates
Resident Ensemble: 6 dates
Black Hills Symphony
Art Museums and Galleries
Dahl Fine Arts Center
Sioux Indian Museum
Public Libraries
4 independent systems
123,924 books; circulation: 440,283
Places Rated Score: 15.10
Places Rated Rank: 320

Reading, PA
Concert Radio
In Philadelphia media market
Lively Arts Calendar
Touring Artists Bookings: 56 dates
Resident Ensembles: 19 dates
Berks Grand Opera
Reading Symphony
Art Museums and Galleries

Freedman Gallery-Albright College
Reading Public Museum & Art Gallery
Public Libraries
16 systems, 3 branches
461,375 books; circulation: 867,467
Places Rated Score: 31.00
Places Rated Rank: 256

Redding, CA
Concert Radio
KFPR-FM
Lively Arts Calendar
Touring Artists Bookings: 4 dates
Resident Ensemble: 4 dates
Shasta Symphony
Art Museums and Galleries
Redding Museum of Art & History
Public Libraries
1 system, 2 branches
232,746 books; circulation: 245,495
Places Rated Score: 12.49
Places Rated Rank: 331

Regina, SK
Lively Arts Calendar
Touring Artists Bookings: 155 dates
Resident Ensembles: 135 dates
Globe Theater
Regina Symphony
Art Museums and Galleries
Dunlop Art Gallery
Legislative Building Galleries
MacKenzie Art Gallery
Rosemont Art Gallery
Public Libraries
2 systems, 10 branches
717,094 books; circulation: 2,133,046
Places Rated Score: 68.04
Places Rated Rank: 95

Reno, NV
Concert Radio
KUNR-FM
Lively Arts Calendar
Touring Artists Bookings: 10 dates
Resident Ensembles: 45 dates
Nevada Opera Association
Reno Chamber Orchestra
Reno Philharmonic
Reno Pops Orchestra
Art Museums and Galleries
The Nevada Museum of Art
Public Libraries
1 system, 8 branches
529,449 books; circulation: 1,300,937
Places Rated Score: 28.04
Places Rated Rank: 270

Richland–Kennewick–Pasco, WA
Concert Radio
KFAE-FM
Lively Arts Calendar
Resident Ensemble: 5 dates
Mid-Columbia Symphony
Public Libraries
2 systems, 10 branches
383,302 books; circulation: 864,263
Places Rated Score: 25.28
Places Rated Rank: 282

Richmond–Petersburg, VA
Concert Radio
WCVE-FM
Lively Arts Calendar
Touring Artists Bookings: 29 dates
Resident Ensembles: 402 dates
Concert Ballet of Virginia
Richmond Ballet
Richmond Philharmonic
Richmond Symphony
Theater IV
TheaterVirginia
Art Museums and Galleries
Virginia Museum of Fine Arts
VCU Anderson Gallery
Public Libraries
7 systems, 38 branches
2,679,032 books; circulation: 6,465,217
Places Rated Score: 81.77
Places Rated Rank: 51

✓ Riverside–San Bernardino, CA
Concert Radio
In Los Angeles media market
KPSC-FM, KVCR-FM
Lively Arts Calendar
Touring Artists Bookings: 233 dates
Resident Ensembles: 73 dates
Desert Sinfonia
Inland Empire Symphony
Redlands Symphony
Riverside Ballet Theater
Riverside County Philharmonic
San Bernardino Civic Light Opera
West Coast Opera Theater
Art Museums and Galleries
Cabot's Old Indian Pueblo Museum
Edward-Dean Museum of Decorative Arts
Palm Springs Desert Museum
Riverside Art Museum
University of California Galleries
Public Libraries
12 systems, 61 branches
3,954,974 books; circulation: 11,168,061
Places Rated Score: 91.25
Places Rated Rank: 32

Roanoke, VA
Concert Radio
WVTF-FM
Lively Arts Calendar
Touring Artists Bookings: 12 dates
Resident Ensembles: 76 dates
Mill Mountain Theater
Opera Roanoke
Roanoke Symphony & Choral Society
Art Museums and Galleries
Art Museum of Western Virginia
Public Libraries
4 systems, 13 branches
713,534 books; circulation: 1,438,867
Places Rated Score: 47.53
Places Rated Rank: 172

Rochester, MN
Concert Radio
KLSE-FM
Lively Arts Calendar
Touring Artists Bookings: 10 dates
Resident Ensemble: 13 dates
Rochester Symphony
Art Museums and Galleries
Rochester Art Center
Public Libraries
2 independent systems
308,750 books; circulation: 1,281,243
Places Rated Score: 49.22
Places Rated Rank: 167

Rochester, NY
Concert Radio
WRUR-FM, WXXI-FM
Lively Arts Calendar
Touring Artists Bookings: 127 dates
Resident Ensembles: 244 dates
Genesee Symphony
GeVa Theater
Opera Theater of Rochester
Rochester Chamber Orchestra
Rochester Philharmonic Orchestra
Art Museums and Galleries
Eastman Museum of Photography
UR Memorial Art Gallery
Public Libraries
61 systems, 16 branches
3,498,510 books; circulation: 9,064,716
Places Rated Score: 78.10
Places Rated Rank: 63

Rockford, IL
Lively Arts Calendar
Touring Artists Bookings: 19 dates
Resident Ensembles: 52 dates
New American Theater
Rockford Symphony
Art Museums and Galleries
Rockford Art Museum
Public Libraries
16 systems, 5 branches
1,067,156 books; circulation: 2,203,317
Places Rated Score: 42.15
Places Rated Rank: 197

Rocky Mount, NC
Concert Radio
In Raleigh–Durham media market
WESQ-FM
Lively Arts Calendar
Touring Artists Bookings: 3 dates
Resident Ensemble: 6 dates
Tar River Choral & Orchestral Society
Art Museums and Galleries
Hobson Pittman Memorial Gallery
Public Libraries
2 systems, 1 branch
252,265 books; circulation: 546,215
Places Rated Score: 27.48
Places Rated Rank: 273

Sacramento, CA
Concert Radio
KXKB-FM, KXPR-FM
Lively Arts Calendar
Touring Artists Bookings: 13 dates
Resident Ensembles: 205 dates
Auburn Civic Symphony
Camellia Symphony
Sacramento Ballet
Sacramento Opera Company
Sacramento Symphony
Sacramento Theater Comapny
Art Museums and Galleries
Crocker Art Museum
Public Libraries
6 systems, 37 branches
2,281,796 books; circulation: 5,096,618
Places Rated Score: 68.45
Places Rated Rank: 92

Saginaw–Bay City–Midland, MI
Concert Radio
WUCX-FM
Lively Arts Calendar
Touring Artists Bookings: 54 dates
Resident Ensembles: 24 dates
Midland Symphony
Saginaw Symphony
Art Museums and Galleries
Arts Midland Galleries
Saginaw Art Museum
Public Libraries

12 systems, 9 branches
1,334,699 books; circulation: 2,780,684
Places Rated Score: 51.50
Places Rated Rank: 151

St. Catharines–Niagara, ON
Lively Arts Calendar
Touring Artists Bookings: 72 dates
Resident Ensembles: 194 dates
Carousel Players
Niagara Symphony
Shaw Festival
Theater Beyond Words
Art Museums and Galleries
Rodman Hall Arts Centre
Public Libraries
10 systems, 22 branches
1,085,510 books; circulation: 2,898,260
Places Rated Score: 69.98

Art Museums and Galleries
Kiehle Gallery
Public Libraries
1 system, 29 branches
629,169 books; circulation: 1,681,428
Places Rated Score: 79.53
Places Rated Rank: 57

Saint John, NB
Lively Arts Calendar
Touring Artists Bookings: 6 dates
Resident Ensemble: 22 dates
Symphony New Brunswick
Art Museums and Galleries
New Brunswick Museum
Public Libraries
1 system, 9 branches
301,266 books; circulation: 591,490
Places Rated Score: 26.71
Places Rated Rank: 278

St. John's, NF
Concert Radio
CBN-FM
Lively Arts Calendar
Touring Artists Bookings: 112 dates
Resident Ensembles: 56 dates
Newfoundland Symphony
RCA Theater
Rising Tide Theater
Art Museums and Galleries
Eastern Edge Gallery
Memorial University Art Gallery
Resource Centre for the Arts
Public Libraries
3 systems, 28 branches
361,986 books; circulation: 694,513
Places Rated Score: 30.71
Places Rated Rank: 258

St. Joseph, MO
Lively Arts Calendar
Touring Artists Bookings: 12 dates
Resident Ensemble: 5 dates
St. Joseph Symphony
Art Museums and Galleries
Albrecht-Kemper Museum of Art

Public Libraries
1 system, 4 branches
430,096 books; circulation: 736,995
Places Rated Score: 50.24
Places Rated Rank: 159

✓ St. Louis, MO–IL
Concert Radio
KFUO-FM, KWMU-FM
Lively Arts Calendar
Touring Artists Bookings: 450 dates
Resident Ensembles: 478 dates
Bellville Philharmonic Society
Black Repertory Company
Brentwood Symphony
Gateway Ballet of St. Louis
Gateway Festival Orchestra
Kirkwood Symphony

Public Libraries
58 systems, 52 branches
9,902,237 books; circulation: 19,418,809
Places Rated Score: 96.04
Places Rated Rank: 18

Salem, OR
Concert Radio
In Portland media market
Lively Arts Calendar
Touring Artists Bookings: 30 dates
Art Museums and Galleries
Bush Barn Art Center
George Putnam University Center
Public Libraries
10 systems, 1 branch
504,572 books; circulation: 2,256,751
Places Rated Score: 41.04
Places Rated Rank: 207

Salinas, CA
Concert Radio
KBOQ-FM, KVRG-AM
Lively Arts Calendar
Touring Artists Bookings: 16 dates
Resident Ensembles: 56 dates
Hidden Valley Opera Ensemble
Monterey Bay Chamber Orchestra
Monterey County Symphony
Art Museums and Galleries
Monterey Penisula Museum of Art
Public Libraries
4 systems, 18 branches
1,113,612 books; circulation: 2,147,786
Places Rated Score: 50.12
Places Rated Rank: 161

Salt Lake City–Ogden, UT
Concert Radio
KUER-FM
Lively Arts Calendar
Touring Artists Bookings: 355 dates
Resident Ensembles: 463 dates
Ballet West
Mormon Symphony
Pioneer Theater Company
Rocky Mountain Symphony
Salt Lake Acting Company
Salt Lake Opera Theater
Utah Opera Company
Utah Symphony
Wasatch Community Symphony
Art Museums and Galleries
Eccles Community Arts Center
Museum of Church History & Art
Salt Lake Art Center
University Museum of Fine Arts
Public Libraries
5 systems, 26 branches
2,659,598 books; circulation: 9,859,814
Places Rated Score: 88.40
Places Rated Rank: 41

San Angelo, TX
Lively Arts Calendar

San Antonio, TX
Concert Radio
KPAC-FM, KRTU-FM
Lively Arts Calendar
Touring Artists Bookings: 67 dates
Resident Ensembles: 102 dates
Mid-Texas Symphony
San Antonio Ballet Company
San Antonio Symphony
Art Museums and Galleries
McNay Art Museum
San Antonio Museum of Art
Public Libraries
11 systems, 21 branches
1,961,874 books; circulation: 3,906,166
Places Rated Score: 54.07
Places Rated Rank: 139

✓ San Diego, CA
Concert Radio
KFSD-FM
Lively Arts Calendar
Touring Artists Bookings: 246 dates
Resident Ensembles: 438 dates
Blackfriars Theater
California Ballet Company
East County Community Orchestra of Tifereth Israel
La Jolla Playhouse
Old Globe Theater
San Diego Civic Light Opera
San Diego Comic Opera Company
San Diego Opera
San Diego Repertory Theater
San Diego Symphony
Art Museums and Galleries
Grossmont College Art Gallery
Mandeville Gallery
Mingei International World Folk Art
Museum of Contemporary Art
Museum of Photographic Arts
San Diego Museum of Art
Timken Museum of Art
Public Libraries
7 systems, 69 branches
4,576,326 books; circulation: 13,149,141
Places Rated Score: 90.59
Places Rated Rank: 36

✓ San Francisco, CA
Concert Radio
KDFC-AM, KKHI-FM
Lively Arts Calendar
Touring Artists Bookings: 363 dates
Resident Ensembles: 1,046 dates
Symphony Orchestras
Marin Symphony
Mid Peninsula Symphony
New Century Chamber Orchestra
Peninsula Symphony
Philharmonia Baroque Orchestra
Redwood Symphony
San Francisco Chamber Symphony
San Francisco Community Orchestra
San Francisco Symphony
Women's Philharmonic
Opera Companies
Marin Opera
Opera Center Singers
Pocket Opera
San Francisco Opera
San Francisco Opera Center
Western Opera Theater
Ballet Companies
Khadra International Folk Ballet
Marin Ballet Company
Peninsula Ballet Theater
San Francisco Ballet
Theater Ballet of San Francisco
Professional Theaters
A Traveling Jewish Theater
American Conservatory Theater
Magic Theater
Marin Theater Company
Art Museums and Galleries
Ansel Adams Photography Center
Arts Council of San Mateo County
Asian Art Museum of San Francisco
California Crafts Museum
Cartoon Art Museum
Exploratorium
Falkirk Cultural Center
Fine Arts Museums of San Francisco
San Francisco Art Institute Galleries
San Francisco Camerawork
San Francisco Museum of Modern Art
Wiegand Gallery
Public Libraries
15 systems, 64 branches
4,209,448 books; circulation: 10,797,634
Places Rated Score: 98.59
Places Rated Rank: 10

✓ San Jose, CA
Concert Radio
KDFC-FM
Lively Arts Calendar
Touring Artists Bookings: 441 dates
Resident Ensembles: 402 dates
American Musical Theater of San Jose
California Theater Center
Hewlett-Packard Symphony
Nova Vista Symphony
Opera San Jose
San Jose Repertory Theater
San Jose Symphony
Santa Clara Ballet Company
South Valley Symphony
TheaterWorks
West Bay Opera
Art Museums and Galleries
De Saisset Museum
Los Gatos Museum
Palo Alto Cultural Center
San Jose Museum of Art
San Jose Museum of Contemporary Art
Stanford University Galleries
State University Art Galleries
Triton Museum of Art
Public Libraries
5 systems, 28 branches
3,383,734 books; circulation: 12,843,903
Places Rated Score: 95.76
Places Rated Rank: 20

San Luis Obispo–Atascadero–Paso Robles, CA
Concert Radio
In Santa Barbra–Santa Maria media market
KCBX-FM
Lively Arts Calendar
Touring Artists Bookings: 51 dates
Resident Ensembles: 18 dates
Pacific Repertory Opera
San Luis Obispo County Symphony
Public Libraries
2 systems, 14 branches
388,314 books; circulation: 1,720,676
Places Rated Score: 32.22
Places Rated Rank: 249

Santa Barbara–Santa Maria–Lompoc, CA
Concert Radio
KDB-FM, KFAC-FM
Lively Arts Calendar
Touring Artists Bookings: 55 dates
Resident Ensembles: 106 dates
PCPA Theaterfest
Santa Barbara Chamber Orchestra
Santa Barbara Civic Light Opera
Santa Barbara Symphony
West Coast Symphony
Art Museums and Galleries
Santa Barbara Museum of Art
University of California Galleries
Public Libraries
3 systems, 12 branches
674,504 books; ciculation: 2,400,458
Places Rated Score: 49.24
Places Rated Rank: 166

Santa Cruz–Watsonville, CA
Concert Radio
In Monterey–Salinas media market
Lively Arts Calendar
Touring Artists Bookings: 78 dates
Resident Ensembles: 50 dates
Cabrillo Music Festival
Shakespeare Santa Cruz
Art Museums and Galleries
Art Museum Santa Cruz County
Public Libraries
2 systems, 9 branches
501,316 books; circulation: 1,526,034
Places Rated Score: 51.09
Places Rated Rank: 154

Santa Fe, NM
Concert Radio
In Albuquerque media market
KSFR-FM
Lively Arts Calendar
Touring Artists Bookings: 26 dates
Resident Ensembles: 66 dates
New Mexico Repertory Theater
Santa Fe Opera
Santa Fe Pro Musica
Art Museums and Galleries
Center for Contemporary Arts
Fuller Lodge Art Center
Governor's Gallery Museum
Institute of American Indian Arts
Museum of Fine Arts
Museum of International Folk Art
Wheelwright Museum of the American Indian
Public Libraries
5 systems, 3 branches
277,495 books; circulation: 945,470
Places Rated Score: 41.03
Places Rated Rank: 209

Santa Rosa, CA
Concert Radio
In San Francisco–Oakland–San Jose media market
KRCB-FM
Lively Arts Calendar
Touring Artists Bookings: 20 dates
Resident Ensembles: 63 dates
Redwood Empire Ballet
Santa Rosa Symphony
Public Libraries
1 system, 11 branches
648,453 books; circulation: 2,472,999
Places Rated Score: 56.09
Places Rated Rank: 123

Sarasota–Bradenton, FL
Concert Radio
In Tampa–St. Petersburg media market
WSPB-AM
Lively Arts Calendar
Touring Artists Bookings: 120 dates
Resident Ensembles: 176 dates
Asolo Center for Peforming Arts
Florida Studio Theater
Florida West Coast Symphoy Orchestra
Sarasota Ballet of Florida
Sarasota Opera Association
Sarasota Pops
Venice Symphony
Art Museums and Galleries
Ringling Museum of Art
Public Libraries
2 systems, 10 branches
715,708 books; circulation: 3,134,267
Places Rated Score: 65.04
Places Rated Rank: 98

Saskatoon, SK
Concert Radio
CBKS-FM
Lively Arts Calendar
Touring Artists Bookings: 4 dates
Resident Ensembles: 112 dates
Persophone Theater
Saskatoon Fringe Festival
Saskatoon Symphony
Shakespeare On The Saskatchwan
Twenty-Fifth Street Theater
Art Museums and Galleries
AKA Gallery
Diefenbaker Centre
Gorden Snelgrove Art Gallery
Mendel Art Gallery
Photographers Gallery
Saskatoon Library Art Gallery
St. Thomas More Art Gallery
Ukrainian Museum of Canada
Public Libraries
2 systems, 45 branches
792,945 books; circulation: 2,755,634
Places Rated Score: 72.34
Places Rated Rank: 75

Savannah, GA
Concert Radio
WSVH-FM
Lively Arts Calendar

Touring Artists Bookings: 15 dates
Resident Ensemble: 55 dates
Savannah Symphony
Art Museums and Galleries
Kiah Museum
Telfair Academy of Arts & Sciences
Public Libraries
1 system, 18 branches
548,493 books; circulation: 1,035,679
Places Rated Score: 42.37
Places Rated Rank: 195

Scranton–Wilkes-Barre–Hazleton, PA
Concert Radio
WVIA-FM
Lively Arts Calendar
Touring Artists Bookings: 259 dates
Resident Ensembles: 135 dates

Touring Artists Bookings: 12 dates
Resident Ensembles: 8 dates
Greenville Symphony
Romanenko Chamber Players
Public Libraries
5 independent systems
170,309 books; circulation: 274,089
Places Rated Score: 1.67
Places Rated Rank: 342

Sheboygan, WI
Concert Radio
In Milwaukee media market
Lively Arts Calendar
Touring Artists Bookings: 14 dates
Resident Ensemble: 8 dates
Sheboygan Symphony
Art Museums and Galleries

Sioux City Art Center
Public Libraries
8 systems, 5 branches
421,535 books; circulation: 873,708
Places Rated Score: 37.32
Places Rated Rank: 226

Sioux Falls, SD
Concert Radio
KCSD-FM, KRSD-FM
Lively Arts Calendar
Touring Artists Bookings: 6 dates
Resident Ensemble: 8 dates
South Dakota Symphony
Art Museums and Galleries
Civic Fine Arts Center
Public Libraries
5 systems, 8 branches

Seattle–Bellevue–Everett, WA
Concert Radio
KING-FM
Lively Arts Calendar
Touring Artists Bookings: 166 dates
Resident Ensembles: 665 dates
Symphony Orchestras
Bellevue Philharmonic Orchestra
Cascade Symphony
Everett Symphony
Northwest Chamber Orchestra
Orchestra Seattle
Seattle Philharmonic Orchestra
Seattle Symphony
Opera Companies
Civic Light Opera
Seattle Opera Association
Ballet Companies
Olympic Ballet Theater
Pacific Northwest Ballet
Professional Theaters
A Contemporary Theater
Alice B. Theater
Intiman Theater Company
Seattle Children's Theater
Seattle Group Theater
Seattle Repertory Theater
The Bathhouse Theater
The Empty Space Theater
University of Washington Theater
Art Museums and Galleries
Bellevue Art Museum
Charles & Emma Frye Art Museum
Edmonds Art Festival Museum
Pacific Arts Center
Seattle Art Museum
University Henry Art Gallery
Public Libraries
5 systems, 81 branches
6,070,689 books; circulation: 23,882,786
Places Rated Score: 96.87
Places Rated Rank: 16

Sharon, PA
Concert Radio
In Youngstown media market
WSAJ-AM, WSAJ-FM
Lively Arts Calendar

Resident Ensembles: 26 dates
Concerts Symphonique de Sherbrooke
Theater du Sang Neuf
Art Museums and Galleries
Bishop's Champlain Art Gallery
Universite de Sherbrooke
Public Libraries
3 systems, 46 branches
256,879 books; circulation: 633,020
Places Rated Score: 22.79
Places Rated Rank: 294

Sherman–Denison, TX
Lively Arts Calendar
Touring Artists Bookings: 38 dates
Resident Ensemble: 5 dates
Sherman Symphony
Public Libraries
6 independent systems
256,896 books; circulation: 533,640
Places Rated Score: 25.19
Places Rated Rank: 283

Shreveport–Bossier City, LA
Concert Radio
KDAQ-FM
Lively Arts Calendar
Touring Artists Bookings: 48 dates
Resident Ensembles: 45 dates
Shreveport Opera
Shreveport Symphony
Art Museums and Galleries
Centenary College Meadows Museum
R.W. Norton Art Gallery
Public Libraries
3 systems, 33 branches
737,529 books; circulation: 1,755,653
Places Rated Score: 39.93
Places Rated Rank: 215

Sioux City, IA–NE
Concert Radio
KWIT-FM
Lively Arts Calendar
Touring Artists Bookings: 5 dates
Resident Ensemble: 12 dates
Sioux City Symphony
Art Museums and Galleries

Art Museums and Galleries
Notre Dame Snite Museum of Art
South Bend Art Center
Public Libraries
3 systems, 8 branches
702,377 books; circulation: 3,014,697
Places Rated Score: 54.76
Places Rated Rank: 133

Spokane, WA
Concert Radio
KPBX-FM, KSVY-FM
Lively Arts Calendar
Touring Artists Bookings: 10 dates
Resident Ensembles: 103 dates
Spokane Ballet
Spokane Symphony
Art Museums and Galleries
Ad Art Gallery
Cheney Cowles Museum
Public Libraries
1 system, 13 branches
911,792 books; circulation: 4,015,775
Places Rated Score: 63.02
Places Rated Rank: 102

Springfield, IL
Concert Radio
WUIS-FM
Lively Arts Calendar
Touring Artists Bookings: 30 dates
Resident Ensembles: 89 dates
Illinois Chamber Orchestra
Illinois Symphony
Springfield Ballet Company
Art Museums and Galleries
Illinois State Museum
Public Libraries
9 systems, 5 branches
510,075 books; circulation: 1,177,213
Places Rated Score: 38.69
Places Rated Rank: 221

Springfield, MA
Concert Radio
WFCR-FM
Lively Arts Calendar
Touring Artists Bookings: 53 dates
Resident Ensembles: 73 dates

Amherst Ballet Theater Company
Commonwealth Opera
Springfield Symphony
StageWest
Art Museums and Galleries
George Smith Art Museum
Jasper Rand Art Museum
Mead Art Museum
Museum of Fine Arts
Smith College Museum of Art
Public Libraries
29 systems, 16 branches
2,245,403 books; circulation: 4,141,095
Places Rated Score: 67.55
Places Rated Rank: 96

Springfield, MO
Concert Radio
KSMU-FM
Lively Arts Calendar
Touring Artists Bookings: 38 dates
Resident Ensembles: 52 dates
Springfield Ballet
Springfield Regional Opera
Springfield Symphony
Art Museums and Galleries
Springfield Art Museum
Public Libraries
3 systems, 6 branches
511,040 books; circulation: 2,069,144
Places Rated Score: 35.99
Places Rated Rank: 233

Stamford–Norwalk, CT
Concert Radio
In New York media market
WSLX-FM
Lively Arts Calendar
Touring Artists Bookings: 184 dates
Resident Ensembles: 133 dates
Connecticut Ballet Theater
Connecticut Grand Opera & Orchestra
Connecticut Philharmonic Orchestra
Greenwich Symphony
New England Lyric Operetta
Norwalk Symphony
Stamford Symphony
Stamford Theater Works
Symphony On The Sound
Art Museums and Galleries
The Bruce Museum
Whitney Museum Fairfield County
Public Libraries
11 systems, 6 branches
1,620,103 books; circulation: 4,186,536
Places Rated Score: 85.90
Places Rated Rank: 44

State College, PA
Concert Radio
In Johnstown–Altoona media market
WPSU-FM
Lively Arts Calendar
Touring Artists Bookings: 35 dates
Resident Ensembles: 36 dates
Nittany Valley Symphony
Pennsylvania Centre Chamber Orchestra
PSU Theater Company
Art Museums and Galleries
PSU Palmer Museum of Art
Public Libraries
4 independent systems
290,890 books; circulation: 752,113
Places Rated Score: 29.33
Places Rated Rank: 264

Steubenville–Weirton, OH–WV
Lively Arts Calendar
Touring Artists Bookings: 12 dates
Public Libraries
5 systems, 8 branches
344,185 books; circulation: 854,759
Places Rated Score: 34.10
Places Rated Rank: 242

Stockton–Lodi, CA
Concert Radio
In Sacramento–Modesto media market
KUOP-FM
Lively Arts Calendar
Touring Artists Bookings: 8 dates
Resident Ensembles: 25 dates
Stockton Opera
Stockton Symphony
Art Museums and Galleries
Haggin Museum
Public Libraries
2 systems, 9 branches
1,063,601 books; circulation: 2,150,016
Places Rated Score: 28.50
Places Rated Rank: 224

Sudbury, ON
Lively Arts Calendar
Resident Ensembles: 40 dates
Sudbury Symphony
Sudbury Theater
Art Museums and Galleries
Laurentian University Museum
Public Libraries
5 systems, 13 branches
331,572 books; circulation: 694,820
Places Rated Score: 20.19
Places Rated Rank: 302

Sumter, SC
Concert Radio
In Columbia media market
WRJA-FM
Lively Arts Calendar
Touring Artists Bookings: 3 dates
Art Museums and Galleries
Sumter Gallery of Art
Public Libraries
1 system, 1 branch
118,472 books; circulation: 323,564
Places Rated Score: 11.66
Places Rated Rank: 332

Syracuse, NY
Concert Radio
WCNY-FM
Lively Arts Calendar
Touring Artists Bookings: 89 dates
Resident Ensembles: 251 dates
Auburn Chamber Orchestra
Onondaga Civic Symphony
Syracuse Opera Company
Syracuse Stage
Syracuse Symphony
Art Museums and Galleries
Everson Museum of Art
Joe & Emily Lowe Art Gallery
Public Libraries
48 systems, 9 branches
1,997,595 books; circulation: 5,413,597
Places Rated Score: 74.09
Places Rated Rank: 70

Tacoma, WA
Concert Radio
In Seattle media market
Lively Arts Calendar
Touring Artists Bookings: 47 dates
Resident Ensembles: 87 dates
Tacoma Actors Guild
Tacoma Opera
Tacoma Performing Dance Company
Tacoma Symphony
Art Museums and Galleries
Tacoma Art Museum
Public Libraries
4 systems, 26 branches
1,952,327 books; circulation: 7,843,826
Places Rated Score: 79.49
Places Rated Rank: 58

Tallahassee, FL
Concert Radio
WFSQ-FM
Lively Arts Calendar
Touring Artists Bookings: 42 dates
Resident Ensembles: 43 dates
Big Bend Community Orchestra
Florida State University Theater
Tallahassee Ballet Company
Tallahassee Symphony
Art Museums and Galleries
FSU Fine Arts Gallery
Public Libraries
2 systems, 5 branches
329,256 books; circulation: 1,201,487
Places Rated Score: 27.20
Places Rated Rank: 276

Tampa–St. Petersburg–Clearwater, FL
Concert Radio
WUSF-FM
Lively Arts Calendar
Touring Artists Bookings: 505 dates
Resident Ensembles: 193 dates
Acanthus Ballet
Florida Lyric Opera & Theater
Florida Orchestra
Spanish Lyric Theater
Tampa Bay Chamber Orchestra
Tampa Bay Opera
Art Museums and Galleries
Florida Gulf Coast Art Center
University Scarfone Gallery
Museum of Fine Arts
Ruth Eckerd Hall
Salvador Dali Museum
Tampa Museum of Art
USF Contemporary Art Museum
Public Libraries
19 systems, 36 branches
2,932,050 books; circulation: 10,604,871
Places Rated Score: 88.77
Places Rated Rank: 40

Terre Haute, IN
Lively Arts Calendar
Touring Artists Bookings: 9 dates
Resident Ensemble: 10 dates
Terre Haute Symphony
Art Museums and Galleries
Sheldon Swope Art Museum
Public Libraries
4 systems, 10 branches
408,386 books; circulation: 993,436
Places Rated Score: 31.03
Places Rated Rank: 255

Texarkana, TX–Texarkana, AR
Concert Radio
In Shreveport media market
KTXK-FM
Lively Arts Calendar
Touring Artists Bookings: 25 dates
Public Libraries
5 independent systems

164,803 books; circulation: 455,925
Places Rated Score: 0.65
Places Rated Rank: 347

Thunder Bay, ON
Lively Arts Calendar
Touring Artists Bookings: 25 dates
Resident Ensembles: 88 dates
Magnus Theater Company Northwest
Thunder Bay Symphony
Art Museums and Galleries
Thunder Bay Art Gallery
Public Libraries
2 systems, 5 branches
328,608 books; circulation: 1,014,698
Places Rated Score: 41.04
Places Rated Rank: 207

Toronto Operetta Theater
Professional Theaters
Air-Conditioned Theater
Autumn Leaf Performance
Bald Ego Theater
Bananafish Company
Best Boys Productions
Buddies in Bad Times Theater
Cahoots Theater Projects
The Canadian Stage Company
Cascade Theater
Children's Dance Theater
Classical Caberet
Comedy On Wry
Company of Sirens
Crow's Theater
Equity Showcase Theater

23 systems, 152 branches
9,529,632 books; circulation: 29,785,512
Places Rated Score: 99.72
Places Rated Rank: 5

Trenton, NJ
Concert Radio
In Philadelphia media market
WPRB-FM, WPRB-FM, WWFM-FM
Lively Arts Calendar
Touring Artists Bookings: 133 dates
Resident Ensembles: 160 dates
Greater Trenton Symphony
McCarter Theater Center
Opera Festival of New Jersey
Princeton Chamber Symphony
Art Museums and Galleries

Spectrum Gallery of Toledo
Public Libraries
14 systems, 25 branches
3,163,567 books; circulation: 7,761,641
Places Rated Score: 80.77
Places Rated Rank: 54

Topeka, KS
Lively Arts Calendar
Touring Artists Bookings: 20 dates
Resident Ensemble: 6 dates
Topeka Symphony
Art Museums and Galleries
Mulvane Art Museum
Public Libraries
3 independent systems
436,653 books; circulation: 1,488,266
Places Rated Score: 44.78
Places Rated Rank: 182

✓ Toronto, ON
Concert Radio
CFMX-FM, CJBC-FM, CJRT-FM
Lively Arts Calendar
Touring Artists Bookings: 1,251 dates
Resident Ensembles: 1,503 dates
Symphony Orchestras
Brampton Symphony
Cathedral Bluffs Symphony
Counterpoint Orchestra
East York Symphony
Esprit Orchestra
Etobicoke Philharmonic Orchestra
Hart House Orchestra
Korean Canadian Symphoy Orchestra
Mississauga Symphony
North York Concert Association
North York Symphony
Oakville Symphony
Pro Arte Orchestra
Royal Conservatory Orchestra
Scarborough Philharmonic Orchestra
Tafelmusik Baroque Orchestra
Toronto Sinfonietta
Toronto Symphony
York Symphony
Opera Companies
Canadian Opera Company
Opera Atelier
Opera in Concert

The Other Theater of Toronto
Pacun Peras The-A-Tro
Petty Rebel Theater
Phyzikal Theater
Platform 9 Theater
Random Acts Theater
Roseneath Theater
Shakespeare in Action
Skylight Theater
Smile Theater Company
Solar Stage
Sound Image Theater
Spend Your Rent Theater
Stiletto Company
Tapestry Musical Theater
Tarragon Theater
Theater Boku-Maru
Theater Centre
Theater Columbus
Theater Counterclockwise
Theater Direct Canada
Theater Francais de Toronto
Theater Gargantua
Theater Passe Muraille
Theater Plus
Theater Smith-Gilmour
Tolmec Dance Theater
Trinity Theater Toronto
Wild Pig Theater
World Miracle Theater
Young People's Theater
Zisis Theater Company
Art Museums and Galleries
Art Gallery at Harbourfront
Art Gallery of Ontario
Art Gallery of York University
Art Metropole
Brampton Library Art Gallery
Centennial Gallery
Gardiner Museum of Ceramic Art
Glendon Gallery
Koffler Gallery
Mississauga Library Art Gallery
Mississauga Springbank Centre
Oakville Galleries
Royal Ontario Museum
Toronto Centre for Contemporary Art
Toronto Sculpture Garden
University of Toronto Gallery
Public Libraries

Lively Arts Calendar
Touring Artists Bookings: 35 dates
Resident Ensemble: 20 dates
Orchestra Symphonique de Trois-Rivieres
Art Museums and Galleries
Galerie d'Art du Parc
Public Libraries
4 independent systems
616,915 books; circulation: 1,310,548
Places Rated Score: 49.35
Places Rated Rank: 164

Tucson, AZ
Concert Radio
KUAT-FM
Lively Arts Calendar
Touring Artists Bookings: 204 dates
Resident Ensembles: 114 dates
Arizona Opera Company
Civic Orchestra of Tucson
Southern Arizona Symphony
Tucson Symphony
University of Arizona Theater
Art Museums and Galleries
Aquary Museum
De Grazia Art Foundation
Tucson Museum of Art
University Museum of Art
Public Libraries
1 system, 17 branches
1,059,800 books; circulation: 5,212,651
Places Rated Score: 56.59
Places Rated Rank: 120

Tulsa, OK
Concert Radio
KOAS-FM
Lively Arts Calendar
Touring Artists Bookings: 265 dates
Resident Ensembles: 161 dates
American Theater Company
Oklahoma Sinfonia/Tulsa Pops
Tulsa Ballet Theater
Tulsa Opera
Tulsa Philharmonic Orchestra
Art Museums and Galleries
Gilcrease Institute of Art
Philbrook Museum of Art
Public Libraries

17 systems, 21 branches
1,274,692 books; circulation: 4,173,467
Places Rated Score: 55.32
Places Rated Rank: 131

Tuscaloosa, AL
Concert Radio
WUAL-FM
Lively Arts Calendar
Touring Artists Bookings: 20 dates
Resident Ensembles: 35 dates
Tuscaloosa Symphony
University Alabama Theater
Art Museums and Galleries
University Moody Gallery
Public Libraries
1 system, 3 branches
191,024 books; circulation: 450,358
Places Rated Score: 18.90
Places Rated Rank: 306

Tyler, TX
Lively Arts Calendar
Touring Artists Bookings: 10 dates
Resident Ensemble: 11 dates
East Texas Symphony
Art Museums and Galleries
Tyler Museum of Art
Public Libraries
2 independent systems
152,823 books; circulation: 245,009
Places Rated Score: 0.01
Places Rated Rank: 350

Utica–Rome, NY
Concert Radio
WUNY-FM
Lively Arts Calendar
Touring Artists Bookings: 95 dates
Resident Ensemble: 8 dates
Utica Symphony
Art Museums and Galleries
Munson-Williams-Proctor Museum
Public Libraries
35 systems, 4 branches
824,707 books; circulation: 1,711,570
Places Rated Score: 33.48
Places Rated Rank: 245

Vallejo–Fairfield–Napa, CA
Concert Radio
In Sacramento–Stockton–Modesto media market
Lively Arts Calendar
Touring Artists Bookings: 25 dates
Resident Ensembles: 27 dates
Napa Valley Symphony
Vallejo Symphony
Public Libraries
5 systems, 7 branches
825,218 books; circulation: 2,402,759
Places Rated Score: 55.93
Places Rated Rank: 125

✓ Vancouver, BC
Concert Radio
CBU-AM
Lively Arts Calendar
Touring Artists Bookings: 913 dates
Resident Ensembles: 716 dates
Symphony Orchestras
Richmond Community Orchestra
Vancouver Philharmonic Orchestra
Vancouver Symphony
Vancouver Youth Symphony
Opera Company
Vancouver Opera
Ballet Company
Ballet British Columbia
Professional Theaters
Arts Club Theater
Axis Theater Company
Carousel Theater Company
Coconut Theater
Fend Players Society
Gateway Theater
Green Thumb Theater
Headlines Theater
Pacific Theater
Playwrights Theater Centre
Tamahnous Theater
Theater la Siezieme
Theater Terrific
Theaterspace/Vancouver Fringe
Touchstone Theater
Vancouver Playhouse
Vancouver Youth Theater Society
Art Museums and Galleries
Burnaby Art Gallery
Canadian Craft Museum
Cartwright Gallery
Charles H. Scott Gallery
Maple Ridge Art Gallery
Place des Arts
Richmond Art Gallery
Simon Fraser Gallery
Surrey Art Gallery
UBC Fine Arts Gallery
Vancouver Art Gallery
Public Libraries
11 systems, 46 branches
2,588,459 books; circulation: 13,957,197
Places Rated Score: 94.58
Places Rated Rank: 23

Ventura, CA
Concert Radio
In Los Angeles media market
KCPB-FM
Lively Arts Calendar
Touring Artists Bookings: 138 dates
Resident Ensemble: 12 dates
New West Chamber Orchestra
Art Museums and Galleries
Carnegie Art Museum
Public Libraries
4 systems, 18 branches
1,440,021 books; circulation: 3,037,685
Places Rated Score: 55.65
Places Rated Rank: 129

Victoria, BC
Lively Arts Calendar
Touring Artists Bookings: 25 dates
Resident Ensembles: 247 dates
Asylum Theater
Belfry Theater
Intrepid Theater Company
Kaleidoscope Theater
New Bastion Theater Company
Pacific Opera Victoria
Victoria Symphony
Art Museums and Galleries
Art Gallery of Greater Victoria
Emily Carr Gallery
Open Space Gallery
UV Maltwood Art Museum
Public Libraries
2 systems, 9 branches
659,937 books; circulation: 2,344,578
Places Rated Score: 58.85
Places Rated Rank: 108

Victoria, TX
Concert Radio
KVRT-FM
Lively Arts Calendar
Touring Artists Bookings: 8 dates
Resident Ensemble: 5 dates
Victoria Symphony
Public Libraries
1 independent system
143,584 books; circulation: 327,116
Places Rated Score: 14.98
Places Rated Rank: 322

Vineland–Millville–Bridgeton, NJ
Concert Radio
In Philadelphia media market
Lively Arts Calendar
Resident Ensemble: 17 dates
Bridgeton Symphony
Public Libraries
5 independent systems
432,172 books; circulation: 392,755
Places Rated Score: 36.36
Places Rated Rank: 231

Visalia–Tulare–Porterville, CA
Lively Arts Calendar
Touring Artists Bookings: 12 dates
Resident Ensemble: 30 dates
Tulare County Symphony
Public Libraries
3 systems, 15 branches
526,187 books; circulation: 861,807
Places Rated Score: 22.26
Places Rated Rank: 295

Waco, TX
Concert Radio
KWBU-FM
Lively Arts Calendar
Touring Artists Bookings: 18 dates
Resident Ensemble: 8 dates
Waco Symphony
Art Museums and Galleries
The Art Center
Public Libraries
4 systems, 4 branches
333,030 books; circulation: 622,122
Places Rated Score: 19.44
Places Rated Rank: 304

✓ Washington, DC–MD–VA–WV
Concert Radio
WETA-FM, WGMS-FM, WGTS-FM, WVEP-FM
Lively Arts Calendar
Touring Artists Bookings: 3,268 dates
Resident Ensembles: 1,048 dates
Symphony Orchestras
Alexandria Symphony
American Chamber Orchestra
Columbus Orchestra
Frederick Symphony
Georgetown Symphony
Jewish Community Center Symphony
Loudoun Symphony
Millbrook Orchestra
National Chamber Orchestra
National Gallery Orchestra
National Symphony
Prince George's Philharmonic
Mid-Atlantic Chamber Orchestra
United States Air Force Concert Band
United States Air Force Symphony
Washington Bach Consort
Washington Chamber Symphony
Washington Philharmonic
Washington Symphony

Opera Companies
National Lyric Opera Company
Opera Americana
Opera Camerata of Washington
Opera Theater of Northern Virginia
Potomac Valley Opera Company
Summer Opera Theater Company
Washington Concert Opera
Washington Opera
Wolf Trap Opera Company
Ballet Companies
Capitol Ballet Company
Washington Ballet
Professional Theaters
Arena Stage
Ford's Theater
Living Stage Theater Company
Olney Theater
Round House Theater

Georgetown University Collection
GWU Dimock Gallery
Hirshhorn Museum & Sculpture Garden
Howard University Gallery of Art
Mary Washington College Belmont Gallery
National Gallery of Art
National Museum American Art
National Museum of African Art
National Museum of Women in the Arts
National Portrait Gallery
Phillips Collection
Studio Gallery
University of Maryland Art Gallery
Public Libraries
16 systems, 137 branches
11,749,664 books; circulation: 34,261,159
Places Rated Score: 99.87
Places Rated Rank: 2

Waterbury, CT
Concert Radio
In Hartford–New Haven media market
Lively Arts Calendar
Resident Ensemble: 11 dates
Waterbury Symphony
Public Libraries
10 systems, 2 branches
621,036 books; circulation: 1,051,940
Places Rated Score: 35.02
Places Rated Rank: 239

Waterloo–Cedar Falls, IA
Concert Radio
In Cedar Rapids–Waterloo–Dubuque media market
KHKE-FM, KUNI-FM
Lively Arts Calendar
Touring Artists Bookings: 6 dates
Resident Ensemble: 22 dates
Waterloo-Cedar Falls Symphony
Art Museums and Galleries
Hearst Center for the Arts
UNI Gallery of Art
Waterloo Museum of Art
Public Libraries

6 independent systems
320,563 books; circulation: 863,411
Places Rated Score: 40.24
Places Rated Rank: 211

Wausau, WI
Concert Radio
WHRM-FM
Lively Arts Calendar
Touring Artists Bookings: 45 dates
Resident Ensemble: 5 dates
Wisconsin Valley Musicians
Art Museums and Galleries
Leigh Yawkey Woodson Art Museum
Public Libraries
1 system, 10 branches
252,733 books; circulation: 619,854
Places Rated Score: 25.64
Places Rated Rank: 281

Piccolo Opera Company
Pope Theater Company
Art Museums and Galleries
Boca Raton Museum of Art
Hibel Museum of Art
International Museum of Cartoon Art
Morikami Museum
Norton Museum of Art
Public Libraries
11 systems, 12 branches
996,633 books; circulation: 4,274,355
Places Rated Score: 69.92
Places Rated Rank: 86

Wheeling, WV–OH
Concert Radio
WVNP-FM
Lively Arts Calendar
Touring Artists Bookings: 95 dates
Resident Ensemble: 33 dates
Wheeling Symphony
Public Libraries
6 systems, 11 branches
545,639 books; circulation: 1,010,392
Places Rated Score: 44.92
Places Rated Rank: 180

Wichita, KS
Concert Radio
KMUW-FM
Lively Arts Calendar
Touring Artists Bookings: 20 dates
Resident Ensemble: 60 dates
Wichita Symphony
Art Museums and Galleries
Coutts Memorial Museum of Art
Edwin Ulrich Museum of Art
Friends University Whittier Gallery
Wichita Art Museum
Public Libraries
25 systems, 11 branches
1,388,757 books; circulation: 2,577,363
Places Rated Score: 47.81
Places Rated Rank: 170

Wichita Falls, TX
Lively Arts Calendar
Touring Artists Bookings: 3 dates
Resident Ensemble: 8 dates
Wichita Falls Symphony
Art Museums and Galleries
Wichita Falls Museum & Art Center
Public Libraries
5 independent systems
196,436 books; circulation: 433,751
Places Rated Score: 17.10
Places Rated Rank: 314

Williamsport, PA
Concert Radio
In Wilkes-Barre–Scranton media market
Lively Arts Calendar
Touring Artists Bookings: 35 dates
Resident Ensemble: 5 dates
Williamsport Symphony

Wilmington Symphony
Art Museums and Galleries
St. John's Museum of Art
Public Libraries
2 systems, 6 branches
339,842 books; circulation: 1,094,595
Places Rated Score: 23.45
Places Rated Rank: 289

Wilmington–Newark, DE–MD
Concert Radio
In Philadelphia media market
Lively Arts Calendar
Touring Artists Bookings: 104 dates
Resident Ensembles: 89 dates
Delaware Symphony
Delaware Theater Company
OperaDelaware
Art Museums and Galleries
Delaware Art Museum
Winterthur Museum
Public Libraries
11 systems, 8 branches
1,028,320 books; circulation: 2,557,279
Places Rated Score: 59.82
Places Rated Rank: 104

Windsor, ON
Concert Radio
CBE-AM
Lively Arts Calendar
Touring Artists Bookings: 32 dates
Resident Ensemble: 32 dates
Windsor Symphony
Art Museums and Galleries
Art Gallery of Windsor
Public Libraries
4 systems, 26 branches
914,766 books; circulation: 1,888,288
Places Rated Score: 49.30
Places Rated Rank: 165

Winnipeg, MB
Concert Radio
CBW-FM
Lively Arts Calendar
Touring Artists Bookings: 29 dates

Resident Ensembles: 396 dates
Manitoba Chamber Orchestra
Manitoba Opera Association
Manitoba Theater Center
Manitoba Theater for Young People
Prairie Theater Exchange
Primus Theater
Royal Winnipeg Ballet
Shakespeare in the Ruins
Theater Projects Manitoba
Winnepeg Jewish Theater
Winnipeg Symphony
Art Museums and Galleries
University of Manitoba Gallery III
Winnipeg Art Gallery
Public Libraries
2 systems, 23 branches
1,277,652 books; circulation: 4,879,394
Places Rated Score: 79.22
Places Rated Rank: 60

Worcester, MA–CT
Concert Radio
In Boston media market
WICN-FM
Lively Arts Calendar
Touring Artists Bookings: 48 dates
Resident Ensembles: 41 dates
Foothills Theater Company
Salisbury Lyric Opera
Art Museums and Galleries
Worcester Art Museum
Public Libraries
34 systems, 5 branches
1,860,103 books; circulation: 2,909,361
Places Rated Score: 68.42
Places Rated Rank: 93

Yakima, WA
Concert Radio
KNWY-FM
Lively Arts Calendar
Touring Artists Bookings: 24 dates
Resident Ensemble: 7 dates
Yakima Symphony
Public Libraries
2 systems, 20 branches
613,751 books; circulation: 918,735
Places Rated Score: 31.26
Places Rated Rank: 254

Yolo, CA
Concert Radio
In Sacramento–Stockton–Modesto media market
Lively Arts Calendar
Touring Artists Bookings: 33 dates
Art Museums and Galleries
UC Nelson Gallery
Public Libraries
1 system, 7 branches
305,074 books; circulation: 662,949
Places Rated Score: 24.67
Places Rated Rank: 285

York, PA
Concert Radio
In Harrisburg–Lancaster–Lebanon–York media market
Lively Arts Calendar
Touring Artists Bookings: 22 dates
Resident Ensemble: 10 dates
York Symphony
Public Libraries
10 systems, 6 branches
317,189 books; circulation: 1,268,812
Places Rated Score: 18.09
Places Rated Rank: 309

Youngstown–Warren, OH
Concert Radio
WYSU-FM
Lively Arts Calendar
Touring Artists Bookings: 147 dates
Resident Ensembles: 27 dates
Warren Camber Orchestra
Youngstown Symphony
Art Museums and Galleries
Butler Institute of American Art
Public Libraries
15 systems, 23 branches
1,426,482 books; circulation: 4,371,243
Places Rated Score: 55.76
Places Rated Rank: 128

Yuba City, CA
Concert Radio
In Sacramento–Stockton–Modesto media market
Lively Arts Calendar
Touring Artists Bookings: 9 dates
Public Libraries
2 systems, 4 branches
203,530 books; circulation: 359,718
Places Rated Score: 15.24
Places Rated Rank: 319

Yuma, AZ
Concert Radio
KAWC-FM
Lively Arts Calendar
Touring Artists Bookings: 20 dates
Art Museums and Galleries
Yuma Fine Arts Association Center
Public Libraries
1 system, 5 branches
165,280 books; circulation: 629,336
Places Rated Score: 8.04
Places Rated Rank: 338

Et Cetera

THE DAVID AND GOLIATH PROPOSITION

Show you the biggest metro areas and you'll be shown the best places to live for the arts: New York, Chicago, Los Angeles, Washington, Toronto, and San Francisco. The consistent relationship between a metro area's size and its arts facilities might make you think that such places as Bangor, ME, and Bismarck, ND—both with populations under 100,000 and ranking 130th and 91st, respectively, in the arts—must resign themselves to being cultural underdogs. But think again.

Pick on Someone Your Own Size

What would happen if Bangor and Bismarck, remembering the old playground cliché, were to say to New York, "Go pick on someone your own size"? By grouping metro areas according to their populations, we are able to explore which ones have a large supply of cultural assets relative to their size and which might be considered artistically deficient. *Places Rated* divides the metro areas into four competitive population groups, based on criteria established by the federal government.

The following lists show how the metro areas rank in the arts when they are measured against similarly sized places:

Metro Areas and the Arts: Some Size Comparisons

Largest (Population over 1,000,000)	
New York, NY	99.99
Washington, DC	99.87
Los Angeles–Long Beach, CA	99.84
Chicago, IL	99.81
Toronto, ON	99.72
Medium Size (Population 250,000 to 999,999)	
Honolulu, HI	89.98
Stamford–Norwalk, CA	85.90
Calgary, AB	84.44
Dayton–Springfield, OH	83.56
Richmond–Petersburg, VA	81.77

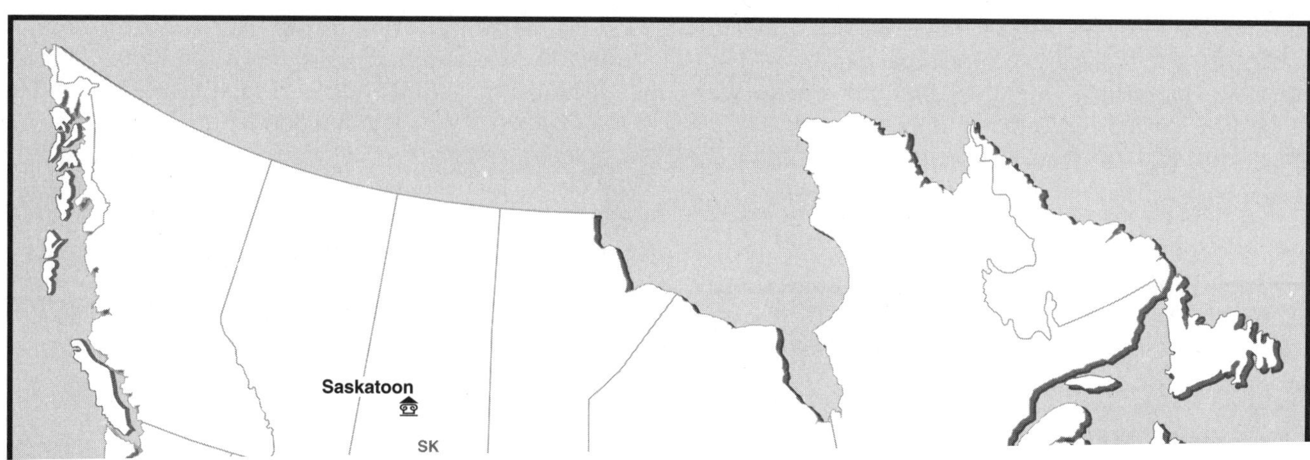

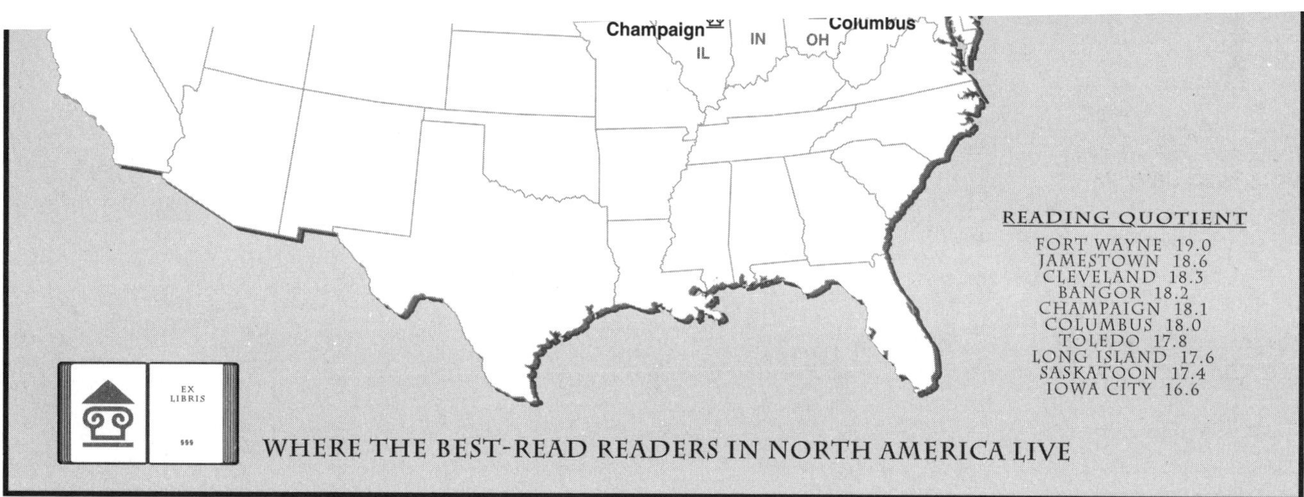

Thomas Nast, Cartographer

Small (Population 100,000 to 249,999)	
Olympia, WA	86.56
St. Cloud, MN	79.53
Fargo–Moorhead, ND–MN	75.21
Saskatoon, SK	72.34
Jamestown, NY	69.60

Smallest (Population under 100,000)	
Bismarck, ND	69.54
Pittsfield, MA	58.46
Jackson, TN	58.20
Bangor, ME	55.40
St. Joseph, MO	50.24

HITTING THE BOOKS

In which states and provinces do people read the most? Where the least? Where are the greatest concentrations of books? Which state or province spends the most money per capita on its libraries and which the least?

Circulation rate is one way to find out which are North America's readingest areas. Library circulation rates—that is, the annual number of checkouts per resident—indicate both how much people read and how successful local libraries are in serving their communities. According to the American Library Association's directory, the annual per capita circulation rate on the continent ranges from a low of fewer than two books per person in Mississippi to a high of nearly ten books per person in Iowa.

Do circulation rates reflect the availability of library volumes, or does the number of public library books reveal the importance that people in an area attach to collecting and disseminating knowledge? It is interesting to note that the two states that provide the greatest number of public library volumes per person—Maine and New Hampshire—are also among the states with the highest circulation rates, whereas four out of five states with the fewest library volumes per capita are among those with the lowest circulation rates.

The Reading Quotient

The number of books on a metro area's library shelves tells only half the story of a place's reading habits; how much use those volumes get, or the metro area's circulation rate, is the other half. When the circulation figure is added to the number of volumes, and that sum is divided by the population served, the result is what *Places Rated* calls the reading quotient, which may serve as a rough indicator of a metro area's reading habits. The metro area average is 6.7.

In metro areas that have reading quotients of 3.0 or less, reading as expressed in visits to the library is not a pastime. But metro areas with reading quotients above 15.0 are places where libraries are used and used often.

Ironically, America—land of plenty, land of high technology—isn't the world's healthiest nation. This country lags behind Canada in life expectancy and in infant mortality, while Canada in turn lags behind Sweden and Japan.

Millions of Americans are uninsured and lack access to the full range of health services. Indeed, almost one-third of all American children aren't covered by any health insurance. In spite of an abundance of physicians packing advanced training and technical support, unfair distribution of medical care remains a central problem.

WHAT THE NUMBERS SAY

Americans continue to get healthier. Judging by two universal measures of population health, infant mortality and life expectancy, the United States is healthier now than it was a generation ago. Why are life expectancy and infant mortality such commonly accepted indicators of a nation's health? First, because these data can be found in almost every developed nation in the form of birth and death certificates.

Second, the quality of postpartum and infant care available in a nation (or state or town) generally reflects the quality of other important health services as well. As for life expectancy, it remains a very broad but meaningful indicator of a nation's ability to provide sanitary food and drinking water, proper immunization and disease screening, and professional medical attention throughout life.

In 1994, infant mortality in America had dropped to its lowest level ever, with data showing 8 deaths per 1,000 live births (compared to 7 per 1,000 live births in Canada). At the same time, life expectancy for children born in 2000 is projected to rise to 76.4 years (79.1 in Canada). This represents an increase of nearly 4 years since 1975, and a gain of 32 years since 1900.

TWO SYSTEMS—INSURANCE, ACCESS, AND THE REST

Unfortunately, not all Americans share in these statistical gains, and the inequality contributes to the modest U.S. health ranking compared with other countries. Black/white. Rich/poor. Urban/rural. Insured/uninsured. Profit/nonprofit. Short-term/long-term care. Consumer/provider. These are the poles of a health-care system that is a business enterprise. To get at the real essence of the system, one needs to look at the providers—the hospitals and the doctors.

HOSPITALS

The word *health* can also mean its opposite, illness. A hospital is not really a health-care institution; its business is to take care of sick people. The truly healthy need little health care except for an occasional shot or checkup; the unhealthy need a lot more.

Not all hospitals handle typical illnesses and emergencies. Many of them exclusively treat chronic diseases or alcohol and drug addiction, or they may be burn centers, psychiatric hospitals, or rehabilitation hospitals. When rating a metro area for its health care, *Places Rated* counts only general hospitals accredited for acute care by the Joint Commission on Accreditation of Healthcare

AMA Physician Categories

The American Medical Association (AMA) classifies a physician as a family practitioner, general practitioner, medical specialist, surgeon, or other specialist by 35 specialties in which the physician reports spending the largest number of his or her professional hours.

General/Family Practitioners

General Practice
Family Practice

Medical Specialists

Allergy
Cardiovascular Diseases
Dermatology
Gastroenterology
Internal Medicine
Pediatrics
Pediatric Allergy
Pediatric Cardiology
Pulmonary Diseases

Surgical Specialists

General Surgery
Neurological Surgery
Obstetrics and Gynecology
Ophthalmology
Orthopedic Surgery
Otolaryngology
Plastic Surgery
Colon and Rectal Surgery
Thoracic Surgery
Urology

Other Specialists

Aerospace Medicine
Anesthesiology
Child Psychiatry
Diagnostic Radiology
Forensic Pathology
Neurology
Occupational Medicine
Psychiatry
Pathology
Physical Medicine and Rehabilitation
General Preventive Medicine
Public Health
Radiology
Therapeutic Radiology

Organizations (JCAHO) or, in Canada, similar institutions certified by the Canadian Council for Health Services Accreditation (CCHSA).

The number of accredited acute-care hospitals and their inpatient beds varies among places. Although the number of hospital beds isn't as valuable an indicator as it was before advances in medicine and pharmacology shortened a hospital stay, it is still a reliable gauge of relative health-care supply.

Hospital Services

Each year, the American Hospital Association (AHA) surveys its thousands of member hospitals, enumerating which of 85 AHA-defined services each institution provides. The number of services a hospital offers is one index of the level of care you may receive there and certainly of the level of technology and specialization in that hospital.

Some of the AHA-defined services (a postoperative recovery room, a blood bank, an intensive-care unit, for example) are basic. Others (a radioactive implant department, a department that provides X-ray radiation therapy, a histopathology laboratory, or a department with organ transplant capabilities), however, are highly specialized. Of course, it really depends on one's situation; if a woman is of child-bearing years, access to genetic counseling services, an obstetrics unit, a neonatal intensive-care unit, and a pediatric inpatient unit may be extremely important.

Quality Care—What's a Consumer to Do?

Many hospitals, pressured by public and private cost-containment efforts, have had to slash services and staff. At the same time, hospitals remain critically short of qualified nurses. No wonder the quality of care is such a concern today. Since it's just about impossible to measure quality of care in any statistical way, how do we judge the skills of a doctor or hospital? Accreditation, with certain caveats, is one way.

Hospital Accreditation

The Joint Commission on Accreditation of Healthcare Organizations (JCAHO) is the private nonprofit body that investigates and certifies hospitals. The JCAHO certification determines which hospitals are eligible for federal funds or state licensure. The commission came under question recently, however, when federal investigations found that 156 JCAHO accredited hospitals in 30 states had serious deficiencies in at least one area of operation. Texas, the state with the most hospitals on this list, had 50 hospitals that were accredited but were found to be deficient in some area by federal standards. At least two hospitals in New York continued to operate under the JCAHO accredited designation for two years after the JCAHO had investigated them and found them deficient.

Since JCAHO assessments have been kept confidential, consumers have no way of knowing how to interpret this discrepancy between JCAHO findings and those of federal investigators. In other words, a patient could only find out whether or not a hospital was accredited—a questionable indicator of quality, considering the extent of deficiencies found over the past few years.

However, starting in 1995, you can buy a performance report from the JCAHO on local hospitals. Hospitals are scored on a scale of 0 to 100 in 28 categories, including dietary services, medication use, and staff preparation. Then each gets an overall score.

A hospital has incentives to qualify for accreditation. It makes it easier to recruit doctors and operate residency programs, and it reduces malpractice liability. Now

General/Family Practitioners: The Top Metro Areas

North of the border, the proportion of physicians who are general practitioners is three times greater than in the United States. Below are ten metro areas, all Canadian, with the greatest number of general practitioners per 100,000 people. The American metro area closest to this group is Sioux Falls, SD, with 87.

Metro Area	General Practitioners per 100,000 people
Victoria, BC	162
Halifax, NS	155
Vancouver, BC	149

Medical Specialists: The Top Metro Areas

Most American physicians specialize. Their number per 100,000 people tends to rise in smaller areas with medical schools and veterans' hospitals, and also where medical care is a basic industry attracting patients from outside. Below are metro areas, all American, with more than 100 medical specialists per 100,000 people. The Canadian metro area closest to the group is London, ON, with 98.

Metro Area	Specialists per 100,000
Rochester, MN	375
Boston, MA–NH	144

that accreditation status is becoming a more public matter, it may also become a useful tool for attracting patients—the consumers of health care.

PHYSICIANS AND THEIR SPECIALTIES

Not every doctor is listed in the yellow pages. Some are hospital administrators, medical school professors, journalists, lawyers, or researchers for pharmaceutical companies. Others work for government public-health services or Department of Defense service branches. Still others are in residency training or are full-time members of hospital staffs. When it comes to the number of physicians per capita, what really counts is the number of doctors who maintain offices and see patients. It's surprising how many of them don't.

Whether in the United States or in Canada, depending on how office-based or fee-for-service physicians spend their professional hours, they can be classified into three groups:

General Practitioners are physicians who treat diseases and injuries, provide preventive care, give routine checkups, prescribe drugs, and perform some surgery. They also refer patients to medical specialists. General practitioners use all accepted methods of medical care.

Medical Specialists focus on specific medical disciplines, such as cardiology, allergy, gastroenterology, and dermatology. Medical specialists (and general practitioners) are likely to give attention to surgical and nonsurgical approaches to treatment. If they decide that surgery is the method of treatment, they refer their patients to surgeons.

Surgical Specialists operate on a regular basis several times a week. In the United States the letters F.A.C.S. (Fellow of the American College of Surgeons) after the surgeon's name indicate that he or she has passed an evaluation of surgical training and skills as well as ethical fitness.

Where Physicians Cluster—One Measure of Health Care

Where doctors end up practicing is partly determined by sentiment, their perceptions of local quality of life, or both. But mainly it's a matter of economics. The physician has invested three to seven years in graduate medical education and frequently has to start out with a monstrous loan to repay.

Some begin work on a hospital staff, develop a practice, then open an office. Others are taken into someone else's practice as a partner or as one of a group of physicians. Still others buy practices from doctors who are preparing to retire. By whatever means they launch themselves professionally, new physicians who wish to specialize are concerned primarily with a place's population size.

Many physicians want to practice near a major hospital and also want to live in a city large enough to provide them with the amenities their incomes allow. In general, larger, more affluent places—Boston, New York, San Francisco, and Toronto, for example—have a greater proportion of health-care facilities, medical specialists, high-tech equipment, and exotic procedures.

On the other hand, small American metro areas tend to have more general and family practitioners than specialists. The common explanation is that the smaller metro areas don't have enough patients to support a large number of specialists. There's not enough business for an allergist to open an office in one out of five smaller metro areas, for example. Doctors in these areas who want to see 30 to 40 patients a day need to be generalists.

Another pattern is for expensive, complex procedures to be available only in major metro areas or in areas with medical schools and veterans' hospitals. You can't get a bone marrow transplant in most metro areas in North America. In Utica, NY, no one performs open-heart surgery. A patient has to go to Syracuse—about 50 miles away—for that. Surgeons, too, tend to cluster in metro areas with medical schools, veterans' hospitals, and ancillary medical centers.

A counter trend in physician clustering is developing, however. Some newly graduated specialists are leaving big cities where things are so competitive that they can't find jobs and where it's simply too expensive for them to set up their own practices. They choose, instead, to go to smaller metro areas—often the towns in which they grew up—to establish a practice and to penetrate the existing referral network of doctors.

Another phenomenon north of the border is the active and successful recruitment of Canadian physicians by American headhunters whose seminars detail the intricacies of emigration and setting up a practice in underserved areas in the United States.

SCORING: HEALTH CARE

What is being judged in this chapter is health care in each metro area, not how sick the resident population is. Moreover, *Places Rated* doesn't assess the quality of health care but its supply. As for the expense of health care to the consumer, see the Costs of Living chapter.

Keeping these distinctions in mind will help the reader avoid assuming that a low score in this chapter means either (1) that the people in a given place are unhealthy and don't live very long, or (2) that if one were to relocate to this place, basic health care—including even such complex emergency surgery as a coronary bypass—would be unavailable or inferior. *Both of these conclusions are incorrect.* A low score in this chapter does indicate, however, that the emphasis in that metro area is probably on basic health care and that the latest techniques and equipment, and personnel trained to implement them, are more likely to be found elsewhere.

In rating metro areas for relative strength in health care, *Places Rated* considers five things:

1. *General/Family Practitioners* per 100,000: physicians who generalize because of the size of the patient base or choose to specialize in family practice.
2. *Medical Specialists* per 100,000: physicians who concentrate on specific medical disciplines such as pediatrics or cardiovascular diseases.
3. *Surgical Specialists* per 100,000: physicians who operate on a regular basis several times a week.

As stated earlier, just as not all MDs see patients, not all hospitals handle typical illnesses and emergencies. In the Short-Term General Hospitals category, *Places Rated* counts only hospitals classified by the AHA or the CHA as acute-care facilities whose patients stay fewer than 30 days.

4. *Accredited General Hospital Beds.* In U.S. metro areas, 91 percent of short-term general hospitals are accredited by the JCAHO. In Canadian metro areas, 94 percent are accredited by the CCHSA. While the lack of accreditation doesn't necessarily mean a facility is substandard, the presence of such accreditation means the hospital has passed rigorous and periodic reviews.

   While the number of hospital beds is dropping throughout North America because of cost-containment policies and the shift to outpatient services, it still is an indicator of health-care supply.
5. *Physician Residency Programs.* One-third of short-term general hospitals in the United States and half of Canada's general hospitals have approved physician training programs. Hospitals with no teaching programs aren't necessarily lagging in quality, but facilities with such programs tend to be larger urban institutions where the interaction between students and faculty encourages the development and use of the latest techniques, equipment, and therapy.

Affluent, big-city metro areas generally score higher in the rankings than the smaller, poorer metro areas. This doesn't mean that a person cannot receive excellent medical care in a rural clinic or, conversely, experience medical care that is bad enough to be life-threatening in even the finest of big-city hospitals. The quality of medical and nursing care most people receive depends on a number of factors, including the patient's ability to pay, blind chance, and human error.

Hospital Services

The American Hospital Association (AHA) classifies hospital services into 85 categories.

Adult day-care program
Alcohol/drug abuse or dependency inpatient unit
Alcohol/drug abuse or dependency outpatient services
Alzheimer's diagnostic/assessment services
Angioplasty
Arthritis treatment center
Birthing room/LDRP room
Blood bank
Burn-care unit
Cardiac catheterization laboratory
Cardiac intensive-care unit

Fitness center
General inpatient care for AIDS/ARC
Genetic counseling/screening services
Geriatric acute-care unit
Geriatric clinics
Health sciences library
Hemodialysis
Histopathology laboratory
HIV/AIDS unit
Home health services
Hospice
Magnetic resonance imaging
Mammography diagnostic
Mammography screening
Medical surgical or other intensive-care unit
Megavoltage radiation therapy
Neonatal intensive-care unit
Noninvasive cardiac assessment services
Obstetrics unit

Occupational health services
Occupational therapy services
Oncology services
Open-heart surgery
Organ/tissue transplant
Organized outpatient services
Organized social work services
Orthopedic surgery
Outpatient social work services
Outpatient surgery services
Patient education

Radioactive implants
Recreational therapy services
Rehabilitation inpatient unit
Rehabilitation outpatient services
Reproductive health services
Respiratory therapy services
Respite care
Senior membership program
Single photon emission computerized tomography (SPECT)
Skilled nursing or other long-term-care facility
Specialized outpatient program for AIDS/ARC
Speech therapy services
Sports medicine clinic/services
Therapeutic radioisotope facility
Trauma center (certified)
Ultrasound
Volunteer services department
Women's health center/services
Worksite health promotion
X-ray radiation therapy

Source: American Hospital Association, *Guide to the Health Care Field.*

RANKINGS: Health Care

Five per capita criteria are used to rate the supply of health care in a metro area: (1) general/family practitioners, (2) medical specialists, (3) surgical specialists, (4) short-term, general hospital beds, and (5) hospitals with physician teaching programs certified by the AMA or Association of Canadian Teaching Hospitals. Places that receive tie scores get the same rank and are listed alphabetically.

Metro Areas from Best to Worst

Places Rated Rank	Places Rated Score	Places Rated Rank	Places Rated Score	Places Rated Rank	Places Rated Score
1. New York, NY	99.94	4. Rochester, MN	99.79	6. Vancouver, BC	99.03
2. Los Angeles–Long Beach, CA	99.93	5. Philadelphia, PA–NJ	99.64	7. Montreal, PQ	98.82
3. Chicago, IL	99.91			8. Toronto, ON	98.61

Places Rated Rank		Places Rated Score
9.	Halifax, NS	97.90
10.	Washington, DC–MD–VA–WV	97.28
11.	Quebec City, PQ	97.27
12.	Sherbrooke, PQ	97.18
13.	Iowa City, IA	97.11
14.	Pittsburgh, PA	96.56
15.	London, ON	96.38
16.	Houston, TX	95.62
17.	Victoria, BC	95.46
18.	Ottawa–Hull, ON–PQ	94.00
19.	Saskatoon, SK	93.81
20.	Detroit, MI	93.61
21.	Minneapolis–St. Paul, MN–WI	93.27
22.	St. John's, NF	93.18
23.	Long Island, NY	92.99
24.	Columbia, MO	92.53
25.	Boston, MA–NH	92.42
26.	San Francisco, CA	92.30
27.	Gainesville, FL	92.18
28.	Edmonton, AB	91.99
29.	Cleveland–Lorain–Elyria, OH	91.87
30.	Seattle–Bellevue–Everett, WA	91.55
31.	Newark, NJ	91.38
32.	Kansas City, MO–KS	91.33
33.	Sioux Falls, SD	89.61
34.	New Orleans, LA	89.58
35.	Miami, FL	89.42
36.	Atlanta, GA	88.86
37.	Hamilton, ON	88.42
38.	Orange County, CA	88.18
39.	Charlottesville, VA	87.79
40.	Regina, SK	86.91
41.	Tampa–St. Petersburg–Clearwater, FL	86.52
42.	Indianapolis, IN	86.44
43.	Winnipeg, MB	85.99
44.	Phoenix–Mesa, AZ	85.92
45.	Lexington, KY	85.26
46.	Little Rock–North Little Rock, AR	85.24
47.	San Diego, CA	85.18
48.	Dallas, TX	84.74
49.	Milwaukee–Waukesha, WI	84.47
50.	Jackson, TN	84.07
51.	Greenville, NC	83.72
52.	Birmingham, AL	82.92
53.	Omaha, NE–IA	82.79
54.	Calgary, AB	82.08
55.	Duluth–Superior, MN–WI	82.05
56.	Riverside–San Bernardino, CA	81.21
57.	San Antonio, TX	80.91
58.	Eau Claire, WI	80.81
59.	Roanoke, VA	80.59
60.	Cincinnati, OH–KY–IN	80.17
61.	Louisville, KY–IN	79.78
62.	Richmond–Petersburg, VA	78.77
63.	Johnson City–Kingsport–Bristol, TN–VA	78.47
64.	Nashville, TN	78.31
65.	Jackson, MS	77.62
66.	Lubbock, TX	77.33
67.	Dayton–Springfield, OH	76.81
68.	Madison, WI	76.72
69.	Spokane, WA	76.55
70.	Trois-Rivieres, PQ	76.40
71.	Denver, CO	76.34
72.	Lowell, MA–NH	75.72
73.	Scranton–Wilkes-Barre–Hazleton, PA	75.31
74.	Toledo, OH	75.18
75.	Oakland, CA	75.15
76.	Raleigh–Durham–Chapel Hill, NC	74.71
77.	Buffalo–Niagara Falls, NY	74.50
78.	Grand Forks, ND–MN	74.37
79.	Thunder Bay, ON	74.10
80.	Wheeling, WV–OH	73.56
81.	Asheville, NC	73.54
82.	Anchorage, AK	73.14
83.	Santa Rosa, CA	73.13
84.	Chicoutimi–Jonquiere, PQ	73.01
85.	Shreveport–Bossier City, LA	72.87
86.	Oklahoma City, OK	72.75
87.	Albuquerque, NM	72.42
88.	Portland–Vancouver, OR–WA	72.28
89.	Memphis, TN–AR–MS	72.21
90.	Wichita, KS	71.41
91.	Augusta–Aiken, GA–SC	69.69
91.	Grand Junction, CO	69.69
93.	Evansville–Henderson, IN–KY	69.63
94.	Williamsport, PA	69.04
95.	Sudbury, ON	68.99
96.	Bismarck, ND	68.91
97.	Ann Arbor, MI	68.62
98.	Hattiesburg, MS	67.64
99.	St. Catharines–Niagara, ON	67.52
100.	La Crosse, WI–MN	67.48
101.	Knoxville, TN	67.43
102.	Fargo–Moorhead, ND–MN	65.97
103.	San Jose, CA	65.82
104.	Saint John, NB	65.80
105.	Burlington, VT	65.71
106.	Charleston–North Charleston, SC	65.35
107.	Fort Wayne, IN	65.27
108.	Rochester, NY	65.05
109.	Springfield, IL	64.75
110.	Victoria, TX	64.31
111.	Lincoln, NE	64.30
112.	Alexandria, LA	64.08
113.	Columbus, OH	63.78
114.	Fort Lauderdale, FL	63.27
115.	Albany–Schenectady–Troy, NY	63.16
115.	Harrisburg–Lebanon–Carlisle, PA	63.16
117.	Bergen–Passaic, NJ	63.03
118.	Sacramento, CA	62.88
119.	Hartford, CT	62.86
120.	Waterloo–Cedar Falls, IA	62.48
121.	Windsor, ON	61.83
122.	Pine Bluff, AR	61.25
123.	Jacksonville, FL	61.23
124.	Charleston, WV	61.09
125.	Santa Fe, NM	61.02
126.	West Palm Beach–Boca Raton, FL	60.76
127.	Tallahassee, FL	60.59
128.	Boulder–Longmont, CO	60.42
129.	Amarillo, TX	60.22
130.	Altoona, PA	59.98
131.	Fayetteville–Springdale–Rogers, AR	59.75
132.	Florence, SC	59.72
133.	Syracuse, NY	59.47
134.	Tucson, AZ	59.31
135.	Fort Collins–Loveland, CO	59.07
136.	Sioux City, IA–NE	58.64
137.	Erie, PA	58.60
138.	Kitchener, ON	58.53
139.	Portland, ME	58.13
140.	Bridgeport, CT	58.06
140.	Danbury, CT	58.06
140.	Stamford–Norwalk, CT	58.06
143.	Greenville–Spartanburg–Anderson, SC	57.72
144.	Tyler, TX	57.61
145.	Allentown–Bethlehem–Easton, PA	57.41
146.	Appleton–Oshkosh–Neenah, WI	57.40
147.	Greensboro–Winston-Salem–High Point, NC	57.22
148.	St. Cloud, MN	57.19
149.	Orlando, FL	56.94
150.	Pueblo, CO	56.50
151.	Monroe, LA	56.35
152.	Galveston–Texas City, TX	56.19
153.	Fitchburg–Leominster, MA	55.99
153.	Worcester, MA–CT	55.99
155.	Salt Lake City–Ogden, UT	55.95
156.	Huntington–Ashland, WV–KY–OH	55.40
157.	Tulsa, OK	55.20
158.	Santa Barbara–Santa Maria–Lompoc, CA	54.86
159.	Enid, OK	54.58
160.	Reno, NV	54.22
161.	Rockford, IL	54.09
162.	New Haven–Meriden, CT	53.97
162.	Waterbury, CT	53.97
164.	South Bend, IN	53.96
165.	Cedar Rapids, IA	53.76
166.	Redding, CA	53.71
167.	Decatur, IL	53.58
168.	Lancaster, PA	53.57
169.	Des Moines, IA	53.29
170.	Middlesex–Somerset–Hunterdon, NJ	53.22
171.	Columbia, SC	52.64
172.	Johnstown, PA	52.63
173.	Yolo, CA	52.61
174.	Pensacola, FL	51.30
175.	Cheyenne, WY	50.52
176.	Gary, IN	50.47
177.	Fort Smith, AR–OK	50.33
178.	Honolulu, HI	50.28
179.	Boise City, ID	49.79
180.	Norfolk–Virginia Beach–Newport News, VA–NC	49.77

Places Rated Rank		Places Rated Score
181.	Tacoma, WA	49.60
182.	Eugene–Springfield, OR	48.88
183.	Fort Worth–Arlington, TX	48.71
184.	Sarasota–Bradenton, FL	48.47
185.	Lake Charles, LA	48.04
186.	Macon, GA	47.41
186.	Wichita Falls, TX	47.41
188.	Ventura, CA	47.15
189.	Montgomery, AL	47.08
190.	Springfield, MO	46.88
191.	Trenton, NJ	46.81
192.	Oshawa, ON	46.51
193.	Corpus Christi, TX	46.34
	Atascadero–Paso Robles, CA	45.09
202.	Kokomo, IN	45.07
203.	Champaign–Urbana, IL	44.73
204.	Wausau, WI	44.44
205.	Beaumont–Port Arthur, TX	44.42
206.	Huntsville, AL	44.36
207.	Providence–Fall River–Warwick, RI–MA	44.33
208.	Lima, OH	43.80
209.	Killeen–Temple, TX	43.72
210.	Kalamazoo–Battle Creek, MI	43.48
211.	Davenport–Moline–Rock Island, IA–IL	42.75
212.	Fresno, CA	42.53
213.	Great Falls, MT	42.38
214.	Texarkana, TX–Texarkana, AR	42.33
215.	Chico–Paradise, CA	42.32
216.	Peoria–Pekin, IL	41.65
217.	Vallejo–Fairfield–Napa, CA	41.01
218.	Billings, MT	40.81
219.	Columbus, GA–AL	40.54
220.	Lewiston–Auburn, ME	40.44
221.	Waco, TX	40.13
222.	Chattanooga, TN–GA	39.34
223.	Baton Rouge, LA	38.94
224.	Rapid City, SD	38.85
225.	Casper, WY	37.94
226.	Dothan, AL	37.76
227.	Bellingham, WA	37.69
228.	Pittsfield, MA	37.63
229.	Austin–San Marcos, TX	37.36
230.	Lafayette, LA	37.09
231.	Lynchburg, VA	37.04
232.	Cumberland, MD–WV	36.71
233.	Wilmington–Newark, DE–MD	36.67
234.	Bangor, ME	36.59
235.	Muncie, IN	36.58
236.	Tuscaloosa, AL	36.45
236.	Yakima, WA	36.45
238.	Daytona Beach, FL	36.29

Places Rated Rank		Places Rated Score
239.	Charlotte–Gastonia–Rock Hill, NC–SC	35.92
240.	Hickory–Morganton–Lenoir, NC	35.79
241.	Modesto, CA	35.50
242.	Glens Falls, NY	35.13
243.	Reading, PA	34.63
244.	Biloxi–Gulfport–Pascagoula, MS	34.44
245.	Sheboygan, WI	34.35
246.	Santa Cruz–Watsonville, CA	34.02
247.	Springfield, MA	33.58
257.	Salinas, CA	29.10
258.	Salem, OR	29.08
259.	Kankakee, IL	28.94
260.	Athens, GA	28.91
261.	Sherman–Denison, TX	28.84
262.	St. Louis, MO–IL	28.67
263.	Dutchess County, NY	28.32
264.	Akron, OH	28.18
265.	Youngstown–Warren, OH	26.58
266.	Savannah, GA	26.56
267.	Owensboro, KY	26.43
268.	Lawrence, KS	26.24
269.	Gadsden, AL	26.20
270.	Elmira, NY	26.01
271.	Monmouth–Ocean, NJ	25.89
272.	Bloomington, IN	25.47
273.	Jersey City, NJ	24.83
274.	San Angelo, TX	24.76
275.	Parkersburg–Marietta, WV–OH	22.42
276.	Wilmington, NC	22.02
277.	Longview–Marshall, TX	21.60
278.	Dubuque, IA	21.59
279.	Fort Myers–Cape Coral, FL	21.56
280.	York, PA	21.55
281.	Decatur, AL	21.42
282.	Myrtle Beach, SC	21.40
283.	Elkhart–Goshen, IN	21.16
284.	Stockton–Lodi, CA	20.86
285.	Benton Harbor, MI	20.50
286.	Bryan–College Station, TX	20.02
287.	Green Bay, WI	19.48
288.	St. Joseph, MO	19.28
289.	Lawrence, MA–NH	19.03
290.	Visalia–Tulare–Porterville, CA	18.81
291.	Binghamton, NY	18.62
292.	Lafayette, IN	18.58
293.	Bremerton, WA	18.55
294.	Topeka, KS	18.44
295.	Joplin, MO	17.95

Places Rated Rank		Places Rated Score
296.	Melbourne–Titusville–Palm Bay, FL	17.90
297.	Lawton, OK	16.92
298.	Las Vegas, NV–AZ	16.88
299.	Merced, CA	16.39
300.	Anniston, AL	16.11
301.	Fayetteville, NC	15.07
302.	Naples, FL	14.75
303.	Rocky Mount, NC	14.73
304.	Sharon, PA	14.42
305.	Portsmouth–Rochester, NH–ME	14.29
314.	Provo–Orem, UT	11.98
315.	Jamestown, NY	11.94
316.	Mansfield, OH	11.34
317.	Lakeland–Winter Haven, FL	11.08
318.	Punta Gorda, FL	10.66
319.	Bakersfield, CA	10.64
320.	Odessa–Midland, TX	10.52
321.	Goldsboro, NC	10.12
322.	Albany, GA	9.96
323.	El Paso, TX	9.92
324.	New London–Norwich, CT–RI	9.35
325.	Fort Pierce–Port St. Lucie, FL	8.98
326.	Colorado Springs, CO	8.46
327.	Brockton, MA	8.32
328.	State College, PA	7.96
329.	Baltimore, MD	7.65
330.	Hamilton–Middletown, OH	6.87
331.	Yuba City, CA	6.53
332.	Steubenville–Weirton, OH–WV	6.36
333.	Racine, WI	6.26
334.	Las Cruces, NM	6.01
335.	Panama City, FL	4.95
336.	Atlantic City–Cape May, NJ	4.91
337.	Newburgh, NY–PA	4.11
338.	Brazoria, TX	3.92
339.	Kenosha, WI	3.48
340.	Hagerstown, MD	3.43
341.	Clarksville–Hopkinsville, TN–KY	3.34
342.	Brownsville–Harlingen–Benito, TX	2.86
343.	Ocala, FL	2.64
344.	Danville, VA	1.92
345.	New Bedford, MA	1.58
346.	Jackson, MI	1.54
347.	Jacksonville, NC	1.38
348.	Yuma, AZ	0.58
349.	Sumter, SC	0.15
350.	Laredo, TX	0.11
351.	Dover, DE	0.00

PLACES PROFILES: Health Care

In the following pages, selected health-care assets for the 351 metro areas are detailed.

Under the heading **General Hospitals** is the total number of short-term general hospitals and their total number of beds. Under that is the number of hospitals accredited by the Joint Commission on Accreditation of Healthcare Organizations (JCAHO) or the Canadian Council on Health Services Accreditation (CCHSA), and the number of hospitals with physician teaching programs.

Under the heading **Hospital Services** are, except for Canadian metro areas, the number of hospitals grouped by range of services offered. A single star (⋆) indicates 1–14 services, two stars (⋆ ⋆) indicate 15–24 services, and three stars (⋆ ⋆ ⋆) indicate 25 or more services.

Under the heading **Office-Based Physicians** (in Canada, **Fee-for-Service Physicians**) are groupings by major professional activity of local doctors who maintain offices and treat patients.

The access rating for each professional group (AA, A, B, or C) is shown in the right-hand column. An AA indicates the best access and C the least and is derived as follows:

1. *General/Family Practitioners.*

A metro area gets a rating of:	if, for every 100,000 people, General/Family Practitioners number:
AA	50 or more
A	between 40 and 49
B	between 30 and 39
C	fewer than 30

2. *Medical Specialists.*

A metro area gets a rating of:	if, for every 100,000 people, General/Family Practitioners number:
AA	55 or more
A	between 42 and 54
B	between 32 and 41
C	fewer than 32

3. *Surgical Specialists.*

A metro area gets a rating of:	if, for every 100,000 people, General/Family Practitioners number:
AA	47 or more
A	40 to 46
B	33 to 39
C	fewer than 33

Anchorage figures are imputed from Alaska totals. For New England metro areas, summary figures for the county in which the central city is located are used in place of cities and towns. For example, figures for New Haven–Meriden, CT, are those for New Haven County, CT, and figures for both Fitchburg–Leominster and Worcester in central Massachusetts are those for Worcester County, MA.

The information is derived from these sources: American Hospital Association, *Guide to the Health Care Field,* 1996; Canadian Healthcare Association, *Guide to Canadian Healthcare Facilities,* 1996; Health and Welfare Canada, Health Information Division, National Physician Database; and U.S. Department of Health and Human Services, Bureau of Health-Care Professions, unpublished "Area Resource File," 1996.

A check mark (✓) in front of a metro area's name highlights it as one of the top 35 places for health care.

Metro Area	General Hospitals	Hospital Services	Office-Based Physicans		Places Rated SCORE	Places Rated RANK
Abilene, TX	3 (465 beds)		50 General/Family Practice	A	**29.12**	**256**
	JCAHO accredited: 2		52 Medical Specialists	A		
		⋆⋆⋆ 3	55 Surgical Specialists	A		
Akron, OH	5 (1,975 beds)		232 General/Family Practice	B	**28.18**	**264**
	JCAHO accredited: 4		289 Medical Specialists	A		
	AMA residency: 3	⋆⋆⋆ 5	260 Surgical Specialists	B		
Albany, GA	2 (613 beds)		18 General/Family Practice	C	**9.96**	**322**
	JCAHO accredited: 2		55 Medical Specialists	A		
	AMA residency: 1	⋆⋆⋆ 2	53 Surgical Specialists	A		
Albany–Schenectady–Troy, NY	13 (3,610 beds)		286 General/Family Practice	B	**63.16**	**115**
	JCAHO accredited: 13	⋆⋆ 1	528 Medical Specialists	AA		
	AMA residency: 5	⋆⋆⋆ 12	398 Surgical Specialists	A		
Albuquerque, NM	11 (2,227 beds)	⋆ 3	333 General/Family Practice	AA	**72.42**	**87**
	JCAHO accredited: 10	⋆⋆ 2	400 Medical Specialists	AA		
	AMA residency: 5	⋆⋆⋆ 6	314 Surgical Specialists	AA		
Alexandria, LA	4 (1,178 beds)		43 General/Family Practice	B	**64.08**	**112**
	JCAHO accredited: 4	⋆⋆ 1	61 Medical Specialists	A		
	AMA residency: 2	⋆⋆⋆ 3	75 Surgical Specialists	AA		
Allentown–Bethlehem–Easton, PA	8 (2,377 beds)		259 General/Family Practice	A	**57.41**	**146**
	JCAHO accredited: 7	⋆⋆ 1	316 Medical Specialists	A		
	AMA residency: 4	⋆⋆⋆ 7	293 Surgical Specialists	AA		

Metro Area	General Hospitals	Hospital Services	Office-Based Physicans		Places Rated SCORE	Places Rated RANK
Altoona, PA	5 (713 beds) JCAHO accredited: 5 AMA residency: 1	 ★★★ 5	75 General/Family Practice 53 Medical Specialists 51 Surgical Specialists	AA B B	**59.98**	**130**
Amarillo, TX	6 (1,302 beds) JCAHO accredited: 5 AMA residency: 4	 ★★ 1 ★★★ 5	71 General/Family Practice 98 Medical Specialists 101 Surgical Specialists	B A AA	**60.22**	**129**
Anchorage, AK	4 (1,578 beds) JCAHO accredited: 3	 ★★ 1 ★★★ 3	180 General/Family Practice 105 Medical Specialists 112 Surgical Specialists	AA A A	**73.14**	**82**
Ann Arbor, MI	11 (2,425 beds) JCAHO accredited: 11 AMA residency: 4	★ 2 ★★★ 9	181 General/Family Practice 434 Medical Specialists 262 Surgical Specialists	B AA AA	**68.62**	**97**
		★★★ 2	71 Surgical Specialists	AA		
Atlanta, GA	42 (10,044 beds) JCAHO accredited: 39 AMA residency: 8	★ 6 ★★ 6 ★★★ 30	790 General/Family Practice 1,799 Medical Specialists 1,543 Surgical Specialists	C A A	**88.86**	**36**
Atlantic City–Cape May, NJ	4 (1,154 beds) JCAHO accredited: 4 AMA residency: 1	★ 1 ★★★ 3	55 General/Family Practice 130 Medical Specialists 125 Surgical Specialists	C B B	**4.91**	**336**
Augusta–Aiken, GA–SC	9 (3,223 beds) JCAHO accredited: 8 AMA residency: 4	 ★★ 2 ★★★ 7	156 General/Family Practice 276 Medical Specialists 244 Surgical Specialists	B AA AA	**69.69**	**92**
Austin–San Marcos, TX	10 (1,712 beds) JCAHO accredited: 8 AMA residency: 1	★ 1 ★★ 3 ★★★ 6	426 General/Family Practice 390 Medical Specialists 370 Surgical Specialists	A B B	**37.36**	**229**
Bakersfield, CA	11 (1,374 beds) JCAHO accredited: 6 AMA residency: 1	★ 3 ★★ 3 ★★★ 5	151 General/Family Practice 190 Medical Specialists 161 Surgical Specialists	C C C	**10.64**	**319**
Baltimore, MD	9 (2,008 beds) JCAHO accredited: 9	 ★★★ 9	377 General/Family Practice 902 Medical Specialists 638 Surgical Specialists	C A B	**7.65**	**329**
Bangor, ME	4 (583 beds) JCAHO accredited: 4 AMA residency: 1	 ★★ 1 ★★★ 3	60 General/Family Practice 68 Medical Specialists 62 Surgical Specialists	A A A	**36.59**	**234**
Barnstable–Yarmouth, MA	2 (375 beds) JCAHO accredited: 2 AMA residency: 1	 ★★★ 2	62 General/Family Practice 116 Medical Specialists 78 Surgical Specialists	B AA B	**13.12**	**311**
Baton Rouge, LA	8 (1,822 beds) JCAHO accredited: 6 AMA residency: 2	★ 3 ★★ 1 ★★★ 4	208 General/Family Practice 251 Medical Specialists 248 Surgical Specialists	B A A	**38.94**	**223**
Beaumont–Port Arthur, TX	9 (1,799 beds) JCAHO accredited: 7 AMA residency: 1	 ★★ 1 ★★★ 8	148 General/Family Practice 127 Medical Specialists 139 Surgical Specialists	B B B	**44.42**	**205**
Bellingham, WA	1 (211 beds) JCAHO accredited: 1	 ★★★ 1	96 General/Family Practice 54 Medical Specialists 56 Surgical Specialists	AA B B	**37.69**	**227**
Benton Harbor, MI	4 (681 beds) JCAHO accredited: 4	 ★★★ 4	55 General/Family Practice 59 Medical Specialists 51 Surgical Specialists	B B C	**20.50**	**285**
Bergen–Passaic, NJ	12 (5,181 beds) JCAHO accredited: 12 AMA residency: 5	 ★★★ 12	250 General/Family Practice 1,255 Medical Specialists 784 Surgical Specialists	C AA A	**63.03**	**117**
Billings, MT	2 (536 beds) JCAHO accredited: 2	 ★★★ 2	41 General/Family Practice 89 Medical Specialists 84 Surgical Specialists	B AA 	**40.81**	**218**

Metro Area	General Hospitals	Hospital Services	Office-Based Physicans		Places Rated SCORE	Places Rated RANK
Biloxi–Gulfport–Pascagoula, MS	9 (2,005 beds)		81 General/Family Practice	C	**34.44**	**244**
	JCAHO accredited: 9	★★ 2	98 Medical Specialists	C		
	AMA residency: 2	★★★ 7	125 Surgical Specialists	B		
Binghamton, NY	2 (751 beds)		94 General/Family Practice	B	**18.62**	**291**
	JCAHO accredited: 2		123 Medical Specialists	A		
		★★★ 2	121 Surgical Specialists	A		
Birmingham, AL	16 (4,853 beds)	★ 5	284 General/Family Practice	B	**82.92**	**52**
	JCAHO accredited: 13	★★ 2	687 Medical Specialists	AA		
	AMA residency: 9	★★★ 9	514 Surgical Specialists	AA		
Bismarck, ND	3 (703 beds)		43 General/Family Practice	A	**68.91**	**96**
	JCAHO accredited: 3		55 Medical Specialists	AA		
	AMA residency: 2	★★★ 3	43 Surgical Specialists	AA		
Bloomington, IN	1 (263 beds)		57 General/Family Practice	AA	**25.47**	**272**
	JCAHO accredited: 1		43 Medical Specialists	B		
		★★★ 1	46 Surgical Specialists	A		
Bloomington–Normal, IL	2 (528 beds)		44 General/Family Practice	B	**13.35**	**308**
	JCAHO accredited: 2		50 Medical Specialists	B		
		★★★ 2	48 Surgical Specialists	B		
Boise City, ID	5 (983 beds)	★ 1	182 General/Family Practice	AA	**49.79**	**179**
	JCAHO accredited: 5		113 Medical Specialists	B		
	AMA residency: 3	★★★ 4	155 Surgical Specialists	A		
✓ **Boston, MA–NH**	20 (6,732 beds)	★ 1	210 General/Family Practice	C	**92.42**	**25**
	JCAHO accredited: 20		1,825 Medical Specialists	AA		
	AMA residency: 11	★★★ 19	1,025 Surgical Specialists	AA		
Boulder–Longmont, CO	3 (369 beds)		208 General/Family Practice	AA	**60.42**	**128**
	JCAHO accredited: 3		118 Medical Specialists	A		
		★★★ 3	100 Surgical Specialists	A		
Brazoria, TX	4 (280 beds)		65 General/Family Practice	B	**3.92**	**338**
	JCAHO accredited: 4	★★ 1	36 Medical Specialists	C		
		★★★ 3	22 Surgical Specialists	C		
Bremerton, WA	2 (337 beds)		103 General/Family Practice	A	**18.55**	**293**
	JCAHO accredited: 2		65 Medical Specialists	C		
	AMA residency: 1	★★★ 2	61 Surgical Specialists	C		
Bridgeport, CT	7 (2,287 beds)		201 General/Family Practice	C	**58.06**	**140**
	JCAHO accredited: 7		764 Medical Specialists	AA		
	AMA residency: 7	★★★ 7	513 Surgical Specialists	AA		
Brockton, MA	5 (1,493 beds)	★ 1	77 General/Family Practice	C	**8.32**	**327**
	JCAHO accredited: 5		189 Medical Specialists	A		
	AMA residency: 3	★★★ 4	134 Surgical Specialists	C		
Brownsville–Harlingen–San Benito, TX	5 (837 beds)	★ 1	64 General/Family Practice	C	**2.86**	**342**
	JCAHO accredited: 5	★★ 1	73 Medical Specialists	C		
		★★★ 3	77 Surgical Specialists	C		
Bryan–College Station, TX	2 (285 beds)		59 General/Family Practice	A	**20.02**	**286**
	JCAHO accredited: 2		52 Medical Specialists	B		
		★★★ 2	44 Surgical Specialists	B		
Buffalo–Niagara Falls, NY	17 (5,678 beds)	★ 1	363 General/Family Practice	B	**74.50**	**77**
	JCAHO accredited: 15	★★ 2	784 Medical Specialists	AA		
	AMA residency: 7	★★★ 14	584 Surgical Specialists	AA		
Burlington, VT	3 (652 beds)		107 General/Family Practice	AA	**65.71**	**105**
	JCAHO accredited: 3		161 Medical Specialists	AA		
	AMA residency: 2	★★★ 3	103 Surgical Specialists	AA		
Calgary, AB	5 (2,075 beds)		701 General/Family Practice	AA	**82.08**	**54**
	CCHSA accredited: 5		475 Medical Specialists	AA		
	ACTH residency: 5		228 Surgical Specialists	C		
Canton–Massillon, OH	5 (1,656 beds)		137 General/Family Practice	B	**29.55**	**255**
	JCAHO accredited: 4		168 Medical Specialists	B		
	AMA residency: 2	★★★ 5	140 Surgical Specialists	B		
Casper, WY	1 (225 beds)		33 General/Family Practice	AA	**37.94**	**225**
	JCAHO accredited: 1		25 Medical Specialists	B		
	AMA residency: 1	★★★ 1	27 Surgical Specialists	A		
Cedar Rapids, IA	2 (898 beds)		101 General/Family Practice	AA	**53.76**	**165**
	JCAHO accredited: 2		54 Medical Specialists	C		
	AMA residency: 2	★★★ 2	64 Surgical Specialists	B		

Metro Area	General Hospitals	Hospital Services	Office-Based Physicans		Places Rated SCORE	Places Rated RANK
Champaign–Urbana, IL	2 (806 beds) JCAHO accredited: 1 AMA residency: 1	 ★★★ 2	73 General/Family Practice 108 Medical Specialists 79 Surgical Specialists	A AA AA	**44.73**	**203**
Charleston, WV	4 (1,327 beds) JCAHO accredited: 4 AMA residency: 1	 ★★★ 4	134 General/Family Practice 132 Medical Specialists 146 Surgical Specialists	AA A AA	**61.09**	**124**
Charleston–North Charleston, SC	9 (2,343 beds) JCAHO accredited: 7 AMA residency: 4	★ 1 ★★ 1 ★★★ 7	227 General/Family Practice 308 Medical Specialists 285 Surgical Specialists	A AA AA	**65.35**	**106**
Charlotte–Gastonia–Rock Hill, NC–SC	10 (3,265 beds) JCAHO accredited: 10	 ★★ 2	445 General/Family Practice 544 Medical Specialists	B A	**35.92**	**239**
✓ **Chicago, IL**	94 (28,531 beds) JCAHO accredited: 90 AMA residency: 34	★ 3 ★★ 3 ★★★ 88	2,602 General/Family Practice 4,969 Medical Specialists 3,271 Surgical Specialists	B AA A	**99.91**	**3**
Chico–Paradise, CA	5 (615 beds) JCAHO accredited: 4	★ 2 ★★★ 3	99 General/Family Practice 72 Medical Specialists 92 Surgical Specialists	AA B AA	**42.32**	**215**
Chicoutimi–Jonquiere, PQ	3 (855 beds) CCHSA accredited: 2 ACTH residency: 1		135 General/Family Practice 68 Medical Specialists 45 Surgical Specialists	AA A C	**73.01**	**84**
Cincinnati, OH–KY–IN	19 (5,516 beds) JCAHO accredited: 18 AMA residency: 8	★ 1 ★★ 1 ★★★ 17	656 General/Family Practice 899 Medical Specialists 745 Surgical Specialists	A AA AA	**80.17**	**60**
Clarksville–Hopkinsville, TN–KY	3 (512 beds) JCAHO accredited: 3	★ 1 ★★★ 2	48 General/Family Practice 40 Medical Specialists 46 Surgical Specialists	C C C	**3.34**	**341**
✓ **Cleveland–Lorain–Elyria, OH**	37 (10,274 beds) JCAHO accredited: 35 AMA residency: 10	★ 1 ★★ 1 ★★★ 35	554 General/Family Practice 1,580 Medical Specialists 1,134 Surgical Specialists	C AA AA	**91.87**	**29**
Colorado Springs, CO	4 (1,292 beds) JCAHO accredited: 4 AMA residency: 1	 ★★★ 4	114 General/Family Practice 153 Medical Specialists 160 Surgical Specialists	C B B	**8.46**	**326**
✓ **Columbia, MO**	4 (1,257 beds) JCAHO accredited: 4 AMA residency: 2	 ★★★ 4	75 General/Family Practice 131 Medical Specialists 115 Surgical Specialists	AA AA AA	**92.53**	**24**
Columbia, SC	6 (2,107 beds) JCAHO accredited: 6 AMA residency: 3	★ 1 ★★★ 5	204 General/Family Practice 234 Medical Specialists 234 Surgical Specialists	A A AA	**52.64**	**171**
Columbus, GA–AL	5 (1,542 beds) JCAHO accredited: 5 AMA residency: 2	★ 2 ★★★ 3	103 General/Family Practice 74 Medical Specialists 93 Surgical Specialists	B C B	**40.54**	**219**
Columbus, OH	14 (4,258 beds) JCAHO accredited: 13 AMA residency: 5	 ★★★ 14	614 General/Family Practice 594 Medical Specialists 575 Surgical Specialists	A B A	**63.78**	**113**
Corpus Christi, TX	8 (1,390 beds) JCAHO accredited: 7 AMA residency: 1	★ 1 ★★ 1 ★★★ 6	169 General/Family Practice 154 Medical Specialists 158 Surgical Specialists	A B A	**46.34**	**193**
Cumberland, MD–WV	4 (566 beds) JCAHO accredited: 4	 ★★ 1 ★★★ 3	35 General/Family Practice 48 Medical Specialists 48 Surgical Specialists	B A AA	**36.71**	**232**
Dallas, TX	37 (8,216 beds) JCAHO accredited: 35 AMA residency: 6	★ 2 ★★ 2 ★★★ 33	858 General/Family Practice 1,260 Medical Specialists 1,306 Surgical Specialists	C A A	**84.74**	**48**

Metro Area	General Hospitals	Hospital Services	Office-Based Physicans		Places Rated SCORE	Places Rated RANK
Danbury, CT	2 (543 beds) JCAHO accredited: 2 AMA residency: 2	★★ 1 ★★★ 1	201 General/Family Practice 764 Medical Specialists 513 Surgical Specialists	C AA AA	**58.06**	**140**
Danville, VA	1 (408 beds) JCAHO accredited: 1 AMA residency: 1	★★★ 1	18 General/Family Practice 40 Medical Specialists 39 Surgical Specialists	C B B	**1.92**	**344**
Davenport–Moline–Rock Island, IA–IL	7 (1,498 beds) JCAHO accredited: 7 AMA residency: 2	★★★ 7	147 General/Family Practice 106 Medical Specialists 130 Surgical Specialists	A C B	**42.75**	**211**
Dayton–Springfield, OH	12 (5,102 beds) JCAHO accredited: 11 AMA residency: 6	★★★ 12	494 General/Family Practice 420 Medical Specialists 378 Surgical Specialists	AA A B	**76.81**	**67**
Daytona Beach, FL	9 (1,841 beds) JCAHO accredited: 9 AMA residency: 1	★★ 1 ★★★ 8	156 General/Family Practice 128 Medical Specialists 149 Surgical Specialists	B C B	**36.29**	**238**
Decatur, AL	4 (477 beds) JCAHO accredited: 4	★ 2 ★★ 1 ★★★ 1	55 General/Family Practice 31 Medical Specialists 42 Surgical Specialists	B C C	**21.42**	**281**
Decatur, IL	2 (717 beds) JCAHO accredited: 2 AMA residency: 2	★★★ 2	60 General/Family Practice 43 Medical Specialists 40 Surgical Specialists	AA B B	**53.58**	**167**
Denver, CO	18 (4,862 beds) JCAHO accredited: 16 AMA residency: 8	★★★ 18	705 General/Family Practice 1,143 Medical Specialists 860 Surgical Specialists	B AA AA	**76.34**	**71**
Des Moines, IA	8 (2,134 beds) JCAHO accredited: 7 AMA residency: 5	★ 2 ★★★ 6	148 General/Family Practice 161 Medical Specialists 159 Surgical Specialists	B B B	**53.29**	**169**
✓ **Detroit, MI**	48 (13,895 beds) JCAHO accredited: 39 AMA residency: 16	★ 3 ★★ 1 ★★★ 44	869 General/Family Practice 2,131 Medical Specialists 1,622 Surgical Specialists	C A B	**93.61**	**20**
Dothan, AL	4 (736 beds) JCAHO accredited: 4	★ 1 ★★ 1 ★★★ 2	42 General/Family Practice 72 Medical Specialists 77 Surgical Specialists	B A AA	**37.76**	**226**
Dover, DE	2 (234 beds) JCAHO accredited: 1	★★ 1 ★★★ 1	15 General/Family Practice 31 Medical Specialists 32 Surgical Specialists	C C C	**0.00**	**351**
Dubuque, IA	2 (524 beds) JCAHO accredited: 2	★★★ 2	14 General/Family Practice 59 Medical Specialists 51 Surgical Specialists	C AA AA	**21.59**	**278**
Duluth–Superior, MN–WI	9 (1,425 beds) JCAHO accredited: 6 AMA residency: 2	★★ 1 ★★★ 8	192 General/Family Practice 107 Medical Specialists 102 Surgical Specialists	AA A A	**82.05**	**55**
Dutchess County, NY	4 (1,087 beds) JCAHO accredited: 4 AMA residency: 2	★★★ 4	75 General/Family Practice 145 Medical Specialists 111 Surgical Specialists	C AA A	**28.32**	**263**
Eau Claire, WI	5 (872 beds) JCAHO accredited: 5 AMA residency: 2	★★★ 5	113 General/Family Practice 62 Medical Specialists 67 Surgical Specialists	AA A AA	**80.81**	**58**
✓ **Edmonton, AB**	12 (3,054 beds) CCHSA accredited: 12 ACTH residency: 6		879 General/Family Practice 512 Medical Specialists 265 Surgical Specialists	AA AA C	**91.99**	**28**
El Paso, TX	7 (1,931 beds) JCAHO accredited: 7 AMA residency: 2	★ 1 ★★ 1 ★★★ 5	145 General/Family Practice 187 Medical Specialists 182 Surgical Specialists	C C C	**9.92**	**323**
Elkhart–Goshen, IN	2 (429 beds) JCAHO accredited: 2	★★★ 2	78 General/Family Practice 37 Medical Specialists 43 Surgical Specialists	A C C	**21.16**	**283**
Elmira, NY	2 (512 beds) JCAHO accredited: 2	★★★ 2	23 General/Family Practice 64 Medical Specialists 48 Surgical Specialists	C AA AA	**26.01**	**270**
Enid, OK	3 (405 beds) JCAHO accredited: 2 AMA residency: 2	★★★ 3	25 General/Family Practice 19 Medical Specialists 27 Surgical Specialists	A B AA	**54.58**	**160**

Metro Area	General Hospitals	Hospital Services	Office-Based Physicans		Places Rated SCORE	Places Rated RANK
Erie, PA	7 (1,472 beds)	★ 1	138 General/Family Practice	A	**58.60**	**137**
	JCAHO accredited: 5	★★ 1	107 Medical Specialists	B		
	AMA residency: 2	★★★ 5	130 Surgical Specialists	A		
Eugene–Springfield, OR	4 (647 beds)		192 General/Family Practice	AA	**48.88**	**182**
	JCAHO accredited: 4	★★ 1	134 Medical Specialists	A		
		★★★ 3	127 Surgical Specialists	A		
Evansville–Henderson, IN–KY	5 (1,547 beds)		181 General/Family Practice	AA	**69.63**	**93**
	JCAHO accredited: 5		133 Medical Specialists	A		
	AMA residency: 2	★★★ 5	130 Surgical Specialists	A		
Fargo–Moorhead, ND–MN	5 (941 beds)	★ 1	80 General/Family Practice	A	**65.97**	**102**
	JCAHO accredited: 3		100 Medical Specialists	AA		
	AMA residency: 3	★★★ 4	83 Surgical Specialists	AA		
[illegible]	[illegible]		[illegible]	[illegible]		
[illegible]	[illegible]	[illegible]	[illegible]	[illegible]	[illegible]	[illegible]
	JCAHO accredited: 3	★★ 2	43 Medical Specialists	B		
		★★★ 1	43 Surgical Specialists	B		
Flint, MI	5 (1,759 beds)	★ 1	156 General/Family Practice	B	**31.56**	**251**
	JCAHO accredited: 4		168 Medical Specialists	B		
	AMA residency: 3	★★★ 4	111 Surgical Specialists	C		
Florence, AL	4 (927 beds)	★ 2	35 General/Family Practice	C	**30.65**	**254**
	JCAHO accredited: 4		58 Medical Specialists	A		
		★★★ 2	63 Surgical Specialists	A		
Florence, SC	4 (744 beds)		61 General/Family Practice	AA	**59.72**	**132**
	JCAHO accredited: 3	★★ 1	60 Medical Specialists	A		
	AMA residency: 1	★★★ 3	62 Surgical Specialists	AA		
Fort Collins–Loveland, CO	3 (409 beds)		162 General/Family Practice	AA	**59.07**	**135**
	JCAHO accredited: 3		55 Medical Specialists	C		
	AMA residency: 2	★★★ 3	86 Surgical Specialists	A		
Fort Lauderdale, FL	19 (5,294 beds)		404 General/Family Practice	C	**63.27**	**114**
	JCAHO accredited: 18		951 Medical Specialists	AA		
	AMA residency: 2	★★★ 19	645 Surgical Specialists	A		
Fort Myers–Cape Coral, FL	5 (1,498 beds)	★ 1	107 General/Family Practice	C	**21.56**	**279**
	JCAHO accredited: 4		167 Medical Specialists	A		
		★★★ 4	166 Surgical Specialists	A		
Fort Pierce–Port St. Lucie, FL	3 (775 beds)		78 General/Family Practice	C	**8.98**	**325**
	JCAHO accredited: 3		113 Medical Specialists	B		
		★★★ 3	110 Surgical Specialists	B		
Fort Smith, AR–OK	4 (955 beds)	★ 1	91 General/Family Practice	A	**50.33**	**177**
	JCAHO accredited: 3		72 Medical Specialists	B		
	AMA residency: 1	★★★ 3	85 Surgical Specialists	A		
Fort Walton Beach, FL	5 (556 beds)		43 General/Family Practice	C	**12.82**	**312**
	JCAHO accredited: 5	★★ 2	56 Medical Specialists	B		
	AMA residency: 1	★★★ 3	48 Surgical Specialists	C		
Fort Wayne, IN	10 (1,899 beds)		264 General/Family Practice	AA	**65.27**	**107**
	JCAHO accredited: 9		139 Medical Specialists	C		
	AMA residency: 3	★★★ 10	179 Surgical Specialists	B		
Fort Worth–Arlington, TX	20 (3,609 beds)	★ 1	492 General/Family Practice	B	**48.71**	**183**
	JCAHO accredited: 16	★★ 2	448 Medical Specialists	C		
	AMA residency: 2	★★★ 17	503 Surgical Specialists	B		
Fresno, CA	13 (1,721 beds)	★ 4	311 General/Family Practice	B	**42.53**	**212**
	JCAHO accredited: 11	★★ 2	337 Medical Specialists	B		
	AMA residency: 3	★★★ 7	284 Surgical Specialists	B		
Gadsden, AL	2 (548 beds)		34 General/Family Practice	B	**26.20**	**269**
	JCAHO accredited: 2		41 Medical Specialists	B		
		★★★ 2	41 Surgical Specialists	A		

Metro Area	General Hospitals	Hospital Services	Office-Based Physicans		Places Rated SCORE	Places Rated RANK
✓ Gainesville, FL	4 (1,714 beds) JCAHO accredited: 4 AMA residency: 3	⋆⋆⋆ 4	130 General/Family Practice 201 Medical Specialists 176 Surgical Specialists	AA AA AA	92.18	27
Galveston–Texas City, TX	4 (1,465 beds) JCAHO accredited: 4 AMA residency: 1	⋆⋆⋆ 4	104 General/Family Practice 120 Medical Specialists 122 Surgical Specialists	A A AA	56.19	153
Gary, IN	8 (2,987 beds) JCAHO accredited: 8 AMA residency: 2	⋆ 2 ⋆⋆⋆ 6	262 General/Family Practice 225 Medical Specialists 225 Surgical Specialists	A B B	50.47	176
Glens Falls, NY	2 (555 beds) JCAHO accredited: 2	⋆⋆⋆ 2	54 General/Family Practice 54 Medical Specialists 52 Surgical Specialists	A A A	35.13	242
Goldsboro, NC	2 (289 beds) JCAHO accredited: 2	⋆⋆ 1 ⋆⋆⋆ 1	40 General/Family Practice 27 Medical Specialists 29 Surgical Specialists	B C C	10.12	321
Grand Forks, ND–MN	5 (737 beds) JCAHO accredited: 2 AMA residency: 1	⋆⋆ 1 ⋆⋆⋆ 4	75 General/Family Practice 32 Medical Specialists 43 Surgical Specialists	AA C A	74.37	78
Grand Junction, CO	4 (755 beds) JCAHO accredited: 2 AMA residency: 1	⋆⋆ 1 ⋆⋆⋆ 3	68 General/Family Practice 38 Medical Specialists 38 Surgical Specialists	AA B B	69.69	91
Grand Rapids–Muskegon–Holland, MI	12 (2,331 beds) JCAHO accredited: 10 AMA residency: 3	⋆⋆ 1 ⋆⋆⋆ 11	308 General/Family Practice 317 Medical Specialists 348 Surgical Specialists	B B B	33.26	248
Great Falls, MT	2 (579 beds) JCAHO accredited: 2	⋆⋆⋆ 2	24 General/Family Practice 46 Medical Specialists 49 Surgical Specialists	C AA AA	42.38	213
Greeley, CO	1 (266 beds) JCAHO accredited: 1 AMA residency: 1	⋆⋆⋆ 1	84 General/Family Practice 44 Medical Specialists 46 Surgical Specialists	AA C C	31.87	250
Green Bay, WI	4 (655 beds) JCAHO accredited: 3	⋆ 1 ⋆⋆⋆ 3	70 General/Family Practice 89 Medical Specialists 93 Surgical Specialists	B A A	19.48	287
Greensboro–Winston-Salem–High Point, NC	13 (3,886 beds) JCAHO accredited: 13 AMA residency: 3	⋆⋆ 3 ⋆⋆⋆ 10	411 General/Family Practice 549 Medical Specialists 501 Surgical Specialists	B A A	57.22	148
Greenville, NC	1 (609 beds) JCAHO accredited: 1 AMA residency: 1	⋆⋆⋆ 1	94 General/Family Practice 118 Medical Specialists 77 Surgical Specialists	AA AA AA	83.72	51
Greenville–Spartanburg–Anderson, SC	12 (2,626 beds) JCAHO accredited: 9 AMA residency: 2	⋆ 1 ⋆⋆ 2 ⋆⋆⋆ 9	454 General/Family Practice 288 Medical Specialists 365 Surgical Specialists	AA B A	57.72	144
Hagerstown, MD	1 (314 beds) JCAHO accredited: 1	⋆⋆⋆ 1	32 General/Family Practice 47 Medical Specialists 51 Surgical Specialists	C B A	3.43	340
✓ Halifax, NS	6 (1,869 beds) CCHSA accredited: 6 ACTH residency: 5		497 General/Family Practice 336 Medical Specialists 152 Surgical Specialists	AA AA AA	97.90	9
Hamilton, ON	6 (2,256 beds) CCHSA accredited: 5 ACTH residency: 5		602 General/Family Practice 473 Medical Specialists 212 Surgical Specialists	AA AA B	88.42	37
Hamilton–Middletown, OH	4 (796 beds) JCAHO accredited: 4	⋆⋆⋆ 4	92 General/Family Practice 88 Medical Specialists 85 Surgical Specialists	C C C	6.87	330
Harrisburg–Lebanon–Carlisle, PA	8 (2,250 beds) JCAHO accredited: 7 AMA residency: 4	⋆⋆ 1 ⋆⋆⋆ 7	312 General/Family Practice 312 Medical Specialists 268 Surgical Specialists	AA A A	63.16	116
Hartford, CT	12 (3,266 beds) JCAHO accredited: 12 AMA residency: 7	⋆ 1 ⋆⋆⋆ 11	307 General/Family Practice 840 Medical Specialists 592 Surgical Specialists	C AA AA	62.86	119
Hattiesburg, MS	3 (695 beds) JCAHO accredited: 2	⋆ 1 ⋆⋆⋆ 2	62 General/Family Practice 50 Medical Specialists 62 Surgical Specialists	AA A AA	67.64	98

Metro Area	General Hospitals	Hospital Services	Office-Based Physicans		Places Rated SCORE	Places Rated RANK
Hickory–Morganton–Lenoir, NC	6 (827 beds) JCAHO accredited: 5	 ★★ 1 ★★★ 5	156 General/Family Practice 71 Medical Specialists 112 Surgical Specialists	AA C B	35.79	240
Honolulu, HI	10 (2,205 beds) JCAHO accredited: 10 AMA residency: 6	★ 3 ★★★ 7	213 General/Family Practice 653 Medical Specialists 441 Surgical Specialists	C AA AA	50.28	178
Houma, LA	5 (666 beds) JCAHO accredited: 5 AMA residency: 1	 ★★ 2 ★★★ 3	49 General/Family Practice 50 Medical Specialists 74 Surgical Specialists	C C B	13.93	306
✓ Houston, TX	50 (13,234 beds) JCAHO accredited: 47 AMA residency: 10	★ 4 ★★ 7 ★★★ 39	1,310 General/Family Practice 1,798 Medical Specialists 1,604 Surgical Specialists	B A A	95.62	16
Huntington–Ashland [illegible]	[illegible]	[illegible]	[illegible]	[illegible]	[illegible]	[illegible]
[illegible]	[illegible] JCAHO accredited: 3 AMA residency: 3	 ★★★ 3	[illegible] 133 Medical Specialists 113 Surgical Specialists	[illegible] AA AA	[illegible]	[illegible]
Jackson, MI	2 (438 beds) JCAHO accredited: 1	 ★★★ 2	36 General/Family Practice 39 Medical Specialists 39 Surgical Specialists	C C C	1.54	346
Jackson, MS	9 (2,773 beds) JCAHO accredited: 7 AMA residency: 5	★ 2 ★★★ 7	188 General/Family Practice 256 Medical Specialists 243 Surgical Specialists	A AA AA	77.62	65
Jackson, TN	2 (816 beds) JCAHO accredited: 2 AMA residency: 1	 ★★★ 2	45 General/Family Practice 61 Medical Specialists 71 Surgical Specialists	AA AA AA	84.07	50
Jacksonville, FL	12 (3,115 beds) JCAHO accredited: 12 AMA residency: 4	 ★★ 1 ★★★ 11	411 General/Family Practice 480 Medical Specialists 431 Surgical Specialists	A A A	61.23	123
Jacksonville, NC	2 (309 beds) JCAHO accredited: 2	 ★★ 1 ★★★ 1	37 General/Family Practice 19 Medical Specialists 30 Surgical Specialists	C C C	1.38	347
Jamestown, NY	4 (652 beds) JCAHO accredited: 2	 ★★ 1 ★★★ 3	40 General/Family Practice 31 Medical Specialists 46 Surgical Specialists	C C C	11.94	315
Janesville–Beloit, WI	3 (493 beds) JCAHO accredited: 3 AMA residency: 1	 ★★★ 3	41 General/Family Practice 71 Medical Specialists 48 Surgical Specialists	C A C	13.39	307
Jersey City, NJ	9 (2,444 beds) JCAHO accredited: 9 AMA residency: 2	★ 2 ★★★ 7	109 General/Family Practice 276 Medical Specialists 190 Surgical Specialists	C A B	24.83	273
Johnson City–Kingsport–Bristol, TN–VA	11 (2,327 beds) JCAHO accredited: 11 AMA residency: 4	 ★★ 3 ★★★ 8	259 General/Family Practice 246 Medical Specialists 217 Surgical Specialists	AA A AA	78.47	63
Johnstown, PA	7 (1,080 beds) JCAHO accredited: 7 AMA residency: 1	 ★★ 1 ★★★ 6	125 General/Family Practice 71 Medical Specialists 80 Surgical Specialists	AA C B	52.63	172
Joplin, MO	5 (744 beds) JCAHO accredited: 2	 ★★★ 5	37 General/Family Practice 45 Medical Specialists 62 Surgical Specialists	C C A	17.95	295
Kalamazoo–Battle Creek, MI	7 (1,438 beds) JCAHO accredited: 7 AMA residency: 2	 ★★★ 7	187 General/Family Practice 208 Medical Specialists 176 Surgical Specialists	A A B	43.48	210
Kankakee, IL	2 (541 beds) JCAHO accredited: 2	 ★★★ 2	41 General/Family Practice 35 Medical Specialists 30 Surgical Specialists	A B C	28.94	259

Metro Area	General Hospitals	Hospital Services	Office-Based Physicans		Places Rated SCORE	Places Rated RANK
✓ **Kansas City, MO-KS**	35 (6,951 beds)	★ 1	604 General/Family Practice	B	**91.33**	**32**
	JCAHO accredited: 29	★★ 1	882 Medical Specialists	A		
	AMA residency: 11	★★★ 33	711 Surgical Specialists	A		
Kenosha, WI	2 (326 beds)		37 General/Family Practice	C	**3.48**	**339**
	JCAHO accredited: 2		39 Medical Specialists	C		
	AMA residency: 1	★★★ 2	31 Surgical Specialists	C		
Killeen-Temple, TX	6 (1,924 beds)		81 General/Family Practice	C	**43.72**	**209**
	JCAHO accredited: 6	★★ 1	134 Medical Specialists	A		
	AMA residency: 3	★★★ 5	99 Surgical Specialists	B		
Kitchener, ON	3 (963 beds)		292 General/Family Practice	AA	**58.53**	**138**
	CCHSA accredited: 3		101 Medical Specialists	C		
			82 Surgical Specialists	C		
Knoxville, TN	9 (2,588 beds)		331 General/Family Practice	AA	**67.43**	**101**
	JCAHO accredited: 9	★★ 1	371 Medical Specialists	AA		
	AMA residency: 2	★★★ 8	334 Surgical Specialists	AA		
Kokomo, IN	3 (499 beds)		54 General/Family Practice	AA	**45.07**	**202**
	JCAHO accredited: 3		25 Medical Specialists	C		
		★★★ 3	31 Surgical Specialists	C		
La Crosse, WI-MN	3 (654 beds)		53 General/Family Practice	A	**67.48**	**100**
	JCAHO accredited: 2	★★ 1	113 Medical Specialists	AA		
	AMA residency: 2	★★★ 2	80 Surgical Specialists	AA		
Lafayette, IN	3 (581 beds)		58 General/Family Practice	B	**18.58**	**292**
	JCAHO accredited: 3		65 Medical Specialists	B		
		★★★ 3	66 Surgical Specialists	B		
Lafayette, LA	12 (1,531 beds)	★ 5	112 General/Family Practice	B	**37.09**	**230**
	JCAHO accredited: 10	★★ 3	122 Medical Specialists	B		
	AMA residency: 1	★★★ 4	132 Surgical Specialists	B		
Lake Charles, LA	6 (887 beds)	★ 1	80 General/Family Practice	A	**48.04**	**185**
	JCAHO accredited: 4	★★ 2	59 Medical Specialists	B		
	AMA residency: 1	★★★ 3	73 Surgical Specialists	A		
Lakeland-Winter Haven, FL	6 (1,291 beds)		109 General/Family Practice	C	**11.08**	**317**
	JCAHO accredited: 6		161 Medical Specialists	B		
		★★★ 6	159 Surgical Specialists	B		
Lancaster, PA	5 (1,203 beds)		305 General/Family Practice	AA	**53.57**	**168**
	JCAHO accredited: 4	★★ 1	103 Medical Specialists	C		
	AMA residency: 1	★★★ 4	123 Surgical Specialists	C		
Lansing-East Lansing, MI	6 (1,430 beds)		165 General/Family Practice	B	**30.92**	**253**
	JCAHO accredited: 5		178 Medical Specialists	B		
	AMA residency: 2	★★★ 6	139 Surgical Specialists	C		
Laredo, TX	2 (382 beds)		29 General/Family Practice	C	**0.11**	**350**
	JCAHO accredited: 2		35 Medical Specialists	C		
		★★★ 2	26 Surgical Specialists	C		
Las Cruces, NM	1 (221 beds)		60 General/Family Practice	B	**6.01**	**334**
	JCAHO accredited: 1		42 Medical Specialists	C		
		★★★ 1	39 Surgical Specialists	C		
Las Vegas, NV-AZ	12 (2,461 beds)	★ 5	263 General/Family Practice	C	**16.88**	**298**
	JCAHO accredited: 10	★★ 3	373 Medical Specialists	B		
	AMA residency: 1	★★★ 4	339 Surgical Specialists	C		
Lawrence, KS	1 (200 beds)		48 General/Family Practice	AA	**26.24**	**268**
	JCAHO accredited: 1		28 Medical Specialists	C		
		★★★ 1	26 Surgical Specialists	C		
Lawrence, MA-NH	9 (1,947 beds)	★ 1	130 General/Family Practice	C	**19.03**	**289**
	JCAHO accredited: 9		398 Medical Specialists	AA		
	AMA residency: 1	★★★ 8	290 Surgical Specialists	A		
Lawton, OK	4 (525 beds)		38 General/Family Practice	B	**16.92**	**297**
	JCAHO accredited: 4	★★ 1	27 Medical Specialists	C		
		★★★ 3	30 Surgical Specialists	C		
Lewiston-Auburn, ME	2 (440 beds)		47 General/Family Practice	A	**40.44**	**220**
	JCAHO accredited: 2		48 Medical Specialists	A		
	AMA residency: 1	★★★ 2	50 Surgical Specialists	AA		
Lexington, KY	12 (2,903 beds)	★ 1	224 General/Family Practice	AA	**85.26**	**45**
	JCAHO accredited: 12	★★ 4	327 Medical Specialists	AA		
	AMA residency: 4	★★★ 7	271 Surgical Specialists	AA		
Lima, OH	4 (658 beds)		87 General/Family Practice	AA	**43.80**	**208**
	JCAHO accredited: 3	★★ 1	37 Medical Specialists	C		
		★★★ 3	51 Surgical Specialists	C		

Metro Area	General Hospitals	Hospital Services	Office-Based Physicans		Places Rated SCORE	Places Rated RANK
Lincoln, NE	4 (901 beds) JCAHO accredited: 4 AMA residency: 4	 ★★★ 4	130 General/Family Practice 104 Medical Specialists 112 Surgical Specialists	AA A AA	**64.30**	**111**
Little Rock–North Little Rock, AR	11 (3,655 beds) JCAHO accredited: 11 AMA residency: 4	★ 2 ★★★ 9	304 General/Family Practice 348 Medical Specialists 343 Surgical Specialists	AA AA AA	**85.24**	**46**
✓ **London, ON**	4 (1,661 beds) CCHSA accredited: 4 ACTH residency: 3		515 General/Family Practice 441 Medical Specialists 170 Surgical Specialists	AA AA AA	**96.38**	**15**
Long Island, NY	28 (11,672 beds) JCAHO accredited: 27 AMA residency: 11	★ 1 ★★ 1 ★★★ 26	798 General/Family Practice 2,761 Medical Specialists 1,719 Surgical Specialists	B AA AA	**92.99**	**23**
[illegible]	[illegible] JCAHO accredited: 20 AMA residency: 7	[illegible] ★★ 1 ★★★ 19	[illegible] General/Family Practice 1,439 Medical Specialists 797 Surgical Specialists	[illegible] AA AA	**[illegible]**	**[illegible]**
Lubbock, TX	6 (1,567 beds) JCAHO accredited: 5 AMA residency: 3	 ★★ 1 ★★★ 5	121 General/Family Practice 156 Medical Specialists 148 Surgical Specialists	AA AA AA	**77.33**	**66**
Lynchburg, VA	3 (852 beds) JCAHO accredited: 2	 ★★★ 3	102 General/Family Practice 68 Medical Specialists 72 Surgical Specialists	AA B B	**37.04**	**231**
Macon, GA	8 (1,272 beds) JCAHO accredited: 8 AMA residency: 1	★ 1 ★★ 2 ★★★ 5	126 General/Family Practice 119 Medical Specialists 153 Surgical Specialists	A B AA	**47.41**	**187**
Madison, WI	5 (1,502 beds) JCAHO accredited: 5 AMA residency: 4	 ★★★ 5	247 General/Family Practice 326 Medical Specialists 218 Surgical Specialists	AA AA AA	**76.72**	**68**
Manchester, NH	9 (1,581 beds) JCAHO accredited: 9 AMA residency: 1	 ★★★ 9	188 General/Family Practice 251 Medical Specialists 208 Surgical Specialists	A A A	**46.19**	**194**
Mansfield, OH	6 (604 beds) JCAHO accredited: 5	 ★★ 1 ★★★ 5	49 General/Family Practice 47 Medical Specialists 52 Surgical Specialists	C C C	**11.34**	**316**
McAllen–Edinburg–Mission, TX	5 (910 beds) JCAHO accredited: 5 AMA residency: 1	 ★★ 1 ★★★ 4	159 General/Family Practice 75 Medical Specialists 80 Surgical Specialists	B C C	**12.40**	**313**
Medford–Ashland, OR	3 (438 beds) JCAHO accredited: 3	 ★★★ 3	71 General/Family Practice 82 Medical Specialists 81 Surgical Specialists	A A AA	**31.21**	**252**
Melbourne–Titusville–Palm Bay, FL	5 (1,118 beds) JCAHO accredited: 4	 ★★ 1 ★★★ 4	161 General/Family Practice 185 Medical Specialists 157 Surgical Specialists	B B B	**17.90**	**296**
Memphis, TN–AR–MS	15 (5,645 beds) JCAHO accredited: 3 AMA residency: 7	★ 2 ★★ 2 ★★★ 11	306 General/Family Practice 620 Medical Specialists 557 Surgical Specialists	C AA AA	**72.21**	**89**
Merced, CA	6 (358 beds) JCAHO accredited: 3 AMA residency: 1	★ 3 ★★ 2 ★★★ 1	79 General/Family Practice 40 Medical Specialists 37 Surgical Specialists	A C C	**16.39**	**299**
✓ **Miami, FL**	26 (8,422 beds) JCAHO accredited: 26 AMA residency: 4	★ 6 ★★ 3 ★★★ 17	992 General/Family Practice 1,631 Medical Specialists 1,182 Surgical Specialists	A AA AA	**89.42**	**35**
Middlesex–Somerset–Hunterdon, NJ	8 (2,999 beds) JCAHO accredited: 7 AMA residency: 6	 ★★ 1 ★★★ 7	359 General/Family Practice 795 Medical Specialists 463 Surgical Specialists	B AA A	**53.22**	**170**

Metro Area	General Hospitals	Hospital Services	Office-Based Physicans		Places Rated SCORE	Places Rated RANK
Milwaukee-Waukesha, WI	21 (5,195 beds) JCAHO accredited: 19 AMA residency: 10	* 2 ** 1 *** 18	599 General/Family Practice 894 Medical Specialists 675 Surgical Specialists	A AA	**84.47**	**49**
✓ **Minneapolis-St. Paul, MN-WI**	32 (7,330 beds) JCAHO accredited: 26 AMA residency: 9	* 5 ** 1 *** 26	1,823 General/Family Practice 1,362 Medical Specialists 1,057 Surgical Specialists	AA A B	**93.27**	**21**
Mobile, AL	9 (2,117 beds) JCAHO accredited: 9 AMA residency: 3	* 1 ** 1 *** 7	162 General/Family Practice 236 Medical Specialists 244 Surgical Specialists	B A AA	**46.08**	**197**
Modesto, CA	6 (1,302 beds) JCAHO accredited: 5	* 3 ** 1 *** 2	194 General/Family Practice 154 Medical Specialists 133 Surgical Specialists	A B C	**35.50**	**241**
Monmouth-Ocean, NJ	10 (3,380 beds) JCAHO accredited: 10 AMA residency: 2	*** 10	181 General/Family Practice 656 Medical Specialists 446 Surgical Specialists	C AA A	**25.89**	**271**
Monroe, LA	5 (992 beds) JCAHO accredited: 4 AMA residency: 1	* 1 *** 4	64 General/Family Practice 68 Medical Specialists 69 Surgical Specialists	A A AA	**56.35**	**152**
Montgomery, AL	9 (1,287 beds) JCAHO accredited: 8 AMA residency: 2	* 1 ** 2 *** 6	116 General/Family Practice 143 Medical Specialists 140 Surgical Specialists	B A A	**47.08**	**189**
✓ **Montreal, PQ**	40 (12,777 beds) CCHSA accredited: 31 ACTH residency: 17		2,899 General/Family Practice 2,352 Medical Specialists 1,063 Surgical Specialists	AA AA B	**98.82**	**7**
Muncie, IN	1 (469 beds) JCAHO accredited: 1 AMA residency: 1	*** 1	57 General/Family Practice 52 Medical Specialists 50 Surgical Specialists	A A A	**36.58**	**235**
Myrtle Beach, SC	3 (562 beds) JCAHO accredited: 3	*** 3	59 General/Family Practice 39 Medical Specialists 59 Surgical Specialists	B C B	**21.40**	**282**
Naples, FL	1 (434 beds) JCAHO accredited: 1	*** 1	62 General/Family Practice 84 Medical Specialists 85 Surgical Specialists	B A AA	**14.75**	**302**
Nashua, NH	9 (1,581 beds) JCAHO accredited: 9 AMA residency: 1	*** 9	188 General/Family Practice 251 Medical Specialists 208 Surgical Specialists	A A A	**46.19**	**194**
Nashville, TN	20 (5,239 beds) JCAHO accredited: 19 AMA residency: 6	* 4 ** 1 *** 15	303 General/Family Practice 730 Medical Specialists 615 Surgical Specialists	C AA AA	**78.31**	**64**
New Bedford, MA	5 (1,278 beds) JCAHO accredited: 5	*** 5	90 General/Family Practice 181 Medical Specialists 147 Surgical Specialists	C B C	**1.58**	**345**
New Haven-Meriden, CT	8 (2,868 beds) JCAHO accredited: 8 AMA residency: 6	** 1 *** 7	121 General/Family Practice 792 Medical Specialists 482 Surgical Specialists	C AA AA	**53.97**	**163**
New London-Norwich, CT-RI	3 (523 beds) JCAHO accredited: 3 AMA residency: 1	*** 3	64 General/Family Practice 120 Medical Specialists 112 Surgical Specialists	C A A	**9.35**	**324**
✓ **New Orleans, LA**	30 (6,454 beds) JCAHO accredited: 26 AMA residency: 10	* 6 ** 3 *** 21	318 General/Family Practice 931 Medical Specialists 854 Surgical Specialists	C AA AA	**89.58**	**34**
✓ **New York, NY**	79 (39,863 beds) JCAHO accredited: 78 AMA residency: 51	* 16 ** 3 *** 60	1,352 General/Family Practice 7,876 Medical Specialists 4,395 Surgical Specialists	C AA AA	**99.94**	**1**
✓ **Newark, NJ**	28 (9,567 beds) JCAHO accredited: 27 AMA residency: 15	*** 28	370 General/Family Practice 1,578 Medical Specialists 1,078 Surgical Specialists	C AA AA	**91.38**	**31**
Newburgh, NY-PA	7 (1,079 beds) JCAHO accredited: 7 AMA residency: 1	** 1 *** 6	50 General/Family Practice 143 Medical Specialists 113 Surgical Specialists	C B C	**4.11**	**337**
Norfolk-Virginia Beach-Newport News, VA-NC	12 (2,634 beds) JCAHO accredited: 12 AMA residency: 3	* 1 ** 1 *** 10	488 General/Family Practice 392 Medical Specialists 381 Surgical Specialists	A B B	**49.77**	**180**

Metro Area	General Hospitals	Hospital Services	Office-Based Physicans		Places Rated SCORE	Places Rated RANK
Oakland, CA	25 (4,892 beds) JCAHO accredited: 25 AMA residency: 5	★ 7 ★★★ 18	719 General/Family Practice 1,439 Medical Specialists 954 Surgical Specialists	B AA A	**75.15**	**75**
Ocala, FL	2 (471 beds) JCAHO accredited: 2	 ★★★ 2	61 General/Family Practice 59 Medical Specialists 64 Surgical Specialists	C C C	**2.64**	**343**
Odessa-Midland, TX	4 (709 beds) JCAHO accredited: 3 AMA residency: 2	 ★★ 1 ★★★ 3	60 General/Family Practice 76 Medical Specialists 87 Surgical Specialists	C B B	**10.52**	**320**
Oklahoma City, OK	19 (3,968 beds) JCAHO accredited: 16 AMA residency: 5	★ 1 ★★ 4 ★★★ 14	409 General/Family Practice 476 Medical Specialists 439 Surgical Specialists	A A A	**72.75**	**86**
	JCAHO accredited: 15 AMA residency: 2	★★ 1 ★★★ 13	601 Medical Specialists 572 Surgical Specialists	A A		
Oshawa, ON	2 (685 beds) CCHSA accredited: 2		168 General/Family Practice 68 Medical Specialists 56 Surgical Specialists	AA C C	**46.51**	**192**
✓ **Ottawa-Hull, ON-PQ**	11 (3,240 beds) CCHSA accredited: 10 ACTH residency: 6		1,035 General/Family Practice 812 Medical Specialists 356 Surgical Specialists	AA AA B	**94.00**	**18**
Owensboro, KY	2 (480 beds) JCAHO accredited: 2	 ★★★ 2	27 General/Family Practice 40 Medical Specialists 48 Surgical Specialists	C A AA	**26.43**	**267**
Panama City, FL	3 (460 beds) JCAHO accredited: 3	 ★★★ 3	31 General/Family Practice 45 Medical Specialists 56 Surgical Specialists	C B A	**4.95**	**335**
Parkersburg-Marietta, WV-OH	4 (749 beds) JCAHO accredited: 3	 ★★ 1 ★★★ 3	51 General/Family Practice 39 Medical Specialists 55 Surgical Specialists	B C B	**22.42**	**275**
Pensacola, FL	7 (1,794 beds) JCAHO accredited: 6 AMA residency: 2	 ★★ 1 ★★★ 6	158 General/Family Practice 155 Medical Specialists 165 Surgical Specialists	A B A	**51.30**	**174**
Peoria-Pekin, IL	5 (1,413 beds) JCAHO accredited: 4 AMA residency: 2	★ 1 ★★★ 4	146 General/Family Practice 153 Medical Specialists 132 Surgical Specialists	A A B	**41.65**	**216**
✓ **Philadelphia, PA-NJ**	72 (20,237 beds) JCAHO accredited: 63 AMA residency: 30	★ 10 ★★ 1 ★★★ 61	1,495 General/Family Practice 3,516 Medical Specialists 2,443 Surgical Specialists	B AA AA	**99.64**	**5**
Phoenix-Mesa, AZ	32 (6,958 beds) JCAHO accredited: 31 AMA residency: 7	★ 4 ★★ 3 ★★★ 25	967 General/Family Practice 1,127 Medical Specialists 1,028 Surgical Specialists	B A A	**85.92**	**44**
Pine Bluff, AR	1 (482 beds) JCAHO accredited: 1 AMA residency: 1	 ★★★ 1	54 General/Family Practice 31 Medical Specialists 37 Surgical Specialists	AA B A	**61.25**	**122**
✓ **Pittsburgh, PA**	38 (13,638 beds) JCAHO accredited: 37 AMA residency: 15	★ 3 ★★★ 35	912 General/Family Practice 1,495 Medical Specialists 1,204 Surgical Specialists	B AA AA	**96.56**	**14**
Pittsfield, MA	4 (612 beds) JCAHO accredited: 4 AMA residency: 1	 ★★★ 4	39 General/Family Practice 110 Medical Specialists 67 Surgical Specialists	C AA AA	**37.63**	**228**
Portland, ME	5 (1,000 beds) JCAHO accredited: 4 AMA residency: 2	 ★★ 1 ★★★ 4	103 General/Family Practice 191 Medical Specialists 159 Surgical Specialists	A AA AA	**58.13**	**139**
Portland-Vancouver, OR-WA	20 (4,361 beds) JCAHO accredited: 19 AMA residency: 6	★ 2 ★★★ 18	577 General/Family Practice 1,022 Medical Specialists 816 Surgical Specialists	B AA AA	**72.28**	**88**

Metro Area	General Hospitals	Hospital Services	Office-Based Physicans		Places Rated SCORE	Places Rated RANK
Portsmouth-Rochester, NH-ME	5 (633 beds)		132 General/Family Practice	B	14.29	305
	JCAHO accredited: 5		131 Medical Specialists	B		
		★★★ 5	120 Surgical Specialists	B		
Providence-Fall River-Warwick, RI-MA	10 (2,817 beds)		181 General/Family Practice	C	44.33	207
	JCAHO accredited: 10		673 Medical Specialists	AA		
	AMA residency: 5	★★★ 10	454 Surgical Specialists	AA		
Provo-Orem, UT	4 (550 beds)		112 General/Family Practice	B	11.98	314
	JCAHO accredited: 3		71 Medical Specialists	C		
		★★★ 4	88 Surgical Specialists	C		
Pueblo, CO	2 (556 beds)		75 General/Family Practice	AA	56.50	151
	JCAHO accredited: 2		63 Medical Specialists	A		
	AMA residency: 1	★★★ 2	65 Surgical Specialists	AA		
Punta Gorda, FL	3 (585 beds)	★ 1	27 General/Family Practice	C	10.66	318
	JCAHO accredited: 3		64 Medical Specialists	A		
		★★★ 2	46 Surgical Specialists	B		
✓ Quebec City, PQ	14 (4,676 beds)		715 General/Family Practice	AA	97.27	11
	CCHSA accredited: 13		566 Medical Specialists	AA		
	ACTH residency: 8		297 Surgical Specialists	A		
Racine, WI	3 (553 beds)		48 General/Family Practice	C	6.26	333
	JCAHO accredited: 3		69 Medical Specialists	B		
		★★★ 3	56 Surgical Specialists	C		
Raleigh-Durham-Chapel Hill, NC	10 (3,917 beds)	★ 2	438 General/Family Practice	A	74.71	76
	JCAHO accredited: 10	★★ 1	761 Medical Specialists	AA		
	AMA residency: 5	★★★ 7	554 Surgical Specialists	AA		
Rapid City, SD	2 (408 beds)		38 General/Family Practice	A	38.85	224
	JCAHO accredited: 2		44 Medical Specialists	A		
		★★★ 2	40 Surgical Specialists	A		
Reading, PA	3 (914 beds)		164 General/Family Practice	A	34.63	243
	JCAHO accredited: 3		135 Medical Specialists	B		
	AMA residency: 2	★★★ 3	134 Surgical Specialists	B		
Redding, CA	3 (448 beds)	★ 1	107 General/Family Practice	AA	53.71	166
	JCAHO accredited: 2		51 Medical Specialists	C		
	AMA residency: 1	★★★ 2	77 Surgical Specialists	AA		
Regina, SK	3 (975 beds)	★	207 General/Family Practice	AA	86.91	40
	JCAHO accredited: 3	★★	80 Medical Specialists	B		
	AMA residency: 3	★★★	71 Surgical Specialists	B		
Reno, NV	4 (1,243 beds)		129 General/Family Practice	A	54.22	161
	JCAHO accredited: 4		142 Medical Specialists	A		
	AMA residency: 2	★★★ 4	169 Surgical Specialists	AA		
Richland-Kennewick-Pasco, WA	4 (395 beds)		65 General/Family Practice	B	13.29	310
	JCAHO accredited: 3	★★ 2	55 Medical Specialists	C		
		★★★ 2	49 Surgical Specialists	C		
Richmond-Petersburg, VA	15 (4,362 beds)	★ 1	418 General/Family Practice	A	78.77	62
	JCAHO accredited: 15	★★ 1	610 Medical Specialists	AA		
	AMA residency: 5	★★★ 13	446 Surgical Specialists	AA		
Riverside-San Bernardino, CA	37 (6,372 beds)	★ 9	910 General/Family Practice	B	81.21	56
	JCAHO accredited: 32	★★ 4	961 Medical Specialists	B		
	AMA residency: 7	★★★ 24	838 Surgical Specialists	C		
Roanoke, VA	4 (1,709 beds)		133 General/Family Practice	AA	80.59	59
	JCAHO accredited: 4		140 Medical Specialists	AA		
	AMA residency: 3	★★★ 4	161 Surgical Specialists	AA		
✓ Rochester, MN	3 (1,251 beds)		82 General/Family Practice	AA	99.79	4
	JCAHO accredited: 3	★★ 1	424 Medical Specialists	AA		
	AMA residency: 2	★★★ 2	210 Surgical Specialists	AA		
Rochester, NY	17 (4,115 beds)		286 General/Family Practice	C	65.05	108
	JCAHO accredited: 17	★★ 2	799 Medical Specialists	AA		
	AMA residency: 5	★★★ 15	473 Surgical Specialists	A		
Rockford, IL	6 (1,128 beds)	★ 1	182 General/Family Practice	AA	54.09	162
	JCAHO accredited: 6	★★ 1	166 Medical Specialists	A		
	AMA residency: 3	★★★ 4	124 Surgical Specialists	B		
Rocky Mount, NC	3 (459 beds)	★ 1	48 General/Family Practice	B	14.73	303
	JCAHO accredited: 3		43 Medical Specialists	C		
		★★★ 2	50 Surgical Specialists	B		

Metro Area	General Hospitals	Hospital Services	Office-Based Physicans		Places Rated SCORE	Places Rated RANK
Sacramento, CA	13 (3,339 beds) JCAHO accredited: 13 AMA residency: 4	★ 3 ★★ 1 ★★★ 9	650 General/Family Practice 756 Medical Specialists 664 Surgical Specialists	A A A	62.88	118
Saginaw–Bay City–Midland, MI	6 (1,610 beds) JCAHO accredited: 6 AMA residency: 4	★★★ 6	168 General/Family Practice 126 Medical Specialists 122 Surgical Specialists	A C C	45.30	200
St. Catharines–Niagara, ON	7 (1,334 beds) CCHSA accredited: 7 ACTH residency: 1		276 General/Family Practice 107 Medical Specialists 95 Surgical Specialists	AA C C	67.52	99
St. Cloud, MN	5 (673 beds) JCAHO accredited: 2	★★ 2 ★★★ 3	104 General/Family Practice 52 Medical Specialists 63 Surgical Specialists	AA B A	57.19	149
Saint John, NB	2 (709 beds) CCHSA accredited: 2		88 General/Family Practice	AA	65.80	104
	AMA residency: 4	★★★ 20	464 Surgical Specialists	C		
Salem, OR	4 (540 beds) JCAHO accredited: 3	★★ 1 ★★★ 3	165 General/Family Practice 84 Medical Specialists 102 Surgical Specialists	AA C B	29.08	258
Salinas, CA	5 (667 beds) JCAHO accredited: 5 AMA residency: 1	★ 1 ★★★ 4	162 General/Family Practice 126 Medical Specialists 124 Surgical Specialists	A B B	29.10	257
Salt Lake City–Ogden, UT	14 (2,792 beds) JCAHO accredited: 12 AMA residency: 6	★ 1 ★★★ 13	385 General/Family Practice 588 Medical Specialists 537 Surgical Specialists	B A A	55.95	156
San Angelo, TX	3 (491 beds) JCAHO accredited: 3	★★★ 3	27 General/Family Practice 48 Medical Specialists 58 Surgical Specialists	C A AA	24.76	274
San Antonio, TX	19 (5,955 beds) JCAHO accredited: 15 AMA residency: 10	★★ 1 ★★★ 18	580 General/Family Practice 678 Medical Specialists 641 Surgical Specialists	A A A	80.91	57
San Diego, CA	26 (6,618 beds) JCAHO accredited: 26 AMA residency: 8	★ 3 ★★★ 23	1,119 General/Family Practice 1,480 Medical Specialists 1,235 Surgical Specialists	A AA A	85.18	47
✓ San Francisco, CA	20 (5,454 beds) JCAHO accredited: 20 AMA residency: 12	★ 1 ★★ 1 ★★★ 18	581 General/Family Practice 1,952 Medical Specialists 1,228 Surgical Specialists	B AA AA	92.30	26
San Jose, CA	14 (4,810 beds) JCAHO accredited: 13 AMA residency: 5	★ 5 ★★★ 9	519 General/Family Practice 1,131 Medical Specialists 836 Surgical Specialists	B AA AA	65.82	103
San Luis Obispo–Atascadero–Paso Robles, CA	6 (526 beds) JCAHO accredited: 5	★★ 2 ★★★ 4	123 General/Family Practice 108 Medical Specialists 100 Surgical Specialists	AA A A	45.09	201
Santa Barbara–Santa Maria–Lompoc, CA	8 (1,038 beds) JCAHO accredited: 8 AMA residency: 1	★ 2 ★★ 2 ★★★ 4	182 General/Family Practice 241 Medical Specialists 205 Surgical Specialists	A AA AA	54.86	159
Santa Cruz–Watsonville, CA	2 (405 beds) JCAHO accredited: 2	★★★ 2	135 General/Family Practice 94 Medical Specialists 100 Surgical Specialists	AA B A	34.02	246
Santa Fe, NM	3 (360 beds) JCAHO accredited: 3	★ 1 ★★★ 2	96 General/Family Practice 67 Medical Specialists 64 Surgical Specialists	AA A AA	61.02	125
Santa Rosa, CA	8 (798 beds) JCAHO accredited: 8 AMA residency: 1	★ 4 ★★★ 4	332 General/Family Practice 208 Medical Specialists 200 Surgical Specialists	AA A AA	73.13	83

Metro Area	General Hospitals	Hospital Services	Office-Based Physicans		Places Rated SCORE	Places Rated RANK
Sarasota–Bradenton, FL	6 (2,195 beds)		216 General/Family Practice	A	**48.47**	**184**
	JCAHO accredited: 6		310 Medical Specialists	AA		
		★★★ 6	285 Surgical Specialists	AA		
✓ **Saskatoon, SK**	3 (997 beds)	★	278 General/Family Practice	AA	**93.81**	**19**
	JCAHO accredited: 3	★★	170 Medical Specialists	AA		
	AMA residency: 3	★★★	94 Surgical Specialists	A		
Savannah, GA	4 (1,266 beds)	★ 1	77 General/Family Practice	C	**26.56**	**266**
	JCAHO accredited: 4	★★ 1	130 Medical Specialists	A		
	AMA residency: 1	★★★ 2	133 Surgical Specialists	AA		
Scranton–Wilkes-Barre–Hazleton, PA	14 (3,417 beds)		311 General/Family Practice	A	**75.31**	**73**
	JCAHO accredited: 13	★★ 1	319 Medical Specialists	A		
	AMA residency: 4	★★★ 13	265 Surgical Specialists	A		
✓ **Seattle–Bellevue–Everett, WA**	25 (5,106 beds)	★ 4	1,514 General/Family Practice	AA	**91.55**	**30**
	JCAHO accredited: 21	★★ 2	1,334 Medical Specialists	AA		
	AMA residency: 8	★★★ 19	1,142 Surgical Specialists	AA		
Sharon, PA	3 (628 beds)		33 General/Family Practice	C	**14.42**	**304**
	JCAHO accredited: 2		35 Medical Specialists	C		
		★★★ 3	47 Surgical Specialists	B		
Sheboygan, WI	3 (421 beds)	★ 1	52 General/Family Practice	A	**34.35**	**245**
	JCAHO accredited: 3		32 Medical Specialists	C		
		★★★ 2	38 Surgical Specialists	B		
✓ **Sherbrooke, PQ**	4 (1,114 beds)		172 General/Family Practice	AA	**97.18**	**12**
	CCHSA accredited: 4		168 Medical Specialists	AA		
	ACTH residency: 4		88 Surgical Specialists	AA		
Sherman–Denison, TX	3 (543 beds)		29 General/Family Practice	C	**28.84**	**261**
	JCAHO accredited: 3		45 Medical Specialists	A		
		★★★ 3	48 Surgical Specialists	AA		
Shreveport–Bossier City, LA	12 (2,370 beds)	★ 4	145 General/Family Practice	B	**72.87**	**85**
	JCAHO accredited: 11	★★ 2	217 Medical Specialists	AA		
	AMA residency: 3	★★★ 6	238 Surgical Specialists	AA		
Sioux City, IA–NE	2 (681 beds)		67 General/Family Practice	AA	**58.64**	**136**
	JCAHO accredited: 2		47 Medical Specialists	B		
	AMA residency: 2	★★★ 2	50 Surgical Specialists	A		
✓ **Sioux Falls, SD**	5 (1,193 beds)		132 General/Family Practice	AA	**89.61**	**33**
	JCAHO accredited: 3	★★ 2	97 Medical Specialists	AA		
	AMA residency: 3	★★★ 3	89 Surgical Specialists	AA		
South Bend, IN	4 (907 beds)		156 General/Family Practice	AA	**53.96**	**164**
	JCAHO accredited: 3		85 Medical Specialists	B		
	AMA residency: 2	★★★ 4	95 Surgical Specialists	B		
Spokane, WA	8 (1,609 beds)	★ 4	279 General/Family Practice	AA	**76.55**	**69**
	JCAHO accredited: 7		209 Medical Specialists	A		
	AMA residency: 3	★★★ 4	191 Surgical Specialists	AA		
Springfield, IL	3 (1,350 beds)	★ 1	72 General/Family Practice	B	**64.75**	**109**
	JCAHO accredited: 3		159 Medical Specialists	AA		
	AMA residency: 2	★★★ 2	128 Surgical Specialists	AA		
Springfield, MA	10 (2,118 beds)		147 General/Family Practice	C	**33.58**	**247**
	JCAHO accredited: 10	★★ 1	379 Medical Specialists	AA		
	AMA residency: 1	★★★ 9	259 Surgical Specialists	A		
Springfield, MO	4 (1,808 beds)		102 General/Family Practice	B	**46.88**	**190**
	JCAHO accredited: 3		166 Medical Specialists	AA		
	AMA residency: 1	★★★ 4	146 Surgical Specialists	AA		
Stamford–Norwalk, CT	7 (2,287 beds)		201 General/Family Practice	C	**58.06**	**140**
	JCAHO accredited: 7		764 Medical Specialists	AA		
	AMA residency: 7	★★★ 7	513 Surgical Specialists	AA		
State College, PA	1 (182 beds)		50 General/Family Practice	B	**7.96**	**328**
	JCAHO accredited: 1		46 Medical Specialists	B		
		★★★ 1	45 Surgical Specialists	B		
Steubenville–Weirton, OH–WV	3 (695 beds)	★ 1	31 General/Family Practice	C	**6.36**	**332**
	JCAHO accredited: 3		43 Medical Specialists	C		
		★★★ 2	30 Surgical Specialists	C		
Stockton–Lodi, CA	6 (1,013 beds)		195 General/Family Practice	B	**20.86**	**284**
	JCAHO accredited: 6		195 Medical Specialists	B		
	AMA residency: 1	★★★ 6	161 Surgical Specialists	C		
Sudbury, ON	3 (743 beds)		123 General/Family Practice	AA	**68.99**	**95**
	CCHSA accredited: 3		58 Medical Specialists	B		
	ACTH residency: 1		56 Surgical Specialists	B		

Metro Area	General Hospitals	Hospital Services	Office-Based Physicans		Places Rated SCORE	Places Rated RANK
Sumter, SC	2 (250 beds) JCAHO accredited: 2	 ★★ 1 ★★★ 1	19 General/Family Practice 23 Medical Specialists 24 Surgical Specialists	C C C	**0.15**	**349**
Syracuse, NY	10 (2,776 beds) JCAHO accredited: 10 AMA residency: 5	★ 1 ★★★ 9	295 General/Family Practice 379 Medical Specialists 335 Surgical Specialists	B A A	**59.47**	**133**
Tacoma, WA	9 (1,848 beds) JCAHO accredited: 8 AMA residency: 3	★ 3 ★★★ 6	304 General/Family Practice 207 Medical Specialists 216 Surgical Specialists	A B B	**49.60**	**181**
Tallahassee, FL	3 (820 beds) JCAHO accredited: 3 AMA residency: 1	★ 1 ★★★ 2	180 General/Family Practice 103 Medical Specialists 112 Surgical Specialists	AA B A	**60.59**	**127**
Thunder Bay, ON	2 (591 beds) CCHSA accredited: 2 ACTH residency: 1		111 General/Family Practice 45 Medical Specialists 42 Surgical Specialists	AA B B	**74.10**	**79**
Toledo, OH	11 (3,058 beds) JCAHO accredited: 10 AMA residency: 5	 ★★★ 11	309 General/Family Practice 316 Medical Specialists 311 Surgical Specialists	AA A AA	**75.18**	**74**
Topeka, KS	2 (664 beds) JCAHO accredited: 2 AMA residency: 1	 ★★★ 2	42 General/Family Practice 92 Medical Specialists 79 Surgical Specialists	C AA AA	**18.44**	**294**
Toronto, ON	34 (11,321 beds) CCHSA accredited: 3 ACTH residency: 11		4,318 General/Family Practice 2,617 Medical Specialists 1,141 Surgical Specialists	AA AA C	**98.61**	**8**
Trenton, NJ	5 (1,627 beds) JCAHO accredited: 5 AMA residency: 3	 ★★★ 5	67 General/Family Practice 299 Medical Specialists 192 Surgical Specialists	C AA AA	**46.81**	**191**
Trois-Rivieres, PQ	3 (819 beds) CCHSA accredited: 3 ACTH residency: 1		114 General/Family Practice 58 Medical Specialists 45 Surgical Specialists	AA A B	**76.40**	**70**
Tucson, AZ	11 (2,322 beds) JCAHO accredited: 11 AMA residency: 4	 ★★ 2 ★★★ 9	270 General/Family Practice 461 Medical Specialists 371 Surgical Specialists	B AA AA	**59.31**	**134**
Tulsa, OK	15 (2,861 beds) JCAHO accredited: 11 AMA residency: 3	★ 4 ★★ 3 ★★★ 8	274 General/Family Practice 337 Medical Specialists 282 Surgical Specialists	B A B	**55.20**	**158**
Tuscaloosa, AL	3 (742 beds) JCAHO accredited: 3 AMA residency: 1	 ★★ 1 ★★★ 2	64 General/Family Practice 66 Medical Specialists 64 Surgical Specialists	A A A	**36.45**	**236**
Tyler, TX	3 (601 beds) JCAHO accredited: 2 AMA residency: 1	★ 1 ★★★ 2	91 General/Family Practice 92 Medical Specialists 92 Surgical Specialists	AA AA AA	**57.61**	**145**
Utica-Rome, NY	6 (1,137 beds) JCAHO accredited: 5 AMA residency: 1	 ★★★ 6	125 General/Family Practice 111 Medical Specialists 122 Surgical Specialists	B B B	**32.51**	**249**
Vallejo-Fairfield-Napa, CA	8 (1,610 beds) JCAHO accredited: 7 AMA residency: 1	★ 1 ★★★ 7	203 General/Family Practice 242 Medical Specialists 174 Surgical Specialists	A A B	**41.01**	**217**
Vancouver, BC	20 (9,221 beds) CCHSA accredited: 20 ACTH residency: 12		2,386 General/Family Practice 1,099 Medical Specialists 589 Surgical Specialists	AA AA B	**99.03**	**6**
Ventura, CA	8 (1,308 beds) JCAHO accredited: 8 AMA residency: 1	★ 1 ★★ 1 ★★★ 6	382 General/Family Practice 292 Medical Specialists 270 Surgical Specialists	AA B B	**47.15**	**188**

Metro Area	General Hospitals	Hospital Services	Office-Based Physicans		Places Rated SCORE	Places Rated RANK
✓ **Victoria, BC**	2 (1,760 beds) CCHSA accredited: 1		465 General/Family Practice 174 Medical Specialists 115 Surgical Specialists	AA AA B	**95.46**	**17**
Victoria, TX	3 (575 beds) JCAHO accredited: 3	 ★★★ 3	46 General/Family Practice 37 Medical Specialists 34 Surgical Specialists	AA A A	**64.31**	**110**
Vineland-Millville-Bridgeton, NJ	2 (531 beds) JCAHO accredited: 2	 ★★★ 2	41 General/Family Practice 66 Medical Specialists 51 Surgical Specialists	C A B	**13.29**	**309**
Visalia-Tulare-Porterville, CA	7 (656 beds) JCAHO accredited: 7	★ 1 ★★ 2 ★★★ 4	136 General/Family Practice 90 Medical Specialists 74 Surgical Specialists	B C C	**18.81**	**290**
Waco, TX	3 (695 beds) JCAHO accredited: 3 AMA residency: 2	 ★★ 1 ★★★ 2	98 General/Family Practice 61 Medical Specialists 70 Surgical Specialists	A C B	**40.13**	**221**
✓ **Washington, DC-MD-VA-WV**	44 (13,551 beds) JCAHO accredited: 44 AMA residency: 19	 ★★ 2 ★★★ 42	1,369 General/Family Practice 3,379 Medical Specialists 2,336 Surgical Specialists	B AA AA	**97.28**	**10**
Waterbury, CT	8 (2,868 beds) JCAHO accredited: 8 AMA residency: 6	 ★★ 1 ★★★ 7	121 General/Family Practice 792 Medical Specialists 482 Surgical Specialists	C AA AA	**58.06**	**140**
Waterloo-Cedar Falls, IA	3 (658 beds) JCAHO accredited: 3 AMA residency: 2	 ★★★ 3	76 General/Family Practice 43 Medical Specialists 52 Surgical Specialists	AA B A	**62.48**	**120**
Wausau, WI	1 (269 beds) JCAHO accredited: 1 AMA residency: 1	 ★★★ 1	78 General/Family Practice 45 Medical Specialists 48 Surgical Specialists	AA B B	**44.44**	**204**
West Palm Beach-Boca Raton, FL	16 (3,893 beds) JCAHO accredited: 15	★ 1 ★★ 2 ★★★ 13	290 General/Family Practice 701 Medical Specialists 569 Surgical Specialists	B AA AA	**60.76**	**126**
Wheeling, WV-OH	6 (1,217 beds) JCAHO accredited: 6 AMA residency: 2	 ★★★ 6	88 General/Family Practice 68 Medical Specialists 74 Surgical Specialists	AA A A	**73.56**	**80**
Wichita, KS	9 (2,435 beds) JCAHO accredited: 7 AMA residency: 4	 ★★★ 9	297 General/Family Practice 239 Medical Specialists 192 Surgical Specialists	AA A B	**71.41**	**90**
Wichita Falls, TX	4 (605 beds) JCAHO accredited: 3 AMA residency: 2	★ 2 ★★★ 2	62 General/Family Practice 52 Medical Specialists 57 Surgical Specialists	A B A	**47.41**	**186**
Williamsport, PA	4 (611 beds) JCAHO accredited: 4 AMA residency: 1	 ★★★ 4	87 General/Family Practice 46 Medical Specialists 51 Surgical Specialists	AA B A	**69.04**	**94**
Wilmington, NC	4 (682 beds) JCAHO accredited: 3 AMA residency: 1	 ★★ 1 ★★★ 3	47 General/Family Practice 119 Medical Specialists 104 Surgical Specialists	C AA AA	**22.02**	**276**
Wilmington-Newark, DE-MD	5 (1,668 beds) JCAHO accredited: 4 AMA residency: 3	 ★★★ 5	208 General/Family Practice 271 Medical Specialists 215 Surgical Specialists	B A B	**36.67**	**233**
Windsor, ON	3 (912 beds) CCHSA accredited: 3 ACTH residency: 2		188 General/Family Practice 94 Medical Specialists 92 Surgical Specialists	AA B B	**61.83**	**121**
Winnipeg, MB	7 (2,642 beds) CCHSA accredited: 7 ACTH residency: 2		630 General/Family Practice 509 Medical Specialists 235 Surgical Specialists	AA AA B	**85.99**	**43**
Worcester, MA-CT	11 (2,082 beds) JCAHO accredited: 11 AMA residency: 4	 ★★ 1 ★★★ 10	252 General/Family Practice 562 Medical Specialists 280 Surgical Specialists	B AA B	**55.99**	**154**
Yakima, WA	4 (476 beds) JCAHO accredited: 3 AMA residency: 2	 ★★ 1 ★★★ 3	108 General/Family Practice 63 Medical Specialists 68 Surgical Specialists	AA C C	**36.45**	**237**
Yolo, CA	2 (164 beds) JCAHO accredited: 2	 ★★ 1 ★★★ 1	111 General/Family Practice 81 Medical Specialists 62 Surgical Specialists	AA AA A	**52.61**	**173**

Metro Area	General Hospitals	Hospital Services	Office-Based Physicans		Places Rated SCORE	Places Rated RANK
York, PA	3 (846 beds) JCAHO accredited: 2 AMA residency: 1	 ★★★ 3	162 General/Family Practice 94 Medical Specialists 92 Surgical Specialists	A C C	21.55	280
Youngstown–Warren, OH	10 (2,390 beds) JCAHO accredited: 7 AMA residency: 3	★ 3 ★★★ 7	145 General/Family Practice 247 Medical Specialists 188 Surgical Specialists	C B C	26.58	265
Yuba City, CA	3 (271 beds) JCAHO accredited: 1	 ★★★ 3	45 General/Family Practice 48 Medical Specialists 41 Surgical Specialists	B B C	6.53	331
Yuma, AZ	1 (213 beds) JCAHO accredited: 1	 ★★★ 1	31 General/Family Practice 35 Medical Specialists 35 Surgical Specialists	C C C	0.58	348

HEALTH CARE IN CANADA

Canada's taxpayer-financed, comprehensive health insurance system had much opposition when *Medicare*, as it's popularly called, came into play nearly three decades ago. Business and industry predicted failure because, if it were to be managed by government, doctors saw it as a threat to their livelihoods and some made plans to move south. Today, most Canadian doctors rate the system as "good to excellent," and business has been brought around because the cost is spread across society on the basis of ability to pay.

How It Works

Canada's health insurance system covers all medically necessary hospital and physician services for everyone. When Canadians need medical care, they make an appointment with the doctor of their choice, pull out the health insurance card issued to them by their province, and ask for treatment. Patients contend with no flurry of forms to fill out. There aren't any. Nor are there deductibles, co-payments, or dollar limits on coverage.

There are forms the physician fills out, but the paperwork is swift and simple. He or she bills the province on a fee-for-service basis under a published schedule negotiated each year by peers in their own medical association and the provincial government.

Almost all hospitals are nonprofit institutions operated by municipalities, religious, or voluntary organizations. The hospital's board and its administrators grapple with tight budgets, but they control spending decisions as long as they don't overspend a figure they negotiate every year with the provincial ministry of health.

Canadians do have to spend their own money on dental care, eyeglasses, and some drugs. About three out of every ten dollars spent on health care comes out of pocket. There are private insurers, but they may not offer coverage that duplicates government programs, only supplemental benefits. Their customers include retired Canadians who winter in Florida, Texas, and the American Southwest.

Money Matters

Canada spends $2,700 and the United States spends $3,600 on health care per capita. American administrative costs make up most of the $900 difference. Under the Canadian system, there are no marketing expenses, no staff to estimate risk and decide who should be denied or offered coverage. Neither doctors nor hospitals have to verify coverage or complete onerous paperwork required by multiple private insurance firms or resolve double-billing problems. Also, Canadian doctors pay relatively low premiums to the nonprofit Medical Protective Association for malpractice insurance.

Problems

For all the attention Canada's health-care system gets in the debate over reform, it isn't likely that the United States will copy the Canadian system. "America, with the world's most expensive health-care system," one expert noted, "has little to learn from a neighbor with the world's *second* most expensive system."

Canada is working out its *own* health-care crisis. As popular as it is with consumers, the system has become a monster to fund. Nearly a third of provincial budgets go to health care, the money coming from general revenues, high sales taxes, and high employer-paid payroll taxes. Two provinces, Alberta and British Columbia, collect premiums from residents.

Critics, many of them Canadian physicians, also

point to crowded hospitals, limited availability of new medical technology, long waiting lists even for lifesaving surgeries, and a reliance on rationing for the system to function.

HEALTHY LIFE/LONGER LIFE

Do you subscribe to the theory of when your time is up, you go? Then you may be surprised at current thinking. Experts now conclude that it's less likely to be a stray bullet or virus that kills you than the way you lead your life.

The most common causes of death at the turn of the century—typhoid fever, cholera, tuberculosis, smallpox, gastroenteritis, and nephritis—have been practically eliminated by scientific advances and improved sanitation. Today, more than 70 percent of the two million Americans who die each year are victims of heart disease, cancer, stroke, cirrhosis of the liver, bronchitis, asthma, and emphysema—the so-called lifestyle diseases that may be aggravated by such behavior as overeating, heavy drinking, smoking, and lack of exercise. To see how your daily habits measure up, take a look at the table "How Healthy Is Your Lifestyle?" The creators of this table warn that some risk factors are more important than others. Thus, an entirely accurate picture of your health may not emerge from practicing self-analysis. However, they add, changing your habits so that you qualify for the low-risk ratings will result in a longer life. The following are some suggestions—certainly not new, but still as healthful as the first time you heard them—that can help you reduce your health risks.

How Healthy Is Your Lifestyle?

Risk Category	No Risk	Slight Risk	Substantial Risk	Heavy Risk	Dangerous Risk
Smoking	No smoking or stopped for at least 10 years	Less than 10 cigarettes, 5 pipes or cigars a day	Half pack a day	1 pack a day	2 packs or more a day
Alcohol	Nondrinker	Stopped Drinker	6 drinks per week	More than 6 drinks per week	More than 2 drinks per day
Trimness	Lean	Slightly plump	Moderately obese	Considerably obese	Grossly obese
Physical activity	Walk more than 2 miles a day or climb 20 or more flights of stairs a day	Walk 1.5–2 miles a day or climb 15–20 flights of stairs a day	Walk only 0.5 to 1.5 miles a day or climb only 5–15 flights of stairs a day	Walk only 2–5 blocks a day or climb 2–4 flights of stairs a day	Walk less than 2 blocks a day or climb less than 2 flights of stairs a day
Prescription drugs	With a doctor's consent, following orders carefully	Take medication daily without side effects	Take medication when needed with few side effects	Use sleeping and nerve pills regularly without doctor's supervision	Without doctor's consent, mix with other drugs or alcohol
Nonprescription drugs	Use occasionally only for short periods; label warnings heeded				Continuing use, drinking or driving despite label warnings
Alcohol and driving—boats, cars, motorcycles, snowmobiles	Never drink; drive only with safety aids—seat belt, helmet, life jacket	Never drive after drinking without safety aids	Drive after 2 drinks with safety aids	Drive after 2 drinks without safety aids	Drive after more than 2 drinks without safety aids
Motor vehicle safety	Always wear seat belt	Wear seat belt more than half the time	Wear seat belt as a driver half the time	Wear seat belt as a passenger half the time	Wear seat belt less than half the time
Water safety—swimming and boating	Qualified expert	Know how to swim and the safety rules	Know how to swim and may swim after 1 drink or nerve drug	Do not know how to swim but use life jacket half the time	Do not know how to swim; never use life jacket
Blood cholesterol	Less than 180	180–220	220–280	280–320	320 and up
Blood pressure	120/80 or less	120/80–140/90	140/90–160/100	160/100–180/105	Above 180/105
Blood sugar	Less than 120 two hours after a meal of syrup and pancakes	Between 110 and 130 two hours after meals; checked each 3 months	Blood sugar more than 150 without diet control	Blood sugar more than 150 without diet control, doctor's care	Diabetes without doctor's care at less than 45 years of age
FOR WOMEN ONLY					
Breast check for lumps	Monthly self-exam and yearly check by physician	Monthly self-exam but no doctor exam	Self-exam 2–3 times a year but no doctor's exam	1 time a year by a doctor	Never
Pap smear	Every year	Every 3 years	Every 4 years	Never	Never; nonmenstrual bleeding

Source: Methodist Hospital of Indianapolis, Inc. Prepared by Pamela Hall under the supervision of Drs. Lewis C. Robbins and Jack H. Hall, developers of the Health Hazard Appraisal System. Used by Permission.

If you haven't yet paid heed to the wisdom of these suggestions, perhaps this will nudge you into a healthier style of living.

Stop smoking and drink only in moderation. Cigarette smokers run twice the risk that nonsmokers do of death from coronary disease. Smoking also contributes to stroke, lung cancer, emphysema, and bronchitis. Likewise, an excess of alcohol can be dangerous, increasing chances of developing cirrhosis of the liver (this condition is found six times as frequently among alcoholics as among nonalcoholics) and cardiovascular problems. Drinking, too, combined with driving, multiplies the risk of dying in an automobile accident; at least half of such accidents in the United States involve drunk

The Top Killers

Below are ten causes—and their death rates per 100,000 people—that account for 82 percent of all deaths. The top three non-accidental causes—heart disease, cancer, and stroke—account for 60 percent of all deaths.

Cause of Death	Rate per 100,000
Heart diseases	144.3
Malignancies	133.1
Accidents	29.4
Cerebrovascular diseases	26.2
Chronic obstructive pulmonary diseases	19.9
Infectious and parasitic diseases	14.7

choosing from a range of meat, poultry, fish, fruits, vegetables, and fiber foods (which have been shown to prevent colon cancer) is highly recommended. A balanced diet can also help you to lose extra weight, which puts added stress on the heart and organs, aggravating disease conditions.

Get regular exercise. Exercise, now seen almost as a miracle drug, can help you maintain proper weight, keep your body in good operating condition, and relieve stress (which contributes to ulcers and high blood pressure). It helps prevent premature aging and degeneration of bone (osteoporosis), muscles, and joints. The use-it-or-lose-it maxim definitely applies here.

Get regular medical care. Be sure to consult your doctor regularly and have whatever checkups or tests he or she recommends, such as a Pap smear, blood pressure, or blood cholesterol tests.

FINDING THE RIGHT DOCTOR

Not all doctors are created equal. The doctor you select and the hospital in which you're treated may be more important in determining the outcome of your illness than the disease you have. When you're selecting a surgeon, for example, you need to know how often the surgeon has done your kind of surgery (more is better) and what the outcome has been. Compare the records of several surgeons to get a sense of what a "good" track record is. Don't forget to trust your intuitions about doctors. How comfortable do you feel with the doctor? Your gut feeling could be the deciding factor.

The American Medical Association is the U.S. licensing body for physicians, but individual states vary in their licensing requirements. Highly populated states like New York and California have large staffs in their state licensing departments that can perform more thor-

Idaho do not have the same investigative resources. But licensing boards alone cannot track down all the bad doctors. Medical schools, where students first enter the doctor track; licensing boards; national, state, and local professional societies; and hospitals (where most doctors have staff privileges) must work together in order to assure that patients are treated by competent, licensed professionals.

The Health Care Financing Administration, which reimburses doctors and hospitals that treat Medicare and Medicaid patients, also has plans to help consumers in their selection of doctors. It will soon begin a long-term project of rating doctors by how well their patients do—as indicated by mortality rates and speed of recovery, for example.

In the meantime, consider the following suggestions. Chances are good that you'll have to choose a new physician at some point; even if you don't move, your doctor might. Finding a replacement for the person in whom you may have put a lot of trust isn't always easy. Give some thought to the kind of doctor you are most comfortable with. Do you want to place complete faith in your physician? Or do you have questions about your treatment? Do you like a cooperative arrangement in which you and your doctor work as a team? It's very important to most people that they have a doctor who will listen to their complaints, worries, and concerns, rather than one who may make patients feel that they're questioning the doctor's authority.

If you're planning to move, you might ask your present doctor if he or she knows anything about doctors in your destination. Or you may get names from the nearest hospital at the new location, from friends you make, from medical societies, and from new neighbors. Given the competition for insured patients, don't be surprised to receive mail from hospitals touting their

Paging Dr. Finder

Learning whether cardiologists, urologists, psychiatrists or other specialists practice in an area needn't mean a drudgerous session with the telephone book's yellow-pages. Call the local hospital's public relations office for a free copy of their Physician Locator or MD Directory. Hospitals in competitive markets know they will more likely have you as a customer when you're ill if they can introduce you early on to a physician who uses their facilities.

These "Dr. Finders" aren't mere telephone contact sheets. Often they are photo galleries of physicians with capsule résumés on their education from college through medical school to residency, their specialties, and their board certifications. You can also learn if they take walk-in patients and whether another doctor will cover for them on their day off. Some of these guides even detail their civic clubs and what they like to do on weekends.

services and the quality of physicians on their referral network.

When you have decided whom you want to contact, call that doctor's office, saying that you are a prospective patient, and ask to speak to the doctor briefly. You may have to agree to call back, but making connection with a professional voice is an important step. If you can't arrange this, if the doctor is "too busy," you probably ought to go to the next name on your list.

When you do make contact, tell the doctor enough about yourself so that he or she has a good idea of who you are and what your problems may be. If the doctor sounds "right" to you, you could ask about fees and emergencies. Or you may wish to save some of these questions for a personal visit. It is important to establish through the initial phone call or visit that you and the doctor will be at ease with each other.

Evaluate the doctor's attitude. If he or she doesn't want to bother with you now, you will probably get that don't-bother-me treatment sooner or later when dealing with specific problems. Make sure that:

- You can openly discuss your feelings and personal concerns about sexual and emotional problems.
- The doctor isn't vague, impatient, or unwilling to answer all your questions about the causes and treatment of your physical problems.
- The doctor takes a thorough history on you and asks about past physical and emotional problems, family medical history, medication you are taking, and other matters affecting your health.
- The doctor doesn't automatically prescribe drugs rather than deal with real causes of your medical problems.
- The doctor has an associate to whom you can turn should your doctor retire or die.

Talk with the doctor about the transfer of your medical records. Some doctors like to have them, especially if there is any specific medical problem or chronic condition. Other doctors prefer to develop new records.

Even if you feel fine, arrange to have a physical or at least a quick checkup. Should an emergency occur, the doctor will have basic information about you and some knowledge of your needs, and you will avoid the stress of trying to work with a doctor who has to learn about you in an emergency.

After "Where's that?" the thing people most often wonder about an unfamiliar place is, "Is there anything to do there?" Wherever they are, people want to make the most of leisure. Consider the billions spent each year on everything from video rentals, insulated jogging clothes, season tickets at the ballpark, European vacations, and down-filled sleeping bags to graphite fishing rods.

Not everyone can take advantage of all the opportunities for recreation. An Aspen ski trip or a Hilton Head golf weekend costs too much for most people. Even a backpacking trip in a national park with cheap camping fees might be out of the question for the dollars and time it takes to get there and back.

Fortunately, there are many other things to do that are inexpensive and nearby. Movies, golf, and good restaurants are available almost anywhere; in fact, people living in smaller metro areas usually have better access to these than residents of bigger ones. On the other hand, zoos and professional sports enhance life in larger places. For more and more people, convenient outdoor recreation in a national forest or on a wild and scenic river is a lucky geographical circumstance; the protected outdoors is a part of the landscape just as developed urban land is. *Places Rated* looks at each of these kinds of recreation in determining the best places to play.

COMMON DENOMINATORS

For scuba diving, the coasts of Florida, California, and Hawaii are best bets. For skiing on powdery snow, British Columbia and Colorado are better than most other areas. Weather and winds turn still other areas into premier places for hang gliding. But there are certain kinds of recreation that you can find everywhere: dining out at a quality restaurant, a round of weekend golf, or movie-going at a downtown picture palace or a multiplex cinema at a suburban mall.

Counting Stars: Good Restaurants

If you're among the one in ten who get out at least once a week for dinner, you may as well go to a worthwhile eatery instead of a portion-controlled Casa de la Maison House where distantly prepared frozen packages of Beef Wellington and Veal Cordon Bleu are microwaved, dished up, and menued at ten times what the restaurant paid for them.

To determine the best metro areas in North America for eating out, *Places Rated* uses the *Mobil Travel Guide,* which rates restaurants across the continent. The ratings are derived from two sources: an extensive review of consumer comments, and the inspection reports of field representatives who dine anonymously at establishments throughout the year.

Restaurants are judged on the basis of their food, service, and ambiance. Ratings range from one star for a "good, better than average" restaurant to five stars for "one of the country's best." Only a very few restaurants receive five stars in any given year; there were just thirteen top-rated restaurants in 1996.

Places Rated gauges access to good restaurants by dividing the resident population by the total number of quality stars awarded by *Mobil Travel Guide* to metro-area restaurants. Four one-star restaurants and one three-star restaurant, for example, would yield seven quality stars.

Counting Holes: Golf Courses

Certainly golf is a common denominator; the game is played in every metro area but one: Jersey City, NJ. When it comes to finding a local golf course on an idle, sunny weekend, there are three options: the private equity course, typically part of a country club open only to members and guests; daily-fee operations open to all players; and city-built and operated courses, again open to everyone.

If you're a golfer who can afford to join a private country club with an 18-hole course, your dues buy one big advantage: you belong to the fortunate 14 percent of golfers who don't have to wait to tee off at a crowded municipal or daily-fee course.

On the other hand, if you're one of nearly 25 million North American golfers who've played a round at a local municipal or daily-fee course, only 6 out of every 10 of the continent's 9,185 regulation courses are open to you. This may be changing; thanks to hard times, membership waiting periods have shortened and initiation fees have plunged at many clubs. However, because access to public golf is still an excellent reflection of recreation opportunities in metro areas, *Places Rated* counts the number of local municipal and daily-fee holes per capita.

The Top Metro Areas for Public Golf

Below are nineteen places, some of them resorts, others industrial areas in the Great Lakes, all having fewer than 1,000 residents per public golf hole.

Metro Area	Pop/Hole
Myrtle Beach, SC	174
Wilmington, NC	373
Barnstable–Yarmouth, MA	444
Jackson, MI	503
Fort Walton Beach, FL	630
Glens Falls, NY	686
Jamestown, NY	755
Ann Arbor, MI	816
Binghamton, NY	836
Utica–Rome, NY	839
Lakeland–Winter Haven, FL	876
Kalamazoo–Battle Creek, MI	894
Canton–Massillon, OH	898
Sharon, PA	913
Sarasota–Bradenton, FL	924
Kankakee, IL	944
Pittsfield, MA	944
Janesville–Beloit, WI	962
Grand Rapids–Muskegon–Holland, MI	963

Source: Derived from unpublished National Golf Foundation data and Woods & Poole Economics, Inc., population forecasts.

Counting Screens: The Movies

In 1948, John Huston won two academy awards—best director and best screenplay—for *The Treasure of Sierra Madre.* His father, Walter, was named best supporting actor for his portrayal of the old prospector in the same film. Jane Wyman won an Oscar for her role in *Johnny Belinda; Hamlet* was best picture, and its star, Lawrence Olivier, best actor.

The 1940s were a time when moviegoing was the thing to do any evening. Popcorn was regularly swept up from the aisles between shows, the next John Wayne or Spencer Tracy film was announced on a large easel in the lobby, usherettes took you to your seat with a red-lensed flashlight, and you always got a Movietone or Warner Pathe newsreel with the show. There were nearly 20,000 movie houses back then. Never again would there be so many.

Places Rated divides the local population by the number of commercial four-wall (as opposed to the fast-disappearing drive-in) theater screens to figure access to movies. Most are in multiplex cinemas run by chain exhibitors like Famous Players, United Artists, Cinemark, or Cineplex Odeon. But the single-screen or twin Bijou or Roxy kind of neighborhood theater is still alive in smaller metro areas.

CROWD PLEASERS

At different times of the year in Los Angeles–Long Beach, CA, you can visit the animals at the Los Angeles Zoo; join the crowds at Six Flags Magic Mountain and the Universal Studios tour; bet on the horses at Hollywood Park or Santa Anita; or take in professional baseball, football, basketball, and hockey, as well as NCAA Division I competition.

Few metro areas have as varied a supply of crowd pleasers as Los Angeles–Long Beach, but some of these opportunities are common in many of the larger metro areas. From Disneyland in Anaheim, CA, to New York's Bronx Zoo, these attractions offer Americans interesting ways to spend their leisure time.

Seeing the Animals: Zoos and Aquariums

The two best metro areas for seeing the animals are Chicago and San Diego. Each has not one but two of the continent's top-ranked zoological parks. Altogether, 118 metro areas have at least one zoo accredited by the American Association of Zoological Parks and Aquariums (AAZPA) or the Canadian counterpart, the CAZPA.

The idea that zoos enhance people's lives is a European one flourishing in America's Midwest. Besides Chicago's two great zoos, the Cincinnati, Cleveland,

The Top Metro Areas for Good Food

Although Santa Fe has 38 restaurants rated by Mobil, the number isn't overwhelming in the face of 322 found in New York. Still, "The City Different" can boast one quality star for every 1,788 residents, the best ratio among metro areas.

Metro Area	Pop/Star
Santa Fe, NM	1,788
Pittsfield, MA	1,846
Barnstable–Yarmouth, MA	1,897
Naples, FL	2,965
Salinas, CA	3,620
Flagstaff, AZ–UT	4,686
West Palm Beach–Boca Raton, FL	5,098
Atlantic City–Cape May, NJ	[illegible]

The Best Metro Areas for Moviegoing

Montreal's Forum, for decades the home ice of the NHL Canadiens, is converting into a cineplex. At 55 screens, it will be North America's largest. Below are eleven metro areas with fewer than 5,000 people per movie screen.

Metro Area	Pop/Screen
New Bedford, MA	2,472
Manchester, NH	2,714
Barnstable–Yarmouth, MA	2,739
Lowell, MA–NH	2,815
Atlantic City–Cape May, NJ	3,090
Charlottesville, VA	3,547
Panama City, FL	4,314

Detroit, Milwaukee, and St. Louis zoological parks are among the best in the United States. It is not coincidental that the working-class citizens of these cities can trace their roots to European countries—particularly Germany—that also have great zoos.

"Postage-stamp collecting" is the name that zoo keepers give to the assembling of colorful animal specimens without regard to whether the animals fit and thrive in a zoo's limited space. This was once a sure way of drawing more patrons and carving out a reputation as an outstanding institution. Today, professionally run zoos have fewer species on exhibit but more specimens of each. The standard phylogenetic exhibits (grouping African lions with Bengal tigers, timber wolves with hyenas) have been replaced with ecological displays (wildlife in desert or mountain environments) and behavioral exhibits (hibernation, burrowing, nocturnalism) that group specimens more creatively and openly.

This isn't to say that zoos no longer maintain large, diverse collections, for the best zoos are those with the biggest animal populations. But today the benchmark of a zoo's quality isn't simply how many animals it can keep or breed; just as important is how creatively and naturally the animals are exhibited.

Aquariums are far less common than zoos; just 23 of the 351 metro areas have one and most of these are in areas with ocean coastlines. Unlike the great zoological parks, which are run municipally or by societies, some of the best aquariums (including Boston's New England Aquarium) are owned and operated for profit by private firms.

A frequent topic of discussion on talk shows, in bars, and at work is where the "good" sports towns are. The question is usually argued from two perspectives: whether a town has winners or whether fans turn out to root for the teams. These two trends are often linked; over the regular seasons, the clubs with the best attendance usually have had some of the best records.

Another way to find the best sports towns is to measure the access that a metro area's fans have to regular-season games. "Game seats per capita" is an elementary measurement used most often in professional sports franchising and marketing, especially at expansion time. This figure is found by multiplying the number of home games played by all the teams in a metro area (for example, 81 baseball; 41 basketball; 8 football) by the combined seating capacity of the teams' playing arenas and then dividing that number by the metro area's population.

Professional Sports. In arriving at a figure for game seats per capita at professional sporting events, *Places Rated* surveyed each of the 174 metro areas with major-league or minor-league teams in any of four sports: baseball, basketball, football, and hockey. For example, the number of regular-season football games played by the Indianapolis Colts multiplied by the RCA Dome's capacity is 480,000. The same calculations yield a figure of 1,037,000 for NBA Pacers basketball and Ice minor-league hockey games played in Market Square Arena, and 995,918 for Indians Triple-A baseball games played at Bush Stadium. The sum of these four figures divided by Indianapolis's metro area population is more than two game seats for everyone in the nine-county metro area. Other metro areas have better averages, and in each of them the presence of a baseball team, with its large stadium and long playing season, makes a good deal of difference.

Baseball's Odyssey

Which major-league baseball team is descended from the old Beaneaters? It's not the Boston Red Sox; in fact, it's not even an American League team. It's the Atlanta Braves.

This is just one of many odd and intriguing changes major-league baseball teams have undergone since 1876, when eight professional clubs joined forces to form the National League. Twenty-five years later, in 1901, the American League began play, also with eight teams. Fifteen of today's American League (AL) and National League (NL) teams have moved to another city and/or changed their name since their founding date.

Atlanta Braves (NL)—*1876,* began as Boston Red Caps; *1883,* renamed Beaneaters; *1907,* renamed Doves; *1909,* renamed Pilgrims; *1936,* renamed Bees; *1941,* renamed Braves; *1953,* moved to Milwaukee and renamed Milwaukee Braves; *1966,* moved to Atlanta and renamed Atlanta Braves.

Baltimore Orioles (AL)—*1901,* began as Milwaukee Brewers; *1902,* moved to St. Louis and renamed St. Louis Browns; *1954,* moved to Baltimore and renamed Baltimore Orioles.

Boston Red Sox (AL)—*1901,* began as Somersets; *1905,* renamed Puritans; *1907,* renamed Red Sox.

California Angels (AL)—*1961,* began as Los Angeles Angels; *1965,* renamed California Angels.

Chicago Cubs (NL)—*1876,* began as White Stockings; *1894,* renamed Colts; *1898,* renamed Orphans; *1899,* renamed Cubs.

Cleveland Indians (AL)—*1901,* began as Bronchos; *1902,* renamed Blues; *1905,* renamed Naps; *1912,* renamed Molly McGuires; *1914,* renamed Indians.

Houston Astros (NL)—*1962,* began as Houston Colt .45's; *1964,* renamed Astros.

Los Angeles Dodgers (NL)—*1890,* began as Brooklyn Bridegrooms; *1898,* renamed Superbas; *1911,* renamed Dodgers; *1958,* moved to Los Angeles and renamed Los Angeles Dodgers.

Milwaukee Brewers (AL)—*1969,* began as Seattle Pilots; *1970,* moved to Milwaukee and renamed Milwaukee Brewers.

Minnesota Twins (AL)—*1901,* began as Washington Senators; *1960,* moved to Minneapolis–St. Paul and renamed Minnesota Twins.

New York Yankees (AL)—*1901,* began as Baltimore Orioles; *1903,* moved to New York and renamed New York Highlanders; *1912,* renamed Yankees.

Oakland A's (AL)—*1901,* began as Philadelphia Athletics; *1955,* moved to Kansas City and renamed Kansas City Athletics; *1968,* moved to Oakland and renamed Oakland Athletics; *1974,* renamed Oakland A's.

Pittsburgh Pirates (NL)—*1887,* began as Alleghenys; *1890,* renamed Innocents; *1891,* renamed Pirates.

San Francisco Giants (NL)—*1879,* began as Troy (NY) Trojans; *1883,* moved to New York City and renamed New York Gothams; *1886,* renamed Giants; *1958,* moved to San Francisco and renamed San Francisco Giants.

Texas Rangers (AL)—*1961,* began as Washington Senators; *1971,* moved to Arlington and renamed Texas Rangers.

The Cincinnati Reds (NL, 1876), Philadelphia Phillies (NL, 1883), St. Louis Cardinals (NL, 1892), Chicago White Sox (AL, 1901), Detroit Tigers (AL, 1901), New York Mets (NL, 1962), Kansas City Royals (AL, 1969), Montreal Expos (NL, 1969), San Diego Padres (NL, 1969), Seattle Mariners (AL, 1977), Toronto Blue Jays (AL, 1977), Colorado Rockies (NL, 1993), and Florida Marlins (NL, 1993) have neither changed their name nor moved.

Collegiate Sports. Among the biggest crowd pleasers around are varsity teams fielded by colleges and universities. The cream of those is generally found among the teams classified Division I (split into Divisions I-A and I-AA for football only) by the National Collegiate Athletic Association (NCAA). Eligibility for this division is based on the quality of a school's typical opponent, or "schedule strength," and game attendance figures.

Nearly 34 million fans attend the 3,251 regular season games played by the 667 colleges and universities with varsity football. Although the 191 Division I-A and I-AA teams play only one-third of these games, they draw 90 percent of the attendance.

Basketball is even more widely available. More than 28 million fans come out for the 11,063 regular season and tournament games played by the 868 schools that field men's varsity basketball teams. The 302 NCAA Division I men's teams play one-third of these games, yet they account for over 80 percent of total attendance. The 864 women's basketball teams draw another 5 million people to 7,305 season and tournament games, and 80 percent of the crowd watches the 293 NCAA Division I teams.

Division I and Canadian Inter-University Athletic Union (CIAU) football, men's and women's basketball, and hockey are on view in 275 of the 351 metro areas, from the Aces of the University of Evansville to the Zips of the University of Akron. Using game seats per capita as the criterion, the best metro area for college football and basketball is Lawrence, KS. The number of University of Kansas Jayhawks games played at home multiplied by the seating capacities of Memorial Stadium (football) and Allen Fieldhouse (basketball) yields a figure of 465,498, or almost seven game seats for everyone in town and in surrounding Douglas County.

OUTDOOR RECREATION ASSETS

To many people, recreation is not something that takes place within four walls or in the middle of a crowded city. Instead, it means turning to the open spaces for fishing, boating, swimming, hiking, running, picnicking, or getting away from it all. Just as some metro areas have more to offer in urban recreation, others undeniably are richer in access to the great outdoors

Coastlines and Inland Water

Sooners boast that Oklahoma has so many impounded lakes of every size that if you were to tip the state to the south a bit, the water would flow out and flood Texas for a good while. And Maryland crabbers point out to newcomers that the true length of estuarine shore reached by the Chesapeake Bay's tide would total more than 8,000 miles if all the bends and kinks were straightened out.

Outdoor Assets: 22 Outstanding Metro Areas

Listed below are places where a third or more of the surface area embraces any of the following outdoor assets: inland and offshore water, federal protected areas, or state/provincial parks.

Anchorage, AK
Bellingham, WA
Boulder–Longmont, CO
Eugene–Springfield, OR
Fort Collins–Loveland, CO
Fresno, CA
Miami, FL
Naples, FL
New Orleans, LA
Provo–Orem, UT

Visalia–Tulare–Porterville, CA

Hockey's Odyssey

The National Hockey League was formed by five team owners in the Windsor Hotel, in Montreal, nearly eighty years ago.

Calgary Flames—*1972,* began as Atlanta Flames; 1980, moved to Calgary and renamed Calgary Flames.

Colorado Avalanche—*1972,* began as Quebec Nordiques of the World Hockey Association; *1979,* joined NHL; *1995,* moved to Denver and renamed Colorado Avalanche.

Dallas Stars—*1967,* began as Minnesota North Stars; *1993,* moved to Dallas and renamed Stars.

Detroit Red Wings—*1926,* began as Cougars; *1929,* renamed Falcons; *1932,* renamed Red Wings.

Edmonton Oilers—*1972,* began as Alberta Oilers of the World Hockey Association; *1973,* renamed Edmonton Oilers; *1979,* joined NHL.

Hartford Whalers—*1972,* began as New England Whalers (Boston) of the World Hockey Association; *1977,* moved to Hartford; *1979,* joined NHL.

New Jersey Devils—*1974,* began as Kansas City Scouts; *1976,* moved to Denver and renamed Colorado Rockies; *1982,* moved to East Rutherford and renamed New Jersey Devils.

Phoenix Coyotes—*1979,* began as Winnipeg Jets; *1996,* moved to Phoenix and renamed Phoenix Coyotes.

Toronto Maple Leafs—*1917,* began as Arenas; *1919,* changed name to St. Patricks; *1926,* changed name to Maple Leafs.

The Anaheim Mighty Ducks (1993), Boston Bruins (1924), Buffalo Sabres (1970), Chicago Black Hawks (1926), Florida Panthers (1993), Los Angeles Kings (1967), Montreal Canadiens (1917), New York Islanders (1972), New York Rangers (1926), Ottawa Senators (1992), Philadelphia Flyers (1967), Pittsburgh Penguins (1967), St. Louis Blues (1967), San Jose Sharks (1991), Tampa Bay Lightening (1992), Vancouver Canucks (1970), and Washington Capitals (1974) have neither changed their name nor moved.

Four of every five North Americans today are congregated together in metro areas within 100 miles of an ocean or Great Lakes coastline; in less than 10 years, the U.S. Department of the Interior predicts that three of every four Americans will live within 50 miles of a coastline. Ocean or Great Lakes coastlines form part of the peripheries of 121 metro areas and 100 percent of another, Honolulu.

National Forests, Parks, and Wildlife Refuges

Some of the most popular outdoor activities—driving for pleasure, walking, picnicking, sightseeing, bird watching, nature walking, and fishing—would probably

built not only for loggers but for everyone. They lead to a wide variety of recreation outlets: ski resorts, marinas, fishing lakes and streams, hiking trails, and campgrounds.

In contrast to the National Forest System, the National Park System is meant expressly for recreation. The founding of Yellowstone National Park in 1872 marked the beginning of the oldest and now the largest national park system in the world. It comprises 354 national parks, preserves, monuments, memorials, battlefields, seashores, riverways, and trails that together cover some 80 million acres.

Whereas the National Park System acts to keep irreplaceable geographical and historical treasures in the public domain, the national wildlife refuges protect native flora and fauna from people. There are 452 of these remarkable sanctuaries throughout the country, embracing more than 89 million acres. Most of them are open to the public for a variety of wildlife activities, particularly photography and nature observation.

In certain refuges at irregular times, fishing and hunting are permitted, depending on the size of the wild populations. Although the majority of the nation's wildlife refuges are located in open, sometimes remote country, they aren't exclusively a rural amenity. Several can be found within metropolitan areas, such as the Nisqually National Wildlife Refuge in Olympia, WA, and San Pablo Bay National Wildlife Refuge in the California metro area of Santa Rosa–Petaluma.

SCORING: RECREATION

Is there more to do in Houston than in Dallas? How do those California rivals—Los Angeles and San Francisco—compare? In recreation, it may be impossible to rank metro areas with absolute fairness. Yet some metro areas seem shortchanged while others seem rich. To compare them, *Places Rated* considers twelve recreation-related elements.

Football's Odyssey

The first NFL franchise in Cleveland belonged not to the Browns but to the Rams, who played such opponents as the Brooklyn Dodgers, Chicago Cardinals, and Pittsburgh Pirates back in the 1930s. Organized professional football began to take shape in 1922 with the establishment of the National Football League, although the early teams seem ragtag compared to today's juggernauts. Through a series of splits and mergers with other leagues over the years, the NFL has remained the dominant pro football organization, and presently consists of 30 teams. The list below recaps the moves and name changes of today's NFL teams since their founding date.

Baltimore Ravens—*1946,* began as Cleveland Browns of the All-America Football Conference; *1946,* joined NFL; *1996,* moved to Baltimore, renamed Ravens.

Detroit Lions—*1930,* began as Portsmouth (OH) Spartans; *1934,* moved to Detroit and renamed Detroit Lions.

Indianapolis Colts—*1952,* defunct Dallas Texans of the All-America Football Conference moved to Baltimore, renamed Baltimore Colts, and joined the NFL; *1983,* moved to Indianapolis and renamed Indianapolis Colts.

Kansas City Chiefs—*1959,* began as Dallas Texans of the American Football League; *1963,* moved to Kansas City and renamed Kansas City Chiefs; *1970,* joined NFL.

Los Angeles Raiders—*1959,* began as Oakland Raiders of the American Football League; *1970,* joined NFL; *1982,* moved to Los Angeles and renamed Los Angeles Raiders. *1995,* moved to Oakland and renamed Oakland Raiders.

Los Angeles Rams—*1937,* began as Cleveland Rams; *1946,* moved to Los Angeles and renamed Los Angeles Rams; *1995,* moved to St. Louis and renamed St. Louis Rams.

New England Patriots—*1959,* began as Boston Patriots of the American Football League; *1970,* joined NFL; *1971,* renamed New England Patriots.

New York Jets—*1959,* began as New York Titans of the American Football League; *1963,* renamed New York Jets; *1970,* joined NFL.

Phoenix Cardinals—*1913,* began as Racine Avenue (Chicago) Cardinals; *1922,* renamed Chicago Cardinals; *1960,* moved to St. Louis and renamed St. Louis Cardinals; *1988,* moved to Phoenix and renamed Phoenix Cardinals.

San Diego Chargers—*1959,* franchised as Los Angeles Chargers of the American Football League; *1961,* moved to San Diego and renamed San Diego Chargers; *1970* joined NFL.

Washington Redskins—*1932,* began as Boston Braves; *1933,* renamed Boston Redskins; *1937,* moved to Washington and renamed Washington Redskins.

The Carolina Panthers (1995), Chicago Bears (1922), Green Bay Packers (1922), New York Giants (1925), Philadelphia Eagles (1933), Pittsburgh Steelers (1933), Dallas Cowboys (1960), Jacksonville Jaguars (1995), Minnesota Vikings (1960), Atlanta Falcons (1965), New Orleans Saints (1966), Seattle Seahawks (1974), and Tampa Bay Buccaneers (1974) began as NFL teams and have neither moved nor changed their team name.

The San Francisco 49ers (1946) are a former All-American Football Conference team that joined the NFL in 1949. The Buffalo Bills (1959), Denver Broncos (1959), Houston Oilers (1959), Miami Dolphins (1965), and Cincinnati Bengals (1967) are former American Football League franchises that merged with the NFL in 1970.

For **Common Denominators** take the number of (1) public golf holes, (2) movie screens, and (3) restaurant quality stars, plus (4) public golf holes per capita, (5) movie screens per capita, and (6) restaurant quality stars per capita. For **Crowd Pleasers** add (7) seats for major- and minor-league professional sports home games and (8) seats for college sports home games. For **Outdoor Assets** add (9) acres of protected recreation land as a percent of total land area, (10) protected land area per capita, (11) circumference of inland lakes, and (12) length of ocean or Great Lakes coastlines.

These elements embrace a lot of information. You might wonder whether they are more than really needed because many, such as total public golf holes and total movie screens, go hand in hand with one another. In other words, they are correlated.

How much can be eliminated? *Factor analysis,* a mathematical procedure, systematically reduces many pieces of information about a set of items (here, pieces of recreation information about a set of metro areas) to fewer pieces of information called "factors." Each factor embodies one or more of the original pieces of information.

For recreation, factor analysis uncovered three critical things. In decreasing order of importance, they are (1) what might be called "bigness," which takes in everything from the total number of public golf holes, good restaurants, and movie theater screens, to game seats for professional and collegiate sports and length of ocean or Great Lakes coastlines. As you might expect, bigness winners start with Chicago, Los Angeles, and New York. Losers include the smaller areas of Flagstaff and Yuma in Arizona, Rapid City, SD, and Grand Junction, CO.

Next is (2) "recreation land," or everything from total acres of state parks and federal protected areas (national parks, forests, and wildlife refuges) as a percent of total land area, to acres of these lands per capita, to the circumference of inland lakes. Flagstaff, a loser in bigness, is a winner here. So are Bellingham, WA, Eugene–Springfield, OR, and Anchorage, AK. Losers include Louisville and Lexington in Kentucky, Columbus, OH, and North Carolina's Triad (Greensboro–Winston-Salem–High Point) and Triangle (Raleigh–Durham–Chapel Hill).

Call the final factor (3) "golf, movies, and good food per capita." Losers include giant New York and Los Angeles, suggesting reservations are needed for dining out in those areas and much time is wasted queuing up for a round of golf or a new Hollywood film. Winners inclue Myrtle Beach, SC, and Barnstable–Yarmouth, MA, two of the country's best-known resorts.

Factor analysis produces a score for each metro area on each of the three factors. These scores are then weighted by their relative importance, *bigness* at 60 percent, *recreation land* at 22 percent, and *golf, movies, and good food per capita* at 18 percent. A metro area's final score is its percentile on a scale of 0 to 100 corresponding to its weighted average. Chicago's is 99.02; Redding, CA's is 50.35; and Altoona, PA's is 0.45. They are respectively the best, average, and worst North American metro areas for recreation.

RANKINGS: Recreation

Twelve criteria are used to derive a metro area's score for recreation. Using a factor analysis technique, these are grouped into three main factors: (1) *bigness,* (2) *recreation land,* and (3) *golf, movies, and good food per capita.* Places that are tied get the same rank and are listed in alphabetical order.

Rank	Metro Area	Score
6.	Washington, DC-MD-VA-WV	97.87
7.	Grand Rapids-Muskegon-Holland, MI	97.83
8.	Toronto, ON	97.66
9.	New York, NY	97.30
10.	Detroit, MI	97.13
11.	Riverside-San Bernardino, CA	96.93
12.	Minneapolis-St. Paul, MN-WI	96.90
13.	Norfolk-Virginia Beach-Newport News, VA-NC	96.72
14.	San Francisco, CA	96.57
15.	Miami, FL	96.56
16.	Milwaukee-Waukesha, WI	96.55
17.	Seattle-Bellevue-Everett, WA	96.49
18.	Tampa-St. Petersburg-Clearwater, FL	96.39
19.	San Diego, CA	96.34
20.	Orlando, FL	96.12
21.	Rochester, NY	95.98
22.	Salt Lake City-Ogden, UT	95.64
23.	Dallas, TX	95.29
24.	Phoenix-Mesa, AZ	95.28
25.	St. Louis, MO-IL	94.89
26.	Las Vegas, NV-AZ	94.74
27.	Vancouver, BC	94.55
28.	Houston, TX	94.34
29.	Barnstable-Yarmouth, MA	92.39
30.	Atlanta, GA	92.37
31.	West Palm Beach-Boca Raton, FL	92.26
32.	Baltimore, MD	91.41
33.	Charleston-North Charleston, SC	91.02
34.	Philadelphia, PA-NJ	90.98
35.	Duluth-Superior, MN-WI	90.86
36.	Portland-Vancouver, OR-WA	90.85
37.	Syracuse, NY	90.61
38.	Pittsburgh, PA	90.21
39.	Jacksonville, FL	89.92
40.	Kansas City, MO-KS	89.73
46.	Honolulu, HI	87.48
47.	Orange County, CA	87.28
48.	Fort Myers-Cape Coral, FL	87.07
49.	Sacramento, CA	87.06
50.	Knoxville, TN	86.95
51.	Buffalo-Niagara Falls, NY	86.84
52.	Cincinnati, OH-KY-IN	86.53
53.	Melbourne-Titusville-Palm Bay, FL	86.13
54.	Fort Lauderdale, FL	85.56
55.	Edmonton, AB	85.42
56.	Daytona Beach, FL	85.40
57.	Mobile, AL	85.14
58.	Tucson, AZ	84.61
59.	Atlantic City-Cape May, NJ	84.51
60.	Tacoma, WA	83.08
61.	Houma, LA	82.88
62.	Monmouth-Ocean, NJ	82.79
63.	Wilmington, NC	82.71
64.	Santa Barbara-Santa Maria-Lompoc, CA	82.37
65.	Biloxi-Gulfport-Pascagoula, MS	81.93
66.	Newark, NJ	81.75
67.	Montreal, PQ	81.32
68.	Flagstaff, AZ-UT	80.35
69.	Kalamazoo-Battle Creek, MI	80.19
70.	Fort Pierce-Port St. Lucie, FL	80.18
71.	Charlotte-Gastonia-Rock Hill, NC-SC	80.05
72.	Myrtle Beach, SC	79.88
73.	Salinas, CA	79.85
74.	Naples, FL	79.70
75.	Lakeland-Winter Haven, FL	79.43
75.	Provo-Orem, UT	79.43
77.	Ventura, CA	79.34
78.	Providence-Fall River-Warwick, RI-MA	79.17
79.	Portland, ME	79.14
80.	Tulsa, OK	78.97
85.	Nashville, TN	75.49
86.	Burlington, VT	75.02
87.	St. John's, NF	74.98
88.	Richmond-Petersburg, VA	74.90
89.	Hartford, CT	74.50
90.	Albany-Schenectady-Troy, NY	74.37
91.	Reno, NV	74.22
92.	Oklahoma City, OK	74.16
93.	Saint John, NB	73.91
94.	Pensacola, FL	73.89
95.	Ann Arbor, MI	73.75
96.	Albuquerque, NM	73.68
97.	Brownsville-Harlingen-San Benito, TX	72.51
98.	Chicoutimi-Jonquiere, PQ	71.85
99.	San Jose, CA	71.83
100.	Greenville-Spartanburg-Anderson, SC	71.71
101.	Akron, OH	71.59
102.	Bellingham, WA	71.27
103.	Savannah, GA	71.04
104.	Halifax, NS	70.35
105.	Austin-San Marcos, TX	70.22
106.	Boulder-Longmont, CO	69.97
107.	Fort Collins-Loveland, CO	69.70
108.	Utica-Rome, NY	69.67
109.	Tallahassee, FL	69.45
110.	Quebec City, PQ	69.09
111.	Birmingham, AL	68.89
112.	San Antonio, TX	68.62
113.	Vallejo-Fairfield-Napa, CA	67.36
114.	Little Rock-North Little Rock, AR	66.62
115.	Erie, PA	66.59
116.	Wilmington-Newark, DE-MD	66.52
117.	Omaha, NE-IA	66.51
118.	Benton Harbor, MI	65.85
119.	Columbia, SC	65.70
120.	Calgary, AB	65.67

Places Rated Rank	Places Rated Score
121. Sudbury, ON	65.05
122. Fresno, CA	64.42
123. Panama City, FL	64.01
124. Winnipeg, MB	63.60
125. Jamestown, NY	63.55
126. Beaumont–Port Arthur, TX	62.47
127. Corpus Christi, TX	62.36
128. Fort Walton Beach, FL	62.34
129. Worcester, MA–CT	62.31
130. Johnson City–Kingsport–Bristol, TN	62.21
131. Indianapolis, IN	62.04
132. Gainesville, FL	61.80
133. Columbus, OH	61.38
134. Scranton–Wilkes-Barre–Hazleton, PA	61.36
135. Santa Rosa, CA	61.24
136. Punta Gorda, FL	61.02
137. Baton Rouge, LA	60.73
138. Bangor, ME	60.33
139. Youngstown–Warren, OH	59.97
140. New Haven–Meriden, CT	59.90
141. Glens Falls, NY	59.52
142. Ottawa–Hull, ON–PQ	58.95
143. Bergen–Passaic, NJ	58.43
144. Hickory–Morganton–Lenoir, NC	58.39
145. Shreveport–Bossier City, LA	58.25
146. Springfield, MA	58.17
147. Toledo, OH	57.84
148. Chattanooga, TN–GA	57.64
149. Peoria–Pekin, IL	57.40
150. San Luis Obispo–Atascadero–Paso Robles, CA	57.28
151. Sheboygan, WI	57.17
152. Saginaw–Bay City–Midland, MI	57.02
153. Raleigh–Durham–Chapel Hill, NC	56.27
154. Ocala, FL	56.18
155. Davenport–Moline–Rock Island, IA–IL	56.05
156. Des Moines, IA	55.50
157. Galveston–Texas City, TX	55.47
158. Harrisburg–Lebanon–Carlisle, PA	54.91
159. Newburgh, NY–PA	54.84
160. Bridgeport, CT	54.74
161. Huntsville, AL	54.60
162. Brockton, MA	54.59
163. Portsmouth–Rochester, NH–ME	53.99
164. Madison, WI	53.72
165. Jackson, MS	53.65
166. Lynchburg, VA	53.60
167. Lafayette, LA	52.28
168. Lawrence, MA–NH	51.99
169. Brazoria, TX	51.89
170. Roanoke, VA	51.28
171. Anchorage, AK	51.22
172. Fayetteville–Springdale–Rogers, AR	51.21
173. Dutchess County, NY	50.96
174. Greensboro–Winston-Salem–High Point, NC	50.71
175. Middlesex–Somerset–Hunterdon, NJ	50.62
176. Redding, CA	50.35
177. Colorado Springs, CO	49.87
178. Victoria, BC	49.80
179. Dayton–Springfield, OH	49.09
180. Kenosha, WI	48.95
181. Augusta–Aiken, GA–SC	48.86
182. Jackson, MI	48.84
183. Gary, IN	48.71
184. Fort Wayne, IN	47.89
185. Huntington–Ashland, WV–KY–OH	47.78
186. Canton–Massillon, OH	47.74
187. Medford–Ashland, OR	47.70
187. Racine, WI	47.70
189. Asheville, NC	47.38
190. Yakima, WA	47.26
191. New London–Norwich, CT–RI	47.22
192. Macon, GA	47.02
193. Lowell, MA–NH	46.97
194. St. Cloud, MN	46.95
195. Decatur, AL	46.83
196. Manchester, NH	46.46
197. Fort Smith, AR–OK	46.36
198. Regina, SK	46.24
199. Pittsfield, MA	46.22
200. Santa Fe, NM	46.10
201. Bloomington, IN	45.49
202. La Crosse, WI–MN	44.83
203. Bremerton, WA	44.57
204. Wichita, KS	44.32
205. New Bedford, MA	44.29
206. Allentown–Bethlehem–Easton, PA	42.46
206. Louisville, KY–IN	43.46
208. Saskatoon, SK	42.13
209. Bakersfield, CA	42.06
210. Santa Cruz–Watsonville, CA	41.70
211. Rapid City, SD	41.44
212. Florence, AL	40.47
213. Binghamton, NY	40.06
214. Alexandria, LA	39.85
215. Bismarck, ND	39.76
216. Hattiesburg, MS	39.43
217. Visalia–Tulare–Porterville, CA	38.64
218. Stamford–Norwalk, CT	38.60
219. Salem, OR	38.59
220. Grand Junction, CO	38.16
221. Spokane, WA	38.15
222. Chico–Paradise, CA	38.13
223. Parkersburg–Marietta, WV–OH	36.40
224. Jacksonville, NC	35.81
225. Springfield, MO	35.51
226. St. Catharines–Niagara, ON	35.27
227. Lancaster, PA	35.25
228. Grand Forks, ND–MN	35.04
229. Columbus, GA–AL	34.89
230. Richland–Kennewick–Pasco, WA	34.46
231. Lansing–East Lansing, MI	34.37
232. Montgomery, AL	34.31
233. Boise City, ID	33.89
234. Reading, PA	33.78
235. Windsor, ON	33.77
236. Fitchburg–Leominster, MA	32.97
237. Eau Claire, WI	31.88
238. Amarillo, TX	31.80
239. Sherbrooke, PQ	31.43
240. Rockford, IL	30.39
241. Charlottesville, VA	30.20
242. Olympia, WA	29.89
243. Nashua, NH	29.72
244. Tuscaloosa, AL	29.52
245. Hamilton, ON	29.45
246. Flint, MI	29.43
247. Green Bay, WI	28.58
248. Evansville–Henderson, IN–KY	27.87
249. Johnstown, PA	27.65
250. Stockton–Lodi, CA	27.40
251. Yuma, AZ	27.18
252. Great Falls, MT	26.44
253. Las Cruces, NM	26.29
254. Hagerstown, MD	26.21
255. Lawrence, KS	25.58
256. Sherman–Denison, TX	25.23
257. El Paso, TX	24.81
258. Dover, DE	24.79
259. Fargo–Moorhead, ND–MN	23.89
260. McAllen–Edinburg–Mission, TX	23.77
261. Merced, CA	23.62
262. Wausau, WI	23.40
263. Killeen–Temple, TX	23.01
264. South Bend, IN	22.70
265. Tyler, TX	22.66
266. London, ON	22.18
267. Lincoln, NE	21.61
268. Waco, TX	21.52
269. Iowa City, IA	21.43
270. Sharon, PA	21.38
271. Greeley, CO	20.93
272. Cedar Rapids, IA	20.73
273. Longview–Marshall, TX	20.58
274. Danbury, CT	20.38
275. Monroe, LA	20.36
276. Columbia, MO	20.27
277. Springfield, IL	20.13
278. Jersey City, NJ	20.08
279. Janesville–Beloit, WI	20.00
280. Lexington, KY	18.83
281. Wichita Falls, TX	18.61
282. Anniston, AL	18.60
283. Sioux Falls, SD	18.20
284. Yuba City, CA	17.96
285. State College, PA	17.44
286. Lawton, OK	17.32
287. Lewiston–Auburn, ME	17.06
288. York, PA	16.73
289. Lake Charles, LA	16.58
290. Terre Haute, IN	16.44
291. Pueblo, CO	15.76
292. Casper, WY	15.63

Places Rated Rank		Places Rated Score
293.	Vineland–Millville–Bridgeton, NJ	15.56
294.	Modesto, CA	15.33
295.	Hamilton–Middletown, OH	15.10
296.	Charleston, WV	14.65
297.	Sioux City, IA–NE	14.42
298.	Oshawa, ON	14.24
299.	Wheeling, WV–OH	14.01
300.	San Angelo, TX	13.61
301.	Billings, MT	13.38
302.	Lima, OH	13.30
303.	Topeka, KS	13.14
304.	Owensboro, KY	12.99

Places Rated Rank		Places Rated Score
313.	Kitchener, ON	10.87
314.	Steubenville–Weirton, OH–WV	10.58
315.	Sumter, SC	10.28
316.	Clarksville–Hopkinsville, TN–KY	10.06
317.	Fayetteville, NC	9.89
318.	Bryan–College Station, TX	9.77
319.	Trois–Rivieres, PQ	9.50
320.	Muncie, IN	8.98
321.	Mansfield, OH	8.54
322.	Gadsden, AL	8.27
323.	Lafayette, IN	7.87
324.	Yolo, CA	7.77

Places Rated Rank		Places Rated Score
333.	Elkhart–Goshen, IN	4.50
334.	Joplin, MO	4.41
335.	Kokomo, IN	4.15
336.	Williamsport, PA	3.86
337.	Rochester, MN	3.84
338.	Athens, GA	3.71
339.	Danville, VA	3.25
340.	Cheyenne, WY	3.19
341.	Abilene, TX	3.12
342.	Victoria, TX	3.05
343.	Laredo, TX	2.89
344.	Florence, SC	2.82

PLACE PROFILES: Recreation

The following profiles are a selective catalogue of recreation features in each metro area.

Common Denominators are options for recreation available everywhere. The *Golf courses* entry shows the number of private, daily-fee, and municipal courses and their total regulation holes. *Good restaurants* tells how many restaurants at each *Mobil Travel Guide* quality level are in a metro area ("4★★" means, for example, that the place has four two-star restaurants). *Movie theaters* shows the number of independently owned theaters and chain-exhibitor theaters and their total screens. The access rating (AA, A, B, or C) for each item is shown in the right-hand column. An AA indicates the best access and C the least and is derived as follows:

1. *Good restaurants.*

A metro area gets a rating of:	If there is one quality star for every:
AA	15,000 or fewer people
A	15,001 to 25,000 people
B	25,001 to 40,000 people
C	40,001 or more people

2. *Public Golf courses.*

A metro area gets a rating of:	If there is one hole for every:
AA	1,500 or fewer people
A	1,501 to 2,250 people
B	2,251 to 4,000 people
C	4,001 or more people

3. *Movie theaters.*

A metro area gets a rating of:	If there is one screen for every:
AA	8,000 or fewer people
A	8,001 to 10,000 people
B	10,001 to 16,000 people
C	16,001 or more people

Crowd Pleasers lists local zoos, aquariums, major- and minor-league baseball, basketball, football, and hockey teams, and NCAA Division I or CIAU, men's and women's basketball, football, and ice hockey teams. If the school doesn't participate in all of these sports, the team's name is followed by one or two letters—(B) or (F) or (H)—for the sport it plays.

Outdoor Recreation Assets counts the metro area's number of offshore and inland water acres and also counts the acreage for all protected land.

American protected lands include all national forest, park, and wildlife refuge acres, plus all state park units located within metro-area counties. Canadian protected lands include all federal parks, natural areas and wildlife areas, plus all provincial parks and natural areas located within metro-area census divisions. A number of abbreviations are used in this section:

MBS	Migratory Bird Sanctuary	NS	National Seashore
NF	National Forest	NWA	National Wildlife Area

NHP	National Historic Park	NWR	National Wildlife Refuge
NHS	National Historic Site	PNA	Provincial Natural Area
NMP	National Military Park	PP	Provincial Park
NM	National Monument	SF	State Forest
NP	National Park	SNA	State Natural Area
NRA	National Recreation Area	SP	State Park
NSR	National Scenic River	SRA	State Recreation Area

Information comes from these sources: American Association of Zoological Parks and Aquariums, *Zoological Parks and Aquariums in the Americas,* 1996; American Baseball League, unpublished data, 1996; American Hockey League, *Media Guide,* 1996; Baseball America, *Directory,* 1996; Canadian Association of Zoological Parks and Aquariums, *Zoos, Aquariums, and Game Farms,* 1996; Canadian Inter-University Athletic Union, *Directory,* 1996; Continental Basketball Association, unpublished data, 1996; Environment Canada, unpublished national conservation area data, 1996; *Film Canada Yearbook,* 1996; International Hockey League, *Media Guide,* 1996; National Association of Collegiate Directors of Athletics, *The 1996–97 National Directory of College Athletics,* 1996; National Association of Professional Baseball Leagues, unpublished data, 1996; National Association of Theater Owners, *Encyclopedia of Exhibition,* 1996; National Basketball Association, unpublished data, 1996; National Collegiate Athletic Association, *National Collegiate Championships,* 1996, *NCAA Basketball,* 1996, and *NCAA Football,* 1996; National Football League, unpublished data, 1996; National Golf Foundation, unpublished data, 1996; National Hockey League, unpublished data, 1996; National League of Professional Baseball Teams, unpublished data, 1996; Fodor's Travel Publications, *Mobil Travel Guide* 1996; Quigley Publishing Company, *Motion Picture Almanac,* 1996; U.S. Department of Agriculture, Forest Service, *Land Areas of the National Forest System,* 1995; U.S. Department of Commerce: Bureau of the Census, unpublished "Coastal Counties of the United States," and unpublished area measurements, 1990; U.S. Department of the Interior, Fish and Wildlife Service, unpublished master deed listing, 1996, and National Park Service, *Index to the National Park System and Related Areas,* 1996, and unpublished master deed listing, 1996.

	Rating
Abilene, TX	
Common Denominators	
Golf courses: 3 private (54 holes), 1 daily fee (9 holes), 1 municipal (18 holes)	**C**
Good restaurants: 1 **	**C**
Movie theaters: 3 Chains (16 screens) 2 Independent (2 screens)	**AA**
Crowd Pleasers	
Aquariums and Zoos	
Abilene Zoo	
Outdoor Assets	
Inland Water Area: 2,560 acres	
State Recreation Area	
Abilene SRA, 1,242 acres	
Places Rated Score: 3.12	Places Rated Rank: 341

	Rating
Akron, OH	
Common Denominators	
Golf courses: 15 private (252 holes), 30 daily fee (459 holes), 4 municipal (72 holes)	**AA**
Good restaurants: 2 *, 3 **, 2 ***	**C**
Movie theaters: 8 Circuit (72 screens), 4 Independent (6 screens)	**A**
Crowd Pleasers	
Aquariums and Zoos	
Akron Zoological Park	
Sea World of Ohio	
NCAA Division I	
Kent State Golden Flashes (B, F)	
University of Akron Zips (B, F)	
Professional Sports	
Cavaliers (NBA Basketball)	
Outdoor Assets	
Inland Water Area: 14,080 acres	
Federal Protected Areas	
Cuyahoga Valley NRA, 15,864 acres	
State Recreation Areas	
Eagle Creek SNA, 441 acres	
Nelson-Kennedy Ledges SP, 167 acres	
Portage Lakes SP, 2,443 acres	
Tinkers Creek SP, 1,143 acres	
West Branch SP, 5,352 acres	
Places Rated Score: 71.59	Places Rated Rank: 101

	Rating
Albany, GA	
Common Denominators	
Golf courses: 4 private (63 holes), 2 daily fee (27 holes), 1 municipal (18 holes)	**B**
Good restaurants: 1 **	**C**
Movie theaters: 2 Chains (15 screens)	**AA**
Crowd Pleasers	
Aquariums and Zoos	
Chehaw Wild Animal Park	
Outdoor Assets	
Inland Water Area: 7,040 acres	
Places Rated Score: 7.49	Places Rated Rank: 325

	Rating
Albany-Schenectady-Troy, NY	
Common Denominators	
Golf courses: 16 private (261 holes), 23 daily fee (315 holes), 7 municipal (117 holes)	**A**
Good restaurants: 9 *, 8 **, 8 ***	**A**
Movie theaters: 7 Chains (39 screens), 4 Independent (6 screens)	**A**
Crowd Pleasers	
NCAA Division I	
Rensselaer Polytechnic Engineers (H)	
Siena College Saints (B, F)	
Professional Sports	
River Rats (AHL Hockey)	
Outdoor Assets	
Inland Water Area: 42,880 acres	
Federal Protected Areas	
Saratoga NHP, 2,886 acres	
State Recreation Areas	
Bennington Battlefield SHS, 208 acres	
Castleton Island SP, 300 acres	
Cherry Plain SP, 175 acres	
Grafton Lakes SP, 2,357 acres	
John Thatcher SP, 1,347 acres	
Mine Kill SP, 500 acres	
Moreau SP, 893 acres	
Peebles Island SP, 142 acres	
Saratoga Spa SP, 2,033 acres	
Schoharie Crossing SHS, 240 acres	
Thompson's Lake Camp SP, 152 acres	
Places Rated Score: 74.37	Places Rated Rank: 90

Rating

Albuquerque, NM
Common Denominators
- Golf courses: 7 private (108 holes), 7 daily fee (108 holes), 5 municipal (72 holes) — **B**
- Good restaurants: 11 *, 14 **, 3 *** — **AA**
- Movie theaters: 10 Chains (66 screens), 4 Independent (7 screens) — **A**

Crowd Pleasers
- Aquariums and Zoos
  - Rio Grande Zoological Park
- Professional sports
  - Dukes (Triple A Baseball)
- NCAA Division I
  - University of New Mexico Lobos (B, F)

Outdoor Assets
- Inland Water Area: 5,760 acres

Rating

- Inland Water Area: 640 acres
- Federal Protected Areas
  - Allegheny Portage Railroad NHS, 627 acres
- State Recreation Area
  - Canoe Creek SP, 959 acres

Places Rated Score: 0.45 Places Rated Rank: 351

Amarillo, TX
Common Denominators
- Golf courses: 2 private (36 holes), 4 daily fee (54 holes), 3 municipal (54 holes) — **A**
- Good restaurants: 1 *, 3 ** — **B**
- Movie theaters: 8 Chains (18 screens) — **B**

Crowd Pleasers
- Aquariums and Zoos
  - Amarillo Zoo
  - Storyland Zoo

Alexandria, LA
Common Denominators
- Golf courses: 2 private (36 holes), 3 daily fee (27 holes), 1 municipal (9 holes) — **B**
- Good restaurants: 1 **, 1 *** — **B**
- Movie theaters: 3 Chains (14 screens), 2 Independent (12 screens) — **AA**

Crowd Pleasers
- Aquariums and Zoos
  - Alexandria Zoo

Outdoor Assets
- Inland Water Area: 24,960 acres
- Federal Protected Areas
  - Kisatchee NF, 100,895 acres
- State Recreation Area
  - Kent House SCA, 4 acres

Places Rated Score: 39.85 Places Rated Rank: 214

Allentown–Bethlehem–Easton, PA
Common Denominators
- Golf courses: 11 private (189 holes), 14 daily fee (216 holes), 2 municipal (36 holes) — **B**
- Good restaurants: 1 **, 2 *** — **C**
- Movie theaters: 7 Chains (35 screens), 5 Independent (5 screens) — **B**

Crowd Pleasers
- NCAA Division I
  - Lafayette College Leopards (B, F)
  - Lehigh University Engineers (B, F)

Outdoor Assets
- Inland Water Area: 7,680 acres
- Federal Protected Areas
  - Appalachian NT, 2,278 acres
  - Delaware Water Gap NRA, 1,168 acres
- State Recreation Areas
  - Beltzville SP, 2,972 acres
  - Hickory Run SP, 15,482acres
  - Jacobsburg SP, 1,167 acres
  - Lehigh Gorge SP, 3,390 acres

Places Rated Score: 42.46 Places Rated Rank: 206

Altoona, PA
Common Denominators
- Golf courses: 3 private (54 holes), 3 daily fee (36 holes) — **B**
- Good restaurants: 1 **, 1 *** — **B**
- Movie theaters: 3 Chains (11 screens) — **B**

Crowd Pleasers

Outdoor Assets

Common Denominators
- Golf courses: 2 daily fee (36 holes), 1 municipal (18 holes) — **C**
- Movie theaters: 5 Chains (22 screens), 2 Independent (2 screens) — **A**

Crowd Pleasers
- Aquariums and Zoos
  - The Alaska Zoo
- NCAA Division I
  - University of Alaska Seawolves (H)

Outdoor Assets
- Water Area
  - Pacific offshore: 14,272 acres
  - Inland: 26,240 acres
- Federal Protected Areas
  - Chugach NF, 275,056 acres
- State Recreation Areas
  - Chugach SP, 495,204 acres

Places Rated Score: 51.22 Places Rated Rank: 171

Ann Arbor, MI
Common Denominators
- Golf courses: 12 private (207 holes), 35 daily fee (558 holes), 5 municipal (90 holes) — **AA**
- Good restaurants: 3 *, 6 **, 2 *** — **B**
- Movie theaters: 7 Chains (33 screens), 4 Independent (4 screens) — **C**

Crowd Pleasers
- Aquariums and Zoos
  - University of Michigan Zoology Museum
- NCAA Division I
  - Eastern Michigan University Eagles (B, F)
  - University of Michigan Wolverines

Outdoor Assets
- Inland Water Area: 26,240 acres
- State Recreation Areas
  - Brighton SRA, 4,913 acres
  - Cambridge SHS, 184 acres
  - Island Lake SRA, 3,272 acres
  - Lake Hudson SRA, 2,650 acres
  - Pinckney SRA, 9,994 acres
  - Waterloo SRA, 6,887 acres
  - WJ Hayes SP, 632 acres

Places Rated Score: 73.75 Places Rated Rank: 95

Anniston, AL
Common Denominators
- Golf courses: 2 private (36 holes), 3 daily fee (54

	Rating
holes), 1 municipal (9 holes)	A
Good restaurants: 2 *, 1 **	B
Movie theaters: 2 Chains (12 screens)	A

Crowd Pleasers
NCAA Division I
Jacksonville State Gamecocks (WB, F)
Outdoor Assets
Inland Water Area: 2,560 acres
Federal Protected Area
Talladega NF, 23,603 acres
Places Rated Score: 18.60 Places Rated Rank: 282

Appleton–Oshkosh–Neenah, WI
Common Denominators

	Rating
Golf courses: 6 private (99 holes), 16 daily fee (261 holes), 2 municipal (36 holes)	AA
Good restaurants: 2 *, 2 **, 1 ***	B
Movie theaters: 5 Chains (35 screens), 4 Independent (4 screens)	A

Crowd Pleasers
Professional sports
Timber Rattlers (Class A Baseball)
Outdoor Assets
Inland Water Area: 141,440 acres
State Recreation Areas
High Cliff SP, 1,145 acres
Wiouwash State Trail, 108 acres
Places Rated Score: 78.65 Places Rated Rank: 81

Asheville, NC
Common Denominators

	Rating
Golf courses: 4 private (72 holes), 4 daily fee (63 holes), 2 municipal (36 holes)	A
Good restaurants: 2 *, 4 **, 3 ***	AA
Movie theaters: 8 Chains (28 screens), 1 Independent (1 screen)	AA

Crowd Pleasers
Aquariums and Zoos
Western North Carolina Nature Center
Professional sports
Tourists (Class A Baseball)
NCAA Division I
University of North Carolina Bulldogs (B)
Outdoor Assets
Inland Water Area: 3,840 acres
Federal Protected Areas
Appalachian NT, 250 acres
Blue Ridge N Parkway, 5,673 acres
Pisgah NF, 85,957 acres
Places Rated Score: 47.38 Places Rated Rank: 189

Athens, GA
Common Denominators

	Rating
Golf courses: 3 private (45 holes), 4 daily fee (72 holes)	A
Good restaurants: 1 *, 1 **	C
Movie theaters: 3 Chains (17 screens), 1 Independent (1 screen)	AA

Crowd Pleasers
Aquariums and Zoos
Memorial Park
NCAA Division I
University of Georgia Bulldogs (B, F)
Outdoor Assets
Inland Water Area: 640 acres
Federal Protected Area
Oconee NF, 157 acres
State Recreation Area
Watson Mill Bridge SP, 600 acres
Places Rated Score: 3.71 Places Rated Rank: 338

✓ Atlanta, GA
Common Denominators

	Rating
Golf courses: 57 private (954 holes), 53 daily fee (882 holes), 13 municipal (225 holes)	B
Good restaurants: 12 *, 36 **, 27 ***, 4 ****	A
Movie theaters: 80 Chains (395 screens), 6 Independent (10 screens)	A

Crowd Pleasers
Aquariums and Zoos
Stone Mountain Park
Zoo Atlanta
Professional sports
Braves (NL Baseball)
Falcons (NFL Football)
Hawks (NBA Basketball)
Knights (IHL Hockey)
Trojans (USBL Basketball)
NCAA Division I
Georgia State University Panthers (B)
Georgia Tech Yellow Jackets (B, F)
Outdoor Assets
Inland Water Area: 55,040 acres
Federal Protected Areas
Chattahoochee River NRA, 4,240 acres
Kennesaw Mountain NBP, 2,880 acres
Martin Luther King Jr. NHS acres
State Recreation Areas
Etowah Indian Mounds SHS, 68 acres
Fort Yargo SP, 1,850 acres
Hard Labor Creek SP, 3,005 acres
John Tanner SP, 136 acres
Panola Mountain SP, 617 acres
Pickett's Mill Battlefield SHS, 765 acres
Red Top Mountain SP, 1,950 acres
Sweetwater Creek SP, 1,986 acres
Places Rated Score: 92.37 Places Rated Rank: 30

Atlantic City–Cape May, NJ
Common Denominators

	Rating
Golf courses: 8 private (117 holes), 10 daily fee (162 holes), 2 municipal (27 holes)	A
Good restaurants: 6 *, 22 **, 5 ***	AA
Movie theaters: 15 Chains (90 screens)	AA

Crowd Pleasers
Aquariums and Zoos
Birch Grove Park Zoo
Professional sports
Seagulls (USBL Basketball)
Outdoor Assets
Water Area
Atlantic offshore: 25,280 acres
Inland: 51,200 acres
Federal Protected Areas
Cape May NWR, 6,217 acres
Edwin Forsythe NWR, 19,909 acres
State Recreation Areas
Cape May Point SP, 190 acres
Cape May Wetlands SNA, 3,715 acres
Corson's Inlet SP, 341 acres
Great Sound SP, 217 acres
North Brigantine SNA, 680 acres
Strathmere SNA, 95 acres
Places Rated Score: 84.51 Places Rated Rank: 59

Augusta–Aiken, GA–SC
Common Denominators

	Rating
Golf courses: 14 private (225 holes), 12 daily fee (180 holes), 1 municipal (18 holes)	B
Good restaurants: 1 **, 2 ***	C
Movie theaters: 8 Chains (32 screens)	C

Crowd Pleasers
Professional sports
Greenjackets (Class A Baseball)
Outdoor Assets
Inland Water Area: 26,240 acres
Federal Protected Area
Sumter NF, 31,056 acres
State Recreation Areas
Aiken SP, 1,067 acres
Mistletoe SP, 1,920 acres

Rating

Redcliffe SP, 350 acres
Places Rated Score: 48.86 — Places Rated Rank: 181

Austin–San Marcos, TX

Common Denominators
- **Golf courses:** 14 private (243 holes), 17 daily fee (270 holes), 10 municipal (144 holes) — **B**
- **Good restaurants:** 6 *, 12 **, 3 *** — **B**
- **Movie theaters:** 20 Chains (104 screens), 1 Independent (2 screens) — **A**

Crowd Pleasers
Aquariums and Zoos
Austin Nature Center
NCAA Division I
Southwest Texas State Bobcats (B, F)
University of Texas Longhorns (B, F)
Outdoor Assets

Rating

Outdoor Assets
Water Area
Atlantic offshore: 22,912 acres
Inland: 87,680 acres
Federal Protected Areas
National Capital Parks, 432 acres
State Recreation Areas
Gunpowder Falls SP, 14,340 acres
Hart-Miller Island SP, 244 acres
Morgan Run SNA, 1,300 acres
North Point SP, 1,310 acres
Patapsco Valley SP, 13,309 acres
Patuxent River SP, 3,469 acres
Rocks SP, 855 acres
Sandy Point SP, 786 acres
Soldier's Delight SNA, 1,815 acres

Bakersfield, CA

Common Denominators
- **Golf courses:** 7 private (117 holes), 7 daily fee (99 holes), 5 municipal (90 holes) — **B**
- **Good restaurants:** 3 *, 1 ** — **C**
- **Movie theaters:** 5 Chains (17 screens), 1 Independent (1 screen) — **C**

Crowd Pleasers
Aquariums and Zoos
The California Living Museum
Professional sports
Dodgers (Class A Baseball)
Outdoor Assets
Inland Water Area: 12,800 acres
Federal Protected Areas
Bitter Creek NWR, 13,935 acres
Kern NWR, 10,618 acres
Los Padres NF, 64,803 acres
Sequoia NF, 312,000 acres
State Recreation Areas
Fort Tejon SHP, 205 acres
Red Rock Canyon SP, 28,000 acres
Tule Elk SR, 946 acres
Places Rated Score: 42.06 — Places Rated Rank: 209

✓ Baltimore, MD

Common Denominators
- **Golf courses:** 40 private (666 holes), 13 daily fee (198 holes), 9 municipal (153 holes) — **C**
- **Good restaurants:** 13 *, 29 **, 14 ***, 1 **** — **A**
- **Movie theaters:** 19 Chains (89 screens), 9 Independent (29 screens) — **C**

Crowd Pleasers
Aquariums and Zoos
Baltimore Zoo
National Aquarium
Professional sports
Bandits (AHL Hockey)
Orioles (AL Baseball)
Ravens (NFL Football)
NCAA Division I
Coppin State College Eagles (B)
Loyola College Greyhounds (B)
Morgan State University Bears (B, F)
Towson State University Tigers (B, F)
University of Maryland Retrievers (B)
U.S. Naval Academy Midshipmen (B, F)

NCAA Division I
University of Maine Black Bears
Outdoor Assets
Inland Water Area: 102,400 acres
Federal Protected Area
Sunkhaze Meadows NWR, 9,337 acres
Places Rated Score: 60.33 — Places Rated Rank: 138

✓ Barnstable–Yarmouth, MA

Common Denominators
- **Golf courses:** 12 private (207 holes), 13 daily fee (207 holes), 7 municipal (126 holes) — **AA**
- **Good restaurants:** 15 *, 19 **, 7 ***, 1 **** — **AA**
- **Movie theaters:** 2 Chains (12 screens), 1 Independent (1 screen) — **AA**

Crowd Pleasers
Aquariums and Zoos
Aquarium of Cape Cod
Outdoor Assets
Water Area
Atlantic offshore: 54,400 acres
Inland: 38,400 acres
Federal Protected Areas
Cape Cod NSeashore, 27,399 acres
Monomoy NWR, 2,702 acres
State Recreation Areas
Hawksnest SP, 218 acres
Nickerson SP, 47 acres
Scusset Beach SRA, 380 acres
South Cape Beach SP, 401 acres
Places Rated Score: 92.39 — Places Rated Rank: 29

Baton Rouge, LA

Common Denominators
- **Golf courses:** 9 private (126 holes), 3 daily fee (54 holes), 6 municipal (90 holes) — **C**
- **Good restaurants:** 4 *, 4 **, 1 ***, 1 **** — **B**
- **Movie theaters:** 5 Chains (31 screens), 1 Independent (4 screens) — **C**

Crowd Pleasers
Aquariums and Zoos
Greater Baton Rouge Zoo
Professional sports
Panthers (ECHL Hockey)
NCAA Division I
Louisiana State Fighting Tigers (B, F)
Southern University Jaguars (B, F)

Rating

Outdoor Assets
Inland Water Area: 59,520 acres
State Recreation Areas
Port Hudson SCA, 899 acres
Tickfaw SP, 1,169 acres
Places Rated Score: 60.73 Places Rated Rank: 137

Beaumont–Port Arthur, TX
Common Denominators
Golf courses: 7 private (117 holes), 6 daily fee (90 holes), 2 municipal (36 holes) **B**
Good restaurants: 2 *, 1 ** **C**
Movie theaters: 8 Chains (24 screens), 3 Independent (6 screens) **B**
Crowd Pleasers
NCAA Division I
Lamar University Cardinals (B)
Outdoor Assets
Water Area
Gulf offshore: 7,680 acres
Inland: 72,320 acres
Federal Protected Areas
Big Thicket NP, 47,738 acres
McFaddin NWR, 41,682 acres
Texas Point NWR, 8,952 acres
State Recreation Areas
Sabine Pass Battleground SHS, 56 acres
Sea Rim SP, 15,094 acres
Village Creek SP, 942 acres
Places Rated Score: 62.47 Places Rated Rank: 126

Bellingham, WA
Common Denominators
Golf courses: 4 private (54 holes), 9 daily fee (135 holes), 1 municipal (18 holes) **AA**
Good restaurants: 2 **, 1 *** **A**
Movie theaters: 3 Chains (6 screens) **C**
Crowd Pleasers
Professional sports
Giants (Class A Baseball)
Outdoor Assets
Water Area
Pacific offshore: 21,056 acres
Inland: 35,200 acres
Federal Protected Areas
Mt. Baker NF, 452,736 acres
North Cascades NP, 281,690 acres
Ross Lake NRA, 107,067 acres
State Recreation Areas
Birch Bay SP, 193 acres
Larrabee SP, 2,389 acres
Peace Arch SP, 20 acres
Places Rated Score: 71.27 Places Rated Rank: 102

Benton Harbor, MI
Common Denominators
Golf courses: 6 private (90 holes), 8 daily fee (135 holes), 2 municipal (18 holes) **AA**
Good restaurants: 2 ** **C**
Movie theaters: 1 Chain (5 screens) **C**
Outdoor Assets
Water Area
Lake Michigan offshore: 64,064 acres
Inland: 5,760 acres
State Recreation Areas
Grand Mere SP, 985 acres
Warren Dunes SP, 1,950 acres
Warren Woods SP, 311 acres
Places Rated Score: 65.85 Places Rated Rank: 118

Bergen–Passaic, NJ
Common Denominators
Golf courses: 20 private (306 holes), 4 daily fee (72 holes), 8 municipal (126 holes) **C**
Good restaurants: 1 *, 2 **, 2 *** **C**

Rating

Movie theaters: 17 Chains (76 screens), 19 Independent (61 screens) **B**
Crowd Pleasers
Aquariums and Zoos
Van Saun Park Zoo
Professional sports
Giants (NFL Football)
Jets (NFL Football)
Nets (NBA Basketball)
New Jersey Devils (NHL Hockey)
NCAA Division I
Fairleigh Dickinson Knights (B)
Outdoor Assets
Inland Water Area: 16,000 acres
Federal Protected Area
Appalachian NT, 26 acres
State Recreation Areas
Greenwood Lake SP, 217 acres
Long Pond Ironworks SP, 1,725 acres
Ringwood SP, 5,237 acres
Wawayanda SP, 4,454 acres
Places Rated Score: 58.43 Places Rated Rank: 143

Billings, MT
Common Denominators
Golf courses: 6 private (90 holes), 2 daily fee (36 holes) **B**
Good restaurants: 3 *, 4 **, 1 *** **AA**
Movie theaters: 4 Chains (22 screens), 1 Independent (1 screen) **AA**
Crowd Pleasers
Aquariums and Zoos
Zoo Montana
Outdoor Assets
Inland Water Area: 8,960 acres
State Recreation Areas
Lake Elmo SP, 120 acres
Pictograph Cave SP, 72 acres
Places Rated Score: 13.38 Places Rated Rank: 301

Biloxi–Gulfport–Pascagoula, MS
Common Denominators
Golf courses: 4 private (63 holes), 13 daily fee (225 holes), 1 municipal (18 holes) **AA**
Good restaurants: 7 *, 4 **, 3 *** **AA**
Movie theaters: 6 Chains (21 screens), 2 Independent (5 screens) **B**
Outdoor Assets
Water Area
Gulf offshore: 47,232 acres
Inland: 31,360 acres
Federal Protected Areas
Desoto NF, 81,495 acres
Grand Bay NWR, 4,611 acres
Gulf Islands NSeashore, 70,219 acres
Mississippi Sandhil Crane NWR, 18,859 acres
State Recreation Areas
Buccaneer SP, 398 acres
Shepard SP, 307 acres
Places Rated Score: 81.93 Places Rated Rank: 65

Binghamton, NY
Common Denominators
Golf courses: 5 private (81 holes), 17 daily fee (261 holes), 3 municipal (54 holes) **AA**
Good restaurants: 1 *, 1 **, 1 *** **C**
Movie theaters: 8 Chains (6 screens) **C**
Crowd Pleasers
Aquariums and Zoos
Ross Park Zoo
Professional sports
Mets (Class AA Baseball)
Rangers (AHL Hockey)
Outdoor Assets
Inland Water Area: 8,320 acres
State Recreation Area
Chenango Valley SP, 1,071 acres
Places Rated Score: 40.06 Places Rated Rank: 213

Rating

Birmingham, AL

Common Denominators
- Golf courses: 23 private (387 holes), 13 daily fee (216 holes), 6 municipal (99 holes) — **B**
- Good restaurants: 3 *, 10 **, 4 *** — **B**
- Movie theaters: 10 Chains (96 screens), 1 Independent (2 screens) — **A**

Crowd Pleasers
- Aquariums and Zoos
  - Birmingham Zoo
- Professional sports
  - Barons (Class AA Baseball)
  - Bulls (ECHL Hockey)
- NCAA Division I
  - Samford University Bulldogs (F, MB)
  - University of Alabama Blazers (B, F)

Rating

- State Recreation Areas
  - Funk's Grove SP, 202 acres
  - Moraine View SP, 1,688 acres

Places Rated Score: 11.19 Places Rated Rank: 310

Boise City, ID

Common Denominators
- Golf courses: 4 private (63 holes), 7 daily fee (108 holes), 6 municipal (81 holes) — **A**
- Good restaurants: 3 *, 1 ** — **C**
- Movie theaters: 1 Chain (6 screens), 2 Independent (4 screens) — **A**

Crowd Pleasers
- Aquariums and Zoos
  - Boise City Zoo
- NCAA Division I

holes) — **AA**
- Good restaurants: 2 ** — **A**
- Movie theaters: 2 Chains (11 screens), 1 Independent (3 screens) — **AA**

Crowd Pleasers
- Aquariums and Zoos
  - Dakota Zoo
- Professional sports
  - Wizards (IBA Basketball)

Outdoor Assets
- Inland Water Area: 34,560 acres
- Federal Protected Areas
  - Florence Lake NWR, 1,468 acres
  - Long Lake NWR, 10,330 acres
- State Recreation Areas
  - Double Ditch SHS, 116 acres
  - Fort Lincoln SP, 1,006 acres
  - Missouri River SNA, 157 acres

Places Rated Score: 39.76 Places Rated Rank: 215

Bloomington, IN

Common Denominators
- Golf courses: 1 private (18 holes), 2 daily fee (36 holes), 1 municipal (18 holes) — **A**
- Good restaurants: 3 *, 1 ** — **A**
- Movie theaters: 5 Chains (20 screens) — **AA**

Crowd Pleasers
- NCAA Division I
  - Indiana University Hoosiers (B, F)

Outdoor Assets
- Inland Water Area: 10,880 acres
- Federal Protected Areas
  - Hoosier NF, 18,974 acres
  - Muscatatuck NWR, 78 acres

Places Rated Score: 45.49 Places Rated Rank: 201

Bloomington-Normal, IL

Common Denominators
- Golf courses: 3 private (45 holes), 4 daily fee (36 holes), 4 municipal (72 holes) — **AA**
- Good restaurants: 1 *, 1 ** — **C**
- Movie theaters: 4 Chains (20 screens) — **AA**

Crowd Pleasers
- Aquariums and Zoos
  - Miller Park Zoo
- NCAA Division I
  - Illinois State University Redbirds (B, F)

Outdoor Assets
- Inland Water Area: 1,920 acres

Boston, MA-NH

Common Denominators
- Golf courses: 51 private (774 holes), 43 daily fee (612 holes), 25 municipal (342 holes) — **B**
- Good restaurants: 14 *, 46 **, 16 ***, 3 **** — **A**
- Movie theaters: 49 Chains (217 screens), 22 Independent (44 screens) — **C**

Crowd Pleasers
- Aquariums and Zoos
  - Metro Parks Zoos
  - New England Aquarium
  - Pine Banks Park
  - Prospect Hill Animal Farm
- Professional sports
  - Bruins (NHL Hockey)
  - Celtics (NBA Basketball)
  - New England Patriots (NFL Football)
  - Red Sox (AL Baseball)
  - Revolution (MLS Soccer)
- NCAA Division I
  - Boston College Eagles
  - Boston University Terriers
  - Harvard University Crimson
  - Northeastern University Huskies

Outdoor Assets
- Water Area
  - Atlantic offshore: 3,840 acres
  - Inland: 28,800 acres
- Federal Protected Areas
  - Boston NHP, 35 acres
  - John Fitzgerald Kennedy NHS acres
- State Recreation Areas
  - Ashland SP, 47 acres
  - Boston Harbor Islands SP, 195 acres
  - Bradley Palmer SP, 721 acres
  - Bristol Blake SP, 200 acres
  - Callahan SP, 819 acres
  - Cochituate SP, 1,126 acres
  - Cushing Memorial SP, 9 acres
  - Dighton Rock SP, 108 acres
  - Ellisville Harbor SP, 101 acres
  - Great Brook Farm SP, 934 acres
  - Halibut Point SP, 56 acres
  - Hopkinton SP, 1,450 acres
  - Horseneck Beach SR, 537 acres
  - Lynn Heritage SP, 5 acres
  - Massasoit SP, 1,500 acres
  - Maudslay SP, 480 acres

Rating

Myles Standish Monument SHS, 32 acres
Pearl Hill SP, 1,000 acres
Pilgrim Memorial SHS, 9 acres
Plum Island SR, 73 acres
Roxbury Heritage SP, 5 acres
Salisbury Beach SR, 520 acres
Sandy Point SR, 73 acres
Seabrook Fish Pier SRA, 4 acres
Squannacook River SNA, 300 acres
Walden Pond SR, 304 acres
Watson Pond SP, 10 acres
Webb Memorial SP, 37 acres
Whitehall SP, 909 acres
Wompatuck SP, 3,500 acres
Places Rated Score: 89.13 Places Rated Rank: 42

Boulder–Longmont, CO
Common Denominators
Golf courses: 2 private (36 holes), 3 daily fee (54 holes), 4 municipal (63 holes) **A**
Good restaurants: 2 *, 3 **, 3 *** **A**
Movie theaters: 7 Chains (37 screens) **AA**
Crowd Pleasers
NCAA Division I
University of Colorado Golden Buffaloes (B, F)
Outdoor Assets
Inland Water Area: 5,760 acres
Federal Protected Areas
Rocky Mountain NP, 27,253 acres
Roosevelt NF, 137,296 acres
State Recreation Area
Eldorado Canyon SP, 845 acres
Places Rated Score: 69.97 Places Rated Rank: 106

Brazoria, TX
Common Denominators
Golf courses: 3 private (54 holes), 6 daily fee (72 holes), 1 municipal (18 holes) **B**
Movie theaters: 4 Chains (7 screens), 2 Independent (4 screens) **C**
Outdoor Assets
Water Area
Gulf offshore: 7,168 acres
Inland: 63,360 acres
Federal Protected Areas
Brazoria NWR, 43,220 acres
San Bernard NWR, 21,784 acres
State Recreation Areas
Christmas Bay SRA, 485 acres
Places Rated Score: 51.89 Places Rated Rank: 169

Bremerton, WA
Common Denominators
Golf courses: 2 private (36 holes), 5 daily fee (81 holes), 2 municipal (36 holes) **A**
Good restaurants: 1 ** **C**
Movie theaters: 2 Chains (4 screens), 3 Independent (6 screens) **B**
Outdoor Assets
Water Area
Pacific offshore: 6,848 acres
Inland: 40,320 acres
State Recreation Areas
Blake Island SP, 476 acres
Camp Calvinwood, 118 acres
Fort Ward SP, 137 acres
Manchester SP, 111 acres
Places Rated Score: 44.57 Places Rated Rank: 203

Bridgeport, CT
Common Denominators
Golf courses: 8 private (126 holes), 2 daily fee (27 holes), 4 municipal (72 holes) **C**
Good restaurants: 4 *, 2 ** **C**
Movie theaters: 8 Chains (51 screens), 4 Independent (4 screens) **AA**

Rating

Crowd Pleasers
Aquariums and Zoos
Beardsley Zoo
Professional sports
Skyhawks (USBL Basketball)
NCAA Division I
Fairfield University Stags (B, H)
Outdoor Assets
Water Area
Atlantic offshore: 11,520 acres
Inland: 19,840 acres
Federal Protected Areas
Appalachian NT, 301 acres
McKinney NWR, 464 acres
State Recreation Areas
American Shakespeare Theatre SP, 12 acres
Bartlett Arboretum SP, 63 acres
Indian Well SP, 153 acres
Osborne Homestead Museum SH, 3 acres
Osbornedale SP, 350 acres
Silver Sands SP, 223 acres
Southford Falls SP, 120 acres
Places Rated Score: 54.74 Places Rated Rank: 160

Brockton, MA
Common Denominators
Golf courses: 3 private (45 holes), 4 daily fee (63 holes), 2 municipal (27 holes) **B**
Good restaurants: 1 * **C**
Movie theaters: 4 Chains (12 screens), 1 Independent (6 screens) **AA**
Outdoor Assets
Water Area
Atlantic offshore: 24,192 acres
Inland: 34,560 acres
Federal Protected Area
Massasoit NWR, 184 acres
State Recreation Areas
Ames Nowell SP, 607 acres
Borderland SP, 1,772 acres
Places Rated Score: 54.59 Places Rated Rank: 162

Brownsville–Harlingen–San Benito, TX
Common Denominators
Golf courses: 4 private (72 holes), 2 daily fee (36 holes), 4 municipal (63 holes) **B**
Good restaurants: 4 *, 4 ** **B**
Movie theaters: 8 Chains (36 screens), 1 Independent (1 screen) **A**
Crowd Pleasers
Aquariums and Zoos
Gladys Porter Zoo
Outdoor Assets
Water Area
Gulf offshore: 6,848 acres
Inland: 168,320 acres
Federal Protected Areas
Laguna Atascosa NWR, 44,922 acres
Lower Rio Grande Valley NWR, 15,452 acres
State Recreation Area
Port Isabel Lighthouse SHS, 1 acre
Places Rated Score: 72.51 Places Rated Rank: 97

Bryan–College Station, TX
Common Denominators
Golf courses: 2 private (36 holes), 1 daily fee (18 holes), 1 municipal (18 holes) **B**
Good restaurants: 1 *, 1 ** **C**
Movie theaters: 8 Chains (31 screens), 1 Independent (1 screen) **AA**
Crowd Pleasers
NCAA Division I
Texas A & M University Aggies (B, F)
Outdoor Assets
Inland Water Area: 3,200 acres
Places Rated Score: 9.77 Places Rated Rank: 318

Rating

Buffalo–Niagara Falls, NY
Common Denominators
Golf courses: 17 private (306 holes), 16 daily fee (2 holes), 15 municipal (234 holes) — **B**
Good restaurants: 7 *, 6 **, 7 *** — **B**
Movie theaters: 14 Chains (64 screens), 1 Independent (1 screen) — **C**
Crowd Pleasers
Aquariums and Zoos
Aquarium of Niagara Falls
Buffalo Zoological Gardens
Professional sports
Bills (NFL Football)
Bisons (Triple A Baseball)
Sabres (NHL Hockey)

Buckhorn Island SP, 895 acres
Earl Brydges Artpark, 197 acres
Evangola SP, 733 acres
Fort Niagara SP, 504 acres
Four Mile Creek SP, 248 acres
Golden Hill SP, 510 acres
Joseph Davis SP, 388 acres
Niagara Reservation SP, 435 acres
Reservoir SP, 132 acres
Whirlpool SP, 109 acres
Wilson–Tuscarora SP, 390 acres
Places Rated Score: 86.84 Places Rated Rank: 51

Burlington, VT
Common Denominators
Golf courses: 1 private (18 holes), 7 daily fee (117 holes) — **AA**
Good restaurants: 5 *, 3 **, 2 *** — **AA**
Movie theaters: 5 Chains (27 screens), 1 Independent (6 screens) — **AA**
Crowd Pleasers
Professional sports
Expos (Class A Baseball)
NCAA Division I
University of Vermont Catamounts (B, H)
Outdoor Assets
Inland Water Area: 159,360 acres
Federal Protected Area
Missisquoi NWR, 6,339 acres
State Recreation Areas
Burton Island SP, 253 acres
Grand Isle SP, 226 acres
Woods Island SP, 125 acres
Places Rated Score: 75.02 Places Rated Rank: 86

Calgary, AB
Common Denominators
Golf courses: 9 private (162 holes), 9 daily fee (1 holes), 7 municipal (99 holes) — **B**
Good restaurants: 7 **, 6 *** — **B**
Movie theaters: 15 Chains (67 screens), 3 Independent (4 screens) — **B**
Crowd Pleasers
Aquariums and Zoos
Calgary Zoo
Professional sports
Cannons (Triple A Baseball)
Flames (NHL Hockey)
Stampeders (CFL Football)

Rating

CIAU
University of Calgary Dinosaurs
Outdoor Assets
Inland Water Area: 21,000 acres
Federal Protected Area
Inglewood MBS, 395 acres
Provincial Recreation Areas
Brag Creek PP, 301 acres
Emerson Creek NA, 479 acres
Fish Creek PP, 1,804 acres
Sheep River Wildlife Sanctuary, 14,295 acres
Threepoint Creek NA, 153 acres
Places Rated Score: 65.67 Places Rated Rank: 120

Canton–Massillon, OH
Common Denominators

Places Rated Score: 47.74 Places Rated Rank: 186

Casper, WY
Common Denominators
Golf courses: 2 private (36 holes), 1 daily fee (9 holes), 1 municipal (18 holes) — **B**
Good restaurants: 2 ** — **A**
Movie theaters: 2 Chains (6 screens) — **B**
Crowd Pleasers
Outdoor Assets
Inland Water Area: 23,040 acres
Federal Protected Areas
Medicine Bow NF, 5,615 acres
Pathfinder NWR, 1,535 acres
State Recreation Areas
Independence Rock SHS, 197 acres
Wilkins SP, 319 acres
Places Rated Score: 15.63 Places Rated Rank: 292

Cedar Rapids, IA
Common Denominators
Golf courses: 3 private (45 holes), 4 daily fee (45 holes), 4 municipal (63 holes) — **A**
Good restaurants: 1 *, 3 ** — **B**
Movie theaters: 7 Chains (26 screens), 1 Independent (1 screen) — **AA**
Crowd Pleasers
Aquariums and Zoos
Beaver Park Zoo
Professional sports
Kernels (Class A Baseball)
Outdoor Assets
Inland Water Area: 4,480 acres
State Recreation Area
Palisades-Kepler SP, 603 acres
Places Rated Score: 20.73 Places Rated Rank: 272

Champaign–Urbana, IL
Common Denominators
Golf courses: 3 private (54 holes), 2 daily fee (36 holes), 2 municipal (36 holes) — **B**
Good restaurants: 2 *, 2 ** — **B**
Movie theaters: 6 Chains (33 screens) — **AA**
Crowd Pleasers
NCAA Division I
University of Illinois Illini (B, F)
Places Rated Score: 0.55 Places Rated Rank: 350

	Rating

Charleston, WV
Common Denominators
Golf courses: 4 private (72 holes), 1 daily fee (18 holes), 3 municipal (45 holes) — C
Good restaurants: 1 *, 2 **, 2 *** — A
Movie theaters: 1 Chain (9 screens), 1 Independent (1 screen) — C
Professional sports
Alley Cats (Class A Baseball)
Outdoor Assets
Inland Water Area: 7,680 acres
Places Rated Score: 14.65 Places Rated Rank: 296

✓ Charleston–North Charleston, SC
Common Denominators
Golf courses: 9 private (153 holes), 21 daily fee (360 holes), 2 municipal (36 holes) — AA
Good restaurants: 1 *, 15 **, 2 *** — AA
Movie theaters: 9 Chains (48 screens), 1 Independent (2 screens) — B
Crowd Pleasers
Aquariums and Zoos
Charles Towne Landing
Professional sports
Riverdogs (Class A Baseball)
South Carolina Stingrays (ECHL Hockey)
NCAA Division I
Charleston Southern University Buccaneers (B, F)
College of Charleston Cougars (B)
The Citadel Bulldogs (MB, F)
Outdoor Assets
Water Area
Atlantic offshore: 20,544 acres
Inland: 160,640 acres
Federal Protected Areas
Ace Basin NWR, 6,528 acres
Cape Romain NWR, 34,049 acres
Fort Sumter NM, 194 acres
Francis Marion NF, 251,139 acres
State Recreation Areas
Charles Towne Landing SP, 664 acres
Drayton Hall SP, 550 acres
Givhans Ferry SP, 888 acres
Hampton Plantation SP, 337 acres
Old Dorchester SP, 325 acres
Old Santee Canal SP, 224 acres
Places Rated Score: 91.02 Places Rated Rank: 33

Charlotte–Gastonia–Rock Hill, NC–SC
Common Denominators
Golf courses: 25 private (441 holes), 29 daily fee (504 holes), 5 municipal (72 holes) — B
Good restaurants: 5 *, 4 **, 5 *** — C
Movie theaters: 27 Chains (131 screens), 5 Independent (21 screens) — A
Crowd Pleasers
Aquariums and Zoos
Dan Nicholas Park Nature Center
Professional sports
Boll Weevils (Class A Baseball)
Carolina Panthers (NFL Football)
Checkers (ECHL Hockey)
Hornets (NBA Basketball)
Knights (Triple A Baseball)
NCAA Division I
Davidson College Wildcats (B, F)
University of North Carolina 49ers (B)
Outdoor Assets
Inland Water Area: 41,600 acres
Federal Protected Area
Kings Mountain NMP, 2,529 acres
State Recreation Areas
Crowder's Mountain SP, 1,966 acres
Kings Mountain SP, 6,100 acres
Places Rated Score: 80.05 Places Rated Rank: 71

Charlottesville, VA
Common Denominators
Golf courses: 8 private (126 holes), 1 municipal (18 holes) — C
Good restaurants: 1 *, 8 **, 1 *** — AA
Movie theaters: 4 Chains (26 screens), 3 Independent (5 screens) — AA
Crowd Pleasers
NCAA Division I
University of Virginia Cavaliers (B, F)
Outdoor Assets
Inland Water Area: 3,840 acres
Federal Protected Areas
Appalachian NT, 984 acres
Blue Ridge NParkwayacres
Shenandoah NP, 30,111 acres
Places Rated Score: 30.20 Places Rated Rank: 241

Chattanooga, TN–GA
Common Denominators
Golf courses: 10 private (171 holes), 9 daily fee (126 holes), 3 municipal (54 holes) — B
Good restaurants: 1 *, 3 **, 1 *** — C
Movie theaters: 6 Chains (34 screens), 1 Independent (1 screen) — A
Crowd Pleasers
Aquariums and Zoos
Tennessee Aquarium
Warner Park Zoo
Professional sports
Lookouts (Class AA Baseball)
NCAA Division I
University of Tennessee Moccasins (B, F)
Outdoor Assets
Inland Water Area: 30,080 acres
Federal Protected Areas
Chattahoochee NF, 18,780 acres
Chickamauga and Chattanooga NMP, 8,102 acres
State Recreation Areas
Booker T Washington SP, 353 acres
Cloudland Canyon SP, 2,219 acres
Harrison Bay SP, 1,199 acres
South Cumberland SRA, 5,803 acres
Places Rated Score: 57.64 Places Rated Rank: 148

Cheyenne, WY
Common Denominators
Golf courses: 2 daily fee (36 holes), 2 municipal (27 holes) — AA
Good restaurants: 1 ** — B
Movie theaters: 2 Chains (9 screens) — A
Crowd Pleasers
Aquariums and Zoos
Lions Park Native Animal Display
Outdoor Assets
Inland Water Area: 1,280 acres
State Recreation Area
Curt Gowdy SP, 1,960 acres
Places Rated Score: 3.19 Places Rated Rank: 340

✓ Chicago, IL
Common Denominators
Golf courses: 95 private (1,620 holes), 93 daily fee (1,548 holes), 95 municipal (1,476 holes) — B
Good restaurants: 73 *, 84 **, 49 ***, 4 ****, 3 ***** — A
Movie theaters: 88 Chains (450 screens), 29 Independent (60 screens) — C
Crowd Pleasers
Aquariums and Zoos
Brookfield Zoo
Cosley Children's Animal Farm
Jurica Natural History Museum
Lincoln Park Zoo
Lords Park Zoo
Phillips Park Zoo
Randall Oaks Park Zoo

	Rating
Shedd Aquarium	
Professional sports	
Bears (NFL Football)	
Blackhawks (NHL Hockey)	
Bulls (NBA Basketball)	
Cubs (NL Baseball)	
K C Cougars (Class A Baseball)	
Rockers (CBA Basketball)	
White Sox (AL Baseball)	
Wolves (IHL Hockey)	
NCAA Division I	
Chicago State University Cougars (B)	
Depaul University Blue Demons (B)	
Loyola University of Chicago Ramblers (B)	
Northeastern Illinois University Golden Eagles (B)	
Northern Illinois University Huskies (B, F)	

Illinois Beach SP, 2,978 acres
McHenry Dam & Lake Defiance SP, 1,690 acres
Moraine Hills SP, 1,763 acres
Shabbona Lake SP, 1,546 acres
Silver Springs SP, 1,314 acres
Places Rated Score: 99.02 Places Rated Rank: 1

Chico–Paradise, CA

Common Denominators	Rating
Golf courses: 2 private (36 holes), 2 daily fee (18 holes), 2 municipal (36 holes)	**B**
Good restaurants: 1 **	**C**
Movie theaters: 4 Chains (15 screens), 1 Independent (1 screen)	**B**

Outdoor Assets
Inland Water Area: 24,320 acres
Federal Protected Areas
Lassen NF, 51,178 acres
North Central Valley NWR, 1,732 acres
Plumas NF, 82,299 acres
Sacramento River NWR, 784 acres
State Recreation Areas
Bidwell-Sacramento River SP, 175 acres
Clay Pit SVRA, 220 acres
Lake Oroville SRA, 31,600 acres
Places Rated Score: 38.13 Places Rated Rank: 222

Chicoutimi–Jonquiere, PQ

Common Denominators	Rating
Golf courses: 2 daily fee (36 holes), 1 municipal (9 holes)	**B**
Movie theaters: 1 Chain (3 screens)	**C**

Outdoor Assets
Inland Water Area: 395,000 acres
Provincial Recreation Areas
Claude-Melancon Ecological Reserve PP, 1,285 acres
Oscar-Villeneuve Ecological Reserve PP, 1,401 acres
Riviere Petit Saguenay Wildlife Sanctuary, 494 acres
Saquenay PP, 70,078 acres
Places Rated Score: 71.85 Places Rated Rank: 98

Cincinnati, OH–KY–IN

Common Denominators	Rating
Golf courses: 30 private (504 holes), 28 daily fee (432 holes), 25 municipal (396 holes)	**A**
Good restaurants: 12 *, 18 **, 7 ***, 1 ****, 1 *****	**A**
Movie theaters: 26 Chains (127 screens), 4 Independent (4 screens)	**B**

Crowd Pleasers
Aquariums and Zoos
Zoo of Cincinnati
Professional sports
Bengals (NFL Football)
Reds (NL Baseball)
NCAA Division I
University of Cincinnati Bearcats (B, F)
Xavier University Musketeers (B)
Outdoor Assets
Inland Water Area: 33,920 acres
Federal Protected Area
William Howard Taft NHS, 2 acres
State Recreation Areas

	Rating
Golf courses: 3 private (54 holes), 2 daily fee (27 holes), 4 municipal (54 holes)	**B**
Movie theaters: 1 Chain (5 screens)	**A**

Crowd Pleasers
NCAA Division I
Austin Peay University Governors (B, F)
Outdoor Assets
Inland Water Area: 5,120 acres
State Recreation Areas
Dunbar Cave SNA, 110 acres
Pennyrile Forest State Resort Park, 863 acres
Places Rated Score: 10.06 Places Rated Rank: 316

✓ Cleveland–Lorain–Elyria, OH

Common Denominators	Rating
Golf courses: 31 private (549 holes), 73 daily fee (1,152 holes), 20 municipal (351 holes)	**AA**
Good restaurants: 6 *, 21 **, 3 ***, 1 ****	**B**
Movie theaters: 41 Chains (175 screens), 17 Independent (27 screens)	**B**

Crowd Pleasers
Aquariums and Zoos
Cleveland Metro Park Zoo
Professional sports
Indians (AL Baseball)
NCAA Division I
Cleveland State University Vikings (B)
Outdoor Assets
Water Area
Lake Erie offshore: 167,744 acres
Inland: 13,440 acres
Federal Protected Area
Cuyahoga Valley NRA, 2,709 acres
State Recreation Areas
Cleveland Lakefront SP, 450 acres
Findley SP, 838 acres
Geneva SP, 698 acres
Headlands Beach SP, 125 acres
Mentor Marsh SNA, 644 acres
Punderson SP, 846 acres
Pymatuning SP, 3,500 acres
Places Rated Score: 98.00 Places Rated Rank: 3

Colorado Springs, CO

Common Denominators	Rating
Golf courses: 11 private (198 holes), 3 daily fee (45 holes), 4 municipal (63 holes)	**C**
Good restaurants: 2 *, 7 **, 3 ***	**A**
Movie theaters: 10 Chains (49 screens)	**A**

	Rating
Crowd Pleasers	
Aquariums and Zoos	
Cheyenne Mountain Zoological Park	
Professional sports	
Sky Sox (Triple A Baseball)	
NCAA Division I	
Colorado College Tigers (H)	
U.S. Air Force Academy Falcons (MB, F, H)	
Outdoor Assets	
Inland Water Area: 1,920 acres	
Federal Protected Area	
Pike NF, 100,597 acres	
Places Rated Score: 49.87	Places Rated Rank: 177

Columbia, MO

Common Denominators	
Golf courses: 4 private (54 holes), 2 daily fee (36 holes), 2 municipal (36 holes)	A
Good restaurants: 3 **	A
Movie theaters: 5 Chains (19 screens)	AA
Crowd Pleasers	
NCAA Division I	
University of Missouri Tigers (B, F)	
Outdoor Assets	
Inland Water Area: 3,840 acres	
Federal Protected Area	
Mark Twain NF, 3,322 acres	
State Recreation Areas	
Finger Lakes SP, 1,132 acres	
Rock Bridge Memorial SP, 2,238 acres	
Places Rated Score: 20.27	Places Rated Rank: 276

Columbia, SC

Common Denominators	
Golf courses: 13 private (225 holes), 12 daily fee (198 holes), 1 municipal (18 holes)	B
Good restaurants: 3 **, 2 ***	C
Movie theaters: 10 Chains (35 screens), 3 Independent (10 screens)	B
Crowd Pleasers	
Aquariums and Zoos	
Riverbanks Zoological Park	
Professional sports	
Bombers (Class A Baseball)	
NCAA Division I	
University of South Carolina Gamecocks (B, F)	
Outdoor Assets	
Inland Water Area: 47,360 acres	
Federal Protected Area	
Congaree Swamp NM, 20,056 acres	
State Recreation Area	
Sesquicentennial SP, 1,445 acres	
Places Rated Score: 65.70	Places Rated Rank: 119

Columbus, GA–AL

Common Denominators	
Golf courses: 4 private (72 holes), 8 daily fee (126 holes), 3 municipal (54 holes)	A
Good restaurants: 3 *, 2 **, 2 ***	A
Movie theaters: 5 Chains (28 screens)	A
Crowd Pleasers	
Professional sports	
Redstixx (Class A Baseball)	
Outdoor Assets	
Inland Water Area: 13,440 acres	
State Recreation Areas	
FD Roosevelt SP, 10,000 acres	
Sprewell Bluff SP, 1,400 acres	
Places Rated Score: 34.89	Places Rated Rank: 229

Columbus, OH

	Rating
Common Denominators	
Golf courses: 34 private (549 holes), 40 daily fee (603 holes), 10 municipal (162 holes)	A
Good restaurants: 16 *, 14 **, 8 ***	A
Movie theaters: 26 Chains (145 screens), 7 Independent (10 screens)	A
Crowd Pleasers	
Aquariums and Zoos	
Columbus Zoological Park	
Professional sports	
Chill (ECHL Hockey)	
Clippers (Triple A Baseball)	
Crew (MLS Soccer)	
NCAA Division I	
Ohio State University Buckeyes	
Outdoor Assets	
Inland Water Area: 17,280 acres	
State Recreation Areas	
Alum Creek SP, 5,213 acres	
Blackhand Gorge SNA, 955 acres	
Buckeye Lake SP, 2,478 acres	
Deer Creek SP, 368 acres	
Delaware SP, 7,411 acres	
Flint Ridge SHS, 515 acres	
Marion SP, 308 acres	
Morris Woods SNA, 104 acres	
Octagon Earthworks SHS, 1,392 acres	
Stage's Pond SNA, 178 acres	
Wahkeena Nature Preserve SHS, 190 acres	
Places Rated Score: 61.38	Places Rated Rank: 133

Corpus Christi, TX

Common Denominators	
Golf courses: 7 private (108 holes), 2 daily fee (36 holes), 3 municipal (54 holes)	C
Good restaurants: 3 *, 2 **	C
Movie theaters: 5 Chains (23 screens)	C
Crowd Pleasers	
Aquariums and Zoos	
Texas State Aquarium	
Outdoor Assets	
Water Area	
Gulf offshore: 4,672 acres	
Inland: 174,720 acres	
State Recreation Areas	
Lake Corpus Christi SRA, 576 acres	
Mustang Island SP, 3,704 acres	
Places Rated Score: 62.36	Places Rated Rank: 127

Cumberland, MD–WV

Common Denominators	
Golf courses: 2 private (36 holes), 3 daily fee (36 holes)	B
Good restaurants: 1 *, 1 **, 1 ***	A
Movie theaters: 1 Chain (3 screens)	B
Outdoor Assets	
Inland Water Area: 3,200 acres	
Federal Protected Area	
Chesapeake and Ohio Canal NHP, 3,095 acres	
State Recreation Area	
Dans Mountain SP, 481 acres	
Rocky Gap SP, 2,983 acres	
Places Rated Score: 4.91	Places Rated Rank: 332

✓ Dallas, TX

Common Denominators	
Golf courses: 43 private (747 holes), 31 daily fee (513 holes), 21 municipal (351 holes)	B
Good restaurants: 6 *, 15 **, 19 ***, 1 ****, 1 *****	B
Movie theaters: 55 Chains (337 screens), 7 Independent (21 screens)	A
Crowd Pleasers	
Aquariums and Zoos	
Dallas Aquarium	
Dallas Zoo	
Professional sports	
Burn (MLS Soccer)	
Cowboys (NFL Football)	
Mavericks (NBA Basketball)	
Stars (NHL Hockey)	

Rating

NCAA Division I
Southern Methodist University Mustangs (B, F)
University North Texas Mean Green Eagles (B, F)
Outdoor Assets
Inland Water Area: 195,200 acres
State Recreation Areas
Cedar Hill SRA, 1,811 acres
Lake Lewisville SRA, 721 acres
Lake Tawakoni SRA, 376 acres
Purtis Creek SRA, 566 acres
Ray Roberts Lake SRA, 3,026 acres
Places Rated Score: 95.29 Places Rated Rank: 23

Danbury, CT
Common Denominators
Golf courses: 6 private (81 holes), 2 daily fee (27 holes), 2 municipal (36 holes) **–**

Places Rated Score: 20.38 Places Rated Rank: 274

Danville, VA
Common Denominators
Golf courses: 5 private (81 holes), 4 daily fee (54 holes) **A**
Movie theaters: 2 Chains (4 screens), 1 Independent (2 screens) **C**
Outdoor Assets
Inland Water Area: 5,120 acres
Places Rated Score: 3.25 Places Rated Rank: 339

Davenport–Moline–Rock Island, IA–IL
Common Denominators
Golf courses: 8 private (126 holes), 9 daily fee (126 holes), 9 municipal (153 holes) **AA**
Good restaurants: 2 *, 7 **, 1 *** **A**
Movie theaters: 6 Chains (29 screens) **B**
Crowd Pleasers
Aquariums and Zoos
Fejervary Zoo
Niabi Zoo
Professional sports
Quad City Mallards (CoHL Hockey)
Quad City River Bandits (Class A Baseball)
Quad City Thunder (CBA Basketball)
Outdoor Assets
Inland Water Area: 23,040 acres
Federal Protected Area
Upper Mississippi NWR, 398 acres
State Recreation Area
Johnson Sauk Trail SP, 1,361 acres
Places Rated Score: 56.05 Places Rated Rank: 155

Dayton–Springfield, OH
Common Denominators
Golf courses: 18 private (306 holes), 13 daily fee (198 holes), 14 municipal (243 holes) **A**
Good restaurants: 8 *, 10 **, 5 *** **A**
Movie theaters: 27 Chains (74 screens), 1 Independent (2 screens) **C**
Crowd Pleasers
Professional sports
Bombers (ECHL Hockey)
NCAA Division I
University of Dayton Flyers (B, F)
Wright State University Raiders (B)
Outdoor Assets

Rating

Inland Water Area: 6,400 acres
State Recreation Areas
Buck Creek SP, 1,910 acres
John Bryan SP, 1,750 acres
Piqua Historical Area SHS, 176 acres
Sycamore SP, 2,295 acres
Places Rated Score: 49.09 Places Rated Rank: 179

Daytona Beach, FL
Common Denominators
Golf courses: 5 private (90 holes), 18 daily fee (306 holes), 5 municipal (90 holes) **AA**
Good restaurants: 2 *, 8 **, 1 *** **A**
Movie theaters: 14 Chains (43 screens) **A**
Crowd Pleasers
Professional sports

State Recreation Areas
Blue Spring SP, 2,192 acres
Bulow Creek SP, 2,577 acres
Bulow Plantation Ruins SHS, 109 acres
De Leon Springs SRA, 401 acres
Flagler Beach SRA, 145 acres
Haw Creek SNA, 3,061 acres
Hontoon Island SP, 1,051 acres
North Peninsula SRA, 442 acres
Tomoka SP, 1,539 acres
Washington Oaks State Gardens, 400 acres
Places Rated Score: 85.40 Places Rated Rank: 56

Decatur, AL
Common Denominators
Golf courses: 2 private (36 holes), 2 daily fee (27 holes), 4 municipal (72 holes) **AA**
Good restaurants: 1 ** **C**
Movie theaters: 3 Chains (20 screens) **AA**
Outdoor Assets
Inland Water Area: 26,880 acres
Federal Protected Areas
Bankhead NF, 90,332 acres
Wheeler NWR, 3,493 acres
State Recreation Area
Joe Wheeler SP, 400 acres
Places Rated Score: 46.83 Places Rated Rank: 195

Decatur, IL
Common Denominators
Golf courses: 2 private (36 holes), 4 municipal (72 holes) **A**
Movie theaters: 2 Chains (12 screens) **A**
Crowd Pleasers
Aquariums and Zoos
Decatur Park Zoo
Outdoor Assets
Inland Water Area: 3,200 acres
State Recreation Areas
Lincoln Trail Homestead SHS, 162 acres
Spitler Woods SP, 202 acres
Places Rated Score: 5.65 Places Rated Rank: 330

Denver, CO
Common Denominators
Golf courses: 24 private (414 holes), 8 daily fee (135 holes), 25 municipal (423 holes) **B**
Good restaurants: 12 *, 13 **, 10 ***, 2 **** **B**
Movie theaters: 39 Chains (207 screens) **A**

Rating

Crowd Pleasers
Aquariums and Zoos
Denver Zoological Gardens
Englewood Childrens Zoo
Professional sports
Broncos (NFL Football)
Colorado Avalanche (NHL Hockey)
Colorado Rockies (NL Baseball)
Nuggets (NBA Basketball)
Rapids (MLS Soccer)
NCAA Division I
University of Denver Pioneers (H)
Outdoor Assets
Inland Water Area: 12,160 acres
Federal Protected Areas
Arapaho NF, 2,057 acres
Pike NF, 244,237 acres
Roosevelt NF, 160 acres
State Recreation Areas
Barr Lake SP, 692 acres
Castlewood Canyon SP, 873 acres
Chatfield SRA, 3,768 acres
Cherry Creek SRA, 3,305 acres
Roxborough SP, 1,620 acres
Places Rated Score: 88.98 Places Rated Rank: 43

Des Moines, IA
Common Denominators
Golf courses: 11 private (153 holes), 11 daily fee (153 holes), 5 municipal (90 holes) **A**
Good restaurants: 10 *, 3 **, 3 *** **A**
Movie theaters: 16 Chains (50 screens), 1 Independent (1 screen) **A**
Crowd Pleasers
Aquariums and Zoos
Blank Park Zoo
Professional sports
Cubs (Triple A Baseball)
NCAA Division I
Drake University Bulldogs (B, F)
Outdoor Assets
Inland Water Area: 18,560 acres
State Recreation Areas
Big Creek SP, 1,536 acres
Lake Ahquabi SP, 770 acres
Margo Frankel Woods SP, 136 acres
Walnut Woods SP, 300 acres
Places Rated Score: 55.50 Places Rated Rank: 156

✓ Detroit, MI
Common Denominators
Golf courses: 50 private (837 holes), 122 daily fee (1,917 holes), 42 municipal (630 holes) **A**
Good restaurants: 4 *, 21 **, 8 ***, 3 **** **C**
Movie theaters: 51 Chains (311 screens), 12 Independent (31 screens) **B**
Crowd Pleasers
Aquariums and Zoos
Belle Isle Zoo and Aquarium
Detroit Zoological Park
Professional sports
Falcons (CoHL Hockey)
Lions (NFL Football)
Pistons (NBA Basketball)
Red Wings (NHL Hockey)
Tigers (AL Baseball)
Vipers (IHL Hockey)
NCAA Division I
University of Detroit Titans (B)
Outdoor Assets
Water Area
Great Lakes offshore: 20,736 acres
Inland: 67,840 acres
Federal Protected Area
Wyandotte NWR, 304 acres
State Recreation Areas
Algonac SP, 1,307 acres
Bald Mountain SRA, 4,637 acres
Dodge Brothers No. 4 SP, 139 acres
Highland SRA, 5,524 acres
Holly SRA, 7,670 acres
Island Lake SRA, 194 acres
Lakeport SP, 566 acres
Maybury SP, 944 acres
Metamora-Hadley SRA, 683 acres
Ortonville SRA, 4,875 acres
Pontiac Lake SRA, 3,700 acres
Proud Lake SRA, 3,614 acres
Seven Lakes SP, 1,410 acres
Sterling SP, 1,000 acres
Wetzel SP, 900 acres
Places Rated Score: 97.13 Places Rated Rank: 10

Dothan, AL
Common Denominators
Golf courses: 4 private (63 holes), 6 daily fee (90 holes) **A**
Good restaurants: 1 * **C**
Movie theaters: 2 Chains (6 screens), 1 Independent (1 screen) **C**
Outdoor Assets
Inland Water Area: 1,920 acres
State Recreation Area
Chattahoochee SP, 596 acres
Places Rated Score: 2.61 Places Rated Rank: 346

Dover, DE
Common Denominators
Golf courses: 3 private (54 holes), 2 daily fee (36 holes) **B**
Good restaurants: 2 *, 3 **, 1 *** **AA**
Movie theaters: 2 Chains (12 screens) **B**
Crowd Pleasers
NCAA Division I
Delaware State College Hornets (B, F)
Outdoor Assets
Water Area
Atlantic offshore: 12,864 acres
Inland: 5,120 acres
Federal Protected Area
Bombay Hook NWR, 15,122 acres
State Recreation Areas
Killens Pond SP, 1,061 acres
Murderkill River Nature Preserve, 140 acres
Places Rated Score: 24.79 Places Rated Rank: 258

Dubuque, IA
Common Denominators
Golf courses: 2 private (36 holes), 3 daily fee (36 holes), 2 municipal (27 holes) **AA**
Good restaurants: 3 *, 1 ** **A**
Movie theaters: 2 Chains (14 screens) **AA**
Outdoor Assets
Inland Water Area: 5,120 acres
Federal Protected Areas
Upper Mississippi NWR, 475 acres
State Recreation Areas
Mines of Spain SP, 1,380 acres
Places Rated Score: 12.05 Places Rated Rank: 308

✓ Duluth–Superior, MN–WI
Common Denominators
Golf courses: 3 private (45 holes), 9 daily fee (99 holes), 10 municipal (135 holes) **AA**
Good restaurants: 2 *, 3 **, 1 *** **A**
Movie theaters: 7 Chains (34 screens), 3 Independent (3 screens) **AA**
Crowd Pleasers
Aquariums and Zoos
Duluth Zoological Gardens
NCAA Division I
University of Minnesota Bulldogs (H)
Outdoor Assets
Water Area

Rating

Lake Superior offshore: 16,384 acres
Inland: 352,000 acres
Federal Protected Areas
Saint Croix Scenic River, 3,128 acres
Superior NF, 686,551 acres
Voyageurs NP, 121,253 acres
State Recreation Areas
Amnicon Falls SP, 825 acres
Bear Head Lake SP, 4,375 acres
Gandy Dancer State Trail, 191 acres
McCarthy Beach SP, 2,311 acres
Pattison SP, 1,374 acres
Saunders Grade State Trail, 336 acres
Soudan Underground Mine SP, 1,300 acres
Places Rated Score: 90.86 Places Rated Rank: 35

Rating

Provincial Recreation Areas
Alsike-Bat Lake NA, 321 acres
Bat Lake NA, 640 acres
Battle Creek NA, 158 acres
Buck Creek NA, 321 acres
Buck Lake NA, 272 acres
Easyford Creek NA, 247 acres
Easyford NA, 321 acres
Genesse NA, 161 acres
Hasse Lake PP, 170 acres
Horseshoe Creek NA, 801 acres
Modeste Creek NA, 1,767 acres
Modeste-Saskatchewan NA, 996 acres
Pembina River PP, 413 acres
Pembina River/Moon Lake NA, 264 acres
Pigeon Lake PP, 1,095 acres

Marist College Red Foxes (B)
Outdoor Assets
Inland Water Area: 15,360 acres
Federal Protected Areas
Appalachian NT, 4,203 acres
Eleanor Roosevelt NHS, 180 acres
Home of Franklin D Roosevelt NHS, 290 acres
Vanderbilt Mansion NHS, 212 acres
State Recreation Areas
Hudson Highlands SP, 697 acres
James Baird SP, 590 acres
Margaret Norrie SP, 330 acres
Ogden Mills SP, 637 acres
Taconic SP, 1,868 acres
Places Rated Score: 50.96 Places Rated Rank: 173

Eau Claire, WI
Common Denominators
Golf courses: 2 private (36 holes), 7 daily fee (90 holes), 2 municipal (27 holes) — AA
Good restaurants: 1 **, 1 *** — B
Movie theaters: 1 Chain (6 screens), 4 Independent (4 screens) — C
Outdoor Assets
Inland Water Area: 24,960 acres
State Recreation Areas
Brunet Island SP, 1,032 acres
Chippewa Moraine Ice Age RA, 2,762 acres
Chippewa River State Trail, 673 acres
Lake Wissota SP, 1,062 acres
Old Abe State Trail, 259 acres
Places Rated Score: 31.88 Places Rated Rank: 237

Edmonton, AB
Common Denominators
Golf courses: 5 private (90 holes), 13 daily fee (180 holes), 16 municipal (243 holes) — A
Good restaurants: 4 **, 8 *** — B
Movie theaters: 15 Chains (73 screens), 6 Independent (19 screens) — A
Crowd Pleasers
Aquariums and Zoos
Valley Zoo
Professional sports
Eskimos (CFL Football)
Trappers (Triple A Baseball)
CIAU
University of Alberta Golden Bears
Outdoor Assets
Inland Water Area: 83,000 acres

Golf courses: [illegible] holes), 4 municipal (63 holes) — C
Good restaurants: 2 *, 5 ** — C
Movie theaters: 7 Chains (32 screens), 2 Independent (4 screens) — C
Crowd Pleasers
Aquariums and Zoos
El Paso Zoo
Professional sports
Diablos (Class AA Baseball)
NCAA Division I
University of Texas Miners (B, F)
Outdoor Assets
Inland Water Area: 1,280 acres
Federal Protected Area
Chamizal NMem, 55 acres
State Recreation Areas
Franklin Mountains SP, 23,867 acres
Hueco Tanks SHS, 860 acres
Places Rated Score: 24.81 Places Rated Rank: 257

Elkhart-Goshen, IN
Common Denominators
Golf courses: 4 private (72 holes), 4 daily fee (63 holes), 2 municipal (36 holes) — A
Good restaurants: 2 **, 1 *** — A
Movie theaters: 3 Chains (10 screens) — C
Outdoor Assets
Inland Water Area: 2,560 acres
Places Rated Score: 4.50 Places Rated Rank: 333

Elmira, NY
Common Denominators
Golf courses: 1 private (18 holes), 2 daily fee (27 holes), 2 municipal (36 holes) — A
Good restaurants: 1 *, 2 **, 1 *** — AA
Movie theaters: 5 Chains (13 screens) — AA
Outdoor Assets
Inland Water Area: 1,920 acres
State Recreation Areas
Mark Twain SP, 462 acres
Newton Battlefield SP, 321 acres
Places Rated Score: 5.88 Places Rated Rank: 329

Enid, OK
Common Denominators
Golf courses: 1 private (18 holes), 1 daily fee (9 holes), 1 municipal (18 holes) — A
Good restaurants: 1 *, 1 ** — A
Movie theaters: 2 Chains (7 screens) — A

Rating

Outdoor Assets
Inland Water Area: 1,280 acres
State Recreation Area
Museum of the Cherokee Strip SHS, 1 acre
Places Rated Score: 0.90 Places Rated Rank: 349

Erie, PA
Common Denominators
Golf courses: 5 private (81 holes), 11 daily fee (153 holes), 4 municipal (63 holes) **AA**
Good restaurants: 1 ** **C**
Movie theaters: 7 Chains (12 screens), 1 Independent (2 screens) **B**
Crowd Pleasers
Aquariums and Zoos
Erie Zoological Park
Professional sports
Seawolves (Class A Baseball)
Outdoor Assets
Water Area
Lake Erie offshore: 47,872 acres
Inland: 5,120 acres
State Recreation Area
Presque Isle SP, 3,209 acres
Places Rated Score: 66.59 Places Rated Rank: 115

Eugene–Springfield, OR
Common Denominators
Golf courses: 3 private (54 holes), 8 daily fee (117 holes), 1 municipal (9 holes) **B**
Good restaurants: 3 *, 7 **, 1 *** **A**
Movie theaters: 8 Chains (28 screens), 1 Independent (2 screens) **B**
Crowd Pleasers
Professional sports
Emeralds (Class A Baseball)
NCAA Division I
University of Oregon Ducks (B, F)
Outdoor Assets
Water Area
Pacific offshore: 6,656 acres
Inland: 40,960 acres
Federal Protected Areas
Siuslaw NF, 246,173 acres
Umpqua NF, 151,248 acres
Willamette NF, 1,032,269 acres
State Recreation Areas
Armitage SP, 5,776 acres
Ben and Kay Dorris SP, 92 acres
Carl Washburne Memorial SP, 1,089 acres
Devil's Elbow SP, 547 acres
Elijah Bristow SP, 848 acres
Jessie Honeyman Memorial SP, 522 acres
Joaquin Miller Forest Wayside, 112 acres
Neptune SP, 303 acres
Willamette River Greenway, 925 acres
Places Rated Score: 78.11 Places Rated Rank: 83

Evansville–Henderson, IN–KY
Common Denominators
Golf courses: 7 private (108 holes), 4 daily fee (63 holes), 3 municipal (45 holes) **B**
Good restaurants: 3 * **C**
Movie theaters: 1 Independent (5 screens) **C**
Crowd Pleasers
Aquariums and Zoos
Mesker Park Zoo
NCAA Division I
University of Evansville Aces (B, F)
Outdoor Assets
Inland Water Area: 29,440 acres
State Recreation Areas
Harmonie SP, 3,465 acres
John James Audubon SP, 619 acres
Places Rated Score: 27.87 Places Rated Rank: 248

Rating

Fargo–Moorhead, ND–MN
Common Denominators
Golf courses: 3 private (54 holes), 3 daily fee (27 holes), 7 municipal (108 holes) **AA**
Good restaurants: 1 *, 3 ** **A**
Movie theaters: 5 Chains (22 screens), 2 Independent (2 screens) **AA**
Crowd Pleasers
Professional sports
Beez (IBA Basketball)
Outdoor Assets
Inland Water Area: 5,760 acres
State Recreation Area
Buffalo River SP, 1,367 acres
Places Rated Score: 23.89 Places Rated Rank: 259

Fayetteville, NC
Common Denominators
Golf courses: 6 private (99 holes), 4 daily fee (72 holes) **C**
Good restaurants: 1 *, 4 ** **B**
Movie theaters: 7 Chains (31 screens) **A**
Crowd Pleasers
Professional sports
Generals (Class A Baseball)
Outdoor Assets
Inland Water Area: 3,200 acres
Places Rated Score: 9.89 Places Rated Rank: 317

Fayetteville–Springdale–Rogers, AR
Common Denominators
Golf courses: 10 private (171 holes), 7 daily fee (99 holes) **B**
Good restaurants: 2 *, 4 **, 1 *** **A**
Movie theaters: 6 Chains (28 screens), 2 Independent (3 screens) **A**
Crowd Pleasers
NCAA Division I
University of Arkansas Razorbacks (B, F)
Outdoor Assets
Inland Water Area: 25,600 acres
Federal Protected Areas
Logan Cave NWR, 124 acres
Ozark NF, 29,998 acres
Pea Ridge NMP, 4,279 acres
State Recreation Areas
Beaver Lake SP, 10,790 acres
Devil's Den SP, 1,047 acres
Prairie Grove SP, 304 acres
Places Rated Score: 51.21 Places Rated Rank: 172

Fitchburg–Leominster, MA
Common Denominators
Golf courses: 1 private (18 holes), 5 daily fee (72 holes), 1 municipal (18 holes) **AA**
Movie theaters: 2 Chains (14 screens), 2 Independent (3 screens) **C**
Outdoor Assets
Inland Water Area: 42,240 acres
State Recreation Areas
Dunn Pond SP, 115 acres
Gardner Heritage SP, 115 acres
Lake Dennison SRA, 4,221 acres
Places Rated Score: 32.97 Places Rated Rank: 236

Flagstaff, AZ–UT
Common Denominators
Golf courses: 2 private (36 holes), 2 daily fee (27 holes), 3 municipal (36 holes) **A**
Good restaurants: 9 *, 5 **, 2 *** **AA**
Movie theaters: 6 Chains (12 screens), 1 Independent (1 screen) **A**
Crowd Pleasers
NCAA Division I
Northern Arizona Lumberjacks (B, F)
Outdoor Assets
Inland Water Area: 101,760 acres

Rating

Federal Protected Areas
Bryce Canyon NP, 8,901 acres
Coconino NF, 1,415,653 acres
Dixie NF, 124,283 acres
Glen Canyon NRA, 492,267 acres
Grand Canyon NP, 662,038 acres
Kaibab NF, 1,527,674 acres
Lake Mead NRA, 83,116 acres
Prescott NF, 43,695 acres
Sitgreaves NF, 284,325 acres
Sunset Crater NM, 3,040 acres
Walnut Canyon NM, 2,012 acres
Wupatki NM, 35,253 acres
Zion NP, 9,391 acres
State Recreation Areas
Coral Pink Sand Dunes SP, 3,730 acres

Rating

Fort Lauderdale, FL
Common Denominators
Golf courses: 15 private (270 holes), 34 daily fee (594 holes), 5 municipal (90 holes) — **A**
Good restaurants: 5 *, 33 **, 22 ***, 1 **** — **AA**
Movie theaters: 25 Chains (188 screens), 7 Independent (23 screens) — **AA**
Crowd Pleasers
Professional sports
Florida Panthers (NHL Hockey)
Outdoor Assets
Water Area
Atlantic offshore: 6,272 acres
Inland: 8,320 acres
State Recreation Areas
Birch SRA, 180 acres

Outdoor Assets
Inland Water Area: 6,400 acres
Federal Protected Area
Manistee NF, 8 acres
Places Rated Score: 29.43 Places Rated Rank: 246

Florence, AL
Common Denominators
Golf courses: 4 private (54 holes), 4 daily fee (54 holes), 2 municipal (27 holes) — **A**
Good restaurants: 2 *, 1 ** — **B**
Movie theaters: 3 Chains (12 screens) — **B**
Outdoor Assets
Inland Water Area: 49,920 acres
Federal Protected Areas
Natchez Trace N Parkway, 4,175 acres
State Recreation Area
Joe Wheeler SP, 2,080 acres
Places Rated Score: 40.47 Places Rated Rank: 212

Florence, SC
Common Denominators
Golf courses: 3 private (54 holes), 3 daily fee (54 holes) — **B**
Movie theaters: 4 Chains (13 screens) — **A**
Outdoor Assets
Inland Water Area: 2,560 acres
State Recreation Area
Lynches River SP, 668 acres
Places Rated Score: 2.82 Places Rated Rank: 344

Fort Collins–Loveland, CO
Common Denominators
Golf courses: 2 private (36 holes), 3 daily fee (45 holes), 5 municipal (81 holes) — **A**
Good restaurants: 3 *, 3 **, 1 *** — **A**
Movie theaters: 7 Chains (14 screens), 3 Independent (6 screens) — **B**
Crowd Pleasers
NCAA Division I
Colorado State University Rams (B, F)
Outdoor Assets
Inland Water Area: 21,120 acres
Federal Protected Areas
Rocky Mountain NP, 144,315 acres
Roosevelt NF, 644,854 acres
State Recreation Areas
Boyd Lake SRA, 197 acres
Lory SP, 2,479 acres
Places Rated Score: 69.70 Places Rated Rank: 107

Miracle (Class A Baseball)
Outdoor Assets
Water Area
Gulf offshore: 11,008 acres
Inland: 151,040 acres
Federal Protected Areas
Ding Darling NWR, 5,174 acres
Matlacha Pass NWR, 512 acres
Pine Island NWR, 548 acres
State Recreation Areas
Cayo Cosia SP, 2,241 acres
Gasparilla Island SRA, 144 acres
Koreshan SHS, 156 acres
Lovers Key SRA, 434 acres
Places Rated Score: 87.07 Places Rated Rank: 48

Fort Pierce–Port St. Lucie, FL
Common Denominators
Golf courses: 20 private (360 holes), 13 daily fee (225 holes), 4 municipal (72 holes) — **AA**
Good restaurants: 7 *, 7 **, 1 *** — **AA**
Movie theaters: 3 Chains (16 screens), 1 Independent (2 screens) — **A**
Crowd Pleasers
Professional sports
Mets (Class A Baseball)
Treasure Coast Tropics (USBL Basketball)
Outdoor Assets
Water Area
Atlantic offshore: 9,536 acres
Inland: 104,960 acres
Federal Protected Area
Hobe Sound NWR, 972 acres
State Recreation Areas
Avalon SP, 570 acres
Dickinson SP, 11,550 acres
Fort Pierce Inlet SRA, 973 acres
St. Lucie Inlet SP, 808 acres
Places Rated Score: 80.18 Places Rated Rank: 70

Fort Smith, AR-OK
Common Denominators
Golf courses: 2 private (36 holes), 6 daily fee (81 holes), 2 municipal (27 holes) — **A**
Good restaurants: 1 *, 2 **, 1 *** — **A**
Movie theaters: 4 Chains (17 screens) — **B**
Outdoor Assets
Inland Water Area: 38,400 acres
Federal Protected Areas

Rating

Ouachita NF, 14,888 acres
Ozark NF, 86,262 acres
State Recreation Areas
Lake Fort Smith SP, 126 acres
Lake Tenkiller SP, 1,190 acres
Sallisaw SP, 90 acres
Places Rated Score: 46.36 Places Rated Rank: 197

Fort Walton Beach, FL
Common Denominators
Golf courses: 4 private (72 holes), 14 daily fee (234 holes), 2 municipal (36 holes) **AA**
Good restaurants: 6 *, 3 ** **AA**
Movie theaters: 3 Chains (13 screens), 3 Independent (9 screens) **AA**
Outdoor Assets
Water Area
Gulf offshore: 5,504 acres
Inland: 38,400 acres
Federal Protected Areas
Choctawhatchee NF, 523 acres
Gulf Islands NSeashore, 3,485 acres
State Recreation Areas
Henderson Beach SRA, 209 acres
Rocky Bayou SRA, 357 acres
Places Rated Score: 62.34 Places Rated Rank: 128

Fort Wayne, IN
Common Denominators
Golf courses: 5 private (90 holes), 25 daily fee (405 holes), 1 municipal (18 holes) **AA**
Good restaurants: 4 **, 1 *** **C**
Movie theaters: 13 Chains (41 screens), 2 Independent (3 screens) **B**
Crowd Pleasers
Aquariums and Zoos
Fort Wayne Children's Zoo
Professional sports
Fury (CBA Basketball)
Komets (IHL Hockey)
Wizards (Class A Baseball)
Outdoor Assets
Inland Water Area: 7,680 acres
State Recreation Area
Ouabache SP, 1,065 acres
Places Rated Score: 47.89 Places Rated Rank: 184

Fort Worth–Arlington, TX
Common Denominators
Golf courses: 18 private (315 holes), 12 daily fee (189 holes), 14 municipal (225 holes) **B**
Good restaurants: 5 *, 10 **, 4 *** **C**
Movie theaters: 24 Chains (170 screens), 3 Independent (4 screens) **A**
Crowd Pleasers
Aquariums and Zoos
Fort Worth Zoological Park
Professional sports
Rangers (AL Baseball)
NCAA Division I
Texas Christian Horned Frogs (B, F)
University of Texas Mavericks (B)
Outdoor Assets
Inland Water Area: 39,040 acres
State Recreation Areas
Acton SHS, 1 acre
Cleburne SRA, 529 acres
Eagle Mountain SRA, 802 acres
Lake Mineral Wells SP, 3,008 acres
Places Rated Score: 78.52 Places Rated Rank: 82

Fresno, CA
Common Denominators
Golf courses: 7 private (126 holes), 8 daily fee (126 holes), 4 municipal (63 holes) **C**
Good restaurants: 2 *, 1 **, 1 *** **C**
Movie theaters: 9 Chains (46 screens) **C**

Rating

Crowd Pleasers
Aquariums and Zoos
Chaffee Zoological Gardens
NCAA Division I
California State University Bulldogs (B)
Outdoor Assets
Inland Water Area: 44,800 acres
Federal Protected Areas
Devils Postpile NM, 798 acres
Inyo NF, 52,296 acres
Kings Canyon NP, 354,828 acres
Sequoia NF, 130,757 acres
Sierra NF, 1,217,995 acres
Yosemite NP, 66,886 acres
State Recreation Areas
Millerton Lake SRA, 6,551 acres
Wassama Round House SHP, 27 acres
Places Rated Score: 64.42 Places Rated Rank: 122

Gadsden, AL
Common Denominators
Golf courses: 4 private (63 holes), 3 daily fee (45 holes) **B**
Movie theaters: 3 Chains (15 screens) **AA**
Outdoor Assets
Inland Water Area: 8,960 acres
Places Rated Score: 8.27 Places Rated Rank: 322

Gainesville, FL
Common Denominators
Golf courses: 2 private (36 holes), 3 daily fee (54 holes), 1 municipal (18 holes) **B**
Good restaurants: 1 **, 1 *** **C**
Movie theaters: 6 Chains (27 screens), 1 Independent (1 screen) **AA**
Crowd Pleasers
Aquariums and Zoos
Santa Fe Community College Teaching Zoo
NCAA Division I
University of Florida Gators (B, F)
Outdoor Assets
Inland Water Area: 60,800 acres
State Recreation Areas
Devil's Millhopper Geological SHS, 63 acres
O'Leno SP, 299 acres
Paynes Prairie State Preserve, 20,678 acres
River Rise SNA, 1,706 acres
San Felasco Hammock SNA, 6,903 acres
Places Rated Score: 61.80 Places Rated Rank: 132

Galveston–Texas City, TX
Common Denominators
Golf courses: 6 private (81 holes), 1 daily fee (18 holes), 2 municipal (36 holes) **C**
Good restaurants: 1 *, 3 **, 1 *** **A**
Movie theaters: 3 Chains (13 screens) **C**
Outdoor Assets
Water Area
Gulf offshore: 24,192 acres
Inland: 63,360 acres
State Recreation Area
Galveston Island SP, 1,950 acres
Places Rated Score: 55.47 Places Rated Rank: 157

Gary, IN
Common Denominators
Golf courses: 10 private (162 holes), 15 daily fee (243 holes), 4 municipal (72 holes) **A**
Good restaurants: 1 **, 2 *** **C**
Movie theaters: 6 Chains (32 screens), 4 Independent (4 screens) **C**
Crowd Pleasers
NCAA Division I
Valparaiso University Crusaders (B, F)
Outdoor Assets
Water Area
Lake Michigan offshore: 14,464 acres
Inland: 4,480 acres

Rating

Federal Protected Area
Indiana Dunes NLakeshore, 9,644 acres
State Recreation Area
Indiana Dunes SP, 2,182 acres
Places Rated Score: 48.71 Places Rated Rank: 183

Glens Falls, NY
Common Denominators
Golf courses: 2 private (36 holes), 14 daily fee (180 holes) **AA**
Good restaurants: 2 *, 3 **, 2 *** **AA**
Movie theaters: 6 Chains (20 screens), 1 Independent (1 screen) **AA**
Crowd Pleasers
Professional sports
Adirondack Red Wings (AHL Hockey)
Outdoor Assets

Common Denominators
Golf courses: 3 private (54 holes), 3 daily fee (54 holes) **A**
Good restaurants: 1 * **C**
Movie theaters: 3 Chains (8 screens) **C**
Outdoor Assets
Inland Water Area: 2,560 acres
State Recreation Area
Cliffs-of-the-Neuse SP, 608 acres
Places Rated Score: 2.30 Places Rated Rank: 347

Grand Forks, ND–MN
Common Denominators
Golf courses: 3 private (36 holes), 7 daily fee (72 holes), 2 municipal (27 holes) **AA**
Good restaurants: 2 ** **B**
Movie theaters: 6 Chains (16 screens), 2 Independent (3 screens) **AA**
Crowd Pleasers
NCAA Division I
University of North Dakota Sioux (H)
Outdoor Assets
Inland Water Area: 18,560 acres
Federal Protected Area
Kelly's Slough NWR, 680 acres
State Recreation Area
Turtle River SP, 784 acres
Places Rated Score: 35.04 Places Rated Rank: 228

Grand Junction, CO
Common Denominators
Golf courses: 1 private (18 holes), 1 daily fee (18 holes), 2 municipal (27 holes) **B**
Good restaurants: 1 *, 2 ** **A**
Movie theaters: 3 Chains (13 screens), 1 Independent (1 screen) **AA**
Outdoor Assets
Inland Water Area: 8,320 acres
Federal Protected Areas
Colorado NM, 20,454 acres
Grand Mesa NF, 252,647 acres
Manti-La Sal NF, 4,542 acres
Uncompahgre NF, 207,256 acres
White River NF, 81,289 acres
State Recreation Areas
Highline SRA, 580 acres
Island Acres SRA, 130 acres
Vega SRA, 898 acres
Places Rated Score: 38.16 Places Rated Rank: 220

Rating

✓ Grand Rapids–Muskegon–Holland, MI
Common Denominators
Golf courses: 18 private (306 holes), 62 daily fee (1,008 holes), 3 municipal (54 holes) **AA**
Good restaurants: 7 *, 16 **, 3 *** **A**
Movie theaters: 15 Chains (95 screens) **B**
Crowd Pleasers
Aquariums and Zoos
John Ball Zoological Gardens
Professional sports
Fury (CoHL Hockey)
Mackers (CBA Basketball)
Whitecaps (Class A Baseball)
Outdoor Assets
Water Area
Lake Michigan offshore: 190,528 acres
Inland: 39.040 acres

Common Denominators
Golf courses: 1 private (18 holes), 2 municipal (36 holes) **B**
Good restaurants: 1 *, 2 ** **A**
Movie theaters: 3 Chains (8 screens) **B**
Outdoor Assets
Inland Water Area: 8,960 acres
Federal Protected Areas
Benton Lake NWR, 11,955 acres
Lewis & Clark NF, 178,658 acres
State Recreation Areas
Giant Springs SP, 280 acres
Sluice Boxes SP, 1,454 acres
Ulm Pishkun SP, 170 acres
Places Rated Score: 26.44 Places Rated Rank: 252

Greeley, CO
Common Denominators
Golf courses: 2 private (36 holes), 1 daily fee (18 holes), 2 municipal (36 holes) **B**
Good restaurants: 1 ** **C**
Movie theaters: 4 Chains (13 screens), 1 Independent (1 screen) **B**
Outdoor Assets
Inland Water Area: 18,560 acres
State Recreation Areas
Barbour Ponds SRA, 50 acres
Fort Vasquez SHS, 1 acre
Places Rated Score: 20.93 Places Rated Rank: 271

Green Bay, WI
Common Denominators
Golf courses: 2 private (18 holes), 11 daily fee (162 holes), 1 municipal (18 holes) **AA**
Good restaurants: 2 *, 1 ** **C**
Movie theaters: 5 Chains (26 screens), 3 Independent (3 screens) **AA**
Crowd Pleasers
Aquariums and Zoos
Bay Beach Wildlife Sanctuary
Northeastern Wisconsin Zoo
Professional sports
Packers (NFL Football)
NCAA Division I
University of Wisconsin Phoenix (B)
Outdoor Assets
Water Area
Lake Michigan offshore: 4,992 acres

Rating

Inland: 5,120 acres
State Recreation Area
Mountain-Bay State Trail, 188 acres
Places Rated Score: 28.58 Places Rated Rank: 247

Greensboro–Winston-Salem–High Point, NC
Common Denominators
Golf courses: 17 private (288 holes), 48 daily fee (774 holes), 13 municipal (216 holes) **AA**
Good restaurants: 7 **, 1 *** **C**
Movie theaters: 19 Chains (79 screens), 5 Independent (11 screens) **B**
Crowd Pleasers
Aquariums and Zoos
Nature Science Center
North Carolina Zoological Park
Professional sports
Bats (Class A Baseball)
Cardinals (USBL Basketball)
Carolina Monarchs (AHL Hockey)
Warthogs (Class A Baseball)
NCAA Division I
North Carolina A & T Aggies (B, F)
University of North Carolina Spartans (B)
Wake Forest Demon Deacons (B, F)
Outdoor Assets
Inland Water Area: 25,600 acres
Federal Protected Areas
Guilford Courthouse NMP, 220 acres
Uwharrie NF, 10,137 acres
State Recreation Areas
Boone's Cave SP, 110 acres
Hanging Rock SP, 5,862 acres
Pilot Mountain SP, 298 acres
Places Rated Score: 50.71 Places Rated Rank: 174

Greenville, NC
Common Denominators
Golf courses: 4 private (72 holes), 4 daily fee (72 holes) **A**
Good restaurants: 1 *, 1 ** **C**
Movie theaters: 4 Chains (12 screens) **B**
Crowd Pleasers
NCAA Division I
East Carolina University Pirates (B, F)
Outdoor Assets
Inland Water Area: 1,920 acres
Places Rated Score: 5.48 Places Rated Rank: 331

Greenville–Spartanburg–Anderson, SC
Common Denominators
Golf courses: 22 private (369 holes), 27 daily fee (459 holes) **A**
Good restaurants: 1 *, 3 **, 3 ***, **C**
Movie theaters: 10 Chains (49 screens), 3 Independent (8 screens) **C**
Crowd Pleasers
Aquariums and Zoos
Greenville Zoo
Professional sports
Braves (Class AA Baseball)
NCAA Division I
Clemson University Tigers (B, F)
Furman University Paladins (B, F)
Wofford College Terriers (F)
Outdoor Assets
Inland Water Area: 46,080 acres
Federal Protected Areas
Cowpens NB, 789 acres
Kings Mountain NMP, 1,416 acres
State Recreation Areas
Caesars Head SP, 7,467 acres
Croft SP, 7,054 acres
Jones Gap SP, 3,346 acres
Keowee Toxaway SP, 1,000 acres
Musgrove Mill SP, 91 acres
Paris Mountain SP, 1,275 acres

Rating

Sadlers Creek SP, 395 acres
Table Rock SP, 3,083 acres
Places Rated Score: 71.71 Places Rated Rank: 100

Hagerstown, MD
Common Denominators
Golf courses: 2 private (27 holes), 1 daily fee (18 holes), 2 municipal (27 holes) **B**
Good restaurants: 2 *, 2 ** **A**
Movie theaters: 4 Chains (16 screens), 1 Independent (1 screen) **AA**
Crowd Pleasers
Professional sports
Suns (Class A Baseball)
Outdoor Assets
Inland Water Area: 5,760 acres
Federal Protected Areas
Antietam NB, 2,393 acres
Appalachian NT, 316 acres
Chesapeake and Ohio Canal NHP, 6,376 acres
Harpers Ferry NHP, 765 acres
State Recreation Areas
Fort Frederick SP, 561 acres
Gathland SP, 117 acres
Greenbrier SP, 1,288 acres
South Mountain SP, 6,087 acres
Washington Monument SP, 147 acres
Places Rated Score: 26.21 Places Rated Rank: 254

Halifax, NS
Common Denominators
Golf courses: 4 private (72 holes), 4 daily fee (72 holes) **C**
Good restaurants: 2 *, 1 **, 1 *** **C**
Movie theaters: 5 Chains (26 screens), 2 Independent (2 screens) **B**
Crowd Pleasers
CIAU
Dalhousie University Tigers (B, H)
St. Mary's University Huskies
Outdoor Assets
Water Area
Atlantic offshore: 55,000 acres
Inland: 39,000 acres
Federal Protected Areas
Musquodoboit Harbour Outer River Estuary, 2,965 acres
Sable Island MBS, 5,807 acres
Provincial Recreation Areas
Clam Harbour Beach PP, 974 acres
Crystal Cresent Beach PP, 452 acres
Eastern Shore Islands WMA, 29,076 acres
Lawrencetown Beach PP, 588 acres
Lewis Lake PP, 371 acres
Martinique Beach Game Sanctuary, 761 acres
Martinique Beach PP, 151 acres
Oakfield PP, 133 acres
Porters Lake PP, 215 acres
Taylors Head PP, 2,014 acres
Waverley Game Sanctuary, 14,075 acres
Places Rated Score: 70.35 Places Rated Rank: 104

Hamilton, ON
Common Denominators
Golf courses: 5 private (81 holes), 4 daily fee (72 holes), 6 municipal (108 holes) **B**
Good restaurants: 1 *, 5 **, 1 *** **C**
Movie theaters: 8 Chains (39 screens), 3 Independent (3 screens) **C**
Crowd Pleasers
Professional sports
Tiger-Cats (CFL Football)
CIAU
McMaster University Marauders
Outdoor Assets
Water Area
Lake Ontario offshore: 12,000 acres

Rating

Inland: 1,200 acres
Places Rated Score: 29.45 Places Rated Rank: 245

Hamilton–Middletown, OH
Common Denominators
Golf courses: 8 private (126 holes), 4 daily fee (54 holes), 6 municipal (108 holes) **A**
Good restaurants: 1 ** **C**
Movie theaters: 6 Chains (12 screens), 3 Independent (8 screens) **C**
Crowd Pleasers
NCAA Division I
Miami University Redskins
Outdoor Assets
Inland Water Area: 1,920 acres
State Recreation Area
Hueston Woods SP, 990 acres

Zoo America Wildlife Park
Professional sports
Bears (AHL Hockey)
Senators (Class AA Baseball)
Outdoor Assets
Inland Water Area: 23,040 acres
Federal Protected Area
Appalachian NT, 5,461 acres
State Recreation Areas
Colonel Denning SP, 273 acres
Fowlers Hollow SP, 104 acres
Kings Gap SP, 1,439 acres
Little Buffalo SP, 830 acres
Memorial Lake SP, 230 acres
Pine Grove Furnace SP, 696 acres
Swatara SP, 1,050 acres
Places Rated Score: 54.91 Places Rated Rank: 158

Hartford, CT
Common Denominators
Golf courses: 18 private (288 holes), 26 daily fee (378 holes), 7 municipal (117 holes) **B**
Good restaurants: 4 *, 8 **, 7 *** **B**
Movie theaters: 12 Chains (81 screens), 5 Independent (6 screens) **C**
Crowd Pleasers
Professional sports
Connecticut Pride (CBA Basketball)
Rock Cats (Class AA Baseball)
Whalers (NHL Hockey)
NCAA Division I
Central Connecticut State Blue Devils (B, F)
University of Hartford Hawks (B)
Outdoor Assets
Water Area
Inland: 25,600 acres
Federal Protected Area
McKinney NWR, 191 acres
State Recreation Areas
Beaver Brook SP, 401 acres
Bolton Notch SP, 70 acres
Brainard Homestead SP, 25 acres
Dart Island SP, 2 acres
Day Pond SP, 180 acres
Devil's Hopyard SP, 860 acres
Dinosaur SP, 70 acres
Gay City SP, 1,569 acres
George D. Seymour SP, 222 acres

Rating

Gillette Castle SP, 184 acres
Haddam Island SP, 14 acres
Haddam Meadows SP, 175 acres
Higganum Reservoir SP, 147 acres
Horseguard SP, 146 acres
Hurd SP, 884 acres
Lamentation Mountain SP, 47 acres
Mansfield Hollow SP, 2,328 acres
Millers Pond SP, 231 acres
Penwood SP, 787 acres
Platt Hill SP, 124 acres
Pomeroy SP, 104 acres
Stratton Brook SP, 148 acres
Sunset Rock SP, 15 acres
Talcott Mountain SP, 557 acres
Tri Mountain SP, 157 acres
Wadsworth Falls SP, 285 acres

(B, F)
Outdoor Assets
Inland Water Area: 3,840 acres
Federal Protected Area
Desoto NF, 50,354 acres
State Recreation Area
Paul Johnson SP, 744 acres
Places Rated Score: 39.43 Places Rated Rank: 216

Hickory–Morganton–Lenoir, NC
Common Denominators
Golf courses: 6 private (90 holes), 13 daily fee (225 holes) **AA**
Good restaurants: 1 ** **C**
Movie theaters: 5 Chains (16 screens), 1 Independent (1 screen) **C**
Crowd Pleasers
Professional sports
Crawdads (Class A Baseball)
Outdoor Assets
Inland Water Area: 17,920 acres
Federal Protected Areas
Blue Ridge NParkway, 964 acres
Pisgah NF, 97,261 acres
State Recreation Area
South Mountain SP, 5,783 acres
Places Rated Score: 58.39 Places Rated Rank: 144

Honolulu, HI
Common Denominators
Golf courses: 16 private (189 holes), 14 daily fee (234 holes), 5 municipal (81 holes) **B**
Movie theaters: 14 Chains (90 screens), 1 Independent (2 screens) **A**
Crowd Pleasers
Aquariums and Zoos
Honolulu Zoo
Waikiki Aquarium
NCAA Division I
University of Hawaii Rainbow Warriors (B, F)
Outdoor Assets
Water Area
Pacific offshore: 96,512 acres
Inland: 12,160 acres
Federal Protected Area
Hawaiian Islands NWR, 1,907 acres
State Recreation Areas
Diamond Head State Monument, 475 acres

Rating

Hanauma Bay Underwater Park, 101 acres
Kaena Point SP, 779 acres
Kahana Valley SP, 5,229 acres
Keaiwa Heiau SRA, 385 acres
Malaekahana SRA, 110 acres
Sacred Falls SP, 1,374 acres
Sand Island SRA, 140 acres
Places Rated Score: 87.48 Places Rated Rank: 46

Houma, LA
Common Denominators
Golf courses: 3 private (45 holes), 3 daily fee (27 holes) **C**
Movie theaters: 3 Chains (10 screens) **C**
Crowd Pleasers
NCAA Division I
Nicholls State University Colonels (B, F)
Outdoor Assets
Water Area
Gulf offshore: 43,008 acres
Inland: 345,600 acres
Federal Protected Area
Jean Lafitte NHP, 5 acres
State Recreation Area
Edward Douglas White SCA, 6 acres
Places Rated Score: 82.88 Places Rated Rank: 61

✓ Houston, TX
Common Denominators
Golf courses: 65 private (1,026 holes), 38 daily fee (594 holes), 10 municipal (180 holes) **C**
Good restaurants: 6 *, 23 **, 19 ***, 2 **** **B**
Movie theaters: 55 Chains (302 screens), 2 Independent (2 screens) **B**
Crowd Pleasers
Aquariums and Zoos
Houston Zoological Gardens
Kipp Aquarium
Professional sports
Aeros (IHL Hockey)
Astros (NL Baseball)
Oilers (NFL Football)
Rockets (NBA Basketball)
NCAA Division I
Prairie View A & M University Panthers (B, F)
Rice University Owls (B, F)
Texas Southern University Tigers (B, F)
University of Houston Cougars (B, F)
Outdoor Assets
Water Area
Gulf offshore: 14,848 acres
Inland: 95,360 acres
Federal Protected Areas
Anahuac NWR, 30,515 acres
Big Thicket NP, 1,474 acres
Sam Houston NF, 47,776 acres
Trinity River NWR, 4,400 acres
State Recreation Areas
Brazos Bend SP, 4,897 acres
Davis Hill SP, 1,735 acres
Lake Houston SP, 4,912 acres
San Jacinto Battleground SHS, 1,005 acres
Places Rated Score: 94.34 Places Rated Rank: 28

Huntington–Ashland, WV–KY–OH
Common Denominators
Golf courses: 5 private (81 holes), 14 daily fee (189 holes) **A**
Good restaurants: 2 **, 1 *** **C**
Movie theaters: 3 Chains (19 screens) **C**
Crowd Pleasers
Professional sports
Blizzard (ECHL Hockey)
NCAA Division I
Marshall University Thundering Herd (B, F)
Outdoor Assets
Inland Water Area: 16,640 acres
Federal Protected Area
Wayne NF, 64,153 acres
State Recreation Areas
Beech Fork SP, 3,981 acres
Carter Caves State Resort Park, 1,350 acres
Grayson Lake SP, 1,222 acres
Greenbo Lake State Resort Park, 3,008 acres
Places Rated Score: 47.78 Places Rated Rank: 185

Huntsville, AL
Common Denominators
Golf courses: 5 private (72 holes), 7 daily fee (117 holes), 2 municipal (36 holes) **A**
Good restaurants: 2 ** **C**
Movie theaters: 5 Chains (43 screens) **AA**
Crowd Pleasers
Professional sports
Stars (Class AA Baseball)
Outdoor Assets
Inland Water Area: 30,080 acres
Federal Protected Area
Wheeler NWR, 5,006 acres
State Recreation Areas
Monte Sano SP, 2,140 acres
Places Rated Score: 54.60 Places Rated Rank: 161

Indianapolis, IN
Common Denominators
Golf courses: 27 private (441 holes), 44 daily fee (666 holes), 16 municipal (234 holes) **A**
Good restaurants: 3 *, 8 **, 3 *** **C**
Movie theaters: 26 Chains (123 screens), 12 Independent (22 screens) **B**
Crowd Pleasers
Aquariums and Zoos
Indianapolis Zoo
Professional sports
Colts (NFL Football)
Ice (IHL Hockey)
Indians (Triple A Baseball)
Pacers (NBA Basketball)
NCAA Division I
Butler University Bulldogs (B, F)
Outdoor Assets
Inland Water Area: 12,160 acres
State Recreation Areas
Fort Harrison SP, 801 acres
Mounds SP, 284 acres
Places Rated Score: 62.04 Places Rated Rank: 131

Iowa City, IA
Common Denominators
Golf courses: 1 private (9 holes), 6 daily fee (63 holes), 1 municipal (18 holes) **AA**
Good restaurants: 2 *, 4 ** **AA**
Movie theaters: 4 Chains (11 screens) **A**
Crowd Pleasers
NCAA Division I
University of Iowa Hawkeyes (B, F)
Outdoor Assets
Inland Water Area: 5,760 acres
State Recreation Area
Lake Macbride SP, 2,180 acres
Places Rated Score: 21.43 Places Rated Rank: 269

Jackson, MI
Common Denominators
Golf courses: 3 private (45 holes), 18 daily fee (270 holes), 2 municipal (36 holes) **AA**
Good restaurants: 2 ** **B**
Movie theaters: 3 Chains (8 screens) **C**
Crowd Pleasers
Aquariums and Zoos
Jackson Zoological Park
Outdoor Assets
Inland Water Area: 10,880 acres

Rating

State Recreation Area
Waterloo SRA, 13,075 acres
Places Rated Score: 48.84 Places Rated Rank: 182

Jackson, MS
Common Denominators
Golf courses: 11 private (171 holes), 5 daily fee (90 holes), 4 municipal (45 holes) **B**
Good restaurants: 1 *, 3 **, 2 *** **B**
Movie theaters: 5 Chains (27 screens), 1 Independent (1 screen) **C**
Crowd Pleasers
Aquariums and Zoos
Jackson Zoological Park
Professional sports
Generals (Class AA Baseball)
NCAA Division I

Golf courses: 2 private (36 holes), 4 daily fee (45 holes) **A**
Good restaurants: 1 * **C**
Movie theaters: 2 Chains (14 screens) **AA**
Outdoor Assets
Inland Water Area: 1,280 acres
State Recreation Area
Pinson Mounds SAP, 1,086 acres
Places Rated Score: 2.80 Places Rated Rank: 345

Jacksonville, FL
Common Denominators
Golf courses: 26 private (441 holes), 19 daily fee (333 holes), 5 municipal (81 holes) **B**
Good restaurants: 17 *, 21 **, 5 ***, 1 **** **AA**
Movie theaters: 18 Chains (100 screens) **A**
Crowd Pleasers
Aquariums and Zoos
Jacksonville Zoological Park
Professional sports
Barracudas (USBL Basketball)
Jaguars (NFL Football)
Lizard Kings (ECHL Hockey)
Suns (Class AA Baseball)
NCAA Division I
Jacksonville University Dolphins (MB)
Outdoor Assets
Water Area
Atlantic offshore: 17,344 acres
Inland: 129,280 acres
Federal Protected Areas
Fort Caroline NMem, 133 acres
Fort Matanzas NM, 228 acres
Timucuan Ecological Historic Peserve, 5,414 acres
State Recreation Areas
Amelia Island SRA, 229 acres
Anastasia SRA, 1,292 acres
Big Talbot Island SP, 1,597 acres
Faver-Dykes SP, 1,450 acres
Fort Clinch SP, 1,153 acres
Fort George Island SHS, 597 acres
Gold Head Branch SP, 2,099 acres
Guana River SP, 2,398 acres
Little Talbot Island SP, 2,633 acres
Places Rated Score: 89.92 Places Rated Rank: 39

Jacksonville, NC
Common Denominators
Golf courses: 3 private (54 holes), 5 daily fee (81 holes) **A**

Rating

Movie theaters: 5 Chains (22 screens) **AA**
Outdoor Assets
Water Area
Atlantic offshore: 5,632 acres
Inland: 33,920 acres
State Recreation Area
Hammocks Beach SP, 892 acres
Places Rated Score: 35.81 Places Rated Rank: 224

Jamestown, NY
Common Denominators
Golf courses: 2 private (36 holes), 14 daily fee (189 holes) **AA**
Good restaurants: 3 **, 1 *** **A**
Movie theaters: 7 Chains (24 screens) **AA**
Crowd Pleasers
Professional sports

Common Denominators
Golf courses: 2 private (36 holes), 9 daily fee (108 holes), 3 municipal (45 holes) **AA**
Good restaurants: 1 ** **C**
Movie theaters: 3 Chains (8 screens), 3 Independent (11 screens) **AA**
Crowd Pleasers
Professional sports
Snappers (Class A Baseball)
Outdoor Assets
Inland Water Area: 3,840 acres
Places Rated Score: 20.00 Places Rated Rank: 279

Jersey City, NJ
Common Denominators
Good restaurants: 1 * **C**
Movie theaters: 4 Chains (26 screens), 5 Independent (16 screens) **B**
Crowd Pleasers
Professional sports
Metro Stars (MLS Soccer)
NCAA Division I
St. Peter's College Peacocks (B, F)
Outdoor Assets
Inland Water Area: 10,240 acres
Federal Protected Area
Statue of Liberty NM, 45 acres
State Recreation Area
Liberty SP, 1,211 acres
Places Rated Score: 20.08 Places Rated Rank: 278

Johnson City–Kingsport–Bristol, TN–VA
Common Denominators
Golf courses: 6 private (108 holes), 9 daily fee (117 holes), 7 municipal (108 holes) **A**
Good restaurants: 4 *, 4 **, 2 *** **B**
Movie theaters: 9 Chains (22 screens), 3 Independent (5 screens) **C**
Crowd Pleasers
Aquariums and Zoos
Bays Mountain Preserve Park
NCAA Division I
East Tennessee State University Buccaneers (B, F)
Outdoor Assets
Inland Water Area: 28,800 acres
Federal Protected Areas
Appalachian NT, 988 acres
Cherokee NF, 194,648 acres

Rating

Jefferson NF, 56,411 acres
State Recreation Areas
Natural Tunnel SP, 649 acres
Roan Mountain SP, 200 acres
Warriors Path SP, 905 acres
Places Rated Score: Places Rated Rank:

Johnstown, PA
Common Denominators
Golf courses: 2 private (36 holes), 17 daily fee (216 holes), 1 municipal (9 holes) **AA**
Good restaurants: 1 *, 3 ** **B**
Movie theaters: 1 Chain (2 screens), 1 Independent (1 screen) **C**
Crowd Pleasers
Professional sports
Chiefs (ECHL Hockey)
NCAA Division I
St. Francis College Red Flash (B, F)
Outdoor Assets
Inland Water Area: 7,040 acres
Federal Protected Areas
Allegheny Portage Railroad NHS, 443 acres
Johnstown Flood NMem, 155 acres
State Recreation Areas
Kooser SP, 250 acres
Laurel Hill SP, 3,935 acres
Laurel Ridge SP, 8,814 acres
Prince Gallitzin SP, 6,249 acres
Places Rated Score: 27.65 Places Rated Rank: 249

Joplin, MO
Common Denominators
Golf courses: 3 private (54 holes), 2 daily fee (27 holes), 3 municipal (54 holes) **A**
Good restaurants: 3 * **C**
Movie theaters: 6 Chains (22 screens) **AA**
Outdoor Assets
Inland Water Area: 1,280 acres
Federal Protected Area
George Washington Carver NM, 210 acres
Places Rated Score: 4.41 Places Rated Rank: 334

Kalamazoo–Battle Creek, MI
Common Denominators
Golf courses: 9 private (153 holes), 27 daily fee (441 holes), 4 municipal (63 holes) **AA**
Good restaurants: 3 *, 3 **, 1 *** **B**
Movie theaters: 11 Chains (45 screens), 1 Independent (1 screen) **A**
Crowd Pleasers
Aquariums and Zoos
Binder Park Zoo
Kalamazoo Nature Center
Professional sports
Battle Cats (Class A Baseball)
Wings (IHL Hockey)
NCAA Division I
Western Michigan University Broncos
Outdoor Assets
Water Area
Lake Michigan offshore: 29,888 acres
Inland: 25,600 acres
State Recreation Areas
Fort Custer SRA, 3,033 acres
Van Buren SP, 326 acres
Places Rated Score: 80.19 Places Rated Rank: 69

Kankakee, IL
Common Denominators
Golf courses: 1 private (18 holes), 5 daily fee (90 holes), 1 municipal (18 holes) **AA**
Good restaurants: 1 * **C**
Movie theaters: 2 Chains (8 screens) **B**
Outdoor Assets
Inland Water Area: 2,560 acres
State Recreation Area
Kankakee River SP, 3,932 acres
Places Rated Score: 10.95 Places Rated Rank: 312

Kansas City, MO–KS
Common Denominators
Golf courses: 27 private (432 holes), 25 daily fee (396 holes), 20 municipal (333 holes) **B**
Good restaurants: 14 *, 27 **, 13 *** **A**
Movie theaters: 31 Chains (187 screens), 4 Independent (4 screens) **A**
Crowd Pleasers
Aquariums and Zoos
Fleming Park Zoo
Kansas City Zoological Gardens
Overland Park Zoo
Professional sports
Blades (IHL Hockey)
Chiefs (NFL Football)
Royals (AL Baseball)
Wiz (MLS Soccer)
NCAA Division I
University of Missouri Kangaroos (B)
Outdoor Assets
Inland Water Area: 50,560 acres
Federal Protected Area
Harry Truman NHS, 7 acres
State Recreation Areas
Battle of Lexington SHS, 106 acres
Confederate Memorial SHS, 192 acres
Hillsdale SP, 2,830 acres
Wallace SP, 502 acres
Watkins Mill SP, 818 acres
Watkins Woolen Mill SHS, 624 acres
Weston Bend SP, 1,133 acres
Places Rated Score: 89.73 Places Rated Rank: 40

Kenosha, WI
Common Denominators
Golf courses: 1 private (18 holes), 5 daily fee (90 holes), 2 municipal (27 holes) **AA**
Good restaurants: 2 **, 1 *** **A**
Movie theaters: 1 Chain (5 screens), 3 Independent (10 screens) **A**
Outdoor Assets
Water Area
Lake Michigan offshore: 30,400 acres
Inland: 3,840 acres
State Recreation Area
Bong SRA, 4,515 acres
Places Rated Score: 48.95 Places Rated Rank: 180

Killeen–Temple, TX
Common Denominators
Golf courses: 4 private (72 holes), 4 daily fee (63 holes), 3 municipal (45 holes) **B**
Good restaurants: 1 *, 2 ** **C**
Movie theaters: 2 Chains (11 screens), 3 Independent (17 screens) **B**
Outdoor Assets
Inland Water Area: 21,120 acres
State Recreation Area
Mother Neff SP, 259 acres
Places Rated Score: 23.01 Places Rated Rank: 263

Kitchener, ON
Common Denominators
Golf courses: 3 private (54 holes), 4 daily fee (63 holes), 3 municipal (54 holes) **B**
Good restaurants: 1 *, 3 **, 5 *** **A**
Movie theaters: 7 Chains (17 screens), 1 Independent (1 screen) **C**
Crowd Pleasers
Aquariums and Zoos
African Lion Safari
CIAU

Rating

University of Waterloo Warriors
Wilfrid Laurier University Golden Hawks
Outdoor Assets
Inland Water Area: 1,200 acres
Provincial Recreation Area
Dumfries Crown Game Preserve, 2,471
Places Rated Score: 10.87 Places Rated Rank: 313

Knoxville, TN
Common Denominators
Golf courses: 9 private (144 holes), 14 daily fee (252 holes), 4 municipal (72 holes) **A**
Good restaurants: 8 *, 14 **, 6 *** **AA**
Movie theaters: 10 Chains (71 screens), 4 Independent (17 screens) **AA**
Crowd Pleasers

State Recreation Areas
Big Ridge SP, 3,642 acres
Norris Dam SP, 2,056 acres
Places Rated Score: 86.95 Places Rated Rank: 50

Kokomo, IN
Common Denominators
Golf courses: 1 private (18 holes), 5 daily fee (72 holes), 1 municipal (18 holes) **AA**
Good restaurants: 1 *, 1 ** **B**
Movie theaters: 2 Chains (13 screens), 1 Independent (1 screen) **AA**
Outdoor Assets
Inland Water Area: 640 acres
Places Rated Score: 4.15 Places Rated Rank: 335

La Crosse, WI–MN
Common Denominators
Golf courses: 1 private (18 holes), 7 daily fee (99 holes), 2 municipal (27 holes) **AA**
Good restaurants: 2 ** **B**
Movie theaters: 3 Chains (13 screens), 3 Independent (3 screens) **AA**
Crowd Pleasers
Aquariums and Zoos
Myrick Park Zoo
Outdoor Assets
Inland Water Area: 23,680 acres
Federal Protected Area
Upper Mississippi NWR, 24,221 acres
State Recreation Areas
Beaver Creek Valley SP, 1,214 acres
Great River State Trail, 270 acres
La Crosse River State Trail, 381 acres
Places Rated Score: 44.83 Places Rated Rank: 202

Lafayette, IN
Common Denominators
Golf courses: 3 private (45 holes), 6 daily fee (99 holes), 1 municipal (18 holes) **AA**
Good restaurants: 1 *** **C**
Movie theaters: 3 Chains (16 screens) **B**
Crowd Pleasers
Aquariums and Zoos
Columbian Park Zoo
NCAA Division I
Purdue University Boilermakers (B, F)
Outdoor Assets

Rating

Inland Water Area: 1,920 acres
Places Rated Score: 7.87 Places Rated Rank: 323

Lafayette, LA
Common Denominators
Golf courses: 4 private (72 holes), 5 daily fee (63 holes), 2 municipal (36 holes) **B**
Good restaurants: 5 *, 5 **, 3 *** **A**
Movie theaters: 7 Chains (22 screens), 1 Independent (4 screens) **C**
Crowd Pleasers
Professional sports
Ice Gators (ECHL Hockey)
NCAA Division I
University of Southwestern Louisiana Ragin' Cajuns (B, F)

Golf courses: 2 private (36 holes), 1 daily fee (18 holes), 2 municipal (36 holes) **B**
Good restaurants: 5 *, 1 **, 2 *** **AA**
Movie theaters: 3 Chains (9 screens) **C**
Crowd Pleasers
NCAA Division I
McNeese State University Cowboys (B, F)
Outdoor Assets
Inland Water Area: 14,720 acres
State Recreation Area
Sam Houston Jones SP, 1,087 acres
Places Rated Score: 16.58 Places Rated Rank: 289

Lakeland–Winter Haven, FL
Common Denominators
Golf courses: 7 private (126 holes), 26 daily fee (441 holes), 4 municipal (63 holes) **AA**
Good restaurants: 3 *, 1 **, 3 *** **B**
Movie theaters: 11 Chains (41 screens) **B**
Crowd Pleasers
Aquariums and Zoos
Cypress Gardens
Professional sports
Tigers (Class A Baseball)
Outdoor Assets
Inland Water Area: 86,400 acres
State Recreation Areas
Lake Arbuckle SP, 2,813 acres
Lake Kissimmee SP, 5,030 acres
Places Rated Score: 79.43 Places Rated Rank: 75

Lancaster, PA
Common Denominators
Golf courses: 6 private (90 holes), 9 daily fee (144 holes), 2 municipal (36 holes) **B**
Good restaurants: 1 *, 5 **, 4 *** **A**
Movie theaters: 7 Chains (18 screens), 3 Independent (3 screens) **C**
Outdoor Assets
Inland Water Area: 22,400 acres
State Recreation Area
Susquehannock SP, 224 acres
Places Rated Score: 35.25 Places Rated Rank: 227

Lansing–East Lansing, MI
Common Denominators
Golf courses: 3 private (45 holes), 26 daily fee (387 holes), 4 municipal (45 holes) **AA**
Good restaurants: 3 *, 1 ** **C**

	Rating
Movie theaters: 4 Chains (26 screens), 2 Independent (5 screens)	A

Crowd Pleasers
Aquariums and Zoos
Potter Park Zoo
NCAA Division I
Michigan State University Spartans
Outdoor Assets
Inland Water Area: 5,120 acres
State Recreation Area
Sleepy Hollow SP, 2,678 acres
Places Rated Score: 34.37 Places Rated Rank: 231

Laredo, TX

Common Denominators	Rating
Golf courses: 1 private (18 holes), 1 municipal (18 holes)	C
Good restaurants: 1 *	C
Movie theaters: 3 Chains (19 screens)	C

Outdoor Assets
Inland Water Area: 12,160 acres
State Recreation Area
Lake Casa Blanca SRA, 742 acres
Places Rated Score: 2.89 Places Rated Rank: 343

Las Cruces, NM

Common Denominators	Rating
Golf courses: 4 private (63 holes), 4 daily fee (63 holes)	B
Good restaurants: 1 *, 2 **, 1 ***	A
Movie theaters: 4 Chains (13 screens)	C

Crowd Pleasers
NCAA Division I
New Mexico State University Aggies (B, F)
Outdoor Assets
Inland Water Area: 4,480 acres
Federal Protected Areas
San Andres NWR, 57,217 acres
White Sands NM, 52,778 acres
State Recreation Area
Leasburg Dam SP, 140 acres
Places Rated Score: 26.29 Places Rated Rank: 253

✓ Las Vegas, NV–AZ

Common Denominators	Rating
Golf courses: 11 private (189 holes), 25 daily fee (405 holes), 6 municipal (108 holes)	B
Good restaurants: 14 *, 9 **, 15 ***, 1 ****	AA
Movie theaters: 11 Chains (77 screens), 2 Independent (2 screens)	C

Crowd Pleasers
Aquariums and Zoos
Zoological Park For The Birds
Professional sports
Stars (Triple A Baseball)
Thunder (IHL Hockey)
NCAA Division I
University of Nevada Runnin' Rebels (B, F)
Outdoor Assets
Inland Water Area: 224,000 acres
Federal Protected Areas
Ashe Meadows NWR, 12,849 acres
Death Valley NM, 107,616 acres
Desert NWR, 828,794 acres
Grand Canyon NP, 517,156 acres
Havasu NWR, 9,382 acres
Humboldt NF, 248,321 acres
Kaibab NF, 5,487 acres
Lake Mead NRA, 1,385,836 acres
Toiyabe NF, 1,560,819 acres
State Recreation Areas
Berlin-Ichthyosaur SP, 1,132 acres
Cattail Cove SP, 480 acres
Floyd Lamb SP, 2,041 acres
Lake Havasu SP, 10,859 acres
Spring Mountain Ranch SP, 17,608 acres
Valley of Fire SP, 34,880 acres
Places Rated Score: 94.74 Places Rated Rank: 26

Lawrence, KS

Common Denominators	Rating
Golf courses: 2 private (36 holes), 3 daily fee (36 holes)	B
Good restaurants: 1 *, 1 ***	A
Movie theaters: 4 Chains (17 screens)	AA

Crowd Pleasers
NCAA Division I
University of Kansas Jayhawks (B, F)
Outdoor Assets
Inland Water Area: 11,520 acres
State Recreation Area
Clinton SP, 1,425 acres
Places Rated Score: 25.58 Places Rated Rank: 255

Lawrence, MA–NH

Common Denominators	Rating
Golf courses: 4 private (63 holes), 11 daily fee (171 holes)	A
Good restaurants: 1 *, 1 **	C
Movie theaters: 4 Chains (13 screens)	C

Crowd Pleasers
NCAA Division I
Merrimack College Warriors (H)
Outdoor Assets
Water Area
Atlantic offshore: 18,752 acres
Inland: 24,320 acres
Federal Protected Area
Parker River NWR, 4,653 acres
State Recreation Areas
Georgetown-Rowley SP, 1,112 acres
Kingston SP, 44 acres
Lawrence Heritage SP, 74 acres
Pawtuckaway SP, 5,500 acres
Places Rated Score: 51.99 Places Rated Rank: 168

Lawton, OK

Common Denominators	Rating
Golf courses: 3 private (54 holes), 1 municipal (18 holes)	C
Good restaurants: 2 **, 1 ***	A
Movie theaters: 3 Chains (13 screens)	A

Outdoor Assets
Inland Water Area: 8,960 acres
Federal Protected Area
Wichita Mountains NWR, 59,019 acres
Places Rated Score: 17.32 Places Rated Rank: 286

Lewiston–Auburn, ME

Common Denominators	Rating
Golf courses: 1 private (18 holes), 4 daily fee (54 holes)	A
Good restaurants: 1 **	C
Movie theaters: 1 Chain (10 screens)	A

Outdoor Assets
Inland Water Area: 17,280 acres
State Recreation Area
Range Ponds SP, 740 acres
Places Rated Score: 17.06 Places Rated Rank: 287

Lexington, KY

Common Denominators	Rating
Golf courses: 12 private (198 holes), 14 daily fee (216 holes), 3 municipal (54 holes)	A
Good restaurants: 8 *, 5 **, 2 ***	A
Movie theaters: 2 Chains (8 screens), 2 Independent (2 screens)	A

Crowd Pleasers
Professional sports
Kentucky Thoroughblades (AHL Hockey)
NCAA Division I
Eastern Kentucky University Colonels (B, F)
University of Kentucky Wildcats (B, F)
Outdoor Assets

Rating

Inland Water Area: 3,840 acres
State Recreation Area
Fort Boonesborough SP, 153 acres
Places Rated Score: 18.83 — Places Rated Rank: 280

Lima, OH
Common Denominators
Golf courses: 3 private (45 holes), 9 daily fee (162 holes) — **AA**
Good restaurants: 1 *, 2 ** — **B**
Movie theaters: 6 Chains (14 screens), 3 Independent (6 screens) — **AA**
Outdoor Assets
Inland Water Area: 1,280 acres
State Recreation Areas
Grand Lake St. Marys SP, 2,802 acres

Folsom Children's Zoo
Pioneer's Prairie Interpretive Museum
NCAA Division I
University of Nebraska Cornhuskers (B, F)
Outdoor Assets
Inland Water Area: 5,120 acres
State Recreation Areas
Bluestem SRA, 742 acres
Branched Oak SRA, 1,180 acres
Conestoga SRA, 486 acres
Olive Creek SRA, 437 acres
Pawnee SRA, 1,804 acres
Stagecoach SRA, 412 acres
Wagon Train SRA, 747 acres
Places Rated Score: 21.61 — Places Rated Rank: 267

Little Rock–North Little Rock, AR
Common Denominators
Golf courses: 15 private (234 holes), 6 daily fee (99 holes), 7 municipal (108 holes) — **B**
Good restaurants: 6 *, 6 **, 1 *** — **B**
Movie theaters: 11 Chains (44 screens) — **B**
Crowd Pleasers
Aquariums and Zoos
Zoo of Arkansas
Professional sports
Arkansas Travelers (Class AA Baseball)
NCAA Division I
University of Arkansas Trojans (MB)
Outdoor Assets
Inland Water Area: 62,080 acres
Federal Protected Area
Ouachita NF, 53,703 acres
State Recreation Areas
Pinnacle Mountain SP, 1,803 acres
Toltec Mounds, 182 acres
Wooly Hollow SP, 399 acres
Places Rated Score: 66.62 — Places Rated Rank: 114

London, ON
Common Denominators
Golf courses: 5 private (90 holes), 5 daily fee (72 holes), 6 municipal (90 holes) — **B**
Good restaurants: 1 *, 4 ** — **C**
Movie theaters: 11 Chains (47 screens), 4 Independent (4 screens) — **A**
Crowd Pleasers
CIAU
University of Western Ontario Mustangs

Rating

Outdoor Assets
Inland Water Area: 6,700 acres
Places Rated Score: 22.18 — Places Rated Rank: 266

✓ Long Island, NY
Common Denominators
Golf courses: 63 private (1,062 holes), 19 daily fee (261 holes), 31 municipal (513 holes) — **B**
Good restaurants: 28 *, 73 **, 30 *** — **AA**
Movie theaters: 18 Chains (82 screens), 12 Independent (32 screens) — **B**
Crowd Pleasers
Professional sports
New York Islanders (NHL Hockey)
Surf (USBL Basketball)
NCAA Division I

State Recreation Areas
Bayard Cutting Arboretum SP, 690 acres
Belmont Lake SP, 459 acres
Bethpage SP, 2,950 acres
Brookhaven SP, 4,274 acres
Caleb Smith SP, 543 acres
Camp Hero SP, 415 acres
Connetoquot River SP, 3,473 acres
Captree SP, 298 acres
Caumsett SP, 1,500 acres
Connetquot River SP, 3,473 acres
Gilgo SP, 1,223 acres
Heckscher SP, 1,657 acres
Hempstead Lake SP, 727 acres
Hither Hills SP, 1,755 acres
Jones Beach SP, 2,413 acres
Massapequa SP, 596 acres
Montauk Downs SP, 171 acres
Montauk Point SP, 861 acres
Napeague SP, 1,364 acres
Orient Beach SP, 363 acres
Planting Fields Arboretum SP, 409 acres
Robert Moses SP, 875 acres
Sunken Meadow SP, 1,266 acres
Wildwood SP, 767 acres
Places Rated Score: 97.93 — Places Rated Rank: 5

Longview–Marshall, TX
Common Denominators
Golf courses: 6 private (72 holes), 7 daily fee (108 holes) — **A**
Good restaurants: 1 *, 1 ** — **C**
Movie theaters: 4 Chains (19 screens), 2 Independent (3 screens) — **A**
Outdoor Assets
Inland Water Area: 14,720 acres
State Recreation Areas
Caddo Lake SP, 7,090 acres
Places Rated Score: 20.58 — Places Rated Rank: 273

✓ Los Angeles–Long Beach, CA
Common Denominators
Golf courses: 32 private (558 holes), 8 daily fee (126 holes), 37 municipal (612 holes) — **C**
Good restaurants: 30 *, 67 **, 38 ***, 5 ****, 1 ***** — **B**
Movie theaters: 120 Chains (550 screens), 13 Independent (15 screens) — **C**
Crowd Pleasers
Aquariums and Zoos

Rating

Mohave Desert Museum
Parnell Park Zoo
The Los Angeles Zoo
Professional sports
Clippers (NBA Basketball)
Dodgers (NL Baseball)
Galaxy (MLS Soccer)
Ice Dogs (IHL Hockey)
Jethawks (Class A Baseball)
Lakers (NBA Basketball)
Los Angeles Kings (NHL Hockey)
NCAA Division I
California State University Forty-Niners (B)
California State University Matadors (B, F)
Loyola Marymount University Lions (B)
Pepperdine University Waves (B)
University of California Bruins (B, F)
University of Southern California Trojans (B, F)
Outdoor Assets
Water Area
Pacific offshore: 41,472 acres
Inland: 28,160 acres
Federal Protected Areas
Angeles NF, 643,572 acres
Los Padres NF, 8,776 acres
Santa Monica Mountains NRA, 10,827 acres
State Recreation Areas
Antelope Valley Poppy SR, 1,745 acres
Castaic Lake SRA, 2,035 acres
Dockweiler SB, 91 acres
Hungry Valley SVRA, 19,000 acres
Kenneth Hahn SRA, 310 acres
Leo Carrillo SB, 2,217 acres
Malibu Creek SP, 6,600 acres
Placerita Canyon SP, 342 acres
Saddleback Butte SP, 2,955 acres
Topanga SP, 9,181 acres
Will Rogers SHP, 186 acres
Places Rated Score: 97.95 Places Rated Rank: 4

Louisville, KY–IN
Common Denominators
Golf courses: 24 private (396 holes), 20 daily fee (279 holes), 9 municipal (135 holes) **B**
Good restaurants: 3 *, 8 **, 5 *** **B**
Movie theaters: 14 Chains (77 screens), 2 Independent (2 screens) **B**
Crowd Pleasers
Aquariums and Zoos
Louisville Zoological Gardens
Professional sports
Redbirds (Triple A Baseball)
River Frogs (ECHL Hockey)
NCAA Division I
University of Louisville Cardinals (B, F)
Outdoor Assets
Inland Water Area: 16,640 acres
State Recreation Areas
Charlestown SP, 1,983 acres
Dream Lake SRA, 1,300 acres
Sawyer SP, 377 acres
Wyandotte Woods SRA, 2,000 acres
Places Rated Score: 43.46 Places Rated Rank: 206

Lowell, MA–NH
Common Denominators
Golf courses: 3 private (36 holes), 6 daily fee (72 holes), 1 municipal (9 holes) **B**
Good restaurants: 1 ** **C**
Movie theaters: 2 Chains (6 screens), 3 Independent (5 screens) **AA**
Crowd Pleasers
Professional sports
Spinners (Class A Baseball)
NCAA Division I
University of Lowell Chiefs (H)

Rating

Outdoor Assets
Inland Water Area: 15,360 acres
Federal Protected Areas
Great Meadows NWR, 3,415 acres
Minute Man NHP, 742 acres
State Recreation Area
Lowell Heritage SP, 35 acres
Places Rated Score: 46.97 Places Rated Rank: 193

Lubbock, TX
Common Denominators
Golf courses: 4 private (63 holes), 2 daily fee (36 holes), 4 municipal (54 holes) **B**
Good restaurants: 2 *, 4 ** **A**
Movie theaters: 7 Chains (34 screens), 1 Independent (1 screen) **AA**
Crowd Pleasers
NCAA Division I
Texas Tech University Red Raiders (B, F)
Outdoor Assets
Inland Water Area: 640 acres
State Recreation Area
Lubbock Lake Landmark SHS, 365 acres
Places Rated Score: 6.07 Places Rated Rank: 327

Lynchburg, VA
Common Denominators
Golf courses: 4 private (63 holes), 7 daily fee (99 holes) **A**
Good restaurants: 1 *, 3 **, 2 *** **A**
Movie theaters: 4 Chains (26 screens) **AA**
Crowd Pleasers
Professional sports
Hillcats (Class A Baseball)
NCAA Division I
Liberty University Flames (B, F)
Outdoor Assets
Inland Water Area: 14,080 acres
Federal Protected Areas
Appalachian NT, 120 acres
Blue Ridge NParkway, 8,678 acres
George Washington NF, 57,728 acres
Jefferson NF, 18,810 acres
State Recreation Area
Smith Mountain Lake SP, 21,506 acres
Places Rated Score: 53.60 Places Rated Rank: 166

Macon, GA
Common Denominators
Golf courses: 7 private (117 holes), 7 daily fee (99 holes), 3 municipal (54 holes) **A**
Good restaurants: 5 **, 1 *** **A**
Movie theaters: 4 Chains (38 screens) **AA**
Crowd Pleasers
Professional sports
Braves (Class A Baseball)
NCAA Division I
Mercer University Bears (B)
Outdoor Assets
Inland Water Area: 8,320 acres
Federal Protected Areas
Bond Swamp NWR, 5,490 acres
Ocmulgee NM, 702 acres
Oconee NF, 16,103 acres
Piedmont NWR, 28,533 acres
State Recreation Area
Jarrell Plantation SHS, 10 acres
Places Rated Score: 47.02 Places Rated Rank: 192

Madison, WI
Common Denominators
Golf courses: 7 private (126 holes), 9 daily fee (144 holes), 4 municipal (63 holes) **A**
Good restaurants: 4 *, 5 **, 2 *** **A**
Movie theaters: 9 Chains (48 screens), 10 Independent (12 screens) **AA**
Crowd Pleasers
Aquariums and Zoos

Rating

Henry Vilas Park Zoo
Professional sports
Monsters (CoHL Hockey)
NCAA Division I
University of Wisconsin Badgers
Outdoor Assets
Inland Water Area: 23,040 acres
State Recreation Areas
Blue Mounds SP, 178 acres
Cross Plains Ice Age SP, 129 acres
Governor Nelson SP, 433 acres
Lake Kegonsa SP, 343 acres
Places Rated Score: 53.72 Places Rated Rank: 164

Manchester, NH
Common Denominators

Clough SP, 2 acres
Places Rated Score: 46.46 Places Rated Rank: 196

Mansfield, OH
Common Denominators
Golf courses: 3 private (54 holes), 9 daily fee (135 holes) — AA
Movie theaters: 4 Chains (17 screens), 2 Independent (2 screens) — A
Outdoor Assets
Inland Water Area: 2,560 acres
State Recreation Areas
Fowler Woods SNA, 133 acres
Malabar Farm SP, 914 acres
Places Rated Score: 8.54 Places Rated Rank: 321

McAllen–Edinburg–Mission, TX
Common Denominators
Golf courses: 3 private (45 holes), 7 daily fee (108 holes), 5 municipal (63 holes) — B
Good restaurants: 3 * — C
Movie theaters: 5 Chains (34 screens) — C
Crowd Pleasers
NCAA Division I
University of Texas, Pan American Broncs (B)
Outdoor Assets
Inland Water Area: 8,960 acres
Federal Protected Areas
Lower Rio Grande Valley NWR, 22,180 acres
Santa Ana NWR, 2,087 acres
State Recreation Area
Bentsen-Rio Grande Valley SP, 588 acres
Places Rated Score: 23.77 Places Rated Rank: 260

Medford–Ashland, OR
Common Denominators
Golf courses: 2 private (27 holes), 5 daily fee (72 holes), 1 municipal (9 holes) — A
Good restaurants: 2 *, 4 **, 1 *** — AA
Movie theaters: 2 Chains (9 screens), 1 Independent (5 screens) — A
Crowd Pleasers
Professional sports
Timberjacks (Class A Baseball)
Outdoor Assets
Inland Water Area: 10,880 acres
Federal Protected Areas
Crater Lake NP, 944 acres
Klamath NF, 26,334 acres

Rating

Rogue River NF, 411,681 acres
Umpqua NF, 10,628 acres
State Recreation Areas
Joseph Stewart SP, 911 acres
Vally of the Rogue SP, 278 acres
Places Rated Score: 47.70 Places Rated Rank: 187

Melbourne–Titusville–Palm Bay, FL
Common Denominators
Golf courses: 7 private (126 holes), 8 daily fee (144 holes), 5 municipal (81 holes) — A
Good restaurants: 3 *, 7 **, 3 *** — A
Movie theaters: 6 Chains (48 screens) — AA
Crowd Pleasers
Aquariums and Zoos
Brevard Zoo

Memphis, TN–AR–MS
Common Denominators
Golf courses: 20 private (324 holes), 9 daily fee (162 holes), 10 municipal (162 holes) — B
Good restaurants: 7 *, 5 **, 5 *** — B
Movie theaters: 14 Chains (77 screens), 3 Independent (33 screens) — A
Crowd Pleasers
Aquariums and Zoos
Memphis Zoo and Aquarium
Professional sports
Chicks (Class AA Baseball)
NCAA Division I
Memphis State University Tigers (B, F)
Outdoor Assets
Inland Water Area: 58,240 acres
Federal Protected Areas
Lower Hatchie NWR, 3,040 acres
Wapanocca NWR, 5,484 acres
State Recreation Areas
Fuller SP, 384 acres
Meeman-Shelby Forest SP, 13,467 acres
Places Rated Score: 76.67 Places Rated Rank: 84

Merced, CA
Common Denominators
Golf courses: 1 private (18 holes), 3 daily fee (45 holes) — C
Good restaurants: 1 *, 1 ** — C
Movie theaters: 3 Chains (13 screens) — C
Crowd Pleasers
Aquariums and Zoos
Applegate Park Zoo
Outdoor Assets
Inland Water Area: 27,520 acres
Federal Protected Areas
Grasslands WMA, 2,464 acres
Kesterson NWR, 10,621 acres
Merced NWR, 4,571 acres
San Luis NWR, 15,322 acres
State Recreation Areas
Great Valley Grasslands SP, 2,826 acres
San Luis Reservoir SRA, 26,026 acres
Places Rated Score: 23.62 Places Rated Rank: 261

✓ Miami, FL
Common Denominators
Golf courses: 8 private (144 holes), 19 daily fee (333 holes), 11 municipal (180 holes) — C

	Rating
Good restaurants: 13 *, 45 **, 25 ***, 3 ****	AA
Movie theaters: 24 Chains (180 screens), 3 Independent (5 screens)	B

Crowd Pleasers
Aquariums and Zoos
Metrozoo-Crandon Park
Miami Seaquarium
Professional sports
Dolphins (NFL Football)
Heat (NBA Basketball)
Marlins (NL Baseball)
NCAA Division I
Florida International University Golden Panthers (B)
University of Miami Hurricanes (B, F)
Outdoor Assets
Water Area
Atlantic offshore: 26,176 acres
Inland: 49,280 acres
Federal Protected Areas
Big Cypress NP, 12,413 acres
Biscayne NP, 169,530 acres
Everglades NP, 469,744 acres
State Recreation Areas
Cape Florida SRA, 406 acres
Oleta River SRA, 853 acres
Places Rated Score: 96.56 Places Rated Rank: 15

Middlesex–Somerset–Hunterdon, NJ
Common Denominators

	Rating
Golf courses: 20 private (342 holes), 8 daily fee (126 holes), 5 municipal (90 holes)	C
Good restaurants: 3 *, 4 **, 3 ***, 1 ****	C
Movie theaters: 17 Chains (57 screens), 6 Independent (18 screens)	B

Crowd Pleasers
NCAA Division I
Rutgers University Scarlet Knights (B, F)
Outdoor Assets
Inland Water Area: 10,240 acres
Federal Protected Area
Morristown NHP, 188 acres
State Recreation Areas
Cheesequake SP, 1,284 acres
D & R Canal SP, 2,620 acres
Pigeon Swamp SP, 1,078 acres
Round Valley SRA, 3,639 acres
Spruce Run SRA, 1,910 acres
Voorhees SP, 626 acres
Places Rated Score: 50.62 Places Rated Rank: 175

✓ Milwaukee–Waukesha, WI
Common Denominators

	Rating
Golf courses: 17 private (288 holes), 31 daily fee (477 holes), 13 municipal (225 holes)	A
Good restaurants: 8 *, 17 **, 11 ***	A
Movie theaters: 25 Chains (132 screens), 29 Independent (47 screens)	A

Crowd Pleasers
Aquariums and Zoos
Milwaukee County Zoological Gardens
Professional sports
Admirals (IHL Hockey)
Brewers (AL Baseball)
Bucks (NBA Basketball)
Packers (NFL Football)
NCAA Division I
Marquette University Warriors (B)
University of Wisconsin Panthers (B)
Outdoor Assets
Water Area
Lake Michigan offshore: 117,056 acres
Inland: 21,120 acres
State Recreation Areas
Glacial Drumlin State Trail, 375 acres
Harrington Beach SP, 636 acres
Pike Lake SP, 678 acres
Places Rated Score: 96.55 Places Rated Rank: 16

✓ Minneapolis–St. Paul, MN–WI
Common Denominators

	Rating
Golf courses: 31 private (522 holes), 73 daily fee (1,161 holes), 29 municipal (477 holes)	A
Good restaurants: 26 *, 29 **, 11 ***	A
Movie theaters: 41 Chains (207 screens), 18 Independent (52 screens)	A

Crowd Pleasers
Aquariums and Zoos
Minnesota Zoo
St. Paul's Como Zoo
Professional sports
Timberwolves (NBA Basketball)
Twins (AL Baseball)
Vikings (NFL Football)
NCAA Division I
University of Minnesota Gophers
Outdoor Assets
Inland Water Area: 192,000 acres
Federal Protected Areas
Lower Saint Croix NS River, 5,595 acres
Minnesota Valley NWR, 5,368 acres
Saint Croix SRiver, 1,906 acres
Sherburne NWR, 29,583 acres
State Recreation Areas
Afton SP, 1,702 acres
Fort Snelling SP, 3,300 acres
Interstate SP, 293 acres
Kinnickinnic SP, 1,242 acres
Lake Maria SP, 1,590 acres
Wild River SP, 6,803 acres
William O'Brien SP, 1,403 acres
Willow River SP, 2,950 acres
Places Rated Score: 96.90 Places Rated Rank: 12

Mobile, AL
Common Denominators

	Rating
Golf courses: 5 private (72 holes), 19 daily fee (306 holes), 4 municipal (72 holes)	AA
Good restaurants: 7 *, 6 **, 4 ***	A
Movie theaters: 6 Chains (40 screens), 1 Independent (1 screen)	B

Crowd Pleasers
Professional sports
Mysticks (ECHL Hockey)
NCAA Division I
University of South Alabama Jaguars (B)
Outdoor Assets
Water Area
Gulf offshore: 45,120 acres
Inland: 87,040 acres
Federal Protected Areas
Bon Secour NWR, 5,893 acres
Grand Bay NWR, 840 acres
State Recreation Area
Gulf SP, 6,150 acres
Places Rated Score: 85.14 Places Rated Rank: 57

Modesto, CA
Common Denominators

	Rating
Golf courses: 3 private (54 holes), 3 municipal (45 holes)	C
Movie theaters: 4 Chains (21 screens)	C

Crowd Pleasers
Professional sports
A's (Class A Baseball)
Outdoor Assets
Inland Water Area: 12,800 acres
Federal Protected Area
San Joaquin River NWR, 1,638 acres
State Recreation Areas
Henry Coe SP, 27,169 acres

Rating

Turlock Lake SRA, 409 acres

Places Rated Score: 15.33 — Places Rated Rank: 294

Monmouth-Ocean, NJ

Common Denominators

Golf courses: 18 private (297 holes), 9 daily fee (153 holes), 7 municipal (126 holes) — **B**

Good restaurants: 1 *, 6 **, 2 *** — **C**

Movie theaters: 18 Chains (90 screens), 2 Independent (5 screens) — **A**

Crowd Pleasers

Aquariums and Zoos

Popcorn Park Zoo

NCAA Division I

Monmouth College Hawks (B, F)

Outdoor Assets

Swan Point SNA, 147 acres

Swimming River SNA, 109 acres

Places Rated Score: 82.79 — Places Rated Rank: 62

Monroe, LA

Common Denominators

Golf courses: 2 private (36 holes), 1 daily fee (9 holes), 2 municipal (27 holes) — **C**

Good restaurants: 1 *, 3 ** — **A**

Movie theaters: 2 Chains (13 screens) — **B**

Crowd Pleasers

Aquariums and Zoos

Louisiana Purchase Zoo

NCAA Division I

Northeast Louisiana University Indians (B, F)

Outdoor Assets

Inland Water Area: 14,080 acres

Federal Protected Area

D'Arbonne NWR, 7,859 acres

Places Rated Score: 20.36 — Places Rated Rank: 275

Montgomery, AL

Common Denominators

Golf courses: 10 private (171 holes), 5 daily fee (81 holes), 1 municipal (18 holes) — **B**

Good restaurants: 2 **, 1 *** — **C**

Movie theaters: 6 Chains (22 screens) — **C**

Crowd Pleasers

Aquariums and Zoos

Montgomery Zoo

NCAA Division I

Alabama State University Hornets (B, F)

Outdoor Assets

Inland Water Area: 34,560 acres

Places Rated Score: 34.31 — Places Rated Rank: 232

Montreal, PQ

Common Denominators

Golf courses: 25 private (414 holes), 20 daily fee (306 holes), 22 municipal (342 holes) — **C**

Good restaurants: 5 *, 6 **, 16 ***, 2 ***** — **C**

Movie theaters: 26 Chains (121 screens), 24 Independent (33 screens) — **C**

Crowd Pleasers

Aquariums and Zoos

Aquarium de Montreal

Insectarium de Montreal

Jardin Zoologique de Montreal

Professional sports

Rating

Alouettes (CFL Football)

Canadiens (NHL Hockey)

Expos (NL Baseball)

CIAU

Concordia University Stingers

McGill University Redmen

Outdoor Assets

Inland Water Area: 8,600 acres

Federal Protected Areas

Ile aux Herons MBS, 1,483 acres

Iles de Contrecoeur NWA, 561 acres

Iles de la Paix MBS, 2,718 acres

Iles de la Paix NWA, 299 acres

Ils St. Ours MBS, 741 acres

Mount St. Hilaire MBS, 2,347 acres

Senneville MBS, 741 acres

NCAA Division I

Ball State University Cardinals (B, F)

Outdoor Assets

Inland Water Area: 1,920 acres

Places Rated Score: 8.98 — Places Rated Rank: 320

Myrtle Beach, SC

Common Denominators

Golf courses: 2 private (36 holes), 59 daily fee (990 holes) — **AA**

Good restaurants: 5 *, 9 **, 1 *** — **AA**

Movie theaters: 5 Chains (23 screens) — **AA**

Crowd Pleasers

NCAA Division I

University of South Carolina Chanticleers (B)

Outdoor Assets

Water Area

Atlantic offshore: 6,976 acres

Inland: 7,680 acres

State Recreation Area

Myrtle Beach SP, 312 acres

Places Rated Score: 79.88 — Places Rated Rank: 72

Naples, FL

Common Denominators

Golf courses: 36 private (630 holes), 9 daily fee (162 holes) — **AA**

Good restaurants: 10 *, 13 **, 10 *** — **AA**

Movie theaters: 2 Chains (16 screens) — **B**

Outdoor Assets

Water Area

Gulf offshore: 12,096 acres

Inland: 58,240 acres

Federal Protected Areas

Big Cypress NP, 410,646 acres

Everglades NP, 39,262 acres

Florida Panther NWR, 22,782 acres

State Recreation Areas

Collier-Seminole SP, 6,423 acres

Delnor-Wiggins Pass SRA, 155 acres

Fakahatchee Strand SNA, 66,367 acres

Places Rated Score: 79.70 — Places Rated Rank: 74

Nashua, NH

Common Denominators

Golf courses: 1 private (18 holes), 8 daily fee (126 holes) — **AA**

Good restaurants: 3 *, 2 ** — **B**

Movie theaters: 3 Chains (10 screens), — **C**

Rating

2 Independent (3 screens)
Outdoor Assets
Inland Water Area: 24,320 acres
State Recreation Areas
Bradford Pines SNA, 5 acres
Hannah Duston SHS, 1 acre
Silver Lake SP, 15 acres
Webster Birthplace SHS, 147 acres
Places Rated Score: 29.72 Places Rated Rank: 243

Nashville, TN
Common Denominators
Golf courses: 19 private (288 holes), 14 daily fee (234 holes), 12 municipal (198 holes) **B**
Good restaurants: 8 *, 12 **, 8 *** **A**
Movie theaters: 7 Chains (37 screens), 2 Independent (2 screens) **AA**
Crowd Pleasers
Professional sports
Sounds (Triple A Baseball)
NCAA Division I
Middle Tennessee State University Blue Raiders (B, F)
Tennessee State University Tigers (B, F)
Vanderbilt University Commodores (B, F)
Outdoor Assets
Inland Water Area: 39,680 acres
Federal Protected Areas
Natchez Trace NParkway, 2,668 acres
Stones River NB, 494 acres
State Recreation Areas
Bledsoe Creek SP, 164 acres
Cedars of Lebanon SP, 832 acres
Long Hunter SP, 2,315 acres
Montgomery Bell SP, 3,782 acres
Radnor Lake SNA, 1,000 acres
Places Rated Score: 75.49 Places Rated Rank: 85

New Bedford, MA
Common Denominators
Golf courses: 2 private (27 holes), 2 daily fee (27 holes), 1 municipal (18 holes) **B**
Good restaurants: 1 ** **C**
Movie theaters: 2 Chains (14 screens), 1 Independent (1 screen) **AA**
Crowd Pleasers
Aquariums and Zoos
Zoo at Buttonwood
Outdoor Assets
Water Area
Atlantic offshore: 6,208 acres
Inland: 24,320 acres
State Recreation Areas
Demarest Lloyd SP, 222 acres
Fort Phoenix SNA, 23 acres
Places Rated Score: 44.29 Places Rated Rank: 205

New Haven–Meriden, CT
Common Denominators
Golf courses: 11 private (180 holes), 5 daily fee (63 holes), 4 municipal (63 holes) **C**
Good restaurants: 4 *, 7 **, 1 *** **A**
Movie theaters: 4 Chains (28 screens), 4 Independent (10 screens) **A**
Crowd Pleasers
Aquariums and Zoos
West Rock Nature Center
Professional sports
Ravens (Class AA Baseball)
NCAA Division I
Yale University Elis
Outdoor Assets
Water Area
Atlantic offshore: 15,104 acres
Inland: 12,800 acres
Federal Protected Area
McKinney NWR, 27 acres
State Recreation Areas
Chatfield Hollow SP, 356 acres
Foster Pond SP, 194 acres
Hammonasset Beach SRA, 919 acres
Qunnipiac SP, 342 acres
Sleeping Giant SP, 1,439 acres
West Peak SP, 177 acres
West Rock Ridge SP, 1,533 acres
Wharton Brook SP, 96 acres
Places Rated Score: 59.90 Places Rated Rank: 140

New London–Norwich, CT–RI
Common Denominators
Golf courses: 6 private (81 holes), 5 daily fee (72 holes), 3 municipal (45 holes) **B**
Good restaurants: 2 *, 6 **, 2 *** **AA**
Movie theaters: 4 Chains (22 screens) **A**
Crowd Pleasers
Aquariums and Zoos
Mohegan Park Zoo
Professional sports
Navigators (Class AA Baseball)
Outdoor Assets
Water Area
Atlantic offshore: 4,480 acres
Inland: 23,040 acres
State Recreation Areas
Bluff Point Coastal Reserve SP, 806 acres
Fort Griswold SHS, 16 acres
Fort Shantok SP, 170 acres
Haley Farm SP, 198 acres
Harkness Memorial SP, 116 acres
Hopemead SP, 60 acres
Hopeville Pond SP, 554 acres
Minnie Island SP, 1 acre
Misquamicut SB, 51 acres
Stoddard Hill SP, 55 acres
Places Rated Score: 47.22 Places Rated Rank: 191

✓ New Orleans, LA
Common Denominators
Golf courses: 15 private (261 holes), 14 daily fee (234 holes), 5 municipal (81 holes) **C**
Good restaurants: 12 *, 22 **, 22 ***, 2 **** **AA**
Movie theaters: 16 Chains (71 screens), 2 Independent (4 screens) **C**
Crowd Pleasers
Aquariums and Zoos
Audubon Zoo
Professional sports
Saints (NFL Football)
Zephyrs (Triple A Baseball)
NCAA Division I
Tulane University of Louisiana Green Wave (B, F)
University of New Orleans Privateers (B)
Outdoor Assets
Water Area
Gulf offshore: 135,232 acres
Inland: 1,173,760 acres
Federal Protected Areas
Bayou Sauvage NWR, 18,000 acres
Bogue Chitto NWR, 27,839 acres
Breton NWR, 9,047 acres
Delta NWR, 45,907 acres
Jean Lafitte NHP, 10,563 acres
State Recreation Areas
Bayou Segnette SP, 580 acres
Fairview-Riverside SP, 99 acres
Fontainebleau SP, 2,809 acres
Fort Pike SCA, 94 acres
Grand Isle East SP, 120 acres
St. Bernard SP, 358 acres
Places Rated Score: 98.60 Places Rated Rank: 2

Rating

New York, NY
Common Denominators
Golf courses: 48 private (828 holes), 6 daily fee (81 holes), 22 municipal (396 holes) — **C**
Good restaurants: 29 *, 145 **, 79 ***, 25 ****, 3 ***** — **AA**
Movie theaters: 49 Chains (187 screens), 29 Independent (77 screens) — **C**
Crowd Pleasers
Aquariums and Zoos
Central Park Children's Zoo
New York Aquarium
New York Zoological Park
Staten Island Zoo
Professional sports
Knicks (NBA Basketball)

Outdoor Assets
Water Area
Atlantic offshore: 6,976 acres
Inland: 97,920 acres
Federal Protected Areas
Appalachian NT, 980 acres
Gateway NRA, 18,733 acres
State Recreation Areas
Appalachian Trail SP, 544 acres
Bear Mountain/Iona SP, 2,533 acres
Blauvelt SP, 590 acres
Clarence Fahnestock SP, 6,799 acres
Clay Pit Pond SP, 258 acres
Fort Montgomery SHS, 150 acres
Franklin D Roosevelt SP, 761 acres
Harriman SP, 23,307 acres
High Tor SP, 565 acres
Hook Mountain SP, 676 acres
Hudson Highlands SP, 4,000 acres
Old Croton Trailway SP, 216 acres
Palisades Parkway SP, 1,839 acres
Rockefeller Preserve SP, 743 acres
Rockland Lake SP, 1,080 acres
Rockwood Hall SP, 151 acres
Tallman Mountain SP, 687 acres

Places Rated Score: 97.30 — Places Rated Rank: 9

Newark, NJ
Common Denominators
Golf courses: 39 private (648 holes), 18 daily fee (243 holes), 15 municipal (252 holes) — **B**
Good restaurants: 5 **, 7 ***, 2 **** — **C**
Movie theaters: 16 Chains (98 screens), 48 Independent (131 screens) — **B**
Crowd Pleasers
Aquariums and Zoos
Turtle Back Zoo
NCAA Division I
Seton Hall University Pirates (B)
Outdoor Assets
Inland Water Area: 23,680 acres
Federal Protected Areas
Appalachian NT, 1,244 acres
Delaware Water Gap NRA, 30,641 acres
Edison NHS, 21 acres
Great Swamp NWR, 7,359 acres
Morristown NHP, 1,495 acres
Wallkill River NWR, 2,071 acres

Rating

State Recreation Areas
Allmuchy SP, 6,966 acres
Cranberry Lake SP, 199 acres
Farney SP, 803 acres
Great Piece Meadow SP, 794 acres
Hacklebarney SP, 873 acres
High Point SP, 14,193 acres
Hopatcong SP, 112 acres
Kittatinny Valley, 1,354 acres
Musconetong SP, 328 acres
Swartswood SP, 1,356 acres
Troy Meadows SNA, 334 acres
Wawayanda SP, 8,968 acres

Places Rated Score: 81.75 — Places Rated Rank: 66

Newburgh, NY–PA

Appalachian NT, 2,677 acres
Delaware Water Gap NRA, 17,383 acres
Wallkill River NWR, 147 acres
State Recreation Areas
Bear Mountain/Iona SP, 2,533 acres
Goose Pond Mountain SP, 1,543 acres
Harriman SP, 23,306 acres
Highland Lakes SP, 3,086 acres
Knox Headquarters SHS, 48 acres
New Windsor SHS, 120 acres
Promised Land SP, 5,700 acres
Storm King SP, 1,874 acres

Places Rated Score: 54.84 — Places Rated Rank: 159

✓ Norfolk–Virginia Beach–Newport News, VA–NC
Common Denominators
Golf courses: 17 private (297 holes), 21 daily fee (351 holes), 13 municipal (216 holes) — **B**
Good restaurants: 18 *, 39 **, 8 *** — **AA**
Movie theaters: 29 Chains (149 screens), 4 Independent (4 screens) — **B**
Crowd Pleasers
Aquariums and Zoos
Bluebird Gap Farm
Lafayette Zoo
Newport News Zoo
Virginia Zoological Park
Professional sports
Hampton Roads Admirals (ECHL Hockey)
Tides (Triple A Baseball)
NCAA Division I
College of William and Mary Tribe (B, F)
Hampton University Pirates (F)
Old Dominion University Monarchs (B)
Outdoor Assets
Water Area
Atlantic offshore: 51,712 acres
Inland: 264,320 acres
Federal Protected Areas
Back Bay NWR, 7,781 acres
Cape Hatteras N Seashore acres
Colonial NHP, 8,842 acres
Currituck NWR, 1,820 acres
Great Dismal Swamp NWR, 82,197 acres
Mackay Island NWR, 7,819 acres
Nansemond NWR, 208 acres
Plum Tree Island NWR, 3,276 acres
State Recreation Areas

Rating

False Cape SP, 4,321 acres
Seashore SP, 2,770 acres
York River SP, 2,505 acres
Places Rated Score: 96.72 Places Rated Rank: 13

Oakland, CA
Common Denominators
Golf courses: 17 private (297 holes), 12 daily fee (198 holes), 11 municipal (189 holes) **C**
Good restaurants: 7 *, 9 **, 8 *** **C**
Movie theaters: 40 Chains (165 screens), 5 Independent (8 screens) **B**
Crowd Pleasers
Aquariums and Zoos
Knowland Park-Oakland Zoo
Walnut Creek Zoo
Professional sports
Athletics (AL Baseball)
Raiders (NFL Football)
Warriors (NBA Basketball)
NCAA Division I
St. Mary's College of California Gaels (WB)
University of California Golden Bears (B, F)
Outdoor Assets
Inland Water Area: 106,240 acres
Federal Protected Areas
John Muir NHS, 335 acres
San Francisco Bay NWR, 12,676 acres
State Recreation Areas
Bethany Reservoir SRA, 608 acres
Franks Tract SRA, 3,515 acres
Lake Del Valle SRA, 3,732 acres
Mount Diablo SP, 20,090 acres
Robert Crown Memorial SB, 132 acres
Places Rated Score: 89.35 Places Rated Rank: 41

Ocala, FL
Common Denominators
Golf courses: 3 private (54 holes), 4 daily fee (63 holes), 3 municipal (45 holes) **A**
Good restaurants: 2 **, 1 *** **B**
Movie theaters: 4 Chains (16 screens), 1 Independent (1 screen) **C**
Outdoor Assets
Inland Water Area: 53,760 acres
Federal Protected Area
Ocala NF, 275,503 acres
State Recreation Areas
Lake Rousseau SRA, 696 acres
Silver River SP, 5,138 acres
Places Rated Score: 56.18 Places Rated Rank: 154

Odessa–Midland, TX
Common Denominators
Golf courses: 6 private (99 holes), 2 daily fee (36 holes), 2 municipal (27 holes) **B**
Good restaurants: 5 *, 2 ** **B**
Movie theaters: 6 Chains (25 screens), 1 Independent (1 screen) **A**
Crowd Pleasers
Professional sports
Angels (Class AA Baseball)
Outdoor Assets
Inland Water Area: 1,920 acres
Places Rated Score: 6.85 Places Rated Rank: 326

Oklahoma City, OK
Common Denominators
Golf courses: 13 private (216 holes), 14 daily fee (216 holes), 12 municipal (216 holes) **B**
Good restaurants: 8 *, 9 **, 8 *** **A**
Movie theaters: 23 Chains (129 screens), 1 Independent (1 screen) **AA**
Crowd Pleasers
Aquariums and Zoos
Aquaticus Aquarium
Oklahoma City Zoo
Professional sports
89ers (Triple A Baseball)
Cavalry (CBA Basketball)
NCAA Division I
University of Oklahoma Sooners (B, F)
Outdoor Assets
Inland Water Area: 35,840 acres
State Recreation Areas
John Miskelley SP, 160 acres
Little River SP, 1,834 acres
Places Rated Score: 74.16 Places Rated Rank: 92

Olympia, WA
Common Denominators
Golf courses: 2 private (36 holes), 4 daily fee (63 holes), 1 municipal (18 holes) **B**
Good restaurants: 1 **, 1 *** **C**
Movie theaters: 3 Chains (16 screens) **B**
Outdoor Assets
Water Area
Puget Sound offshore: 2,180 acres
Inland: 30,080 acres
Federal Protected Areas
Nisqually NWR, 1,983 acres
Snoqualmie NF, 612 acres
State Recreation Areas
Elbow Lake SP, 320 acres
Millersylvania Memorial SP, 843 acres
Nisqually, 140 acres
Tolmie SP, 106 acres
Places Rated Score: 29.89 Places Rated Rank: 242

Omaha, NE–IA
Common Denominators
Golf courses: 12 private (189 holes), 17 daily fee (243 holes), 10 municipal (144 holes) **A**
Good restaurants: 4 *, 9 **, 7 *** **A**
Movie theaters: 16 Chains (72 screens), 1 Independent (2 screens) **A**
Crowd Pleasers
Aquariums and Zoos
Henry Doorly Zoo
Professional sports
Racers (CBA Basketball)
Royals (Triple A Baseball)
NCAA Division I
Creighton University Bluejays (B, F)
Outdoor Assets
Inland Water Area: 20,480 acres
Federal Protected Area
De Soto NWR, 595 acres
State Recreation Areas
Fort Atkinson SHP, 154 acres
Lake Manawa SP, 1,529 acres
Louisville SRA, 142 acres
Mahoney SP, 479 acres
Platte River SP, 413 acres
Schramm Park SRA, 326 acres
Two Rivers SRA, 302 acres
Wilson Island SRA, 577 acres
Places Rated Score: 66.51 Places Rated Rank: 117

Orange County, CA
Common Denominators
Golf courses: 23 private (387 holes), 12 daily fee (216 holes), 8 municipal (144 holes) **C**
Good restaurants: 15 *, 26 **, 12 *** **B**
Movie theaters: 56 Chains (246 screens), 5 Independent (12 screens) **A**
Crowd Pleasers
Aquariums and Zoos
Orange County Zoo
Santa Ana Zoo
Professional sports
Angels (AL Baseball)

Rating

Mighty Ducks (NHL Hockey)
NCAA Division I
California State University Titans (B)
University of California Anteaters (B)
Outdoor Assets
Water Area
Pacific offshore: 9,472 acres
Inland: 6,400 acres
Federal Protected Area
Cleveland NF, 54,343 acres
State Recreation Areas
Chino Hills SP, 3,115 acres
Crystal Cove SP, 2,300 acres
Huntington SB, 164 acres
San Clemente SB, 110 acres
Places Rated Score: 87.28 — Places Rated Rank: 47

Professional sports
Cobras (Class A Baseball)
Cubs (Class AA Baseball)
Magic (NBA Basketball)
Solar Bears (IHL Hockey)
NCAA Division I
University of Central Florida Knights (B, F)
Outdoor Assets
Inland Water Area: 333,440 acres
Federal Protected Areas
Lake Woodruff NWR, 280 acres
Ocala NF, 84,105 acres
State Recreation Areas
Hontoon Island SP, 599 acres
Lake Griffin SRA, 255 acres
Lake Louisa SP, 4,211 acres
Lower Wekiva River SNA, 12,407 acres
Rock Springs Run State Reserve, 13,871 acres
Tosohatchee SNA, 30,349 acres
Wekiwa Springs SP, 7,705 acres
Places Rated Score: 96.12 — Places Rated Rank: 20

Oshawa, ON

Common Denominators
Golf courses: 1 private (18 holes), 2 daily fee (36 holes) — **C**
Movie theaters: 2 Chains (14 screens) — **C**
Outdoor Assets
Water Area
Lake Ontario offshore: 16,500 acres
Inland: 4,500 acres
Provincial Recreation Areas
Darlington PP, 516 acres
Scugog Island Provincial Wildlife Area, 450 acres
Places Rated Score: 14.24 — Places Rated Rank: 298

Ottawa-Hull, ON-PQ

Common Denominators
Golf courses: 12 private (198 holes), 11 daily fee (180 holes), 5 municipal (81 holes) — **B**
Good restaurants: 5 *, 5 **, 2 *** — **C**
Movie theaters: 13 Chains (52 screens), 3 Independent (3 screens) — **C**
Crowd Pleasers
Professional sports
Lynx (Triple A Baseball)
Rough Riders (CFL Football)
Senators (NHL Hockey)
CIAU
Carleton University Ravens

Rating

University of Ottawa Gees Gees
Outdoor Assets
Inland Water Area: 15,000 acres
Federal Protected Areas
Beckett Creek MBS, 247 acres
Ile Carillon MBS, 1,236 acres
Provincial Recreation Area
Carillon PP, 3,501 acres
Fitzroy PP, 457 acres
Rideau River PP, 242 acres
Shirley Bay Crown Game Preserve, 4,569 acres
Places Rated Score: 58.95 — Places Rated Rank: 142

Owensboro, KY

Common Denominators
Golf courses: 2 private (36 holes), 2 daily fee (27 holes), 2 municipal (27 holes) — **A**

holes), 1 municipal (18 holes) — **AA**
Good restaurants: 5 *, 4 ** — **AA**
Movie theaters: 4 Chains (23 screens), 1 Independent (1 screen) — **AA**
Outdoor Assets
Water Area
Gulf offshore: 9,600 acres
Inland: 76,160 acres
State Recreation Area
St. Andrews SRA, 1,268 acres
Places Rated Score: 64.01 — Places Rated Rank: 123

Parkersburg-Marietta, WV-OH

Common Denominators
Golf courses: 2 private (36 holes), 8 daily fee (126 holes) — **AA**
Good restaurants: 1 *, 2 ** — **B**
Movie theaters: 3 Chains (18 screens), 1 Independent (1 screen) — **AA**
Outdoor Assets
Inland Water Area: 9,600 acres
Federal Protected Areas
Ohio River Islands NWR, 45 acres
Wayne NF, 37,891 acres
State Recreation Area
Blennerhassett SHS, 500 acres
Places Rated Score: 36.40 — Places Rated Rank: 223

Pensacola, FL

Common Denominators
Golf courses: 5 private (81 holes), 11 daily fee (189 holes), 1 municipal (18 holes) — **A**
Good restaurants: 7 *, 3 **, 1 *** — **A**
Movie theaters: 5 Chains (20 screens), 2 Independent (8 screens) — **C**
Crowd Pleasers
Professional sports
Knights (ECHL Hockey)
Outdoor Assets
Water Area
Gulf offshore: 9,088 acres
Inland: 138,880 acres
Federal Protected Areas
Choctawhatchee NF, 108 acres
Gulf Islands N Seashore, 25,573 acres
State Recreation Areas
Big Lagoon SRA, 698 acres
Blackwater River SP, 590 acres
Perdido Key SRA, 285 acres
Places Rated Score: 73.89 — Places Rated Rank: 94

	Rating

Peoria–Pekin, IL

Common Denominators

	Rating
Golf courses: 7 private (108 holes), 6 daily fee (90 holes), 7 municipal (126 holes)	A
Good restaurants: 1 *, 1 **, 2 ***	B
Movie theaters: 8 Chains (49 screens), 1 Independent (1 screen)	AA

Crowd Pleasers
- Aquariums and Zoos
  - Glen Oak Zoo
  - Wildlife Prairie Park
- Professional sports
  - Chiefs (Class A Baseball)
  - Rivermen (ECHL Hockey)
  - Rivermen (IHL Hockey)
- NCAA Division I
  - Bradley University Braves (B)

Outdoor Assets
- Inland Water Area: 22,400 acres
- State Recreation Areas
  - Jubilee College SP, 3,500 acres
  - Mackinaw River State Wildlife Area, 1,423 acres
  - Powerton Lake State Fish & Wildlife Area, 1,426 acres
  - Rock Island Trail SP, 392 acres
  - Spring Lake State Fish & Wildlife Area, 2,032 acres
  - Woodford State Fish & Wildlife Area, 2,901 acres

Places Rated Score: 57.40 Places Rated Rank: 149

✓ Philadelphia, PA–NJ

Common Denominators

	Rating
Golf courses: 82 private (1,350 holes), 56 daily fee (918 holes), 13 municipal (234 holes)	C
Good restaurants: 11 *, 44 **, 39 ***, 1 ****, 1 *****	A
Movie theaters: 44 Chains (244 screens), 26 Independent (64 screens)	C

Crowd Pleasers
- Aquariums and Zoos
  - Philadelphia Zoological Garden
  - Thomas Kean State Aquarium
- Professional sports
  - 76ers (NBA Basketball)
  - Eagles (NFL Football)
  - Flyers (NHL Hockey)
  - Phantoms (AHL Hockey)
  - Phillies (NL Baseball)
- NCAA Division I
  - Drexel University Dragons (B)
  - La Salle University Explorers (B)
  - St. Joseph's University Hawks (B)
  - Temple University Owls (B, F)
  - University of Pennsylvania Quakers (B, F)
  - Villanova University Wildcats

Outdoor Assets
- Water Area
  - Atlantic offshore: 1,536 acres
  - Inland: 51,200 acres
- Federal Protected Areas
  - Edwin Forsythe NWR, 2,372 acres
  - Hopewell Furnace NHS, 320 acres
  - John Heinz NWR, 919 acres
  - Supawna Meadows NWR, 2,855 acres
  - Valley Forge NHP, 3,001 acres
- State Recreation Areas
  - Benjamin Rush SP, 275 acres
  - Delaware Canal SP, 487 acres
  - Evansburg SP, 3,349 acres
  - Fort Mott SP, 104 acres
  - Fort Washington SP, 493 acres
  - French Creek SP, 875 acres
  - Marsh Creek SP, 1,705 acres
  - Neshaminy SP, 336 acres
  - Nockamixon SP, 5,283 acres
  - Parvin SP, 1,135 acres
  - Rancocas SP, 1,252 acres
  - Ridley Creek SP, 2,607 acres
  - Tyler SP, 1,711 acres
  - Warren Grove SRA, 617 acres
  - White Clay Creek SP, 1,254 acres

Places Rated Score: 90.98 Places Rated Rank: 34

✓ Phoenix–Mesa, AZ

Common Denominators

	Rating
Golf courses: 39 private (693 holes), 81 daily fee (1,350 holes), 13 municipal (225 holes)	A
Good restaurants: 20 *, 44 **, 19 ***, 6 ****	AA
Movie theaters: 52 Chains (270 screens), 3 Independent (5 screens)	A

Crowd Pleasers
- Aquariums and Zoos
  - Phoenix Zoo
- Professional sports
  - Cardinals (NFL Football)
  - Coyotes (NHL Hockey)
  - Firebirds (Triple A Baseball)
  - Roadrunners (IHL Hockey)
  - Suns (NBA Basketball)
- NCAA Division I
  - Arizona State University Sun Devils (B, F)

Outdoor Assets
- Inland Water Area: 16,000 acres
- Federal Protected Areas
  - Casa Grande NM, 472 acres
  - Coronado NF, 23,312 acres
  - Hohokam Pima NM, 1acres
  - Tonto NF, 857,509 acres
- State Recreation Areas
  - Lost Dutchman SP, 292 acres
  - Oracle WR, 4,000 acres
  - Pichaco Peak SP, 3,440 acres

Places Rated Score: 95.28 Places Rated Rank: 24

Pine Bluff, AR

Common Denominators

	Rating
Golf courses: 2 private (36 holes), 1 daily fee (9 holes), 2 municipal (27 holes)	B
Good restaurants: 1 *	C
Movie theaters: 3 Chains (6 screens)	C

Outdoor Assets
- Inland Water Area: 18,560 acres

Places Rated Score: 11.02 Places Rated Rank: 311

Pittsburgh, PA

Common Denominators

	Rating
Golf courses: 56 private (909 holes), 82 daily fee (1,251 holes), 5 municipal (72 holes)	A
Good restaurants: 1 *, 14 **, 18 ***	B
Movie theaters: 42 Chains (170 screens), 11 Independent (16 screens)	C

Crowd Pleasers
- Aquariums and Zoos
  - Pittsburgh Aviary
  - The Pittsburgh Zoo
- Professional sports
  - Penguins (NHL Hockey)
  - Pirates (NL Baseball)
  - Steelers (NFL Football)
- NCAA Division I
  - Duquesne University Dukes (B, F)
  - Robert Morris College Colonials (B, F)
  - University of Pittsburgh Panthers (B, F)

Outdoor Assets
- Inland Water Area: 35,840 acres
- Federal Protected Areas
  - Fort Necessity NB, 894 acres
  - Friendship Hill NHS, 661 acres
  - Ohio River Islands NWR, 55 acres
- State Recreation Areas
  - Hillman SP, 3,654 acres
  - Jennings SP, 297 acres
  - Keystone SP, 1,187 acres
  - Laurel Mountain SP, 493 acres
  - Laurel Ridge SP, 5,886 acres
  - Linn Run SP, 613 acres

Rating

Moraine SP, 16,132 acres
Ohiopyle SP, 18,719 acres
Raccoon Creek SP, 7,572 acres
Places Rated Score: 90.21 Places Rated Rank: 38

Pittsfield, MA

Common Denominators
Golf courses: 3 private (54 holes), 7 daily fee (90 holes) **AA**
Good restaurants: 3 *, 12 **, 5 ***, 1 **** **AA**
Movie theaters: 3 Chains (10 screens) **AA**
Crowd Pleasers
Professional sports
Mets (Class A Baseball)
Outdoor Assets
Inland Water Area: 9,600 acres
Federal Protected Area

Golf courses: 5 private (90 holes), 10 daily fee (126 holes), 3 municipal (36 holes) **AA**
Good restaurants: 6 *, 9 **, 2 *** **AA**
Movie theaters: 4 Chains (26 screens), 1 Independent (1 screen) **AA**
Crowd Pleasers
Professional sports
Mountain Cats (USBL Basketball)
Pirates (AHL Hockey)
Sea Dogs (Class AA Baseball)
Outdoor Assets
Water Area
Atlantic offshore: 12,096 acres
Inland: 122,880 acres
Federal Protected Area
Rachel Carson NWR, 186 acres
State Recreation Areas
Crescent Beach SP, 244 acres
Scarboro Beach SP, 5 acres
Sebago Lake SP, 1,342 acres
Two Lights SP, 41 acres
Wolfe's Neck Woods SP, 244 acres
Places Rated Score: 79.14 Places Rated Rank: 79

Portland–Vancouver, OR–WA

Common Denominators
Golf courses: 16 private (288 holes), 31 daily fee (423 holes), 7 municipal (117 holes) **B**
Good restaurants: 7 *, 18 **, 12 *** **A**
Movie theaters: 32 Chains (91 screens), 19 Independent (29 screens) **C**
Crowd Pleasers
Aquariums and Zoos
Metro Washington Park Zoo
Professional sports
Rockies (Class A Baseball)
Trail Blazers (NBA Basketball)
NCAA Division I
University of Portland Pilots (WB)
Outdoor Assets
Inland Water Area: 68,480 acres
Federal Protected Areas
Fort Vancouver NHS, 202 acres
Gifford Pinchot NF, 1,180 acres
Mt. Hood NF, 616,483 acres
Ridgefield NWR, 5,150 acres
Siuslaw NF, 25,500 acres
Steigerwald Lake NWR, 627 acres
Tualatin River NWR, 170 acres

Rating

Willamette NF, 856 acres
State Recreation Areas
Ainsworth SP, 156 acres
Battle Ground Lake SP, 280 acres
Benson SP, 272 acres
Bonnie Lure SP, 94 acres
Crown Point SP, 307 acres
Dabney SP, 135 acres
George Joseph SP, 150 acres
Guy Talbot SP, 378 acres
John Yeon SP, 284 acres
Mary Young SP, 133 acres
McLoughlin SP, 216 acres
Milo McIver SP, 952 acres
Molalla River SP, 567 acres
Paradise Point SP, 92 acres

Portsmouth–Rochester, NH–ME

Common Denominators
Golf courses: 4 private (63 holes), 10 daily fee (135 holes) **A**
Good restaurants: 5 *, 7 **, 2 *** **AA**
Movie theaters: 7 Chains (20 screens), 1 Independent (6 screens) **AA**
Crowd Pleasers
NCAA Division I
University of New Hampshire Wildcats
Outdoor Assets
Water Area
Atlantic offshore: 4,352 acres
Inland: 29,440 acres
Federal Protected Area
Great Bay NWR, 1,054 acres
State Recreation Areas
Fort Constitution SHS, 2 acres
Fort McClary SHS, 27 acres
Fort Stark SHS, 10 acres
Hampton Beach SP, 50 acres
Jenness Beach SB, 1 acre
John Paul Jones SHS, 2 acres
North Hampton SB, 3 acres
Odiorne Point SP, 370 acres
Portsmouth Fish Pier SRA, 3 acres
Rye Harbor SP, 63 acres
Vaughn Woods SHS, 165 acres
Wallis Sands SB, 9 acres
Wentworth-Coolidge SHS, 64 acres
Places Rated Score: 53.99 Places Rated Rank: 163

Providence–Fall River–Warwick, RI–MA

Common Denominators
Golf courses: 19 private (297 holes), 23 daily fee (279 holes), 5 municipal (63 holes) **B**
Good restaurants: 2 *, 10 **, 3 *** **B**
Movie theaters: 11 Chains (62 screens), 6 Independent (10 screens) **C**
Crowd Pleasers
Aquariums and Zoos
Capron Park Zoo
Roger Williams Park Zoo
Slater Memorial Park
Professional sports
Bruins (AHL Hockey)
Red Sox (Triple A Baseball)
NCAA Division I
Brown University Bears

Rating

Providence College Friars (B, H)
University of Rhode Island Rams (B, F)
Outdoor Assets
Water Area
Atlantic offshore: 12,480 acres
Inland: 61,440 acres
Federal Protected Areas
Block Island NWR, 48 acres
Ninigret NWR, 407 acres
Pettaquamscutt Cove NWR, 159 acres
Trustom Pond NWR, 642 acres
State Recreation Areas
Beavertail SP, 153 acres
Burlingame SP, 2,100 acres
Charlestown Beachway SB, 62 acres
Colt SP, 464 acres
Diamond Hill SP, 373 acres
East Beach SB, 174 acres
Fall River Heritage SP, 9 acres
Fishermen's Memorial SP, 91 acres
Fort Wetherill SP, 100 acres
Goddard Memorial SP, 489 acres
Haines Memorial SP, 102 acres
Lincoln Woods SP, 627 acres
Salty Brine SB, 1 acre
Scarborough SB, 42 acres
Wheeler SB, 27 acres
World War II Memorial SP, 14 acres
Places Rated Score: 79.17 Places Rated Rank: 78

Provo–Orem, UT
Common Denominators
Golf courses: 2 private (36 holes), 1 daily fee (9 holes), 5 municipal (90 holes) **B**
Good restaurants: 2 * **C**
Movie theaters: 5 Chains (21 screens), 8 Independent (9 screens) **B**
Crowd Pleasers
NCAA Division I
Brigham Young University Cougars (B, F)
Outdoor Assets
Inland Water Area: 91,520 acres
Federal Protected Areas
Ashley NF, 3,797 acres
Manti-La Sal NF, 91,293 acres
Timpanogos Cave NM, 250 acres
Uinta NF, 392,055 acres
State Recreation Areas
Utah Lake SP, 308 acres
Places Rated Score: 79.43 Places Rated Rank: 75

Pueblo, CO
Common Denominators
Golf courses: 1 private (18 holes), 1 daily fee (18 holes), 4 municipal (63 holes) **A**
Good restaurants: 2 *, 1 **, 1 *** **A**
Movie theaters: 3 Chains (5 screens) **C**
Crowd Pleasers
Aquariums and Zoos
Pueblo Zoo
Outdoor Assets
Inland Water Area: 5,760 acres
Federal Protected Area
San Isabel NF, 32,761 acres
State Recreation Areas
Pueblo SRA, 9,045 acres
Places Rated Score: 15.76 Places Rated Rank: 291

Punta Gorda, FL
Common Denominators
Golf courses: 2 private (36 holes), 8 daily fee (144 holes) **AA**
Good restaurants: 2 * **C**
Movie theaters: 2 Chains (12 screens) **C**
Crowd Pleasers

Rating

Professional sports
Rangers (Class A Baseball)
Outdoor Assets
Water Area
Gulf offshore: 2,752 acres
Inland: 78,080 acres
Federal Protected Area
Island Bay NWR, 20 acres
State Recreation Areas
Don Pedro Island SRA, 133 acres
Port Charlotte Beach SRA, 213 acres
Places Rated Score: 61.02 Places Rated Rank: 136

Quebec City, PQ
Common Denominators
Golf courses: 2 private (36 holes), 10 daily fee (153 holes), 2 municipal (36 holes) **B**
Good restaurants: 4 *, 8 **, 8 *** **A**
Movie theaters: 5 Chains (22 screens), 2 Independent (3 screens) **C**
Crowd Pleasers
Aquariums and Zoos
Aquarium du Quebec
Jardin Zoologique de Quebec
CIAU
Universite Laval Rouge Et Or (B, H)
Outdoor Assets
Inland Water Area: 63,000 acres
Federal Protected Areas
Cap Tourmente NWA, 5,510 acres
St-Vallier MBS, 988 acres
Provincial Recreation Area
Jacques Cartier PP, 165,705 acres
Laurentides Wildlife Sanctuary, 1,967,163 acres
Riviere Sainte-Anne Wildlife Sanctuary, 988 acres
Places Rated Score: 69.09 Places Rated Rank: 110

Racine, WI
Common Denominators
Golf courses: 2 private (36 holes), 2 daily fee (36 holes), 9 municipal (126 holes) **AA**
Good restaurants: 3 *, 3 ** **A**
Movie theaters: 2 Chains (11 screens), 1 Independent (1 screen) **C**
Crowd Pleasers
Aquariums and Zoos
Racine Zoo
Outdoor Assets
Water Area
Lake Michigan offshore: 28,928 acres
Inland: 4,480 acres
Places Rated Score: 47.70 Places Rated Rank: 187

Raleigh–Durham–Chapel Hill, NC
Common Denominators
Golf courses: 20 private (324 holes), 28 daily fee (468 holes) **B**
Good restaurants: 10 *, 10 **, 3 *** **B**
Movie theaters: 18 Chains (84 screens), 2 Independent (4 screens) **B**
Crowd Pleasers
Professional sports
Bulls (Class A Baseball)
Icecaps (ECHL Hockey)
Mudcats (Class AA Baseball)
NCAA Division I
Duke University Blue Devils (B, F)
North Carolina State University Wolfpack (B, F)
University of North Carolina Tarheels (B, F)
Outdoor Assets
Inland Water Area: 41,600 acres
State Recreation Areas
Eno River SP, 1,965 acres
Falls Lake SRA, 1,100 acres
Jordan Lake SRA, 1,475 acres
Umstead SP, 5,334 acres
Places Rated Score: 56.27 Places Rated Rank: 153

Rating

Rapid City, SD
Common Denominators
Golf courses: 2 private (36 holes), 2 daily fee (27 holes), 2 municipal (27 holes) — **A**
Good restaurants: 4 *, 1 ** — **AA**
Movie theaters: 3 Chains (14 screens), 1 Independent (1 screen) — **AA**
Crowd Pleasers
Aquariums and Zoos
Bear Country USA
Professional sports
Black Hills Posse (IBA Basketball)
Outdoor Assets
Inland Water Area: 5,120 acres
Federal Protected Areas
Badlands NP, 94,755 acres

Professional sports
Phillies (Class AA Baseball)
Outdoor Assets
Inland Water Area: 3,840 acres
Federal Protected Areas
Appalachian NT, 1,380 acres
Hopewell Furnace NHS, 528 acres
State Recreation Areas
French Creek SP, 6,470 acres
Nolde Forest SP, 666 acres
Places Rated Score: 33.78 — **Places Rated Rank: 234**

Redding, CA
Common Denominators
Golf courses: 3 private (45 holes), 5 daily fee (63 holes) — **B**
Movie theaters: 4 Chains (26 screens), 1 Independent (1 screen) — **AA**
Outdoor Assets
Inland Water Area: 39,680 acres
Federal Protected Areas
Lassen NF, 248,007 acres
Lassen Volcanic NP, 66,862 acres
Shasta NF, 470,018 acres
Trinity NF, 30,626 acres
Whiskeytown-Shasta-Trinity NRA, 42,459 acres
State Recreation Areas
Ahjumawi Lava Springs SP, 6,000 acres
Castle Crags SP, 4,350 acres
McArthur-Burney Falls Memorial SP, 850 acres
Places Rated Score: 50.35 — **Places Rated Rank: 176**

Regina, SK
Common Denominators
Golf courses: 1 private (18 holes), 2 daily fee (27 holes), 10 municipal (135 holes) — **AA**
Movie theaters: 2 Chains (10 screens), 2 Independent (2 screens) — **C**
Crowd Pleasers
Professional sports
Roughriders (CFL Football)
CIAU
University of Regina Cougars (B, H)
Outdoor Assets
Inland Water Area: 32,000 acres
Federal Protected Areas
Wascana Lake MBS, 321 acres
Provincial Recreation Areas
Condie Nature Refuge, 719 acres
Echo Valley PP, 1,594 acres
Mclean, 131 acres
Rowan's Ravine PP, 672 acres
Valeport, 148 acres
Valley Centre, 200 acres
Wascana Trails, 324 acres
White Butte Trails, 1,065 acres
Places Rated Score: 46.24 — **Places Rated Rank: 198**

Reno, NV
Common Denominators
Golf courses: 1 private (18 holes), 4 daily fee (63 holes), 5 municipal (81 holes) — **A**
Good restaurants: 2 *, 5 **, 2 *** — **A**
Movie theaters: 5 Chains (24 screens) — **B**
Crowd Pleasers

Places Rated Score: 74.22 — **Places Rated Rank: 91**

Richland-Kennewick-Pasco, WA
Common Denominators
Golf courses: 1 private (18 holes), 3 daily fee (54 holes), 2 municipal (36 holes) — **A**
Good restaurants: 2 *, 2 ** — **B**
Movie theaters: 4 Chains (8 screens), 1 Independent (1 screen) — **C**
Outdoor Assets
Inland Water Area: 51,200 acres
Federal Protected Area
Umatilla NWR, 1,466 acres
State Recreation Areas
Crow Butte SP, 1,312 acres
Lyons Ferry SP, 1,150 acres
Palouse Falls SP, 83 acres
Pasco/Fish Lake Trail, 680 acres
Potholes SP, 3,737 acres
Sacajawea SP, 284 acres
Places Rated Score: 34.46 — **Places Rated Rank: 230**

Richmond-Petersburg, VA
Common Denominators
Golf courses: 17 private (306 holes), 14 daily fee (243 holes), 1 municipal (18 holes) — **B**
Good restaurants: 9 *, 9 **, 5 *** — **A**
Movie theaters: 15 Chains (68 screens), 2 Independent (2 screens) — **B**
Crowd Pleasers
Aquariums and Zoos
Maymont
Professional sports
Braves (Triple A Baseball)
Renegades (ECHL Hockey)
NCAA Division I
University of Richmond Spiders (B, F)
Virginia Commonwealth University Rams (B)
Outdoor Assets
Inland Water Area: 52,480 acres
Federal Protected Areas
James River NWR, 4,147 acres
Petersburg NB, 1,538 acres
Presquile NWR, 1,329 acres
Richmond NBP, 766 acres
State Recreation Area
Pocahontas SP, 7,778 acres
Places Rated Score: 74.90 — **Places Rated Rank: 88**

	Rating

✓ Riverside–San Bernardino, CA

Common Denominators
- Golf courses: 62 private (1,017 holes), 60 daily fee (999 holes), 12 municipal (189 holes) — **B**
- Good restaurants: 14 *, 28 **, 13 *** — **B**
- Movie theaters: 37 Chains (229 screens), 5 Independent (12 screens) — **B**

Crowd Pleasers
- Aquariums and Zoos
  - Hi-Desert Nature Museum
  - Moonridge Zoo
  - The Living Desert
- Professional sports
  - Mavericks (Class A Baseball)
  - Quakes (Class A Baseball)
  - Stampede (Class A Baseball)
  - Storm (Class A Baseball)

Outdoor Assets
- Inland Water Area: 90,240 acres
- Federal Protected Areas
  - Angeles NF, 10,656 acres
  - Cleveland NF, 78,293 acres
  - Coachella Valley NWR, 3,536 acres
  - Death Valley NP, 81,152 acres
  - Joshua Tree NM, 708,109 acres
  - Joshua Tree NP, 74,426 acres
  - Mojave Desert NP, 1,450,000 acres
  - San Bernardino NF, 670,381 acres
- State Recreation Areas
  - Anza-Borrego Desert SP, 35,177 acres
  - California Citrus SHP, 400 acres
  - Chino Hills SP, 7,071 acres
  - Lake Elsinore SRA, 2,976 acres
  - Lake Perris SRA, 8,800 acres
  - Mount San Jacinto SP, 13,522 acres
  - Providence Mountains SRA, 5,250 acres
  - Salton Sea SRA, 9,400 acres
  - Silverwood Lake SRA, 2,400 acres

Places Rated Score: 96.93 — Places Rated Rank: 11

Roanoke, VA

Common Denominators
- Golf courses: 5 private (81 holes), 6 daily fee (99 holes), 1 municipal (9 holes) — **A**
- Good restaurants: 1 *, 5 **, 2 *** — **AA**
- Movie theaters: 5 Chains (22 screens) — **B**

Crowd Pleasers
- Aquariums and Zoos
  - Mill Mountain Zoo
- Professional sports
  - Avalanche (Class A Baseball)
  - Express (ECHL Hockey)

Outdoor Assets
- Inland Water Area: 1,920 acres
- Federal Protected Areas
  - Appalachian NT, 3,597 acres
  - Blue Ridge N Parkway, 5,683 acres
  - George Washington NF, 13,032 acres
  - Jefferson NF, 68,514 acres

Places Rated Score: 51.28 — Places Rated Rank: 170

Rochester, MN

Common Denominators
- Golf courses: 1 private (18 holes), 3 daily fee (54 holes), 1 municipal (18 holes) — **A**
- Good restaurants: 3 *, 3 **, 1 *** — **AA**
- Movie theaters: 4 Chains (19 screens) — **AA**

Outdoor Assets
- Inland Water Area: 640 acres

Places Rated Score: 3.84 — Places Rated Rank: 337

✓ Rochester, NY

Common Denominators
- Golf courses: 21 private (351 holes), 50 daily fee (810 holes), 6 municipal (90 holes) — **AA**
- Good restaurants: 10 *, 10 **, 13 *** — **A**
- Movie theaters: 17 Chains (97 screens), 5 Independent (9 screens) — **C**

Crowd Pleasers
- Aquariums and Zoos
  - Seneca Park Zoo
- Professional sports
  - Americans (AHL Hockey)
  - Clippers (Class A Baseball)
  - Red Wings (Triple A Baseball)

Outdoor Assets
- Water Area
  - Lake Ontario offshore: 121,344 acres
  - Inland: 28,800 acres
- Federal Protected Area
  - Iroquois NWR, 10,819 acres
- State Recreation Areas
  - Chimney Bluffs SP, 597 acres
  - Darien Lakes SP, 1,845 acres
  - Ganondagan SHS, 245 acres
  - Hamlin Beach SP, 1,224 acres
  - Harriet Spencer SP, 678 acres
  - Lakeside Beach SP, 734 acres
  - Letchworth SP, 10,000 acres
  - Old Erie Canal SP, 300 acres

Places Rated Score: 95.98 — Places Rated Rank: 21

Rockford, IL

Common Denominators
- Golf courses: 6 private (99 holes), 4 daily fee (54 holes), 8 municipal (135 holes) — **A**
- Good restaurants: 2 *, 1 **, 1 *** — **C**
- Movie theaters: 8 Chains (34 screens) — **B**

Crowd Pleasers
- Professional sports
  - Cubbies (Class A Baseball)
  - Lightning (CBA Basketball)

Outdoor Assets
- Inland Water Area: 6,400 acres
- State Recreation Areas
  - Castle Rock SP, 1,995 acres
  - Franklin Creek SP, 520 acres
  - Lowden SP, 207 acres
  - Lowden-Miller State Forest, 2,234 acres
  - Rock Cut SP, 3,092 acres
  - White Pines Forest SP, 385 acres

Places Rated Score: 30.39 — Places Rated Rank: 240

Rocky Mount, NC

Common Denominators
- Golf courses: 3 private (45 holes), 3 daily fee (45 holes) — **B**
- Movie theaters: 4 Chains (11 screens) — **C**

Outdoor Assets
- Inland Water Area: 2,560 acres

Places Rated Score: 1.20 — Places Rated Rank: 348

Sacramento, CA

Common Denominators
- Golf courses: 12 private (207 holes), 13 daily fee (189 holes), 9 municipal (153 holes) — **C**
- Good restaurants: 6 *, 12 **, 6 *** — **B**
- Movie theaters: 17 Chains (79 screens), 3 Independent (3 screens) — **C**

Crowd Pleasers
- Aquariums and Zoos
  - Folsom Zoo
  - Roseville City Zoo
  - Sacramento City Zoo
- Professional sports
  - Kings (NBA Basketball)
- NCAA Division I
  - California State University Hornets (B, F)

Outdoor Assets
- Inland Water Area: 131,840 acres
- Federal Protected Areas
  - Eldorado NF, 545,411 acres
  - Tahoe NF, 275,894 acres

Rating

Toiyabe NF, 31 acres
State Recreation Areas
Auburn SRA, 42,000 acres
Bliss SP, 1,237 acres
Brannan Island SRA, 336 acres
Burton Creek SP, 1,981 acres
Emerald Bay SP, 593 acres
Folsom Lake SRA, 17,718 acres
Lake Valley SRA, 150 acres
Marshall Gold Discovery SHP, 280 acres
Prairie City SVRA, 836 acres
Sugar Pine Point SP, 2,011 acres
Washoe Meadows SP, 620 acres

Places Rated Score: 87.06 — Places Rated Rank: 49

Saginaw–Bay City–Midland, MI

Common Denominators

Water Area
Lake Huron offshore: 11,584 acres
Inland: 12,800 acres
Federal Protected Area
Shiawassee NWR, 9,042 acres
State Recreation Area
Bay City SP, 196 acres

Places Rated Score: 57.02 — Places Rated Rank: 152

St. Catharines–Niagara, ON

Common Denominators
Golf courses: 3 private (45 holes), 6 daily fee (90 holes), 7 municipal (108 holes) — A
Good restaurants: 2 *, 5 **, 1 *** — B
Movie theaters: 6 Chains (18 screens), 3 Independent (5 screens) — C
Crowd Pleasers
Professional sports
Stompers (Class A Baseball)
CIAU
Brock University Badgers
Outdoor Assets
Water Area
Lake Ontario offshore: 21,000 acres
Inland: 890 acres
Provincial Recreation Area
Short Hills PP, 1,633

Places Rated Score: 35.27 — Places Rated Rank: 226

St. Cloud, MN

Common Denominators
Golf courses: 2 private (27 holes), 10 daily fee (117 holes), 1 municipal (18 holes) — AA
Good restaurants: 1 ** — C
Movie theaters: 2 Independent (3 screens) — A
Crowd Pleasers
Professional sports
Rockin' Rollers (IBA Basketball)
NCAA Division I
St. Cloud State University Huskies (H)
Outdoor Assets
Inland Water Area: 32,000 acres

Places Rated Score: 46.95 — Places Rated Rank: 194

Saint John, NB

Common Denominators
Golf courses: 2 private (36 holes), 1 daily fee (18 holes), 1 municipal (9 holes) — C

Rating

Movie theaters: 3 Chains (10 screens), 2 Independent (2 screens) — B
Crowd Pleasers
Aquariums and Zoos
Cherry Brook Zoo
Professional sports
Flames (AHL Hockey)
Outdoor Assets
Water Area
Bay of Fundy offshore: 65,000 acres
Inland: 54,000 acres
Federal Protected Area
Grand Manan MBS, 618 acres
Provincial Recreation Areas
Becaguimec WMA, 27,532 acres
Herring Cove PP, 1,048 acres
Lepreau River WMA, 60,184 acres

holes), 1 municipal (18 holes)
Movie theaters: 2 Chains (8 screens) — C
Crowd Pleasers
Aquariums and Zoos
Pippy Park Zoo
Professional sports
Maple Leafs (AHL Hockey)
CIAU
Memorial University of Newfoundland Sea Hawks (MB, H)
Outdoor Assets
Water Area
Atlantic offshore: 76,000 acres
Inland: 25,000 acres
Provincial Recreation Areas
Avalon Wilderness Reserve, 264,397 acres
Baccalieu Island Ecological Reserve PP, 2,990 acres
Backside Pond PP, 1,389 acres
Bellevue Beach PP, 358 acres
Butter Pot PP, 4,329 acres
Cape St. Mary's Seabird Ecological Reserve PP, 3,113 acres
Cataracts PP, 425 acres
Chance Cove PP, 5,110 acres
Fitzgerald's Pond PP, 2,009 acres
Gushue's Pond PP, 442 acres
Hawk Hill Ecological Reserve PP, 324 acres
Holyrood Pond PP, 558 acres
Jack's Pond PP, 1,485 acres
La Manche PP, 3,445 acres
Marine Drive PP, 1,935 acres
Mistaken Point Ecological Reserve PP, 618 acres
Witless Bay Seabird Ecological Reserve, 348 acres

Places Rated Score: 74.98 — Places Rated Rank: 87

St. Joseph, MO

Common Denominators
Golf courses: 2 private (36 holes), 2 municipal (36 holes) — B
Good restaurants: 1 *, 1 ** — B
Movie theaters: 3 Chains (9 screens) — AA
Outdoor Assets
Inland Water Area: 3,840 acres
State Recreation Area
Lewis & Clark SP, 121

Places Rated Score: 5.99 — Places Rated Rank: 328

Rating

✓ St. Louis, MO–IL
Common Denominators
Golf courses: 36 private (585 holes), 70 daily fee (1,044 holes), 14 municipal (180 holes) — **A**
Good restaurants: 16 *, 26 **, 21 ***, 1 **** — **A**
Movie theaters: 15 Chains (63 screens), 7 Independent (16 screens) — **B**
Crowd Pleasers
Aquariums and Zoos
Forest Park Zoo
Professional sports
Blues (NHL Hockey)
Cardinals (NL Baseball)
Rams (NFL Football)
NCAA Division I
St. Louis University Billikens (B)
Outdoor Assets
Inland Water Area: 98,560 acres
Federal Protected Area
Jefferson National Expansion NM, 91 acres
State Recreation Areas
Castlewood SP, 1,780 acres
Cuivre River SP, 6,351 acres
Edmund Babler Memorial SP, 2,439 acres
Eldon Hazlett SP, 3,000 acres
Frank Holton SP, 1,180 acres
Horsehoe Lake SP, 2,850 acres
Mastodon SP, 425 acres
Meramec SP, 4,114 acres
Mississippi River State Fish & Wildlife, 24,386 acres
Pere Marquette SP, 7,900 acres
Robertsville SP, 1,172 acres
Sandy Creek Bridge SHS, 206 acres
South Shore SP, 800 acres
Places Rated Score: 94.89 Places Rated Rank: 25

Salem, OR
Common Denominators
Golf courses: 2 private (36 holes), 10 daily fee (153 holes) — **A**
Good restaurants: 2 *, 1 *** — **C**
Movie theaters: 7 Chains (9 screens), 6 Independent (6 screens) — **C**
Outdoor Assets
Inland Water Area: 8,320 acres
Federal Protected Areas
Ankeny NWR, 2,796 acres
Baskett Slough NWR, 2,492 acres
Mt. Hood NF, 65,915 acres
Siuslaw NF, 1,479 acres
Willamette NF, 135,375 acres
State Recreation Areas
Champoeg SP, 615 acres
Detroit Lake SP, 104 acres
North Santiam SP, 120 acres
Silver Falls SP, 8,546 acres
Van Duzer Forest Corridor Wayside, 463 acres
Willamette Mission SP, 1,686 acres
Willamette River Greenway, 1,109 acres
Places Rated Score: 38.59 Places Rated Rank: 219

Salinas, CA
Common Denominators
Golf courses: 8 private (144 holes), 10 daily fee (180 holes), 3 municipal (45 holes) — **A**
Good restaurants: 17 *, 15 **, 16 ***, 2 **** — **AA**
Movie theaters: 10 Chains (34 screens), 1 Independent (1 screen) — **AA**
Crowd Pleasers
Aquariums and Zoos
Monterey Bay Aquarium
Outdoor Assets
Water Area
Pacific offshore: 27,904 acres
Inland: 8,320 acres
Federal Protected Areas
Los Padres NF, 305,907 acres
Pinnacles NM, 1,283 acres
Salinas River NWR, 364 acres
State Recreation Areas
Andrew Molera SP, 4,786 acres
Asilomar Conference and SB, 106 acres
Carmel River SB, 106 acres
Garrapata SP, 2,800 acres
Julia Pfeiffer Burns SP, 3,583 acres
Marina SB, 170 acres
Pfeiffer Big Sur SP, 821 acres
Point Lobos SR, 1,325 acres
Salinas River SB, 246 acres
Zmudowski SB, 177 acres
Places Rated Score: 79.85 Places Rated Rank: 73

✓ Salt Lake City–Ogden, UT
Common Denominators
Golf courses: 7 private (117 holes), 9 daily fee (144 holes), 21 municipal (342 holes) — **B**
Good restaurants: 3 *, 10 ** — **C**
Movie theaters: 28 Chains (130 screens), 9 Independent (13 screens) — **A**
Crowd Pleasers
Aquariums and Zoos
Hogle Zoological Garden
Professional sports
Buzz (Triple A Baseball)
Grizzlies (IHL Hockey)
Jazz (NBA Basketball)
NCAA Division I
University of Utah Utes (B, F)
Weber State University Wildcats (B, F)
Outdoor Assets
Inland Water Area: 309,120 acres
Federal Protected Areas
Cache NF, 67,707 acres
Wasatch NF, 133,211 acres
State Recreation Areas
Antelope Island SP, 25,790 acres
Jordan River Parkway SP, 440 acres
Saltaire Beach SP, 3,115 acres
This Is The Place SP, 1,646 acres
Veterans Cemetary SHS, 30 acres
Places Rated Score: 95.64 Places Rated Rank: 22

San Angelo, TX
Common Denominators
Golf courses: 2 private (36 holes), 1 daily fee (18 holes), 2 municipal (18 holes) — **B**
Good restaurants: 4 ** — **AA**
Movie theaters: 3 Chains (13 screens) — **AA**
Outdoor Assets
Inland Water Area: 11,520 acres
Places Rated Score: 13.61 Places Rated Rank: 300

San Antonio, TX
Common Denominators
Golf courses: 14 private (234 holes), 9 daily fee (162 holes), 8 municipal (144 holes) — **C**
Good restaurants: 16 *, 13 **, 6 *** — **B**
Movie theaters: 19 Chains (145 screens), 1 Independent (2 screens) — **B**
Crowd Pleasers
Aquariums and Zoos
San Antonio Zoological Gardens and Aquarium
Sea World of Texas
Professional sports
Missions (Class AA Baseball)
Spurs (NBA Basketball)
NCAA Division I
University of Texas Roadrunners (B)
Outdoor Assets
Inland Water Area: 17,280 acres
Federal Protected Area

Rating

San Antonio Missions NHP, 258 acres
State Recreation Areas
Guadalupe River SP, 1,000 acres
Jose Antonio Navarro SHS, 1 acre
Rancho De Las Cabras SHS, 99 acres
Places Rated Score: 68.62 Places Rated Rank: 112

✓ San Diego, CA
Common Denominators
Golf courses: 25 private (450 holes), 29 daily fee (486 holes), 7 municipal (126 holes) — **C**
Good restaurants: 15 *, 39 **, 35 *** — **AA**
Movie theaters: 37 Chains (206 screens), 9 Independent (22 screens) — **B**
Crowd Pleasers
Aquariums and Zoos

Water Area
Pacific offshore: 17,152 acres
Inland: 34,560 acres
Federal Protected Areas
Cabrillo NM, 137 acres
Cleveland NF, 290,095 acres
Sweetwater Marsh NWR, 316 acres
Tijuana Slough NWR, 407 acres
State Recreation Areas
Anza-Borrego Desert SP, 522,097 acres
Border Field SP, 680 acres
Cuyamaca Rancho SP, 24,677 acres
Ocotillo Wells SVRA, 42,000 acres
Palomar Mountain SP, 1,897 acres
San Onofre SB, 3,036 acres
Silver Strand SB, 428 acres
South Carlsbad SB, 135 acres
Torrey Pines SR, 1,082 acres
Places Rated Score: 96.34 Places Rated Rank: 19

✓ San Francisco, CA
Common Denominators
Golf courses: 13 private (234 holes), 7 daily fee (108 holes), 8 municipal (135 holes) — **C**
Good restaurants: 28 *, 72 **, 28 ***, 8 **** — **AA**
Movie theaters: 48 Chains (184 screens), 9 Independent (12 screens) — **A**
Crowd Pleasers
Aquariums and Zoos
San Francisco Zoological Gardens
Steinhart Aquarium
Professional sports
49ers (NFL Football)
Giants (NL Baseball)
San Jose Sharks (NHL Hockey)
Spiders (IHL Hockey)
NCAA Division I
University of San Francisco Dons (B)
Outdoor Assets
Water Area
Pacific offshore: 34,432 acres
Inland: 158,080 acres
Federal Protected Areas
Farallon NWR, 91 acres
Fort Point NHS, 29 acres
Golden Gate NRA, 30,014 acres
Marin Islands NWR, 132 acres
Muir Woods NM, 523 acres
Point Reyes N Seashore, 64,505 acres

Rating

San Francisco Bay NWR, 2,865 acres
State Recreation Areas
Angel Island SP, 740 acres
Ano Nuevo SR, 4,000 acres
Big Basin Redwoods SP, 908 acres
Burleigh Murray Ranch, 1,128 acres
Butano SP, 3,200 acres
Candlestick Point SRA, 252 acres
China Camp SP, 1,512 acres
Half Moon Bay SB, 170 acres
Montara SB, 680 acres
Mount Tamalpais SP, 6,300 acres
Olompali SHP, 200 acres
Pescadero SB, 638 acres
Pomponio SB, 410 acres
Portola SP, 2,800 acres

8 Independent (23 screens)
Crowd Pleasers
Aquariums and Zoos
Palo Alto Junior Museum
San Jose Baby Zoo
Professional sports
Clash (MLS Soccer)
Giants (Class A Baseball)
NCAA Division I
San Jose State University Spartans (B, F)
Santa Clara University Broncos (B)
Stanford University Cardinal (B, F)
Outdoor Assets
Inland Water Area: 8,320 acres
Federal Protected Area
San Francisco Bay NWR, 3,566 acres
State Recreation Areas
Castle Rock SP, 50 acres
Henry Coe SP, 41,038 acres
Places Rated Score: 71.83 Places Rated Rank: 99

San Luis Obispo–Atascadero–Paso Robles, CA
Common Denominators
Golf courses: 2 private (36 holes), 3 daily fee (54 holes), 3 municipal (45 holes) — **B**
Good restaurants: 2 *, 8 **, 1 *** — **AA**
Movie theaters: 5 Chains (24 screens), 3 Independent (4 screens) — **A**
Crowd Pleasers
Aquariums and Zoos
Charles Paddock Zoo
NCAA Division I
California State Polytechnic University Mustangs (WB, F)
Outdoor Assets
Water Area
Pacific offshore: 18,752 acres
Inland: 12,160 acres
Federal Protected Areas
Golden Gate NRA, 28 acres
Los Padres NF, 188,944 acres
State Recreation Areas
Hearst San Simeon SHM, 149 acres
Montana De Oro SP, 8,400 acres
Morro Bay SP, 2,749 acres
Morro Strand SB, 117 acres
Pismo Dunes SVRA, 2,500 acres
Pismo SB, 1,051 acres

Rating

San Simeon SP, 541 acres
Places Rated Score: 57.28 Places Rated Rank: 150

Santa Barbara–Santa Maria–Lompoc, CA
Common Denominators
Golf courses: 8 private (144 holes), 6 daily fee (90 holes), 1 municipal (18 holes) **B**
Good restaurants: 2 *, 7 **, 5 ***, 1 **** **AA**
Movie theaters: 11 Chains (37 screens), 2 Independent (3 screens) **A**
Crowd Pleasers
Aquariums and Zoos
Santa Barbara Zoological Gardens
NCAA Division I
University of California Gauchos (B)
Outdoor Assets
Water Area
Pacific offshore: 66,496 acres
Inland: 8,320 acres
Federal Protected Areas
Channel Islands NP, 63,552 acres
Los Padres NF, 629,118 acres
State Recreation Areas
Carpinteria SB, 84 acres
El Capitan SB, 133 acres
Gaviota SP, 2,790 acres
La Purisima Mission SHP, 967 acres
Point Sal SB, 84 acres
Refugio SB, 155 acres
Places Rated Score: 82.37 Places Rated Rank: 64

Santa Cruz–Watsonville, CA
Common Denominators
Golf courses: 5 daily fee (90 holes), 1 municipal (18 holes) **B**
Good restaurants: 3 **, 3 *** **A**
Movie theaters: 6 Chains (16 screens), 4 Independent (9 screens) **A**
Outdoor Assets
Water Area
Pacific offshore: 10,304 acres
Inland: 640 acres
Federal Protected Area
Ellicott Slough NWR, 133 acres
State Recreation Areas
Big Basin Redwoods SP, 17,092 acres
Castle Rock SP, 3,650 acres
Forest of Nisene Marks SP, 10,121 acres
Henry Cowell Redwoods SP, 4,300 acres
New Brighton SB, 94 acres
Sunset SB, 324 acres
Twin Lakes SB, 110 acres
Wilder Ranch SP, 4,505 acres
Places Rated Score: 41.70 Places Rated Rank: 210

Santa Fe, NM
Common Denominators
Golf courses: 2 private (27 holes), 1 daily fee (18 holes), 1 municipal (18 holes) **B**
Good restaurants: 11 *, 15 **, 11 ***, 1 **** **AA**
Movie theaters: 3 Chains (14 screens), 2 Independent (2 screens) **A**
Outdoor Assets
Inland Water Area: 1,280 acres
Federal Protected Areas
Bandelier NM, 7,309 acres
Pecos NM, 87 acres
Santa Fe NF, 275,608 acres
State Recreation Areas
Hyde Memorial SP, 350 acres
Santa Fe River SP, 5 acres
Places Rated Score: 46.10 Places Rated Rank: 200

Santa Rosa, CA
Common Denominators

Rating

Golf courses: 2 private (27 holes), 7 daily fee (108 holes), 5 municipal (81 holes) **B**
Good restaurants: 11 *, 14 **, 6 *** **AA**
Movie theaters: 5 Chains (27 screens), 3 Independent (7 screens) **B**
Outdoor Assets
Water Area
Pacific offshore: 10,432 acres
Inland: 18,560 acres
Federal Protected Area
San Pablo Bay NWR, 249 acres
State Recreation Areas
Annadel SP, 5,000 acres
Armstrong Redwoods SR, 752 acres
Austin Creek SRA, 4,236 acres
Bothe-Napa Valley SP, 203 acres
Fort Ross SHP, 3,315 acres
Jack London SHP, 802 acres
Kruse Rhododendron SR, 317 acres
Robert Louis Stevenson SP, 1,538 acres
Salt Point SP, 5,970 acres
Sonoma Coast SB, 5,000 acres
Sugarloaf Ridge SP, 2,514 acres
Places Rated Score: 61.24 Places Rated Rank: 135

Sarasota–Bradenton, FL
Common Denominators
Golf courses: 23 private (396 holes), 29 daily fee (486 holes), 7 municipal (117 holes) **AA**
Good restaurants: 18 *, 22 **, 13 *** **AA**
Movie theaters: 13 Chains (62 screens), 2 Independent (4 screens) **A**
Crowd Pleasers
Professional sports
Red Sox (Class A Baseball)
Sharks (USBL Basketball)
Outdoor Assets
Water Area
Gulf offshore: 13,824 acres
Inland: 56,960 acres
Federal Protected Areas
De Soto NMem, 25 acres
Passage Key NWR, 36 acres
State Recreation Areas
Benjamin Memorial SHS, 17 acres
Lake Manatee SRA, 556 acres
Myakka River SP, 28,875 acres
Oscar Scherer SRA, 1,377 acres
Places Rated Score: 88.54 Places Rated Rank: 44

Saskatoon, SK
Common Denominators
Golf courses: 2 private (36 holes), 2 daily fee (36 holes), 8 municipal (108 holes) **A**
Movie theaters: 5 Chains (13 screens), 4 Independent (4 screens) **C**
Crowd Pleasers
Aquariums and Zoos
Forestry Farm Zoo
CIAU
University of Saskatchewan Huskies
Outdoor Assets
Inland Water Area: 47,000 acres
Federal Protected Areas
Bradwell NWA, 304 acres
Last Mountain Lake MBS, 11,713 acres
Last Mountain Lake NWA, 38,553 acres
Prairie NWA, 7,448 acres
Stalwart NWA, 3,608 acres
Sutherland MBS, 321 acres
Provincial Recreation Areas
Blackstrap PP, 1,300 acres
Coldwell Park, 259 acres
Elbow Harbour, 482 acres
Etter's Beach, 363 acres
Otapasoo Trails, 321 acres

Rating

Pike Lake PP, 1,236 acres
Places Rated Score: 42.13 — Places Rated Rank: 208

Savannah, GA
Common Denominators
Golf courses: 10 private (171 holes), 5 daily fee (81 holes), 3 municipal (45 holes) — **A**
Good restaurants: 5 *, 9 **, 3 *** — **AA**
Movie theaters: 6 Chains (38 screens) — **AA**
Crowd Pleasers
Aquariums and Zoos
Oatland Island Education Center
Professional sports
Sand Gnats (Class A Baseball)
Outdoor Assets
Water Area

Rating

San Juan Islands NWR, 65 acres
Snoqualmie NF, 518,722 acres
State Recreation Areas
Black Diamond SP, 163 acres
Bridle Trails SP, 480 acres
Cama Beach, 224 acres
Camano Island SP, 134 acres
Dash Point SP, 230 acres
Deception Pass SP, 2,515 acres
Everett Jetty SP, 160 acres
Federation Forest SP, 619 acres
Flaming Geyser SP, 667 acres
Fort Casey SP, 421 acres
Fort Ebey SP, 644 acres
Hanging Gardens SP, 369 acres
Iron Horse West SP, 613 acres

Scranton–Wilkes-Barre–Hazleton, PA
Common Denominators
Golf courses: 12 private (207 holes), 23 daily fee (324 holes), 2 municipal (27 holes) — **A**
Good restaurants: 3 *, 1 *** — **C**
Movie theaters: 6 Chains (39 screens), 8 Independent (21 screens) — **A**
Crowd Pleasers
Professional sports
Red Barons (Triple A Baseball)
Outdoor Assets
Inland Water Area: 21,760 acres
Federal Protected Area
Steamtown NHS, 1 acre
State Recreation Areas
Archbald Pothole SP, 153 acres
Frances Slocum SP, 1,035 acres
Lackawanna SP, 1,411 acres
Lehigh Gorge SP, 271 acres
Nescopeck SP, 2,981 acres
Ricketts Glen SP, 11,258 acres
Places Rated Score: 61.36 — Places Rated Rank: 134

✓ Seattle–Bellevue–Everett, WA
Common Denominators
Golf courses: 21 private (333 holes), 25 daily fee (378 holes), 13 municipal (225 holes) — **B**
Good restaurants: 8 *, 26 **, 30 ***, 2 **** — **AA**
Movie theaters: 41 Chains (157 screens), 8 Independent (8 screens) — **B**
Crowd Pleasers
Aquariums and Zoos
Seattle Aquarium
Woodland Park Zoological Gardens
Professional sports
Aquasox (Class A Baseball)
Mariners (AL Baseball)
Seahawks (NFL Football)
Supersonics (NBA Basketball)
NCAA Division I
University of Washington Huskies (B, F)
Outdoor Assets
Water Area
Pacific offshore: 31,040 acres
Inland: 71,040 acres
Federal Protected Areas
Ebey's Landing NHR, 1,379 acres
Mt. Baker NF, 463,134 acres

Places Rated Score: 96.49 — Places Rated Rank: 17

Sharon, PA
Common Denominators
Golf courses: 4 private (63 holes), 9 daily fee (135 holes) — **AA**
Good restaurants: 1 *, 3 ** — **A**
Movie theaters: 3 Chains (8 screens) — **C**
Outdoor Assets
Inland Water Area: 7,040 acres
State Recreation Area
Goddard SP, 2,857
Places Rated Score: 21.38 — Places Rated Rank: 270

Sheboygan, WI
Common Denominators
Golf courses: 1 private (18 holes), 7 daily fee (108 holes) — **AA**
Good restaurants: 2 **, 1 *** — **A**
Movie theaters: 2 Chains (10 screens) — **B**
Outdoor Assets
Water Area
Lake Michigan offshore: 48,192 acres
Inland: 2,560 acres
State Recreation Areas
Kohler-Andrae SP, 962
Old Wade House SP, 243
Places Rated Score: 57.17 — Places Rated Rank: 151

Sherbrooke, PQ
Common Denominators
Golf courses: 3 daily fee (45 holes), 2 municipal (27 holes) — **A**
Movie theaters: 2 Chains (4 screens), 2 Independent (4 screens) — **C**
Crowd Pleasers
CIAU
Bishop's University Gaiters
Outdoor Assets
Inland Water Area: 45,000 acres
Provincial Recreation Areas
Mount-Orford PP, 14,423
Tantare Ecological Reserve, 3,684
Places Rated Score: 31.43 — Places Rated Rank: 239

Sherman–Denison, TX
Common Denominators
Golf courses: 1 private (18 holes), 3 daily fee (54 holes) — **A**

	Rating
Movie theaters: 4 Chains (16 screens)	AA

Outdoor Assets
Inland Water Area: 29,440 acres
State Recreation Areas
Eisenhower Birthplace SHS, 6
Eisenhower SRA, 457
Places Rated Score: 25.23 Places Rated Rank: 256

Shreveport–Bossier City, LA
Common Denominators

	Rating
Golf courses: 9 private (126 holes), 4 daily fee (54 holes), 3 municipal (45 holes)	B
Good restaurants: 2 *, 3 **, 1 ***	B
Movie theaters: 7 Chains (33 screens), 1 Independent (4 screens)	B

Crowd Pleasers
Professional sports
Captains (Class AA Baseball)
Storm (CBA Basketball)
NCAA Division I
Centenary College Gentlemen (MB)
Outdoor Assets
Inland Water Area: 65,920 acres
Federal Protected Area
Kisatchee NF, 12,456 acres
State Recreation Areas
Bickham Dickson SP, 585 acres
Lake Bistineau SP, 750 acres
Places Rated Score: 58.25 Places Rated Rank: 145

Sioux City, IA–NE
Common Denominators

	Rating
Golf courses: 2 private (27 holes), 9 daily fee (90 holes), 1 municipal (18 holes)	AA
Good restaurants: 2 *	C
Movie theaters: 4 Chains (16 screens)	AA

Outdoor Assets
Inland Water Area: 5,120 acres
Places Rated Score: 14.42 Places Rated Rank: 297

Sioux Falls, SD
Common Denominators

	Rating
Golf courses: 3 private (45 holes), 7 daily fee (90 holes), 4 municipal (63 holes)	AA
Good restaurants: 1 **	C
Movie theaters: 3 Chains (20 screens), 1 Independent (1 screen)	AA

Crowd Pleasers
Aquariums and Zoos
Great Plains Zoo
Professional sports
Sky Force (CBA Basketball)
Outdoor Assets
Inland Water Area: 3,200 acres
State Recreation Areas
Beaver Creek SNA, 160 acres
Big Sioux SRA, 430 acres
Newton Hills SP, 948 acres
Palisades SP, 157 acres
Places Rated Score: 18.20 Places Rated Rank: 283

South Bend, IN
Common Denominators

	Rating
Golf courses: 4 private (72 holes), 5 daily fee (72 holes), 3 municipal (54 holes)	A
Good restaurants: 2 *, 6 **, 1 ***	A
Movie theaters: 5 Chains (28 screens)	A

Crowd Pleasers
Aquariums and Zoos
Potawatomi Zoo
Professional sports
Silver Hawks (Class A Baseball)
NCAA Division I
University of Notre Dame Fighting Irish
Outdoor Assets
Inland Water Area: 2,560 acres
State Recreation Area
Potato Creek SP, 3,815 acres
Places Rated Score: 22.70 Places Rated Rank: 264

Spokane, WA
Common Denominators

	Rating
Golf courses: 2 private (36 holes), 4 daily fee (63 holes), 7 municipal (126 holes)	A
Good restaurants: 4 *, 1 **, 1 ***	C
Movie theaters: 12 Chains (24 screens)	C

Crowd Pleasers
Aquariums and Zoos
Inland Northwest Zoo
Professional sports
Indians (Class A Baseball)
NCAA Division I
Eastern Washington University Eagles (B, F)
Gonzaga University Bulldogs (B)
Outdoor Assets
Inland Water Area: 10,880 acres
Federal Protected Area
Turnbull NWR, 15,468 acres
State Recreation Areas
Centennial Trail SP, 374 acres
Mount Spokane SP, 13,821 acres
Pasco/Fish Lake Trail, 255 acres
Riverside SP, 7,188 acres
Spokane Plains Battlefield SHS, 1 acre
Spokane River Cent Trail, 376 acres
Places Rated Score: 38.15 Places Rated Rank: 221

Springfield, IL
Common Denominators

	Rating
Golf courses: 2 private (36 holes), 6 daily fee (99 holes), 4 municipal (54 holes)	AA
Good restaurants: 3 **, 1 ***	A
Movie theaters: 5 Chains (27 screens), 1 Independent (1 screen)	AA

Crowd Pleasers
Aquariums and Zoos
Henson Robinson Zoo
Outdoor Assets
Inland Water Area: 6,400 acres
Federal Protected Area
Lincoln Home NHS, 12 acres
State Recreation Area
Sangchris Lake SP, 1 acre
Places Rated Score: 20.13 Places Rated Rank: 277

Springfield, MA
Common Denominators

	Rating
Golf courses: 9 private (153 holes), 17 daily fee (252 holes), 7 municipal (108 holes)	A
Good restaurants: 1 *, 5 **, 4 ***	B
Movie theaters: 10 Chains (38 screens), 4 Independent (5 screens)	B

Crowd Pleasers
Aquariums and Zoos
Forest Park Children's Zoo
Museum of Zoology
Professional sports
Falcons (AHL Hockey)
NCAA Division I
University of Massachusetts Minutemen (B, F)
Outdoor Assets
Inland Water Area: 20,480 acres
Federal Protected Area
Springfield Armory NHS, 21 acres
State Recreation Area
C.M. Gardner SP, 29 acres
Chicopee Memorial SP, 574 acres
Deer Hill SP, 259 acres
Elwell SP, 1 acre
Hampton Ponds SP, 42 acres
Holyoke Heritage SP, 9 acres
Holyoke Range SP, 1,936 acres
Lake Lorraine SP, 2 acres

Rating

Mt. Tom SR, 1,800 acres
Red Bridge SP, 42 acres
Robinson SP, 811 acres
Skinner SP, 390 acres
Springfield Heritage SP, 1 acre
Places Rated Score: 58.17 Places Rated Rank: 146

Springfield, MO
Common Denominators
Golf courses: 5 private (90 holes), 7 daily fee (117 holes), 2 municipal (36 holes) — A
Good restaurants: 2 *, 2 **, 1 *** — B
Movie theaters: 8 Chains (51 screens), 2 Independent (2 screens) — AA
Crowd Pleasers
Aquariums and Zoos

Stamford–Norwalk, CT
Common Denominators
Golf courses: 18 private (306 holes), 1 daily fee (18 holes), 4 municipal (72 holes) — B
Good restaurants: 5 *, 10 **, 5 ***, 1 **** — AA
Movie theaters: 15 Chains (40 screens) — C
Outdoor Assets
Water Area
Long Island Sound offshore: 11,520 acres
Inland: 19,840 acres
State Recreation Areas
Mianus SP, 335 acres
Sherwood Island SP, 234 acres
Places Rated Score: 38.60 Places Rated Rank: 218

State College, PA
Common Denominators
Golf courses: 3 private (9 holes), 5 daily fee (81 holes) — A
Good restaurants: 2 **, 1 *** — A
Movie theaters: 4 Chains (15 screens), 2 Independent (2 screens) — AA
Crowd Pleasers
NCAA Division I
Pennsylvania State University Nittany Lions (B, F)
Outdoor Assets
Inland Water Area: 2,560 acres
State Recreation Areas
Bald Eagle SP, 5,900
Black Moshannon SP, 3,394
McCall Dam SP, 8
Penn Roosevelt SP, 41
Poe Paddy SP, 23
Poe Valley SP, 620
Places Rated Score: 17.44 Places Rated Rank: 285

Steubenville–Weirton, OH–WV
Common Denominators
Golf courses: 4 private (63 holes), 7 daily fee (99 holes), 1 municipal (9 holes) — AA
Movie theaters: 1 Chain (6 screens), 1 Independent (2 screens) — C
Outdoor Assets
Inland Water Area: 5,760 acres
State Recreation Areas
Jefferson Lake SP, 906 acres
Quaker Meeting House SHS, 5 acres
Tomlinson Run SP, 1,398 acres
Places Rated Score: 10.58 Places Rated Rank: 314

Rating

Stockton–Lodi, CA
Common Denominators
Golf courses: 8 private (126 holes), 2 daily fee (27 holes), 3 municipal (54 holes) — C
Good restaurants: 2 ** — C
Movie theaters: 6 Chains (36 screens), 1 Independent (4 screens) — C
Crowd Pleasers
Aquariums and Zoos
Micke Grove Zoo
Professional sports
Ports (Class A Baseball)
NCAA Division I
University of the Pacific Tigers (B, F)
Outdoor Assets
Inland Water Area: 17,280 acres

Laurentian University Voyageurs (B, H)
Outdoor Assets
Inland Water Area: 186,000 acres
Federal Protected Area
Fielding MBS, 3,212 acres
Provincial Recreation Areas
Chapleau Crown Game Preserve, 2,004,114 acres
Chapleau–Nemegosenda River PP, 20,176 acres
Chutes PP, 267 acres
Eighteen Mile Island Wilderness Area, 482 acres
Fairbank PP, 259 acres
Fairy Point Wilderness Area, 640 acres
Five Mile Lake PP, 1,127 acres
Halfway Lake PP, 11,688 acres
Ivanhoe Lake PP, 3,926 acres
Killarney Wilderness PP, 119,844 acres
La Cloche PP, 18,404 acres
Lake Shore Esker, 69 acres
Marrows Shoreline, 109 acres
Mashkinonje PP, 2,323 acres
Missinaibi PP, 108,875 acres
Mississagi River PP, 48,960 acres
Moose Pass Ridges, 1,362 acres
Northshore Peninsula, 153 acres
Silver Peak, 754 acres
The Shoals PP, 26,301 acres
Wakami Lake PP, 21,760 acres
Wanapitei PP, 6,672 acres
Whitefish Falls Wilderness Area, 267 acres
Windy Lake PP, 292 acres
Places Rated Score: 65.05 Places Rated Rank: 121

Sumter, SC
Common Denominators
Golf courses: 2 private (36 holes), 3 daily fee (54 holes), 1 municipal (9 holes) — A
Good restaurants: 1 ** — C
Movie theaters: 3 Chains (7 screens) — C
Outdoor Assets
Inland Water Area: 10,880 acres
State Recreation Areas
Poinsett SP, 1,000 acres
Thomas Sumter SHS, 5 acres
Woods Bay SP, 924 acres
Places Rated Score: 10.28 Places Rated Rank: 315

Syracuse, NY
Common Denominators

	Rating
Golf courses: 17 private (279 holes), 48 daily fee (693 holes), 2 municipal (36 holes)	AA
Good restaurants: 8 *, 18 **, 6 ***	AA
Movie theaters: 8 Chains (52 screens), 5 Independent (6 screens)	A

Crowd Pleasers
Aquariums and Zoos
Burnet Park Zoo
Professional sports
Chiefs (Triple A Baseball)
Crunch (AHL Hockey)
Doubledays (Class A Baseball)
NCAA Division I
Colgate University Red Raiders
Syracuse University Orange (B, F)
Outdoor Assets
Water Area
Lake Ontario offshore: 21,568 acres
Inland: 88,960 acres
State Recreation Areas
Battle Island SP, 235 acres
Chittenango Falls SP, 193 acres
Clark Reservation, 326 acres
Fair Haven Beach SP, 739 acres
Fillmore Glen SP, 941 acres
Fort Ontario SHS, 36 acres
Green Lakes SP, 1,400 acres
Long Point SP, 229 acres
Lorenzo Mansion SHS, 85 acres
Mexico Point Boat Launch SP, 20 acres
Old Erie Canal SP, 301 acres
Otisco Lake Boat Launch SP, 4 acres
Owasco Lake Marine Park, 1 acres
Selkirk Shores SP, 980 acres
South Shore Boat Launch SP, 12 acres
Places Rated Score: 90.61 Places Rated Rank: 37

Tacoma, WA

Common Denominators

	Rating
Golf courses: 8 private (126 holes), 10 daily fee (153 holes), 4 municipal (63 holes)	B
Good restaurants: 4 **, 3 ***	B
Movie theaters: 7 Chains (36 screens), 3 Independent (3 screens)	C

Crowd Pleasers
Aquariums and Zoos
Port Defiance Zoo and Aquarium
Professional sports
Raniers (Triple A Baseball)
Outdoor Assets
Water Area
Pacific offshore: 1,024 acres
Inland: 73,600 acres
Federal Protected Areas
Mount Ranier NP, 206,441 acres
Nisqually NWR, 808 acres
Snoqualmie NF, 124,579 acres
State Recreation Areas
Dash Point SP, 168 acres
Haley Property, 178 acres
Joemma Beach, 122 acres
Kopachuck SP, 113 acres
Nisqually, 441 acres
Pensrose Point SP, 152 acres
Places Rated Score: 83.08 Places Rated Rank: 60

Tallahassee, FL

Common Denominators

	Rating
Golf courses: 5 private (72 holes), 3 daily fee (54 holes), 3 municipal (36 holes)	B
Good restaurants: 1 *, 3 **	B
Movie theaters: 8 Chains (34 screens)	AA

Crowd Pleasers
Aquariums and Zoos
Tallahassee Junior Museum
Professional sports
Tiger Sharks (ECHL Hockey)
NCAA Division I
Florida A & M Rattlers (B, F)
Florida State University Seminoles (B, F)
Outdoor Assets
Inland Water Area: 30,080 acres
Federal Protected Area
Appalachicola NF, 104,490 acres
State Recreation Areas
Lake Talquin SRA, 607 acres
Maclay State Gardens, 985 acres
Places Rated Score: 69.45 Places Rated Rank: 109

✓ Tampa–St. Petersburg–Clearwater, FL

Common Denominators

	Rating
Golf courses: 41 private (711 holes), 59 daily fee (1,017 holes), 7 municipal (126 holes)	A
Good restaurants: 26 *, 24 **, 16 ***	A
Movie theaters: 38 Chains (193 screens), 2 Independent (7 screens)	A

Crowd Pleasers
Aquariums and Zoos
Busch Gardens
CMSC Aquarium
Lowry Park Zoological Garden
Professional sports
Blue Jays (Class A Baseball)
Buccaneers (NFL Football)
Cardinals (Class A Baseball)
Lightning (NHL Hockey)
Mutiny (MLS Soccer)
Phillies (Class A Baseball)
Windjammers (USBL Basketball)
Yankees (Class A Baseball)
NCAA Division I
University of South Florida Bulls (B)
Outdoor Assets
Water Area
Gulf offshore: 40,000 acres
Inland: 97,280 acres
Federal Protected Areas
Chassahowitzka NWR, 6,707 acres
Egmont Key NWR, 328 acres
State Recreation Areas
Anclote Key SNA, 287 acres
Caladesi Island SP, 631 acres
Egmont Key SP, 381 acres
Hillsborough River SP, 3,738 acres
Honeymoon Island SRA, 2,400 acres
Little Manatee River SRA, 2,010 acres
Places Rated Score: 96.39 Places Rated Rank: 18

Terre Haute, IN

Common Denominators

	Rating
Golf courses: 2 private (27 holes), 3 daily fee (36 holes), 4 municipal (63 holes)	A
Good restaurants: 2 *	C
Movie theaters: 3 Chains (6 screens)	C

Crowd Pleasers
NCAA Division I
Indiana State University Sycamores (B, F)
Outdoor Assets
Inland Water Area: 8,320 acres
State Recreation Area
Shakamak SP, 942 acres
Places Rated Score: 16.44 Places Rated Rank: 290

Texarkana, TX–Texarkana, AR

Common Denominators

	Rating
Golf courses: 3 private (36 holes), 1 daily fee (18 holes)	C
Movie theaters: 2 Chains (8 screens)	C

Outdoor Assets
Inland Water Area: 30,720 acres
Places Rated Score: 12.14 Places Rated Rank: 306

Rating

Thunder Bay, ON

Common Denominators
- Golf courses: 2 private (18 holes), 1 daily fee (18 holes), 4 municipal (54 holes) — **A**
- Good restaurants: 1 ** — **C**
- Movie theaters: 4 Chains (17 screens) — **AA**

Crowd Pleasers
- Aquariums and Zoos
  - Chippewa Park Zoo
- Professional sports
  - Senators (CoHL Hockey)
- CIAU
  - Lakehead University Nor'westers (B, H)

Outdoor Assets

- Clearwater Lake, 1,035 acres
- Craigs Pit Nature Reserve PP, 1,310 acres
- Devon Road Mesa Nature Reserve PP, 148 acres
- Divide Ridge Nature Reserve PP, 581 acres
- Edward Island Nature Reserve PP, 1,483 acres
- Fraleigh Lake Nature Reserve PP, 2,039 acres
- Geikie Island Crown Game Preserve, 13,657 acres
- Grassy Lake, 445 acres
- Gravel River Nature Reserve PP, 1,310 acres
- Joeboy Lake, 1,243 acres
- Kabitotikwia River Nature Reserve PP, 4,856 acres
- Kaiashk Provincial Nature Reserve PP, 568 acres
- Kakabeka Falls PP, 1,038 acres
- Kaministiquia Spillway, 484 acres
- Kashabowie PP, 5,078 acres
- Klotz Lake PP, 294 acres
- Lake Nipigon PP, 3,603 acres
- Le Pate Nature Reserve PP, 618 acres
- Little Greenwater Lake Nature Reserve PP, 603 acres
- Livingstone Point Nature Reserve PP, 4,448 acres
- Mac Leod PP, 183 acres
- Matawin River Nature Reserve PP, 6,462 acres
- Michipicoten Island PP, 90,785 acres
- Middlebrun Bay, 1,045 acres
- Middle Falls PP, 2,241 acres
- Neys PP, 8,513 acres
- Ouimet Canyon Nature Reserve PP, 1,920 acres
- Outer Barn Island Wilderness Area, 161 acres
- Pantagruel Creek Nature Reserve PP, 5,436 acres
- Pickeral Lake, 242 acres
- Pigeon River Clay Plain Nature Reserve PP, 7,092 acres
- Porphyry Island Nature Reserve PP, 264 acres
- Prairie River Mouth Nature Reserve PP, 939 acres
- Rainbow Falls PP, 1,421 acres
- Red Sucker Point Nature Reserve PP, 890 acres
- Sedgman Lake Nature Reserve PP, 14,109 acres
- Shesheeb Bay Nature Reserve PP, 680 acres
- Sibley PP, 60,379 acres
- Sifting Creek, 1,722 acres
- Silver Falls PP, 8,058 acres
- Sleeping Giant Wilderness Area, 633 acres
- Thompson Island Nature Reserve PP, 358 acres
- Wabakimi Wilderness PP, 383,005 acres
- West Bay Nature Reserve PP, 2,768 acres
- White Lake PP, 4,265 acres
- Windigo Bay Nature Reserve PP, 20,509 acres

Places Rated Score: 88.31 — Places Rated Rank: 45

Rating

Toledo, OH

Common Denominators
- Golf courses: 8 private (144 holes), 13 daily fee (216 holes), 5 municipal (72 holes) — **A**
- Good restaurants: 2 *, 4 **, 1 *** — **C**
- Movie theaters: 9 Chains (47 screens), 3 Independent (4 screens) — **B**

Crowd Pleasers
- Aquariums and Zoos
  - Toledo Zoological Gardens
- Professional sports
  - Mud Hens (Triple A Baseball)
  - Storm (ECHL Hockey)
- NCAA Division I
  - Bowling Green State University Falcons

- Harrison Lake SP, 142 acres
- Irwin Prairie SNA, 187 acres
- Mary Jane Thurston SP, 104 acres
- Maumee Bay SP, 1,736 acres

Places Rated Score: 57.84 — Places Rated Rank: 147

Topeka, KS

Common Denominators
- Golf courses: 3 private (54 holes), 2 daily fee (36 holes), 3 municipal (45 holes) — **A**
- Good restaurants: 1 *, 3 **, 1 *** — **A**
- Movie theaters: 5 Chains (22 screens) — **AA**

Crowd Pleasers
- Aquariums and Zoos
  - Gage Park Zoo

Outdoor Assets
- Inland Water Area: 3,840 acres
- Federal Protected Area
  - Brown/Board of Education NHS, 2 acres

Places Rated Score: 13.14 — Places Rated Rank: 303

✓ Toronto, ON

Common Denominators
- Golf courses: 35 private (587 holes), 33 daily fee (531 holes), 16 municipal (252 holes) — **C**
- Good restaurants: 17 *, 30 **, 23 ***, 5 **** — **B**
- Movie theaters: 54 Chains (249 screens), 18 Independent (19 screens) — **C**

Crowd Pleasers
- Aquariums and Zoos
  - Metropolitan Toronto Zoo
- Professional sports
  - Argonauts (CFL Football)
  - Blue Jays (AL Baseball)
  - Maple Leafs (NHL Hockey)
  - Raptors (NBA Basketball)
- CIAU
  - Ryerson Polytechnical Institute Rams (B, H)
  - University of Toronto Varsity Blues
  - York University Yeowomen

Outdoor Assets
- Water Area
  - Lake Ontario offshore: 103,000 acres
  - Inland: 82,000 acres
- Federal Protected Area
  - Wye Marsh NWA, 116 acres
- Provincial Recreation Areas
  - Awenda PP, 7,208 acres
  - Bass Lake PP, 96 acres
  - Boyne Valley PP, 1,072 acres

Rating

Bronte Creek PP, 1,581 acres
Duclos Point Nature Reserve PP, 274 acres
Earl Rowe PP, 771 acres
Forks Of The Credit PP, 645 acres
Giant Tombs Island, 983 acres
Holland Marsh PWA, 1,416 acres
Macey Lake Bog, 168 acres
Matchedash Bay PWA, 556 acres
McRae Point PP, 341 acres
Mono Cliffs PP, 1,559 acres
Nipissing Modern Shoreline E, 193 acres
Nipissing Modern Shoreline W, 198 acres
Noisy River Nature Reserve PP, 964 acres
Relict Prairie, 430 acres
Scott's Falls Nature Reserve PP, 1,013 acres
Springwater PP, 116 acres
Tiny Marsh PWA, 1,401 acres
Wasaga Beach PP, 3,818 acres
Wye Marsh PWA, 2,271 acres

Places Rated Score: 97.66 — Places Rated Rank: 8

Trenton, NJ

Common Denominators
- Golf courses: 6 private (99 holes), 2 daily fee (36 holes), 3 municipal (54 holes) — **B**
- Good restaurants: 7 ** — **A**
- Movie theaters: 6 Chains (29 screens), 7 Independent (21 screens) — **C**

Crowd Pleasers
- Professional sports
  - Thunder (Class AA Baseball)
- NCAA Division I
  - Princeton University Tigers
  - Rider College Broncs (B)

Outdoor Assets
- Inland Water Area: 1,920 acres
- State Recreation Areas
  - D & R Canal SP, 1,030 acres
  - Princeton Battle Monument SHS, 2 acres
  - Princeton Battlefield SP, 85 acres
  - Trenton Battle Monument SHS, 1 acres
  - Washington Crossing SP, 991 acres

Places Rated Score: 11.49 — Places Rated Rank: 309

Trois-Rivieres, PQ

Common Denominators
- Golf courses: 4 private (63 holes), 1 municipal (18 holes) — **C**
- Movie theaters: 1 Independent (1 screen) — **C**

Crowd Pleasers
- CIAU
  - Universite du Quebec Les Patriotes (H)

Outdoor Assets
- Inland Water Area: 32,000 acres

Places Rated Score: 9.50 — Places Rated Rank: 319

Tucson, AZ

Common Denominators
- Golf courses: 12 private (189 holes), 17 daily fee (279 holes), 7 municipal (126 holes) — **A**
- Good restaurants: 9 *, 13 **, 11 ***, 3 **** — **AA**
- Movie theaters: 15 Chains (73 screens) — **B**

Crowd Pleasers
- Aquariums and Zoos
  - Reid Park Zoo
- Professional sports
  - Toros (Triple A Baseball)
- NCAA Division I
  - University of Arizona Wildcats (B, F)

Outdoor Assets
- Inland Water Area: 1,280 acres
- Federal Protected Areas
  - Buenos Aires NWR, 113,642 acres
  - Cabeza Prieta NWR, 416,242 acres
  - Coronado NF, 390,426 acres
  - Organ Pipe Cactus NM, 329,316 acres
  - Saguaro NM, 83,945 acres
- State Recreation Area
  - Catalina SP, 5,511 acres

Places Rated Score: 84.61 — Places Rated Rank: 58

Rating

Tulsa, OK

Common Denominators
- Golf courses: 11 private (171 holes), 11 daily fee (144 holes), 9 municipal (162 holes) — **B**
- Good restaurants: 3 *, 12 **, 3 *** — **A**
- Movie theaters: 13 Chains (68 screens), 1 Independent (1 screen) — **B**

Crowd Pleasers
- Aquariums and Zoos
  - Tulsa Zoological Park
- Professional sports
  - Drillers (Class AA Baseball)
- NCAA Division I
  - University of Tulsa Golden Hurricane (MB, F)

Outdoor Assets
- Inland Water Area: 94,720 acres
- State Recreation Areas
  - Fred Drummond Home SHS, 1 acres
  - Heyburn SP, 438 acres
  - Lake Keystone SP, 715 acres
  - Osage Hills SP, 1,199 acres
  - Sequoyah Bay SP, 303 acres
  - Wah-Sha-She SP, 807 acres
  - Walnut Creek SP, 1,429 acres

Places Rated Score: 78.97 — Places Rated Rank: 80

Tuscaloosa, AL

Common Denominators
- Golf courses: 4 private (72 holes), 2 daily fee (36 holes) — **C**
- Good restaurants: 1 *, 2 ** — **B**
- Movie theaters: 2 Chains (18 screens) — **A**

Crowd Pleasers
- NCAA Division I
  - University of Alabama Crimson Tide (B, F)

Outdoor Assets
- Inland Water Area: 17,280 acres
- Federal Protected Area
  - Talladega NF, 10,645 acres
- State Recreation Area
  - Lake Lurleen SP, 1,625 acres

Places Rated Score: 29.52 — Places Rated Rank: 244

Tyler, TX

Common Denominators
- Golf courses: 4 private (72 holes), 6 daily fee (108 holes) — **A**
- Good restaurants: 1 *, 2 ** — **B**
- Movie theaters: 8 Chains (25 screens) — **AA**

Outdoor Assets
- Inland Water Area: 13,440 acres
- State Recreation Area
  - Tyler SP, 986 acres

Places Rated Score: 22.66 — Places Rated Rank: 265

Utica-Rome, NY

Common Denominators
- Golf courses: 9 private (117 holes), 26 daily fee (351 holes), 2 municipal (27 holes) — **AA**
- Good restaurants: 4 *, 4 **, 2 *** — **A**
- Movie theaters: 4 Chains (19 screens), 1 Independent (1 screen) — **B**

Crowd Pleasers
- Aquariums and Zoos
  - Utica Zoo
- Professional sports
  - Blizzard (CoHL Hockey)
  - Blue Marlins (Class A Baseball)

Outdoor Assets
- Inland Water Area: 58,240 acres
- Federal Protected Area
  - Fort Stanwix NM, 16 acres
- State Recreation Areas

Rating

Delta Lake SP, 400 acres
Herkimer Home SHS, 151 acres
Hinckley Reservoir SRA, 2,782 acres
Nicks Lake SRA, 320 acres
Old Erie Canal SP, 300 acres
Oriskany Battlefield SHS, 83 acres
Pixley Falls SP, 375 acres
Verona Beach SP, 1,735 acres

Places Rated Score: 69.67 Places Rated Rank: 108

Vallejo–Fairfield–Napa, CA

Common Denominators
Golf courses: 6 private (108 holes), 6 daily fee (81 holes), 7 municipal (108 holes) **B**
Good restaurants: 10 *, 13 **, 5 ***, 2 **** **AA**

Sugarloaf Ridge SP, 139 acres

Places Rated Score: 67.36 Places Rated Rank: 113

✓ Vancouver, BC

Common Denominators
Golf courses: 11 private (198 holes), 10 daily fee (162 holes), 21 municipal (333 holes) **B**
Good restaurants: 4 *, 9 **, 17 *** **A**
Movie theaters: 25 Chains (109 screens), 9 Independent (9 screens) **C**

Crowd Pleasers
Aquariums and Zoos
Stanley Park Zoological Gardens
Vancouver Public Aquarium
Professional sports
Canadians (Triple A Baseball)
Canucks (NHL Hockey)
Grizzlies (NBA Basketball)
Lions (CFL Football)
CIAU
Simon Fraser University Clansmen (B, F)
University of British Columbia Thunderbirds

Outdoor Assets
Water Area
Strait of Georgia offshore: 35,000 acres
Inland: 76,000 acres
Federal Protected Areas
Alaksen NWA, 741 acres
Reifel MBS, 1,601 acres
Widgeon Valley NWA, 309 acres
Provincial Recreation Areas
Bowen Island Ecological Reserve, 981 acres
Cypress PP, 7,443 acres
Davis Lake PP, 474 acres
Golden Ears Provincial Park, 137,378 acres
Mount Judge Howay PP, 15,271 acres
Mount Seymour PP, 8,668 acres
Pitt-Addington Marsh WMA, 10,027 acres
Pitt Polder Ecological Reserve, 217 acres
Rolley Lake PP, 284 acres
U.B.C. Endowment Lands Ecological Reserve, 222 acres

Places Rated Score: 94.55 Places Rated Rank: 27

Ventura, CA

Common Denominators
Golf courses: 10 private (162 holes), 6 daily fee (108 holes), 6 municipal (99 holes) **B**
Good restaurants: 1 *, 4 **, 2 *** **C**

Rating

Movie theaters: 16 Chains (91 screens), 3 Independent (6 screens) **AA**

Outdoor Assets
Water Area
Pacific offshore: 22,400 acres
Inland: 7,680 acres
Federal Protected Areas
Angeles NF, 1,474 acres
Bitter Creek NWR, 122 acres
Channel Islands NP, 702 acres
Hopper Mountain NWR, 2,471 acres
Los Padres NF, 557,232 acres
Santa Monica Mountains NRA, 7,830 acres
State Recreation Areas
Emma Wood SB, 116 acres
Mandalay SB, 92 acres

2 Independent (2 screens)

Crowd Pleasers
Aquariums and Zoos
Crystal Garden
Sealand of the Pacific
CIAU
University of Victoria Vikes

Outdoor Assets
Water Area
Strait of Juan de Fuca offshore: 30,000 acres
Inland: 8,500 acres
Federal Protected Areas
Esquimalt Lagoon MBS, 321 acres
Shoal Harbour MBS, 371 acres
Victoria Harbour MBS, 4,201 acres
Provincial Recreation Areas
Beaumont Marine PP, 143 acres
Botanical Beach PP, 867 acres
Brackman Island Ecological Reserve, 86 acres
China Beach PP, 151 acres
D'Arcy Island PP, 208 acres
Dionisio Point PP, 351 acres
Discovery Island Marine PP, 151 acres
French Beach PP, 146 acres
Galiano Island Ecological Reserve, 74 acres
Goldstream PP, 813 acres
John Dean PP, 430 acres
Matheson Lake PP, 400 acres
Montague Harbour PP, 240 acres
Mount Maxwell Ecological Reserve, 161 acres
Mount Maxwell PP, 492 acres
Mount Tuam Ecological Reserve, 628 acres
Oak Bay Islands Ecological Reserve, 507 acres
Princess Margaret Marine PP, 1,320 acres
Race Rocks Ecological Reserve, 544 acres
Ruckle PP, 1,201 acres
San Juan Ridge Ecological Reserve, 242 acres
Satellite Channel Ecological Reserve, 848 acres
Saturna Island Ecological Reserve, 324 acres
Sidney Spit Marine PP, 986 acres
Sooke Potholes PP, 17 acres
Wallace Island Marine PP, 178 acres
Winter Cove PP, 225 acres

Places Rated Score: 49.80 Places Rated Rank: 178

Victoria, TX

Common Denominators
Golf courses: 2 private (36 holes), 2 municipal (27 holes) **B**

	Rating
Good restaurants: 1 *	C
Movie theaters: 3 Chains (14 screens), 1 Independent (1 screen)	AA

Crowd Pleasers
Aquariums and Zoos
The Texas Zoo
Outdoor Assets
Inland Water Area: 3,840 acres
Places Rated Score: 3.05 Places Rated Rank: 342

Vineland–Millville–Bridgeton, NJ
Common Denominators

	Rating
Golf courses: 3 daily fee (45 holes)	B
Movie theaters: 3 Chains (9 screens)	C

Crowd Pleasers
Aquariums and Zoos
Cohanzick Zoo
Outdoor Assets
Water Area
Atlantic offshore: 11,072 acres
Inland: 9,600 acres
State Recreation Area
Bear Swamp East SNA, 1,415 acres
Places Rated Score: 15.56 Places Rated Rank: 293

Visalia–Tulare–Porterville, CA
Common Denominators

	Rating
Golf courses: 1 private (18 holes), 4 daily fee (63 holes), 3 municipal (36 holes)	B
Good restaurants: 1 **, 1 ***	C
Movie theaters: 6 Chains (15 screens), 3 Independent (6 screens)	C

Crowd Pleasers
Professional sports
Oaks (Class A Baseball)
Outdoor Assets
Inland Water Area: 9,600 acres
Federal Protected Areas
Blue Ridge NWR, 897 acres
Inyo NF, 190,798 acres
Kings Canyon NP, 107,018 acres
Pixley NWR, 6,348 acres
Sequoia NF, 698,977 acres
Sequoia NP, 402,299 acres
State Recreation Area
Colonel Allensworth SHP, 240 acres
Places Rated Score: 38.64 Places Rated Rank: 217

Waco, TX
Common Denominators

	Rating
Golf courses: 2 private (36 holes), 2 daily fee (36 holes), 2 municipal (36 holes)	B
Good restaurants: 3 *, 2 **	B
Movie theaters: 7 Chains (13 screens)	A

Crowd Pleasers
Aquariums and Zoos
Central Texas Zoo
NCAA Division I
Baylor University Bears (B, F)
Outdoor Assets
Inland Water Area: 11,520 acres
Places Rated Score: 21.52 Places Rated Rank: 268

✓ Washington, DC–MD–VA–WV
Common Denominators

	Rating
Golf courses: 63 private (1,026 holes), 43 daily fee (711 holes), 25 municipal (423 holes)	C
Good restaurants: 47 *, 132 **, 76 ***, 2 ****	AA
Movie theaters: 61 Chains (226 screens), 9 Independent (23 screens)	A

Crowd Pleasers
Aquariums and Zoos
Catoctin Mountain Zoological Park
National Aquarium
National Zoological Park
Professional sports
Bay Sox (Class AA Baseball)
Keys (Class A Baseball)
P W Cannons (Class A Baseball)
Redskins (NFL Football)
United (MLS Soccer)
Washington Capitals (NHL Hockey)
Wizards (NBA Basketball)
NCAA Division I
American University Eagles (B)
George Mason University Patriots (B)
George Washington University Colonials (B)
Georgetown University Hoyas (B, F)
Howard University Bison (B, F)
Mount St. Mary's College Mountaineers (B)
University of Maryland Terps (B, F)
Outdoor Assets
Water Area
Atlantic offshore: 16,576 acres
Inland: 95,360 acres
Federal Protected Areas
Appalachian NT, 7,323 acres
Arlington House–Robert E Lee NM, 28 acres
Blue Ridge N Parkway, 1 acre
Catoctin Mountain Park, 5,696 acres
Chesapeake and Ohio Canal NHP, 4,474 acres
Constitution Gardens, 52 acres
Featherstone NWR, 326 acres
Ford's Theatre NHS, 1 acre
Fort Washington Park, 341 acres
Frederick Douglass NHS, 8 acres
Fredericksburg and Spotsylvania NMP, 5,373 acres
George Washington NF, 6,270 acres
George Washington N Parkway, 7,089 acres
Greenbelt Park, 1,175 acres
Harpers Ferry NHP, 1,394 acres
Korean War Veterans NM, 2 acres
Lincoln NMem, 107 acres
Lyndon B. Johnson NM Grove, 17 acres
Manassas NBP, 4,356 acres
Mason Neck NWR, 1,487 acres
Monocacy NB, 1,015 acres
National Capital Parks, 6,051 acres
National Mall, 146 acres
Pennsylvania Avenue NHS, 1 acre
Piscataway Park, 4,216 acres
Prince William Forest Park, 17,410 acres
Rock Creek Park, 1,754 acres
Shenandoah NP, 13,690 acres
Theodore Roosevelt Island, 88 acres
Thomas Jefferson NM, 18 acres
Thomas Stone NHS, 322 acres
Vietnam Veterans NM, 2 acres
Washington Monument, 106 acres
White House, 18 acres
Wolf Trap Farm Park, 130 acres
State Recreation Areas
Caledon NA, 2,579 acres
Calvert Cliffs SP, 1,313 acres
Cunningham Falls SP, 4,946 acres
Gambrill SP, 1,137 acres
Gathland SP, 23 acres
George Washington's Grist Mill SHS, 7 acres
Lake Anna SP, 2,000 acres
Leesylvania SP, 500 acres
Mason Neck SP, 3,608 acres
Merkle Wildlife Sanctuary, 1,670 acres
Patuxent River SP, 3,177 acres
Rosaryville SP, 982 acres
Seneca Creek SP, 6,109 acres
Sky Meadows SP, 1,618 acres
Smallwood SP, 629 acres
South Mountain SP, 2,356 acres
Places Rated Score: 97.87 Places Rated Rank: 6

Rating

Waterbury, CT
Common Denominators
Golf courses: 5 private (72 holes), 5 municipal (72 holes) — **B**
Good restaurants: 2 *, 2 ** — **B**
Movie theaters: 2 Chains (10 screens) — **C**
Outdoor Assets
Inland Water Area: 12,800 acres
State Recreation Areas
Black Rock SP, 443 acres
George C. Waldo SP, 150 acres
Kettletown SP, 492 acres
Whittemore Glen SP, 242 acres
Places Rated Score: 12.09 — Places Rated Rank: 307

Waterloo–Cedar Falls, IA

George Wyth Memorial SHS, 494 acres
Places Rated Score: 12.75 — Places Rated Rank: 305

Wausau, WI
Common Denominators
Golf courses: 1 private (18 holes), 6 daily fee (90 holes) — **AA**
Good restaurants: 3 *, 3 ** — **AA**
Movie theaters: 2 Chains (9 screens), 1 Independent (1 screen) — **B**
Outdoor Assets
Inland Water Area: 19,840 acres
State Recreation Areas
Mountain-Bay State Trail, 232 acres
Rib Mountain SP, 1,051 acres
Places Rated Score: 23.40 — Places Rated Rank: 262

✓ West Palm Beach–Boca Raton, FL
Common Denominators
Golf courses: 103 private (1,800 holes), 17 daily fee (297 holes), 11 municipal (189 holes) — **A**
Good restaurants: 10 *, 37 **, 36 ***, 3 **** — **AA**
Movie theaters: 16 Chains (118 screens) — **A**
Crowd Pleasers
Aquariums and Zoos
Dreher Park Zoo
South Florida Aquarium
Professional sports
Expos (Class A Baseball)
Florida Beachdogs (CBA Basketball)
NCAA Division I
Florida Atlantic University Owls (B)
Outdoor Assets
Water Area
Atlantic offshore: 6,208 acres
Inland: 163,840 acres
Federal Protected Area
Loxahatchee NWR, 2,550 acres
State Recreation Area
MacArthur Beach SP, 225 acres
Places Rated Score: 92.26 — Places Rated Rank: 31

Wheeling, WV–OH
Common Denominators
Golf courses: 3 private (54 holes), 3 daily fee (27 holes), 4 municipal (63 holes) — **A**
Good restaurants: 1 **, 1 *** — **B**
Movie theaters: 1 Independent (1 screen) — **C**
Crowd Pleasers
Aquariums and Zoos
Oglebay Good Children's Zoo
Professional sports
Thunderbirds (ECHL Hockey)
Outdoor Assets
Inland Water Area: 7,680 acres
State Recreation Areas
Barkcamp SP, 1,115 acres
Grave Creek Mound SP, 7 acres
Places Rated Score: 14.01 — Places Rated Rank: 299

Wichita, KS
Common Denominators
Golf courses: 10 private (162 holes), 9 daily fee (117 holes), 8 municipal (117 holes) — **A**
Good restaurants: 3 **, 2 *** — **C**

Cheney SP, 203 acres
El Dorado SP, 3,800 acres
Places Rated Score: 44.32 — Places Rated Rank: 204

Wichita Falls, TX
Common Denominators
Golf courses: 1 private (18 holes), 4 daily fee (54 holes), 2 municipal (36 holes) — **AA**
Good restaurants: 2 * — **C**
Movie theaters: 5 Chains (18 screens) — **AA**
Outdoor Assets
Inland Water Area: 13,440 acres
Places Rated Score: 18.61 — Places Rated Rank: 281

Williamsport, PA
Common Denominators
Golf courses: 1 private (18 holes), 2 municipal (36 holes) — **B**
Movie theaters: 3 Chains (11 screens) — **B**
Outdoor Assets
Inland Water Area: 5,760 acres
State Recreation Areas
Little Pine SP, 2,158 acres
Susquehanna SP, 20 acres
Upper Pine Bottom SP, 5 acres
Places Rated Score: 3.86 — Places Rated Rank: 336

Wilmington, NC
Common Denominators
Golf courses: 4 private (72 holes), 30 daily fee (540 holes), 1 municipal (18 holes) — **AA**
Good restaurants: 9 *, 12 ** — **AA**
Movie theaters: 6 Chains (20 screens) — **B**
Crowd Pleasers
Aquariums and Zoos
North Carolina Aquarium
Professional sports
Roosters (Class AA Baseball)
NCAA Division I
University of North Carolina Seahawks (B)
Outdoor Assets
Water Area
Atlantic offshore: 16,960 acres
Inland: 37,760 acres
State Recreation Area
Carolina Beach SP, 1,773 acres
Places Rated Score: 82.71 — Places Rated Rank: 63

	Rating

Wilmington-Newark, DE-MD

	Rating
Common Denominators	
Golf courses: 11 private (189 holes), 5 daily fee (90 holes), 2 municipal (36 holes)	**C**
Good restaurants: 7 *, 8 **, 8 ***	**AA**
Movie theaters: 7 Chains (49 screens)	**B**

Crowd Pleasers
- Aquariums and Zoos
  - Brandywine Zoo
- Professional sports
  - Blue Rocks (Class A Baseball)
- NCAA Division I
  - University of Delaware Blue Hens (B, F)

Outdoor Assets
- Water Area
  - Atlantic offshore: 5,376 acres
  - Inland: 34,560 acres
- State Recreation Areas
  - Bellevue SP, 328 acres
  - Brandywine Creek SP, 873 acres
  - Carpenter SP, 1,164 acres
  - Elk Neck SP, 2,188 acres
  - Fail Hill SNA, 5,613 acres
  - Fletcher Brown SP, 2 acres
  - Flint Woods Nature Preserve, 138 acres
  - Fort Delaware SP, 288 acres
  - Fort DuPont SP, 323 acres
  - Fox Point SP, 171 acres
  - Lums Pond SP, 1,777 acres
  - Port Penn Interpretive Center, 7 acres
  - White Clay Creek Preserve, 593 acres
  - White Clay Creek SP, 1,009 acres

Places Rated Score: 66.52 Places Rated Rank: 116

Windsor, ON

	Rating
Common Denominators	
Golf courses: 3 private (54 holes), 5 daily fee (81 holes), 5 municipal (72 holes)	**A**
Good restaurants: 7 **	**A**
Movie theaters: 5 Chains (16 screens)	**C**

Crowd Pleasers
- CIAU
  - University of Windsor Lancers

Outdoor Assets
- Water Area
  - Lake St. Claire offshore: 17,000 acres
  - Inland: 1,500 acres
- Federal Protected Areas
  - Pinafore Park MBS, 988 acres
  - Point Pelee NP, 3,830 acres
- Provincial Recreation Areas
  - Aylmer Provincial Wildlife Area, 371 acres
  - East Sister Island Nature Res Prov Pk, 131 acres
  - Fingal Provincial Wildlife Area, 724 acres
  - Fish Point Nature Reserve Provincial Pk, 272 acres
  - Holiday Beach PP, 227 acres
  - John Pearce PP, 168 acres
  - Lighthouse Point Nature Reserve Prov Pk, 237 acres
  - Miner Crown Game Preserve, 1,436 acres
  - Nr-Zone 1 (port Burwell Pp), 220 acres
  - Ojibway Prairie Nature Reserve Prov Pk, 161 acres
  - Peche Island PP, 378 acres
  - Port Burwell PP, 561 acres
  - Yarmouth Crown Game Preserve, 3,257 acres

Places Rated Score: 33.77 Places Rated Rank: 235

Winnipeg, MB

	Rating
Common Denominators	
Golf courses: 8 private (126 holes), 7 daily fee (108 holes), 3 municipal (54 holes)	**C**
Good restaurants: 1 **, 1 ***	**C**
Movie theaters: 8 Chains (35 screens), 3 Independent (5 screens)	**C**

Crowd Pleasers
- Aquariums and Zoos
  - Assiniboine Park Zoo
- Professional sports
  - Blue Bombers (CFL Football)
  - Cyclone (IBA Basketball)
- CIAU
  - University of Manitoba Bisons
  - University of Winnipeg Wesmen (B, H)

Outdoor Assets
- Inland Water Area: 85,000 acres
- Federal Protected Areas
  - Pope NWA, 77 acres
  - Rockwood NWA, 79 acres
- Provincial Recreation Areas
  - Beaudry PP, 2,170 acres
  - Birds Hill PP, 8,700 acres
  - Libau Bog Ecological Reserve, 460 acres
  - Patricia Beach PP, 153 acres

Places Rated Score: 63.60 Places Rated Rank: 124

Worcester, MA-CT

	Rating
Common Denominators	
Golf courses: 6 private (90 holes), 15 daily fee (207 holes), 3 municipal (36 holes)	**A**
Good restaurants: 2 **, 2 ***	**C**
Movie theaters: 6 Chains (16 screens), 3 Independent (4 screens)	**B**

Crowd Pleasers
- Aquariums and Zoos
  - Greenhill Farm Nature Center
  - New England Science Center
- Professional sports
  - Ice Cats (AHL Hockey)
- NCAA Division I
  - College of the Holy Cross Crusaders

Outdoor Assets
- Inland Water Area: 42,240 acres
- Federal Protected Area
  - Oxbow NWR, 711 acres
- State Recreation Area
  - Blackstone River and Canal SHS, 1,005 acres
  - Buffumville SRA, 400 acres
  - Campbell's Falls SP, 5 acres
  - Holland Pond SRA, 35 acres
  - Moore SP, 595 acres
  - Purgatory Chasm SP, 533 acres
  - Quaddick SP, 116 acres
  - Quinsigamond SP, 51 acres
  - Rutland SP, 396 acres
  - Streeter Point SRA, 10 acres
  - Wachusett Mountain SR, 2,849 acres
  - Wells SP, 1,470 acres

Places Rated Score: 62.31 Places Rated Rank: 129

Yakima, WA

	Rating
Common Denominators	
Golf courses: 2 private (36 holes), 5 daily fee (81 holes)	**B**
Good restaurants: 1 **, 1 ***	**C**
Movie theaters: 4 Chains (21 screens), 2 Independent (5 screens)	**A**

Crowd Pleasers
- Professional sports
  - Bears (Class A Baseball)
  - Sun Kings (CBA Basketball)

Outdoor Assets
- Inland Water Area: 10,240 acres
- Federal Protected Areas
  - Gifford Pinchot NF, 37,552 acres
  - Snoqualmie NF, 466,543 acres
  - Toppenish NWR, 1,979 acres
- State Recreation Areas
  - Fort Simcoe SP, 200 acres
  - Yakima Sportsmans SP, 246 acres

Places Rated Score: 47.26 Places Rated Rank: 190

	Rating
Yolo, CA	
Common Denominators	
Golf courses: 2 private (36 holes), 2 daily fee (27 holes), 1 municipal (18 holes)	B
Good restaurants: 1 *, 1 **	C
Movie theaters: 4 Chains (16 screens)	A
Outdoor Assets	
Inland Water Area: 6,400 acres	
State Recreation Area	
Woodland Opera House SHP, 1	
Places Rated Score: 7.77 Places Rated Rank: 324	

York, PA
Common Denominators

Places Rated Score: 16.73 Places Rated Rank: 286

	Rating
Youngstown–Warren, OH	
Common Denominators	
Golf courses: 7 private (117 holes), 39 daily fee (540 holes), 4 municipal (63 holes)	AA
Good restaurants: 1 *, 1 **, 2 ***	C
Movie theaters: 5 Chains (32 screens), 5 Independent (8 screens)	C
Crowd Pleasers	
NCAA Division I	
Youngstown State University Penguins (B, F)	
Outdoor Assets	
Inland Water Area: 18,560 acres	
State Recreation Areas	
Beaver Creek SP, 3,038 acres	
Guilford Lake SP, 92 acres	
Kyle Woods SNA, 82 acres	
Mosquito Creek SP, 3,961 acres	
Museum of Ceramics SHS, 1 acres	
Youngstown Center Industry/Labor SHS, 1 acres	
Places Rated Score: 59.97 Places Rated Rank: 139	

	Rating
Yuba City, CA	
Common Denominators	
Golf courses: 1 private (18 holes), 3 daily fee (36 holes), 1 municipal (18 holes)	B
Movie theaters: 1 Chain (8 screens), 1 Independent (1 screen)	C

	Rating
Golf courses: 1 private (18 holes), 4 daily fee (63 holes), 1 municipal (18 holes)	A
	A
Good restaurants: 1 *, 2 **	B
Movie theaters: 2 Chains (12 screens)	B
Outdoor Assets	
Inland Water Area: 3,200 acres	
Federal Protected Areas	
Cabeza Prieta NWR, 443,800 acres	
Kofa NWR, 528,481 acres	
State Recreation Area	
Yuma Territorial Prison SHS, 9 acres	
Places Rated Score: 27.18 Places Rated Rank: 251	

Et Cetera

LOOKING FOR THE BEST SKIING?

Draw a line on a map of North America separating regions with the best conditions for skiing from those with poor conditions or none at all and you'd have a jagged northward arc. It starts in North Carolina's Great Smokey Mountains and extends upward to Atlantic Canada, west to the foothills of the Rockies, then south along the Rocky Mountain cordillera to northern New Mexico and Arizona. Next it would reappear in the California Sierra Nevada, dropping southwest to end in the San Bernardino National Forest an hour and a half out of Los Angeles.

Although ski areas exist as far south as Alabama and Georgia, the ideal conditions are found north of this imaginary curve in the rolling, rugged terrain and predictable winter weather that everyone except skiers would call bad.

By definition, a ski area is more than a snow-covered hill or mountain. It also has developed trails and lift machinery. Usually, too, there is a lodge for meals and overnight stays. If the area is large and popular, it also has *aprè-ski*—nighttime entertainment from music to movies to disco—that is as critical as fresh snow and challenging runs to many skiers.

Of the 610 ski areas in North America, half are found in nine states and provinces that border the St. Lawrence River and the Great Lakes—Michigan, Minnesota, New Hampshire, New York, Ontario, Pennsylvania, Quebec, Vermont, and Wisconsin—owing to harsh, long winters and large, outdoorsy urban populations.

Vertical Rise . . .

The perpendicular distance from the base to the highest skiable point on a hill or mountain is a ski area's vertical. British Columbia's 26 ski areas average 1,824 feet, whereas Nebraska's single ski area has a rise of

The Top Ski Areas for Vertical Rise

Ski Area	Height
Whistler/Blackcomb Mountains, BC	5,280
Jackson Hole, WY	4,139
Aspen Highlands, CO	3,800
Panorama, BC	3,800
Snowmass at Aspen, CO	3,615
Heavenly Valley, CA	3,600
Steamboat, CO	3,600
Telluride, CO	3,522
Sunshine Village, AB	3,514
Sun Valley, ID	3,400
Beaver Creek, CO	3,340
Aspen, CO	3,267
Lake Louise, AB	3,250
Vail, CO	3,250
Whiteface Mountain, NY	3,216
Killington, VT	3,175
Crystal Mountain, WA	3,100
Mammoth Mountain, CA	3,100
Mt. Bachelor, OR	3,100
Park City, UT	3,100
Snowbird, UT	3,100
Tod Mountain, BC	3,100
Nakiska, AB	3,082

Source: Inter-Ski Services, *The White Book of Ski Areas.*

only 200 feet. Although vertical rise has little to do with the quality of trails, it is a good indication of length of the runs and the mountain's challenge. More than one optimistic ski-area promoter has stretched the distance a bit—some, allegedly, by measuring from the top of the tallest tree on the crest to the surface of the highway below the base lodge.

. . . and Longest Runs . . .

The highest vertical is found at British Columbia's Whistler area, but the longest run is at Killington, in Vermont. The longest run is the lengthiest continuous trail on the mountain, from the top to the runout, which is usually in the base lodge's parking lot.

The Top Ski Areas for Lift Capacity

Ski Area	Skiers per Hour
Squaw Valley, CA	47,370
Mammoth Mountain, CA	46,000
Vail, CO	35,020
Keystone Mountain/The Outback, CO	32,817
Heavenly Valley, CA	31,000
Killington, VT	30,827
Alpental/Ski Acres/Snoqualmie, WA	30,000
Steamboat, CO	29,327
Winter Park, CO	28,310
Copper Mountain, CO	28,250
Mount Snow, VT	26,685
Breckenridge, CO	24,430
Whistler/Blackcomb Mountains, BC	23,850
Sun Valley, ID	23,580
Stratton Mountain, VT	22,120
Alpine Valley, MI	21,330
Sunday River, ME	21,000
Snowmass at Aspen, CO	20,535
Seven Springs, PA	20,400
Afton Alps, MN	20,000
Mount St. Louis Moonstone, ON	20,000

Source: Inter-Ski Services, *The White Book of Ski Areas.*

The Longest Ski Runs

Ski Area	Length
Killington Ski Resort, VT	10.2 miles
Jackson Hole, WY	7
Whistler–Blackcomb Mountains, BC	7
Heavenly Valley, CA	5.5
Taos Ski Valley, NM	5.2
Tod Mountain, BC	5.2
Lake Louise, AB	5
Mission Ridge, WA	5
Sunshine Village, AB	5
Okemo Mountain, VT	4.5
Red Mountain Ski Area, BC	4.5
Vail, CO	4.5
Snowmass at Aspen, CO	4.1
Kimberley Ski Resort, BC	4

Source: Inter-Ski Services, *The White Book of Ski Areas.*

. . . and Lift Capacities

A ski area's lift capacity is the number of people its lifts can move up the mountain in one hour. Lifts can be elementary rope or cable tows, bars (T-bars, J-bars, pomalifts, or platterpulls), chairs, trams, or gondolas. Whatever the mix of lifts at a ski resort, the total lift capacity is a good indication of how developed the ski area is and often of how efficient the lift lines are. Twenty-one North American ski areas have lift capacities of at least 20,000 skiers per hour. At Squaw Valley and at Mammoth Mountain in the California Sierras, nearly 50,000 skiers per hour can be moved up the mountain.

WHERE ARE THE BEST SPORTS TOWNS?

Ask 100 sports fans to describe the ideal sports town and you'll probably get 100 different answers. Being able to attend a game easily is not the only thing a fan wants. Rooting for the home team is fun, but rooting for a winning home team is ecstasy. In the lists that follow, *Places Rated* looks at the metro areas with the winning teams.

Major-League Title Towns

For baseball fans in the mid-1970s, the place to be was Oakland as the A's hauled in three straight World Series championships. In the 1960s, football fans found a warm welcome in frosty Green Bay, where the Packers took five NFL championships over a seven-year span. No baseball team can really be called a dominant World Series champ for the 1980s. Neither has any football team topped the Packers' record for the 1960s, but the Pittsburgh Steelers, with four Super Bowl wins, the San Francisco 49ers, with three, and the Washington Redskins, with two, inspired devotion among fans in the late

1970s and throughout the 1980s. The Dallas Cowboys have dominated much of the 1990s.

Basketball lovers from the 1960s through the 1980s, on the other hand, wouldn't have been far wrong if they backed the Boston Celtics, winners of more titles than any other team in NBA history. With all their tradition and mystique—and the renowned parquet floor of the Boston Garden where they played—they left many opponents bewitched, bothered, and bewildered. Still, in the 1980s the Los Angeles Lakers didn't do too badly either, with more championships in that decade than any other team. In the 1990s, the Chicago Bulls and the Houston Rockets have been the teams to watch.

Super Bowl: Bears, 1986
NHL Stanley Cup: Black Hawks, 1934, 1938, 1961

Cincinnati, OH-KY-IN
World Series: Reds, 1919, 1940, 1975, 1976, 1990

Cleveland, OH
World Series: Indians, 1920, 1948
NFL Championship: Rams, 1945; Browns, 1950, 1954, 1955, 1964

Dallas, TX
Super Bowl: Cowboys, 1972, 1978, 1993, 1994, 1995
AFL Championship: Texans, 1962

Denver, CO
NHL Stanley Cup: Colorado Avalanche, 1996

Detroit, MI
World Series: Tigers, 1935, 1945, 1968, 1984
NBA Championship: Pistons, 1989, 1990

a little more toward the roots, we also list the winning teams from the leagues that preceded the modern NFL (the National Football League, 1933–1969, and American Football League, 1960–1969) and the NBA (the Basketball Association of America, 1947–1949). The NFL and AFL champions of 1966, 1967, and 1968 met in the Super Bowls of 1967, 1968, and 1969, before the formation of the modern NFL; for those years, we name the winners of both the individual league championships and the Super Bowl.

If a team has changed names or towns, we list it with the name it used and in the town it played at the time it won the championship.

Professional Championships in the Metro Areas

Anaheim–Santa Ana, CA
NFL Championship: Los Angeles Rams, 1951

Atlanta, GA
World Series: Braves, 1995

Baltimore, MD
World Series: Orioles, 1966, 1970, 1983
Super Bowl: Colts, 1971
NFL Championship: Colts 1958, 1959, 1968
BAA Championship: Bullets, 1948

Bergen–Passaic, NJ
NHL Stanley Cup: Devils, 1995

Boston, MA
World Series: Somersets, 1903; Red Sox, 1912, 1914, 1915, 1916, 1918
NBA Championship: Celtics, 1957, 1959, 1960, 1961, 1962, 1963, 1964, 1965, 1966, 1968, 1969, 1974, 1976, 1981, 1984, 1986
NHL Stanley Cup: Bruins, 1929, 1939, 1941, 1970, 1972

Buffalo, NY
AFL Championship: Bills, 1964, 1965

Calgary, AB
CFL Grey Cup: Stampeders, 1948, 1971, 1992
NHL Stanley Cup: Flames, 1989

Chicago, IL
World Series: White Sox, 1906, 1917; Cubs, 1907, 1908
NBA Championship: Bulls, 1991, 1992, 1993, 1996
NFL Championship: Bears, 1933, 1940, 1941, 1943, 1946; Cardinals, 1947; Bears, 1963

Hamilton, ON
CFL Grey Cup: Alerts, 1912; Tigers, 1913, 1915, 1925, 1929, 1932; Flying Wildcats, 1943; Tiger-Cats, 1953, 1957, 1963, 1965, 1967, 1972, 1986

Houston, TX
AFL Championship: Oilers, 1960, 1961
NBA Championship: Rockets, 1994, 1995

Kansas City, MO
Super Bowl: Chiefs, 1970
AFL Championship: Chiefs, 1966, 1969
World Series: Royals, 1985

Los Angeles–Long Beach, CA
World Series: Dodgers, 1959, 1963, 1965, 1981, 1988
Super Bowl: Raiders, 1984
NFL Championship: Rams, 1951
NBA Championship: Lakers, 1972, 1980, 1982, 1985, 1987, 1988

Miami, FL
Super Bowl: Dolphins, 1973, 1974

Milwaukee, WI
World Series: Braves, 1957
NBA Championship: Bucks, 1971

Minneapolis–St. Paul, MN
NFL Championship: Minnesota Vikings, 1969
BAA Championship: Minneapolis Lakers, 1949
NBA Championship: Minneapolis Lakers, 1950, 1952, 1953, 1954
World Series: Twins, 1987, 1991

Montreal, PO
CFL Grey Cup: M.A.A.A., 1931; HMCS St. Hyacinthe-Connacona, 1944; Alouettes, 1949, 1970, 1974, 1977
NHL Stanley Cup: Canadiens, 1924; Maroons, 1926; Canadiens, 1930, 1931; Maroons, 1935; Canadiens, 1944, 1946, 1953, 1956, 1957, 1958, 1959, 1960, 1965, 1966, 1968, 1969, 1971, 1973, 1976, 1977, 1978, 1979, 1986

Nassau–Suffolk, NY
NHL Stanley Cup: New York Islanders, 1980, 1981, 1982, 1983

New York, NY
World Series: Giants, 1905, 1921, 1922, 1933, 1954; Yankees, 1923, 1927, 1928, 1932, 1936, 1937, 1938, 1939, 1941, 1943, 1947, 1949, 1950, 1951, 1952, 1953, 1956, 1958, 1961, 1962, 1977, 1978; Brooklyn Dodgers, 1955; Mets, 1969, 1986
Super Bowl: Jets, 1969; Giants, 1987, 1991
AFL Championship: Jets, 1968
NFL Championship: Giants, 1934, 1938, 1944, 1956
NBA Championship: Knickerbockers, 1970, 1973
NHL Stanley Cup: Rangers, 1928, 1933, 1940

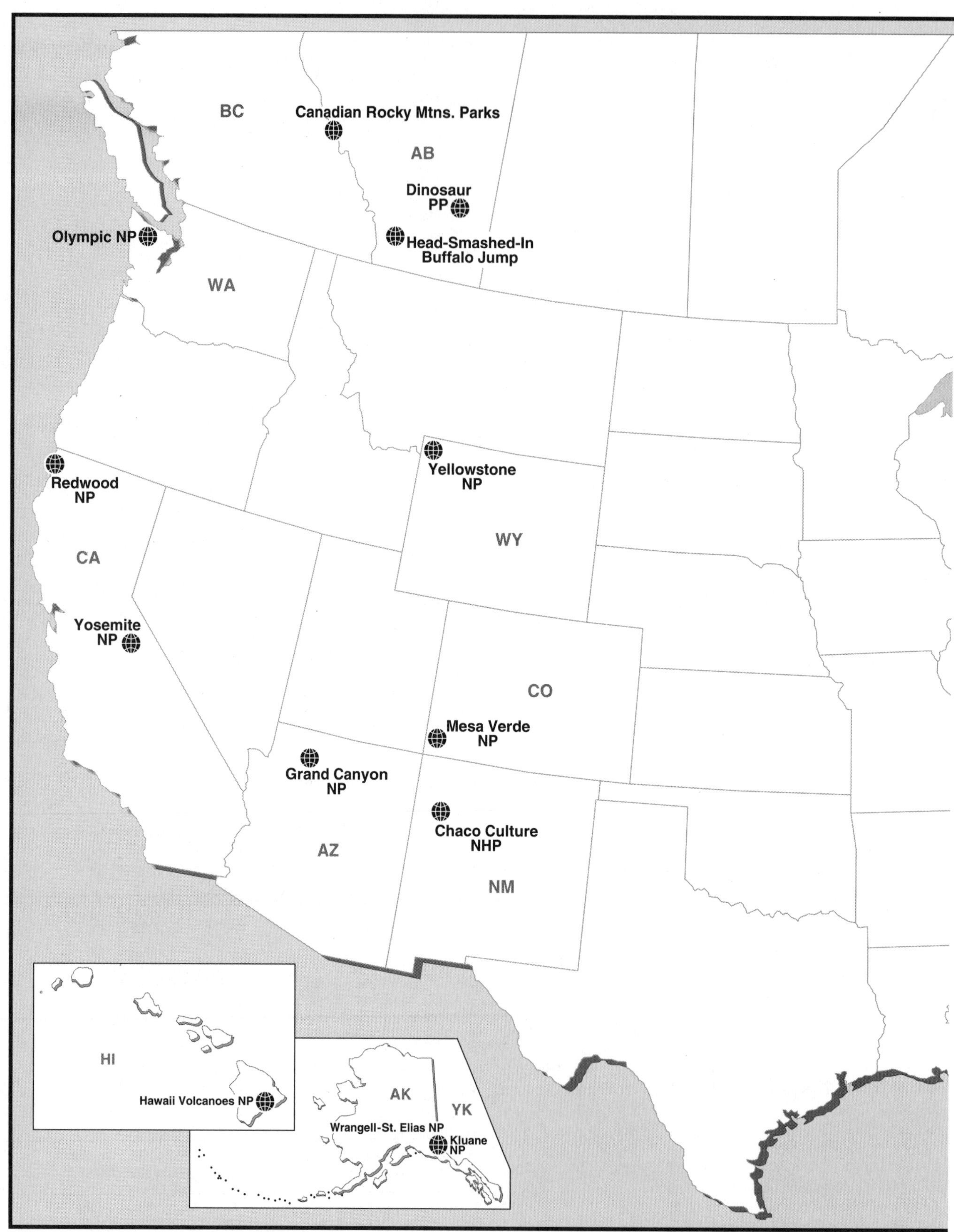
BC
Canadian Rocky Mtns. Parks
AB
Dinosaur PP
Head-Smashed-In Buffalo Jump
Olympic NP
WA
Redwood NP
Yellowstone NP
WY
CA
Yosemite NP
CO
Mesa Verde NP
Grand Canyon NP
Chaco Culture NHP
AZ
NM
HI
Hawaii Volcanoes NP
AK
YK
Wrangell-St. Elias NP
Kluane NP

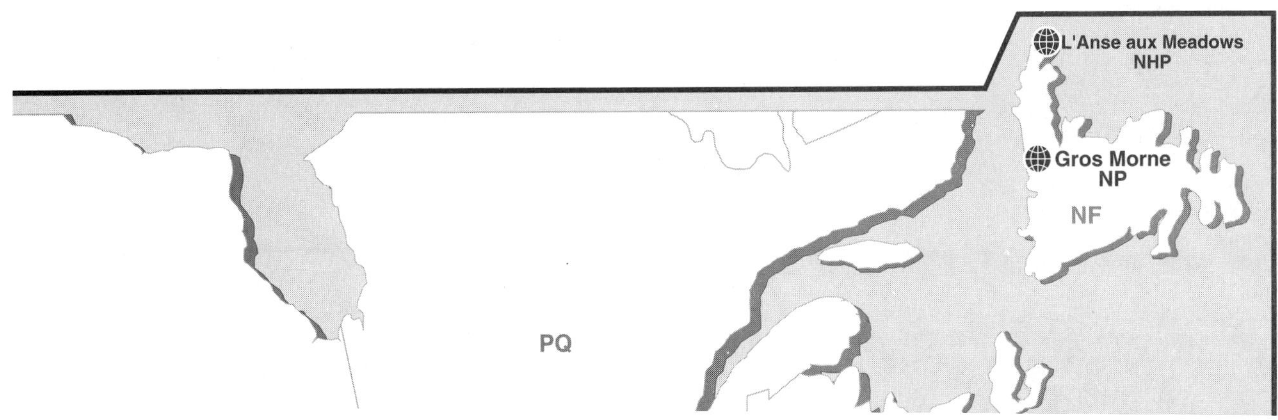

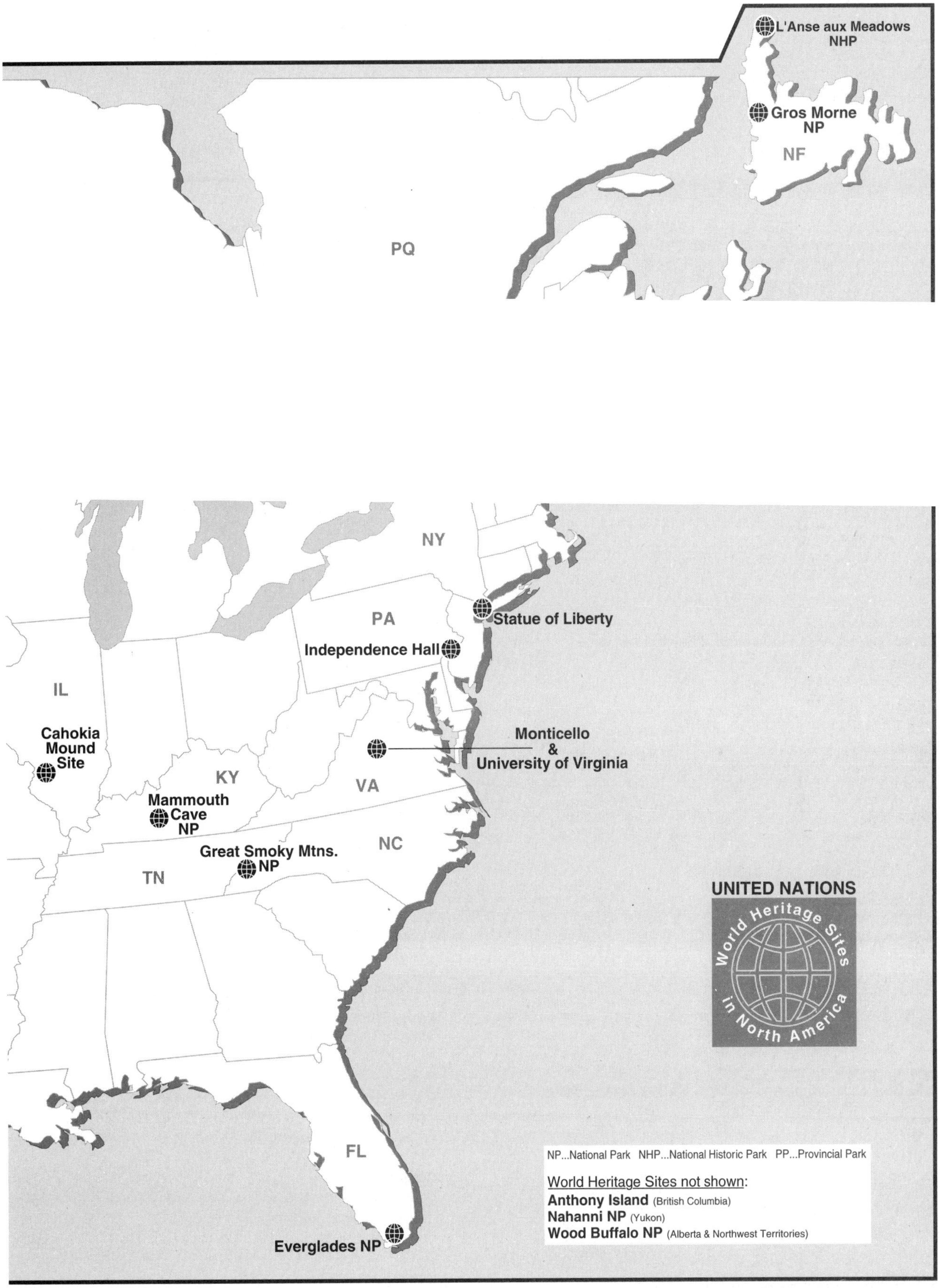

L'Anse aux Meadows NHP
Gros Morne NP
NF
PQ
NY
PA
Statue of Liberty
Independence Hall
IL
Cahokia Mound Site
Monticello & University of Virginia
KY
VA
Mammouth Cave NP
Great Smoky Mtns. NP
NC
TN
UNITED NATIONS
World Heritage Sites in North America
FL
Everglades NP
NP...National Park NHP...National Historic Park PP...Provincial Park
World Heritage Sites not shown:
Anthony Island (British Columbia)
Nahanni NP (Yukon)
Wood Buffalo NP (Alberta & Northwest Territories)

Thomas Nast, Cartographer

Oakland, CA
World Series: Athletics, 1972, 1973; A's, 1974, 1989
Super Bowl: Raiders, 1977, 1981
AFL Championship: Raiders, 1967
NBA Championship: Golden State Warriors, 1975

Ottawa–Hull, ON–PQ
CFL Grey Cup: Senators, 1925, 1926; Rough Riders, 1940, 1951, 1960, 1968, 1969, 1973, 1976
NHL Stanley Cup: Senators, 1920, 1921, 1923, 1927

Philadelphia, PA
World Series: Athletics, 1910, 1911, 1913, 1929, 1930; Phillies, 1980
NFL Championship: Eagles, 1948, 1949, 1960
BAA Championship: Warriors, 1947
NBA Championship: Warriors, 1956; 76ers, 1967, 1983
NHL Stanley Cup: Flyers, 1974, 1975

Pittsburgh, PA
World Series: Pirates, 1909, 1925, 1960, 1971, 1979
Super Bowl: Steelers, 1975, 1976, 1979, 1980
NHL Stanley Cup: Penguins, 1991, 1992

Portland, OR
NBA Championship: Trail Blazers, 1977

Regina, SK
CFL Grey Cup: Roughriders, 1966, 1989

Rochester, NY
NBA Championship: Royals, 1951

St. Louis, MO–IL
World Series: Cardinals, 1926, 1931, 1934, 1942, 1944, 1946, 1964, 1967, 1982
NBA Championship: Hawks, 1958

San Diego, CA
AFL Championship: Chargers, 1963

San Francisco, CA
Super Bowl: 49ers, 1982, 1985, 1989, 1990

Seattle, WA
NBA Championship: Supersonics, 1979

Syracuse, NY
NBA Championship: Nationals, 1955

Toronto, ON
CFL Grey Cup: Argonauts, 1914, 1921, 1933, 1937, 1938, 1945, 1946, 1947, 1950, 1952, 1983, 1991; Balmy Beach, 1927, 1930; U of Toronto, 1909, 1910, 1911, 1920; RCAF Hurricanes, 1942
NHL Stanley Cup: Arenas, 1918; St. Patricks, 1922; Maple Leafs, 1932, 1942, 1945, 1947, 1948, 1949, 1951, 1962, 1963, 1964, 1967
World Series: Blue Jays, 1992, 1993

Vancouver, BC
CFL Grey Cup: Lions, 1964, 1985, 1994

Victoria, BC
NHL Stanley Cup: Cougars, 1925

Washington, DC–MD–VA
World Series: Senators, 1924
Super Bowl: Redskins, 1983, 1988, 1992
NFL Championship: Redskins, 1937, 1942
NBA Championship: Bullets, 1978

Winnipeg, MB
CFL Grey Cup: Winnipegs, 1935; Blue Bombers, 1939, 1941, 1958, 1959, 1961, 1962, 1984, 1988, 1990

Collegiate Title Towns

The 1996–1997 academic year marks the 113th season of American college athletic championships that began all the way back when Harvard University's J. S. Clark captured the first singles title in college tennis in 1883. Founded in 1906, the National Collegiate Athletic Association (NCAA) began sponsoring college athletic championships in 1921, beginning with its first outdoor track meet. It was not until 1981, however, that the association initiated women's championships. Over the years, some 600 colleges and universities have been named national champions in each of the NCAA's three divisions. What follows are 67 metro areas with Division I champions since 1980.

Many NCAA sports, such as basketball and volleyball, have both men's and women's championships. An M or W after the sport in the list below indicates whether the title was in men's or women's competition. Sports such as baseball, football, ice hockey, and wrestling are played at the championship level by men only, whereas field hockey and softball championships are for women only; accordingly, no M or W designation is given for those sports. Ski teams are coed.

NCAA Division I Championships in the Metro Areas

Albany–Schenectady–Troy, NY
Rensselaer Polytechnic Institute: Ice Hockey, 1985

Ann Arbor, MI
University of Michigan: Basketball (M), 1989; Swimming and Diving (M), 1995

Athens, GA
University of Georgia: Baseball, 1990; Football (Division I-A), 1980; Gymnastics (W), 1987, 1989, 1993; Tennis (M), 1985, 1987; Tennis (W), 1994

Atlanta, GA
Georgia Institute of Technology: Football (Division I-A), 1990

Austin, TX
University of Texas: Baseball, 1983; Basketball (W), 1986; Cross Country (W), 1986; Gymnastics (W), 1987; Indoor Track (W), 1986, 1988, 1990; Outdoor Track (W), 1986; Swimming and Diving (M), 1981, 1988, 1989, 1990, 1991; Swimming and Diving (W), 1984, 1985, 1986, 1987, 1988, 1990, 1991; Tennis (W), 1993, 1995; Volleyball (W), 1988

Baltimore, MD
Johns Hopkins University: Lacrosse (M), 1980, 1984, 1985, 1987

Bangor, ME
University of Maine, Orono; Ice Hockey, 1993

Baton Rouge, LA
Louisiana State University: Baseball, 1991, 1993; Indoor Track (W) 1987, 1989, 1991, 1993, 1994, 1995; Outdoor Track (M), 1989, 1990; Outdoor Track (W), 1987, 1988, 1989, 1990, 1991, 1992, 1993, 1994, 1995

Bloomington, IN
Indiana University: Basketball (M), 1981, 1987; Soccer (M), 1982, 1983, 1988

Boise City, ID
Boise State University: Football (Division I-AA), 1980

Boston, MA
Harvard University: Ice Hockey, 1989
Boston University: Ice Hockey, 1995

Boulder–Longmont, CO
University of Colorado: Football (Division I-A), 1990; Skiing, 1982, 1991, 1995

Bryan–College Station, TX
Texas A & M University: Softball, 1983, 1987

Burlington, VT
University of Vermont: Skiing, 1980, 1989, 1990, 1992, 1994

Charlottesville, VA
University of Virginia: Cross Country (W), 1981, 1982; Lacrosse (W), 1993; Soccer (M), 1989, 1991, 1992, 1993, 1994

Columbus, OH
Ohio State University: Gymnastics (M), 1985

Dallas, TX
Southern Methodist University: Indoor Track (M), 1983; Outdoor Track (M), 1983, 1986

Denver, CO
University of Denver: Gymnastics (W), 1983

El Paso, TX
University of Texas, El Paso: Cross Country (M), 1980, 1981, 1983; Indoor Track (M), 1980, 1981, 1982; Outdoor Track (M), 1980, 1981, 1982

Eugene–Springfield, OR
University of Oregon: Cross Country (W), 1983, 1987; Outdoor Track (M), 1984; Outdoor Track (W), 1985

Fayetteville, AR
University of Arkansas: Basketball (M), 1994; Cross Country (M), 1986, 1987, 1991, 1992, 1993; Indoor Track (M), 1984, 1985, 1986, 1987, 1988, 1989, 1990, 1991, 1992, 1993, 1995, 1995; Outdoor Track (M), 1988, 1992, 1993, 1994, 1995

Fort Worth–Arlington, TX
Texas Christian University: Golf (W), 1983

...: Football (Division I-A), 1981; Soccer, 1984, 1987
Furman University: Football (Division I-AA), 1988

Honolulu, HI
University of Hawaii: Volleyball (W), 1982, 1983, 1987

Houston, TX
University of Houston: Golf (M), 1982, 1984, 1985

Iowa City, IA
University of Iowa: Field Hockey, 1986; Wrestling, 1980, 1981, 1982, 1983, 1984, 1985, 1986, 1991, 1992, 1993, 1995

Knoxville, TN
University of Tennessee: Basketball (W), 1987, 1989, 1991; 1996; Outdoor Track (M), 1991

Lansing–East Lansing, MI
Michigan State University: Ice Hockey, 1986

Las Vegas, NV
University of Nevada: Basketball (M), 1990

Lawrence, KS
Kansas University: Basketball (M), 1988

Lexington–Fayette, KY
University of Kentucky: Basketball (M), 1996; Cross Country (W), 1988;

Lincoln, NE
University of Nebraska: Gymnastics (M), 1980, 1981, 1982, 1983, 1988, 1994; Indoor Track (W), 1983, 1984

Los Angeles–Long Beach, CA
California State University, Long Beach: Volleyball (M), 1991; Volleyball (W), 1989, 1993
California State University, Northridge: Gymnastics (W), 1982 *Pepperdine University:* Baseball, 1992; Volleyball (M), 1985, 1986, 1992
University of California, Los Angeles: Basketball (M) 1995; Golf (M), 1988; Golf (W), 1991; Gymnastics (M), 1984, 1987; Outdoor Track (M), 1987, 1988; Outdoor Track (W), 1982, 1983; Soccer, 1985, 1990; Softball, 1982, 1984, 1985, 1988, 1989, 1990, 1992, 1995; Swimming and Diving (M), 1982; Tennis (M), 1982, 1984; Volleyball (M), 1981, 1982, 1983, 1984, 1987, 1989; Volleyball (W), 1984, 1990, 1991, 1993, 1995
University of Southern California: Basketball (W), 1983, 1984; Outdoor Track (W), 1982, 1983; Tennis (M), 1991, 1993, 1994; Tennis (W), 1983, 1985; Volleyball (W), 1981; Volleyball (M), 1980, 1988, 1990

Louisville, KY–IN
University of Louisville: Basketball (M), 1980, 1986

Madison, WI
University of Wisconsin: Cross Country (M), 1984; Cross Country (W), 1984, 1985; Ice Hockey, 1981, 1983, 1990

Miami, FL
University of Miami: Baseball, 1982, 1985; Football (Division I-A), 1983, 1987, 1989; Golf (W), 1984

Monroe, LA
Northeast Louisiana University: Football (Division I-AA), 1987

New York, NY
Columbia University: Fencing, 1992, 1993

Norfolk–Virginia Beach–Newport News, VA
Old Dominion University: Field Hockey, 1982, 1983, 1984, 1988, 1990, 1991, 1992; Basketball (W), 1985

Oakland, CA
University of California, ...

...: Lacrosse (W), 1984
Villanova University: Basketball (M), 1985; Cross Country (W), 1989, 1990, 1991, 1992, 1993, 1994

Phoenix, AZ
Arizona State University: Baseball, 1981; Golf (M), 1990; Golf (W), 1990, 1993, 1994, 1995; Gymnastics (M), 1986; Wrestling, 1988

Provo–Orem, UT
Brigham Young University: Football (Division I-A), 1984; Golf (M), 1981

Raleigh–Durham–Chapel Hill, NC
Duke University: Basketball, 1991, 1992; Soccer, 1986
North Carolina State University: Basketball (M), 1983
University of North Carolina: Basketball (M), 1982, 1993; Basketball (W), 1994; Field Hockey, 1989; Lacrosse (M), 1981, 1982, 1986, 1991; Soccer (W), 1982, 1983, 1984, 1986, 1987, 1988, 1990, 1991, 1992, 1993, 1994

Salt Lake City–Ogden, UT
University of Utah: Gymnastics (W), 1982, 1983, 1984, 1985, 1986, 1990, 1992, 1994, 1995; Skiing, 1981, 1983, 1984, 1986, 1987, 1988, 1993

San Francisco, CA
University of San Francisco: Soccer (M), 1980

San Jose, CA
San Jose State University: Golf (W), 1987, 1989, 1991, 1992 *Stanford University:* Baseball, 1987, 1988; Basketball (W), 1990, 1992; Golf (M), 1994; Gymnastics, 1992, 1993, 1995; Swimming and Diving (M), 1985, 1986, 1987, 1992, 1993, 1994; Swimming and Diving (W), 1983, 1989, 1992, 1993, 1994, 1995; Tennis (M), 1980, 1981, 1983, 1986, 1988, 1989, 1990, 1992, 1995; Tennis (W), 1982, 1984, 1986, 1987, 1988, 1989, 1990, 1991; Volleyball (W) 1992, 1994; Water Polo (M), 1980, 1981, 1993, 1994
University of Santa Clara: Soccer (M), 1989

Seattle, WA
University of Washington: Football (Division I-A), 1992

South Bend–Mishawaka, IN
University of Notre Dame: Fencing, 1994; Football (Division I-A), 1988

State College, PA
Pennsylvania State University: Fencing, 1990, 1991, 1995; Football (Division I-A), 1982, 1986; Volleyball (M), 1994

Stockton, CA
University of the Pacific: Volleyball (W), 1985, 1986

Syracuse, NY
Syracuse University: Lacrosse (M), 1983, 1988, 1989, 1990, 1993, 1995

Tallahassee, FL
Florida State University: Indoor Track (W), 1985; Outdoor Track (W), 1984

Toledo, OH
Bowling Green University: Ice Hockey, 1984

Trenton, NJ
Princeton University: Lacrosse (M), 1992, 1994; Lacrosse (W), 1994

Tucson, AZ
University of Arizona: Baseball, 1980, 1986; Golf (M), 1992; Softball (W), 1991, 1993, 1994

Tulsa, OK
University of Tulsa: Golf (W), 1982, 1988

Tuscaloosa, AL
University of Alabama: Football (Division I-A); Gymnastics (W), 1988, 1991

Washington, DC–MD–VA–WV
George Mason University: Soccer (W), 1985
Georgetown University: Basketball (M), 1984
University of Maryland: Field Hockey, 1987, 1993; Lacrosse (W), 1992, 1995

Wichita, KS
Wichita State University: Baseball, 1989

Wilmington, DE–NJ–MD
University of Delaware: Lacrosse (W), 1983

Youngstown, OH
Youngstown State University: Football (Division I-AA), 1991, 1993, 1994

Source: National Collegiate Athletic Association, College Champions, 1993.

In Division I-A Football, the NCAA recognizes as unofficial national champion the team selected each year by the Associated Press poll of sportswriters and the United Press International poll of coaches.

CIAU Championships in the Metro Areas

Canadian college athletes get only three years to play in interuniversity competition. Because there are no athletic scholarships, many football and hockey stars are playing at American universities. Still, rivalry among institutions here goes back to the mid-nineteenth century; Canadian football predates American football by several years, and ice hockey, the national sport, was invented here.

Calgary, ON
University of Calgary: Football, 1983, 1985, 1988, 1995

Edmonton, AB
University of Alberta: Basketball, 1994, 1994; Ice Hockey, 1992

Kitchener, ON
Wilfred Laurier University: Football, 1991

London, ON
University of Western Ontario: Football, 1989, 1994; Basketball, 1991

Montreal, PQ
Concordia University: Basketball, 1990
McGill University: Football, 1987

St. Catharines–Niagara, ON
Brock University: Basketball, 1992

Saskatoon, SK
University of Saskatchewan: Ice Hockey, 1983; Football, 1990

Toronto, ON
University of Toronto: Ice Hockey, 1984; Football, 1993
York University: Ice Hockey, 1985, 1988, 1989

Trois-Rivieres, PQ
University de Quebec: Ice Hockey, 1987, 1991

Vancouver, BC
University of British Columbia: Football, 1986

Victoria, BC
University of Victoria: Basketball, 1983, 1984, 1985, 1986

Winnipeg, MB
University of Manitoba: Basketball (W), 1996
University of Winnipeg: Basketball (W), 1994, 1995

PUTTING IT ALL

Question: Where will you find a mild climate, inexpensive living, extensive health-care facilities, a low crime rate, a wide range of transportation options, excellent opportunities for higher education, a wide choice of recreational pursuits, a generous helping of the arts, and a bright job outlook?

Answer: The best place to live. But if you think about the odds of finding these qualities in one place, it all sounds too good to be true. Does such a place exist?

To meet all the requirements, this ideal place would resemble San Francisco or Oakland, where the weather is moderated by the warm Pacific Ocean and the temperature seldom varies much from a mild 65 degrees. The place's overall costs of living might resemble that of Texarkana, a small metro area astride the Arkansas and Texas border.

This ideal place would need to be large enough to match Boston's variety of higher education options, New York's array of arts attractions, Toronto's public transit system, Chicago's ease of travel to other parts of the continent, and Philadelphia's supply of physicians and health-care facilities.

Yet this place would also need to be small if it were to have a crime rate as low as Johnstown, PA. For quality and variety of man-made and natural recreation amenities, the standard set by Miami would have to be met. Finally, our ideal location would have to present individuals with employment prospects as bright as those of Atlanta.

Obviously, this ideal spot is fictional. You can explore the geography long and hard, but you will never find the single metro area that combines all of the "bests" in each of *Places Rated's* nine categories. Moreover, because one person's long-sought heaven can be another's purgatory, one can argue that there really is no such thing as the ideal metro area.

If you can move anywhere you wish, choosing your destination is still not easy. The best strategy is to focus on your own preferences and needs (the section "Decisions, Decisions" at the front of the book can help you identify what these preferences and needs might be). Having said as much, we can still try to discover which of North America's 351 metro areas come closest to the ideal.

FINDING THE BEST PLACES IN NORTH AMERICA

Nearly a quarter century ago, the Environmental Protection Agency rated 243 American metro areas for livability by such diverse factors as unemployment rates, crime rates, and per capita contributions to charity. Their

If You Read This Chapter First

Readers who've skipped ahead to see how it all comes out may be surprised by many of the results shown in the cumulative table on the following pages. If you are curious how a metro area is scored in a particular category, see the explanation of the scoring system in the appropriate chapter.

Places Rated's categories include five relating to facilities (health care, education, recreation, transportation, and the arts) and four relating to indicators (climate, crime, costs of living, and jobs). Smaller metro areas do better on the indicators (these places typically have lower crime rates and lower costs of living), while larger places score higher on facilities. Climate favors neither large places nor small ones. Because *Places Rated*'s emphasis is on facilities, larger metro areas have an edge.

When you review the rankings in each of the chapters, be sure to note the close groupings of scores. With such close results, ranking metro areas from 1 to 351 may give the impression of greater differences among them than actually exist. Remember, too, that throughout this almanac the unit of comparison is not the incorporated city but the officially defined metropolitan area, typically made up of cities, towns, and other minor civil divisions in New England and Canada, and one or more counties in the rest of the United States.

method for determining the best all-around city was very simple: The scores for each place in each of the factors were averaged for a final score.

Places Rated's method is no different. El Paso, for example, has a score of 88.04 in costs of living, 69.19 in transportation, 86.56 in job outlook, 42.06 in higher education options, 71.95 in climate mildness, 69.56 in crime, 23.43 in the arts, 9.92 in health care, and 24.81 in recreation. The mean of all these scores is 53.54, slightly better than the metro area average.

Because the system is based on scores, the higher the mean score, the better the metro area is judged to be all-around. (El Paso places 131st overall among the metro areas.) The map on the preceding pages locates the 35 metro areas that rise to the top as the best places to live in North America.

The list of top 35 metro areas in this edition of *Places Rated Almanac* closely resembles that of the previous (1993) edition. Although their rankings have changed somewhat, 20 were in the top 35 before. Of the 15 newcomers to the list, 7 were among the previous top 50.

By no means are top-rated places untarnished. Twenty-three score near the bottom in one or more of *Places Rated's* nine categories. More importantly, not one metro area scores in the upper half in all of them.

Back to the point: There isn't an ideal haven in North America. In spite of a blot or two, many areas come close through a combination of strengths. Whether their strengths are vital or unimportant, or whether their blots are knockout factors or trivial, is for you to decide.

The Most Normal Metro Areas

"Will it play in Peoria?" goes the principle in motion picture marketing. Add some more guidelines: "Will it whither in Wichita? Can it sell in Spokane?"

Below are the seven metro areas whose scores across all of *Places Rated*'s nine categories differ the least from the average. In other words, these are the most normal metro areas among all 351 in North America.

Metro Area	Average Percentile Difference from Normal
Wichita, KS	10.11
Spokane, WA	10.53
Des Moines, IA	10.53
Boise City, ID	11.56
Lansing–East Lansing, MI	11.68
Davenport–Moline–Rock Island, IA–IL	11.82
Tulsa, OK	12.28
Peoria–Pekin, IL	12.90

WHY HAVE THE RANKINGS CHANGED?

Readers may note differences in the final rankings for metro areas profiled in *Places Rated's* 1993 edition and this one. There are five reasons for this:

New scoring methods. Scores in each chapter have been normalized into percentiles such that the 50th

The Most Abnormal Metro Areas

Many high-ranking metro areas have combinations of superior and dismal rankings in *Places Rated*'s nine factors. New York City is the classic example of an uneven performance. It finishes among the top ten in five categories: transportation, health care, the arts, recreation, and options for higher education. Anyone who knows New York can appreciate these rankings. But what of its miserable showings in costs of living (4.31), jobs (0.01), and crime (0.06)? For most people, high costs of living, dangerous streets, and poor prospects for employment growth could cancel out this super-city's finer points.

Here are the six metro areas whose scores across all of *Places Rated*'s nine categories differ the most from the average. In other words, these are the most abnormal metro areas among all 351 in North America.

Metro Area	Average Percentile Difference from Normal
Los Angeles–Long Beach, CA	46.90
Chicago, IL	44.18
New York, NY	43.77
San Diego, CA	40.92
Oakland, CA	40.82
San Francisco, CA	39.96

percentile is the average for all metro areas. *Factor analysis*, a mathematical procedure that systematically reduces many pieces of information about a set of items to fewer pieces of information called "factors," is used for the first time.

New scoring elements. The scoring in all nine chapters has been further refined by additional data elements. For example, the number of domestic airline markets reachable nonstop from the local airport has been added to the Transportation chapter for a fuller picture of a metro area's air travel assets. In the Education chapter, graduate student enrollment in local universities carries more weight than

Time series data. Local population figures (for deriving per capita access to public golf courses, for example), prices (for measuring living costs), and household incomes have increased at varying rates since the previous edition was published.

New geography. Each summer, the federal government identifies new metro areas, if any, based on a specific set of population criteria. Since *Places Rated's* 1993 edition, five new areas have come into being and boundary changes affecting nearly 30 areas in New England and other parts of the northeast have been announced.

lower ranking.

RANKINGS: Putting It All Together

The following table recaps each metro area's score in *Places Rated's* nine categories. Scores range from 0 to 100 and are normalized such that the 50th percentile point is the average for all metro areas. Scores that are among the top 35 in each category are highlighted.

The mean of these nine scores is also shown, as is the overall rank. Abilene's mean score, 39.04 (the sum of its scores in each category divided by nine), ranks it 277th overall among the 351 metro areas. Akron's mean score of 55.75 ranks it 105th. Atlanta's mean score of 75.07 ranks it 7th. Lower mean scores indicate worse metro areas and higher mean scores indicate better metro areas. The highest possible score would be 100, meaning a perfect score in all nine categories.

Metro Area	Cost of Living	Transport	Jobs	Education	Climate	Crime	Arts	Health Care	Recreation	Mean Score	Overall Rank
Abilene, TX	93.46	24.30	22.42	34.69	64.01	49.54	30.71	29.12	3.12	**39.04**	**277**
Akron, OH	37.37	78.78	45.67	73.61	29.64	62.59	74.33	28.18	71.59	**55.75**	**105**
Albany, GA	79.23	11.21	25.22	27.74	68.93	9.35	35.53	9.96	7.49	**30.52**	**343**
Albany–Schenectady–Troy, NY	22.95	83.87	52.43	81.01	26.72	77.81	72.06	63.16	74.37	**61.60**	**60**
Albuquerque, NM	23.19	76.74	75.96	67.51	57.94	4.47	69.31	72.42	73.68	**57.91**	**89**
Alexandria, LA	97.01	9.23	32.40	13.65	68.92	11.38	40.36	64.08	39.85	**41.88**	**253**
Allentown–Bethlehem–Easton, PA	26.78	60.20	34.52	72.91	35.89	90.09	51.65	57.41	42.46	**52.43**	**141**
Altoona, PA	81.77	20.27	25.93	7.21	34.06	94.70	21.27	59.98	0.45	**38.40**	**284**
Amarillo, TX	93.14	42.10	34.52	33.20	51.66	35.66	36.58	60.22	31.80	**46.54**	**207**

Vancouver
30
2
Seattle—Bellevue—
Everett
Portland—Vancouver
16
6
Minneapolis—
St. Paul
San
Francisco
20
17
Oakland
11
San Jose
26
Salt Lake City—Ogden
18
Denver
9
San Diego
Phoenix—Mesa
5
Dallas
22
San Antonio
27
Houston
3
Los Angeles—
Long Beach
34
13
Riverside—
San Bernardino
1
Orange
County

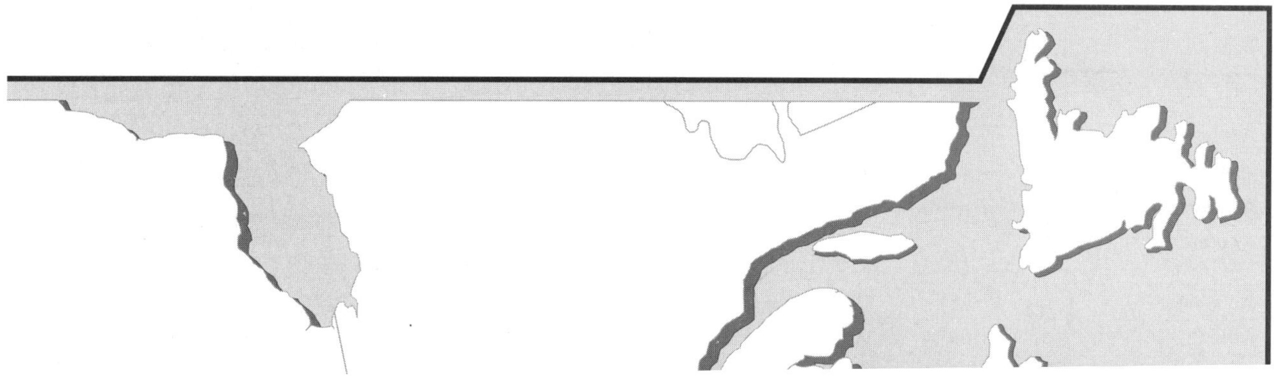

Toronto 15

Milwaukee—Waukesha 28

Detroit 21

Long Island 12

Philadelphia 10

23 Chicago

25 Cleveland—Lorain—Elyria

Pittsburgh 14

4 Washington

Cincinnati 19

32 Raleigh—Durham—Chapel Hill

7 Atlanta

PUTTING IT ALL TOGETHER

PLACES RATED ALMANAC

TOP 35
METROPOLITAN AREAS

New Orleans 35

Orlando 29

Tampa—St. Petersburg—Clearwater 8

Fort Lauderdale 33

24 Miami

(1) ....ranks among bottom 35 in one or more categories

Houston............newcomer to the TOP 35

Thomas Nast, Cartographer

Metro Area	Cost of Living	Transport	Jobs	Education	Climate	Crime	Arts	Health Care	Recreation	Mean Score	Overall Rank
Anchorage, AK	19.16	47.39	57.13	44.14	32.69	30.69	32.12	73.14	51.22	**43.08**	**238**
Ann Arbor, MI	20.97	78.23	61.25	94.34	28.45	72.03	57.84	68.62	73.75	**61.72**	**58**
Anniston, AL	96.29	5.36	30.94	23.96	62.05	25.37	35.95	16.11	18.60	**34.96**	**321**
Appleton-Oshkosh-Neenah, WI	62.34	52.51	64.68	51.71	14.59	92.78	47.06	57.40	78.65	**57.97**	**88**
Asheville, NC	56.72	17.51	42.15	47.07	60.62	73.86	42.23	73.54	47.38	**51.23**	**152**
Athens, GA	60.54	88.99	30.96	67.98	64.87	36.27	38.57	28.91	3.71	**46.76**	**201**
✓Atlanta, GA	42.61	92.55	100.00	86.09	65.20	11.95	95.97	88.86	92.37	**75.07**	**7**
Atlantic City-Cape May, NJ	14.08	87.78	40.07	29.93	51.62	10.66	39.18	4.91	84.51	**40.30**	**268**
Augusta-Aiken, GA-SC	70.22	4.93	75.52	44.18	64.93	42.67	46.61	69.69	48.86	**51.96**	**145**
Austin-San Marcos, TX	37.98	70.56	98.62	82.20	73.75	37.87	64.11	37.36	70.22	**63.63**	**45**
Bakersfield, CA	44.57	29.47	49.08	25.22	85.68	19.52	24.54	10.64	42.06	**36.75**	**304**
Baltimore, MD	15.58	97.86	62.80	94.95	56.80	3.91	98.89	7.65	91.41	**58.87**	**80**
Bangor, ME	62.25	47.18	28.96	89.80	26.15	91.76	55.40	36.59	60.33	**55.38**	**110**
Barnstable-Yarmouth, MA	6.48	63.09	35.94	31.28	59.45	44.13	79.68	13.12	92.39	**47.28**	**197**
Baton Rouge, LA	71.61	14.07	64.34	26.18	68.24	0.02	43.22	38.94	60.73	**43.04**	**240**
Beaumont-Port Arthur, TX	93.85	18.31	29.84	20.16	70.73	16.24	28.66	44.42	62.47	**42.74**	**243**
Bellingham, WA	29.64	83.51	44.39	46.78	83.13	78.30	57.05	37.69	71.27	**59.08**	**78**
Benton Harbor, MI	76.41	44.77	30.66	34.72	26.78	11.64	71.82	20.50	65.85	**42.57**	**245**
Bergen-Passaic, NJ	1.93	87.79	29.36	66.72	39.17	78.20	89.76	63.03	58.43	**57.15**	**96**
Billings, MT	83.55	48.05	30.04	18.89	27.35	79.65	23.17	40.81	13.38	**40.54**	**266**
Biloxi-Gulfport-Pascagoula, MS	88.46	36.74	58.16	1.25	72.80	67.41	33.55	34.44	81.93	**52.75**	**138**
Binghamton, NY	37.80	34.95	20.63	21.29	26.95	91.14	43.87	18.62	40.06	**37.26**	**296**
Birmingham, AL	41.31	62.81	64.06	73.40	61.31	12.52	55.07	82.92	68.89	**58.03**	**86**
Bismarck, ND	84.20	35.47	32.16	35.91	8.69	91.63	69.54	68.91	39.76	**51.81**	**147**
Bloomington, IN	66.74	70.80	43.31	58.46	34.80	78.08	44.53	25.47	45.49	**51.96**	**145**
Bloomington-Normal, IL	52.48	79.02	44.84	79.19	24.31	91.16	38.53	13.35	11.19	**48.23**	**182**
Boise City, ID	42.63	61.26	78.09	49.82	49.12	78.86	38.95	49.79	33.89	**53.60**	**129**
Boston, MA-NH	3.23	93.79	10.33	99.75	46.46	32.15	99.42	92.42	89.13	**62.96**	**49**
Boulder-Longmont, CO	8.31	79.04	66.42	51.31	50.00	77.46	59.13	60.42	69.97	**58.01**	**87**
Brazoria, TX	79.85	55.15	53.70	18.83	74.77	83.52	23.80	3.92	51.89	**49.49**	**174**
Bremerton, WA	28.52	49.57	30.35	27.31	82.49	84.01	37.32	18.55	44.57	**44.74**	**222**
Bridgeport, CT	15.89	91.41	33.77	68.10	47.11	40.91	70.83	58.06	54.74	**53.42**	**132**
Brockton, MA	15.51	41.84	32.46	74.75	39.96	37.88	37.88	8.32	54.59	**38.23**	**286**
Brownsville-Harlingen-San Benito, TX	91.02	21.13	49.82	25.92	88.82	34.72	6.54	2.86	72.51	**43.70**	**230**
Bryan-College Station, TX	97.09	4.27	53.86	35.63	73.99	50.53	9.56	20.02	9.77	**39.41**	**275**
Buffalo-Niagara Falls, NY	37.98	81.30	35.22	82.20	26.45	39.05	94.01	74.50	86.84	**61.95**	**55**
Burlington, VT	25.38	48.55	43.32	87.37	18.53	76.00	18.44	65.71	75.02	**50.92**	**157**
Calgary, AB	27.21	83.64	42.62	33.62	17.74	49.82	84.44	82.08	65.67	**54.09**	**125**
Canton-Massillon, OH	47.63	76.01	30.30	46.83	29.64	64.66	75.15	29.55	47.74	**49.72**	**172**
Casper, WY	99.17	11.00	22.99	4.92	22.81	54.81	41.48	37.93	15.63	**34.53**	**325**
Cedar Rapids, IA	52.29	49.81	36.24	75.37	18.08	78.11	51.07	53.76	20.73	**48.38**	**181**
Champaign-Urbana, IL	48.23	80.60	55.35	64.30	25.41	50.89	50.68	44.73	0.55	**46.75**	**202**
Charleston, WV	65.97	54.65	26.49	54.72	50.28	78.63	48.02	61.09	14.65	**50.50**	**162**
Charleston-North Charleston, SC	59.88	19.15	59.83	54.83	71.55	19.18	54.10	65.35	91.02	**54.99**	**116**
Charlotte-Gastonia-Rock Hill, NC-SC	31.54	87.72	94.92	80.96	64.94	5.34	82.43	35.92	80.05	**62.65**	**52**

Metro Area	Cost of Living	Transport	Jobs	Education	Climate	Crime	Arts	Health Care	Recreation	Mean Score	Overall Rank
Charlottesville, VA	28.19	23.85	39.72	68.23	56.94	84.02	53.55	87.79	30.20	**52.50**	**140**
Chattanooga, TN-GA	82.01	16.62	42.55	48.68	57.26	28.19	15.02	39.34	57.64	**43.03**	**241**
Cheyenne, WY	88.67	29.92	22.26	6.73	30.88	85.38	29.75	50.52	3.19	**38.59**	**281**
✓Chicago, IL	10.02	98.92	91.47	98.19	24.69	4.97	99.81	99.91	99.02	**69.67**	**23**
Chico-Paradise, CA	30.50	17.89	39.86	41.80	85.07	66.86	16.89	42.32	38.13	**42.15**	**250**
Chicoutimi-Jonquiere, PQ	41.71	19.06	15.25	33.39	6.03	86.03	13.78	73.01	71.85	**40.01**	**270**
✓Cincinnati, OH-KY-IN	29.70	91.63	85.36	77.75	38.07	58.44	92.35	80.17	86.53	**71.11**	**19**
Corpus Christi, TX	74.33	25.58	40.64	14.68	85.62	20.73	23.89	46.34	62.36	**43.80**	**229**
Cumberland, MD-WV	64.06	4.79	21.85	40.65	42.56	86.90	26.45	36.71	4.91	**36.54**	**307**
✓Dallas, TX	43.88	62.20	99.99	89.98	62.87	5.00	93.32	84.74	95.29	**70.81**	**22**
Danbury, CT	6.68	65.05	33.77	15.34	36.59	91.93	54.01	58.06	20.38	**42.42**	**248**
Danville, VA	95.46	10.90	21.59	19.27	58.12	91.38	20.01	1.92	3.25	**35.77**	**311**
Davenport-Moline-Rock Island, IA-IL	74.22	59.07	32.50	61.67	21.89	49.95	52.52	42.75	56.05	**50.07**	**168**
Dayton-Springfield, OH	41.62	71.00	39.86	84.94	31.08	52.24	83.56	76.81	49.09	**58.91**	**79**
Daytona Beach, FL	55.20	79.17	55.69	76.02	79.91	28.06	43.68	36.29	85.40	**59.94**	**70**
Decatur, AL	82.42	2.43	33.87	44.16	56.77	84.73	27.07	21.42	46.83	**44.41**	**225**
Decatur, IL	69.86	17.91	13.27	29.43	25.56	44.88	42.04	53.58	5.65	**33.58**	**336**
✓Denver, CO	22.82	94.95	98.93	92.18	40.33	36.56	90.70	76.34	88.98	**71.31**	**18**
Des Moines, IA	50.01	54.48	56.06	77.52	18.89	62.86	53.96	53.29	55.50	**53.62**	**128**
✓Detroit, MI	27.72	92.68	94.63	91.67	28.30	15.85	96.60	93.61	97.13	**70.91**	**21**
Dothan, AL	90.10	3.46	40.57	28.37	59.93	43.72	11.14	37.76	2.61	**35.30**	**314**
Dover, DE	36.53	2.74	36.76	36.19	56.83	58.25	4.11	0.00	24.79	**28.47**	**349**
Dubuque, IA	86.52	33.02	33.19	51.75	16.10	86.61	43.67	21.59	12.05	**42.72**	**244**
Duluth-Superior, MN-WI	87.76	24.80	36.99	69.03	7.68	88.46	68.31	82.05	90.86	**61.77**	**57**
Dutchess County, NY	22.84	80.57	22.02	68.50	35.55	83.44	44.62	28.32	50.96	**48.54**	**179**
Eau Claire, WI	83.08	15.84	37.43	32.85	10.40	91.76	41.51	80.81	31.88	**47.28**	**197**
Edmonton, AB	28.52	80.30	45.55	51.21	12.90	37.74	77.14	91.99	85.42	**56.75**	**97**
El Paso, TX	89.38	64.19	86.56	42.06	71.95	69.56	23.43	9.92	24.81	**53.54**	**131**
Elkhart-Goshen, IN	88.04	29.75	53.56	21.33	22.56	82.75	40.22	21.16	4.50	**40.43**	**267**
Elmira, NY	54.16	26.71	25.84	5.81	29.69	8.25	44.64	26.01	5.88	**25.22**	**350**
Enid, OK	99.06	6.52	22.79	0.28	44.29	34.50	13.69	54.58	0.90	**30.73**	**341**
Erie, PA	77.85	49.37	31.85	52.48	29.21	84.41	39.44	58.60	66.59	**54.42**	**121**
Eugene-Springfield, OR	37.02	47.12	33.72	53.57	83.09	71.28	47.31	48.88	78.11	**55.57**	**108**
Evansville-Henderson, IN-KY	82.53	38.44	38.27	39.13	41.34	62.15	68.97	69.63	27.87	**52.04**	**144**
Fargo-Moorhead, ND-MN	76.13	57.11	36.26	65.42	6.06	91.62	75.21	65.97	23.89	**55.30**	**113**
Fayetteville, NC	85.46	27.80	38.43	30.87	65.43	7.96	33.69	15.07	9.89	**34.96**	**321**
Fayetteville-Springdale-Rogers, AR	82.55	25.71	68.26	42.16	49.56	89.58	13.57	59.75	51.21	**53.59**	**130**
Fitchburg-Leominster, MA	14.75	57.90	35.16	59.19	33.94	34.62	49.44	55.99	32.97	**41.55**	**255**
Flagstaff, AZ-UT	24.87	20.57	37.32	23.12	44.31	63.30	28.34	45.88	80.35	**40.90**	**262**

Metro Area	Cost of Living	Transport	Jobs	Education	Climate	Crime	Arts	Health Care	Recreation	Mean Score	Overall Rank
Flint, MI	60.51	84.94	22.22	71.56	26.66	6.87	41.94	31.56	29.43	**41.74**	**254**
Florence, AL	90.61	0.35	43.30	39.43	56.77	88.18	14.21	30.65	40.47	**44.89**	**220**
Florence, SC	91.77	11.44	31.90	27.37	66.76	11.88	12.98	59.72	2.82	**35.18**	**316**
Fort Collins–Loveland, CO	38.12	81.16	60.43	50.54	36.57	88.28	40.07	59.06	69.70	**58.21**	**84**
✓Fort Lauderdale, FL	30.38	86.40	90.74	68.53	87.35	6.60	84.32	63.27	85.56	**67.02**	**33**
Fort Myers–Cape Coral, FL	26.03	50.91	69.79	7.21	81.51	51.66	42.42	21.56	87.07	**48.68**	**178**
Fort Pierce–Port St. Lucie, FL	73.27	17.61	53.06	40.41	84.65	35.51	32.85	8.98	80.18	**47.39**	**195**
Fort Smith, AR–OK	97.49	2.88	54.31	1.74	51.52	74.21	3.86	50.33	46.36	**42.52**	**246**
Fort Walton Beach, FL	49.53	23.17	43.45	17.66	69.36	82.15	0.00	12.82	62.34	**40.05**	**269**
Fort Wayne, IN	83.58	45.15	61.58	62.76	25.27	75.90	78.75	65.26	47.89	**60.68**	**65**
Fort Worth–Arlington, TX	61.39	45.39	99.39	77.08	62.87	13.26	80.16	48.71	78.52	**62.97**	**48**
Fresno, CA	37.52	63.80	64.08	58.29	84.07	5.96	35.82	42.53	64.42	**50.72**	**159**
Gadsden, AL	94.29	17.81	32.46	21.32	58.15	16.54	33.45	26.19	8.27	**34.28**	**329**
Gainesville, FL	61.25	36.54	48.73	59.55	74.61	0.90	52.35	92.18	61.80	**54.21**	**123**
Galveston–Texas City, TX	74.49	59.78	51.37	50.66	76.66	19.12	27.61	56.19	55.47	**52.37**	**142**
Gary, IN	44.80	92.72	27.72	65.43	25.60	26.00	73.07	50.47	48.71	**50.50**	**162**
Glens Falls, NY	44.05	37.13	26.95	8.87	18.51	80.87	34.72	35.13	59.52	**38.42**	**283**
Goldsboro, NC	78.29	43.26	27.75	32.05	65.89	41.23	13.83	10.12	2.30	**34.97**	**320**
Grand Forks, ND–MN	91.96	61.21	22.96	61.22	5.84	90.05	58.26	74.37	35.04	**55.66**	**107**
Grand Junction, CO	60.67	25.35	37.42	22.00	34.36	74.64	30.58	69.69	38.16	**43.65**	**231**
Grand Rapids–Muskegon–Holland, MI	51.03	54.94	89.17	78.35	22.61	56.98	70.57	33.26	97.83	**61.64**	**59**
Great Falls, MT	87.14	45.79	22.35	0.54	27.94	60.96	20.85	42.38	26.44	**37.15**	**297**
Greeley, CO	42.12	83.13	44.70	65.69	32.99	69.92	41.62	31.87	20.93	**48.11**	**183**
Green Bay, WI	39.40	53.56	56.40	61.36	15.82	86.39	39.52	19.48	28.58	**44.50**	**224**
Greensboro–Winston-Salem–High Point, NC	31.86	81.36	85.44	77.47	59.83	38.84	65.62	57.22	50.71	**60.93**	**64**
Greenville, NC	75.72	1.85	59.59	50.95	66.21	28.86	55.81	83.72	5.48	**47.58**	**189**
Greenville–Spartanburg–Anderson, SC	52.77	48.29	77.95	65.88	66.93	19.83	57.09	57.72	71.71	**57.57**	**92**
Hagerstown, MD	27.16	74.79	31.25	13.28	38.92	90.29	36.59	3.43	26.21	**37.99**	**290**
Halifax, NS	17.88	77.25	29.12	69.90	42.25	28.36	56.10	97.90	70.35	**54.35**	**122**
Hamilton, ON	10.52	93.41	32.74	52.79	23.46	66.09	77.85	88.42	29.45	**52.75**	**138**
Hamilton–Middletown, OH	38.36	61.88	38.55	57.22	35.99	63.70	47.56	6.87	15.10	**40.58**	**265**
Harrisburg–Lebanon–Carlisle, PA	47.79	64.81	63.12	78.55	42.44	82.48	43.47	63.16	54.91	**60.08**	**67**
Hartford, CT	16.49	83.19	36.38	80.31	35.49	57.90	95.67	62.86	74.50	**60.31**	**66**
Hattiesburg, MS	89.02	5.14	34.18	60.04	62.99	84.95	0.13	67.64	39.43	**49.28**	**176**
Hickory–Morganton–Lenoir, NC	73.81	74.11	62.28	40.78	61.65	75.78	34.99	35.79	58.39	**57.51**	**93**
Honolulu, HI	0.28	28.92	42.73	73.15	97.74	69.79	89.98	50.28	87.48	**60.04**	**68**
Houma, LA	94.71	0.10	28.66	3.18	74.65	68.21	16.38	13.93	82.88	**42.52**	**246**
✓Houston, TX	51.35	87.74	99.98	71.20	74.44	25.69	93.19	95.62	94.34	**77.06**	**3**
Huntington–Ashland, WV–KY–OH	93.25	27.88	26.40	59.40	48.18	88.61	37.30	55.40	47.78	**53.80**	**127**
Huntsville, AL	39.46	13.96	62.99	80.16	58.24	45.66	27.73	44.36	54.60	**47.46**	**192**
Indianapolis, IN	48.65	81.97	84.56	75.53	29.65	40.03	91.03	86.44	62.04	**66.66**	**36**
Iowa City, IA	49.77	42.30	37.14	62.67	21.03	75.87	51.36	97.11	21.43	**50.96**	**156**
Jackson, MI	53.29	21.48	24.14	32.65	25.60	29.31	30.57	1.54	48.84	**29.71**	**347**
Jackson, MS	84.02	35.61	53.65	69.65	59.40	20.98	45.17	77.62	53.65	**55.53**	**109**

Metro Area	Cost of Living	Transport	Jobs	Education	Climate	Crime	Arts	Health Care	Recreation	Mean Score	Overall Rank
Jackson, TN	80.28	5.27	37.03	58.89	52.02	2.38	58.20	84.07	2.80	**42.33**	**249**
Jacksonville, FL	34.19	70.71	80.67	40.36	75.67	1.03	70.86	61.22	89.92	**58.29**	**83**
Jacksonville, NC	75.80	3.26	31.42	1.45	69.43	81.25	9.30	1.38	35.81	**34.34**	**328**
Jamestown, NY	52.20	50.23	22.15	42.57	29.73	88.06	69.60	11.94	63.55	**47.78**	**187**
Janesville-Beloit, WI	85.41	27.50	24.93	47.00	18.89	78.94	52.78	13.39	20.00	**40.98**	**259**
Jersey City, NJ	10.98	74.04	25.60	37.90	47.24	7.17	62.44	24.83	20.08	**34.48**	**327**
Johnson City-Kingsport-Bristol, TN-VA	78.72	12.46	50.09	54.77	58.66	89.73	41.17	78.47	62.21	**58.48**	**82**
[illegible]	[illegible]	[illegible]	[illegible]	[illegible]	[illegible]	[illegible]	[illegible]	[illegible]	[illegible]	[illegible]	[illegible]
Kitchener, ON	11.65	93.89	39.73	47.13	23.05	82.53	64.86	58.53	10.87	**48.03**	**184**
Knoxville, TN	71.13	35.80	75.02	62.01	56.15	25.49	56.25	67.43	86.95	**59.58**	**73**
Kokomo, IN	85.83	50.91	27.95	35.06	29.08	79.14	49.04	45.07	4.15	**45.14**	**216**
La Crosse, WI-MN	64.79	50.73	38.27	75.66	16.46	91.76	41.11	67.48	44.83	**54.57**	**119**
Lafayette, IN	74.81	27.32	46.82	57.23	26.35	83.10	43.63	18.58	7.87	**42.86**	**242**
Lafayette, LA	88.86	14.76	51.52	25.90	68.69	60.38	28.13	37.09	52.28	**47.51**	**190**
Lake Charles, LA	93.18	11.10	29.57	3.93	69.03	17.56	17.67	48.04	16.58	**34.07**	**331**
Lakeland-Winter Haven, FL	55.67	72.45	36.41	73.32	79.17	5.93	1.63	11.08	79.43	**46.12**	**209**
Lancaster, PA	31.29	70.12	31.59	59.91	44.72	92.13	30.98	53.57	35.25	**49.95**	**169**
Lansing-East Lansing, MI	49.84	48.39	49.51	81.49	23.89	55.41	44.83	30.92	34.37	**46.52**	**208**
Laredo, TX	92.00	16.17	77.35	18.34	84.63	25.28	1.60	0.11	2.89	**35.37**	**313**
Las Cruces, NM	60.27	43.47	45.84	42.50	65.71	49.38	0.02	6.01	26.29	**37.72**	**293**
Las Vegas, NV-AZ	27.32	82.42	98.20	22.40	74.33	22.60	46.05	16.88	94.74	**53.88**	**126**
Lawrence, KS	71.33	57.98	31.77	92.27	33.31	58.68	29.24	26.24	25.58	**47.38**	**196**
Lawrence, MA-NH	17.36	57.40	22.42	65.19	36.14	48.42	59.48	19.03	51.99	**41.94**	**252**
Lawton, OK	95.28	9.89	31.79	5.36	52.43	40.51	1.00	16.92	17.32	**30.06**	**345**
Lewiston-Auburn, ME	50.53	5.62	27.41	34.37	30.42	89.95	16.31	40.44	17.06	**34.68**	**323**
Lexington, KY	55.42	37.74	61.66	85.66	44.24	36.04	50.65	85.26	18.83	**52.83**	**137**
Lima, OH	50.57	5.97	27.90	28.19	27.60	24.18	46.03	43.80	13.30	**29.73**	**346**
Lincoln, NE	68.46	84.60	48.83	85.98	20.57	42.01	58.42	64.30	21.61	**54.98**	**117**
Little Rock-North Little Rock, AR	67.28	59.38	65.21	68.00	54.80	1.48	41.81	85.24	66.62	**56.65**	**98**
London, ON	12.68	88.91	40.24	70.72	20.68	65.05	63.77	96.38	22.18	**53.40**	**133**
✓Long Island, NY	1.44	71.01	65.36	95.34	54.47	85.40	98.85	92.99	97.93	**73.64**	**12**
Longview-Marshall, TX	91.19	4.57	39.94	45.00	62.60	37.15	20.41	21.60	20.58	**38.12**	**287**
✓Los Angeles-Long Beach, CA	6.57	94.30	8.48	97.91	97.68	0.42	99.84	99.93	97.95	**67.01**	**34**
Louisville, KY-IN	54.85	69.42	68.43	64.42	43.86	59.14	71.06	79.78	43.46	**61.60**	**60**
Lowell, MA-NH	15.76	49.16	22.70	25.54	36.10	44.13	51.23	75.71	46.97	**40.81**	**263**
Lubbock, TX	92.61	51.08	40.82	47.57	61.27	45.41	21.82	77.33	6.07	**49.33**	**175**
Lynchburg, VA	79.24	25.67	36.45	65.49	59.71	82.46	25.93	37.04	53.60	**51.73**	**149**
Macon, GA	83.84	2.22	27.94	55.70	66.12	46.22	54.20	47.41	47.02	**47.85**	**186**
Madison, WI	15.94	49.29	67.23	79.00	16.33	78.30	71.65	76.72	53.72	**56.46**	**102**
Manchester, NH	14.39	27.96	33.08	93.09	30.43	85.79	42.07	46.19	46.46	**46.61**	**204**

Metro Area	Cost of Living	Transport	Jobs	Education	Climate	Crime	Arts	Health Care	Recreation	Mean Score	Overall Rank
Mansfield, OH	51.92	4.64	22.36	6.20	29.65	35.39	50.48	11.34	8.54	**24.50**	**351**
McAllen-Edinburg-Mission, TX	96.77	5.38	67.35	8.71	87.91	35.63	18.21	12.40	23.77	**39.57**	**273**
Medford-Ashland, OR	42.67	22.23	43.49	2.50	73.73	69.11	40.10	31.21	47.70	**41.42**	**256**
Melbourne-Titusville-Palm Bay, FL	60.72	57.96	56.32	68.05	82.30	27.21	51.81	17.90	86.13	**56.49**	**101**
Memphis, TN-AR-MS	60.74	82.19	82.28	58.04	56.53	9.64	59.70	72.21	76.67	**62.00**	**54**
Merced, CA	43.06	24.06	37.26	8.65	84.41	61.84	17.32	16.39	23.62	**35.18**	**316**
✓Miami, FL	22.39	84.56	73.35	81.33	87.53	0.00	91.69	89.42	96.56	**69.65**	**24**
Middlesex-Somerset-Hunterdon, NJ	4.38	91.41	88.41	64.22	41.05	86.41	90.28	53.22	50.62	**63.33**	**47**
✓Milwaukee-Waukesha, WI	19.64	90.33	66.34	83.18	24.57	56.89	92.98	84.47	96.55	**68.33**	**28**
✓Minneapolis-St. Paul, MN-WI	27.52	95.22	99.95	90.03	10.76	64.09	97.96	93.27	96.90	**75.08**	**6**
Mobile, AL	78.50	38.23	52.95	55.41	67.23	27.91	44.28	46.08	85.14	**55.08**	**115**
Modesto, CA	36.10	22.76	48.77	24.77	85.81	19.02	27.40	35.50	15.33	**35.05**	**318**
Monmouth-Ocean, NJ	6.22	83.41	60.54	52.95	53.91	86.11	82.89	25.89	82.79	**59.41**	**76**
Monroe, LA	94.71	20.09	29.04	9.10	55.30	17.36	29.85	56.35	20.36	**36.91**	**302**
Montgomery, AL	61.67	18.62	41.38	64.73	65.34	34.75	21.65	47.08	34.31	**43.28**	**233**
✓Montreal, PQ	16.86	98.11	71.89	75.37	16.16	48.46	98.21	98.82	81.32	**67.24**	**31**
Muncie, IN	82.51	71.13	30.98	63.88	31.69	86.27	17.99	36.57	8.98	**47.78**	**188**
Myrtle Beach, SC	50.01	19.88	63.23	10.60	64.11	9.11	23.07	21.39	79.88	**37.92**	**292**
Naples, FL	10.18	31.86	62.59	6.75	82.00	35.93	32.09	14.74	79.70	**39.54**	**274**
Nashua, NH	12.81	42.45	33.08	63.91	32.45	95.58	47.38	46.19	29.72	**44.84**	**221**
Nashville, TN	51.77	74.36	96.19	83.10	51.65	14.37	70.93	78.31	75.49	**66.24**	**37**
New Bedford, MA	27.37	68.83	25.98	17.98	51.80	21.87	35.97	1.58	44.29	**32.85**	**338**
New Haven-Meriden, CT	12.19	96.72	21.85	91.04	47.11	34.32	81.11	53.97	59.90	**55.36**	**111**
New London-Norwich, CT-RI	13.24	27.53	31.48	31.90	45.88	86.82	58.39	9.35	47.22	**39.09**	**276**
New Orleans, LA	72.86	77.56	42.86	71.11	73.28	1.55	73.28	89.58	98.60	**66.74**	**35**
New York, NY	4.31	98.34	0.01	99.65	53.09	0.06	99.99	99.94	97.30	**61.41**	**62**
Newark, NJ	4.49	96.59	8.40	93.01	48.55	18.49	97.54	91.38	81.75	**60.02**	**69**
Newburgh, NY-PA	16.34	38.48	36.85	34.65	39.20	81.27	33.39	4.11	54.84	**37.68**	**294**
Norfolk-Virginia Beach-Newport News, VA-NC	32.79	67.87	70.98	69.94	64.85	44.68	79.35	49.77	96.72	**64.11**	**42**
✓Oakland, CA	3.28	80.86	94.29	97.20	96.83	10.49	97.50	75.15	89.35	**71.66**	**17**
Ocala, FL	76.36	2.34	63.23	1.46	77.09	10.57	14.02	2.64	56.18	**33.77**	**334**
Odessa-Midland, TX	79.89	23.43	44.05	24.97	68.59	31.19	21.65	10.52	6.85	**34.57**	**324**
Oklahoma City, OK	80.04	60.89	60.23	83.58	49.51	20.38	69.77	72.75	74.16	**63.48**	**46**
Olympia, WA	32.41	75.79	48.29	38.53	80.01	84.03	86.56	45.55	29.89	**57.90**	**90**
Omaha, NE-IA	55.54	77.26	47.38	86.58	21.45	51.42	75.57	82.79	66.51	**62.72**	**50**
✓Orange County, CA	2.87	84.50	99.97	95.80	96.84	54.03	95.01	88.18	87.28	**78.28**	**1**
✓Orlando, FL	43.18	80.72	99.90	72.21	79.22	7.54	79.03	56.94	96.12	**68.32**	**29**
Oshawa, ON	14.67	95.60	34.31	15.37	32.42	83.67	31.99	46.51	14.24	**40.98**	**259**
Ottawa-Hull, ON-PQ	11.75	92.70	50.79	56.15	16.11	62.56	73.97	94.00	58.95	**57.44**	**94**
Owensboro, KY	82.35	7.49	29.34	41.90	48.29	88.66	19.20	26.43	12.99	**39.63**	**272**
Panama City, FL	62.60	4.76	35.51	12.19	74.18	29.89	15.70	4.94	64.01	**33.75**	**335**
Parkersburg-Marietta, WV-OH	89.86	9.01	23.35	42.05	44.98	93.37	50.23	22.42	36.40	**45.74**	**214**
Pensacola, FL	53.63	43.02	47.74	33.52	73.26	13.38	23.22	51.30	73.89	**45.88**	**211**
Peoria-Pekin, IL	67.85	48.10	29.83	74.40	21.68	49.22	57.00	41.65	57.40	**49.68**	**173**

Metro Area	Cost of Living	Transport	Jobs	Education	Climate	Crime	Arts	Health Care	Recreation	Mean Score	Overall Rank
✓Philadelphia, PA-NJ	15.12	98.40	67.79	94.87	49.39	51.11	99.15	99.64	90.98	**74.05**	**10**
✓Phoenix-Mesa, AZ	25.41	85.03	99.93	87.45	81.91	24.30	90.95	85.92	95.28	**75.13**	**5**
Pine Bluff, AR	96.84	39.54	25.09	13.87	56.77	10.77	17.29	61.25	11.02	**36.94**	**301**
✓Pittsburgh, PA	34.40	95.10	45.04	85.83	33.20	83.52	92.68	96.56	90.21	**72.95**	**14**
Pittsfield, MA	33.72	37.42	18.59	1.66	28.66	82.59	58.46	37.63	46.22	**38.33**	**285**
Portland, ME	25.04	41.12	49.49	82.99	34.75	78.93	52.51	58.13	79.14	**55.79**	**104**
✓Portland-Vancouver, OR-WA	11.50	85.09	98.87	87.80	79.99	36.89	85.47	72.28	90.85	**72.08**	**16**
Racine, WI	55.62	50.64	27.71	0.00	24.47	58.84	39.29	6.26	47.70	**34.50**	**326**
✓Raleigh-Durham-Chapel Hill, NC	18.42	79.27	99.49	85.70	64.82	45.30	80.99	74.71	56.27	**67.22**	**32**
Rapid City, SD	85.40	20.82	30.73	16.88	24.94	68.18	15.10	38.85	41.44	**38.04**	**289**
Reading, PA	39.15	69.37	25.44	60.60	35.56	82.18	31.00	34.63	33.78	**45.75**	**212**
Redding, CA	47.54	24.31	36.08	47.32	81.06	66.98	12.49	53.71	50.35	**46.65**	**203**
Regina, SK	32.88	75.59	30.27	70.62	4.94	24.91	68.04	86.91	46.24	**48.93**	**177**
Reno, NV	14.46	74.73	40.26	57.07	66.79	45.29	28.04	54.22	74.22	**50.56**	**161**
Richland-Kennewick-Pasco, WA	53.03	24.48	38.25	2.26	68.47	70.82	25.28	13.29	34.46	**36.70**	**305**
Richmond-Petersburg, VA	29.97	68.51	79.75	66.62	55.39	49.72	81.77	78.77	74.90	**65.04**	**41**
✓Riverside-San Bernardino, CA	22.44	76.80	99.81	86.86	94.01	8.04	91.25	81.21	96.93	**73.04**	**13**
Roanoke, VA	66.21	33.20	30.62	53.01	58.20	77.22	47.53	80.59	51.28	**55.32**	**112**
Rochester, MN	42.94	35.87	36.67	32.78	9.37	91.43	49.22	99.79	3.84	**44.66**	**223**
Rochester, NY	35.01	73.88	60.13	74.69	29.35	74.88	78.10	65.05	95.98	**65.23**	**40**
Rockford, IL	49.57	21.50	30.84	10.59	19.44	37.70	42.15	54.09	30.39	**32.92**	**337**
Rocky Mount, NC	68.28	48.18	41.77	44.10	65.66	36.20	27.48	14.73	1.20	**38.62**	**279**
Sacramento, CA	20.61	70.09	98.91	72.66	88.05	23.62	68.45	62.88	87.06	**65.81**	**38**
Saginaw-Bay City-Midland, MI	70.63	19.99	30.06	52.12	25.57	36.24	51.50	45.30	57.02	**43.16**	**237**
St. Catharines-Niagara, ON	14.43	73.91	24.44	26.19	30.35	79.00	69.98	67.52	35.27	**46.79**	**200**
St. Cloud, MN	61.64	94.42	55.40	74.23	7.95	86.48	79.53	57.19	46.95	**62.64**	**53**
Saint John, NB	25.48	32.82	28.59	0.00	26.98	88.12	26.71	65.80	73.91	**40.93**	**261**
St. John's, NF	19.96	70.22	27.34	15.93	42.25	87.50	30.71	93.18	74.98	**51.34**	**151**
St. Joseph, MO	86.33	71.48	20.82	42.21	26.12	65.02	50.24	19.28	5.99	**43.05**	**239**
St. Louis, MO-IL	20.79	95.25	70.93	90.00	35.03	25.63	96.04	28.67	94.89	**61.91**	**56**
Salem, OR	36.84	70.08	45.36	78.95	81.48	66.14	41.04	29.08	38.59	**54.17**	**124**
Salinas, CA	3.10	36.77	58.58	52.79	96.50	47.41	50.12	29.10	79.85	**50.47**	**164**
✓Salt Lake City-Ogden, UT	27.20	93.17	98.82	70.86	29.07	61.79	88.40	55.95	95.64	**68.99**	**26**
San Angelo, TX	96.29	16.59	28.85	5.97	66.03	47.73	31.45	24.76	13.61	**36.81**	**303**
✓San Antonio, TX	87.68	81.14	94.25	57.32	74.88	20.15	54.07	80.91	68.62	**68.78**	**27**
✓San Diego, CA	4.91	87.26	99.96	86.92	96.92	19.96	90.59	85.18	96.34	**74.23**	**9**
✓San Francisco, CA	1.09	86.33	55.61	96.62	98.12	13.38	98.59	92.30	96.57	**70.96**	**20**
✓San Jose, CA	1.23	85.28	90.02	94.48	93.79	65.11	95.76	65.82	71.83	**73.70**	**11**

Metro Area	Cost of Living	Transport	Jobs	Education	Climate	Crime	Arts	Health Care	Recreation	Mean Score	Overall Rank
San Luis Obispo–Atascadero–Paso Robles, CA	5.81	16.83	46.90	30.59	96.93	74.45	32.22	45.09	57.28	**45.12**	**217**
Santa Barbara–Santa Maria–Lompoc, CA	4.15	58.54	51.12	72.11	96.68	66.85	49.24	54.86	82.37	**59.55**	**74**
Santa Cruz–Watsonville, CA	1.92	66.96	46.13	66.14	96.34	44.35	51.09	34.02	41.70	**49.85**	**170**
Santa Fe, NM	9.41	65.15	45.98	71.34	53.09	37.63	41.03	61.02	46.10	**47.86**	**185**
Santa Rosa, CA	3.36	65.34	73.75	54.67	93.74	68.33	56.09	73.13	61.24	**61.07**	**63**
Sarasota–Bradenton, FL	28.26	82.45	77.46	45.87	83.27	18.20	65.04	48.46	88.54	**59.73**	**72**
Saskatoon, SK	34.22	67.03	36.27	87.80	8.14	54.35	72.34	93.81	42.13	**55.12**	**114**
Savannah, GA	43.14	37.61	36.55	40.06	74.90	24.41	42.37	26.56	71.04	**44.07**	**228**
Scranton–Wilkes-Barre–Hazleton, PA	63.34	35.51	24.35	80.30	41.17	93.47	57.21	75.31	61.36	**59.11**	**77**
✓Seattle–Bellevue–Everett, WA	9.01	83.40	99.72	88.86	89.03	44.35	96.87	91.55	96.49	**77.70**	**2**
Sharon, PA	82.59	6.47	24.50	40.10	33.70	92.58	1.67	14.42	21.38	**35.27**	**315**
Sheboygan, WI	70.91	87.81	33.91	6.08	28.42	91.00	54.21	34.35	57.17	**51.54**	**150**
Sherbrooke, PQ	14.28	25.67	23.48	80.74	15.94	77.89	22.79	97.18	31.43	**43.27**	**234**
Sherman–Denison, TX	96.77	0.36	29.25	14.04	54.38	58.76	25.19	28.84	25.23	**36.98**	**299**
Shreveport–Bossier City, LA	89.18	33.51	23.30	19.11	59.62	10.00	39.93	72.87	58.25	**45.09**	**218**
Sioux City, IA-NE	51.30	39.27	29.60	31.65	16.17	28.94	37.32	58.64	14.42	**34.15**	**330**
Sioux Falls, SD	82.85	50.30	44.65	27.34	9.22	86.22	42.45	89.61	18.20	**50.09**	**167**
South Bend, IN	81.96	54.17	32.63	77.16	27.88	50.74	54.76	53.96	22.70	**50.66**	**160**
Spokane, WA	51.79	66.97	44.42	64.57	49.98	54.44	63.02	76.55	38.15	**56.65**	**98**
Springfield, IL	65.42	61.47	26.53	58.58	26.34	27.00	38.69	64.75	20.13	**43.21**	**235**
Springfield, MA	17.21	87.69	17.99	93.67	35.62	24.04	67.55	33.58	58.17	**48.39**	**180**
Springfield, MO	72.95	26.67	67.96	79.10	38.02	75.63	35.99	46.88	35.51	**53.19**	**135**
Stamford–Norwalk, CT	1.66	82.70	33.77	2.44	43.64	79.99	85.90	58.06	38.60	**47.42**	**193**
State College, PA	47.32	18.80	38.42	63.23	30.89	93.56	29.33	7.96	17.44	**38.55**	**282**
Steubenville–Weirton, OH-WV	95.16	1.53	17.74	41.22	36.71	89.17	34.10	6.36	10.58	**36.95**	**300**
Stockton–Lodi, CA	21.73	6.03	42.73	36.75	88.57	8.71	38.50	20.86	27.40	**32.36**	**339**
Sudbury, ON	16.47	54.67	28.44	20.34	8.19	65.09	20.19	68.98	65.05	**38.60**	**280**
Sumter, SC	82.18	5.18	32.19	49.95	70.40	8.89	11.66	0.15	10.28	**30.10**	**344**
Syracuse, NY	46.58	78.93	29.62	83.76	25.88	85.21	74.09	59.47	90.61	**63.79**	**43**
Tacoma, WA	31.83	67.37	73.95	51.76	80.79	20.88	79.49	49.60	83.08	**59.86**	**71**
Tallahassee, FL	39.71	38.68	53.83	68.52	68.71	0.09	27.20	60.59	69.45	**47.42**	**193**
✓Tampa–St. Petersburg–Clearwater, FL	53.35	87.05	99.36	80.24	78.84	3.14	88.77	86.52	96.39	**74.85**	**8**
Terre Haute, IN	80.35	3.14	32.66	57.68	30.92	92.36	31.03	46.18	16.44	**43.42**	**232**
Texarkana, TX–Texarkana, AR	99.30	4.65	28.77	18.98	63.27	35.37	0.65	42.33	12.14	**33.94**	**332**
Thunder Bay, ON	13.31	59.27	23.38	23.24	7.45	39.25	41.04	74.10	88.31	**41.04**	**258**
Toledo, OH	48.32	60.08	26.64	62.84	26.78	40.40	80.77	75.18	57.84	**53.21**	**134**
Topeka, KS	89.10	85.69	30.67	12.67	28.93	6.24	44.78	18.44	13.14	**36.63**	**306**
✓Toronto, ON	3.77	98.29	82.89	71.41	25.40	71.62	99.72	98.61	97.66	**72.15**	**15**
Trenton, NJ	15.49	96.53	36.66	87.01	44.45	47.73	73.68	46.81	11.49	**51.09**	**153**
Trois-Rivieres, PQ	29.55	3.68	25.29	41.78	12.02	79.57	49.35	76.40	9.50	**36.35**	**309**
Tucson, AZ	33.52	62.53	87.55	44.85	79.62	15.13	56.59	59.31	84.61	**58.19**	**85**
Tulsa, OK	69.55	51.72	65.31	35.58	47.04	32.86	55.32	55.20	78.97	**54.62**	**118**

Metro Area	Cost of Living	Transport	Jobs	Education	Climate	Crime	Arts	Health Care	Recreation	Mean Score	Overall Rank
Tuscaloosa, AL	78.39	49.86	45.31	83.36	61.67	10.18	18.90	36.45	29.52	**45.96**	**210**
Tyler, TX	93.04	3.39	40.15	45.66	68.86	25.86	0.01	57.61	22.66	**39.69**	**271**
Utica-Rome, NY	51.68	68.62	19.61	78.59	23.39	91.40	33.48	32.51	69.67	**52.11**	**143**
Vallejo-Fairfield-Napa, CA	11.58	52.91	55.48	56.25	90.38	35.00	55.93	41.01	67.36	**51.77**	**148**
✓Vancouver, BC	3.15	74.93	71.76	73.15	81.49	19.47	94.58	99.03	94.55	**68.01**	**30**
Ventura, CA	3.36	70.04	78.72	70.27	97.52	71.48	55.65	47.15	79.34	**63.73**	**44**
Victoria, BC	3.49	68.28	43.94	24.96	84.86	46.25	58.85	95.46	49.80	**52.88**	**136**
Victoria, TX	[illegible]	[illegible]	[illegible]	[illegible]	[illegible]	[illegible]	[illegible]	[illegible]	[illegible]	[illegible]	[illegible]
Waterloo-Cedar Falls, IA	94.63	41.39	33.36	37.76	15.25	73.89	40.24	62.48	12.75	**45.75**	**212**
Wausau, WI	83.02	30.57	42.47	10.35	12.89	94.43	25.64	44.44	23.40	**40.80**	**264**
West Palm Beach-Boca Raton, FL	21.59	65.70	89.21	41.17	84.67	2.99	69.92	60.76	92.26	**58.70**	**81**
Wheeling, WV-OH	94.62	2.87	27.78	57.55	37.39	95.09	44.92	73.56	14.01	**49.75**	**171**
Wichita, KS	65.51	59.45	53.12	50.11	34.20	32.28	47.81	71.41	44.32	**50.91**	**158**
Wichita Falls, TX	97.86	21.19	34.48	3.67	53.71	21.08	17.10	47.41	18.61	**35.01**	**319**
Williamsport, PA	78.24	19.72	22.27	30.57	32.90	92.82	28.37	69.04	3.86	**41.98**	**251**
Wilmington, NC	43.03	12.66	49.82	28.21	69.59	18.37	23.45	22.02	82.71	**38.87**	**278**
Wilmington-Newark, DE-MD	22.67	94.11	50.26	69.28	51.28	69.27	59.82	36.67	66.52	**57.76**	**91**
Windsor, ON	16.79	95.58	26.46	31.45	28.34	75.97	49.30	61.83	33.77	**46.61**	**204**
Winnipeg, MB	16.36	85.57	32.48	60.33	3.40	31.88	79.22	85.99	63.60	**50.98**	**155**
Worcester, MA-CT	12.74	71.64	35.16	92.80	33.95	83.22	68.42	55.99	62.31	**57.36**	**95**
Yakima, WA	61.38	19.88	30.75	6.21	57.72	29.92	31.26	36.45	47.26	**35.65**	**312**
Yolo, CA	12.76	74.60	56.39	49.38	87.61	40.65	24.67	52.60	7.77	**45.16**	**215**
York, PA	43.37	22.00	44.10	25.13	44.33	91.37	18.09	21.55	16.73	**36.30**	**310**
Youngstown-Warren, OH	75.14	16.20	28.17	47.61	29.55	80.07	55.76	26.58	59.97	**46.56**	**206**
Yuba City, CA	49.18	32.61	33.21	19.98	86.17	27.77	15.24	6.53	17.96	**32.07**	**340**
Yuma, AZ	53.31	17.17	40.48	5.04	89.29	35.16	8.04	0.58	27.18	**30.69**	**342**

Appendix

Metropolitan Complexes (MCs) & Their Metro Area Parts

North America's 351 metro areas stand on their own as centers for employment and culture, but many are also blended with other metro areas by commuting workers and by print and broadcasting media.

Places Rated identifies 177 of these, grouped into 59 metropolitan complexes using at least three of four criteria: (1) their boundaries are contiguous; (2) they are parts of the same television market as defined by The A. C. Nielsen Company in the U.S. or the Bureau of Broadcast Measurement in Canada; (3) their daily newspapers, according to the Standard Rate and Data Service, significantly invade each others' turf; and (4) many of their workers commute from one to another.

Albany–Glens Falls, NY
Albany–Schenectady–Troy
Glens Falls

Albuquerque–Santa Fe, NM
Albuquerque
Santa Fe

Allentown–Reading, PA
Allentown–Bethlehem–Easton
Reading

Atlanta–Athens, GA
Athens
Atlanta

Birmingham–Tuscaloosa–Gadsden, AL
Birmingham
Gadsden
Tuscaloosa

Boston–Worcester–Lawrence, MA–NH–ME–CT
Barnstable–Yarmouth, MA
Boston, MA–NH
Brockton, MA
Fitchburg–Leominster, MA
Lawrence, MA–NH
Lowell, MA–NH
Manchester, NH
Nashua, NH
New Bedford, MA
Portsmouth–Rochester, NH–ME
Worcester, MA–CT

Buffalo–Niagara Region, NY–ON
Buffalo–Niagara Falls, NY
Jamestown, NY
St. Catharines–Niagara, ON

Cedar Rapids–Iowa City, IA
Cedar Rapids
Iowa City

Charlotte–Gastonia–Hickory, NC–SC
Charlotte–Gastonia–Rock Hill, NC–SC
Hickory–Morganton–Lenoir, NC

Chicago–Tri-State, IL–IN–WI
Chicago, IL
Gary, IN
Kankakee, IL
Kenosha, WI

Cincinnati–Hamilton, OH–KY–IN
Cincinnati, OH–KY–IN
Hamilton–Middletown, OH

Cleveland–Akron, OH
Akron
Canton–Massillon
Cleveland–Lorain–Elyria

Colorado Springs–Pueblo, CO
Colorado Springs
Pueblo

Dallas–Fort Worth, TX
Dallas
Fort Worth–Arlington

Denver–Eastern Slope, CO
Boulder–Longmont
Denver
Fort Collins–Loveland
Greeley

Detroit–Ann Arbor–Flint, MI–ON
Ann Arbor, MI
Detroit, MI
Flint, MI
Windsor, ON

El Paso–Las Cruces, TX–NM
El Paso, TX
Las Cruces, NM

Fort Myers–Naples–Punta Gorda, FL
Fort Myers–Cape Coral
Naples
Punta Gorda

Fresno–Visalia, CA
Fresno
Visalia–Tulare–Porterville

Green Bay–Fox Valley, WI
Appleton–Oshkosh–Neenah
Green Bay

Harrisburg–Lancaster–York, PA
Harrisburg–Lebanon–Carlisle
Lancaster
York

Houston–Galveston–Brazoria, TX
Brazoria
Galveston–Texas City
Houston

Huntington–Charleston, WV–OH
Charleston, WV
Huntington–Ashland, WV–OH

Huntsville–Decatur, AL
Decatur
Huntsville

Indianapolis–Muncie–Bloomington, IN
Bloomington
Indianapolis
Kokomo
Muncie

Johnstown–Altoona, PA
Altoona
Johnstown

Kansas City–Lawrence, MO–KS
Kansas City, MO–KS
Lawrence, KS
St. Joseph, MO
Topeka, KS

Little Rock–Pine Bluff, AR
Little Rock–North Little Rock
Pine Bluff

Los Angeles–Riverside–Orange

Brownsville–Harlingen
McAllen–Edinburg–Mission

Miami–Fort Lauderdale, FL
Fort Lauderdale
Miami

Milwaukee–Racine–Sheboygan, WI
Milwaukee–Waukesha
Racine
Sheboygan

Minneapolis–St. Paul–St. Cloud, MN–WI
Minneapolis–St. Paul, MN–WI
St. Cloud, MN

Mobile–Pensacola–Fort Walton, AL–FL
Fort Walton Beach, FL
Mobile, AL
Pensacola, FL

Modesto–Stockton–Merced, CA
Merced
Modesto
Stockton–Lodi

Nashville–Clarkesville, TN–KY
Clarkesville–Hopkinsville, TN–KY
Nashville, TN

New Orleans–Biloxi, LA–MS
Biloxi–Gulfport–Pascagoula, MS
New Orleans, LA

New York–Tri-State, NY–NJ–CT
Bergen–Passaic, NJ
Bridgeport, CT
Danbury, CT
Dutchess County, NY
Jersey City, NJ
Long Island, NY
Middlesex–Somerset–Hunterdon, NJ
Monmouth–Ocean, NJ
New Haven–Meriden, CT
New York, NY

Daytona Beach
Melbourne–Titusville–Palm Bay
Orlando

Peoria–Bloomington, IL
Bloomington–Normal
Peoria–Pekin

Philadelphia–Wilmington–Atlantic City, PA–NJ–DE–MD
Atlantic City–Cape May, NJ
Philadelphia, PA–NJ
Vineland–Millville–Bridgeton, NJ
Wilmington–Newark, DE–MD

Portland–Salem, OR–WA
Portland–Vancouver, OR–WA
Salem, OR

Raleigh–Rocky Mount, NC
Goldsboro
Raleigh–Durham–Chapel Hill
Rocky Mount

Sacramento–Yolo, CA
Sacramento
Yolo
Yuba City

Salt Lake City–Provo, UT
Provo–Orem
Salt Lake City–Ogden

San Francisco–Oakland–San Jose, CA
Oakland
San Francisco
San Jose
Santa Cruz–Watsonville
Santa Rosa
Vallejo–Fairfield–Napa

Seattle–Tacoma–Bremerton, WA
Bremerton
Olympia
Seattle–Bellevue–Everett
Tacoma

South Bend–Michiana, IN–MI

Tampa–St. Petersburg–Clearwater

Toronto–Ontario Shore, ON
Hamilton
Kitchener
Oshawa
Toronto

Vancouver–Bellingham, BC–WA
Bellingham, WA
Vancouver, BC

Waco–Killeen, TX
Killeen–Temple
Waco

Washington–Baltimore, DC–MD–VA–WV
Baltimore, MD
Hagerstown, MD
Washington, DC–MD–VA–WV

West Palm Beach–Fort Pierce, FL
Fort Pierce–Port St. Lucie
West Palm Beach–Boca Raton

Wheeling–Steubenville, WV–OH
Steubenville–Wierton, OH–WV
Wheeling, WV

Youngstown–Sharon, OH–PA
Sharon, PA
Youngstown–Warren, OH

Metropolitan Contacts & Place Finder

Each metropolitan area's listing includes contact information for its largest daily newspaper, its Convention and Visitors Bureau (CVB), and its Chamber of Commerce (C/C). Following that is a listing of cities, towns, and unincorporated places with populations over 5,000 within metro area boundaries. Whenever these boundaries cross state or provincial lines, the postal abbreviation for each state or province is also given.

Abilene, TX

Abilene Reporter-News
N. 100 Cypress St.
Abilene 79601
(915) 673-4271

Abilene CVB
1101 N. First St.
Abilene 79604
(915) 676-2557

Abilene C/C
325 Hickory
Abilene 79604
(915) 677-7241

Abilene, 110,035

Akron, OH

Akron Beacon Journal
44 E. Exchange St.
Akron 44328
(216) 996-3000

Akron/Summit CVB
Cascade Plaza
Akron 44308
(216) 376-4255

Akron Regional Development Board
Cascade Plaza
Akron 44308
(216) 376-5550

Akron, 221,886
Aurora, 10,688
Barberton, 27,784
Cuyahoga Falls, 48,870
Fairlawn, 6,411
Green, 20,587
Hudson, 5,161
Hudson Village, 5,161
Kent, 28,676
Macedonia, 8,166
Munroe Falls, 5,776
Norton, 11,784
Portage Lakes, 13,373
Ravenna, 12,537
Stow, 30,184
Streetsboro, 10,614
Tallmadge, 15,316
Twinsburg, 12,442

Albany, GA

Albany Herald
126 North Washington St.
Albany 31701
(912) 888-9300

Albany CVB & C/C
225 W. Broad Ave.
Albany 31701
(912) 434-8700

Albany, 81,062

Albany-Schenectady-Troy, NY

Albany Times Union
645 Albany-Shaker Rd.
Albany 12211
(518) 454-5694

Albany County CVB
52 S. Pearl St.
Albany 12207
(518) 434-1218

Albany-Colonie Regional C/C
540 Broadway
Albany 12207
(518) 434-1214

Albany, 104,828
Amsterdam, 20,065
Ballston Spa, 5,586
Cobleskill, 5,407
Cohoes, 15,873
Colonie, 7,599
Delmar, 8,360
East Glenville, 6,518
Latham, 10,131
Loudonville, 10,822
Mechanicville, 5,439
Rensselaer, 8,516
Roessleville, 10,753
Rotterdam, 21,228
Saratoga Springs, 26,117
Schenectady, 64,274
Scotia, 7,491
Troy, 52,606
Watervliet, 10,317
Westmere, 6,750

Albuquerque, NM

Albuquerque Journal/Tribune
7777 Jefferson NE
Albuquerque 87109
(505) 823-7777

Albuquerque CVB
121 Tijeras NE
Albuquerque 87102
(505) 842-9919

Greater Albuquerque C/C
401 Second St. NW
Albuquerque 87125
(505) 764-3700

Albuquerque, 411,994
Belen, 7,295
Bernalillo, 6,758
Corrales, 5,871
Los Lunas, 7,319
North Valley, 12,507
Paradise Hills, 5,513
Rio Rancho, 41,492
Sandia, 6,742
South Valley, 35,701

Alexandria, LA

Alexandria Daily Town Talk
1201 Third St.
Alexandria 71306
(318) 487-6397

Alexandria-Pineville Area CVB
1470 MacArthur Dr.
Alexandria 71306
(318) 443-7050

Central Louisiana C/C
802 Third St.
Alexandria 71306
(318) 442-6671

Alexandria, 45,982
Pineville, 12,012

Allentown-Bethlehem-Easton, PA

Morning Call
101 N. Sixth St.
Allentown 18101
(610) 820-6500

Lehigh Valley CVB
P.O. Box 20785
Lehigh Valley 18002
(610) 882-9201

Allentown-Lehigh County C/C
462 Walnut St.
Allentown 18102
(610) 437-9661

Allentown, 105,339
Bangor, 5,710
Bethlehem, 72,822
Catasauqua, 6,742
Easton, 27,725
Emmaus, 12,146
Fullerton, 13,127
Hellertown, 6,026
Jim Thorpe, 5,513
Lehighton, 6,137
Middletown, 6,866
Nazareth, 5,814
Northampton, 9,069
Palmerton, 5,463
Wilson, 7,961

Altoona, PA

Altoona Mirror
301 Cayuga Ave.
Altoona 16602
(814) 946-7411

Altoona-Blair County CVB
1231 Eleventh Ave.
Altoona 16601
(814) 943-4184

Altoona–Blair County C/C
1212 Twelfth Ave.
Altoona 16601
(814) 943-8151

Altoona, 52,531
Hollidaysburg, 5,634
Tyrone, 5,791

Amarillo, TX

Amarillo Globe–Times
900 S. Harrison St.
Amarillo 79101

Amarillo, 165,036
Canyon, 11,756

Anchorage, AK

Anchorage Daily News
1001 Northway Dr.
Anchorage 99508
(907) 257-4200

Anchorage CVB
1600 A Street
Anchorage, 99501
(907) 276-4118

Anchorage C/C
441 W. Fifth Ave.
Anchorage 99501
(907) 272-7588

Anchorage, 253,649

Ann Arbor, MI

Ann Arbor News
340 E. Huron St.
Ann Arbor 48104
(313) 994-6876

Ann Arbor CVB
211 E. Huron St.
Ann Arbor 48104
(313) 995-7281

Ann Arbor Area C/C
211 E. Huron St.
Ann Arbor 48104
(313) 665-4433

Adrian, 22,556
Ann Arbor, 108,817
Brighton, 6,451
Howell, 9,097
Saline, 7,350
Tecumseh, 7,942
Ypsilanti, 23,607

Anniston, AL

Anniston Star
216 W. Tenth St.
Anniston 36201
(205) 236-1558

Calhoun County CVB
801 Noble St.
Anniston 36202
(205) 237-3536

Calhoun County C/C
1330 Quintard
Anniston 36202
(205) 237-3536

Anniston, 27,206
Jacksonville, 10,987
Oxford, 10,422
Piedmont, 6,004
Saks, 11,138

(414) 734-3358

Fox Cities C/C & Industry
227 S. Walnut St.
Appleton 54913
(414) 734-7101

Appleton, 69,594
Kaukauna, 11,910
Kimberly, 5,546
Little Chute, 9,843
Menasha, 15,557
Neenah, 24,378
Oshkosh, 56,229

Asheville, NC

Asheville Citizen–Times
14 O'Henry Ave.
Asheville 28801
(704) 252-5611

Asheville Area CVB
151 Haywood St.
Asheville 28802
(704) 258-6112

Asheville Area C/C
151 Haywood St.
Asheville 28802
(704) 258-6101

Asheville, 64,261
Black Mountain, 5,915

Athens, GA

Athens Banner Herald/News
1 Press Place
Athens 30601
(706) 549-0123

Athens CVB
P.O. Box 948
Athens 30603
(706) 546-1805

Athens Area C/C
220 College Ave.
Athens 30601
(706) 549-6800

Athens, 89,181
Gaines School, 11,354

Atlanta, GA

Atlanta Constitution–Journal
72 Marietta St.
Atlanta 30303
(404) 526-5092

Atlanta CVB
233 Peachtree St.
Atlanta 30303
(404) 521-6600

Atlanta Area C/C
235 International Blvd. NW
Atlanta 30303
(404) 880-9000

College Park, 22,470
Conley, 5,528
Conyers, 8,468
Covington, 11,379
Decatur, 18,043
Doraville, 8,004
Douglasville, 13,677
Druid Hills, 12,174
Duluth, 12,602
Dunwoody, 26,302
East Point, 32,607
Fair Oaks, 6,996
Fayetteville, 7,017
Forest Park, 16,372
Gresham Park, 9,000
Griffin, 22,405
Hapeville, 5,480
Kennesaw, 10,410
Lawrenceville, 21,252
Lilburn, 10,011
Lithia Springs, 11,403
Loganville, 5,682
Mableton, 25,725
Marietta, 50,290
Monroe, 13,289
Morrow, 5,402
Mountain Park, 11,025
Newnan, 15,293
Norcross, 7,288
North Atlanta, 27,812
North Decatur, 13,936
North Druid Hills, 14,170
Panthersville, 9,874
Peachtree City, 25,082
Powder Springs, 10,545
Redan, 24,376
Riverdale, 10,170
Roswell, 54,908
Sandy Springs, 67,842
Scottdale, 8,636
Smyrna, 32,406
Snellville, 14,453
Stone Mountain, 6,955
Sugar Hill, 8,358
Tucker, 25,781
Union City, 10,818
Villa Rica, 7,792
Vinings, 7,417
Winder, 9,040
Woodstock, 5,297

Atlantic City–Cape May, NJ

The Press
22 Devins Ln.
Pleasantville 08232
(609) 645-1234

Greater Atlantic City CVB
2314 Pacific Ave.
Atlantic City 08401
(609) 348-7100

Greater Atlantic City C/C
1301 Atlantic Ave.
Atlantic City 08401
(609) 345-5600

Absecon, 7,541
Atlantic City, 36,563
Brigantine, 11,996
Buena Vista, 8,277
Dennis, 6,106
Egg Harbor, 25,717
Galloway, 24,789
Hamilton, 17,722
Hammonton, 12,312
Linwood, 7,511
Lower, 21,689
Margate City, 8,460
Middle, 16,125
Mullica, 5,838
North Wildwood, 5,003
Northfield, 7,519
Ocean City, 15,022
Pleasantville, 17,073
Somers Point, 11,491
Upper, 11,535
Ventnor City, 10,790
Villas, 8,136

Augusta–Aiken, GA–SC

Augusta Chronicle
725 Broad St.
Augusta 30901
(706) 724-0851

Augusta–Richmond County CVB
32 Eighth St.
Augusta 30901
(800) 726-0243

Metro Augusta C/C
600 Broad St. Plaza
Augusta 30903
(706) 821-1300

Aiken, SC, 24,929
Augusta, GA, 43,459
Belvedere, SC, 6,133
Evans, GA, 13,713
Fort Gordon, GA, 9,140
Martinez, GA, 24,738
North Augusta, SC, 17,618
South Augusta, GA, 55,998
Thomson, GA, 7,920
West Augusta, GA, 27,637

Austin–San Marcos, TX

Austin American-Statesman
305 S. Congress St.
Austin 78704
(512) 445-3500

Austin CVB
201 E. Second St.
Austin 78701
(512) 478-0099

Greater Austin C/C
Eleventh Street at Brazos
Austin 78767
(512) 478-9383

Anderson Mill, 9,299
Austin, 514,013
Brushy Creek, 5,833
Cedar Park, 6,582
Elgin, 5,018
Georgetown, 17,598
Jollyville, 14,094
Lockhart, 9,942
Pflugerville, 7,489
Round Rock, 41,435
San Marcos, 31,019
Taylor, 12,120
Wells Branch, 7,094

Bakersfield, CA

Bakersfield Californian
1707 Eye St.
Bakersfield 93301
(805) 395-7500

Greater Bakersfield CVB
1033 Truxtun Ave.
Bakersfield 93301
(805) 325-5051

Greater Bakersfield C/C
1033 Truxtun Ave.
Bakersfield 93301
(805) 327-4421

Arvin, 10,161
Bakersfield, 191,060
California City, 9,583
Delano, 27,684
Golden Hills, 5,423
Greenacres, 7,379
Lamont, 11,517
McFarland, 7,295
Oildale, 26,553
Ridgecrest, 29,398
Rosamond, 7,430
Shafter, 9,803
Taft, 6,518
Tehachapi, 6,799
Wasco, 18,099

Baltimore, MD

Baltimore Sun
501 N. Calvert St.
Baltimore 21278
(410) 332-6000

Baltimore Area CVB
100 Light St.
Baltimore 21202
(800) 343-3468

Greater Baltimore Committee
111 S. Calvert St.
Baltimore 21202
(410) 727-2820

Aberdeen, 13,458
Annapolis, 35,169
Arbutus, 19,750
Arnold, 20,261
Baltimore, 702,979
Bel Air, 9,919
Bel Air North, 14,880
Bel Air South, 26,421
Bowleys Quarters, 5,595
Brooklyn Park, 10,987
Cape St. Claire, 7,878
Carney, 25,578
Catonsville, 35,233
Cockeysville, 18,668
Columbia, 75,883
Crofton, 12,781
Dundalk, 65,800
Edgemere, 9,226
Edgewood, 23,903
Eldersburg, 9,720
Elkridge, 12,953
Ellicott City, 41,396
Essex, 40,872
Fallston, 5,730
Ferndale, 16,355
Fort Meade, 12,509
Garrison, 5,045
Glen Burnie, 37,305
Green Haven, 14,416
Havre de Grace, 9,782
Jessup, 5,324
Joppatowne, 11,084
Lake Shore, 13,269
Linthicum, 7,547
Lochearn, 25,240
Londontowne, 6,992
Maryland City, 6,813
Mays Chapel, 10,132
Middle River, 24,616
Milford Mill, 22,547
North Laurel, 15,008
Odenton, 12,833
Overlea, 12,137
Owings Mills, 9,474
Parkville, 31,617
Parole, 10,054
Pasadena, 10,012
Perry Hall, 22,723
Pikesville, 24,815
Pumphrey, 5,483
Randallstown, 26,277
Reisterstown, 19,314
Riviera Beach, 11,376
Rosedale, 18,703
Rossville, 9,492
Severn, 24,499
Severna Park, 25,879
South Gate, 27,564
Towson, 49,445
Westminster, 14,512
White Marsh, 8,183
Woodlawn, 32,907

Bangor, ME

Bangor Daily News
491 Main St.
Bangor 04401
(207) 990-8000

Greater Bangor C/C
519 Main St.
Bangor 04401
(207) 947-0307

Bangor, 32,004
Brewer, 8,735
Hampden, 6,030
Old Town, 8,152
Orono, 9,463

Barnstable–Yarmouth, MA

Cape Cod Times
319 Main St.
Hyannis 02601
(508) 775-7337

Cape Cod C/C
P.O. Box 16
Hyannis 02601
(508) 362-3225

Barnstable, 42,579
Brewster, 9,242
Chatham, 6,269

(504) 383-1111

Baton Rouge CVB
New State Capitol
Baton Rouge 70821
(504) 383-1826

Greater Baton Rouge C/C
564 Laurel St.
Baton Rouge 70821
(504) 381-7125

Baker, 13,145
Baton Rouge, 227,482
Brownfields, 5,229
Denham Springs, 9,066
Donaldsonville, 7,919
Gardere, 7,209
Gonzales, 7,958
Merrydale, 10,395
Oak Hills Place, 5,479
Port Allen, 6,182
Shenandoah, 13,429
Village St. George, 6,242
Zachary, 9,432

Beaumont–Port Arthur, TX

Beaumont Enterprise
380 Main St.
Beaumont 77701
(409) 833-3311

Beaumont CVB
801 Main St.
Beaumont 77704
(409) 880-3750

Beaumont C/C
450 Bowie St.
Beaumont 77701
(409) 838-6581

Beaumont, 115,022
Bridge City, 8,443
Groves, 16,835
Lumberton, 7,092
Nederland, 16,926
Orange, 19,901
Port Arthur, 58,795
Port Neches, 13,493
Silsbee, 6,620
Vidor, 11,356

Bellingham, WA

Bellingham Herald
1155 N. State St.
Bellingham 98225
(360) 676-2600

Bellingham/Whatcom CVB
904 Potter St.
Bellingham 98227
(800) 487-2032

Bellingham/Whatcom C/C
1801 Roeder Ave.
Bellingham 98227
(360) 734-1330

Lake Michigan CVB
185 E. Main St.
Benton Harbor 49023
(616) 925-6100

Cornerstone Alliance
185 E. Main St.
Benton Harbor 49023
(616) 925-6101

Benton Harbor, 13,186
Benton Heights, 5,465
Fair Plain, 8,051
Niles, 12,394
St. Joseph, 9,131

Bergen–Passaic, NJ

The Record
150 River St.
Hackensack 07601
(201) 646-4000

Gateway Regional Tourism Council
317 Pennsylvania Ave.
Paterson 07503
(201) 881-2783

Meadowlands C/C
201 Rt. 17 N
Rutherford 07070
(201) 393-0707

Allendale, 6,076
Bergenfield, 24,885
Bloomingdale, 7,824
Bogota, 7,906
Carlstadt, 5,530
Cliffside Park, 20,836
Clifton, 74,002
Closter, 8,194
Cresskill, 7,622
Dumont, 17,358
East Rutherford, 7,874
Edgewater, 5,423
Elmwood Park, 17,811
Emerson, 6,859
Englewood, 24,889
Englewood Cliffs, 5,785
Fair Lawn, 31,184
Fairview, 10,569
Fort Lee, 32,067
Franklin Lakes, 10,318
Garfield, 26,443
Glen Rock, 11,352
Hackensack, 37,441
Haledon, 7,203
Hasbrouck Heights, 11,721
Hawthorne, 18,077
Hillsdale, 9,924
Leonia, 8,596
Little Falls, 11,294
Little Ferry, 9,943
Lodi, 22,602
Lyndhurst, 18,262

Park Ridge, 8,494
Passaic, 56,042
Paterson, 138,290
Pompton Lakes, 11,003
Prospect Park, 5,401
Ramsey, 14,513
Ridgefield, 10,118
Ridgefield Park, 12,516
Ridgewood, 24,614
Ringwood, 13,239
River Edge, 10,899
River Vale, 9,410
Rochelle Park, 5,587
Rutherford, 17,721
Saddle Brook, 13,296
Teaneck, 37,825
Tenafly, 13,289
Totowa, 10,378
Upper Saddle River, 7,539
Waldwick, 9,925
Wallington, 10,487
Wanaque, 10,128
Washington, 9,245
Wayne, 47,025
West Milford, 25,430
West Paterson, 11,371
Westwood, 10,304
Wood-Ridge, 7,802
Woodcliff Lake, 5,535
Wyckoff, 15,372

Billings, MT

Billings Gazette
401 N. Broadway
Billings 59101
(406) 657-1200

Billings CVB
815 S. 27th St.
Billings 59107
(406) 245-4112

Billings Area C/C
815 S. 27th St.
Billings 59107
(406) 245-4111

Billings, 86,578
Laurel, 6,343

Biloxi–Gulfport–Pascagoula, MS

The Sun Herald
205 DeBuys Rd.
Gulfport 39507
(601) 896-2100

Mississippi Beach CVB
135 Court House Rd.
Gulfport 39506
(601) 896-6700

Mississippi Gulf Coast C/C
1401 20th Ave.
Gulfport 39502
(601) 863-2933

Bay St. Louis, 9,442
Biloxi, 47,832
D'Iberville, 7,608
Gautier, 11,470
Gulf Hills, 5,004
Gulfport, 43,023
Long Beach, 16,806
Moss Point, 17,975
Ocean Springs, 16,411
Orange Grove, 15,676
Pascagoula, 29,043
Pass Christian, 5,751
St. Martin, 6,349
Waveland, 6,400

Binghamton, NY

Press & Sun-Bulletin
Vestal Pkwy. E
Binghamton 13902
(607) 798-1234

Broome County CVB
49 Court St.
Binghamton 13902
(607) 772-8851

Broome County C/C
P.O. Box 995
Binghamton 13902
(607) 772-8861

Binghamton, 51,144
Endicott, 13,457
Endwell, 12,602
Johnson City, 15,961
Waverly, 5,055

Birmingham, AL

Birmingham News/Post-Herald
2200 Fourth Ave. N
Birmingham 35203
(205) 325-2222

Birmingham CVB
2200 Ninth Ave. N
Birmingham 35203
(205) 252-9826

Birmingham Area C/C
2027 First Ave. N
Birmingham 35202
(205) 323-5461

Alabaster, 17,260
Bessemer, 31,822
Birmingham, 264,527
Center Point, 22,658
Fairfield, 12,387
Forestdale, 10,395
Fultondale, 6,378
Gardendale, 9,917
Helena, 5,673
Homewood, 23,869
Hoover, 41,964
Hueytown, 15,425
Irondale, 9,704
Leeds, 10,027
Midfield, 5,400
Moody, 5,635
Mountain Brook, 20,143
Oneonta, 5,024
Pelham, 12,048
Pell City, 9,230
Pleasant Grove, 8,990
Tarrant, 8,029
Trussville, 8,459
Vestavia Hills, 19,854

Bismarck, ND

Bismarck Tribune
707 E. Front St.
Bismarck 58504
(701) 223-2500

Bismark–Mandan CVB
523 N. Fourth St.
Bismarck 58502
(701) 222-4309

Bismarck–Mandan C/C
P.O. Box 1675
Bismarck 58502
(701) 223-5660

Bismarck, 52,592
Mandan, 15,827

Bloomington, IN

Herald-Times
1900 S. Walnut St.
Bloomington 47401
(812) 332-4401

Bloomington/Monroe County CVB
2855 N. Walnut St.
Bloomington 47404
(812) 334-8901

Greater Bloomington C/C
400 W. Seventh St.
Bloomington 47404
(812) 336-6381

Bloomington, 62,560

Bloomington–Normal, IL

The Pantagraph
301 W. Washington
Bloomington 61701
(309) 829-9411

Bloomington–Normal CVB
210 S. East St.
Bloomington 61701
(309) 829-1642

C/C of Bloomington–Normal Area
210 S. East St.
Bloomington 61702
(309) 829-6344

Bloomington, 55,570
Normal, 42,749

Boise City, ID

Idaho Statesman
1200 N. Curtis Rd.
Boise 83706
(208) 377-6200

Boise CVB
168 N. Ninth St.
Boise 83702
(208) 344-7778

Boise Area C/C
300 N. Sixth St.
Boise 83701
(208) 344-5515

Boise City, 145,987
Caldwell, 23,970
Garden City, 7,981
Meridian, 14,566
Nampa, 35,333

Boston, MA–NH

Boston Globe
135 Morrissey Blvd.
Boston 02107
(617) 929-2000

Boston Herald
300 Harrison Ave.
Boston 02106
(617) 426-3000

Greater Boston CVB
Prudential Plaza
Boston 02199
(617) 536-4100

Greater Boston C/C
1 Beacon St.
Boston 02108
(617) 227-4500

Acton, 18,371
Amesbury, 15,980
Arlington, 43,624
Ashland, 12,888
Ayer, 7,107
Bedford, 12,765
Bellingham, 15,246
Belmont, 24,339
Berkley, 5,473
Beverly, 38,755
Blackstone, 8,468
Boston, 547,725
Braintree, 33,798
Brookline, 52,716
Burlington, 23,179
Cambridge, 99,890
Canton, 20,039
Carver, 11,184
Chelsea, 25,726
Cohasset, 7,503
Concord, 17,563
Danvers, 24,569
Dedham, 23,546
Dighton, 5,761
Dover, 5,500
Duxbury, 14,556
Everett, 34,139
Foxborough, 15,532
Framingham, 63,366
Franklin, 25,818
Gloucester, 29,098
Hamilton, 7,572
Hanover, 12,554
Harvard, 11,215

Hingham, 20,052
Holbrook, 11,117
Holliston, 13,393
Hopedale, 5,733
Hopkinton, 10,704
Hudson, 17,414
Hull, 10,747
Ipswich, 12,421
Kingston, 10,256
Lancaster, 6,521
Lexington, 29,108
Lincoln, 8,249
Littleton, 7,530
Lynn, 78,312
Lynnfield, 11,290

Milford, 25,209
Millis, 7,967
Milton, 25,788
Natick, 30,817
Needham, 28,080
Newbury, 6,384
Newburyport, 16,838
Newton, 85,358
Norfolk, 10,412
North Reading, 12,849
Norton, 15,775
Norwell, 9,591
Norwood, 28,607
Peabody, 47,993
Pembroke, 16,022
Plainville, 7,465
Plymouth, 48,997
Quincy, 84,040
Randolph, 30,126
Reading, 22,853
Revere, 41,843
Rockland, 16,703
Rockport, 7,854
Rowley, 5,162
Salem, 37,497
Salisbury, 7,042
Saugus, 25,949
Scituate, 17,223
Seabrook, NH, 6,607
Sharon, 16,542
Shirley, 7,142
Somerville, 68,940
Southborough, 7,274
Stoneham, 22,017
Stoughton, 27,050
Stow, 5,535
Sudbury, 15,290
Swampscott, 13,743
Taunton, 51,624
Topsfield, 5,919
Townsend, 9,041
Upton, 5,335
Wakefield, 25,176
Walpole, 21,872
Waltham, 54,791
Wareham, 20,120
Watertown, 31,437
Wayland, 12,355
Wellesley, 27,036
Weston, 10,301
Westwood, 13,329
Weymouth, 54,859
Wilmington, 19,193
Winchester, 20,652
Winthrop, 17,953
Woburn, 36,374
Wrentham, 10,186

Boulder–Longmont, CO

Daily Camera
1048 Pearl St.
Boulder 80302
(303) 442-1202

Gunbarrel, 9,388
Lafayette, 17,276
Longmont, 56,264
Louisville, 17,403

Brazoria, TX

Brazosport Facts
720 S. Main
Clute 77531
(409) 265-7411

Brazoria C/C
908 S. Brooks
Brazoria 77422
(409) 798-6100

Alvin, 21,537
Angleton, 18,687
Clute, 9,739
Freeport, 12,097
Lake Jackson, 25,083
Pearland, 24,935

Bremerton, WA

The Sun
545 Fifth St.
Bremerton 98310
(360) 377-3711

Bremerton–Kitsap County CVB
120 Washington Ave.
Bremerton 98310
(206) 479-3588

Bremerton Area C/C
837 Fourth St.
Bremerton 98310
(360) 479-3579

Bremerton, 42,319
East Port Orchard, 5,409
Parkwood, 6,853
Port Orchard, 5,735
Poulsbo, 5,586
Silverdale, 7,660

Bridgeport, CT

Connecticut Post
410 State St.
Bridgeport 06604
(203) 333-0161

Greater Fairfield Tourism
297 West Ave.
Norwalk 06850
(203) 854-7826

Bridgeport Business Council
10 Middle St.
Bridgeport 06601
(203) 335-3800

Stratford, 50,236
Trumbull, 32,805

Brockton, MA

Brockton Enterprise
60 Main St.
Brockton 02401
(508) 586-6200

Metro South C/C
60 School St.
Brockton 02401
(508) 586-0500

Abington, 14,467
Bridgewater, 23,041
Brockton, 87,411
East Bridgewater, 12,005
Easton, 20,756
Halifax, 6,935
Hanson, 9,612
Lakeville, 8,816
Middleborough, 18,613
Raynham, 10,443
West Bridgewater, 6,455
Whitman, 13,439

Brownsville–Harlingen–San Benito, TX

Brownsville Herald
1135 E. Van Buren
Brownsville 78520
(210) 542-4301

Valley Morning Star
1310 S. Commerce
Harlingen 78550
(210) 423-5511

Brownsville CVB
650 FM 802
Brownsville 78523
(210) 546-3722

Brownsville C/C
650 E. Elizabeth St.
Brownsville 78522
(210) 546-3938

Brownsville, 112,904
Harlingen, 55,522
La Feria, 5,152
San Benito, 23,317

Bryan–College Station, TX

Bryan College Station Eagle
1729 Briarcrest Dr.
Bryan 77802
(409) 776-4444

Bryan/College Station CVB
715 University Dr. E
College Station 77840
(409) 260-9899

Bryan/College Station C/C
4001 E. 29th St.
College Station 77802
(409) 260-5200

Bryan, 60,756
College Station, 57,273

Buffalo–Niagara Falls, NY

Buffalo News
News Plaza
Buffalo 14203
(716) 849-4444

Greater Buffalo CVB
107 Delaware Ave.
Buffalo 14202
(716) 852-0512

Greater Buffalo Partnership
300 Main Place Tower
Buffalo 14202
(716) 852-7100

Buffalo, 312,965
Cheektowaga, 84,387
Depew, 17,975
East Aurora, 6,864
Hamburg, 10,356
Kenmore, 16,622
Lackawanna, 20,151
Lancaster, 13,521
Lockport, 25,706
Niagara Falls, 60,517
North Tonawanda, 32,934
South Lockport, 7,112
Tonawanda, 65,284
West Seneca, 47,866
Williamsville, 5,401

Burlington, VT

Burlington Free Press
191 College St.
Burlington 05401
(802) 860-3441

Lake Champlain Regional C/C
209 Battery St.
Burlington 05402
(802) 863-3489

Burlington, 38,306
Colchester, 15,711
Essex, 17,250
Jericho, 5,026
Milton, 8,922
St. Albans, 7,650
Shelburne, 6,314
South Burlington, 13,170
Swanton, 5,894
Williston, 6,273
Winooski, 6,219

Calgary, AB

Calgary Herald
215 16th St. SE
Calgary T2E 7P5
(403) 235-7100

Calgary Sun
2615 Twelfth St. NE
Calgary T2E 7W9
(403) 250-4200

Calgary TCB
237 Eighth Ave. SE
Calgary T2G 2C4
(403) 263-8510

Calgary C/C
517 Centre St. S
Calgary T2G 2C4
(403) 750-0440

Airdrie, 14,259
Calgary, 771,768
Cochrane, 6,238

Canton–Massillon, OH

The Repository
500 Market Ave. S
Canton 44702
(216) 454-5611

Canton/Stark County CVB
229 Wells Ave. NW
Canton 44703
(216) 454-1440

Canton C/C
229 Wells Ave. NW
Canton 44703
(216) 456-7253

Alliance, 23,605
Canton, 84,188
Louisville, 8,290
Massillon, 31,293
North Canton, 15,357
Perry Heights, 9,055

Casper, WY

Casper Star Tribune
170 Star Ln.
Casper 82604
(307) 266-0500

Casper Area CVB
P.O. Box 399
Casper 82602
(307) 234-5312

Casper Area C/C
500 N. Center St.
Casper 82601
(307) 234-5311

Casper, 49,192

Cedar Rapids, IA

Cedar Rapids Gazette
500 Third Ave. SE
Cedar Rapids 52401
(319) 398-8211

Cedar Rapids Area CVB
119 First Ave. SE
Cedar Rapids 52301
(319) 398-5009

Cedar Rapids Area C/C
424 First Ave. NE
Cedar Rapids 52407
(319) 398-5317

Cedar Rapids, 113,438
Hiawatha, 5,133
Marion, 22,551

Champaign–Urbana, IL

Champaign News Gazette
15 Main St.
Champaign 61820
(217) 351-5252

Champaign Urbana CVB
40 E. University Ave.
Champaign 61820
(217) 351-4134

Champaign County C/C
100 Trade Center Dr.
Champaign 61820
(217) 359-1791

Champaign, 66,888
Rantoul, 7,698
Urbana, 37,546

Charleston, WV

Charleston Gazette/Mail
1001 E. Virginia St.
Charleston 25301
(304) 348-5140

Charleston CVB
200 Civic Center Dr.
Charleston 25301
(304) 344-5076

Charleston Regional C/C
106 Capitol St.
Charleston 25301
(304) 345-0770

Charleston, 56,553
Cross Lanes, 10,878
Dunbar, 8,482
Hurricane, 5,539
Nitro, 6,681
St. Albans, 10,823
South Charleston, 13,409
Teays Valley, 8,436

Charleston–North Charleston, SC

Charleston Post & Courier
134 Columbus St.
Charleston 29403
(803) 577-7111

Charleston Trident CVB
81 Mary St.
Charleston 29402
(803) 853-8000

Charleston Trident C/C
81 Mary St.
Charleston 29402
(803) 577-2510

Charleston, 76,854
Goose Creek, 27,454
Hanahan, 12,886
Ladson, 10,494
Moncks Corner, 6,103
Mount Pleasant, 34,425
North Charleston, 67,720
Summerville, 22,516

Charlotte–Gastonia–Rock Hill, NC–SC

Charlotte Observer
600 S. Tryon St.
Charlotte 28202

Belmont, NC, 8,602
Bessemer City, NC, 5,488
Charlotte, NC, 437,797
Cherryville, NC, 5,640
Concord, NC, 30,894
Fort Mill, NC, 5,461
Gastonia, NC, 59,093
Kannapolis, NC, 30,661
Lincolnton, NC, 9,196
Matthews, NC, 14,901
Mint Hill, NC, 11,632
Monroe, NC, 19,428
Mount Holly, NC, 8,402
Rock Hill, SC, 47,006
Salisbury, NC, 27,800
South Gastonia, NC, 5,487
York, SC, 7,610

Charlottesville, VA

Daily Progress
685 W. Rio Rd.
Charlottesville 22901
(804) 978-7210

Charlottesville–Albemarle County C/C
P.O. Box 1564
Charlottesville 22902
(804) 295-3141

Charlottesville, 41,034
Commonwealth, 5,538
Rio, 5,133
University Heights, 6,900

Chattanooga, TN–GA

Chattanooga Free Press
400 E. Eleventh St.
Chattanooga 37401
(423) 756-6900

Chattanooga Area CVB
1001 Market St.
Chattanooga 37402
(423) 756-8688

Chattanooga Area C/C
1001 Market St.
Chattanooga 37402
(423) 756-2121

Chattanooga, TN, 152,259
East Brainerd, TN, 11,594
East Ridge, TN, 21,147
Fairview, GA, 6,444
Fort Oglethorpe, GA, 5,900
Harrison, TN, 7,191
La Fayette, GA, 7,066
Middle Valley, TN, 12,255
Red Bank, TN, 11,817
Signal Mountain, TN, 7,658
Soddy–Daisy, TN, 8,928

Cheyenne, WY

Wyoming Tribune-Eagle

Cheyenne, 53,559

Chicago, IL

Chicago Sun Times
401 N. Wabash Ave.
Chicago 60611
(312) 321-3000

Chicago Tribune
435 N. Michigan Ave.
Chicago 60611
(312) 222-3232

Chicago CVB
McCormick Pl.
Chicago 60616
(312) 567-8500

Chicagoland C/C
200 N. LaSalle St.
Chicago 60601
(312) 580-6900

Addison, 32,815
Algonquin, 14,542
Alsip, 19,257
Antioch, 6,712
Arlington Heights, 77,438
Aurora, 112,313
Barrington, 9,830
Bartlett, 29,920
Batavia, 19,357
Beach Park, 10,169
Bellwood, 21,722
Bensenville, 17,295
Berkeley, 5,188
Berwyn, 46,751
Bloomingdale, 20,662
Blue Island, 21,762
Bolingbrook, 46,371
Boulder Hill, 8,894
Bridgeview, 14,705
Broadview, 8,816
Brookfield, 19,270
Buffalo Grove, 39,806
Burbank, 28,494
Burr Ridge, 9,232
Calumet City, 38,223
Calumet Park, 8,881
Carol Stream, 36,905
Carpentersville, 23,649
Cary, 13,109
Channahon, 7,602
Chicago, 2,731,743
Chicago Heights, 33,713
Chicago Ridge, 14,000
Cicero, 74,823
Clarendon Hills, 7,491
Country Club Hills, 16,556
Countryside, 6,015
Crest Hill, 12,121
Crestwood, 11,163
Crete, 7,522
Crystal Lake, 29,587
Darien, 24,577

Forest Park, 15,041
Fox Lake, 8,009
Frankfort, 7,863
Frankfort Square, 6,227
Franklin Park, 17,896
Gages Lake, 8,349
Geneva, 14,682
Glen Ellyn, 25,517
Glencoe, 8,705
Glendale Heights, 29,551
Glenview, 37,836
Glenwood, 9,249
Goodings Grove, 14,054
Grayslake, 8,136
Gurnee, 19,428
Hanover Park, 35,381
Harvard, 6,668
Harvey, 30,651
Harwood Heights, 7,698
Hawthorn Woods, 5,617
Hazel Crest, 14,049
Hickory Hills, 13,446
Highland Park, 29,309
Hillside, 7,757
Hinsdale, 16,357
Hoffman Estates, 48,625
Homewood, 20,061
Inverness, 7,564
Island Lake, 5,250
Itasca, 7,331
Joliet, 79,492
Justice, 12,086
La Grange, 15,885
La Grange Park, 12,980
Lake Bluff, 6,125
Lake Forest, 18,771
Lake in the Hills, 9,558
Lake Zurich, 17,586
Lansing, 29,396
Lemont, 9,643
Libertyville, 19,757
Lincolnwood, 12,168
Lindenhurst, 9,153
Lisle, 20,460
Lockport, 10,386
Lombard, 40,495
Long Grove, 5,118
Lynwood, 7,874
Lyons, 10,040
Marengo, 5,175
Markham, 13,262

Matteson, 12,389
Maywood, 27,513
McHenry, 18,019
Melrose Park, 20,644
Midlothian, 14,972
Mokena, 9,288
Morris, 11,077
Morton Grove, 22,303
Mount Prospect, 53,605
Mundelein, 23,995
Naperville, 101,163
New Lenox, 12,080
Niles, 29,451
Norridge, 14,079
North Aurora, 6,620
North Chicago, 34,909
North Riverside, 6,001
Northbrook, 33,476
Northlake, 12,638
Oak Brook, 9,325
Oak Forest, 28,016
Oak Lawn, 56,690
Oak Park, 54,385
Orland Hills, 5,902
Orland Park, 43,918
Palatine, 39,985
Palos Heights, 11,689
Palos Hills, 18,165
Park City, 5,092
Park Forest, 25,297
Park Ridge, 36,454
Plainfield, 5,027
Plano, 5,464
Prospect Heights, 15,635
Richton Park, 11,514
River Forest, 11,980
River Grove, 9,961
Riverdale, 14,976
Riverside, 9,050
Robbins, 7,590
Rolling Meadows, 22,952
Romeoville, 14,775
Roselle, 21,593
Round Lake Beach, 18,821
St. Charles, 24,787
Sandwich, 6,164
Sauk Village, 10,374
Schaumburg, 73,521
Schiller Park, 10,967
Shorewood, 7,330
Skokie, 58,980
South Elgin, 8,235
South Holland, 21,673
Steger, 8,748
Stickney, 6,008
Streamwood, 35,116
Summit, 10,109
Sycamore, 10,809
Tinley Park, 41,091
University Park, 6,935
Vernon Hills, 18,830
Villa Park, 22,220
Warrenville, 12,693
Wauconda, 7,456
Waukegan, 67,751
West Chicago, 16,207
Westchester, 17,330
Western Springs, 12,464
Westmont, 21,765
Wheaton, 54,298
Wheeling, 30,863
Willowbrook, 8,967
Wilmette, 27,547
Wilmington, 5,683
Winfield, 8,154
Winnetka, 12,899
Winthrop Harbor, 6,878
Wonder Lake, 6,664
Wood Dale, 12,989
Woodridge, 28,233
Woodstock, 15,872
Worth, 11,578
Zion, 21,436

Chico–Paradise, CA

Chico Enterprise-Record
400 E. Park Ave.
Chico 95928
(916) 891-1234

Greater Chico C/C
500 Main St.
Chico 95927
(916) 891-5556

Chico, 43,642
Magalia, 8,987
Oroville, 13,120
Oroville East, 8,462
Palermo, 5,260
Paradise, 26,389
South Oroville, 7,463
Thermalito, 5,646

Chicoutimi–Jonquiere, PQ

Le Quotidien
1051 boul. Talbot
Chicoutimi G7H 4A3
(418) 545-4474

Chicoutimi Tourism
2525 boul. Talbot
Chicoutimi G7H 4A3
(418) 698-3167

Chicoutimi C/C
31 rue Racine
Chicoutimi G7J 1E4
(418) 543-5941

Chicoutimi, 63,632
Jonquiere, 56,843
La Baie, 21,029
Laterriere, 5,173

Cincinnati, OH–KY–IN

Cincinnati Enquirer
312 Elm St.
Cincinnati 45202
(513) 721-2700

Greater Cincinnati CVB
300 W. Sixth St.
Cincinnati 45202
(513) 621-2142

Greater Cincinnati C/C
300 Carew Tower
Cincinnati 45202
(513) 579-3100

Alexandria, KY, 5,869
Bellevue, KY, 6,798
Blue Ash, OH, 12,352
Bridgetown North, OH, 11,748
Burlington, KY, 6,070
Cheviot, OH, 9,561
Cincinnati, OH, 358,170
Covedale, OH, 6,669
Covington, KY, 41,830
Dayton, KY, 6,316
Deer Park, OH, 6,063
Dent, OH, 6,416
Dry Run, OH, 5,389
Edgewood, KY, 8,629
Elsmere, KY, 6,986
Erlanger, KY, 15,996
Finneytown, OH, 13,096
Florence, KY, 21,792
Forest Park, OH, 19,275
Forestville, OH, 9,185
Fort Mitchell, KY, 7,041
Fort Thomas, KY, 16,120
Fort Wright, KY, 6,666
Franklin, OH, 11,436
Groesbeck, OH, 6,684
Harrison, OH, 7,697
Highland Heights, KY, 5,049
Independence, KY, 11,793
Kenwood, OH, 7,469
Landen, OH, 9,263
Lebanon, OH, 11,646
Loveland, OH, 12,136
Mack South, OH, 5,767
Madeira, OH, 9,039
Mason, OH, 13,284
Milford, OH, 5,954
Montgomery, OH, 10,100
Mount Healthy, OH, 7,577
Newport, KY, 18,388
North College Hill, OH, 10,211
Northbrook, OH, 11,471
Northgate, OH, 7,864
Norwood, OH, 22,376
Reading, OH, 11,753
St. Bernard, OH, 5,215
Sharonville, OH, 13,969
Silverton, OH, 5,488
Springboro, OH, 8,380
Springdale, OH, 10,633
Taylor Mill, KY, 7,310
Village of Indian Hill, OH, 5,325
Villa Hills, KY, 7,558
White Oak, OH, 12,430
Wyoming, OH, 8,074

Clarksville–Hopkinsville, TN–KY

Leaf-Chronicle
200 Commerce St.
Clarksville 37040
(615) 552-1808

Clarksville–Montgomery County Tourist Comm.
180 Holiday Rd.
Clarksville 37040
(615) 648-0001

Clarkesville Area C/C
312 Madison St.
Clarkesville 37041
(615) 647-2331

Clarksville, TN, 92,116
Hopkinsville, KY, 32,283

Cleveland–Lorain–Elyria, OH

Cleveland Plain Dealer
1801 Superior Ave.
Cleveland 44114
(216) 344-4500

Cleveland CVB
3100 Terminal Tower
Cleveland 44113
(216) 621-4111

Greater Cleveland C/C
200 Tower City Center
Cleveland 44114
(216) 621-3300

Amherst, 11,101
Ashtabula, 22,005
Avon, 8,197
Avon Lake, 16,570
Bay Village, 16,755
Beachwood, 11,265
Bedford, 14,598
Bedford Heights, 11,828
Berea, 18,795

Euclid, 53,251
Fairview Park, 17,526
Garfield Heights, 30,870
Geneva, 6,754
Highland Heights, 7,509
Independence, 6,613
Kirtland, 6,185
Lakewood, 57,063
Lorain, 70,919
Lyndhurst, 15,582
Maple Heights, 26,171
Mayfield Heights, 18,437
Medina, 21,897
Mentor, 50,058
Mentor-on-the-Lake, 8,500
Middleburg Heights, 14,477
North Madison, 8,699
North Olmsted, 34,577
North Ridgeville, 22,420
North Royalton, 27,092
Oberlin, 8,312
Olmsted Falls, 7,015
Painesville, 16,280
Parma, 85,792
Parma Heights, 21,117
Pepper Pike, 6,160
Richmond Heights, 9,577
Rocky River, 20,253
Seven Hills, 12,041
Shaker Heights, 30,548
Sheffield Lake, 10,213
Solon, 20,470
South Euclid, 23,364
Strongsville, 40,135
University Heights, 14,257
Vermilion, 11,367
Wadsworth, 16,836
Warrensville Heights, 15,739
Westlake, 30,370
Wickliffe, 13,785
Willoughby, 21,398
Willoughby Hills, 8,471
Willowick, 14,498

Colorado Springs, CO

Colorado Springs Gazette Telegraph
30 S. Prospect St.
Colorado Springs 80903
(719) 632-5511

Colorado Springs CVB
104 S. Cascade Ave.
Colorado Springs 80903
(719) 635-7507

Colorado Springs C/C
2 N. Cascade Ave.
Colorado Springs 80903
(719) 635-1551

Black Forest, 8,143
Cimarron Hills, 11,160
Colorado Springs, 316,480
Fort Carson, 11,309
Fountain, 12,289

300 S. Providence Rd.
Columbia 65205
(314) 875-1231

Columbia C/C
300 S. Providence Rd.
Columbia 65205
(314) 874-1132

Columbia, 74,072

Columbia, SC

The State
1401 Shop Rd.
Columbia 29201
(803) 771-6161

Greater Columbia CVB
301 Gervais St.
Columbia 29201
(803) 254-0480

Greater Columbia C/C
930 Richland St.
Columbia 29202
(803) 733-1110

Cayce, 10,495
Columbia, 104,101
Dentsville, 11,839
Forest Acres, 7,192
Irmo, 12,795
Oak Grove, 7,173
Red Bank, 5,950
St. Andrews, 25,692
Seven Oaks, 15,722
West Columbia, 12,091
Woodfield, 8,862

Columbus, GA–AL

Columbus Ledger-Enquirer
17 W. Twelfth St.
Columbus 31902
(706) 324-5526

Columbus CVB
801 Front Ave.
Columbus 31902
(800) 999-1613

Columbus C/C
901 Front Ave.
Columbus 31902
(706) 327-1566

Columbus, GA, 186,470
Phenix City, AL, 28,912

Columbus, OH

Columbus Dispatch

Bexley, 13,384
Blacklick Estates, 10,080
Circleville, 12,083
Columbus, 635,913
Delaware, 21,857
Dublin, 21,757
Gahanna, 30,971
Grandview Heights, 7,292
Grove City, 22,682
Heath, 7,551
Hilliard, 16,722
Huber Ridge, 5,255
Lancaster, 35,808
Lincoln Village, 9,958
London, 8,386
Newark, 45,263
Pickerington, 6,658
Reynoldsburg, 28,884
Upper Arlington, 36,083
Westerville, 34,833
Whitehall, 21,095
Worthington, 15,045

Corpus Christi, TX

Corpus Christi Caller-Times
820 Lower N. Broadway
Corpus Christi 78401
(512) 884-2011

Corpus Christi Area CVB
1201 N. Shoreline Blvd.
Corpus Christi 78401
(512) 882-5604

Corpus Christi Area C/C
1201 N. Shoreline Blvd.
Corpus Christi 78401
(512) 881-1888

Aransas Pass, 8,359
Corpus Christi, 275,419
Ingleside, 7,709
Mathis, 5,757
Portland, 13,642
Robstown, 13,292
Sinton, 5,561

Cumberland, MD–WV

Cumberland Times
19 Baltimore St.
Cumberland 21502
(301) 722-4600

Allegany County C/C
Bell Tower Bldg.
Cumberland 21502
(301) 722-2820

Cumberland, MD, 23,901
Frostburg, MD, 7,758
Keyser, WV, 5,932

Dallas, TX

Dallas Morning News
400 S. Record
Dallas 75202
(214) 977-8222

Dallas CVB
1201 Elm St.
Dallas 75270
(214) 746-6680

Dallas C/C
1201 Elm St.
Dallas 75270
(214) 746-6600

Addison, 9,399
Allen, 27,188
Athens, 11,092
Balch Springs, 18,963
Carrollton, 94,261
Cedar Hill, 24,905
The Colony, 26,475
Commerce, 6,857
Coppell, 24,416
Corinth, 5,593
Dallas, 1,022,830
Denton, 69,210
DeSoto, 34,904
Duncanville, 36,442
Ennis, 14,302
Farmers Branch, 24,607
Flower Mound, 27,907
Forney, 5,062
Frisco, 10,789
Garland, 194,218
Glenn Heights, 5,078
Grand Prairie, 108,908
Greenville, 22,630
Highland Park, 8,655
Highland Village, 9,770
Irving, 164,917
Kaufman, 5,772
Lancaster, 23,491
Lewisville, 51,143
McKinney, 26,524
Mesquite, 113,631
Midlothian, 5,485
Plano, 157,394
Richardson, 78,989
Rockwall, 13,695
Rowlett, 31,141
Sachse, 7,650
Seagoville, 10,057
Terrell, 13,030
University Park, 22,413
Waxahachie, 19,599
Wylie, 9,937

Danbury, CT

News-Times
333 Main St.
Danbury 06810
(203) 744-5100

Housatonic Valley District
72 West St.
Danbury 06813
(203) 743-0546

Greater Danbury C/C
72 West St.
Danbury 06810
(203) 743-5565

Bethel, 18,216
Brookfield, 14,801
Danbury, 64,675
New Fairfield, 13,777
New Milford, 25,387
Newtown, 21,027
Redding, 8,293
Ridgefield, 21,993

Danville, VA

Danville Register & Bee
700 Monument St.
Danville 24541
(804) 793-2311

Danville Area C/C
635 Main St.
Danville 24543
(804) 793-5422

Danville, 54,227

Davenport–Moline–Rock Island, IA–IL

Quad-City Times
500 E. Third St.
Davenport 52801
(319) 383-2200

Quad Cities CVB
2021 River Dr.
Moline IL 61204
(309) 788-7801

Davenport C/C
101 W. Second St.
Davenport 52801
(319) 355-4753

Bettendorf, IA, 30,640
Davenport, IA, 96,964
East Moline, IL, 20,220
Geneseo, IL, 6,601
Kewanee, IL, 12,772
Milan, IL, 5,778
Moline, IL, 43,472
Rock Island, IL, 40,657
Silvis, IL, 7,011

Dayton–Springfield, OH

Dayton Daily News
Fourth & Ludlow Sts.
Dayton 45401
(513) 225-2424

Dayton/Montgomery County CVB
1 Chamber Plaza
Dayton 45402
(513) 226-8211

Dayton Area C/C
1 Chamber Plaza
Dayton 45402
(513) 226-1445

Beavercreek, 37,739
Bellbrook, 7,120
Centerville, 21,741
Dayton, 178,540
Drexel, 5,143
Englewood, 11,276
Fairborn, 29,927
Fort McKinley, 9,740
Germantown, 5,023
Huber Heights, 40,673
Kettering, 59,357
Miamisburg, 18,121
Moraine, 6,087
New Carlisle, 6,078
Northridge, 9,448
Northview, 10,337
Oakwood, 8,735
Piqua, 20,781
Shiloh, 11,607
Springfield, 70,388
Tipp City, 6,500
Trotwood, 8,779
Troy, 20,405
Union, 5,414
Vandalia, 13,997
West Carrollton City, 14,386
Xenia, 24,058

Daytona Beach, FL

News-Journal
901 Sixth St.
Daytona Beach 32117
(904) 252-1511

Daytona Beach Area CVB
126 E. Orange Ave.
Daytona Beach 32114
(904) 255-0416

Daytona Beach–Halifax Area C/C
126 E. Orange Ave.
Daytona Beach 32114
(904) 255-0981

Daytona Beach, 64,644
De Bary, 7,176
De Land, 18,054
Deltona, 50,828
Edgewater, 18,070
Holly Hill, 11,328
New Smyrna Beach, 17,778
Orange City, 6,141
Ormond Beach, 31,751
Ormond-By-The-Sea, 8,157
Palm Coast, 14,287
Port Orange, 39,530
South Daytona, 12,316

Decatur, AL

Decatur Daily
201 First Ave. SE
Decatur 35601
(205) 340-2366

Decatur CVB
719 Sixth Ave. SE
Decatur 35602
(205) 350-2028

Decatur C/C
515 Sixth Ave. NE
Decatur 35602
(205) 353-5312

Decatur, 52,465
Hartselle, 11,664

Decatur, IL

Decatur 62525
(217) 422-2200

Decatur, 83,105

Denver, CO

Denver Post
1560 Broadway
Denver 80202
(303) 820-1010

Rocky Mountain News
400 W. Colfax Ave.
Denver 80204
(303) 892-5000

Denver Metro CVB
225 W. Colfax Ave.
Denver 80202
(303) 892-1113

Greater Denver C/C
1445 Market St.
Denver 80202
(303) 534-8500

Applewood, 11,069
Arvada, 95,445
Aurora, 250,717
Brighton, 16,017
Castle Rock, 12,048
Castlewood, 24,392
Cherry Hills Village, 5,775
Columbine, 22,397
Commerce City, 17,714
Denver, 493,559
Derby, 6,043
Edgewater, 5,143
Englewood, 32,724
Evergreen, 7,582
Federal Heights, 10,231
Gateway, 7,510
Golden, 13,983
Greenwood Village, 8,407
Highlands Ranch, 10,181
Ken Caryl, 24,391
Lakewood, 126,031
Littleton, 37,819
Northglenn, 27,489
Parker, 8,037
Sheridan, 5,640
Sherrelwood, 16,636
Southglenn, 43,087
Thornton, 63,079
Welby, 10,218
Westminster, 87,046
Westminster East, 5,197
Wheat Ridge, 30,889

Des Moines, IA

Des Moines Register
715 Locust St.
Des Moines 50309
(515) 284-8000

Greater Des Moines CVB

Ankeny, [illegible]
Clive, 7,951
Des Moines, 193,965
Indianola, 12,554
Johnston, 5,279
Norwalk, 6,240
Perry, 6,897
Urbandale, 28,250
West Des Moines, 37,243
Windsor Heights, 5,347

Detroit, MI

Detroit Free Press/News
321 Lafayette
Detroit 48226
(313) 222-6400

Metro Detroit CVB
100 Renaissance Ctr.
Detroit 48243
(313) 259-4334

Greater Detroit C/C
600 W. Lafayette Blvd.
Detroit 48226
(313) 964-4000

Allen Park, 30,158
Auburn Hills, 18,884
Berkley, 16,561
Beverly Hills, 10,877
Birmingham, 20,505
Bloomfield, 42,137
Canton, 57,047
Center Line, 8,148
Clawson, 14,258
Clinton, 85,866
Dearborn, 86,187
Dearborn Heights, 58,288
Detroit, 992,038
Ecorse, 11,538
Farmington, 10,286
Farmington Hills, 79,144
Ferndale, 23,222
Flat Rock, 8,171
Fraser, 14,085
Garden City, 31,030
Grosse Ile, 9,781
Grosse Pointe, 5,406
Grosse Pointe Farms, 10,141
Grosse Pointe Park, 12,602
Grosse Pointe Woods, 17,548
Hamtramck, 16,484
Harper Woods, 14,263
Harrison, 24,685
Hazel Park, 18,931
Highland Park, 20,053
Holly, 6,093
Huntington Woods, 6,440
Inkster, 29,597
Lambertville, 7,860
Lapeer, 8,731
Lincoln Park, 40,450
Livonia, 100,415
Madison Heights, 31,914
Marysville, 8,893
Melvindale, 10,827

River Rouge, 10,588
Riverview, 13,485
Rochester, 7,494
Rochester Hills, 66,267
Romulus, 22,993
Roseville, 51,592
Royal Oak, 68,431
St. Clair, 5,481
St. Clair Shores, 63,834
Shelby, 48,655
South Lyon, 7,202
South Monroe, 5,266
Southfield, 79,789
Southgate, 29,594
Sterling Heights, 119,505
Taylor, 68,541
Temperance, 6,542
Trenton, 19,799
Troy, 79,029
Utica, 5,139
Walled Lake, 6,769
Warren, 142,625
Waterford, 66,692
Wayne, 19,291
West Bloomfield, 54,843
Westland, 85,221
Wixom, 9,807
Wolverine Lake, 5,139
Woodhaven, 11,926
Wyandotte, 29,524

Dothan, AL

Dothan Eagle
227 N. Oates
Dothan 36303
(205) 792-3141

Dothan Area CVB
3311 Ross Clark Circle
Dothan 36304
(205) 794-6622

Dothan Area C/C
706 Honeysuckle Rd.
Dothan 36302
(334) 792-5138

Daleville, 5,331
Dothan, 55,793
Fort Rucker, 7,593
Ozark, 13,205

Dover, DE

Delaware State News
Webbs Ln. & New Burton Rd.
Dover 19901
(302) 674-3600

Kent County Tourism
9 E. Lockerman St.
Dover 19901
(302) 734-1737

Central Delaware C/C
Treadwater Tower
Dover 19902
(302) 678-0892

Dover, 28,876
Smyrna, 5,700

Dubuque, IA

Dubuque Telegraph Herald
801 Bluff St.
Dubuque 52001
(319) 588-5611

Dubuque Area C/C
770 Town Clock Plaza
Dubuque 52004
(319) 557-9200

Dubuque, 59,084

Duluth–Superior, MN–WI

Duluth News-Tribune
424 W. First St.
Duluth 55802
(218) 723-5281

Duluth CVB
100 Lake Place Dr.
Duluth 55802
(218) 722-4012

Duluth Area C/C
118 E. Superior St.
Duluth 55802
(218) 722-5501

Chisholm, MN, 5,196
Duluth, MN, 83,990
Hermantown, MN, 8,031
Hibbing, MN, 17,663
Superior, WI, 27,546
Virginia, MN, 9,148

Dutchess County, NY

Poughkeepsie Journal
85 Civic Center Plaza
Poughkeepsie 12601
(914) 454-2010

Poughkeepsie Area C/C
110 Main St.
Poughkeepsie 12601
(914) 454-1700

Arlington, 11,948
Beacon, 13,530
Myers Corner, 5,599
Poughkeepsie, 29,439

Eau Claire, WI

Leader-Telegram
701 S. Farwell
Eau Claire 54701
(715) 834-3471

Eau Claire Area CVB
2127 Brackett Ave.
Eau Claire 54701
(715) 831-2346

Eau Claire Area C/C
3625 Gateway Dr.
Eau Claire 54701
(715) 834-1204

Altoona, 6,500
Chippewa Falls, 13,377
Eau Claire, 58,476

Edmonton, AB

Edmonton Journal
10006 10 St.
Edmonton T5J 0S1
(403) 429-5100

Edmonton Sun
4990 92 Ave. NW
Edmonton T6B 3A1
(403) 468-0100

Edmonton Tourism
104-9797 Jasper Ave.
Edmonton T5J 1N9
(403) 496-8401

Edmonton C/C
600 10123 99 St.
Edmonton T5J 3H1
(403) 426-4620

Beaumont, 6,039
Edmonton, 649,666
Fort Saskatchewan, 11,975
Leduc, 14,573
Morinville, 6,733
St. Albert, 46,808
Spruce Grove, 13,627
Stony Plain, 8,510

El Paso, TX

El Paso Times
300 N. Campbell St.
El Paso 79901
(905) 546-6100

El Paso CVB
1 Civic Center Plaza
El Paso 79901
(915) 534-0697

Greater El Paso C/C
10 Civic Center Plaza
El Paso 79901
(915) 534-0500

El Paso, 579,307
Fabens, 5,599
Socorro, 26,556

Elkhart–Goshen, IN

Elkhart Truth
421 S. Second St.
Elkhart 46516
(219) 294-1661

Elkhart County CVB
219 Caravan Dr.
Elkhart 46514
(219) 262-8161

Greater Elkhart C/C
418 S. Main St.
Elkhart 46516
(219) 293-1531

Dunlap, 5,705
Elkhart, 44,840
Goshen, 25,346
Nappanee, 5,563

Elmira, NY

Star-Gazette
201 Baldwin St.
Elmira 14901
(607) 734-5151

Chemung County C/C
215 E. Church St.
Elmira 14901
(607) 734-5138

Elmira, 33,200
Horseheads, 6,845
Southport, 7,753
West Elmira, 5,218

Enid, OK

Enid News & Eagle
227 W. Broadway
Enid 73701
(405) 233-6600

Greater Enid C/C
210 Kenwood Blvd.
Enid 73702
(405) 237-2494

Enid, 45,851

Erie, PA

Erie Morning News/Daily Times
205 W. Twelfth St.
Erie 16534
(814) 870-1600

Erie County CVB
1006 State St.
Erie 16501
(814) 454-7191

Erie Area C/C
1006 State St.
Erie 16501
(814) 454-7191

Corry, 7,384
Edinboro, 7,897
Erie, 108,398
Northwest Harborcreek, 6,662

Eugene–Springfield, OR

Register-Guard
975 High St.
Eugene 97401
(503) 485-1234

Eugene–Springfield CVB
305 W. Seventh Ave.
Eugene 97440
(503) 484-5308

Eugene Area C/C
1401 Willamette St.
Eugene 97440
(503) 484-1314

Cottage Grove, 7,918
Eugene, 118,122
Florence, 6,075
North Springfield, 5,451

Evansville CVB
623 Walnut St.
Evansville 47708
(812) 425-5403

Metro Evansville C/C
100 NW Second St.
Evansville 47708
(812) 425-8147

Boonville, IN, 7,159
Evansville, IN, 129,452
Henderson, KY, 26,862
Mount Vernon, IN, 7,887

Fargo–Moorhead, ND–MN

The Forum
101 N. Fifth St.
Fargo 58102
(701) 235-7311

Fargo–Moorhead CVB
2001 44th St. SW
Fargo 58103
(701) 282-3654

Fargo–Moorhead C/C
321 N. Fourth St.
Fargo 58108
(701) 237-5678

Fargo, ND, 79,715
Moorhead, MN, 33,072
West Fargo, ND, 13,771

Fayetteville, NC

Fayetteville Observer-Times
458 Whitfield St.
Fayetteville 28306
(910) 323-4848

Fayetteville Area CVB
515 Ramsey St.
Fayetteville 28301
(910) 483-5312

Fayetteville Area C/C
519 Ramsey St.
Fayetteville 28302
(910) 483-8133

Fayetteville, 83,999
Hope Mills, 9,517
Spring Lake, 7,569

Fayetteville–Springdale–Rogers, AR

Northwest Arkansas Times
212 N. East Ave.
Fayetteville 72701
(501) 442-1710

Fayetteville C/C
123 W. Mountain St.
Fayetteville 72702

Sentinel & Enterprise
808 Main St.
Fitchburg 01420
(508) 343-6911

North Central Massachusetts C/C
110 Erdman Way
Leominster 01453
(508) 840-4300

Ashburnham, 5,756
Fitchburg, 36,726
Gardner, 20,330
Leominster, 38,240
Lunenburg, 9,468
Templeton, 6,572
Westminster, 6,553
Winchendon, 9,248

Flagstaff, AZ–UT

Arizona Daily Sun
417 W. Santa Fe Ave.
Flagstaff 86001
(520) 774-4545

Flagstaff C/C
101 E. Route 66
Flagstaff 86001
(520) 774-9542

Flagstaff, AZ, 50,708
Page, AZ, 7,162
Tuba City, AZ, 7,323

Flint, MI

Flint Journal
200 E. First St.
Flint 48502
(810) 766-6100

Flint Area CVB
400 N. Saginaw St.
Flint 48502
(810) 232-8901

Flint Area C/C
316 W. Water St.
Flint 48503
(810) 232-7101

Beecher, 14,465
Burton, 27,428
Davison, 5,689
Fenton, 9,363
Flint, 138,164
Flushing, 8,505
Grand Blanc, 7,655

Florence, AL

Times Daily
219 W. Tennessee St.
Florence 35630
(205) 766-3434

Sheffield, 10,278
Tuscumbia, 8,344

Florence, SC

Florence Morning News
141 S. Irby St.
Florence 29501
(803) 669-1771

Greater Florence C/C
610 W. Palmetto St.
Florence 29503
(803) 665-0515

Florence, 32,387
Lake City, 7,347

Fort Collins–Loveland, CO

Fort Collins Coloradoan
1212 Riverside Ave.
Fort Collins 80524
(970) 224-7730

Fort Collins CVB
420 S. Howes St.
Fort Collins 80522
(970) 482-5822

Fort Collins Area C/C
225 S. Meldrum St.
Fort Collins 80522
(970) 482-3746

Fort Collins, 98,954
Loveland, 43,967

Fort Lauderdale, FL

Sun-Sentinel
200 E. Las Olas Blvd.
Fort Lauderdale 33301
(305) 356-4000

Greater Ft. Lauderdale CVB
200 E. Los Olas Blvd.
Fort Lauderdale 33301
(305) 765-4467

Greater Fort Lauderdale C/C
512 NE Third Ave.
Fort Lauderdale 33301
(305) 462-6000

Broadview Park, 6,109
Browardale, 6,257
Coconut Creek, 29,664
Cooper City, 28,076
Coral Springs, 92,612
Dania, 13,940
Davie, 57,156
Deerfield Beach, 46,848
Fort Lauderdale, 162,842
Hallandale, 29,980
Hollywood, 124,992
Lauderdale Lakes, 27,645
Lauderhill, 52,023
Lighthouse Point, 10,480
Margate, 47,450
Melrose Park, 6,477
Miramar, 47,985
North Andrews Gardens, 9,002
North Lauderdale, 27,413
Oakland Park, 29,159
Parkland, 7,307
Pembroke Park, 5,302
Pembroke Pines, 81,498
Pine Island Ridge, 5,244
Plantation, 74,748
Pompano Beach, 75,719
Pompano Beach Highlands, 17,915
Riverland, 5,376
Sunrise, 75,038
Tamarac, 47,816
Washington Park, 6,930
Wilton Manors, 11,863

Fort Myers–Cape Coral, FL

News-Press
Martin Luther King Jr. Blvd.
Fort Myers 33901
(941) 335-0200

Lee County CVB
2180 W. First St.
Fort Myers 33901
(941) 338-3501

Greater Fort Myers C/C
2310 Edwards Dr.
Fort Myers 33901
(941) 332-3625

Bonita Springs, 13,600
Cape Coral, 84,968
Cypress Lake, 10,491
Forest Island Park, 5,988
Fort Myers, 50,489
Fort Myers Beach, 9,284
Fort Myers Shores, 5,460
Iona, 9,565
Lehigh Acres, 13,611
McGregor, 6,504
North Fort Myers, 30,027
San Carlos Park, 11,785
Sanibel, 5,528
Villas, 9,898
Whiskey Creek, 5,061

Fort Pierce–Port St. Lucie, FL

The Tribune
600 Edwards Rd.
Fort Pierce 34982
(407) 461-2050

St. Lucie County Tourist Development Council
2300 Virginia Ave.
Fort Pierce 34982
(407) 462-1533

Fort Pierce–St. Lucie County C/C
2200 Virginia Ave.
Fort Pierce 34982
(407) 461-2700

Fort Pierce, 36,775
Hobe Sound, 11,507
Jensen Beach, 9,884
Lakewood Park, 7,211
Port St. Lucie, 70,399
Port Salerno, 7,786
Stuart, 12,588

Fort Smith, AR–OK

Southwest Times Record
920 Rogers Ave.
Fort Smith 72901
(501) 785-7700

Fort Smith CVB
North B & Clayton Expwy.
Fort Smith 72901
(501) 783-8889

Fort Smith C/C
612 Garrison Ave.
Fort Smith 72902
(501) 783-6118

Fort Smith, AR, 74,480
Greenwood, AR, 5,760
Sallisaw, OK, 7,086
Van Buren, AR, 16,892

Fort Walton Beach, FL

Northwest Florida Daily News
200 Racetrack Rd. NW
Fort Walton Beach 32547
(904) 863-1111

Emerald Coast CVB
1540 Hwy. 98 E
Fort Walton Beach 32548
(904) 651-7132

Greater Fort Walton Beach C/C
34 S. Miracle Strip Pkwy.
Fort Walton Beach 32548
(904) 244-8191

Crestview, 14,438
Destin, 10,431
Fort Walton Beach, 24,207
Lake Lorraine, 6,779
Niceville, 11,864
Ocean City, 5,422
Valparaiso, 6,534
Wright, 18,945

Fort Wayne, IN

Fort Wayne Journal-Gazette/News-Sentinel
600 W. Main St.
Fort Wayne 46802
(219) 461-8333

Fort Wayne/Allen County CVB
1021 S. Calhoun St.
Fort Wayne 46802
(219) 424-3701

Greater Fort Wayne C/C
826 Ewing St.
Fort Wayne 46802
(219) 424-1435

Auburn, 9,975
Bluffton, 9,248
Columbia City, 7,896
Decatur, 9,860
Fort Wayne, 183,359
Garrett, 5,607
Huntington, 16,943
New Haven, 10,974

Fort Worth–Arlington, TX

Fort Worth Star-Telegram
400 W. Seventh St.
Fort Worth 76102
(817) 390-7400

Fort Worth CVB
415 Throckmorton St.
Fort Worth 76102
(817) 336-8792

Fort Worth C/C
777 Taylor St.
Fort Worth 76102
(817) 336-2491

Arlington, 286,922
Azle, 9,644
Bedford, 44,846
Benbrook, 20,995
Burleson, 18,133
Cleburne, 23,213
Colleyville, 18,549
Crowley, 7,311
Eagle Mountain, 5,847
Euless, 39,963
Everman, 5,791
Forest Hill, 12,089
Fort Worth, 451,814
Grapevine, 36,679
Haltom City, 34,475
Hurst, 35,256
Keller, 18,820
Kennedale, 5,261
Mansfield, 19,191
North Richland Hills, 55,471
Rendon, 7,658
Richland Hills, 8,452
River Oaks, 6,747
Saginaw, 9,170
Southlake, 12,345
Watauga, 23,179
Weatherford, 17,915
White Settlement, 16,502

Fresno, CA

Fresno Bee
1626 E Street
Fresno 93786
(209) 441-6111

Fresno CVB
808 M Street
Fresno 93721
(209) 233-0837

Fresno C/C
2331 Fresno St.
Fresno 93716

Orange Cove, 6,222
Parlier, 7,933
Reedley, 16,883
Sanger, 17,941
Selma, 16,417

Gadsden, AL

Gadsden Times
401 Locust
Gadsden 35901
(205) 549-2000

Gadsden–Etowah CVB
1500 Noccalula Rd.
Gadsden 35902
(205) 549-0351

Gadsden–Etowah C/C
1 Commerce Sq.
Gadsden 35902
(205) 543-3472

Attalla, 7,544
Gadsden, 46,550
Glencoe, 5,126
Rainbow City, 7,778
Southside, 5,619

Gainesville, FL

Gainesville Sun
2700 SW 13th St.
Gainesville 32608
(904) 378-1411

Alachua County VCB
30 E. University Ave.
Gainesville 32601
(904) 374-5231

Gainesville Area C/C
30 E. University Ave.
Gainesville 32602
(904) 334-7100

Alachua, 5,443
Gainesville, 87,806

Galveston–Texas City, TX

Galveston County Daily News
8522 Teichman
Galveston 77553
(409) 744-3611

Galveston CVB
2106 Seawall Blvd.
Galveston 77550
(409) 763-4312

Galveston C/C
2106 Seawall Blvd.
Galveston 77550
(409) 763-5326

Gary, IN

Post-Tribune
1065 Broadway
Gary 46402
(219) 881-3000

Greater Gary C/C
504 Broadway
Gary 46402
(219) 885-7407

Cedar Lake, 9,460
Chesterton, 9,663
Crown Point, 18,027
Dyer, 11,930
East Chicago, 32,592
Gary, 114,256
Griffith, 18,544
Hammond, 82,837
Highland, 22,613
Hobart, 24,214
Lake Station, 14,181
Lowell, 7,072
Merrillville, 27,652
Munster, 20,402
Portage, 31,046
St. John, 7,108
Schererville, 24,486
South Haven, 6,112
Valparaiso, 25,940
Whiting, 5,174

Glens Falls, NY

Post-Star
Lawrence & Cooper Sts.
Glens Falls 12801
(518) 792-3131

Adirondack Regional C/C
136 Warren St.
Glens Falls 12801
(800) 487-6867

Glens Falls, 13,562
Glens Falls North, 7,978
Hudson Falls, 7,592
West Glens Falls, 5,964

Goldsboro, NC

News-Argus
310 N. Berkeley Blvd.
Goldsboro 27534
(919) 778-2211

Wayne County C/C
308 N. William St.
Goldsboro 27533
(919) 734-2241

Goldsboro, 45,012
Mount Olive, 5,872

Grand Forks, ND–MN

202 N. Third St.
Grand Forks 58206
(701) 772-7271

Crookston, MN, 7,888
East Grand Forks, MN, 9,013
Grand Forks, ND, 50,168

Grand Junction, CO

Daily Sentinel
734 S. Seventh St.
Grand Junction 81501
(970) 256-4256

Grand Junction Area C/C
360 Grand Ave.
Grand Junction 81501
(970) 242-3214

Clifton, 12,671
Fruitvale, 5,222
Grand Junction, 31,758
Orchard Mesa, 5,977
Redlands, 9,355

Grand Rapids–Muskegon–Holland, MI

Grand Rapids Press
155 Michigan, NW
Grand Rapids 49503
(616) 459-1400

Grand Rapids Area CVB
245 Monroe NW
Grand Rapids 49503
(616) 459-8288

Grand Rapids Area C/C
Waters Bldg.
Grand Rapids 49503
(616) 771-0300

Allendale, 6,950
Comstock Park, 6,530
Cutlerville, 11,228
East Grand Rapids, 10,243
Forest Hills, 16,690
Grand Haven, 12,857

Grand Rapids, 190,395
Grandville, 16,950
Holland, 31,558
Hudsonville, 6,829
Jenison, 17,882
Kentwood, 39,896
Muskegon, 40,639
Muskegon Heights, 14,017
Northview, 13,712
Norton Shores, 22,061
Walker, 18,835
Wyoming, 63,688
Zeeland, 6,107

Great Falls, MT

Great Falls Tribune
205 River Dr. S
Great Falls 59405
(406) 791-1444

Great Falls Area C/C
815 Second St. S
Great Falls 59404
(406) 761-4434

Great Falls, 58,202

Greeley, CO

Greeley Tribune
501 Eighth Ave.
Greeley 80631
(303) 352-0211

Greeley CVB
1407 Eighth Ave.
Greeley 80631
(970) 352-3567

Greeley–Weld C/C
1407 Eighth Ave.
Greeley 80631
(970) 352-3566

Evans, 7,023
Fort Lupton, 5,649
Greeley, 64,189
Windsor, 5,950

Green Bay, WI

Green Bay Press-Gazette
435 E. Walnut St.
Green Bay 54301
(414) 435-4411

Green Bay Area CVB
1901 S. Oneida St.
Green Bay 54307
(414) 494-9508

Green Bay Area C/C
400 S. Washington St.
Green Bay 54305
(414) 437-8704

Ashwaubenon, 17,271
Bellevue, 7,541
De Pere, 18,876
Green Bay, 102,708
Howard, 10,197

Greensboro–Winston-Salem–High Point, NC

Greensboro News & Record
200 E. Market St.
Greensboro 27401
(910) 373-7000

Winston-Salem Journal
N. Marshal St.
Winston Salem 27101
(910) 727-7211

Greensboro Area CVB
317 S. Greene St.
Greensboro 27401
(910) 274-2283

Greensboro Area C/C
125 S. Elm St.
Greensboro 27402
(910) 275-8675

Archdale, 11,379
Asheboro, 18,461
Burlington, 43,804
Clemmons, 6,196
Elon College, 5,277
Graham, 10,981
Greensboro, 196,167
High Point, 72,207
Kernersville, 13,180
Lewisville, 6,871
Lexington, 18,546
Mebane, 5,181
Thomasville, 17,671
Trinity, 5,469
Winston-Salem, 155,128

Greenville, NC

Greenville Daily Reflector-Morning
209 Cotanche St.
Greenville 27858
(919) 752-6166

Pitt–Greenville C/C
302 S. Greene St.
Greenville 27834
(919) 752-4101

Ayden, 5,007
Greenville, 49,326

Greenville–Spartanburg–Anderson, SC

Greenville News/Piedmont
305 S. Main St.
Greenville 29601
(864) 298-4100

Greater Greenville CVB
500 E. North St.
Greenville 29603
(864) 233-0462

Greater Greenville C/C
24 Cleveland St.
Greenville 29603
(864) 242-1050

Anderson, 29,722
Belton, 5,945
Berea, 13,535
Clemson, 11,116
Easley, 19,653
Gaffney, 15,962
Gantt, 13,891
Greenville, 59,808
Greer, 12,005
Homeland Park, 6,569
Mauldin, 13,127
Parker, 11,072
Sans Souci, 7,612
Simpsonville, 12,962
Spartanburg, 45,721
Taylors, 19,619
Wade Hampton, 20,014
Welcome, 6,560

Hagerstown, MD

Hagerstown Herald-Mail
100 Summit Ave.
Hagerstown 21740
(301) 733-5131

Hagerstown–Washington County C/C
111 W. Washington St.
Hagerstown 21740
(301) 739-2015

Hagerstown, 38,510
Halfway, 8,873
Long Meadow, 5,594

Halifax, NS

Chronicle-Herald/Mail-Star
1650 Argyle St.
Halifax B3J 2B4
(902) 426-2898

Tourism Halifax
Duke & Barrington Sts.
Halifax B3J 3K8
(902) 421-8736

Halifax Board of Trade
P.O. Box 5127
Halifax B3L 4M7
(902) 420-0223

Bedford, 15,149
Dartmouth, 69,995
Halifax, 114,746

Hamilton, ON

The Spectator
44 Frid St.
Hamilton L8P 4M3
(905) 526-3333

Greater Hamilton Tourist Centre
127 King St. E
Hamilton L8N 1B1
(905) 546-2667

Hamilton & District C/C
555 Bay St. N
Hamilton L8L 1H1
(905) 522-1151

Ancaster, 26,365
Burlington, 140,628
Dundas, 23,312
Flamborough, 32,661
Grimsby, 19,824
Hamilton, 325,979
Stoney Creek, 55,657

Hamilton–Middletown, OH

Middletown Journal
52 S. Broad
Middletown 45044
(513) 422-3611

Hamilton CVB
201 Dayton St.
Hamilton 45011
(513) 844-1500

Greater Hamilton C/C
201 Dayton St.
Hamilton 45011
(513) 844-1500

Patriot/Evening News
812 Market St.
Harrisburg 17105
(717) 255-8100

Harrisburg–Hershey–Carlisle CVB
114 Walnut St.
Harrisburg 17108
(717) 232-1378

Capital Region C/C
114 Walnut St.
Harrisburg 17108
(717) 232-4121

Camp Hill, 7,942
Carlisle, 18,976
Colonial Park, 13,777
Enola, 5,961
Harrisburg, 54,238
Hershey, 11,860
Lebanon, 25,515
Linglestown, 5,862
Lower Allen, 6,329
Mechanicsburg, 9,951
Middletown, 9,401
New Cumberland, 7,995
Palmyra, 6,979
Progress, 9,654
Shippensburg, 6,346
Steelton, 5,039

Hartford, CT

Hartford Courant
285 Broad St.
Hartford 06115
(860) 241-6200

Greater Hartford CVB
1 Civic Center Plaza
Hartford 06103
(860) 728-6789

Greater Hartford C/C
250 Constitution Plaza
Hartford 06103
(860) 525-4451

Avon, 14,335
Berlin, 17,719
Bloomfield, 19,224
Bristol, 60,647
Burlington, 8,066
Canton, 8,482
Colchester, 12,222
Coventry, 10,949
Cromwell, 12,400
Durham, 6,097
East Haddam, 7,540
East Hampton, 10,973
East Hartford, 49,402
East Windsor, 10,120
Ellington, 11,239
Enfield, 45,281
Farmington, 22,345
Glastonbury, 29,357

New Hartford, 5,930
Newington, 29,354
Plainville, 17,392
Plymouth, 11,845
Portland, 8,623
Rocky Hill, 16,881
Simsbury, 22,485
Somers, 9,439
South Windsor, 23,359
Southington, 39,351
Stafford, 11,071
Suffield, 11,575
Tolland, 11,625
Vernon, 28,990
West Hartford, 59,465
Wethersfield, 25,919
Willington, 6,361
Winchester, 11,576
Windham, 21,036
Windsor, 28,241
Windsor Locks, 12,357

Hattiesburg, MS

Hattiesburg American
825 N. Main St.
Hattiesburg 39401
(601) 582-4321

Hattiesburg CVB
P.O. Box 16122
Hattiesburg 39404
(601) 268-3221

Hattiesburg Area C/C
607 Adeline St.
Hattiesburg 39403
(601) 545-3301

Hattiesburg, 47,692
Petal, 8,233
West Hattiesburg, 5,450

Hickory–Morganton–Lenoir, NC

Hickory Daily Record
1100 Park Pl.
Hickory 28602
(704) 322-4510

Greater Hickory CVB
470 Hwy. 70 SW
Hickory 28603
(704) 323-2861

Catawba County C/C
470 Hwy. 70 SW
Hickory 28603
(704) 328-6111

Conover, 7,042
Hickory, 29,577
Lenoir, 14,646
Morganton, 17,370
Newton, 10,978
St. Stephens, 8,734

Honolulu 96815
(808) 923-1811

Honolulu C/C
1132 Bishop St.
Honolulu 96813
(808) 949-5531

Ahuimanu, 8,387
Aiea, 8,906
Aliamanu, 8,835
Ewa Beach, 14,315
Halawa, 13,408
Heeia, 5,010
Honolulu, 385,881
Kailua, 36,818
Kaneohe, 35,448
Laie, 5,577
Maili, 6,059
Makaha, 7,990
Makakilo City, 9,828
Mililani, 29,359
Nanakuli, 9,575
Pearl City, 30,993
Village Park, 7,407
Wahiawa, 17,386
Waianae, 8,758
Waimalu, 29,967
Waipahu, 31,435
Waipio, 11,812
Waipio Acres, 5,304

Houma, LA

The Courier
3030 Barrow St.
Houma 70360
(504) 879-1557

Houma–Terrebonne C/C
1700 St. Charles St.
Houma 70361
(504) 876-5600

Bayou Cane, 15,876
Cut Off, 5,325
Houma, 31,311
Larose, 5,772
Raceland, 5,564
Thibodaux, 14,212

Houston, TX

Houston Chronicle
801 Texas Ave
Houston 77002
(713) 220-7171

Houston Post
4747 Southwest Fwy.
Houston 77027
(713) 840-5600

Greater Houston CVB
801 Congress Ave.
Houston 77002
(713) 227-3101

Greater Houston Partnership
1200 South St.
Houston 77002
(713) 651-2100

Aldine, 11,133
Baytown, 67,454
Bellaire, 14,668
Channelview, 25,564
Cleveland, 8,052
Cloverleaf, 18,230
Conroe, 30,890
Dayton, 5,693
Deer Park, 29,805
First Colony, 18,327
Galena Park, 10,222
Highlands, 6,632
Houston, 1,702,086
Humble, 13,098
Jacinto City, 10,084
Jersey Village, 5,369
Katy, 8,659
Kingwood, 37,350
La Porte, 30,922
Liberty, 7,856
Mission Bend, 14,195
Missouri City, 45,324
Pasadena, 129,292
Pecan Grove, 9,502
Richmond, 12,611
Rosenberg, 21,526
Seabrook, 7,533
South Houston, 14,729
Spring, 33,111
Stafford, 10,532
Sugar Land, 30,871
Tomball, 7,798
Town West, 6,166
West University Place, 13,851
The Woodlands, 29,205

Huntington–Ashland, WV–KY–OH

Huntington Herald-Dispatch
946 Fifth Ave.
Huntington 25701
(304) 526-4000

Cabell–Huntington CVB
210 Eleventh St.
Huntington 25708
(304) 525-7334

Huntington Regional C/C
522 Ninth St.
Huntington 25716
(304) 525-5131

Ashland, KY, 23,962
Flatwoods, Ky, 7,843
Huntington, WV, 53,788
Ironton, OH, 12,718
Pea Ridge, WV, 6,535
Westwood, KY, 5,300

Huntsville, AL

Huntsville Times/News
2317 Memorial Pkwy.
Hunstville 35801
(205) 532-4000

Huntsville–Madison County CVB
700 Monroe St.
Huntsville 35801
(205) 551-2231

C/C of Huntsville and Madison County
225 Church St. NW
Huntsville 35804
(205) 535-2000

Athens, 18,705
Huntsville, 160,326
Madison, 20,241

Indianapolis, IN

Indianapolis Star/News
307 N. Pennsylvania St.
Indianapolis 46204
(317) 633-1240

Indianapolis CVB
1 Hoosier Dome
Indianapolis 46225
(317) 639-4282

Indianapolis C/C
320 N. Meridian St.
Indianapolis 46204
(317) 464-2200

Alexandria, 6,004
Anderson, 60,846
Beech Grove, 13,031
Brownsburg, 8,649
Carmel, 31,411
Edinburgh, 5,003
Elwood, 9,823
Fishers, 18,524
Franklin, 15,337
Greenfield, 13,025
Greenwood, 30,332
Indianapolis 752,279
Lawrence, 27,876
Lebanon, 12,771
Martinsville, 12,341
Mooresville, 6,092
Noblesville, 20,054
Plainfield, 15,634
Shelbyville, 17,445
Speedway, 12,255
Zionsville, 6,229

Iowa City, IA

Iowa City Press-Citizen
1725 N. Dodge St.
Iowa City 52245
(319) 337-3181

Iowa City/Coralville CVB
325 E. Washington St.
Iowa City 52240
(319) 337-6593

Iowa City Area C/C
325 E. Washington St.
Iowa City 52240
(319) 337-9637

Coralville, 11,654
Iowa City, 60,655

Jackson, MI

Jackson Citizen Patriot
214 S. Jackson St.
Jackson 49201
(517) 787-2300

Jackson CTB
6007 Ann Arbor Rd.
Jackson 49201
(517) 764-4441

Greater Jackson C/C
209 E. Washington Ave.
Jackson 49201
(517) 782-8221

Jackson, 38,303

Jackson, MS

Clarion-Ledger
311 E. Pearl St.
Jackson 39205
(601) 961-7000

Metro Jackson CVB
921 N. President St.
Jackson 39215
(601) 960-1892

Metro Jackson C/C
201 S. President St.
Jackson 39225
(601) 948-7575

Brandon, 12,917
Canton, 10,767
Clinton, 23,047
Jackson, 193,097
Madison, 12,255
Pearl, 20,519
Ridgeland, 14,087

Jackson, TN

Jackson Sun
245 W. Lafayette
Jackson 38301
(901) 427-3333

The Jackson Chamber
197 Auditorium St.
Jackson 38301
(901) 423-2200

Jackson, 52,343

Jacksonville, FL

Florida Times-Union
1 Riverside Ave.
Jacksonville 32202
(904) 359-4111

Jacksonville & Beaches CVB
3 Independent Dr.
Jacksonville 32202
(904) 798-9149

Jacksonville C/C
3 Independent Dr.
Jacksonville 32202
(904) 366-6600

Atlantic Beach, 12,215
Fernandina Beach, 10,338
Fruit Cove, 5,904
Jacksonville, 665,070
Jacksonville Beach, 18,162
Lakeside, 29,137
Middleburg, 6,223
Neptune Beach, 6,593
Orange Park, 10,335

1 Marine Blvd. N
Jacksonville 28541
(919) 347-3141

Half Moon, 6,306
Jacksonville, 79,494
New River Station, 9,732
Piney Green, 8,999

Jamestown, NY

The Post-Journal
15 W. Second St.
Jamestown 14701
(716) 487-1111

Jamestown Area C/C
101 W. Fifth St.
Jamestown 14701
(716) 484-1101

Dunkirk, 13,902
Fredonia, 10,415
Jamestown, 34,388

Janesville-Beloit, WI

Janesville Gazette
1 S. Parker Dr.
Janesville 53547
(608) 754-3311

Forward Janesville
20 S. Main St.
Janesville 53545
(608) 757-3161

Beloit, 36,644
Janesville, 56,862
Milton, 5,141

Jersey City, NJ

The Jersey Journal
30 Journal Sq.
Jersey City 07306
(201) 863-2000

Hudson County C/C
574 Summit Ave.
Jersey City 07306
(201) 653-7400

Bayonne, 62,270
Guttenberg, 8,414
Harrison, 13,172
Hoboken, 33,363
Jersey City, 226,022
Kearny, 35,825
North Bergen, 50,763
Secaucus, 15,370
Union City, 56,308
Weehawken, 12,385
West New York, 36,558

Johnson City-Kingsport-Bristol, TN-VA

Washington County C/C
603 E. Market St.
Johnson City 37601
(423) 461-8000

Abingdon, VA, 7,681
Bloomingdale, TN, 10,953
Bristol, TN, 18,069
Bristol, VA, 24,956
Church Hill, TN, 5,856
Colonial Heights, TN, 6,716
Elizabethton, TN, 12,380
Erwin, TN, 5,145
Johnson City, TN, 51,573
Kingsport, TN, 38,476

Johnstown, PA

Tribune Democrat
425 Locust St.
Johnstown 15907
(814) 532-5050

Cambria County Tourist Council
111 Market St.
Johnstown 15901
(814) 536-7993

Greater Johnstown C/C
111 Market St.
Johnstown 15901
(814) 536-5108

Johnstown, 27,318
Somerset, 6,566
Westmont, 5,721

Joplin, MO

Joplin Globe
117 E. Fourth St.
Joplin 64801
(417) 623-3480

Joplin CVB
211 S. Main St.
Joplin 64801
(417) 625-4790

Joplin Area C/C
320 E. Fourth St.
Joplin 64801
(417) 624-4150

Carthage, 11,062
Joplin, 42,892
Neosho, 9,633
Webb City, 7,730

Kalamazoo-Battle Creek, MI

Kalamazoo Gazette
401 S. Burdick
Kalamazoo 49007

Albion, 10,197
Battle Creek, 55,053
Eastwood, 6,340
Kalamazoo, 81,644
Marshall, 7,082
Portage, 42,526
South Haven, 5,697
Springfield, 5,745
Westwood, 8,957

Kankakee, IL

Daily Journal
8 Dearborn Sq.
Kankakee 60901
(815) 937-3300

Kankakee Area C/C
4 Dearborn Sq.
Kankakee 60901
(815) 933-7721

Bourbonnais, 15,750
Bradley, 11,221
Kankakee, 29,859
Manteno, 5,158

Kansas City, MO-KS

Kansas City Star
1729 Grand Blvd.
Kansas City 64108
(816) 234-4141

Greater Kansas City CVB
1100 Main St.
Kansas City 64105
(800) 767-7700

Greater Kansas City C/C
2600 Commerce Towers
Kansas City 64105
(816) 221-2424

Belton, MO, 20,691
Blue Springs, MO, 40,931
Bonner Springs, KS, 7,118
Excelsior Springs, MO, 10,985
Gladstone, MO, 27,675
Grandview, MO, 25,373
Harrisonville, MO, 8,461
Independence, MO, 111,669

Kansas City, KS, 142,630
Kansas City, MO, 443,877
Lansing, KS, 7,967
Leavenworth, KS, 42,250
Leawood, KS, 24,852
Lee's Summit, MO, 47,029
Lenexa, KS, 36,990
Liberty, MO, 21,763
Merriam, KS, 13,095
Mission, KS, 9,145
Olathe, KS, 72,455
Overland Park, KS, 125,225
Paola, KS, 5,527
Prairie Village, KS, 23,056
Raymore, MO, 6,156
Raytown, MO, 29,939
Richmond, MO, 5,656
Roeland Park, KS, 7,530
Shawnee, KS, 40,471

Kenosha, WI

Kenosha News
715 58th St.
Kenosha 53141
(414) 656-6297

Kenosha Area C/C
800 55th St.
Kenosha 53141
(414) 654-7308

Kenosha, 85,122
Pleasant Prairie, 13,345

Killeen–Temple, TX

Killeen Daily Herald
1809 Florence St.
Killeen 76541
(817) 634-2125

Temple Daily Telegram
10 S. Third St.
Temple 76501
(817) 778-4444

Greater Killeen CVB
1 Santa Fe Plaza
Killeen 76540
(817) 526-9552

Greater Killeen C/C
1 Santa Fe Plaza
Killeen 76540
(817) 526-9551

Belton, 13,942
Copperas Cove, 28,417
Fort Hood, 18,559
Gatesville, 11,976
Harker Heights, 17,847
Killeen, 82,856
Temple, 52,087

Kitchener, ON

Kitchener–Waterloo Record
225 Fairway Rd. S
Kitchener N2A 2N7
(519) 894-2231

Kitchner VCB
2848 King St. E
Kitchener N2G 2N9
(519) 748-0800

C/C of Kitchener and Waterloo
67 King St. E
Kitchener N2G 2K4
(519) 742-4760

Cambridge, 104,256
Kitchener, 183,546
Waterloo, 82,558

Knoxville, TN

Knoxville News-Sentinel
208 W. Church Ave.
Knoxville 37902
(423) 523-3131

Knoxville Area CVB
500 Henley St.
Knoxville 37901
(423) 523-7264

Greater Knoxville C/C
301 E. Church Ave.
Knoxville 37915
(423) 637-4550

Alcoa, 6,655
Clinton, 10,223
Eagleton Village, 5,169
Farragut, 13,694
Halls, 6,450
Knoxville, 169,311
Lenoir City, 8,660
Loudon, 5,556
Maryville, 22,469
Oak Ridge, 28,209
Powell, 7,534
Sevierville, 10,204
Seymour, 5,104

Kokomo, IN

Kokomo Tribune
300 N. Union St.
Kokomo 46904
(317) 459-3121

Howard County CVB
112 N. Washington St.
Kokomo 46901
(317) 457-6803

Kokomo/Howard County C/C
106 N. Washington St.
Kokomo 46901
(317) 457-5301

Kokomo, 46,027

La Crosse, WI–MN

La Crosse Tribune
401 N. Third St.
La Crosse 54601
(608) 782-9701

La Crosse Area CVB
410 E. Veterans Memorial Dr.
La Crosse 54602
(608) 782-2367

La Crosse Area C/C
712 Main St.
La Crosse 54602
(608) 784-4880

La Crosse, WI, 50,877
Onalaska, WI, 12,684

Lafayette, IN

Journal & Courier
217 N. Sixth St.
Lafayette 47901
(317) 423-5511

Greater Lafayette CVB
301 Frontage Rd.
Lafayette 47903
(317) 448-0000

Greater Lafayette C/C
122 N. Third St.
Lafayette 47902
(317) 742-4041

Frankfort, 15,975
Lafayette, 45,877
West Lafayette, 24,777

Lafayette, LA

Lafayette Advertiser
221 Jefferson St.
Lafayette 70501
(318) 235-8511

Lafayette Parish CVB
1400 NW Evangeline Thrwy.
Lafayette 70505
(318) 232-3809

Greater Lafayette C/C
804 E. St. Mary Blvd.
Lafayette 70503
(318) 233-2705

Breaux Bridge, 7,058
Carencro, 5,840
Crowley, 14,487
Eunice, 11,426
Lafayette, 102,281
Opelousas, 19,305
Rayne, 8,878
St. Martinville, 8,063
Scott, 5,641

Lake Charles, LA

Lake Charles American Press
4900 Highway 90 E.
Lake Charles 70601
(318) 433-3000

Southwest Louisiana CVB
1211 N. Lakeshore Dr.
Lake Charles 70601
(318) 436-9588

Chamber of Southwest Louisiana
120 Pujo St.
Lake Charles 70601
(318) 433-3632

Lake Charles, 72,424
Moss Bluff, 8,039
Prien, 6,448
Sulphur, 21,575
Westlake, 5,126

Lakeland–Winter Haven, FL

The Ledger
401 S. Missouri Ave.
Lakeland 33801
(941) 687-7000

Lakeland C/C
35 Lake Morton Dr.
Lakeland 33802
(941) 688-8551

Auburndale, 9,439
Bartow, 14,995
Combee Settlement, 5,463
Crystal Lake, 5,300
Cypress Gardens, 9,188
Gibsonia, 5,168
Haines City, 12,459
Inwood, 6,824
Jan Phyl Village, 5,308
Lake Wales, 10,255

Lancaster 17603
(717) 291-8600

Pennsylvania Dutch CVB
501 Greenfield Rd.
Lancaster 17601
(717) 299-8902

Lancaster C/C
100 S. Queen St.
Lancaster 17608
(717) 397-3531

Columbia, 11,535
Elizabethtown, 10,337
Ephrata, 12,711
Lancaster, 57,721
Lititz, 8,390
Manheim, 5,216
Millersville, 8,321
Mount Joy, 8,405
Willow Street, 5,817

1ansing–East Lansing, MI

Lansing State Journal
120 E. Lenawee
Lansing 48919
(517) 377-1000

Greater Lansing CVB
119 Pere Marquette
Lansing 48901
(517) 487-6801

Lansing Regional C/C
510 W. Washtenaw
Lansing 48901
(517) 487-6340

Charlotte, 8,474
East Lansing, 50,322
Grand Ledge, 7,670
Haslett, 10,230
Holt, 11,744
Lansing, 119,590
Mason, 7,011
Okemos, 20,216
St. Johns, 7,705
Waverly, 15,614

Laredo, TX

Laredo Morning Times
111 Esperanza Dr.
Laredo 78041
(210) 728-2500

City of Laredo CVB
P.O. Box 579
Laredo 78040
(210) 712-1231

Laredo–Webb County C/C
2310 San Bernardo Ave.
Laredo 78040
(210) 722-9895

Las Cruces 88001
(505) 524-8522

Las Cruces C/C
760 W. Picacho
Las Cruces 88004
(505) 524-1968

Anthony, 5,160
Las Cruces, 71,043
Sunland Park, 9,101

Las Vegas, NV–AZ

Las Vegas Sun/Review-Journal
800 S. Valley View Blvd.
Las Vegas 89107
(702) 385-3111

Las Vegas CVB
3150 Paradise Rd.
Las Vegas 89109
(702) 733-2323

Las Vegas C/C
2301 E. Sahara Ave.
Las Vegas 89109
(702) 733-2323

Boulder City, AZ, 13,092
Bullhead City, 27,175
East Las Vegas, NV, 11,087
Enterprise, NV, 6,412
Henderson, NV, 101,997
Kingman, AZ, 15,943
Lake Havasu City, AZ, 31,895
Las Vegas, NV, 327,878
Mohave Valley, AZ, 6,962
North Las Vegas, NV, 64,536
Pahrump, NV, 7,424
Paradise, NV, 124,682
Spring Valley, NV, 51,726
Sunrise Manor, NV, 95,362
Winchester, NV, 23,365

Lawrence, KS

Lawrence Journal-World
609 New Hampshire St.
Lawrence 66044
(913) 843-1000

Lawrence CVB
734 Vermont
Lawrence 66044
(913) 865-4411

Lawrence C/C
734 Vermont St.
Lawrence 66044
(913) 843-4411

Lawrence, 71,721

Lawrence, MA–NH

Eagle Tribune

(508) 686-0900

Andover, MA, 31,317
Atkinson, NH, 5,724
Boxford, MA, 7,112
Derry, NH, 31,921
Georgetown, MA, 7,210
Groveland, MA, 5,540
Hampstead, NH, 7,504
Haverhill, MA, 52,962
Kingston, NH, 5,786
Lawrence, MA, 63,117
Merrimac, MA, 5,803
Methuen, 40,964
North Andover, MA, 24,532
Plaistow, NH, 7,655
Raymond, NH, 9,472
Salem, NH, 26,708
Windham, NH, 9,877

Lawton, OK

Lawton Constitution
P.O. Box 2069
Lawton 73502
(405) 335-3062

Lawton C/C
607 C Avenue
Lawton 73502
(405) 355-3541

Lawton, 86,078

Lewiston–Auburn, ME

Sun-Journal
104 Park St.
Lewiston 04243
(207) 784-5411

Androscoggin County C/C
179 Lisbon St.
Lewiston 04240
(207) 783-2249

Auburn, 23,364
Lewiston, 37,385
Lisbon, 9,488

Lexington, KY

Lexington Herald-Leader
100 Midland Ave.
Lexington 40508
(606) 231-3100

Greater Lexington CVB
430 W. Vine St.
Lexington 40507
(800) 848-1224

Greater Lexington C/C
330 E. Main St.
Lexington 40587
(606) 254-4447

Berea, 10,609
Georgetown, 12,926
Lexington–Fayette, 237,612
Nicholasville, 16,121
Paris, 8,928
Richmond, 23,842
Versailles, 7,934
Winchester, 16,919

Lima, OH

Lima News
121 E. High St.
Lima 45801
(419) 223-1010

Lima/Allen County CVB
147 N. Main St.
Lima 45801
(419) 222-6045

West Central Ohio Reg. Development
147 N. Main St.
Lima 45801
(419) 222-6045

Delphos, 7,289
Lima, 44,374
St. Marys, 9,019
Wapakoneta, 10,304

Lincoln, NE

Lincoln Journal-Star
926 P Street
Lincoln 68508
(402) 475-4200

Lincoln CVB
1221 N Street
Lincoln 68508
(402) 434-5335

Lincoln C/C
1221 N Street
Lincoln 68508
(402) 476-7511

Lincoln, 203,076

Little Rock–North Little Rock, AR

Arkansas Democrat-Gazette
Capitol Ave. & Scott St.
Little Rock 72201
(501) 378-3400

Little Rock CVB
P.O. Box 3232
Little Rock 72203
(501) 376-4782

Greater Little Rock C/C
1 Spring St.
Little Rock 72201
(501) 374-4871

Benton, 21,891
Bryant, 7,596
Cabot, 11,757
Conway, 33,946
Jacksonville, 29,584
Little Rock, 178,136
Maumelle, 8,269
North Little Rock, 62,197
Sherwood, 20,453

London, ON

London Free Press
369 York St.
London N6B 3M2
(519) 679-1111

London VCB
300 York St.
London N6B 3M2
(519) 661-5001

London C/C
244 Pall Mall St.
London N6A 1P4
(519) 432-7551

London, 332,009
St. Thomas, 30,639
Westminster, 7,620

Long Island, NY

Newsday
235 Pinelawn Rd.
Melville 11747
(516) 843-2020

Long Island Assn.
80 Hauppauge Rd.
Commack L.I. 11725
(516) 499-4400

Albertson, 5,166
Amityville, 9,347
Babylon, 12,250
Baldwin, 22,719
Baldwin Harbor, 7,899
Bay Shore, 21,279
Bayport, 7,702
Bayville, 7,341
Baywood, 7,351
Bellmore, 16,438
Bethpage, 15,761
Bohemia, 9,556
Brentwood, 45,218
Carle Place, 5,107
Cedarhurst, 5,656
Center Moriches, 5,987
Centereach, 26,720
Centerport, 5,333
Central Islip, 26,028
Commack, 36,124
Copiague, 20,769
Coram, 30,111
Deer Park, 28,840
Dix Hills, 25,849
East Hills, 7,037
East Islip, 14,325
East Massapequa, 19,550
East Meadow, 36,909
East Northport, 20,411
East Patchogue, 20,195
East Rockaway, 10,156
East Shoreham, 5,461
Elmont, 28,612
Elwood, 10,916
Farmingdale, 8,297
Farmingville, 14,842
Floral Park, 16,400
Fort Salonga, 9,176
Franklin Square, 28,205
Freeport, 39,900
Garden City, 22,000
Garden City Park, 7,437
Glen Cove, 23,873
Great Neck, 8,755
Great Neck Plaza, 5,848
Greenlawn, 13,208
Hampton Bays, 7,893
Hauppauge, 19,750
Hempstead, 44,730
Hewlett, 6,620
Hicksville, 40,174
Holbrook, 25,273
Holtsville, 14,972
Huntington, 18,243
Huntington Station, 28,247
Inwood, 7,767
Island Park, 5,026
Islip, 18,924
Islip Terrace, 5,530
Jericho, 13,141
Kings Park, 17,773
Lake Grove, 11,103
Lake Ronkonkoma, 18,997
Lakeview, 5,476
Lawrence, 6,560
Levittown, 53,286
Lindenhurst, 26,787
Long Beach, 34,216
Lynbrook, 19,595
Malverne, 9,246
Manhasset, 7,718
Manorhaven, 5,781
Manorville, 6,198
Massapequa, 22,018
Massapequa Park, 17,971
Mastic, 13,778
Mastic Beach, 10,293
Medford, 21,274
Melville, 12,586
Merrick, 23,042
Middle Island, 7,848
Miller Place, 9,315
Mineola, 18,629
Mount Sinai, 8,023
Nesconset, 10,712
New Cassel, 10,257
New Hyde Park, 9,716
North Amityville, 13,849
North Babylon, 18,081
North Bay Shore, 12,799
North Bellmore, 19,707
North Bellport, 8,182
North Lindenhurst, 10,563
North Massapequa, 19,365
North Merrick, 12,113
North New Hyde Park, 14,359
North Patchogue, 7,374
North Valley Stream, 14,574
North Wantagh, 12,276
Northport, 7,610
Oakdale, 7,875
Oceanside, 32,423
Old Bethpage, 5,610
Oyster Bay, 6,687

Patchogue, 11,357
Plainedge, 8,739
Plainview, 26,207
Port Jefferson, 7,365
Port Jefferson Station, 7,232
Port Washington, 15,387
Ridge, 11,734
Riverhead, 8,814
Rockville Centre, 25,060
Rocky Point, 8,596
Ronkonkoma, 20,391
Roosevelt, 15,030
Roslyn Heights, 6,405
St. James, 12,703
Salisbury, 12,226

Stony Brook, 13,726
Syosset, 18,967
Terryville, 10,275
Uniondale, 20,328
Valley Stream, 34,629
Wading River, 5,317
Wantagh, 18,567
West Babylon, 42,410
West Hempstead, 17,689
West Hills, 5,849
West Islip, 28,419
Westbury, 13,226
Wheatley Heights, 5,027
Williston Park, 7,761
Woodbury, 8,008
Woodmere, 15,578
Wyandanch, 8,950

Longview-Marshall, TX

Longview News Journal
320 E. Methvin St.
Longview 75601
(903) 757-3311

Longview CVB
100 Grand Blvd.
Longview 75604
(903) 753-3282

Longview C/C
410 N. Center St.
Longview 75601
(903)237-4000

Gilmer, 5,034
Gladewater, 6,660
Kilgore, 11,361
Longview, 73,265
Marshall, 23,324
White Oak, 5,643

Los Angeles–Long Beach, CA

Los Angeles Times
Times Mirror Sq.
Los Angeles 90053
(213) 237-5000

Los Angeles CVB
633 W. Fifth St.
Los Angeles 90024
(213) 624-7301

Los Angeles Area C/C
404 S. Bixel St.
Los Angeles 90051
(213) 629-0602

Agoura Hills, 25,364
Alhambra, 84,411
Alondra Park, 12,215
Altadena, 42,658
Arcadia, 50,654

Citrus, 9,481
Claremont, 34,125
Commerce, 12,356
Compton, 96,477
Covina, 44,643
Cudahy, 23,041
Culver City, 39,286
Del Aire, 8,040
Diamond Bar, 58,828
Downey, 99,889
Duarte, 22,454
East Compton, 7,967
East La Mirada, 9,367
East Los Angeles, 126,379
East Pasadena, 5,910
East San Gabriel, 12,736
El Monte, 104,661
El Segundo, 15,585
Gardena, 53,479
Glendale, 178,481
Glendora, 51,957
Hacienda Heights, 52,354
Hawaiian Gardens, 13,223
Hawthorne, 75,329
Hermosa Beach, 18,859
Huntington Park, 55,712
Inglewood, 110,085
La Canada Flintridge, 19,834
La Habra Heights, 6,743
La Mirada, 46,342
La Puente, 39,027
La Verne, 33,107
Ladera Heights, 6,316
Lake Los Angeles, 7,977
Lakewood, 79,416
Lancaster, 119,186
Lawndale, 28,911
Lennox, 22,757
Lomita, 20,706
Long Beach, 433,852
Los Angeles, 3,448,613
Lynwood, 64,809
Manhattan Beach, 33,288
Marina del Rey, 7,431
Maywood, 27,349
Monrovia, 38,764
Montebello, 61,519
Monterey Park, 57,921
Norwalk, 100,744
Palmdale, 103,423
Palos Verdes Estates, 13,944

Paramount, 52,209
Pasadena, 134,170
Pico Rivera, 62,566
Pomona, 143,870
Quartz Hill, 9,626
Rancho Palos Verdes, 43,833
Redondo Beach, 64,236
Rolling Hills Estates, 8,293
Rosemead, 52,024
Rowland Heights, 42,647
San Dimas, 35,645
San Fernando, 22,998
San Gabriel, 37,982
San Marino, 13,509
Santa Clarita, 123,676

Valinda, 18,735
Vincent, 13,713
Walnut, 32,345
Walnut Park, 14,722
West Athens, 8,859
West Carson, 20,143
West Compton, 5,451
West Covina, 103,298
West Hollywood, 34,443
West Puente Valley, 20,254
Westlake Village, 8,615
Westmont, 31,044
Whittier, 79,813
Willowbrook, 32,772

Louisville, KY–IN

Courier-Journal
525 W. Broadway
Louisville 40202
(502) 582-4156

Louisville CVB
400 S. First St.
Louisville 40202
(800) 626-5646

Louisville Area C/C
600 W. Main St.
Louisville 40202
(502) 625-0000

Buechel, KY, 7,081
Charlestown, IN, 6,555
Clarksville, IN, 21,586
Douglass Hills, KY, 5,546
Fairdale, KY, 6,563
Fern Creek, KY, 16,406
Highview, KY, 14,814
Hillview, KY, 6,967
Jeffersontown, KY, 24,314
Jeffersonville, IN, 23,588
Louisville, KY, 270,308
Lyndon, KY, 8,146
Middletown, KY, 5,012
Mount Washington, KY, 7,662
New Albany, IN, 37,920
Newburg, KY, 21,647
Oak Park, IN, 5,630
Okolona, KY, 18,902
Pleasure Ridge Park, KY, 25,131
St. Dennis, KY, 10,326

St. Matthews, KY, 15,511
Scottsburg, IN, 6,192
Sellersburg, IN, 6,091
Shepherdsville, IN, 5,573
Shively, KY, 15,168
Valley Station, KY, 22,840

Lowell, MA–NH

Lowell Sun
15 Kearney Sq.
Lowell 01852
(508) 458-7100

Northern Middlesex CVB
45 Palmer St.
Lowell 01853
(508) 937-9300

Northern Middlesex C/C
45 Palmer St.
Lowell 01852
(508) 937-9300

Billerica, MA, 38,853
Chelmsford, MA, 33,617
Dracut, MA, 27,576
Groton, MA, 8,714
Lowell, MA, 96,054
Pelham, NH, 9,919
Pepperell, MA, 10,850
Tewksbury, MA, 28,946
Tyngsborough, MA, 9,637
Westford, MA, 18,407

Lubbock, TX

Lubbock Avalanche–Journal
710 Avenue J
Lubbock 79401
(806) 762-8844

Lubbock C/C
14 & Avenue K
Lubbock 79401
(806) 763-4666

Lubbock, 194,467
Slaton, 5,963

Lynchburg, VA

News & Advance
101 Wyndale Dr.
Lynchburg 24501
(804) 385-5400

Lynchburg Visitor Center
Twelfth & Church Sts.
Lynchburg 24504
(804) 847-1811

Greater Lynchburg C/C
2015 Memorial Ave.
Lynchburg 24501
(804) 845-5966

Bedford, 6,570
Forest, 5,624
Lynchburg, 66,491
Madison Heights, 11,700
Timberlake, 10,314

Macon, GA

Macon Telegraph
120 Broadway
Macon 31201
(912) 744-4200

Macon–Bibb County CVB
200 Cherry St.
Macon 31208
(800) 768-3401

Greater Macon C/C
305 Coliseum Dr.
Macon 31298
(912) 741-8000

Fort Valley, 8,359
Macon, 109,191
Perry, 10,206
Warner Robins, 47,694

Madison, WI

Wisconsin State Journal/ Capital Times
1901 Fish Hatchery Rd.
Madison 53713
(608) 252-6100

Greater Madison CVB
615 E. Washington Ave.
Madison 53701
(608) 255-2538

Greater Madison C/C
615 E. Washington Ave.
Madison 53701
(608) 256-8348

De Forest, 5,284
Fitchburg, 17,043
Madison, 194,586
McFarland, 5,733
Middleton, 14,449
Monona, 8,446
Stoughton, 10,319
Sun Prairie, 17,408
Verona, 6,286
Waunakee, 7,185

Manchester, NH

Union Leader
100 William Loeb Dr.
Manchester 03109
(603) 668-4321

Greater Manchester C/C
889 Elm St.
Manchester 03101
(603) 666-6600

Bedford, 14,106
Goffstown, 16,586
Hooksett, 9,308
Londonderry, 21,313
Manchester, 96,640
Weare, 6,957

Mansfield, OH

News Journal
70 W. Fourth St.
Mansfield 44903
(419) 522-3311

Mansfield/Richland County CVB
52 Park Ave. W
Mansfield 44902
(419) 525-1301

Mansfield–Richland Area C/C
55 N. Mulberry St.
Mansfield 44902
(419) 522-3211

Bucyrus, 13,198
Crestline, 5,029
Galion, 11,768
Mansfield, 53,192
Shelby, 10,184

McAllen–Edinburg–Mission, TX

McAllen Monitor
1101 Ash St.
McAllen 78501
(210) 686-4343

McAllen C/C
10 N. Broadway
McAllen 78502
(210) 682-2871

Alamo, 10,483
Donna, 14,478
Edinburg, 36,479
Elsa, 6,076
McAllen, 95,299
Mercedes, 14,342
Mission, 38,437
Pharr, 36,576
San Juan, 13,091
Weslaco, 25,184

Medford–Ashland, OR

Mail Tribune
111 N. Fir St.
Medford 97501
(541) 776-4411

Greater Medford CVB
304 S. Central Ave.
Medford 97501
(541) 779-4847

Chamber of Medford/Jackson County
101 W. Eighth
Medford 97501
(541) 779-4847

Ashland, 16,951
Central Point, 8,566
Medford, 52,611
White City, 5,891

Melbourne–Titusville–Palm Bay, FL

Florida Today
Gannett Plaza
Melbourne 32940
(407) 242-3500

Florida's Space Coast Office of Tourism
2725 St. Johns St.
Melbourne 32940
(407) 633-2111

Melbourne–Palm Bay Area C/C
1005 E. Strawbridge Ave.
Melbourne 32901
(407) 724-5400

Cape Canaveral, 8,024
Cocoa, 20,220
Cocoa Beach, 12,068
Cocoa West, 6,160
Indian Harbour Beach, 7,255
Melbourne, 68,024

Merritt Island, 32,886
Micco, 8,757
Mims, 9,412
Palm Bay, 75,139
Port St. John, 8,933
Rockledge, 17,743
Satellite Beach, 10,643
South Patrick Shores, 10,249
Titusville, 41,061
West Melbourne, 9,235

Memphis, TN–AR–MS

Commercial Appeal
495 Union Ave.
Memphis 38103

Bartlett, TN, 32,769
Collierville, TN, 19,544
Covington, TN, 8,962
Germantown, TN, 35,816
Horn Lake, MS, 11,871
Marion, AR, 5,603
Memphis, TN, 614,289
Millington, TN, 17,080
Southaven, MS, 19,329
West Memphis, AR, 27,517

Merced, CA

Merced Sun-Star
3033 N. G Street
Merced 95340
(209) 722-1511

Merced CVB
690 W. 16th St.
Merced 95340
(209) 384-3334

Merced C/C
690 W. 16th St.
Merced 95340
(209) 384-3333

Atwater, 23,367
Livingston, 9,110
Los Banos, 17,937
Merced, 60,348
Winton, 7,559

Miami, FL

Miami Herald
1 Herald Plaza
Miami 33132
(305) 350-2111

Greater Miami CVB
701 Brickell Ave.
Miami 33131
(305) 539-3001

Greater Miami C/C
1601 Biscayne Blvd.
Miami 33132
(305) 350-7700

Andover, 6,251
Aventura, 14,914
Brownsville, 15,607
Carol City, 53,331
Coral Gables, 41,750
Coral Terrace, 23,255
Cutler, 16,201
Cutler Ridge, 21,268
Florida City, 6,669
Gladeview, 15,637
Glenvar Heights, 14,823
Golden Glades, 25,474
Goulds, 7,284
Hammocks, 10,897
Hialeah, 194,120
Hialeah Gardens, 14,393

Miami Beach, 90,153
Miami Lakes, 12,750
Miami Shores, 10,850
Miami Springs, 13,786
Naranja, 5,790
Norland, 22,109
North Bay Village, 5,432
North Miami, 53,504
North Miami Beach, 38,324
Ojus, 15,519
Olympia Heights, 37,792
Opa-Locka, 16,343
Opa-Locka North, 6,568
Palm Springs North, 5,300
Palmetto Estates, 12,293
Perrine, 15,576
Pinewood, 15,518
Princeton, 7,073
Richmond Heights, 8,583
Scott Lake, 14,588
South Miami, 10,864
South Miami Heights, 30,030
Sunny Isles, 11,772
Sunset, 15,810
Sweetwater, 14,494
Tamiami, 33,845
West Little River, 33,575
West Miami, 5,699
Westchester, 29,883
Westview, 9,668
Westwood Lakes, 11,522

Middlesex–Somerset–Hunterdon, NJ

Home News
35 Kennedy Blvd.
East Brunswick 08816
(908) 246-5500

Hunterdon County C/C
2200 Route 31
Lebanon 08833
(908) 735-5955

Middlesex County C/C
1091 Aaron Rd.
North Brunswick 08902
(908) 821-1700

Somerset County C/C
64 W. End Ave.
Somerville 08876
(908) 725-1552

Avenel, 15,504
Bedminster, 8,201
Bernards, 18,672
Bernardsville, 6,914
Bound Brook, 9,486
Branchburg, 13,449
Bridgewater, 37,455
Carteret, 19,130
Clinton, 12,090
Colonia, 18,238

Madison Park, 7,490
Manville, 10,483
Metuchen, 13,008
Middlesex, 13,364
Milltown, 7,212
Monroe, 21,281
Montgomery, 11,209
New Brunswick, 41,266
North Brunswick 31,287
North Plainfield, 19,197
Old Bridge, 22,151
Perth Amboy, 40,467
Piscataway, 49,259
Plainsboro, 15,536
Raritan, 17,172
Readington, 14,718
Sayreville, 36,405
Somerset, 22,070
Somerville, 12,193
South Amboy, 7,867
South Brunswick, 30,932
South Plainfield, 20,981
South River, 13,857
Spotswood, 8,140
Union, 5,335
Warren, 12,393
Watchung, 5,089
Woodbridge, 17,434

Milwaukee–Waukesha, WI

Milwaukee Journal/Sentinel
333 W. State St.
Milwaukee 53203
(414) 224-2000

Greater Milwaukee CVB
510 W. Kilbourn Ave.
Milwaukee 53203
(414) 273-7223

Metro Milwaukee Assn. of Comm.
756 N. Milwaukee St.
Milwaukee 53202
(414) 273-3000

Brookfield, 36,814
Brown Deer, 11,897
Cedarburg, 10,661

Cudahy, 18,264
Delafield, 6,325
Elm Grove, 6,258
Fox Point, 7,008
Franklin, 21,726
Germantown, 16,231
Glendale, 13,204
Grafton, 9,665
Greendale, 14,624
Greenfield, 32,051
Hales Corners, 7,412
Hartford, 8,956
Hartland, 7,921
Menomonee Falls, 28,448
Mequon, 21,478
Milwaukee, 617,044
Muskego, 19,970
New Berlin, 35,933
Oak Creek, 19,298
Oconomowoc, 11,776
Pewaukee, 5,799
Port Washington, 9,950
St. Francis, 8,947
Shorewood, 13,522
South Milwaukee, 20,206
Sussex, 6,233
Waukesha, 60,138
Wauwatosa, 47,694
West Allis, 61,259
West Bend, 27,216
Whitefish Bay, 14,067

Minneapolis–St. Paul, MN–WI

St. Paul Pioneer Press
345 Cedar St.
St. Paul 55101
(612) 222-5011

Star Tribune
425 Portland Ave.
Minneapolis 55488
(612) 673-4000

Greater Minneapolis CVB
33 S. Sixth St.
Minneapolis 55402
(612) 348-4313

St. Paul CVB
101 Northwest Center
St. Paul 55101
(612) 297-6986

Greater Minneapolis C/C
81 S. Ninth St.
Minneapolis 55402
(612) 370-9132

St. Paul Area C/C
55 E. Fifth St.
St. Paul 55101
(612) 223-5000

Andover, MN, 19,998
Anoka, MN, 16,686
Apple Valley, MN, 39,788
Arden Hills, MN, 9,050
Blaine, MN, 41,592
Bloomington, MN, 85,185
Brooklyn Center, MN, 27,558
Brooklyn Park, MN, 58,786
Buffalo, MN, 7,633
Burnsville, MN, 55,081
Cambridge, MN, 6,178
Champlin, MN, 20,552
Chanhassen, MN, 15,131
Chaska, MN, 13,494
Circle Pines, MN, 5,215
Columbia Heights, MN, 18,175
Coon Rapids, MN, 62,364
Corcoran, MN, 5,871
Cottage Grove, MN, 26,829
Crystal, MN, 22,892
Eagan, MN, 56,992
East Bethel, MN, 9,625
Eden Prairie, MN, 47,941
Edina, MN, 46,516
Elk River, MN, 13,118
Falcon Heights, MN, 5,691
Farmington, MN, 6,688
Forest Lake, MN, 6,792
Fridley, MN, 26,236
Golden Valley, MN, 20,635
Ham Lake, MN, 10,395
Hastings, MN, 16,371
Hopkins, MN, 15,743
Hudson, WI, 6,908
Hugo, MN, 5,189
Inver Grove Heights, MN, 24,501
Lake Elmo, MN, 6,295
Lakeville, MN, 33,423
Lino Lakes, MN, 11,667
Little Canada, MN, 9,404
Mahtomedi, MN, 6,729
Maple Grove, MN, 46,651
Maplewood, MN, 33,561
Mendota Heights, MN, 10,777
Minneapolis, MN, 354,590
Minnetonka, MN, 50,778
Monticello, MN, 6,181
Mound, MN, 10,006
Mounds View, MN, 12,990
New Brighton, MN, 21,606
New Hope, MN, 21,137
New Richmond, WI, 6,258
North St. Paul, MN, 12,654
Oakdale, MN, 23,441
Orono, MN, 7,293
Plymouth, MN, 60,143
Prior Lake, MN, 13,280
Ramsey, MN, 15,701
Richfield, MN, 34,430
River Falls, WI, 11,521
Robbinsdale, MN, 14,050
Rosemount, MN, 9,863
Roseville, MN, 33,075
St. Anthony, MN, 7,650
St. Louis Park, MN, 42,490
St. Paul, MN, 262,071
St. Paul Park, MN, 5,265
Savage, MN, 13,879
Shakopee, MN, 13,048
Shoreview, MN, 26,953
Shorewood, MN, 7,491
South St. Paul, MN, 19,570
Spring Lake Park, MN, 6,267
Stillwater, MN, 15,956
Vadnais Heights, MN, 13,255
West St. Paul, MN, 18,859
White Bear Lake, MN, 24,487
Woodbury, MN, 29,154

Mobile, AL

Mobile Register
304 Government St.
Mobile 36602
(334) 433-1551

Mobile Dept. of Tourism
150 S. Royal St.
Mobile 36633
(334) 434-7305

Mobile Area C/C
451 Government St.
Mobile 36652
(334) 433-6951

Bay Minette, 8,455
Chickasaw, 6,419
Daphne, 14,479
Fairhope, 10,524
Foley, 6,572
Mobile, 204,490
Prichard, 33,263
Saraland, 12,234
Satsuma, 5,629
Theodore, 6,509
Tillmans Corner, 17,988

Modesto, CA

Modesto Bee
1325 H Street
Modesto 95354
(209) 578-2000

Modesto CVB
1114 J Street
Modesto 95353
(209) 577-5757

Modesto C/C
1114 J Street
Modesto 95353
(209) 577-5757

Ceres, 29,933
Modesto, 176,357
Newman, 5,261
Oakdale, 13,765
Patterson, 9,607
Riverbank, 12,018
Turlock, 46,360
Waterford, 6,185

Monmouth–Ocean, NJ

Asbury Park Press
3601 Highway 66
Neptune 07753
(908) 922-6000

Monmouth County Tourism
27 E. Main St.
Freehold 07728
(908) 431-7476

Ocean Township C/C
1602 Lawrence
Oakhurst 07755
(908) 493-8181

Aberdeen, 17,601
Asbury Park, 15,606
Barnegat, 13,237
Beachwood, 9,983
Belmar, 5,905
Brick, 70,708
Colts Neck, 9,785
Crestwood Village, 8,030
Dover, 81,550
Eatontown, 13,017
Fair Haven, 5,580
Freehold, 25,856
Gilford Park, 8,668
Hazlet, 22,021
Holiday City South, 5,452
Holmdel, 13,161
Howell, 42,317
Jackson, 36,151
Keansburg, 11,743
Keyport, 7,497
Lacey, 23,897
Lakewood, 46,909
Lincroft, 6,193
Little Egg Harbor, 14,284

Little Silver, 6,078
Long Branch, 27,878
Manalapan, 33,287
Manasquan, 5,650
Manchester, 37,426
Marlboro, 31,630
Matawan, 9,779
Middletown, 68,355
Millstone, 6,073
Mystic Island, 7,400
Neptune, 28,825
Neptune City, 5,166
Ocean, 26,864
Ocean Acres, 5,587
Oceanport, 5,975
Plumsted, 6,684

Union Beach, 6,113
Wall, 22,090
West Freehold, 11,166
West Long Branch, 7,818
Yorketown, 6,313

Monroe, LA

New Star
411 N. Fourth St.
Monroe 71201
(318) 322-5161

Monroe–West Monroe CVB
1333 State Farm Dr.
Monroe 71211
(318) 387-5691

Monroe C/C
300 Washington St.
Monroe 71201
(318) 323-3461

Claiborne, 8,300
Monroe, 57,049
West Monroe, 14,350

Montgomery, AL

Montgomery Advertiser
200 Washington Ave.
Montgomery 36104
(334) 262-1611

Montgomery CVB
401 Madison Ave.
Montgomery 36101
(334) 262-0013

Montgomery Area C/C
41 Commerce St.
Montgomery 36101
(334) 262-0013

Millbrook, 6,904
Montgomery, 195,471
Prattville, 24,118
Tallassee, 5,841
Wetumpka, 5,314

Montreal, PQ

Gazette
250 rue St. Antoine Ouest
Montreal H2Z 1H5
(514) 987-2222

La Presse
7 rue St. Jacques
Montreal H2Y 1K9
(514) 285-7306

Le Journal de Montreal
4545 rue Frontenac
Montreal H2H 2R7
(514) 521-4545

Anjou, 37,135
Beaconsfield, 19,737
Beauharnois, 6,313
Beloeil, 18,890
Blainville, 28,900
Bois-des-Filion, 7,665
Boisbriand, 27,617
Boucherville, 36,119
Brossard, 71,439
Candiac, 12,554
Carignan, 5,929
Chambly, 18,730
Charlemagne, 5,813
Chateauguay, 41,398
Cote-Saint-Luc, 28,536
Delson, 7,060
Deux-Montagnes, 15,393
Dollard-des-Ormeaux, 50,257
Dorion, 6,312
Dorval, 16,975
Greenfield Park, 16,847
Hampstead, 9,740
Hudson, 5,182
Kirkland, 21,403
L'Ile-Perrot, 9,452
La Plaine, 15,008
La Prairie, 18,972
Lachenaie, 19,776
Lachine, 35,278
LaSalle, 71,282
Laval, 341,264
Le Gardeur, 18,215
LeMoyne, 5,142
Longueuil, 132,994
Lorraine, 9,394
Mascouche, 30,073
Mercier, 9,100
Mirabel, 21,852
Mont-Royal, 17,899
Mont-Saint-Hilaire, 13,953
Montreal, 1,009,940
Montreal-Nord, 79,937
Notre-Dame-de-l'Ile-Perrot, 6,358
Otterburn Park, 7,447
Outremont, 22,563
Pierrefonds, 57,299
Pincourt, 10,058
Pointe-Claire, 28,982
Repentigny, 57,909
Rosemere, 13,586
Roxboro, 5,565

Saint-Basile-le-Grand, 11,290
Saint-Bruno-de-Montarville, 24,356
Saint-Constant, 24,100
Saint-Eustache, 41,925
Saint-Hubert, 81,037
Saint-Lambert, 21,709
Saint-Laurent, 77,040
Saint-Lazare, 12,924
Saint-Leonard, 69,606
Sainte-Anne-des-Plaines, 12,520
Sainte-Catherine, 12,468
Sainte-Julie, 25,509
Sainte-Marthe-sur-le-Lac, 8,592
Sainte-Therese, 28,696
Terrebonne, 47,575

(317) 747-5700

Muncie/Delaware County CVB
425 N. High
Muncie 47305
(317) 284-2701

Muncie–Delaware County C/C
401 S. High St.
Muncie 47305
(317) 288-6681

Muncie, 71,407
Yorktown, 5,178

Myrtle Beach, SC

Sun News
914 Frontage Rd. E
Myrtle Beach 29577
(803) 626-8555

Myrtle Beach Area CVB
710 21st Ave. N
Myrtle Beach 29577
(803) 448-1629

Myrtle Beach Area C/C
1301 N. Kings Hwy.
Myrtle Beach 29578
(803) 626-7445

Conway, 11,053
Garden City, 6,305
Myrtle Beach, 28,047
North Myrtle Beach, 9,012
Red Hill, 6,112
Socastee, 10,426

Naples, FL

Naples Daily News
1075 Central Ave.
Naples 33940
(941) 263-4470

Naples Area Tourism Bureau
P.O. Box 10129
Naples 33941
(941) 262-2713

Naples Area C/C
3620 Tamiami Trail N
Naples 33940
(941) 262-6141

East Naples, 22,951
Golden Gate, 14,148
Immokalee, 14,120
Marco, 9,493
Naples, 21,273
Naples Park, 8,002
North Naples, 13,422

Nashua, NH

The Telegraph
17 Executive Drive
Hudson 03061
(603) 882-2741

Greater Nashua C/C
188 Main St.
Nashua 03060
(603) 881-8333

Amherst, 9,471
Hollis, 6,300
Hudson, 21,291
Litchfield, 6,696
Merrimack, 24,095
Milford, 12,536
Nashua, 79,631

Nashville, TN

Nashville Banner/Tennessean
1100 Broadway
Nashville 37203
(615) 259-8800

Nashville CVB
161 Fourth Ave. N
Nashville 37219
(615) 259-4747

Nashville Area C/C
161 Fourth Ave. N
Nashville 37219
(615) 259-4700

Brentwood, 21,246
Dickson, 10,986
Franklin, 25,323
Gallatin, 20,957
Goodlettsville, 11,919
Green Hill, 6,763
Hendersonville, 36,625
La Vergne, 11,027
Lebanon, 18,945
Mount Juliet, 6,184
Murfreesboro, 56,194
Nashville, 504,505
Portland, 5,708
Smyrna, 16,860
Springfield, 14,023

New Bedford, MA

New Bedford Standard-Times
25 Elm St.
New Bedford 02740
(508) 997-7411

New Bedford Area C/C
794 Purchase St.
New Bedford 02742
(508) 999-5231

Acushnet, 9,904
Dartmouth, 27,868
Fairhaven, 16,279
Freetown, 8,466
Mattapoisett, 5,861
New Bedford, 94,623

New Haven–Meriden, CT

New Haven Register
40 Sargent Dr.
New Haven 06511
(203) 789-5440

Greater New Haven CVB
1 Long Wharf
New Haven 06511
(203) 777-8551

Greater New Haven C/C
195 Church St.
New Haven 06510
(203) 787-6735

Branford, 28,473
Cheshire, 26,414
Clinton, 12,717
East Haven, 27,343
Guilford, 20,676
Hamden, 52,417
Killingworth, 5,361
Madison, 16,338
Meriden, 56,928
New Haven, 119,604
North Branford, 13,690
North Haven, 22,745
Orange, 12,773
Wallingford, 41,586
West Haven 52,848
Woodbridge, 8,053

New London–Norwich, CT–RI

The Day
47 Eugene O'Neill Dr.
New London 06320
(860) 442-2200

C/C of Southeastern Connecticut
105 Huntington St.
New London 06320
(860) 443-8332

East Lyme, CT, 15,717
Griswold, CT, 10,408
Groton, CT, 44,300
Hopkinton, RI, 7,425
Ledyard, CT, 14,650
Montville, CT, 16,808
New London, CT, 22,792
North Stonington, CT, 5,042
Norwich, CT, 35,504
Old Lyme, CT, 6,902
Old Saybrook, CT, 9,642
Plainfield, CT, 14,454
Preston, CT, 5,477
Stonington, CT, 16,584
Waterford, CT, 17,948
Westerly, RI, 22,334

New Orleans, LA

Times-Picayune
3800 Howard Ave.
New Orleans 70125
(504) 826-3279

Greater New Orleans CVB
1520 Sugar Bowl Dr.
New Orleans 70112
(504) 566-5011

The Chamber/New Orleans & River
301 Camp St.
New Orleans 70130
(504) 527-6900

Arabi, 8,787
Avondale, 5,813
Belle Chasse, 8,512
Bridge City, 8,327
Chalmette, 31,860
Covington, 8,317
Destrehan, 8,031
Estelle, 14,091
Gretna, 17,371
Harahan, 9,630
Harvey, 21,222
Jefferson, 14,521
Kenner, 72,891
Lacombe, 6,523
Laplace, 24,194
Mandeville, 9,362
Marrero, 36,671
Meraux, 8,849
Metairie, 149,428
New Orleans, 484,149
Reserve, 8,847
River Ridge, 14,800
St. Rose, 6,259
Slidell, 29,669
Terrytown, 23,787
Timberlane, 12,614
Violet, 8,574
Waggaman, 9,405
Westwego, 10,928

New York, NY

New York Daily News
450 W. 33rd St.
New York 10001
(212) 210-2100

New York Post
1211 Avenue of the Americas
New York 10036
(212) 815-8000

New York Times
229 W. 43rd St.
New York 10036
(212) 556-1234

New York CVB
2 Columbus Circle & 59th St.
New York 10019
(212) 397-8222

New York C/C & Ind.
1 Battery Park Plaza
New York 10004
(212) 493-7500

Airmont, 7,835
Briarcliff Manor, 7,328
Bronxville, 6,119
Chestnut Ridge, 7,462
Congers, 8,003
Croton, 7426
Croton-on-Hudson, 7,426
Dobbs Ferry, 10,230
Eastchester, 18,537
Greenville, 9,528
Harrison, 23,251

Hartsdale, 9,587
Hastings-on-Hudson, 8,336
Haverstraw, 9,973
Hillcrest, 6,447
Irvington, 6,652
Lake Carmel, 8,489
Larchmont, 6,299
Mahopac, 7,755
Mamaroneck, 17,660
Monsey, 13,986
Mount Ivy, 6,013
Mount Kisco, 9,379
Mount Vernon, 65,862
Nanuet, 14,065
New City, 33,673
New Rochelle, 66,764

Rye Brook, 7,839
Scarsdale, 16,966
Spring Valley, 23,103
Stony Point, 10,587
Suffern, 11,363
Tappan, 6,867
Tarrytown, 10,370
Thiells, 5,204
Thornwood, 7,025
Tuckahoe, 6,567
Valley Cottage, 9,007
West Haverstraw, 9,648
White Plains, 49,771
Yonkers, 183,490
Yorktown Heights, 7,690

Newark, NJ

Star Ledger
1 Star Ledger Plaza
Newark 07102
(201) 877-4141

Newark/Meadowlands CVB
40 Clinton St.
Newark 07102
(201) 622-3010

Metro Newark C/C
1 Newark Center
Newark 07102
(201) 242-6237

Andover, 5,586
Belleville, 34,213
Berkeley Heights, 11,980
Blairstown, 5,509
Bloomfield, 45,061
Boonton, 8,704
Budd Lake, 7,272
Butler, 7,508
Byram, 8,622
Caldwell, 7,549
Caldwell Borough, 7,625
Cedar Grove, 12,053
Chatham, 9,597
Chester, 6,254
Clark, 14,629
Cranford, 22,624
Denville, 13,936
Dover, 14,498
East Hanover, 9,926

East Orange, 72,847
Elizabeth, 106,298
Fairfield, 7,615
Fanwood, 7,196
Florham Park, 8,817
Frankford, 5,263
Franklin, 5,227
Glen Ridge, 7,076
Hackettstown, 8,315
Hanover, 11,688
Hardyston, 5,469
Hillside, 21,044
Hopatcong, 16,044
Irvington, 59,774
Jefferson, 18,277
Kenilworth, 7,658

Morris, 20,192
Morris Plains, 5,392
Morristown, 16,406
Mount Olive, 22,034
Mountainside, 6,867
New Providence, 12,044
Newark, 258,751
Newton, 7,760
North Caldwell, 6,706
Nutley, 27,099
Orange, 29,925
Passaic, 56,042
Parsippany–Troy Hills, 48,478
Pequannock, 13,548
Phillipsburg, 15,845
Plainfield, 44,793
Rahway, 25,760
Randolph, 21,972
Rockaway, 6,491
Roselle, 20,572
Roselle Park, 12,907
Roxbury, 21,632
Scotch Plains, 21,160
South Orange, 16,390
South Orange Village, 16,289
Sparta, 16,481
Springfield, 13,420
Summit, 20,192
Union, 50,024
Vernon, 22,686
Verona, 13,597
Wantage, 10,065
Washington, 16,588
West Caldwell, 10,422
West Orange, 39,103
Westfield, 29,340
Wharton, 5,393
White Meadow Lake, 8,002

Newburgh, NY–PA

Times Herald-Record
40 Mulberry St.
Middletown 10940
(914) 343-2181

Eastern Orange County C/C
47 Grand St.
Newburgh 12550
(914) 562-5100

Goshen, NY, 5,301
Kiryas Joel, NY, 8,616
Middletown, NY, 24,797
Monroe, NY, 6,935
New Windsor, NY, 8,898
Newburgh, NY, 25,705
Orange Lake, NY, 5,196
Port Jervis, NY, 9,626
Scotchtown, NY, 8,765
Walden, NY, 6,716
Warwick, NY, 6,377
Washingtonville, NY, 5,600

Norfolk–Virginia Beach–Newport News,

Hampton Roads C/C
420 Bank St.
Norfolk 23510
(804) 622-2312

Chesapeake, VA, 180,577
Gloucester Point, VA, 8,509
Hampton, VA, 139,628
Newport News, VA, 179,127
Norfolk, VA–NC, 241,426
Poquoson, VA, 11,684
Portsmouth, VA, 103,464
Smithfield, VA, 6,070
Suffolk, VA, 54,922
Virginia Beach, VA, 430,295
Williamsburg, VA, 12,560

Oakland, CA

The Tribune
66 Jack London Sq.
Oakland 94607
(510) 208-6300

Oakland CVB
1000 Broadway
Oakland 94607
(510) 839-9001

Oakland C/C
475 14th St.
Oakland 94612
(510) 874-4800

Alameda, 78,672
Alamo, 12,277
Albany, 16,877
Antioch, 73,019
Ashland, 16,590
Berkeley, 99,830
Blackhawk, 6,199
Brentwood, 9,347
Castro Valley, 48,619
Cherryland, 11,088
Clayton, 8,711
Concord, 111,889
Danville, 38,710
Discovery Bay, 5,351
Dublin, 26,140
El Cerrito, 22,540
El Sobrante, 9,852

Emeryville, 6,545
Fairview, 9,045
Fremont, 183,575
Hayward, 115,590
Hercules, 19,615
Lafayette, 23,997
Livermore, 63,362
Martinez, 32,688
Moraga, 16,193
Newark, 39,568
Oakland, 366,926
Oakley, 18,374
Orinda, 17,415
Piedmont, 11,581
Pinole, 18,455
Pittsburg, 52,036
Pleasant Hill, 31,635
Pleasanton, 57,682
Richmond, 87,944
Rodeo, 7,589
San Leandro, 69,490
San Lorenzo, 19,987
San Pablo, 26,880
San Ramon, 39,904
Union City, 55,383
Walnut Creek, 62,030
West Pittsburg, 17,453

Ocala, FL

Ocala Star Banner
2121 SW 19th Ave.
Ocala 32674
(904) 867-4010

Ocala–Marion County C/C
110 E. Silver Springs Blvd.
Ocala 34470
(904) 629-8051

Ocala, 53,225
Silver Springs Shores, 6,421

Odessa–Midland, TX

Odessa American
222 E. Fourth St.
Odessa 79761
(915) 337-4661

Midland Reporter-Telegram
201 E. Illinois
Midland 79701
(915) 682-5311

Odesssa CVB
400 W. Fourth St.
Odessa 79760
(915) 332-9112

Odessa C/C
129 N. Grant Ave.
Odessa 79761
(915) 332-9111

Midland, 96,163
Odessa, 94,763
West Odessa, 16,568

Oklahoma City, OK

Daily Oklahoman
9000 N. Broadway
Oklahoma City 73114
(405) 475-3311

Oklahoma City CVB
123 Park Ave.
Oklahoma City 73102
(405) 278-8913

Oklahoma City C/C
123 Park Ave.
Oklahoma City 73102
(405) 278-8900

Bethany, 19,967
Choctaw, 9,078
Del City, 23,753
Edmond, 61,224
El Reno, 15,799
Guthrie, 10,597
Midwest City, 53,473
Moore, 42,593
Mustang, 11,577
Norman, 87,290
Oklahoma City, 463,201
Purcell, 5,211
Shawnee, 27,879
Tecumseh, 6,267
The Village, 10,864
Warr Acres, 9,517
Yukon, 21,689

Olympia, WA

The Olympian
1268 E. Fourth Ave.
Olympia 98506
(360) 754-5400

Olympia/Thurston County C/C
1000 Plum St. SE
Olympia 98507
(360) 357-3362

Lacey, 22,788
Olympia, 39,724
Tumwater, 11,513

Omaha, NE–IA

Omaha World-Herald
1334 Dodge St.
Omaha 68102
(402) 444-1000

Greater Omaha CVB
1819 Farnam St.
Omaha 68183
(402) 444-4660

Greater Omaha C/C
1301 Harney St.
Omaha 68102
(402) 346-5000

Bellevue, NE, 41,274
Blair, NE, 7,099
Chalco, NE, 7,337
Council Bluffs, IA, 54,850
La Vista, NE, 10,634
Omaha, NE, 345,033
Papillion, NE, 10,817
Plattsmouth, NE, 6,780
Ralston, NE, 6,462

Orange County, CA

Orange County Register
625 N. Grand Ave.
Santa Ana 92701
(714) 835-1234

Anaheim Area CVB
800 W. Katella Ave.
Anaheim 92802
(714) 999-8999

Orange County C/C
1City Blvd. W
Orange 92668
(714) 634-2900

Aliso Viejo, 7,612
Anaheim, 282,133
Brea, 34,672
Buena Park, 72,671
Costa Mesa, 98,427
Cypress, 46,419
Dana Point, 33,455
El Toro, 62,685
El Toro Station, 6,869
Fountain Valley, 55,467
Fullerton, 116,863
Garden Grove, 147,958
Huntington Beach, 189,220
Irvine, 125,624
La Habra, 53,664
La Palma, 16,008
Laguna Beach, 23,923
Laguna Hills, 46,731
Laguna Niguel, 56,681
Los Alamitos, 12,013
Mission Viejo, 83,813
Newport Beach, 70,668
Orange, 116,785
Placentia, 43,002
Rancho Santa Margarita, 11,390
Rossmoor, 9,893
San Clemente, 45,149
San Juan Capistrano, 29,092
Santa Ana, 290,827
Seal Beach, 24,932
Stanton, 30,139
Tustin, 58,480
Tustin Foothills, 24,358
Villa Park, 6,655
Westminster, 79,751
Yorba Linda, 61,497

Orlando, FL

Orlando Sentinel
633 N. Orange Ave.
Orlando 32801
(407) 420-5000

Orlando/Orange County CVB
8445 International Dr.
Orlando 32819
(407) 363-5892

Greater Orlando C/C
75 E. Ivanhoe Blvd.
Orlando 32802
(407) 425-1234

Altamonte Springs, 36,281
Apopka, 15,617
Azalea Park, 8,926
Bay Hill, 5,346
Belle Isle, 5,601
Buena Ventura Lakes, 14,148
Casselberry, 20,547
Clermont, 8,631
Conway, 13,159
Doctor Phillips, 7,963
Eustis, 15,107
Fairview Shores, 13,192
Fern Park, 8,294
Forest City, 10,638
Goldenrod, 6,602
Kissimmee, 36,407
Lady Lake, 14,488
Lake Mary, 6,990
Leesburg, 19,417
Lockhart, 11,636

Longwood, 15,772
Maitland, 8,811
Mount Dora, 8,850
Oak Ridge, 15,388
Ocoee, 14,981
Orlando, 176,948
Orlovista, 5,990
Oviedo, 13,805
Pine Castle, 8,276
Pine Hills, 35,322
St. Cloud, 14,770
Sanford, 34,461
Sky Lake, 6,202
South Apopka, 6,360
Tavares, 8,295

(905) 723-3474

Oshawa C/C
5250 Richmond St. E
Oshawa L1N 7Y2
(905) 728-1683

Newcastle, 64,039
Oshawa, 133,287
Whitby, 75,750

Ottawa-Hull, ON-PQ

Ottawa Citizen
1101 Baxter Rd.
Ottawa K2C 3P2
(613) 829-9100

Ottawa Sun
380 Hunt Club Rd.
Ottawa K1V 8S6
(613) 739-7000

Ottawa TCA
111 Lisgar St.
Ottawa K1M 2G5
(613) 237-5150

Aylmer, PQ, 35,163
Buckingham, PQ, 12,156
Gatineau, PQ, 105,815
Gloucester, ON, 112,072
Hull, PQ, 62,077
Kanata, ON, 46,556
Masson, PQ, 6,601
Nepean, ON, 118,205
Ottawa ON, 322,966
Vanier, ON, 17,643

Owensboro, KY

Owensboro Messenger-Inquirer
1401 Frederica St.
Owensboro 42301
(502) 926-0123

Owensboro-Daviess County Tourist Commission
326 St. Elizabeth
Owensboro 42301
(800) 489-1131

Owensboro-Daviess County C/C
335 Frederica St.
Owensboro 42302
(502) 926-1860

Owensboro, 53,645

Panama City, FL

News Herald
501 W. Eleventh St.
Panama City 32401
(904) 763-7621

Panama City, 37,991
Parker, 5,560
Springfield, 9,967
Upper Grand Lagoon, 7,855

Parkersburg-Marietta, WV-OH

Parkersburg Sentinel
519 Juliana St.
Parkersburg 26101
(304) 485-1891

Parkersburg CVB
215 First St.
Parkersburg 26101
(304) 428-1131

Greater Parkersburg Area C/C
214 E. Eighth St.
Parkersburg 26101
(304) 422-3588

Belpre, OH, 6,954
Marietta, OH, 15,157
Parkersburg, WV, 33,102
Vienna, WV, 11,030

Pensacola, FL

Pensacola News Journal
P.O. Box 12710
Pensacola 32574
(904) 435-8500

Pensacola CVB
1401 E. Gregory St.
Pensacola 32501
(904) 434-1235

Pensacola Area C/C
117 W. Garden St.
Pensacola 32593
(904) 438-4081

Bellview, 19,386
Brent, 21,624
Ensley, 16,362
Ferry Pass, 26,301
Gonzalez, 7,669
Gulf Breeze, 6,369
Milton, 8,756
Myrtle Grove, 17,402
Pace, 6,277
Pensacola, 60,025
Warrington, 16,040
West Pensacola, 22,107

Peoria-Pekin, IL

Peoria Journal Star
1 News Plaza
Peoria 61643
(309) 686-3000

Peoria CVB
403 NE Jefferson St.
Peoria 61603

Pekin, 32,409
Peoria, 112,878
Peoria Heights, 6,805
Washington, 10,393
West Peoria, 5,314

Philadelphia, PA-NJ

Philadelphia Inquirer/Daily News
400 N. Broad St.
Philadelphia 19130
(215) 854-2000

Philadelphia CVB
1515 Market St.
Philadelphia 19102
(215) 636-1667

Greater Philadelphia C/C
1234 Market St.
Philadelphia 19107
(215) 545-1234

Ambler, PA, 6,870
Ardmore, PA, 7,325
Audubon, NJ, 6,328
Barrington, NJ, 6,581
Bellmawr, NJ, 12,279
Berlin, NJ, 5,626
Blackwood, NJ, 5,120
Blue Bell, PA, 6,091
Boothwyn, PA, 5,069
Bordentown, NJ, 7,843
Bristol, PA, 10,814
Brookhaven, PA, 8,346
Broomall, PA, 10,930
Brown Mills, NJ, 11,429
Burlington, NJ, 9,878
Camden, NJ, 82,866
Carneys Point, NJ, 7,686
Cherry Hill, NJ, 69,319
Chester, PA, 39,467
Chesterfield, NJ, 5,257
Cinnaminson, NJ, 14,583
Clayton, NJ, 6,787
Clementon, NJ, 5,606
Clifton Heights, PA, 7,024
Coatesville, PA, 11,838
Collingdale, PA, 9,092
Collingswood, NJ, 14,352
Conshohocken, PA, 8,322

Croydon, PA, 9,967
Darby, PA, 11,054
Delran, NJ, 13,587
Deptford, NJ, 24,600
Downingtown, PA, 8,224
Doylestown, PA, 8,637
Drexel Hill, PA, 29,744
East Greenwich, NJ, 5,414
East Norriton, PA, 13,324
Eastampton, NJ, 6,907
Edgewater Park, NJ, 8,388
Evesham, NJ, 38,633
Fairless Hills, PA, 9,026
Florence, NJ, 10,076
Folcroft, PA, 7,264
Folsom, PA, 8,173
Fort Dix, NJ, 10,205
Franklin, NJ, 14,984
Glassboro, NJ, 17,384
Glendora, NJ, 5,201
Glenolden, PA, 7,276
Glenside, PA, 8,704
Gloucester, NJ, 57,625
Gloucester City, NJ, 12,364
Haddon, NJ, 14,642
Haddon Heights, NJ, 7,561
Haddonfield, NJ, 11,583
Harleysville, PA, 7,405
Harrison, NJ, 6,894
Hatboro, PA, 7,672
Horsham, PA, 15,051
Kennett Square, PA, 5,451
King of Prussia, PA, 18,406
Kulpsville, PA, 5,183
Lansdale, PA, 16,916
Lansdowne, PA, 11,661
Levittown, PA, 55,362
Lindenwold, NJ, 18,482
Logan, NJ, 5,599
Lumberton, NJ, 6,618
Mantua, NJ, 10,558
Maple Glen, PA, 5,881
Maple Shade, NJ, 19,211
Marlton, NJ, 10,228
Medford, NJ, 21,264
Media, PA, 5,817
Monroe, NJ, 27,925
Montgomeryville, PA, 9,114
Moorestown, NJ, 16,212
Morrisville, PA, 10,264
Mount Holly, NJ, 10,639
Mount Laurel, NJ, 35,048
Nether Providence, PA, 13,229
Norristown, PA, 32,069
North Hanover, NJ, 9,400
Norwood, PA, 5,933
Oreland, PA, 5,695
Palmyra, NJ, 6,851
Paoli, PA, 5,603
Paulsboro, NJ, 6,527
Pemberton, NJ, 26,043
Penn Wynne, PA, 5,807
Pennsauken, NJ, 34,733
Pennsville, NJ, 12,218
Perkasie, PA, 9,280
Philadelphia, PA, 1,524,249
Phoenixville, PA, 15,654
Pine Hill, NJ, 10,571
Pitman, NJ, 9,366
Pittsgrove, NJ, 8,323
Plymouth Meeting, PA, 6,241
Pottstown, PA, 23,130
Prospect Park, PA, 6,871
Quakertown, PA, 9,345
Radnor, PA, 28,705
Ramblewood, PA, 6,181
Richboro, PA, 5,332
Ridley Park, PA, 7,376
Riverside, NJ, 7,974
Runnemede, NJ, 8,927
Salem, NJ, 6,953
Sanatoga, PA, 5,534
Shamong, NJ, 5,661
Sharon Hill, PA, 5,875
Somerdale, NJ, 5,364
Souderton, PA, 6,612
Southampton, NJ, 10,664
Springfield, PA, 24,160
Stratford, NJ, 7,575
Swarthmore, PA, 6,148
Tabernacle, NJ, 8,291
Trooper, PA, 5,137
Upper Providence, PA, 9,727
Voorhees, NJ, 26,745
Washington, NJ, 44,289
Waterford, NJ, 11,386
West Chester, PA, 18,867
West Deptford, NJ, 20,207
West Goshen, PA, 8,948
West Norriton, PA, 15,209
Westampton, NJ, 6,319
Williamstown, NJ, 10,891
Willingboro, NJ, 36,291
Willow Grove, PA, 16,325
Winslow, NJ, 36,118
Woodbury, NJ, 10,572
Woodlyn, PA, 10,151
Wyndmoor, PA, 5,682
Yeadon, PA, 12,094

Phoenix–Mesa, AZ

Arizona Republic/Phoenix Gazette
120 E. Van Buren St.
Phoenix 85004
(602) 271-8235

Phoenix & Valley CVB
1 Arizona Center
Phoenix 85004
(602) 254-6500

Phoenix Metro C/C
34 W. Monroe St.
Phoenix 85003
(602) 254-5521

Apache Junction, 21,354
Avondale, 20,650
Buckeye, 5,093
Casa Grande, 21,088
Chandler, 119,227
Coolidge, 7,150
El Mirage, 5,317
Eloy, 7,390
Florence, 7,623
Fountain Hills, 14,289
Gilbert, 51,074
Glendale, 168,439
Goodyear, 6,894
Guadalupe, 5,563
Mesa, 313,649
Paradise Valley, 13,784
Peoria, 70,139
Phoenix, 1,048,949
Scottsdale, 152,439
Sun City, 38,126
Sun City West, 15,997
Sun Lakes, 6,578
Surprise, 9,394
Tempe, 144,289
Wickenburg, 5,343

Pine Bluff, AR

Pine Bluff Commercial
300 Beech St.
Pine Bluff 71601
(501) 534-3400

Greater Pine Bluff C/C
121 W. Sixth Ave.
Pine Bluff 71611
(501) 535-0110

Pine Bluff, 57,971

Pittsburgh, PA

Pittsburgh Post-Gazette
3450 Blvd. of the Allies
Pittsburgh 15222
(412) 263-1100

Greater Pittsburgh CVB
4 Gateway Ctr.
Pittsburgh 15222
(412) 281-7712

Greater Pittsburgh C/C
3 Gateway Ctr.
Pittsburgh 15222
(412) 392-4500

Aliquippa, 13,744
Ambridge, 8,086
Arnold, 5,868
Avalon, 5,836
Baden, 5,325
Baldwin, 21,367
Beaver Falls, 11,145
Bellevue, 8,942
Bethel Park, 34,287
Brentwood, 10,527
Bridgeville, 5,217
Butler, 16,895
California, 5,736
Canonsburg, 9,769
Carnegie, 9,166
Castle Shannon, 9,107
Charleroi, 5,073
Clairton, 9,750
Connellsville, 9,242
Coraopolis, 6,663
Crafton, 6,990
Donora, 5,711
Dormont, 9,656
Duquesne, 7,877
Economy, 9,166
Fernway, 9,072
Forest Hills, 6,934
Fox Chapel, 5,517
Franklin Park, 10,293
Glassport, 5,455
Greensburg, 16,646
Hampton, 15,568
Harrison, 11,763
Jeannette, 11,191
Jefferson, 10,061
Kennedy, 7,152
Latrobe, 9,285
Lower Burrell, 12,361
McCandless, 28,781
McKees Rocks, 7,743
McKeesport, 25,121
Monaca, 6,840
Monessen, 9,476
Monongahela, 5,053
Mount Lebanon, 33,362
Munhall, 12,578
Monroeville, 29,061
Murrysville, 18,468

New Brighton, 6,775
New Kensington, 16,148
North Braddock, 6,784
North Versailles, 12,302
Oakmont, 6,880
O'Hara, 9,096
Penn Hills, 51,430
Pittsburgh, 358,883
Pleasant Hills, 8,870
Plum, 26,092
Robinson, 10,830
Ross, 33,482
Scott, 17,118
Scottdale, 5,183
Shaler, 30,533

White Oak, 8,752
Whitehall, 14,081
Wilkins, 7,487
Wilkinsburg, 20,305

Pittsfield, MA

Berkshire Eagle
75 S. Church St.
Pittsfield 01201
(413) 447-7311

Berkshire VB
Berkshire Common
Pittsfield 01201
(800) 237-5747

Central Berkshire C/C
66 West St.
Pittsfield 01201
(413) 499-4000

Adams, 9,072
Dalton, 7,194
Lee, 5,798
Lenox, 5,149
Pittsfield, 46,437

Portland, ME

Portland Press Herald
390 Congress St.
Portland 04101
(207) 780-9000

Greater Portland CVB
305 Commercial St.
Portland 04101
(207) 772-5800

Greater Portland Reg. C/C
145 Middle St.
Portland 04101
(207) 772-2811

Buxton, 6,754
Cape Elizabeth, 9,244
Cumberland, 6,032
Falmouth, 8,426
Freeport, 6,784
Gorham, 13,331
Gray, 6,432
Old Orchard Beach, 7,815
Portland, 61,982
Scarborough, 13,750
South Portland, 22,596
Standish, 8,433
Westbrook, 15,737
Windham, 13,406
Yarmouth, 8,450

Portland–Vancouver, OR–WA

The Oregonian
1320 SW Broadway

(360) 694-2588

Aloha, OR, 34,284
Battle Ground, WA, 5,146
Beaverton, OR, 59,367
Camas, WA, 8,451
Canby, OR, 9,855
Cascade Park East, WA, 6,996
Cascade Park West, WA, 6,656
Cedar Hills, OR, 9,294
Cedar Mill, OR, 9,697
Cornelius, OR, 7,586
Ellsworth North, WA, 5,796
Evergreen, WA, 11,249
Five Corners, WA, 6,776
Forest Grove, OR, 15,520
Gladstone, OR, 10,798
Gresham, OR, 78,594
Hazel Dell North, WA, 6,924
Hazel Dell South, WA, 5,796
Hazelwood, OR, 11,480
Hillsboro, OR, 44,470
Jennings Lodge, OR, 6,530
Lake Oswego, OR, 33,134
Lake Shore, WA, 6,268
McMinnville, OR, 20,293
Milwaukie, OR, 20,410
Minnehaha, WA, 9,661
Newberg, OR, 14,631
Oak Grove, OR, 12,576
Oak Hills, OR, 6,450
Oatfield, OR, 15,348
Orchards North, WA, 6,479
Orchards South, WA, 12,956
Oregon City, OR, 16,099
Portland, OR, 450,777
Raleigh Hills, OR, 6,066
Rockcreek, OR, 8,282
St. Helens, OR, 8,605
Salmon Creek, WA, 11,989
Tigard, OR, 35,509
Troutdale, OR, 9,457
Tualatin, OR, 18,477
Vancouver, WA, 51,847
Vancouver Mall, WA, 6,938
Washougal, WA, 5,817
West Linn, OR, 18,569
West Slope, OR, 7,959
Wilsonville, OR, 9,735

Portsmouth–Rochester, NH–ME

Foster's Daily Democrat
333 Central Ave.
Dover 03820
(603) 742-4455

Greater Portsmouth C/C
500 Market St.
Portsmouth 03802
(603) 436-1118

Greater Rochester C/C
88 Hancock St.

Kittery, ME, 9,434
Newmarket, NH, 6,848
Portsmouth, NH, 19,594
Rochester, NH, 27,023
Somersworth, NH, 11,769
South Berwick, ME, 6,248
Stratham, NH, 5,599
York, ME, 10,142

Providence–Fall River–Warwick, RI–MA

Providence Journal-Bulletin
75 Fountain St.
Providence 02902
(401) 277-7000

Greater Providence CVB
30 Exchange Ter.
Providence 02903
(401) 274-1637

Greater Providence C/C
30 Exchange Ter.
Providence 02903
(401) 521-5000

Attleboro, MA, 38,863
Barrington, RI, 15,951
Bristol, RI, 21,865
Burrillville, RI, 16,986
Central Falls, RI, 15,210
Charlestown, RI, 7,055
Coventry, RI, 32,110
Cranston, RI, 77,323
Cumberland, RI, 30,398
East Greenwich, RI, 11,843
East Providence, RI, 50,059
Exeter, RI, 6,227
Fall River, MA, 89,425
Glocester, RI, 9,781
Jamestown, RI, 5,336
Johnston, RI, 27,683
Lincoln, RI, 19,063
Narragansett, RI, 15,483
North Attleborough, MA, 26,375
North Kingstown, RI, 24,065
North Providence, RI, 32,378
North Smithfield, RI, 10,567
Pawtucket, RI, 69,002
Providence, RI, 150,639

Rehoboth, MA, 9,240
Richmond, RI, 5,816
Scituate, RI, 10,211
Seekonk, MA, 13,166
Smithfield, RI, 20,035
Somerset, MA, 17,442
South Kingstown, RI, 26,228
Swansea, MA, 15,572
Tiverton, RI, 14,824
Warren, RI, 11,177
Warwick, RI, 86,006
West Warwick, RI, 28,471
Westport, MA, 14,110
Woonsocket, RI, 40,752

Provo–Orem, UT

Daily Herald
1555 N. 200 West
Provo 84604
(801) 373-5050

Provo/Orem C/C
51 S. University Ave.
Provo 84603
(801) 379-2555

American Fork, 18,194
Highland, 5,909
Lehi, 10,535
Orem, 74,402
Payson, 10,837
Pleasant Grove, 15,813
Provo, 88,519
Spanish Fork, 13,522
Springville, 15,762

Pueblo, CO

Pueblo Chieftain
825 W. Sixth St.
Pueblo 81003
(719) 544-3520

Pueblo C/C
302 N. Santa Fe Ave.
Pueblo 81002
(719) 542-1704

Pueblo, 100,471

Punta Gorda, FL

Charlotte Sun Herald
23170 Harbor View
Charlotte Harbor 33980
(941) 629-2855

Charlotte County C/C
326 W. Marion Ave.
Punta Gorda 33950
(941) 639-2222

Port Charlotte, 41,535
Punta Gorda, 12,102

Quebec City, PQ

Le Journal de Quebec
450 rue Bechard
Vanier G1M 2E9
(418) 683-1573

Le Soleil
390 rue St. Vallier Est
Quebec City G1K 3P7
(418) 847-3233

City Region TCB
60 rue d'Auteuil
Quebec City G1R 4C4
(418) 692-2471

C/C du Quebec
17 rue St-Louis
Quebec City G5R 2V3
(418) 543-5941

Beauport, 74,707
Cap-Rouge, 15,953
Charlesbourg, 71,871
Charny, 11,244
L'Ancienne-Lorette, 16,572
Levis-Lauzon, 40,802
Loretteville, 13,965
Quebec, 167,762
Saint-Jean-Chrysostome, 16,472
Saint-Nicolas, 8,989
Saint-Redempteur, 6,624
Saint-Romuald, 9,611
Sainte-Foy, 71,940
Sillery, 12,133
Val-Belair, 21,048
Vanier, 11,348

Racine, WI

Journal Times
212 Fourth St.
Racine 53403
(414) 634-3222

Racine County CVB
345 Main St.
Racine 53403
(414) 634-3294

Racine Area C/C
300 Fifth St.
Racine 53403
(414) 634-1931

Burlington, 9,184
Racine, 86,014

Raleigh–Durham–Chapel Hill, NC

News & Observer
215 S. McDowell St.
Raleigh 27602
(919) 829-4500

Greater Raleigh CVB
225 Hillsborough St.
Raleigh 27602
(919) 834-5901

Greater Raleigh C/C
800 S. Salisbury St.
Raleigh 27602
(919) 664-7000

Apex, 5,762
Carrboro, 13,763
Cary, 60,775
Chapel Hill, 46,614
Clayton, 5,481
Durham, 143,439
Fuquay-Varina, 5,196
Garner, 17,116
Hillsborough, 6,650
New Hope, 5,694
Raleigh, 236,707
Selma, 6,333
Siler City, 5,018
Smithfield, 8,686
Wake Forest, 6,946

Rapid City, SD

Rapid City Journal
507 Main St.
Rapid City 57701
(605) 394-8300

Rapid City CVB & C/C
444 Mt. Rushmore Rd. N
Rapid City 57709
(800) 487-3223

Rapid City, 57,609
Rapid Valley, 5,968

Reading, PA

Reading Eagle & Reading Times
345 Penn St.
Reading 19601
(215) 371-5000

Reading/Berks County CVB
VF Outlet Village
Reading 19610
(215) 375-4086

Berks County C/C
645 Penn St.
Reading 19603
(215) 376-6766

Kutztown, 5,593
Reading, 78,246
Shillington, 5,074
Wyomissing, 7,295

Redding, CA

Record Searchlight
1101 Twin View Blvd.
Redding 96003
(916) 243-2424

Redding CVB
777 Auditorium Dr.
Redding 96001
(916) 225-4101

Greater Redding C/C
747 Auditorium Dr.
Redding 96001
(916) 225-4433

Anderson, 8,825
Redding, 72,906

Regina, SK

The Leader-Post
1964 Park St.
Regina S4N 6B2
(306) 565-8211

Regina CVB
Victoria Ave. E
Regina S4P 3H1
(306) 789-5099

Regina C/C
2145 Albert St.
Regina S4P 2V1
(306) 757-4658

Regina, 184,582

Reno, NV

Reno Gazette-Journal
955 Kuenzli St.
Reno 89502
(702) 788-6200

Reno–Sparks CVB
4590 S. Virginia St.
Reno 89502
(702) 827-7601

Greater Reno–Sparks C/C
133 N. Sierra St.
Reno 89503

(509) 582-1500

Tri-Cities CVB
6951 W. Grandridge Blvd.
Kennewick 99336
(800) 666-1929

Richland C/C
515 Lee Blvd.
Richland 99352
(509) 946-1651

Kennewick, 48,100
Pasco, 23,226
Richland, 35,740
West Pasco, 7,312
West Richland, 5,836

Richmond–Petersburg, VA

Richmond Times-Dispatch
333 E. Grace St.
Richmond 23219
(804) 649-6000

Metro Richmond CVB
550 E. Marshall
Richmond 23219
(800) 365-7272

Metropolitan Richmond C/C
201 E. Franklin St.
Richmond 23241
(804) 648-1234

Ashland, 5,982
Bellwood, 6,178
Bensley, 5,093
Bon Air, 16,413
Chester, 14,986
Colonial Heights, 16,447
Dumbarton, 8,526
East Highland Park, 11,850
Ettrick, 5,290
Fort Lee, 6,895
Glen Allen, 9,010
Highland Springs, 13,823
Hopewell, 24,453
Lakeside, 12,081
Laurel, 13,011
Mechanicsville, 22,027
Montrose, 6,405
Petersburg, 40,934
Richmond, 201,108
Tuckahoe, 42,629

Riverside–San Bernardino, CA

Press-Enterprise
3512 14th St.
Riverside 92501
(909) 684-1200

San Bernardino County Sun
399 N. D Street
San Bernardino 92401
(909) 889-9666

Apple Valley, 51,994
Banning, 23,452
Barstow, 19,854
Beaumont, 10,644
Big Bear Lake, 5,775
Bloomington, 15,116
Blythe, 9,826
Canyon Lake, 7,938
Cathedral City, 34,734
Cherry Valley, 5,945
Chino, 64,781
Chino Hills, 27,608
Coachella, 18,608
Colton, 41,239
Corona, 92,898
Crestline, 8,594
Desert Hot Springs, 14,406
East Hemet, 17,611
Fontana, 103,737
Glen Avon, 12,663
Grand Terrace, 11,623
Hemet, 41,614
Hesperia, 59,131
Highland, 39,215
Home Gardens, 7,780
Indio, 39,455
La Quinta, 17,241
Lake Arrowhead, 6,539
Lake Elsinore, 22,726
Lakeland Village, 5,159
Loma Linda, 18,478
Los Serranos, 7,099
Mentone, 5,675
Mira Loma, 15,786
Montclair, 28,544
Moreno Valley, 139,311
Murrieta, 33,067
Muscoy, 7,541
Needles, 5,202
Norco, 24,639
Ontario, 134,825
Palm Desert, 26,555
Palm Desert Country, 5,626
Palm Springs, 39,635
Pedley, 8,869
Perris, 30,356
Rancho Cucamonga, 114,799
Rancho Mirage, 10,355
Redlands, 64,526
Rialto, 83,519
Riverside, 241,644
Rubidoux, 24,367
San Bernardino, 181,718
San Jacinto, 20,719
Sun City, 14,930
Temecula, 39,645
Twentynine Palms, 13,505
Upland, 61,827
Valle Vista, 8,751
Victorville, 50,123
Wildomar, 10,411
Woodcrest, 7,796
Yucaipa, 36,558
Yucca Valley, 13,701

Roanoke, VA

310 First St. SW
Roanoke 24011
(540) 983-0700

Cave Spring, 24,053
Hollins, 13,180
Roanoke, 96,643
Salem, 24,218
Vinton, 7,628

Rochester, MN

Rochester Post-Bulletin
18 First Ave. SE
Rochester 55904
(507) 285-7600

Rochester CVB
150 S. Broadway
Rochester 55904
(507) 288-4332

Rochester Area C/C
220 S. Broadway
Rochester 55904
(507) 288-1122

Rochester, 75,769
Stewartville, 5,033

Rochester, NY

Democrat & Chronicle/Times Union
55 Exchange Blvd.
Rochester 14614
(716) 232-7100

Greater Rochester Visitors Association
126 Andrews St.
Rochester 14604
(716) 546-3070

Rochester Area C/C
55 St. Paul St.
Rochester 14604
(716) 454-2220

Albion, 6,901
Batavia, 16,079
Brighton, 34,455

Brockport, 8,689
Canandaigua, 11,205
Dansville, 5,175
East Rochester, 6,572
Fairport, 5,997
Geneseo, 7,651
Geneva, 14,268
Greece, 15,632
Hilton, 5,500
Irondequoit, 52,322
Le Roy, 5,172
Medina, 6,992
Newark, 9,982
Rochester, 231,170
Webster, 5,509

Rockford, IL

Register Star
99 E. State St.
Rockford 61104
(815) 987-1200

Rockford Area CVB
211 N. Main St.
Rockford 61101
(815) 963-8112

Rockford Area C/C
515 N. Court St.
Rockford 61110
(815) 987-8100

Belvidere, 17,782
Loves Park, 16,734
Machesney Park, 20,029
Rochelle, 9,336
Rockford, 143,263

Rocky Mount, NC

Rocky Mount Telegram
150 Howard St.
Rocky Mount 27804
(919) 446-5161

Rocky Mount Area C/C
437 Falls Rd.
Rocky Mount 27802
(919) 442-5112

Rocky Mount, 51,940
Tarboro, 10,800

Sacramento, CA

Sacramento Bee
2100 Q Street
Sacramento 95816
(916) 321-1000

Sacramento CVB
1421 K Street
Sacramento 95814
(916) 264-7777

Sacramento Metro C/C
917 Seventh St.
Sacramento 95814
(916) 552-6800

Auburn, 11,866
Cameron Park, 11,897
Carmichael, 48,702
Citrus Heights, 107,439
El Dorado Hills, 6,395
Elk Grove, 17,483
Fair Oaks, 26,867
Florin, 24,330
Folsom, 39,603
Foothill Farms, 17,135
Galt, 12,872
La Riviera, 10,986
Laguna, 9,828
Lincoln, 8,055
Loomis, 6,116
North Auburn, 10,301
North Highlands, 42,105
Orangevale, 26,266
Placerville, 9,301
Rancho Cordova, 48,731
Rio Linda, 9,481
Rocklin, 26,218
Rosemont, 22,851
Roseville, 53,019
Sacramento, 373,964
South Lake Tahoe, 22,116

Saginaw–Bay City–Midland, MI

Saginaw News
203 S. Washington Ave.
Saginaw 48607
(517) 752-7171

Saginaw County CVB
901 S. Washington Ave.
Saginaw 48601
(517) 752-7165

Saginaw County C/C
901 Swanson Rd.
Saginaw 48609
(517) 752-7161

Bay City, 38,389
Bridgeport, 8,569
Buena Vista, 8,196
Carrollton, 6,521
Midland, 39,568
Saginaw, 70,607
Shields, 6,634

St. Catharines–Niagara, ON

The Standard
17 Queen St.
St. Catharines L2E 2L2
(905) 684-7251

Niagara Falls VCB
4673 Ontario Ave.
Niagara Falls L2E 3R1
(905) 356-6061

St. Catharines & District C/C
11 King St.
St. Catharines L2R 6Z4
(905) 684-2361

Fort Erie, 28,385
Lincoln, 19,649
Niagara Falls, 77,669
Niagara-on-the-Lake, 13,220
Pelham, 14,331
Port Colborne, 19,001
St. Catharines, 133,388
Thorold, 18,708
Welland, 50,113

St. Cloud, MN

St. Cloud Times
3000 Seventh St. N
St. Cloud 56303
(320) 255-8700

St. Cloud Area CVB
30 Sixth Ave. S
St. Cloud 56302
(320) 251-2941

St. Cloud Area C/C
30 Sixth Ave. S
St. Cloud 56302
(320) 251-2940

St. Cloud, 50,785
Sartell, 6,457
Sauk Rapids, 9,113
Waite Park, 5,355

Saint John, NB

Telegraph-Journal/Times-Globe
210 Crown St.
Saint John E2L 2X7
(506) 632-8888

Saint John CVB
P.O. Box 1971
Saint John E2L 4R5
(506) 658-2990

Saint John Board of Trade
P.O. Box 6037
Saint John E2L 4R5
(506) 634-8111

Quispamsis, 9,687
Saint John, 73,860

St. John's, NF

Evening Telegram
Columbus Drive
St. John's A1E 2B8
(709) 364-6300

St. John's Tourist Commission
New Gower St.
St. John's A1C 1J4
(709) 729-8106

St. John's Board of Trade
P.O. Box 5127
St. John's A1C 5V5

Conception Bay South, 19,689
Goulds, 7,651
Mount Pearl, 27,136
St. John's, 95,504
Torbay, 5,539

St. Joseph, MO

News-Press
825 Edmond
St. Joseph 64502
(816) 271-8500

St. Joseph CVB
P.O. Box 445
St. Joseph 64502
(816) 233-6689

St. Joseph Area C/C
3003 Frederick Ave.
St. Joseph 64506
(816) 232-4461

St. Joseph, 71,711

St. Louis, MO–IL

Post-Dispatch
900 N. Tucker Blvd.
St. Louis 63101
(314) 340-8000

St. Louis CVC
10 S. Broadway
St. Louis 63102
(314) 421-1023

Downtown St. Louis C/C
500 N. Broadway
St. Louis 63102
(314) 436-6500

Breckenridge Hills, MO, 5,329
Brentwood, MO, 8,196
Bridgeton, MO, 17,776
Cahokia, IL, 16,959
Centreville, IL, 7,205
Chesterfield, MO, 42,298
Clayton, MO, 13,705
Collinsville, IL, 23,657
Columbia, IL, 5,950
Concord, MO, 19,859
Crestwood, MO, 11,164
Creve Coeur, MO, 12,071
De Soto, MO, 6,240
Dellwood, MO, 5,308
Des Peres, MO, 8,416
East Alton, IL, 7,103
East St. Louis, IL, 37,438
Edwardsville, IL, 16,015
Ellisville, MO, 7,171
Fairview Heights, IL, 16,174
Ferguson, MO, 22,587
Festus, MO, 8,400
Florissant, MO, 51,398
Glasgow Village, MO, 5,199
Glen Carbon, IL, 10,029
Glendale, MO, 6,050
Godfrey, IL, 5,436
Granite City, IL, 32,671
Hazelwood, MO, 15,792
Highland, IL, 8,447
Jennings, MO, 15,990
Jerseyville, IL, 7,793
Kirkwood, MO, 28,284
Ladue, MO, 8,591
Lake St. Louis, MO, 8,293
Lemay, MO, 18,005
Manchester, MO, 6,671
Maplewood, MO, 10,237
Maryland Heights, MO, 26,031
Mascoutah, IL, 6,376
Mehlville, MO, 27,557
Murphy, MO, 9,342
Normandy, MO, 5,127
Northwoods, MO, 5,118
Oakville, MO, 31,750
O'Fallon, IL, 20,061
O'Fallon, MO, 18,296
Olivette, MO, 7,476
Overland, MO, 18,315
Pine Lawn, MO, 5,289
Richmond Heights, MO, 10,452
Rock Hill, MO, 5,314
St. Ann, MO, 14,698
St. Charles, MO, 56,339
St. John, MO, 7,690
St. Louis, MO, 368,215
St. Peters, MO, 46,408
Sappington, MO, 10,917
Shrewsbury, MO, 6,309
Spanish Lake, MO, 20,322
Sullivan, MO, 5,956
Swansea, IL, 8,202
Town and Country, MO, 9,219
Troy, IL, 6,787
Union, MO, 6,386
University City, MO, 40,778
Washington, MO, 11,333

(503) 399-6611

Salem CVB
1313 Mill St. SE
Salem 97301
(503) 581-4326

Salem Area C/C
220 Cottage St. NE
Salem 97301
(503) 581-1466

Dallas, 10,676
Four Corners, 12,156
Hayesville, 14,318
Keizer, 26,968
Monmouth, 6,425
Salem, 115,912
Silverton, 6,122
Stayton, 5,845
Woodburn, 13,953

Salinas, CA

Monterey County Herald
Eight Upper Ragsdale Drive
Monterey 93940
(408) 372-3311

Monterey Peninsula CVB
380 Alvarado St.
Monterey 93942
(408) 649-1770

Salinas Area C/C
119 E. Alisal St.
Salinas 93902
(408) 424-7611

Castroville, 5,272
Del Monte Forest, 5,069
Gonzales, 5,436
Greenfield, 8,350
King City, 8,586
Marina, 15,433
Monterey, 29,812
Pacific Grove, 16,521
Prunedale, 7,393
Salinas, 119,814
Seaside, 32,186
Soledad, 9,019

Salt Lake City–Ogden, UT

Salt Lake Tribune/Deseret News
143 S. Main St.
Salt Lake City 84111
(801) 237-2011

Salt Lake CVB
180 S. West Temple St.
Salt Lake City 84101
(801) 521-2822

Salt Lake Area C/C
175 E. 400 South
Salt Lake City 84111

Kaysville, 16,869
Kearns, 28,374
Layton, 49,200
Little Cottonwood Creek Valley, 5,042
Magna, 17,829
Midvale, 12,083
Millcreek, 32,230
Mount Olympus, 7,413
Murray, 33,361
North Ogden, 13,081
North Salt Lake, 7,294
Ogden, 67,763
Oquirrh, 7,593
Riverdale, 6,867
Riverton, 14,404
Roy, 27,369
Salt Lake City, 171,849
Sandy, 85,406
South Jordan, 16,911
South Ogden, 12,972
South Salt Lake, 11,196
Sunset, 5,347
Syracuse, 5,270
Union, 13,684
Washington Terrace, 8,742
West Jordan, 49,979
West Valley City, 94,663
White City, 6,506
Woods Cross, 5,378

San Angelo, TX

San Angelo Standard-Times
34 W. Harris Ave.
San Angelo 76903
(915) 653-1221

San Angelo CVB
500 Rio Concho Dr.
San Angelo 76903
(915) 653-3163

San Angelo C/C
500 Rio Concho Dr.
San Angelo 76903
(915) 655-4136

San Angelo, 88,726

San Antonio, TX

San Antonio Express-News
Ave. E & Third St.
San Antonio 78205
(210) 225-7411

San Antonio CVB
121 Alamo Plaza
San Antonio 78298
(210) 270-8701

Greater San Antonio C/C
602 E. Commerce
San Antonio 78296
(210) 229-2100

Alamo Heights, 6,731
Canyon Lake, 9,975
Converse, 11,383
Floresville, 5,917
Kirby, 9,035
Leon Valley, 10,361
Live Oak, 10,957
New Braunfels, 31,153
San Antonio, 998,905
Schertz, 12,693
Seguin, 19,865
Universal City, 13,637
Windcrest, 5,309

San Diego, CA

San Diego Union Tribune
350 Camino de la Raina
San Diego 92112
(619) 299-3131

San Diego CVB
401 B Street
San Diego 92101
(619) 232-3101

Greater San Diego C/C
402 W. Broadway
San Diego 92101
(619) 232-0124

Alpine, 9,695
Bonita, 12,542
Bostonia, 13,670
Carlsbad, 65,461
Chula Vista, 149,255
Coronado, 21,831
El Cajon, 92,658
Encinitas, 57,029
Escondido, 116,349
Fallbrook, 22,095
Imperial Beach, 25,736
La Mesa, 54,316
Lakeside, 39,412
Lemon Grove, 24,527
National City, 57,538
Oceanside, 146,229
Poway, 47,923
Ramona, 13,040
Rancho San Diego, 6,977
San Diego, 1,151,977
San Diego Country Estates, 6,874
San Marcos, 44,442
Santee, 55,222
Solana Beach, 12,835
Spring Valley, 55,331
Vista, 79,816

San Francisco, CA

San Francisco Chronicle
901 Mission St.
San Francisco 94103
(415) 777-1111

San Francisco Examiner
110 Fifth St.
San Francisco 94103
(415) 777-2424

San Francisco CVB
201 Third St.
San Francisco 94101
(415) 391-2000

San Francisco C/C
465 California St.
San Francisco 94104
(415) 392-4511

Atherton, 7,651
Belmont, 25,152
Burlingame, 27,648
Corte Madera, 8,458
Daly City, 94,036
East Palo Alto, 25,845
Fairfax, 7,125
Foster City, 29,472
Half Moon Bay, 9,734
Hillsborough, 11,228
Kentfield, 6,030
Larkspur, 10,945
Menlo Park, 29,755
Mill Valley, 13,190
Millbrae, 20,869
North Fair Oaks, 13,912
Novato, 48,796
Pacifica, 39,507
Redwood City, 67,786
San Anselmo, 12,094
San Bruno, 40,554
San Carlos, 28,075
San Francisco, 734,676
San Mateo, 87,836
San Rafael, 48,645
Sausalito, 7,218
South San Francisco, 56,576
Tiburon, 7,871
Woodside, 5,313

San Jose, CA

San Jose Mercury News
750 Ridder Park Dr.
San Jose 95190
(408) 920-5000

San Jose CVB
333 W. San Carlos St.
San Jose 95110
(408) 295-9601

San Jose Metro C/C
180 S. Market St.
San Jose 95113
(408) 291-5250

Campbell, 37,314
Cupertino, 42,691
East Foothills, 14,898
Gilroy, 33,620
Los Altos, 28,205
Los Altos Hills, 7,660
Los Gatos, 29,228
Milpitas, 55,927
Morgan Hill, 26,768
Mountain View, 65,812
Palo Alto, 56,925
San Jose, 816,884
Santa Clara, 94,562
Saratoga, 29,855
Stanford, 18,097
Sunnyvale, 119,584

San Luis Obispo–Atascadero–Paso Robles, CA

San Luis Obispo County Telegram-Tribune
3825 S. Higuera St.
San Luis Obispo 93401
(805) 781-7800

San Luis Obispo County VCB
1041 Chorro St.
San Luis Obispo 93401
(805) 541-8001

San Luis Obispo C/C
1039 Chorro St.
San Luis Obispo 93401
(805) 781-2777

Arroyo Grande, 15,147
Atascadero, 24,232
Cambria, 5,382
Morro Bay, 9,351
Nipomo, 7,109
Oceano, 6,169
Paso Robles, 20,948
Pismo Beach, 7,937
San Luis Obispo, 40,308

Santa Barbara–Santa Maria–Lompoc, CA

Santa Barbara News Press
715 Ana Capa
Santa Barbara 93101
(805) 564-5200

Santa Barbara CVB
510 State St.
Santa Barbara 93101
(805) 966-9223

Santa Barbara County C/C
504 State St.
Santa Barbara 93101
(805) 965-3023

Carpinteria, 13,657
Guadalupe, 5,602
Isla Vista, 20,395
Lompoc, 41,516
Santa Barbara, 85,626
Santa Maria, 65,932
Solvang, 5,149
Vandenberg Village, 5,971

Santa Cruz–Watsonville, CA

Santa Cruz County Sentinel
207 Church St.
Santa Cruz 95060
(408) 423-4242

Santa Cruz County CVC
701 Front St.
Santa Cruz 95060
(408) 425-1235

Santa Cruz Area C/C
1543 Pacific Ave.
Santa Cruz 95060
(408) 423-1111

Aptos, 9,061
Ben Lomond, 7,884
Boulder Creek, 6,725
Capitola, 9,967
Felton, 5,350
Freedom, 8,361
Interlaken, 6,404
Live Oak, 15,212
Opal Cliffs, 5,940
Rio del Mar, 8,919
Santa Cruz, 48,497
Scotts Valley, 9,687
Soquel, 9,188
Twin Lakes, 5,379
Watsonville, 32,091

Santa Fe C/C
P.O. Box 1928
Santa Fe 87504
(505) 983-7317

Los Alamos, 11,455
Santa Fe, 62,514
White Rock, 6,192

Santa Rosa, CA

Santa Rosa Press Democrat
427 Mendocino Ave.
Santa Rosa 95401
(707) 546-2020

Sonoma County CVB
5000 Roberts Lake Rd.
Santa Rosa 95401
(707) 586-8100

Boyes Hot Springs, 5,973
Cloverdale, 5,535
Cotati, 6,484
Healdsburg, 9,155
Petaluma, 45,956
Rohnert Park, 38,548
Roseland, 8,779
Santa Rosa, 116,962
Sebastopol, 7,253
Sonoma, 8,198
Windsor, 13,371

Sarasota–Bradenton, FL

Bradenton Herald
102 Manatee Ave.
Bradenton 34205
(941) 748-0411

Sarasota Herald Tribune
801 S. Tamiami Trail
Sarasota 34236
(941) 953-7755

Sarasota CVB
655 N. Tamiami Trail
Sarasota 34236
(941) 957-1878

Sarasota C/C
1819 Main St.
Sarasota 34236
(941) 955-8188

Bayshore Gardens, 17,062
Bee Ridge, 6,406
Bradenton, 46,750
Englewood, 10,079
Fruitville, 9,808
Gulf Gate Estates, 11,622
Holmes Beach, 5,460
Laurel, 8,245
Longboat Key, 6,092
Memphis, 6,760

Venice, 16,722
Venice Gardens, 7,701

Saskatoon, SK

Star-Phoenix
204 Fifth Ave. N
Saskatoon S7K 2P2
(306) 664-8340

Tourism Saskatoon
102–310 Idylwyld Dr. N
Saskatoon S7K 1M6
(306) 242-1206

Saskatoon C/C
345 Third Ave. S
Saskatoon S7K 1M6
(306) 244-2151

Saskatoon, 195,790

Savannah, GA

Savannah Morning News/ Evening Press
111 W. Bay St.
Savannah 31401
(912) 236-9511

Savannah Area CVB
222 W. Oglethorpe Ave.
Savannah 31401
(800) 444-2427

Savannah Area C/C
222 W. Oglethorpe Ave.
Savannah 31401
(912) 944-0444

Garden City, 7,679
Georgetown, 5,554
Savannah, 140,597
Wilmington Island, 11,230

Scranton–Wilkes-Barre–Hazleton, PA

Scranton Times/Tribune
Penn Ave. & Spruce St.
Scranton 18503
(717) 348-9100

Times Leader
15 N. Main St.
Wilkes Barre 18701
(717) 829-7100

Wilkes-Barre Citizens Voice
75 N. Washington St.
Wilkes Barre 18711
(717) 821-2000

Greater Hazleton CVB
1 S. Church St.
Hazleton 18201
(717) 455-1509

Greater Scranton C/C

Edwardsville, 5,349
Exeter, 5,747
Hazleton, 24,664
Kingston, 13,806
Moosic, 5,280
Nanticoke, 11,983
Old Forge, 8,791
Olyphant, 5,298
Pittston, 9,390
Plymouth, 6,861
Scranton, 77,964
Swoyersville, 5,521
Taylor, 6,961
West Pittston, 5,574
Wilkes-Barre, 45,645

Seattle–Bellevue–Everett, WA

Seattle Times/Post-Intelligencer
1120 John St.
Seattle 98109
(206) 464-2111

Seattle–King County CVB
520 Pike St.
Seattle 98101
(206) 461-5840

Greater Seattle C/C
1301 Fifth Ave.
Seattle 98101
(206) 389-7200

Auburn, 36,484
Bellevue, 84,239
Bothell, 13,045
Brier, 6,429
Burien, 25,089
Des Moines, 18,811
East Renton Highlands, 13,218
Edmonds, 30,341
Enumclaw, 8,750
Esperance, 11,236
Everett, 76,685
Federal Way, 67,554
Harbour Pointe, 9,107
Issaquah, 8,207
Kenmore, 8,917
Kent, 41,125

Kingsgate, 14,259
Kirkland, 42,256
Lake Forest North, 8,002
Lakeland North, 14,402
Lakeland South, 9,027
Lea Hill, 6,876
Lynnwood, 30,558
Martha Lake, 10,155
Marysville, 11,714
Mercer Island, 20,947
Mill Creek, 7,993
Monroe, 5,143
Mountlake Terrace, 19,646
Mukilteo, 9,288
Newport Hills, 14,736
Normandy Park, 7,030
North Hill, 5,706
North Marysville, 18,711
Oak Harbor, 18,706
Pacific, 6,169
Pine Lake, 13,940
Redmond, 39,761
Renton, 43,531
Richmond Highlands, 26,037
Sahalee, 13,951
Seatac, 24,108
Seattle, 520,947
Sheridan Beach, 6,518
Snohomish, 7,205
Tukwila, 12,581
West Lake Sammamish, 6,087
West Lake Stevens, 12,453
Woodinville, 23,654
Woodmont Beach, 7,493

Sharon, PA

Sharon Herald
52 S. Dock St.
Sharon 16146
(412) 981-6100

Mercer County Tourist Agency
1 W. State St.
Sharon 16146
(412) 981-5881

Shenango Valley C/C
1 W. State St.
Sharon 16146
(412) 981-5880

Farrell, 6,554
Greenville, 6,732
Grove City, 9,046
Hermitage, 16,235
Sharon, 17,184

Sheboygan, WI

Sheboygan Press
632 Center Ave.
Sheboygan 53081
(414) 457-7711

Sheboygan Area CVB
712 Riverfront Dr.
Sheboygan 53081
(414) 457-9495

Sheboygan County C/C
631 New York Ave.
Sheboygan 53081
(414) 457-9491

Plymouth, 7,654
Sheboygan, 50,368
Sheboygan Falls, 6,340

Sherbrooke, PQ

La Tribune
1950 rue Roy
Sherbrooke J1K 218
(819) 564-5450

Sherbrook Tourism
48 rue de Pot
Sherbrook J1H 1R4
(819) 564-8331

C/C de Sherbrook
390 King Oest
Sherbrook J1H 1R4
(819) 822-6151

Rock Forest, 16,726
Sherbrooke, 77,612

Sherman–Denison, TX

Sherman Democrat
603 S. Sam Rayburn Fwy.
Sherman 75090
(903) 893-8181

Denison Herald
331 W. Woodard
Denison 75020
(903) 465-7171

Sherman CVB & C/C
1815 S. Sam Rayburn Fwy.
Sherman 75090
(903) 893-1184

Denison, 21,498
Sherman, 31,539

Shreveport–Bossier City, LA

The Times
222 Lake St.
Shreveport 71101
(318) 459-3200

Shreveport–Bossier CVB
629 Spring St.
Shreveport 71101
(318) 222-9392

Shreveport C/C
400 Edwards St.
Shreveport 71120
(318) 677-2500

Bossier City, 54,419
Minden, 13,814
Red Chute, 5,431
Shreveport, 196,982
Springhill, 5,467

Sioux City, IA–NE

Sioux City Journal
Sixth & Pavonia St.
Sioux City 51102
(712) 279-5072

Sioux City Tourism Bureau
801 Fourth St.
Sioux City 51102
(712) 279-4800

Sioux City C/C
101 Pierce St.
Sioux City 51101
(712) 258-7578

Sioux City, IA, 82,735
South Sioux City, NE, 10,285

Sioux Falls, SD

Argus Leader
200 S. Minnesota Ave
Sioux Falls 57102
(605) 331-2200

Sioux Falls CVB & C/C
200 N. Phillips Ave.
Sioux Falls 57102
(605) 336-1620

Sioux Falls, 109,174

South Bend, IN

South Bend Tribune
225 W. Colfax Ave.
South Bend 46626
(219) 235-6161

South Bend/Mishawaka CVB & C/C
401 E. Colfax Ave.
South Bend 46634
(219) 234-0051

Granger, 20,241
Mishawaka, 43,843
South Bend, 105,092

Spokane, WA

Spokesman–Review
999 Riverside Ave.
Spokane 99201
(509) 459-5000

Spokane CVB
926 W. Sprague
Spokane 99204
(800) 248-3230

Spokane Area C/C
W. 1020 Riverside Ave.
Spokane 99201
(509) 624-1393

Cheney, 8,867
Country Homes, 5,126
Dishman, 9,671
Fairwood, 5,807
Opportunity, 22,326
Spokane, 192,781
Veradale, 7,836

Springfield, IL

State-Journal Register
1 Copley Plaza
Springfield 62705
(217) 788-1300

Springfield CVB
109 N. Seventh
Springfield 62701
(217) 789-2361

Greater Springfield C/C
3 S. Old State Capitol Plaza
Springfield 62701
(217) 525-1173

Chatham, 6,837
Springfield, 105,938

Springfield, MA

Union-News
1860 Main St.
Springfield 01103
(413) 788-1000

Greater Springfield CVB
34 Boland Way
Springfield 01103
(413) 787-1549

Greater Springfield C/C
1350 Main St.
Springfield 01103

Monson, 8,242
Northampton, 28,879
Palmer, 12,189
South Hadley, 17,039
Southwick, 8,163
Springfield, 149,164
Ware, 9,783
West Springfield, 26,786
Westfield, 38,186
Wilbraham, 12,553

Springfield, MO

News-Leader
651 Booneville Ave.
Springfield 65806
(417) 836-1100

Springfield CVB
3315 E. Battlefield Rd.
Springfield 65804
(417) 881-5301

Springfield Area C/C
320 N. Jefferson Ave.
Springfield 65801
(417) 862-5567

Nixa, 6,086
Ozark, 5,409
Republic, 6,724
Springfield, 149,727

Stamford–Norwalk, CT

The Advocate
75 Tresser Blvd.
Stamford 06901
(203) 964-2200

Greater Norwalk C/C
101 East Ave.
Norwalk 06852
(203) 866-2521

Stamford C/C
1 Landmark Sq.
Stamford 06901
(203) 359-4761

Darien, 18,900
Greenwich, 57,516
New Canaan, 18,568
Norwalk, 78,710
Stamford, 107,199
Weston, 9,237
Westport, 25,001
Wilton, 16,704

State College, PA

Centre Daily Times
3400 E. College Ave.
State College 16801

Bellefonte, 7,128
Park Forest Village, 6,703
State College, 39,587

Steubenville–Weirton, OH–WV

Herald-Star
401 Herald Sq.
Steubenville 43952
(614) 283-4711

Jefferson County C/C
630 Market St.
Steubenville 43952
(614) 282-6227

Steubenville, OH, 21,384
Toronto, OH, 6,040
Weirton, WV, 21,482

Stockton–Lodi, CA

The Record
530 E. Market St.
Stockton 95202
(209) 943-6397

Stockton–San Joaquin County CVB
46 W. Fremont St.
Stockton 95202
(209) 943-1988

Greater Stockton C/C
445 W. Weber Ave.
Stockton 95203
(209) 547-2770

August, 6,376
Country Club, 9,325
Garden Acres, 8,547
Lathrop, 8,746
Lodi, 52,423
Manteca, 44,180
Ripon, 8,561
Stockton, 222,633
Tracy, 44,736

Sudbury, ON

The Star
33 MacKenzie St.
Sudbury P3C 4Y1
(705) 674-5271

Sudbury & District C/C
100 Elm St.
Sudbury P3C 1T4
(705) 673-7133

Nickel Centre, 13,024
Onaping Falls, 5,119
Rayside–Balfour, 15,637

Sumter 29151
(800) 688-4748

Greater Sumter C/C
215 N. Washington St.
Sumter 29151
(803) 775-1231

Sumter, 42,773

Syracuse, NY

Post-Standard/Herald-Journal
1 Clinton Sq.
Syracuse 13221
(315) 470-0011

Syracuse CVB
572 S. Salina St.
Syracuse 13202
(315) 470-1801

Greater Syracuse C/C
572 S. Salina St.
Syracuse 13202
(315) 470-1800

Auburn, 30,793
Baldwinsville, 6,599
Chittenango, 5,244
De Witt, 8,244
Fairmount, 12,266
Fulton, 13,008
Mattydale, 6,418
North Syracuse, 7,533
Oneida, 11,208
Oswego, 18,715
Solvay, 6,651
Syracuse, 159,895
Westvale, 5,952

Tacoma, WA

Tacoma Morning News Tribune
1950 S. State
Tacoma 98405
(206) 597-8742

Tacoma–Pierce County VCB
906 Broadway
Tacoma 98401
(800) 272-2662

Tacoma–Pierce County C/C
950 Pacific Ave.
Tacoma 98401
(206) 627-2175

Artondale, 7,141
Bonney Lake, 10,227
Elk Plain, 12,197
Fircrest, 5,404
Fort Lewis, 22,224
Lakewood, 58,412
Midland, 5,587
Milton, 5,693
Parkland, 20,882
Prairie Ridge, 8,278
Puyallup, 26,896
South Hill, 12,963
Spanaway, 15,001
Steilacoom, 6,037
Summit, 6,312
Sumner, 7,038
Tacoma, 183,060
University Place, 27,701
Waller, 6,415

Tallahassee, FL

Tallahassee Democrat
277 N. Magnolia Dr.
Tallahassee 32301
(904) 599-2100

Tallahassee Area CVB
200 W. College Ave.
Tallahassee 32301
(904) 413-9201

Tallahassee C/C
100 N. Duval St.
Tallahassee 32302
(904) 224-8116

Quincy, 7,582
Tallahassee, 133,718

Tampa–St. Petersburg–Clearwater, FL

St. Petersburg Times
490 First Ave.
St. Petersburg 33701
(813) 893-8111

Tampa Tribune
202 S. Parker St.
Tampa 33606
(813) 259-7711

Tampa/Hillsborough CVA
111 E. Madison St.
Tampa 33601
(813) 223-1112

Greater Tampa C/C
801 E. Kennedy Blvd.
Tampa 33601
(813) 228-7777

Apollo Beach, 6,025
Bayonet Point, 21,860
Beacon Square, 6,265
Bloomingdale, 13,912
Brandon, 57,985
Brooksville, 8,798
Carrollwood, 7,195
Carrollwood Village, 15,051
Clearwater, 99,838
Dade City, 5,677
Del Rio, 8,248
Dunedin, 34,136
Egypt Lake, 14,580
Elfers, 12,356
Gibsonton, 7,706
Greater Northdale, 16,318
Gulfport, 11,618
Highpoint, 13,818
Holiday, 19,360
Hudson, 7,344
Jasmine Estates, 17,136
Lake Magdalene, 15,973
Land O' Lakes, 7,892
Largo, 67,721
Lealman, 21,748
Lutz, 10,552
Mango, 8,700
New Port Richey, 15,092
New Port Richey East, 9,683
Oldsmar, 9,462
Palm Harbor, 50,256
Pinellas Park, 45,068
Plant City, 22,990
Riverview, 6,478
Ruskin, 6,046
St. Petersburg, 238,585
St. Petersburg Beach, 8,925
Safety Harbor, 15,926
Seffner, 5,371
Seminole, 8,777
South Pasadena, 5,414
Spring Hill, 31,117
Sun City Center, 8,326
Tampa, 285,523
Tarpon Springs, 19,384
Temple Terrace, 16,355
Town 'n' Country, 60,946
Treasure Island, 7,107
University West, 23,760
West Park, 10,347
Zephyrhills, 7,647

Terre Haute, IN

Tribune-Star
721 Wabash Ave.
Terre Haute 47807
(812) 231-4200

Terre Haute CVB
643 Wabash Ave.
Terre Haute 47807
(812) 234-5555

Greater Terre Haute C/C
643 Wabash Ave.
Terre Haute 47808
(812) 232-2391

Brazil, 8,192
Clinton, 5,074
Terre Haute, 60,200

Texarkana, TX–Texarkana, AR

Texarkana Gazette
315 Pine St.
Texarkana 75501
(903) 794-3311

Texarkana C/C
819 State Line Ave.
Texarkana 75501
(903) 792-7191

New Boston, TX, 5,119
Texarkana, AR, 22,922
Texarkana, TX, 32,460
Wake Village, TX, 5,317

Thunder Bay, ON

Times-News/Chronicle-Journal
75 S. Cumberland St.
Thunder Bay P7B 1A3
(807) 343-6200

Tourism Thunder Bay
520 Leith St.
Thunder Bay P7C 1M9
(800) 667-8386

Thunder Bay C/C
857 N. May St.
Thunder Bay P7C 3S2
(807) 622-9642

Thunder Bay, 113,960

Toledo, OH

Toledo Blade
541 Superior St.
Toledo 43660
(419) 245-6000

Greater Toledo CVB
401 W. Jefferson Ave.
Toledo 43604
(419) 321-6404

Toledo C/C
218 Huron St.
Toledo 43604
(419) 243-8191

Bowling Green, 27,853
Maumee, 15,911
Northwood, 5,639
Oregon, 18,276
Perrysburg, 13,848
Rossford, 6,013
Sylvania, 18,703
Toledo, 322,550
Wauseon, 6,604

Topeka, KS

Capital-Journal
616 SE Jefferson
Topeka 66607
(913) 295-1111

Topeka CVB
120 SE Sixth
Topeka 66603
(913) 234-1031

Greater Topeka C/C
120 E. Sixth Ave.
Topeka 66603
(913) 234-2644

Topeka, 120,646

Toronto, ON

Globe and Mail
444 Front St. W.
Toronto
(416) 585-5000

Toronto Sun
333 King St. E
Toronto M5A 3X5
(416) 947-2222

Toronto Star
1 Yonge St.
Toronto M5E 1E5
(416) 367-2000

Metro Toronto CVA
207 Queen's Quay W
Toronto M5J 2P5
(416) 203-2501

Metro Toronto Board of Trade
1 First Canadian Place
Toronto M5X 1C1
(416) 366-6811

Ajax, 77,131
Aurora, 37,508
Bradford–West Gwillimbury, 21,918
Brampton, 276,756

Orangeville, 21,112
Pickering, 87,158
Richmond Hill, 112,044
Scarborough, 557,194
Toronto, 649,958
Vaughan, 155,614
Whitchurch–Stouffville, 21,298
York, 143,761

Trenton, NJ

The Times
500 Perry St.
Trenton 08605
(609) 396-3232

Trenton CVB
Lafayette & Barrack Sts.
Trenton 08625
(609) 777-1770

Mercer County C/C
214 W. State St.
Trenton 08608
(609) 393-4143

East Windsor, 22,599
Ewing, 34,185
Hamilton, 87,025
Hightstown, 5,083
Hopewell, 12,374
Lawrence, 27,491
Lawrenceville, 6,446
Princeton, 12,997
Trenton, 84,441
Twin Rivers, 7,715
Washington, 7,235
West Windsor, 18,641
White Horse, 9,397

Trois–Rivieres, PQ

Le Nouvelliste
1920 rue Bellefeuille
Trois Rivieres G9A 3Y2
(819) 376-2501

Trois Rivieres Tourism & Congress
1563 rue Notre Dame
Trois Rivieres G9A 4X8
(819) 375-1122

Trois Rivieres & District C/C
168 Bonaventure
Trois Rivieres G9A 2A9

Becancour, 11,217
Cap-de-la-Madeleine, 34,292
Trois-Rivieres, 48,252
Trois-Rivieres-Ouest, 24,371

Tucson, AZ

Arizona Daily Star/Tucson Citizen
4850 S. Park Ave.
Tucson 85714

Flowing Wells, 14,013
Green Valley, 13,231
Oro Valley, 7,084
South Tucson, 5,866
Tucson, 434,726

Tulsa, OK

Tulsa World
318 S. Main
Tulsa 74103
(918) 581-8300

Tulsa CVB
616 S. Boston Ave.
Tulsa 74119
(918) 585-1201

Metro Tulsa C/C
616 S. Boston Ave.
Tulsa 74119
(918) 585-1201

Bixby, 10,751
Broken Arrow, 65,679
Claremore, 15,569
Coweta, 6,972
Glenpool, 7,607
Jenks, 8,042
Owasso, 12,982
Sand Springs, 16,496
Sapulpa, 18,486
Skiatook, 5,291
Tulsa, 374,851
Wagoner, 7,229

Tuscaloosa, AL

Tuscaloosa News
2001 Sixth St.
Tuscaloosa 35401
(205) 345-0505

Tuscaloosa CVB
P.O. Box 032167
Tuscaloosa 35403
(205) 391-9200

C/C of West Alabama
2200 University Blvd.
Tuscaloosa 35402
(205) 758-7589

Northport, 20,229
Tuscaloosa, 79,797

Tyler, TX

Tyler Morning Telegraph
410 W. Erwin
Tyler 75702
(903) 597-8111

Tyler Area CVB & C/C
407 N. Broadway
Tyler 75710
(903) 592-1662

Tyler, 80,194

P.O. Box 551
Utica 13503
(315) 724-7222

Utica Area C/C
258 Genesee St.
Utica 13502
(315) 724-3151

Herkimer, 7,883
Ilion, 8,736
Little Falls, 5,720
Rome, 44,233
Utica, 64,095

Vallejo–Fairfield–Napa, CA

Vallejo Times-Herald
440 Curtola Parkway
Vallejo 94590
(707) 644-1141

Daily Republic
1250 Texas St.
Fairfield 94533
(707) 425-4646

Napa Valley Register
1615 Second St.
Napa 94559
(707) 226-3711

Vallejo CVB
301 Georgia St.
Vallejo 94590
(707) 642-3653

Vallejo C/C
2 Florida St.
Vallejo 94590
(707) 644-5551

American Canyon, 7,706
Benicia, 27,026
Dixon, 11,570
Fairfield, 83,776
Napa, 63,444
St. Helena, 5,294
Suisun City, 27,360
Vacaville, 83,008
Vallejo, 111,484

Vancouver, BC

Province/Vancouver Sun
2250 Granville St.
Vancouver V6H 3G1
(604) 732-2513

Tourism Vancouver
4 Bentall Centre
Vancouver V6C 3L6
(800) 888-8835

Vancouver Board of Trade
400–999 Canada Place
Vancouver V6C 3C1

Burnaby, 168,091
Coquitlam, 96,198
Delta, 95,801
Langley, 76,607
Maple Ridge, 59,159
New Westminster, 45,974
North Vancouver, 79,949
Pitt Meadows, 13,920
Port Coquitlam, 43,281
Port Moody, 18,973
Richmond, 141,013
Surrey, 300,906
Vancouver, 499,280
West Vancouver, 40,229
White Rock, 17,768

Ventura, CA

Ventura County Star
5250 Ralson St.
Ventura 93003
(805) 650-2900

Ventura VCB
89-C S. California St.
Ventura 93001
(805) 648-2076

Greater Ventura C/C
785 S. Seaward Ave.
Ventura 93001
(805) 648-2875

Camarillo, 56,734
El Rio, 6,419
Fillmore, 12,399
Mira Monte, 7,744
Moorpark, 29,018
Ojai, 7,697
Oxnard, 145,863
Port Hueneme, 22,969
Santa Paula, 25,694
Simi Valley, 106,949
Thousand Oaks, 110,981
Ventura, 96,769

Victoria, BC

Times-Colonist
2621 Douglas St.
Victoria V8T 4M2
(604) 380-5211

Tourism Victoria
812 Wharf St.
Victoria V8W 1T3
(604) 382-2127

Victoria C/C
525 Fort St.
Victoria V8W 1E8
(604) 383-7191

Central Saanich, 15,484
Colwood, 15,102
Esquimalt, 15,986
North Saanich, 11,731
Oak Bay, 18,084
Saanich, 105,774
Sidney, 10,892
Victoria, 74,178
View Royal, 6,711

Victoria, TX

Victoria Advocate
311 E. Constitution
Victoria 77901
(512) 575-1451

Victoria CVB
700 Main Center
Victoria 77902
(512) 573-5277

Victoria C/C
700 Main Center
Victoria 77901
(512) 573-5277

Victoria, 60,584

Vineland–Millville–Bridgeton, NJ

Daily Journal
891 E. Oak Rd.
Vineland 08360
(609) 825-3456

Bridgeton Evening News
100 E. Commerce St.
Bridgeton 08302
(609) 451-1000

Greater Vineland C/C
Seventh & Wood Sts.
Vineland 08360
(609) 691-7400

Bridgeton, 19,038
Fairfield, 6,632
Maurice River, 6,629
Millville, 26,528
Upper Deerfield, 6,744
Vineland, 54,673

Visalia–Tulare–Porterville, CA

Visalia Times-Delta
330 N. West St.
Visalia 93291
(209) 734-5821

Tulare C/C
260 N. L Street
Tulare 93274
(209) 686-1547

Visalia C/C
720 W. Mineral King
Visalia 93291
(209) 734-5877

Dinuba, 13,553
Earlimart, 5,881
East Porterville, 5,790
Exeter, 8,532
Farmersville, 7,603
Lindsay, 8,543
Orosi, 5,486
Porterville, 32,427
Tulare, 38,564
Visalia, 85,073
Woodlake, 5,839

y-2Waco, TX

Waco Tribune Herald
900 Franklin Ave.
Waco 76701
(817) 757-5757

Waco CVB
100 Washington Ave.
Waco 76702
(817) 753-3622

Greater Waco C/C
Civic Center Plaza
Waco 76700
(817) 752-6551

Bellmead, 8,726
Hewitt, 10,438
Robinson, 7,303
Waco, 105,892
Woodway, 8,869

Washington, DC–MD–VA–WV

Washington Post
1150 15th St. NW
Washington 20071
(202) 334-6000

Washington Times
3600 New York Ave. NE
Washington 20002
(202) 636-3000

Washington D.C. CVB
1212 New York Ave. NW
Washington 20005
(202) 789-7000

District of Columbia C/C
1301 Pennsylvania Ave. NW
Washington 20004
(202) 638-3222

Adelphi, MD, 13,524
Alexandria, VA, 112,879
Annandale, VA, 50,975
Aquia Harbour, VA, 6,308
Arlington, VA, 170,936
Aspen Hill, MD, 45,494
Bailey's Crossroads, VA, 19,507
Ballenger Creek, MD, 5,546
Belle Haven, VA, 6,427
Beltsville, MD, 14,476
Bethesda, MD, 62,936
Bladensburg, MD, 7,857
Bowie, MD, 39,345
Brunswick, MD, 5,193
Bull Run, VA, 5,525
Burke, VA, 57,734
Burtonsville, MD, 5,853
Calverton, MD, 7,585
Camp Springs, MD, 16,392
Centreville, VA, 26,585
Chantilly, VA, 29,337
Chesapeake Ranch Estates, MD, 5,423
Cheverly, MD, 6,475
Chevy Chase, MD, 8,559
Chillum, MD, 31,309
Clinton, MD, 19,987
Cloverly, MD, 7,904
Colesville, MD, 18,819
College Park, MD, 21,320
Coral Hills, MD, 11,032

Countryside, VA, 8,349
Culpeper, VA, 9,453
Dale City, VA, 47,170
Damascus, MD, 9,817
District Heights, MD, 7,075
Dunn Loring, VA, 6,509
East Riverdale, MD, 14,187
Fairfax, VA, 20,654
Fairland, MD, 19,828
Falls Church, VA, 9,181
Forestville, VA, 16,731
Fort Belvoir, VA, 8,590
*Fort Hunt, 12,989
Fort Washington, MD, 24,032
Franconia, VA, 19,882

Green Valley, MD, 9,424
Greenbelt, MD, 20,711
Groveton, VA, 19,997
Herndon, VA, 17,839
Hillandale, MD, 8,151
Hillcrest Heights, MD, 17,136
Huntington, VA, 7,489
Hyattsville, MD, 14,532
Hybla Valley, VA, 15,491
Idylwood, VA, 14,710
Jefferson, VA, 25,782
Kentland, MD, 7,967
Kettering, MD, 9,901
La Plata, MD, 6,796
Lake Barcroft, VA, 8,686
Lake Ridge, VA, 23,862
Landover, MD, 5,052
Langley Park, MD, 14,345
Largo, MD, 9,475
Laurel, MD, 21,567
Leesburg, VA, 19,777
Lincolnia, VA, 13,041
Lorton, VA, 15,385
Manassas, VA, 31,873
Manassas Park, VA, 7,351
Mantua, VA, 6,804
Marlow Heights, MD, 5,885
Marlton, MD, 5,523
Martinsburg, WV, 14,921
McLean, VA, 38,168
Merrifield, VA, 8,399
Mitchellville, MD, 12,593
Montclair, VA, 11,399
Montgomery Village, MD, 32,315
Mount Rainier, MD, 7,795
Mount Vernon, VA, 27,485
New Carrollton, MD, 11,672
Newington, VA, 17,965
North Bethesda, MD, 29,656
North Kensington, MD, 8,607
North Potomac, MD, 18,456
North Springfield, VA, 8,996
Oakton, VA, 24,610
Olney, MD, 23,019
Palmer Park, MD, 7,019
Pimmit Hills, VA, 6,019
Potomac, MD, 45,634
Redland, MD, 16,145
Reston, VA, 48,556
Riverdale, MD, 5,041
Rockville, MD, 47,078
Rosaryville, MD, 8,976

Rose Hill, VA, 12,675
Rossmoor, MD, 6,182
St. Charles, MD, 28,717
Seat Pleasant, MD, 5,626
Seven Corners, VA, 7,280
Silver Spring, MD, 76,046
South Kensington, MD, 8,777
South Laurel, MD, 18,591
Springfield, VA, 23,706
Sterling, VA, 20,512
Sudley, VA, 7,321
Sugarland Run, VA, 9,357
Takoma Park, MD, 16,932
Temple Hills, MD, 6,865
Tysons Corner, VA, 13,124

Yorkshire, VA, [illegible]

Waterbury, CT

Waterbury Republican-American
389 Meadow St.
Waterbury 06702
(203) 574-3636

Waterbury Region CVB
83 Bank St.
Waterbury 06721
(203) 597-9527

Greater Waterbury C/C
83 Bank St.
Waterbury 06721
(203) 757-0701

Middlebury, 6,239
Naugatuck, 30,968
Prospect, 8,334
Southbury, 17,678
Thomaston, 7,152
Waterbury, 103,523
Watertown, 21,208
Wolcott, 14,327
Woodbury, 8,495

Waterloo–Cedar Falls, IA

Waterloo Courier
501 Commercial St.
Waterloo 50701
(319) 291-1400

Waterloo CVB
215 E. Fourth St.
Waterloo 50704
(319) 233-8432

Waterloo C/C
215 E. Fourth St.
Waterloo 50704
(319) 233-8431

Cedar Falls, 33,908
Waterloo, 66,537

Wausau, WI

Wausau Daily Herald
Scott St.
Wausau 54401
(715) 842-2101

Wausau Area CVB
300 Third St.
Wausau 54402
(715) 845-6232

Wausau Area C/C
300 Third St.
Wausau 54402
(715) 845-6231

West Palm Beach 33405
(407) 820-4445

Palm Beach County CVB
1555 Palm Beach Lakes Blvd.
West Palm Beach 33401
(407) 471-3995

C/C of the Palm Beaches
401 N. Flagler Dr.
West Palm Beach 33401
(407) 833-3711

Belle Glade, 16,413
Boca Del Mar, 17,754
Boca Raton, 66,422
Boynton Beach, 51,230
Century Village, 8,363
Delray Beach, 51,026
Hamptons at Boca Raton, 11,686
Greenacres City, 22,940
Jupiter, 27,572
Kings Point, 12,422
Lake Park, 7,502
Lake Worth, 31,537
Lantana, 9,048
North Palm Beach, 10,993
Pahokee, 6,845
Palm Beach, 9,682
Palm Beach Gardens, 28,082
Palm Springs, 9,272
Riviera Beach, 26,658
Royal Palm Beach, 19,373
Sandalfoot Cove, 14,214
Villages of Oriole, 5,698
Wellington, 20,670
West Palm Beach, 75,456

Wheeling, WV–OH

Morning Intelligencer/News-Register
1500 Main St.
Wheeling 26003
(304) 266-0100

Wheeling CVB
1233 Main St.
Wheeling 26003
(304) 233-7710

Wheeling Area C/C
1233 Main St.
Wheeling 26003
(304) 233-2575

Bellaire, OH, 5,724
Martins Ferry, OH, 7,937
Moundsville, WV, 10,801
St. Clairsville, OH, 5,035
Wheeling, WV, 33,969

Wichita, KS

Wichita Eagle
825 E. Douglas
Wichita 67202
(316) 268-6000

Wichita CVB
100 S. Main St.
Wichita 67202
(316) 265-2800

Wichita Area C/C
350 W. Douglas Ave.
Wichita 67202
(316) 265-7771

Augusta, 8,439
Derby, 16,588
El Dorado, 12,032
Haysville, 8,561
Mulvane, 5,101
Newton, 17,012
Park City, 5,375
Wichita, 310,236

Wichita Falls, TX

Times Record News
1301 Lamar
Wichita Falls 76301
(817) 767-8341

Wichita Falls CVB
1300 Seventh St.
Wichita Falls 76301
(817) 723-9989

Wichita Falls Board of Commerce
218 hamilton Bldg.
Wichita Falls 76301
(817) 723-2741

Burkburnett, 10,292
Iowa Park, 6,359
Wichita Falls, 97,766

Williamsport, PA

Williamsport Sun-Gazette
252 W. Fourth St.
Williamsport 17701
(717) 326-1551

Lycoming County Tourism Agency
848 W. Fourth St.
Williamsport 17701
(717) 321-1201

Williamsport-Lycoming C/C
454 Pine St.
Williamsport 17701
(717) 326-1971

Montoursville, 5,234
South Williamsport, 6,655
Williamsport, 31,854

Wilmington, NC

Wilmington Morning Star
1003 S. 17th St.
Wilmington 28401
(910) 343-2000

Greater Wilmington C/C
505 Nutt St.
Wilmington 28401
(910) 762-2611

Long Beach, 5,618
Masonboro, 7,010
Seagate, 5,444
Smith Creek, 7,461
Wilmington, 62,651

Wilmington-Newark, DE-MD

News Journal
950 W. Basin Rd.
New Castle 19720
(302) 324-2500

Greater Wilmington CVB
1300 Market St.
Wilmington 19801
(302) 652-4089

New Castle County C/C
P.O. Box 11247
Wilmington 19850
(302) 378-6582

Brookside, DE, 15,307
Claymont, DE, 9,800
Edgemoor, DE, 5,853
Elkton, MD, 9,809
Elsmere, DE, 5,542
New Castle, DE, 5,131
Newark, DE, 27,386
Pike Creek, DE, 10,163
Stanton, DE, 5,028
Talleyville, DE, 6,346
Wilmington, DE, 72,799
Wilmington Manor, DE, 8,568

Windsor, ON

Windsor Star
167 Ferry St.
Windsor N9A 4M5
(519) 255-5711

Windsor CVB
333 Riverside Dr. W
Windsor N9A 5K6
(519) 255-6531

Windsor & District C/C
500 Riverside Dr. W
Windsor N9A 5K6
(519) 256-2641

Essex, 7,289
Tecumseh, 13,087
Windsor, 187,299

Winnipeg, MB

Free Press
1355 Mountain Ave.
Winnipeg R2X 3B6
(204) 697-7000

Winnipeg Sun
1700 Church Ave.
Winnipeg R2X 3A2
(204) 694-2022

Tourism Winnipeg
320–25 Forks Market Rd.
Winnipeg R3C 4L9
(800) 665-0204

Winnipeg C/C
500–167 Lombard Ave.
Winnipeg R0C 3G0
(204) 944-8484

Winnipeg, 634,296

Worcester, MA-CT

Telegram & Gazette
P.O. Box 15012
Worcester 01615
(508) 777-1111

Worcester County CVB
33 Waldo St.
Worcester 01608
(508) 753-2920

Worcester Area C/C
33 Waldo St.
Worcester 01608
(508) 753-2924

Auburn, MA, 15,226
Charlton, MA, 11,638
Clinton, MA, 12,845
Douglas, MA, 6,510
Dudley, MA, 9,554
Grafton, MA, 13,398
Holden, MA, 15,265
Leicester, MA, 10,105
Millbury, MA, 12,327
Northborough, MA, 12,752
Northbridge, MA, 13,207
Oxford, MA, 13,298
Rutland, MA, 5,446
Shrewsbury, MA, 26,101
Southbridge, MA, 16,122
Spencer, MA, 11,679
Sterling, MA, 7,041
Sturbridge, MA, 8,046
Sutton, MA, 7,565
Thompson, NH, 8,754
Uxbridge, MA, 11,497
Webster, MA, 16,227
West Boylston, MA, 6,600
Westborough, MA, 15,165
Worcester, MA, 165,387

Yakima, WA

Yakima Herald-Republic
114 N. Fourth St.
Yakima 98901
(509) 248-1251

Yakima Valley VCB
10 N. Eighth St.
Yakima 98901
(800) 221-0751

Greater Yakima C/C
10 N. Ninth St.
Yakima 98907
(509) 248-2021

Grandview, 9,148
Selah, 5,549
Sunnyside, 12,808
Toppenish, 8,748
West Valley, 6,594
Yakima, 61,976

Yolo, CA

Davis Enterprise
315 G Street
Davis 95616
(916) 756-0800

Davis Visitors Center & C/C
228 B Street
Davis 95616
(916) 756-5160

Davis, 48,275
West Sacramento, 30,103
Winters, 5,143

Weigelstown, 8,665
York, 45,657

Youngstown–Warren, OH

The Vindicator
Vindicator Sq.
Youngstown 44503
(216) 747-1471

Youngstown–Warren Regional C/C
1200 Stambaugh
Youngstown 44503
(216) 744-2131

Yuba–Sutter C/C
429 Tenth St.
Marysville 95901
(916) 743-6501

Linda, 13,033
Marysville, 13,177
Olivehurst, 9,738
South Yuba City, 8,816
Yuba City, 32,441

York County CVB
1 Market Way E
York 17401
(717) 848-4001

York County C/C
1 Market Way E
York 17401
(717) 848-4000

East York, 8,487
Hanover, 14,937
Parkville, 6,014
Red Lion, 7,822
Shiloh, 8,245

Newton Falls, 5,043
Niles, 21,365
Salem, 12,841
Struthers, 12,212
Warren, 50,343
Youngstown, 91,775

Yuba City, CA

Appeal-Democrat
1530 Ellis Lake Drive
Marysville 95901
(916) 741-2345

Yuma CVB
377 S. Main St.
Yuma 85366
(520) 783-0071

Yuma County C/C
377 S. Main St.
Yuma 85366
(520) 782-2567

Fortuna Foothills, 7,737
San Luis, 5,643
Somerton, 7,177
Yuma, 67,185

List of Tables, Maps, and Diagrams

Putting It All Together

Appendix

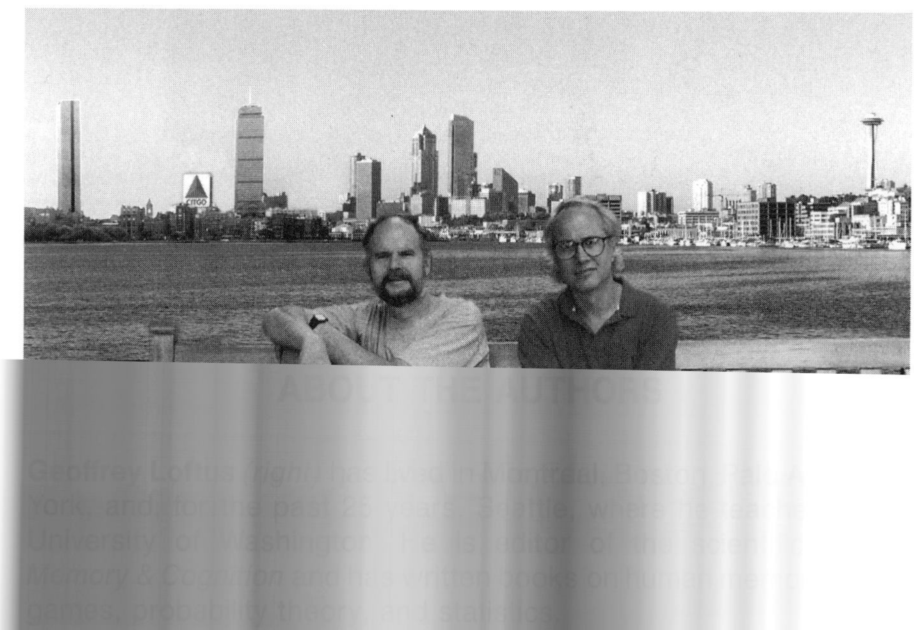

Boston/Seattle montage, Susan Loftus

ABOUT THE AUTHORS

Geoffrey Loftus *(right)* has lived in Montreal, Boston, Palo Alto, New York, and, for the past 25 years, Seattle, where he teaches at the University of Washington. He is editor of the scientific journal *Memory & Cognition* and has written books on human memory, video games, probability theory, and statistics.

David Savageau *(left)* has lived in Denver, South Bend, St. Louis, and Indianapolis, and now resides near Boston. He is a columnist for *Expansion Management* magazine and author of the best-selling *Retirement Places Rated*.